# The Zohar

by
## Rav Shimon bar Yochai
### From The Book of Avraham

with
The Sulam Commentary

by
## Rav Yehuda Ashlag

The First Ever Unabridged
English Translation with Commentary

Published by
## The Kabbalah Centre International Inc.
## Dean Rav S. P. Berg Shlita

Edited and Compiled by
Rabbi Michael Berg

Kabbalah Centre Publishing is a registered DBA of
The Kabbalah Centre International, Inc.

For further information:

The Kabbalah Centre
155 E. 48th St., New York, NY 10017
1062 S. Robertson Blvd., Los Angeles, CA 90035

1.800.Kabbalah  www.kabbalah.com

First Printing 2001
Revised Edition 2003
Fifth Printing 2015

Printed in USA

ISBN: 978-157189-239-3

With much love and appreciation to the
Rav and Karen
all the teachers
and all my friends at the Center

May the Light of the *Zohar* surround them and their
family, the world and my family
with love, peace, and spiritual fulfillment.

Hayim and Rivka Menda
Benjamin Menda
Tal and Ari Menda
Denise Abravanel
Sami and Nadine Abravanel
Lily Rose Abravanel

## APPLYING THE POWER OF THE ZOHAR

The Zohar is a book of great mystical power and wisdom. It is Universally recognized as the definitive work on the Kabbalah – and it is also so Much more.

The Zohar is a wellspring of spiritual energy, a fountainhead of metaphysical power that not only reveals and explains, but literally brings blessing, protection, and well-being into the lives of all those who read or peruse its sacred texts. All that is required is worthy desire, the certainty of a trusting heart, and an open and receptive mind. Unlike other books, including the great spiritual texts of other traditions, The Zohar is written in a kind of code, through which metaphors, parables, and cryptic language at first conceal but ultimately reveal the forces of creation.

As electrical current is concealed in wire and cable before disclosing itself as an illuminated light bulb, the spiritual Light of the Creator is wrapped in allegory and symbolism throughout the Aramaic text of the Zohar. And while many books contain information and knowledge, the Zohar both expresses and embodies spiritual Light. The very letters on its pages have the power to bring spiritual wisdom and positive energy into every area of our lives.

As we visually scan the Aramaic texts and study the accompanying insights that appear in English, spiritual power is summoned from above – and worlds tremble as Light is sent forth in response.

It's primary purpose is not only to help us acquire wisdom, but to draw Light from the Upper Worlds and to bring sanctification into our lives. Indeed, the book itself is the most powerful of all tools for cleansing the soul and connecting to the Light of the Creator. As you open these pages, therefore, do not make understanding in the conventional sense your primary goal.

Although you may not have a knowledge of Aramaic, look first at the Aramaic text before reading the English. Do not be discouraged by difficulties with comprehension. Instead, open your heart to the spiritual transformation the Zohar is offering you.

Ultimately, the Zohar is an instrument for refining the individual soul – for removing darkness from the earth – and for bringing well being and blessing to our fellow man.

Its purpose is not only to make us intellectually wise, but to make us spiritually pure.

## Torah

Also known as the Five Books of Moses, the Torah is considered to be the physical body of learning, whereas the Zohar is the internal soul. The literal stories of the Torah conceal countless hidden secrets.` The Zohar is the Light that illuminates all of the Torah's sublime mysteries.

| | |
|---|---|
| Beresheet | Genesis |
| Shemot | Exodus |
| Vayikra | Leviticus |
| Bemidbar | Numbers |
| Devarim | Deuteronomy |

## Prophets

| | |
|---|---|
| Amos | Amos |
| Chagai | Haggai |
| Chavakuk | Habakkuk |
| Hoshea | Hosea |
| Malachi | Malachi |
| Melachim | Kings |
| Michah | Micah |
| Nachum | Nahum |
| Ovadyah | Obadiah |
| Shmuel | Samuel |
| Shoftim | Judges |
| Tzefanyah | Zephaniah |
| Yechezkel | Ezekiel |
| Yehoshua | Joshua |
| Yeshayah | Isaiah |
| Yirmeyah | Jeremiah |
| Yoel | Joel |
| Yonah | Jonah |
| Zecharyah | Zechariah |

## Writings

| | |
|---|---|
| Daniel | Daniel |
| Divrei Hayamim | Chronicles |
| Eicha | Lamentations |
| Ester | Esther |
| Ezra | Ezra |
| Nechemiah | Nehemiah |
| Iyov | Job |
| Kohelet | Ecclesiastes |
| Mishlei | Proverbs |
| Rut | Ruth |

| | |
|---|---|
| Sir Hashirim | Songs of Songs |
| Tehilim | Psalms |

## The Ten Sfirot – Emanations

To conceal the blinding *Light* of the Upper World, and thus create a tiny point into which our universe would be born, ten *curtains* were fabricated. These ten *curtains* are called Ten Sfirot. Each successive Sfirah further reduces the emanation of *Light*, gradually dimming its brilliance to a level almost devoid of *Light* – our physical world known as *Malchut*. The only remnant of Light remaining in this darkened universe is a *pilot light* which sustains our existence. This Light is the life force of a human being and the force that gives birth to stars, sustains suns and sets everything from swirling galaxies to busy ant hills in motion. Moreover, the Ten Sfirot act like a prism, refracting the Light into many *colors* giving rise to the diversity of life and matter in our world.

The Ten Sfirot are as follows:

| | |
|---|---|
| Keter | Crown |
| Chochmah | Wisdom |
| Binah | Understanding |
| Da'at | Knowledge |
| Zeir Anpin | Small Face, |
| | (includes the next six Sfirot): |
| Chesed | Mercy (Chassadim - plural) |
| Gvurah | Judgment (Gvurot - Plural) |
| Tiferet | Splendor |
| Netzach | Victory (Eternity) |
| Hod | Glory |
| Yesod | Foundation |
| Malchut | Kingdom |

## The Partzufim - Spiritual forms

One complete structure of the Ten Sfirot creates a *Partzuf* or Spiritual Form. Together, these forces are the building blocks of all reality. As water and sand combine to create cement, the Ten Sfirot

combine to produce a Spiritual Form [Partzuf]. Each of the Spiritual Forms below are therefore composed of one set of Ten Sfirot.

These Spiritual Forms are called:

| | |
|---|---|
| Atik | Ancient |
| Atik Yomin | Ancient of Days |
| Atika Kadisha | Holy Ancient |
| Atik of Atikin | Anceint of Ancients |
| Aba | Father |
| Arich Anpin | Long Face |
| Ima | Mother |
| Nukva | Female |
| Tevunah | Intelligence |
| Yisrael Saba | Israel Grandfather |
| Zachar | Male |

These names are not meant to be understood literally. Each represents a unique spiritual force and building block, producing a substructure and foundation for all the worlds make up reality.

## The Five Worlds

All of the above Spiritual Forms [Partzufim] create one spiritual world. There are Five Worlds in total that compose all reality, therefore, five sets of the above Spiritual Forms are required.

Our physical world corresponds to the world of: Asiyah – Action

| | |
|---|---|
| Adam Kadmon | Primordial Man |
| Atzilut | Emanation |
| Briyah | Creation |
| Yetzirah | Formation |
| Asiyah | Action |

## The Five Levels of the soul

| | |
|---|---|
| Nefesh | First, Lowest level of Soul |
| Ruach | Second level of Soul |
| Neshamah | Third level of Soul |
| Chayah | Fourth level of Soul |
| Yechidah | Highest, fifth level of Soul |

## Names of God

As a single ray of white sunlight contains the seven colors of the spectrum, the one Light of the Creator embodies many diverse spiritual forces. These different forces are called *Names of God*. Each Name denotes a specific attribute and spiritual power. The Hebrew letters that compose these Names are the interface by which these varied Forces act upon our physical world. The most common Name of God is the Tetragrammaton (the four letters, *Yud Hei Vav Hei* יהוה.) Because of the enormous power that the Tetragrammaton transmits, we do not utter it aloud. When speaking of the Tetragrammaton, we use the term *Hashem* which means, *The Name*.

Adonai, El, Elohim, Hashem, Shadai, Eheyeh, Tzevaot, Yud Hei Vav Hei

## People

| | |
|---|---|
| Er | The son of Noach |
| Rabbi Elazar | The son of Rabbi Shimon bar Yochai |
| Rabbi Shimon bar Yochai | Author of the Zohar |
| Shem, Cham, Yefet | Noach's children |
| Shet | Seth |
| Ya'akov | Jacob |
| Yishai | Jesse (King David's father) |
| Yitzchak | Isaac |
| Yosef | Joseph |
| Yitro | Jethro |
| Yehuda | Judah |

## Angels

Angels are distinct energy components, part of a vast communication network running through the upper worlds. Each unique Angel is responsible for transmitting various forces of influence into our physical universe.

Adriel, Ahinael, Dumah (name of Angel in charge of the dead), Gabriel, Kadshiel, Kedumiel, Metatron, Michael, Rachmiel,

Raphael, Tahariel, Uriel

## Nations

Nations actually represent the inner attributes and character traits of our individual self. The nation of Amalek refers to the doubt and uncertainty that dwells within us when we face hardship and obstacles. Moab represents the dual nature of man. Nefilim refers to the sparks of Light that we have defiled through our impure actions, and to the negative forces that lurk within the human soul as a result of our own wrongful deeds.

Amalek, Moab, Nefilim

## General

| | |
|---|---|
| Aba | Father |
| | Refers to the male principle and positive force in our universe. Correlates to the proton in an atom. |
| Arvit | The Evening prayer |
| Chayot | Animals |
| Chupah | Canopy (wedding ceremony) |
| Et | The |
| Avadon | Hell |
| Gehenom | Hell |
| Sheol | Hell |
| | The place a soul goes for purification upon leaving this world. |
| Ima | Mother |
| | The female principle and minus force in our universe. Correlates to the electron in an atom. |
| Kiddush | Blessing over the wine |
| Klipah | Shell (negativity) |
| Klipot | Shells (Plural) |
| Kriat Sh'ma | The Reading of the Sh'ma |
| Mashiach | Messiah |
| Minchah | The Afternoon prayer |
| Mishnah | Study |
| Mochin | Brain, Spiritual levels of Light |
| Moed | A designated time or holiday |
| Negev | The south of Israel |
| Nukva | Female |

| | |
|---|---|
| Partzuf | Face |
| Shacharit | The Morning prayer |
| Shamayim | Heavens (sky) |
| Shechinah | The Divine presence, The female aspect of the Creator |
| Tefilin | Phylacteries |
| The Dinur river | The river of fire |
| Tzadik | Righteous person |
| Zion | Another name for Jerusalem |
| Yisrael | The land of Israel |
| | The nation of Israel or an individual Israelite |
| Zohar | Splendor |

## The Hebrew vowels

Chirik א, Cholam וא א, Kamatz א, Patach א, Segol א, Sh'va א, Shuruk וא א, Tzere א.

## The Twelve Tribes

Asher, Dan, Ephraim, Gad, Issachar, Judah, Levi, Menasheh, Naphtali, Reuben, Shimon, Zebulun

## Jewish Holidays

| | |
|---|---|
| Rosh Hashanah | The Jewish New Year |
| Yom Kippur | Day of Atonement |
| Sukkot | Holiday of the Booths |
| Shmini Atzeret | The day of Convocation |
| Simchat Torah | Holiday on which we dance with the Torah |
| Pesach | Passover |
| Shavout | Holiday of the Weeks |

# כרך יא

פרשת תרומה, ספרא דצניעותא

# Vol. XI

**Trumah, Safra De'tzniuta**

# A Prayer from The Ari

### To be recited before the study of the Zohar

Ruler of the universe, and Master of all masters, The Father of mercy and forgiveness, we thank You, our God and the God of our fathers, by bowing down and kneeling, that You brought us closer to Your Torah and Your holy work, and You enable us to take part in the secrets of Your holy Torah. How worthy are we that You grant us with such big favor, that is the reason we plead before You, that You will forgive and acquit all our sins, and that they should not bring separation between You and us.

And may it be your will before You, our God and the God of our fathers, that You will awaken and prepare our hearts to love and revere You, and may You listen to our utterances, and open our closed heart to the hidden studies of Your Torah, and may our study be pleasant before Your Place of Honor, as the aroma of sweet incense, and may You emanate to us Light from the source of our soul to all of our being. And, may the sparks of your holy servants, through which you revealed Your wisdom to the world, shine.

May their merit and the merit of their fathers, and the merit of their Torah, and holiness, support us so we shall not stumble through our study. And by their merit enlighten our eyes in our learning as it is stated by King David, The Sweet Singer of Israel: "Open my eyes, so that I will see wonders from Your Torah" (Tehilim 119:18). Because from His mouth God gives wisdom and understanding.

"May the utterances of my mouth and the thoughts of my heart find favor before You, God, my Strength and my Redeemer" (Tehilim 19:15).

# TRUMAH

## Names of the articles

## 1. "Who is she that looks out like the dawn"

### A synopsis

This section opens with the verse, "And The Creator spoke to Moses, saying, 'Speak to the children of Yisrael that they bring Me an offering, of every man whose heart prompts him...'" Rabbi Chiya points out that The Creator put all other nations under His ministers but chose to oversee Yisrael Himself, having a wish to be specially connected to them.

Rabbi Shimon then explains that in the text, "Who is she that looks out like the dawn, fair as the moon, clear as the sun, and terrible as an army with banners," "she" is the secret of the lower world joined to the higher world. He goes on to say that the upper worlds were united in Leah and the lower worlds were united in Rachel, yet that it was Jacob who united the two worlds in his love for and marriage to them both. When it was written, "Rachel envied her sister," the meaning was that the whole longing and desire of the lower world is to be like the upper world and to inherit its position. Between the worlds, those who sought to lust after them both would perish, having found neither Understanding nor Faith. And when we read, "For Yah has chosen Jacob to himself," we see that God has completed Yisrael above and below in perfection.

### The Relevance of this Passage

In a true offering to God ('Speak to the children of Yisrael that they bring Me an offering'"), a man sacrifices an aspect of his innate negative nature, for this is how we connect to the Light of the Creator. This passage uproots our selfish tendencies so that we enjoin ourselves to the Divine Radiance.

Jacob also cautions us to recognize the dangers of lusting after the fleeting pleasures of the material world. A desire for eternal fulfillment – the love of family, of friends, and of God – is thus wakened in our souls. Our consciousness is raised by virtue of the Light that shines through the story of Jacob and his love for Leah and Rachel. This love elevates the entire world, connecting us to the source of all Light.

וַיְדַבֵּר יְיָ' אֶל מֹשֶׁה לֵאמֹר. דַּבֵּר אֶל בְּנֵי יִשְׂרָאֵל וְיִקְחוּ לִי תְּרוּמָה .1 מֵאֵת כָּל אִישׁ אֲשֶׁר יִדְּבֶנּוּ לִבּוֹ וְגוֹ'. רַבִּי חִיָּיא פָּתַח, כִּי יַעֲקֹב בָּחַר לוֹ יָהּ יִשְׂרָאֵל לִסְגוּלָתוֹ, כַּמָּה חֲבִיבִין יִשְׂרָאֵל קָמֵי קוּדְשָׁא בְּרִיךְ הוּא, דְּאִתְרְעֵי בְּהוּ, וּבָעָא לְאִתְדַּבְּקָא בְּהוּ, וּלְאִתְקַשְׁרָא עִמְּהוֹן. וְעָבֵד לְהוֹן

עַמָּא יְחִידָאי בְּעָלְמָא, דִּכְתִיב וּמִי כְעַמְּךָ כְּיִשְׂרָאֵל גּוֹי אֶחָד בָּאָרֶץ, וְאִינּוּן אִתְרְעוּ בֵּיהּ, וְאִתְקַשְּׁרָן בֵּיהּ. הה"ד, כִּי יַעֲקֹב בָּחַר לוֹ יָהּ. וּכְתִיב כִּי חֵלֶק יְיָ' עַמּוֹ. וְיָהַב לִשְׁאָר עַמִּין שׁוּלְטָנִין רַבְרְבָן מְמָנָן עֲלַיְיהוּ, וְהוּא נָטִיל לְחוּלָקֵיהּ יִשְׂרָאֵל.

**1.** "And Hashem spoke to Moses, saying, 'Speak to the children of Yisrael that they bring Me an offering, of every man whose heart prompts him…'" (Shemot 25:1-2). Rabbi Chiya opened the discussion saying: "For Yah has chosen Jacob to Himself, Yisrael for His peculiar possession" (Tehilim 135:4). How beloved are Yisrael before the Holy One, blessed be He, who desires them, and wants to be attached to them and connect Himself with them to make them a single nation in the world, as it is written: "And what one nation in the earth is like Your people Yisrael?" (II Shmuel 7:23). They wanted Him and were attached to Him, as it says, "For Yah has chosen Jacob to Himself" and, "For Hashem's portion is His people" (Devarim 32:9). He gave ministers and officers to the other nations and took Yisrael to His part.

**2.** ר"ש פָּתַח, מִי זֹאת הַנִּשְׁקָפָה כְּמוֹ שָׁחַר יָפָה כַלְּבָנָה בָּרָה כַּחַמָּה אֲיֻמָּה כַּנִּדְגָּלוֹת. מִי זֹאת, רָזָא דִּתְרֵין עָלְמִין מִתְחַבְּרָן כַּחֲדָא, וְדָא הוּא עוֹלָם וְעוֹלָם. מִ"י: הָא אוֹקִימְנָא דַּרְגָּא עִלָּאָה לְעֵילָּא, שֵׁירוּתָא דְּקַיְימָא בִּשְׁאֶלְתָּא, וְאִקְרֵי מִ"י, כד"א שְׂאוּ מָרוֹם עֵינֵיכֶם וּרְאוּ מִי בָרָא אֵלֶּה. זֹא"ת: דַּרְגָּא תַּתָּאָה לְתַתָּא, עָלְמָא תַּתָּאָה. וְתַרְוַוייהוּ, תְּרֵין עָלְמִין בְּחִבּוּרָא חֲדָא, בְּקִשּׁוּרָא חֲדָא כַּחֲדָא.

**2.** Rabbi Shimon opened the discussion saying: "Who is she that looks out like the dawn, fair as the moon, clear as the sun, and terrible as an army with banners?" (Shir Hashirim 6:10). "Who (Heb. *mi*) is she (Heb. *zot*)"? *Mi zot* is the secret of two worlds that unite, which are a world and a world. THIS IS, AS IS WRITTEN: "FOREVER AND EVER (LIT. 'FROM THE WORLD TO THE WORLD')" (I DIVREI HAYAMIM 16:36), WHICH ARE BINAH AND MALCHUT. 'Who' is the supernal level above, the beginning of all things which may be examined, and is named 'Mi', WHICH IS BINAH, as it says, "Lift up your eyes on high, and behold who created these" (Yeshayah 40:26). "She (Heb. *zot*)" is a lower level below, which is the lower world,

THAT IS TO SAY MALCHUT. They are two worlds joined by one connection, by one tie, together – THROUGH THE ELEVATION OF MALCHUT INTO BINAH, WHICH IS HOW SHE ATTAINED THE MOCHIN OF BINAH.

3. הַנִּשְׁקָפָה: כַּד מִתְחַבְּרָן תַּרְוַויְיהוּ כַּחֲדָא. כְּמוֹ שָׁחַר: כַּד בַּעְיָיא שַׁחֲרוּתָא לְאַנְהָרָא וּלְבָתַר אִתְנְהִיר כְּסִיהֲרָא, כַּד בָּטַשׁ בָּהּ נְהִירוּ דְשִׁמְשָׁא. וּלְבָתַר כְּשִׁמְשָׁא, כַּד קַיְימָא סִיהֲרָא בִּשְׁלִימוּ. אֲיוּמָה: תַּקִּיפָא, לְאַגָּנָא עַל כֹּלָּא. דְּהָא כְּדֵין אִית לָהּ שְׁלִימוּ וּתְקִיפוּ, לְמֶעְבַּד חֵילָא.

3. "That looks out": THAT IS, when both of them are attached as one, MALCHUT "looks out like the dawn," when the dawn wants to illuminate, and she is "fair as the moon" in which the sun's light, WHICH IS ZEIR ANPIN, illuminates. Then She is "clear as the sun," as clear as the sun's light when the moon is full; THAT IS, WHEN MALCHUT IS FACE-TO-FACE WITH ZEIR ANPIN WHICH IS CALLED 'SUN'. "Terrible as an army with banners": This is when She is strong to protect all, being at that point furnished with perfection and power to perform great feats.

4. וְנַטְלָא חֵילָא מֵעָלְמָא עִלָּאָה, עַל יְדָא דְיַעֲקֹב שְׁלֵימָא, דְּחַבֵּר לוֹן כַּחֲדָא. חַבֵּר לוֹן כַּחֲדָא לְעֵילָא. וְחִבֵּר לוֹן כַּחֲדָא לְתַתָּא. וּמִתַּמָּן נַפְקוּ, תְּרֵיסַר שִׁבְטִין קַדִּישִׁין, כְּגַוְונָא דִלְעֵילָא. יַעֲקֹב דַּהֲוָה שְׁלִים, אָעִיל רְחִימוּ בִּתְרֵין עָלְמִין, כְּמָה דְאוֹקִימְנָא. שְׁאָר בְּנֵי נָשָׁא דְעַבְדִין כְּדֵין מַגְלִין עֶרְיָין לְעֵילָא וְתַתָּא, גָּרִים דְּבָבוּ בִּתְרֵין עָלְמִין, וְגָרִים פְּרוּדָא, הה"ד וְאִשָּׁה אֶל אֲחֹתָהּ לֹא תִקַּח לִצְרֹ"ר, דְּאִתְעֲבִידוּ מָארֵי דְבָבוּ דָּא לְדָא.

4. And MALCHUT receives strength – THAT IS, MOCHIN – from the supernal word, WHICH IS BINAH, by means of Jacob, the whole man, who united them together. BY ELEVATING MAYIN NUKVIN ('FEMALE WATERS'), HE HAS ELEVATED MALCHUT INTO BINAH AND THEY GOT CONNECTED ONE WITH THE OTHER. He connected them together above, SO THAT BINAH RECEIVED THE SHAPE OF MALCHUT, AND IS THE SECRET OF LEAH. He also connected them together below, SO THAT MALCHUT

ACQUIRED THE SHAPE OF BINAH, AND IS THE SECRET OF RACHEL. And the twelve holy tribes came out from there in the likeness of above; IN OTHER WORDS, AS THE TWELVE ASPECTS THAT EXIST IN THE UPPER MALCHUT. Jacob, who was whole, brought love into the two worlds, as we have stated THAT HE WEDDED TWO SISTERS – LEAH AND RACHEL – WHO ARE THE SECRET OF THE TWO WORLDS OF BINAH AND MALCHUT. Other men who do such a thing merely commit sexual misconduct both above and below and cause antagonism in both worlds and engender separation BETWEEN ZEIR ANPIN AND LEAH AND BETWEEN ZEIR ANPIN AND RACHEL, SINCE HE UNITES WITH LEAH FROM THE CHEST ABOVE AND WITH RACHEL FROM THE CHEST BELOW. It is written: "Neither shall you take a wife to her sister, as her rival" (Vayikra 18:18), so that they became RIVALS AND full of hatred toward each other.

5. וְאִי תֵּימָא וַתְּקַנֵּא רָחֵל בַּאֲחוֹתָהּ. הָכִי הוּא וַדַּאי דְּהָא עָלְמָא תַּתָּאָה, כָּל תִּיאוּבְתֵּהּ לָאו אִיהוּ, אֶלָּא בְּגִין לְמֶיהֱוֵי כְּגַוְונָא דְּעָלְמָא עִלָּאָה, וּלְמֵירַת דּוּכְתָּהָא. בְּדוּכְתָּא אַחֲרָא קִנְאַת סוֹפְרִים אַסְגִּיאַת חָכְמְתָא, וְהָכָא קִנְאַת סוֹפְרִין, בְּגִין דְּאִית סֵפֶר וְסֵפֶר, אַסְגִּיאוּ מְשִׁיכוּ דְּחָכְמְתָא לְגַבַּיְיהוּ.

5. If you say, WHAT IS THE MEANING OF: "Rachel envied her sister" (Beresheet 30:1)? THE TEXT TALKS ABOUT THE TWO WORLDS, LEAH AND RACHEL, WHO ARE THE ASPECT OF BINAH AND MALCHUT, WHO ARE INCLUDED TOGETHER. WHAT KIND OF JEALOUSY IS THERE HERE? HE REPLIES: It is surely so, for the whole desire of the lower world, RACHEL, is to be in the semblance of the upper world, LEAH, WHO IS BINAH, and to inherit its position. In other places, IT STATES, 'When scholars compete, Wisdom mounts,' so THERE IS ALSO envy between scholars, since there are books and then there are *books,* ABA AND IMA, FROM WHOM CHOCHMAH IS DRAWN. THEREFORE, BY COMPETITION BETWEEN THESE SCHOLARS, they draw an enormous amount of Wisdom.

6. וְעַכ"ד, אֲפִילוּ יַעֲקֹב לָא אַשְׁלִים לְגַבַּיְיהוּ כַּדְקָא חֲזֵי. שְׁאָר בְּנֵי עָלְמָא, גַּרְמִין דְּבָבוּ, וְגַרְמִין פֵּרוּדָא, וּמְגַלִּין עֲרָיִין דְּכֹלָּא, עֲרָיִין דְּעֵילָּא וְתַתָּא. וּבְרָזָא דָּא אִית רָזָא דַּעֲרָיִין, עֲרָיִין דְּאִימָא וּבְרָתָא, וְכֹלָּא בְּרָזָא

חֲדָא. מִי זֹאת אִתְקְרוּן אֲחָתָן, בְּגִין דְּאִינּוּן בְּאַחְוָה וּבִרְחִימוּ, וּבְחִבּוּרָא
דִּרְעוּתָא. וְאִקְרוּן אִמָּא וּבְרַתָּא. מַאן דְּגַלֵּי עֶרְיָיתְהוֹן, לֵית לֵיהּ חוּלָקָא
לְעָלְמָא דְּאָתֵי, וְלֵית לֵיהּ חוּלָקָא בִּמְהֵימְנוּתָא.

6. Notwithstanding all this, Jacob could not even succeed in bringing perfect harmony between them as would be desirable, but other men caused enmity and separation through incest both above and below. In this secret is included the secret of nakedness, THAT IS the nakedness of the Mother and the Daughter, WHICH ARE BINAH AND MALCHUT, and everything, BOTH THE TWO SISTERS AND THE MOTHER AND HER DAUGHTER pertain to the same secret. This is because 'who (Heb. *mi*)' and 'she (Heb. *zot*)' are considered sisters, as they are united in love and sisterly affection and in the connection of intention. They are ALSO called 'Mother and Daughter', BECAUSE BINAH IS CALLED 'MOTHER' AND MALCHUT IS HER DAUGHTER. He who uncovers their nakedness, THAT IS TO SAY, THE JUDGMENTS THAT ARE IN THEM, shall have no portion in the World to Come, WHICH IS BINAH, and shall have no portion in the Faith, WHICH IS MALCHUT.

7. ת"ח, כִּי יַעֲקֹב בָּחַר לוֹ יָהּ, רָזָא עִלָּאָה לְעֵילָּא. כֵּיוָן דְּאַשְׁלִים, וְאִקְרֵי
יִשְׂרָאֵל, כְּדֵין לִסְגֻלָּתוֹ, נָטִיל כֹּלָּא בְּכָל סִטְרִין, וְנָטִיל לְעֵילָּא וְנָטִיל
לְתַתָּא, וְאִשְׁתְּלִים בְּכֹלָּא.

7. Come and see: "For Yah has chosen Jacob to Himself" is the supernal secret above, FOR HE CLEAVED ABOVE TO ABA AND IMA IN THEIR LIGHT OF CHASSADIM, WHICH ARE TERMED 'YAH (*YUD-HEI*)'. Since he has completed EVERYTHING and is now named Yisrael, he is His peculiar possession, WHICH IS MALCHUT CALLED 'PECULIAR POSSESSION', FOR THEN he takes everything in all the aspects, THE RIGHT AND THE LEFT. He takes above, IN ABA AND IMA WHO ILLUMINATE CHASSADIM, and he takes below, IN YISRAEL SABA AND TEVUNAH WHO ILLUMINATE CHOCHMAH. And he attains perfection in everything, BOTH IN CHOCHMAH AND IN THE CHASSADIM.

## 2. When the Holy One, blessed be He, created the world

### A Synopsis

Rabbi Shimon says that when the Holy One created the world He engraved on the upper and the lower worlds the letters of His Holy Name, which hold the secret of the supernal lights. The upper world is concealed in one of these letters; it ascends by means of the secret of infinity, and from this concealment emerges a thin and hidden light. In this light exists its counterpart, the glorious light of creation. When first it was struck, the supernal world emerged and was filled with a light so great that it would be too terrifying for those below to see. In this unknown concealed world live six thousand 'myriads' – which are supernal inhabitants and hosts and camps. Only Jacob, who possessed Malchut as his own, received permission to rise to the higher world. And, we learn, Malchut is illuminated by the light of Bina from above. The lower world always has a secret desire for the higher world, being unable to experience it directly as Jacob did.

### The Relevance of this Passage

The letters inscribed below connect us to letters of the Holy Name ‏.ה.ו.ה.י‎, which embody the primordial forces of Creation. This awesome luminosity is normally far too intense for a mortal to behold. However, through Jacob – who personifies control over physical existence – we have a key to unlock the gate to the upper world. Through Jacob, we acquire the vessel necessary to hold this divine energy that shines so brightly in the distant heavens.

‏8. א״ר שִׁמְעוֹן, הָא תָּנֵינָן, דְּכַד בָּרָא קוּדְשָׁא בְּרִיךְ הוּא עָלְמָא, גָּלִיף בְּגִלִיפוֹי דְּרָזֵי מְהֵימְנוּתָא, גּוֹ טְהִירִין בְּרָזִין עִלָּאִין, וְגָלִיף לְעֵילָא וְגָלִיף לְתַתָּא, וְכֹלָּא בְּרָזָא חֲדָא, בְּרָזָא דְּגִלוּפֵי דִּשְׁמָא קַדִּישָׁא ידו״ד, דְּשָׁלִיט בְּאַתְוֵוֹי עֵילָא וְתַתָּא. וּבְרָזָא דָּא אִשְׁתַּכְלָלוּ עָלְמִין, עָלְמָא עִלָּאָה וְעָלְמָא תַּתָּאָה.‎

**8.** Rabbi Shimon said: We learned that when the Holy One, blessed be He, WHO IS BINAH, created the world, WHICH IS MALCHUT, He engraved His engravings of the secret of the Faith, WHICH IS MALCHUT, into the lights which are the secret of the supernal beings. And He engraved above, IN BINAH, and engraved below, IN MALCHUT; everything is in the secret of the engraving of the Holy Name, YUD HEI VAV HEI that controls by means of its letters above and below, THAT IS, IN BINAH AND MALCHUT, WHICH

ARE THE FIRST *Hei* AND THE LAST *Hei* OF YUD HEI VAV HEI, SINCE
BOTH OF THEM ARE OF THE SAME SHAPE, WHICH IS *Hei*. The worlds
were brought to completion by means of this secret, both the superior world,
WHICH IS BINAH, and the lower world, WHICH IS MALCHUT.

9. עָלְמָא עִלָּאָה אִשְׁתַּכְלַל בְּרָזָא דְּאָת י', נְקוּדָה עִלָּאָה קַדְמָאָה,
דְּנָפְקָא מִגּוֹ דְּסָתִים וְגָנִיז דְּלָא יְדִיעַ, וְלָא קַיְּימָא לְמִנְדַּע, וְלָא אִתְיְידַע
כְּלָל, סְלִיקוּ דְּרָזָא דְּאֵין סוֹף, וּמִגּוֹ סְתִימוּ דָּא, נָהִיר נְהִירוּ חַד דָּקִיק
וְסָתִים, כָּלִיל בְּגַוֵּיהּ כְּלָלָא דְּכָל נְהוֹרִין. וּבְהַהוּא נְהִירוּ נָהִיר סָתִים, בָּטַשׁ
בֵּיהּ מַאן דְּלָא בָּטַשׁ. נָהִיר בֵּיהּ מַאן דְּלָא נָהִיר. וּכְדֵין, אַפִּיק חַד
נְהִירוּ, דְּאִיהוּ עֲדוּנָא לְעֲדוּנָא, לְאִשְׁתַּעְשְׁעָא, לְאִתְגַּנְזָא נְהִירוּ דָּקִיק,
וְסָתִים בְּגוֹ הַהוּא נְהִירוּ.

9. The upper world is included in the secret of the letter *Yud* OF YUD HEI
VAV HEI, WHICH INCLUDES ARICH ANPIN AND ABA AND IMA, NAMELY
the first upper dot, WHICH IS ARICH ANPIN that emerges from the
concealed, the hidden and that which is not known and is not known at all
and will not be known. It ascends by MEANS OF the secret of infinity, THE
PARTZUF OF ATIK, and from this concealment, FROM ARICH ANPIN, shines
a thin and hidden light WHICH IS SUPERNAL ABA AND IMA THAT HAVE
TWO ASPECTS OF YESOD: 1) A NARROW PATH AND 2) A CONCEALED WAY,
including in itself the generality of all the lights. And in this concealed WAY,
THAT IS IN ABA AND IMA, one strikes it who did not yet strike BEFORE,
WHEN IT WAS IN SUPERNAL ABA AND IMA. That which did not illuminate in
him now illuminates in him. It then produced one light, which is a delight of
delight (NAMELY CHOCHMAH OF CHOCHMAH), AND IT IS for pleasure, and
to hide the thin light, which is concealed in that light.

10. וְהַהוּא נְהִירוּ דְּאִיהוּ עֲדוּנָא לְעֲדוּנָא, סָתִים, אִתְקַיְּימוּ וְאִשְׁתַּכְלָלוּ
בֵּיהּ שִׁית רְשִׁימִין, דְּלָא יְדִיעָן, בַּר לְהַהוּא נְהוֹרָא דָּקִיק כַּד עָאל
לְאִתְגַּנְזָא, עֲדוּנָא בְּעֲדוּנָא נָהִיר בִּנְהִירוּ.

10. Within this light, which is delight of delight and is concealed, six
unknown impressions materialized and were completed THROUGH THE
CENTRAL COLUMN. THEY ARE NOT REVEALED IN ORDER TO ILLUMINATE,

except when that thin light OF ABA AND IMA enters to be concealed, FOR THEN the delight of delight illuminates in its light.

**11.** וְהַאי נְהִירוּ דְּנָפַק מִגּוֹ נְהִירוּ דָּקִיק אִיהוּ דְחִילָא וְאֵמְתָּנִי וְתַקִּיפָא יַתִּירָא, וְאִתְפַּשַּׁט הַאי וְאִתְעֲבֵיד עָלְמָא חֲדָא, דְּנָהִיר לְכָל עָלְמִין. עָלְמָא סְתִימָא דְּלָא יְדִיעַ כְּלָל, וּבְגַוֵּיהּ דַּיְירִין שִׁית רִבּוֹא אֶלֶף, דְּאִינוּן דַּיְירִין וְחֵילִין וּמַשִׁירְיָין עִלָּאִין.

**11.** This light that emerges TO THOSE BELOW from the thin light is awesome and frightful and very strong. AND THIS THIN LIGHT spreads and becomes one world, WHICH IS SUPERNAL ABA AND IMA that illuminates all the worlds. It is a concealed world that is wholly unknown and 60,000,000 of supernal inhabitants and hosts and camps live in them.

**12.** וְכֵיוָן דְּאַפִּיק לוֹן וְאִשְׁתַּכְלָלוּ כַּחֲדָא כְּדֵין אִיהוּ חִבּוּרָא חֲדָא. וְאִינוּן רָזָא דְאָת וי״ו, דְּאִתְחַבַּר בְּהַהוּא עָלְמָא סְתִימָא, וּכְדֵין כְּתִיב, כִּי יַעֲקֹב בָּחַר לוֹ יָהּ. כַּד נָפִיק וי״ו, וְאִשְׁכְּלַל מִגּוֹ יָ״ה, כְּדֵין יִשְׂרָאֵל לִסְגֻלָּתוֹ.

**12.** Once YUD brought them out, they become one joint, YUD-HEI. They are the secret of the letter Vav, which has become attached to that concealed world; AND THIS VAV ALLUDES TO JACOB, as it is written: "For Yah has chosen Jacob to Himself." JACOB CLEAVED UNTO THE MENTIONED NAME YUD-HEI. When the Vav emerges and becomes accomplished through Yud-Hei, MEANING THAT THE LETTER VAV HAS BECOME INDEPENDENT WITH THE MOCHIN OF YUD-HEI AND HAS THE FIRST THREE SFIROT, then it is written: "Yisrael for His peculiar possession," AND IS CALLED YISRAEL RATHER THAN JACOB.

**13.** שְׁאָר בְּנֵי עָלְמָא, לָא אִתְיְיהִיב לוֹן רְשׁוּ לְסַלְּקָא הָכִי, אֶלָּא לִסְגֻלָּתוֹ, אֲתַר דְּנָטִיל וְכָנִישׁ כֹּלָּא. וְדָא אִיהוּ דַּרְגָּא לְתַתָּא, וּמִגּוֹ דָא, נָטְלִין לְעֵילָא, בִּסְתִימוּ דִרְעוּ, אֲבָל לָא בְּאִתְגַּלְיָא, כְּמָה דְנָטִיל יַעֲקֹב, הֲהֲ״ד וְיִקְחוּ לִי תְּרוּמָה.

**13.** None of the other people in the world, EXCEPT FOR JACOB, received permission to rise TO BINAH, TO CLEAVE UNTO YUD-HEI LIKE JACOB, but

to His peculiar possession ALONE, which is the place that receives and gathers everything, which is the lower level, NAMELY MALCHUT. From within MALCHUT they receive THE LIGHT OF CHASSADIM of above IN BINAH, WHICH IS THE ASPECT OF LEAH in a hidden desire, but not openly as Jacob does. This is the meaning of: "That they bring Me an offering."

## 3. "How great is Your goodness, which You have laid up"

### A Synopsis

Rabbi Yehuda opens the discussion by reciting this verse: "How great is your goodness, which You have laid up for those who fear You; which You have performed for those who trust in You in the sight of the sons of men!" He goes on to discuss the various levels and worlds and he reveals the code words that speak of their wondrous roles in the process of creation. For instance, there is the highest level, which is 'the secret of the higher world,' and is called "who"; then there is the lowest level, which is 'the secret of the lower world', and is called "what." Although the Sfirah of Chochmah is connected to the lower world through the quality of Binah, it does not become revealed until it is completed here in Malchut, the earthly kingdom. The word "what" is "mah," we're told, which is contained in Chochmah.

Next, we learn that the foundation of the world is laid upon goodness that is distributed by God, and the Light that is concealed in this foundation is a testament to the goodness with which He crafted the whole world as well as the souls and spirits. The tabernacle was made with the same divine secret as the secret of the whole world – the image of the world above manifested in the world below. This, we're told, is Understanding manifested in the Kingdom.

### The Relevance of this Passage

We come to this earth for "what" we may learn, and in the university of this universe, we study to grow, transform, and become perfected. This endeavor is the manner in which we express our Godly nature, and thus become (co)-creators of our wisdom and Light, which are purposely concealed in this realm. Our meditation here completes our own unique role in creation: the tasks that we have been sent into the world to perform in order to facilitate our personal transformation.

In addition, the vast mysteries of the Tabernacle are revealed here. By virtue of all this great energy, the tasks of all mankind are now completed and the final correction is achieved through the Light of the Zohar. World peace and immortality are now attained in a kind, compassionate, and merciful process.

14. וְיִקְחוּ לִי תְּרוּמָה. רַבִּי יְהוּדָה פָּתַח, מַה רַב טוּבְךָ אֲשֶׁר צָפַנְתָּ לִירֵאֶיךָ פָּעַלְתָּ לַחוֹסִים בָּךְ נֶגֶד בְּנֵי אָדָם. הַאי קְרָא הָא אוּקְמוּהָ וְאִתְּמַר. אֲבָל רָזָא דָּא, הָא אוּקְמוּהָ בּוּצִינָא קַדִּישָׁא, גּוֹ רָזִין עִלָּאִין.

**14.** "That they bring Me an offering" (Shemot 25:1-2): Rabbi Yehuda

opened the discussion with the verse, "How great is Your goodness, which
You have laid up for those who fear You; which You have performed for
those who trust in You in the sight of the sons of men!" (Tehilim 31:20).
This passage has been explained and we have learned it. This secret was
established by the holy luminary as part of supernal secrets.

15. דַּרְגָּא עִלָּאָה, דְּאִיהוּ רָזָא דְּעָלְמָא עִלָּאָה, אִקְרֵי מִ"י. דַּרְגָּא תַּתָּאָה,
דְּאִיהוּ רָזָא דְּעָלְמָא תַּתָּאָה, אִקְרֵי מַ"ה. וְתָנֵינָן, אַל תִּקְרֵי מַ"ה אֶלָּא
מֵאָה, בְּגִין דְּכָל דַּרְגִּין עִלָּאִין בְּאַשְׁלָמוּתְהוֹן הָכָא אִינּוּן.

**15.** The highest level, which is the secret of the highest world, NAMELY
BINAH, is called 'mi (Eng. 'who')'. The lower level, which is the secret of
the lower world, WHICH IS MALCHUT, is called 'mah (Eng. 'what')'. We
learned THAT IT IS WRITTEN: "WHAT (HEB. 'MAH') DOES HASHEM YOUR
ELOHIM REQUIRE OF YOU?" (DEVARIM 10:12). Do not pronounce it as
'mah', but rather as 'me'ah (Eng. 'one hundred')'', because all the levels are
sublime in perfection THERE ARE FIFTY OF THEM, here IN MALCHUT.
THEREFORE, IT IS CALLED 'ONE HUNDRED'.

16. תּוּ אֲמַאי אִקְרֵי מַ"ה. אֶלָּא אע"ג דְּמָשִׁיכוּ עִלָּאָה אִתְמְשַׁךְ, לָא
אִתְגַּלְיָא עַד דְּאִשְׁתְּלִים הָכָא, דְּאִיהוּ אֲתָר סוֹפָא דְּכָל דַּרְגִּין, סוֹפָא
דְּאַמְשָׁכוּתָא דְּכֹלָּא, וְקַיְּימָא בְּאִתְגַּלְיָא. וְאע"ג דְּאִתְגַּלְיָא יַתִּיר מִכֹּלָּא,
קַיְּימָא לִשְׁאֵלָא, מַ"ה. מַה חָמֵית, מַה יָדַעְתְּ, כד"א כִּי לֹא רְאִיתֶם כָּל
תְּמוּנָה.

**16.** Another REASON why MALCHUT is called 'Mah': Although the pull
from above OF CHOCHMAH is conducted BY WAY OF THE HIGHER LEVELS,
BINAH AND ZEIR ANPIN, it is not revealed until it is completed here IN
MALCHUT. This is the last place of all the levels and the end of all the
continuance, and it stands revealed IN THE ILLUMINATION OF CHOCHMAH.
Even though it is more revealed than all of them, one is allowed to ask what
(Heb. mah), as in what did you see and what do you know, as is written:
"For you saw no manner of form" (Devarim 4:15).

17. וּבְגִין כָּךְ, מָה, רַב טוּבְךָ, דָּא אִיהוּ יְסוֹדָא דְּעָלְמָא, דְּאִקְרֵי רַב טוּב.

כד"א וְרַב טוּב לְבֵית יִשְׂרָאֵל בְּגִין דְּהַאי רַב טוּב. אוֹר קַדְמָאָה, אִקְרֵי טוֹב סְתָם, וְהָכָא כְּלִילָן דְּכַר וְנוּקְבָּא כַּחֲדָא. אֲשֶׁר צָפַנְתָּ, דְּהַאי אִתְגְּנִיז, כִּגְוּוֹנָא דְּאוֹר קַדְמָאָה, דְּאִתְגְּנִיז וְאִתְטַמַּר. פָּעַלְתָּ: דְּהָכָא אִיהוּ אוּמָנוּתָא דְּכֹלָּא, אוּמָנוּתָא דְּכָל עָלְמָא, אוּמָנוּתָא דְּנִשְׁמָתִין וְרוּחִין.

**17.** Therefore, it is written: "How (Heb. *mah*) great is Your goodness," WHERE MAH IS MALCHUT. "How great is Your goodness" is the foundation of the world, NAMELY YESOD OF ZEIR ANPIN, which is called 'great goodness', as written: "And the great goodness toward the House of Yisrael" (Yeshayah 63:7). This is because the first light THAT IS INCLUDED IN YESOD is merely called 'good'. Male and female are included here, SINCE THE FEMALE, WHO IS ALSO CALLED 'MAH' (SINCE CHOCHMAH IS REVEALED IN HER), IS ALSO INCLUDED HERE, AS IT IS WRITTEN: "HOW GREAT IS YOUR GOODNESS." IT IS THEREFORE WRITTEN "GREAT" BECAUSE IT POINTS TOWARD THE ILLUMINATION OF CHOCHMAH. "Which You have laid up": This light is concealed, just as the first light was hidden and kept FOR THE RIGHTEOUS. "You have performed," because here, IN MALCHUT THAT IS CALLED 'MAH', BECAUSE OF THE INCLUSION OF BINAH IN IT, is the craftsmanship of everything, the craftsmanship of the whole world and the craftsmanship of the souls and spirits.

18. בְּרָזָא דָּא עָבֵיד קוּדְשָׁא בְּרִיךְ הוּא אוּמָנוּתָא דְּכָל עָלְמָא, וְרָזָא דָּא בְּרֵאשִׁית בָּרָא אֱלֹהִים אֵת הַשָּׁמַיִם וְאֵת הָאָרֶץ. בְּרָזָא דָּא אִתְעֲבֵיד מַשְׁכְּנָא וְאִתְבְּנֵי, דְּאִיהוּ בְּדִיּוּקְנָא דְּעָלְמָא דִּלְעֵילָא, וּבְדִיּוּקְנָא דְּעָלְמָא תַּתָּאָה, הה"ד וְיִקְחוּ לִי תְּרוּמָה. לִי. תְּרוּמָה. תְּרֵין דַּרְגִּין, דְּאִינּוּן חַד, דְּמִתְחַבְּרָן כַּחֲדָא.

**18.** The Holy One, blessed be He, made the craftsmanship of the whole world, in this secret OF BINAH BEING COMPRISED IN MALCHUT. This is the secret of the verse: "In the beginning Elohim created the heaven and the earth" (Beresheet 1:1). The tabernacle was made and built by this means, which is the image of the world above, WHICH IS BINAH, and in the image of the lower world, WHICH IS MALCHUT. This is what is meant by: "That they bring Me an offering," and "Me an offering" ARE two levels, BINAH AND MALCHUT, which are one when combined together.

## 4. The balsam tree and the palanquin

### A Synopsis

Rabbi Shimon, Rabbi Elazar, Rabbi Aba and Rabbi Yosi are sitting one day under the pleasant shade of some trees. Rabbi Shimon opens the discussion by saying, "King Solomon made himself a palanquin from the woods of Levanon." He goes on to speak of the palanquin as 'the lower chamber', which God called 'the Garden of Eden', and built for Himself in order to commune with the souls of the righteous – for they are recorded there and it is there too that they are crowned. Disembodied souls, we're told, are filled with the delights of the river of the pure balsam tree. Rabbi Shimon states that the balsam tree is the upper chamber, covered and hidden, which represents Binah. 'Palanquin' is the lower chamber that has no support until it is held up by the upper chamber.

A discussion between the rabbis follows on the secret of one hundred, which is hidden in the names for 'Palanquin' and 'Balsam tree', whose forms are comparable. Those who do not have a body in this world are suckled by the river of light that emerges from the pure balsam, while those who do have a body delight in the palanquin, which is the earthly garden. Rabbi Shimon then says that "King Solomon" means Zeir Anpin, God, with his attributes, which are the male world. The king without attributes refers to the Messiah, the female world. He concludes by saying that "The cedars of Levanon that He planted," and of which the palanquin was built and completed, were Chesed, Gvurah, Tiferet, Netzach, Hod and Yesod.

### The Relevance of this Passage

This marvelously informative discussion speaks to us of the two forms of the Garden of Eden that God has made for us: the garden on earth, where we may rest and be comforted, and the higher garden that awaits us after death, where we may commune with Him. Our souls give to and take from the qualities of the garden, emitting fragrance from our good deeds and in turn absorbing the exquisite fragrance of the garden.

By our thoughtful reading, our entire world is nourished by His Light. Our life is scented with the aroma of the garden, and the fragrance of Eden now emanates throughout the world, ushering in the arrival of the Messianic age.

19. וְיִקְחוּ לִי תְּרוּמָה וְגוֹ'. רַבִּי שִׁמְעוֹן וְרַבִּי אֶלְעָזָר וְר' אַבָּא וְר' יוֹסִי, הֲווֹ יַתְבֵי יוֹמָא חַד, תְּחוֹת אִילָנֵי, בְּבִקְעָתָא גַּבֵּי יַמָּא דְגִנּוֹסָר. אָמַר רַבִּי

שִׁמְעוֹן, כַּמָּה יָאֶה צִלָּא דָּא, דְּחַפְיָא עֲלָן מִגּוֹ אִילָנֵי, וַאֲנָן צְרִיכִין לְאַעְטְרָא הַאי אֲתָר בְּמִלֵּי דְּאוֹרַיְיתָא.

**19.** "That they bring Me an offering..." (Shemot 25:2): Rabbi Shimon, Rabbi Elazar, Rabbi Aba, and Rabbi Yosi were sitting one day under some trees in the valley next to the Sea of Genosar, THAT IS, THE SEA OF GALILEE. Rabbi Shimon said: How pleasant is this shade from the trees that covers us, and we are obliged to adorn this place with the words of Torah.

20. פָּתַח רַבִּי שִׁמְעוֹן וְאָמַר, אַפִּרְיוֹן עָשָׂה לוֹ הַמֶּלֶךְ שְׁלֹמֹה מֵעֲצֵי הַלְּבָנוֹן. הַאי קְרָא הָא אוֹקִימְנָא לֵיהּ וְאִתְּמַר, אֲבָל אַפִּרְיוֹן, דָּא הֵיכָלָא דִּלְתַתָּא, דְּאִיהוּ כְּגַוְונָא דְּהֵיכָלָא עִלָּאָה, וְקוּדְשָׁא בְּרִיךְ הוּא קָרָא לֵיהּ גִּנְתָּא דְּעֵדֶן, דְּאִיהוּ נָטַע לֵיהּ לַהֲנָאָתֵיהּ, וְכִסּוּפָא דִּילֵיהּ לְאִשְׁתַּעְשְׁעָא בֵּיהּ גּוֹ אִינּוּן נִשְׁמָתִין דְּצַדִּיקַיָּיא, דְּתַמָּן כֻּלְּהוּ קַיְימִין וּרְשִׁימִין בְּגַוֵּיהּ. אִינּוּן נִשְׁמָתִין דְּלֵית לוֹן גּוּפָא בְּהַאי עָלְמָא, כֻּלְּהוּ סַלְּקִין וּמִתְעַטְּרָן תַּמָּן, וְאִית לוֹן דּוּכְתִּין לְמֶחֱמֵי, לְאִתְעַנְּגָא גּוֹ עֲנוּגָא עִלָּאָה דְּאִקְרֵי נֹעַם יְיָ'. וְתַמָּן אִתְמַלְּיָין מִכָּל כִּסּוּפִין דְּנַהֲרֵי דְּאֲפַרְסְמוֹנָא דַּכְיָא.

**20.** Rabbi Shimon opened the discussion saying: "King Solomon made himself a palanquin from the woods of Lebanon" (Shir Hashirim 3:9). We have established and learned this passage. Still, palanquin is the lower chamber, MALCHUT, which is similar to the upper chamber, BINAH. The Holy One, blessed be He, called it the Garden of Eden, which He plants for His pleasure, and His desire is to amuse Himself in it with the souls of the righteous, for they all stand there and are recorded there. The souls that do not have a body in this world all ascend and are crowned there. They have places to see and to delight in the supernal delight that is called the pleasantness of Hashem, and there they are filled with all the delights of the river of the pure balsam tree.

21. אֲפַרְסְמוֹן: דָּא הֵיכָלָא עִלָּאָה טְמִירָא גְּנִיזָא. אַפִּרְיוֹן: דָּא הֵיכָלָא דִּלְתַתָּא, דְּלֵית בֵּיהּ סָמֶךְ, עַד דְּאִסְתְּמִיךְ מִגּוֹ הֵיכָלָא עִלָּאָה. וּבְגִין כָּךְ אָת סָמֶךְ אִיהוּ סָתִים בְּכָל סִטְרוֹי, כְּגַוְונָא דָּא אָת ס סְתִימָא.

**21.** The balsam tree is the upper chamber, which is covered and hidden, WHICH IS BINAH. The palanquin is the lower chamber, MALCHUT, which has no support (Heb. *somech*) until it is supported from the upper chamber. Therefore, the letter *Samech* is closed on all sides, like a square. It is a closed letter.

**22.** מַה בֵּין הַאי לְהַאי. אֶלָּא בְּשַׁעֲתָא דְּסָתִים וְאִתְגְּנִיז בְּגַוֵּיהּ, גּוֹ נְהוֹרָא עִלָּאָה לְעֵילָּא, כְּדֵין אִיהִי קַיְּימָא, בְּדִיּוּקְנָא דְּאָת סָמֶךְ סָתִים בְּגַוֵּיהּ, וְאִתְגְּנִיז בֵּיהּ, לְסַלְּקָא לְעֵילָּא. וּבְשַׁעֲתָא דְּהַדְרָא וְיָתְבָא רְבִיעָא עַל בְּנִין לְתַתָּא לְיַנְקָא לוֹן, כְּדֵין אִיהִי קַיְּימָא בְּדִיּוּקְנָא דְּאָת ם רְבִיעָא סְתִימָא לְגוֹ אַרְבַּע סִטְרִין דְּעָלְמָא.

**22.** What is the difference BETWEEN THE BALSAM TREE AND THE PALANQUIN? When the supernal light above is hidden and concealed in it, BINAH assumes in the form of the letter *Samech*, IN WHICH THE LIGHT is concealed. It is hidden in it in order to ascend above. When she returns and settles, she sits over her children below to nurse them. Then it dons the form of the letter final *Mem*, which lies and is closed to all four directions of the world, WHICH ARE CHESED, GVURAH, TIFERET, AND MALCHUT, FOR CHESED AND GVURAH ARE SOUTH AND NORTH AND TIFERET AND MALCHUT ARE EAST AND WEST.

**23.** וְעַל דָּא, דָּא אִיהוּ אֲפַרְסָמוֹן, וְדָא הוּא אַפִּרְיוֹן. וּבַאֲתָר תְּרֵין אַתְוָון ס"מ, קַיְּימָא י', בְּרָזָא דִּבְרִית, דְּאִיהוּ זַמִּין לְנַטְלָא כֹּלָּא, רָזָא דְּאִינּוּן מְאָה בִּרְכָאן, שִׁתִּין וְאַרְבְּעִין. שִׁתִּין, לָקֳבֵל שִׁית סְטְרִין, דְּנַפְקֵי מֵאָת ס'. אַרְבְּעִין, לָקֳבֵל ד' סְטְרֵי עָלְמָא, וְכֹלָּא אַשְׁלִימוּ לִמְאָה. וְאָת יוֹ"ד, אִיהוּ אַשְׁלִים לְרָזָא דִּמְאָה, כְּגַוְונָא דִּלְעֵילָּא. וע"ד, דָּא אֲפַרְסָמוֹן, וְדָא אַפִּרְיוֹן.

**23.** Hence, one is a balsam tree and the other a palanquin, BECAUSE A PALANQUIN (HEB. *APIRION*), WHICH IS MALCHUT, IS PERFECTED SIMILAR TO THE BALSAM TREE (HEB. *APHARSEMON*), WHICH IS BINAH, AND THEY HAVE THE SAME FORM instead of the two letters, *Samech* and final *Mem*, THAT ARE IN APHARSEMON, there is a *Yud* IN APIRION, in the secret of the covenant, and it will eventually receive all FROM THE *SAMECH*

(= 60) AND FINAL *MEM* (= 40), which is the secret of the one hundred blessings. *Samech* and final *Mem* ARE sixty and forty, with sixty corresponding to the six corners that emerge from the *Samech* and forty corresponding to the four directions of the world. The letter *Yud* OF APIRION ALSO completes the secret of one hundred, THAT IS, *YUD* (= 10) SFIROT, EACH COMPOSED OF TEN - like the supernal *SAMECH* AND FINAL *MEM* IN APHARSEMON - WHICH IS BINAH. Therefore, one is apharsemon and the other an apirion, AND THEIR FORMS ARE EQUAL!

24. אִינּוּן נַהֲרֵי נָפְקִין מֵאֲפַרְסָמוֹן דָּא, וְנִשְׁמָתִין עִלָּאִין, דְּלֵית לוֹן גּוּפָא בְּהַאי עָלְמָא, יַנְקִין מֵהַהוּא נְהִירוּ דְּנָפִיק מֵאִינּוּן נַהֲרֵי אֲפַרְסָמוֹנָא דַּכְיָא, וּמִתְעַנְּגֵי בְּעִנּוּגָא דָּא עִלָּאָה, וְנִשְׁמָתִין דְּאִית לוֹן גּוּפָא בְּהַאי עָלְמָא, סַלְקִין וְיַנְקִין מֵהַהוּא נְהִירוּ דְּאַפִּרְיוֹן דָּא, וְנַחְתִּין. וְאִלֵּין יַהֲבֵי וְנַטְלֵי. יַהֲבֵי רֵיחָא, מֵאִינּוּן עוֹבָדִין דְּכַשְׁרָאן, דְּמִשְׁתַּדְּלֵי בְּהוּ בְּהַאי עָלְמָא. וְנַטְלֵי מֵהַהוּא רֵיחָא דְּאִשְׁתְּאַר בֵּיהּ בְּגִנְתָּא, כד"א כְּרֵיחַ שָׂדֶה אֲשֶׁר בֵּרְכוֹ יְיָ', רֵיחָא דְּאִשְׁתְּאַר בֵּיהּ בְּהַהוּא חַקְלָא. וְכֻלְּהוּ קַיְימֵי בְּהַהִיא גִּנְתָּא, אִלֵּין מִתְעַנְּגֵי לְעֵילָּא, וְאִלֵּין מִתְעַנְּגֵי לְתַתָּא.

24. They are the rivers that emerge from that balsam, and the supernal souls that do not have a body in this world nurse from the light that emerges from the pure balsam and delight in this supernal delight. The souls that have a body in this world ascend and nurse from this palanquin and descend. These give and take, giving the fragrance from those good deeds in which they endeavored in this world and taking from that fragrance that remained in the Garden of Eden, as it is written: "Like the smell of a field which Hashem has blessed" (Beresheet 27:27), meaning the fragrance that remained in that field. They all stand in that Garden. Those THAT DO NOT HAVE A BODY IN THIS WORLD delight above IN THE BALSAM WHICH IS BINAH IN THE GARDEN, and those THAT HAVE A BODY IN THIS WORLD, delight below IN THE PALANQUIN, WHICH IS MALCHUT IN THE GARDEN.

25. עָשָׂה לוֹ הַמֶּלֶךְ שְׁלֹמֹה, עָשָׂה לוֹ, לְגַרְמֵיהּ. וְאִי תֵּימָא, הָא נִשְׁמָתִין דְּצַדִּיקַיָּא מִשְׁתַּעַשְׁעָן בֵּיהּ, וְאַתְּ אַמְרַתְּ עָשָׂה לוֹ. הָכִי הוּא וַדַּאי. בְּגִין דְּהַאי אַפִּרְיוֹן וְכָל אִינּוּן נִשְׁמָתִין דְּצַדִּיקַיָּא, כֻּלְּהוּ קַיְימֵי לְאִשְׁתַּעְשְׁעָא

בְּהוּ קוּדְשָׁא בְּרִיךְ הוּא. הַמֶּלֶךְ שְׁלֹמֹה, מַלְכָּא דִשְׁלָמָא דִילֵיה, וְדָא אִיהוּ מַלְכָּא עִלָּאָה הַמֶּלֶךְ סְתָם, דָּא מַלְכָּא מְשִׁיחָא. דָּא עָלְמָא דִּדְכוּרָא, וְדָא עָלְמָא דְּנוּקְבָּא. מֵעֲצֵי הַלְּבָנוֹן אִינּוּן אִילָנִין נְטִיעָן, דְּעָקַר לוֹן קוּדְשָׁא בְּרִיךְ הוּא, וְשָׁתִיל לוֹן בַּאֲתָר אַחֲרָא, וְאַלֵּין אִקְרוּן אַרְזֵי לְבָנוֹן, כד"א, אַרְזֵי לְבָנוֹן אֲשֶׁר נָטָע. וְלָא אִתְבְּנֵי הַאי אַפִּרְיוֹן, וְלָא אִשְׁתַּכְלָל אֶלָּא בְּהוּ.

**25.** "King Solomon made himself," for his own benefit. HE QUESTIONS: The souls of the pious delight with it, yet you say "made himself"? HE ANSWERS: It is certainly so, because this palanquin and these souls of the righteous all exist so that the Holy One, blessed be He, can amuse Himself with them, SO WE SEE THAT HE MADE IT FOR HIMSELF. "King Solomon" (Heb. *Shlomo*) is the King that the peace (Heb. *shalom*) is His, namely the supernal King, ZEIR ANPIN. 'The King' without attributes refers to Messiah, WHICH IS MALCHUT. The one is the male world and the other the female world. "From the woods of Lebanon": THESE ARE the trees and plants that the Holy One, blessed be He, uprooted and planted in a different place. THEY ARE THE SEVEN SFIROT OF MALE AND FEMALE THAT WERE IN MALCHUT WITH THE QUALITY OF JUDGMENT, WHICH HE UPROOTED AND REPASTED IN BINAH, IN THE SECRET OF MALCHUT OF THE QUALITY OF MERCY. These are called the cedars of Lebanon, as it is written: "The cedars of Lebanon that He planted" (Tehilim 104:16). This palanquin was built and completed with them alone.

## 5. "The woods of Lebanon" are the six days of Creation

### A Synopsis

Here we read an alternative explanation of "the woods of Lebanon" – that they are the six days of creation. The six attributes of Chesed, Gvurah, Tiferet, Netzach, Hod and Yesod all in their turn entered and mated with the palanquin, producing in this fashion the manifested world in six days. Then, we learn, this palanquin became sanctified until it ascended the crown of rest and was given a supernal name, 'Shabbat'. Rabbi Shimon tells us that we have to see we are sitting in the shadow of The Creator within that palanquin.

### The Relevance of this Passage

Again and again in the Zohar, we see that each interpretation of Scripture leads us back to the knowledge that God has placed His own qualities into the creation that He made for us. From our mundane perspective, the upper world consists of six Sfirot [dimensions] rolled into one, called *Zeir Anpin*. This realm is the repository of all our wisdom and fulfillment. The love we feel, the joy we experience, the serenity we seek, all originate there.

*Zeir Anpin* also embodies the supernal Light of Shabbat. Access to this realm can be achieved through inner transformation and various tools, such as the Zohar. On Shabbat, however, this Light is freely given as a gift to all Creation. These words of Zohar open up the gates to Zeir Anpin, causing the Light of the cosmic Sabbath to shine the moment our eyes fall upon them.

26. תּוּ מֵעֲצֵי הַלְּבָנוֹן, אִלֵּין שִׁית יוֹמִין דִּבְרֵאשִׁית דְּכָל יוֹמָא וְיוֹמָא, מְסַדֵּר בְּהַאי אַפִּרְיוֹן, סִדּוּרָא דְּאִתְחֲזֵי לֵיהּ: סִדּוּרָא קַדְמָאָה. אִתְנְגִיד מִסִּטְרָא דִּימִינָא, אוֹר קַדְמָאָה דְּאִתְגְּנִיז, וְאִתְנְטִיל מִסִּטְרָא דִּימִינָא, וְעָאל בְּהַאי אַפִּרְיוֹן עַל יְדָא דִּיסוֹדָא חַד, וְעָבִיד בֵּיהּ שִׁמּוּשָׁא. לְבָתַר אַפִּיק הַהוּא אַפִּרְיוֹן חַד דְּיוּקְנָא כְּגַוְונָא דְּהַאי אוֹר, וְדָא הוּא רָזָא דִּכְתִיב, יְהִי אוֹר וַיְהִי אוֹר. כֵּיוָן דְּאָמַר יְהִי אוֹר, אַמַּאי כְּתִיב וַיְהִי אוֹר, לָא אִצְטְרִיךְ קְרָא לְמִכְתַּב, אֶלָּא וַיְהִי כֵן, מַהוּ וַיְהִי אוֹר. אֶלָּא, דְּהַהוּא אוֹר אַפִּיק, אוֹר אַחֲרָא דְּאִתְחֲזֵי לֵיהּ, וְדָא אִיהוּ יוֹמָא קַדְמָאָה, מֵאִינוּן עֲצֵי הַלְּבָנוֹן.

26. Another explanation of "the woods of Lebanon": These are the six days of creation, for each day is arranged on this palanquin in the system that

applies to it. EVERY ATTRIBUTE OF CHESED, GVURAH, TIFERET, NETZACH, HOD AND YESOD OF ZEIR ANPIN THAT ARE COMPLETED THROUGH BINAH BESTOWS ONE PART IN THE EDIFICE OF MALCHUT THAT IS CALLED 'PALANQUIN'. The first system: The first light that was concealed is drawn from the right side OF BINAH, and it takes from the right side OF ZEIR ANPIN who enters this palanquin upon one foundation and cohabits with it. Afterwards, the palanquin produces an image that is suitable for this light, WHICH IS THE ATTRIBUTE OF CHESED OF THE PALANQUIN. This is the secret of what is written: "Let there be light, and there was light" (Beresheet 1:3). After it said, "Let there be light," why add, "And there was light"? It could have just been written: 'And it was so.' Wherefore does it say, "And there was light"? It means that this light brought forth a different light that was suitable for it, and this was the first day of these woods of Lebanon.

27. סְדּוּרָא תִּנְיָינָא: אִתְנְגִיד מִסִּטְרָא דִשְׂמָאלָא, פְּרִישׁוּ דְּמַיָּא, בִּנְגִידוּ דְאֶשָּׁא תַּקִּיפָא, וְאִתְנְטִיל מִסִּטְרָא דִשְׂמָאלָא, וְעָאל בְּהַאי אַפִּרְיוֹן, וְעָבֵיד בֵּיהּ שִׁמּוּשָׁא, וְאַפְרִישׁ בֵּין מַיִּין דְּבִסְטַר יְמִינָא, וּבֵין אִינּוּן מַיִּין דְּבִסְטַר שְׂמָאלָא. לְבָתַר אַפִּיק הַהוּא אַפִּרְיוֹן, חַד דְּיוּקְנָא, כְּגַוְונָא דִּילֵיהּ. וְדָא אִיהוּ רָזָא דִּכְתִיב, בֵּין הַמַּיִם אֲשֶׁר מִתַּחַת לָרָקִיעַ וּבֵין הַמַּיִם אֲשֶׁר מֵעַל לָרָקִיעַ וַיְהִי כֵן. וְדָא אִיהוּ יוֹמָא תִּנְיָינָא מֵאִינּוּן עֲצֵי הַלְּבָנוֹן.

27. The second system: The separation of the waters is drawn from the left side OF BINAH by the drawing of a strong fire, taken from the left side OF ZEIR ANPIN. It enters into the palanquin, mates with it and divides between the water on the right side and the water on the left side. Afterwards, the palanquin brought forth an image similar to this, AND THE ATTRIBUTE OF GVURAH OF THE PALANQUIN WAS BUILT. This is the secret of the verse: "The waters which were under the firmament from the waters which were above the firmament, and it was so" (Ibid. 7). This is the second day of these woods of Lebanon.

28. סְדּוּרָא תְּלִיתָאָה: אִתְנְגִיד מִסִּטְרָא דְּאֶמְצָעִיתָא, וּמִסִּטְרָא דִּימִינָא, חַד יוֹמָא תְּלִיתָאָה, דְּעָבֵיד שְׁלָמָא בְּעָלְמָא. וּמִתַּמָּן אִתְמְשִׁיכוּ אִיבִּין

לְכֹלָּא, וְדָא עָבֵיד שִׁמּוּשָׁא בְּהַאי אַפִּרְיוֹן, וְאַפִּיק זִינָא לְזִינֵיהּ. זִינָא
לְעוֹבָדִין סַגִּיאִין, זִינָא דְּאִתְחֲזֵי לֵיהּ, וְכָל דְּשָׁאִין וַעֲשָׂבִין וְאִילָנִין
בְּכַמָּה חֵילִין. וְאִשְׁתְּאַר דְּיוּקְנֵיהּ תַּמָּן, וְאַפִּיק זִינָא הַהוּא אַפִּרְיוֹן,
כְּהַהוּא גַּוְונָא מַמָּשׁ, וְדָא אִיהוּ יוֹמָא תְּלִיתָאָה, דְּאִתְכְּלִיל מִב׳ סִטְרִין,
מֵאִינּוּן עֲצֵי הַלְּבָנוֹן.

**28.** The third system: A certain third day is drawn from the central side and the right side, MEANING THE ATTRIBUTE OF TIFERET OF ZEIR ANPIN, WHICH IS THE CENTRAL COLUMN that makes peace in the world BETWEEN THE TWO COLUMNS, RIGHT AND LEFT, whence fruits proceed to everyone. And it cohabits with this palanquin and draws forth a species after its kind, a species that does many actions like the kinds that fit it accordingly, MEANING all the vegetation and grasses and trees in many strengths, and its image remains IN THE PALANQUIN. That palanquin brings forth a species exactly identical to it THAT CAME FORTH FROM THE CENTRAL COLUMN, AND THE ATTRIBUTE OF TIFERET OF THE PALANQUIN IS BUILT. This is the third day that includes both sides, RIGHT AND LEFT, of these woods of Lebanon.

**29.** סִדּוּרָא רְבִיעָאָה: אִתְנְגִיד וְאִתְנְהִיר נְהִירוּ דְּשִׁמְשָׁא, לְאַנְהָרָא
לְהַאי אַפִּרְיוֹן, גּוֹ חָשׁוּךְ דִּילֵיהּ, וְעָאל בֵּיהּ לְאַנְהָרָא, וְלָא עָבֵיד בֵּיהּ
שִׁמּוּשָׁא. עַד יוֹמָא חֲמִשָׁאָה, דְּאַפִּיק הַאי אַפִּרְיוֹן הַהוּא שִׁמּוּשָׁא
דִּנְהִירוּ, דְּעָאל בֵּיהּ בְּיוֹמָא רְבִיעָאָה, וְאַפִּיק הַהוּא אַפִּרְיוֹן בְּהַהוּא
גַּוְונָא מַמָּשׁ דְּהַהוּא נְהִירוּ, וְדָא אִיהוּ יוֹמָא רְבִיעָאָה חַד מֵאִינּוּן עֲצֵי
הַלְּבָנוֹן.

**29.** The fourth system: The light of the sun is drawn and illuminates this palanquin in the midst of its darkness. It enters to illuminate but does not cohabit with it, until the fifth day. THEN the palanquin brings forth the cohabitation of the illumination that entered it on the fourth day, and the palanquin brings forth the exact likeness of that light. THE ATTRIBUTE OF NETZACH OF THE PALANQUIN IS BUILT IN THIS WAY. This is the fourth day, which is one of the woods of Lebanon.

**30.** סִדּוּרָא חֲמִישָׁאָה: אִתְנְגִיד חַד מְשִׁיכוּ, דִּרְחִישׁוּ דְּמַיָּא, וְעָבֵיד

שְׁמוּשָׁא לְאַפְקָא הַהוּא נְהִירוּ, דְּסִדּוּרָא דְּיוֹמָא רְבִיעָאָה, וְעָבֵיד בְּהַאי אַפְרְיוֹן שְׁמוּשָׁא, וְאַפִּיק זִמְנִין לְזִינֵיהּ, אִינוּן דְּאִתְחֲזֵי כְּהַהוּא גַּוְונָא מַמָּשׁ, וְהַאי יוֹמָא שִׁמֵּשׁ הַהוּא שְׁמוּשָׁא, יַתִּיר מִכָּל שְׁאַר יוֹמִין. וְכֹלָּא תַּלְיָא עַד יוֹמָא שְׁתִיתָאָה, דְּאַפִּיק אַפְרְיוֹן כָּל מַה דַּהֲוָה גָּנִיז בֵּיהּ, דִּכְתִיב, תּוֹצֵא הָאָרֶץ נֶפֶשׁ חַיָּה לְמִינָהּ וְגוֹ'. וְדָא אִיהוּ יוֹמָא חֲמִישָׁאָה, חַד מֵאִינוּן עֲצֵי הַלְּבָנוֹן.

**30.** The fifth system: One drawing of the swarming of the water was brought forth, and mated so as to bring forth that light from the system of the fourth day. It cohabited with that palanquin ON THE FIFTH DAY, and brought forth species according to its very own kind. This day OF THE WOODS OF LEBANON did that action more than in the other days, BECAUSE IT PERFECTED THE ATTRIBUTE OF HOD IN THE PALANQUIN WITH THE SWEETENED JUDGMENTS OF BINAH. It was all suspended until the sixth day, for the palanquin brought forth all that was hidden in it, as it is written: "Let the earth bring forth living creatures after their kind" (Ibid. 24). This is the fifth day, ONE day of the woods of the Lebanon.

31. סִדּוּרָא שְׁתִיתָאָה: דָּא אִיהוּ יוֹמָא, דְּאַתְקִין כָּל הַאי אַפְרְיוֹן, וְלֵית לֵיהּ תִּקּוּנָא, וְלֵית לֵיהּ תֶּקְפָּא, בַּר מֵהַאי יוֹמָא, כַּד אָתָא הַאי יוֹמָא, אִתְתָּקַן הַאי אַפְרְיוֹן, בְּכַמָּה רוּחִין, בְּכַמָּה נִשְׁמָתִין, בְּכַמָּה עוּלֵימָתָן שַׁפִּירָן בְּחֵיזוּ. אִינוּן דְּאִתְחֲזוּן לְמֵיתַב בְּהֵיכְלָא דְּמַלְכָּא. אוּף אִיהוּ אִתְתָּקַן בְּשַׁפִּירוּ כָּל שְׁאַר יוֹמִין דַּהֲווֹ בְּקַדְמֵיתָא, וְאַתְקִין לוֹן בְּתִיאוּבְתָּא חֲדָא, בִּרְעוּתָא בְּחֶדְוָה, תִּקּוּנָא דִּלְעֵילָּא וְתַתָּא.

**31.** The sixth system: It is the day that perfected the entire palanquin. THE PALANQUIN has no perfection and power except through that day, WHICH IS YESOD OF ZEIR ANPIN, BECAUSE THE PALANQUIN DOES NOT RECEIVE ANYTHING FROM THOSE ABOVE EXCEPT THROUGH YESOD OF ZEIR ANPIN. When that day came, the palanquin became perfected with many spirits, with many souls, and with many beautiful maidens, WHO ARE SEVEN CHAMBERS THAT SERVE MALCHUT, those ones worthy to sit in the King's chamber. YESOD also was perfected with the beauty of all the days that preceded, BECAUSE YESOD INCLUDES ALL THE FIVE DAYS, CHESED,

GVURAH, TIFERET, NETZACH AND HOD. And it perfected them with one wish, with desire, joy, and perfection of above and below.

32. כְּדֵין אִתְקַדָּשׁ הַאי אַפִּרְיוֹן, בְּקִדּוּשִׁין עִלָּאִין וְאִתְעַטָּר בְּעִטְרוֹי, עַד דְּסָלִיק בִּסְלִיקוּ דְּעִטְרָא דִּנְיָיחָא, וְאִקְרֵי שְׁמָא עִלָּאָה, שְׁמָא קַדִּישָׁא, דְּאִיהִי שַׁבָּת. נַיְיחָא דְּכֹלָּא, תִּיאוּבְתָּא דְּכֹלָּא, דִּבְקוּתָא דְּכֹלָּא, דְּעֵילָא וְתַתָּא כַּחֲדָא. וּכְדֵין כְּתִיב, אַפִּרְיוֹן עָשָׂה לוֹ הַמֶּלֶךְ שְׁלֹמֹה מֵעֲצֵי הַלְּבָנוֹן.

**32.** Then this palanquin became sanctified with supernal sanctities and adorned with its crowns, until it ascended with the rising of the crown of rest and was given a supernal Name, the Holy Name, which is Shabbat. This is the tranquillity of all, the desire of all and the cleaving of all, of above and below together, of which it is written: "King Solomon made himself a palanquin from the woods of Lebanon."

33. אָמַר רַבִּי שִׁמְעוֹן, מַאן דְּזָכֵי בְּהַהוּא אַפִּרְיוֹן, זָכֵי בְּכֹלָּא, זָכֵי לְמֵיתַב בְּנָיְיחָא דְּצִלָּא דְּקוּדְשָׁא בְּרִיךְ הוּא, כד"א, בְּצִלּוֹ חִמַּדְתִּי וְיָשַׁבְתִּי. וְהַשְׁתָּא דְּיָתִיבְנָא בְּצִלָּא דִּנְיָיחָא דָּא, אִית לָן לְאִסְתַּכְּלָא דְּלָא יַתְבֵינָן אֶלָּא בְּצִלָּא דְּקוּדְשָׁא בְּרִיךְ הוּא, גּוֹ הַהוּא אַפִּרְיוֹן. וְאִית לָן לְאַעֲטְרָא הַאי אֲתָר, בְּעִטְרִין עִלָּאִין, עַד דְּיִתְעָרוּן אִילָנֵי דְּהַהוּא אַפִּרְיוֹן, לְמֵיתֵי עֲלָן בְּצִלָּא אַחֲרָא.

**33.** Rabbi Shimon said: The one who merits that palanquin merits everything. He merits to sit and rest in the shadow of Hashem, as it is written: "I sat down under His shadow with great delight" (Shir Hashirim 2:3). Now that I sit in the shadow of this rest, we have to see that we are sitting in the shadow of the Holy One, blessed be He, within that palanquin. But we have to adorn this place with supernal crowns, until the trees of that palanquin are aroused to come to us with a different shadow.

## 6. "That they bring Me an offering"

### A Synopsis
The section title passage summarizes one single great truth, which Rabbi Shimon explains to us: that for one to aspire toward divine union, he must strive with all his heart and soul and with self-purification, and pay the necessary price. We also hear that he is prompted to do this by the heart of God in himself, that he may increase his worthiness by turning a wicked person from the path of evil. In doing so he causes the subjugation of the Other Side, causes God to be elevated in his honor, and thence causes the world to be preserved both above and below. Such a righteous one, we're told, shall enter in through the twelve gates.

### The Relevance of this Passage
Perfection comes partly through striving and steadfast self-transformation with the right intent; yet there is more to bettering ourselves. We can increase our merit by tutoring the wicked, helping them to be free of evil.

Through our meditation upon these verses, we grasp in our hearts the source of all goodness from whence we sprang. The evil tendencies of the wicked are abolished and the Other Side is immobilized. We are now free to attain unity with the Light of the Creator.

34. פָּתַח רַבִּי שִׁמְעוֹן בְּרֵישָׁא וְאָמַר, וְיִקְחוּ לִי תְּרוּמָה מֵאֵת כָּל אִישׁ אֲשֶׁר יִדְּבֶנּוּ לִבּוֹ תִּקְחוּ אֶת תְּרוּמָתִי. וְיִקְחוּ לִי, הַאי מַאן דְּבָעֵי לְאִשְׁתַּדְּלָא בְּמִצְוָה, וּלְאִשְׁתַּדְּלָא בֵּיה בְּקוּדְשָׁא בְּרִיךְ הוּא, אִצְטְרִיךְ דְּלָא יִשְׁתָּדַל בֵּיה בְּרֵיקַנְיָּיא וּבְמַגָּנָא, אֶלָּא אִצְטְרִיךְ לֵיה לְבַר נָשׁ לְאִשְׁתַּדְּלָא בֵּיה כַּדְקָא יֵאוֹת כְּפוּם חֵילֵיה. וְהָא אוֹקִימְנָא מִלָּה דָּא בְּכַמָּה אַתְרֵי, יֵאוֹת לְמֶיסַב בַּר נָשׁ הַהוּא אִשְׁתַּדְּלוּתָא דְּקוּדְשָׁא בְּרִיךְ הוּא. כד"א אִישׁ כְּמַתְּנַת יָדוֹ וְגו'.

34. Rabbi Shimon opened the discussion saying: "That they bring Me an offering, of every man whose heart prompts him to give" (Shemot 25:2). "That they bring Me" POINTS OUT that if one wishes to undertake a precept and to aspire towards the Holy One, blessed be He, it is necessary that the person not strive in vain and empty handed, but rather that he makes efforts as befitting, and according to, his strengths. We have established this in many places, AND SO it is good for a person to strive after the Holy One,

blessed be He, as it is written: "Every man shall give as he is able, according to the blessing of Hashem your Elohim which He has given you" (Devarim 16:17).

35. וְאִי תֵּימָא, הָא כְּתִיב לְכוּ שִׁבְרוּ וֶאֱכֹלוּ וּלְכוּ שִׁבְרוּ בְּלֹא כֶסֶף וּבְלֹא מְחִיר יַיִן וְחָלָב, דְּהָא אִיהוּ בְּמַגָּנָא, וְאִיהוּ אִשְׁתַּדְּלוּתָא דְקוּדְשָׁא בְּרִיךְ הוּא. אֶלָּא אִשְׁתַּדְּלוּתָא דְאוֹרַיְיתָא, כָּל מַאן דְּבָעֵי זָכֵי בָּהּ. אִשְׁתַּדְּלוּתָא דְקוּדְשָׁא בְּרִיךְ הוּא לְמִנְדַע לֵיהּ, כָּל מַאן דְּבָעֵי זָכֵי בֵּיהּ, בְּלָא אַגְרָא כְּלָל. אֲבָל אִשְׁתַּדְּלוּתָא דְקוּדְשָׁא בְּרִיךְ הוּא דְקַיְימָא בְּעוֹבָדָא, אָסִיר לְנַטְלָא לֵיהּ לְמַגָּנָא וּבְרֵיקַנְיָיא, בְּגִין דְּלָא זָכֵי בְּהַהוּא עוֹבָדָא כְּלָל, לְאַמְשָׁכָא עֲלֵיהּ רוּחָא דְקוּדְשָׁא, אֶלָּא בַּאֲגַר שָׁלִים.

35. And if you ask, Is it not written: "Come, buy, and eat; come, buy wine and milk without money and without a price" (Yeshayah 55:1)? So we see that it is free, and that is the striving after the Holy One, blessed be He, BECAUSE WINE AND MILK MEAN THE TORAH, WHICH IS REFERRED TO IN THIS WAY. HE ANSWERS: Anybody who desires to endeavor for Torah merits it. The striving after the Holy One, blessed be He, is to know Him; for anyone who desires it will merit it without any payment whatsoever. But if the striving after the Holy One, blessed be He, is in the form of an action, it is prohibited to perform that action empty handed and in vain, because one will not merit the drawing down of a spirit of holiness unless he pays in full.

36. בְּסִפְרָא דְחַרְשֵׁי, דְּאוֹלִיף אַשְׁמְדָאי לִשְׁלֹמֹה מַלְכָּא, כָּל מַאן דְּבָעֵי לְאִשְׁתַּדְּלָא לְאַעְבְּרָא מִנֵּיהּ רוּחַ מְסָאֲבָא, וּלְאַכְפְּיָיא רוּחָא אַחֲרָא. הַהוּא עוֹבָדָא דְּבָעֵי לְאִשְׁתַּדְּלָא בֵּיהּ, בָּעֵי לְמִקְנֵי לֵיהּ בַּאֲגַר שָׁלִים, בְּכָל מַה דְּיִבְעוּן מִנֵּיהּ, בֵּין זְעֵיר בֵּין רַב, בְּגִין דְּרוּחַ מְסָאֲבָא, אִיהוּ אִזְדַּמַּן תָּדִיר בְּמַגָּנָא וּבְרֵיקַנְיָיא, וְאִזְדַּבַּן בְּלָא אַגְרָא, וְאָנִיס לִבְנֵי נָשָׁא לְמִשְׁרֵי עֲלַיְיהוּ, וּמְפַתֵּי לוֹן לְדַיְירָא עִמְּהוֹן, בְּכַמָּה פִּתּוּיִין, בְּכַמָּה אָרְחִין, סָטֵי לוֹן לְשַׁוְּואָה דִּיּוּרֵיהּ עִמְּהוֹן.

36. In the books of sorcery that Asmodeus, THE KING OF THE DEMONS, taught King Solomon IT IS WRITTEN THAT whoever wants to endeavor to

remove from himself the impure spirit and to subdue the other spirit OF THE OTHER SIDE, must buy in full payment the action in which he wishes to endeavor, and he should give whatever is requested of him, whether a little or a lot. The spirit of impurity is always ready freely and for nothing and is saleable without payment, because he compels people upon whom he dwells and entices them to dwell with him. He tempts them to make their habitation with him in many ways.

37. וְרוּחַ קוּדְשָׁא לָאו הָכִי, אֶלָא בַּאֲגַר שָׁלִים, וּבְאִשְׁתַּדְלוּתָא רַב סַגִּי, וּבְאִתְדַּכְּאוּתָא דְּגַרְמֵיהּ וּבְאִתְדַּכְּאוּתָא דְּמַשְׁכָּנֵיהּ, וּבִרְעוּתָא דְּלִבֵּיהּ וְנַפְשֵׁיהּ. וּלְוָאי דְּיָכִיל לְמִרְוַוח לֵיהּ, דִּישַׁוֵּי מָדוֹרֵיהּ עִמֵּיהּ. וְעַכ״ד דְּיָהַךְ בְּאֹרַח מֵישָׁר, דְּלָא יִסְטֵי לִימִינָא וְלִשְׂמָאלָא, וְאִי לָאו, מִיָּד אִסְתַּלָּק מִנֵּיהּ, וְאִתְרְחַק מִנֵּיהּ. וְלָא יָכִיל לְמִרְוַוח לֵיהּ כְּדִבְקַדְמֵיתָא.

37. The spirit of holiness is not this way, but only with full payment and great endeavor, and by purifying himself and purifying his habitation with the desire of his heart and soul. AND EVEN THEN, fortunate is he who merits that he will place its habitation with him. With all this, HE MUST go in the straight path, neither turning right nor left. If he does not, He separates itself immediately and distances itself from him, and he will not again be able to merit it as he did originally.

38. וְעַל דָּא כְּתִיב, וְיִקְחוּ לִי תְּרוּמָה מֵאֵת כָּל אִישׁ, מֵהַהוּא דְּאִקְרֵי אִישׁ, דְּאִתְגַּבַּר עַל יִצְרֵיהּ. וְכָל מַאן דְּאִתְגַּבַּר עַל יִצְרֵיהּ, אִקְרֵי אִישׁ. אֲשֶׁר יִדְּבֶנּוּ לִבּוֹ, מַאי אֲשֶׁר יִדְּבֶנּוּ לִבּוֹ. אֶלָא. דְּיִתְרְעֵי בֵּיהּ קוּדְשָׁא בְּרִיךְ הוּא, כד״א לְךָ אָמַר לִבִּי. צוּר לְבָבִי. וְטוֹב לֵב. וַיִּיטַב לִבּוֹ. כֻּלְּהוּ בְּקוּדְשָׁא בְּרִיךְ הוּא קָאֲמַר. אוּף הָכָא אֲשֶׁר יִדְּבֶנּוּ לִבּוֹ. מִנֵּיהּ תִּקְחוּ אֶת תְּרוּמָתִי, דְּהָא תַּמָּן אִשְׁתְּכַח וְלָאו בַּאֲתָר אַחֲרָא.

38. In reference to this, it is written: "That they bring Me an offering, of every man..." MEANING one called 'man' who has overcome his inclination, for whoever overcomes his inclination is called 'man'. "Whose heart prompts him": HE QUESTIONS: What does "whose heart prompts him" mean? HE ANSWERS: Rather that the Holy One, blessed be He, takes pleasure in him, as it is written: "Of You my heart has said" (Tehilim 27:8);

"the strength of my heart" (Tehilim 73:26), "of a merry heart" (Mishlei 15:15) and "His heart was merry" (Rut 3:7). They all refer to the Holy One, blessed be He, MEANING THE HEART OF THE HOLY ONE, BLESSED BE HE, THAT IS, HIS GOODWILL. Here also, "Whose heart prompts him" IS THE HEART OF THE HOLY ONE, BLESSED BE HE. From Him "shall you take My offering," because there is where THE HOLY ONE, BLESSED BE HE is found, FOR HE DWELLS IN HIM and in no other place.

**39.** וּמְנָא יַדְעִינָן דְּהָא קוּדְשָׁא בְּרִיךְ הוּא אִתְרָעֵי בֵּיהּ, וְשַׁוֵּי מָדוֹרֵיהּ בֵּיהּ. כַּד חַמֵּינָן דִּרְעוּתָא דְּהַהוּא בַּר נָשׁ, לְמִרְדַּף וּלְאִשְׁתַּדְּלָא אֲבַתְרֵיהּ דְּקוּדְשָׁא בְּרִיךְ הוּא בְּלִבֵּיהּ וּבְנַפְשֵׁיהּ וּבִרְעוּתֵיהּ, וַדַּאי תַּמָּן יַדְעִינָן דְּשַׁרְיָא בֵּיהּ שְׁכִינְתָּא. כְּדֵין בָּעֵינָן לְמִקְנֵי הַהוּא בַּר נָשׁ, בְּכֶסֶף שְׁלִים, לְאִתְחַבְּרָא בַּהֲדֵיהּ וּלְמֵילַף מִנֵּיהּ. וְעַל דָּא קַדְמָאֵי הֲווֹ אַמְרֵי, וּקְנֵה לְךָ חָבֵר, בַּאֲגַר שְׁלִים בָּעֵי לְמִקְנֵי לֵיהּ, בְּגִין לְמִזְכֵּי בִּשְׁכִינְתָּא. עַד הָכָא בָּעֵי לְמִרְדַּף בָּתַר זַכָּאָה וּלְמִקְנֵה לֵיהּ.

**39.** How do we know that the Holy One, blessed be He, wants him and places His dwelling place in him? IT IS when we see that the desire of the person IS to endeavor to pursue the Holy One, blessed be He, with his heart and soul and desire. We are certain then that the Shechinah dwells there. Then we should pay in full to befriend him and to learn from him. About this, the ancients said, '…and acquire for yourself a friend.' You must buy him for a full price in order to merit the Shechinah THAT DWELLS IN HIM. This is how far it is necessary to pursue a righteous man and purchase him.

**40.** אוּף הָכִי, הַהוּא זַכָּאָה בָּעֵי לְמִרְדַּף בָּתַר חַיָּיבָא, וּלְמִקְנֵי לֵיהּ בַּאֲגַר שְׁלִים, בְּגִין דְּיֶעְבַּר מִנֵּיהּ הַהוּא זוּהֲמָא, וְיִתְכַּפְיָא סִטְרָא אַחֲרָא, וְיַעֲבִיד לְנַפְשֵׁיהּ, בְּגִין דְּיִתְחֲשַׁב עֲלֵיהּ, כְּאִילּוּ הוּא בָּרָא לֵיהּ. וְדָא אִיהוּ שְׁבָחָא דְּיִסְתַּלַּק בֵּיהּ יְקָרָא דְּקוּדְשָׁא בְּרִיךְ הוּא, יַתִּיר מִשְּׁבָחָא אַחֲרָא, וְאִסְתַּלְּקוּתָא דָּא יַתִּיר מִכֹּלָּא. מַאי טַעְמָא. בְּגִין דְּאִיהוּ גָּרִים לְאַכְפְיָא סִטְרָא אַחֲרָא, וּלְאִסְתַּלְּקָא יְקָרָא דְּקוּדְשָׁא בְּרִיךְ הוּא. וְעַל דָּא כְּתִיב בְּאַהֲרֹן, וְרַבִּים הֵשִׁיב מֵעָוֹן. וּכְתִיב בְּרִיתִי הָיְתָה אִתּוֹ.

**40.** In the same way, the righteous one must pursue the wicked person and purchase him for a full price in order to remove from him that filth, subdue the Other Side and build him, for it is considered as though he created him. This is a praise with which the glory of the Holy One, blessed be He, will be elevated, more than with any other praise, and this elevation is quite in excess! What is the reason? Because he caused the Other Side to be subdued and to elevate the honor of the Holy One, blessed be He, as it is written about Aaron: "And turned many away from iniquity" (Malachi 2:6) and also, "My covenant was with him" (Ibid. 5).

41. תָּא חֲזֵי, כָּל מַאן דְּאָחִיד בִּידָא דְּחַיָּיבָא, וְאִשְׁתָּדַּל בֵּיה, לְמִשְׁבַּק אָרְחָא בִּישָׁא, אִיהוּ אִסְתַּלָּק בִּתְלַת סְלוּקִין, מַה דְּלָא אִסְתַּלָּק הָכִי בַּר נָשׁ אַחֲרָא. גָּרִים לְאַכְפַּיָּיא סִטְרָא אַחֲרָא. וְגָרִים דְּאִסְתַּלָּק קוּדְשָׁא בְּרִיךְ הוּא בִּיקָרֵיה. וְגָרִים לְקַיְּימָא כָּל עָלְמָא בְּקִיּוּמֵיה לְעֵילָא וְתַתָּא. וְעַל הַאי בַּר נָשׁ כְּתִיב, בְּרִיתִי הָיְתָה אִתּוֹ הַחַיִּים וְהַשָּׁלוֹם. וְזָכֵי לְמֶחֱמֵי בְּנִין לִבְנוֹי, וְזָכֵי בְּהַאי עָלְמָא, וְזָכֵי לְעָלְמָא דְּאָתֵי. כָּל מָארֵי דִינִין, לָא יַכְלִין לְמֵידָן לֵיה, בְּהַאי עָלְמָא וּבְעָלְמָא דְּאָתֵי. עָאל בִּתְרֵיסַר תַּרְעֵי, וְלֵית מַאן דְּיִמְחֵי בִּידֵיה. וְעַל דָּא כְּתִיב, גִּבּוֹר בָּאָרֶץ יִהְיֶה זַרְעוֹ דּוֹר יְשָׁרִים יְבֹרָךְ. הוֹן וָעֹשֶׁר בְּבֵיתוֹ וְצִדְקָתוֹ עוֹמֶדֶת לָעַד. זָרַח בַּחֹשֶׁךְ אוֹר לַיְשָׁרִים וְגוֹ'.

**41.** Come and see: Everyone who holds the hand of the wicked person and endeavors to help him leave the path of evil is elevated in three elevations, to which another person cannot rise. He causes the subjugation of the Other Side, he causes the Holy One, blessed be He, to be elevated in His honor and he causes the world to be preserved both above and below. About this person, it is written: "My covenant was with him for life and peace" and he merits to see the children of his children, and gains merit in this world and in the World to Come. All the accusers will not be able to judge him in this world and in the World to Come. He enters through the twelve gates THAT ARE IN THE FIRMAMENT, and there is nothing to prevent him. It is written: "His seed shall be mighty upon earth; the generation of the upright shall be blessed. Wealth and riches shall be in his house, and his righteousness endures forever. Light rises in the darkness for the upright: He is gracious and full of compassion, and just..." (Tehilim 112:2-4).

## 7. The three colors in the flame

### A Synopsis

This section deals with the three colors that can be distinguished inside a flame. One rises up, while another seems to dip down. The other one is usually visible, but appears to be concealed when the sun shines. There is one color that ascends above and emerges, and that color is whiter than white.

Through this analogy, we learn how our prayers cause the white light to ascend to the crown, and how all the Sfirot join to each other with light above and below, and then join with all the candles. Only then are all combined with the righteous one, who is called 'good'. Whosoever causes the wicked to return to the right path is now worthy, we are told. This recognition is then witnessed by the angels who supervise the world. Next, the overseer appears, bringing with him the image of that person; and, we read, there is no righteous person in this world who does not have his image thus engraved above. The King then blesses the image of that righteous one, and four camps of supernal angels take it and depart, whence they go, however, we are not told.

The Zohar next recounts the seventy keys belonging of treasures owned by the overseer's Master, and then of seventy concealed worlds. After this, we learn that those who help the poor merit much good in return, as well as many supernal treasures, but these rewards are nothing like those merited by someone who redeems the wicked.

Now we learn when the children of Yisrael reach the Kedushah in the prayer, the third color in the flame emerges and shines. We are next told that the sanctification we recite is the same as the praise we give to the supernal angels, and we give this praise both so that we may be sanctified ourselves and so that we may earn their friendship. Sanctification in the Holy Language may only be recited when ten men are present , because the Shechinah joins the sanctification. Prayer, we are told, has great strength and is often able to break the power of the Other Side. Concluding the discourse, Rabbi Shimon blesses the other rabbis.

### The Relevance of this Passage

Just as the seven colors of the rainbow emerge from a single beam of white sunlight, our reading unites all the spiritual forces into their original state: a ray of pure Light emanating from the Creator.

This union produces a luminescence that brightens our entire existence. We steer this Light towards the wicked, the evil who dwell among us, as well as the wicked tendencies in ourselves, thus purging immoral impulses and subjugating the Other Side, the Satan, which is

the root of personal and global negativity. This Light also emancipates the poor, annulling the force of poverty so all may now partake of God's goodness.

42. בְּאִדְּרָא עִלָּאָה, קַיְימִין תְּלַת גַּוְונִין. וְאִינוּן לָהֲטִין גּוֹ שַׁלְהוֹבָא חֲדָא, וְהַהוּא שַׁלְהוֹבָא נָפְקָא מִסִּטְרָא דְּדָרוֹם דְּאִיהוּ יְמִינָא. וְאִינוּן גַּוְונִין מִתְפָּרְשָׁן לִתְלַת סִטְרִין. חַד סָלִיק לְעֵילָא. וְחַד נָחִית לְתַתָּא. וְחַד דְּאִתְחֲזֵי, וְגָנִיז בְּשַׁעֲתָא דְּשִׁמְשָׁא נָהִיר.

**42.** In the upper chamber, WHICH IS MALCHUT, there are three colors, WHICH ARE NETZACH, HOD AND YESOD, that glitter inside one flame, and that flame emerges from the south side which is right. These colors separate to three sides. One ascends above, SHINING FROM BELOW UP, AND IT IS NETZACH, one descends below, SHINING FROM ABOVE DOWN, AND IT IS HOD, and one is visible, but is concealed when the sun shines. IT IS THE ILLUMINATION OF CHOCHMAH IN CHASSADIM THAT IS PRODUCED BY YESOD THAT SHINES ONLY AT NIGHT, WHICH IS THE DOMINION OF NUKVA, BUT NOT BY DAY, WHICH IS THE DOMINION OF ZEIR ANPIN.

43. גַּוְונָא חֲדָא הַהוּא דְּסָלִיק לְעֵילָא, נָפְקָא, וְהַהוּא גַּוְונָא אִיהוּ גָּוֶון חִוָּור, יַתִּיר מֵחִוָּורוּ אַחֲרָא. וְעָאל בְּהַהוּא שַׁלְהוֹבָא וְאִצְטְבַע זְעֵיר, וְלָא אִצְטְבַע, וְקַיְימָא הַהוּא גָּוֶון לְעֵילָא עַל רֵישָׁא דְּהַהוּא אִדְּרָא. וּבְשַׁעֲתָא דְּיִשְׂרָאֵל עָאלִין לְבֵי כְּנִשְׁתָּא וּמְצַלָּן צְלוֹתְהוֹן, כַּד מָטָאן לְגָאַל יִשְׂרָאֵל, וְסַמְכִין גְּאוּלָה לִתְפִלָּה, כְּדֵין הַאי גָּוֶון חִוָּור, אִסְתַּלָּק עַל רֵישָׁא דְּאִדְּרָא, וְאִתְעֲבֵיד לֵיהּ כִּתְרָא.

**43.** There is one color that ascends above, WHICH IS NETZACH, and emerges, and that color is white, much whiter than any other kind of white. It enters that flame and becomes slightly colored, FOR IT INCLUDES SOME JUDGMENTS OF THE FLAME, yet does not become colored, MEANING THAT NO COLOR IS NOTICEABLE IN IT, WHICH IS JUDGMENT. That color is situated above on the top of that chamber, NAMELY ON TOP OF MALCHUT, when Yisrael come to synagogue and pray their prayers, when they reach: 'Who redeemed Yisrael' and bring redemption and Amidah prayer close together, BY NOT INTERRUPTING IN BETWEEN. THROUGH THIS, THEY

CAUSE YESOD, WHICH IS CALLED 'REDEMPTION', TO GET CLOSE TO MALCHUT, WHICH IS CALLED 'PRAYER'. Then that white color, WHICH IS NETZACH, ascends to the top of the chamber, WHICH IS MALCHUT, and becomes its crown.

44. וְכָרוֹזָא נָפִיק וְאָמַר, זַכָּאִין אַתּוּן עַמָּא קַדִּישָׁא, דְּעַבְדֵי טוֹב קָמֵיהּ דְּקוּדְשָׁא בְּרִיךְ הוּא, וְרָזָא דָּא, וְהַטּוֹב בְּעֵינֶיךָ עָשִׂיתִי, דְּסָמִיךְ גְּאוּלָה לִתְפִלָּה. בְּגִין דְּהָא בְּהַהִיא שַׁעֲתָא דְּמָטוּ לִתְהִלּוֹת לָאֵל עֶלְיוֹן, דְּסָלִיק הַאי גָּוֶון עַל רֵישָׁא דְּהַהוּא אִדְרָא, אִתְּעַר הַאי צַדִּיק, לְאִתְחַבְּרָא בַּאֲתַר דְּאִצְטְרִיךְ, בִּרְחִימוּ בַּחֲבִיבוּ בְּחֶדְוָה בִּרְעוּתָא. וְכָל שַׁיְיפִין כֻּלְּהוּ, מִתְחַבְּרָן בְּתִיאוּבְתָּא חֲדָא אִלֵּין בְּאִלֵּין, עִלָּאִין בְּתַתָּאִין, וּבוּצִינִין כֻּלְּהוּ נָהֲרִין וּמִתְלַהֲטִין, וְכֻלְּהוֹן קַיְימָא בְּחַבּוּרָא חֲדָא בְּהַאי צַדִּיק דְּאִקְרֵי טוֹב, כד"א אִמְרוּ צַדִּיק כִּי טוֹב, וְדָא מְחַבֵּר לְכֻלְּהוּ בְּחַבּוּרָא חֲדָא. כְּדֵין כֹּלָּא בִּלְחִישׁוּ עֵילָא וְתַתָּא, בִּנְשִׁיקִין דִּרְעוּתָא, וְקַיְימָא מִלָּה בְּחַבּוּרָא דְּבֵי אִדְרָא.

44. A proclamation is made: Blessed are you the holy nation that do good, MEANING THAT THEY CAUSE THE UNITY OF YESOD THAT IS CALLED 'GOOD' before the Holy One, blessed be He. This is the secret of: "And have done that which is good in your eyes" (Yeshayah 38:3), WHICH MEANS that he brought redemption close to prayer. When they reach 'Praises to the supernal El,' that color, NETZACH, ascends upon the top of the chamber, and the righteous one is aroused, WHICH IS YESOD OF ZEIR ANPIN, to unite where it should with love and affection and with joy and desire. All the limbs, NAMELY ALL THE SFIROT, join each other with the same desire, those of above with those of below, and all the candles, NAMELY ALL THE LEVELS, shine and glitter. They are all combined with the righteous one who is called 'good', as it is written: "Say of the righteous that it shall be well (also: 'good') with him" (Yeshayah 3:10). It joins them all in one union and all is silent above and below with the kisses of desire. It is all found in the union of the chamber, NAMELY THE SECRET OF THE EMBRACE.

45. כֵּיוָן דְּמָטוּ לְשִׂים שָׁלוֹם, כְּדֵין עָבִיד שִׁמּוּשָׁא הַהוּא נָהָר דְּנָפִיק מֵעֵדֶן בְּאִדְרָא דָּא, וּכְדֵין בַּעְיָין כֹּלָּא לְנָפְקָא מִקַּמֵי מַלְכָּא, וְלָא

אִצְטְרִיךְ בַּר נָשׁ, וְלָא אַחֲרָא, לְאִשְׁתַּכְּחָא תַּמָּן, וְלָא לְמִשְׁאַל שְׁאֶלְתִּין, אֶלָּא אִצְטְרִיךְ לְמִנְפַּל עַל אַנְפִּין. מ"ט. בְּגִין דְּהַהִיא שַׁעְתָּא שַׁעֲתָא דְּשִׁמּוּשָׁא הֲוֵי, וּבָעֵי כָּל בַּר נָשׁ לְמִכְסַף מִקַּמֵּי מָארֵיהּ, וּלְחַפְיָא אַנְפּוֹי בְּכִסּוּפָא סַגִּי, וּלְאַכְלְלָא נַפְשֵׁיהּ בְּהַהוּא שִׁמּוּשָׁא דְּנַפְשִׁין, דְּאִתְכְּלִיל הַהוּא אִדְרָא מֵעֵילָא וּמִתַּתָּא בְּנַפְשִׁין וְרוּחִין. כְּדֵין גַּוֶון אַחֲרָא, דְּנָחִית לְתַתָּא, קָאֵים וְאָחִיד בְּשִׁפּוּלֵי דְּהַאי אִדְרָא.

**45.** As soon as 'Give peace' is reached, WHICH IS THE LAST BLESSING OF THE AMIDAH AND THE ATTRIBUTE OF YESOD, the river that emerges from Eden, WHICH IS YESOD, cohabits with this chamber, WHICH IS MALCHUT, and all must leave the presence of the King. No person needs to be present there, nor make their requests, but it is just necessary to fall on the face, THAT IS TO SAY THE PRAYER OF FALLING ON THEIR FACES. What is the reason? That is the time of cohabitation, and everyone must be embarrassed before his Master and cover his face with great embarrassment to include himself in that cohabitation of the souls, for this chamber is included from above and from below with souls and spirits. Then another color that descends below, NAMELY HOD, gets up and attaches itself to the end of this room.

**46.** וְכָרוֹזָא נָפִיק וְקָארֵי וְאָמַר, עִלָּאִין וְתַתָּאִין אַסְהִידוּ סַהֲדוּתָא, מַאן אִיהוּ דְּעָבִיד נַפְשָׁאן וְזַכֵּי לְחַיָּיבַיָּא, הַהוּא דְּאִתְחֲזֵי לְאַעַטְרָא לֵיהּ, בְּעִטְרָא דְּמַלְכוּתָא עַל רֵישֵׁיהּ, הַהוּא דְּאִתְחֲזֵי לְעָאלָא הַשְׁתָּא קַמֵּי מַלְכָּא וּמַטְרוֹנִיתָא, דְּהָא מַלְכָּא וּמַטְרוֹנִיתָא שָׁאֲלֵי עָלֵיהּ.

**46.** Another proclamation is made: Those of above and those of below bear witness. Whoever creates souls and exonerates the wicked, MEANING HE WHO CAUSES THEM TO RETURN TO THE RIGHT PATH, is worthy to be adorned with the Crown of Royalty on his head. That is the one who is now worthy to come before the King and Queen, because the King and Queen are inquiring about him.

**47.** כְּדֵין אִזְדַּמַּן תְּרֵין סָהֲדִין, מֵאִינּוּן עֵינֵי יְיָ' דִּמְשַׁטְּטֵי בְּכָל עָלְמָא, וְקַיְימִין בָּתַר פַּרְגּוֹדָא, וְסָהֲדָן סַהֲדוּתָא דָא, וְאָמְרֵי, הָא אֲנָן סַהֲדִין עַל

פְּלָנְיָא בַּר פְּלָנְיָא. דָּא אִיהוּ עָבִיד נַפְשָׁן לְתַתָּא, נַפְשָׁאן דְּחַיָּיבַיָּא דַּהֲווֹ
מִסִּטְרָא אָחֳרָא. כְּדֵין אִתְיָקַר קוּדְשָׁא בְּרִיךְ הוּא בְּחֶדְוָה שְׁלֵימָתָא זַכָּאה
חוּלָקֵיהּ, דְּהָא אֲבוֹי יִדְכַּר בְּגִינֵיהּ לְטַב.

**47.** Then appear two witnesses of the eyes of Hashem that roam the entire
world, NAMELY THE ANGELS WHO SUPERVISE THE WORLD, who stand
behind the curtain, and bear this testimony, saying, 'We witnessed that
so-and-so, son of so-and-so, acquired souls below, souls of the wicked who
were on the Other Side.' Then the Holy One, blessed be He, is glorified
with complete joy. Blessed is his portion, for his father is also mentioned for
good because of him, BECAUSE THEY HAVE TESTIFIED ABOUT
SO-AND-SO, SON OF SO-AND-SO.

**48.** בֵּיהּ שַׁעֲתָא אִזְדְּמַן חַד מְמָנָא, דְּאִיהוּ גִּזְבָּרָא עַל דִּיּוּקְנִין דְּצַדִּיקַיָּא,
בְּרָזָא דְשִׁמּוּשָׁא דְּאַתְוָון, דְּאִתְקְרֵי בְּרָזָא יְהוֹדִי״עָם, בְּכִתְרָא דְשִׁמּוּשָׁא
דִּשְׁמָא קַדִּישָׁא. וְרָמִיז קוּדְשָׁא בְּרִיךְ הוּא לְהַהוּא מְמָנָא, וְאַיְיתֵי
דִּיּוּקְנֵיהּ דְּהַהוּא ב״נ דְּעָבִיד נַפְשָׁאן דְּחַיָּיבַיָּא וְקָאִים לֵיהּ קַמֵּי מַלְכָּא
וּמַטְרוֹנִיתָא.

**48.** At that moment, there appears an overseer who is the treasurer of the
images of the righteous in the secret of cohabitation of the letters, MEANING
THE PAIRING OF THE LETTERS OF THE NAME, called 'Yehodiam', WHICH
IS SPELLED WITH THE LETTERS *YUD-HEI-VAV* OF THE NAME. IT IS IN
THE SECRET OF the crown of the pairing OF THE LETTERS *YUD* AND *HEI*
of the Holy Name, WHICH IS DA'AT. And the Holy One, blessed be He,
gestures to that minister, and brings the image of that person who made over
the souls of the wicked to stand before the King and Queen.

**49.** וַאֲנָא אַסְהֲדְנָא עֲלֵי שְׁמַיָּא וְאַרְעָא דְּבַהֲהִיא שַׁעֲתָא מַסְרִין לֵיהּ
הַהוּא דִּיּוּקְנָא. דְּהָא לֵית לָךְ כָּל צַדִּיקָא בְּהַאי עָלְמָא, דְּלָא חָקִיק
דִּיּוּקְנֵיהּ לְעֵילָא, תְּחוֹת יְדָא דְּהַהוּא מְמָנָא. וּמַסְרִין בִּידֵיהּ ע׳ מַפְתְּחָן
דְּכָל גִּנְזַיָּא דְּמָארֵיהּ בְּהוּ. כְּדֵין מַלְכָּא בָּרִיךְ לְהַהוּא דִּיּוּקְנָא, בְּכָל
בִּרְכָּאן דְּבָרִיךְ לְאַבְרָהָם, כַּד עָבֵד נַפְשָׁאן דְּחַיָּיבַיָּא.

**49.** Rabbi Shimon said: I bring witness upon me the heavens and the earth that at that moment they give to Him the image OF THE RIGHTEOUS ONE, because there is no righteous person in this world that does not have his image engraved above unless under the jurisdiction of this overseer. And seventy keys of all the treasures of his Master, WHICH IS THE SECRET OF THE SEVEN LOWER SFIROT OF CHOCHMAH, are given over into the hand OF THE RIGHTEOUS ONE. The King then blesses the image OF THAT RIGHTEOUS ONE with all the blessings that He blessed Abraham when he made over the souls of the wicked, AS IN THE SECRET OF THE VERSE: "THE SOULS THEY HAD ACQUIRED IN CHARAN" (BERESHEET 12:5).

50. וְקוּדְשָׁא בְּרִיךְ הוּא רָמִיז לד' מַשְׁרְיָין עִלָּאִין, וְנַטְלִין לְהַהוּא דְיוּקְנָא, וְאַזְלִין עִמֵיהּ, וְאִיהוּ עָאל לְע׳ עָלְמִין גְּנִיזִין, דְּלָא זָכֵי בְּהוּ בַּר נָשׁ אַחֲרָא, בַּר אִינוּן גְּנִיזִין דְּעַבְדֵי נַפְשֵׁיהוֹן דְּחַיָּיבַיָּא. וְאִלְמָלֵי הֲווֹ יַדְעֵי בְּנֵי נָשָׁא, כַּמָּה תּוֹעַלְתָּא וּזְכוּ וְזַכָּאן בְּגִינַיְיהוּ כַּד זָכוּ לְהוֹן. הֲווֹ אַזְלֵי אֲבַתְרַיְיהוּ, וְרַדְפֵי לוֹן כְּמַאן דְּרָדִיף בָּתַר חַיִּין.

**50.** The Holy One, blessed be He, gestures to four camps of supernal ANGELS, who take that image and go with it. He enters seventy concealed worlds that no other person EXCEPT HIM merited, because these worlds are concealed and are only for those who made over the souls of the wicked. If people knew how much benefit and merit they would acquire when they merit them WITH REPENTANCE, they would go after them and pursue them as one who pursues life.

51. מִסְכְּנָא זָכֵי לִבְנֵי נָשָׁא בְּכַמָּה טָבָאן, בְּכַמָּה גְּנִיזִין עִלָּאִין, וְלָאו אִיהוּ כְּמַאן דְּזָכֵי בְּחַיָּיבַיָּא. מַה בֵּין הַאי לְהַאי. אֶלָּא מַאן דְּאִשְׁתַּדַּל בָּתַר מִסְכְּנָא, אִיהוּ אַשְׁלִים חַיִּין לְנַפְשֵׁיהּ, וְגָרִים לֵיהּ לְאִתְקַיְּימָא, וְזָכֵי בְּגִינֵיהּ, לְכַמָּה טָבָאן לְהַהוּא עָלְמָא. וּמַאן דְּאִשְׁתַּדַּל בָּתַר חַיָּיבַיָּא, אִיהוּ אַשְׁלִים יַתִּיר. עָבִיד לְסִטְרָא אַחֲרָא דֶּאֱלֹהִים אֲחֵרִים דְּאִתְכַּפְיָא, וְלָא שַׁלְטָא, וְאַעֲבַר לֵיהּ מְשֻׁלְטָנוּתֵיהּ. עָבִיד דְּאִסְתַּלַּק קוּדְשָׁא בְּרִיךְ הוּא עַל כּוּרְסֵי יְקָרֵיהּ. עָבִיד לְהַהוּא חַיָּיבָא, נַפְשָׁא אַחֲרָא. זַכָּאָה חוּלָקֵיהּ.

**51.** A poor person causes people to merit much good and many supernal treasures, but not like one who brings merit to the wicked. What is the difference between them? Simply, he who works for and does charity with the poor enlivens his soul, enables him to live and merits because he has done much good in this world. But he who endeavors after the wicked, TO RETURN THEM TO REPENT, accomplishes even more, because he causes the other Elohim of the Other Side to become subdued and removes him from his dominion. He causes the Holy One, blessed be He, to become elevated upon His Throne of Glory and makes a new soul for that wicked one. Happy is his share.

**52.** גְּוּונָא אַחֲרָא, דְּאִתְחֲזֵי וְלָא אִתְחֲזֵי, בְּשַׁעֲתָא דְּמָטָאן יִשְׂרָאֵל לִקְדוּשָׁה דְּסִידְרָא, כְּדֵין הַאי גְּוּונָא דְּגָנִיז, וְנָפִיק, בְּגִין דְּהַאי אִיהוּ קְדוּשָׁתָא דְּקָא מְקַדְּשֵׁי יִשְׂרָאֵל יַתִּיר עַל מַלְאֲכֵי עִלָּאֵי, דְּאִינוּן חַבְרִים בַּהֲדַיְיהוּ. וְהַאי גְּוּונָא נָהִיר וְאִתְחֲזֵי בְּשַׁעֲתָא דְּיִשְׂרָאֵל מְקַדְּשֵׁי קְדוּשָׁתָא דָּא, עַד דִּמְסַיְּימֵי יִשְׂרָאֵל, בְּגִין דְּלָא יִשְׁגְּחוּן מַלְאָכִים עִלָּאִין, וְיַעֲנִישׁוּ לוֹן לְעֵילָא, וְלָא יְקַטְרְגוּן עֲלַיְיהוּ.

**52.** The other color, NAMELY THE THIRD COLOR, is visible yet not visible WHEN THE SUN SHINES. When Yisrael reach the Kedushah (lit. 'sanctification') in the prayer, NAMELY THE SANCTIFICATION IN THE PRAYER: "BUT TO ZION A REDEEMER SHALL COME" (YESHAYAH 59:20), that THIRD color which was concealed emerges, because this sanctification is sanctified by the children of Yisrael even more than the supernal angels who are comrades with them. That color shines and is seen at the time that the children of Yisrael say this sanctification until they finish it, so that the supernal angels should not notice and punish them above and should not accuse them.

**53.** כְּדֵין כְּרוֹזָא נָפִיק וְאָמַר, עִלָּאִין וְתַתָּאִין אָצִיתוּ, מַאן אִיהוּ גַּס רוּחָא בְּמִלֵּי דְּאוֹרַיְיתָא, מַאן אִיהוּ דְּכָל מִלּוֹי בְּגִין לְמִגְבַּהּ בְּמִלֵּי דְּאוֹרַיְיתָא בְּגִין דְּתַנֵּינָן, דְּבַר נָשׁ בָּעֵי לְמֶהֱוֵי שָׁפִיל בְּהַאי עָלְמָא בְּמִלֵּי דְּאוֹרַיְיתָא, דְּהָא לֵית גַּבְהוּ בְּאוֹרַיְיתָא, אֶלָּא בְּעָלְמָא דְּאָתֵי.

**53.** Then a proclamation is issued: Those above and those below who are haughty with the words of Torah, listen carefully. Who is he that all his

words are only to be proud with the words of Torah? As we learned man needs to be humble in the world with the words of Torah, because there is no pride due to the Torah except in the World to Come.

54. בְּקְדוּשָׁתָא דָא, בָּעֵינָן לְאִסְתַּמְּרָא, וּלְאַגְנְזָא לָהּ בֵּינָנָא, בְּגִין דְּנִתְקַדֵּשׁ גּוֹ קְדוּשָׁה בְּרֵישָׁא וּבְסוֹפָא. יַתִּיר מֵאִינּוּן קְדוּשִׁין דְּאָמְרֵי בַּהֲדָן מַלְאֲכֵי עִלָּאֵי. קְדוּשָׁה דְּאֲנָן מְקַדְּשֵׁי בִּשְׁבָחָא דְּאֲנָן מְשַׁבְּחָן לְמַלְאֲכֵי עִלָּאֵי, וּבְגִין שְׁבָחָא דָא, שַׁבְקִין לָן לְמֵיעַאל גּוֹ תַּרְעֵי עִלָּאֵי, וְעַל דָּא אֲנָן אַמְרִין קְדוּשָׁה דָא בְּלִשׁוֹן הַקֹּדֶשׁ, וְשַׁבְקִין לָן בִּרְחִימוּ, לְמֵיעַאל תַּרְעִין דִּלְעֵילָּא, מִגּוֹ דְּאֲנָן מְשַׁבְּחִין לוֹן בְּסִדּוּרָא דִלְהוֹן. וּבְגִין כָּךְ, אֲנָן נַטְלִין קְדוּשָׁן יַתִּיר, וְעָאלִין תַּרְעִין עִלָּאִין.

54. We must be guarded and conceal this sanctification among us in order that we become holy with sanctification in the beginning and in the end, more than with these sanctifications that the supernal angels say with us. The sanctification that we recite IN THE AMIDAH IS the praise that we praise the supernal angels, who permit us to enter the supernal gates for this praise. Therefore, we recite this sanctification in the Holy Language, WHICH IS THE LANGUAGE THAT THE MINISTERING ANGELS USE, and they leave us to come with love into the gates of above because we praise them in their system. NAMELY, WE SAY, 'AND ONE CRIED TO ANOTHER, AND SAID,' so we receive a great sanctification and enter into the highest gates.

55. וְאִי תֵּימָא רְמָאוּתָא הִיא. לָאו הָכִי. אֶלָּא מַלְאֲכֵי עִלָּאֵי אִינּוּן קַדִּישִׁין יַתִּיר מִינָן, וְאִינּוּן נַטְלֵי קְדוּשָׁתָא יַתִּיר, וְאִלְמָלֵא דְּאֲנָן נַטְלִין וּמַשְׁכִין עֲלָן קְדוּשָׁאן אִלֵּין, לָא נֵיכוּל לְמֶהֱוֵי חַבְרִים בַּהֲדַיְיהוּ, וִיקָרָא דְקוּדְשָׁא בְּרִיךְ הוּא לָא יִשְׁתְּלִים עֵילָּא וְתַתָּא בְּזִמְנָא חֲדָא. וְעַל דָּא אֲנָן מִשְׁתַּדְּלִין לְמֶהֱוֵי עִמְּהוֹן חַבְרִים, וְיִסְתַּלָּק יְקָרָא דְקוּדְשָׁא בְּרִיךְ הוּא עֵילָּא וְתַתָּא בְּזִמְנָא חֲדָא.

55. And if you say that WHAT WE PRAISE THEM is deception, and THAT IT IS NOT WITH A WHOLE HEART BUT ONLY TO RECEIVE SANCTIFICATION, this is not so. The supernal angels are holier than us, and they receive more sanctification. If it were not for the fact that we take and draw upon

ourselves these sanctifications THROUGH THE PRAISE WE GIVE THEM, we could not be friends with them. And the glory of the Holy One, blessed be He, would not be complete above and below at one time, BECAUSE WE WOULD NOT BE ABLE TO RECEIVE SUPERNAL SANCTIFICATION. Therefore, we endeavor to be friends with them THROUGH THE PRAISE WE GIVE THEM, and the glory of the Holy One, blessed be He, should rise above and below at the same time.

56. קְדוּשָׁה דִּי בְּסוֹפָא, אִיהִי תַּרְגוּם, כְּמָה דְּאוֹקִימְנָא. וְדָא אֲפִילוּ יָחִיד יָכִיל לוֹמַר לָהּ, אִינוּן מִלֵּי דְּתַרְגוּם. אֲבָל מִלִּין דְּלָשׁוֹן הַקֹּדֶשׁ דִּקְדוּשָׁה, לָאו אִינוּן אֶלָּא בַּעֲשָׂרָה, בְּגִין דְּלָשׁוֹן הַקֹּדֶשׁ שְׁכִינְתָּא מִתְחַבְּרָא בַּהֲדֵיהּ. וּבְכָל קְדוּשָׁה דִּשְׁכִינְתָּא אַתְיָא, לָאו אִיהוּ אֶלָּא בַּעֲשָׂרָה. דִּכְתִיב, וְנִקְדַּשְׁתִּי בְּתוֹךְ בְּנֵי יִשְׂרָאֵל וְגוֹ', בְּנֵי יִשְׂרָאֵל אִינוּן לָשׁוֹן הַקֹּדֶשׁ וַדַּאי, וְלָא שְׁאָר עַמִּין דְּאִית לוֹן לִישָׁן אַחֲרָא.

56. The sanctification which is at the end, IN "AND A REDEEMER SHALL COME TO ZION," is translated, as we have established. Even a solitary man may say this SINCE they are words of translation, but the sanctification that is in the Holy Language may be recited only when ten are present, because the Shechinah joins the sanctification. When the Shechinah is present, any sanctification is only recited by ten, as it is written: "But I will be hallowed among the children of Yisrael" (Vayikra 22:32). The children of Yisrael certainly speak in the Holy Language, unlike the other nations that speak a different language.

57. וְאִי תֵּימָא, הָא קְדוּשָׁתָא דְּקַדִּישׁ, דְּאִיהוּ תַּרְגוּם, אַמַּאי לָאו אִיהוּ בְּיָחִיד. ת"ח, קְדוּשָׁתָא דָּא, לָאו אִיהוּ כִּשְׁאָר קְדוּשָׁאן דְּאִינוּן מְשַׁלְשְׁלִין. אֲבָל קְדוּשָׁתָא דָּא, אִיהִי סַלְקָא בְּכָל סִטְרִין, לְעֵילָא וְתַתָּא וּבְכָל סִטְרֵי מְהֵימְנוּתָא, וְתַבְרָא מַנְעוּלִין וְגוּשְׁפַּנְקָן דְּפַרְזְלָא, וּקְלִיפִין בִּישִׁין, לְאִסְתַּלְּקָא יְקָרָא דְּקוּדְשָׁא בְּרִיךְ הוּא עַל כֹּלָּא, וַאֲנָן בָּעֵינָן לְמֵימַר לָהּ בְּלִישָׁנָא דְּסִטְרָא אַחֲרָא, וּלְאַתָּבָא בְּחֵילָא תַּקִּיף, אָמֵן יְהֵא שְׁמֵיהּ רַבָּא מְבָרַךְ, בְּגִין דְּיִתְבַּר חֵילָא דְּסִטְרָא אַחֲרָא, וְיִסְתַּלַּק קוּדְשָׁא בְּרִיךְ הוּא בִּיקָרֵיהּ עַל כֹּלָּא. וְכַד אִתְּבַר בִּקְדוּשָׁתָא דָּא חֵילָא דְּסִטְרָא

אָחֳרָא, קוּדְשָׁא בְּרִיךְ הוּא אִסְתַּלָּק בִּיקָרֵיה, וְאַדְכַּר לִבְנוֹי, וְאַדְכַּר
לִשְׁמֵיה. וּבְגִין דְּקוּדְשָׁא בְּרִיךְ הוּא אִסְתַּלָּק בִּיקָרֵיה בִּקְדוּשָׁתָא דָּא,
לָאו אִיהוּ אֶלָּא בַּעֲשָׂרָה.

**57.** And if you ask: Why isn't the sanctification of Kaddish, which is in Aramaic, recited alone? HE ANSWERS: Come and see, this sanctification, MEANING KADDISH, is not like the other kinds of sanctification which are tripled, but this sanctification is in all the sides, above and below and in all sides of the Faith. It breaks even locks and rings of iron and evil Klipot, so that the glory of the Holy One, blessed be He, shall ascend above all. We must say it in the language of the Other Side, and answer, 'Amen. May His Great Name be blessed' with great strength, in order to break the power of the Other Side. Then, the Holy One, blessed be He, should ascend in His glory over all. When power of the Other Side is broken with this sanctification, the Holy One, blessed be He, becomes elevated in His glory, and He remembers His children and His name. Because the Holy One, blessed be He, ascends in His glory through this sanctification, it can be recited only among ten.

**58.** וּבְלִישָׁנָא דָּא, עַל כָּרְחֵיה דְּסִטְרָא אַחֳרָא אִתְכַּפְיָא, וְאִתְתְּבַר
חֵילֵיה, וְאִסְתַּלָּק יְקָרָא דְּקוּדְשָׁא בְּרִיךְ הוּא, וְתָבַר מַנְעוּלִין וְגוּשְׁפַּנְקָן
וְשַׁלְשְׁלָאן תַּקִּיפִין, וּקְלִיפִין בִּישִׁין, וְאַדְכַּר קוּדְשָׁא בְּרִיךְ הוּא לִשְׁמֵיה
וְלִבְנוֹי. זַכָּאִין אִינּוּן עַמָּא קַדִּישָׁא דְּקוּדְשָׁא בְּרִיךְ הוּא יָהַב לָן אוֹרַיְיתָא
קַדִּישָׁא, לְמִזְכֵּי בָּה לְעָלְמָא דְּאָתֵי.

**58.** The Other Side is subdued against his will by this language OF ARAMAIC, and its power is broken. The glory of the Holy One, blessed be He, ascends and breaks locks and rings and strong chains and evil Klipot, and the Holy One, blessed be He, remembers His name and children. Blessed are they, the holy people, that the Holy One, blessed be He, gives them the Holy Torah to merit through it the World to Come.

**59.** אר"ש לְחַבְרַיָּיא, זַכָּאִין אַתּוּן לְעָלְמָא דְּאָתֵי, וְכֵיוָן דְּשָׁרֵינָן מִלִּין
דְּכִתְרָא דְּמַלְכוּתָא עִלָּאָה אֵימָא אֲנָא בְּגִינַיְיכוּ וְקוּדְשָׁא בְּרִיךְ הוּא יָהִיב

לְכוֹן אַגְרָא בְּהַהוּא עָלְמָא. וְהַהוּא הֶבֶל דְּפוּמַיְיכוּ, יִסְתַּלֵּק לְעֵילָא,
כְּאִילוּ אַתּוּן מִתְעָרִין מִלִּין אִלֵּין.

**59.** Rabbi Shimon said to the friends: Blessed are you in the World to Come. Since I started the words of the supernal Crown of Royalty, I will say MORE and only for you. May the Holy One, blessed be He, grant you reward in that world, and may the breath of your mouths ascend above as though you yourselves said these words.

## 8. "Gold, and silver, and brass"

### A Synopsis

Rabbi Shimon opens the discussion with the verse, "And this is the offering which you shall take of them; gold, and silver, and brass." This passage is both toward the upper side, which is the side of holiness or the right side, and the lower side, which is the 'other side' or the 'left side'. When God created the world and the tabernacle, he made them opposite, so that while they are both silver and gold, the world is begun from silver, or right, while the tabernacle is begun from gold, or left.

### The Relevance of this Passage

Good and evil are undeniable forces that live within us. This truth is revealed by way of the metal metaphor (gold, silver, and brass), whose purpose is to help us become truly cognizant of their influence. Our inner aspect of good now emerges as our dominant feature, and we, finally, uproot and eliminate the evil component forever. As our own negative traits are toppled, the macrocosmic force of evil is conquered in equal measure.

60. פָּתַח וְאָמַר וְזֹאת הַתְּרוּמָה אֲשֶׁר תִּקְחוּ מֵאִתָּם זָהָב וָכֶסֶף וּנְחֹשֶׁת. הַאי קְרָא אִיהוּ לְסִטְרָא עִלָּאָה, וְאִיהוּ לְסִטְרָא תַּתָּאָה. אִיהוּ לְסִטְרָא עִלָּאָה, בְּסִטְרָא דִקְדוּשָׁה. וְאִיהוּ לְסִטְרָא תַּתָּאָה, בְּסִטְרָא אַחֲרָא. ת"ח, כַּד בָּרָא קוּדְשָׁא בְּרִיךְ הוּא עָלְמָא, שָׁארֵי לְמִבְרֵי מִסִּטְרָא דְכַסְפָּא, דְאִיהוּ יְמִינָא, בְּגִין דְהַהוּא כַּסְפָּא הֲוָה מִלְּעֵילָא. וּבְעוֹבָדָא דְמַשְׁכְּנָא, דְאִיהוּ כְּגַוְונָא דִילֵיהּ, שָׁארֵי מִסִּטְרָא דִשְׂמָאלָא, וּלְבָתַר מִסִּטְרָא דִימִינָא. בְּגִין דְמַשְׁכְּנָא מִסִּטְרָא דִשְׂמָאלָא הֲוָה, וְע"ד שָׁארֵי הָכָא מִסִּטְרָא דִשְׂמָאלָא, וְהָתָם מִסִּטְרָא דִימִינָא, וְזֹאת הַתְּרוּמָה וְגו'.

60. He opened the discussion with the verse: "And this is the offering which you shall take of them; gold, and silver, and brass" (Shemot 25:3). This passage is both toward the upper side and the lower side, AND HE EXPLAINS the upper side means the side of holiness, NAMELY THE RIGHT SIDE, and the lower side MEANS another side, WHICH MEANS THE LEFT SIDE, BECAUSE THE TABERNACLE WAS FIRST BUILT FROM THE LEFT SIDE AND WAS AFTERWARDS JOINED TO THE RIGHT SIDE. Come and see: When the Holy One, blessed be He, created the world, He started to create from the

side of silver, which is right, because silver is higher THAN GOLD, BECAUSE SILVER IS CHESED AND RIGHT, AND GOLD IS GVURAH AND THE ATTRIBUTE OF THE LEFT. In the construction of the tabernacle, which is similar TO MALCHUT, He started from the left side, WHICH IS GOLD, and then from the right side, WHICH IS SILVER, since the tabernacle is from the left side. Therefore, it starts here from the left side, FROM GOLD, and there BY THE CREATION OF THE WORLD from the right side, as it is written: "And this is the offering…"

## 9. "Evening, and morning, and at noon"

### A Synopsis

This section tells us of the spirits of the night and why they are much to be feared. They are nourished, we learn, in the darkness, when the leftovers of the sacrifice are burned and the smoke rises up, twisting toward a hole in the north (keri) from which they emerge. The overseer of these spirits, we are told, is named Sangirya, and they come out only when they need to feast on the smoke of sacrificial fires. The purpose of the evening prayer is to protect us from fear of the night. On Shabbat, this prayer is not necessary because there is no fear of hell nor of other judgments on that night. At midnight, when the north wind is aroused, it attacks all the habitations of these evil spirits, breaks through to the Other Side and enters in there, floating above and below. This breaks the power of the spirits and they no longer rule in their realm. Then, we learn, God enters to amuse Himself with the righteous in the Garden of Eden. When morning comes it completes the outpouring of good to all the worlds; it waters the Garden, and in this action protects the whole world. The rabbis go on to discuss the letters that appear in the eastern sky before dawn. One pillar is thrust into the southern edge of the firmament's canopy that is over the Garden; and in this pillar there is one branch, and in this branch are three birds who are aroused to sing in praise.

### The Relevance of this Passage

This is where we ignite the Light of the three daily prayers, the energy of Shabbat, and the primordial power of the 42-Letter Name of God. Much good is accomplished through the energy that is awakened here. First, the negative forces that, throughout history, have risen after dark are now battered and broken by this awesome display of Light. All judgments are halted. The fires that have blazed in Hell for millennia are doused. Our dreams of the night are forever shielded from the negative forces (Lilit) that have caused man to discharge and waste his semen since the dawn of human existence.

These negative forces have used this squandered life force to sustain their own negative existence. Thus, this force of negativity is now rendered powerless. Our soul achieves dominion over the Evil Inclination, and we help others achieve this same mastery simply by meditating upon them with a loving heart.

Second, the cosmic morning (the age of Messiah) now dawns. The blissful melody of birds in morning song fills us with untold joy. Balance is restored to our lives and to the world. This portion completes our spiritual evolution, for that is the ultimate wish and desire of the author of this all-powerful book.

61. וּכְתִיב עֶרֶב וָבֹקֶר וְצָהֲרַיִם וְגוֹ', הַאי קְרָא אוּקְמוּהָ וְאִתְּמַר, אֲבָל הָכָא עִדָּן עִדָּנִין הוּא דִּצְלוֹתָא דְּכָל יוֹמָא. וְחַבְרַיָּיא אִתְעֲרוּ בְּהָנֵי תְּלַת זִמְנִין. עֶרֶב, דָּא הִיא אַסְפַּקְלַרְיָאה דְּלָא נָהֲרָא. וָבֹקֶר, דָּא הִיא אַסְפַּקְלַרְיָאה דְּנָהֲרָא. וְצָהֲרַיִם, אֲתָר דְּאִתְקְרֵי חֹשֶׁךְ אִיהוּ, דְּאָחִיד בַּעֲרֶב, וְקַיְימָא דָּא עִם דָּא.

61. It is written: "Evening, and morning, and at noon" (Tehilim 55:18). We have established and learned this passage. These are the daily times of prayer, and the friends remarked about these three times THAT evening is the mirror that does not shine, WHICH IS MALCHUT. Morning is the mirror that shines, WHICH IS ZEIR ANPIN, and noon is the place that is called darkness, WHICH IS GVURAH, and is attached to evening, WHICH IS MALCHUT. They stand one with the other, BECAUSE THE LEFT IS ATTACHED TO MALCHUT.

62. וּמַה דְּאִתְּמַר צָהֲרַיִם, דְּאִיהוּ תּוּקְפָּא דְּשִׁמְשָׁא. לִישָׁנָא מַעַלְיָא נָקַט. וְהָכִי אִיהוּ אָרְחָא, לְבַר נָשׁ אוּכָם, קָרָאן לֵיהּ חִוּוֹר, וְלִישָׁנָא מַעַלְיָא נָקַט, וּלְזִמְנִין לְחִוּוֹר קָרָאן לֵיהּ אוּכָם, דִּכְתִיב כִּי אִשָּׁה כוּשִׁית לָקַח הֲלֹא כִבְנֵי כוּשִׁיִּים אַתֶּם לִי וְגוֹ'.

62. We learned that noon is the strength of the sun and is simply a flowery language, because that is the way that a black person is referred to as white, for a flowery language is used. Sometimes white is called black, as it is written: "For he had taken a Kushite (Eng. 'black') woman" (Bemidbar 12:1) and "Are you not as much mine as the children of the Kushite?" (Amos 9:7).

63. עֶרֶב דָּא, צְלוֹתָא דְּעַרְבִית. וּבְגִין דִּבְעֶרֶב דָּא אִתְעֲרַב בֵּיהּ סִטְרָא אַחֲרָא, דְּחָשִׁיךְ נְהוֹרֵיהּ, וְשַׁלְטָא בְּלֵילְיָא, שַׁוּוּ לֵיהּ רְשׁוּת, וְלֵית לֵיהּ זְמַן קָבַע, אֵימוּרִין וּפְדָרִין מִתְאַכְּלִין בְּהַאי זִמְנָא, וּמִכָּאן אִתְזְנוּ כַּמָּה חֲבִילֵי טְהִירִין, דְּנָפְקִין וְשַׁלְטִין בְּלֵילְיָא.

63. Evening refers to Arvit (Eng. 'the evening prayer') and the Other Side is mixed with the evening, since its light has darkened and ruled by night. Therefore, they made it optional. THE EVENING SERVICE does not have a

set time, BECAUSE IT CORRESPONDS TO the portions and fats THAT WERE LEFT OVER FROM THE SACRIFICES and are consumed at this time, ALL NIGHT ON THE ALTAR. Many legions of spirits that go out and dominate the night are nourished from them, BECAUSE THE EXTERNALS ARE NOURISHED FROM THE LEFTOVERS OF THE OFFERING.

64. וְאִי תֵּימָא, אִי הָכִי, הָא תָּנֵינָן, דְּכָל אִינּוּן מָארֵי סִטְרָא אַחֲרָא דְּרוּחַ מִסְאֲבָא, לָא שַׁלְטֵי בְּאַרְעָא קַדִּישָׁא, וְהָא מִתְעָרֵי לוֹן יִשְׂרָאֵל בְּהַאי, וְאָסִיר לְאִתְעָרָא לוֹן לְשַׁרְיָא עַל אַרְעָא קַדִּישָׁא.

**64.** If you ask: Have we not learned that all these members of the spirit of impurity of the Other Side do not dominate in the Holy Land? And that Yisrael arouse themselves in this, TO CHASE THEM AWAY, and it is forbidden to entice them to dwell in the Holy Land?

65. אֶלָּא בְּלֵילְיָא, הַהוּא תְּנָנָא סָלִיק, וְלָא סָלִיק כְּגַוְונָא דְּקָרְבְּנָא אַחֲרָא, דַּהֲוָה סָלִיק תְּנָנָא בְּאֹרַח מֵישָׁר, וְהָכָא הֲוָה סָלִיק הַהוּא תְּנָנָא לְחַד נוּקְבָּא דְּצָפוֹן, דְּתַמָּן כָּל מָדוֹרִין דְּרוּחִין בִּישִׁין, וְכֵיוָן דְּהַהוּא תְּנָנָא סָלִיק וְעָקִים אֹרַח לְהַהוּא סִטְרָא כֻּלְּהוּ הֲווֹ מִתְזָנִין וְקַיְימִין וְעָאלִין בְּדוּכְתַּיְיהוּ, וְלָא הֲווֹ נָפְקִין וְשַׁלְטִין בְּעָלְמָא.

**65.** HE ANSWERS: During the night, that smoke OF THE PORTIONS AND FATS rises, but doesn't rise like THE SMOKE OF any other offering, for the smoke rises in a straight line. Yet here that smoke rises to a hole in the north, where the habitation of the evil spirits is, and since the smoke would rise and twist to that side, they would all be nourished and stand and enter their places. They would not go out FROM THERE to dominate the world.

66. חַד מְמַנָּא קַיְימָא לְהַהוּא סִטְרָא, עַל הַהוּא נוּקְבָּא דְּצָפוֹן, בְּכָל אִינּוּן חֲבִילֵי טְהִירִין, סַנְגִּירִי"א שְׁמֵיהּ, וּבְשַׁעֲתָא דְּהַהוּא תְּנָנָא עָקִים אָרְחֵיהּ וְסָלִיק, הַאי מְמַנָּא וְשִׁתִּין אֶלֶף רִבּוֹא מַשְׁרְיָין אַחֲרָנִין, כֻּלְּהוּ מִתְעַתְּדָן לְקַבְּלָא לֵיהּ, וּלְאִתְּזָנָא מִנֵּיהּ, וְקַיְימִין בְּהַהוּא נוּקְבָּא, וְעָאלִין בְּחַד פִּתְחָא דְּאִקְרֵי קְרִי, וְדָא אִיהוּ רָזָא דִּכְתִיב, וְאִם תֵּלְכוּ עִמִּי קֶרִי וְגוֹ',

-47-

וּכְתִיב, וְהָלַכְתִּי עִמָּכֶם בַּחֲמַת קֶרִי, בְּהַהוּא רוּגְזָא דְּנָפִיק מִפִּתְחָא דְּקֶרִי.

**66.** There was one overseer there at that side over that hole in the north over all these groups of spirits, and his name was Sangirya. When that smoke would twist his way and ascend, this overseer, and sixty million other encampments, were all waiting to accept it and be nourished from it. They would stand in that hole THAT IS IN THE NORTH, and enter through one entrance called 'keri'. This is the secret of that which is written: "And if you walk contrary (Heb. *keri*) to me" (Vayikra 26:21) and that which is written: "Then I will walk contrary to you also in fury" (Ibid. 28), MEANING with that anger that goes forth from the entrance CALLED 'keri'.

67. וְאִלֵּין אִינּוּן דִּמְשַׁטְּטֵי בְּלֵילְיָא, וּבְשַׁעֲתָא דְּנִשְׁמָתִין נָפְקִין לְסַלְּקָא, לְאִתְחֲזָאָה לְעֵילָּא, אִינּוּן נָפְקִין, וּמְקַטְרְגָן לוֹן, וְלָא יַכְלִין לְסַלְּקָא וּלְאִתְחֲזָאָה לְעֵילָּא, בַּר אִינּוּן חֲסִידֵי קַדִּישִׁין עֶלְיוֹנִים, דְּאִינּוּן בַּקְעִין רְקִיעִים וַאֲוִירִים וְסַלְּקִין. וְאִלֵּין חֲבִילֵי טְהִירִין נָפְקִין, וּמוֹדִיעִין מִלִּין כְּדִיבִין לִבְנֵי נָשָׁא, וְאִתְחֲזִיָּין לוֹן בְּדִיּוּקְנִין אַחֲרָנִין, וְחַיְיכָאן בְּהוּ, עַד דְּאוֹשְׁדִין זַרְעָא, וְאִקְרוּן מָארֵיהוֹן דְּקֶרִי, בְּגִין דְּאִינּוּן דְּנָפְקִין מִפִּתְחָא דְּקֶרִי, גַּרְמֵי לוֹן.

**67.** There are those who float around during the night, IF THEY ARE NOT BEING NOURISHED FROM THE SMOKE AS MENTIONED EARLIER. When the souls emerge from the entrance to appear above, they go out and accuse them, so they are not able to ascend and appear above, except for those holy supernal pious ones who split the firmaments and airs and ascend. These camps of spirits go forth and inform people with falsehoods, and appear to them in other FEMALE forms and seduce them until they discharge semen. They are called men who have nocturnal emission of semen (Heb. *keri*), because it causes those who go forth from the entrance called 'keri' TO BE CALLED MEN OF NOCTURNAL EMISSION.

68. וּבְשַׁעֲתָא דְּמִתְאַכְּלֵי אֲמוּרִין וּפַדְרִין, הַהוּא תְּנָנָא הֲוֵי רַוֵּי לוֹן, וְזָן לוֹן, כְּפוּם יְקָרָא דִּלְהוֹן הָכִי מְזוֹנָא דִּלְהוֹן, מַה דְּאִתְחֲזֵי לוֹן. וּבְהַאי, לָא נַפְקָן, וְלָא מְשַׁטְּטֵי בְּאַרְעָא קַדִּישָׁא.

-48-

**68.** During the time that the portions and fats were consumed ON THE ALTAR, that smoke would give them drink and nourish them, according to their stature and according to their needs. Therefore, they would not go forth and float over the Holy Land.

69. עֶרֶב: כד"א, וְגַם עֶרֶב רַב עָלָה אִתָּם, דְּכָל אִינוּן חֲבִילֵי טְהִירִין, אִינוּן מִתְעָרְבֵי בְּשׁוּלְטָנוּ דְּלֵילְיָא. וְע"ד לָא שַׁוְּיוּהָא חוֹבָא לִצְלוֹתָא דְּעַרְבִית, דְּלֵית מַאן דְּיָכִיל לְאַתְקְנָא לָהּ כְּיַעֲקֹב, דְּאִיהוּ הֲוָה מָארֵי מַשְׁכְּנָא, וּמְתַקֵּן לֵיהּ כַּדְקָא יֵאוֹת.

**69.** Evening (Heb. *erev*) is called so, as it is written: "And a mixed multitude (Heb. *erev rav*) went up also with them" (Shemot 12:38), WHICH MEANS A MIXTURE, because all these groups of spirits mingle according to the rule of the night. Therefore, they did not make the evening prayer obligatory, because there was nobody who could correct it like Jacob, who was the master of the tabernacle, WHICH IS MALCHUT, and corrected it properly.

70. וְאע"ג דְּאִיהוּ רְשׁוּ, צְלוֹתָא דָּא אִיהוּ לְאַגָּנָא עָלָן מִגּוֹ פַּחַד בַּלֵּילוֹת, מִגּוֹ פַּחַד דְּכַמָּה סִטְרִין דְּגֵיהִנָּם, דְּהָא בְּהַהִיא שַׁעֲתָא טַרְדֵי לְחַיָּיבַיָּא בַּגֵּיהִנָּם, עַל חַד תְּרֵין מִבִּימָמָא. וּבג"כ, מְקַדְּמֵי יִשְׂרָאֵל לְמֵימַר וְהוּא רַחוּם, דְּאִיהוּ בְּגִין פַּחַד דְּגֵיהִנָּם. וּבְשַׁבָּת דְּלָא אִשְׁתְּכַח פַּחַד דִּינָא דְּגֵיהִנָּם, וְלָא דִּינָא אַחֲרָא, אָסִיר לְאַתְעָרָא לֵיהּ, דְּאִתְחֲזֵי דְּהָא לֵית רְשׁוּ לְשַׁבָּת לְאַעְבְּרָא דִּינָא מֵעָלְמָא.

**70.** Even though it is obligatory, the purpose of the prayer is to protect us from the fear of the nights and the fear of many kinds of Gehenom, because at that time the wicked are punished twice as much as during the day. Therefore, Yisrael hasten to say, "But He was full of compassion" (Tehilim 78:38), for fear of Gehenom. On Shabbat, when there is neither fear of Gehenom nor fear of other Judgments, it is forbidden to awaken it, NAMELY TO SAY, "BUT HE WAS FULL OF COMPASSION," because it would look as though the Shabbat does not have the power to remove Judgment from the world. SO IT IS NECESSARY TO SAY, "AND HE IS COMPASSIONATE."

71. וְפַחַד דְּקַטְרוּגָא דְּנִשְׁמָתִין, כַּד בָּעָאן לְסַלְקָא לְעֵילָא, לְאִתְחֲזָאָה קַמֵּי מָארֵיהוֹן. וּבְג״כ אֲנָן מַקְדִּימִים, שׁוֹמֵר אֶת עַמּוֹ יִשְׂרָאֵל לָעַד אָמֵן. פַּחַד דְּכַמָּה מַזִּיקִין וְקַטְרוּגִין דְּמִשְׁתַּכְּחֵי בְּלֵילְיָא, וְאִית לוֹן רְשׁוּ לְנַזְקָא, לְמַאן דְּנָפִיק מִתְּרַע בֵּיתֵיהּ לְבַר, וּבְג״כ אֲנָן מַקְדִּימִים, וּשְׁמוֹר צֵאתֵנוּ וּבוֹאֵנוּ.

71. There is fear of accusation against the souls when they wish to ascend above to appear before their Master; therefore, we hasten TO SAY '…who guards His nation Yisrael forever. Amen,' MEANING from the fear of many demons and accusers that are prevalent during the night. They have the ability to harm one who goes out of the entrance of his house. Therefore, we first SAY, 'And guard our coming and our going forth.'

72. וְעַל כָּל דָּא, מִגּוֹ דְּחִילוּ דְּכָל דָּא, אֲנָן מַפְקִידִינָן גּוּפִין רוּחִין וְנִשְׁמָתִין, לְמַלְכוּתָא עִלָּאָה, דִּי שׁוּלְטָנוּ דְּכֹלָּא בִּידָהָא. וְעַל דָּא צְלוֹתָא דְּעַרְבִית, בְּכָל לֵילְיָא וְלֵילְיָא. הַשְׁתָּא דְּקָרְבְּנִין וּמַדְבְּחָן לָא אִשְׁתְּכָחוּ, אֲנָן עַבְדֵּינָן כָּל תִּקּוּנִין דְּאֲנָן עַבְדִּין עַל רָזָא דְּנָא.

72. Because of the fear of all this, AS MENTIONED, we deposit our bodies and spirits and souls to the supernal Malchut, for all the dominion is in Her hands. Therefore, the evening prayer is to be recited every single night. Now that offerings and altars are not in existence, we do all the corrections that we do by these means OF THE SMOKE OF THE OFFERINGS.

73. בְּפַלְגּוּ לֵילְיָא, כַּד רוּחַ צָפוֹן אִתְּעַר, בָּטַשׁ בְּכָל אִינּוּן מְדוֹרִין דְּרוּחִין בִּישִׁין, וְתָבַר סִטְרָא אַחֲרָא, וְעָאל וְשָׁאט לְעֵילָא וְתַתָּא, וְכָל אִינּוּן חֲבִילֵי טְהִירִין עַיְילִין לְדוּכְתַּיְיהוּ, וְאִתְּבַּר חֵילַיְיהוּ וְלָא שַׁלְטִין. וּכְדֵין קוּדְשָׁא ב״ה עָאל לְאִשְׁתַּעְשְׁעָא עִם צַדִּיקַיָּא בְּגִנְתָּא דְּעֵדֶן, וְהָא אִתְּמַר.

73. At midnight, when the north wind is aroused, WHICH IS THE LEFT COLUMN THAT COMES THEN TO ITS PERFECTION, it smites all the habitations of the evil spirits, breaks the Other Side and enters and floats above and below. All these groups of spirits enter their place and their

power is broken, so they do not dominate. Then the Holy One, blessed be He, enters to amuse Himself with the righteous in the Garden of Eden, as we have already learned.

74. כַּד אָתֵי צַפְרָא, נְהוֹרָא דִּשְׁרָגָא דְּשָׁלְטָא בְּלֵילְיָא, אִתְגְּנִיז מִקַּמֵּי נְהוֹרָא דִּימָמָא, כְּדֵין בֹּקֶר שַׁלְטָא, וְאִתְעֲבַר שׁוּלְטָנוּ דְּעֶרֶב, הַאי בֹּקֶר, אִיהוּ בֹּקֶר דְּאוֹר קַדְמָאָה, הַאי בֹּקֶר, אַשְׁלִים טִיבוּ לְעָלְמִין כֻּלְּהוּ. מִנֵּיהּ אִתְּזָנוּ עִלָּאִין וְתַתָּאִין. הַאי אַשְׁקֵי לְגִנְתָּא. הַאי אִיהוּ נְטִירוּ דְּכָל עָלְמָא.

74. When the morning comes, the light of the candle that dominates during the night, WHICH IS THE ILLUMINATION OF THE LEFT, is concealed before the light of day, WHICH IS THE LIGHT OF CHASSADIM. Then the morning dominates, WHICH IS YESOD, and the domination of evening is removed, WHICH IS MALCHUT. This morning is the morning of the primordial light. This morning completes the good to all the worlds, and the upper and the lower worlds are nourished from it. It waters the Garden, WHICH IS MALCHUT, and this protects the whole world.

75. הָכָא רָזָא לְיַדְעֵי מִדִּין, מַאן דְּבָעֵי לְמֵיפַק לְאָרְחָא, יְקוּם בְּנַגְהָא, וְיִשְׁגַּח בְּאִסְתַּכְּלוּתָא לְפוּם שַׁעֲתָא, לְסְטַר מִזְרָח, וְיֶחֱמֵי כְּחֵיזוּ דְּאַתְוָון דְּבַטְשֵׁי בִּרְקִיעָא, דָּא סָלִיק וְדָא נָחִית. וְאִלֵּין אִינוּן נְצִיצוּ דְּאַתְוָון, דְּאִתְבְּרוּן בְּהוּ שְׁמַיָּא וְאַרְעָא.

75. Here is the secret for those who understand measurements. One who wishes to go out on a journey should arise when it is still night, watch closely according to the hour toward the east and see the appearance of the letters that strike in the sky. One rises and another falls. These are the sparkling of the letters with which the heavens and earth were created.

76. אִי אִיהוּ יָדַע בְּרָזָא דְּאִינוּן אַתְוָון, דְּאִינוּן רָזָא דִּשְׁמָא קַדִּישָׁא, דְּאַרְבְּעִין וּתְרֵין אַתְוָון, וְיִדְכַּר לוֹן כַּדְקָא חֲזֵי, בִּרְעוּתָא דְּלִבָּא. יֶחֱמֵי גּוֹ נְהִירוּ דְּנַגְהָא דִּרְקִיעָא שִׁית יוֹדִי"ן, תְּלַת לִסְטַר יְמִינָא, וּתְלַת לִסְטַר שְׂמָאלָא. וּתְלַת וָוִין, דְּסַלְקִין וְנַחְתִּין וְנַצְצֵי בִּרְקִיעָא. וְאִינוּן אַתְוָון

דְּבִרְכַּת כֹּהֲנִים, וּכְדֵין יְצַלֵּי צְלוֹתֵיה, וְיִפּוּק לְאָרְחָא, וַדַּאי שְׁכִינְתָּא אַקְדִּימַת עִמֵּיה, זַכָּאָה חוּלְקֵיה.

**76.** If one knows the secret of these letters, which is the secret of the Holy Name of 42 letters, he will mention them properly with a willing heart and will see six *Yuds* in the shine of the brightness of the firmament, three to the right side and three to the left, and three *Vavs* that rise and fall and sparkle in the sky. They are the letters of the Priests' Blessings. THERE ARE SIX *YUDS* IN THEM, NAMELY IN THE FIRST WORDS OF THE PASSAGES, "HASHEM BLESS YOU (HEB. *YEVARECHECHA*)…MAKE HIS COUNTENANCE (HEB. *YA'ER*)…TURN HIS COUNTENANCE (HEB. *YISA*)" (BEMIDBAR 6:24) AND THREE *VAVS* OF: "…AND (*VAV*) GUARD YOU…AND (*VAV*) BE GRACIOUS TO YOU…AND (*VAV*) GRANT YOU" (IBID.). THE *YUDS* are DIVIDED INTO TWO COLUMNS, RIGHT AND LEFT, AND THE *VAVS* ARE THE SECRET OF THE CENTRAL COLUMN THAT UNITES THEM. Then he should pray his prayer and go out on his way, for it is certain that the Shechinah has preceded him. Happy is his position.

77. כַּד אָתֵי הַאי בֹּקֶר, עַמּוּדָא חַד נָעִיץ בְּסִטְרָא דָרוֹם, לְגוֹ מְתִיחוּ דִרְקִיעָא, דְּעַל גַּבֵּי גִּנְתָּא. בַּר מֵהַהוּא עַמּוּדָא, דְּאִיהוּ נָעִיץ בְּאֶמְצָעוּ דְגִנְתָּא. וְעַמּוּדָא דָא, אִיהוּ נָהִיר בִּנְהִירוּ דִּתְלַת גְּוָונִין, מְרֻקָמָא דְּאַרְגְּוָונָא. בְּהַהוּא עַמּוּדָא, קַיְימָא עַנְפָּא חֲדָא, בְּהַהוּא עַנְפָּא, אִתְעֲתָּדוּ תְּלַת צִפֳּרִין, מִתְעָרִין צִפְצְפָא לְשַׁבְּחָא.

**77.** When this morning arrives, one pillar, WHICH IS TIFERET, is thrust in the south side of the spread of the firmament that is over the Garden, MEANING THAT IT LEANS TOWARD CHESED. It is outside of the pillar that is thrust in the center of the Garden. This pillar shines with the shine of three hues, WHICH ARE CHESED, GVURAH AND TIFERET, woven TOGETHER in THE COLOR purple. In this pillar, WHICH IS TIFERET, there is one branch, WHICH IS YESOD. And in this branch are gathered three birds, WHICH ARE THE THREE COLUMNS THAT SHINE IN MALCHUT, FOR THE ILLUMINATION OF CHOCHMAH IN IT IS CALLED 'A BIRD'. They arouse chirping praise.

## 10. "The watchman said, 'The morning comes'"

### A Synopsis

This extremely long section is hardly capable of being summarized, so dense is it with details and instructions for the time and order of prayers. It begins charmingly with a bird, which opens the discussion by giving praise for the morning. Then we hear of the phrase, "Watchman, what of the night?" which the exiled children of Yisrael called out to the Creator. Then the passage continues on to say that the secret of "The burden of Dumah" is that prophecy is transmitted to the prophets in six grades – vision, revelation, sight, appearance, word, and burden. And this particular prophecy of Dumah was not able to be revealed. The secret of Faith is such that grades shine from within grades. The text then describes what kind of prophecy is associated with each grade. Next, we learn that the Watchman of the night is Matatron, about whom it is written, "So he who waits on his Master shall be honored." In the morning the holy people need to join and come to synagogue, we're told, and most blessed is he who arrives first, for he ascends to the level of righteousness. The psalms and praises of David, we next learn, are designed to awaken love above and below, to build perfection and to arouse joy. Warning is then given to those who would speak of worldly matters in the synagogue. While the children of Yisrael are reciting, we're told, three camps of supernal angels gather. There then follows details of the order of prayers, and, after, a long description of the letters of the words of praise and their numerical significance. Next we are reminded again that the sanctification of the Holy Tongue must be said by no fewer than ten, and that those prayers to be said alone are said in Aramaic. Finally, the section comes to a close, exclaiming: "Happy is the portion of Yisrael that become sanctified with the supernal sanctification, because they cleave unto above'."

### The Relevance of this Passage

The seemingly simple act of dialing a friend long distance involves a complex communication network. Cables and wires must be laid, and a host of intricate equipment must be in place to ensure easy and reliable communication. Prayer works a lot like that. This passage of Zohar ensures that all our prayers, and the spiritual connections that we will make here, are as simple as making a telephone call.

In the act of describing the metaphysical circuitry of the upper world, these verses install all the cables and wiring on our behalf. All we must do to set the entire communications network into action is read or meditate upon this text. This is the equivalent of dialing a correct telephone number.

78. פָּתַח חַד וְאָמַר, הַלְלוּיָהּ הַלְלוּ עַבְדֵי יְיָ' הַלְלוּ אֶת שֵׁם יְיָ'. פָּתַח תִּנְיָינָא וְאָמַר, יְהִי שֵׁם יְיָ' מְבוֹרָךְ מֵעַתָּה וְעַד עוֹלָם. פָּתַח תְּלִיתָאָה וְאָמַר, מִמִּזְרַח שֶׁמֶשׁ עַד מְבוֹאוֹ מְהוּלָל שֵׁם יְיָ'. כְּדֵין כָּרוֹזָא קָדִים וְקָרֵי אִתְעַתְדוּ קַדִּישֵׁי עֶלְיוֹנִין, אִינוּן דִּמְשַׁבְּחָן לְמָארֵיהוֹן, אִתְתַּקְנוּ בְּשִׁבְחָא דִימָמָא. כְּדֵין אִתְפָּרְשׁוּן יְמָמָא מִן לֵילְיָא. זַכָּאָה חוּלָקֵיהּ, מַאן דְּקָם בְּצַפְרָא, מִגּוֹ תוּשְׁבַּחְתָּא דְאוֹרַיְיתָא, דְּלָעֵי בְּלֵילְיָא. בְּהַהוּא זִמְנָא צְלוֹתָא דְּצַפְרָא.

78. The first BIRD opened the discussion saying: "Haleluyah, Give praise, servants of Hashem, praise the Name of Hashem" (Tehilim 113:1). THIS IS THE SECRET OF THE RIGHT COLUMN THAT IS IN MALCHUT, WHICH ILLUMINATES CHASSADIM. THEREFORE, IT SAYS: "PRAISE THE NAME OF HASHEM," AN INVITATION TO PRAISE THE NAME OF HASHEM, WHICH IS MALCHUT, AFTER SOME TIME, MEANING AFTER THE CHOCHMAH IN HER WILL ILLUMINATE WHEN SHE WILL BE ATTIRED IN CHASSADIM. The second bird opened the discussion saying: "Blessed be the Name of Hashem from this time forth and for ever more" (Ibid. 2). THIS IS THE SECRET OF THE SHINING OF THE LEFT COLUMN THAT GIVES FORTH THE ILLUMINATION OF CHOCHMAH, WHENCE IS THE ESSENCE OF MALCHUT. AND THEREFORE IT SAYS: "BLESSED BE THE NAME OF HASHEM FROM THIS TIME" THAT SHINES IMMEDIATELY IN MALCHUT, WHICH IS CALLED 'THE NAME OF HASHEM'. The third bird opened the discussion saying: "From this rising of the sun to its setting, praised is the Name of Hashem" (Ibid. 2), WHICH IS THE SECRET OF THE SHINING OF THE CENTRAL COLUMN THAT RECEIVES FROM THE ESSENCE OF TIFERET, THAT IS CALLED 'SUN'. Then a proclamation soon cries, Prepare yourselves supernal Holy Ones, those who praise their Master. Prepare yourselves with the praises of the day. Then the day is separated from the night. Blessed is the portion of he who rises in the morning from the midst of the praise of the Torah with which he was occupied during the night. That is time for the morning prayer.

79. כְּתִיב, אָמַר שׁוֹמֵר אָתָא בֹקֶר וְגַם לָיְלָה אִם תִּבְעָיוּן בְּעָיוּ שֵׁבוּ אֵתָיוּ, הַאי קְרָא אוּקְמוּהַּ לֵיהּ, עַל גָּלוּת דְּיִשְׂרָאֵל, דְּיַתְבֵי גּוֹ בְּנֵי שֵׂעִיר, וְיִשְׂרָאֵל אַמְרֵי לְקוּדְשָׁא בְּרִיךְ הוּא, שׁוֹמֵר, מַה מִלֵּילְיָא, מַה תְּהֵא עֲלָן

מִן גָּלוּתָא דָא, דְּדַמֵּי לַחֲשׁוֹכָא דְּלֵילְיָא. מַה כְּתִיב, אָמַר שׁוֹמֵר, דָּא
קוּדְשָׁא בְּרִיךְ הוּא, אָתָא בֹקֶר, כְּבָר נְהִירְנָא לְכוּ בְּגָלוּתָא דְּמִצְרַיִם,
וְאַסִּיקְנָא לְכוּ וְקָרִיבַת יַתְכוֹן לְפוּלְחָנִי, וְאוֹרַיְיתָא יָהֲבִית לְכוֹן, בְּגִין
דְּתִזְכּוּן לְחַיֵּי עָלְמָא. שְׁבַקְתּוּן אוֹרַיְיתִי, וְגַם לָיְלָה, אָעִילְנָא לְכוּ
בְּגָלוּתָא דְּבָבֶל, וְאַסִּיקְנָא לְכוּ. שְׁבַקְתּוּן אוֹרַיְיתִי כְּמִלְּקַדְּמִין, אָעִילְנָא
לְכוּ בְּגָלוּתָא כְּמִלְּקַדְּמִין. אִם תִּבְעָיוּן בָּעֲיוּ כד״א, דִּרְשׁוּ מֵעַל סֵפֶר יְיָ׳
וְקָרָאוּ, וְתַמָּן תִּשְׁכְּחוּן בַּמֶּה תַּלְיָא גָלוּתָא דִּלְכוֹן, וּגְאוּלָה דִּלְכוֹן, וְכַד
תִּבְעָיוּן בָּהּ, הִיא תֵּימָא וְתַכְרִיז קַמַּיְיכוּ. שׁוּבוּ אֱתָיוּ. שׁוּבוּ בִּתְשׁוּבָה
שְׁלֵימָתָא, וּמִיַּד אֱתָיוּ וְאַקְרִיבוּ לְגַבָּאי.

**79.** It is written: "The watchman said, 'The morning comes, and also the night. If you will inquire, inquire: return, come'" (Yeshayah 21:12). This passage was established to refer to those exiles of Yisrael, who were living among the children of Seir. Yisrael said to the Holy One, blessed be He, "Watchman, what of the night?" (Ibid. 11). What will come of us from this exile that is like the darkness of night? It is written: "The watchman said," and this is the Holy One, blessed be He. "The morning comes": I have already shone upon you during the exile in Egypt, I have raised you and brought you to My service and I gave you the Torah in order that you merit eternal life. You have forsaken My Torah. "And also night": I have brought you to Exile of Babylon and raised you, but you forsook My Torah as before. I brought you again into exile. "If you inquire, inquire" as it is written: "Seek out of the Book of the Hashem, and read" (Yeshayah 34:16). You will find there just what your exile and deliverance are dependent on. If you inquire of it, it will say and proclaim you to "return, come" in complete repentance, and immediately you will come and get close to Me.

80. וּבְהַאי קְרָא כְּתִיב, מַשָּׂא דוּמָה. וְרָזָא דָא, בְּשִׁית דַּרְגִּין דִּנְבוּאָה
אִתְּמַר לִנְבִיאֵי. בְּמַחֲזֶ״ה. בַּחֲזוֹ״ן. בְּחֶזְיוֹ״ן. בְּחָזוּ״ת. בַּדָּבָ״ר. בְּמַשָּׂ״א.
וְכֻלְּהוּ חֲמִשָׁה כֻּלְּהוּ כְּמַאן דְּחָמֵי בָּתַר כּוֹתָלָא, הַהוּא נְהִירוּ דִּנְהוֹרָא.
וּמִנַּיְיהוּ, כְּמַאן דְּחָמֵי נְהוֹרָא דְּשִׁמְשָׁא מִגּוֹ עֲשָׁשִׁיתָא. אֲבָל מַשָּׂא, הֲוֵי,
כַּד מָטֵי הַהוּא נְהוֹרָא בְּטוֹרַח סַגִּי וְאִיטְרַח מִלּוֹי עֲלוֹי, דְּלָא יָכִיל
לְאִתְגַּלְיָיא לֵיהּ, כד״א, לָשׂוּם אֶת מַשָּׂא כָּל הָעָם הַזֶּה עָלָי. וּבְג״כ,

מַשָּׂא.

**80.** In this passage, it is written: "The burden of Dumah" (Yeshayah 21:11). The secret is that prophecy is transmitted to the prophets in six grades, vision, revelation, sight, appearance, word, and burden, and all of them are as one who looks from behind the wall at a shine of the light. It is as though some of them see the light of the sun through a lamp OF GLASS. But this is a burden, as light comes through great effort, because it was difficult for him and he could not reveal it, as it is written: "That You lay the burden of this whole people on me" (Bemidbar 11:11). Therefore, this is CALLED 'burden'.

81. וְהָכָא מַשָּׂא דּוּמָה טוֹרַח סַגִּיאָה, דְּלָא יָכִיל לְאִתְגַּלְיָיא וְאִיהוּ נְבוּאָה בִּלְחִישׁוּ, וְקָיְימָא בִּלְחִישׁוּ. אֵלַי קוֹרֵא מִשֵּׂעִיר הָכָא לָא אִתְגַּלְיָא מַאן אָמַר אֵלַי קוֹרֵא מִשֵּׂעִיר. אִי קוּדְשָׁא בְּרִיךְ הוּא, אִי נְבִיאָה מְהֵימְנָא. אֲבָל נְבוּאָה דָא וַדַּאי קָיְימָא בִּלְחִישׁוּ, גּוֹ רָזָא דִּמְהֵימְנוּתָא עִלָּאָה, וּמִגּוֹ רָזָא סְתִימָאָה, נְבִיאָה מְהֵימְנָא אָמַר, דְּלֵיהּ הֲוָה קָרָא קָלָא בְּרָזָא דִּמְהֵימְנוּתָא, וְאָמַר אֵלַי קוֹרֵא מִשֵּׂעִיר. כד"א, וְזָרַח מִשֵּׂעִיר לָמוֹ. וְלָא כְּתִיב וְזָרַח לְשֵׂעִיר, בְּגִין דְּרָזָא דִּמְהֵימְנוּתָא הָכִי אִיהוּ, דַּרְגִּין מִגּוֹ דַּרְגִּין, אִלֵּין פְּנִימָאִין מֵאִלֵּין, קְלִיפָה, גּוֹ קְלִיפָה וּמוֹחָא גּוֹ מוֹחָא.

**81.** Here IT IS WRITTEN the burden of Dumah, WHICH MEANS great effort, BECAUSE THE PROPHECY was not able to be revealed. It is a secretive prophecy and remains in secrecy. "One calls to Me out of Seir" (Yeshayah 21:11): It is not revealed whether the Holy One, blessed be He, or the faithful prophet SAID, "ONE CALLS TO ME OUT OF SEIR." This prophecy definitely is secret in the midst of the supernal Faith. And from the depth of secrecy, said the faithful prophet, to whom the voice of the secret of the Faith, WHICH IS MALCHUT, called and said, "One calls to me out of Seir," as it is written: "And rose from Seir to them" (Devarim 33:2) instead of, 'And rose to Seir.' This is because the secret of Faith is such that grades shine from within grades, the ones, inside the others, a shell within a shell, one part the inner to another part within which it lies. THEREFORE, IT IS WRITTEN: "FROM SEIR," MEANING THAT IT BECAME REVEALED FROM THE MIDST OF THE KLIPAH (ENG. 'SHELL') OF SEIR.

82. וְהָא אוֹקִימְנָא, דִּכְתִּיב, וְהִנֵּה רוּחַ סְעָרָה בָּאָה מִן הַצָּפוֹן, הָא

דַּרְגָּא חַד. עָנָן גָּדוֹל, הָא דַּרְגָּא אַחֲרָא. וְאֵשׁ מִתְלַקַּחַת, הָא דַּרְגָּא
תְּלִיתָאָה. וְנֹגַהּ לוֹ סָבִיב, הָא דַּרְגָּא רְבִיעָאָה. וּלְבָתַר וּמִתּוֹכָהּ כְּעֵין
הַחַשְׁמַל. וּלְבָתַר וּמִתּוֹכָהּ דְּמוּת אַרְבַּע חַיּוֹת הָא דַּרְגִּין גּוֹ דַּרְגִּין.

**82.** But we have established that it is written: "And, behold, a storm wind came out of the north" (Yechezkel 1:4). This is one grade, while "a great cloud" (Ibid.) is a second grade, "and a fire flaring up" (Ibid.) is a third grade, "and a brightness was about it" (Ibid.) is a fourth grade, and afterwards "And out of the midst of it, as it were the color of electrum" (Ibid.), after which "out of the midst of it came the likeness of four living creatures." (Ibid. 5) These are the grades within grades.

83. אוֹף הָכָא, כַּד אִתְגַּלְּיָיא קוּדְשָׁא בְּרִיךְ הוּא לְיִשְׂרָאֵל, לָא אִתְגַּלְּיָיא
אֶלָּא מִגּוֹ דַּרְגִּין אִלֵּין. מִסִּינַי בָּא, דַּרְגָּא דַּהֲוָה טְמִירָא יַתִּיר, וּלְבָתַר
אִצְטְרִיךְ לְאִתְגַּלְּיָא. וְאָמַר וְזָרַח מִשֵּׂעִיר, הָא דַּרְגָּא אַחֲרָא, דְּאִיהוּ
בְּאִתְגַּלְּיָיא יַתִּיר, קְלִיפָא דְּשַׁרְיָא עַל גַּבֵּי מוֹחָא. וּלְבָתַר הוֹפִיעַ מֵהַר
פָּארָן, הָא דַּרְגָּא אַחֲרָא. וּלְבָתַר וְאָתָה מֵרִבְבוֹת קֹדֶשׁ, דָּא שְׁבָחָא
דְּכֹלָּא, דְּאַף עַל גַּב דְּאִתְגַּלְּיָיא מִכָּל אִלֵּין דַּרְגִּין, מֵהַהוּא אֲתַר דְּהוּא
עִקָּרָא דְּכֹלָּא, שָׁרֵי לְאִתְגַּלָּאָה מִנֵּיהּ. מַאן אֲתַר אִיהוּ. מֵרִבְבוֹת קֹדֶשׁ
אִיהוּ, אִינּוּן דַּרְגִּין עִלָּאִין לְעֵילָּא, אוֹף הָכָא אֵלַי קוֹרֵא מִשֵּׂעִיר,
מֵהַהוּא דַּרְגָּא דְּקָאָמַרָן, דְּאִתְדָּבַק לְעֵילָּא.

**83.** Here also, when the Holy One, blessed be He, became revealed to Yisrael, He did so only from within these grades, and "came from Sinai" (Devarim 33:2). This is the grade that is exceedingly concealed. Afterwards it must be revealed that it said, "And rose from Seir": This is another grade that is more revealed, a shell that envelops the fruit. Then, "He shone forth from Mount Paran" (Ibid.), which is another grade and "He came from holy multitudes" (Ibid.), which is a praise to them all. For even though He became revealed in all these grades, IT IS CONSIDERED THAT He started being revealed from a place which is the essence of all. Which place is it? "Holy multitudes," which are the highest levels above. Here also: "One calls to me out of Seir," meaning from that level that we said ABOVE: "AND ROSE FROM SEIR TO THEM," as he was cleaved to the above.

‏84. שׁוֹמֵר מַה מִלַּיְלָה שׁוֹמֵר מַה מֵלֵיל. שׁוֹמֵר דָּא מְטַטְרוֹ"ן, וּכְתִיב,
וְשׁוֹמֵר אֲדוֹנָיו יְכֻבָּד, וְדָא רָזָא דְּשַׁלְטָא בְּלֵילְיָא. מַה מִלַּיְלָה שׁוֹמֵר מַה
מֵלֵיל, מַה בֵּין הַאי לְהַאי. אֶלָּא, כֹּלָּא חַד, אֲבָל בְּחוּלָקָא דָּא, שַׁלְטָא
סִטְרָא אַחֲרָא. וּבְחוּלָקָא דָּא, לָא שַׁלְטָא כְּלָל. לֵיל, אִצְטְרִיךְ לִנְטוּרָא,
דִּכְתִיב לֵיל שִׁמּוּרִים הוּא, וְעַל דָּא חָסֵר ה', וְדָא אִיהוּ כַּד עָאל לֵילְיָא,
עַד דְּאִתְפְּלַג. מִפַּלְגּוּ לֵילְיָא וּלְהָלְאָה, שַׁלְטָא לַיְלָה דִּכְתִיב בָּהּ וַיְהִי
בַּחֲצִי הַלָּיְלָה. הוּא הַלַּיְלָה הַזֶּה. וְלַיְלָה כַּיּוֹם יָאִיר וְגוֹ'. וּבְגִין כָּךְ,
שׁוֹמֵר מַה מִלַּיְלָה שׁוֹמֵר מַה מֵלֵיל.

**84.** "Watchman, what of the night. Watchman, what of the night?" The watchman is Metatron, ABOUT WHOM it is written: "So he who waits on his Master shall be honored" (Mishlei 27:18). This means the ruler of the night. "What of the night (Heb. *laylah*)? Watchman, what of the night (Heb. *leyl*)?" What is the difference between them, BETWEEN LAYLAH AND LEYL? HE ANSWERS: It is all one; THEY ARE BOTH NIGHT AND DARK, just as the Other Side dominates in this part OF LEYL, it does not dominate at all in this part OF LAYLAH. Leyl needs guarding, as it is written: "It is a night (Heb. *leyl*) of watchfulness" (Shemot 12:42). Therefore, it is spelled without *Hei*, BECAUSE *HEI* DENOTES THE PERFECTED MALCHUT. From nightfall until midnight, THE FIRST HALF OF THE NIGHT UNTIL MIDNIGHT, IS CALLED 'LEYL'. Laylah with *HEI* dominates from midnight and further, as it is written: "And it came to pass, that at midnight (Heb. *laylah*)" (Ibid. 29), "this is Hashem's watchnight" (Ibid. 42) and "but the night (*laylah*) shines like the day" (Tehilim 139:12). Therefore, THE PASSAGE SAYS: "Watchman, what of the (Laylah) night. Watchman, what of the (Heb. *leyl*) night?"

‏85. אָמַר שׁוֹמֵר. אַשְׁכַּחְנָא בְּסִפְרָא דְּאָדָם, מַה בֵּין וַיֹּאמֶר לְאָמַר.
וַיֹּאמֶר לְעֵילָא, וְאָמַר לְתַתָּא, וְאֶל מֹשֶׁה אָמַר. מַאן אָמַר, אָמַר שׁוֹמֵר,
דָּא מְטַטְרוֹן. אָתָא בֹקֶר, דָּא צְלוֹתָא דְּשַׁחֲרִית דְּאִיהוּ שָׁלְטָנוּ דִּימָמָא,
הַהוּא דְּשַׁלִּיט עַל לֵילְיָא. וְאִי תֵּימָא דְּאִיהוּ אָתֵי בִּלְחוֹדוֹי, וְאִתְפְּרַשׁ
דְּכַר מִנּוּקְבָּא, הָא כְּתִיב וְגַם לַיְלָה, תַּרְוַוייְהוּ כַּחֲדָא, וְלָא מִתְפָּרְשִׁין
דָּא מִן דָּא לְעָלְמִין. וְקָלָא דָּא קָרֵי בְּמִלִּין אִלֵּין, אָתָא בֹקֶר וְגַם לַיְלָה
תַּרְוַוייְהוּ זְמִינִין לְגַבַּייְכוּ.

**85.** "The watchman said" (Yeshayah 21:12): I found in the Book of Adam, what is the difference between *Vayomer* (Eng. 'and he said') and *Amar* (Eng. 'he said')? Vayomer is above, WHICH IS ZEIR ANPIN, and Amar is below, THAT IS METATRON, AS IT IS WRITTEN: "And he said (Heb. *amar*) to Moses" (Shemot 24:1). Who said? The watchman, who is Metatron. "The morning comes," namely the morning prayer which is the dominion of the day, that which dominates the night. If you say that the morning came alone and the male, WHICH IS THE MORNING, is separated from the female, WHICH IS NIGHT, then behold it is written: "And also night" for both of them are together, and never separate. This voice cries out these words: "The morning comes, and also night" and both of them are ready for you.

86. מִכָּאן וּלְהָלְאָה אִם תִּבְעָיוּן בְּעָיוּ. אִם תִּבְעוּן בָּעוּתְכוֹן בִּצְלוֹ קַמֵּי מַלְכָּא קַדִּישָׁא, בְּעָיוּ, צַלּוּ וּבְעוּ בָּעוּתְכוֹן, וְתוּבוּ לְגַבֵּי מָארֵיכוֹן. אָתָיוּ, כְּמַאן דְּזַמִּין לְקַבְּלָא לִבְנוֹי, וּלְרַחֲמָא עֲלַיְיהוּ. אוּף הָכִי קוּדְשָׁא בְּרִיךְ הוּא, בֹּקֶר וְגַם לַיְלָה, קָרָא וְאָמַר אָתָיוּ. זַכָּאָה עַמָּא קַדִּישָׁא, דְּמָארֵיהוֹן בָּעֵי עֲלוֹן, וְקָרָא לוֹן לְקָרְבָא לוֹן לְגַבֵּיהּ.

**86.** From here and further, 'if you will inquire, inquire.' If you will inquire during prayer before the King, request, pray, and ask your petitions and 'return' to your Master. 'Come' like one who invites his children to accept them and have Mercy on them. So the Holy One, blessed be He, morning and night, called, and said, "Come…" Blessed are the holy people, whose Master seeks them and calls to bring them close.

87. כְּדֵין עַמָּא קַדִּישָׁא, בָּעָאן לְאִתְחַבְּרָא, וּלְאַעֲלָא בְּבֵי כְנִישְׁתָּא. וְכָל מַאן דְּאַקְדִּים בְּקַדְמֵיתָא, אִתְחַבַּר בִּשְׁכִינְתָּא בְּחַבּוּרָא חֲדָא. תָּא חֲזֵי, הַהוּא קַדְמָאָה דְּאִשְׁתְּכַח בְּבֵי כְנִישְׁתָּא, זַכָּאָה חוּלְקֵיהּ, דְּאִיהוּ קַיְימָא בְּדַרְגָּא דְּצַדִּיק בַּהֲדֵי שְׁכִינְתָּא. וְדָא אִיהוּ רָזָא וּמְשַׁחֲרַי יִמְצָאָנְנִי. הָא סָלִיק בִּסְלִיקוּ עִלָּאָה. וְאִי תֵּימָא, הָא תָּנֵינָן בְּשַׁעֲתָא דְּקוּדְשָׁא בְּרִיךְ הוּא אָתֵי לְבֵי כְנִישְׁתָּא, וְלָא אַשְׁכַּח תַּמָּן עֲשָׂרָה, מִיַּד כּוֹעֵס. וְאַתְּ אָמַרְתְּ הַהוּא חַד דְּאַקְדִּים, אִתְחַבַּר בִּשְׁכִינְתָּא, וְקַיְּימָא בְּדַרְגָּא דְּצַדִּיק.

**87.** Then the holy people needs to join and come to the synagogue, and whoever comes first joins with the Shechinah in one union. Come and see

that first one to be present in the synagogue. Blessed is his portion, for he stands in the level of the righteous in relation to the Shechinah, and this is the secret of: "And those who seek me early shall find me" (Mishlei 8:17). Such a person rises to the highest level. And if you say, we learned the Holy One, blessed be He, immediately becomes angry when He comes to the synagogue and does not find ten people, yet you say that the one who precedes becomes joined with the Shechinah, and is in the level of righteous?

88. אֶלָּא, לְמַלְכָּא דְּשָׁדַר לְכָל בְּנֵי מָתָא, דְּיִשְׁתַּכְּחוּן עִמֵּיה בְּיוֹם פְּלָן, בְּדוּךְ פְּלָן. עַד דַּהֲווֹ מְזַמְּנֵי גַּרְמַיְיהוּ אִינּוּן בְּנֵי מָתָא, אַקְדִּים חַד וְאָתָא לְהַהוּא אֲתָר. בֵּין כָּךְ וּבֵין כָּךְ אָתָא מַלְכָּא, אַשְׁכַּח לְהַהוּא בַּר נָשׁ דְּאַקְדִּים תַּמָּן, אָמַר לֵיהּ, פְּלָן בְּנֵי מָתָא אָן אִינּוּן. אָמַר לֵיהּ, מָארִי, אֲנָא אַקְדִּימְנָא מִנַּיְיהוּ, וְהָא אִינּוּן אָתָאן אֲבַתְרַאי לְפִקּוּדָא דְּמַלְכָּא. כְּדֵין, טָב בְּעֵינֵי מַלְכָּא, וְיָתִיב תַּמָּן בַּהֲדֵיהּ, וְאִשְׁתָּעֵי עִמֵּיה, וְאִתְעָבֵיד רְחִימָא דְּמַלְכָּא. בֵּין כָּךְ וּבֵין כָּךְ, אָתוּ כָּל עַמָּא, וְאִתְפַּיַּיס מַלְכָּא עִמְּהוֹן, וְשָׁדַר לוֹן לִשְׁלָם. אֲבָל אִי אִינּוּן בְּנֵי מָתָא לָא אַתְיָין, וְחַד לָא אַקְדִּים לְאִשְׁתָּעֵי קָמֵי מַלְכָּא, לְאִתְחֲזָאָה בְּגִינַיְיהוּ דְּהָא כֻּלְּהוּ אַתְיָין. מִיָּד כָּעִיס וְרָגִיז מַלְכָּא.

88. HE ANSWERS: This is similar to a king who sent a message to all the inhabitants of a city that they should gather with him at a certain time at a certain place. Before the inhabitants of the city could prepare themselves, one person came first to that place. In the meantime, the king arrived and found that person who came early. THE KING said to him: You, where are the inhabitants of the city? He said to him: My master, I came earlier than they and they are coming after me by the king's order. This pleased the king, who sat with him and spoke to him, and they became friends. In the meantime, all the people came and the king accepted them and then sent them away in peace. But if these people would not have come, and one would not have preceded them to speak before the king AND TO SAY that they are all coming, he would immediately get angry and wrathful.

89. אוּף הָכָא, כֵּיוָן דְּחַד אַקְדִּים, וְאִשְׁתְּכַח בְּבֵי כְנִישְׁתָּא, וּשְׁכִינְתָּא אַתְיָא וְאַשְׁכַּח לֵיהּ, כְּדֵין אִתְחֲשִׁיב כְּאִלּוּ כֻּלְּהוּ אִשְׁתְּכָחוּ תַּמָּן. דְּהָא

דָּא אוֹרִיךְ לוֹן תַּמָּן. מִיַּד אִתְחַבְּרַת עִמֵּיהּ שְׁכִינְתָּא, וְיַתְבֵי בְּזֵווּגָא חַד,
וְאִשְׁתְּמוֹדַע בַּהֲדֵיהּ, וְאוֹתִיב לֵיהּ בְּדַרְגָּא דְּצַדִּיק. וְאִי חַד לָא אַקְדִּים
וְלָא אִשְׁתְּכַח תַּמָּן, מַה כְּתִיב, מַדּוּעַ בָּאתִי וְאֵין אִישׁ. וְאֵין עֲשָׂרָה לָא
כְּתִיב, אֶלָּא וְאֵין אִישׁ, לְאִתְחַבְּרָא בַּהֲדָאי, לְמֶהֱוֵי גַּבָּאי, כד"א אִישׁ
הָאֱלֹהִים לְמֶהֱוֵי בְּדַרְגָּא דְּצַדִּיק.

**89.** In this case also, since one preceded and is present in the synagogue, and the Shechinah arrives and finds him, it is considered as though they are all present there, because he is waiting for them there. Immediately, the Shechinah joins with him. They sit together, and she becomes acquainted with him and sets him into the level of righteous. But if one did not precede and was not there, it is written: "Why, when I came, was there no man?" (Yeshayah 50:2). It does not say, 'And there were not ten men,' but rather "Was there no man?" MEANING ONE to join with Me and to be near Me, as it is written: "the man of Elohim" (Devarim 33:1), which means to be in the level of righteous.

90. וְלֹא עוֹד, אֶלָּא דְּאִשְׁתְּמוֹדַע בַּהֲדֵיהּ, וְשָׁאִיל עֲלוֹי, אִי יוֹמָא חַד לָא
אָתֵי, כְּמָה דְּאוֹקִימְנָא, דִּכְתִיב מִי בָכֶם יְרֵא יְיָ' שׁוֹמֵעַ בְּקוֹל עַבְדּוֹ. וְהָא
אִתְעָרְנָא בְּהַאי דִּכְתִיב, אֵלַי קוֹרֵא מִשֵּׂעִיר, דְּהָא דַּרְגָּא בָּתַר דַּרְגָּא
דַּרְגָּא גוֹ דַּרְגָּא, הַהוּא שׁוֹמֵר, קוֹרֵא בְּחֵילָא בְּכָל יוֹמָא וְיוֹמָא, וְדָא
אִיהוּ שׁוֹמֵעַ בְּקוֹל עַבְדּוֹ, עַבְדּוֹ, דָּא מְטַטְרוֹן. וּבְגִין כָּךְ, זַכָּאָה אִיהוּ
מַאן דְּאַקְדִּים לְבֵי כְּנִשְׁתָּא, לְסַלְּקָא בְּהַהוּא דַּרְגָּא עִלָּאָה דְּקָאמְרָן.

**90.** And He also makes an acquaintance with him, and inquires if he does not come one day, as we have established, as it is written: "Who is there among you that fears Hashem, that obeys the voice of His servant" (Ibid. 10). We have already observed that which is written: "One calls to me out of Seir," that there is a grade over a grade and a grade within a grade. THEREFORE, the watchman, EVEN THOUGH "ONE CALLS TO ME OUT OF SEIR" REFERS TO METATRON, calls with strength daily: "THE MORNING COMES, AND ALSO NIGHT," THUS SUMMONING TO THE MORNING PRAYER SUCH A PERSON THAT THE HOLY ONE, BLESSED BE HE, INQUIRES ABOUT IN THE PHRASES, "WHO IS THERE AMONG YOU THAT FEARS HASHEM," and "that obeys the voice of His servant," who is Metatron, AND

COMES TO THE HOUSE OF PRAYER. SO THE HOLY ONE, BLESSED BE HE, INQUIRES ABOUT HIM IF HE DOES NOT COME, AND SAYS, "WHO IS THERE AMONG YOU THAT FEARS HASHEM..." Therefore, blessed is he who hastens to the synagogue, to ascend to this level, NAMELY TO THE LEVEL OF THE RIGHTEOUS.

91. כַּד אָתֵי צַפְרָא, וְצִבּוּרָא אִשְׁתְּכָחוּ בְּבֵי כְּנִישְׁתָּא, בָּעוּ לְאִשְׁתַּכְּחָא בְּשִׁירִין וְתוּשְׁבְּחָן דְּדָוִד. וְהָא אוֹקִימְנָא, דְּסִדוּרָא אִיהוּ לְאַתְעָרָא רְחִימוּ לְעֵילָּא וְתַתָּא, לְאַתְקָנָא תִּקּוּנִין, וּלְאַתְעָרָא חֶדְוָה. דְּהָא בְּגִין דָּא לֵיוָאֵי מִתְעָרֵי לְאַתְעָרָא רְחִימוּ וְחֶדְוָה לְעֵילָּא, בְּאִינּוּן שִׁירִין וְתוּשְׁבְּחָן.

91. When the morning arrives and the congregation is present in the synagogue, they should be immersed in the psalms and songs of David. We have established that it is arranged so as to awaken love above and below to build perfection and to arouse joy. So the Levites work at awakening love and joy above with these psalms and songs.

92. וּמַאן דְּמִשְׁתָּעֵי בְּבֵי כְּנִישְׁתָּא בְּמִלִּין דְּחוֹל, וַוי לֵיה, דְּאַחְזֵי פְּרוֹדָא, וַוי לֵית דְּגָרַע מֵהֵימְנוּתָא. וַוי לֵיה דְּלֵית לֵיה חוּלָקָא בֶּאֱלָהָא דְּיִשְׂרָאֵל. דְּאַחְזֵי דְּהָא לֵיה אֱלָהָא, וְלָא אִשְׁתְּכַח תַּמָּן, וְלָא דָּחִיל מִנֵּיה, וְאַנְהִיג קְלָנָא בְּתִקּוּנָא עִלָּאָה דִּלְעֵילָּא.

92. Regarding one who speaks worldly talk in the synagogue: Woe to him for he shows dissension, woe to him for he lessens the Faith and woe to him for he has no part in the Elohim of Yisrael, because he shows THROUGH THIS that there is no Elohim, and that He is not present there. Also, he does not fear Him and he acts shamefully against the supernal perfection of above, BECAUSE A SYNAGOGUE IS SET AGAINST THE SUPERNAL MALCHUT.

93. דְּהָא בְּשַׁעֲתָא דְּיִשְׂרָאֵל מְסַדְּרֵי בְּבֵי כְּנִישְׁתָּא, סִדּוּרָא דְּשִׁירִין וְתוּשְׁבְּחָן וְסִדּוּרָא דִּצְלוֹתָא, כְּדֵין מִתְכַּנְּשֵׁי תְּלַת מַשִּׁרְיָין דְּמַלְאֲכֵי עִלָּאֵי. מַשִּׁרְיָיתָא חֲדָא, אִינּוּן מַלְאָכִין קַדִּישִׁין דְּקָא מְשַׁבְּחָן לְקוּדְשָׁא בְּרִיךְ הוּא בִּימָמָא, בְּגִין דְּאִית אַחֲרָנִין דְּקָא מְשַׁבְּחָן לְקוּדְשָׁא בְּרִיךְ

הוּא בְּלֵילְיָא. וְאִלֵּין אִינּוּן דְּקָא מְשַׁבְּחָן לְקוּדְשָׁא בְּרִיךְ הוּא, וְאַמְרִין שִׁירִין וְתוּשְׁבְּחָן בַּהֲדַיְיהוּ דְּיִשְׂרָאֵל בִּימָמָא.

**93.** When Yisrael are reciting in the synagogue the sequence of psalms and praises and the order of prayer, three camps of supernal angels gather. One camp represents the holy angels who praise the Holy One, blessed be He, during the day. There are others who praise the Holy One, blessed be He, during the night and those who praise the Holy One, blessed be He, and say psalms and praises with Yisrael during the day.

94. מַשִׁרְיָיתָא תִּנְיָינָא, אִינּוּן מַלְאָכִין קַדִּישִׁין, דְּמִשְׁתַּכְּחֵי בְּכָל קְדוּשָׁה וּקְדוּשָׁה דְּיִשְׂרָאֵל, מְקַדְּשֵׁי לְתַתָּא. וּבְשׁוּלְטָנָא דִּלְהוֹן, כָּל אִינּוּן דְּמִתְעָרִין בְּכָל אִינּוּן רְקִיעִין, בְּהַהִיא צְלוֹתָא דְּיִשְׂרָאֵל. מַשִׁרְיָיתָא תְּלִיתָאָה אִינּוּן עוּלֶמְתָן עִלָּאִין. דְּקָא מִתְתַּקְנֵי עִם מַטְרוֹנִיתָא, וּמְתַקְּנֵי לָהּ לְאַעֲלָא לָהּ קַמֵּי מַלְכָּא, וְאִלֵּין אִינּוּן מַשִׁרְיָין עִלָּאִין עַל כֻּלְּהוּ.

**94.** The second camp represents the holy angels that are present in every sanctification that Yisrael recite below, and under their dominion are all those who are aroused in all the firmaments with that prayer of Yisrael. The third camp represents the supernal Maidens, WHO ARE THE SEVEN SPIRITS OF THE SEVEN SANCTUARIES OF BRIYAH, that are prepared together with Malchut, and they perfect Malchut in order to bring her before the King. These are the highest camps above all others.

95. וְכֻלְּהוּ מִתְתַּקְנֵי, בְּסִדּוּרָא דְּיִשְׂרָאֵל דְּמִתַּתְקְנֵי לְתַתָּא, בְּאִינּוּן שִׁירִין וְתוּשְׁבְּחָן, וּבְהַהִיא צְלוֹתָא דְּקָא מְצַלּוּ יִשְׂרָאֵל. כֵּיוָן דְּאַלֵּין תְּלַת מַשִׁרְיָין מִזְדַּמְּנָן, כְּדֵין יִשְׂרָאֵל פַּתְחֵי שִׁירָתָא, וְזַמְרֵי קַמֵּי מָארֵיהוֹן. וְהַהִיא מַשִׁרְיָיתָא חֲדָא, דִּי מְמַנָּא לְשַׁבְּחָא לְמָארֵיהוֹן בִּימָמָא, אִזְדַּמְּנָן עֲלַיְיהוּ, וְזַמְרֵי עִמְּהוֹן כַּחֲדָא, בְּאִינּוּן שְׁבָחֵי דְּדָוִד מַלְכָּא, וְהָא אוּקִימְנָא מִלֵּי.

**95.** They are all perfected with the prayer sequence of Yisrael, who prepare themselves below with these psalms and praises and with that prayer that they recite. As soon as these three camps are gathered, the children of

Yisrael start to sing before their Master. That one camp, which is appointed to praise its Master during the day, gathers with the children of Yisrael and sings together these praises of King David, as we have established.

‎96. בְּהַהוּא זִמְנָא דִמְסַיְּימֵי יִשְׂרָאֵל שְׁבָחֵי דְּאִינוּן תּוּשְׁבְּחָן דְּדָוִד, כְּדֵין תּוּשְׁבַּחְתָּא דְּשִׁירָתָא, דְּיַמָּא, כְּמָה דְּאוּקִימְנָא. וְאִי תֵּימָא, הַאי תּוּשְׁבַּחְתָּא אֲמַאי אִיהִי בְּתִקּוּנָא בַּתְרַיְיתָא בָּתַר שְׁבָחֵי דְּדָוִד, וְהָא תּוֹרָה שֶׁבִּכְתָב, אַקְדִּימַת לְתוֹרָה שֶׁבְּעַל פֶּה, וְאַקְדִּימַת לַנְּבִיאִים, וְאַקְדִּימַת לַכְּתוּבִים, וּכְמָה דְּאַקְדִּימַת, הָכִי אִצְטְרִיךְ לְאַקְדְּמָא.

96. When Yisrael complete the praises of the hymns of David, they say the praise of the Song of the Red Sea, as we have established. And if you ask: Why is this praise in the last service after the praises of David? Does not the Written Torah precede the Oral Torah, the Prophets and the Writings, and is it not proper to place it first?

‎97. אֶלָּא, מִגּוֹ דְּכ"י לָא אִתַּתְקָנַת אֶלָּא מִתּוֹרָה שֶׁבִּכְתָב, מִשּׁוּם הָכִי אִצְטְרִיךְ לוֹמַר לָהּ בְּשֵׁירוּתָא דְּתִקּוּנָהָא, וְהַאי תּוּשְׁבַּחְתָּא מְעַלְיָא, מִכָּל שְׁאָר תּוּשְׁבְּחָן דְּעָלְמָא. וְאִיהִי לָא אִתַּתְקָנַת מִכֻּלְּהוּ, כְּמָה דְּאִתַּתְקָנַת מִתּוּשְׁבַּחְתָּא דָּא. וּבְגִין דָּא, אִיהִי סָמוּךְ לִצְלוֹתָא דִמְיוּשָׁב, כְּמָה דְּאוֹקִימְנָא.

97. The Congregation of Yisrael, WHICH IS MALCHUT, is perfected by the Written Torah; therefore, it is necessary to say the Song at the beginning of the prayers, NAMELY CLOSE TO THE PRAYER THAT IS RECITED SITTING DOWN. This praise is more valuable than all the praises in the world. She, MALCHUT, is not perfected by all of them as it is perfected by this praise. Therefore it is adjacent to the prayer that is recited sitting down, NAMELY THE PRAYER OF HE WHO FORMS LIGHT, as explained.

‎98. בָּהּ שַׁעֲתָא כַּד שִׁירָתָא דְּיַמָּא אִתְּמַר, מִתְעַטְּרָא כְּנֶסֶת יִשְׂרָאֵל בְּהַהוּא כִּתְרָא, דְּזַמִּין קוּדְשָׁא בְּרִיךְ הוּא לְאַעַטְּרָא לְמַלְכָּא מְשִׁיחָא, וְהַהוּא כִּתְרָא גְּלִיפָא מְחַקְּקָא בִּשְׁמָהָן קַדִּישִׁין, כְּמָה דְּאִתְעַטַּר קוּדְשָׁא

בְּרִיךְ הוּא הַהוּא יוֹמָא דְּאַעְבָּרוּ יִשְׂרָאֵל יַת יַמָּא, וְאַטְבַּע לְכָל מַשְׁרְיָין דְּפַרְעֹה וּפָרְשׁוֹהִי. בְּג״ד, בָּעֵי ב״נ לְשַׁוָּואָה רְעוּתֵיהּ בְּהַאי שִׁירָתָא. וְכָל מַאן דְּזָכֵי לָהּ בְּהַאי עָלְמָא, זָכֵי לְמֶחֱמֵי לְמַלְכָּא מְשִׁיחָא בְּתִקּוּנֵי הַהוּא כִּתְרָא, וּבַחֲגִירוּ דְּזַיְינֵיהּ, וְזַכֵּי לְשַׁבְּחָא הַאי שִׁירָתָא תַּמָּן, וְהָא אוּקִימְנָא מִלֵּי.

**98.** When the Song of the Sea is recited, the Congregation of Yisrael is adorned with the crown that the Holy One, blessed be He, is going to crown King Messiah. That crown is decorated and engraved with the Holy Names just as the Holy One, blessed be He, was crowned on the day that Yisrael crossed the sea and He drowned all the camps of Pharaoh and his horsemen. Therefore, a person has to direct his will to this song. Everyone who merits it in this world, merits to see Messiah with the perfection of that crown, the weapons with which he is girded, and merits to praise the song there. We have established these matters.

99. כֵּיוָן דְּמָטֵי ב״נ לְיִשְׁתַּבַּח נָטַל קוּדְשָׁא בְּרִיךְ הוּא הַהוּא כִּתְרָא, וְשַׁוֵּי לֵיהּ קָמֵיהּ, וכ״י שָׁרִיאַת לְאִתְתַּקְּנָא לְמֵיתֵי קָמֵי מַלְכָּא עִלָּאָה. וְאִצְטְרִיךְ לְאַכְלְלָא לָהּ, בִּתְלֵיסַר מְכִילָן דְּרַחֲמֵי עִלָּאֵי, דְּמִנְּהוֹן אִתְבְּרְכַת. וְאִינוּן תְּלֵיסַר בּוּסְמִין עִלָּאִין, כד״א, נֵרְדְּ וְכַרְכֹּם קָנֶה וְקִנָּמוֹן וְגוֹ', וְהָכָא אִינוּן, שִׁיר, וּשְׁבָחָה, הַלֵּל, וְזִמְרָה, עֹז, וּמֶמְשָׁלָה, נֶצַח, גְּדוּלָה, וּגְבוּרָה, תְּהִלָּה, וְתִפְאֶרֶת, קְדוּשָׁה. הָא תְּרֵיסַר. וּלְבָתַר לְחַבְּרָא לָהּ בַּהֲדַיְיהוּ, וְלוֹמַר וּמַלְכוּת, וַהֲווֹ תְּלֵיסַר. בְּגִין דְּאִיהִי מִתְבָּרְכָא מִנַּיְיהוּ.

**99.** As soon as the person reaches the Praise (May Your name be praised), the Holy One, blessed be He, takes that crown and places it before him. The Congregation of Yisrael, THAT IS MALCHUT, starts to prepare Herself to come before the supernal King, THAT IS ZEIR ANPIN. It is necessary to include it in the thirteen supernal attributes of Mercy, from which She is blessed, and there are thirteen kinds of supernal spices, as it is written: "Nard and saffron; columns and cinnamon…" (Shir Hashirim 4:14). They are, song and praise; adoration and melody; might and dominion; victory; grandeur and power; glory, splendor, and holiness. These are twelve until

She joins with them to say: 'And sovereignty (lit. 'Malchut')'. They become thirteen now, because she is blessed from them.

 .100 וְעַל דָּא אִצְטְרִיךְ, בְּשַׁעֲתָא דְּאִתְכְּלִילַת בֵּינַיְיהוּ, לְשַׁוְּואָה לִבָּא וּרְעוּתָא בְּהַאי, וְלָא לִישְׁתָּעֵי כְּלָל, דְּלָא לְפַסּוֹק בֵּינַיְיהוּ. וְאִי פָּסִיק בֵּינַיְיהוּ, מִתְּחוֹת גַּדְפֵּי כְּרוּבַיָּיא נָפִיק חַד שַׁלְהוֹבָא, וְקָארֵי בְּחֵילָא וְאָמַר, פְּלַנְיָא דִּי פָּסִיק גָּאוּתָא דְּקוּדְשָׁא בְּרִיךְ הוּא, יִשְׁתְּצֵי וְיִתְפְּסַק, דְּלָא יֶחֱמֵי גָּאוּתָא דְּמַלְכָּא קַדִּישָׁא, כד"א וּבַל יִרְאֶה גֵּאוּת ה', בְּגִין דְּאִלֵּין תְּלֵיסַר אִינּוּן גֵּאוּת יְיָ'.

**100.** Therefore, at the time WHEN MALCHUT is combined among them, THE THIRTEEN ATTRIBUTES, one should to pay attention to it and not talk at all or interrupt between them. If he interrupts between them, a flame emerges from under the wings of the Cherubs, cries aloud and says: So-and-so who interrupted the majesty of the Holy One, blessed be He, shall decrease and HIS LIFE shall be interrupted, so that he does not see the majesty of the Holy King. It is written: "And will not behold the majesty of Hashem" (Yeshayah 26:10), as these thirteen are the majesty of Hashem.

.101 מִכָּאן וּלְהָלְאָה אֵל הַהוֹדָאוֹת כו', דָּא מַלְכָּא עִלָּאָה דִּשְׁלָמָא כֹּלָּא דִּילֵיהּ, כד"א שִׁיר הַשִּׁירִים אֲשֶׁר לִשְׁלֹמֹה, לְמַלְכָּא דִּשְׁלָמָא דִּילֵיהּ, בְּגִין דְּכָל הָנֵי שְׁבָחָן אִינּוּן לְגַבָּהּ דכנ"י כַּד מִשְׁתַּבְּחָא בְּמַשְׁרְיָיתָא דִּלְתַתָּא. מִתַּמָּן וּלְהָלְאָה, יוֹצֵר אוֹר וּבוֹרֵא חֹשֶׁךְ עוֹשֶׂה שָׁלוֹם וּבוֹרֵא אֶת הַכֹּל. וְהָא אִתְּעַרְנָא בֵּיהּ, וְאִתְּעָרוּ חַבְרַיָּיא דְּהָנֵי אִינּוּן תִּיקוּנִין דְּעָלְמָא עִלָּאָה.

**101.** From 'El worthy of thanksgiving...' and further, this is the supernal King, that all peace is His, as it is written: "The song of songs, which is Solomon's (Heb. *Shlomo*)" (Shir Hashirim 1:1), MEANING of the King that the peace (Heb. *shalom*) is His, WHICH IS ZEIR ANPIN. This is because all the EARLIER praises were addressed to the Congregation of Yisrael, WHICH IS MALCHUT, which is praised via the lower camps. From "forms light and creates darkness..." (Yeshayah 45:7) and further, I have explained and the friends have explained that this is perfection of the upper world, WHICH IS ZEIR ANPIN.

102. אָ"ל בָּרוּ"ךְ: תִּקּוּנֵי דְעָלְמָא תַּתָּאָה, דְּאִינּוּן כ"ב אַתְוָון זְעִירִין, בְּגִין דְּאִית אַתְוָון רַבְרְבָן, וְאַתְוָון זְעִירִין. אַתְוָון זְעִירִין, מֵעָלְמָא תַּתָּאָה. אַתְוָון רַבְרְבָן, מֵהַהוּא עָלְמָא דְּאָתֵי.

**102.** THE ALPHABET AT THE INITIALS OF THE WORDS: 'Blessed Hashem, great in knowledge...' are the corrections of the lower world, WHICH IS MALCHUT, that are, IN THE INITIALS, 22 small letters, as there are large letters and small letters. Small letters are in the lower world, THAT IS MALCHUT, and the large letters are in the World to Come, WHICH IS BINAH.

103. בְּכֹלָּא אִינּוּן רַבְרְבָן, אִינּוּן רַבְרְבָן בְּגַרְמַיְיהוּ. כַּד אַתְיָין יְחִידָאִין אִינּוּן רַבְרְבָן דְּכַר פְּשִׁיטָן יַתִּיר, אִינּוּן אַתְיָין כָּל אָת וְאָת בִּרְתִּיכָא דְּחַזֵּי לֵיהּ, כְּגוֹן שְׁבָחָא דְּשַׁבָּת דְּאִינּוּן אַתְוָון דְּשֶׁבַח, אֵל אָדוֹן עַל כָּל הַמַּעֲשִׂים, בָּרוּךְ וּמְבוֹרָךְ בְּפִי כָּל נְשָׁמָה. אִלֵּין אַתְוָון בַּחֲמֵשׁ חֲמֵשׁ תֵּיבִין, דְּאִינּוּן חַמְשִׁין תַּרְעִין דְּעָלְמָא דְּאָתֵי.

**103.** They are great in everything, MEANING BECAUSE OF TWO REASONS. They are large LETTERS essentially even when on their own and they are large, when these letters expand further, each letter comes with its own fitting Chariot, namely the song of praise of Shabbat, for these are letters of praise: '(*Aleph*) Almighty El, Master over all works; (*Bet*) Blessed is He, and He is blessed by the mouth of every soul.' These letters expand into five words each, BECAUSE IN THIS PRAYER, THERE ARE FIVE WORDS IN EVERY PHRASE they correspond to the fifty gates of the World to Come, WHICH IS BINAH, WHICH ARE THE FIVE SFIROT, KETER, CHOCHMAH, BINAH, TIFERET AND MALCHUT, EACH COMPRISED OF TEN.

104. תְּרֵין אַתְוָון אָחֳרָנִין דִּי בְּסוֹפָא: שׁ"ת. אִינּוּן בְּשִׁית שִׁית תֵּיבִין, דְּאִינּוּן שִׁית סִטְרִין דְּעָלְמָא דְּאָתֵי, וְנַפְקֵי מִתַּמָּן. כְּגוֹן: שֶׁבַח יִתְּנוּ לוֹ כָּל צְבָא מָרוֹם. תִּפְאֶרֶת וּגְדוּלָה שְׂרָפִים וְאוֹפַנִּים וְחַיּוֹת הַקּוֹדֶשׁ.

**104.** The last two letters are at the end of the praise: 'ALMIGHTY EL' THAT ARE *Shin-Tav*, and come with six words each. They CORRESPOND to the six

extremities, CHESED, GVURAH, TIFERET NETZACH, HOD AND YESOD, of the World to Come, WHICH IS BINAH. And they emerge from these.

105. אִלֵּין תְּרֵין אַתְוָון, בְּשִׁית שִׁית תְּרֵין אַתְוָון קַדְמָאֵי, בְּחָמֵשׁ חָמֵשׁ. כֻּלְּהוּ שְׁאַר אַתְוָון דִּי בְּאֶמְצָעִיתָא, כֻּלְּהוּ בְּאַרְבַּע אַרְבַּע, בְּגִין דְּאִינּוּן בְּרָזָא דִרְתִיכָא עִלָּאָה, דְּאִינּוּן אַתְוָון קַדְמָאֵי וְאִינּוּן דִּבְסוֹפָא, אִינּוּן שְׁלִימוּ דְכ״ב אַתְוָון, בְּגִין דְּאִית בְּהוּ כ״ב תֵּיבִין, לָקֳבֵל כ״ב אַתְוָון עִלָּאִין. אִשְׁתָּאֲרוּ תַּמְנֵיסַר אַתְוָון אַחֲרָנִין, דְּקָא סַלְקִין בִּרְתִיכַיְיהוּ לְאַרְבַּע אַרְבַּע, לְשַׁבְעִין וּתְרֵין תֵּיבִין, דְּאִינּוּן רָזָא דִשְׁמָא מְפָרַשׁ, גְּלִיפָא קַדִּישָׁא דְע״ב אַתְוָון, דְּקוּדְשָׁא בְּרִיךְ הוּא מִתְעַטַּר בְּהוּ. וּשְׁמָא דָא, אִיהוּ מְעַטְּרָא לכ״י, וְסָלִיק בְּרָזָא דָא, לְאִתְעַטְּרָא בְּהוּ גּוֹ שְׁלֵימוּתָא דִשְׁכִינְתָּא.

**105.** These two letters, SHIN AND TAV, each have six LETTERS, while the two first letters, ALEPH AND BET – each have five LETTERS. All the other letters that are in the middle have four LETTERS each. This is because they are in the secret of the supernal Chariot, because the first letters ALEPH-BET, WHICH ARE TEN, and SHIN-TAV at the end, WHICH ARE TWELVE, are together the complete 22 supernal letters, as they contain 22 words against the supernal 22 supernal letters, WHICH ARE IN BINAH. Another eighteen letters remain THAT ARE IN THE MIDDLE and ascend in their Chariots, MEANING EXPAND to four WORDS each, WHICH ARE TOGETHER 72 words BECAUSE FOUR TIMES EIGHTEEN EQUALS 72. This is the secret of the Holy Name fully pronounced, the holy engraving of Ayin-Bet (72) letters with which the Holy One, blessed be He, adorns Himself. With this Name, He adorns the Congregation of Yisrael, WHICH IS MALCHUT, and ascends through this secret to adorn Himself with them in the perfection of the Shechinah.

106. וְסִימָנִיךְ דְּאִלֵּין אַתְוָון, דְּקָא מִתְעַטְּרָן בְּשַׁבְחָא עִלָּאָה, דָּא קַדְמָאֵי וְסוֹפֵי, דְּסַלְקִין בְּעִטְרַיְיהוּ אִינּוּן א״ת ב״שׁ. אָלֶף בְּחָמֵשׁ. תָּי״ו בְּשִׁי״ת. בֵּית בַּחֲמֵשׁ. שִׁי״ן בְּשִׁית. בְּג״כ רָזָא דְאָ״ת ב״שׁ כְּלָלָא דְכ״ב אַתְוָון, דְּאִינּוּן עֲטָרָה דִתְלָתִין וּתְרֵין שְׁבִילִין.

**106.** You may derive it from the fact that these letters become adorned in the supernal Praise. The first ones, WHICH ARE ALEPH-BET, and the last ones, WHICH ARE SHIN-TAV ascend with their crowns and are the Atbash cipher in which *Aleph* (first) is exchanged with *Tav* (last) and *Bet* (second) with *Shin* (second to last). *Aleph* EXPANDS into five LETTERS NAMELY THE PHRASE 'ALMIGHTY EL,' *Tav* into six LETTERS, NAMELY 'SPLENDOR (TIFERET) AND GREATNESS...' *Bet* into five LETTERS, NAMELY 'BLESSED IS HE...' and *Shin* into six LETTERS, NAMELY 'PRAISE (HEB. *SHEVACH*) GIVE TO HIM...' Therefore, the secret of the Atbash cipher THAT IS IN THE PRAISE OF 'ALMIGHTY EL,' is that they contain 22 words. The inclusion of the 22 letters OF ZEIR ANPIN are the crown to the 32 paths of CHOCHMAH. FOR THE 32 PATHS OF CHOCHMAH ARE THE 22 LETTERS OF ZEIR ANPIN, WHICH ROSE TO BINAH THAT CONTAINS TEN SFIROT. TWENTY-TWO PLUS TEN EQUALS 32 PATHS OF CHOCHMAH, THAT IS, BINAH, WHICH BECAME CHOCHMAH. AND THE 22 LETTERS OF THE ATBASH CIPHER IN THE HYMN 'EL ADON' ALLUDE TO ZEIR ANPIN WITHIN BINAH.

107. וְסִימָן דְּאִינּוּן אַתְוָון אָחֳרָנִין דְּסַלְקִין בִּרְתִיכַיְיהוּ, ג״ר. שָׁאֲרֵי בְּגִימֶ״ל, וְסַיִּים בְּרֵי״שׁ, וְכֻלְּהוּ רָזָא דִּרְתִיכָא קַדִּישָׁא. א״ת ב״שׁ, רָזָא דִּשְׁמָא קַדִּישָׁא. ג״ר, רָזָא דִּרְתִיכָא קַדִּישָׁא, דְּסַלְקָא לְע״ב, וְאִתְעֲבִיד מִנַּיְיהוּ שְׁמָא קַדִּישָׁא, לְאִתְעַטְּרָא כ״י, מִגּוֹ רְתִיכָא עִלָּאָה.

**107.** The sign of the other letters, BESIDES ALEPH-TAV AND BET-SHIN, that ascend in their Chariots are *Gimel-Resh*, as they start with Gimel (third), NAMELY 'HIS GREATNESS (HEB. *GODLO*) AND GOODNESS FILL THE WORLD' and end in *Resh* (third in reverse order), namely: 'HE SAW (HEB. *RA'AH*) AND PERFECTED THE FORM OF THE MOON.' They are all the secret of the Holy Chariot. *Aleph-Tav* and *Bet-Shin*, WHICH ARE IN THE HYMN 'ALMIGHTY EL,' is the secret of the Holy Name YUD HEI VAV HEI, BEING ZEIR ANPIN THAT ASCENDED TO BINAH. *Gimel-Resh* OF 'ALMIGHTY EL' ARE THE EIGHTEEN LETTERS from Gimel until *Resh*, and is the secret of the Holy Chariot that totals THE SUM *Ayin-Bet* (72), MEANING CHESED, GVURAH AND TIFERET THAT CONTAIN THE PASSAGES: "AND... REMOVED, AND IT CAME...AND...STRETCHED OUT" (SHEMOT 14: 19- 21). Then the Holy Name was made to adorn the Congregation of Yisrael, WHICH IS MALCHUT, from the supernal Chariot, FOR MALCHUT RECEIVES 72

WORDS OF CHESED, GVURAH AND TIFERET, WHICH MAKE A SUPERNAL
CHARIOT.

108. וּבְגִין כָּךְ הַהוּא שְׁמָא דְּע״ב כְּלִילָא בְּרָזָא דַּאֲבָהָן, יְמִינָא
וּשְׂמָאלָא וְאֶמְצָעִיתָא. וְאִיהִי מִתְעַטְּרָא בְּהוּ, לְמֶהֱוֵי שְׁמָא קַדִּישָׁא.
וְלָאו שְׁמָא עִלָּאָה, כְּאִינּוּן שְׁמָהָן עִלָּאִין, דְּעָלְמָא עִלָּאָה, דְּאִתְאֲחָדָן
לְעֵילָּא לְעֵילָּא. וְאע״ג דְּהַאי שְׁמָא עִלָּאָה אִיהוּ, אֲבָל רָזָא דִּילֵיהּ, דָּוִד
מַלְכָּא, דְּמִתְעַטְּרָא בַּאֲבָהָן.

108. Therefore, that name of *Ayin-Bet* (72) is included in the secret of the
patriarchs, WHICH ARE THREE COLUMNS, Right, Left, and Central, AND
MALCHUT is adorned with them to become a Holy Name. It is not a
supernal Name like the Supernal Names of the Supernal World, WHICH IS
ZEIR ANPIN, that are joined high above IN BINAH, AND THEY ARE NOT
DRAWN DOWN. Even though this Name is Supernal, FOR IT IS THREE
COLUMNS, WHICH ARE CHESED, GVURAH AND TIFERET OF ZEIR
ANPIN, its secret is King David, MEANING MALCHUT, that becomes
adorned with the Patriarchs, WHICH ARE CHESED, GVURAH AND TIFERET
OF ZEIR ANPIN.

109. שְׁמָא דְּמ״ב אַתְוָון רָזָא דִּילֵיהּ אֲבָהָן, דְּקָא מִתְעַטְּרָן בְּעָלְמָא
עִלָּאָה. וְעָלְמָא עִלָּאָה בְּמַה דִּלְעֵילָּא. וְעַל דָּא, סָלִיק וְלָא נָחִית, אִתְעַטָּר
גּוֹ מַחֲשָׁבָה עִלָּאָה. זַכָּאָה חוּלָקָא דְּמַאן דְּיָדַע לֵיהּ, וְאִזְדְּהַר בֵּיהּ.

109. The secret of the name of *Mem-Bet* (42) letters is the Patriarchs, THAT
ARE CHESED GVURAH AND TIFERET OF ZEIR ANPIN, WHICH IS THE
SECRET OF THE 22 LETTERS that become adorned in the upper world,
WHICH ARE THE TEN SFIROT OF BINAH. The upper world becomes
adorned with that which is higher THAN IT, WHICH ARE THE TEN SFIROT
OF CHOCHMAH, FOR THE 22 OF ZEIR ANPIN PLUS THE TEN OF BINAH
AND THE TEN OF CHOCHMAH EQUAL 42. Therefore, it ascends but does
not descend, FOR IT DOES NOT PROVIDE CHOCHMAH FROM ABOVE DOWN
TO MALCHUT. THIS IS BECAUSE it becomes adorned in supernal Thought.
Happy is the portion of he who knows the significance OF THE NAME OF
*MEM-BET* (42 LETTERS), and is careful about it.

110. שְׁמָא דְּעַ"ב אַתְוֹון, דָּוִד דְּקָא מִתְעַטְּרָא בַּאֲבָהָן, וְרָזָא דִילֵיהּ
סָלִיק וְנָחִית, בְּגַוְונָא דָא מצפ"ץ, שְׁמָא דִּתְלֵיסַר מְכִילִין דְּרַחֲמֵי. אִינּוּן
תְּרֵיסַר, רָזָא דִּרְתִּיכָא קַדִּישָׁא, דְּנָפִיק מֵחַד, דְּשַׁרְיָא עָלַיְיהוּ וּבְגִין כַּךְ
שְׁמָא דְּעַ"ב סָלִיק וְנָחִית, סָלִיק מִסִּטְרָא דָא, וְנָחִית מִסִּטְרָא דָא. שְׁמָא
דִּתְלֵיסַר מְכִילָן, סָלִיק מִסִּטְרָא דָא, וְנָחִית מִסִּטְרָא דָא, וְהַהוּא דְּנָחִית
בְּגִין לְאַמְשָׁכָא טִיבוּ לְתַתָּא. וְעַל דָּא, א"ת ב"ש ג"ר ד"ק ה"צ ו"פ ז"ע
ח"ס ט"ן י"ם כ"ל. אַתְוֹון קַדְמָאֵי סַלְקִין בְּחוּשְׁבָּנָא, וְאַתְוֹון אַחֲרָנִין
נַחְתֵּי בְּחוּשְׁבָּנָא, בְּגִין לְאַמְשָׁכָא טִיבוּ דִלְעֵילָא לְתַתָּא.

110. It is David, NAMELY MALCHUT, that becomes adorned with the patriarch, WHICH ARE CHESED, GVURAH AND TIFERET OF ZEIR ANPIN, FOR CHESED, GVURAH AND TIFERET OF ZEIR ANPIN IS THE SECRET OF THE 72 WORDS THAT ARE IN THE THREE PASSAGES: "AND…REMOVED …AND IT CAME…AND…STRETCHED OUT," THAT IS, PROVIDE CHOCHMAH TO MALCHUT. Its secret ascends and descends; THAT IS, PROVIDES DOWN TO MALCHUT, thus: *Mem-Pe-Mem-Tzadi* THIS IS THE SECRET OF YUD HEI VAV HEI IN THE SIDES OF THE HEAD OF ARICH ANPIN, WHICH BECOMES, THROUGH THE ATBASH CIPHER, *MEM-TZADI-PE-TZADI* which is the name from which the thirteen attributes of Mercy are drawn. These are twelve in the secret of the Holy Chariot, NAMELY CHOCHMAH, BINAH, TIFERET, AND MALCHUT, FOR EACH ONE HAS THREE COLUMNS, AND SO EQUAL TWELVE that emerge from one that rests over them, WHICH IS *MEM-TZADI-PE-TZADI*. THEY AMOUNT TO THIRTEEN, AND IT ASCENDS AND DESCENDS TO PROVIDE CHOCHMAH FROM ABOVE DOWNWARDS. Therefore, the Name of *Ayin-Bet* (72) ascends and descends. It ascends FROM THE RIGHT SIDE WHICH IS CHESED, GVURAH AND TIFERET OF ZEIR ANPIN, and descends FROM THE LEFT SIDE WHICH IS MALCHUT THAT RECEIVES CHESED, GVURAH AND TIFERET LIKE the name of the thirteen aspects of Mercy that ascends from this side and descends from that side. It descends in order to draw goodness downwards TO MALCHUT. Therefore, in THE ALPHABET WHERE *Aleph=Tav, Bet=Shin, Gimel=Resh, Dalet=Kof, Hei=Tzadi, Vav=Pe, Zayin=Ayin, Chet=Samech, Tet=Nun, Yud=Mem, Caf=Lamed*, the first letters go up in numerical value BECAUSE *BET* IS HIGHER IN WORTH THAN *ALEPH,* AND *GIMEL* THAN *BET,* AND *DALET* THAN *GIMEL*…AND SO ON. The last letters descend in numerical value, AS *SHIN* IS LESS THAN *TAV* AND *RESH* THAN *SHIN* AND *KOF* THAN

RESH. THAT MEANS THAT THEY RISE FROM ONE SIDE AND DESCEND FROM ONE ANOTHER AND THE PURPOSE OF THE DESCENT IS to draw goodness from above down.

111. שְׁמָא דְמ"ב, אִיהוּ מִתְעַטְּרָא לִרְתִיכָא עִלָּאָה. שְׁמָא דְּע"ב, אִיהוּ מִתְעַטְּרָא לִרְתִיכָא תַּתָּאָה. זַכָּאָה חוּלָקֵיהּ מַאן דְּמִשְׁתַּדֵּל לְמִנְדַּע לְמָארֵיהּ, זַכָּאָה אִיהוּ בְּעָלְמָא דֵּין וּבְעָלְמָא דְּאָתֵי.

111. The Name *Mem-Bet* (42) adorns the supernal Chariot, NAMELY SUPERNAL CHOCHMAH-BINAH, AS MENTIONED ABOVE. The Name *Ayin-Bet* (72) adorns the lower Chariot, NAMELY MALCHUT, AS MENTIONED ABOVE. Happy is the portion of the one who endeavors to know his Master. Happy is he in this world and happy is he in the World to Come.

112. וּבְגִין כָּךְ, תּוּשְׁבַּחְתָּא דְּשַׁבָּת דְּקָא מְשַׁבְּחָא לְמַלְכָּא דִּשְׁלָמָא דִּילֵיהּ. מְשַׁבַּח לֵיהּ בִּשְׁמָא דְּע"ב, וּבכ"ב תֵּיבִין, רָזָא דְּכ"ב אַתְוָון, בְּגִין דְּתִתְעַטֵּר בֵּיהּ לְסַלְקָא לְעֵילָא בְּתוּשְׁבַּחְתָּא דָּא. וְעַל דָּא, אֵל אָדוֹן, תּוּשְׁבַּחְתָּא דְּעָלְמָא דְּאָתֵי אִיהוּ, וּפְרִיחוּ דִּרְתִיכָא קַדִּישָׁא עִלָּאָה, דְּמִתְעַטְּרָא לְסַלְקָא לְעֵילָא, וּפְרִיחוּ דִּכְנֶסֶת יִשְׂרָאֵל, דְּמִתְעַטְּרָא לְסַלְקָא גּוֹ רְתִיכָא עִלָּאָה.

112. This is why this hymn is sung on Shabbat, 'EL ADON (ALMIGHTY EL)', that praises the King that peace be upon Him, praises Him with the Name *Ayin-Bet* (72) IN THE EIGHTEEN LETTERS BETWEEN *GIMEL* TO *RESH* and with the 22 words THAT ARE IN THE FOUR LETTERS OF *ALEPH-TAV*, *BET-SHIN*. This is the secret of the 22 letters, in order to become adorned with it so as to ascend above, TO BINAH, by this Name. Therefore, 'Almighty El' is the praise of the World to Come, WHICH IS BINAH, and the ascension of the Supernal Holy Chariot, WHICH IS CHESED, GVURAH AND TIFERET OF ZEIR ANPIN, that becomes adorned to ascend above TO BINAH. The ascension of the Congregation of Yisrael, WHICH IS MALCHUT, becomes adorned to ascend AND RECEIVE from the supernal Chariot, WHICH IS CHESED, GVURAH AND TIFERET OF ZEIR ANPIN.

113. אָ״ת בָּ״שׁ, סַלְקִין וְנַחְתִּין, כְּמָה דְּאִתְּמַר. אָ״ל בָּ״ם סַלְקִין וְלָא
נַחְתִּין, וְסִימָנִיךְ, דָּא שַׁבָּ״ת בִּלְחוֹדוֹי. וְדָא שַׁבָּ״ת וְיוֹם הַכִּפּוּרִים,
דְּסַלְקָא רָזָא לְעֵילָא לְעֵילָא, עַד דְּמִתְעַטְּרָא כֹּלָא בְּאֵין סוֹף.

113. THE LETTERS OF the Atbash cipher ascend and descend, as we have
established THAT THE LAST LETTERS THAT ARE IN THEM DESCEND. THE
LETTERS OF the Albam cipher ascend but do not descend, FOR ALSO THE
LAST LETTERS THAT ARE IN THEM ASCEND, BECAUSE THE WORTH OF
*LAMED* ASCENDS TO THE WORTH OF *MEM* AND AFTERWARD TO *NUN* AND
TO *SAMECH* - THEREFORE, THEY DO NOT DESCEND TO PROVIDE TO
BELOW. You may derive this from the fact that the one, THE ATBASH
CIPHER, is only on Shabbat, WHICH IS MALCHUT, AND THEY PROVIDE
BELOW. But THE ALBAM CIPHER is Shabbat and Yom Kippur, BEING
MALCHUT THAT ASCENDS TO BINAH, WHICH IS THE SECRET OF YOM
KIPPUR that ascends in the secret higher and higher FROM BINAH TO
CHOCHMAH, until everything becomes adorned in the secret of the endless
AND IS NOT PROVIDING BELOW.

114. אֵל בָּרוּךְ, דָּא סְדוּרָא דְּאַתְוָון זְעֵירִין, וְתִקּוּנֵי כ״י בְּכָל יוֹמָא
בִּצְלוֹתָא. וּבְגִין דְּאִינּוּן אַתְוָון זְעֵירִין, לֵית רְוָוחָא בֵּינַיְיהוּ, וְאִינּוּן
תִּקּוּנֵי עוּלֵימָתָן דְּאַתְיָין עִם מַטְרוֹנִיתָא לְגַבֵּי מַלְכָּא עִלָּאָה.

114. 'The blessed El' THAT IS AT THE END OF THE PRAISE 'HE WHO
ILLUMINATES THE EARTH AND THOSE WHO DWELL UPON IT' is in the
order of the ALPHABET OF small letters, WHICH ARE MALCHUT, which are
the corrections of the Congregation of Yisrael, WHICH IS MALCHUT, daily
in prayer. Because they are small letters, there is no space between them,
MEANING THAT THEY DO NOT EXPAND EACH ONE TO REVEAL MANY
WORDS, AS IN THE PRAISE OF 'ALMIGHTY EL' ON SHABBAT. They are the
perfection of the world, WHICH ARE THE SEVEN CHAMBERS OF BRIYAH
that come with the Queen, WHICH IS MALCHUT, to the supernal King, WHO
IS ZEIR ANPIN.

115. קְדוּשָׁא דָּא דְּקָא מְקַדְּשֵׁי מַלְאֲכֵי עִלָּאֵי, לָאו אִיהוּ בְּיָחִיד. וְהָא
אוּקִימְנָא, כָּל קְדוּשָׁה דְּאִיהוּ בִּלְשׁוֹן הַקּוֹדֶשׁ, יָחִיד אָסִיר לֵיהּ לְמֵימַר.
תַּרְגּוּם, לְעוֹלָם בְּיָחִיד, וְלָא בְּסַגִּיאִין, וְיָחִיד אִיהוּ תִּקּוּנָא דִּילֵיהּ וַדַּאי,

וְלָא סַגִּיאִין. וְסִימָן לְרָזָא דָּא, שְׁנַיִם מִקְרָא וְאֶחָד תַּרְגּוּם. שְׁנַיִם לִישָׁנָא דְּסַגִּיאִין אִיהוּ, דְּוַדַּאי קְדוּשָּׁה דְּלָשׁוֹן הַקּוֹדֶשׁ אָסִיר אִיהִי בְּיָחִיד. קְדוּשַּׁת תַּרְגּוּם אָסִיר אִיהוּ בְּסַגִּיאִין, אֶלָּא בְּיָחִיד לְעוֹלָם. אֶחָד תַּרְגּוּם תָּנֵינָן, וְלָא תְּרֵין וְלָא יַתִּיר. תַּרְגּוּם אַתְיָא לְמִיעוּטָא, וְהָכִי אִצְטְרִיךְ. לָשׁוֹן הַקּוֹדֶשׁ אַתְיָא לְרִבּוּיָיא, וְהָכִי אִצְטְרִיךְ. דְּמַעֲלִין בַּקּוֹדֶשׁ וְלָא מוֹרִידִין. וּבְתַרְגּוּם מוֹרִידִין וְלָא מַעֲלִין. אֶחָד תָּנֵינָן, וְלָא יַתִּיר, וְלָא מַעֲלִין כְּלָל.

**115.** The sanctification that the supernal angels make, NAMELY THE SANCTIFICATION IN THE BLESSING OF 'WHO FORMS' AND IN THE PRAYER OF AMIDAH, is not said when alone. We have established that the single person is prohibited to recite any sanctification that is in the Holy Tongue. AND SANCTIFICATION in the Aramaic LANGUAGE is always recited by one alone and not in quorum, for this is definitely the correction for one but not for the quorum. The sign for this is the expression, 'read the scripture twice and the Aramaic translation once,' because two is plural, AND THE ALLUSION IS that assuredly the sanctification of the Holy Tongue, WHICH IS SCRIPTURE, is prohibited to be recited alone, ONLY IN PUBLIC, NAMELY A QUORUM OF TEN. Sanctification in the Aramaic LANGUAGE is lacking in public, AND IT IS TO BE SAID always only when alone. We learned that (one) the Aramaic translation once and not with two or more, AND THE REASON IS that the Aramaic translation has come to lessen, and so it must be. But the Holy Tongue increases, and it must be so because 'one should increase, not lessen, the importance of holy matters.' We decrease rather than increase in Aramaic translation. We learned 'one' and not more, because one does not increase at all.

116. קְדוּשָׁא דָּא, קְדוּשָׁתָא דְּאִתְקַדְּשַׁת שְׁכִינְתָּא, וְכָל אִינּוּן רְתִיכִין דִּילָהּ, לְאִתְתַּקְנָא לְגַבֵּי מַלְכָּא עִלָּאָה. וּבְגִין דְּאִיהִי קְדוּשַׁת עָלְמָא תַּתָּאָה, אִיהִי מְיוּשָּׁב וְלָא בַּעֲמִידָה. קְדוּשָׁה אַחֲרָא דְּאַהֲדוּרֵי צְלוֹתָא, אִיהִי קְדוּשָׁתָא דְּעָלְמָא עִלָּאָה, וּבְגִין כָּךְ אִיהִי בַּעֲמִידָה, בְּגִין לְאַמְשָׁכָא לָהּ לְתַתָּא, וְכָל מַלּוֹי דְּעָלְמָא עִלָּאָה, אִיהוּ בַּעֲמִידָה וְלָא מְיוּשָּׁב.

**116.** This sanctification THAT IS IN THE BLESSING 'WHO FORMS' IS NOT SIMPLE NARRATIVE, but is rather sanctification that sanctifies the

Shechinah and all Her Chariots in order to become perfected before the supernal King. Because it is the sanctification of the lower world, WHICH IS MALCHUT, it is said sitting and not standing. The other sanctification THAT IS SAID during the repetition of the Amidah prayer is the sanctification of the upper world, WHICH IS ZEIR ANPIN. Therefore, it is SAID standing in order to draw THE SANCTIFICATION downwards, while all the words relating to the upper world, WHICH IS ZEIR ANPIN, are recited standing and not sitting.

117. וּבְכָל הָנֵי קְדוּשָׁתֵי, יִשְׂרָאֵל מִתְקַדְּשֵׁי בְּהוּ לְתַתָּא. וְעַ"ד יִשְׂרָאֵל מִתְקַדְּשֵׁי בִּקְדוּשָׁה דִּרְתִיכָא תַּתָּאָה מְיוּשָׁב. וּבִקְדוּשָׁה דִּרְתִיכָא עִלָּאָה מְעוֹמָד. קְדוּשָׁה אַחֲרָא, אִיהִי תּוֹסֶפֶת קְדוּשָׁה, בְּגִינֵי כָּךְ אִיהִי בָּתַר צְלוֹתָא. וּבְגִין דְּאִיהִי תּוֹסֶפֶת קְדוּשָׁה, עַל קָדוּשָׁן אַחֲרָנִין, אִיהִי לְבָתַר צְלוֹתָא. וּבְגִין דְּכָל חַד וְחַד בָּעֵי לְאַמְשָׁכָא עֲלֵיהּ מֵהַהוּא תּוֹסֶפֶת, אִתְתָּקַּן לְכָל יָחִיד וְיָחִיד קְדוּשַׁת תַּרְגּוּם.

117. Yisrael become sanctified through all these sanctifications below. Therefore, they are endowed with the sanctification of the lower Chariot, WHICH IS MALCHUT, when seated, and with the sanctification of the upper Chariot, WHICH IS ZEIR ANPIN, when they stand. The other sanctification, WHICH IS IN, "BUT TO ZION A REDEEMER SHALL COME" (YESHAYAH 59:20), is an additional sanctification. Therefore, it is after the Amidah prayer, since it is an additional sanctification on the other sanctifications. Since each one has to draw upon himself from that addition, a translated Aramaic sanctification was arranged for each individual.

118. וְאִי תֵּימָא הָא אִית בָּהּ קְדוּשַׁת לָשׁוֹן הַקֹּדֶשׁ. הַהוּא לַצְבּוּר, לְאִתְקַדְּשָׁא כֻּלְּהוּ בִּכְלָל, בְּהַהוּא תּוֹסֶפֶת קְדוּשָׁה. וּבְגִין דְּיָחִיד לֵית לֵיהּ רְשׁוּת, לְאוֹמְרָהּ בִּלְשׁוֹן הַקֹּדֶשׁ, וּלְאִתְקַדְּשָׁא יְחִידָאי, אַתְקִינוּ לָהּ בִּלְשׁוֹן תַּרְגּוּם, וְאִיהוּ בְּיָחִיד, לְאִתְקַדְּשָׁא כָּל חַד וְחַד בְּהַהוּא תּוֹסֶפֶת, לְאַמְשָׁכָא עֲלֵיהּ קְדוּשָׁה יַתִּיר. זַכָּאָה חוּלָקֵיהוֹן דְּיִשְׂרָאֵל, דְּקָא מִתְקַדְּשֵׁי בִּקְדוּשֵׁי עִלָּאֵי, בְּגִין דְּאִינּוּן דְּבֵקִין לְעֵילָּא, דִּכְתִיב וְאַתֶּם הַדְּבֵקִים בַּיְיָ' אֱלֹהֵיכֶם חַיִּים כֻּלְּכֶם הַיּוֹם.

**118.** And if you ask, But it does contain ALSO sanctification in the Holy Tongue. That is for the Congregation, that they all be sanctified generally with that additional translated sanctification. Since the individual is not permitted to say it in the Holy Tongue and become sanctified singularly, they prepared it in the Aramaic tongue. IT IS for the single one so that each and every one should become sanctified with that addition to draw upon himself more sanctification. Happy is the portion of Yisrael that become sanctified with the supernal sanctification, because they cleave unto above, as it is written: "But you that did cleave of Hashem, your Elohim, are alive every one of you this day" (Devarim 4:4).

## 11. "a bed, and a table, and a chair, and a lamp"

### A Synopsis

The section opens with the verse, "Behold now, I perceive that this is a holy man of Elohim, who passes us by continually. Let us make a little upper chamber'" Employing the lyrical language of metaphor, this is a reference to the upper world, Zeir Anpin, who continually sanctifies above as He sanctifies us below. We learn how we perfect Him for His gratification with our order of songs and praises, and with prayer. The "bed" is in the order of the Evening Prayer and its perfection. The "table" is in the order of the offerings, songs and prayers of the morning. The "chair" is the order of the prayer recited while sitting, and the unity we strive to perfect. The blessings that we recite are the "lamp." Next, we're told how these things were supplied and perfected by Jacob, by King David, by Abraham and by Isaac. Holy people who constantly wish to prepare before the upper world, we finally learn, should therefore recite 'a bed, a table, a chair' and 'a lamp', so that there might be perfection daily, both above and below.

### The Relevance of this Passage

To partake of water, a man requires a vessel, or cup, to hold the fluid while he drinks. In like fashion, Light needs a vessel before it can express itself in our physical domain. Therein lies one purpose of the Daily Prayers.

The words of wisdom set forth below expound upon the construction of a Vessel (prayer) so that Light and blessing may be received in our world. Thus, this knowledge perfects and prepares our own souls and the global vessel so that we, and all mankind, may be the recipients of Divine Light. This effect is now achieved through the lofty spiritual influence of the patriarchs Abraham, Isaac, Jacob, and King David, whose names channel the energy that brings preparation and perfection to our souls.

119. כְּתִיב הִנֵּה נָא יָדַעְתִּי כִּי אִישׁ אֱלֹהִים קָדוֹשׁ הוּא עוֹבֵר וְגוֹ', וּכְתִיב נַעֲשֶׂה נָא עֲלִיַּת קִיר קְטַנָּה וְגוֹ', בְּהַאי קְרָא אִית לָן סְמָךְ בְּעָלְמָא לְסִדּוּרָא דִּצְלוֹתָא. הִנֵּה נָא יָדַעְתִּי, דָּא אִיהוּ רְעוּתָא דְּאִצְטְרִיךְ בַּר נָשׁ לְשַׁוָּאָה בְּגַוֵּיהּ בִּצְלוֹתָא. כִּי אִישׁ אֱלֹהִים קָדוֹשׁ הוּא, דָּא אִיהוּ עָלְמָא עִלָּאָה, דְּאִיהוּ יָתִיב עַל כּוּרְסֵי יְקָרֵיהּ, וְכָל קַדּוּשָׁאן נָפְקִין מִנֵּיהּ, וְאִיהוּ מְקַדֵּשׁ לְכֻלְּהוּ עָלְמִין. עוֹבֵר עָלֵינוּ תָּמִיד, מֵהַהוּא קְדוּשָׁה דְּאִיהוּ מְקַדֵּשׁ לְכָל עָלְמִין לְעֵילָא, אִיהוּ מְקַדֵּשׁ לָן בְּהַאי עָלְמָא. דְּהָא לֵית

קְדוּשָׁה לְעֵילָא, אֶלָּא אִי אִית קְדוּשָׁא לְתַתָּא, כד״א וְנִקְדַּשְׁתִּי בְּתוֹךְ בְּנֵי יִשְׂרָאֵל.

**119.** It is written: "Behold now, I perceive that this is a holy man of Elohim, who passes by us continually. Let us make a little upper chamber..." (II Melachim 4:9-10). In this passage, we have a slight allusion to the sequence of prayer. "Behold now, I perceive" is desire, and a person must put into his prayer that "this is a holy man of Elohim." This is the upper world, NAMELY ZEIR ANPIN, who sits on His Throne of Glory. All sanctifications emanate from Him, and He sanctifies all the worlds. "Passes by us continually," MEANING THAT He sanctifies the world above and He sanctifies us in this world from that sanctification. There is no sanctification above unless there is sanctification below, as it is written: "But I will be hallowed Yisrael" (Vayikra 22:32).

120. וְהוֹאִיל וְכַךְ הוּא, נַעֲשֶׂה נָא עֲלִיַּת קִיר קְטַנָּה, דָּא אִיהוּ סְדוּרָא דְּתִקּוּנָא דִּשְׁכִינְתָּא, דְּאִיהִי עֲלִיַּת קִיר, כד״א וַיַּסֵּב חִזְקִיָּהוּ פָּנָיו אֶל הַקִּיר. קְטַנָּה: בְּגִין דְּאִיהִי זְעֵירָא, כד״א עִיר קְטַנָּה. וְנָשִׂים לוֹ שָׁם בְּתִקּוּנָא דָּא דְּאֲנָן מְתַקְּנִין, וּבְסִדּוּרָא דִּילָן בְּשִׁירִין וְתוּשְׁבְּחָן וּבִצְלוֹתָא, אֲנָן מְתַקְּנִין לְגַבֵּיהּ, לְנַיְיחָא דִּילֵיהּ. מִטָּה וְשֻׁלְחָן וְכִסֵּא וּמְנוֹרָה. אַרְבַּע אִלֵּין, כֻּלְּהוּ בִּשְׁכִינְתָּא אִינּוּן. וְאִיהִי בְּכָל תִּקּוּנִין אִלֵּין מִתְתַּקְּנָן, לְגַבֵּי עָלְמָא עִלָּאָה בְּסִדּוּרָא דְּאֲנָן מְסַדְּרִין.

**120.** Since this is so, "let us make a little upper chamber," which is the order of the perfection of the Shechinah, who is CALLED "a little upper chamber...with walls," as it is written: "And Chizkiyah turned his face toward the wall" (Yeshayah 38:2). 'Little', because it is small, as it is written: "A little city" (Kohelet 9:14). "And let us set for him there" (II Melachim 4:10), through this perfection that we are arranging. We perfect Him, ZEIR ANPIN, for His gratification with our sequence of songs and praises and with prayer. "A bed, and table, and a chair, and a lamp" (Ibid.): All these four are in the Shechinah, for She is prepared with all these tools toward the upper world, WHICH IS ZEIR ANPIN, in the order that we set out.

121. בְּסִדּוּרָא דִּצְלוֹתָא דְּעַרְבִית, וּבְתִקּוּנָא דִּילֵיהּ, הָא מִטָּה. בְּסִדּוּרָא

דְּאִינּוּן קָרְבָּנִין וְעָלָוָון, דְּאֲנָן מְסַדְּרִין בְּצַפְרָא דְּאִינּוּן שִׁירִין וְתוּשְׁבְּחָן, הָא שֻׁלְחָן. וּבְהַהוּא סִדּוּרָא דִּצְלוֹתָא דִּמְיוּשָׁב, וּבְתִקּוּנָא דְּק״ש, בְּהַהוּא יִחוּדָא דְּאֲנָן מְתַקְּנִין הָא כֻּרְסְיָא. בְּהַהוּא סִדּוּרָא דִּצְלוֹתָא דִּמְעוֹמָד, וּבְאִינּוּן קְדוּשָׁאן, וְתוֹסֶפֶת קְדוּשָׁה, וּבִרְכָּאן, דְּאֲנָן מְסַדְּרִין הָא מְנוֹרָה.

**121.** In the order of the evening prayer and in its perfection is the bed, and in the order of the offerings and burnt offerings that we set out in the morning and these songs and prayers is the table. In the order of the prayer recited while sitting down, and in the perfection of the reading of Sh'ma, in that unity which we strive to perfect is a chair. In the order of the standing prayer and these sanctifications THAT ARE IN 'WHO FORMS' AND IN THE REPETITION OF THE AMIDAH BY THE CANTOR, and the additional sanctification THAT IS IN "AND A REDEEMER SHALL COME TO ZION," and the blessings that we recite are the lamp.

**122.** זַכָּאָה אִיהוּ בַּר נָשׁ, דְּדָא שַׁוֵּי בִּרְעוּתֵיהּ, לְאַשְׁלָמָא לְגַבֵּי מָארֵיהּ בְּכָל יוֹמָא, וּלְאַתְקְנָא הַאי עֲלִיַּת קִיר קְטַנָּה, לְגַבֵּי מָארֵיהּ בְּהַנֵּי תִּקּוּנִין. כְּדֵין וַדַּאי קוּדְשָׁא בְּרִיךְ הוּא יְהֵא אוּשְׁפִּיזֵיהּ בְּכָל יוֹמָא. זַכָּאָה אִיהוּ בְּהַאי עָלְמָא, וְזַכָּאָה אִיהוּ בְּעָלְמָא דְּאָתֵי. בְּגִין דְּאִלֵּין אַרְבַּע, אִינּוּן תִּקּוּנֵי דִּשְׁכִינְתָּא, לְאִתְתַּקְּנָא לְגַבֵּי בַּעְלָהּ. בְּאַרְבַּע תִּקּוּנִין אִלֵּין, אִתְתַּקְּנַת בְּשַׁפִּירָהָא, בְּחֶדְוָותָא, בְּחֶזְוָותָא, ע״י דְּעַמָּא קַדִּישָׁא בְּכָל יוֹמָא.

**122.** Happy is the man that concentrates his wish on this, to be perfect before his Master every day and to perfect this little upper chamber, WHICH IS THE SHECHINAH, TO HIS MASTER, with these constructions OF A BED, A TABLE, A CHAIR, AND A LAMP. Then the Holy One, blessed be He, will surely be his guest every day. Happy is he in this world and happy is he in the World to Come, because these four are the tools of the Shechinah with which to become ready for her husband, ZEIR ANPIN. She becomes ready in these four tools with beauty, with joy and in appearance through the holy people every day.

**123.** מִטָּה אִתְיְהִיבַת לֵיהּ לְיַעֲקֹב לְאִתְתַּקְּנָא, וְע״ד יַעֲקֹב אַתְקִין צְלוֹתָא דְּעַרְבִית. שֻׁלְחָן אַתְקִין דָּוִד מַלְכָּא, בְּאִינּוּן שִׁירִין וְתוּשְׁבְּחָן

דְּאִיהוּ אַתְקִין, כד"א תַּעֲרֹךְ לְפָנַי שֻׁלְחָן נֶגֶד צוֹרְרָי. כֻּסֵּא אַתְקִין אַבְרָהָם, בְּאִתְקַשְׁרוּתָא דִּילֵיהּ, דְּעָבִיד טִיבוּ וּשְׁלִימוּ דְּנִשְׁמָתִין לְכָל בְּנֵי עָלְמָא, וְלֵית תִּקּוּנָא דְּכֻּסֵּא, אֶלָּא בְּחֶסֶד דְּאַבְרָהָם, כד"א וְהוּכַן בַּחֶסֶד כֻּסֵּא.

**123.** The bed was given to be prepared by Jacob. Therefore, Jacob composed the evening prayer. The table was prepared by King David through the songs and praises that he composed, as it is written: "You prepare a table before me in the presence of my enemies" (Tehilim 23:5). A chair was prepared by Abraham by his attachment, by his doing kindness and perfection of the souls of all the inhabitants of the world. The perfection of the chair is only through the kindness of Abraham, as it is written: "And in Mercy a throne was established" (Yeshayah 16:5).

124. מְנוֹרָה אַתְקִין יִצְחָק, דְּאַקְדִּישׁ שְׁמָא דְּקוּדְשָׁא בְּרִיךְ הוּא לְעֵינֵיהוֹן דְּכָל עָלְמָא, וְנָהִיר נְהִירוּ דְּבוּצִינָא עִלָּאָה בְּהַהִיא קְדוּשָׁה. בְּגִינֵי כָּךְ, צְרִיכִין עַמָּא קַדִּישָׁא, לוֹמַר תָּדִיר וּלְשַׁוָּאָה רְעוּתְהוֹן, לְסַדְּרָא לְגַבֵּי עָלְמָא עִלָּאָה, דְּאִיהוּ מָארֵיהּ דְּבֵיתָא, אִישׁ הָאֱלֹהִים, מִטָּה וְשֻׁלְחָן וְכֻסֵּא וּמְנוֹרָה, לְמֶהֱוֵי שְׁלִימוּ בְּכָל יוֹמָא, עֵילָּא וְתַתָּא.

**124.** The lamp was built by Isaac, who sanctified the Name of the Holy One, blessed be He, before the eyes of the whole world, and illuminated the light of the supernal candle with that sanctification. Therefore the holy people, who constantly wish to prepare the upper world, WHICH IS ZEIR ANPIN, the Master of the house, the man of Elohim, should recite 'a bed, a table, a chair' and 'a lamp,' so that there might be perfection daily, above and below.

## 12. "Sh'ma Yisrael" and 'Blessed be the Name'

### A Synopsis

When the children of Yisrael are declaring the union of the secret of Sh'ma Yisrael, we learn, one light emerges from concealment in the upper world. This light is then battered into a 'hard spark', which itself is finally divided into seventy lights. These are illuminated in the seventy branches of the Tree of Life, and the Tree emanates fragrance and gives forth spices. At the same time, all the trees in the Garden of Eden emanate fragrance and praise their Master. All the supernal limbs, the Sfirot, join in one aspiration and one desire to be unified as one without any separation. Following this, we learn of the secret and joyous mating of Malchut, the Queen, with Zeir Anpin, and are told of the significance of the four keys, and of the four letters on them, which when they are gathered together cause the union. The union above, we learn once more, is mirrored by the union below. It is not possible to refer openly to Malchut as 'one' — in case the evil eye is aroused — but in the time to come, the Other Side will separate from her, and will in fact be removed from the world. Then, and only then, will Malchut be called 'one'. By her union to Zeir Anpin in silence and in secret, though, she is now removed from that Other Side. The secret of the upper world, we're then told, is the heart of Jacob, and the secret of the lower world is the heart of his sons. Rabbi Hamnuna Saba (the elder), we discover, has said that the awakening of this union between Malchut and Zeir Anpin is beautiful. Lastly, we are reminded there is a commandment to study the Torah every day. The Torah is the Tree of Life, and he who studies it deserves to be bound with the supernal Torah.

### The Relevance of this Passage

The Zohar ignites the seventy Lights that illuminate the seventy branches of the Tree of Life by revealing holy secrets pertaining to the Tetragrammaton .ה.ו.ה.י. This Light enjoins Malchut (our world) with Zeir Anpin (upper world), our body with our soul, which now elevates us above and beyond the sphere of influence of the Other Side.

125. בְּשַׁעֲתָא דְּקָא מְיַחֲדֵי יִשְׂרָאֵל, יְחוּדָא דְּרָזָא דִּשְׁמַע יִשְׂרָאֵל, בִּרְעוּתָא שְׁלִים, כְּדֵין נַפְקֵי מִגּוֹ סְתִימוּ דְּעָלְמָא עִלָּאָה, חַד נְהִירוּ, וְהַהוּא נְהִירוּ בָּטַשׁ גּוֹ בּוּצִינָא דְּקַרְדִּינוּתָא, וְאִתְפְּלַג לְע' נְהוֹרִין, וְאִינּוּן ע' נְהוֹרִין, בְּע' עַנְפִין דְּאִילָנָא דְּחַיֵּי.

**125.** When Yisrael are declaring the union of the secret of Sh'ma Yisrael with complete desire, one light, WHICH IS THE PATH OF ABA, emerges from the concealment of the upper world, NAMELY THE UPPER ABA AND IMA. This light is battered into the hard spark, WHICH IS YESOD OF IMA, and is divided into seventy lights THAT RADIATE FROM THEM THE MOCHIN OF YISRAEL–SABA AND TEVUNAH, WHICH ARE THE LOWER SEVEN SFIROT OF ABA AND IMA, CHESED, GVURAH, TIFERET NETZACH, HOD, YESOD AND MALCHUT, EACH COMPOSED OF TEN. And these seventy lights ILLUMINATED in the seventy branches of the Tree of Life, NAMELY IN CHESED, GVURAH, TIFERET, NETZACH, HOD, YESOD AND MALCHUT OF ZEIR ANPIN, EACH CONTAINING TEN.

126. כְּדֵין, הַהוּא אִילָנָא סָלִיק רֵיחִין ובוּסְמִין, וְכָל אִילָנֵי דְגִנְתָּא דְעֵדֶן, כֻּלְּהוּ סַלְּקִין רֵיחִין, ומְשַׁבְּחָן לְמָארֵיהוֹן, דְּהָא כְּדֵין אִתְתַּקְּנַת מַטרוֹנִיתָא, לְאַעֲלָא לַחוּפָּה בַּהֲדֵי בַּעְלָהּ, כָּל אִינּוּן שַׁיְיפִין עִלָּאִין, כֻּלְּהוּ מִתְחַבְּרָן בְּתִיאוֹבְתָּא חֲדָא, ובִרְעוּתָא חֲדָא, לְמֶהֱוֵי חַד בְּלָא פֵּרוּדָא כְּלָל. וּכְדֵין בַּעְלָהּ אִתְתָּקַּן לְגַבָּהּ לְאַעֲלָא לַחוּפָּה בְּיִחוּדָא חַד, לְאִתְיַיחֲדָא בְּמַטרוֹנִיתָא.

**126.** Then that Tree, WHICH IS ZEIR ANPIN, emanates fragrances and spices, NAMELY THE LIGHT OF CHOCHMAH THAT IS CALLED 'FRAGRANCE'. All the trees that are in the Garden of Eden, WHICH IS MALCHUT, emanate fragrances and praise their Master, ZEIR ANPIN, for Malchut is then prepared to enter the marriage canopy with her husband, ZEIR ANPIN. All the supernal limbs, WHICH ARE THE SFIROT OF ZEIR ANPIN, join in one aspiration and one desire to be one without any separation. Then her husband, ZEIR ANPIN, is prepared to enter the marriage canopy in one union to unite with Malchut.

127. וְעַ״ד אֲנַן מִתְּעָרֵי לֵיהּ, וְאַמְרִינָן שְׁמַע יִשְׂרָאֵל, אַתְקִין גַּרְמָךְ, הָא בַּעְלִיךְ יֵיתֵי לְגַבִּיךְ בְּתִקּוּנוֹי, זַמִּין לְקַבְּלָךְ. יְיָ׳ אֱלֹהֵינוּ יְיָ׳ אֶחָד, בְּיִחוּדָא חֲדָא, בִּרְעוּתָא חֲדָא, בְּלָא פֵּרוּדָא, דְּכָל אִינּוּן שַׁיְיפִין כֻּלְּהוּ אִתְעֲבִידוּ חַד, וְעַיְילִין בְּחַד תִּיאוֹבְתָּא.

**127.** Therefore we stimulate her, MALCHUT, and we say Sh'ma Yisrael, MEANING MALCHUT, FOR THE CHILDREN OF YISRAEL ARE INCLUDED IN HER. WE SAY TO MALCHUT, Prepare yourself, for your husband, ZEIR ANPIN, will come to you adorned and he is prepared toward you. "Hashem our Elohim, Hashem is One" (Devarim 6:4). HASHEM IS ABA, OUR ELOHIM IS IMA, HASHEM IS ZEIR ANPIN AS IT IS WRITTEN BEFORE US. They are one, MEANING in one union with one desire without separation, and all these limbs OF ZEIR ANPIN, NAMELY HIS SFIROT, become one and enter with one longing, MEANING IN YESOD OF ZEIR ANPIN.

128. כֵּיוָן דְּאַמְרֵי יִשְׂרָאֵל יְיָ׳ אֶחָד בְּאִתְעָרוּתָא דְּשִׁית סְטְרִין, כְּדֵין כָּל אִינּוּן שִׁית סְטְרִין, אִתְעֲבֵידוּ חַד וְעָאלִין בְּחַד תִּיאוּבְתָּא, וְרָזָא דָא ו׳ חַד פְּשִׁיטוּ בִּלְחוֹדוֹי, בְּלָא דְּבֵקוּתָא אַחֲרָא לְגַבֵּיהּ, אֶלָּא אִיהוּ בִּלְחוֹדוֹי פָּשִׁיט מִכֹּלָּא, וְאִיהוּ חַד.

**128.** As soon as Yisrael say, "Hashem is One," WHICH ALLUDES TO ZEIR ANPIN AS MENTIONED ABOVE, with the stimulus of the six sides, THAT RECEIVE FROM ABA AND IMA, THE SECRET OF "HASHEM OUR ELOHIM" AS THEY BECAME ONE, AS MENTIONED. Then all these six sides become one and enter to one longing, WHICH IS YESOD. This is the secret of *Vav*, WHICH ALLUDES TO ZEIR ANPIN, WHICH IS THE SECRET OF one expansion. JUST LIKE THE LETTER *VAV* THAT IS SHAPED LIKE A LINE with nothing attached to it, MEANING THAT THE ILLUMINATION OF CHASSADIM OF THE RIGHT DOMINATES IT, AND THERE IS NO ATTACHMENT FROM THE REVELATION OF CHOCHMAH IN THE LEFT. Only it itself spreads AND IS COMBINED of them all, EVEN FROM THE LEFT, and it is one. EVEN THOUGH IT IS COMBINED ALSO FROM THE ILLUMINATION OF CHOCHMAH, WHICH IS THE SECRET OF ONE, STILL ONLY THE RIGHT DOMINATES IT, WHICH IS THE ILLUMINATION OF CHASSADIM ALONE.

129. בְּהַהִיא שַׁעֲתָא, מַטְרוֹנִיתָא מִתְתַּקְּנָא וּמִתְקַשְּׁטָא, וְעַיְילִין לָהּ שַׁמָּשָׁהָא בִּלְחִישׁוּ סַגִּי, לְגַבֵּי בַּעְלָהּ, וְאַמְרֵי בָּרוּךְ שֵׁם כְּבוֹד מַלְכוּתוֹ לְעוֹלָם וָעֶד. דָּא אִיהוּ בִּלְחִישׁוּ, דְּהָכִי אִצְטְרִיךְ לְאַעֲלָא לָהּ לְגַבֵּי בַּעְלָהּ. זַכָּאָה עַמָּא דְּיַדְעֵי דָּא, וּמְסַדְּרֵי סִדּוּרָא עִלָּאָה דִּמְהֵימְנוּתָא.

**129.** At that time, Malchut prepares and adorns Herself. The attendants, MEANING THE MAIDENS as written, bring her in great secrecy to her

husband, ZEIR ANPIN, and say, 'Blessed be the Name of the glory of His kingdom forever and ever.' This is in secret because this is the way that it is necessary to bring Her to Her husband, ZEIR ANPIN. Happy are the people who know this and perform the supernal order of the Faith, WHICH IS MALCHUT.

130. בְּהַהִיא שַׁעֲתָא דְאִתְחַבְּרוּ בַּעֲלָה וּמַטְרוֹנִיתָא כַּחֲדָא, כְּדֵין כָּרוֹזָא נָפִיק מִסִּטְרָא דְּדָרוֹם, אִתְעָרוּ חֵילִין וּמַשְׁרְיָין דְּגַלֵּי רְחִימוּתָא לְגַבֵּי מָארֵיכוֹן.

130. At the time that the husband OF THE QUEEN, THAT IS ZEIR ANPIN, and the Queen join as one, a proclamation emerges from the south side, WHICH IS CHESED, Awaken, hosts and camps that manifested the love of their Master, MEANING THOSE THAT CAUSED THIS UNION.

131. כְּדֵין אִתְּעַר חַד מְמָנָא עִלָּאָה, בּוֹאֵ"ל שְׁמֵיהּ, רַב מַשִׁרְיָין, וּבִידֵיהּ אַרְבַּע מַפְתְּחָן, דְּנָטִיל מד' סִטְרֵי עָלְמָא, וְחַד מַפְתְּחָא אִתְרְשִׁים בְּאָת י', וּמַפְתְּחָא אַחֲרָא אִתְרְשִׁים בְּאָת ה'. וְחַד מַפְתְּחָא אִתְרְשִׁים בְּאָת ו'. וְאַנַּח לְהוּ תְּחוֹת אִילָנָא דְּחַיֵּי. אִינּוּן תְּלַת מַפְתְּחָן, דְּאִתְרְשִׁימוּ בִּתְלַת אַתְוָון אִלֵּין, אִתְעֲבִידוּ חַד. כֵּיוָן דְּאִתְעֲבִידוּ חַד, הַהוּא מַפְתְּחָא אַחֲרָא, סָלִיק וְקָאִים וְאִתְחַבַּר בְּהַהוּא אַחֲרָא כְּלָלָא דִּתְלַת, וְכָל אִינּוּן מַשְׁרְיָין וְחַיָּילִין עַיְילִין לְאִינּוּן תְּרֵין מַפְתְּחָן גּוֹ גִּנְתָּא וְכֻלְּהוּ מִיַחֲדֵי כְּגַוְונָא דִּלְתַתָּא.

131. Then a supernal overseer, the minister of the camps whose name is Boel, becomes aroused. In his hands are four keys, which he received from the four directions of the world, CHESED, GVURAH, TIFERET AND MALCHUT. One key is marked with the letter *Yud*, one is marked with the letter *Hei* and another key is marked with the letter *Vav*. He places them under the Tree of Life, WHICH IS ZEIR ANPIN. These three keys that are marked with these three letters become one. As soon as they become one, that last key, WHICH IS THE LAST *HEI*, ascends and stands and combines with the other key that includes the three KEYS. All camps and hosts enter these two keys in the Garden, WHICH ARE *VAV-HEI*, and they all combine as below, MEANING LIKE YISRAEL.

132. יְדֹוָ״ד: דָּא רְשִׁימוּ דְּאָת י׳, רֵישָׁא עִלָּאָה דִּבְשְׁמָא קַדִּישָׁא. אֱלֹהֵינוּ: דָּא אִיהוּ רָזָא דִּרְשִׁימוּ דְּאָת ה׳ עִלָּאָה, אָת תִּנְיָינָא דִּבְשְׁמָא קַדִּישָׁא. יְדֹוָ״ד: דָּא מְשִׁיכוּ דְּאִתְמְשַׁךְ לְתַתָּא, בְּרָזָא דִּרְשִׁימוּ דְּאָת ו׳, דְּאִינּוּן תְּרֵין וְאַתְוָון אִתְמְשָׁכוּ לְמֶהֱוֵי בְּאֲתַר דָּא, וְאִיהוּ אֶחָד. כָּל הָנֵי תְּלָתָא אִינּוּן חַד, בְּיִחוּדָא חַד.

132. NOW THE ZOHAR EXPLAINS THE SECRET OF THE WORDS OF "SH'MA YISRAEL." THE FIRST Yud Hei Vav Hei is the mark of the letter *Yud* that is in the Holy Name, WHICH ALLUDES TO ABA. "Our Elohim" is the secret of the mark of the upper *Hei* of the Holy Name THAT ALLUDES TO IMA. THE SECOND Yud Hei Vav Hei is the drawing OF MOCHIN FROM ABA AND IMA that are drawn below in the secret of the mark of the letter *Vav* OF THE HOLY NAME THAT ALLUDES TO ZEIR ANPIN. These two letters, *YUD* AND *HEI*, are drawn to be in this place, MEANING IN THE *VAV*, WHICH IS ZEIR ANPIN. It is one, for all these three, WHICH ARE ABA AND IMA AND ZEIR ANPIN, are one in one unity.

133. כֵּיוָן דְּכָל דָּא אִתְעֲבֵיד חַד בְּיִחוּדָא חַד, וְאִשְׁתְּאַר כֹּלָּא בְּרָזָא דְּאָת ו׳ שְׁלִים, מֵרֵישָׁא דְּמַבּוּעָא, וּמֵהֵיכָלָא פְּנִימָאָה, וְיָרִית לְאַבָּא וְאִימָּא, כְּדֵין עַיְילִין לְמַטְרוֹנִיתָא בַּהֲדֵיהּ, דְּהָא הַשְׁתָּא אִיהוּ שְׁלִים בְּכָל טִיבוּ עִלָּאָה, וְיָכִיל לְאַתְזְנָא לָהּ, וּלְמֵיהַב לָהּ מְזוֹנָא וְסִפּוּקָא כַּדְקָא יָאוֹת. וְכָל אִינּוּן שַׁיְיפִין דִּילֵיהּ כֻּלְּהוּ חַד. כְּדֵין עַיְילִין לָהּ לְגַבֵּיהּ, בִּלְחִישׁוּ. אֲמַאי בִּלְחִישׁוּ. בְּגִין דְּלָא יִתְעָרַב זָר בְּהַהִיא חֶדְוָה, כד״א וּבְשִׂמְחָתוֹ לֹא יִתְעָרַב זָר.

133. All these have become one in one unity and everything remains in the secret of the letter *Vav*, FOR ALL THE MOCHIN HAVE REMAINED IN ZEIR ANPIN, WHICH IS THE SECRET OF *VAV*. He is whole from the source of the fountain, WHICH IS ABA, and from the inner chamber, THAT IS IMA, and He inherits Aba and Ima. Then they bring into Him the Queen, NAMELY MALCHUT, because He is now complete with all the supernal good, and can nourish her and give her food and sustenance as befitting. All His limbs, WHICH ARE THE SFIROT, are all one and then they bring her in secret. Why in secret? In order that a stranger should not intrude on this joy, as it is

written: "And no stranger shares its joy" (Mishlei 14:10), MEANING SO THAT THE OTHER SIDE SHOULD NOT BE DRAWN TO NURTURE FROM THE ILLUMINATION OF THE UNION.

134. כֵּיוָן דְּאִיהוּ אִתְיַחַד לְעֵילָּא בְּשִׁית סִטְרִין. אוֹף הָכִי אִיהִי אִתְיַחֲדַת לְתַתָּא בְּשִׁית סִטְרִין אָחֲרָנִין. בְּגִין לְמֶהֱוֵי אֶחָד לְעֵילָּא, וְאֶחָד לְתַתָּא, כד"א יִהְיֶה יְיָ' אֶחָד וּשְׁמוֹ אֶחָד. אֶחָד לְעֵילָּא בְּשִׁית סִטְרִין, דִּכְתִיב שְׁמַע יִשְׂרָאֵל יְיָ' אֱלֹהֵינוּ יְיָ' אֶחָד. הָא שִׁית תֵּיבִין, לָקֳבֵל שִׁית סִטְרִין. אֶחָד לְתַתָּא בְּשִׁית סִטְרִין, בשכמל"ו, הָא שִׁית סִטְרִין אָחֲרָנִין בְּשִׁית תֵּיבִין. יְיָ' אֶחָד לְעֵילָּא, וּשְׁמוֹ אֶחָד לְתַתָּא.

134. Since ZEIR ANPIN becomes united above in six sides, MALCHUT also becomes united below in six other sides, WHICH ARE CHESED, GVURAH, TIFERET, NETZACH, HOD AND YESOD OF THE MOCHIN. So there will be one above and one below, as it is written: "Hashem shall be One, and His Name One" (Zecharyah 14:9), NAMELY ZEIR ANPIN. "And His Name One" is MALCHUT THAT IS CALLED 'NAME', one above in six sides, as written: "Hear Yisrael, Hashem our Elohim, Hashem is One" (Devarim 6:4). There are six words corresponding to six sides. Blessed be the Name of the glory of His kingdom forever and ever: Here are six other sides in six words. Hashem is One above, IN ZEIR ANPIN, and His Name is One below IN MALCHUT.

135. וְאִי תֵּימָא, הָא כְּתִיב אֶחָד לְעֵילָּא, וּלְתַתָּא לָא כְּתִיב אֶחָד. וְעַד הוּא אֶחָד, בְּחִלּוּפֵי אַתְוָון. אַתְוָון דִּדְכוּרָא לָא מִתְחַלְּפֵי, אַתְוָון דְּנוּקְבָּא מִתְחַלְּפֵי, דְּהָא שְׁבָחָא דִּדְכוּרָא עַל נוּקְבָּא. וּבְגִין דְּלָא תִּשְׁלוֹט עַיִן הָרַע, אֲנָן מְחַלְּפֵי אַתְוָון, דְּלָא אַמְרִינָן אֶחָד בְּאִתְגַּלְיָיא. וּבִזִמְנָא דְּאָתֵי, דְּיִתְעֲבַר עַיִן הָרַע מֵעָלְמָא, וְלָא תִּשְׁלוֹט, כְּדֵין יִתְקְרֵי אֶחָד בְּאִתְגַּלְיָיא. בְּגִין דְּהַשְׁתָּא דְּהַהוּא סִטְרָא אָחֳרָא אִתְדַּבַּק בַּהֲדָהּ, לָאו אִיהִי אֶחָד, אֶלָּא דַּאֲנָן מְיַחֲדִין לָהּ בִּלְחִישׁוּ, בְּרָזָא דְּאַתְוָון אָחֲרָנִין, וְאַמְרֵי וָעֶד.

135. If you ask, yet it is only written 'one' above IN ZEIR ANPIN, NAMELY IN "SH'MA YISRAEL," but below, IN MALCHUT, NAMELY IN 'BLESSED BE

THE NAME OF THE GLORY OF HIS KINGDOM FOREVER AND EVER,' 'one' is not written. HE ANSWERS: 'And ever (Heb. *vaed*, Vav-Ayin-Dalet)' is 'one (Heb. *echad*, Aleph-Chet-Dalet)' when the letters are interchanged, because Aleph is exchanged with Vav and Chet changes with Ayin AND VAED BECOMES ECHAD. The male letters do not change, but the female letters do, for this shows the praise the male has over the female. In order that the evil eye should not dominate, WHICH IS THE OTHER SIDE, we interchange the letters, for we don't say 'one' openly, BUT RATHER 'AND EVER.' In the future, when the evil eye will be removed from the world and will not dominate, MALCHUT will be called 'One' openly. Now that the Other Side is attached to it, IN THE SECRET: "AND HER FEET GO DOWN TO DEATH" (MISHLEI 5:5), She is not one. But we unite Her silently in the secret of THE INTERCHANGE OF other letters, and say 'and ever' INSTEAD OF 'ONE'.

136. אֲבָל בְּזִמְנָא דְּאָתֵי, דְּיִתְפְּרַשׁ הַהוּא סִטְרָא מִינָהּ, וְיִתְעֲבַר מֵעָלְמָא, כְּדֵין יִתְקְרֵי אֶחָד וַדַּאי, דְּלָא יְהֵא בַּהֲדָהּ שׁוּתָּפוּ וּדְבִיקוּ אַחֲרָא, כד״א בַּיּוֹם הַהוּא יִהְיֶה יְיָ׳ אֶחָד וּשְׁמוֹ אֶחָד, בְּאִתְגַּלְיָא בַּהֲדַיָא, וְלָא בִּלְחִישׁוּ, וְלָא בְּרָזָא.

136. However, in the time to come, the Other Side will separate from Her and will be removed from the world. Then MALCHUT will be called 'one', for there will not be any other partnership or attachment, as written: "On that day Hashem shall be one, and His Name One." EVEN MALCHUT THAT IS CALLED 'HIS NAME' SHALL BE 'ONE' revealed with Him, WITH ZEIR ANPIN, and not in whispering or in secret.

137. וְעַל דָּא, אֲנָן מְיַחֲדִין לָהּ מֵהַהוּא סִטְרָא אַחֲרָא, כְּמַאן דְּזַמִּין לְאַחֲרָא לְמֶיהֱוֵי סָהִיד דִּילֵיהּ. בְּגִין דְּדָא אִיהוּ סָהִיד דִּילָן, וְסִטְרָא אַחֲרָא לָאו אִיהוּ סָהֲדָא לְגַבָּן. וּכְדֵין אִיהִי אִתְפְּרִישַׁת מֵהַהוּא סִטְרָא. כֵּיוָן דְּאָתַת, אֲנָן מַעֲלִין לָהּ לַחוּפָּה לְגַבֵּי בַּעְלָהּ, מַלְכָּא עִלָּאָה, בְּכָל רְעוּתָא וְכַוְּונָא דְּלִבָּא, וְעַל דָּא אִיהוּ אֶחָד.

137. Therefore, we unite Her NOW TO REMOVE HER from that Other Side, as one invites someone to be his witness; NAMELY, ZEIR ANPIN BECOMES HER WITNESS THAT SHE IS ONE. Because ZEIR ANPIN is our witness and

the Other Side is not a witness by us, She is then separated from the OTHER Side. Since she has come TO ZEIR ANPIN, we elevate Her to the marriage canopy to Her husband, the supernal King WHO IS ZEIR ANPIN, with full desire and intention of the heart. Therefore, She is one.

138. בְּשַׁעֲתָא דְּאִיהִי אָתַת בְּעוּלֵימְתָהָא, וּבָעַאת לְאִתְפַּרְשָׁא מִסִּטְרָא אַחֲרָא, לָא אָתַת, אֶלָּא כְּמַאן דְּאִזְדַּמְּנַת לְמֶחֱמֵי בִּיקָרָא דְּמַלְכָּא וְלָא יַתִּיר, וְהָכִי מַכְרְיֵזֵי דְּיִזְדַּמְּנוּן לְמֶחֱמֵי בִּיקָרָא דְּמַלְכָּא. כד"א צְאֶנָה וּרְאֶינָה בְּנוֹת צִיּוֹן בַּמֶּלֶךְ שְׁלֹמֹה, פּוּקוּ לְמֶחֱמֵי בִּיקָרָא דְּמַלְכָּא, כְּדֵין סִטְרָא אַחֲרָא לָא נִיחָא לֵיהּ לְמֶחֱמֵי, וְאִתְפָּרַשׁ מִינָהּ. כֵּיוָן דְּאָתַת. כָּל אִינּוּן שַׁמָּשָׁהָא, עַיְילִין לָהּ לַחוּפָּה בַּהֲדֵי מַלְכָּא עִלָּאָה, בִּלְחִישׁוּ בְּרָזָא. דְּאִלְמָלֵא לָאו הָכִי, לָא יִתְפְּרַשׁ מִינָהּ הַהוּא סִטְרָא אַחֲרָא וְיִתְעָרַב חֶדְוָותָא. אֲבָל בְּזִמְנָא דְּאָתֵי, דְּיִתְפְּרַשׁ מִינָהּ הַהִיא סִטְרָא אַחֲרָא, כְּדֵין בַּיּוֹם הַהוּא יִהְיֶה יְיָ' אֶחָד וּשְׁמוֹ אֶחָד.

**138.** When She comes with her maidens, WHO ARE THE SEVEN CHAMBERS OF BRIYAH, and wishes to separate from the Other Side, she comes only as one who is invited to see the glory of the King and not more. It is thus announced, that they will come to behold the glory of the King, as written: "Go forth, daughters of Zion, and behold King Solomon" (Shir Hashirim 3:11), MEANING go out to see the glory of the king. The Other Side does not want to see her and separates FROM MALCHUT. When She arrives, all Her attendants, NAMELY THE MAIDENS, bring Her in to the marriage canopy with the supernal King, WHO IS ZEIR ANPIN, in silence and in secret. If it were not so, the Other Side would not separate from Her, and the joy would have been confused. But in the time to come, when the Other Side will be separated from Her, then "on that day Hashem shall be one, and His Name One."

139. כֵּיוָן דְּעָאלַת לַחוּפָּה, וְאִיהִי בַּהֲדֵי מַלְכָּא. עִלָּאָה, כְּדֵין אֲנָן מִתְעָרֵי חֶדְוָה דִּימִינָא וּשְׂמָאלָא, כד"א וְאָהַבְתָּ אֵת יְיָ' אֱלֹהֶיךָ בְּכָל לְבָבְךָ וְגוֹ'. וְהָיָה אִם שָׁמוֹעַ וְגוֹ'. בְּלָא דְּחִילוּ כְּלָל, דְּהָא סִטְרָא אַחֲרָא לָא יִתְקָרַב תַּמָּן, וְלֵית לֵיהּ רְשׁוּ.

**139.** Since She has entered the marriage canopy and is with the supernal King, WHO IS ZEIR ANPIN, we arouse the joy OF MOCHIN of the right and left, as it is written: "And you shall love Hashem your Elohim with all your heart…" (Devarim 6:5), WHICH IS THE RIGHT; "And it shall to pass, if you hearken…" (Devarim 11:13) IS THE LEFT. And this will be without any fear OF THE OTHER SIDE whatsoever, because the Other Side will not approach there, as it has no permission.

140. כַּלָּה, כָּל זִמְנָא דְּבָעָאן לְאַעֲלָא לָהּ לְגַבֵּי מַלְכָּא, לְחֶדְוָה דְשִׁמּוּשָׁא, אִצְטְרִיךְ בִּלְחִישׁוּ בְּרָזָא, בְּגִין דְּלָא יִשְׁתְּכַח בְּרַגְלֵי צַעֲדָהָא, רְמֶז דְּסִטְרָא בִּישָׁא, וְלָא יִתְדְּבַּק בַּהֲדָהּ, וְלָא יִשְׁתַּכְּחוּן בִּבְנֵי, רְמֶז פְּסוּל כְּלַל.

**140.** As long as they want to bring the bride, WHO IS MALCHUT, unto the KING for the celebration of union, it must be in silence and in secret, in order that there should not be found in her footsteps any hint of the evil side. Any hint of disqualification should neither cleave unto her, nor should it be found among her children, NAMELY YISRAEL BELOW.

141. וְהָכִי אָמַר יַעֲקֹב לִבְנוֹי, שֶׁמָּא חַס וְשָׁלוֹם אֵירַע פְּסוּל בְּעַרְסִי, כְּדֵין אִינּוּן אָמְרוּ, כְּמָה דְּלֵית בְּלִבָּךְ אֶלָּא אֶחָד, כַּךְ וְכוּ' לֵית לָן דְּבִיקוּ בְּסִטְרָא אַחֲרָא כְּלַל, דְּהָא פְּרִישָׁא הֲוָה מֵעַרְסָךְ, וַאֲנָן בְּיִחוּדָא לְגַבֵּי מַלְכָּא עִלָּאָה, וְלֵית לָן דְּבִיקוּ כְּלַל בְּסִטְרָא אַחֲרָא, דְּהָא בִּפְרִישׁוּ מִסִּטְרָא אַחֲרָא הֲוָה רְעוּתָא וּמַחֲשַׁבְתָּא דִּילָן.

**141.** Jacob said to his sons: 'Perhaps, heaven forbid, there has occurred a flaw in my bed.' His sons said: 'Just as there is only one in your heart, we have no attachment with the Other Side at all, because it is separated from your bed and we are united with the supernal King, ZEIR ANPIN. We have no attachment at all with the Other Side, because our desires and thoughts are to separate from the Other Side.'

142. כֵּיוָן דְּיָדַע דְּסִטְרָא אַחֲרָא לָא אִתְדְּבַּק תַּמָּן כְּלַל כְּדֵין עָאלַת אִתְּתָא, לְגַבֵּי בַּעְלָהּ בִּלְחִישׁוּ, בְּרָזָא דְּיִחוּדָא דְּשִׁית סִטְרִין. פָּתַח וְאָמַר,

בשכמל"ו דְּהָא אִיהִי בְּרָזָא דְּאֶחָד, בְּעוֹלֵימְתָהָא, בְּלָא עִרְבּוּבָא כְּלָל
וְלָא שׁוּתָפוּ דִּסְטְרָא אַחֲרָא.

**142.** As soon as JACOB knew that the Other Side was not attached there at all, the wife, WHO IS MALCHUT, then entered to her husband, ZEIR ANPIN, in silence, in the secret of the unity of the six sides THAT ARE IN "SH'MA YISRAEL." JACOB opened by saying: 'Blessed be the Name of the glory of His kingdom forever and ever,' for She is in the secret of one with her maidens, without any mixing and without partnership of the Other Side.

143. וְתָא חֲזֵי, בְּהַהִיא שַׁעֲתָא, יַעֲקֹב וּבְנוֹי הֲווֹ בְּדִיּוּקְנָא עִלָּאָה לְתַתָּא
בַּהֲדֵי שְׁכִינְתָּא. יַעֲקֹב הֲוָה בְּרָזָא דְּשִׁית סִטְרִין דְּעָלְמָא עִלָּאָה, בְּרָזָא
חַד. בְּנוֹי הֲווֹ בְּדִיּוּקְנָא דְּשִׁית סִטְרִין דְּעָלְמָא תַּתָּאָה. וְאִיהוּ בָּעָא
לְגַלָּאָה לוֹן הַהוּא קֵץ, כְּמָה דְּאוֹקִימְנָא, דְּאִית קֵץ וְאִית קֵץ, אִית קֵץ
הַיָּמִין, וְאִית קֵץ הַיָּמִים. קֵץ הַיָּמִין: דָּא מַלְכוּת קַדִּישָׁא רָזָא
דִּמְהֵימְנוּתָא רָזָא דְּמַלְכוּ דִּשְׁמַיָּא. קֵץ הַיָּמִים: דָּא רָזָא דְּמַלְכוּ חַיָּיבָא
רָזָא דִּסְטְרָא אַחֲרָא דְּאִקְרֵי קֵץ כָּל בָּשָׂר. וְהָא אוֹקִימְנָא.

**143.** Come and see: At that time, Jacob and his sons below assumed a supernal image with the Shechinah. Jacob was in the secret of the six sides of the upper world in the secret of one, NAMELY ZEIR ANPIN, and his sons were in the image of the six sides of the lower world, NAMELY MALCHUT. And JACOB wanted to reveal to them that end, WHICH IS MALCHUT, MEANING TO MAKE THE UNION OPENLY AND NOT IN SILENCE. As we have established that there is an end and an end; there is 'the end of days' and there is 'the end of days (also: 'of the right')'. The end of the right is Malchut of Holiness, the secret of the Faith and the secret of the Kingdom of Heaven. The end of days is the secret of the wicked kingdom, the secret of the Other Side that is called: "The end of all flesh" (Beresheet 6:13), as we have already established.

144. כֵּיוָן דְּחָמָא דְּאִסְתַּלָּקַת שְׁכִינְתָּא מִנֵּיהּ וְכוּ'. אִינּוּן אָמְרוּ כְּמָה
דְּלֵית בְּלִבָּךְ אֶלָּא אֶחָד, דְּאַנְתְּ בְּרָזָא דְּעָלְמָא עִלָּאָה, וְאִיהוּ אֶחָד. אוּף

אֲנָן, דְּאֲנָן בְּרָזָא דְּעָלְמָא תַּתָּאָה, אִיהוּ אֶחָד. וְעַל דָּא אַדְכָּרוּ תְּרֵי
לְבָבוֹת, רָזָא דְּעָלְמָא עִלָּאָה, דְּאִיהוּ לִבָּא דְּיַעֲקֹב, וְרָזָא דְּעָלְמָא תַּתָּאָה,
דְּאִיהוּ לִבָּא דִּבְנוֹי, כְּדֵין אָעִיל לָהּ בִּלְחִישׁוּ.

**144.** As soon as he saw that the Shechinah left him..., BECAUSE HE
WANTED TO MAKE THE UNION OPENLY – THAT IS – TO REVEAL THE END,
they, THE TRIBES, said, Just as in your heart there is only one for you
pertain to the secret of the upper world which is one, so we also, who
pertain to the secret of the lower world, WHICH IS MALCHUT, IN OUR
HEART THERE IS ONLY ONE. Therefore, there are mentioned here two hearts,
MEANING THERE IS NOT IN OUR HEART JUST AS THERE IS NOT IN YOUR
HEART, because the secret of the upper world, ZEIR ANPIN, is the heart of
Jacob. And the secret of the lower world THAT IS MALCHUT is the heart of
the sons. Thus, they bring Her, MALCHUT, silently.

**145.** וְכַמָּה דְּאִינּוּן אִתְיַיחֲדוּ רָזָא דְּעָלְמָא עִלָּאָה בְּאֶחָד, וְרָזָא דְּעָלְמָא
תַּתָּאָה בְּאֶחָד. אוּף הָכִי אֲנָן צְרִיכִין לְיַחֲדָא עָלְמָא עִלָּאָה בְּאֶחָד,
וּלְיַחֲדָא עָלְמָא תַּתָּאָה בְּרָזָא דְּאֶחָד. דָּא בְּשִׁית סִטְרִין, וְדָא בְּשִׁית
סִטְרִין. וּבְגִין כָּךְ, שִׁית תֵּיבִין הָכָא, בְּרָזָא דְּשִׁית סִטְרִין. וְשִׁית תֵּיבִין
הָכָא, בְּרָזָא דְּשִׁית סִטְרִין, יְיָ' אֶחָד וּשְׁמוֹ אֶחָד. זַכָּאָה עַדְבֵיהּ וְחוּלְקֵיהּ
מַאן דְּיִשַׁוֵּי רְעוּתֵיהּ לְהַאי, בְּעָלְמָא דֵין, וּבְעָלְמָא דְּאָתֵי.

**145.** As the upper world was unified in the secret of one, and the lower
world in the secret of one, so are we obliged to unite the upper world in one
and unite the lower world in the secret of one, each of them with six ends.
Therefore, there are six words here IN SH'MA YISRAEL in the secret of six
ends and six words here, IN 'BLESSED IS THE NAME...' in the secret of six
ends, NAMELY "Hashem is one and His Name One." Happy is he who has
put his heart into this, and happy are his lot and portion in this world and in
the World to Come.

**146.** רַב הַמְנוּנָא סָבָא אָמַר הָכִי, דָּא אִתְעֲרוּתָא דְּיִחוּדָא שַׁפִּיר אִיהוּ,
דְּרָזָא דִּבְרִירָא דְּמִלְּתָא הָא אוֹקִימְנָא. וּמִלִּין אִלֵּין זְמִינִין לְאִתְעַתְּדָא
קַמֵּי עַתִּיק יוֹמִין, בְּלָא כִּסּוּפָא כְּלָל.

**146.** Rav Hamnuna Saba (the elder) said thus: THE ORDER OF the awakening of this union is beautiful, for we have established the secret of the clarification of the matter. And these words will be placed before Atik Yomin without any shame at all.

רעיא מהימנא

**147.** פְּקוּדָא לִלְמוֹד תּוֹרָה בְּכָל יוֹמָא, דְּאִיהִי רָזָא דִּמְהֵימְנוּתָא עִלָּאָה, לְמִנְדַּע אָרְחֵיהּ דְּקוּדְשָׁא בְּרִיךְ הוּא. דְּכָל מַאן דְּאִשְׁתְּדַּל בְּאוֹרַיְיתָא, זָכֵי בְּהַאי עָלְמָא, וְזָכֵי בְּעָלְמָא דְּאָתֵי, וְאִשְׁתְּזִיב מִכָּל קַטְרוּגִין בִּישִׁין. בְּגִין דְּאוֹרַיְיתָא רָזָא דִּמְהֵימְנוּתָא אִיהִי, דְּמַאן דְּאִתְעַסַּק בָּהּ, אִתְעַסַּק בִּמְהֵימְנוּתָא עִלָּאָה, קוּדְשָׁא בְּרִיךְ הוּא אַשְׁרֵי שְׁכִינְתֵּיהּ בְּגַוֵּיהּ דְּלָא תַּעְדֵי מִנֵּיהּ.

### Ra'aya Meheimna (the Faithful Shepherd)

**147.** It is a commandment to study Torah every day, for it is the secret of the supernal Faith with which to know the ways of the Holy One, blessed be He. Everyone who is occupied with Torah merits in this world and merits in the World to Come, and is saved from all the evil accusers, because Torah is the secret of the Faith, and he who is occupied with it is occupied with the supernal Faith. The Holy One, blessed be He, causes His Shechinah to dwell in him, so she would not turn away from him.

**148.** מַאן דְּיָדַע מִלָּה דְּאוֹרַיְיתָא, אִצְטְרִיךְ לְמִרְדַּף אֲבַתְרֵיהּ, וּלְאוֹלְפָא הַאי מִלָּה מִנֵּיהּ, לְקַיְּימָא רָזָא דִּכְתִיב, מֵאֵת כָּל אִישׁ אֲשֶׁר יִדְּבֶנּוּ לִבּוֹ תִּקְחוּ אֶת תְּרוּמָתִי. אוֹרַיְיתָא אִילָנָא דְּחַיֵּי אִיהוּ, לְמֵיהַב חַיִּין לְכֹלָּא. מַאן דְּאִתְתְּקַף בְּאוֹרַיְיתָא, אִתְתְּקַף בְּאִילָנָא דְּחַיֵּי, כְּד"א עֵץ חַיִּים הִיא לַמַּחֲזִיקִים בָּהּ.

**148.** We should pursue one who knows a subject of Torah and learn from him that subject, to fulfill the secret of what is written: "Of every man whose heart prompts him to give you shall you take My offering" (Shemot 25:2). The Torah is the Tree of Life that gives life to everyone who becomes

mighty in Torah, who becomes mighty in the Tree of Life, as it is written: "She is a Tree of Life to those who lay hold on her" (Mishlei 3:18).

149. וְכַמָּה רָזִין עִלָּאִין אוֹקִימְנָא בְּמַאן דְּאִשְׁתָּדַּל בְּאוֹרַיְיתָא, דְּזָכֵי לְאִתְקַשְּׁרָא בְּאוֹרַיְיתָא דִּלְעֵילָא. בְּהַאי עָלְמָא לָא שָׁכִיךְ, וְלָא שָׁכִיךְ בְּעָלְמָא דְּאָתֵי, וַאֲפִילוּ בְּקִבְרָא שִׂפְוָותֵיה מְרַחֲשָׁן אוֹרַיְיתָא, כד"א דּוֹבֵב שִׂפְתֵי יְשֵׁנִים.

עד כאן רעיא מהימנא

149. We have established many supernal secrets concerning he who is occupied with Torah, in that he merits to be bound with the supernal Torah, WHICH IS ZEIR ANPIN. He neither takes respite from it in this world, nor does he take respite in the World to Come, and his lips move gently in Torah even in the grave, as it is written: "Causing the sleepers' lips to murmur" (Shir Hashirim 7:11).

**End of Ra'aya Meheimna (the Faithful Shephered)**

## 13. "That they bring Me an offering"

## 13. "That they bring Me an offering"

### A Synopsis

Frequently in the Zohar, the Rabbis seem to be reinterpreting one verse: "That they bring Me an offering," Again, Rabbi Hamnuna Saba (the elder) opens the discussion on this topic, speaking of the union of Zeir Anpin with Malchut, and of their mutual agreement to offer Malchut a chance to dwell among the children of Yisrael. Malchut is thus the offering spoken of earlier. Rabbi Yeba Saba (the elder) says that even though they take Her, they can only take Her with the permission and approval of Her husband. It is necessary to perform for Him a service of love, and then with His love, "take My offering". This is what happens during the service of prayer. The explanation is followed by a listing of the holy days and of the gifts that accompany each of them. These gifts are gold and silver, and brass, and blue, and purple, and scarlet. After this is the secret of the ten days of Atonement, and their special gifts. And so Malchut is taken and established in her place among those living on earth.

### The Relevance of this Passage

During the High Holy Days, specifically between Rosh Hashanah (gold) and Yom Kippur (silver), the dimension of Malchut climbs into the realm of Keter, the highest level of the spiritual atmosphere. Hence, Kabbalistically, atonement signifies not repentance, but rather "at-one- ment," which is union and oneness between the upper and lower worlds. As we acknowledge and uproot our negative traits (the true meaning of "sacrifice" or "offering") and cleanse our souls, we rise to higher spiritual heights. Our sins (scarlet colored) are purified so that we become "white as snow."

This passage ignites the cleansing power of the Ten Days of Atonement right now. This power eradicates all immoral qualities from our nature. It cleanses all the iniquities of humanity, making our souls as white as the wintry snow.

In the physical world, this cleansing occurs each and every year during Rosh Hashanah and Yom Kippur. But because the Zohar is above time and place, above physicality, because this mystical tome deals with the mysteries of the soul and the secrets of secrets, the effect and results are sweeping – universal, macrocosmic, and in the now.

Our actions here are the ultimate atonement and Final Redemption for human civilization, thanks to the righteousness and power of the rabbis cited here and throughout the Zohar.

150. פָּתַח וְאָמַר וְיִקְחוּ לִי תְּרוּמָה, הָכָא אִיהוּ יִחוּדָא בִּכְלָלָא חֲדָא,

עֵילָא וְתַתָּא. וְיִקְחוּ תְּרוּמָה לָא כְּתִיב, אֶלָּא וְיִקְחוּ לִי תְּרוּמָה, עֵילָא וְתַתָּא בִּכְלָלָא חֲדָא, בְּלָא פֵּרוּדָא כְּלַל.

**150.** He opened the discussion saying: "That they bring Me an offering" (Shemot 25:2). Here is the unification of above, ZEIR ANPIN, and of below, MALCHUT, under one principle. BECAUSE 'ME' IS ZEIR ANPIN AND 'AN OFFERING' IS MALCHUT. It is not written: 'that they bring an offering,' but rather "that they bring Me an offering," FOR THIS SHOWS above and below in one principle without any separation at all.

**151.** מֵאֵת כָּל אִישׁ אֲשֶׁר יִדְּבֶנּוּ לִבּוֹ תִּקְחוּ אֶת תְּרוּמָתִי. הַאי קְרָא, הָכִי אִצְטְרִיךְ לֵיהּ לְמֵימַר, כָּל אִישׁ אֲשֶׁר יִדְּבֶנּוּ לִבּוֹ, מַאי מֵאֵת כָּל אִישׁ. אֶלָּא רָזָא הָכָא לְאִינּוּן מָרֵי מִדִּין. זַכָּאִין אִינּוּן צַדִּיקַיָּא, דְּיַדְעֵי לְשַׁוָּואָה רְעוּתָא דְּלִבְּהוֹן לְגַבֵּי מַלְכָּא עִלָּאָה קַדִּישָׁא, וְכָל רְעוּתָא דְּלִבְּהוֹן לָאו אִיהוּ לְגַבֵּי עָלְמָא דָא, וּבְכִסּוּפָא בַּטְלָה דִּילֵיהּ. אֶלָּא יַדְעֵי וּמִשְׁתַּדְּלֵי לְשַׁוָּואָה רְעוּתְהוֹן וּלְאִתְדַּבְּקָא לְעֵילָּא, בְּגִין לְאַמְשְׁכָא רְעוּתָא דְּמָארֵיהוֹן לְגַבַּיְיהוּ מֵעֵילָּא לְתַתָּא.

**151.** "Of every man whose heart prompts him to give you shall take My offering" (Ibid.): HE QUESTIONS: This passage should have said, 'Every man whose heart prompts him,' wherefore "of every man"? HE ANSWERS: Here is the secret for those who understand measurements. Happy are those righteous ones who know how to place the desire of their heart before the supernal Holy King. The entire desire of their heart is not for this world and its vain desire, but rather they know and endeavor to place their desire and to cleave unto above, in order to draw to them the desire of their Master from above to below.

**152.** וּמַאן אֲתָר נַטְלֵי הַהוּא רְעוּתָא דְּמָארֵיהוֹן לְאַמְשְׁכָא לֵיהּ לְגַבַּיְיהוּ. נַטְלִין מֵאֲתָר חַד עִלָּאָה קַדִּישָׁא, דְּמִנֵּיהּ נָפְקִין כָּל רְעוּתִין קַדִּישִׁין. וּמַאן אִיהוּ. כָּל אִישׁ. דָּא צַדִּיק, דְּאִתְקְרֵי כֹּל, כד"א וְיִתְרוֹן אֶרֶץ בַּכֹּל הִיא. עַל כֵּן כָּל פִּקּוּדֵי כֹל יִשָּׁרְתִּי. אִישׁ: כד"א אִישׁ צַדִּיק. דָּא אִיהוּ צַדִּיק, מָארֵיהּ דְּבֵיתָא, דִּרְעוּתֵיהּ תָּדִיר לְגַבֵּי מַטְרוֹנִיתָא,

כְּבַעֲלָה דְּרָחִים לְאִתְּתֵיה תָּדִיר. יִדְּבְנוּ לִבּוֹ אִיהוּ רָחִים לָהּ. וְלִבּוֹ דְּאִיהִי
מַטְרוֹנִיתָא דִּילֵיהּ, יִדְּבְנוּ לְאִתְדַּבְּקָא בֵּיהּ.

**152.** From which place do they take that desire of their Master to draw to them? They take from one place that is holy and lofty, where all the holy desires are. And who is it? IT IS 'every man', which refers to the Righteous, NAMELY YESOD OF ZEIR ANPIN, who is called 'every', as written: "Moreover, land has an advantage for everyone" (Kohelet 5:8). "Therefore I esteem all your precepts" (Tehilim 119:128). 'Man' is as written: "a just man" (Beresheet 6:9). This is the Righteous, the Master of the house, NAMELY YESOD, WHO IS THE MASTER OF MALCHUT THAT IS CALLED 'HOUSE'. His desire is always for the Matron, WHICH IS MALCHUT, like a husband who loves his wife always. "Whose heart prompts him," MEANING that he loves her and his heart, namely his Matron, MEANING MALCHUT THAT IS CALLED 'HEART', shall prompt him to cleave unto her.

153. וְאַף עַל גַּב דִּרְחִימוּ סַגִּי דָּא בְּדָא, דְּלָא מִתְפָּרְשָׁן לְעָלְמִין, מֵהַהוּא כָּל אִישׁ, מָארֵיהּ בֵּיתָא, מָארֵיהּ דְּמַטְרוֹנִיתָא, מִנֵּיהּ תִּקְחוּ אֶת תְּרוּמָתִי. אָרְחֵיהּ דְּעָלְמָא, מַאן דְּבָעֵי לְנַסְבָא אִתְּתֵיה דְּב"נ מִנֵּיהּ אִיהוּ קָפִיד וְלָא שָׁבִיק לָהּ. אֲבָל קוּדְשָׁא בְּרִיךְ הוּא לָאו הָכִי, כְּתִיב וְזֹאת הַתְּרוּמָה, זוֹ כְּנֶסֶת יִשְׂרָאֵל, אע"ג דְּכָל רְחִימוּ דִּילָהּ לְגַבֵּיה, וּרְחִימוּ דִּילֵיהּ לְגַבָּהּ. מִנֵּיהּ נַטְלִין לָהּ לְאַשְׁרָאָה בֵּינַיְיהוּ, מֵהַהוּא אֲתָר עִלָּאָה, דְּכָל רְחִימוּ דְּאִתְּתָא וּבַעֲלָהּ שַׁרְיָא. מִתַּמָּן תִּקְחוּ אֶת תְּרוּמָתִי, זַכָּאָה חוּלָקֵיהוֹן דְּיִשְׂרָאֵל, וְזַכָּאִין כֻּלְּהוּ דְּזָכוּ לְהַאי.

**153.** Even though THEY HAVE great love between them, and they never separate, STILL IN ALL, from 'every man' THAT IS YESOD, the Master of the house, THAT IS the husband of the Queen, you "shall take My offering" WHICH IS MALCHUT. The way of the world is that if someone wants to take the wife away from a man, he is indignant and does not leave her. But the Holy One, blessed be He, is not so, for it is written: "And this is the offering" (Shemot 25:3), which is the Congregation of Yisrael, NAMELY MALCHUT, even though all her love is to Him and all His love is to her. They take her from Him to cause her to dwell among them from that lofty place where all the love of a wife and her husband dwell, NAMELY YESOD.

From there, you "shall take My offering." Happy is the portion of Yisrael, and happy are they all that merited this.

154. וְזֹאת הַתְּרוּמָה אֲשֶׁר תִּקְחוּ מֵאִתָּם. וְאִי תֵּימָא, אִי הָכִי, אֲשֶׁר תִּקְחוּ מֵאִתּוֹ מִבָּעֵי לֵיהּ מַאי מֵאִתָּם. מֵאֵת תְּרֵין שְׁמָהָן אִלֵּין.

**154.** "And this is the offering which you shall take of them": If you ask, '...which you shall take of him' should have been said, MEANING FROM YESOD AS MENTIONED ABOVE, what is the meaning of "of them"? HE ANSWERS: From these two names, WHICH ARE YESOD AND MALCHUT TOGETHER, MEANING THAT HE SHOULD NOT TAKE HER OF HER OWN, BUT RATHER THE ASPECT OF THEM BOTH TOGETHER. IT IS THEREFORE WRITTEN "OF THEM."

155. תּוּ רַב יֵיבָא סָבָא אָמַר, מֵאִתָּם: מֵאֵת ם׳, דְּאִיהוּ רָזָא דְּעָלְמָא עִלָּאָה. אֲתָר מָדוֹרֵיהּ דְּהַאי צַדִּיק, דְּאִיהוּ אִתְעַטָּר מֵאֵת ס׳, וּמִתַּמָּן נָטִיל חַיִּין, לְאַתְזְנָא לְעָלְמִין כֻּלְּהוּ. וְכֹלָּא מִלָּה חֲדָא, רָזָא לְחַכִּימִין אִתְיְהִיבַת, זַכָּאָה חוּלָקֵיהוֹן.

**155.** Rav Yeba Saba (the elder) said "of them" MEANS from final *Mem*, which is the secret of the Supernal World, NETZACH, HOD, YESOD AND MALCHUT OF BINAH. THE YESOD OF BINAH CALLED 'YISRAEL-SABA AND TEVUNAH', the dwelling place of that righteous who is adorned with *Samech*, WHICH IS THE SECRET SUPERNAL ABA AND IMA, WHICH ARE CHOCHMAH, BINAH, DA'AT, CHESED, GVURAH AND TIFERET OF BINAH. For he receives life from them to feed all the worlds. AND FROM THIS YESOD OF BINAH WILL THEY RECEIVE THE OFFERING WHICH IS MALCHUT. It is all one thing. The secret is given to the wise and happy is their portion.

156. דְּאע״ג דְּאִינוּן נַטְלִין לָהּ, לָא יַכְלִין לְנַטְלָא לָהּ, אֶלָּא בִּרְשׁוּ דְּבַעְלָהּ, וּבִרְעוּ דִּילֵיהּ, וּלְמֶעְבַּד פּוּלְחָנָא דִּרְחִימוּ לְגַבֵּיהּ, וּכְדֵין בִּרְחִימוּ דִּילֵיהּ תִּקְחוּ אֶת תְּרוּמָתִי. וְכָל דָּא, בְּאִינוּן פּוּלְחָנֵי דִּצְלוֹתָא, וְתִקּוּנָא וְסִדּוּרָא דְּיִשְׂרָאֵל מְסַדְּרִין בְּכָל יוֹמָא. ד״א מֵאִתָּם, מִכְּלָלָא

דְּשִׁית סִטְרִין עִלָּאִין וְכֹלָּא חַד.

**156.** Even though they take Her, MALCHUT, they can do so only with the permission of her husband, ZEIR ANPIN, and with His approval. It is necessary to perform a service of love toward Him, and then with His love, "take My offering," WHICH IS MALCHUT. We do all this during the service of prayer, and the improvements that Yisrael perform daily. Another explanation: "Of them" means from the principle of the six supernal extremities OF ZEIR ANPIN. THEREFORE, IT IS WRITTEN "OF THEM" IN PLURAL.

157. מֵאִתָּם, מֵאִינוּן זִמְנֵי וְשַׁבָּתֵּי, וְכֹלָּא רָזָא חֲדָא. זָהָב וָכֶסֶף וּנְחֹשֶׁת וּתְכֵלֶת וְאַרְגָּמָן וְתוֹלַעַת שָׁנִי. זָהָב, בְּרָזָא דְּיוֹמָא דְּרֹאשׁ הַשָּׁנָה, דְּאִיהוּ יוֹמָא דְּזַהֲבָא, יוֹמָא דְּדִינָא, וְשַׁלְטָא הַהוּא סִטְרָא, כד"א מִצָּפוֹן זָהָב יֶאֱתֶה. וָכֶסֶף, דָּא יוֹם הַכִּפּוּרִים, דְּמִתְלַבְּנָן חוֹבֵיהוֹן דְּיִשְׂרָאֵל כְּתַלְגָּא, כד"א אִם יִהְיוּ חֲטָאֵיכֶם כַּשָּׁנִים כַּשֶּׁלֶג יַלְבִּינוּ. וּכְתִיב כִּי בַיּוֹם הַזֶּה יְכַפֵּר עֲלֵיכֶם לְטַהֵר אֶתְכֶם.

**157.** "Of them": Of these holidays and Shabbatot SHALL YOU TAKE THEM, and it is all one secret. THEY ARE THE SECRET OF "gold, and silver, and brass, and blue, and purple, and scarlet..." (Shemot 25:3). Gold is in the secret of the day of Rosh Hashanah (the Jewish New Year), which is the day of gold, NAMELY the Day of Judgment. That side OF LEFT dominates, as it is written: "Gold comes out of the north" (Iyov 37:22) AND NORTH IS LEFT. Silver refers to Yom Kippur, when the sins of Yisrael become white like snow, as it is written: "Though your sins be like scarlet, they shall be as white as snow" (Yeshayah 1:18). AND SILVER IS ALSO COLORED WHITE. It is also written "For on that day will He forgive you, to cleanse you" (Vayikra 16:30).

158. וּנְחֹשֶׁת. יוֹמֵי דְּקׇרְבְּנִין דְּחַג, דְּאִינוּן רְתִיכֵי דְּעַמִּין עכו"ם, וְאִינוּן אִקְרוּן רָזָא דְּהָרֵי נְחֹשֶׁת, וּבְגִין כָּךְ מִתְמַעֲטִין בְּכָל יוֹמָא וְאַזְלִין. וּתְכֵלֶת, דָּא פֶּסַח, שׁוּלְטָנוּ דְּרָזָא דִּמְהֵימְנוּתָא, רָזָא דְּגַוְונָא תְּכֵלָא, וּבְגִין דְּהִיא תְּכֵלָא, לָא שַׁלְטָא עַד דְּשֵׁיצִיאַת וְקַטִּילַת כָּל בּוּכְרֵי דְּמִצְרָאֵי, כד"א וְעָבַר יְיָ' לִנְגֹּף אֶת מִצְרַיִם. בג"כ, כָּל גַּוְונִין טָבִין

בְּחֶלְמָא, בַּר מִן תְּכֶלָא.

**158.** "And brass" refers to the offerings on Sukkot (holiday of booths), which are the Chariots of the heathen peoples, FOR WE OFFER SEVENTY BULLOCKS FOR THEM and they are called 'the secret of the brass mountains'. Therefore, THE BULLOCKS ON SUKKOT progressively lessen every day. "And blue" is Pesach (Passover), for the dominion of the secret of Faith, NAMELY MALCHUT, is the secret of the color blue. It is blue THAT HINTS TO JUDGMENTS, BECAUSE BLUE (HEB. *TECHELET*) IS THE DERIVATIVE OF KLAYAH (ENG. 'DESTRUCTION'). It did not dominate until it killed and destroyed all the first-born of Egypt, as it is written: "And Hashem will pass through to smite Egypt" (Shemot 12:23). Therefore, all the colors are good in a dream except blue.

159. וְאַרְגָּמָן, דָּא שָׁבוּעוֹת, רָזָא דְּאַרְגְּוָונָא, דְּתוֹרָה שֶׁבִּכְתָב דְּאִתְיְהִיבַת בֵּיהּ, כְּלִילָא מִתְּרֵין סִטְרִין, מִימִינָא וּמִשְׂמָאלָא, כד"א מִימִינוֹ אֵשׁ דָּת לָמוֹ, וְדָא אִיהוּ אַרְגָּמָן. וְתוֹלַעַת שָׁנִי, דָּא אִיהוּ ט"ו בְּאָב, דִּבְנוֹת יִשְׂרָאֵל הֲווֹ נַפְקִי בְּמָאנֵי מִלַּת, כד"א הָאֱמֻנִים עֲלֵי תוֹלָע.

**159.** "And purple" is Shavuot (holiday of the Weeks), which is the secret of purple, because the Written Torah, which was given through it, is combined of two sides, right and left, as it is written: "From His right hand went a fiery law for them" (Devarim 33:2). This is purple, WHICH IS COMPOSED OF MANY COLORS. "And scarlet" is the fifteenth day of Av, when the daughters of Yisrael used to go out in garments of scarlet, as it is written: "That were brought up in scarlet" (Eichah 4:5).

160. עַד הָכָא, שִׁית סִטְרִין, מִכָּאן וּלְהָלְאָה רָזָא דִּי' יְמֵי תְּשׁוּבָה. וְשֵׁשׁ, וְעִזִּים, וְעוֹרוֹת אֵילִם מְאָדָּמִים. וְעוֹרוֹת תְּחָשִׁים. וַעֲצֵי שִׁטִּים. וְשֶׁמֶן לַמָּאוֹר. וּבְשָׂמִים לְשֶׁמֶן הַמִּשְׁחָה וְלִקְטוֹרֶת הַסַּמִּים. וְאַבְנֵי שׁוֹהַם. וְאַבְנֵי מִלּוּאִים. עַד הָכָא תִּשְׁעָה, לָקֳבֵל תִּשְׁעָה יוֹמִין וְיוֹם הַכִּפּוּרִים אַשְׁלִים לַעֲשָׂרָה.

**160.** Until here, IT CORRESPONDS TO six sides, NAMELY "GOLD, AND SILVER, AND BRASS, AND BLUE, AND PURPLE, AND SCARLET." From here

and further is the secret of the ten days of Atonement, which are "fine linen, and goats' hair, and rams' skins dyed red, and badger skins, and Acacia wood, oil for the light, spices for the anointing oil, and for the sweet incense, onyx stones, and stones to be set" (Shemot 25:4-6). Until here are nine corresponding to nine days, which Yom Kippur completes to ten.

161. וּמִכָּל אִלֵּין, אֲנָן נַטְלִין תְּרוּמַת יְיָ', בְּכָל זִמְנָא וְזִמְנָא, בְּגִין לְאַשְׁרָאָה עֲלָן. בְּר״ה אֲנָן נַטְלִין תְּרוּמַת יְיָ', וְאִיהוּ רָזָא דר״ה, דְּאַתְיָא מִסְּטְרָא דְּדַהֲבָא. בְּיוֹם הַכִּפּוּרִים אֲנָן נַטְלִין לָהּ, וְאִיהִי יוֹם הַכִּפּוּרִים דִּירְתָא בְּרַתָּא לְאִימָּא. בְּסֻכּוֹת אֲנָן נַטְלִין לָהּ, וְאִיהִי סוּכָּה סוֹכֶכֶת וְאַגִּינַת עֲלָן, וּכְתִיב בַּיּוֹם הַשְּׁמִינִי עֲצֶרֶת תִּהְיֶה לָכֶם וְדָא אִיהִי תְּרוּמַת יְיָ'.

161. We take the offering of Hashem, MEANING MALCHUT, from all these, IN THE SECRET OF THE PASSAGE: "AND THIS IS THE OFFERING WHICH YOU SHALL TAKE OF THEM" (SHEMOT 25:3). We take it at every time, MEANING AT ALL THE HOLY DAYS, in order to cause it to dwell over us. At Rosh Hashanah, we take the offering of Hashem, which is the secret of New Year that comes from the side of Gold, WHICH IS GVURAH, BECAUSE MALCHUT IS GVURAH. On Yom Kippur, we take Her for She is the Yom Kippur, because the daughter, WHICH IS MALCHUT, inherits Her mother, WHICH IS BINAH, THAT IS CALLED 'YOM KIPPUR'. On Sukkot (Eng. 'the Festival of Tabernacles'), we take Her for She is a tabernacle that covers and shields us. It is written: "On the eighth day you shall have a solemn assembly" (Bemidbar 29:35). This is the offering of Hashem, NAMELY MALCHUT THAT IS CALLED 'ASSEMBLY'.

162. בְּפֶסַח אוֹף הָכִי אֲנָן נַטְלִין לָהּ, וְאִיהִי פֶּסַח. וְהָא אוֹקִימְנָא, רָזָא דִּגְוָון דִּנְהוֹרָא תִּכְלָא. בִּשְׁבוּעוֹת אֲנָן נַטְלִין לָהּ, וְאִיהִי שְׁתֵּי הַלֶּחֶם. וּכְתִיב וַיְדַבֵּר אֱלֹהִים אֵת כָּל הַדְּבָרִים הָאֵלֶּה לֵאמֹר, וַאֲנָן נַטְלִין מִתּוֹרָה שֶׁבִּכְתָב, תּוֹרָה שֶׁבְּעַל פֶּה. ט״ו בְּאָב, אִיהוּ קַיְימָא בְּחֶדְוָה, עַל בְּנוֹת יִשְׂרָאֵל. כָּל שְׁאָר יוֹמִין, אִינּוּן לְתִקּוּנָא דִּילָהּ. וְעַל דָּא אֲשֶׁר תִּקְחוּ מֵאִתָּם כְּתִיב.

**162.** On Pesach also, we take Her and She is CALLED 'Pesach'. We have already established that She is the secret of the color of the light of blue. We take Her on Shavuot, and She is the two loaves of bread. BY THE GIVING OF THE TORAH, it is written: "And Elohim spoke all these words, saying..." (Shemot 20:1). We take the Oral Torah, WHICH IS MALCHUT, from the Written Torah. On the fifteenth day of Av, MALCHUT stands in joy upon the daughters of Yisrael, and all the other days are there to establish MALCHUT. Therefore, it is written: "You shall take of them" IN PLURAL.

## 14. Just as they (Kegavna)

### A Synopsis

This section deals with the secret of Shabbat. Malchut is called 'Shabbat' when she is united in the secret of one, so that Zeir Anpin should dwell upon her. Then the Holy Throne of Glory is united. We are reminded again of how, when the Shabbat enters, she unites and separates from the Other Side. The people bless her with joy, and must never address her with a verse of judgment, for all judgments are suspended. It would not be good to awaken the prosecutors below, who have fled to conceal themselves in holes beneath the sand of the great abyss because of the holiness of the Shabbat. Rather the holy people should be having goodwill and great love, so that they should arouse blessings above and below together.

### The Relevance of this Passage

The merging of lower and upper worlds is, perhaps, the most predominant theme that weaves itself throughout the Zohar. And nowhere else, we are told, is this unification more readily attainable than on the day of Sabbath. This passage provides the image of an egg as both symbol and analogy to illustrate this recurring theme. Fragile yet strong, the shell will only break when the time is right for birth. Enclosed in their shell, the white and the yolk can safely unite in secret. And later, by the splitting of the shell, new life arises from that union.

On Sabbath, the secret union takes place safe from harm, safe from evil. Afterward, the fruit of this blessed union comes to life among us. The great Light and unity of Shabbat shines in full splendor as we contemplate this profound Kabbalistic narrative. Judgments flee from our midst and the Other Side is expelled from our lives. The cosmic equivalent of the weekday Sabbath, the Age of Messiah, dawns as our eyes touch these words and our souls embrace these truths.

163. כְּגַוְונָא דְּאִינּוּן מִתְיַיחֲדִין לְעֵילָּא בְּאֶחָד, אוֹף הָכִי אִיהִי, אִתְיַיחֲדַת לְתַתָּא בְּרָזָא דְּאֶחָד, לְמֶהֱוֵי עִמְּהוֹן לְעֵילָּא חַד לָקֳבֵל חַד, קוּדְשָׁא בְּרִיךְ הוּא אֶחָד לְעֵילָּא, לָא יָתִיב עַל כּוּרְסְיָיא דִּיקָרֵיה, עַד דְּאִיהִי אִתְעֲבִידַת בְּרָזָא דְּאֶחָד כְּגַוְונָא דִּילֵיהּ, לְמֶהֱוֵי אֶחָד בְּאֶחָד. וְהָא אוֹקִימְנָא רָזָא דַּיְיָ׳ אֶחָד וּשְׁמוֹ אֶחָד.

163. Just as THE SIX EXTREMITIES OF ZEIR ANPIN unite above, MEANING FROM THE CHEST OF ZEIR ANPIN AND ABOVE, unto one, MEANING THAT

THERE IS NO PARTNERSHIP WITH THE OTHER SIDE, MALCHUT also unites below, MEANING FROM THE CHEST OF ZEIR ANPIN AND LOWER, in the secret of one, in order to be with them above, one in correspondence with one. For the Holy One, blessed be He, WHO IS ZEIR ANPIN, who is one above, does not sit on His Throne of Glory, WHICH IS MALCHUT, until She also becomes in the secret of one like Him IN ORDER so it would be One in One. We have already established the secret of "Hashem is One and His Name One", FOR HASHEM IS ZEIR ANPIN AND HIS NAME IS MALCHUT AND THEY ARE ONE IN ONE.

164. רָזָא דְּשַׁבָּת, אִיהִי שַׁבָּת, דְּאִתְאַחֲדַת בְּרָזָא דְּאֶחָ"ד, לְמִשְׁרֵי עֲלָה רָזָא דְּאֶחָד. צְלוֹתָא דְּמַעֲלֵי שַׁבְּתָא, דְּהָא אִתְאַחֲדַת כּוּרְסַיָּיא יַקִּירָא קַדִּישָׁא, בְּרָזָא דְּאֶחָ"ד, וְאִתְתַּקָּנַת לְמִשְׁרֵי עֲלָה מַלְכָּא קַדִּישָׁא עִלָּאָה.

**164.** This is the secret of Shabbat. MALCHUT IS CALLED 'Shabbat' WHEN She is united in the secret of one, so that ZEIR ANPIN should dwell upon Her, which is the secret of one. AND THIS IS THE SECRET OF the prayer of Shabbat eve, because then the Holy Throne of Glory, WHICH IS MALCHUT in the secret of one, is united into one. This was established so that the supernal Holy King, WHO IS ZEIR ANPIN, shall dwell upon Her.

165. כַּד עַיֵּיל שַׁבְּתָא, אִיהִי אִתְיַחֲדַת וְאִתְפָּרְשַׁת מִסִּטְרָא אַחֲרָא, וְכָל דִּינִין מִתְעַבְּרִין מִינָה, וְאִיהִי אִשְׁתְּאָרַת בְּיִחוּדָא דִּנְהִירוּ קַדִּישָׁא, וְאִתְעַטְּרַת בְּכַמָּה עִטְרִין לְגַבֵּי מַלְכָּא קַדִּישָׁא, וְכָל שׁוּלְטָנֵי רוּגְזִין וּמָארֵי דְּדִינָא כֻּלְּהוּ עַרְקִין, וְלֵית שׁוּלְטָנוּ אַחֲרָא בְּכֻלְּהוּ עָלְמִין.

**165.** When the Shabbat enters, She unites and separates from the Other Side. All the Judgments pass away from Her, and She remains united with the holy light and becomes adorned with many crowns before the Holy King. All the dominions of anger and the instigators of Judgment flee, and there is no other dominion in all the worlds, EXCEPT HER.

166. וְאַנְפָּהָא נְהִירִין בִּנְהִירוּ עִלָּאָה, וְאִתְעַטְּרַת לְתַתָּא בְּעַמָּא קַדִּישָׁא, וְכֻלְּהוּ מִתְעַטְּרָן בְּנִשְׁמָתִין חַדְתִּין. כְּדֵין שֵׁירוּתָא דִּצְלוֹתָא, לְבָרְכָא לָה

בְּחֶדְוָה, בִּנְהִירוּ דְּאַנְפִּין, וְלוֹמַר בָּרְכוּ אֶת יְיָ' הַמְבוֹרָךְ. אֶת יְיָ' דַּיְיקָא, בְּגִין לְמִפְתַּח לְגַבָּהּ בִּבְרָכָה.

**166.** And Her face, MEANING HER FIRST THREE SFIROT, shines with the supernal light and becomes adorned with the holy nation below, for they all become adorned from Her with new souls. Then the prayer begins of blessing Her with joy, with shining face and saying, 'Bless the blessed Hashem;' the particle 'Et' before Hashem is precise, WHICH IS MALCHUT THAT IS CALLED 'ET', in order to address Her with a blessing.

167. וְאָסִיר לְעַמָּא קַדִּישָׁא לְמִפְתַּח לְגַבָּהּ בְּפָסוּקָא דְּדִינָא, כְּגוֹן וְהוּא רַחוּם וְגוֹ', בְּגִין דְּהָא אִתְפָּרְשַׁת מֵרָזָא דְּסִטְרָא אַחֲרָא, וְכָל מָארֵי דְּדִינִין אִתְפָּרְשׁוּ וְאִתְעֲבָרוּ מִינָהּ. וּמַאן דְּאִתְעַר הַאי לְתַתָּא, גָּרִים לְאַתְעָרָא הָכִי לְעֵילָא. וְכֻרְסְיָיא קַדִּישָׁא לָא יָכְלָא לְאִתְעַטְּרָא בַּעֲטָרָא דִּקְדוּשָׁה, דְּכָל זִמְנָא דְּמִתְעָרֵי לְתַתָּא אִינוּן מָארֵיהוֹן דְּדִינָא, דַּהֲווֹ מִתְעַבְּרָן וַהֲווֹ אַזְלֵי כֻּלְהוּ לְאִתְטַמְּרָא גּוֹ נוּקְבָּא דְּעַפְרָא דִּתְהוֹמָא רַבָּא, כֻּלְהוּ תַּיְיבִין לְאַשְׁרָאָה בְּדוּכְתַּיְיהוּ וְאִתְרְחֲקַת בְּהוּ אֲתָר קַדִּישָׁא דְּבָעָאת נַיְיחָא.

**167.** It is prohibited for the holy people to start addressing Her with a Judgment passage, such as: "But He was full of compassion…" (Tehilim 78:38), because She has already separated from the secret of Other Side. All the prosecutors have separated and passed away from Her, and one who arouses Judgment below causes a similar arousal above. The Holy Throne, WHICH IS MALCHUT, cannot then become adorned with the Holy Crown, for the prosecutors below are aroused, THAT HERETOFORE were absent, and all went to conceal themselves in the hole of sand of the great abyss, BECAUSE OF THE HOLINESS OF THE SHABBAT. NOW THAT THEY WERE AROUSED FROM BELOW, they all return to dwell in their place AS DURING THE WEEKDAYS, and the Holy Place is distanced by them, WHICH IS MALCHUT, that seeks rest.

168. וְלָא תֵּימָא דְּדָא אִיהוּ בִּלְחוֹדוֹי, אֶלָּא לֵית אִתְעָרוּתָא לְעֵילָא לְאִתְעָרָא, עַד דְּיִשְׂרָאֵל מִתְעָרֵי לְתַתָּא, כְּמָה דְּאוּקִימְנָא, דִּכְתִיב בַּכֵּסֶה

לְיוֹם חַגֵּנוּ. לְיוֹם חַג לָא כְּתִיב, אֶלָּא לְיוֹם חַגֵּנוּ. וְעַ"ד אָסִיר לְעַמָּא
קַדִּישָׁא, דְּקָא מִתְעַטְּרָן בְּעִטְרִין קַדִּישִׁין דְּנִשְׁמָתִין, בְּגִין לְאִתְעֲרָא
נַיְיחָא, דְּאִינּוּן יִתְעֲרוּן דִּינָא, אֶלָּא כֻּלְּהוּ בִּרְעוּ וּרְחִימוּ סַגִּי, דְּיִתְעֲרוּן
בִּרְכָּאן עֵילָא וְתַתָּא כַּחֲדָא.

**168.** Do not say that only this One BECOMES AROUSED ABOVE BY THOSE BELOW, but rather there is no one aroused above unless Yisrael awaken below, as we have established in the passage: "At the full moon on our feast day" (Tehilim 81:4). It does not say 'the feast day' but rather "our feast day;" THAT IS BECAUSE THE HOLINESS OF THE HOLY DAY BECOMES AWAKENED ABOVE THROUGH THE CHILDREN OF YISRAEL WHO SANCTIFY IT BELOW, AND IT IS THEREFORE OUR FEAST DAY. Therefore, it is forbidden for the holy people, who adorn themselves with the holy crowns of souls in order to arouse rest, to arouse Judgment. They should all be rather having goodwill and great love, so that they should arouse blessings above and below together.

## 15. 'Bless the blessed Hashem'

### A Synopsis

Blessings from the source of life, The Creator, flow to Malchut, filling and watering her forever and ever. Therefore it is incumbent upon the entire nation to make the blessing at the commencement of the Shabbat, for when they begin to bless, a voice goes through all the firmaments that become sanctified with the holiness of the commencement of the Shabbat. We learn that as the blessing and sanctification takes place below, it also takes place above in many supernal camps. So the children of Israel become adorned with the crowns of the holy souls. That night is the time for the Sages to perform marital duties, for adorned with these holy souls, they will produce holy children. We read how the souls of the righteous and other holy spirits move back and forth between the Garden of Eden and the upper Garden. The scripture speaks of the adornment of souls, whereby the courageous forefathers return in spirit to fill the living with their souls. At midnight on Shabbat Eve, when the Sages awake to perform marital duties, there is a supernal spirit with which they became adorned when the day was sanctified. While they are sleeping, other souls wish to ascend and see the glory of the King, the supernal spirit that descended at the commencement of the Shabbat takes that soul, and so they ascend. The other souls bathe in the spices that are in the Garden of Eden, and see there whatever they see. We read that Rabbi Hamnuna Saba (the elder) was filled with joy at the commencement of Shabbat, to see the supernal angels and the ascending and descending souls.

### The Relevance of this Passage

Here the beauty of the commencement of the Shabbat is profoundly stirred within our souls. It connects us, richly, to the weekly expression of energy, while igniting the cosmic Sabbath in the world. The joy of Rabbi Hamnuna Saba is kindled in our hearts, and our visual embrace of this passage draws down righteous souls into this world.

Kabbalah holds that the highest of souls and finest grade of Light cascade from higher to lower, to our earthly sphere, after midnight on Shabbat when a man and woman join together in love. Thus, by virtue of this mystical knowledge, intimate relations between husband and wife are imbued with divinity, bringing holiness to the entire world. The accumulative Light resulting from the marital duties of the righteous souls all through the ages shines now, in full radiance.

169. בָּרְכוּ אֶת יְיָ'. אֶת דַּיְיקָא. כִּדְקָאמְרָן, דָּא שַׁבָּת דְּמַעֲלֵי שַׁבַּתָּא. בָּרוּךְ יְיָ' הַמְבוֹרָךְ, דָּא אֲפִיקוּ דְּבִרְכָאן מִמְּקוֹרָא דְּחַיֵּי, וַאֲתָר דְּנָפִיק

מִנֵּיהּ כָּל שַׁקְיוּ, לְאַשְׁקָאָה לְכֹלָּא. וּבְגִין דְּאִיהוּ מְקוֹרָא בְּרָזָא דְאָת
קַיְּימָא, קָרֵינָן לֵיהּ הַמְבוֹרָךְ, אִיהוּ מַבּוּעָא דְּבֵירָא. כֵּיוָן דִּמְטוּ תַּמָּן, הָא
וַדַּאי בֵּירָא אִתְמַלְיָא, דְּלָא פַּסְקִין מֵימוֹי לְעָלְמִין.

**169.** 'Bless (*Et*) Hashem': 'Et' is concise, FOR IT ALLUDES TO MALCHUT, WHICH IS CALLED 'ET (ENG. 'THE')'. As we have established ABOVE, 'ET (THE)' is the Shabbat at the entrance of the Shabbat, NAMELY SHABBAT EVE, WHICH IS THE ASPECT OF MALCHUT. Blessed be the blessed Hashem: BLESSED is the source of blessings from the source of life, and the place from which all waterings go forth to water everything, NAMELY YESOD OF BINAH. It is the source THAT PROVIDES in the secret of the sign of the covenant, NAMELY IN YESOD OF ZEIR ANPIN, which we call 'the blessed,' for it is the fountain of the well. YESOD IS THE FOUNTAIN OF MALCHUT THAT IS CALLED 'WELL'. When THE BLESSINGS reach there TO YESOD OF ZEIR ANPIN, the well certainly becomes filled, for the water never stops flowing, NAMELY CHASSADIM THAT ARE CALLED 'WATER'.

170. וְעַל דָּא לָא אַמְרֵינָן, בָּרוּךְ אֶת יְיָ' הַמְבוֹרָךְ, אֶלָּא בָּרוּךְ יְיָ',
דְּאִלְמָלֵא לָא מָטֵי הָתָם נְבִיעוּ מִמְּקוֹרָא עִלָּאָה, לָא אִתְמַלְיָא בֵּירָא
כְּלָל, וְעַל דָּא הַמְבוֹרָךְ, אֲמַאי אִיהוּ הַמְבוֹרָךְ. בְּגִין דְּאִיהוּ אַשְׁלִים
וְאַשְׁקֵי לְעוֹלָם וָעֶד. עוֹלָם וָעֶד דָּא אִיהוּ שַׁבָּת דְּמַעֲלֵי שַׁבַּתָּא, וַאֲנָן
תַּקְעִין בִּרְכָּאן בְּאֲתַר דְּאִקְרֵי מְבוֹרָךְ. וְכֵיוָן דִּמְטָאן הָתָם, כֻּלְּהוּ לְעוֹלָם
וָעֶד, וְדָא אִיהוּ בָּרוּךְ יְיָ' הַמְבוֹרָךְ. עַד הָכָא, מָטוֹן בִּרְכָּאן מֵעָלְמָא
עִלָּאָה, וְכֻלְּהוּ לְעוֹלָם וָעֶד, לְאִתְבָּרְכָא וּלְאִתְשַׁקָּאָה, וּלְמֶהֱוֵי שְׁלִים
כְּדְקָא יֵאוּת, מַלְיָא מִכָּל סִטְרִין.

**170.** Therefore, it does not say, 'Blessed be (*Et*) Hashem who is blessed,' but rather 'Blessed be Hashem.' If the flow from the upper source, YESOD OF BINAH, would not reach there, TO YESOD OF ZEIR ANPIN, then the well would not become filled at all, WHICH IS MALCHUT, BECAUSE MALCHUT CAN RECEIVE ONLY FROM YESOD OF ZEIR ANPIN. Therefore, WE SAY 'who is Blessed', THAT IS YESOD OF ZEIR ANPIN. Why is He Blessed? It is because it fills and waters 'forever and ever'. Forever and ever is the Shabbat of the entrance of Shabbat, NAMELY MALCHUT, and we bring the

blessings to the place called 'Blessed', THAT IS YESOD OF ZEIR ANPIN. When they arrive there, they are all DRAWN forever and ever, WHICH IS MALCHUT. This is the meaning of: 'Blessed be Hashem who is blessed' until here, MEANING UNTIL YESOD OF ZEIR ANPIN THAT IS CALLED 'BLESSED', reach the blessing of the upper world, WHICH IS BINAH, and they are all drawn to 'forever (lit. 'for the world') and ever,' WHICH IS MALCHUT, so it would become blessed and watered and to be filled properly, full on all sides.

171. בָּרוּךְ: דָּא מְקוֹרָא עִלָּאָה, דְּכָל בִּרְכָּן נָפְקִין מִנֵּיהּ. וְכַד סִיהֲרָא אִשְׁתְּלִים, קָרֵינָן לָהּ הָכִי לְגַבֵּי תַּתָּאֵי, אֲבָל בָּרוּךְ מְקוֹרָא עִלָּאָה כִּדְקַאמְרָן. יְיָ: דָּא אֶמְצָעִי דְּכָל סִטְרִין עִלָּאִין. הַמְבוֹרָךְ: דָּא שְׁלָמָא דְּבֵיתָא, מַבּוּעָא דְּבֵירָא, לְאַשְׁלְמָא וּלְאַשְׁקָאָה כֹּלָּא. לְעוֹלָם וָעֶד: דָּא עָלְמָא תַּתָּאָה, דְּאִצְטְרִיךְ לְאִתְבָּרְכָא. וּמִשְׁחָא וּרְבוּ דְּבָרוּךְ יְיָ וְהַמְבוֹרָךְ, כֹּלָּא אִיהוּ לְעוֹלָם וָעֶד.

171. NOW THE ZOHAR EXPLAINS THE SECRET OF EVERY WORD OF: 'BLESSED BE HASHEM WHO IS BLESSED' INDIVIDUALLY, AND SAYS, 'Blessed' is the upper source, WHICH IS YESOD OF BINAH, from which all the blessings emerge. When the moon is full, we call it ALSO BLESSED, in relation to those below, but this 'blessed' is the upper source as we have said. 'Hashem' is the center of all the upper sides, NAMELY ZEIR ANPIN, WHICH IS THE CENTRAL COLUMN. 'Who is blessed' is household peace, WHICH IS YESOD OF ZEIR ANPIN THAT IS CALLED 'PEACE', the fountain of the well, to fill and water everything. 'Forever and ever' is the lower world that needs to be blessed and the oil and greatness, MEANING THE BOUNTY, that is drawn by 'Blessed be Hashem' and 'who is blessed'. It is all FOR THE BENEFIT OF 'forever and ever', WHICH IS MALCHUT.

172. וְעַל דָּא, בְּרָכָה דָּא, אִצְטְרִיכוּ כָּל עַמָּא לְבָרְכָא, וּבְמַעֲלֵי שַׁבַּתָּא, בִּרְעוּ דְּלִבָּא, וּבְחֶדְוָה בָּעוּ לְמִשְׁרֵי בְּשֵׁרוּתָא בְּבִרְכָה דָּא, לְאִתְבָּרְכָא הַאי שַׁבָּת דְּמַעֲלֵי שַׁבַּתָּא, מֵעַמָּא קַדִּישָׁא כַּדְקָא יָאוֹת. בְּהַאי בְּרָכָה.

172. Therefore, it is incumbent upon the entire nation to make this blessing at the commencement of the Shabbat. We must start at the beginning with

this blessing with the desire of the heart and joy, so that this Shabbat of the commencement of the Shabbat, WHICH IS SHABBAT EVE, NAMELY MALCHUT, is blessed by the Holy Nation properly with this blessing.

173. כַּד שָׁרָאן יִשְׂרָאֵל לְבָרְכָא, קָלָא אָזְלָא בְּכֻלְּהוּ רְקִיעִין, דְּמִתְקַדְּשֵׁי בִּקְדוּשָׁא דְּמַעֲלֵי שַׁבַּתָּא. זַכָּאִין אַתּוּן עַמָּא קַדִּישָׁא, דְּאַתּוּן מְבָרְכֵי וּמְקַדְּשֵׁי לְתַתָּא, בְּגִין דְּיִתְבָּרְכוּן וְיִתְקַדְּשׁוּן לְעֵילָא, כַּמָּה מַשִׁרְיָין עִלָּאִין קַדִּישִׁין, זַכָּאִין אִינּוּן בְּהַאי עָלְמָא, וְזַכָּאִין אִינּוּן בְּעָלְמָא דְּאָתֵי, וְלָא מְבָרְכֵי יִשְׂרָאֵל בִּרְכָה דָּא, עַד דְּמִתְעַטְּרָן בְּעִטְרִין דְּנִשְׁמָתִין קַדִּישִׁין כִּדְקָאמְרָן. זַכָּאָה עַמָּא דְּזַכֵּי לוֹן בְּעָלְמָא דֵּין, לְמִזְכֵּי לוֹן לְעָלְמָא דְּאָתֵי.

173. When Yisrael begin to bless, a voice goes through all the firmaments that become sanctified with the holiness of the commencement of the Shabbat. Happy are you, the Holy Nation, that you bless and sanctify below, in order that many holy supernal camps become blessed and become sanctified above. Happy are they in this world and happy are they in the World to Come. Yisrael do not make this blessing until they become adorned with the crowns of the holy souls, as we have said. Happy is the nation that merits in this world, so that they merit in the World to Come.

174. בְּהַאי לֵילְיָא שִׁמּוּשָׁא דְּחַכִּימִין, בְּאִלֵּין נִשְׁמָתִין קַדִּישִׁין דְּמִתְעַטְּרָן בְּהוּ, וְאע"ג דְּהָא אוֹקִימְנָא וְכֹלָּא חַד. וּבְכָל אֲתָר דְּתִשְׁכַּח לְחַכִּימִין בְּהַאי מִלָּה, בְּסִטְרָא דָּא, וּלְזִמְנִין בְּסִטְרָא דָּא כֹּלָּא אִיהוּ חַד, וְהָנֵי מִילֵי הָא אוֹקִימְנָא אֲבָל בְּזִמְנָא דָּא, דְּמִתְעַטְּרָן כֻּלְּהוּ בְּנִשְׁמָתִין וְרוּחִין חַדְתִּין יְתֵירִין קַדִּישִׁין, כְּדֵין אִיהִי זִמְנָא דְּשִׁמּוּשָׁא דִּלְהוֹן, בְּגִין דְּלֶיהֱוֵי נְגִידוּ לְהַהוּא שִׁמּוּשָׁא, בִּנְגִידוּ דִּקְדוּשָׁה, בְּנַיְיחָא עִלָּאָה, וְיִפְּקוּן בְּנַיְיהוּ קַדִּישִׁין כִּדְקָא חֲזִי.

174. That night is the time for Sages to perform marital duties, when they become adorned with these holy souls. Even though we have already established this, it is all one. In every place this subject is found about the Sages, sometimes in one way and sometimes in another way, it all amounts

to the same thing, and we have already established this subject. When they all become adorned with new holy souls and spirits, that are additional TO THOSE OF THE WEEK DAYS, it is their time to perform marital duties, in order to draw upon this union a flow of holiness, in supernal rest. This should produce holy children, as is proper.

175. רָזָא דָּא לְחַכִּימִין אִתְיְיהִיבַת. בְּשַׁעֲתָא דְּאִתְפְּלִיג לֵילְיָא, בְּלֵילְיָא דָּא, קוּדְשָׁא בְּרִיךְ הוּא בָּעֵי לְאַעֲלָא בְּגִנְתָּא דִּלְעֵילָּא. וְרָזָא דָּא, בְּיוֹמֵי דְּחוֹל קוּדְשָׁא בְּרִיךְ הוּא עָאל בְּגִנְתָּא דְּעֵדֶן דִּלְתַתָּא, לְאִשְׁתַּעְשְׁעָא עִם צַדִּיקַיָּא דְּשַׁרְיָין תַּמָּן, וּבְשַׁבָּת, בְּהַהוּא לֵילְיָא דְּשַׁבַּתָּא, קוּדְשָׁא בְּרִיךְ הוּא עָאל בְּגִנְתָּא דִּלְעֵילָּא, בְּרָזָא דִּמְקוֹרָא עִלָּאָה.

175. This secret was given to the Sages. At midnight of this night, OF SHABBAT, the Holy One, blessed be He, desires to enter the Garden of Eden. This secret is that the Holy One, blessed be He, enters the Lower Garden of Eden, WHICH IS IN THE WORLD ASIYAH, on the weekdays to amuse Himself with the righteous who dwell there. On Shabbat and on the eve of Shabbat, the Holy One, blessed be He, enters the Upper Garden of Eden, WHICH IS IN THE WORLD BRIYAH, in the secret of the Supernal Source, WHICH IS BINAH. BECAUSE THE THREE WORLDS, BRIYAH, YETZIRAH AND ASIYAH, ARE AS BINAH, TIFERET, AND MALCHUT, AND BRIYAH IS AS BINAH.

176. בְּגִין דִּבְיוֹמֵי דְּחוֹל, כָּל נִשְׁמָתִין דְּצַדִּיקַיָּא כֻּלְּהוּ, בְּגִנְתָּא דִּי בְאַרְעָא שַׁרְיָין. וְכַד אִתְקַדַּשׁ יוֹמָא בְּמַעֲלֵי שַׁבַּתָּא, כָּל אִינּוּן מַשִׁרְיָין דְּמַלְאָכִין קַדִּישִׁין דִּי מְמַנָּן גּוֹ גִּנְתָּא דִּלְתַתָּא, כֻּלְּהוּ סַלְּקָן לְהָנֵי נִשְׁמָתִין, דְּשַׁרְיָין גּוֹ גִּנְתָּא דִּלְתַתָּא, לְעֵילָּא לְגַבֵּי הַהוּא רְקִיעָא דְּקַיְּימָא עַל גִּנְתָּא, וּמִתַּמָּן אִזְדַּמְנוּ רְתִיכִין קַדִּישִׁין, דְּסַחֲרָאן כּוּרְסֵי יְקָרָא דְּמַלְכָּא, וְסַלְּקִין לוֹן לְכָל אִינּוּן נִשְׁמָתִין, בְּגִנְתָּא דִּלְעֵילָּא.

176. During the weekdays, all the souls of the righteous dwell in the terrestrial Garden of Eden. When the day becomes sanctified at the commencement of the Shabbat, all these camps of holy angels that are appointed in the Lower Garden of Eden elevate these souls that dwell in the

Lower Garden of Eden, to bring them to that firmament that stands over the Garden of Eden. FOR SINCE THEY ARE FROM THE WORLD OF ASIYAH, THEY HAVE NO PERMISSION TO RISE HIGHER THAN THIS. Holy Chariots that surround the Throne of Glory of the King, WHICH IS BRIYAH, come from there and elevate all these souls to the Upper Garden of Eden, WHICH IS IN BRIYAH.

177. כֵּיוָן דְּאִלֵּין רוּחִין סַלְּקִין, כְּדֵין רוּחִין אָחֳרָנִין קַדִּישִׁין, נַחְתִּין, לְאִתְעַטְּרָא בְּהוּ עַמָּא קַדִּישָׁא. אִלֵּין סַלְּקִין, וְאִלֵּין נַחְתִּין.

177. When these spirits ascend TO THE UPPER GARDEN OF EDEN, other holy spirits descend TO THIS WORLD, to become adorned with the Holy People. These ascend TO THE UPPER GARDEN OF EDEN, and those descend TO BECOME ADORNED WITH THE HOLY PEOPLE, MEANING JUST AS THERE IS ELEVATION TO THE SOULS THAT ARE IN THE GARDEN OF EDEN, SO IS THERE AN ELEVATION FOR THE HOLY PEOPLE, FOR THEY BECOME ADORNED WITH AN ADDITIONAL SOUL.

178. וְאִי תֵּימָא, הָא גִּנְתָּא דִּבְאַרְעָא, בְּיוֹמָא דְּשַׁבַּתָּא יָתְבָא בְּרֵיקַנְיָיא בְּלָא נִשְׁמָתִין דְּצַדִּיקַיָּא. לָאו הָכִי. אֶלָּא נִשְׁמָתִין אַזְלִין, וְנִשְׁמָתִין אַתְיָין. נִשְׁמָתִין סַלְּקִין, וְנִשְׁמָתִין נַחְתִּין. נִשְׁמָתִין אַזְלִין מִגּוֹ גִּנְתָּא, וְנִשְׁמָתִין אַתְיָין לְגוֹ גִּנְתָּא. כָּל אִינּוּן נִשְׁמָתִין דְּצַדִּיקַיָּא, דְּמִתְלַבְּנָן בְּיוֹמֵי דְחוֹל, וְעַד לָא עָאלוּ לְגוֹ גִּנְתָּא, בְּשַׁעֲתָא דְּאִלֵּין נָפְקִין, אִלֵּין עָאלִין וְגִנְתָּא לָא אִשְׁתְּאַר בְּרֵיקַנְיָיא. בְּרָזָא דְּלֶחֶם הַפָּנִים בְּיוֹם הִלָּקְחוֹ.

178. And if you ask: But then during the Shabbat day, is the terrestrial Garden of Eden empty of the souls of the righteous? It is not so. Rather souls go and souls come, souls ascend and souls descend, souls go from the Garden and other souls come into the Garden. All these souls of the righteous, who cleanse themselves TO PURIFY THEMSELVES during the weekdays and have still not entered THE LOWER GARDEN of Eden, will enter the LOWER Garden OF EDEN at the moment that these souls leave THE GARDEN OF EDEN TO THE UPPER GARDEN OF EDEN. The Garden does not remain empty, and it is like the shew-bread on the day it is taken, THAT THEY PLACE OTHERS IN THEIR PLACE.

179. וְאִי תֵּימָא, כַּד אָהַדְרוּ בְּיוֹמֵי דְחוֹל. בְּמָה אִתְמַשְׁכָן דּוּכְתֵּי לְאָרְכָּא וּפוּתְיָא וְרוּמָא, בְּגִנְתָּא, וְלָא אִתְיְדַע. כְּגַוְונָא דְרָזָא דְאָרֶץ הַצְּבִי, דַּהֲוָה אִתְמְשַׁךְ לְכָל סִטְרִין וְלָא אִתְיְדַע. כְּגַוְונָא דִּצְבִי, דְּכָל מַה דְּאִתְרַבֵּי, מַשְׁכֵיהּ אִתְרַבֵּי לְכָל סְטָר, וְלָא אִתְיְידַע. וְאִית כְּמָה נִשְׁמָתִין, דְּכֵיוָן דְּסַלְקִין, תּוּ לָא נַחְתִּין.

179. And if you ask: When the souls return FROM THE UPPER GARDEN OF EDEN TO THE LOWER GARDEN OF EDEN during the weekdays, how do the places expand in length and breadth and height in the Garden, UNTIL IT CAN ACCOMMODATE THEM ALL, yet it is not noticeable? HE ANSWERS: It is like the Land of the Deer (the land of Yisrael) that was stretched in all directions, yet it was not noticeable. Like a deer, as much as it grows, its skin grows with it to every side, yet it is not noticeable. There are many souls that no longer descend FROM THERE, once they have ascended TO THE UPPER GARDEN OF EDEN, AND THEY REMAIN THERE ALSO DURING THE WEEKDAYS.

180. נִשְׁמָתִין סַלְקִין, וְנִשְׁמָתִין נַחְתִּין, לְאִתְעַטְּרָא בְּהוּ עַמָּא קַדִּישָׁא. וּבְמַעֲלֵי שַׁבַּתָּא, גִּלְגּוּלָא דְּנִשְׁמָתִין אִיהוּ, אִלֵּין אַזְלִין, וְאִלֵּין אַתְיָין, אִלֵּין סַלְקִין וְאִלֵּין נַחְתִּין. מַאן חָמֵי כַּמָּה רְתִיכִין קַדִּישִׁין, דִּי מְשַׁטְטֵי לְכָאן וּלְכָאן. כֻּלְּהוּ בְּחֶדְוָה, כֻּלְּהוּ בִּרְעוּ, בְּאִלֵּין נִשְׁמָתִין לְאַעְטְרָא לְעַמָּא קַדִּישָׁא, לְאַעְטְרָא לְכַמָּה צַדִּיקַיָּיא, גִּנְתָּא דְעֵדֶן לְתַתָּא, עַד שַׁעֲתָא דְּכָרוֹזָא קָאִים, וְקָארֵי מְקוּדָשׁ מְקוּדָשׁ. כְּדֵין נַיְיחָא שְׁכִיחַ, וּשְׁכִיכוּ לְכֹלָּא. וְחַיָּיבֵי גֵיהִנָּם כֻּלְּהוּ מִשְׁתַּכְּחֵי בְּדוּכְתַּיְיהוּ, וְאִית לוֹן נַיְיחָא. וְנִשְׁמָתִין כֻּלְּהוּ מִתְעַטְּרָן, אִלֵּין לְעֵילָּא וְאִלֵּין לְתַתָּא. זַכָּאָה עַמָּא, דְּחוּלְקָא דָּא לְהוֹן.

180. Souls ascend and souls descend so that the Holy People should adorn themselves with them. At the commencement of the Shabbat, MEANING BEFORE THE DAY HAS BEEN SANCTIFIED, THERE IS a turning of souls. Some are going and some are coming, some ascend while others descend. Who has seen how many Holy Chariots float here and there, all of them in joy, all of them with good will? These souls ARE FOR the adorning of the

Holy People, to adorn many righteous in the Lower Garden of Eden, AND THIS CONTINUES until the moment that an announcer proclaims, 'Sanctified, sanctified.' Then rest and quiet is prevalent for all, while the wicked in Gehenom all become quiet in their place and have rest. All the souls become adorned, MEANING THAT THEY ATTAIN THE FIRST THREE SFIROT, those above and those below. Happy are the people that possess this portion.

181. בְּפַלְגוּת לֵילְיָא דְּמַעֲלֵי שַׁבְּתָא, דְּחַכִּימִין מִתְעָרִין לְשִׁמּוּשָׁא דִּלְהוֹן, הַהוּא רוּחָא עִלָּאָה, דְּמִתְעַטְּרָן בֵּיהּ, כַּד יוֹמָא אִתְקַדַּשׁ, בְּשַׁעֲתָא דְּאִינּוּן נַיְימֵי בְּעַרְסַיְיהוּ, וְנִשְׁמָתִין אַחֲרָנִין דִּלְהוֹן, בָּעָאן לְסַלְּקָא לְמֶחֱמֵי בִּיקָרָא דְּמַלְכָּא, כְּדֵין הַהוּא רוּחַ עִלָּאָה דְּנָחִית בְּמַעֲלֵי שַׁבְּתָא, נָטִיל הַהִיא נִשְׁמְתָא, וְסַלְּקִין לְעֵילָּא, וְאִתְסַחְיָיא נִשְׁמָתָא אַחֲרָא בְּבוּסְמִין דְּגִנְתָּא דְּעֵדֶן, וְתַמָּן חָמֵי מַה דְּחָמֵי.

181. At midnight of Shabbat Eve, when the Sages awake to perform marital duties, there is a Supernal Spirit with which they become adorned when the day was sanctified. While they are sleeping in their beds and their other souls wish to ascend and see the glory of the King, the Supernal Spirit that descended at the commencement of the Shabbat takes that soul and they ascend. The other souls bathe in the spices that are in the Garden of Eden, and see there whatever they see.

182. וְכַד נַחְתָּא לְאַשְׁרָאָה בְּדוּכְתָּהָא בְּפַלְגוּת לֵילְיָא, הַהִיא נִשְׁמְתָא תָּבָאת לְדוּכְתָּהָא. וּבָעֵי לְאִינּוּן חַכִּימִין לוֹמַר, חַד פְּסוּקָא דְּאִתְעֲרוּתָא, דְּהַהוּא רוּחָא עִלָּאָה קַדִּישָׁא דְּעֶטְרָא דְּשַׁבְּתָא, כְּגוֹן, רוּחַ יְיָ' אֱלֹהִים עָלַי יַעַן מָשַׁח יְיָ', אוֹתִי לְבַשֵּׂר עֲנָוִים וְגוֹ'. בְּלֶכְתָּם יֵלֵכוּ וּבְעָמְדָם יַעֲמֹדוּ וּבְהִנָּשְׂאָם מֵעַל הָאָרֶץ וְגוֹ', אֶל אֲשֶׁר יִהְיֶה שָׁם הָרוּחַ לָלֶכֶת יֵלֵכוּ וְגוֹ'. בְּגִין דְּמִתְעַטְּרָן בְּהַהוּא רוּחָא, בְּאִתְעֲרוּתָא דִּלְהוֹן בְּחֶדְוָה דְּשִׁמּוּשָׁא, וִיהֵא נְגִידוּ דְּהַהוּא רוּחַ עִלָּאָה דְּשַׁבְּתָא, בְּהַהוּא שִׁמּוּשָׁא דְּמִצְוָה.

182. When THE SPIRIT descends to dwell in its place at midnight, that soul also returns to its place. The Sages must say a passage of arousal of that supernal Holy Spirit of the Shabbat crown, namely: "The spirit of Hashem

Elohim was upon me; because Hashem has anointed me to announce good tidings to the meek..." (Yeshayah 61:1). "When those moved, these moved; and when those stood still, these stood still; and when those were lifted up from the earth" (Yechezkel 1:21) and "wherever the spirit was minded to go, they went" (Ibid. 12), because they adorn themselves with that spirit, with their awakening to the gladness of the mating. There should be the drawing of that Supernal Spirit of Shabbat in that copulation of merit.

183. רַב הַמְנוּנָא סָבָא, כַּד הֲוָה סָלִיק מִנַּהֲרָא בְּמַעֲלֵי שַׁבַּתָּא, הֲוָה יָתִיב רִגְעָא חֲדָא, וְזָקִיף עֵינוֹי, וַהֲוָה חַדֵּי, דַּהֲוָה יָתִיב, לְמֶחֱמֵי חֶדְוָה דְּמַלְאֲכֵי עִלָּאֵי. אִלֵּין סַלְּקִין, וְאִלֵּין נַחְתִּין. וּבְכָל מַעֲלֵי שַׁבַּתָּא, יָתִיב בַּר נָשׁ בְּעוֹלָם הַנְּשָׁמוֹת. זַכָּאָה אִיהוּ מַאן דְּיָדַע בְּרָזִין דְּמָארֵיהּ.

183. When Rav Hamnuna Saba (the elder) rose from the river at the commencement of Shabbat, he would sit for a moment and raise his eyes, and he was happy. He would say that he was sitting to see the joy of the supernal angels, those ascending and these descending. Man sits in the world of souls during the entire TIME OF THE commencement of the Shabbat. Happy is he who knows the secrets of his Master.

## 16. "The heavens declare the glory of El"

### A Synopsis

This reading links the joy of the day of Shabbat with the source of the heavenly illumination and the supernal Book. It begins by quoting, "The heavens declare the glory of El; and the firmament proclaims his handiwork." Rabbi Hamnuna Saba (the elder) explains that "declare" means the heavens illuminate and sparkle in the glitter of supernal light. Every single ring (the Sfirot in Malchut) lights up and sparkles from that light. He explains that "the firmament" is the fountain of the well and the river that flows from Eden. When the supernal Dew of that crystal is drawn and flows, everything becomes perfected with the Holy Letters. We then read of the meaning in "Day to day utters speech", and "And night to night expresses knowledge," and then "Their line is gone out through all the earth" "And their words to the end of the world". We read of the holy sun, which is like a tent containing all the higher and lower levels. It shines "like a bridegroom coming out of his canopy," and Rabbi Hamnuna Saba (the elder) explains that the canopy is Eden. The moon herself is an expression of the light from the sun and carries also that greater illumination from the source. The Torah is the same expression of Wisdom in the Kingdom, Chochmah in Malchut, and "The Torah of The Creator is perfect." It is composed of phrases containing five words each. During the Shabbat day everything is properly completed in the secret of Shabbat above and below, and on this day, Light is increased in everything. Thus, David recited the verse: "The heavens declare," inspired by the imminent illumination of the Holy Spirit, and by the pre-eminence of the Shabbat Day over all other days.

### The Relevance of this Passage

We learn how the great Source of all Light gives expression through the heavenly bodies, through the Shabbat, and through the Torah. This supernal Light spills downward upon us when our eyes touch the words, revealing these lofty, luminous mysteries. This illumination perfects our souls and completes the world, allowing the cosmic Sabbath (the Age of Messiah) to commence with the boundless sweet mercy.

184. כַּד נָהִיר יְמָמָא בְּיוֹמָא דְּשַׁבַּתָּא, סְלִיקוּ דְּחֶדְוָה סָלִיק בְּכֻלְּהוּ עָלְמִין, בְּנַיְיחָא בְּחֶדְוָה. כְּדֵין הַשָּׁמַיִם מְסַפְּרִים כְּבוֹד אֵל וּמַעֲשֵׂי יָדָיו מַגִּיד הָרָקִיעַ. מַאן שָׁמַיִם. אִלֵּין שָׁמַיִם, דְּשְׁמָא עִלָּאָה אִתְחֲזֵי בָּה, דְּשְׁמָא קַדִּישָׁא אִתְרְשִׁים בְּהוּ.

**184.** When the day of Shabbat dawns, the joy ascends in all the worlds with satisfaction and gladness. Then "The heavens declare the glory of El; and the firmament proclaims His handiwork" (Tehilim 19:2). Who are the heavens? They are these heavens, NAMELY ZEIR ANPIN, in which the supernal Name is visible, WHICH IS IMA, and in which the Holy Name is marked, WHICH IS ABA, MEANING HEAVENS IS ZEIR ANPIN THAT CONTAINS THE MOCHIN OF ABA AND IMA.

185. מְסַפְּרִים, מַאי מְסַפְּרִים, אִי תֵּימָא כְּמַאן דְּמִשְׁתָּעֵי סְפּוּר דְּבָרִים. לָאו הָכִי. אֶלָּא דְּנָהֲרִין וּנְצִיצִין בְּנְצִיצוּ דִּנְהוֹרָא עִלָּאָה, וְסַלְּקִין בִּשְׁמָא, דְּכָלִיל בִּנְהִירוּ דִּשְׁלִימוּ עִלָּאָה.

**185.** HE QUESTIONS: What is THE MEANING OF "declare (also: 'tell')?" If you say it is like one who is telling a story, it is not so. But rather they illuminate and sparkle in the glitter of the supernal light, and ascend in the Name that is included in the shine of the supernal perfection, NAMELY IN THE NAME YUD HEI VAV HEI, WHICH CONTAINS *YUD-HEI*, WHICH ARE SUPERNAL PERFECTION, BEING ABA AND IMA.

186. וּמַאן אִיהוּ סְפּוּר. דְּנִצְצֵי בִּנְהִירוּ דִּשְׁלִימוּ דְּסֵפֶר עִלָּאָה. וּבְגִין כַּךְ, סַלְּקִין בִּשְׁמָא שְׁלִים, וְנַהֲרִין בִּנְהִירוּ שְׁלִים, וְנָצְצֵי בִּנְצִיצוּ שְׁלִים. אִינְהוּ מְנַצְצֵי וְנַהֲרֵי בְּגַרְמַיְיהוּ, מִגּוֹ נְהִירוּ דְּנִצְצֵי דְּסֵפֶר עִלָּאָה, וְנַהֲרֵי לְכָל סְטַר וְסִטְרָא דְּמִתְדַּבְּקָן בֵּיהּ, דְּהָא מִנַּיְיהוּ, מֵהַהוּא סְפִירוּ וּנְהִירוּ, נָהִיר כָּל עִזְקָא וְעִזְקָא, וְנָצִיץ בִּנְצִיצוּ, בְּגִין דִּבְהַאי יוֹמָא מִתְעַטְּרָן שָׁמַיִם, וְסַלְּקִין בִּשְׁמָא קַדִּישָׁא, יַתִּיר מִשְׁאָר יוֹמִין.

**186.** HE QUESTIONS: What is the tale, FOR IT SAYS, "THE HEAVENS TELL"? HE ANSWERS: They sparkle in the shine of the supernal Book, WHICH IS ABA, AND THAT WHICH IS DRAWN FROM THE BOOK IS CALLED 'A TALE'. Therefore, they ascend in a complete Name, WHICH IS YUD HEI VAV HEI, and they illuminate with a complete light, IN THE RIGHT COLUMN. They sparkle in a complete sparkle, IN THE LEFT COLUMN. They sparkle and illuminate by themselves from the light of the sparkle of the supernal Book, and sparkle and illuminate in every side to which they are attached, because every single ring lights up and sparkles, ALL THE SFIROT IN MALCHUT THAT ARE CALLED 'RINGS', from that shine and from the

light, because on this day the heavens, WHICH ARE ZEIR ANPIN, become adorned and ascend in the Holy Name, YUD HEI VAV HEI, more than on the other days.

187. וּמַעֲשֵׂה יָדָיו, הַהוּא טַלָּא עִלָּאָה, דְּנָהִיר מִכָּל סִטְרִין גְּנִיזִין, דְּאִיהוּ מַעֲשֵׂה יָדָיו, וְתִקּוּנָא דִּילֵיהּ, דְּמִתַּתְקְנָא בְּיוֹמָא דָא מִכָּל שְׁאָר יוֹמִין.

187. "His handiwork" MEANS the supernal Dew that illuminates from all the concealed sides, which are the works of His hands, OF ZEIR ANPIN, and His establishment that is established on this day more than on all the other days.

188. מַגִּיד הָרָקִיעַ. מַאי מַגִּיד. מָשִׁיךְ וְנָגִיד לְתַתָּא, מֵרֵישָׁא דְּמַלְכָּא, מַלְיָא מִכָּל סִטְרוֹי. הָרָקִיעַ, הַהוּא רָקִיעַ, דְּאִיהוּ מַבּוּעָא דְּבֵירָא. וְדָא אִיהוּ הַהוּא נָהָר דְּנָפִיק מֵעֵדֶן, וְדָא אִיהוּ דְּנָגִיד וּמָשִׁיךְ לְתַתָּא, נְגִידוּ דְּטַלָּא עִלָּאָה, דְּנָהִיר וְנָצִיץ בְּנִצִיצוּ מִכָּל סִטְרִין. וְדָא רָקִיעַ אַנְגִּיד לֵיהּ בִּמְשִׁיכוּ דִּרְחִימוּ וְתִיאוּבְתָּא, לְאַשְׁקָאָה שַׁקְיוּ דְּחֶדְוָה, לְמַעֲלֵי שַׁבַּתָּא.

188. "The firmament proclaims": HE QUESTIONS: What means "proclaims"? HE ANSWERS THAT ITS MEANING IS THAT He draws THE DEW and it flows down INTO YESOD from the head of the King, NAMELY FROM HIS FIRST THREE SFIROT THAT ARE CALLED 'THE HEAD OF ZEIR ANPIN', and it becomes filled from all sides. "The firmament" is the fountain of the well, NAMELY YESOD THAT PROVIDES THE WELL, WHICH IS MALCHUT, and this is the river that emerges from Eden. This is the one that draws and spills downward the flow of the supernal Dew that illuminates and sparkles from all sides. This firmament draws it with a drawing of love and longing to water a potion of joy to Shabbat Eve, WHICH IS MALCHUT.

189. וְכַד נָגִיד וּמָשִׁיךְ הַהוּא טַלָּא דִּבְדוֹלְחָא, כֹּלָּא מַלְיָא וּשְׁלִים בְּאַתְווֹי קַדִּישִׁין, בְּכָל אִינּוּן שְׁבִילִין קַדִּישִׁין. כֵּיוָן דְּכֹלָּא אִתְחַבָּר בֵּיהּ, אִתְעֲבֵיד בֵּיהּ אָרְחָא לְאַשְׁקָאָה וּלְבָרְכָא לְתַתָּא.

189. When the dew of that crystal is drawn and flows, FROM THE HEAD OF ZEIR ANPIN, everything becomes filled and perfected with the Holy Letters,

NAMELY the 22 LETTERS, in all the holy paths. Since everything is attached to Him, a way to water and bless below, TO MALCHUT, is formed within Him.

190. יוֹם לְיוֹם: יוֹמָא לְיוֹמָא, וְעִזְקָא לְעִזְקָא. הַשְׁתָּא מִשְׁתָּעֵי קְרָא בְּאֹרַח פְּרָט, הֵיךְ שָׁמַיִם מְסַפְּרִים וּמִתְקָנִין בִּסְפִירוּ וּבְנִצִיצוּ עִלָּאָה לְהַאי כָּבוֹד, וְהֵיךְ נָגִיד וּמָשִׁיךְ הַהוּא רְקִיעָא, נְגִידוּ דְּטַלָּא עִלָּאָה. וְאָמַר, יוֹם לְיוֹם יַבִּיעַ אֹמֶר. יוֹמָא לְיוֹמָא, וְדַרְגָּא לְדַרְגָּא, אוֹחֵי לְאִתְכַּלְּלָא דָּא בְּדָא, וּלְאִתְנַהֲרָא דָּא מִן דָּא, מֵהַהוּא סְפִירוּ דִּמְנַצְצֵי וּמְנַהֲרֵי שָׁמַיִם, לְהַאי כָּבוֹד. יַבִּיעַ: כד"א מַבָּע אִתְעֲבֵיד וְגוֹ'. אוֹחֵי לְאִנְהֲרָא דָּא מִן דָּא, וּלְאִתְנַצְצָא דָּא מִן דָּא, מֵהַהוּא סְפִירוּ וּנְצִיצוּ.

**190.** "Day to day utters speech" (Ibid. 3): THIS MEANS THAT day PROVIDES to day and ring PROVIDES to ring, AS EVERY SFIRAH OF ZEIR ANPIN THAT IS CALLED 'DAY' AND 'RING' PROVIDES TO THE SFIRAH THAT CORRESPONDS TO IT IN MALCHUT. The passage is now talking in particulars about how the heavens, THAT IS ZEIR ANPIN, tell and perfect with supernal gleam and sparkle this glory, WHICH IS MALCHUT THAT IS CALLED 'GLORY', and how that firmament draws and causes a flow from the supernal Dew. So it says, "Day to day utters speech," meaning day to day and level to level will hasten to combine with each other, and illuminate one from the other from that gleam that the heavens sparkle and illuminate upon that glory, WHICH IS MALCHUT. *Yabia* (Eng. 'utter') is as in 'Maba (Eng. 'quickly') done'. THE TRANSLATION OF: "AND THE THINGS THAT SHALL COME UPON THEM MAKE HASTE" (DEVARIM 32:35) USES '*MABA*' AND '*YABIYA*' AND MEANS THAT they hasten to illuminate one from the other and to sparkle one from another from that gleam and sparkle OF ZEIR ANPIN THAT IS CALLED 'HEAVENS'.

191. אָמַ"ר: כְּלָלָא דְּאַתְוָון וּשְׁבִילִין דְּנָפְקִין מֵאַבָּא וְאִימָא, וְהַהוּא רֵישָׁא דְּנָפִיק מִנַּיְיהוּ, דְּאִיהוּ בְּרָא בּוּכְרָא, אָלֶף: אַבָּא. וְכַד אִיהוּ סָלִיק וְנָחִית, אִתְחַבְּרַת מ' בַּהֲדֵי א', וְאִיהוּ אֵם. ר': רֵישָׁא בּוּכְרָא. כַּד מִתְחַבְּרָן אַתְוָון כֻּלְּהוּ, אֲמַר. דָּא נְהִירוּ דְּאַבָּא וְאִימָא וּבְרָא בּוּכְרָא, וְנַהֲרִין דָּא בְּדָא בְּחִבּוּרָא חֲדָא. שַׁלְטָא בְּיוֹמָא דְּשַׁבַּתָּא. וְעַ"ד כֹּלָּא

אִתְכְּלִיל דָּא בְּדָא, בְּגִין לְמֶהֱוֵי חַד. וּבְגִין כַּךְ אוֹחוּ דָּא בְּדָא, הַהוּא
אֲמַר שְׁלִיטוּ עִלָּאָה, לְמֶהֱוֵי כֹּלָּא חַד.

**191.** "Speech (Heb. *omer*, Aleph-Mem-Resh)" IN THE PASSAGE "DAY TO
DAY UTTERS SPEECH" MEANS the whole of the letters and paths that
emanate from Aba and Ima and that head, NAMELY THE FIRST THREE
SFIROT THAT ARE CALLED 'HEAD', that emanates from them, which is the
first-born son, NAMELY ZEIR ANPIN THAT IS CALLED 'FIRST-BORN SON'.
The *Aleph* of 'omer' alludes to Aba. When he ascends and descends,
NAMELY WHEN HE REPLENISHES THE SMALLNESS OF IMA, FROM WHICH
LIGHT ASCENDS FROM BELOW UP, AND THE GREATNESS OF IMA, FROM
WHICH LIGHT DESCENDS FROM ABOVE DOWN, then the *Mem* OF OMER,
which is Ima, is joined with the *Aleph*. The *Resh* OF OMER alludes to the
first-born son, WHICH IS ZEIR ANPIN. When all these letters combine, they
are 'omer,' which is the light of Aba and Ima and the first-born son, and
they illuminate to each other in one bond. They dominate on the Shabbat
Day. Therefore, they are all included in each other in order to be one,
BECAUSE ZEIR ANPIN ASCENDS AND BECOMES ATTIRED WITH ABA AND
IMA. Therefore, THE THREE LETTERS OF OMER hasten TO PROVIDE to
each other, which are the supernal Dominion, in order that everything should
be one.

192. וְכַד כָּל הַאי אִתְנְגִיד וְאִתְמְשַׁךְ לְהַאי רָקִיעַ, כְּדֵין אִיהוּ אַשְׁקֵי
וְאַנְהִיר לְתַתָּא, לְהַאי כְּבוֹד אֵל, לְמֶעְבַּד תּוֹלְדִין בְּדִיוּקְנָא דְּאִינּוּן
שָׁמַיִם, דְּנָהֲרִין לְהַהוּא כְּבוֹד אֵל.

**192.** When all this is drawn and flows to this firmament, WHICH IS YESOD
OF ZEIR ANPIN, it waters and illuminates below "the glory of El", WHO IS
MALCHUT, in order to create offspring in the images OF THE LIGHTS of
these heavens, WHICH IS ZEIR ANPIN that illuminates "the glory of El"
(Ibid. 2).

193. וְלַיְלָה לְלַיְלָה יְחַוֶּה דָּעַת, רְתִיכִין דִּילָהּ דְּאִינּוּן גּוּפָא דְּכָרְסַיָּיא,
וְכֻלְּהוּ אִקְרוּן לֵילוֹת, כד"א אַף לֵילוֹת יִסְּרוּנִי כִלְיוֹתָי. רְתִיכָא עִלָּאָה,
אִתְקְרֵי יָמִים, יוֹם לְיוֹם. רְתִיכָא תַּתָּאָה, אִקְרֵי לֵילוֹת, לַיְלָה לְלַיְלָה.

**193.** "And night to night expresses knowledge" (Ibid. 3), MEANING Her Chariots, which are the body of the throne, WHICH IS MALCHUT. They are called 'nights', as it is written: "My reins also admonish me in the nights" (Tehilim 16:7). The SFIROT OF the supernal Chariot, WHICH IS ZEIR ANPIN, are called 'days' as in, "Day to day," while THE SFIROT OF the Lower Chariot, WHICH IS MALCHUT, are called 'nights': "Night to night."

**194.** יְחַוֶּה. דַּעַת, יְחַוֶּה: יְחַיֶּה. יְחַיֶּה תּוֹלְדִין, דְּאִינּוּן שָׁמַיִם. וְאִי תֵּימָא, יְחַוֶּה לָאו יְחַיֶּה. תָּ"ח, כְּתִיב וַיִּקְרָא הָאָדָם שֵׁם אִשְׁתּוֹ חַוָּה, כִּי הִיא הָיְתָה אֵם כָּל חָי. חַוָּה וְחַיָּה בְּמִלָּה חֲדָא סַלְּקִין. וְעַל דְּאִסְתְּלַק י', וְעָיֵיל ו', דְּאִיהוּ כִּדְקָא יֵאוֹת, דְּהָא ו' אִיהוּ חַיִּין וַדַּאי, וְעַל דָּא חַוָּה וְחַיָּה, י' נָטְלָא חַיִּין מִן ו'. אוּף הָכָא, יְחַוֶּה, יְחַיֶּה.

**194.** "Expresses knowledge": "*Yechaveh* (Eng. 'expresses')" MEANS "*Yechayeh*" (Eng. 'to give life'), for it will bring to life offspring FROM THE LIGHTS THAT HE RECEIVED from the heavens. If you say that Yechaveh does not mean Yechayeh, come and see: "And the man called the name of his wife Eve; because she was the mother of all living (Heb. *chay*)" (Beresheet 3:20). SO WE SEE that Eve and Chayah are the same, for the *Yud* is removed FROM CHAYAH and the *Vav* enters IN ITS PLACE. This is as it should be, as the *Vav* surely signifies life BECAUSE THE *VAV* ALLUDES TO ZEIR ANPIN THAT IS THE TREE OF LIFE. Therefore of Eve and Chayah EVE IS THE MAIN, because the *Yud* of CHAYAH takes life from the *Vav* OF EVE. THEREFORE, SHE IS CALLED 'EVE (CHAVAH)' AND NOT CHAYAH. Here also, Yachaveh MEANS Yachayeh.

**195.** דַּעַת: דָּא אִיהוּ רָזָא דְּשָׁמַיִם. מַה שָׁמַיִם שִׁית סִטְרִין, אוּף הָכָא שִׁית סִטְרִין, בְּאִינּוּן תּוֹלְדִין דְּקָא יְחַיֶּה כְּגַוְונָא דִּילֵיהּ, וְעַל דָּא יוֹם לְיוֹם אִתְכְּלִיל בְּדַרְגָּא עִלָּאָה אֲמַ"ר. וְלַיְלָה לְלַיְלָה בְּרָזָא דִּדְכוּרָא, דְּקָא נָהִיר לָהּ דְּאִיהוּ שָׁמַיִם, דַּעַת.

**195.** "Knowledge" IN THE PASSAGE: "AND NIGHT TO NIGHT EXPRESSES KNOWLEDGE" is the secret of the heavens, NAMELY ZEIR ANPIN, as the heavens have six sides. Also here, NIGHT PROVIDES TO NIGHT with six ends through the offspring that the night enlivens, WHICH ARE similar TO

THE SIX EXTREMITIES OF ZEIR ANPIN. Therefore, "day to day" is included in the highest level 'Omer', WHICH IS ABA AND IMA AS MENTIONED. "And night to night" IS INCLUDED IN THE HIGHEST LEVEL in the secret of the male that illuminates her; that is, heaven and knowledge, WHICH IS ZEIR ANPIN.

196. וּבְגִין דְּהַאי אָמֵר רָזָא עִלָּאָה אִיהוּ, וְלָא כִּשְׁאָר אֲמִירָן, אַהֲדָר קְרָא עָלֵיהּ וְאָמַר, אֵין אֹמֶר וְאֵין דְּבָרִים, כִּשְׁאָר אֲמִירָן דְּעָלְמָא. אֶלָּא הַאי אָמֵר, רָזָא עִלָּאָה אִיהוּ, בְּדַרְגִּין עִלָּאִין, דְּלֵית תַּמָּן אֲמִירָן וּדְבָרִים, וְלָא אִשְׁתְּמָעוּ, כִּשְׁאָר דַּרְגִּין דְּאִינּוּן רָזָא דִּמְהֵימְנוּתָא, דְּאִינּוּן קָלָא דְּמִשְׁתְּמַע, אֲבָל הָנֵי לָא אִשְׁתְּמָעוּ לְעָלְמִין, וְהַיְינוּ דִּכְתִּיב בְּלִי נִשְׁמַע קוֹלָם.

196. This 'Omer' is a supernal secret, NAMELY ABA AND IMA, and is not like other sayings; therefore, the Torah repeats it and says, "There is no speech nor are there words" (Tehilim 19:4). It is not like the other sayings of the world, but rather 'Omer (Eng. 'speech')' is a supernal secret in the highest levels, where there are no speeches nor words, MEANING THAT CHOCHMAH IS CONCEALED IN THEM AND DOES NOT SHINE BECAUSE THE ILLUMINATION OF CHOCHMAH IS CALLED 'SPEECH'. They are not heard like the other levels, which are in the secret of Faith THAT IS MALCHUT, which are an audible voice, MEANING THAT CHOCHMAH IS REVEALED IN HER. But 'OMER', WHICH IS ABA AND IMA, is never heard. This is what is meant by: "Their voice is not heard" (Ibid.), WHICH MEANING IS THAT THE CHOCHMAH IS CONCEALED IN THEM AND IS NOT HEARD, BECAUSE CHOCHMAH IS REVEALED ONLY IN MALCHUT ALONE.

197. אֲבָל בְּכָל הָאָרֶץ יָצָא קַוָּם, אע"ג דְּאִינּוּן טְמִירִין עִלָּאִין, דְּלָא אִתְיְידְעוּ לְעָלְמִין, נְגִידוּ וּמְשִׁיכוּ דִּלְהוֹן, אִתְמְשַׁךְ וְאִתְנְגִיד לְתַתָּא. וּבְגִין הַהוּא מְשִׁיכוּ, אִית לָן מְהֵימְנוּתָא שְׁלֵימָתָא, בְּהַאי עָלְמָא, וְכָל בְּנֵי עָלְמָא מִשְׁתָּעוּ רָזָא דִּמְהֵימְנוּתָא דְּקוּדְשָׁא בְּרִיךְ הוּא, בְּאִינּוּן דַּרְגִּין, כְּאִילּוּ אִתְגַּלְּיָין, וְלָא הֲווֹ טְמִירִין וּגְנִיזִין, וְהַיְינוּ וּבִקְצֵה תֵבֵל מִלֵּיהֶם, מֵרֵישָׁא דְּעָלְמָא, עַד סַיְיפֵי עָלְמָא מִשְׁתָּעָאן אִינּוּן חַכִּימֵי לִבָּא, בְּאִינּוּן דַּרְגִּין גְּנִיזִין, אע"ג דְּלָא אִתְיְידְעוּ.

197. "Their line is gone out through all the earth" (Ibid. 5): Even though they, ABA AND IMA are supernal and concealed, and are never known, MEANING THAT CHOCHMAH DOES NOT BECOME REVEALED IN THEM, STILL IN ALL, their flow and drawing is drawn and flows downward TO MALCHUT THAT IS CALLED 'EARTH', MEANING THAT THE CHOCHMAH THAT IS CONCEALED IN THEM IS DRAWN TO MALCHUT. We have complete Faith in this world, NAMELY MALCHUT WITH THE ILLUMINATION OF CHOCHMAH THAT IS CALLED 'COMPLETE FAITH' because of this drawing. All the people of the world speak of the secret of the Faith of the Holy One, blessed be He, WHICH IS MALCHUT, of these levels, NAMELY IN CHOCHMAH OF THE LEVELS ABA AND IMA, as if they were revealed EVEN ABOVE IN ABA AND IMA, instead of hidden and concealed there, hence: "And their words to the end of the world" (Ibid.). From the beginning of the world until the end of the world, the scholars discuss these concealed levels, even though they are not known IN THEIR PLACE IN ABA AND IMA, SINCE THEY ARE REVEALED IN MALCHUT, AS EXPLAINED.

198. אֲבָל בְּמָה אִשְׁתְּמוֹדְעָן, בְּגִין דְּלַשֶּׁמֶשׁ שָׂם אֹהֶל בָּהֶם, בְּגִין שִׁמְשָׁא קַדִּישָׁא, דְּאִיהוּ מַשְׁכְּנָא מֵאִינוּן דַּרְגִּין עִלָּאִין קַדִּישִׁין, וְאִיהוּ נְהוֹרָא, דְּנָטִיל כָּל נְהוֹרִין גְּנִיזִין, וְהַהוּא מְשִׁיכוּ דִּלְהוֹן, וּבְגִינֵיהּ אִתְחֲזֵי מְהֵימְנוּתָא בְּכָל עָלְמָא.

198. But in what are they known, THOSE LEVELS OF CHOCHMAH THAT ARE IN ABA AND IMA? "In them He has set a tent for the sun" (Ibid.), because the holy sun, WHICH IS ZEIR ANPIN, is the abode to these supernal holy levels OF ABA AND IMA. It is light that takes all the concealed lights. That drawing is theirs and the Faith is revealed to the whole world due to it. ZEIR ANPIN IS THE ABODE OF CHOCHMAH IN LEVELS OF ABA AND IMA, AND ZEIR ANPIN PROVIDES IT TO MALCHUT THAT IS CALLED 'FAITH', SO THAT THE FAITH IS SEEN THROUGHOUT THE WHOLE WORLD BECAUSE CHOCHMAH IS CALLED 'SIGHT'.

199. מַאן דְּנָטִיל לְשִׁמְשָׁא, כְּמַאן דְּנָטִיל לְכֻלְּהוּ דַּרְגִּין. בְּגִין דְּשִׁמְשָׁא אִיהוּ אֹהֶל דְּאִתְכְּלִיל בְּהוֹן, וְנָטִיל כֹּלָּא, וְאִיהוּ נָהִיר לְכָל אִינוּן גְּווֹנֵי נְהוֹרִין לְתַתָּא. וְעַל דָּא וְהוּא כְּחָתָן יוֹצֵא מֵחֻפָּתוֹ, בִּנְהִירוּ וּנְצִיצוּ דְּכָל נְהוֹרִין גְּנִיזִין, דְּכֻלְּהוּ בְּתִיאוּבְתָּא בִּרְעוּתָא שְׁלִים, יָהֲבֵי לֵיהּ רְעוּתַיְיהוּ

וּנְהִירוּ דִּלְהוֹן, כְּמָה דִּלְחָתָן אִית רְעוּ וְתִיאוּבְתָּא דְּכַלָּה לְמֵיהַב לָהּ נִבְזְבְּזָן וּמַתְּנָן. וְעַל דָּא וְהוּא כְּחָתָן יוֹצֵא מֵחֻפָּתוֹ.

**199.** He who receives the sun is like one who has received all the levels, because the sun is like a tent, in which the levels are included in it. It receives everything and illuminates to all the kinds of lights below, TO MALCHUT. Therefore, he is "like a bridegroom coming out of his canopy" (Ibid. 6) with the shines and glitterings of all the concealed lights FROM ALL THE LEVELS. For they all give him their desire and their lights with complete pleasure and will, just as a groom has desire and pleasure to give his bride gifts and presents. Therefore, he is "like a bridegroom coming out of his canopy."

200. מַאן חֻפָּתוֹ. דָּא עֵדֶן. וְרָזָא דָּא, וְנָהָר יוֹצֵא מֵעֵדֶן. עֵדֶן, דָּא אִיהוּ חוּפָּא דְּחַפְיָא עַל כֹּלָּא. יָשִׂישׂ כַּגִּבּוֹר. יָשִׂישׂ, מִסִּטְרָא דְּאוֹר קַדְמָאָה דְּלָא אִשְׁתְּכַח בֵּיהּ דִּינָא כְּלָל. כְּגִבּוֹר, מִסִּטְרָא דִּגְבוּרָה, וְאע״ג דִּגְבוּרָה אִיהִי דִּינָא שְׁלִים, כְּגִבּוֹר כְּתִיב, וְלָא גִּבּוֹר, בְּגִין דְּאַמְתִּיק דִּינָא בְּחֶסֶד, וְנָטִיל כֹּלָּא כַּחֲדָא, בְּתִיאוּבְתָּא וּרְעוּתָא שְׁלִים. וְכָל דָּא, לָרוּץ אֹרַח. כד״א הַנּוֹתֵן בַּיָּם דָּרֶךְ לְאַשְׁקָאָה וּלְאַשְׁלָמָא נְהִירוּ דְּסִיהֲרָא בְּכָל סִטְרִין, וּלְמִפְתַּח בָּהּ אֹרַח לְאַנְהָרָא לְתַתָּא.

**200.** HE QUESTIONS: What is "His canopy"? HE SAYS: This is Eden, WHICH IS CHOCHMAH, and this is the secret of: "And a river went out of Eden" (Beresheet 2:10). Eden is a canopy that covers all, MEANING THAT IT COVERS AND SHIELDS FROM ALL KLIPOT "and rejoices like a strong man to run a race" (Tehilim 19:6). "Rejoices" comes from the side of primordial light THAT SERVED DURING THE SIX DAYS OF CREATION BEFORE IT WAS CONCEALED, in which there is no Judgment at all. "Like a strong man" is from the side of Gvurah, and although Gvurah (Might) is wholly Judgment, it is written: "Like a strong (mighty) man" instead of 'a strong man.' This is because he has sweetened the Judgment in Chesed and has taken everything together, BOTH CHOCHMAH AND CHESED, with complete desire and pleasure. And all this IS "to run a race (lit. 'way')" as it is written: "Who makes a way in the sea" (Yeshayah 43:16). HE MAKES A WAY IN MALCHUT THAT IS CALLED 'SEA', in order to water and fill the shine of the moon,

WHICH IS MALCHUT in all the sides, NAMELY ON THE RIGHT AND ON THE LEFT, and to open in it "a way" to illuminate below.

201. מִקְצֵה הַשָּׁמַיִם מוֹצָאוֹ, מִסַּיְיפֵי אִלֵּין שָׁמַיִם עִלָּאִין דְּקָאֲמָרָן, אִיהוּ אַפִּיק, בְּגִין דִּבְסִיּוּמָא דְּגוּפָא, אִיהוּ אַפִּיק, וּבְהַהוּא אֲתָר אִשְׁתְּמוֹדַע בֵּין דְּכַר לְנוּקְבָּא. וְדָא הוּא דִּכְתִּיב, וּלְמִקְצֵה הַשָּׁמַיִם וְעַד קְצֵה הַשָּׁמָיִם. קְצֵה הַשָּׁמַיִם דָּא עָלְמָא עִלָּאָה. וּלְמִקְצֵה הַשָּׁמָיִם, דָּא שְׁלָמָא דִּילֵיהּ. כְּמָה דְּהַאי נָטִיל כָּל נְהוֹרִין, וְכֻלְּהוּ בֵּיהּ, אוּף הָכִי הַאי, נָטִיל כָּל נְהוֹרִין, וְכֻלְּהוּ בֵּיהּ, וְאִיהוּ נָפִיק מִקְצֵה הַשָּׁמַיִם.

**201.** "His going forth is from the end of the heavens…" (Devarim 4:32), MEANING that from the end of these supernal heavens, WHICH IS ZEIR ANPIN, he brings forth THE PROVISION, because at the end of TIFERET THAT IS CALLED 'body', WHICH IS YESOD He brings forth HIS PROVISION, as at that place there is a difference between male and female. This is what is written: "And from the end of the heavens to the end of the heavens" (Devarim 4:32). "The end of the heavens" is the upper world, NAMELY ZEIR ANPIN THAT IS CALLED 'HEAVENS'. "To the end of the heavens" is His peace, WHICH IS YESOD. Just as this one, ZEIR ANPIN, receives all the lights and they are all in Him, so does that one, YESOD, take all the lights and they are all in it. It goes forth from the end of the heavens.

202. וּתְקוּפָתוֹ: דְּסָחֲרָא בְּכָל אִינּוּן סִטְרִין קַדִּישִׁין, דְּאִתְחֲזוּן לְאִתְנַהֲרָא וּלְאִתְשַׁקְאָה וּלְנַצְצָא מִנֵּיהּ. וְאֵין נִסְתָּר, לֵית מַאן דְּאִתְחַפְיָא מֵהַהוּא נְהִירוּ, דְּהָא לְכֻלְּהוּ אַנְהִיר בִּכְלָלָא חֲדָא, לְכָל חַד וְחַד כְּמָה דְּאִתְחֲזֵי לֵיהּ.

**202.** "And His circuit" (Tehilim 19:7) MEANS that He encircles all the holy sides that are worthy of being illuminated and worthy to be watered and to glitter from Him. "And there is nothing hid" (Ibid.) MEANS there is none that can be covered from this light, because it lights under one principle to each and every one as is fitting for it.

203. וְכַד כֻּלְּהוּ אִשְׁתְּלִימוּ וְאִתְנְהִירוּ מִגּוֹ שִׁמְשָׁא, כְּדֵין סִיהֲרָא מִתְעַטְּרָא בִּגְוָונָא דְּאִימָּא עִלָּאָה, שְׁלִימָא בְּנִי תַּרְעִין, וְדָא אִיהוּ דִּכְתִּיב

תּוֹרַת יְיָ' תְּמִימָה, דְּהָא כְּדֵין אִיהִי תְּמִימָה, מִכָּל סִטְרִין, בְּרָזָא דַּחֲמֵשׁ
דַּרְגִּין, כְּגַוְונָא דְּאִימָא עִלָּאָה, דְּאִינוּן חָמֵשׁ רָזָא דְּחַמְשִׁין.

**203.** When they are perfected and illuminating from the sun, the moon, WHICH IS MALCHUT, becomes adorned like the supernal Ima, and becomes completed in fifty gates LIKE HER. This is the meaning of the verse: "The Torah of Hashem is perfect" (Ibid. 8), for it is now perfect from all the sides in the secret of the five levels, CHESED, GVURAH, TIFERET, NETZACH, AND HOD, like supernal Ima. These five are the secret of the fifty GATES OF BINAH, BECAUSE EACH ONE IS COMPOSED OF TEN.

**204.** וּבְגִינֵי כָּךְ, אִיהִי אַתְיָא בַּחֲמֵשׁ חֲמֵשׁ תֵּיבִין, בְּגִין לְאַשְׁלְמָא לְרָזָא
דְּחַמְשִׁין. תּוֹרַת יְיָ' תְּמִימָה מְשִׁיבַת נָפֶשׁ, הָא חֲמֵשׁ. עֵדוּת יְיָ' נָאֱמָנָה
מַחְכִּימַת פֶּתִי, הָא חֲמֵשׁ. פִּקּוּדֵי יְיָ' יְשָׁרִים מְשַׂמְּחֵי לֵב, הָא חֲמֵשׁ.
מִצְוַת יְיָ' בָּרָה מְאִירַת עֵינַיִם, הָא חֲמֵשׁ. יִרְאַת יְיָ' טְהוֹרָה עוֹמֶדֶת לָעַד,
הָא חֲמֵשׁ. מִשְׁפְּטֵי יְיָ' אֱמֶת צָדְקוּ יַחְדָּו, הָא חֲמֵשׁ. וְכֻלְּהוּ אַתְיָין
בַּחֲמֵשׁ חֲמֵשׁ, לְאִתְכַּלְּלָא כְּגַוְונָא דְּאִימָא עִלָּאָה.

**204.** Therefore, it is composed of PHRASES CONTAINING five words each, in order to complete the secret of fifty. "The Torah of Hashem is perfect, restoring the soul" (Ibid.): Here are five. "The testimony of Hashem is sure, making wise the simple" (Ibid.): Here are five. "The statutes of Hashem are right, rejoicing the heart" (Ibid.): Here are five. "The commandment of Hashem is pure, enlightening the eyes" (Ibid. 9): Here are five. "The fear of Hashem is clean, enduring forever" (Ibid. 10): Here are five. "The Judgments of Hashem are true, and are righteous altogether" (Ibid.): Here are five. FOR ALL THESE NAMES, THE TORAH, testimony, STATUTES ...ARE THE NAMES OF MALCHUT. They all come in multiples of five, in order to be included IN FIFTY just like supernal Ima.

**205.** וְעַל דָּא, יְהֹוָ"ה יְהֹוָ"ה שִׁית זִמְנִין, לָקֳבֵל שִׁית סִטְרִין עִלָּאִין,
דְּאִינוּן רָזָא דִּשְׁמָא עִלָּאָה, וְעַל דָּא, סִיהֲרָא אִתְמַלְּיָא וְאִשְׁתְּלִים
בְּסִדּוּרָא עִלָּאָה כְּדְקָא יֵאוֹת, וְדָא אִיהוּ בְּיוֹמָא דְּשַׁבַּתָּא, דְּכֹלָּא
אִשְׁתְּלִים כְּדְקָא יֵאוֹת, בְּרָזָא דְּשַׁבַּתָּא עֵילָא וְתַתָּא.

**205.** Therefore, IN THE PASSAGES, Yud Hei Vav Hei IS WRITTEN six times, for they correspond to the six supernal extremities, which are the secret of the supernal Name, WHICH IS ZEIR ANPIN. The moon becomes full from them, WHICH IS MALCHUT, and becomes perfected in the supernal order properly. This occurs during the Shabbat Day, when everything is properly completed in the secret of Shabbat above, IN ZEIR ANPIN, and below, IN MALCHUT.

206. וְע"ד בְּיוֹמָא דָא, אִתּוֹסָף נְהִירוּ בְּכֹלָּא, כִּדְקָאמְרָן. שָׁמַיִם נַטְלֵי מִמְּקוֹרָא דְּחַיֵּי בְּקַדְמֵיתָא, וְאִינּוּן מְנַהֲרֵי וּמְתַקְּנֵי לִכְבוֹד עִלָּאָה, מֵרָזָא דְּסֵפֶר עִלָּאָה, אַבָּא דְּכֹלָּא. וּמֵרָזָא דְּסֵפֶר, אִימָּא עִלָּאָה. וְאִיהוּ, מֵרָזָא דְּסִפּוּר. וּבְגִין כַּךְ, מְסַפְּרִים, כִּדְקָאמְרָן. בְּרָזָא דִּתְלַת שְׁמָהָן אִלֵּין, דְּשַׁלְטִין בְּיוֹמָא דְּשַׁבַּתָּא, עַל כָּל שְׁאַר יוֹמִין.

**206.** On this day, light is increased in everything, as we have said. The heavens, WHICH IS ZEIR ANPIN, first receive from the source of life, WHICH IS ABA AND IMA. They, THE HEAVENS, illuminate and construct the supernal glory, WHICH IS MALCHUT, from the secret of the supernal Book, which is Aba of them all and from the secret of the Book WHICH IS supernal Ima. And He, NAMELY ZEIR ANPIN THAT IS CALLED 'HEAVENS', is derived from the secret of the tale. Therefore, IT IS WRITTEN: "Declare (also: 'tell')," as we have said. It is in the secret of the three names, NAMELY, BOOK (HEB. SEFER), SCRIBE (HEB. SOFER), TALE (HEB. SIPUR), NAMELY ABA, IMA, AND ZEIR ANPIN, who dominate on the Shabbat Day over all the other days.

207. וּבְגִינֵי כַּךְ תּוּשְׁבַּחְתָּא דָא, קָאָמַר דָּוִד בְּרוּחַ קֻדְשָׁא, עַל נְהִירוּ וּנְצִיצוּ וְשׁוּלְטָנוּ דְּיוֹמָא דְּשַׁבַּתָּא עַל כָּל שְׁאַר יוֹמִין בְּגִין רָזָא דִּשְׁמָא עִלָּאָה, דְּקָא נָהִיר בִּנְהִירוּ, וְנָצִיץ בִּנְצִיצוּ, וְאִשְׁתְּלִים בִּשְׁלִימוּ עֵילָא וְתַתָּא. וּכְדֵין תּוֹרַת יְיָ' תְּמִימָה, שַׁבָּת דְּמַעֲלֵי שַׁבַּתָּא, בְּרָזָא חֲדָא כִּדְקָאמְרָן.

**207.** Therefore, David recited this praise: "THE HEAVENS DECLARE" inspired by the Holy Spirit, about the shine and sparkle and domination of the Shabbat Day over all the other days. Because the secret of the supernal

Name, ZEIR ANPIN, illuminates with light and sparkles with sparkles and becomes complete above and below. Then "the Torah of Hashem is perfect," which is the Shabbat of Shabbat Eve, NAMELY MALCHUT, which is of the same secret WITH ZEIR ANPIN, as we have said.

## 17. "Rejoice in Hashem, you righteous"

### A Synopsis

The scholars decreed that praises on Shabbat should start with the psalms of David, which rise to illuminate and bless the heavens and the river that comes out of Eden. All is performed as it should be performed, though, and on this day even the sun illuminates properly.

### The Relevance of this Passage

David signifies our physical existence. He is Malchut. Thus, David's psalms elevate our lower world (Malchut) into the heavens (Zeir Anpin) when they are recited at the commencement of each new Shabbat. For us, our own souls – and all existence – are now elevated by the sacred texts that speak these hidden truths.

208. וְאַתְקִינוּ חַבְרַיָּיא שֵׁירוּתָא דְּתוּשְׁבַּחְתֵּי, מֵאִינוּן תּוּשְׁבְּחָתָן דְּדָוִד, מֵרָזָא דָּא הַשָּׁמַיִם, דְּאִיהוּ נָטִיל בְּרֵישָׁא, וְנָהִיר לְכָל שְׁאָר. וּלְבָתַר הַהוּא נָהָר דְּנָפִיק מֵעֵדֶן, וְדָא אִיהוּ רָזָא, רַנְּנוּ צַדִּיקִים בַּיְיָ׳ בְּגִין דְּהַאי נָהָר כָּנִישׁ וְנָטִיל כֹּלָּא מֵרָזָא דִּשְׁמַיִם, בְּרָזָא עִלָּאָה, וּמְקוֹרָא דְּחַיֵּי, כֹּלָּא כַּדְקָא יֵאוֹת בְּיוֹמָא דָא. וְשִׁמְשָׁא אַתְקִין לְאַנְהֲרָא כַּדְקָא יֵאוֹת, בְּיוֹמָא דָא.

208. And the friends decreed that the praises start with the praises of David, with this secret OF THE PRAISE "THE HEAVENS DECLARE..." The heaven, WHICH IS ZEIR ANPIN, takes first and illuminates all the rest. Afterwards the river that comes out of Eden, WHICH IS YESOD, TAKES and this is the secret of: "Rejoice in Hashem, you righteous" (Tehilim 33:1), FOR THIS PRAISE IS THE ASPECT OF YESOD. This river gathers and takes everything from the secret of the heavens, WHICH IS ZEIR ANPIN, in the supernal secret, WHICH IS CHASSADIM, and the source of life, WHICH IS THE ILLUMINATION OF CHOCHMAH, and all as is proper on this day. The sun, WHICH IS ZEIR ANPIN, perfects YESOD to illuminate properly on this day.

## 18. "Of David, when he changed his demeanor"

### A Synopsis

This verse explains that the phrase refers to the moon, that is separated on this day from the Other Side, and joins with the sun. It contains the 22 letters that the sun brings into the moon.

### The Relevance of this Passage

The 22 letters of the Hebrew alphabet signify 22 primeval forces of energy that combined together in countless configurations to conceive all Creation. They are the instruments of the Divine, tools to fashion supernal and mundane worlds, along with the diversity of life forms that inhabit them. Accordingly, this passage offers us nothing less than the Light of Creation. This illumination separates our souls from the Other Side, our Evil Inclination. Our prayers are strengthened, our spirit is renewed, and our existence is brightened so that darkness, never again, dominates our world and our souls.

209. וּלְבָתַר סִיהֲרָא דְקָא מִתְפָּרְשַׁת מִסִּטְרָא אַחֲרָא בְּיוֹמָא דָא, בְּגִין לְאִתְנְהָרָא מִן שִׁמְשָׁא, וְדָא אִיהוּ לְדָוִד בְּשַׁנּוֹתוֹ אֶת טַעֲמוֹ וְגוֹ'. וּלְבָתַר דְּאִתְפָּרְשַׁת מִנֵּיה, הָא אִתְחַבְּרַת בְּשִׁמְשָׁא. וְתוּשְׁבַּחְתָּא דָא בְּכ"ב אַתְוָון, דְּאָעִיל בָּה שִׁמְשָׁא בְּסִיהֲרָא. וְתוּשְׁבַּחְתָּא דָא, פְּרִישׁוּ דְּסִיהֲרָא מִסִּטְרָא אַחֲרָא, וְתוּשְׁבַּחְתָּא דְּכ"ב אַתְוָון בִּנְהִירוּ דְּשִׁמְשָׁא.

**209.** Afterwards, ONE SHOULD SAY THE PRAISE, WHICH IS THE SECRET OF the moon, WHICH IS MALCHUT, that is separated from the Other Side on this day, in order to shine from the sun. It is written: "Of David, when he changed his demeanor..." (Tehilim 34:1). After it was separated from the Other Side, it joined with the sun, WHICH IS ZEIR ANPIN. This praise is in THE ORDER OF the 22 letters AT THE BEGINNINGS OF THE VERSES, that the sun brings them into the moon. This praise also CONTAINS the separation of the moon from the Other Side, and the praise of the 22 letters that the sun brings into the moon.

19. "A prayer of Moses"

### A Synopsis

When we read "A prayer of Moses, the man of the Elohim," we are to understand that this refers to the union of Malchut and Zeir Anpin, the Lower realm with the Upper. In that joining of a wife to her husband there is the spreading of the right and left hands, Chesed and Gvurah, to receive her. Here we can understand how the union of the lower world and the upper world is mirrored in the union of husband and wife, and of how Mercy and Gvurah work together to form powerful unions of all kinds.

### The Relevance of this Passage

Our own relationships are enriched and imbued with tremendous blessing as the Zohar reveals the mysteries concerning the union of the upper and lower worlds. Any time this unification is achieved, darkness is expelled from our personal existence. Our connection to Moses and the wisdom of Torah is made complete. Our intimate relations now engender unification of the upper and lower world, culminating in the full radiance of the Light of the Creator. All of this is achieved by virtue of Moses and our visual embrace of the verses that speak his name.

210. וּלְבָתַר אִתְחַבְּרוּתָא וּסְלִיקוּ דְּמַטְרוֹנִיתָא עִם בַּעְלָה. וְדָא אִיהוּ תְּפִלָּה לְמֹשֶׁה אִישׁ הָאֱלֹהִים. אִתְחַבְּרוּתָא וְאִתְדַּבְּקוּתָא דְּאִתְּתָא בְּבַעְלָה, לְפָרְשָׂא יְמִינָא וּשְׂמָאלָא לְקַבְּלָא לָה, וּלְמֶהֱוֵי כַּחֲדָא בְּחִבּוּרָא חֲדָא.

210. Afterwards the Queen elevates and joins with Her husband, ZEIR ANPIN, and it is written: "A prayer of Moses, the man of Elohim" (Tehilim 90:1), BECAUSE PRAYER IS MALCHUT AND MOSES IS THE SECRET OF ZEIR ANPIN. FOR THIS SHOWS the joining and cleaving of the wife to her husband, WHICH IS "A PRAYER OF MOSES," and the spreading of the right and left hands, CHESED AND GVURAH to receive her and to be together in one bond.

## 20. "Sing to Hashem a new song"

### A Synopsis
"Sing to The Creator a new song; for He has done marvelous things."
It is said that the milk cows transporting the ark rose to recite this
praise. And in the higher realm the living creatures that carry the
throne to raise it above also recite this praise. We read that it is called
a 'new' song for each renewal of the new moon when it illuminates
from the sun. They praised Him with this praise when they carried the
ark and were going up to Bet Shemesh, the sun, and the elevation of
the throne to ascend above is on Shabbat.

### The Relevance of this Passage
Here we understand that the power of the Ark and the effulgent Light
that it emits has imbued senseless creatures, milk cows, with the
ability to rise above their inborn nature and sing praise to the Creator.
Clearly all possibilities exist within the infinite realm of the Light. As
such, this wisdom uplifts us above our own base nature so that we
now recognize and embody the Divinity imbued into this seemingly
chaotic world.

211. וְדָא אִיהוּ מִזְמוֹר שִׁירוּ לַיְיָ' שִׁיר חָדָשׁ. תּוּשְׁבַּחְתָּא דָּא הָא
אוֹקִימְנָא. אֲבָל אע"ג דְּאִתְּעַרְנָא בֵּיהּ, אִתְּעָרוּ דְּחַבְרַיָּיא דְּקָא אִתְּעָרוּ,
שַׁפִּיר אִיהוּ, דְּהַנְהוּ פָּרוֹת עָלוֹת כַּד הֲווֹ נַטְלֵי אֲרוֹנָא, אִתְּעָרוּ בְּהַאי
תּוּשְׁבַּחְתָּא, כד"א וַיִּשַּׁרְנָה הַפָּרוֹת בַּדֶּרֶךְ. וּמַה שִׁירָה הֲווֹ אַמְרֵי. מִזְמוֹר
שִׁירוּ לַיְיָ' שִׁיר חָדָשׁ כִּי נִפְלָאוֹת עָשָׂה. רָזָא דָּא אִיהוּ כְּגַוְונָא דִּלְעֵילָּא.
בְּשַׁעֲתָא דְּאִינּוּן חַיּוֹת נַטְלֵי כֻּרְסְיָיא, לְאַרְמָא לֵיהּ לְעֵילָּא, אִינּוּן אַמְרֵי
תּוּשְׁבַּחְתָּא דָּא.

211. It is written: "A Psalm, Sing to Hashem a new song" (Tehilim 98:1).
We have already established this praise. Although we have observed it, the
observations of the friends who observed about this is THAT THEY SAID that
the cows that were transporting the ark rose to recite this praise, as it is
written: "And the cows took the straight (also: 'sang') way" (I Shmuel
6:12). What was the song that they were reciting? It was: "Sing to Hashem a
new song; for He has done marvelous things." This secret is similar to
above for at the time the living creatures carry the throne, WHICH IS
MALCHUT to raise it above, TO ZEIR ANPIN they recite this praise.

212. וְאִי תֵּימָא, אֲמַאי כְּתִיב הָכָא חָדָשׁ, וְהָא תָּדִיר קָאמְרֵי תּוּשְׁבַּחְתָּא דָא. אֶלָּא וַדַּאי חָדָשׁ אִיהוּ, וְחָדָשׁ לָא אִקְרֵי, אֶלָּא בְּאִתְחַדְּתוּתָא דְּסִיהֲרָא, כַּד אִתְנְהִירַת מִן שִׁמְשָׁא, כְּדֵין אִיהוּ חָדָשׁ, וְדָא אִיהוּ שִׁיר חָדָשׁ. הוֹשִׁיעָה לּוֹ יְמִינוֹ וּזְרוֹעַ קָדְשׁוֹ, הָא אִתְעָרוּתָא דִּימִינָא וּשְׂמָאלָא לְקַבְּלָא לָהּ.

212. If you ask: Why is it written here "new", FOR IT IS WRITTEN "A NEW SONG"? Are they not constantly saying this praise? HE ANSWERS: Certainly it is new, for it is called 'new' only with the renewal of the moon, WHICH IS MALCHUT, when it illuminates from the sun, WHICH IS ZEIR ANPIN. Then it is new, and this is "a new song," FOR EACH TIME MALCHUT ASCENDS TO PAIR WITH ZEIR ANPIN, SHE IS TRANSFORMED TO BECOME NEW, IN ACCORDANCE WITH THE SECRET, THAT EVERY TIME SHE REVERTS TO BEING A VIRGIN. "His right hand, and His holy arm have gained Him the victory" (Tehilim 98:1): This is the arousal of right and left, WHICH ARE CHESED AND GVURAH, to receive Her.

213. וְתוּשְׁבַּחְתָּא דָא, כַּד נַטְלֵי אֲרוֹנָא, קָא מְשַׁבְּחָאן לָהּ. כַּד סַלְקִין לְבֵית שֶׁמֶשׁ. כְּגַוְונָא דַּעֲגָלוֹת סַלְקִין לְבֵית שֶׁמֶשׁ. וְכֹלָּא בְּרָזָא חַד סַלְקִין, בְּגִין דִּבְשַׁבָּת אִיהוּ סְלִיקוּ דְכוּרְסְיָיא, לְסַלְקָא לְעֵילָא. תִּקּוּנָא דְּתוּשְׁבַּחְתָּא דָא בְּשַׁבָּת אִלֵּין תּוּשְׁבְּחָן כֻּלְּהוּ אַתְקִינוּ בְּשַׁבָּת, לְשַׁבְּחָא לֵיהּ עַמָּא יְחִידָא בְּעָלְמָא.

213. They did praise Him with this praise when they carried the ark and were going up to Bet Shemesh, like the wagons (also: 'heifers'), WHICH IS THE SECRET OF THE LIVING CREATURES. They went up to Bet Shemesh, WHICH IS THE SECRET OF ZEIR ANPIN THAT IS CALLED 'SHEMESH (ENG. 'SUN')', and it all amounts to the same, for the elevation of the Throne, WHICH IS MALCHUT, to ascend above occurs on Shabbat. THEREFORE, the order of this praise is on the Shabbat. All these praises were composed for Shabbat, for the unique nation of the world to praise Him.

## 21. "A Psalm, a song for the Shabbat day"

### A Synopsis

We learn that, like the candle which cannot be seen in the daylight, the lower world cannot approach the light of the upper world. The Shabbat day is the upper world and the Shabbat Eve is the lower world. "A Psalm, a song for the Shabbat day," was the praise said by Adam at the time he was expelled from the Garden of Eden, and the Shabbat came and shielded him. We read that all the praises of Shabbat, which is the glory of the day, are higher than on all the other days.

### The Relevance of this Passage

Adam (we, the Vessel) had a burning desire to be the cause of his (our) own fulfillment, the creator of his own Light. But as candlelight cannot be seen in the presence of the sun, Adam (we) left the luminous perfection of the Garden to enter our disordered dimension of darkness, Malchut, where the Light is concealed. Man, through his own labor and effort, can rekindle the Light, and thus shares in the divine act of Creation: He becomes God(like)! Keeping the Sabbath, learning Torah, and igniting the Light of the Zohar are the fundamental ways in which we achieve this purpose. Thus, our life's work is being accomplished and completed as we read these words. Our efforts here provide the finishing touches to the spiritual evolution and final ascent of man. Therein lies the ultimate power of the Zohar.

214. מִזְמוֹר שִׁיר לְיוֹם הַשַּׁבָּת, תּוּשְׁבַּחְתָּא דָּא, אָדָם הָרִאשׁוֹן קָאֲמַר לָהּ, בְּשַׁעֲתָא דְּאִתְתְּרַךְ מִגִּנְתָא דְּעֵדֶן, וְאָתָא שַׁבָּת וְאַגִּין עֲלֵיהּ. וְאוּקְמוּהָ חַבְרַיָּיא, תּוּשְׁבַּחְתָּא דָּא, עָלְמָא תַּתָּאָה קָא מְשַׁבַּח לְגַבֵּי עָלְמָא עִלָּאָה, יוֹמָא דְּאִיהוּ כּוּלּוֹ שַׁבָּת, מַלְכָּא, דִּשְׁלָמָא דִּילֵיהּ. וְדָא אִיהוּ מִזְמוֹר שִׁיר, וְלָא כְּתִיב מַאן קָאֲמַר לֵיהּ, כְּמָה דְּאוֹקִימְנָא.

214. "A Psalm, a song for the Shabbat day" (Tehilim 92:1): This praise was said by Adam at the time he was expelled from the Garden of Eden, and the Shabbat came and protected him. The friends have established this already. This is the praise that the lower world, WHICH IS MALCHUT, says to the upper world, which is a day that is wholly Shabbat, which is the King that the Peace is His, NAMELY ZEIR ANPIN. This is: "A Psalm, a song...," but the utterer is not mentioned BECAUSE IT ALLUDES TO MALCHUT, FOR EVERY PLACE WHERE IT IS UNSPECIFIED IT ALLUDES TO MALCHUT, AS WRITTEN ABOVE.

215. לְיוֹם הַשַּׁבָּת, יוֹמָא עִלָּאָה, שַׁבָּת עִלָּאָה. דָּא שַׁבָּת וְדָא שַׁבָּת, מַה בֵּין הַאי לְהַאי. אֶלָּא, שַׁבָּת סְתָם, דָּא שַׁבָּת דְּמַעֲלֵי שַׁבַּתָּא. יוֹם הַשַּׁבָּת, דָּא שַׁבָּת דִּלְעֵילָּא. דָּא יוֹם, וְדָא לַיְלָה. וְשָׁמְרוּ בְּנֵי יִשְׂרָאֵל אֶת הַשַּׁבָּת, הָא לֵילְיָא, רָזָא דְּנוּקְבָּא. זָכוֹר אֶת יוֹם הַשַּׁבָּת, הָא יוֹם, רָזָא דִּדְכוּרָא. וּבְגִין כָּךְ מִזְמוֹר שִׁיר לְיוֹם הַשַּׁבָּת.

215. "For the Shabbat day": NAMELY the supernal Day, the supernal Shabbat, WHICH IS ZEIR ANPIN. The one is Shabbat and the other is Shabbat, so what is the difference between the one and the other? HE ANSWERS: unspecified Shabbat is the Shabbat of Shabbat Eve, NAMELY MALCHUT. Shabbat day is the supernal Shabbat, NAMELY ZEIR ANPIN. The one is day, ZEIR ANPIN, and the other is night, MALCHUT: "Wherefore the children of Yisrael shall keep the Shabbat" (Shemot 31:16) refers to night, the secret of the female. "Remember the Shabbat day" (Shemot 20:8) refers to day, the secret of the male, NAMELY ZEIR ANPIN. Therefore, IT IS SAID: "A psalm, a song for the Shabbat day," FOR MALCHUT PRAISES ZEIR ANPIN THAT IS CALLED 'THE SHABBAT DAY'.

216. וְאַשְׁכְּחָן בְּכַמָּה אֲתָר, דְּעָלְמָא תַּתָּאָה לָא סָלִיק בִּשְׁמָא, וְאַתְיָא סְתָם, כְּגוֹן הַאי, וּכְגוֹן וַיִּקְרָא אֶל מֹשֶׁה, וּכְגוֹן וְאֶל מֹשֶׁה אָמַר עֲלֵה אֶל יְיָ'. כֻּלְּהוּ סָתִים שְׁמָא, וְלָא סָלִיק בֵּיהּ. בְּגִין דְּאִית בֵּיהּ דַּרְגָּא עִלָּאָה, וּלְגַבֵּי דַּרְגָּא עִלָּאָה אִיהוּ לָא סָלִיק בִּשְׁמָא. נְהוֹרָא דִּשְׁרָגָּא, לָא סָלִיק בִּימָמָא, בִּנְהוֹרָא דְּשִׁמְשָׁא, וְעַ"ד לָא סָלִיק בִּשְׁמָא. וְכָל אִלֵּין תּוּשְׁבְּחָן, דְּשַׁבָּת, דְּאִיהִי כְּבוֹד יוֹם, אִיהוּ תּוּשְׁבַּחְתָּא עִלָּאָה, עַל כָּל שְׁאָר יוֹמִין.

216. We have found in many places that the lower world, WHICH IS MALCHUT, is not mentioned by name, and is unspecified WITHOUT A NAME, such as: "A PSALM, A SONG FOR THE SHABBAT DAY," IN WHICH THE NAME OF THE AUTHOR IS NOT MENTIONED. For example: "And...called to Moses" (Vayikra 1:1) as well as: "And He said to Moses, 'Come up to Hashem'" (Shemot 24:1). In all of these, the name is concealed and is not mentioned, because there is a supernal level contained in it, NAMELY ZEIR ANPIN, and She is not mentioned by name near the supernal level. The light of a candle is not noticed during the day in the sunlight. Therefore, She is not mentioned by name. All the praises of Shabbat, which is the glory of the day, are higher than on all the other days.

## 22. "The soul of every living being"

### A Synopsis
We read how the soul flies from the life of the worlds, the Yesod of Zeir Anpin, and is blessed by Him as it emerges and flies downwards. And the soul has permission to bless Malchut. The souls fly downwards and bless Malchut at the commencement of Shabbat. We learn that Malchut receives blessings during the weekdays from the other souls that bless Her from below. During the Shabbat Day, She receives blessings from the upper souls that bless Her with 45 words. All this praise and all these words are known limbs that add up to the proper completion of the Shabbat.

### The Relevance of this Passage
All the blessings (spiritual energy) of the weekday and the Sabbath fill our souls, completing our connection to the Light of the Creator. In turn, we ignite the merciful arrival of the cosmic Sabbath (the age of Messiah), and a unified humanity embraces the world of immortality and boundless delight.

217. נִשְׁמַת כָּל חַי, הָא חַבְרַיָּיא אִתְּעָרוּ בֵּיה מִלִּין דִּקְשׁוֹט. אֲבָל אִית לָן לְאַדְכְּרָא, הַאי נִשְׁמָתָא דְּפַרְחָא מֵהַהוּא חַי הָעוֹלָמִים. וּבְגִין דְּאִיהִי דִּילֵיה, דְּמִנֵּיה נַפְקָן כָּל בִּרְכָאן, וְשַׁרְיָין בֵּיה, וְהוּא אַשְׁקֵי וּמְבָרֵךְ לְתַתָּא, הַאי נִשְׁמָתָא דְּנָפְקָא מִנֵּיה, אִית לָהּ רְשׁוּ לְבָרְכָא לְהַאי אֲתָר.

**217.** 'The soul of every living being': The friends have said true words about it. We must remember that the soul flies from the life of the worlds, WHICH IS YESOD OF ZEIR ANPIN. Because it is his, all the blessings emanate from him and dwell in him, and he waters and blesses downward, MALCHUT, this soul that emerges from him, and has permission to bless this place, MALCHUT.

218. וְעַל דָּא פַּרְחִין נִשְׁמָתִין מֵהַהוּא חַי', בְּמַעֲלֵי שַׁבַּתָּא. אִינּוּן נִשְׁמָתִין דְּאִינּוּן פַּרְחָאן, מַמָּשׁ מְבָרְכִין לְהַאי אֲתָר דְּאִקְרֵי שֵׁם מִתַּתָּא. וְהַהוּא אֲתָר דְּנַפְקֵי מִנֵּיה מְבָרֵךְ לֵיה לְעֵילָא, וְהַאי שֵׁם מְקַבְּלָא בִּרְכָאן, מִתַּתָּא וּמֵעֵילָא, וְאִתְכְּלִילַת מִכָּל סְטָרִין.

**218.** Therefore, the souls fly from that living, WHICH IS YESOD OF ZEIR ANPIN, at the commencement of Shabbat. These souls that fly actually bless that place that is called 'Name' below, NAMELY MALCHUT, FOR WHICH REASON IT IS SAID: 'THE SOUL OF EVERY LIVING BEING WILL BLESS YOUR NAME,' NAMELY MALCHUT THAT IS CALLED 'NAME'. The place from which THE SOULS emerge, WHICH IS YESOD, blesses MALCHUT from above, so we see that this 'Name' receives blessings from below and from above, and is included from all sides.

219. בְּיוֹמֵי דְחוֹל, אִיהִי מְקַבְּלָא בִּרְכָאן, מִשְׁאָר נִשְׁמָתִין, דְּקָא מְבָרְכִין לָהּ מִתַּתָּא. בְּיוֹמָא דְשַׁבָּת, אִיהִי מְקַבְּלָא בִּרְכָאן מֵאִינוּן נִשְׁמָתִין עִלָּאִין, דְּקָא מְבָרְכָאן לָהּ בְּאַרְבְּעִין וַחֲמֵשׁ תֵּיבִין, כְּחוּשְׁבַּן מ"ה. כְּמָה דְאוֹקִימְנָא, בְּרָזָא מ"ה, וּבְרָזָא מ"י. דָּא עָלְמָא עִלָּאָה, וְדָא עָלְמָא תַּתָּאָה. נִשְׁמַת כָּל חַי עַד הָאַחֲרוֹנִים, מ"ה. וּמִן וְאִילוּ פִּינוּ מָלֵא שִׁירָה עַד וּמִלְפָנִים, סַלְקָא תּוּשְׁבַּחְתָּא אַחֲרָא חַמְשִׁין תֵּיבִין. וְאע"ג דְּלָא קַיְּימָא תַּמָּן מִלָּה בְּחוּשְׁבָּנָא, סַלְקָא חוּשְׁבָּנָא רָזָא מ"י. וּמִתַּמָּן וּלְהָלְאָה סַלְקָא תּוּשְׁבַּחְתָּא אַחֲרָא לְחֶשְׁבּוֹן מְאָה תֵּיבִין, תַּשְׁלוּמִין דְּכֹלָּא, וְחַד רְתִיכָא עַל מַה דְּשַׁרְיָא הַהוּא שְׁלֵימָא עִלָּאָה.

**219.** During the weekdays, MALCHUT receives blessings from the other souls that bless Her from below. During the Shabbat Day, She receives blessings from the upper souls OF ATZILUT that bless Her with 45 words, like the numerical value OF THE NAME of 45, as we have established in the secret of Mah (= 45) and Mi (= 50). For this MI is the upper world, BINAH, and MAH is the lower world, MALCHUT. 'The soul of every living being': Until the last WORD contains 45 WORDS, and from 'Were our mouths as full of song' until THE WORD 'before us' it is a different praise, which is composed of fifty words. This is not a word that indicates calculating, MEANING THAT THERE IS NO END OF SUBJECT TO POINT OUT A SPECIFIC SUM, BECAUSE THE WORD 'BEFORE US' IS IN THE MIDDLE OF SUBJECT. WITH ALL THIS, the sum adds up to the secret of 'Mi,' NAMELY FIFTY WORDS. A different praise starts from that point onward that amounts to the sum of a hundred words, UNTIL 'BY THE MOUTH OF THE UPRIGHT YOU SHALL BE EXALTED,' which is the completion of all, NAMELY THE GREATNESS OF MALCHUT THAT CONTAINS TEN SFIROT WITH EACH ONE

CONTAINING TEN, EQUALING ONE HUNDRED. This is one Chariot, upon which dwells the supernal wholeness, WHICH IS ZEIR ANPIN.

220. וְכָל שְׁבָחָא דָּא, וְכָל מִלִּין אִלֵּין, כֻּלְּהוּ שַׁיְיפִין יְדִיעָן, בְּחוּשְׁבָּנָא לְתַשְׁלוּמָא דְּשַׁבָּת, וּלְאִשְׁתַּלְּמָא מִנַּיְיהוּ, כַּדְקָא חֲזֵי. זַכָּאָה עַמָּא, דְּיַדְעֵי לְסַדְּרָא שְׁבָחָא דְּמָרֵיהוֹן, כַּדְקָא יֵאוֹת. מִכָּאן וּלְהָלְאָה סְדוּרָא דִּצְלוֹתָא כְּמָה דְּאִתְתַּקְּנַת.

220. All this praise and all these words are certain limbs, MEANING GRADES, that add up to the completion of the Shabbat, with which to be completed properly. Happy is the nation that knows how to arrange the praise of its Master properly. From here and further, it is the order of prayer as was arranged.

## 23. "But be not You, Hashem, far from me"

### A Synopsis

We read how when King David was arranging the praise of the King he included "But be not You, The Creator, far from me, my Strength, haste You to help me." This is because when Malchut ascends to become adorned with Zeir Anpin, it is in the upper world and from there it is necessary to elevate it to infinity in order that it should all be bound together high above. During the order of praise, the children of Yisrael do not permit Malchut to ascend from them. We read that the Holy One ascends higher and higher to infinity, but immediately returns to His place because the children of Yisrael below are joined with Him. It is necessary to join with the Holy One and hold onto Him so that no person is forsaken by Him even for one moment. Now Rabbi Elazar says to his father, Rabbi Shimon that they must leave the Garden of Eden and travel in the ways of the guards of the Tree of Life; he asks his father to prepare the way.

### The Relevance of this Passage

The upper and lower realms are linked so that blessings may now flow to us unobstructed. A constant connection to the Light is attained through the energy arising here, which acts as an umbilical cord, so that in these, our darkest days, we may call down the Light to illumine our way and end pain, suffering, and evil.

221. כְּתִיב וְאַתָּה יְיָ' אַל תִּרְחָק אֱיָלוּתִי לְעֶזְרָתִי חוּשָׁה. דָוִד מַלְכָּא אָמַר דָא, בְּשַׁעֲתָא דַהֲוָה מְתַקֵן וּמְסַדֵר תּוּשְׁבַּחְתָּא דְמַלְכָּא, בְּגִין לְחַבְּרָא שִׁמְשָׁא בְּסִיהֲרָא. כֵּיוָן דַהֲוָה מְתַקֵן וּמְסַדֵר שְׁבָחִין דִילֵיהּ לְאִתְחַבְּרָא, אָמַר וְאַתָּה יְיָ' אַל תִּרְחָק.

221. It is written: "But be not You, Hashem, far from me; my Strength, haste You to help me" (Tehilim 22:20). King David said this when he was preparing and arranging the praise of the King, in order to join the sun, THAT IS ZEIR ANPIN, with the moon, WHICH IS MALCHUT. Since he was preparing and arranging the praises of THE KING to the bond, he said, "But be not You, Hashem, far from me..."

222. וְאַתָּה יְיָ' רָזָא דְחַבְרוּתָא חֲדָא בְּלָא פְרוּדָא. אַל תִּרְחָק, כֵּיוָן דְאִיהִי סַלְקָא לְאִתְעַטְּרָא בְּבַעְלָהּ, וְכֹלָּא בְּעָלְמָא עִלָּאָה, וּמִתַּמָּן בָּעֵי

-138-

לְסַלְקָא לְאֵין סוֹף, לְאִתְקַשְׁרָא כֹּלָּא לְעֵילָּא לְעֵילָּא, וּבְג״כ אַל תִּרְחָק, לְאִסְתַּלְקָא מִינָן, לְשַׁבְקָא לָן.

**222.** "But be not You, Hashem": This is the secret of being bound together without separation. BECAUSE 'YOU' IS MALCHUT, 'HASHEM' IS ZEIR ANPIN; therefore, "be not far," since She is ascending to become adorned with her husband. It is all in the upper world, and from there it is necessary to elevate it to the endless light, in order that it should all be bound together high above. Therefore, HE SAYS, "Be not far" to ascend from us and leave us.

**223.** וּבְגִין כָּךְ, בְּגוֹ סְדוּרָא דְתוּשְׁבַּחְתָּא, בָּעָאן יִשְׂרָאֵל לְאִתְכְּלָלָא תַּמָּן, וּלְאִתְדַּבְּקָא בַּהֲדַיְיהוּ מִתַּתָּא, דְּאִלְמָלֵא יִבְעֵי לְאִסְתַּלְקָא הַאי כָּבוֹד, הָא יִשְׂרָאֵל לְתַתָּא אֲחִידָן בֵּיהּ וְתַקְפִין בֵּיהּ, דְּלָא שַׁבְקֵי לֵיהּ לְאִתְרַחֲקָא מִנַּיְיהוּ. וְע״ד צְלוֹתָא בִּלְחַשׁ, כְּמַאן דְּמַלִּיל בְּרָזָא עִם מַלְכָּא, וּבְעוֹד דְּאִיהוּ בְּרָזָא עִמֵּיהּ, לָא אִתְרַחֲקָא מִנֵּיהּ כְּלָל.

**223.** During the order of praise, Yisrael have to be included there and join with ZEIR ANPIN AND MALCHUT from below, so that if this glory, WHICH IS MALCHUT, wishes to go up from there, the children of Yisrael below are joined to Her and hold onto Her. And they do not permit Her to go away from them. Therefore, the prayer is silent, as one who is speaking secretly with the King, because She doesn't become far from Him at all as long as She is with Him in secret. THEN SHE IS COMPLETELY INCLUDED IN ZEIR ANPIN AND, EVEN THOUGH ZEIR ANPIN ASCENDS TO THE ENDLESS LIGHT, HE DOES NOT BECOME FAR FROM US, BECAUSE HE IMMEDIATELY RETURNS TO HIS PLACE, AS IT IS WRITTEN BEFORE US.

**224.** אֱיָלוּתִי, מָה אַיָּל וּצְבִי, בְּשַׁעֲתָא דְּאַזְלֵי וּמִרְחֲקֵי, מִיַּד אַהֲדְרָן לְהַהוּא אֲתָר דְּשַׁבְקֵי, אוּף קוּדְשָׁא בְּרִיךְ הוּא, אע״ג דְּאִסְתַּלָּק לְעֵילָּא לְעֵילָּא בְּאֵין סוֹף, מִיַּד אַהֲדָר לְאַתְרֵיהּ. מ״ט. בְּגִין דְּיִשְׂרָאֵל לְתַתָּא אִתְאַחֲדָן בֵּיהּ, וְלָא שַׁבְקִין לֵיהּ לְאִתְנַשְׁיָא, וּלְאִתְרַחֲקָא מִנַּיְיהוּ. וְע״ד, אֱיָלוּתִי לְעֶזְרָתִי חוּשָׁה.

**224.** "My strength (Heb. *eyaluti*)" (Tehilim 22:20): *eyaluti* MEANS that just like a stag (Heb. *eyal*) or deer when they go and leave, they return

immediately to the place they left, so is the Holy One, blessed be He. Even though He ascends higher and higher to the endless world, He immediately returns to His place. Why? Because Yisrael below are joined with Him and do not leave Him so He would be forgotten and removed from them. For this, IT IS SAID, "My strength, haste You to help me."

**225.** וּבְגִין כַּךְ בָּעֵינָן לְאִתְאַחֲדָא בֵּיהּ בְּקוּדְשָׁא בְּרִיךְ הוּא, וּלְאַחֲדָא בֵּיהּ, כְּמַאן דְּאַמְשִׁיךְ מֵעֵילָא לְתַתָּא, דְּלָא יִשְׁתְּבַק בַּר נָשׁ מִנֵּיהּ, אֲפִילוּ שַׁעֲתָא חֲדָא. וְע״ד כַּד סָמִיךְ גְּאוּלָה לִתְפִלָּה, בָּעֵי לְאַחֲדָא בֵּיהּ, וּלְאִשְׁתְּעֵי בַּהֲדֵיהּ בִּלְחִישׁוּ, בְּרָזָא, דְּלָא יִתְרְחַק מִינָן, וְלָא יִשְׁתְּבַק מִינָן, וְע״ד כְּתִיב וְאַתֶּם הַדְּבֵקִים בַּיְיָ׳ אֱלֹהֵיכֶם חַיִּים כֻּלְּכֶם הַיּוֹם. אַשְׁרֵי הָעָם שֶׁכָּכָה לּוֹ אַשְׁרֵי הָעָם שֶׁיְיָ׳ אֱלֹהָיו.

**225.** Therefore, it is necessary to join with the Holy One, blessed be He, and hold onto Him like one who draws from above to below, so that no person is forsaken by Him even for one moment. Therefore, when one connects redemption close to prayer, NAMELY THE BLESSING: "WHO DELIVERED YISRAEL" TO THE AMIDAH, he has to become engrossed in it and speak to Him in silence, so He does not become distanced from him, and does not leave us. Therefore, it is written: "But you who did cleave of Hashem your Elohim are alive, every one of you this day" (Devarim 4:4). "Happy is that people, that is in such a case: happy is that people, whose Elohim is Hashem" (Tehilim 144:15).

**226.** בְּהַהִיא שַׁעֲתָא, קָם רַבִּי שִׁמְעוֹן וְחַבְרַיָּיא אוּף הָכִי קָמוּ וְאַזְלוּ. אָמַר רַבִּי אֶלְעָזָר לְרַבִּי שִׁמְעוֹן אֲבוּי, אַבָּא, עַד הָכָא הֲוֵינָא יַתְבֵי בְּצִלָּא דְּאִילָנָא דְּחַיֵּי בְּגִנְתָּא דְּעֵדֶן. מִכָּאן וּלְהָלְאָה דַּאֲנָן אָזְלִין, אִצְטְרִיךְ לָן לְמֵיהַךְ בְּאָרְחוֹי דְּנַטְרִין אִילָנָא דָא. אָמַר לֵיהּ, אַנְתְּ תִּשְׁרֵי בְּשֵׁירוּתָא לְמִפְתַּח בְּאָרְחָא.

**226.** At the moment that Rabbi Shimon rose, the friends also rose and left. Rabbi Elazar said to Rabbi Shimon, his father: Father, until now we sat in the shade of the Tree of Life in the Garden of Eden. From now and further that we are traveling, we must go in the ways that guard this Tree. He said to him: You start first to open the way.

## 24. "Gold, and silver, and brass"

### A Synopsis

It is impossible to summarize the content of this long and difficult section, which contains a myriad of details explaining the meaning of all the colors and objects referred to in "That they bring Me an offering..." It speaks of gold and silver and brass, blue and purple and scarlet, fine linen and goats' skins and rams' skins dyed red and badgers' skins, acacia wood, oil for the light, onyx stones and stones to be set. The passage goes on to emphasize the importance of the numbers 24 and 25 and 49, and then discusses the prayers which should be made standing and which lying down.

### The Relevance of this Passage

When we read of the many offerings that people made on the altars to the Holy One, we realize, by comparison, how little we are tempted to offer Him today. This unwillingness is planted within us by Satan, for the truthful offerings and sacrifices are actually the negative traits and nefarious qualities implanted within us by the Other Side.

As we now offer our dishonorable traits upon the sacrificial altar, our sins are cleansed and judgments are annulled. The number 49 is spoken of signifying the Sfirah of Binah. From our perspective, here in Malchut (earth), Binah is the fountainhead of spiritual energy. Thus, our souls ascend to this lofty spiritual height to nourish ourselves and bring divinity and boundless mercy to this mundane level of existence.

227. פָּתַח וְאָמַר, וְיִקְחוּ לִי תְּרוּמָה, כְּמָה דְּאִתְּמַר. בְּמַאי אִיהִי תְּרוּמָה. בְּרָזָא דְּזָהָב, דְּהָא מִתַּמָן אִתְזָנַת בְּקַדְמֵיתָא, בְּגִין דְּאִיהִי גְּבוּרָה תַּתָּאָה, דְּאַתְיָא מִסִּטְרָא דְּזָהָב. וְאַף עַל גַּב דְּאַתְיָא מִסִּטְרָא דְּזָהָב, כָּל עִקָּר לָא אִשְׁתְּאָרַת, אֶלָּא בְּסִטְרָא דְּכֶסֶף, דְּאִיהוּ יְמִינָא.

**227.** He opened the discussion saying: "That they bring Me an offering..." (Shemot 25:2), MEANING THAT IT IS MALCHUT THAT IS JOINED WITH ZEIR ANPIN, as we have learned. What makes it an offering? IT IS in the secret of Gold, WHICH IS THE LEFT COLUMN, because it is nourished originally from there as it is the lower Gvurah that comes from the side of Gold. FROM THERE IS THE ILLUMINATIONS OF CHOCHMAH BECAUSE MALCHUT IS BUILT FROM THE LEFT COLUMN. Even though She comes from the side of Gold, She perseveres only by the side of silver, which is the Right COLUMN, NAMELY, BY THE ILLUMINATION OF CHASSADIM.

228. וְרָזָא דָּא כּוֹס שֶׁל בְּרָכָה, דְּאִצְטְרִיךְ לְקַבְּלָא לֵיהּ בִּימִינָא
וּבִשְׂמָאלָא, וְכָל עִקָּר לָא אִשְׁתְּאַר אֶלָּא בִּימִינָא. וּשְׂמָאלָא אִתְּעַר
יְמִינָא, וְלָא אִתְדְּבַק בֵּיהּ, בְּגִין דְּאִיהוּ אִתְיְיהִיב בֵּין יְמִינָא וּשְׂמָאלָא,
וּשְׂמָאלָא אִתְאֲחִיד תְּחוֹתֵיהּ, וִימִינָא אִתְאֲחִיד בֵּיהּ לְעֵילָא, כד"א
שְׂמֹאלוֹ תַּחַת לְרֹאשִׁי וִימִינוֹ תְּחַבְּקֵנִי. זָהָב וָכֶסֶף, כד"א לִי הַכֶּסֶף וְלִי
הַזָּהָב, וְהָא אִתְּמַר.

228. This is the secret of the Cup of Blessing THAT ALLUDES TO MALCHUT THAT IS CALLED 'CUP'. One should accept it with the right and left hands, but it remains only in the right. The left arouses the right, FOR IT PROVIDES THE SHINE OF CHOCHMAH THAT IS IN IT. It does not become attached, because THE CUP is given between right and left, and the left joins AND IS INCLUDED under THE RIGHT. The right becomes joined above, IN ZEIR ANPIN, as it is written: "His left hand is under my head, and his right hand embraces me" (Shir Hashirim 2:6). Gold and silver are as in the verse: "The silver is mine, and the gold is mine" (Chagai 2:8), MEANING THE RIGHT AND LEFT OF ZEIR ANPIN. BUT IN MALCHUT, GOLD IS FIRST AND THEN SILVER, BECAUSE SHE IS BUILT FROM THE LEFT COLUMN WHICH IS GOLD, as has already been explained.

229. וּנְחוֹשֶׁת, דָּא אִיהוּ גָּוֶון כְּגַוְונָא דְּזָהָב, בְּגִין דְּאִצְטַבַּע מִגַּוֶון זָהָב
וּמִגַּוֶון דִּכְסַף. וְעַל דָּא דָּא מִזְבַּח הַנְּחֹשֶׁת קָטָן. אֲמַאי אִיהוּ קָטָן. כד"א כִּי
הַמִּזְבֵּחַ אֲשֶׁר לִפְנֵי יְיָ' קָטֹן מֵהָכִיל אֶת הָעוֹלָה וְגוֹ'. כד"א וְדָוִד הוּא
הַקָּטָן. וְאע"ג דְּאִיהוּ קָטָן, כֹּלָּא אִתְאֲחִיד בְּגַוֵּיהּ. וְאִי תֵּימָא מִזְבֵּחַ
אַחֲרָא, אִקְרֵי קָטָן. לָאו הָכִי. דְּלָאו קָטָן בַּר הַאי, דִּכְתִּיב אֶת הַמָּאוֹר
הַגָּדוֹל לְמֶמְשֶׁלֶת הַיּוֹם וְאֶת הַמָּאוֹר הַקָּטָן לְמֶמְשֶׁלֶת הַלָּיְלָה. וְדָא אִיהוּ
הַמָּאוֹר הַקָּטָן. הַמָּאוֹר הַגָּדוֹל, דָּא מִזְבֵּחַ הַפְּנִימִי דְּאִיהוּ מִזְבַּח הַזָּהָב.

229. "And brass" (Shemot 25:3): Its color is similar to gold, because it is colored from the color gold and the color silver, WHICH IS MALCHUT THAT IS RECEIVED IN THE RIGHT AND LEFT OF ZEIR ANPIN, WHICH ARE GOLD AND SILVER AS MENTIONED EARLIER. Therefore, the brass altar was small, as it is written: "For the altar that was before Hashem was too small to accommodate the offering…" (I Melachim 8:64), and: "And David was the

smallest" (I Shmuel 17:14), MEANING MALCHUT WHICH IS CALLED "THE
LESSER LUMINARY" (BERESHEET 1:16). Even though it is small,
everything is included in it. If you ask why the other altar, NAMELY THE
INNER ONE, is called 'small', IT IS BECAUSE IT WAS ONLY ONE CUBIT BY
ONE CUBIT. It is not so, FOR IT IS NOT DEPENDENT UPON MEASURE, for
the only one which is small is the one about which it is written: "The greater
luminary to rule the day, and the lesser luminary to rule the night." This
one, THE BRASS ALTAR, is the lesser luminary; the greater luminary is the
inner altar, which is the gold altar.

230. וּתְכֵלֶת דָּא אִיהוּ תְּכֵלֶת דְּצִיצִית. תְּכֵלֶת דָּא אִיהוּ כֻּרְסְיָיא, רָזָא
דִּתְפִלָּה דִּיַד. תְּכֵלֶת דָּא אִיהוּ כֻּרְסְיָיא, דְּדַיְינִין בֵּיהּ דִּינֵי נְפָשׁוֹת. בְּגִין
דְּאִית כֻּרְסְיָיא דְּדַיְינִין בֵּיהּ דִּינֵי מָמוֹנוֹת, וְאִית כֻּרְסְיָיא דְּדַיְינִין בֵּיהּ
דִּינֵי נְפָשׁוֹת. וְעַל דָּא, כָּל גַּוְונִין טָבִין לְחֶלְמָא, בַּר גָּוֶון תְּכֵלָא, בְּגִין
דְּיִנְדַּע דְּהָא נִשְׁמָתֵיהּ סַלְקָא בְּדִינָא. וְכַד נִשְׁמְתָא סַלְקָא בְּדִינָא, גּוּפָא
אִתְדָּן לְאִשְׁתְּצָאָה וְאִצְטְרִיךְ הַהוּא חֶלְמָא, לְרַחֲמִין סַגִּיאִין.

230. "And blue" (Ibid.): This is the blue wool of the Tzitzit (Eng. 'fringes').
Blue wool is the Throne, the secret of the hand Tefilin, WHICH IS
MALCHUT. Blue wool is the Throne OF JUSTICE, on which criminal law,
life and death, is judged, MEANING MALCHUT IN THE SIDE OF SEVERE
JUDGMENT. There is a throne upon which monetary laws are judged,
WHICH IS THE SECRET OF WEAK JUDGMENT, and there is a throne upon
which criminal law is judged, WHICH IS THE SECRET OF SEVERE
JUDGMENT. AND BLUE IS THE SEVERE JUDGMENT THAT IS IN
MALCHUT. Therefore, all the colors are acceptable in a dream except for
blue, for this notifies one that his soul is to be judged. When the soul is
being judged, the body is sentenced to destruction, and that dream needs
great Mercy.

231. תְּכֵלֶת דָּא אִיהוּ כֻּרְסְיָיא, דִּכְתִיב בֵּיהּ כְּמַרְאֵה אֶבֶן סַפִּיר דְּמוּת
כִּסֵּא, וּכְתִיב וְנֹגַהּ לוֹ סָבִיב. בְּגִין דְּעַבְדִין בֵּיהּ כְּרִיכִין לְצִיצִית, וְכַד נֹגַהּ
לוֹ, אִתְהַדָּר לְגָוֶון יָרוֹק, כְּגָוֶון כַּרְתִּי. מֵהַהִיא שַׁעֲתָא וְאֵילָךְ, אִשְׁתְּרֵי
זִמְנָא דְּק"שׁ, דְּהָא אִשְׁתְּנֵי גָּוֶון תְּכֵלָא מִכְּמָה דַּהֲוָה, וּבְגִין כָּךְ אָסִיר
לְמֵידַן דִּינֵי נְפָשׁוֹת בַּלַּיְלָה, בְּגִין דְּשַׁלְטָא הַהוּא גָּוֶון תְּכֵלָא בְּהַהוּא

זִמְנָא, וְאִתְיְהִיב רְשׁוּ לְמֶחֱטַף נַפְשָׁא בְּלָא מִשְׁפָּט. דְּהָא מִשְׁפָּט לָא שָׁלְטָא בְּהַהוּא זִמְנָא.

**231.** Blue wool is the Throne, about which is written: "The likeness of a throne, in appearance like a sapphire stone… A brightness round about him" (Yechezkel 1:26-27). When it is used for loops for the Tzitzit (Eng. 'fringes'), THE BRIGHTNESS ILLUMINATES IT. When the brightness illuminates it, it becomes the color green, AS WHITE BECOMES MORE VISIBLE IN IT, FOR THIS IS THE SECRET OF THE BRIGHTNESS THAT LIGHTS UP TOWARD MORNING. From then on the time starts to read the reading of Sh'ma, because the color of blue has changed from what it was; NAMELY, TO THE COLOR GREEN WHICH IS WEAK JUDGMENT. It is therefore prohibited to judge life and death law at night, because the color blue dominates at that time and permission is given to snatch a soul without trial, MEANING THE OTHER SIDE HAS POWER THEN TO CONFUSE THE MINDS OF THE JUDGES, because the Judgment, WHICH IS ZEIR ANPIN WHICH IS MERCY, does not dominate at that time.

**232.** כַּד אָתֵי צַפְרָא, וְאִתְּעַר יְמִינָא דִּלְעֵילָּא, נָפִיק הַהוּא נְהוֹרָא, וּמָטֵי עַד הַאי תִּכְלָא, וְאִשְׁתָּנֵי מִכְּמָה דַּהֲוָה, וּכְדֵין שָׁלְטָא עָלֵיהּ, וְאִתְדַּבָּק בֵּיהּ כֻּרְסְיָיא אַחֲרָא קַדִּישָׁא. מֵהַהִיא שַׁעֲתָא וְאֵילָךְ, זִמְנָא דְּק"ש.

**232.** When morning arrives, the right of above awakens, that light emerges and reaches this blue. It changes from what it was, and then the RIGHT dominates it and a different holy throne then attaches to it, OF MERCY. From that moment on is the time to recite the reading of Sh'ma.

**233.** וְאַרְגָּמָן, דָּא כְּנוּפְיָא דִּכְלִילָא כָּל גְּוֹונִין כַּחֲדָא. וְתוֹלַעַת שָׁנִי, כְּתִיב שָׁנִי, וּכְתִיב שָׁנִים, דִּכְתִיב כִּי כָל בֵּיתָהּ לָבוּשׁ שָׁנִים. אֶלָּא הַאי אִיהוּ גָּוֹון אִקְרֵי שָׁנִי, דְּנָטִיל כָּל גְּוֹונִין בֵּיהּ, וְכֹלָּא אִיהוּ חַד, שָׁנִי וְשָׁנִים. שָׁנִים: כַּד כֻּלְּהוּ כְּלִילָן בֵּיהּ כַּחֲדָא. שָׁנִי: דְּנָפִיק מִכֻּרְסְיָיא עִלָּאָה, דְּשַׁלְטָא עַל תְּכֵלֶת מִסִּטְרָא דִּימִינָא, וְדָא אִיהוּ אַפּוֹטְרוֹפּוֹסָא דְיִשְׂרָאֵל, דִּכְתִיב בֵּיהּ מִיכָאֵל שַׂרְכֶם. תּוֹלַעַת: דְּחֵילֵיהּ בְּפוּמֵיהּ, כְּתוֹלַעַת, דְּמִתְבַּר כֹּלָּא וְעָקַר כֹּלָּא.

233. "And purple": This is all the colors gathered together, WHICH IS ZEIR ANPIN, MEANING THE CENTRAL COLUMN THAT INCLUDES ALL THE THREE COLUMNS WHICH ARE WHITE, RED, AND GREEN. "And scarlet": It is written "scarlet (lit. 'worm of *shani*')" and 'scarlet' in: "For all her household are clothed with scarlet (Heb. *shanim*)" (Mishlei 31:21). This here is the color called 'scarlet', which includes all the colors. And shani and shanim are one, as shanim IS CALLED when they are all included in it together. Shani emerges from the supernal Throne, WHICH IS ZEIR ANPIN, WHICH IS THE THRONE FOR BINAH, that dominates blue from the right side. This is the guardian of Yisrael, of whom it is written: "Michael your prince" (Daniel 10:21). HE IS CALLED 'a worm', because his strength is in his mouth, like a worm that breaks everything and uproots everything.

234. תּוֹלַעַת שָׁנִי וָשֵׁשׁ, תְּרֵין גַּוְונִין כַּחֲדָא, דִּימִינָא וּשְׂמָאלָא, חִיוָּר וְסוּמָק. וָשֵׁשׁ: בּוּצָא אִיהוּ. דְּשִׁית חוּטִין מִתְחַבְּרָן, וְדָא אִיהוּ דִכְתִיב, וּגְוִיָּתוֹ כְתַרְשִׁישׁ. וּבְאִלֵּין תְּרֵין, כְּלִילָן תְּרֵין אָחֳרָנִין.

234. "And scarlet, and fine linen" (Shemot 25:3): These are two colors together of right and left, which are white and red AND THEY ARE BOTH IN YESOD, BECAUSE THE JUDGMENTS IN MALCHUT ARE INCLUDED IN YESOD. "Fine linen (Heb. *shesh*)" is linen in which six (Heb. *shesh*) threads are combined, NAMELY YESOD. This is the meaning of: "His body also was like the beryl" (Ibid. 6), WHO IS THE ANGEL GABRIEL. This is because in these two, WHICH ARE CHESED AND GVURAH THAT ARE IN YESOD, are included two others, WHICH ARE MICHAEL AND GABRIEL. MICHAEL IS IN SCARLET AND GABRIEL IN FINE LINEN.

235. וְעִזִּים: גְּבוּרָאן תַּתָּאֵי דִלְבַר, לְחַפְיָא עַל פְּנִימָאֵי. וְכֹלָא אִצְטְרִיךְ, וְאִצְטְרִיךְ לְמֵיהַב דּוּכְתָּא לְכֹלָא, דְּהָא מִסִּטְרָא דְּדַהֲבָא קָאַתְיָין. וְעוֹרוֹת אֵלִים מְאָדָּמִים, מְשִׁיכוּ דִּתְרֵין סִטְרִין, דִּימִינָא וּשְׂמָאלָא, לְחַפְיָא בְּדוּכְתָּא אָחֳרָא.

235. "And goats' skins" (Ibid. 3): They are lower Gvurot in the exterior; THEY ARE TIFERET AND MALCHUT THAT ARE IN THE KLIPAH OF NOGAH (ENG. 'BRIGHTNESS') OF BRIYAH that cover the internal ones THAT ARE IN HOLINESS. Everything is necessary, because it is necessary to give place for

everything. They come from the side of gold, FOR THEY ARE DRAWN FROM THE SIDE OF GVURAH THAT IS CALLED 'GOLD'. "And rams' skins dyed red" (Ibid. 5): They are drawn from two sides, right and left, WHICH ARE CHOCHMAH AND BINAH OF THE KLIPAH OF NOGAH in order to cover in another place THE HOLINESS, BECAUSE THE GOATS' SKINS COVER OVER THE ASPECTS THAT CORRESPOND TO THEM IN HOLINESS AND RAMS' SKINS DYED RED COVER OVER THE ASPECTS THAT CORRESPOND TO THEM IN HOLINESS.

236. וְעוֹרוֹת תְּחָשִׁים, סִטְרָא חֲדָא אִית דְּרַבֵּי גּוֹ סִטְרָא אַחֲרָא בְּחוּרְבָּא, וְלָא בְּיִשּׁוּבָא אִשְׁתְּכַח, וְדָא אִיהוּ סִטְרָא דַּכְיוּ, וְאִקְרֵי תַּחַשׁ.

236. "And badgers' skins": There is one aspect that grows in the Other Side, in the wilderness and is not found in inhabited places. This is the aspect of purity and is called 'badger', WHICH IS MALE AND FEMALE NOGAH OF ATZILUT THAT GROWS IN THE MIDST OF THREE KLIPOT, WHICH ARE A STORM WIND, A GREAT CLOUD, AND A FIRE FLARING UP.

237. בְּסִפְרָא דִּשְׁלֹמֹה מַלְכָּא אִית גּוֹ הַאי מִזְבַּח הַנְּחֹשֶׁת דְּקָאמְרָן, רָזִין עִלָּאִין. דְּהָא מִזְבַּח אֲדָמָה כְּתִיב, מִזְבַּח אֲדָמָה תַּעֲשֶׂה לִי וְגוֹ' וְדָא אִיהוּ רָזָא כְּדְקָא יֵאוֹת. נְחֹשֶׁת, כַּד שַׁלְטִין טוּרִין אַחֲרָנִין, וְאִיהִי צְרִיכָא לְמֵיזַן לוֹן, אִצְטְבַע בְּהַאי גּוֹוָן לְמֵיזַן לוֹן. וְאִינוּן אִקְרוּן הָרֵי נְחֹשֶׁת.

237. In the Book of King Solomon there are high secrets concerning the brass altar as we said. About the earthen altar it is written: "An altar of earth you shall make to Me" (Shemot 20:21). This is a regular secret, WHICH IS MALCHUT. When other mountains dominate AND MALCHUT has to nourish them, She becomes colored in this color OF BRASS in order to nourish them. FOR THEN MALCHUT IS CALLED 'THE BRASS ALTAR' and they are called 'brass mountains'.

238. וְאִינוּן הָרֵי נְחֹשֶׁת אִתְמְשַׁךְ עֲלַיְיהוּ רוּחָא חֲדָא מִגּוֹ הַאי מִזְבֵּחַ, וְכַד הַאי מִזְבֵּחַ אִסְתַּלָּק בְּסִלּוּקוּ אַחֲרָא, כְּדֵין אִסְתַּלָּק אָת נ', דְּאִיהוּ מִזְבֵּחַ קַדִּישָׁא, וְאִשְׁתְּאַר רוּחָא דְּאִלֵּין טוּרֵי נְחֹשֶׁת. וְכַד הַהוּא רוּחָא אִסְתְּלִיק בְּקִיּוּמֵיהּ, אִקְרֵי תַּחַשׁ, דְּהָא אִסְתַּלָּק מִנֵּיהּ אָת נ'.

**238.** One spirit is drawn from this altar upon these brass mountains, MALCHUT, WHICH IS THE LETTER *Nun* OF NECHOSHET (*Nun-Chet -Shin-Tav*). When this altar ascends in a different ascension, the letter *Nun* also ascends, which is the holy altar. And the spirit of these brass mountains remains, WHICH IS THE LETTERS *CHET-SHIN-TAV*. When the spirit starts rising, it is called 'a badger' (Heb. *tachash*, Tav-Chet-Shin), because the letter *Nun* has gone up from it.

239. וְהַאי אִתְפְּרַשׁ, לְכַמָּה רוּחִין אַחֲרָנִין, וְאִקְרוּן אוּף הָכִי, וְעַל דָּא אִקְרֵי הַהוּא עַמָּא, תַּחַשׁ. כד"א וְאֶת תַּחַשׁ וְאֶת מַעֲכָה. אִינּוּן הֲווֹ יַדְעֵי בְּהָא חַיָּה דְּמַשְׁכְּנָא, דְּאִקְרֵי עַל שְׁמֵהוֹן.

**239.** This spirit TACHASH is divided into many other spirits and this nation was therefore called 'Tachash', as it is written: "And Tachash and Ma'achah" (Beresheet 22:24). They used to have knowledge of this animal, TACHASH, that was in the tabernacle and is named after them.

240. וַעֲצֵי שִׁטִּים, אִלֵּין אִינּוּן רָזִין קַדִּישִׁין, דְּאִינּוּן לוּחֵי מַשְׁכְּנָא, וְאִינּוּן אִקְרוּן בְּרָזָא דִּלְהוֹן. כְּתִיב עֲצֵי שִׁטִּים עוֹמְדִים, וּכְתִיב שְׂרָפִים עוֹמְדִים.

**240.** "And Acacia wood" (Shemot 25:5): These are the holy secrets of these holy boards of the Tabernacle, which are named after their secret, NAMELY ACACIA WOOD. IN RELATION TO THE BOARDS, it is written: "Acacia wood standing up" (Shemot 26:15) and "Serafim stood above" (Yeshayah 6:2) TO TEACH THAT THE BOARDS ARE THE SECRET OF SERAFIM.

241. מִכָּאן וּלְהָלְאָה שֶׁמֶן לַמָּאוֹר, מְשִׁיכוּ דְּמִשַׁח רְבוּת קַדִּישָׁא לְאַמְשָׁכָא עֲלַיְיהוּ. אַבְנֵי שֹׁהַם וְאַבְנֵי מִלּוּאִים, אִלֵּין אַבְנֵי קַדְשָׁא, יְסוֹדֵי דְּמַקְדְּשָׁא, בִּרְתִיכִין קַדִּישִׁין אִלֵּין, אִזְדַּמְּנָן בִּלְחוֹדַיְיהוּ, לִיקָר וּלְשַׁבְחָא, בִּלְבוּשׁ יְקָר, לְעַיְינָא כַּהֲנָא בְּהוּ תַּמָּן, וּלְאַדְכְּרָא תְּרֵיסַר שְׁבָטִין, וְע"ד תְּרֵיסַר אַבְנִין כְּמָה דְּאִתְּמַר.

**241.** From here and further, "oil for the light" is the drawing of the holy oil of greatness to flow upon them; NAMELY, THE MOCHIN OF THE FIRST

THREE SFIROT. "Onyx stones and stones to be set" (Shemot 25:7): These are the holy stones, the foundations of the tabernacle, FOR THEY ARE THE SECRET OF THE FOUR ANGELS, MICHAEL, GABRIEL, URIEL AND RAPHAEL. FOR EACH ONE OF THEM INCLUDES THREE COLUMNS WHICH ARE THE TWELVE THAT CARRY THE CHARIOT, WHICH IS MALCHUT. In these holy Chariots, these TWELVE HERETOFORE MENTIONED come on their own to glorify and praise in a precious garment, NAMELY THE BREASTPLATE, so the priest should concentrate there on them and mention these twelve tribes. Therefore, there are twelve stones, as we have learned.

242. תְּלֵיסַר זִינִין אִינּוּן, בַּר י״ב אַבְנִין יַקִּירִין אִלֵּין, וְכֻלְּהוּ סַלְקִין לכ״ה אַתְוָון, בְּרָזָא עִלָּאָה דְּיִחוּדָא. וְלָקֳבֵל אִלֵּין, גָּלִיף וְאַתְקִין מֹשֶׁה, כ״ה אַתְוָון בְּרָזָא דִּפְסוּקָא דְּיִחוּדָא, דִּכְתִיב שְׁמַע יִשְׂרָאֵל יְדֹוָד אֱלֹהֵינוּ יְדֹוָד אֶחָד. וְאִינּוּן כ״ה אַתְוָון, גְּלִיפָן מְחַקְּקָן בְּרָזָא דִּלְעֵילָּא.

242. There are thirteen kinds, NAMELY GOLD, SILVER, ETC., besides these twelve precious stones THAT ARE THE STONES TO BE SET. Together, they add up to 25, the 25 letters in the supernal mystery of unison. Corresponding to these, Moses engraved and arranged 25 letters in the secret of the verse of unison, as it is written, "Hear, O Yisrael, Hashem our Elohim, Hashem is One" (Devarim 6:4), which contains 25 letters engraved and carved in the supernal secret.

243. יַעֲקֹב בָּעָא לְאַתְקְנָא לְתַתָּא, בְּרָזָא דְּיִחוּדָא, וְאַתְקִין בְּכ״ד אַתְוָון, וְאִינּוּן בָּרוּךְ שֵׁם כְּבוֹד מַלְכוּתוֹ לְעוֹלָם וָעֶד. וְלָא אַשְׁלִים לְכ״ה אַתְוָון, בְּגִין דְּעַד לָא אִתְתָּקַן מַשְׁכְּנָא. כֵּיוָן דְּאִתְתָּקַן מַשְׁכְּנָא, מִלָּה קַדְמָאָה דַּהֲוָה נָפִיק מִנֵּיהּ, כַּד אִשְׁתְּלִים, לָא מַלִיל אֶלָּא בְּכ״ה אַתְוָון, לְאַחֲזָאָה דְּהָא אִשְׁתְּלִים דָּא כְּגַוְונָא דִּלְעֵילָּא, דִּכְתִיב וַיְדַבֵּר יְיָ׳ אֵלָיו מֵאֹהֶל מוֹעֵד לֵאמֹר. הָא כ״ה אַתְוָון.

243. Jacob wanted to prepare below, IN MALCHUT, in the secret of unison, so he prepared 24 letters, which are: 'Blessed is the Name of the glory of His kingdom forever and ever.' He did not complete to 25 letters, because the tabernacle was not yet completed, WHICH CORRESPONDS TO MALCHUT. As soon as the tabernacle was completed and the first thing to

emerge was completed, he spoke only with 25 letters to show that it was completed similarly to above, WHICH IS ZEIR ANPIN. As it is written: "And Hashem called to Moses, and spoke to him out of the Tent of Meeting, saying" (Vayikra 1:1), which contains 25 letters.

244. וְעַ״ד כ״ה זִינִין לְאַשְׁלְמָא תִּקּוּנָא דְּמַשְׁכְּנָא וְכָל הָנֵי אַתְוָון, אוֹקִימְנָא בְּאִינּוּן אַתְוָון גְּלִיפָן, דְּאוֹלִיפְנָא מִמַּר. וּבְגִין דְּמַשְׁכְּנָא אִשְׁתְּלִים בְּרָזִין אַלֵּין, אִקְרֵי כ״ה, בְּיִחוּדָא דִּשְׁלִימוּ דְּמַשְׁכְּנָא, וְעַ״ד וַחֲסִידֶיךָ יְבָרְכוּכָה כְּתִיב, רָזָא דִּשְׁלִימוּ דְּכָל מַשְׁכְּנָא וְתִקּוּנָא דִּילֵיהּ. כ״ה, לְקָבֵל כ״ב אַתְוָון, וְאוֹרַיְיתָא וּנְבִיאִים וּכְתוּבִים, דְּאִינּוּן כְּלָלָא חֲדָא, וְרָזָא חֲדָא.

244. Therefore, there were 25 kinds with which to complete the preparation of the tabernacle, and we established all these letters to be the engraved letters, about which I learned from Master. Once the tabernacle was completed with these secrets, it is called 'koh' (Caf-Hei = 25) in the complete unison of the Tabernacle, WHICH IS MALCHUT. Therefore, it is written: "And Your pious ones shall bless You (Heb. yevarchuchah)" (Tehilim 145:10), WHICH CONTAINS THE LETTERS 'YEVARCHU (ENG. 'BLESS') CAF-HEI', for CAF-HEI is the secret of the completion of the entire tabernacle and its preparation, AS EXPLAINED IN THE ADJACENT ESSAY. Caf-Hei corresponds to 22 letters and the Torah, the Prophets and the Writings, which are under one rule and one secret.

245. בְּשַׁעֲתָא דְּיִשְׂרָאֵל קָא מְחַיְּדֵי יְחוּדָא בְּהַאי קְרָא, בְּרָזָא דְּכ״ה אַתְוָון, דְּאִינּוּן שְׁמַע יִשְׂרָאֵל יְיָ׳ אֱלֹהֵינוּ יְיָ׳ אֶחָד, וּבִשְׁכְמל״ו, דְּאִינּוּן כ״ד אַתְוָון, וִיכַוֵּין כָּל חַד בְּהוּ, אַתְוָון מִתְחַבְּרָן כַּחֲדָא, וְסַלְּקִין בְּחִבּוּרָא חַד מ״ט תַּרְעִין, בְּרָזָא דְיוֹבְלָא. וּכְדֵין אִצְטְרִיךְ לְסַלְּקָא עַד וְלָא יַתִּיר. וּכְדֵין אִתְפַּתְחוּ תַּרְעִין, וְחָשִׁיב קוּדְשָׁא בְּרִיךְ הוּא לְהַהוּא בַּר נָשׁ, כְּאִילּוּ קַיֵּים אוֹרַיְיתָא כֻּלָּה, דְּאִיהִי אַתְיָא בְּמ״ט פָּנִים.

245. Yisrael declare the unity with this passage in the secret of the 25 letters, which are, "Hear, O Yisrael: Hashem our Elohim; Hashem is one" together with 'Blessed is the Name of the glory of His kingdom forever and

ever,' which contains 24 letters and concentrate on each one of them. Then all the letters join together and, in one bond, amount to 49 gates in the secret of Jubilee', WHICH IS BINAH, BECAUSE 25 AND 24 EQUAL 49. It is necessary to mount UNTIL BINAH but not higher. And then the 49 gates of BINAH are opened and the Holy One, blessed be He, considers for the person as though he has fulfilled the whole Torah that comes in 49 aspects.

246. וְעַל דָּא אִצְטְרִיךְ לְכַוְּונָא לִבָּא וּרְעוּתָא בְּכָ"ה וּבכ"ד, וּלְסַלְקָא לוֹן בִּרְעוּתָא דְלִבָּא, לְמ"ט תַּרְעִין דְּקָאמְרָן. כֵּיוָן דְּאִתְכַּוַּון בְּהַאי, יִתְכַּוֵּון בְּהַהוּא יִחוּדָא דְּאָמַר מַר, שְׁמַע יִשְׂרָאֵל וּבשכמל"ו כְּלָלָא דְכָל אוֹרַיְיתָא כֻּלָּה. זַכָּאָה חוּלְקֵיה מַאן דְּיִתְכַּוֵּון בְּהוּ, דְּוַדַּאי כְּלָלָא אִיהוּ דְּכָל אוֹרַיְיתָא דְּעֵילָא וְתַתָּא. וְדָא אִיהוּ רָזָא דְּאָדָם שְׁלִימָא, דִּדְכַר וְנוּקְבָּא, וְרָזָא דְּכָל מְהֵימְנוּתָא.

246. Therefore, the person has to concentrate the heart and will on 25 and 24 and elevate them with a willing of the heart to the 49 gates that we mentioned. After he has concentrated on this, he should concentrate on that unison that my master said, WHO IS RABBI SHIMON, that "Hear, O Yisrael" and 'Blessed is the Name...' are the inclusion of the entire Torah. Happy is the portion of he who concentrates on them, for it is certainly the entirety of the whole Torah above and below. This is the secret of the complete man, male and female, BECAUSE SH'MA YISRAEL IS THE ASPECT MALE AND 'BLESSED IS THE NAME' IS THE ASPECT OF FEMALE, and this is the secret of the entire Faith.

247. מַחֲלוֹקֶת דְּשַׁמַּאי וְהִלֵּל בִּקִימָה וּבִשְׁכִיבָה, דִּכְתִּיב בְּשָׁכְבְּךָ וּבְקוּמֶךָ, דְּשַׁמַּאי סָבַר בָּעֶרֶב דְּקָא כְּלִילָא נוּקְבָא בְּשָׁלְטָנָהָא, אִצְטְרִיךְ לְגַבֵּי נוּקְבָא דְּקָא יַטּוּ וְיִקְרָאוּ. וּבַבֹּקֶר, דְּקָא שַׁלְטָא דְּכוּרָא בְּשׁוּלְטָנוּתָא דְּעָלְמָא עִלָּאָה, אִצְטְרִיךְ לְמֵיקָם קַמֵּיה דִּדְכוּרָא, כְּמָה דְּאִצְטְרִיךְ בִּתְפִלָּה מְעוּמָד, וּבְכָל אֲתָר דִּדְכוּרָא אַתְיָא.

247. There is an argument between Shammai and Hillel about rising up and lying down, for it is written: "When you lie down, and when you rise up" (Devarim 6:7). Shammai holds that in the evening the female rules, so in relation to the female it is necessary to turn and recite THE SH'MA,

MEANING LYING DOWN. In the morning, when the male, ZEIR ANPIN, dominates with the domination of the upper world, it is necessary to rise up and read before the male, just as it is necessary during Amidah prayer, WHICH MUST BE STANDING. So in every place that relates to the male, IT IS IN STANDING.

248. וּבֵית הַלֵּל סָבַר, אִלְמָלֵא אִשְׁתְּכַח דָּא לְחוֹד וְדָא לְחוֹד, הָכִי אִצְטְרִיךְ. אֲבָל כֵּיוָן דַּאֲנַן מְחַבְּרָן לוֹן כַּחֲדָא, בְּחִבּוּרָא בְּמ״ט פָּנִים, ומ״ט תַּרְעִין, לָא אִצְטְרִיכְנָא לְאַפְרָשָׁא דָּא לְחוֹד וְדָא לְחוֹד, אֶלָּא לְאַשְׁגָּחָא דְּכֹלָּא אִיהוּ חַד, בְּלָא פְּרוּדָא. וּכְמָה דְּאִזְדַּמַּן לֵיהּ לְבַר נָשׁ, הָכִי יֵימָא, דְּהָא תַּרְוַויְיהוּ בְּחִבּוּרָא חֲדָא, כְּמָה דְּנַיְחָא לוֹן, וְהָכִי אִצְטְרִיךְ לְאִתְחֲזָאָה.

248. The house of Hillel holds that if this one would be alone, ZEIR ANPIN, and this one alone, MALCHUT, then it should have been so, TO DIVIDE IT THUS THAT THIS ONE SHOULD BE STANDING AND THIS ONE LYING. But since we join ZEIR ANPIN AND MALCHUT together, in the union of 49 versions and 49 gates, WHICH ARE THE 25 OF "SH'MA" AND THE 24 OF 'BLESSED IS THE NAME...' AS MENTIONED ABOVE, we do not have to separate this one on its own and that one on its own, but rather see that everything is one without division. FOR THERE SHOULD BE NO DIVISION BETWEEN THE READING OF SH'MA IN THE MORNING AND THE READING OF SH'MA IN THE EVENING. However, as to the person finds himself, so he should recite it, EITHER STANDING OR LYING DOWN, because they are both in one bond as they please. This is the way it should be presented.

249. וְעַל דָּא דְּכוּרָא, בְּשִׁית סִטְרִין, בַּקְּרָא דִשְׁמַע יִשְׂרָאֵל, דְּאִינוּן שִׁית תֵּיבִין. וְנוּקְבָּא בְּשִׁית סִטְרִין בשכמל״ו. דְּאִינוּן שִׁית תֵּיבִין אַחֲרָנִין, וְסַלְקִין בְּחִבּוּרָא חֲדָא, בְּרָזָא דְּמ״ט תַּרְעִין, וַהֲלָכָה כְּבֵית הַלֵּל בְּכָל אֲתָר.

249. Therefore, the male, ZEIR ANPIN, is in six sides of the passage: "Sh'ma Yisrael," which are six other words CORRESPONDING TO THE SIX SIDES OF GREATNESS THAT HE RECEIVES FROM ABA AND IMA. And the female is in the six sides of: 'Blessed is the Name,' which are the six words

CORRESPONDING TO THE SIX SIDES OF GREATNESS THAT SHE RECEIVES FROM ZEIR ANPIN. They BOTH rise in one bond in the secret of 49 gates, and the law is always according to the house of Hillel.

## 25. "Who raised up one from the east"

### A Synopsis

Rabbi Shimon begins by explaining that the "Who" in the scripture refers to the supernal world, Binah. The entire secret of the Faith (Malchut) begins from Zeir Anpin, from where the Light becomes revealed. The discussion moves to righteousness, which rules over all the worlds to guide them and to maintain them as necessary. Righteousness never turns away from Zeir Anpin and never keeps silence. Rabbi Shimon ends by saying that the Holy One has illuminated the way because of Elazar, Rabbi Shimon's son, who calls to the supernal Light and is not silent.

### The Relevance of this Passage

Like the moon, Malchut is barren, lacking any Light of her own. For this reason, Malchut never turns away from Zeir Anpin, so that she may constantly catch the Light the shines from this supernal sphere. Man, unaware of this cosmic truth, has constantly turned away from the Light, seduced by the illusionary pleasures presented to him by the Other Side.

Here we become cognizant of our Malchut nature, the realization that we have no Light of our own. And as the moon is compelled to faithfully face the sun to receive her light, the entire realm of Malchut is suddenly propelled by the calling and righteousness of Rabbi Elazar. She (Malchut) turns on her spiritual axis and comes face to face with the upper world to receive the full radiance of Light emanating from the Creator.

250. רַבִּי שִׁמְעוֹן אָרִים יְדוֹי וּבְרִיךְ לְרַבִּי אֶלְעָזָר בְּרֵיה. פָּתַח וְאָמַר, מִי הֵעִיר מִמִּזְרָח וְגוֹ'. הַאי קְרָא אוֹקִימְנָא וְאִתְּמַר, אֲבָל רָזָא דְחָכְמְתָא אִיהוּ, מִ"י רָזָא דְּעָלְמָא עִלָּאָה אִיהוּ, דְּהָא מִתַּמָּן נָפְקָא שֵׁירוּתָא, לְאִתְגַּלְיָא רָזָא דִמְהֵימְנוּתָא, וְהָא אוֹקִימְנָא.

250. Rabbi Shimon raised his hands and blessed Rabbi Elazar, his son. He opened the discussion saying: "Who (Heb. *mi*) raised up one from the east..." (Yeshayah 41:2). We have established and learned this passage. Yet the secret of the Wisdom is that Mi is the secret of the Supernal World, BINAH, for from there emanates the beginning of the revelation of the secret of the Faith, WHICH IS MALCHUT, as we have already established.

251. תּוּ. מִ"י טְמִירָא דְּכָל טְמִירִין, דְּלָא אִתְיְדַע וְלָא אִתְגַּלְיָיא כְּלָל.

גַּלֵּי יְקָרֵיהּ לְאִשְׁתְּמוֹדְעָא, מֵהַהוּא אֲתָר דְּאִקְרֵי מִזְרָח, דְּהָא מִתַּמָּן שֵׁירוּתָא דְּכָל רָזָא דִּמְהֵימְנוּתָא, וּנְהוֹרָא לְאִתְגַּלְיָיא. וּלְבָתַר צֶדֶק יִקְרָאֵהוּ לְרַגְלוֹ, דְּהָא צֶדֶק, גַּלֵּי גְּבוּרְתָּא עִלָּאָה, וְשׁוּלְטָנֵיהּ דְּקוּדְשָׁא בְּרִיךְ הוּא, וְלְהַאי צֶדֶק אַשְׁלְטֵיהּ עַל עָלְמִין כֻּלְּהוּ, לְדַבְּרָא לוֹן, וּלְאַתְקָנָא לוֹן, כִּדְקָא יָאוֹת. וְעַ״ד, יִתֵּן לְפָנָיו גּוֹיִם וּמְלָכִים יַרְדְּ, דְּהָא כָּל מַלְכִין דְּעָלְמָא, בִּרְשׁוּתָא דְּהַאי צֶדֶק קַיְימִין, כד״א וְהוּא יִשְׁפּוֹט תֵּבֵל בְּצֶדֶק.

**251.** Moreover, Mi is the most concealed of all the concealments that are unknown and not revealed at all. It revealed its glory to be known from that place which is called 'east', NAMELY ZEIR ANPIN, for the entire secret of the Faith, WHICH IS MALCHUT, begins from there and the light becomes revealed, BECAUSE ALL THE REVELATION THAT IS IN MALCHUT, SHE RECEIVES FROM ZEIR ANPIN, and afterwards: "Whom righteousness met wherever he set his foot" (Ibid.), because righteousness, THAT IS MALCHUT, reveals the supernal Gvurah, and the rule of the Holy One, blessed be He, WHICH IS ZEIR ANPIN. And he allowed this righteousness to rule over all the worlds to guide them and to maintain them properly. Therefore, He "gave the nations before him, and made him rule over His kings" (Ibid.), because all the kings of the world are under the authority of this righteousness, as it is written: "And He will judge the world in righteousness" (Tehilim 9:9).

**252.** תּוּ, צֶדֶק יִקְרָאֵהוּ לְרַגְלוֹ, מַאן קָרֵי לְמַאן. אֶלָּא, צֶדֶק אִיהוּ קָארֵי תָּדִיר לְאַסְפַּקְלַרְיָאה דְּנָהֲרָא, וְלָא שָׁכִיךְ לְעָלְמִין, וְצֶדֶק קָאִים תָּדִיר לְרַגְלוֹי, דְּלָא אִתְעֲדֵי מִתַּמָּן, וְקָארֵי וְלָא שָׁכִיךְ, הה״ד, אֱלֹהִים אַל דֳּמִי לָךְ אַל תֶּחֱרַשׁ וְאַל תִּשְׁקֹט אֵל. וְהַשְׁתָּא קוּדְשָׁא בְּרִיךְ הוּא אַנְהַר לָן אָרְחָא דָּא בְּגִין אֶלְעָזָר בְּרִי דְּקָרֵי לִנְהוֹרָא עִלָּאָה וְלָא שָׁכִיךְ. זַכָּאָה חוּלָקֵהוֹן דְּצַדִּיקַיָּיא בְּעָלְמָא דֵּין וּבְעָלְמָא דְּאָתֵי.

**252.** "Whom righteousness met (lit. 'called') wherever he set his foot": HE QUESTIONS: Who called whom? DID EAST CALL RIGHTEOUSNESS OR DID RIGHTEOUSNESS CALL EAST? HE ANSWERS: But righteousness always

calls to the mirror that illuminates, WHICH IS ZEIR ANPIN THAT IS CALLED 'EAST', and is never silent, and righteousness always stands at his feet. MALCHUT CLOTHES NETZACH, HOD AND YESOD OF ZEIR ANPIN THAT ARE CALLED 'FEET', for she never turns away from there and she cries and is not silent. This is what is written: "Do not keep silence, Elohim, do not hold your peace, and be still, El" (Tehilim 83:2). Now the Holy One, blessed be He, has illuminated this way for us because of Elazar, my son, for he calls to the supernal Light and he is not silent. Happy is the portion of the righteous in this world and in the World to Come.

## 26. "Elohim, You are my El; earnestly I seek You"

### A Synopsis

Rabbi Aba recites the verse, "A psalm of David, when he was in the wilderness of Judah," and then goes on to explain that David sang and praised his Master even though he was in pain and was being pursued. We are reminded that the Holy Spirit does not dwell from above until the person arouses it from below by concentrating his energies. While he was in Judah, David praised a great and precious praise, "Elohim, You are my El," which contains three levels. These are the levels above in Binah, Zeir Anpin, and Malchut. The text goes on to speak of the "black light" in the context of "earnestly I seek you." David also merited the white light that illuminates (from Zeir Anpin). We read how "My soul thirsts for You, my flesh longs for You," as one hungry for food and thirsty for water "in a dry and thirsty land, where no water is."

### The Relevance of this Passage

King David, we are told, was being pursued by his son who was intent on murdering him. David found himself in the wilderness, experiencing great pain. Yet, he sang. He sang to the Light with all his heart. He composed psalms and offered praise to his Creator. And he did all this with untold joy in his heart.

Today, man is similarly lost in the wilderness of spiritual darkness. Employing the wonders of David's psalms, and drawing on his courage and spiritual fortitude, we rouse joy and happiness in our hearts. This joy is not a coping mechanism to see us through our darkest moments. Happiness is not about making the best of a bad situation. On the contrary, the joy and happiness that now manifest to us are the tools that call down the white Light that illuminates from Zeir Anpin. And the brilliance immediately removes all the darkness, liberating mankind from the direst of straits of this physical existence.

253. ר' אַבָּא פָּתַח קְרָא וְאָמַר, מִזְמוֹר לְדָוִד בִּהְיוֹתוֹ בְּמִדְבַּר יְהוּדָה. מַאי שְׁנָא מִכָּל שְׁאָר תּוּשְׁבְּחָן, דְּלָא קָאָמַר בְּאָן אֲתָר שַׁבַּח לוֹן דָּוִד מַלְכָּא, ומ"ש הָכָא דְּקָאָמַר בִּהְיוֹתוֹ בְּמִדְבַּר יְהוּדָה. אֶלָּא לָא דָא בִּלְחוֹדוֹי, דְּהָא אוּף הָכִי נַמֵּי, בְּשַׁנּוֹתוֹ אֶת טַעְמוֹ לִפְנֵי אֲבִימֶלֶךְ. בְּבָא הַזַּיִּפִים. וְכֵן כֻּלְּהוּ. לְאַחֲזָאָה לְכָל בְּנֵי עָלְמָא, שְׁבָחֵיהּ דְּדָוִד, דְּאע"ג דִּבְצַעֲרָא הֲוָה, וַהֲווֹ רַדְפֵי אֲבַתְרֵיהּ, הֲוָה מִשְׁתַּדַּל לוֹמַר שִׁירִין וְתוּשְׁבְּחָן לְקוּדְשָׁא בְּרִיךְ הוּא.

**253.** Rabbi Aba opened the scripture and said: "A psalm of David, when he was in the wilderness of Judah" (Tehilim 63:1). HE QUESTIONS: What is the difference from all the other praises, in which it doesn't say where King David recited them, but here it says, "…when he was in the wilderness of Judah"? HE ANSWERS: This is really not the only one, because there is also, "When he changed his demeanor before Avimelech" (Tehilim 34:1) and also, "When the Zifim came" (Tehilim 54:2). This is to show to all the people of the world the praise of David. Even though he was in pain and they were pursuing him, he endeavored to recite songs and praises to his Master.

**254.** וְאע״ג דִּבְרוּחַ קַדְשָׁא הֲוָה אָמַר, רוּחַ קַדְשָׁא לָא הֲוֵי שָׁארֵי עֲלוֹי, עַד דְּאִיהוּ אִשְׁתַּדַּל לְמִשְׁרֵי עֲלוֹי. וְכֵן בְּכָל אֲתָר, לָא שַׁרְיָא רוּחַ קַדְשָׁא דִּלְעֵילָא, עַד דְּיִתְּעַר עֲלֵיהּ בַּר נָשׁ מִתַּתָּא. וְדָוִד אע״ג דְּקָא רַדְפֵי אֲבַתְרֵיהּ, וַהֲוָה בְּצַעֲרֵיהּ, לָא הֲוָה שָׁבִיק שִׁירִין וְתוּשְׁבְּחָן מִפּוּמֵיהּ, וּלְשַׁבְּחָא לְמָארֵיהּ עַל כֹּלָּא.

**254.** He would say it through the Holy Spirit, yet the Holy Spirit did not dwell upon him until he endeavored that it should dwell upon him. And always, the Holy Spirit does not dwell from above until the person arouses it from below. Even though they were pursuing David and he was in pain, he did not forsake the songs and praises from his mouth and HE DID NOT INTERRUPT his praising of his Master above any other thing.

**255.** וְאִי תֵּימָא, הָא דְּתָנֵינָן, מִזְמוֹר לְדָוִד, אוֹ לְדָוִד מִזְמוֹר, וְהָכָא שָׁרַת עֲלֵיהּ רוּחַ קַדְשָׁא בְּקַדְמֵיתָא, בְּגִין דְּאָמַר מִזְמוֹר לְדָוִד. אֶלָּא, אִי אִיהוּ לָא הֲוָה מְכַוֵּין גַּרְמֵיהּ בְּקַדְמֵיתָא, לָא שָׁרַת עֲלֵיהּ רוּחַ קַדְשָׁא.

**255.** If you ask that we learned, "A psalm of David" SHOWS THAT FIRST THE HOLY SPIRIT DWELT UPON HIM AND AFTERWARD HE RECITED POETRY, or "To David a psalm" SHOWS THAT FIRST HE RECITED POETRY AND AFTERWARDS THE HOLY SPIRIT DWELT UPON HIM. Here the Holy Spirit dwelt first, because he said, "A psalm of David." SO IT SEEMS THAT IT WAS WITHOUT ENDEAVORING? HE ANSWERS: But if he did not consecrate himself first, the Holy Spirit would not dwell upon him.

256. מִזְמוֹר דָּא רוּחַ קַדְשָׁא. אֲמַאי אִקְרֵי הָכִי. בְּגִין דְּאִיהִי, מְשַׁבַּחַת תָּדִיר לְמַלְכָּא עִלָּאָה דְּכָל זִמְנָא הֲוָה קָא מְשַׁבַּחַת וּמְזַמְּרַת, וְלָא שָׁכִיךְ. כֵּיוָן דְּאָתָא דָוִד אַשְׁכַּח גּוּפָא מִתְתַּקְּנָא כַּדְקָא יֵאוֹת, וְשָׁרַת עֲלֵיהּ, וַהֲווֹ מְגַלֵּי בְּהַאי עָלְמָא, לְשַׁבָּחָא וּלְזַמְּרָא לְמַלְכָּא, וְכֹלָּא, בְּגִין דְּיִתְתַּקַּן הַאי עָלְמָא, כְּגַוְונָא דִלְעֵילָּא.

256. "A psalm" is the Holy Spirit THAT IS CALLED 'A PSALM'. Why is it called so? Because MALCHUT, WHICH IS THE HOLY SPIRIT, constantly praises the supernal King, ZEIR ANPIN, for at all times She praises and sings and is not silent. When David came and found the body OF MALCHUT, MEANING HER SIX ENDS, properly prepared and she dwelt upon him, he revealed in this world his praise and song to the King, ZEIR ANPIN, and all this in order to prepare this world similar to the world of above.

257. לְדָוִד. גְּבַר שְׁלִים בְּתִקּוּנוֹי, גְּבַר מִתְתַּקְּנָא, גְּבַר זַכָּאָה. דָּוִד וַדַּאי דְּלָא אִשְׁתַּנֵּי לְעָלְמִין. בִּהְיוֹתוֹ בְמִדְבַּר יְהוּדָה, דָּא שְׁבָחָא דְּדָוִד, אע"ג דִּבְצַעֲרֵיהּ הֲוָה, אע"ג דַּהֲווֹ רַדְפֵי אֲבַתְרֵיהּ. וּמַאי תּוּשְׁבַּחְתָּא קָאֲמַר. תּוּשְׁבַּחְתָּא דְּאִיהוּ רַב וְיַקִּירָא.

257. "To David," MEANING a man who is complete in his exertions, a perfected man, a righteous man. David certainly did not ever change. FOR HE WAS THE SAME, BOTH AT TIME OF PEACE AND TIME OF GRIEF. "When he was in the wilderness of Judah": This is the praise of David, even though he was in his pain and even though they were pursuing him, HE SANG AND PRAISED HASHEM. Which praise did he say? A praise that is great and precious.

258. וּשְׁבָחָא דִּילֵיהּ מַאי אִיהִי. אֱלֹהִים אֵלִי אַתָּה אֲשַׁחֲרֶךָּ. אֱלֹהִים סְתָם. כֵּיוָן דְּאָמַר אֱלֹהִים, אֲמַאי אֵלִי. אֶלָּא הַהוּא דַּרְגָּא דִּילֵיהּ. תְּלַת דַּרְגִּין הָכָא: אֱלֹהִים. אֵלִי. אַתָּה. וְאַף עַל גַּב דְּאִינּוּן תְּלַת שְׁמָהָן, חַד דַּרְגָּא אִיהוּ, בְּרָזָא דֶּאֱלֹהִים חַיִּים. אֱלֹהִים: לְעֵילָּא, אֱלֹהִים חַיִּים. אֵלִי: קְצֵה הַשָּׁמַיִם עַד קְצֵה הַשָּׁמַיִם. אַתָּה: דַּרְגָּא דִּילֵיהּ. וְאַף עַל גַּב דְּכֹלָּא חַד, וּבִשְׁמָא חַד סָלִיק.

**258.** What is the superiority OF THIS PRAISE? IT IS "Elohim, You are my El; earnestly I seek You" (Tehilim 63:2). HE QUESTIONS: Just Elohim MEANS THE ELOHIM OF ALL, since he said "Elohim." Why did he add "my El"? HE ANSWERS: But this SHOWS his level, because there are three levels here, "Elohim," "my El," and "You." Even though they are three names, they are one level in the secret of Living Elohim. "Elohim" IS above IN BINAH THAT IS CALLED 'Living Elohim'. "My El" is the end of the heavens to the end of the heavens, NAMELY ZEIR ANPIN and "You" is his level, NAMELY MALCHUT. Even though it is all one and it amounts to one name ACCORDING TO THE LITERAL MEANING OF THE PASSAGE, STILL IN ALL THEY ALLUDE TO THREE LEVELS.

259. אֲשַׁחֲרֶךָ, אִי כְּמַשְׁמָעוֹ דִּילֵיהּ, שַׁפִּיר. אֲבָל אֲשַׁחֲרֶךָ, אַתְקִין נְהוֹרָא דְּנָהִיר בְּשַׁחֲרוּתָא. דְּהָא נְהוֹרָא דְּקַיְּימָא בְּשַׁחֲרוּתָא, לָא נָהִיר עַד דְּיִתְתַּקְנוּן לֵיהּ לְתַתָּא. וּמַאן דְּאַתְקִין נְהוֹרָא שַׁחֲרָא דָּא, אַף עַל גַּב דְּאִיהִי אוּכְמָא, זָכֵי לִנְהוֹרָא חִוָּורָא דְּנָהִיר, וְדָא אִיהִי נְהוֹרָא אִסְפָּקְלַרְיָא דְּנָהֲרָא, וְדָא אִיהוּ בַּר נָשׁ דְּזָכֵי לְעָלְמָא דְּאָתֵי.

**259.** "I seek You (Heb. *ashacharecha*)." (Tehilim 65:2). If we follow the literal meaning, it is beautiful AND NEEDS NO EXPLANATION, but THERE IS A SECRET HERE. Ashacharecha MEANS that he prepared the light that illuminates during blackness (Heb. *shacharut*), WHICH IS THE SECRET OF THE LIGHT OF CHOCHMAH. DUE TO LACK OF CHASSADIM, IT CANNOT ILLUMINATE. THEREFORE, IT IS CALLED 'BLACK LIGHT', because the light that is found in blackness does not illuminate until it is mended below, MEANING UNTIL MAYIN NUKVIN (FEMALE WATERS) ARE ELEVATED AND CHASSADIM ARE DRAWN, SO THAT CHOCHMAH CAN BE ATTIRED WITH THEM. THEN IT ILLUMINATES, AS WRITTEN THERE. The one that mends this blackness, even though he is black, merits the white light that illuminates. For this is the light of the mirror that illuminates, WHICH IS ZEIR ANPIN, and such a person will merit the World to Come.

260. וְרָזָא דָּא וּמְשַׁחֲרֵי יִמְצָאֻנְנִי, וּמְשַׁחֲרַי: דְּמִתְתַּקְּנִין נְהוֹרָא מְשַׁחֲרֵי אוּכְמָא. יִמְצָאֻנְנִי, יִמְצָאוּנִי לָא כְּתִיב, אֶלָּא יִמְצָאֻנְנִי, דְּזָכֵי לִתְרֵין נְהוֹרִין. לִנְהוֹרָא דְּשַׁחֲרָא אוּכְמָא, וְלִנְהוֹרָא חִוָּורָא דְּנָהֲרָא. וְזָכֵי לְאִסְפָּקְלַרְיָאה דְּלָא נָהִיר, וּלְאִסְפָּקְלַרְיָאה דְּנָהִיר. וְדָא אִיהוּ יִמְצָאֻנְנִי.

וְעַל דָּא אָמַר דָּוִד אֲשַׁחֲרֶךָ, אַתְקִין נְהוֹרָא דְּשַׁחֲרָא אוּכָמָא, לְנַהֲרָא
עֲלֵיהּ נְהוֹרָא חִוְּורָא דְּנָהֲרָא.

**260.** This is the secret of: "And those who seek me early (Heb. *meshacharai*) shall find me (Heb. *yimtza'uneni*)" (Mishlei 8:17). Meshacharai MEANS that they prepare the light of meshacharai, NAMELY THE black (Heb. *shachor*) LIGHT. 'Yimtza'uneni' instead of the common 'yimtzauni' SHOWS that he merits two lights, the light of blackness, WHICH IS THE CHOCHMAH THAT IS IN MALCHUT THAT DOES NOT ILLUMINATE BECAUSE OF THE LACK OF CHASSADIM, and the white light illuminating, WHICH IS ZEIR ANPIN THAT ATTIRES THE CHOCHMAH THAT IS IN MALCHUT WITH CHASSADIM, SO SHE ILLUMINATES. SO WE FIND THAT he merits the mirror that does not illuminate, WHICH IS MALCHUT, and the mirror that illuminates, WHICH IS ZEIR ANPIN; hence 'yimtza'uneni,' MEANING TWO LIGHTS. Therefore, David said, "I seek You (Heb. *ashacharecha*)," because he installed the black light, WHICH IS MALCHUT, so that the white light that illuminates could shine on him, WHICH IS ZEIR ANPIN SO THAT THE CHOCHMAH IN MALCHUT WOULD BE ATTIRED IN THE CHASSADIM OF ZEIR ANPIN. THEN MALCHUT IS MENDED AND ILLUMINATES.

261. צָמְאָה לְךָ נַפְשִׁי כָּמַהּ לְךָ בְשָׂרִי, כְּמַאן דְּכָפִין לְמֵיכַל וְצָחֵי
לְמִשְׁתֵּי. בְּאֶרֶץ צִיָּה וְעָיֵף בְּלִי מָיִם, בְּגִין דְּאִיהוּ מִדְבַּר, וְלָאו אִיהוּ
אֲתָר דְּיִשׁוּבָא, וְלָאו אִיהוּ אֲתָר דְּקֻדְשָׁא. וּבְגִין כָּךְ אִיהוּ אֲתָר בְּלִי מָיִם.
וּכְמָה דְּאֲנַן כַּפְין וְצָחָאן לְגַבָּךְ בַּאֲתָר דָּא, כֵּן בַּקֹּדֶשׁ חֲזִיתִיךָ וְגוֹ'. וַאֲנַן
כְּמָה דְּאֲנַן צָחָאן לְגַבֵּי דְּמַר, לְמִשְׁתֵּי בְּצָחוּתָא מָלֵוי בַּאֲתָר דָּא, אוּף
הָכִי צָחֵינָן לְמִשְׁתֵּי בְּצָחוּתָא מָלֵוי, בְּבֵי מַקְדְּשָׁא, אֲתָר דְּאִקְרֵי קֹדֶשׁ.
אָמַר ר"ש לְר' אַבָּא, מַאן דְּשָׁארֵי מִלָּה הַשְׁתָּא יֵימָא.

**261.** "My soul thirsts for You, my flesh longs for You" (Tehilim 63:2); NAMELY, as one hungry for food and thirsty for water "in a dry and thirsty land, where no water is," (Ibid.), MEANING MALCHUT UNDER THE DOMINATION OF THE LEFT, WHICH IS A BLACK LIGHT, AS MENTIONED ABOVE, DUE TO A LACK OF CHASSADIM CALLED 'WATER' for then it is a wasteland and not a place of habitation, nor a holy place. Therefore, IT IS CONSIDERED a place without water. THEREFORE DAVID IMPROVED HER

AND DREW WATER TO HER FROM ZEIR ANPIN, AS MENTIONED ABOVE. As we are hungry and thirsty for you, FOR CHASSADIM, in this place, so "I have seen You in the sanctuary," BECAUSE HUNGER AND THIRST CAUSE THE ELEVATION OF MAYIN NUKVIN (FEMALE WATERS), THE DRAWING OF CHASSADIM FROM ZEIR ANPIN AND THE CLOTHING OF THE BLACK LIGHT OF MALCHUT. THEN SHE RETURNS TO HOLINESS AND ILLUMINATES. RABBI ABA SAID TO RABBI SHIMON: Just as we are thirsty for Master to drink thirstily his words in this place, so are we thirsty to drink His words thirstily in the Temple, the place that is called 'Holy'. Rabbi Shimon said to Rabbi Aba: Let him who started speaking, speak now AS WELL.

## 27. "That they bring Me an offering"

### A Synopsis

Rabbi Aba explains that before Moses constructed the tabernacle, the people were afraid that the Holy One would not stay with them, even though He had performed for them, through Moses, miracles and wonders. This is because if a king is among his people but without his queen, it is not certain that he will remain. But on the day that Moses completed the tabernacle, the Shechinah descended to the earth. Yet before the Shechinah descended, an accuser appeared, and she became covered with darkness to prevent her from descending. We read that fifteen hundred myriads of accusing angels gathered against her, because all their glow and all their light was concentrated in her, and if she descended her light would become darkened. Yet at that moment she broke the darkness and the demons, descended to the earth and ruled over all. The hosts and camps of angels suffered great pain on the day that Moses' bride descended to the earth. The text goes on to explain that here in the world the work of the tabernacle is like the work of the body, that it should be suitable to include the spirit within it. The comparison is made of the Shechinah to the brain in the body. The Holy Spirit, the Shechinah, is fashioned in the body so that it should include within itself another high, delicate spirit that illuminates, which is Zeir Anpin attired in the Shechinah. Lastly the text speaks of the outer shell of the world and the inner shell of the skull, within which are impurities.

### The Relevance of this Passage

Often, when we begin the spiritual path, miracles and wonders appear before our eyes. But, in truth, miracles cannot support us, long term, in our spiritual work and journey. Miracles do provide an intense flash of Light, for a moment, for a particular situation, but this Light does not continue to glow enduringly. Consequently, we now tie ourselves to the Shechinah and our connection to the Light becomes constant. This is what the Tabernacle achieved for the Israelites in the desert. And this is precisely what we accomplish here.

262. פָּתַח ר' אַבָּא וְאָמַר, וְיִקְחוּ לִי תְּרוּמָה מֵאֵת כָּל אִישׁ וְגו'. מֹשֶׁה בְּשַׁעֲתָא דְּקוּדְשָׁא בְּרִיךְ הוּא אַחֲמֵי לֵיהּ עוֹבָדָא דְּמַשְׁכְּנָא, הֲוָה קָשֶׁה קָמֵיהּ, וְלָא יָכִיל לְמֵיקַם בֵּיהּ, וְהָא אוּקְמוּהָ. וְהַשְׁתָּא אִית לָן לְמִקְשֵׁי הָכָא, אִי תְּרוּמָה דָּא, יָהֲבָה קוּדְשָׁא בְּרִיךְ הוּא לְמֹשֶׁה בִּלְחוֹדוֹי, הֵיךְ יָהֲבָה לְאַחֲרָא, וְאָמַר דְּלִבְנֵי יִשְׂרָאֵל יִקְחוּ הַאי תְּרוּמָה.

**262.** Rabbi Aba opened the discussion saying, "...that they bring Me an offering: of every man..." (Shemot 25:2). When the Holy One, blessed be He, showed Moses the construction of the tabernacle, he found it difficult and could not grasp it, as we have already established. Now we can ask here if this offering, WHICH IS MALCHUT, was given by the Holy One, blessed be He, to Moses alone, how could He give it to another? How could He say that the children of Yisrael should take this offering?

263. אֶלָּא וַדַּאי לְמֹשֶׁה יָהֲבָהּ, וְלָא יָהֲבָהּ לְאַחֲרָא. לְמַלְכָּא דַּהֲוָה בְּגוֹ עַמֵּיהּ, וְלָא הֲוַת מַטְרוֹנִיתָא עִמֵּיהּ דְּמַלְכָּא. כָּל זִמְנָא דְּמַטְרוֹנִיתָא לָא הֲוַת עִמֵּיהּ דְּמַלְכָּא, לָא מִתְיָאֲשֵׁי עַמָּא בֵּיהּ, וְאִינּוּן לָא יַתְבִין לְרַחֲצָן. כֵּיוָן דְּאָתַת מַטְרוֹנִיתָא, כָּל עַמָּא חֲדָאן, וְיַתְבֵי בְּרוּחֲצָנוּ. כַּךְ בְּקַדְמֵיתָא, אע״ג דְּקוּדְשָׁא בְּרִיךְ הוּא עָבַד לוֹן נִסִּין וְאָתִין ע״י דְּמֹשֶׁה, לָא מִתְיָאֲשֵׁי עַמָּא. כֵּיוָן דְּאָמַר קוּדְשָׁא בְּרִיךְ הוּא וְיִקְחוּ לִי תְּרוּמָה, וְנָתַתִּי מִשְׁכָּנִי בְּתוֹכְכֶם. מִיַּד אִתְיָאֲשׁוּ כֻּלְּהוּ, וְחַדוּ בְּפוּלְחָנָא דְּקוּדְשָׁא בְּרִיךְ הוּא, הה״ד וַיְהִי בְּיוֹם כַּלּת מֹשֶׁה דְּנַחְתַּת כַּלַּת מֹשֶׁה לְאַרְעָא.

**263.** HE ANSWERS: Surely that He gave it to Moses and did not give it to another. THIS IS LIKE a king who was among his people, but the queen was not with the king. As long as the queen was not with the king, the people were not certain THAT HE WOULD REMAIN WITH THEM. They did not sit securely, but all the people rejoice and sit securely when the queen arrives. Thus, in the beginning, even though the Holy One, blessed be He, performed for them miracles and wonders through Moses, the people were still not certain THAT THE HOLY ONE, BLESSED BE HE, WOULD REMAIN WITH THEM. When the Holy One, blessed be He, said, "...that they bring Me an offering" and "I will set My tabernacle among you" (Vayikra 26:11), they are immediately certain THAT THE HOLY ONE, BLESSED BE HE, WOULD BE WITH THEM. So they rejoiced in the service of the Holy One, blessed be He. This is what is meant by: "And it came to pass on the day that Moses had finished (Heb. *kalot*)" (Bemidbar 7:1), that Moses' *kalah* (Eng. 'bride') descended to the earth. THEREFORE, KALOT IS SPELLED WITHOUT *VAV* TO POINT OUT THE SUPERNAL BRIDE, WHO IS MALCHUT, WHO DESCENDED TO EARTH TO DWELL IN YISRAEL.

264. וְאִי תֵּימָא, וַיְהִי בְּכָל אֲתָר לָאו אִיהוּ אֶלָּא לִישָׁנָא דְּצַעֲרָא, וְהָכָא

כְּתִיב וַיְהִי בְּיוֹם. אֶלָּא, בְּהַהוּא יוֹמָא דִשְׁכִינְתָּא נַחְתַּת לְאַרְעָא, אִשְׁתְּכַח מְקַטְרְגָא לְגַבָּה, וְחַפְיָא הַהוּא חָשׁוּךְ קַבֵּל לְגַבָּה, בְּגִין דְּלָא תֵּיחוֹת. וְתָנֵינָן, אֶלֶף וַחֲמֵשׁ מְאָה רִבּוֹא מַלְאָכִין מְקַטְרְגִין, אִשְׁתְּכָחוּ לְגַבָּה בְּגִין דְּלָא תֵּיחוֹת.

**264.** If you ask, anytime it is written: "And it came to pass," it is an expression of pain and here it is written: "And it came to pass on the day." HE ANSWERS: On that day that the Shechinah descended to the earth, there appeared an accuser, and She was covered with darkness to prevent Her from descending. We learned that fifteen millions of accusing angels gathered against Her in order to stop Her descent.

265. וּבְהַהוּא זִמְנָא אִשְׁתְּכָחוּ כָּל כְּנוּפְיָא דְּמַלְאֲכֵי עִלָּאֵי קָמֵי קוּדְשָׁא בְּרִיךְ הוּא. אָמְרוּ קַמֵּיה, מָארֵי דְּעָלְמָא, כָּל זִיוָא וְכָל נְהוֹרָא דִּילָן בִּשְׁכִינַת יְקָרָךְ אִיהוּ, וְהַשְׁתָּא תֵּיחוֹת לְגַבֵּי תַּתָּאֵי. בְּהַהִיא שַׁעֲתָא אִתַּתְקְפַת שְׁכִינְתָּא, וְתַבְרַת הַהוּא חָשׁוּךְ קַבֵּל, כְּמַאן דִּמְתַבַּר גְּזִיזִין תַּקִּיפִין, וְנַחְתַּת לְאַרְעָא. כֵּיוָן דְּחָמוּ כֻּלְּהוּ כַּךְ, פְּתָחוּ וְאָמְרוּ יְיָ' אֲדוֹנֵינוּ מָה אַדִּיר שִׁמְךָ בְּכָל הָאָרֶץ. אַדִּיר וַדַּאי, דְּתַבְרַת כַּמָּה גְּזִיזִין וְחֵילִין תַּקִּיפִין, וְנַחְתַּת לְאַרְעָא, וְשַׁלִּיטַת בְּכֹלָּא. וְעַ"ד כְּתִיב וַיְהִי, צַעֲרָא דְּקַבִּילוּ כַּמָּה חַיָּילִין וּמַשִׁירְיָין, בְּיוֹמָא דְּכַלַּת מֹשֶׁה נַחְתַּת לְאַרְעָא.

**265.** At that time, all the groups of the supernal angels were gathered before the Holy One, blessed be He. They said before Him, 'Master of the Universe, all our shine and all our light is in the Shechinah of Your glory. Now You are going to descend to those below'–MEANING THAT THE LIGHT OF CHOCHMAH IN HER WILL SPREAD FROM ABOVE DOWNWARDS, AND THEN HER LIGHT WILL BECOME DARK. At that moment, the Shechinah became strengthened, MEANING THAT SHE BECAME UNITED WITH ZEIR ANPIN AND INCLUDED IN HIS DECISION, SO THAT THE SHINE OF THE LEFT WILL ALWAYS ILLUMINATE ONLY FROM BELOW UPWARDS. Then She broke the darkness and gloom as one breaks strong spears, MEANING THE GREAT DEMONS, and descended to earth. As soon as they saw this, they started saying: "Hashem our lord, how majestic is Your Name in all the earth" (Tehilim 8:2). Assuredly, it is majestic, for She broke many strong spears and forces, descended to the earth and dominated everything. It is

written: "And it came to pass," which POINTS OUT the pain that many hosts and camps of angels suffered on the day that Moses' bride descended to the earth.

266. וּבְגִין כַּךְ וְיִקְחוּ לִי תְּרוּמָה וְגוֹ'. וְיִקְחוּ לִי וּתְרוּמָה לָא כְּתִיב, אֶלָּא וְיִקְחוּ לִי תְּרוּמָה, לְאַחֲזָאָה דְּכֹלָּא חַד בְּלָא פְּרוּדָא. וְעוֹבָדָא דְּמַשְׁכְּנָא כְּגַוְונָא דִּלְעֵילָּא, דָּא לָקֳבֵל דָּא, לְאִתְכַּלְּלָא שְׁכִינְתָּא מִכָּל סִטְרִין עֵילָּא וְתַתָּא, הָכָא בְּהַאי עָלְמָא עוֹבָדָא דִּילֵיהּ, כְּעוֹבָדָא דְּגוּפָא, לְאִתְכַּלְּלָא רוּחָא בְּגַוֵּיהּ, וְדָא אִיהִי שְׁכִינְתָּא, דְּאִתְכְּלִילַת לְעֵילָּא וְתַתָּא, וְאִיהִי רוּחַ קֻדְשָׁא.

266. Therefore, it is written: "…that they bring Me an offering." It is not written: '…that they bring Me and an offering' but rather "that they bring Me an offering" to show that it is all one without separation, THAT THE SHECHINAH CALLED 'OFFERING' IS ONE WITH 'ME' WITHOUT SEPARATION. The work of the tabernacle is in the likeness of above, one corresponding to the other, in order to include the Shechinah in all the sides, above and below. Here in the world, the work OF THE TABERNACLE is like the work of the body, THAT IT SHOULD BE SUITABLE to include the spirit within it. This is the Shechinah that is included above and below, and She is the Holy Spirit.

267. וּלְעוֹלָם אִתְמַשְּׁכַת וְעָאלַת גּוֹ רָזָא דְּגוּפָא, לְאַשְׁרָאָה מוֹחָא גּוֹ קְלִיפָא כֹּלָּא כְּמָה דְּאִתְחֲזֵי. הַאי רוּחָא דְּקֻדְשָׁא, אִתְעֲבֵיד בְּגוּפָא, לְאִתְכַּלְּלָא בְּגַוֵּיהּ רוּחַ אַחֲרָא עִלָּאָה, דָּקִיק וְנָהִיר, וְכֹלָּא הָכִי אִתְאֲחִיד וְאִתְכְּלִיל דָּא בְּדָא, וְעָאל דָּא בְּדָא, עַד דְּאִתְאֲחִיד בְּהַאי עָלְמָא, דְּאִיהוּ קְלִיפָה בַּתְרָאָה דִּלְבַר.

267. THE SHECHINAH is always drawn and enters the secret of the body, WHICH IS THE TABERNACLE, so that the brain should dwell in the shell, FOR THE TABERNACLE AND ITS VESSELS ARE LIKE A SHELL TO THE SHECHINAH, WHICH IS THE BRAIN. Everything is as is befitting. This Holy Spirit, NAMELY THE SHECHINAH, is fashioned in the body so that it should include within itself another high, delicate spirit that illuminates, WHICH IS ZEIR ANPIN THAT IS ATTIRED IN THE SHECHINAH. Everything is tied and

included one within the other, and they enter one into the other until they unite and become attired in this world, which is the last peel on the exterior.

268. קְלִיפָה תַּקִיפָא אִיהִי לְגוֹ מִקְלִיפָה דְּהַאי עָלְמָא. כְּגַוְונָא דֶאֱגוֹזָא, דְּהַאי קְלִיפָה דִּלְבַר לָאו אִיהִי תַּקִיפָא, קְלִיפָה דְּאִיהִי לְגוֹ מִינָּהּ, אִיהִי קְלִיפָה תַּקִיפָא. אוֹף הָכִי לְעֵילָא, קְלִיפָה תַּקִיפָא, אִיהִי רוּחָא אַחֲרָא דְּשַׁלְטָא בְּגוּפָא. לְגוֹ מִנֵּיהּ, אִיהִי קְלִיפָה קְלִישָׁא. לְגוֹ מִנֵּיהּ מוֹחָא.

268. The strong Klipah OF IMPURITY is within the Klipah of this world. Just as in a nut, the external shell is not hard, NAMELY THE GREEN SHELL THAT IS ON THE NUT WHICH IS SOFT. The more inner shell is a strong shell HARD AS WOOD, SO THE GLOBE OF THE EARTH ITSELF IS A LIGHT SHELL AND THE SHELL THAT IS WITHIN IT IS HARD. It is also so above, in that the strong Klipah is another spirit that dominates the body. More inside there is a soft Klipah and even more inside there is the brain, WHICH IS THE SHECHINAH, WHICH IS THE SECRET OF THE NEFESH. AND WITHIN IT IS ZEIR ANPIN, WHICH IS THE SECRET OF THE RUACH, AS MENTIONED ABOVE.

## 28. An opening and a light cover over the Holy Land

### A synopsis

We learn that the hard shell which encompasses the world has an opening over the Holy Land, as long as people are performing the proper service. We are told that the Klipah clogs the brain. Then the discussion moves to an analogy between the shell that covers the world and the shell that covers the brain. When the children of Yisrael were pushed away from the Holy Land, the opening was covered with a holy cover, a delicate curtain, to guard against the Klipah's incursion. The cover prevents the holy presence from descending to earth but it also prevents the strong Klipah from dominating that place. We next learn that the souls of Yisrael who expire there ascend, but the souls of other nations who expire there revolve and finally reach their own side of the impurity. If someone is buried on the day that his soul departs from him in the Holy Land, we are told, the spirit of impurity has no dominion over him at all. The sacrificial limbs and fat must be burned at night on the altar so that the smoke will roll around to the hole in the north and nourish the Other side, to keep them there. The spirit of impurity cannot dominate the bodies of the righteous that do not take any pleasure in the world. He whose soul departs outside of the Holy Land and who had his body defiled by the impure spirit, the impure spirit is absorbed inside it, remaining there until it returns to dust. The impure spirit never dominated Joseph's body, however. Jacob did not die, and his body remained intact and was embalmed. This, we learn, is because he was the bodily vehicle for the supernal image, or in other words a Chariot for Tiferet.

### The Relevance of this Passage

From this portion we shield ourselves from the negative forces that attempt to dominate our lives. In addition, a portal to the upper world is created, raising our consciousness. Our senses of awareness, our intuition, our mental faculties are heightened, and we see and understand, at last, all that we did not see or grasp before. The power of the ancient sacrifices is resurrected to nourish all the dark forces, keeping them at bay, while the purifying Light embodied by Jacob shines brightly, perfecting the body and refining the soul. This Light vanquishes the Angel of Death and the entire armada of the Other Side. The Light of the land of Israel permeates our entire world, so that in addition to Jacob's Light, the Resurrection of the Dead will take place with extreme mercy and loving kindness.

269. בְּאַרְעָא קַדִּישָׁא, מִתַּתְקְנָא כֹּלָּא בְּגַוְונָא אַחֲרָא, דְּהָא קְלִיפָה

תַּקִיפָא אִתְּבְּרַת מֵהַהוּא אֲתָר, וְלָא שַׁלְטָא בֵּיהּ כְּלָל. קְלִיפָה תַּקִיפָא אִתְּבְּרַת תְּבִיר, וְאִתְפַּתְּחַת מֵהַאי סִטְרָא וּמֵהַאי סִטְרָא.

**269.** In the Holy Land, everything is construed in a different way because the strong Klipah THAT IS ATTIRED IN THE EARTH is broken from that place, and does not dominate over it at all. The strong Klipah breaks MORE AND MORE and opens from this side and that side, UNTIL AN ENTRANCE IS FORMED THERE.

270. וְהַהִיא פְּתִיחוּ הֲוָה בְּאַרְעָא קַדִּישָׁא, בְּכָל זִמְנָא דְּפָלְחִין פּוּלְחָנָא כְּדְקָא יֵאוֹת. כֵּיוָן דְּגָרְמוּ חוֹבִין, מְשִׁיכוּ הַהוּא פְּתִיחוּ לְהַאי סִטְרָא וּלְהַאי סִטְרָא, עַד דְּאִתְקְרֵב קְלִיפָה, כֹּלָּא כַּחֲדָא. כֵּיוָן דְּאִסְתִּים קְלִיפָה לְמוֹחָא, כְּדֵין שַׁלְטָא הַהִיא קְלִיפָה עֲלַיְיהוּ וְדָחָה לוֹן לְבַר מֵהַהוּא דּוּכְתָּא.

**270.** That entrance is in the Holy Land, as long as they are doing the proper service. Due to sins, THE STRONG KLIPAH ON THE SIDES OF the entrance is drawn BACK to this side and that side, until THE SIDES OF the Klipah join together. AND THIS OCCURS ONLY AT THE TIME OF THE DESTRUCTION OF THE TEMPLE, AS WRITTEN BEFORE US. Since the Klipah clogs the brain, the Klipah dominates over them, OVER YISRAEL, and pushes them out of this place.

271. וְעַכ״ד אע״ג דְּדָחָה לוֹן לְבַר, לָא יָכִיל הַהִיא קְלִיפָה תַּקִיפָא לְשַׁלְטָאָה בְּהַהוּא דּוּכְתָּא קַדִּישָׁא, דְּלָאו אַתְרֵיהּ אִיהוּ. וְאִי תֵּימָא, אִי הָכִי, הוֹאִיל וְלָא יָכִיל הַהִיא קְלִיפָה תַּקִיפָא לְשַׁלְטָאָה בְּהַהוּא דּוּכְתָּא קַדִּישָׁא, אֲמַאי קַיְימָא חָרוּב, דְּהָא חָרְבָּא לָא הֲוֵי בְּעָלְמָא, אֶלָּא מִסִּטְרָא דְּהַהִיא קְלִיפָה תַּקִיפָא.

**271.** Even though it pushed them outside, that strong Klipah cannot dominate in that holy place, NAMELY IN THE HOLY LAND, because it is not its place. If you ask: If Klipah cannot dominate in that holy place, why does it stand desolate, for there is no destruction in the world but for that strong Klipah?

272. אֶלָּא וַדַּאי כַּד אִתְחָרַב לָא אִתְחָרַב אֶלָּא מֵהַהוּא סִטְרָא, בְּשַׁעְתָא דְּאַסְתִּים לְמוֹחָא, וְקוּדְשָׁא בְּרִיךְ הוּא עָבֵד דְּלָא תִּשְׁלוֹט הַהִיא קְלִיפָה תַּקִּיפָא עַל הַהוּא דּוּכְתָּא. וְכַד דָּחָה לוֹן לְיִשְׂרָאֵל מִנֵּיהּ, הַהִיא קְלִיפָה אִתְהַדְרַת וְאִתְפַּתְּחַת כְּמִלְקַדְמִין. וּבְגִין דְּעַמָּא קַדִּישָׁא לָא הֲווֹ תַּמָּן, חַפְיָא עַל הַהוּא פְּתִיחוּ, חוּפָּאָה קַדִּישָׁא דְּפָרוֹכְתָּא קְלִישָׁא, לְנַטְרָא הַהוּא אֲתָר, דְּלָא יִסְתּוֹם לֵיהּ הַהִיא קְלִיפָה תַּקִּיפָא, וְאָחִיד בְּכָל סִטְרוֹי.

272. HE ANSWERS: Assuredly when it was destroyed, it was destroyed only from that side OF THE STRONG KLIPAH, when it clogged the brain, and the Holy One, blessed be He, caused it so that the strong Klipah would not dominate over this place. And when THE KLIPAH pushed away Yisrael from it, that Klipah returned and it reopened as before. Since the holy nation was not there, BECAUSE IT WAS IN EXILE, that opening was covered with a holy cover of a delicate curtain to guard that place, so that the strong Klipah could not clog it. And THE COVER is attached on all sides TO GUARD IT.

273. לְמֶהֱוֵי רְבוּת קֻדְשָׁא עַל אַרְעָא כְּמִלְקַדְמִין, לָא יָכִיל, דְּהָא הַהוּא חוּפָּאָה קְלִישָׁא אָחִיד, דְּלָא יֵחוּת לְתַתָּא, דְּהָא עַמָּא קַדִּישָׁא לָאו תַּמָּן. וְע"ד לָא אִתְבְּנֵי חָרְבַּן, מִיּוֹמָא דְּאִתְחֲרִיבוּ. לְשַׁלְטָאָה הַהִיא קְלִיפָה תַּקִּיפָא, לָא יַכְלָא, דְּהָא הַהוּא חוּפָּאָה קְלִישָׁא אָחִיד בֵּיהּ בְּכָל סִטְרוֹי בְּהַהוּא פְּתִיחוּ דְּלָא תִּשְׁלוֹט תַּמָּן, וְלָא תַּסְתִּים מוֹחָא, בְּהַהוּא חוּפָּאָה דְּפָרוֹכְתָּא קְלִישָׁא, דְּאִיהוּ מִגּוֹ מְשִׁיכוּ דְּפָרוֹכְתָּא קַדִּישָׁא דִּלְעֵילָּא, דְּנָטִיר הַהוּא אֲתָר.

273. That there should be a holy presence on the earth as originally is not possible, because that delicate cover is attached there so that it should not go down, because the holy nation is not there. Therefore, the desolation has not been rebuilt from the day THE EARTH was destroyed. It is not possible for the strong Klipah to dominate, because that light cover is attached on all sides of that opening so that THE KLIPAH should not dominate and should not clog the brain. That light cover, which is from the drawing of the Holy Curtain of above, guards that place.

274. וּבְגִין כָּךְ, כָּל אִינּוּן נִשְׁמָתִין דִּשְׁאַר עַמִּין, דְּדַיְירִין בְּאַרְעָא, כַּד

נָפְקִין מֵהַאי עָלְמָא, לָא מְקַבְּלָא לוֹן, וְדָחֵי לוֹן לְבַר, וְאַזְלִין וְשָׁטָאן וּמִתְגַּלְגְּלִין בְּכַמָּה גִּלְגּוּלִין, עַד דְּנַפְקֵי מִכָּל אַרְעָא קַדִּישָׁא, וְסַחֲרָן לְסִטְרַיְיהוּ, בִּמְסָאֲבוּ דִּלְהוֹן. וְכָל אִינּוּן נִשְׁמָתִין דְּיִשְׂרָאֵל דְּנָפְקִין תַּמָּן, סַלְּקִין, וְהַהוּא חוּפָּאָה קְלִישָׁא מְקַבְּלָא לוֹן, וְעָאלִין לְקַדִּישָׁא עִלָּאָה, בְּגִין דְּכָל זִינָא אַזְלָא לְזִינֵיהּ.

**274.** Therefore, when all the souls of the other nations that live in the land of Yisrael depart from the world, THE LAND does not accept them and pushes them outside. They go and float and revolve in many evolutions until they exit from the entire Holy Land, and they circle UNTIL THEY REACH their side of their impurity. All the souls of Yisrael who expire there, ascend. That delicate cover accepts them and enter the supernal Holiness, as every kind seeks its own kind.

**275.** וְנִשְׁמָתֵיהוֹן דְּיִשְׂרָאֵל דְּנָפְקֵי לְבַר מֵאַרְעָא, בִּרְשׁוּתָא דְּהַהִיא קְלִיפָא תַּקִּיפָא, אַזְלָא וְסַחֲרָא וּמִתְגַּלְגְּלָא, עַד דְּתָבַת לְדוּכְתָּהָא, וְעָאלַת לַאֲתָר דְּאִתְחֲזֵי לָהּ. זַכָּאָה חוּלָקֵיהּ, מַאן דְּנִשְׁמָתֵיהּ נָפְקָא בִּרְשׁוּ קַדִּישָׁא, בְּהַהוּא פְּתִיחוּ דְּאַרְעָא קַדִּישָׁא.

**275.** The souls of Yisrael who die outside the land of Yisrael, in the domain of that strong Klipah, EACH ONE circles and rolls until it returns to its place and enters the place suitable for it. Happy is the portion of one whose soul departs in the Holy Domain and in that opening in the Holy Land.

**276.** מַאן דְּנִשְׁמָתֵיה נַפְקַת בְּאַרְעָא קַדִּישָׁא, אִי אִתְקְבַר בְּהַהוּא יוֹמָא, לָא שַׁלְטָא עֲלֵיהּ רוּחָא מְסָאֲבָא כְּלָל. וְעַ"ד כְּתִיב בִּצְלִיבָא, כִּי קָבוֹר תִּקְבְּרֶנּוּ בַּיּוֹם הַהוּא וְלֹא תְטַמֵּא אֶת אַדְמָתְךָ. בְּגִין דְּבַלֵּילְיָא אִתְיְהִיב רְשׁוּ לְרוּחַ מְסָאֲבָא לְמִשְׁטַטָא. וְאַע"ג דְּאִתְיְהִיב לוֹן רְשׁוּ, לָא עָאלִין בְּאַרְעָא קַדִּישָׁא, בַּר אִי אַשְׁכְּחָן תַּמָּן מָנָא לְאַעֲלָא בֵּיהּ.

**276.** If someone is buried on the day that his soul departs in the Holy Land, the spirit of impurity has no dominion over him at all. Therefore, it says about one who is hanged, "But you shall surely bury him that day: that your

land be not defiled" (Devarim 21:23). At night, permission is given to the spirits of impurity to hover about and, although permission is given to them, they cannot enter the Holy Land unless they find there a vessel into which to enter, NAMELY A DEAD BODY.

277. אֵבְרִין וּפְדָרִין דְּמִתְאַכְּלָן בְּלֵילְיָא, לְאַתְזְנָא זִינִין אַחֲרָנִין, לָאו דְּעַיְילִין בְּאַרְעָא, וְלָא לְאַמְשָׁכָא לוֹן בְּאַרְעָא, אֶלָּא, בְּגִין דְּלָא תִּשְׁלוֹט סְטְרָא אַחֲרָא גּוֹ אַרְעָא, וְלָא יִתְמַשְׁכָא לְאַעֲלָא תַּמָּן. וּבְגִין כָּךְ, תְּנָנָא מִנַּיְיהוּ הֲוָה סָלִיק עֲקִימָא, וּמִתְגַּלְגְּלָא לְבַר, וְאָזִיל בִּבְהִילוּ, עַד דְּעָאל לְנוּקְבָּא דְּצָפוֹן, דְּתַמָּן מְדוֹרִין דְּכָל סִטְרִין אַחֲרָנִין, וְתַמָּן עָאל תְּנָנָא, וְכֻלְּהוּ אִתְזָנוּ תַּמָּן.

277. The limbs and fat are burned at night ON THE ALTAR to nourish WITH THEIR SMOKE the other kinds, WHICH ARE THE OTHER SIDE. THAT DOES not MEAN that they enter the land TO BE NOURISHED BY THE SMOKE, nor does it draw them into the land. It is rather THE OPPOSITE, in order that the Other Side should not dominate in the land and they should not be drawn to enter there. Therefore, the smoke, OF THE LIMBS AND FAT, would ascend in a crooked WAY and roll outside OF THE LAND OF YISRAEL. It would travel hastily until it entered the hole in the north where lie the habitations of all those of the Other Side. The smoke enters there, and they are all nourished there.

278. תְּנָנָא דִּימָמָא, הֲוָה סָלִיק לְדוּכְתֵּיהּ בְּאֹרַח מֵישָׁר, וְאִתְזָן מַה דְּאִתְזָן. וּמֵהַהוּא פְּתִיחוּ, אִתְזָנוּ כָּל סִטְרֵי קְלִיפָה תַּקִּיפָא, דְּאִיהִי לְבַר מֵאַרְעָא קַדִּישָׁא, וּמֵהַהִיא תְּנָנָא גַּסָּה כְּמָה דְּאוֹקִימְנָא.

278. The smoke OF THE OFFERINGS that ascend during the day would ascend to its place above in a direct path and there was that that was nourished from it, MEANING AS IT IS WRITTEN: "FOR A SWEET SAVOR, AN OFFERING MADE BY FIRE TO HASHEM" (SHEMOT 29:41). From that opening, MEANING THE HOLE IN THE NORTH SIDE, all sides of the strong Klipah are nourished, which is outside of the Holy Land, and they are nourished from that coarse smoke OF THE LIMBS AND FAT, as we have established.

279. גּוּפֵיהוֹן דְּצַדִּיקַיָּיא, דְּלָא אִתְמְשָׁכוּ בְּהַאי עָלְמָא בָּתַר הֲנָאִין דְּהַהִיא קְלִיפָה תַּקִּיפָא, לָא שַׁלְטָא עָלַיְיהוּ רוּחַ מְסָאֲבוּ כְּלָל, דְּהָא לָא אִשְׁתַּתָּפוּ אֲבַתְרֵיהּ כְּלוּם בְּהַאי עָלְמָא. כְּמָה דְגוּפָא דְרַשִׁיעַיָּיא אִתְמְשָׁךְ בְּהַאי עָלְמָא בָּתַר הַהִיא קְלִיפָה תַּקִּיפָא, וַהֲנָאִין וְעִנּוּגִין דִּילֵיהּ וְתִיקּוּנִין דִּילֵיהּ, הָכִי אִסְתָּאַב, בָּתַר דְּנַפְקַת נִשְׁמָתֵיהּ מִנֵּיהּ.

**279.** The spirit of impurity does not dominate the bodies of the righteous that were not drawn in this world after the pleasures AND LUST of that strong Klipah, because they did not join with it at all in this world. As the body of the wicked is drawn in this world after that strong Klipah and after its pleasures, delights and embellishments, thus is he defiled after his soul leaves him.

280. גּוּפֵיהוֹן דְּצַדִּיקַיָּא, דְּלָא מִתְעַנְּגֵי בְּהַאי עָלְמָא, אֶלָּא מִתַּעֲנוּגֵי דְּמִצְוָה, וּסְעוּדָתֵי שַׁבָּתִין וְחַגִּין וּזְמַנִּין, הַהוּא רוּחַ מְסָאֲבָא לָא יָכִיל לְשַׁלְּטָאָה עָלַיְיהוּ, דְּהָא לָא אִתְעַנְּגוּ מִדִּילֵיהּ כְּלוּם. וְהוֹאִיל וְלָא נָטְלוּ מִדִּילֵיהּ, לֵית לֵיהּ רְשׁוּ עָלַיְיהוֹן כְּלָל. זַכָּאָה אִיהוּ מַאן דְּלָא אִתְהֲנֵי מִדִּילֵיהּ כְּלוּם.

**280.** That spirit of impurity cannot dominate the bodies of the righteous that do not have any pleasure in this world, except for the pleasure in performing a commandment and the meals of Shabbat and Holy Days and Festivals, because they have derived no pleasure from it at all and have taken nothing from it. He has our rule over them. Happy is he who has not gained any pleasure from it at all.

281. מַאן דְּנִשְׁמָתֵיהּ נָפְקָא לְבַר מֵאַרְעָא קַדִּישָׁא, וְהַהוּא גּוּפָא אִסְתָּאַב בְּהַהוּא רוּחַ מְסָאֲבוּ, הַהוּא רוּחַ מְסָאֲבוּ אִשְׁתָּאִיב בְּגַוֵּיהּ, עַד דְּתָב לֵיהּ עַפְרָא. וְאִי הַהוּא גּוּפָא, דְּאִשְׁתָּאִיב בֵּיהּ הַהוּא רוּחַ מְסָאֲבָא, סַלְּקִין לֵיהּ לְאִתְקַבְּרָא גּוֹ אַרְעָא קַדִּישָׁא, עֲלֵיהּ כְּתִיב, וַתָּבֹאוּ וַתְּטַמְּאוּ אֶת אַרְצִי וְנַחֲלָתִי שַׂמְתֶּם לְתוֹעֵבָה. אַרְצִי, דְּלָא שַׁלְטָא עֲלָהּ רוּחַ מְסָאֲבוּ, בְּהַהוּא גּוּפָא דִּלְכוֹן, דְּאִשְׁתָּאִיב בֵּיהּ רוּחַ מְסָאֲבוּ, דְּקָא מַיְיתִין לְקַבְרָא לֵיהּ בְּאַרְצִי, אַתּוּן מְסָאֲבִין לָהּ, לְאִסְתָּאֲבָא בֵּיהּ. אִי לָא דְּעָבִיד קוּדְשָׁא

בְּרִיךְ הוּא אַסְוָותָא לְאַרְעָא, דְּהָא כֵּיוָן דְּאִתְבַּלֵּי הַהוּא גּוּפָא, נָשִׁיב
קוּדְשָׁא בְּרִיךְ הוּא רוּחָא מִלְעֵילָא, וְדָחֵי לֵיהּ לְהַהוּא רוּחַ מְסָאֲבָא לְבַר,
דְּהָא אִיהוּ חָס עַל אַרְעֵיהּ.

**281.** He whose soul departs outside of the Holy Land and had his body
defiled by the impure spirit, the impure spirit is absorbed in it until it returns
to dust. If that body that has swallowed that impure spirit is brought up to be
buried in the Holy Land, it is written of it: "But when you entered, you
defiled My land, and made My heritage an abomination" (Yirmeyah 2:7). It
is "My land" as the impure spirit did not have power over it, with that body
of yours, in which the impure spirit is absorbed, that you are bringing to
bury in My land. You defile it in being defiled in it, IN THE IMPURE BODY,
were it not for the Holy One, blessed be He, making a remedy for the land.
As soon as that body decays, the Holy One, blessed be He, causes a wind to
blow from above and push the impure spirit outside, because He has pity
upon the Land.

**282.** יוֹסֵף, לָא שַׁלִּיט עַל גּוּפֵיהּ רוּחַ מְסָאֲבָא לְעָלְמִין, אע״ג דְּנִשְׁמָתֵיהּ
נָפְקַת בִּרְשׁוּ אַחֲרָא. מ״ט. בְּגִין דְּלָא אִתְמְשִׁיךְ בְּחַיּוֹי בָּתַר רוּחַ
מְסָאֲבָא. וְעִם כָּל דָּא, לָא בָּעָא דְּגוּפֵיהּ יְסַלְּקוּן לֵיהּ לְאִתְקַבְּרָא בְּאַרְעָא
קַדִּישָׁא, אֶלָּא אָמַר, וְהַעֲלִיתֶם אֶת עַצְמוֹתַי, וְלָא גוּפִי.

**282.** The impure spirit never dominated Joseph's body, even though his soul
departed in a foreign domain, NAMELY OUTSIDE OF THE LAND OF
YISRAEL. What is the reason? It is because he was not drawn after the
impure spirit during his lifetime. Still in all, he did not want them to bring
up his body to be buried in the Holy Land, but rather said, "And you shall
carry up my bones" (Beresheet 50:25), but not my body.

**283.** יַעֲקֹב לָא מִית, וְגוּפֵיהּ אִתְקַיַּים בְּקִיּוּמָא תָּדִיר, וְלָא דָּחִיל לְסִטְרָא
אַחֲרָא, דְּהָא עַרְסֵיהּ הֲוָה שָׁלִים, בִּשְׁלִימוּ דִּנְהוֹרָא עִלָּאָה, בִּנְהִירוּ
דִּתְרֵיסַר שִׁבְטִין, וּבְשִׁבְעִים נֶפֶשׁ, בְּגִין כָּךְ לָא דָּחִיל לְסִטְרָא אַחֲרָא,
וְלָא יָכִיל לְשַׁלְטָאָה עֲלֵיהּ. וְתוּ, דְּאִיהוּ גוּפָא דְּדִיּוּקְנָא עִלָּאָה, דְּשַׁפִּירוּ
דִּילֵיהּ אָחִיד לְכָל סִטְרִין, וְכָל אִינּוּן שַׁיְיפִין דְּאָדָם קַדְמָאָה הֲווֹ אֲחִידָן

בֵּיהּ. וְעַ"ד כְּתִיב בֵּיהּ, וְשָׁכַבְתִּי עִם אֲבוֹתַי וּנְשָׂאתַנִי מִמִּצְרַיִם, גּוּפָא
שְׁלִים. וְעַ"ד וַיַּחַנְטוּ הָרוֹפְאִים אֶת יִשְׂרָאֵל, דְּגוּפֵיהּ יְהֵא קָאִים בְּקִיּוּמָא.
וְהָכִי אִצְטְרִיךְ. שְׁאַר בְּנֵי עָלְמָא דְּנַפְקַת נִשְׁמָתַיְיהוּ בְּאַרְעָא קַדִּישָׁא,
נַפְשָׁא וְגוּפָא אִשְׁתְּזִיב מִכֹּלָּא.

**283.** Jacob did not die, and his body remained intact constantly. Jacob did not fear the Other Side because his bed was perfect in the perfection of the supernal Light, in the illumination of the twelve tribes and seventy souls. Therefore, he did not fear the Other Side for it could not dominate him and because he was also the body of the supernal Image, MEANING THAT HE WAS A CHARIOT FOR TIFERET, and his beauty was attached in all the sides. All the limbs of Adam were attached to him. Therefore, it is written of him: "But I will lie with my fathers, and you shall carry me out of Egypt" (Beresheet 47:30), MEANING a whole body. Therefore, "the physicians embalmed Yisrael" (Beresheet 50:2) so that his body would remain intact, and this is the way it should BE. The other people of the world whose souls departed in the Holy Land, their souls and bodies are spared from everything.

## 29. Nefesh, Ruach, Neshamah

### A Synopsis

This section explains the three levels of the soul of man and the corresponding three levels in the supernal realm. These levels are Nefesh, Ruach, and Neshamah. The Nefesh is present in the grave until the body decays into dust. The Ruach is the one that enters the terrestrial Garden of Eden and is shaped there in the form of the body belonging to this world. Neshamah ascends immediately to her place, the place from whence she emerged, Malchut. We learn that until the Neshamah ascends to and becomes attached to the Throne, the Ruach does not become crowned in the Garden of Eden of the Earth and the Nefesh does not settle in its place. As soon as the Neshamah ascends, they all can rest. When people pray at the cemetery, the Nefesh awakens, then floats to awaken Ruach, who ascends and awakens the Neshamah. Then the Holy One has mercy on the world. We read how the three are bonded as one : the Nefesh is the throne for the Ruach, while Neshamah takes out the Ruach, gives it power, dominates it and illuminates it with the light of life. After death, at the time that the Neshamah becomes adorned above in the Holy Crown, the Ruach is standing in the supernal Light during Shabbat, New Moons and Festivals. Then when the Ruach descends from the supernal Light to dwell in the Garden of Eden, the Nefesh stands in the grave and becomes attired in the form that the body had originally, and praises the Holy One. If people gave themselves permission they could see these forms on the graves thanking and praising the Holy One. During the day of Rosh Hashanah when the world is being judged and the Throne of Judgment stands by the supernal King to judge the world, every single Nefesh hovers and beseeches Mercy for the living. Sometimes they notify the living of their verdicts in a vision at night, and then the living repent. The text goes on to tell how Yedomiam is the appointed angel who oversees the taking of souls. Then we read of the correspondence between these three levels of soul in man and the three levels in the four worlds of Asiyah, Yetzirah, Briyah and Atzilut. The moon is the Nefesh of Atzilut, and it illuminates all the chariots and camps of the three lower worlds even as the Nefesh of man illuminates the limbs and bones of the body. The text says: Happy are the righteous to merit three rests in the World to Come.

### The Relevance of this Passage

This profound portion raises our consciousness to the highest level of our souls (Neshamah). The ascension assures a peaceful and merciful transition into the world to come. Our meditation awakens the force of

mercy, causing supernal compassion to spill down upon creation. Transformation of our nature and positive change in the world is achieved through a path of mercy as opposed to one of torment.

All judgments are hereby rescinded upon the merit of the righteous throughout history.

284. תְּלַת שְׁמָהָן אִקְרֵי נִשְׁמָתָא דְּבַר נָשׁ, נֶפֶשׁ, רוּחָא, וְנִשְׁמָתָא. וְכֻלְּהוּ כְּלִילָן דָּא בְּדָא, וּבִתְלַת דּוּכְתֵּי אִשְׁתְּכַח חֵילַיְיהוּ. נֶפֶשׁ דָּא, אִשְׁתְּכַחַת גּוֹ קִבְרָא, עַד דְּגוּפָא אִתְבְּלֵי בְּעַפְרָא, וּבְדָא מִתְגַּלְגְּלַת הַאי עָלְמָא, לְאִשְׁתַּכְּחָא גּוֹ חַיָּיא, וּלְמִנְדַּע בְּצַעֲרָא דִּלְהוֹן, וּבְשַׁעֲתָא דִּי אִצְטְרִיכוּ, בָּעָאת רַחֲמֵי עֲלַיְיהוּ.

284. The soul of man is called by three names, which are Nefesh, Ruach, and Neshamah. They are all combined with each other, and their strength is found in three places. The Nefesh is present in the grave until the body decays into dust, and so it rolls around in this world to be among the living and to be acquainted with their pain. At a time of need, it pleads for Mercy for them.

285. רוּחָא דָּא, אִיהוּ דְּעָאל בְּגִנְתָּא דִּי בְּאַרְעָא, וְאִצְטַיַּיר תַּמָּן, בְּדִיּוּקְנָא דְּגוּפָא דְּהַאי עָלְמָא, בְּחַד מַלְבּוּשָׁא דְּמִתְלַבְּשָׁא תַּמָּן. וְדָא אִתְהֲנֵי תַּמָּן בַּהֲנָאִין וְכִסּוּפִין בְּזִיוָא דְּבְגִנְתָּא. וּבְשַׁבַּתֵּי וְיַרְחֵי וּזְמַנֵי, סַלְקָא לְעֵילָא, וְאִתְהֲנֵי תַּמָּן, וְתָב לְאַתְרֵיה. וְעַ"ד כְּתִיב, וְהָרוּחַ תָּשׁוּב אֶל הָאֱלֹהִים אֲשֶׁר נְתָנָהּ. תָּשׁוּב וַדַּאי, בְּהָנֵי זִמְנִין דְּקָאמְרָן.

285. The Ruach is the one that enters the terrestrial Garden of Eden and is shaped there in the form of the body from this world, in a garment that it dons there. It experiences these pleasures and delights that are in the shine of the Garden of Eden. And it ascends above, TO THE UPPER GARDEN OF EDEN, on the Shabbat and beginning of new months and Festivals, and it delights there and returns to its place. Therefore, it is written: "And the spirit (Heb. *ruach*) returns to the Elohim who gave it" (Kohelet 12:7). It shall surely return, MEANING during these times that we have mentioned.

286. נְשָׁמָה אִיהִי סַלְקָא מִיָּד לְאַתְרָהָא, לְהַהוּא אֲתָר דְּנָפְקַת מִתַּמָּן,

וְדָא אִיהִי דְּבְגִינָה אִתְנְהִירַת בּוּצִינָא, לְאַנְהֲרָא לְעֵילָא. דָּא לָא נַחְתַּת
לְתַתָּא לְעָלְמִין, בְּדָא אִתְכְּלִילַת, מַאן דְּאִתְכְּלִילַת מִכָּל סִטְרִין מֵעֵילָא
וּמִתַּתָּא. וְעַד דְּהַאי לָא סַלְקָא לְאִתְקַשְּׁרָא בְּכוּרְסַיָּיא, לָא מִתְעַטְּרָא
רוּחַ בְּגִנְתָּא דִּי בְּאַרְעָא, וְנֶפֶשׁ לָא מִתְיַשְּׁבָא בְּדוּכְתָּהָא. כֵּיוָן דְּאִיהִי
סַלְקָא, כֻּלְּהוּ אִית לְהוּ נַיְיחָא.

**286.** Neshamah ascends immediately to its place, to that place from where it emerged, NAMELY TO MALCHUT, FROM WHICH THE NESHAMAH IS BORN. It is for it that the candle illuminates, WHICH IS MALCHUT, to illuminate above. BECAUSE THE SOULS OF THE RIGHTEOUS ASCEND BY MAYIN NUKVIN (FEMALE WATERS) TO ZEIR ANPIN AND MALCHUT, THEY BECOME PAIRED THROUGH THEM. This one never descends below. In this is included whoever is included, NAMELY MALCHUT, from all the sides from above and below, BECAUSE MALCHUT COMPRISES THE SOULS OF THE RIGHTEOUS. Until THE NESHAMAH ascends to and becomes attached to the Throne, WHICH IS THE WORLD OF BRIYAH, the Ruach is not crowned in the terrestrial Garden of Eden and the Nefesh does not settle in its place. As soon as THE NESHAMAH ascends, they all can rest, FOR THEY ARRIVE AT THEIR PLACE.

287. וְכַד אִצְטְרִיךְ לִבְנֵי עָלְמָא, כַּד אִינוּן בְּצַעֲרָא, וְאָזְלֵי לְבֵי קִבְרֵי,
הַאי נֶפֶשׁ אִתְּעַרַת, וְאִיהִי אַזְלָא וּמְשַׁטְטָא, וְאִתְּעֲרַת לְרוּחַ, וְהַהוּא רוּחַ
אִתְּעַר לְגַבֵּי אֲבָהָן, וְסָלִיק וְאִתְּעַר לְגַבֵּי נִשְׁמָה, וּכְדֵין, קֻדְשָׁא בְּרִיךְ
הוּא חַיִּיס עַל עָלְמָא, וְהָא אוֹקִימְנָא. וְאַף עַל גַּב דְּהָא אִתְּעֲרוּ מִלִּין
אִלֵּין דְּנִשְׁמָתָא בְּגַוְונִין אַחֲרָנִין, כֻּלְּהוּ סַלְקִין בְּמַתְקְלָא, דָּא, וְדָא אִיהוּ
בְּרִירָה דְּמִלָּה, וְכֹלָּא חַד.

**287.** And MERCY is needed for the inhabitants of the world. When they are in sorrow and they go TO PRAY at the cemetery, this Nefesh awakens. It goes and floats and awakens Ruach, and that Ruach awakens toward the Patriarchs, ascends and awakens the Neshamah. Then the Holy One, blessed be He, has Mercy on the world as we have already established. Even though they have explained the subject of the Neshamah in other ways, MEANING THAT NEFESH IS IN ASIYAH, RUACH IN YETZIRAH, AND NESHAMAH IN

BRIYAH, they all amount to this format. This is the clarification of the matter, and it is all one.

288. וְכַד נִשְׁמְתָא אִתְעַכְּבַת מִלְסַלְּקָא לְדוּכְתָּהָא, רוּחָא אַזְלָא וְקַיְימָא בְּפִתְחָא דְּגִנְתָּא דְּעֵדֶן, וְלָא פַּתְחִין לָה פִּתְחָא, וְאָזְלָא וּמְשַׁטְטָא, וְלֵית מָאן דְּיַשְׁגַּח בָּהּ. נֶפֶשׁ אַזְלָא וּמְשַׁטְטָא בְּעָלְמָא, חָמַאת לְגוּפָא דְּסַלְקָא תּוֹלָעִין, וּבְהַהוּא דִּינָא דְּקִבְרָא, וּמִתְאַבְּלַת עֲלֵיהּ, כְּמָה דְּאוּקְמוּהָ דִּכְתִּיב, אַךְ בְּשָׂרוֹ עָלָיו יִכְאָב וְנַפְשׁוֹ עָלָיו תֶּאֱבָל. וְכֹלָּא אִיהוּ בְּעוֹנָשָׁא. עַד דְּנִשְׁמָה אִתְקְשָׁרַת בְּדוּכְתָּהָא לְעֵילָּא, וּכְדֵין כּוּלְּהוּ מִתְקַשְּׁרִין בְּדוּכְתַּיְיהוּ.

288. When the Neshamah is detained from ascending to its place, the Ruach goes and stands by the entrance of the LOWER Garden of Eden, but they do not open the entrance for it. It goes and drifts and no one pays attention. The Nefesh goes through the world and sees the body becoming wormy and judged in the grave, NAMELY THE THRASHING IN THE GRAVE, and it mourns for it as we have established, as it is written: "Only when his flesh is on him does he feel pain, and while his soul (Heb. *nefesh*) is within him does he mourn" (Iyov 14:22). Everyone is punished until the Neshamah is bound in its place above. Then they all become bound in their place.

289. בְּגִין דְּכָל הָנֵי תְּלַת, קִשּׁוּרָא חֲדָא אִינּוּן, כְּגַוְונָא דִּלְעֵילָּא, בְּרָזָא דְּנֶפֶשׁ רוּחַ וּנְשָׁמָה, דְּכֹלָּא חַד, וְקִשּׁוּרָא חַד. נֶפֶשׁ: לֵית לָה נְהוֹרָא מִגַּרְמָהּ כְּלוּם, וְדָא אִיהוּ דְּמִשְׁתַּתְּפָא בְּרָזָא דְּגוּפָא חַד, לְאַעְנְגָא וּלְמֵיזָן לֵיהּ, בְּכָל מָה דְּאִצְטְרִיךְ, כד"א וַתִּתֵּן טֶרֶף לְבֵיתָהּ וְחֹק לְנַעֲרוֹתֶיהָ. בֵּיתָהּ, דָּא אִיהוּ גוּפָא, דְּאִיהִי זָנָא לֵיהּ. וְנַעֲרוֹתֶיהָ, אִלֵּין אִינּוּן שַׁיְיפִין דְּהַאי גוּפָא.

289. All these three are one bond, similar to above in the secret of Nefesh, Ruach, and Neshamah, WHICH ARE MALCHUT, ZEIR ANPIN, AND BINAH OF ATZILUT, for they are all one and one bond: The Nefesh, WHICH IS MALCHUT, has no independent light, which is why it participates in the secret of one body, WHICH IS THE THREE WORLDS, BRIYAH, YETZIRAH AND ASIYAH, THAT MALCHUT DONS AS A SOUL DOES A BODY to delight

and nourish it in all its needs. About this, it is written: "And gives food to her household, and a portion to her maidens" (Mishlei 31:15). "Her household" refers to the body which She nourishes, and "her maidens" are the limbs of that body, NAMELY THE SFIROT OF BRIYAH, YETZIRAH AND ASIYAH.

290. רוּחַ: דָּא אִיהוּ דְּרָכִיב עַל הַאי נֶפֶשׁ, וְשָׁלִיט עֲלָהּ, וְנָהִיר לָהּ בְּכָל מָה דְּאִצְטְרִיךְ, וְנֶפֶשׁ אִיהוּ כֻּרְסְיָּיא לְהַאי רוּחַ. נְשָׁמָה: אִיהִי דְּאַפִּיקַת לְהַאי רוּחָא, וּשְׁלִיטַת עֲלֵיהּ, וְנָהִירַת לֵיהּ בְּהַהוּא נְהוֹרָא דְּחַיִּין, וְהַהוּא רוּחַ תַּלְיָא בְּהַאי נְשָׁמָה, וְאִתְנְהִיר מִנָּהּ בְּהַהוּא נְהוֹרָא דְּנָהִיר. הַהוּא נֶפֶשׁ, תַּלְיָא בְּהַאי רוּחַ, וְאִתְנְהִירַת מִנֵּיהּ, וְאִתְּזָנַת מִנֵּיהּ, וְכֹלָּא קְשׁוּרָא חַד.

290. Ruach is the one who rides on the Nefesh and dominates it, and illuminates it with all that it needs, NAMELY ZEIR ANPIN. The Nefesh is the throne for this Ruach. It is Neshamah who takes out this Ruach, gives it power, dominates it and illuminates it with that light of life, NAMELY BINAH. That Ruach depends upon this Neshamah and shines from it with the light that it illuminates upon it. That Nefesh is dependent upon this Ruach. It shines from it and is nourished by it. And they are all one bond.

291. וְעַד דְּהַאי נְשָׁמָה עִלָּאָה, לָא סַלְקָא גּוֹ נְבִיעוּ דְּעַתִּיקָא דְּעַתִּיקִין. סְתִימָא דְּכָל סְתִימִין, וְאִתְמַלְיָא מִנֵּיהּ, בְּגִין דְּלָא פָּסִיק. רוּחַ דָּא לָא עָאל בְּגִנְתָּא דְּעֵדֶן, דְּאִיהוּ נֶפֶשׁ, וּלְעוֹלָם רוּחַ לָא שַׁרְיָא אֶלָּא בְּגִנְתָּא דְּעֵדֶן, וּנְשָׁמָה לְעֵילָא. נֶפֶשׁ לָא אִתְיַשְׁבַת בְּדוּכְתָּהָא גּוֹ גוּפָא לְתַתָּא.

291. That supernal Neshamah, NAMELY BINAH, ascends into the flow from the most ancient of all and the most concealed, and it is filled WITH LIGHT from it because it does not stop ILLUMINATING. AND AS LONG AS THE NESHAMAH DOES NOT RETURN TO ITS PLACE, this Ruach does not enter the Garden of Eden which is the Nefesh, NAMELY MALCHUT. The Ruach dwells only in the Garden of Eden, BECAUSE ZEIR ANPIN AND MALCHUT UNITE THE ONE WITH THE OTHER, and the Neshamah is above. Also, the Nefesh, WHICH IS MALCHUT, is not settled in its place in the body below,

WHICH IS BRIYAH, YETZIRAH AND ASIYAH, AS LONG AS THE NESHAMAH
DOES NOT RETURN TO ITS PLACE ABOVE.

292. כְּגַוְונָא דָא, כֹּלָּא לְתַתָּא הָכִי מִתְפָּרְשָׁן בְּבַר נָשׁ, וְאע"ג דְּכֻלְּהוּ
קְשׁוּרָא חֲדָא, נְשָׁמָה סַלְקָא לְעֵילָּא, גּוֹ נְבִיעוּ דְּבֵירָא. רוּחַ עָאל בְּגִנְתָּא
דְּעֵדֶן, כְּגַוְונָא דִּלְעֵילָּא. נֶפֶשׁ אִתְיַשְּׁבָא גּוֹ קַבְרָא. וְאִי תֵּימָא, נֶפֶשׁ
לְעֵילָּא, דְּאִתְיַשְּׁבַת גּוֹ גּוּפָא בְּקַבְרָא, אָן הוּא קַבְרָא. אֶלָּא גּוֹ הַהוּא
קְלִיפָה תַּקִּיפָא, וְע"ד, נֶפֶשׁ כְּגַוְונָא דָא לְתַתָּא, וְכֹלָּא דָא כְּגַוְונָא דָא.
וּבְגִין כָּךְ, תְּלַת דַּרְגִּין מִתְפָּרְשָׁן, וְאִינוּן קְשׁוּרָא חֲדָא וְרָזָא חֲדָא.

292. In the same way, it is all explained in man BELOW. Even though THE
NEFESH, RUACH, AND NESHAMAH THAT ARE IN MAN are all one bond,
the Neshamah ascends above with the flow from the pit, NAMELY YESOD
OF MALCHUT. The Ruach enters the Lower Garden of Eden similar to
above, AS ZEIR ANPIN ENTERS THE GARDEN OF EDEN OF ATZILUT,
WHICH IS MALCHUT. The Nefesh settles in the grave. And if you ask, in
relation to the Nefesh above, WHICH IS MALCHUT, WILL YOU ALSO SAY
that it settles in the body in the grave? Where then is the grave ABOVE? HE
ANSWERS: But rather in that strong Klipah, BECAUSE PERTAINING TO
MALCHUT, IT IS SAID, "HER FEET GO DOWN TO DEATH" (MISHLEI 5:5),
FOR SHE BECOMES ATTIRED AT HER END IN THE STRONG KLIPAH,
WHICH IS THE ASPECT OF DEATH AND GRAVE. Therefore, the lower
Nefesh is similar to this below, and they all resemble one another.
Therefore, THE NESHAMAH is divided into three levels, NAMELY NEFESH,
RUACH, AND NESHAMAH. They are one bond and one secret.

293. וּבְכָל זִמְנָא דְּגַרְמֵי אִשְׁתְּכָחוּ גּוֹ קַבְרָא, הַאי נֶפֶשׁ אִשְׁתְּכָחַת תַּמָּן.
רָזָא הָכָא לְאִינוּן דְּיַדְעֵי אֹרַח קְשׁוֹט, דַּחֲלֵי חַטָּאָה. בְּשַׁעֲתָא דְּנִשְׁמְתָא
מִתְעַטְּרָא לְעֵילָּא, גּוֹ עִטְרָא קַדִּישָׁא, וְרוּחָא קָאִים בִּנְהִירוּ עִלָּאָה,
בְּשַׁבָּתֵי וְיַרְחֵי וּזְמַנֵּי, הַאי נֶפֶשׁ בְּשַׁעֲתָא דְּרוּחַ נַחְתָּא מִגּוֹ נְהִירוּ עִלָּאָה,
לְדַיְירָא בְּגִנְתָּא דְּעֵדֶן נָהִיר וְנָצִיץ, אִיהוּ קַיְּימָא גּוֹ קַבְרָא וְאִתְגַּלְּיִמַת
בְּדִיּוּקְנָא, דַּהֲוַת גּוֹ גּוּפָא בְּקַדְמֵיתָא, וְכָל אִינוּן גַּרְמֵי בְּהַהוּא דִּיּוּקְנָא
סַלְקָן, וּמְשַׁבְּחָאן וְאוֹדָן לְקוּדְשָׁא בְּרִיךְ הוּא, הה"ד כָּל עַצְמוֹתַי
תֹּאמַרְנָה יְיָ' מִי כָמוֹךְ. אוֹמְרוֹת לָא כְּתִיב, אֶלָּא תֹּאמַרְנָה.

**293.** As long as the bones are STILL in the grave, BEFORE THEY HAVE DECAYED, that Nefesh is present there. And here is the secret for those who know the true way, for those who fear sin. At the time that the Neshamah is adorned above in the Holy Crown, WHICH IS MALCHUT, the Ruach is standing in the supernal Light during Shabbat, the first day of the month and Festivals. When the Ruach descends from the supernal Light to dwell in the Garden of Eden and illuminates and sparkles, the Nefesh stands in the grave and is attired in the form that the body had originally. All the bones take that form and praise and acknowledge the Holy One, blessed be He, as written: "All my bones shall say, 'Hashem, who is like You'" (Tehilim 35:10). It does not write 'say,' but rather "shall say" MEANING IN THE GRAVE.

294. וְאִלְמָלֵי אִתְיְהִיב רְשׁוּ לְעֵינָא לְמֶחֱמֵי וְחָמֵי בְּלֵילְיָא דְעָיֵיל שַׁבְּתָא, וְלֵילֵי יַרְחֵי וְזִמְנֵי, כְּדִיוּקְנִין עַל גַּבֵּי קִבְרֵי, אוֹדָן וּמְשַׁבְּחָן לְקוּדְשָׁא בְּרִיךְ הוּא. אֲבָל טִפְּשׁוּ דִּבְנֵי נָשָׁא, קָא מְעַכְּבָא לְהוּ, דְּלָא יַדְעִין, וְלָא מַשְׁגִּיחִין עַל מַה קַיְימִין בְּהַאי עָלְמָא, וְלָא חַשְׁשִׁין לְאַשְׁגָּחָא בִּיקָרָא דְּמַלְכָּא עִלָּאָה בְּהַאי עָלְמָא, כ״ש לְאַשְׁגָּחָא בִּיקָרָא דְּהַהוּא עָלְמָא, וְעַל מָה קַיְימָא, וְאֵיךְ מִתְפָּרְשָׁן מִלִּין.

**294.** If permission would be given to the eye to see, it could see the like of forms on the graves that acknowledge and praise the Holy One, blessed be He, on the eve of the commencement of the Shabbat and the night of the first day of the month and Festivals. But the foolishness of man prevents them FROM SEEING. They do not know and do not pay attention to what is existent in this world. They do not bother to observe the honor of the supernal King in this world, and most certainly to observe the honor of that SUPERNAL World, and upon what it is based, and how the things are explained.

295. בְּיוֹמָא דר״ה, דְּעָלְמָא אִתְּדָן, וְכֻרְסְיָא דְדִינָא קַיְימָא, לְגַבֵּי מַלְכָּא עִלָּאָה, לְמֵידָן עָלְמָא. כָּל נֶפֶשׁ וְנֶפֶשׁ מְשַׁטְטָן, וּבָעָאן רַחֲמֵי עַל חַיֵּי. בְּלֵילְיָא דְּנָפְקָא יוֹמָא דְדִינָא, אַזְלִין וְקָא מְשַׁטְטִין לְמִשְׁמַע וּלְמִנְדַּע מָאן הוּא דִּינָא דְּאִתְּדָן עַל עָלְמָא, וּלְזִמְנִין דְּקָא מוֹדִיעִין בְּחֶזְוָוא לְחַיָּיא, כד״א בַּחֲלוֹם חֶזְיוֹן לַיְלָה בִּנְפוֹל תַּרְדֵּמָה עַל אֲנָשִׁים וְגוֹ׳, אָז

יִגְלֶה אֹזֶן אֲנָשִׁים וּבְמוֹסָרָם יַחְתּוֹם. מַאי מוֹסְרָם. דָּא נֶפֶשׁ, דְּאִיהִי קַיְימָא וְחָתִים לִבְנֵי נָשָׁא מִלִּין, לְקַבְּלָא מוּסָר.

**295.** During the day of Rosh Hashanah, when the world is being judged and the Throne of Judgment stands by the supernal King to judge the world, every single Nefesh hovers and beseeches Mercy for the living PEOPLE. During the night of the end of the Day of Judgment, they go and hover to hear and know the verdict that was decided for the world. Sometimes they notify the living in a vision, as it is written: "In a dream, in a night vision when a deep sleep falls upon men…then He opens the ears of man, and with discipline seals their instruction" (Iyov 33:15-16). What is "with discipline"? This is the Nefesh who stands and establishes things for people so that they should accept discipline, MEANING THAT IT NOTIFIES THEM OF THEIR VERDICT IN A VISION AT NIGHT AND THEN THEY REPENT.

296. בְּלֵילְיָא בַּתְרָאָה דְּחַגָּא, דְּקָא נַפְקָן פִּתְקִין מִבֵּי מַלְכָּא, וְהַהוּא צֵל אַעֲדִיאוּ מִבְּנֵי גְּרִיעוּ דְּהַאי עָלְמָא, הַהוּא נֶפֶשׁ דְּקָאמְרָן, אַזְלָא וּמְשַׁטְּטָא, וְחַד מְמַנָּא סָרְכָא, בְּרָזָא גְּלִיפָא בְּעִזְקָא בִּכְתַב מְפָרַשׁ, יְדוּמִיעָ״ם, דְּפָקִיד בִּכְתַב דְּזִיוָא גְּלִיפָא, וּבְגוֹ חֶזְוָון עִלָּאִין. בְּהַהוּא לֵילְיָא נָחִית, וְכַמָּה אֶלֶף אַלְפִין וְרִבּוֹא רִבְוָון עִמֵּיהּ, וְנַטְלִין לְהַהוּא צֵל מִכָּל חַד וְחַד, וְסַלְּקִין, לֵיהּ לְעֵילָּא.

**296.** During the last night of the Festival, the sentences emerge from the house of the King, and that shadow is removed from the people who are to be removed from this world. THEN that Nefesh that we mentioned goes and floats ABOVE. An appointed angel, who supervises the secret of the engraving on the seal in clear writing, MEANING OVER THE WRITING IN THE AFOREMENTIONED VERDICTS, whose name is Yedomiam, authorizes the writing of the engraved light and, within supernal Visions, descends during that night. Many thousands upon thousands and ten thousands upon ten thousands go with him. They take that shadow from each one WHO WAS SENTENCED TO DEATH, and bring it up above.

297. וְהַהִיא נֶפֶשׁ דְּקָאמְרָן, אַזְלָא וּמְשַׁטְּטָא וְחָמְאת לְהַהוּא צֵל, וְתָב לְאַתְרֵיהּ גּוֹ קִבְרָא, וְקָא מַכְרֶזֶת לִשְׁאָר מֵתַיָּיא, פְּלוֹנִי אָתֵי לְגַבָּן, פְּלוֹנִי

אָתֵי לְגַבָּן. אִי זַכָּאָה טָבָא אִיהוּ, כֻּלְּהוּ חַדָּאן, וְאִי לָאו, כֻּלְּהוּ אָמְרֵי וַוי. כַּד סַלְּקִין הַהוּא צֵל, סַלְּקִין לֵיהּ לְגַבֵּי הַהוּא עֶבֶד מְהֵימָן, דִּשְׁמֵיהּ מְטַטְרוֹ"ן, וְנָטִיל הַהוּא צֵל לְגַבֵּיהּ, וְסַלִּיק לֵיהּ לְאַתְרֵיהּ, כד"א, כְּעֶבֶד יִשְׁאַף צֵל, יִשְׁאַף צֵל וַדַּאי.

**297.** The Nefesh that we mentioned goes and floats and sees that shadow, AND KNOWS WHO IS GOING TO DIE, and returns to Her place at the grave. It proclaims to the other dead, So-and-so is coming to us, so-and-so is coming to us. If he is righteous and good, they all rejoice and if not they all say, Woe. When they elevate that shadow, they elevate it to the faithful servant whose name is Metatron, who takes that shadow near him and elevates it to its place, as it is written: "As a servant earnestly desires the shadow" (Iyov 7:2). Certainly, he earnestly desires the shadow.

**298.** מֵהַהִיא שַׁעֲתָא וְאֵילָךְ, מִתְתַּקְנָא דּוּכְתָּא לְהַהִיא נִשְׁמָה דְּהַהוּא בַּר נָשׁ, וְדוּכְתָּא לְרוּחַ בְּגִנְתָּא דְּעֵדֶן. וְדוּכְתָּא לְנֶפֶשׁ לְנַיְיחָא וּלְאִתְהַנָּאָה, בְּשַׁעֲתָא דְּמִשַׁטְּטָא וְאַזְלָא. בְּגִין דְּאִית נֶפֶשׁ דְּלֵית לָהּ נַיְיחָא. וְאִית נֶפֶשׁ דְּאִשְׁתְּצִיאַת עִם גּוּפָא.

**298.** From that moment and further, the place for that Neshamah of the men is prepared, MEANING IN YESOD OF MALCHUT OF ATZILUT, as is a place for Ruach in the LOWER Garden of Eden and a place for Nefesh to rest and enjoy during the time that it floats and goes. For there is a Nefesh that has no rest, and there is a Nefesh that perishes with the body.

**299.** וְהַאי אִיהִי דְּלֵית לָהּ נַיְיחָא, וְהַאי אִיהִי דִּכְתִּיב בָּהּ, וְאֶת נֶפֶשׁ אוֹיְבֶיךָ יְקַלְּעֶנָּה בְּתוֹךְ כַּף הַקָּלַע. דְּדָא אִיהִי אַזְלָא וּמְשַׁטְּטָא וּמִתְגַּלְגְּלָא בְּכָל עָלְמָא, וְלֵית לָהּ נַיְיחָא כָּל יְמָמָא וְלֵילֵי, וְדָא אִיהוּ עוֹנָשָׁא יַתִּיר מִכֹּלָּא וְהַהִיא דְּתִשְׁתְּצֵי עִם גּוּפָה, וְתִשְׁתְּצֵי מֵאֲתַר אַחֲרָא, הַהִיא דִּכְתִּיב בָּהּ, וְנִכְרְתָה הַנֶּפֶשׁ הַהִיא מִלְּפָנַי אֲנִי יְיָ'. מַאן מִלְּפָנַי. דְּלָא שַׁרְיָא עֲלָהּ רוּחָא. וְכַד רוּחָא לָא שַׁרְיָא עֲלָהּ, לֵית לָהּ שׁוּתָּפוּ כְּלָל בְּמַה דִּלְעֵילָּא, וְלָא יַדְעַת מֵאִינּוּן מִלִּין דְּהַהוּא עָלְמָא כְּלָל, וְהַאי אִיהִי נֶפֶשׁ כִּבְעִירֵי.

**299.** The one that has no rest is the one about whom it is written: "And the soul (Heb. *Nefesh*) of your enemies, them shall he sling out, as out of the hollow of a sling" (I Shmuel 25:29). This is the one that goes and floats and rolls throughout the whole world, and has no rest at all days and nights. This is the hardest punishment of all. The Nefesh that perishes with the body is cut out from a different place, as it is written: "That Nefesh will be cut off from My presence, I am Hashem" (Vayikra 22:3). What is "from My presence?" It means that the Ruach does not dwell upon it and when the Ruach does not dwell upon it, it has no connection at all with that which is above. It does not know at all of these things in that world. And this Nefesh is like an animal.

‏300. נֶפֶשׁ דְּאִית לָהּ נַיְיחָא, הַאי אִיהִי כַּד אַזְלָא וּמְשַׁטְּטָא, אִתְעֲרַעת בְּהַאי מְמַנָּא יְדוּמִיעַ״ם, וּבְאִינּוּן סַרְכִין דִּילֵיהּ, וְנַטְלִין לָהּ, וְאַעֲלִין לָהּ בְּכָל פִּתְחֵי גַּן עֵדֶן, וְאַחְזְיָין לָהּ יְקָרָא דְּצַדִּיקַיָּא, וִיקָרָא דְּהַהוּא רוּחַ דִּילָהּ, וְאִיהִי מִתְדַּבְּקָא בֵּיהּ בְּנַיְיחָא, גּוֹ הַהוּא לְבוּשָׁא, וּכְדֵין יַדְעַת בְּאִינּוּן מִלִּין דְּעָלְמָא.

**300.** A Nefesh that has rest meets this appointed Angel Yedomiam and his officers when it goes and floats. They take and elevate it to all the entrances of the Garden of Eden, show it the honor of the righteous and the honor of its Ruach, and it cleaves unto THE RUACH in rest within that garment OF THAT RUACH. Then it knows about the things of the UPPER World.

‏301. וְכַד הַהוּא רוּחַ סַלְקָא לְאִתְעַטְּרָא גּוֹ נְשָׁמָה עִלָּאָה לְעֵילָּא, הַהִיא נֶפֶשׁ מִתְקַשְּׁרָא בְּהַהוּא רוּחַ, וְאִתְנְהִירַת מִנֵּיהּ, כְּסִיהֲרָא כַּד אִתְנְהִירַת מִשִּׁמְשָׁא. וְרוּחַ מִתְקַשְּׁרָא גּוֹ הַהִיא נִשְׁמְתָא. וְהַהִיא נִשְׁמְתָא מִתְקַשְּׁרָא, גּוֹ סוֹף מַחֲשָׁבָה, דְּאִיהִי רָזָא דְּנֶפֶשׁ דִּלְעֵילָּא.

**301.** When that Ruach ascends to be attired with the supernal Neshamah above, the Nefesh joins that Ruach and illuminates from it, like the moon when it illuminates from the sun. And the Ruach is connected with that Neshamah. That Neshamah becomes bound into the end of thought, MEANING THE END OF ATZILUT THAT IS CALLED IN ITS ENTIRETY 'THOUGHT', MEANING CHOCHMAH, BECAUSE IN GENERAL, THE FOUR WORLDS, ATZILUT, BRIYAH, YETZIRAH AND ASIYAH, ARE CHOCHMAH,

BINAH, TIFERET, AND MALCHUT, which is the secret of the Nefesh of above, NAMELY MALCHUT OF ATZILUT THAT IS CALLED 'NEFESH'.

302. וְהַהִיא נֶפֶשׁ, אִתְקְשָׁרַת גּוֹ הַהוּא רוּחַ עִלָּאָה, וְהַהוּא רוּחַ אִתְקְשַׁר גּוֹ הַהִיא נִשְׁמָה עִלָּאָה. וְהַהִיא נִשְׁמְתָא אִתְקַשְּׁרַת בְּאֵין סוֹף. וּכְדֵין אִיהוּ נַיְיחָא דְּכֹלָּא, וְקִשּׁוּרָא דְּכֹלָּא עֵילָא וְתַתָּא, כֹּלָּא בְּרָזָא חֲדָא, וְגַוְוּנָא חֲדָא.

302. That Nefesh, NAMELY MALCHUT OF ATZILUT, is connected with the supernal Ruach, WHICH IS ZEIR ANPIN, and that Ruach is connected with the supernal Neshamah, WHICH IS BINAH. That Neshamah is connected with the endless (Heb. *Ein Sof*), MEANING THAT IT BECOMES BOUND WITH ARICH ANPIN, AS MENTIONED, AND ARICH ANPIN WITH THE ENDLESS. Then there is rest for all, and everything is connected above and below all in one secret and in the same manner.

303. וּכְדֵין דָּא אִיהוּ נַיְיחָא דְּנֶפֶשׁ דִּלְתַתָּא, וְעַל דָּא כְּתִיב, וְהָיְתָה נֶפֶשׁ אֲדֹנִי צְרוּרָה בִּצְרוֹר הַחַיִּים אֶת יְיָ' אֱלֹהֶיךָ. בְּגַוְוֹנָא חֲדָא, וּבְרָזָא חֲדָא, דְּהַהוּא אֶת, דָּא כְּגַוְוֹנָא דָא.

303. Then there is repose for the Nefesh below. About this, it is written: "And may the soul (*Nefesh*) of my master be bound in the bond of life with (Heb. *et*) Hashem your Elohim" (I Shmuel 25:29), MEANING THAT THEY ARE BOUND AND ATTACHED in one way and by one secret with 'Et,' WHICH IS MALCHUT OF ATZILUT. FOR THE NEFESH IS CONNECTED WITH THE RUACH IN THE LOWER GARDEN OF EDEN; AND THE RUACH WITH NESHAMAH WHICH IS IN MALCHUT OF ATZILUT, the ones corresponding to the others, AS NEFESH, RUACH AND NESHAMAH OF A MAN ARE SIMILAR TO NEFESH, RUACH, AND NESHAMAH OF ATZILUT AS MENTIONED.

304. כַּד נַחְתָּא סִיהֲרָא, רָזָא דְּנֶפֶשׁ עִלָּאָה, נְהוֹרָא מִכָּל סִטְרִין. אִיהִי נַהֲרָא לְכָל רְתִיכִין וּמַשִׁרְיָין, וְעָבֵיד לוֹן גּוּפָא חֲדָא שְׁלִימָא, דְּנָהִיר בִּנְהִירוּ בְּזִיוָא עִלָּאָה. אוּף הָכִי כְּגַוְוֹנָא דָּא, נַחְתָּא הַאי נֶפֶשׁ תַּתָּאָה,

נְהִירָא מִכָּל סִטְרִין מִגּוֹ נְהִירוּ דְּנִשְׁמָה, וּמִגּוֹ נְהִירוּ דְּרוּחַ, וְנַחְתָּא
וְנַהֲרָא לְכָל אִינּוּן רְתִיכִין וּמַשְׁרְיָין, דְּאִינּוּן שַׁיְיפִין וְגַרְמִין, וְעָבִיד לוֹן
גּוּפָא שְׁלֵימָא, דְּנָהִיר בִּנְהִירוּ.

**304.** When the moon descends, WHICH IS MALCHUT, which is the secret of the supernal Nefesh OF ATZILUT, it illuminates on all sides. It illuminates all the Chariots and camps OF ANGELS IN BRIYAH, YETZIRAH AND ASIYAH, and makes them into one whole body that illuminates with the light of the supernal shine. Here also, the Lower Nefesh OF MAN descends and illuminates in all directions from the shine of the Neshamah, and from the Shine of Ruach, and descends and illuminates all the Chariots and camps, which are the limbs and bones OF THE MAN'S BODY. And it makes them into a whole body that illuminates in its own light.

**305.** הֲדָא הוּא דִּכְתִיב, וְהִשְׂבִּיעַ בְּצַחְצָחוֹת נַפְשֶׁךָ, נַפְשָׁךְ מַמָּשׁ, וּלְבָתַר
וְעַצְמוֹתֶיךָ יַחֲלִיץ, דְּעָבִיד מִנַּיְיהוּ גּוּפָא שְׁלֵימָא, וְנָהִיר בִּנְהִירוּ, וְקָם
וְאוֹדֵי וּמְשַׁבַּח לְקוּדְשָׁא בְּרִיךְ הוּא, כְּמָה דְּאִתְּמַר דִּכְתִיב, כָּל עַצְמוֹתַי
תֹּאמַרְנָה יְיָ' מִי כָמוֹךְ. וְדָא אִיהוּ נַיְיחָא דְּנֶפֶשׁ וַדַּאי מִכָּל סִטְרִין.

**305.** This is what is meant by: "And satisfy your soul (*Nefesh*) in drought" (Yeshayah 58:11), actually your Nefesh. Afterwards, "and make strong your bones" for the Nefesh illuminates the bones and makes of them a whole body that illuminates with the light. It arises, acknowledges and praises the Holy One, blessed be He, as we learned, and it is written: "All my bones shall say, 'Hashem, who is like You'" (Tehilim 35:10) and this is the rest for the Nefesh from all sides.

**306.** זַכָּאִין אִינּוּן צַדִּיקַיָּיא, דְּדַחֲלִין לְמָארֵיהוֹן בְּעָלְמָא דֵּין, לְמִזְכֵּי
בִּתְלַת נַיְיחֵי לְעָלְמָא דְּאָתֵי. אָתָא רַבִּי שִׁמְעוֹן וּבִרְכֵיהּ לְרַבִּי אַבָּא.
אָמַר רַבִּי שִׁמְעוֹן, זַכָּאִין אַתּוּן בָּנַי, וְזַכָּאָה אֲנָא דְּעֵינַי חָמוּ בְּכַךְ. כַּמָּה
דּוּכְתִּין עִלָּאִין מִתַּתְקְנָן לָן, וּנְהִירִין לָן, לְעָלְמָא דְּאָתֵי.

**306.** Happy are the righteous who fear their Master in this world, to merit three rests, WHICH ARE NEFESH, RUACH, AND NESHAMAH, in the World

to Come. Rabbi Shimon came and blessed Rabbi Aba. Rabbi Shimon said: Happy are you, my children, and happy am I, that my eyes saw this, that many supernal places are prepared for us, and illuminate for us for the World to Come.

## 30. "A song of ascents. They who trust in Hashem"

### A Synopsis

Rabbi Shimon says, "A song of ascents. They who trust in the Creator shall be like Mount Tzion, which cannot be removed, but abides forever." We learn that "ascents" means levels upon levels in the 'secret of fifty years below and the fifty gates of Binah above'. "They who trust in The Creator" are the righteous. The rabbis go on to talk about "But the righteous are bold as a lion." Then they travel on to a city, and after dark Rabbi Shimon expresses his happiness for a perfect day and a perfect night during which they have indeed merited the World to Come.

### The Relevance of this Passage

This section is hard to understand on the surface, yet bubbling underneath is a pure divine teaching masked in metaphors. Trust in the Creator is, perhaps, the most difficult trait a man can evolve. Trust does not pertain to blind faith. Trust is connected to vision that is vast, sweeping, able to perceive the cause and effect principle at work in our lives. Trust includes the ability to observe order beneath chaos, the wisdom to recognize blessing within adversity, the self-honesty to detect the cause behind calamity. It encompasses awareness of the divinity, design, and purpose behind life's joys, and all of its obstacles.

It is true that when affliction and hardship strike, doubts begin to surface in a man's mind. He becomes uncertain about the reality of the Creator. He questions the justice in the universe. He fears for his own future. Thus, we learn that if we have trust, we shall be stable as the mountain, we shall be able to ascend to our own greatest heights. Our moments of pain will be brief, and we shall experience the perfection that is the Light of the Creator, now and in the World to Come. This mystical passage ignites trust, truth, and certainty within our hearts, vanishing forever the doubts that have tainted the hearts of men through all the ages.

307. פָּתַח וְאָמַר, שִׁיר הַמַּעֲלוֹת הַבּוֹטְחִים בַּיְיָ׳ כְּהַר צִיּוֹן לֹא יִמּוֹט לְעוֹלָם יֵשֵׁב, הַאי קְרָא אוּקְמוּהָ. אֲבָל שִׁיר הַמַּעֲלוֹת תּוּשְׁבַּחְתָּא דְּקָאמְרֵי אִינּוּן דַּרְגִּין קַדִּישִׁין עִלָּאִין, מִסִּטְרָא דְּגִבּוּרָן עִלָּאִין, וְאִינּוּן כְּגַוְונָא דִּלְוָאֵי לְתַתָּא, וְאִינּוּן מַעֲלוֹת, דַּרְגִּין עַל דַּרְגִּין, וּפַלְחִין בְּרָזָא דְּחַמְשִׁין שְׁנִין. וְהַאי אִיהוּ שִׁיר הַמַּעֲלוֹת הַבֹּטְחִים בַּיְיָ׳ כְּהַר צִיּוֹן דָּא אִינּוּן צַדִּיקַיָּיא, דְּאִינּוּן מִתְרַחֲצָן בֵּיהּ בְּעוֹבָדִין דִּלְהוֹן.

**307.** He opened the discussion saying: "A song of ascents. They who trust in Hashem shall be like Mount Zion, which cannot be removed, but abides forever" (Tehilim 125:1). This passage has been established, but these are holy supernal levels from the sides of supernal Gvurot THAT ARE IN BINAH. They are similar to the Levites below, who are THE ASPECT OF ascents, MEANING levels upon levels in the secret of fifty years OF WHICH IS WRITTEN, "AND FROM THE AGE OF FIFTY YEARS THEY SHALL GO OUT OF THE RANKS OF THE SERVICE" (BEMIDBAR 8:25), WHICH ALLUDES TO THE FIFTY GATES OF BINAH. This is: "A song of ascents. They who trust in Hashem shall be like Mount Zion," these are the righteous, who trust in Him BY MERIT of their GOOD deeds.

308. כד"א וְצַדִּיקִים כִּכְפִיר יִבְטָח. וְאִי תֵּימָא הָא צַדִּיקַיָּיא לָא מִתְרַחֲצָן בְּעוֹבָדֵיהוֹן כְּלַל, וְתָדִיר דַּחֲלִין, כְּאַבְרָהָם, דִּכְתִיב בֵּיה וַיְהִי כַּאֲשֶׁר הִקְרִיב לָבֹא מִצְרָיְמָה וְגוֹ'. כְּיִצְחָק, דִּכְתִיב בֵּיה, כִּי יָרֵא לֵאמֹר אִשְׁתִּי. כְּיַעֲקֹב, דִּכְתִיב בֵּיה, וַיִּירָא יַעֲקֹב מְאֹד וַיֵּצֶר לוֹ. וְאִי הָנֵי לָא אִתְרְחִיצוּ בְּעוֹבָדֵיהוֹן, כָּל שֶׁכֵּן שְׁאַר צַדִּיקֵי עָלְמָא, וְאַתְּ אָמַרְתְּ וְצַדִּיקִים כִּכְפִיר יִבְטָח.

**308.** It is written: "But the righteous are bold as a lion" (Mishlei 28:1). HE QUESTIONS: The righteous do not depend upon their deeds at all and they are constantly in fear, like Abraham, as it is written of him, "And it came to pass, when he was come near to enter to Egypt..." (Beresheet 12:11). Like Isaac, of them it is written: "For he feared to say, 'She is my wife'" (Beresheet 26:7). As Jacob, of whom it is written: "Then Jacob was greatly afraid and distressed" (Beresheet 32:8). If they did not depend upon their deeds, certainly the other righteous of the world did not, yet you say, "But the righteous are bold as a lion."

309. אֶלָּא וַדַּאי, כִּכְפִיר כְּתִיב, דְּהָא מִכָּל אִינּוּן שְׁמָהָן, לָא כְּתִיב אֶלָּא כְּפִיר, וְלָא כְּתִיב, לָא אַרְיֵה, וְלָא שָׁחַל, וְלָא שַׁחַץ, אֶלָּא כְּפִיר. דְּאִיהוּ חַלְשָׁא וּזְעֵירָא מִכֻּלְּהוּ. וְלָא אִתְרְחִיץ בְּחֵילֵיהּ, אע"ג דְּאִיהוּ תַּקִּיף. כַּךְ צַדִּיקַיָּיא לָא אִתְרְחִיצוּ בְּעוֹבָדֵיהוֹן הַשְׁתָּא, אֶלָּא כִּכְפִיר. אע"ג דְּיַדְעִין דְּתַקִּיף חֵילָא דְּעוֹבָדֵיהוֹן לָא אִתְרַחֲצָן אֶלָּא כִּכְפִיר, וְלָא יַתִּיר.

**309.** HE ANSWERS: But certainly it is written, "as a lion (Heb. *kfir*)" (Mishlei 28:1), because of all the synonyms OF THE LION, only the name Kfir is used. That is the weakest and smallest of them all, who does not depend upon his strength even though he is strong, because the righteous do not depend upon their present deeds but rather like a Kfir. Though they know that the strength of their good deeds is strong, they do not depend on it, but are rather like a Kfir, and not more.

310. וּבְגִינֵי כַּךְ הַבֹּטְחִים בַּיְיָ׳ כְּהַר צִיּוֹן וְגוֹ׳, לָא כִּכְפִיר וְלָא כְּאַרְיֵה, וְלָאו כְּכָלְהוּ שְׁמָהָן. אֶלָּא כְּהַר צִיּוֹן, וְאוּקְמוּהָ מַה הַר צִיּוֹן אִיהוּ תַּקִּיף, וְלָא יָמוֹט תָּדִיר, אוּף הָכִי בְּהַהוּא זִמְנָא, לֶהֱווֹ כְּהַר צִיּוֹן. וְלָא כְּהַשְׁתָּא, דְּלָא אִתְרְחִיצוּ אֶלָּא כִּכְפִיר, דְּדָחִיל וְלָא אִתְרְחִיץ בְּחֵילֵיהּ. וְאַתּוּן בְּנֵי קַדִּישֵׁי עֶלְיוֹנִין, רָחֲצָנוּתָא דִּלְכוֹן כְּהַר צִיּוֹן, וַדַּאי זַכָּאִין אַתּוּן בְּעָלְמָא דֵּין וּבְעָלְמָא דְּאָתֵי.

**310.** And therefore, it IS WRITTEN: "They who trust in Hashem shall be like Mount Zion…" not like a young lion and not like a lion and not like any OF HIS names, but rather "like Mount Zion." They explained that just as Mount Zion is firm and will never decline, IN THE TIME TO COME, they will also be like Mount Zion, not as now when they are only bold like a Kfir (young lion), who fears and does not trust his strength. And you, the children of supernal Holy Ones, your trust is certainly like Mount Zion. Fortunate are you in this and the next world.

311. אָזְלוּ, כַּד מָטוּ לְמָתָא, אִתְחֲשָׁךְ לֵילְיָא. אָמַר ר׳ שִׁמְעוֹן, כְּמָה דְּיוֹמָא דָּא, אַנְהִיר לָן בְּהַאי אָרְחָא, לְמִזְכֵּי בֵּיהּ בְּעָלְמָא דְּאָתֵי, אוּף הָכִי הַאי לֵילְיָא, יַנְהִיר לָן, לְמִזְכֵּי לָן לְעָלְמָא דְּאָתֵי, וּלְאַעֲטָרָא מִלִּין דִּימָמָא בְּלֵילְיָא דָּא, קָמֵי עַתִּיק יוֹמִין דְּהָא כְּיוֹמָא דָּא שָׁלִים, לָא יִשְׁתְּכַח בְּכָל דָּרִין אַחֲרָנִין. זַכָּאָה חוּלָקָנָא בְּעָלְמָא דֵּין, וּבְעָלְמָא דְּאָתֵי.

**311.** They traveled on. When they reached the city, it became dark. Rabbi Shimon said: Just as this day shone upon us, so we will merit the World to Come, this night will also light us, so we shall merit the World to Come,

and crown this night with the words that we said during the day before Atik Yomin. Such a perfect day is not to be found in all the other generations. Happy is our portion in this world and in the World to Come.

312. עָאלוּ לְבֵיתֵיה דר״ש, וְרַבִּי אֶלְעָזָר וְרַבִּי אַבָּא וְרַבִּי יוֹסֵי עִמְּהוֹן. בָּתוּ עַד דְּאִתְפְּלַג לֵילְיָא. כֵּיוָן דְּאִתְפְּלַג לֵילְיָא, אָמַר רַבִּי שִׁמְעוֹן לְחַבְרַיָּא, עִידָן אִיהוּ לְאַעְטְרָא רְתִיכָא קַדִּישָׁא לְעֵילָא, בְּאִשְׁתַּדְלוּתָא דִּילָן. אָמַר לֵיה לְרַבִּי יוֹסֵי, אַנְתְּ דְּלָא אִשְׁתְּמָעוּ מִילָךְ בְּהַאי יוֹמָא בֵּינָנָא, אַנְתְּ הֱוֵי שֵׁירוּתָא, לְאַנְהָרָא לֵילְיָא, דְּהָא הַשְׁתָּא עִידָן רְעוּתָא אִיהוּ, לְאַנְהָרָא עֵילָא וְתַתָּא.

312. They entered the house of Rabbi Shimon. Rabbi Elazar and Rabbi Aba and Rabbi Yosi were with them, and they slept until midnight. At midnight, Rabbi Shimon said to the friends: Now is the time to crown the Holy Chariot above with our efforts. He said to Rabbi Yosi: Your words were not heard among us today. You shall be the first to illuminate the night because now is an auspicious time to illuminate above and below.

## 31. "The song of songs, which is Solomon's"

### A Synopsis

Rabbi Yosi says that King Solomon was inspired to create this song when the Temple was built, and all the worlds above and below were completed in one action, but only when the moon (Malchut) was first fully completed. Moses made the tabernacle in the wilderness so that the Shechinah could descend to earth, and on that day another tabernacle, that of the youth Metatron, was erected above. Everything was completed the day that the Song of Songs (Shir Hashirim) was revealed to the world, and so it is considered to be the Holy of Holies, the chamber in the Temple, the portal to the upper world, that only the High priest may enter. The text goes on to tell of the Cup of Blessing, and the significance of the right and left hands which take the cup. Then we read that the Shir Hashirim includes everything, the history and story of everything there ever was or will be. Another explanation offered suggests that the Hashirim are the Patriarchs, which represent the Holy Chariot. At this time, we learn of a deeper secret, that if one dreams of black grapes growing (but not in the growing season) it is known that a decree of death has been declared against the dreamer. Then Rabbi Yosi tries to understand how if everything below is mirrored above, the serpent and death can possibly be above. Returning to "A song of ascents," he explains that this means the songs of the Supreme Angels, who are divided into ascents and levels, and they sing to David, who is Malchut, to demand of him food and sustenance. As soon as King Solomon came, he recited a song that the great ones of the Upper World recite to the Supreme King. The songs of all the people of the world were in the lower chariots, but only King Solomon's song was in the Supreme Chariots. King David and his son Solomon sang their songs differently; David endeavored to correct the worlds and to beautify the Queen with them, while Solomon endeavored to bring her to the groom, introducing words of love between them in order to join them together. David paired the Queen in this world below; while Solomon paired the Queen in a perfect union above. The passage speaks then of three thousand proverbs, three thousand parables, a thousand and five poems, and the number five. In the end, the reason that prayers and petitions are necessary is so that the place from whence the light emerges, which is Zeir Anpin, should illuminate and become prepared, because when that place is restored, then everything below, in Malchut, is readied for the appearance of God.

### The Relevance of this Passage

Days, weeks, months, years could be spent trying to interpret this one extremely long and complex passage. Yet perhaps its complexity is its

message: to release us from our stubborn adherence to the intellect and turn us toward the divine languages of music and poetry, which are better able than ordinary language to speak of deep things. We know that Zohar's narrative arouses the spiritual forces of which it speaks. Thus, references to the serpent and death ignite sacred sparks that safeguard us from these deadly forces.

And the Angel of Death, himself, dies through the Light that shines here. We draw sustenance in the name of David, ending poverty. Protection and the Light of the Final Redemption are aroused through the Temple. Blessing is bestowed upon us at the hand of the Cup of Blessing. We ignite untold joy by virtue of Solomon's Song of Songs. And we propagate goodness throughout the world through the medium of the white grapes.

313. פָּתַח רַבִּי יוֹסִי וְאָמַר, שִׁיר הַשִּׁירִים אֲשֶׁר לִשְׁלֹמֹה. שִׁירָתָא דָא אִתְּעַר לָה שְׁלֹמֹה מַלְכָּא, כַּד אִתְבְּנֵי בֵּי מַקְדְּשָׁא, וְעָלְמִין כֻּלְּהוּ אִשְׁתְּלִימוּ, עֵילָא וְתַתָּא בִּשְׁלִמוּתָא חֲדָא. וְאע"ג דְּחַבְרַיָּיא פְּלִיגָן בְּהַאי, שִׁירָתָא דָא לָא אִתְּמַר, אֶלָּא בִּשְׁלִימוּ, כַּד סִיהֲרָא אִתְמַלְיָא בִּשְׁלִימוּ, וּבֵי מַקְדְּשָׁא אִתְבְּנֵי כְּגַוְונָא דִלְעֵילָא בְּשַׁעֲתָא דְּאִתְבְּנֵי בֵּי מַקְדְּשָׁא לְתַתָּא, לָא הֲוָה חֶדְוָה קַמֵּיה קוּדְשָׁא בְּרִיךְ הוּא, מִיּוֹמָא דְּאִתְבְּרֵי עָלְמָא, כְּהַהוּא יוֹמָא.

313. Rabbi Yosi opened the discussion saying: "The song of songs, which is Solomon's" (Shir Hashirim 1:1). King Solomon was inspired to this song when the Temple was built, and all the worlds above and below were completed in one completion. Even though the friends disagree AS TO WHEN IT WAS SAID, THE MAIN OPINION IS THAT IT WAS SAID WHEN THE TEMPLE WAS BUILT. But this song was recited whole only when the moon, WHICH IS MALCHUT, was fully completed, and the Temple was built in the likeness of above. When the Temple was built below, there was no joy before the Holy One, blessed be He, from the day that the world was created, like that day.

314. מִשְׁכָּן דְּעָבֵד מֹשֶׁה בְּמַדְבְּרָא, לְנַחְתָּא שְׁכִינְתָּא לְאַרְעָא, בְּהַהוּא יוֹמָא מִשְׁכָּן אַחֲרָא אִתְקַם עִמֵּיה לְעֵילָא, כְּמָה דְּאוּקְמוּהָ דִּכְתִיב הוּקַם הַמִּשְׁכָּן, הַמִּשְׁכָּן: מִשְׁכָּן אַחֲרָא דְּאִתְקַם עִמֵּיה, וְדָא מִשְׁכָּן דְּנַעַר

מְטַטְרוֹ"ן, וְלָא יַתִּיר. בֵּית רִאשׁוֹן כַּד אִתְבְּנֵי, בֵּית רִאשׁוֹן אַחֲרָא אִתְבְּנֵי עֲמֵיהּ, וְאִתְקַיַּים בְּעָלְמִין כֻּלְּהוּ, וְאַנְהִיר לְכָל עָלְמִין, וְאִתְבַּסַּם עָלְמָא, וְאִתְפְּתָחוּ כָּל מַשְׁקוֹפֵי עִלָּאִין לְאַנְהֲרָא, וְלָא הֲוָה חֶדְוָה בְּכָל עָלְמִין כְּהַהוּא יוֹמָא, כְּדֵין פָּתְחוּ עִלָּאֵי וְתַתָּאֵי וְאָמְרוּ שִׁירָתָא, וְהַיְינוּ שִׁיר הַשִּׁירִים. שִׁירָתָא דְּאִינּוּן מְנַגְּנִין דִּמְנַגְּנָן לְקוּדְשָׁא בְּרִיךְ הוּא.

**314.** Moses made the tabernacle in the wilderness, so that the Shechinah could descend to earth. On that day, another tabernacle was erected above, as was explained, as it is written: "The tabernacle was erected" (Shemot 40:17). "The Tabernacle" comes to imply another tabernacle that was erected with it, and that is the tabernacle of the youth Metatron, and not higher. When the first Temple was built, another first Temple was built with it, WHICH IS MALCHUT, WHEN IT WAS IN THE GRADE OF BINAH. It existed in all the worlds and illuminated all the worlds, and the world became fragrant and all the supernal apertures were opened to shine. There was no joy in the world like on that day, and then those above and those below opened and said a song, the Song of Songs, the Songs that the musicians play to the Holy One, blessed be He.

315. דָּוִד מַלְכָּא אָמַר שִׁיר הַמַּעֲלוֹת, שְׁלֹמֹה מַלְכָּא אָמַר שִׁיר הַשִּׁירִים, שִׁיר מֵאִינּוּן מְנַגְּנִין. מָה בֵּין הַאי לְהַאי, דְּהָא אִשְׁתְּמַע דְּכֹלָּא חַד. אֶלָּא וַדַּאי כֹּלָּא חַד, אֲבָל בְּיוֹמֵי דְּדָוִד מַלְכָּא, לָא הֲווֹ כָּל אִינּוּן מְנַגְּנִין מִתְתַּקְנָן בְּדוּכְתַּיְיהוּ, לְנַגְּנָא כַּדְקָא יֵאוֹת, וּבֵי מַקְדְּשָׁא לָא אִתְבְּנֵי, וּבְג"כ לָא אִתְתַּקָּנוּ לְעֵילָּא בְּדוּכְתַּיְיהוּ. דְּהָא כְּמָה דְּאִית תִּקּוּנֵי דְמִשְׁמָרוֹת בְּאַרְעָא, אוּף הָכִי בִּרְקִיעָא, וְקַיְימִין אִלֵּין לָקֳבֵל אִלֵּין.

**315.** King David recited, "A song of ascents" (Tehilim 125:1) and King Solomon recited, "The Song of Songs," MEANING a song of those who play music. What is the difference between them, for it seems that they are all the same? HE ANSWERS: Certainly it is all one, but in the days of King David, all the musicians were not in their places to play music properly, because the Temple was not built yet. Therefore, they were not prepared above in their places. For as there are watches arranged on the earth, so it is in heaven, and they stand one corresponding to the other. AND THE WATCHES

BELOW WERE AS YET NOT PREPARED PROPERLY BECAUSE THE TEMPLE
WAS NOT BUILT.

316. וּבְיוֹמָא דְּאִתְבְּנֵי בֵּי מַקְדְּשָׁא, אִתְתָּקְנוּ כֻּלְּהוּ בְּדוּכְתַּיְיהוּ, וְשַׁרְגָּא
דְּלָא נַהֲרָא שָׁרִיאַת לְאַנְהֲרָא. וְשִׁירָתָא דָּא אִתְתָּקְנַת לְגַבֵּי מַלְכָּא
עִלָּאָה, מַלְכָּא דִּשְׁלָמָא דִּילֵיהּ. וְתוּשְׁבַּחְתָּא דָּא אִיהִי מְעַלְיָא, מִכָּל
תּוּשְׁבְּחָא קַדְמָאֵי. יוֹמָא דְּאִתְגְּלֵי תוּשְׁבַּחְתָּא דָּא בְּאַרְעָא, הַהוּא יוֹמָא
אִשְׁתְּכַח שְׁלִימוּ בְּכֹלָּא, וְע"ד אִיהוּ קֹדֶשׁ קָדָשִׁים.

316. On the day that the Temple was built, they were all fixed in their place,
MEANING THE WATCHES, and the candle, WHICH IS MALCHUT, that did not
illuminate started to illuminate. This song, THE SONG OF SONGS, was
arranged for the supernal King, the King that the peace is His, ZEIR ANPIN.
This praise towered above all first praises. The day that this praise was
revealed to the world was found completed in everything and so "THE
SONG OF SONGS" is considered the Holy of Holies.

317. בְּסִפְרָא דְּאָדָם קַדְמָאָה, הֲוָה כְּתִיב בֵּיהּ. בְּיוֹמָא דְּיִתְבְּנֵי בֵּי
מַקְדְּשָׁא, יִתְעֲרוּן אֲבָהָן שִׁירָתָא, עֵילָא וְתַתָּא. וּבְגִין כַּךְ אַשְׁכַּחְנָא שִׁין
מֵאַתְוָון רַבְרְבָן. וְאִלֵּין אִינוּן דְּקָא אִתְעָרוּ, לָאו דְּאִינּוּן מְנַגְּנָן, אֶלָּא
דְּאִינּוּן מִתְעָרֵי לְגַבֵּי עֵילָא. שִׁיר דְּאִינּוּן שִׁירִין רַבְרְבָן, דִּמְמָנָן עַל
עָלְמִין כֻּלְּהוּ.

317. In the Book of Adam, it was written: On the day that the Temple will
be built, the Patriarchs will inspire song above and below. Therefore, we
find that the *Shin* OF SHIR HASHIRIM is one of the large letters, FOR THE
THREE BRANCHES ALLUDE TO THE THREE PATRIARCHS. These
PATRIARCHS are the ones who inspire the song. They do not actually play
music, BECAUSE ONLY MALCHUT DOES, but they awaken the above by the
song of these great songs that are appointed over all the worlds, NAMELY OF
BINAH.

318. וְתָנֵינָן, בְּהַהוּא יוֹמָא קָם יַעֲקֹב שְׁלִימָא, וְעָאל בְּגִנְתָּא דְּעֵדֶן,
בְּחֵידוּ, עַל דּוּכְתֵּיהּ. כְּדֵין גִּנְתָּא דְּעֵדֶן, שָׁארֵי לְנַגְּנָא, וְכָל אִינוּן בּוּסְמִין

דְּגִנְתָּא. מַאן גָּרִים שִׁירָתָא דָּא, וּמַאן אָמַר לָהּ. הֲוֵי אֵימָא דָּא יַעֲקֹב,
דְּאִלְמָלֵא אִיהוּ לָא עָאל בְּגִנְתָּא דְּעֵדֶן, לָא אָמַר גִּנְתָּא שִׁירָתָא.

**318.** We have learned that the perfect Jacob arose on that day and entered the Garden of Eden joyously to his place. Then the Garden of Eden, WHICH IS MALCHUT, started to sing and all the spices in the Garden of Eden SANG. Who brought the singing and who recited it? You must admit that Jacob brought this about. For had he not entered, then the Garden of Eden would not have sung. SO WE SEE THAT JACOB BROUGHT IT, AND THE GARDEN OF EDEN, WHICH IS MALCHUT, RECITED IT.

319. שִׁירָתָא דָּא שִׁירָתָא, דְּאִיהִי כְּלָלָא דְּכָל אוֹרַיְיתָא. שִׁירָתָא דְּעִלָּאֵי
וְתַתָּאֵי מִתְעָרֵי לְגַבָּהּ. שִׁירָתָא דְּאִיהִי בְּגַוְונָא דְּעָלְמָא דִּלְעֵילָּא, דְּאִיהוּ
שַׁבָּת עִלָּאָה. שִׁירָתָא דִּשְׁמָא קַדִּישָׁא עִלָּאָה, אִתְעַטַּר בְּגִינֵיהּ. וְעַ"ד
אִיהוּ קֹדֶשׁ קָדָשִׁים. מ"ט. בְּגִין דְּכָל מִלּוֹי בִּרְחִימוּ וּבְחֶדְוָה כֹּלָּא. בְּגִין
דְּכוֹס שֶׁל בְּרָכָה אִתְיְהִיב בִּימִינָא, כֵּיוָן דְּאִתְיְהִיב בִּימִינָא, כְּדֵין כָּל
חֵידוּ וְכָל רְחִימוּ אִשְׁתְּכַח. וּבְגִין כָּךְ בִּרְחִימוּ וּבְחֶדְוָה כָּל מִלּוֹי.

**319.** This song is a song that includes the whole Torah, a song with which those above and those below became inspired. It is a song which is similar to above, which is the supernal Shabbat, WHICH IS BINAH, a song that the Supernal Holy Name, WHICH IS MALCHUT, becomes crowned by. Therefore, it is the Holy of Holies. What is the reason? Because all its words are in the love and the joy of all, and the Cup of Blessing, WHICH IS MALCHUT, is given with the right hand, WITH CHESED. Since it is given with the right hand, then all joy and love are present. Therefore, all its words are with love and with joy.

320. בְּזִמְנָא דְּהַאי יְמִינָא אִתְהַדַּר לַאֲחוֹרָא, כד"א הֵשִׁיב אָחוֹר יְמִינוֹ,
כְּדֵין כּוֹס שֶׁל בְּרָכָה אִתְיְהִיב בִּשְׂמָאלָא. כֵּיוָן דְּאִתְיְהִיב בִּשְׂמָאלָא,
שָׁרִיאוּ עִלָּאֵי וְתַתָּאֵי לְמִפְתַּח עֲלֵיהּ קִינָה. וּמַאי קָאַמְרֵי. אֵיכָה, אִי כֹּה,
אִי כּוֹס שֶׁל בְּרָכָה, דְּאֲתָר עִלָּאָה דַּהֲוֵית יָתְבָא בְּגַוֵּיהּ אִתְמְנַע וְאִתְגְּרַע
מִנָּהּ בְּגִינֵי כָּךְ שִׁיר הַשִּׁירִים, דַּהֲוָה מִסִּטְרָא דְּיִמִינָא, כָּל מִלּוֹי רְחִימוּ

וְחֶדְוָה. אֵיכָה, דְּחָסִיר יְמִינָא, וְאִשְׁתְּכַח שְׂמָאלָא, כָּל מִלּוֹי אִינוּן
קַנְטוּרִין וְקִינִין.

**320.** When this right hand is turned back, as it is written: "He has drawn back His right hand" (Eichah 2:3), then the Cup of Blessing, WHICH IS MALCHUT, is given with the left hand, WHERE THE JUDGMENTS ARE BECAUSE OF A LACK OF CHASSADIM. Since it is given with the left hand, those above and those below start to lament Her. And what do they say, "How (Heb. *eichah*)?" WHICH ARE THE LETTERS *ei* (Eng. 'where') *koh*, MEANING where is the Cup of Blessing, WHICH IS MALCHUT THAT IS CALLED 'KOH'. The place above wherein She would sit, NAMELY THE PLACE OF BINAH, was withheld and removed from Her. Therefore, all the words of Shir Hashirim, which is of the right side, are of love and joy. All the words of Eichah, in which the right is missing, and only the left is present, are grievances and lamentations.

321. וְאִי תֵּימָא, הָא כָּל חִידוּ, וְכָל חֶדְוָה, וְכָל שִׁיר, מִסִּטְרָא דִשְׂמָאלָא
אִיהוּ, וְעַל דָּא לֵיוָאֵי מִסִּטְרָא דִשְׂמָאלָא מְנַגְּנֵי שִׁירָתָא. אֶלָּא, כָּל חִידוּ
דְּאִשְׁתְּכַח מִסִּטְרָא דִשְׂמָאלָא, לָא אִשְׁתְּכַח אֶלָּא בְּזִמְנָא דִימִינָא
אִתְדְּבָּק בַּהֲדֵיהּ. וּבְזִמְנָא דִימִינָא אִתְּעַר וְאִתְדְּבָּק בַּהֲדֵיהּ, כְּדֵין הַהוּא
חֶדְוָה מִימִינָא, אִיהוּ דְּקָא אוֹטִיב לְרֻתְחָא, וְכַד רֻתְחָא אִשְׁתְּכַךְ, וְחִדוּ
אִיהוּ מִסִּטְרָא דִימִינָא, כְּדֵין חֶדְוָה שְׁלֵימָתָא אָתֵי מֵהַאי סִטְרָא.

**321.** If you ask: Every joy and every jubilation and every song is from the left side. Therefore, Levites who are of the left side play the song. SO HOW CAN YOU SAY THAT IT IS JUDGMENTS AND LAMENTATIONS? HE ANSWERS: Any time there is joy from the left side, it is present only when the right is joined with it, MEANING THAT THE CHOCHMAH IN THE LEFT BECOMES ATTACHED WITH CHASSADIM OF THE RIGHT. When the right becomes aroused and joins with it, then that joy in the right improves and pacifies the anger OF THE LEFT, BECAUSE ALL THE ANGER AND JUDGMENTS THAT ARE IN THE LEFT ARE BECAUSE OF THE LACK OF CHASSADIM, WHICH IS FROM THE RIGHT. When the anger is pacified and there is joy from the right side, then a complete joy comes from that side, FROM THE LEFT, BECAUSE AFTER BECOMING ATTIRED WITH

CHASSADIM, THE CHOCHMAH IN THE LEFT ALSO ILLUMINATES. AND THE JOY IS COMPLETE.

**322.** וְכַד יְמִינָא לָא אִשְׁתְּכַח, רְתִחָא דִשְׂמָאלָא נָפִישׁ, וְלָא שְׁכִיךְ, וְלָא אוֹטִיב, וְלָא חַדֵּי. כְּדֵין אִיכָה, אֵי כָּה. כּוֹס שֶׁל בְּרָכָה מָה תְּהֵא עֲלֵיהּ, דְּקָא יָתְבָא בִּשְׂמָאלָא, וּרְתִחָא נָפִישׁ, וְלָא שְׁכִיךְ. וַדַּאי קַנְטוּרִין וְקִינִין מִתְעָרִין.

**322.** When the right is not present, the anger in the left increases, BECAUSE THE RIGHT is not pacifying and is not improving and is not causing joy. Then, it IS SAID Eichah, WHICH ARE THE LETTERS *Ei* (Eng. 'where') *koh*, NAMELY the Cup of Blessing THAT IS CALLED 'KOH'. What will become of it, for it sits in the left, and the anger is increasing and is not pacified? Certainly complaints and lamentations are aroused.

**323.** אֲבָל שִׁיר הַשִּׁירִים, וַדַּאי כּוֹס שֶׁל בְּרָכָה דְּאִתְיְהִיב בִּימִינָא, וְאִתְמְסַר בְּגַוֵּויהּ, וְעַל דָּא כָּל רְחִימוּ וְכָל חֶדְוּ אִשְׁתְּכַח. וּבְגִין כַּךְ כָּל מִלּוֹי בִּרְחִימוּ וּבְחֶדְוָה, וְלָא אִשְׁתְּכַח בִּשְׁאַר כָּל שִׁירִין דְּעָלְמָא הָכִי. וּבְגִין דָּא מִסִּטְרָא דַּאֲבָהָן אִתְּעַר שִׁירָתָא דָא.

**323.** As to Shir Hashirim, certainly the Cup of Blessing was ALREADY given with the right hand and handed over to it. Every love and every joy is present. Therefore, all its words are with love and joy, and it is not so in all the other songs in the world. Therefore, the song was inspired by the Patriarchs.

**324.** יוֹמָא דְּאִתְגְּלֵי שִׁירָתָא דָא, הַהוּא יוֹמָא נַחְתַּת שְׁכִינְתָּא לְאַרְעָא, דִּכְתִיב וְלָא יָכְלוּ הַכֹּהֲנִים לַעֲמוֹד לְשָׁרֵת וְגוֹ'. מַאי טַעֲמָא. בְּגִין כִּי מָלֵא כְבוֹד יְיָ' אֶת בֵּית יְיָ'. בְּהַהוּא יוֹמָא מַמָּשׁ, אִתְגַּלְיַאת תּוּשְׁבַּחְתָּא דָא, וְאָמְרָהּ שְׁלֹמֹה בְּרוּחַ קֻדְשָׁא.

**324.** This song was revealed on the day the Shechinah descended to earth, as it is written: "So that the priests could not stand and minister..." (I Melachim 8:11). Why? "For the glory of Hashem had filled the House of

Hashem" (Ibid.). On that very day, the praise of SHIR HASHIRIM was revealed, and Solomon said it through the Holy Spirit.

325. תּוּשְׁבַּחְתָּא דְּשִׁירָתָא דָּא, אִיהִי כְּלָלָא דְּכָל אוֹרַיְיתָא. כְּלָלָא דְּכָל עוֹבָדָא דִּבְרֵאשִׁית, כְּלָלָא דְּרָזָא דַּאֲבָהָן, כְּלָלָא דְּגָלוּתָא דְּמִצְרַיִם. וְכַד נָפְקוּ יִשְׂרָאֵל מִמִּצְרַיִם, וְתוּשְׁבַּחְתָּא דְּיַמָּא. כְּלָלָא דְּיוּ"ד אֲמִירָן. וְקִיּוּמָא דְּהַר סִינַי. וְכַד אָזְלוּ יִשְׂרָאֵל בְּמַדְבְּרָא, עַד דְּעָאלוּ לְאַרְעָא, וְאִתְבְּנֵי בֵּי מַקְדְּשָׁא. כְּלָלָא דְּעִטּוּרָא דִּשְׁמָא קַדִּישָׁא עִלָּאָה, בִּרְחִימוּ וּבְחֶדְוָה. כְּלָלָא דְּגָלוּתְהוֹן דְּיִשְׂרָאֵל בֵּינֵי עַמְמַיָּא, וּפוּרְקָנָא דִּלְהוֹן. כְּלָלָא דִּתְחִיַּית הַמֵּתִים, עַד יוֹמָא דְּאִיהִי שַׁבָּת לַיְיָ'. מַאי דַּהֲוָה, וּמַאי דַּהֲוֵי, וּמַאי דְּזַמִּין לְמֶהֱוֵי, לְבָתַר בְּיוֹמָא שְׁבִיעָאָה, כַּד יְהֵא שַׁבָּת לַיְיָ', כֹּלָּא אִיהוּ בְּשִׁיר הַשִּׁירִים.

325. The praise of this song, SHIR HASHIRIM, is the inclusion of the entire Torah, the inclusion of the whole creation, the inclusion of the secret of the Patriarchs, the inclusion of the Exile in Egypt, the Deliverance of the children of Yisrael from Egypt and the Song of the Sea, NAMELY, "THEN SANG MOSES" (SHEMOT 15:1), the inclusion of the Ten Commandments, the existence of Mount Sinai, AND INCLUDES FROM THE TIME that Yisrael traveled in the wilderness until they came to the Land of Yisrael and the Temple was built. Also, the inclusion of the crowning of the Holy Name with love and joy, the inclusion of the exile of Yisrael among the nations and the redemption, the inclusion of the Resurrection of the Dead until the day that is the Shabbat to Hashem, NAMELY THE DAY THAT IS COMPLETELY SHABBAT OF THE TIME TO COME, whatever is and whatever was and whatever will be afterwards during the seventh day, NAMELY THE SEVENTH MILLENNIUM, when it will be Shabbat to Hashem. It is all in Shir Hashirim.

326. וְעַל דָּא תָּנֵינָן, כָּל מַאן דְּאַפִּיק פְּסוּקָא דְּשִׁיר הַשִּׁירִים, וְאָמַר לֵיהּ בְּבֵי מִשְׁתְּיָא. אוֹרַיְיתָא אִיהִי חֲגִירַת שָׂק, וְסַלְקָא לְגַבֵּי קוּדְשָׁא בְּרִיךְ הוּא, וְאָמְרָה קַמֵּיהּ, עָבְדוּ לִי בָּנַיִךְ מָחוֹךְ בְּבֵי מִשְׁתְּיָא. וַדַּאי אוֹרַיְיתָא סַלְּקָת וְקָאַמְרַת הָכִי, בְּגִין דָּא אִצְטְרִיךְ לְנַטְרָא, וּלְסַלְּקָא עֲטָרָא עַל רֵישֵׁיהּ דְּבַר נָשׁ, כָּל מִלָּה וּמִלָּה דְּשִׁיר הַשִּׁירִים.

**326.** Therefore we have learned that anyone who selects a passage from Shir Hashirim and says it in an ale-house, the Torah girds a sack and ascends before the Holy One, blessed be He, and says before Him, Your children have made me a joke in an ale-house. Certainly, the Torah ascends and says thus. Therefore, one should be careful, and place a crown upon the head of the person out of every single word of Shir Hashirim.

327. וְאִי תֵּימָא אֲמַאי אִיהִי בֵּין הַכְּתוּבִים, הָכִי הוּא וַדַּאי, בְּגִין דְּאִיהוּ שִׁיר תּוּשְׁבַּחְתָּא דִּכְנֶסֶת יִשְׂרָאֵל, קָא מִתְעַטְּרָא לְעֵילָא. וּבְגִין כָּךְ, כָּל תּוּשְׁבְּחָן דְּעָלְמָא, לָא סַלְקָא רְעוּתָא לְגַבֵּי קוּדְשָׁא בְּרִיךְ הוּא, כְּתוּשְׁבַּחְתָּא דָא.

**327.** And if you ask: Why is it among the Writings, AND NOT IN THE PROPHETS? HE ANSWERS: It is certainly so, THAT ITS PLACE IS IN THE WRITINGS, because it is the song of praise of the Congregation of Yisrael, WHICH IS MALCHUT that is crowned above, FROM BINAH. AND MALCHUT IS A PART OF THE WRITINGS. Therefore, none of the praises in the world are as pleasing before the Holy One, blessed be He, as this praise.

328. הָכִי אוֹלִיפְנָא, שִׁיר, חַד. הַשִּׁירִים, תְּרֵין. אֲשֶׁר, הָא תְּלַת. וְרָזָא דָא, דְּאִתְיְהִיב כּוֹס שֶׁל בְּרָכָה וְאִתְנְטִיל בֵּין יְמִינָא וּשְׂמָאלָא. וְכֹלָּא אִתְּעַר לְגַבֵּי מַלְכָּא דִּשְׁלָמָא דִּילֵיהּ. וּבַהַאי אִסְתַּלָּק רְעוּתָא לְעֵילָא לְעֵילָא בְּרָזָא דְּאֵין סוֹף. רְתִיכָא קַדִּישָׁא הָכָא אִשְׁתְּכַח. דְּהָא אַבָהָן אִינוּן רְתִיכָא, דָּוִד מַלְכָּא אִתְחַבַּר עִמְּהוֹן, אִינוּן אַרְבַּע רָזָא דִּרְתִיכָא קַדִּישָׁא עִלָּאָה. וּבְגִין כָּךְ, אַרְבַּע תֵּיבִין בְּהַאי קְרָא קַדְמָאָה, רָזָא דִּרְתִיכָא קַדִּישָׁא שְׁלֵימָתָא.

**328.** We have learned that "*Shir*" (Eng. 'a song') is one, "*Hashirim*" (Eng. 'of Songs') is second and "*asher*" (Eng. 'which is') is third. This is the secret why the Cup of Blessing, WHICH IS MALCHUT, was given and is taken between the right and left hands, WHICH IS THE SECRET OF THE TWO COLUMNS RIGHT AND LEFT, CHESED AND GVURAH. It is all inspired toward the King that the Peace is His, WHO IS THE CENTRAL COLUMN, TIFERET, THAT CORRESPONDS TO THEM AND THE THREE MENTIONED

EARLIER. Desire ascends in this higher and higher, in the secret of the Endless Light. The Holy Chariot is present here, because the Patriarchs, NAMELY CHESED, GVURAH AND TIFERET THAT ARE MENTIONED ABOVE, WHICH IS THE SECRET OF THREE SONGS, are the Chariot. King David joins with them, and they are four, which is the secret of the Supreme Holy Chariot. Therefore, there are four words in this first passage, NAMELY, "THE SONG OF SONGS, WHICH IS SOLOMON'S," the secret of the Holy complete Chariot.

329. תּוּ רָזָא דָּא, שִׁיר: דָּא רָזָא דְּדָוִד מַלְכָּא, דְּאִיהוּ רָזָא לְסַלְּקָא בְּשִׁיר. הַשִּׁירִים: אִלֵּין אֲבָהָן, רָזָא דִּמְמָנָן רַבְרְבָן, רְתִיכָא שְׁלֵימָתָא כַּדְקָא יֵאוֹת. אֲשֶׁר לִשְׁלֹמֹה: רָזָא מַאן דְּרָכִיב עַל רְתִיכָא שְׁלֵימָתָא דָּא.

329. To further explain this secret, "Shir" is the Secret of King David, being the secret of Shir. "Hashirim" are the Patriarchs, being the secret of the great appointees, the proper complete Chariot. "Which is Solomon's" is the secret of he who rides on this complete Chariot, NAMELY BINAH.

330. וּבְהַאי קְרָא אִשְׁתְּכַח שְׁלִימוּ דְּרָזָא, מִן הָעוֹלָם וְעַד הָעוֹלָם, רָזָא דְּכָל מְהֵימְנוּתָא. וְכֹלָּא אִיהוּ רְתִיכָא שְׁלֵימָתָא לְמַאן דִּידִיעַ, וּלְמַאן דְּלָא אִתְיְדַע, וְלֵית מַאן דְּקָאֵים לְמִנְדַּע בֵּיהּ. וְעַל דָּא אִתְּמַר הַאי קְרָא בְּד' תֵּיבִין, רָזָא דִּרְתִיכָא שְׁלֵימָתָא מִכָּל סִטְרִין. מִכָּאן וּלְהָלְאָה, רָזָא לְחַכִּימִין אִתְמְסָר.

330. The whole of the secret of: "Forever and ever (lit. 'from the world and to the world')" (I Divrei Hayamim 16:36), WHICH MEANS FROM BINAH TO MALCHUT, is found in this passage, which is the secret of the whole Faith. It is all a complete Chariot for the one who is known, and for the one who is not known, which is not to be known nor comprehended. Therefore, there are four words in the passage, which is the secret of the Chariot that is complete from all sides, BOTH FROM THE RIGHT AND FROM THE LEFT. From here and further, NAMELY HIGHER THAN ABA AND IMA, the secret was given over to the sages.

331. וְתוּ אִית בֵּיהּ רָזָא פְּנִימָאָה, דְּתָנֵינָן, מַאן דְּחָמֵי עֲנָבִין בְּחֶלְמֵיהּ,

אִי חִוּוָרִין אִינוּן טָבִין. אוּכְמִין, בְּזִמְנָן טָבִין, דְּלָא בְּזִמְנָן צְרִיכִין רַחֲמֵי. מַאי שְׁנָא חִוּוָרֵי, וּמַאי שְׁנָא אוּכְמֵי, וּמַאי שְׁנָא בְּזִמְנָן, וּמַאי שְׁנָא דְּלָא בְּזִמְנָן. וְתוּ, תָּנֵינָן אָכְלָן לְאִינוּן אוּכְמֵי, מוּבְטַח לֵיהּ דְּהוּא בֶּן עָלְמָא דְּאָתֵי, אֲמַאי.

**331.** It also has a deeper secret, for we have learned that if one sees grapes in his dream and they are white, they are good, MEANING THAT THE DREAM ALLUDES TO GOOD. If they are black and if they are in season, MEANING THE SEASON OF GRAPE GROWING, they are good. If not in season, then Mercy is needed, BECAUSE THEY ALLUDE TO AN EVIL DECREE. HE QUESTIONS: What difference is there if they are white or they are black, and what difference is there if they are in season or are not in season? We also learned that if one eats the black grapes, he is assured to be of the World to Come. Why?

332. אֶלָּא תָּנֵינָן, אִילָנָא דְּחָב בֵּיהּ אָדָם קַדְמָאָה, עֲנָבִין הֲווֹ, דִּכְתִּיב עֲנָבֵמוֹ עִנְבֵי רוֹשׁ. וְאִלֵּין אִינוּן עֲנָבִין אוּכְמִין, בְּגִין דְּאִית עֲנָבִין אוּכְמִין, וְאִית עֲנָבִין חִוּוָרִין. חִוּוָרִין טָבִין, דְּהָא מִסְטָר דְּחַיֵּי אִינוּן. אוּכְמִין צְרִיכִין רַחֲמֵי, דְּהָא מִסְטְרָא דְּמוֹתָא אִינוּן. בְּזִמְנָן טָבִין, מַאי טַעֲמָא. בְּגִין דְּבִזְמְנָא דְּחִוּוָרֵי שַׁלְטָן, דְּהָא בְּהַהוּא זִמְנָא כֹּלָּא אִצְטְרִיךְ לְתִקּוּנָא, וְכֹלָּא אִיהוּ שַׁפִּיר, וְכֹלָּא תִּקּוּנָא חֲדָא, אוּכְמָא וְחִוּוָרָא. וּבְזִמְנָא דְּחִוּוָרֵי לָא שַׁלְטָאן, וְאוּכְמֵי אִתְחֲזוּן, לְמִינְדַע דְּהָא בְּדִינָא דְּמוֹתָא סָלִיק, וְאִצְטְרִיךְ רַחֲמֵי, דְּהָא אִילָנָא דְּחָב בֵּיהּ אָדָם קַדְמָאָה, וְגָרִים מוֹתָא לֵיהּ וּלְכָל עָלְמָא חָמָא.

**332.** HE ANSWERS: We have learned that the tree with which Adam sinned was grapes, as it is written: "Their grapes are grapes of gall" (Devarim 32:32), which are black grapes. There are black grapes and white grapes, and the white ones are good because they are of the side of life, BECAUSE WHITE ALLUDES TO CHESED, WHICH IS ZEIR ANPIN THAT IS CALLED 'THE TREE OF LIFE'. The black ones need Mercy, because they are of the side of death and BECAUSE BLACK ALLUDES TO THE TREE OF KNOWLEDGE OF GOOD AND EVIL, WHEREIN IS DEATH. In their season, MEANING WHEN THEY ARE RIPE, they are good, EVEN THOUGH THEY ARE

BLACK. What is the reason? At the time that the white ones dominate, everything becomes improved because at that time, they all are fixed and everything is nice. It is all in the same procedure, the white ones and black ones. When the white ones are not dominating and the black ones appear in the dream, BUT NOT IN THE GROWING SEASON OF GRAPES, it is known that a decree of death has been decreed against him. And he needs Mercy, for he has seen the Tree with which Adam had sinned, and caused death for himself and the whole world.

333. הָכָא אִית לְאִסְתַּכְּלָא, וְאִי לָאו דְּמַר הָכָא, לָא אֵימָא. תָּנֵינָן דְּעָלְמָא דָּא, אִיהוּ כְּגַוְונָא דְּעָלְמָא דִּלְעֵילָּא, וְעָלְמָא דִּלְעֵילָּא כָּל מַה דַּהֲוָה בְּהַאי עָלְמָא, הָכִי אִיהוּ לְעֵילָּא, אִי נָחָשׁ גָּרִים מוֹתָא לְאָדָם לְתַתָּא, לְעֵילָּא אֲמַאי. אִי תֵּימָא, לְאַתְּתָא, דְּבְגִין נָחָשׁ אַגְרַע נְהוֹרָא, דְּהָא סִיהֲרָא גָּרַע נְהוֹרָא לְזִמְנִין, וּבְהַהוּא זִמְנָא אִיהִי מֵיתַת. דְּכוּרָא אֲמַאי. דְּאִי נֵימָא דְּסִיהֲרָא בְּעֵיטוֹ דְּהַאי נָחָשׁ מֵיתַת, בִּגְרִיעוּ דִּנְהוֹרָא. הָא תָּנֵינָן, דְּלָא בְּגִין נָחָשׁ הֲוָה. אֶלָּא דְּאָמְרָה סִיהֲרָא קַמֵּי קוּדְשָׁא בְּרִיךְ הוּא וְכוּ', הָא לָא הֲוָה בְּגִין נָחָשׁ. וְאִי תֵּימָא דְּבַעְלָהּ הָכִי הוּא, חַ"ו דִּגְרִיעוּ הֲוֵי לְעֵילָּא.

333. We should make an observation, and if Master, RABBI SHIMON, were not present, I would not say this. We have learned that this world is similar to the world above, and as for the world above, everything that is in this world is also in the world above. HE QUESTIONS: If it is the serpent who brought death to Adam below, then why did he bring it above, NAMELY TO THE SUPREME ADAM THAT IS THE SECRET OF ZEIR ANPIN AND MALCHUT? If you say that the light of the woman, THAT IS MALCHUT, is lessened as the moon which light is lessened at times, and at that time she IS CONSIDERED as though she were dead, WE SHOULD THEN ASK about the male THAT IS ZEIR ANPIN. Why IS DEATH CONNECTED TO HIM? AND ALSO, if you say that the moon, WHICH IS MALCHUT, died by the counsel of the serpent, which is the lessening of the light, we have learned that the lessening of its light was not because of the serpent, but rather because the moon said before the Holy One, blessed be He, 'IT IS NOT POSSIBLE FOR TWO KINGS TO USE ONE CROWN'. THIS OCCURRED ON THE FOURTH DAY OF CREATION, so we can see that it was not because of the serpent. If you

say that her husband, WHICH IS ZEIR ANPIN, is BEING LESSENED OF THE LIGHT WHICH IS CALLED 'DEATH', heaven forbid that there is lessening above.

334. אֶלָּא כָּל דָּא סִתְרֵי אוֹרַיְיתָא, וְנָחָשׁ בְּכֹלָּא אַתְקִין גְּרִיעוּ. ת"ח וְהָכִי אוֹלִיפְנָא, כָּל מָה דְּעָבַד קוּדְשָׁא בְּרִיךְ הוּא עֵילָּא וְתַתָּא, כֹּלָּא בְּרָזָא דִּדְכַר וְנוּקְבָּא אִיהוּ, וְכַמָּה דַּרְגִּין אִינּוּן לְעֵילָּא, מְשַׁנְיָין אִלֵּין מֵאִלֵּין. וּמִדַּרְגָּא עַד דַּרְגָּא רָזָא דְּאָדָם, וְאִינּוּן דַּרְגִּין דְּאִינּוּן זִינָא חֲדָא, עָבַד לוֹן קוּדְשָׁא בְּרִיךְ הוּא דִּיּוּקְנָא דְּחַד גּוּפָא, עַד דְּסַלְּקִין בְּרָזָא דְּאָדָם.

334. HE ANSWERS: All these are secrets of the Torah, and the snake caused a lessening in everything. Come and see: We learned everything that the Holy One, blessed be He, made above and below is all as male and female. There are many levels above that are different from each other, and from level to level is contained the secret of man. The Holy One, blessed be He, made these levels that are the same in the form of one body, until they reached the secret of man, NAMELY MALE AND FEMALE.

335. וְתָנֵינָן, בְּיוֹמָא תִּנְיָינָא דְּעוֹבָדָא דִּבְרֵאשִׁית, דְּאִתְבְּרֵי בֵּיהּ גֵּיהִנָּם, אִתְעֲבִיד חַד גּוּפָא בְּרָזָא דְּאָדָם, וְאִינּוּן שַׁיְיפִין מְמָנָן דְּמִתְקַרְבִין לְאֶשָׁא, וּמֵתִין וּמֵהַדְרָן כְּמִלְּקַדְמִין. וְדָא בְּגִין דְּאִינּוּן אִתְקְרִיבוּ לְגַבֵּי הַאי חִוְיָא, וְאִיהוּ אָדָם קַדְמָאָה דְּאִתְפַּתָּה גּוֹ מַשְׁכְּנָא בְּהַאי חִוְיָא, וְע"ד מִית, וְחִוְיָא גָּרִים לֵיהּ מוֹתָא דְּאִיהוּ קָרִיב לֵיהּ.

335. We learned of the second day of Creation that Gehenom was created then, and one body was made in the secret of man. THE SIX ENDS OF THE GOOD THAT WAS IN KLIPAH OF NOGAH (ENG. 'BRIGHTNESS') WERE FORMED INTO A BODY, WHICH INCLUDES ALSO MALCHUT AS ITS FEMALE. Its limbs, NAMELY THE ANGELS, that are appointed, THAT ARE INCLUDED IN IT, come close to fire, NAMELY TO THE KLIPAH OF FLAMING FIRE, and they die and return TO LIFE as before. That is because they approached this serpent and this is the supernal Adam who was tempted in his habitation, NAMELY BY HIS FEMALE THAT IS CALLED 'HABITATION' (TABERNACLE). THE TABERNACLE WAS ENTICED by this serpent, and therefore he died. The serpent caused his death because he approached him, AND THIS IS EXACTLY LIKE THE LOWER MAN.

336. וּבְכָל אֲתַר אָדָם דְּכַר וְנוּקְבָּא אִיהוּ, אֲבָל אָדָם דְּאִיהוּ קַדִּישָׁא
עִלָּאָה, אִיהוּ שַׁלְטָא עַל כֹּלָּא, דָּא יָהִיב מְזוֹנָא וְחַיִּין לְכֹלָּא. וְעכ"ד
בְּכֹלָּא מָנַע נְהוֹרָא הַאי חִוְיָא תַּקִּיפָא. כַּד מַסְאִיב מִשְׁכְּנָא נוּקְבָּא
דְּהַהוּא אָדָם כִּדְקָאָמַר מִיתַת, וּדְכוּרָא מִית, וְסַלְּקִין כְּמִלְּקַדְמִין. וְעַל
דָּא כֹּלָּא כְּגַוְונָא דִלְעֵילָּא.

336. Man always MEANS male and female, EVEN IN THE LEVELS OF ATZILUT. But man, who is the Supernal Holy One, NAMELY ZEIR ANPIN OF ATZILUT who dominates everything, gives life and sustenance to everything. Even so, this strong serpent withheld the light, in the entire LEVEL OF ADAM. When the tabernacle, WHICH IS the female of that man WHO IS THE GOOD PART IN NOGAH, became impure, as we have said, she died and the male died too. And they return TO LIFE as before. Therefore, everything BELOW is similar to above.

337. אֲכַל אִינּוּן עֲנָבִין אוּכָמִין, מוּבְטַח לֵיהּ דְּהוּא בֶּן עָלְמָא דְּאָתֵי,
בְּגִין דְּשֵׁיצֵי, וְשָׁלִיט עַל הַהוּא אֲתַר, וְאִתְגַּבַּר עֲלֵיהּ, וְאַדְּק לֵיהּ, כד"א
אָכְלָא וּמַדְּקָא. כֵּיוָן דְּאִעֲבַר הַהִיא קְלִיפָה תַּקִּיפָא, הָא אִתְקְרַב לְגַבֵּי
עָלְמָא דְּאָתֵי, וְלֵית מַאן דִּמְחֵי בִּידֵיהּ. וְעַל דָּא, מַאן דְּחָמֵי בְּחֶלְמֵיהּ
דְּאִינּוּן עֲנָבִין אוּכָמִין אָכַל וּמְהַדֵּק מוּבְטַח לֵיהּ וְכוּ'.

337. If one eats these black grapes IN HIS DREAM, then he is certain that he will be part of the World to Come. It is because he destroys THEM and he dominates that place, NAMELY THE KLIPAH, FOR HE HAS EATEN THEM, overcomes it and grinds it, as it is written: "It devoured and broke in pieces" (Daniel 7:7). Once that strong Klipah is removed, he is closer to the World to Come and there is no one to prevent him. Therefore one who sees in his dream that he ate those black grapes and crushed them, is certain to have the World to Come.

338. כְּגַוְונָא דָּא, לָא הֲוֵי שִׁיר בְּבֵיתָא דְּדָוִד, עַד דְּאִתְעַבָּרוּ אִינּוּן עֲנָבִין
אוּכָמִין, וְשַׁלְטָא עֲלַיְיהוּ, וּכְדֵין אִתְּמַר שִׁיר הַשִּׁירִים, כְּמָה דְּאִתְּמַר.
וַאֲפִילוּ בְּאֲתַר דָּא אִקְרֵי עֲנָבִים, כד"א כַּעֲנָבִים בַּמִּדְבָּר וְגוֹ', וְאִלֵּין
אִינּוּן עֲנָבִים חִוָּורִין.

**338.** Similar to this, there was no song in the House of David, WHICH IS MALCHUT, until these black grapes were removed. He dominated them and then Shir Hashirim was recited, as we have learned. Even in this place, IN MALCHUT, they are called 'grapes', as it is written: "I found Yisrael like grapes in the wilderness…" (Hoshea 9:10). THE CHILDREN OF YISRAEL ARE THE ASPECTS OF MALCHUT, and these, THAT ARE IN THE PASSAGE, are white grapes.

339. שִׁירָתָא דָּא אִיהִי מְעַלְיָא עַל כָּל שְׁאַר שִׁירִין דְּקַדְמָאֵי. כָּל שִׁירִין דְּקַדְמָאֵי אָמְרוּ, לָא סְלִיקוּ אֶלָּא גּוֹ שִׁירִין דְּמַלְאֲכֵי עִלָּאֵי אַמְרֵי. וְאע״ג דְּהָא אוּקְמוּהָ, אֲבָל כְּתִיב שִׁיר הַמַּעֲלוֹת לְדָוִד, שִׁיר הַמַּעֲלוֹת שִׁיר דְּמַלְאֲכֵי עִלָּאֵי אַמְרֵי. דְּאִינּוּן מַעֲלוֹת וְדַרְגִּין. אַמְרֵי לְמַאן. לְדָוִד. לְבַקְשָׁא טַרְפָּא וּמְזוֹנָא מִנֵּיהּ.

**339.** This song is superior to all the songs of the ancient. All the songs recited by the ancient were equal only to the songs that the Angels recited, even though they established it IN A DIFFERENT MANNER, it is written: "A song of ascents to David." "A song of ascents" MEANS the songs that those supreme angels say, who are divided into grades and levels. To whom do they say it? "To David," WHO IS MALCHUT, to request of him food and sustenance.

340. תּוּ שִׁיר הַמַּעֲלוֹת, כד״א עַל עֲלָמוֹת שִׁיר. עַל כֵּן עֲלָמוֹת אֲהֵבוּךָ. לְדָוִד, בְּגִין דָּוִד מַלְכָּא עִלָּאָה, דְּאִיהוּ מְשַׁבַּח תָּדִיר לְמַלְכָּא עִלָּאָה.

**340.** Another EXPLANATION: "A song of ascents (Heb. *Shir Hamaalot*)" is as it is written, "A song to Alamot" (Tehilim 46:1) and "therefore do the virgins (Heb. *alamot*) love you" (Shir Hashirim 1:3), WHICH IS THE SECRET OF THE CHAMBERS OF BRIYAH THAT ARE CALLED 'ALAMOT'. THE VERSE WRITES THAT THIS IS THE SONG OF THE ALAMOT, BECAUSE "*HAMA'ALOT*" (ENG. 'ASCENTS') IS SPELLED WITH THE SAME LETTERS AS HA'ALAMOT (ENG. 'THE MAIDENS'). "To David," MEANING for the Supreme King David WHO IS MALCHUT, who constantly praises the Supreme King, WHO IS ZEIR ANPIN.

341. כֵּיוָן דְּאָתָא שְׁלֹמֹה מַלְכָּא, אָמַר שִׁיר דְּאִיהוּ עִלָּאָה לְעֵילָא.

דְּרַבְרְבֵי עָלְמָא עִלָּאִין, קָאמְרֵי לְגַבֵּי מַלְכָּא עִלָּאָה, דִּשְׁלָמָא כֹּלָּא
דִּילֵיהּ. כֻּלְּהוּ דְּאָמְרֵי שִׁירָתָא, לָא סְלִיקוּ בְּהַהִיא שִׁירָתָא לוֹמַר, אֶלָּא
הַהוּא שִׁירָתָא דְּמַלְאֲכֵי עִלָּאֵי קָאמְרֵי. בַּר שְׁלֹמֹה מַלְכָּא, דִּסְלִיק
בְּהַהִיא שִׁירָתָא לְמַה דְּרַבְרְבִין עִלָּאִין עַמּוּדֵי עָלְמָא קָאמְרֵי. כָּל בְּנֵי
עָלְמָא בִּרְתִיכִין תַּתָּאִין, שְׁלֹמֹה מַלְכָּא בִּרְתִיכִין עִלָּאִין.

**341.** As soon as King Solomon came, he recited a song that is elevated above, which the great ones of the Upper World, CHESED, GVURAH AND TIFERET OF ZEIR ANPIN THAT IS CALLED 'THE UPPER WORLD' recite to the Supreme King that all the peace is His, WHO IS BINAH, WHENCE ALL THE LIGHTS OF MALE AND FEMALE AND BRIYAH, YETZIRAH AND ASIYAH COME FROM. ITS CHESED, GVURAH AND TIFERET ARE CALLED 'GREAT ONES', NAMELY FIRST THREE SFIROT, IN COMPARISON TO ITS NETZACH, HOD AND YESOD WHICH ARE SMALL AND THE ASPECT OF SIX EXTREMITIES. All of them who recited songs had their songs ascend only as high as that song that the supreme angels recited, except for King Solomon, who ascended with this song to what the Supreme Great Ones, the pillars of the World, CHESED, GVURAH AND TIFERET OF ZEIR ANPIN, recited. All the people of the world, THEIR SONGS WERE in the lower Chariots; NAMELY, OF THE NUKVA BELOW THE CHEST OF ZEIR ANPIN. But King Solomon's SONG WAS in the Supreme Chariots, IN CHESED, GVURAH, TIFERET AND MALCHUT ABOVE THE CHEST OF ZEIR ANPIN, WHICH ARE A CHARIOT TO BINAH.

**342.** וְאִי תֵּימָא, מֹשֶׁה דְּסָלִיק בְּדַרְגָּא דִּנְבוּאָה וּבַחֲבִיבוּ לְגַבֵּי קוּדְשָׁא
בְּרִיךְ הוּא, עַל כָּל בְּנֵי עָלְמָא, הַהִיא שִׁירָתָא דְּקָאמַר בִּרְתִיכִין תַּתָּאִין
הֲוָה, וְלָא סָלִיק יַתִּיר. תָּא חֲזֵי, שִׁירָתָא דְּקָאמַר מֹשֶׁה, סָלִיק לְעֵילָא
וְלָא לְתַתָּא. אֲבָל לָא אָמַר שִׁירָתָא כִּשְׁלֹמֹא מַלְכָּא, וְלָא הֲוָה ב״נ
דְּסָלִיק בְּשִׁירָתָא כִּשְׁלֹמֹה.

**342.** If you ask: Yet Moses ascended by the level of prophecy and love to the Holy One, blessed be He, beyond all the inhabitants of the world. WOULD YOU SAY that that song which he said pertained to the lower Chariots and did not rise higher? HE ANSWERS: Come and see, the song that Moses recited ascended above, TO ZEIR ANPIN, and not below, TO

NUKVA. But he did not recite poetry like King Solomon, and no one ascended by a poem like Solomon.

343. מֹשֶׁה סָלִיק בְּתוּשְׁבַּחְתֵּיה לְעֵילָא, וְתוּשְׁבַּחְתָּא דִּילֵיה הֲוָה, לְמֵיהַב תּוּשְׁבְּחָן וְהוֹדָאָן לְמַלְכָּא עִלָּאָה, דְּשֵׁזִיב לוֹן לְיִשְׂרָאֵל, וְעָבֵיד לוֹן נִסִּין וּגְבוּרָאן בְּמִצְרַיִם, וְעַל יַמָּא. אֲבָל דָּוִד מַלְכָּא, וּשְׁלֹמֹה בְּרֵיה, אָמְרוּ שִׁירָתָא בִּגְוָונָא אַחֲרָא. דָּוִד אִשְׁתַּדַּל לְאַתְקְנָא עוּלְמְתָן, וּלְקַשְׁטָא לוֹן בְּמַטְרוֹנִיתָא, לְאִתְחֲזָאָה מַטְרוֹנִיתָא וְעוּלְמְתָהָא בְּשַׁפִּירוּ, וְעַל דָּא אִשְׁתַּדַּל בְּאִינּוּן שִׁירִין וְתוּשְׁבְּחָן דִּגְבֵּייהוּ, עַד דְּאַתְקִין וְקַשִּׁיט כֻּלְּהוּ עוּלְמְתָן וּמַטְרוֹנִיתָא.

343. Moses ascended with his song above, TO ZEIR ANPIN, and the purpose of his praise was to give praises and thankfulness to the Supreme King, WHO IS ZEIR ANPIN, who saved Yisrael and performed for them miracles and mighty deeds in Egypt and on the Sea. But King David and his son Solomon said songs in a different manner. David endeavored to correct the maidens, NAMELY THE CHAMBERS OF BRIYAH, WHICH ARE THE PORTIONS OF NETZACH, HOD AND YESOD OF MALCHUT, FOR WITHOUT THEM THERE ARE NO FIRST THREE SFIROT TO MALCHUT, and to beautify the Queen with them, WHICH IS MALCHUT. He did this so that the Queen and her maidens should appear in beauty. Therefore, he strove through these songs and praises by them, until he improved and beautified all the maidens and the Queen.

344. כֵּיוָן דְּאָתָא שְׁלֹמֹה, אַשְׁכַּח לְמַטְרוֹנִיתָא מִתְקַשְּׁטָא, וְעוּלְמְתָהָא בְּשַׁפִּירוּ, אִשְׁתַּדַּל לְמֵיעַל לָה לְגַבֵּי חָתָן, וְאָעֵיל הֶחָתָן לַחוּפָּה בְּמַטְרוֹנִיתָא, וְאָעֵיל מִלִּין דִּרְחִימוּ בֵּינַיְיהוּ, בְּגִין לְחַבְּרָא לוֹן כַּחֲדָא, וּלְמֶהֱוֵי תַּרְוַויְיהוּ בִּשְׁלִימוּ חֲדָא בְּחֲבִיבוּ שְׁלִים. וְעַל דָּא שְׁלֹמֹה סָלִיק בְּתוּשְׁבַּחְתָּא עִלָּאָה, עַל כָּל בְּנֵי עָלְמָא.

344. As soon as Solomon arrived, he found the Queen adorned and her maidens beautified. He endeavored to bring her to the groom, WHO IS ZEIR ANPIN, and brought the groom to the marriage canopy with the Queen, WHICH IS THE SECRET OF THE DRAWING OF THE SIX EXTREMITIES OF

GREATNESS. Then he introduced words of love between them in order to join them together, MEANING TO DRAW THE FIRST THREE SFIROT OF GREATNESS, so they would both be as one whole with perfect love. Therefore, Solomon surpassed in supreme praise the whole world.

345. מֹשֶׁה, זַוֵּוג לְמַטְרוֹנִיתָא בְּהַאי עָלְמָא לְתַתָּא, לְמֶהֱוֵי בְּהַאי עָלְמָא בְּזִוּוּגָא שְׁלִים בְּתַתָּאֵי. שְׁלֹמֹה, זַוֵּוג לָהּ לְמַטְרוֹנִיתָא בְּזִוּוּגָא שְׁלֵימָא לְעֵילָּא, וְאָעִיל חֲתָן לְחוּפָּה בְּקַדְמֵיתָא, וּלְבָתַר עָאל לְתַרְוַוְיְיהוּ בְּהַאי עָלְמָא, וְזַמִּין לוֹן בְּחֶדְוָה בְּבֵי מַקְדְּשָׁא דְּאִיהוּ בָּנָה.

345. Moses paired the Queen in this world below, FROM THE CHEST DOWN OF ZEIR ANPIN, WHICH IS ONLY THE ASPECT OF SIX EXTREMITIES, to be in this world in complete union among those below, MEANING IN THE ASPECTS OF TIFERET, NETZACH, HOD AND YESOD ALONE. Solomon joined the Queen to a perfect union above, NAMELY FROM THE CHEST UP OF ZEIR ANPIN, and brought the groom to the canopy before the marriage. Afterwards he brought them both into this world into the Temple that he built, MEANING THAT HE EXTENDED THE UNION FROM THE CHEST DOWN. AND SO WE FIND THAT MOSES DREW UNTO MALCHUT ONLY THE ASPECT OF SIX EXTREMITIES, BUT SOLOMON DREW THE FIRST THREE SFIROT, AFTER THE SIX EXTREMITIES WERE ALREADY PREPARED BY MOSES.

346. וְאִי תֵּימָא, הֵיךְ עָיֵיל מֹשֶׁה לְמַטְרוֹנִיתָא בִּלְחוֹדָהָא בְּהַאי עָלְמָא, דְּהָא אִתְחֲזֵי פֵּרוּדָא. ת"ח, קוּדְשָׁא בְּרִיךְ הוּא זַוֵּוג לָהּ בְּמֹשֶׁה בְּקַדְמֵיתָא, וְאִיהוּ הֲוַות כַּלַּת מֹשֶׁה, כְּמָה דְּאִתְּמַר. כֵּיוָן דְּאִזְדַּוְוגַת בֵּיהּ בְּמֹשֶׁה, נַחְתַּת בְּהַאי עָלְמָא. בְּזִוּוּגָא דְּהַאי עָלְמָא, וְאִתְתַּקְּנַת בְּהַאי עָלְמָא, מַה דְּלָא הֲוַות מִקַּדְמַת דְּנָא, וּלְעוֹלָם לָא הֲוַות בְּפֵרוּדָא.

346. If you ask: How could Moses bring the Queen alone to this world, SINCE THE UNION WAS IN THE ASPECT OF TIFERET, NETZACH, HOD AND YESOD OF ZEIR ANPIN, WHICH BELONG TO MALCHUT AND ONLY THE ASPECT OF CHESED, GVURAH AND TIFERET IS DESIGNATED FOR ZEIR ANPIN? For it seems like a separation. HE ANSWERS, Come and see: The Holy One, blessed be He, first united her with Moses, WHO WAS A CHARIOT TO THE ASPECT OF THE CHEST AND UP OF ZEIR ANPIN, and she

was the bride of Moses, as we have learned. As soon as she was united with Moses AND SHE RECEIVED FROM HIM THE SWEETNESS THAT IS ABOVE THE CHEST OF ZEIR ANPIN, she descended into the union of this world, WHICH IS SIX ENDS, and was fixed in this world, which is something she did not achieve beforehand. But she never was separated.

347. אֲבָל לָא הֲוָה בַּר נָשׁ בְּעָלְמָא מִיוֹמָא דְּאִתְבְּרֵי אָדָם, דְּיָעֵיל רְחִימוּ וְחָבִיבוּ, וּמִלִּין דְּזִוּוּגָא לְעֵילָּא, בַּר שְׁלֹמֹה מַלְכָּא, דְּאִיהוּ אַתְקִין זִוּוּגָא דִּלְעֵילָּא בְּקַדְמֵיתָא, וּלְבָתַר זַמִּין לוֹן כַּחֲדָא בְּבֵיתָא דְּאַתְקִין לוֹן. זַכָּאִין אִינּוּן דָּוִד וּשְׁלֹמֹה בְּרֵיהּ, דְּאִינּוּן אַתְקִינוּ זִוּוּגָא דִּלְעֵילָּא. מִיוֹמָא דְּאָמַר לֵהּ קוּדְשָׁא בְּרִיךְ הוּא לְסִיהֲרָא, זִילִי וְאַזְעִירִי גַּרְמֵיךְ, לָא אִזְדַּוְּוגַת בְּזִוּוּגָא שְׁלִים בְּשִׁמְשָׁא, בַּר כַּד אָתָא שְׁלֹמֹה מַלְכָּא.

347. But there was not a person in the world since the day that Adam was created who brought love and amiability and words of marriage above except for King Solomon, who prepared the marriage of above FROM THE CHEST OF ZEIR ANPIN first, FOR HE DREW CHOCHMAH FROM THERE. Afterwards he invited them together to the house that He prepared for them, MEANING ALSO TO THE UNION OF THE ASPECT OF BELOW THE CHEST TO THE DRAWING OF CHASSADIM. Happy are David and his son, Solomon, for they prepared the marriage of above, NAMELY IN THE ASPECT OF THE FIRST THREE SFIROT. Since the day the Holy One, blessed be He, told the moon, WHICH IS MALCHUT, 'Go and diminish yourself,' it did not have a complete union with the sun, THAT IS ZEIR ANPIN, except when King Solomon came.

348. שִׁיר הַשִּׁירִים, הָא הָכָא חָמֵשׁ דַּרְגִּין, לְאִתְדַּבְּקָא בְּעָלְמָא דְּאָתֵי. שִׁיר, חַד. הַשִּׁירִים, תְּרֵין, הָא תְּלַת. אֲשֶׁר, הָא אַרְבְּעָה. לִשְׁלֹמֹה, הָא חֲמִשָׁה. בְּחַמְשָׁאָה אִיהוּ. דְּהָא יוֹמָא דְּחַמְשִׁין, רָזָא דְּיוֹבְלָא אִיהוּ.

348. In Shir Hashirim, there are five levels present with which to become joined in the World to Come, WHICH IS BINAH. 'Song' is one, 'of Songs' is two, making three, 'which is' makes four and 'Solomon's' makes five. FOR THERE ARE TWO LEVELS IN THE SMALL MALE AND FEMALE FROM THE CHEST DOWN OF ZEIR ANPIN, AND TWO LEVELS OF THE GREAT MALE

AND FEMALE, FROM THE CHEST UP OF ZEIR ANPIN. AND AFTER THEM IS
BINAH, SO WE FIND THAT BINAH is in the fifth level, for it is the fiftieth
day, the secret of Jubilee, NAMELY BINAH.

349. ת״ח, זוּוּגָא דִּלְעֵילָא לָא יָכִיל שְׁלֹמֹה לְאַתְקְנָא, אֶלָּא בְּגִין
דְּאִשְׁתְּכַח זוּוּגָא לְתַתָּא, מִקַּדְמַת דְּנָא. וּמַאן אִיהוּ. זוּוּגָא דְּמֹשֶׁה. דְּאִי
לָא הֲוֵי זוּוּגָא דְּנָא, לָא אִתְתָּקַן זוּוּגָא דִּלְעֵילָא. וְכֹלָּא בְּרָזָא עִלָּאָה
אִיהוּ, לְחַכִּימֵי לִבָּא.

**349.** Come and see: Solomon was able to prepare the marriage of above IN
THE ASPECT OF THE FIRST THREE SFIROT, only due to the already existing
marriage below, OF THE ASPECT OF SIX ENDS. Whose is THE MARRIAGE
OF BELOW? It is the marriage of Moses, for had there not been this marriage
BEFOREHAND, then the marriage above would not have been. It is all part of
the supernal secret for the wise-hearted.

350. כְּתִיב וַיְדַבֵּר שְׁלֹשֶׁת אֲלָפִים מָשָׁל וַיְהִי שִׁיר חֲמִשָּׁה וָאָלֶף, הַאי
קְרָא אוּקְמוּהָ חַבְרַיָּיא. אֲבָל וַיְדַבֵּר שְׁלֹשֶׁת אֲלָפִים מָשָׁל, וַדַּאי עַל כָּל
מִלָּה וּמִלָּה דְּאִיהוּ הֲוָה אָמַר, הֲוֹו בֵּיהּ תְּלַת אֶלֶף מְשָׁלֵי, כְּגוֹן סִפְרָא
דְּקֹהֶלֶת, דְּאִיהוּ בְּרָזָא עִלָּאָה, וְאִיהוּ בְּאֹרַח מָשָׁל, דְּלֵית בֵּיהּ קְרָא
דְּלָאו אִיהוּ בְּחָכְמְתָא עִלָּאָה, וּבְאֹרַח מָשָׁל, אֲפִילּוּ קְרָא זְעֵירָא דְּבֵיהּ.

**350.** It is written: "And he spoke three thousand proverbs, and his poems
were a thousand and five" (I Melachim 5:12). This passage was explained
by the friends. Yet "he spoke three thousand proverbs." It is certain that
every single thing that he said contained three thousand proverbs. For
example, the Book of Kohelet is in the supreme secret and is written in a
form of parable, for it contains no passage that is without supreme Wisdom
and is allegorical, even its smallest verses.

351. דְּכַד הֲוָה מָטֵי רַב הַמְנוּנָא סָבָא קַדְמָאָה לְהַאי קְרָא, שָׂמַח בָּחוּר
בְּיַלְדוּתֶךָ וִיטִיבְךָ לִבְּךָ בִּימֵי בְּחוּרוֹתֶךָ הֲוָה בָּכִי. וְאָמַר וַדַּאי הַאי קְרָא
יָאוֹת הוּא, וְאִיהוּ בְּאֹרַח מָשָׁל, וּמַאן יָכִיל לְמֶעְבַּד דְּרָשָׁא בְּמָשָׁל דָּא.
וְאִי אִיהוּ דְּרָשָׁא לֵית בֵּיהּ דְּרָשָׁא, אֶלָּא כְּמָה דַּחֲמֵינָן בְּעֵינִין. וְאִי

חָכְמְתָא אִיהוּ, מַאן יָכִיל לְמִנְדַע לָה.

**351.** When Rav Hamnuna Saba (the elder) the first reached this passage: "Rejoice, young man, in your youth; and let your heart cheer you in the days of your youth" (Kohelet 11:9), he would weep and say, Certainly this passage is beautiful, and it is by way of parable, who can expound upon this parable? If it is interpreted, there is no interpretation THAT IS POSSIBLE TO MEDITATE UPON but SUPERFICIALLY, according to what we see with our eyes. If it is Wisdom, then who can know it?

**352.** מִיַּד הֲוָה תָּב וְאָמַר, כְּתִיב, אֵלֶּה תּוֹלְדוֹת יַעֲקֹב יוֹסֵף בֶּן שְׁבַע עֶשְׂרֵה שָׁנָה וְגוֹ', הַאי קְרָא דְּקֹהֶלֶת, אִיהוּ מָשָׁל לְחָכְמְתָא דִּקְרָא דָּא דְּאוֹרַיְיתָא, וְדָא מָשָׁל לְדָא. שְׂמַח בָּחוּר בְּיַלְדוּתֶךָ, וְהוּא נַעַר. וִיטִיבְךָ לִבְּךָ, הָיָה רֹעֶה אֶת אֶחָיו בַּצֹּאן. בִּימֵי בְחוּרוֹתֶיךָ, אֶת בְּנֵי בִלְהָה וְאֶת בְּנֵי זִלְפָּה נְשֵׁי אָבִיו. וְדַע כִּי עַל כָּל אֵלֶּה, וַיָּבֵא יוֹסֵף אֶת דִּבָּתָם רָעָה. יְבִיאֲךָ אֱלֹהִים בַּמִּשְׁפָּט, אֵלֶּה תּוֹלְדוֹת יַעֲקֹב יוֹסֵף. יוֹסֵף אִתְכְּלִיל בְּיַעֲקֹב, וְרָזִין דְּסִתְרֵי תוֹרָה, מַאן יָכִיל לְמִנְדַּע לוֹן.

**352.** Immediately he said again, It is written: "These are the generations of Jacob. Joseph being seventeen years old..." (Beresheet 37:2). This passage of Kohelet is a parable to the wisdom in this passage in the Torah, and one is comparable to the other. "Rejoice, young man, in your youth" CORRESPONDS TO "and the lad". THE PASSAGE: "And let your heart cheer you" CORRESPONDS TO "was feeding the flock with his brethren" (Ibid.). THE PASSAGE "in the days of your youth" CORRESPONDS TO "with the sons of Bilhah, and with the sons of Zilpah, his father's wives" (Ibid.). THE PASSAGE: "But know you, that for all these things" (Kohelet 11:9) CORRESPONDS TO "and Joseph brought to his father their evil report" (Beresheet 37:2). THE PASSAGE: "Elohim will bring you into Judgment" CORRESPONDS TO: "These are the generations of Jacob. Joseph..." because Joseph is included in Jacob, WHO IS CALLED 'JUDGMENT'. Who can know the secrets of the Torah?

**353.** וְהַאי מָשָׁל אִתְפָּשַׁט לִתְלַת אֶלֶף מְשָׁלִים, וְכֻלְּהוּ בְּהַאי מָשָׁל, בְּשַׁעֲתָא דְּיוֹסֵף אִתְכְּלִיל בְּיַעֲקֹב, תְּלַת אֶלֶף אִינּוּן, בְּאַבְרָהָם יִצְחָק

וְיַעֲקֹב, דְּכֵלְהוּ בְּהַאי מָשָׁל בְּרָזָא דְחָכְמְתָא. וְכָאן, כַּמָּה טַיָּיעִין אִינּוּן בְּטוֹעֲנִין דִּטְמִירוּ, בְּהוּ דַיָּירֵי תְרִיסִין, דְּלֵית לְהוֹן חוּשְׁבָּנָא לִטְמִירִין דְּחָכְמְתָא.

353. This parable expands to three thousand parables, TO THREE COLUMNS, and they are all in this parable at the time that Joseph was included in Jacob, because there are three thousand in Abraham, Isaac and Jacob, THE SECRET OF CHESED, GVURAH AND TIFERET, WHICH ARE THREE COLUMNS. JACOB BY HIMSELF IS COMPRISED OF THEM ALL AND BY HIMSELF HAS THREE COLUMNS, AS MENTIONED BEFORE. THEREFORE, WHEN JOSEPH WAS INCLUDED IN JACOB, THEY WERE ALL IN JOSEPH. For all of them, ALL THE THREE COLUMNS, are in this parable in the secret of wisdom. Here, IN THE THREE THOUSAND PARABLES, many are the merchants who carry THE MERCHANDISE of mystery, MEANING THAT MANY WISE MEN HAVE MANY SECRETS IN THIS. There are those who carry shields, MEANING WEAR SHIELDS AGAINST THE OTHER SIDE WHO DRAW THEM FROM THE CENTRAL COLUMN, and there is no end to the secrets of Wisdom CONTAINED HEREIN.

354. וַיְהִי שִׁירוֹ חֲמִשָּׁה וָאָלֶף, הָכִי אוּקִימְנָא, וַיְהִי שִׁירוֹ שֶׁל מָשָׁל, וְכֹלָּא חַד, בֵּין מַאן דְּאָמַר וַיְהִי שִׁירוֹ דִּשְׁלֹמֹה, בֵּין מַאן דְּאָמַר וַיְהִי שִׁירוֹ שֶׁל מָשָׁל, כֹּלָּא אִיהוּ חַד, וְכֹלָּא אִיהוּ קָאָמַר, וַיְהִי שִׁירוֹ, דָּא שִׁיר הַשִּׁירִים. וְכִי חֲמִשָּׁה וָאָלֶף אִיהוּ שִׁיר הַשִּׁירִים. וַדַּאי הָכִי הוּא, חֲמִשָּׁה אִינּוּן תַּרְעִין וּפִתְחִין דְּמִתְפַּתְּחֵי בְּמַלְכָּא דִּשְׁלָמָא דִילֵיהּ. וְאִינּוּן חֲמֵשׁ מֵאָה שְׁנִין דְּאִילָנָא דְּחַיֵּי. חַמְשִׁין שְׁנִין דְּיוֹבְלָא.

354. "And his poems were a thousand and five." This is what we established: "And his poems" of the parable "WERE A THOUSAND AND FIVE." It is all one, whether we say that they are the poems of Solomon or whether we say they were the poems of the parable. It is all one and the meaning of it all is that: "And his poems" is Shir Hashirim. HE QUESTIONS: Is Shir Hashirim a thousand and five? HE ANSWERS: Certainly it is so! "Five" are the gates and entrances that open to the King that the Peace is His, WHICH IS ZEIR ANPIN. They are the five hundred years of the Tree of Life, WHICH IS ZEIR ANPIN, FOR THEY ARE THE FIVE

SFIROT, KETER, CHOCHMAH, BINAH, TIFERET NAD MALCHUT, THAT
ARE DRAWN TO HIM FROM IMA. AND THEY ARE the fifty years of Jubilee,
WHICH IS BINAH, THAT ARE DRAWN TO ZEIR ANPIN.

355. וְאָלֶף, דָּא אִיהוּ אִילָנָא דְּחַיֵּי, חָתָן דְּנָפִיק מִסְטְרֵיהּ, וְאִיהוּ יָרִית
כָּל אִינוּן חֲמִשָּׁה, לְמֵיתֵי לְגַבֵּי כַּלָּה. יוֹמֵי דְּקוּדְשָׁא בְּרִיךְ הוּא אֶלֶף
שְׁנִין אִיהוּ, וְדָא אִיהוּ נָהָר דְּנָגִיד וְנָפִיק מֵעֵדֶן. יוֹסֵף זַכָּאָה. דְּאִקְרֵי
צַדִּיק, עַל שְׁמָא דְּסִיהֲרָא. כְּמָה דְּאִתְנִי בָּהּ קוּדְשָׁא בְּרִיךְ הוּא. וּבְגִין כָּךְ
שִׁיר הַשִּׁירִים, קֹדֶשׁ קָדָשִׁים.

355. "A thousand" is the Tree of Life, ZEIR ANPIN. The groom that
emerges from his side, WHICH IS YESOD THAT EMERGES FROM THE TREE
OF LIFE, WHICH IS ZEIR ANPIN, inherits all the five THAT ARE IN THE
TREE OF LIFE, to bring them to the bride, THAT IS MALCHUT. The day of
the Holy One, blessed be He, lasts one thousand years, NAMELY, WHEN
ZEIR ANPIN CLOTHES SUPREME ABA AND IMA SO THAT EACH OF THEIR
SFIROT ARE IN THE SECRET OF ONE THOUSAND, AND THEN ALSO THE
SIX SFIROT, CHESED, GVURAH, TIFERET, NETZACH, HOD AND YESOD
OF ZEIR ANPIN, THAT ARE CALLED 'SIX DAYS', EACH DAY IN THE SECRET
OF ONE THOUSAND YEARS. THUS EVEN YESOD HAS ONE THOUSAND
YEARS. This is the river that comes out of Eden, BECAUSE YESOD THAT IS
CALLED 'RIVER' EMERGES FROM EDEN, WHICH IS SUPREME ABA AND
IMA, that is called 'Joseph the Righteous', MEANING YESOD OF THE
GREATNESS OF ZEIR ANPIN THAT IS CALLED 'RIGHTEOUS' after the moon,
WHICH IS MALCHUT THAT IS CALLED 'RIGHTEOUSNESS'. FOR THEY ARE
JOINED as the Holy One, blessed be He, conditioned Her, MEANING IN THE
SECRET OF THE PASSAGE: "IF MY COVENANT BE NOT DAY AND NIGHT, IT
WERE AS IF I HAD NOT APPOINTED THE ORDINANCES OF HEAVEN AND
EARTH" (YIRMEYAH 33:25). Therefore, Shir Hashirim is the Holy of
Holies, FOR THERE ARE DRAWN INTO HER THE MOCHIN OF ABA AND IMA
THAT ARE SO CALLED, AS IT IS WRITTEN BEFORE US.

356. וְלֵית לָךְ קְרָא בְּשִׁיר הַשִּׁירִים, דְּלָא אִית בֵּיהּ רָזָא דְּחֲמִשָּׁה וְאָלֶף
וַדַּאי. שִׁיר הַשִּׁירִים וַדַּאי הָכִי הוּא. חֲמֵשׁ דַּרְגִּין אִינוּן בְּהַאי קְרָא, כְּמָה
דְּאִתְּמַר. וְאִי תֵּימָא, הָאָלֶף אַמַּאי לָא אִדְכַּר הָכָא. וַדַּאי הַהוּא אֶלֶף
טְמִירָא הֲוָה, וּטְמִירָא אִיהוּ עַד דְּאִתְחַבְּרַת אִתְּתָא בְּבַעְלָהּ. וְעַל דָּא

אִשְׁתָּדַּל שְׁלֹמֹה, לְמֵיתֵי הַהוּא אֶלֶף לְגַבֵּי כַּלָּה, בִּטְמִירוּ דְּגוּשְׁפַנְקָא דְּחָכְמְתָא עִלָּאָה.

**356.** There is no passage in Shir Hashirim that does not contain the secret of one thousand and five. THE PASSAGE: 'The Song of Songs' is certainly so, because these are five levels in this passage, as we have learned, IN THAT IT CONTAINS FIVE WORDS CORRESPONDING TO THE FIVE LEVELS KETER, CHOCHMAH, BINAH, TIFERET AND MALCHUT. If you ask about the thousand, WHICH IS YESOD, Why is IT NOT MENTIONED IN THIS PASSAGE? It is because that thousand is certainly hidden until a wife is joined with her husband, ZEIR ANPIN AND MALCHUT. This is what Solomon endeavored, to bring this thousand to the bride in the secret of the seal of supernal Chochmah, WHICH IS YESOD OF MALCHUT. FOR IN IT IS SEALED AND REVEALED SUPERNAL CHOCHMAH.

357. כֵּיוָן דְּעָבֵד קֹדֶשׁ הַקֳּדָשִׁים לְתַתָּא, גָּנִיז וְטָמִיר, וְעָאל רָזָא דְּקֹדֶשׁ הַקֳּדָשִׁים לְתַמָּן, לְמֶעְבַּד גְּנִיזוּ דְּשִׁמּוּשָׁא שְׁלִים, עֵילָא וְתַתָּא כַּדְקָא יָאוֹת. קֹדֶשׁ הַקֳּדָשִׁים אִיהוּ לְעֵילָא, רָזָא דְּחָכְמְתָא עִלָּאָה, וְיוֹבְלָא. כְּגַוְונָא דָּא יַרְתִּין חָתָן וְכַלָּה, יְרוּתָא דְּאַבָּא וְאִמָּא.

**357.** As soon as he made the Holy of Holies below, IN THE TEMPLE, hidden and concealed, he brought in there the secret of the Holy of Holies, WHICH ARE THE TWO CHERUBS IN THE SECRET OF ZEIR ANPIN AND MALCHUT THAT ARE CALLED 'HOLY OF HOLIES', IN ORDER TO make the mystery of the complete union above, IN ABA AND IMA, and below IN ZEIR ANPIN AND MALCHUT, in a proper manner. The Holy of Holies above is the secret of supernal Chochmah and Jubilee, WHICH IS BINAH. Similarly, the groom and bride, WHO ARE ZEIR ANPIN AND MALCHUT, inherit the inheritance of Aba and Ima, MEANING CHOCHMAH AND JUBILEE, AND ARE ALSO CALLED 'HOLY OF HOLIES'.

358. וְאִתְהַדְּרוּ אַחֲסָנַת יְרוּתָא בְּגַוְונָא אַחֲרָא. יְרוּתָא דְּאַבָּא, יָרְתָא בְּרַתָּא, בְּסְלִיקוּ דִּשְׁמָא קַדִּישָׁא דָּא, וְאִתְקְרֵי אוּף הָכִי קֹדֶשׁ, חָכְמָה. יְרוּתָא דְּאִמָּא, יָרִית בְּרָא, וְאִקְרֵי קָדָשִׁים, בְּגִין דְּנָטִיל כָּל אִינּוּן קָדָשִׁים עִלָּאִין, וְכָנִישׁ לוֹן לְגַבֵּיהּ. וּבָתַר יָהִיב לוֹן, וְאָעִיל לוֹן לְגַבֵּי כַּלָּה.

**358.** The inherited possession is returned in a different manner. The inheritance of Aba, WHICH IS SUPERNAL CHOCHMAH DRAWN FROM CONCEALED CHOCHMAH OF ABA AND IMA, is inherited by the daughter, WHO IS MALCHUT, FOR ONLY IN HER IS CHOCHMAH REVEALED. When this Holy Name ascends, MEANING DURING THE ASCENSION OF MALCHUT THAT IS CALLED 'NAME', TO ABA AND IMA, THEN CHOCHMAH IS REVEALED IN HER, and She is also called 'Holy', WHICH IS Chochmah, LIKE ABA. The inheritance of Ima, WHICH IS BINAH, WHICH IS CHASSADIM IN THE SECRET OF: "BECAUSE HE DELIGHTS IN CHESED" (MICHAH 7:18) is inherited by the son and is called 'Holies'. This is because he takes all these Supernal Holies, BOTH THE CHOCHMAH OF ABA AND THE CHASSADIM OF IMA, and gathers them unto him, BUT THE CHOCHMAH IS COVERED AND ONLY CHASSADIM DOMINATES HIM. THEREFORE, IT SEEMS THAT HE INHERITS ONLY FROM IMA AND NOT FROM ABA. Afterwards, he gives them, NAMELY CHOCHMAH AND CHASSADIM, and brings them to the bride, WHO IS MALCHUT, AND CHOCHMAH IS REVEALED IN HER. THEREFORE, IT SEEMS THAT SHE INHERITS ABA, FOR HE POSSESSES SUPERNAL CHOCHMAH FROM CONCEALED CHOCHMAH OF ARICH ANPIN THAT IS THE SOURCE OF CHOCHMAH. THEREFORE, SHE IS CALLED 'HOLY' AFTER HIM.

359. וְעַל דָּא אָמַר שִׁיר הַשִּׁירִים. שִׁיר, לְגַבֵּי קֹדֶשׁ. הַשִּׁירִים, לְגַבֵּי קֳדָשִׁים, לְמֶהֱוֵי כֹּלָּא קֹדֶשׁ קָדָשִׁים, בְּרָזָא חֲדָא כְּמָה דְּאִתְחֲזֵי. אֲשֶׁר לִשְׁלֹמֹה הָא אִתְּמַר לְמַלְכָּא דִּשְׁלָמָא דִּילֵיהּ.

**359.** Therefore he said, "The song of songs." "Song" relates to Holy, THAT IS ABA, "of songs" to Holies, WHICH ARE IMA so that everything will be in the secret of Holy of Holies in one secret as appropriate. "Which is Solomon's," as we have learned THAT ITS MEANING IS, which is of the King that the peace is His, WHICH IS ZEIR ANPIN.

360. וְאִי תֵּימָא שְׁבָחָא דָּא דִּילֵיהּ הוּא. לָא תֵּימָא הָכִי, אֶלָּא שְׁבָחָא בַּאֲתָר עִלָּאָה אִיהוּ סַלְּקָא. אֲבָל הָכָא הוּא רָזָא. כַּד מִתַּתְקְנָן דְּכַר וְנוּקְבָא כַּחֲדָא, תְּחוֹת מַלְכָּא עִלָּאָה, כְּדֵין הַהוּא מַלְכָּא אִסְתַּלִּיק לְעֵילָּא, וְאִתְמַלְיָא מִכָּל קְדוּשִׁין, וּמִכָּל בִּרְכָּאן, דְּנַגְדָּן לְתַתָּא, וְאִתְמַלֵּי וְאָרִיק לְתַתָּא, וְדָא אִיהוּ תִּיאוּבְתֵּיהּ דְּמַלְכָּא עִלָּאָה, כַּד אִתְמַלֵּי קְדוּשָׁן

וּבְרְכָאן, וְאָרִיק לְתַתָּא.

**360.** If you say that this praise, MEANING THIS MOCHIN MENTIONED IN THE SHIR HASHIRIM, is OF ZEIR ANPIN, FOR IT SAYS: "WHICH IS SOLOMON'S" THAT IS ZEIR ANPIN, do not say this. Rather the praise ascends to a high place, NAMELY TO BINAH, but there is a secret IN THE WORDS: "WHICH IS SOLOMON'S." For when the Male and the Female are readied together, ZEIR ANPIN AND MALCHUT under the supernal King, WHO IS BINAH, then that King, WHO IS ZEIR ANPIN, ascends above TO BINAH and is filled there with all the sanctifications and all the blessings that are drawn down, and projects them down, NAMELY TO MALCHUT. This is the desire of the supernal King, ZEIR ANPIN, to be filled with sanctifications and blessings to project downwards, TO MALCHUT.

361. וְעַל דָּא אִיהוּ צְלוֹתִין וּבָעוּתִין, דְּיִתְתָּקַן וְאִתְמַלְיָא הַהוּא מַבּוּעָא עִלָּאָה. דְּכֵיוָן דְּאִיהוּ מִתְתָּקַן כַּדְקָא יָאוֹת, מֵחֵיזוּ דִּילֵיהּ, וּמֵחֵיזוּ דְּהַהוּא תִּקּוּנָא, מִתַּתְקְנָא עָלְמָא תַּתָּאָה, וְעוּלֵמְתָהָא. וְלָא אִצְטְרִיךְ עָלְמָא תַּתָּאָה לְאִתְתַּקְנָא, אֶלָּא מֵחֵיזוּ דְּעָלְמָא עִלָּאָה. סִיהֲרָא, לֵית לָהּ חֵיזוּ מִגַּרְמָהָא כְּלָל, בַּר כַּד אִתְתָּקַן בְּשִׁמְשָׁא וְאַנְהִיר, וּמֵחֵיזוּ דְּשִׁמְשָׁא וְתִקּוּנָא דִּילֵיהּ אִתְתַּקְנַת סִיהֲרָא וְאִתְנְהִירַת.

**361.** The prayers and beseeching THAT WE SAY are for this, that the supernal Spring, ZEIR ANPIN, would be fixed and filled. When it is prepared properly THEN from its appearance, NAMELY CHOCHMAH THAT IS CALLED 'SIGHT', and from the appearance of that fixture, NAMELY THE PREPARATION OF THE ASPECT OF THE CENTRAL COLUMN, the lower world, WHICH IS MALCHUT, and its maidens, WHICH ARE THE CHAMBERS OF BRIYAH, are corrected. The lower world does not have to be fixed BY BINAH, AS IN ITS SMALLNESS, but by the appearance of the Supernal World, ZEIR ANPIN, AND NOT FROM BINAH. The moon, WHICH IS MALCHUT, does not appear on its own at all, MEANING AFTER IT WAS DIMINISHED OF THE LIGHTS THAT IT RECEIVED FROM BINAH, except for when it is made ready by the sun, THAT IS ZEIR ANPIN, AND THEN it shines. It is from the light of the sun and its constructing that the moon is repaired and shines.

362. מַה דְּאִצְטְרִיךְ צְלוֹתִין וּבָעוּתִין, דְּיִתְנְהַר וְיִתְתָּקַן הַהוּא אֲתָר

דְּנָפְקָא מִנֵּיהּ נְהוֹרָא, דְּכֵיוָן דְּהַהוּא אֲתָר מִתְתַּקְנָא, מֵחֵיזוּ דִּילֵיהּ, אִתְתַּקַּן כָּל מַאן דִּלְתַתָּא. וּבְגִין כָּךְ תּוּשְׁבַּחְתָּא דְּקָאָמַר שְׁלֹמֹה, לָא אִשְׁתָּדַל אֶלָּא בְּגִין מַלְכָּא דִּשְׁלָמָא דִּילֵיהּ, דְּיִתְתַּקַּן. כֵּיוָן דְּאִיהוּ אִתְתַּקַּן, מֵחֵיזוּ דִּילֵיהּ, כֹּלָּא יִתְתַּקַּן. וְאִי אִיהוּ לָא אִתְתַּקַּן, לֵית לֵהּ תִּקּוּנָא לְסִיהֲרָא לְעָלְמִין, וּבְגִין כָּךְ אֲשֶׁר לִשְׁלֹמֹה. דְּיִתְתַּקַּן וְיִתְמַלֵּי כַּדְקָא יֵאוֹת בְּקַדְמֵיתָא, כְּמָה דְאִתְּמַר.

362. The reason that prayers and petitions are necessary is that the place from which the light emerges, WHICH IS ZEIR ANPIN, should illuminate and become prepared, because when that place is restored, then everything below, IN MALCHUT, is readied from His appearance. Therefore, when Solomon recited the song he did not strive TO RESTORE except for the sake of the King that the peace is His, WHICH IS ZEIR ANPIN, that He will be restored. Once He is restored, everything is mended through His appearance. If He is not restored, then the moon, WHICH IS MALCHUT, will never be renewed. Therefore, it is written: "Which is Solomon's," WHO IS ZEIR ANPIN, so that he should become restored and full properly as before, as we have learned.

## 32. "Of every man whose heart prompts him to give"

### A Synopsis

When Wisdom was drawn down to the world, it became entrenched in Malchut, in the kingdom on earth, and in speech where its purpose was to bring righteousness. This world, and the supernal angels, take nourishment from the spirit of righteousness. The text tells of how many times this spirit was removed by the wicked of the world and how many times it was perfected again, by Noah, by Abraham, by Isaac, by Jacob, by Moses and by Solomon. The Holy One told Moses to make Him a tabernacle so that He had a place to dwell among the children of Yisrael. "That they bring Me an offering," refers, we are reminded, to Shechinah, the spirit of Malchut. When Solomon came, he perfected that spirit of Malchut with the perfection of above, of Understanding; he started to rectify the appearance of the Upper World, which is Zeir Anpin, in order to rectify from that the appearance of the lower world, which is Malchut. This is the meaning of "Which is Solomon's" – Solomon represents Zeir Anpin.

### The Relevance of this Passage

We can use this story of our repeated cycles of lapsing into sin and then being rectified to illuminate our own world. Just as often as we err and fall from grace, we can also become righteous again through prayer and a renewed effort to succeed. The righteous souls of antiquity, Noah, Abraham, Isaac, Jacob, Moses, Solomon, whose own souls out-balance all the souls of the wicked combined, are with us now, rectifying our iniquities and correcting all the sins of the entire world.

The sum total of Light revealed by all the righteous souls, past and present, floods our existence, prompting the final ascent and redemption of man. Never again will humanity fall and stumble into darkness, for that is the power of the Zohar. And because these great sages possess a deep love for their neighbor that shines brighter than a galaxy of stars, our ascent is sweetened with immeasurable kindness and compassion. For that reason, we should take a moment and appreciate this great gift, giving thanks to all Creation for the opportunity to live during these times.

363. וְיִקְחוּ לִי תְּרוּמָה מֵאֵת כָּל אִישׁ וְגוֹ׳, רָזָא דְּרָזִין לְיַדְעֵי חָכְמְתָא, כַּד אִסְתַּלָּק בִּרְעוּתָא דְּסִתְרָא דְּכָל סִתְרִין לְמֶעְבַּד יְקָרָא לִיקָרֵיהּ, אַנְשִׁיב רוּחָא מִנְּקוּדָה עִלָּאָה, דְּנָגִיד מִלְעֵילָא לְתַתָּא, וְשַׁוֵּי תִּקּוּנֵיהּ, לְאִתְיַשְּׁבָא בְּהַאי עָלְמָא. אֲמַאי. בְּגִין דְּאִי לָא יְהֵא עִקְּרָא וְשָׁרְשָׁא

בְּהַאי עָלְמָא, לָא יְהֵא מָאנָא לְאַרְקָא בְּהַאי עָלְמָא כְּלָל. וְאִי לָא יָרִיק
לְהַאי עָלְמָא, מִיָּד אִתְאֲבִיד, וְלָא יָכִיל לְקַיְּימָא אֲפִילּוּ רִגְעָא חֲדָא.
אֲבָל בְּגִין דְּתִקּוּנֵיהּ אִיהוּ מֵהַאי עָלְמָא אִתְמְלֵי מִסִּטְרָא חֲדָא לְאַרְקָא
לְהַאי עָלְמָא, וּמִסִּטְרָא אַחֲרָא לְאַרְקָא לְמַלְאֲכֵי עִלָּאֵי. וְכֹלָּא אִתְּזָנוּ
מִנֵּיהּ כַּחֲדָא.

**363.** "That they bring Me an offering, of every man…" (Shemot 25:2). It is a most secret secret to those who know Wisdom that when it entered the will of the secret of secrets, THAT IS KETER, to glorify its glory, it blew a spirit from the supernal point, WHICH IS CHOCHMAH, MEANING THE SPIRIT OF CHOCHMAH, that is drawn from above down, TO MALCHUT. CHOCHMAH IS REVEALED IN NO SFIRAH BUT MALCHUT ALONE, and it performed THERE its rectification, in order to settle in this world. Why DID IT PERFORM THIS RECTIFICATION THERE? It is because if the root and source of this world would not BE RECTIFIED IN MALCHUT, there would be no vessel by which to provide to this world at all. If it would not provide to this world, THE WORLD would be lost immediately and would not be able to exist even one moment. But because it made the rectification IN MALCHUT from this world, MALCHUT is filled from one side to provide this world, and from the other side to provide for the supernal angels, and they all gain nourishment from it together.

364. שְׁלִימוּ דְּתִקּוּנָא דְּהַאי רוּחָא, רוּחֵיהוֹן דְּצַדִּיקַיָּא בְּהַאי עָלְמָא.
רוּחָא דָא אִשְׁתְּלִים, בְּזִמְנָא דַּחֲנוֹךְ וְיֶרֶד וּמַהֲלַלְאֵל הֲווֹ בְּעָלְמָא וְכַד
אַסְגִּיאוּ חַיָּיבֵי עָלְמָא, הַהוּא אַעֲדוּ שְׁלִימוּ מִנֵּיהּ. לְבָתַר דְּאִתְאֲבִידוּ,
אָתָא נֹחַ וְאַשְׁלִים לֵיהּ. אָתָא דּוֹר הַפְּלָגָה, אַעֲדוּ הַהוּא שְׁלִימוּ מִנֵּיהּ.
אָתָא אַבְרָהָם וְאַשְׁלִים לֵיהּ. אָתוּ אַנְשֵׁי סְדוֹם וְאַעֲדוּ לֵיהּ. אָתָא יִצְחָק
וְאַשְׁלִים לֵיהּ. אָתוּ פְּלִשְׁתִּים וְחַיָּיבֵי דָּרָא וְאַעֲדוּ לֵיהּ מִנֵּיהּ. אָתָא יַעֲקֹב
וּבְנוֹי, עַרְסָא שְׁלֵימָא, וְאַשְׁלִימוּ לֵיהּ.

**364.** The perfecting of the rectification of this spirit, WHICH IS THE LIGHT OF MALCHUT AS MENTIONED ABOVE, is the spirit of the righteous in this world. This spirit was perfected in the time that Enoch, Yered, and Mahalalel were in the world, and when the wicked of the world increased,

that perfection was removed from it, FROM THE SPIRIT. After they perished IN THE FLOOD, Noah came and brought perfection. Then came the generation of separation and perfection was removed from it, FROM THE SPIRIT. Then Abraham came and perfected it. When the people of Sodom came and removed it, Isaac came and perfected it. The Philistines and the wicked of the generation came and removed THE PERFECTION from it. Then Jacob and his sons came, FOR THEY WERE a perfect bed WITHOUT A FLAW, and perfected it.

365. נָפְקוּ מֵאַרְעָא קַדִּישָׁא וְנַחְתוּ לְמִצְרַיִם, וּבְגִינַיְיהוּ אִתְעַכְּבַת תַּמָּן. וּבְגִין דְּאָהַדְרוּ תַּמָּן יִשְׂרָאֵל לְעוֹבָדִין דְּמִצְרָאֵי, אִתְכַּפְיָא וְאִתְעֲדֵי הַהוּא שְׁלִימוּ, עַד דְּנָפְקוּ מִמִּצְרָיִם, וְאָתוּ לְמֶעְבַּד מַשְׁכְּנָא. אָמַר קוּדְשָׁא בְּרִיךְ הוּא, רְעוּתִי לְדַיְירָא בֵּינַיְיכוּ, אֲבָל לָא יָכִילְנָא עַד דְּתִתְקְנוּן הַהוּא רוּחָא דִּילִי, דְּיִשְׁרֵי בְּגַוַּוַיְיכוּ. הה"ד, וְעָשׂוּ לִי מִקְדָּשׁ וְשָׁכַנְתִּי בְּתוֹכָם.

**365.** They went out of the Holy Land and descended to Egypt, and THE SPIRIT remained IN EGYPT for them. While there, Yisrael reverted to the actions of the Egyptians, THE SPIRIT was subdued and that perfection was removed from it until they left Egypt. They came to make a tabernacle and the Holy One, blessed be He, said, 'It is My desire to dwell among you, but I cannot until you restore that spirit of Mine, NAMELY THE LIGHT OF MALCHUT AS MENTIONED ABOVE, to dwell among you.' This is what is meant by: "And let them make Me a sanctuary; that I may dwell among them" (Shemot 25:8).

366. וְדָא אִיהוּ רָזָא דִּכְתִיב, וְיִקְחוּ לִי תְּרוּמָה. אָמַר מֹשֶׁה לְקוּדְשָׁא בְּרִיךְ הוּא מַאן יָכִיל לְמֵיסַב לָה וּלְמֶעְבַּד לָה. א"ל, מֹשֶׁה, לָא כְּמָה דְּאַתְּ חָשִׁיב, אֶלָּא מֵאֵת כָּל אִישׁ אֲשֶׁר יִדְּבֶנּוּ לִבּוֹ וְגוֹ', מֵהַהוּא רְעוּתָא וְרוּחָא דִּלְהוֹן, תִּסְבּוּן לָה, וְתַשְׁלְמוּן לָה.

**366.** This is the secret of the verse: "That they bring Me an offering," NAMELY THE SHECHINAH, THE SPIRIT OF MALCHUT. Moses said to the Holy One, blessed be He, 'Who can take it and make it?' He said to him, Moses, it is not as you think, but "of every man whose heart prompts him to give…", meaning that you shall take it and perfect it from their desire and their spirit.

367. כַּד אָתָא שְׁלֹמֹה, אַתְקִין לְהַהוּא רוּחָא בִּשְׁלִימוּ דִּלְעֵילָא, דְּהָא מִן
יוֹמָא דְּאִשְׁתְּלִים לְתַתָּא בְּיוֹמוֹי דְּמֹשֶׁה, לָא אַעֲדִיאוּ הַהוּא שְׁלִימוּ
מִנֵּיהּ. כֵּיוָן דְּאָתָא שְׁלֹמֹה, אִשְׁתְּדַּל לְאַשְׁלְמָא לֵיהּ לְעֵילָא, וְשָׁארֵי
לְאַתְקְנָא חֵיזוּ דְּעָלְמָא עִלָּאָה, לְאִתְתַּקְנָא מֵהַהוּא חֵיזוּ עָלְמָא תַּתָּאָה,
וְדָא אִיהוּ אֲשֶׁר לִשְׁלֹמֹה.

367. When Solomon came, he perfected that spirit OF MALCHUT with the perfection of above, OF BINAH, because from the time that it was perfected below in the days of Moses, that perfection FROM BELOW was not removed from it. When Solomon came, he endeavored to perfect it from above and started to rectify the appearance of the Upper World, WHICH IS ZEIR ANPIN, in order to rectify from that appearance the lower world, WHICH IS MALCHUT. This is the meaning of: "Which is Solomon's," WHO IS ZEIR ANPIN.

## 33. The kisses

### A Synopsis

First, we learn that when the Torah was given to the children of Yisrael in the form of the Ten Commandments, every commandment made a sound; that sound was divided into seventy sounds which all illuminated and sparkled in the beauty and rectitude before the eyes of all Yisrael. Each person fully accepted the many commandments of the Torah and also the many punishments of the Torah. Then the sound returned and kissed him on the mouth. Each longed to see the one light that received within itself all the other colored lights, and God promised that this would happen. The text then speaks of the colors that the Light receives, which are gold, silver and brass, corresponding to Gvurah, Mercy and Beauty. We read then of another explanation for the kisses received by Yisrael, wherein the four letters of the word for love, *Ahavah*, join together in a kiss. When their Light spreads to this world, these four spirits produce one fruit, which is a spirit composed of four spirits, and this ascends and splits firmaments, before ascending further to sit near the Sanctuary of Love, whence comes all love. That spirit is also called 'love', and when it rises it causes the sanctuary to become joined above with the Sanctuary of Desire, whence are the kisses. We read next of how that spirit meets Akhtriel, the Appointed Angel who presides over the tides that come from the thirteen rivers of the pure balsam tree. These tides are called "many waters". The Song of Songs says, "Many waters cannot quench love nor can the floods drown it." When the spirit enters the Sanctuary of Love, the love of the supernal kisses becomes aroused. We are told finally of the most concealed light that illuminates everything, and the awakening of the rising of kisses that depends on it. "For your loves are better than wine", we learn, refers to the living Elohim, which is the wine that gives life and delight to all.

### The Relevance of this Passage

Ten Commandments signify the Ten Sfirot, the ten-dimensional structure through which the Light of the Creator refracts and flows, enroute to our world. We connect our souls to the myriad colors, the Lights and the sounds that once lit up Sinai brighter than a billion blazing suns. Love, the mysterious force that links us to one another and to God, resonates in the supernal Sanctuary of Love and in our hearts to illuminate all our days and nights. Speak to me of love, says the poet, and I will show you the beginning and the middle and the end of all things, and the wellspring of your very existence.

By truly opening our hearts to this message and to the wonders of the Song of Songs, this passage furnishes all that God wishes for us –

endless life and unending joy along a path teeming with sweetness, tenderness, and mercy. The full dimension of Sinai's Light is therefore replenished, kissing our souls in an everlasting embrace.

368. וְזֹאת הַתְּרוּמָה, הָא אִתְּמַר, דְּכַד קוּדְשָׁא בְּרִיךְ הוּא אִתְגְּלֵי עַל טוּרָא דְּסִינַי, כַּד אִתְיְהִיבַת אוֹרַיְיתָא לְיִשְׂרָאֵל בְּעֶשֶׂר אֲמִירָן. כָּל אֲמִירָה וַאֲמִירָה עָבִיד קָלָא, וְהַהוּא קָלָא אִתְפְּרַשׁ לְע׳ קַלִין, וַהֲווֹ כֻּלְּהוּ נְהִירִין וְנָצְצִין לְעֵינַיְיהוּ דְּיִשְׂרָאֵל כֻּלְּהוּ, וַהֲווֹ חָמָאן עַיְינִין בְּעַיְינִין זִיו יְקָרָא דִּילֵיהּ, הֲדָא הוּא דִכְתִיב וְכָל הָעָם רוֹאִים אֶת הַקּוֹלֹת. רוֹאִים וַדַּאי.

368. "And this is the offering" (Shemot 25:3). We have learned that when the Holy One, blessed be He, was revealed on Mount Sinai and the Torah was given to Yisrael with the Ten Commandments, every commandment made a sound. FOR SPEECH, THE SECRET OF CHOCHMAH, BROUGHT FORTH A SOUND WHICH IS THE SECRET OF CHESED. That sound was divided into seventy sounds and they all illuminated and sparkled before the eyes of all Yisrael, who saw His splendor eye-to-eye. This is what is meant by: "And all the people perceived the thundering (also: 'see the sounds')" (Shemot 20:15). They certainly saw, MEANING THAT THE MOCHIN OF CHOCHMAH WAS REVEALED IN IT, WHICH IS THE SECRET OF SIGHT EVEN THOUGH ESSENTIALLY IT IS THE SECRET OF CHASSADIM.

369. וְהַהוּא קָלָא הֲוָה אַתְרֵי בֵּיהּ בְּכָל חַד וְחַד מִיִּשְׂרָאֵל, וְאָמַר לוֹן, תְּקַבְּלְנִי עֲלָךְ, בְּכַךְ וְכַךְ פִּקּוּדִין דִּבְאוֹרַיְיתָא, וְאָמְרוּ הֵין. אַהְדָּר לֵיהּ עַל רֵישֵׁיהּ, וּמִתְגַּלְגְּלָא עֲלֵיהּ, וַהֲוָה אַתְרֵי בֵּיהּ, וְאָמַר לֵיהּ, תְּקַבְּלְנִי עֲלָךְ בְּכַךְ עוֹנָשִׁין דִּבְאוֹרַיְיתָא, וַהֲוָה אָמַר הֵין. לְבָתַר אַהְדָּר הַהוּא קָלָא, וְנָשִׁיק לֵיהּ בְּפוּמֵיהּ, הה״ד יִשָּׁקֵנִי מִנְּשִׁיקוֹת פִּיהוּ.

369. That sound HAD THREE COLUMNS AND adjured each one of Yisrael, and said to him, 'Accept me upon you with this many commandments of the Torah,' WHICH IS THE SECRET OF THE RIGHT COLUMN. They said, 'Yes,' and it turned upside down, rolled over him, and adjured him saying, 'Accept me upon you with this many punishments of the Torah,' WHICH IS THE SECRET OF THE LEFT COLUMN. And he would say yes. Afterwards, that

sound returned and kissed him on his mouth. This is what is meant by: "Let him kiss me with the kisses of his mouth" (Shir Hashirim 1:2), FOR THIS IS THE SECRET OF THE CENTRAL COLUMN AND THE ASPECT OF THE FIRST THREE SFIROT.

370. וּכְדֵין כָּל מָה דַּהֲווֹ חֲמָאן יִשְׂרָאֵל בְּהַהוּא זִמְנָא, הֲווֹ חֲמָאן גּוֹ חַד נְהוֹרָא, דְּקַבִּיל כָּל אִינּוּן נְהוֹרִין אַחֲרָנִין, וַהֲווֹ תָּאֲבִין לְמֶחֱמֵי. אָמַר לוֹן קוּדְשָׁא בְּרִיךְ הוּא, הַהוּא נְהוֹרָא דְּחָמֵיתוּ בְּטוּרָא דְסִינַי, דְּקַבִּיל כָּל אִינּוּן גְּווֹנֵי נְהוֹרִין, וְתִיאוּבְתָּא דִּלְכוֹן עָלֵיהּ, תְּקַבְּלוּן לָהּ וְתִסְבוּן לָהּ לְגַבַּיְיכוּ, וְאִינּוּן גְּווֹנִין דְּאִיהִי מְקַבְּלָא, אִלֵּין אִינּוּן זָהָב וָכֶסֶף וּנְחֹשֶׁת וְגוֹ'.

370. Yisrael saw everything at that time within one light, NAMELY MALCHUT, which received within itself all the other lights, WHICH ARE CHESED, GVURAH AND TIFERET. They longed to see it. The Holy One, blessed be He, said to them, The light that you saw at Mount Sinai that received all these colored lights, to which you aspired, WHICH IS MALCHUT, you shall receive it and take it to you. The colors that the light receives are gold, WHICH IS GVURAH, silver, WHICH IS CHESED, brass, WHICH IS TIFERET, ETC. WHICH IS THE SECRET OF THE THREE COLUMNS.

371. דָּבָר אַחֵר יִשָּׁקֵנִי מִנְּשִׁיקוֹת פִּיהוּ, מַאי קָא חָמָא שְׁלֹמֹה מַלְכָּא, דְּאִיהוּ אָעִיל מִלֵּי דִרְחִימוּ בֵּין עָלְמָא עִלָּאָה לְעָלְמָא תַּתָּאָה, וְשֵׁירוּתָא דְּתוּשְׁבַּחְתָּא דִּרְחִימוּ דְּאָעִיל בֵּינַיְיהוּ, יִשָּׁקֵנִי אִיהוּ. אֶלָּא הָא אוּקְמוּהָ וְהָכִי אִיהוּ, דְּלֵית רְחִימוּ דִּדְבֵיקוּת דְּרוּחָא בְּרוּחָא, בַּר נְשִׁיקָה. וּנְשִׁיקָה בְּפוּמָא, דְּאִיהִי מַבּוּעָא דְרוּחָא, וּמַפְּקָנוּ דִּילֵיהּ. וְכַד נַשְׁקִין דָּא לְדָא, מִתְדַּבְּקָן רוּחִין אִלֵּין בְּאִלֵּין, וַהֲווֹ חַד, וּכְדֵין אִיהוּ רְחִימוּ חַד.

371. Another explanation OF THE PASSAGE: "Let him kiss me with the kisses of his mouth": What did King Solomon see that he brought words of love between the Upper World, WHICH IS ZEIR ANPIN, and the lower world, WHICH IS MALCHUT? The beginning of the praise of love that he brought among them is "Let him kiss me." HE ANSWERS: We have learned that there is not love of the cleaving of spirit with spirit except through

kissing, and kissing is with the mouth, which is the spring of the spirit (or: 'breath') and its outlet. When they kiss each other, the spirits cleave one unto the other and become one, and then it is one love.

372. בְּסִפְרָא דְּרַב הַמְנוּנָא סָבָא קַדְמָאָה, הֲוָה אָמַר עַל הַאי קְרָא, נְשִׁיקָה דִּרְחִימוּ אִתְפְּשַׁט לְד' רוּחִין, וְד' רוּחִין מִתְדַּבְּקָן כַּחֲדָא, וְאִינּוּן גּוֹ רָזָא דִּמְהֵימְנוּתָא וְסַלְּקִין בְּד' אַתְוָון, וְאִינּוּן אַתְוָון דִּשְׁמָא קַדִּישָׁא תַּלְיָן בְּהוּ, וְעִלָּאִין וְתַתָּאִין תַּלְיָין בְּהוּ. וְתוּשְׁבַּחְתָּא דְּשִׁיר הַשִּׁירִים תַּלְיָי בְּהוּ. וּמַאן אִיהוּ. אהב"ה. וְאִינּוּן רְתִיכָא עִלָּאָה. וְאִינּוּן חַבְרוּתָא וּדְבֵקוּתָא וּשְׁלִימוּ דְּכֹלָּא.

**372.** In the book of Rav Hamnuna Saba (the elder) the first, it is said about this passage that a kiss of love spreads in four directions, the four directions join together, and they are in the secret of Faith, WHICH IS MALCHUT. THE FOUR DIRECTIONS come through four letters, from which are the letters which form the Holy Name. The upper and lower originate from them, and the praise of Shir Hashirim come from them. Who are they? They are THE FOUR LETTERS OF Ahavah (Aleph-Hei-Bet-Hei, =love), they are a supernal Chariot, CHESED AND GVURAH, TIFERET AND MALCHUT, and they are the connection and cleaving and perfection of everything.

373. אִלֵּין אַתְוָון. ד' רוּחִין אִינּוּן. וְאִינּוּן רוּחִין דִּרְחִימוּ וְחֶדְוָה דְּכָל שַׁיְיפֵי גוּפָא בְּלָא עֲצִיבוּ כְּלָל. ד' רוּחִין אִינּוּן בִּנְשִׁיקָה, כָּל חַד וְחַד כָּלִיל בְּחַבְרֵיהּ. וְכַד הַאי רוּחָא כָּלִיל בְּאַחֲרָא, וְהַהוּא אַחֲרָא כָּלִיל בְּהַאי. אִתְעָבֵידוּ תְּרֵין רוּחִין כַּחֲדָא. וּכְדֵין מִתְחַבְּרָן בְּדִבּוּקוּ חַד, אִינּוּן אַרְבַּע בִּשְׁלִימוּ, וְנַבְעִין דָּא בְּדָא, וְאִתְכְּלִילוּ דָּא בְּדָא.

**373.** These FOUR letters, *ALEPH, HEI, BET, AND HEI,* are four spirits. They are the FOUR spirits of love and joy of all the limbs of the body without any sadness at all. For when the four spirits are in a kiss, each one is combined with the other, MEANING THE SPIRIT OF ZEIR ANPIN IS COMBINED WITH MALCHUT AND THE SPIRIT OF MALCHUT IS COMBINED WITH ZEIR ANPIN. When this spirit is included in the other spirit and the other spirit is included in this spirit, they become IN EACH ONE two spirits united, MEANING THE

ESSENTIAL SPIRIT AND THE OTHER WHICH IS INCLUDED IN IT. Then they join in one cleaving and they are four in all, TWO OF ZEIR ANPIN AND TWO OF MALCHUT. They flow between each other and are included together.

374. וְכַד מִתְפַּשְּׁטָן, אִתְעֲבֵיד מֵאִינּוּן אַרְבַּע רוּחִין חַד אִיבָּא, וְאִיהוּ רוּחָא חֲדָא דְּכָלִיל מִד' רוּחִין. וְדָא סָלִיק וּבָקַע רְקִיעִין, עַד דְּסָלִיק וְיָתִיב לְגַבֵּי חַד הֵיכָלָא. דְּאִתְקְרֵי הֵיכָלָא דְּאַהֲבָה, וְאִיהוּ הֵיכָלָא דְּכָל רְחִימוּ תַּלְיָא בֵּיהּ. וְהַהִיא רוּחָא הָכִי אִקְרֵי אַהֲבָה, וְכַד הַאי רוּחָא סָלִיק אִתְּעַר לְהַהוּא הֵיכָלָא, לְאִתְחַבְּרָא לְעֵילָּא.

374. When THEIR LIGHT spreads TO THIS WORLD, these four spirits produced one fruit, which is a spirit composed of four spirits. This one ascends AGAIN and splits firmaments until it ascends and sits near a certain sanctuary called 'the Sanctuary of Love', the sanctuary from whence every love comes. That spirit is also called 'love' and when it rises, it stimulates that sanctuary to become joined above.

375. ד' אַתְוָון אִינּוּן, לְגַבֵּי ד' רוּחִין. וְאִינּוּן אַהֲבָה. וְאִיבָּא דִּלְהוֹן אַהֲבָה. כַּד מִתְחַבְּרָן דָּא בְּדָא, מִיַּד אִתְּעַר דָּא בִּסְטַר דָּא וְדָא בִּסְטַר דָּא. א'. מִיַּד נָפִיק ה', וְאִתְחַבַּר בָּא', מִתְדַּבַּק בִּדְבִיקוּ בִּרְחִימוּ. וְאִתְּעָרוּ תְּרֵין אַתְוָון אַחֲרָנִין, ב' ה', וְאִתְכְּלִילוּ רוּחִין בְּרוּחִין בִּדְבִיקוּ דִּרְחִימוּ, וּפָרְחִין אִלֵּין אַתְוָון מִנַּיְיהוּ, בְּהַהוּא רוּחָא דְּסָלִיק, וּמִתְעַטְּרָן בֵּיהּ כִּדְקָא יָאוּת.

375. The four letters correspond to the four spirits MENTIONED ABOVE, and they are THE FOUR LETTERS Ahavah (Aleph-Hei-Bet-Hei, = love), BECAUSE THE SPIRIT OF ZEIR ANPIN IS ALEPH AND THE SPIRIT OF MALCHUT THAT IS INCLUDED IN ZEIR ANPIN IS HEI. THE SPIRIT OF MALCHUT IS HEI AND THE SPIRIT OF ZEIR ANPIN THAT IS INCLUDED IN MALCHUT IS BET, and their fruit is CALLED 'love', AS MENTIONED EARLIER. When they join with each other, ZEIR ANPIN WITH MALCHUT IN THE JOINING OF KISSING, they are aroused, the one to the aspect of the other. THE SPIRIT OF MALCHUT BECOMES STIMULATED AND INCLUDED IN THE SPIRIT OF ZEIR ANPIN AND the other to the aspect of the former.

THE SPIRIT OF ZEIR ANPIN BECOMES INCLUDED IN THE SPIRIT OF MALCHUT AND, THEREFORE, *Aleph* WHICH IS THE SPIRIT OF ZEIR ANPIN, immediately produces *Hei*, WHICH IS THE SPIRIT OF MALCHUT THAT IS COMBINED WITH HIM, and joins with that *Aleph* with cleaving and love. And two other letters become aroused: *Hei*, WHICH IS THE SPIRIT OF MALCHUT, with *Bet*, WHICH IS THE SPIRIT OF ZEIR ANPIN THAT IS INCLUDED IN MALCHUT. Spirits are included in spirits with the cleaving of love, and these letters *ALEPH-HEI-BET-HEI* fly from them, AND THEY COME with that spirit that ascends AS MENTIONED ABOVE, WHICH IS THEIR FRUIT. THEREFORE, IT IS NAMED 'LOVE' AFTER THEM and they become adorned with it properly, AND IT IS INCLUDED IN THOSE FOUR SPIRITS.

376. כֵּיוָן דְּאָזִיל וְסָלִיק הַהוּא אַהֲבָה שְׁלֵימָא, כְּלִילָא בְּכָל אִינוּן אַרְבַּע רוּחִין, פָּגַע בְּחַד מְמָנָא עִלָּאָה רַבְרְבָא, דִּי מְמָנָא עַל אֶלֶף וּתְשַׁע מֵאָה וְתִשְׁעִין רְקִיעִין, וְאִיהוּ מְמָנָא עַל נְגִידוּ דִּתְלֵיסַר נַהֲרֵי אֲפַרְסְמוֹנָא דַּכְיָא, דְּנַגְדָּא מֵרָזָא דְּטַלָּא דִּלְעֵילָא. וְהַהוּא נְגִידוּ אִתְקְרֵי מַיִם רַבִּים. כֵּיוָן דְּפָגַע לְגַבֵּי הַהוּא רַב מַשִׁרְיָין קָאִים לְגַבֵּיהּ, וְלָא יָכִיל לְאַעְכְּבָא לֵיהּ, וְעָבַר בְּהוּ עַד דְּאָעִיל לְגַבֵּי הֵיכָל אַהֲבָ"ה.

376. After that, love rises, MEANING THE SPIRIT THAT IS BORN FROM THE FOUR SPIRITS OF THE KISSES, and is combined with all those four spirits. It meets a supernal minister, the officer that is appointed over 1,990 firmaments. He is appointed over the flows that are drawn from the thirteen rivers of the pure balsam trees that are drawn from the supernal dew. And those flows, WHICH ARE THE SECRET OF THE LIGHTS OF CHASSADIM, are called 'many waters'. When the spirit meets that officer of the camps, he stands against it but cannot detain it, so it, THE RIVERS OF PURE BALSAM, crosses over through them until it enters the sanctuary of love.

377. עַל דָּא אָמַר שְׁלֹמֹה, בְּסִיּוּם שְׁבָחֵיהּ, מַיִם רַבִּים לֹא יוּכְלוּ לְכַבּוֹת אֶת הָאַהֲבָה. מַיִם רַבִּים: אִלֵּין מַיִם עִלָּאִין דְּנַגְדִּין מִגּוֹ טַלָּא עִלָּאָה. וּנְהָרוֹת לֹא יִשְׁטְפוּהָ: אִלֵּין אִינוּן נַהֲרֵי אֲפַרְסְמוֹנָא דַּכְיָא, דְּאִינוּן תְּלֵיסַר. הַהוּא מְמָנָא אִיהוּ מַלְאָכָא דְּשָׁלִיחַ מִן קֳדָם יְיָ', וְדָא אִיהוּ רַב מַשִׁרְיָין דְּקָשִׁיר כִּתְרִין לְמָארֵיהּ, רָזָא אַבְכַתְרִיאֵ"ל, מְעַטֵּר עִטְרִין

לְמָארֵיה, בִּשְׁמָא גְּלִיפָא מְחַקְקָא, יְהֹוָה יָה צְבָאוֹת.

**377.** Referring to this, Solomon said at the end of his praise OF SHIR HASHIRIM, "Many waters cannot quench love" (Shir Hashirim 8:7). "Many waters": These are the supernal waters that are drawn from the supernal dew, MEANING THE MANY CHASSADIM, while "nor can the floods drown it" (Ibid.) are the rivers of pure balsam which are thirteen AND ALL THOSE DO NOT EXTINGUISH THE GREAT LOVE OF THE RIGHT TO THE LEFT, AS MENTIONED EARLIER. That minister is an angel, a messenger from Hashem, and he is the head of the camps that puts crowns to his Master. It is the secret of Ach'tariel, who fashions crowns for his Master with the engraved Name Yud Hei Vav Hei *Yah Tzva'ot*.

**378.** כֵּיוָן דְּאָעִיל לְגַבֵּי הֵיכָל אַהֲבָה, אִתְּעַר רְחִימוּ דִּנְשִׁיקִין עִלָּאִין, דִּכְתִיב וַיִּשַּׁק יַעֲקֹב לְרָחֵל, לְמֶהֱוֵי נְשִׁיקִין דִּרְחִימוּ עִלָּאָה כַּדְקָא יָאוֹת, וְאִינּוּן נְשִׁיקִין שֵׁירוּתָא דְּאִתְּעָרוּ דְּכָל רְחִימוּ, וְאִתְדַּבְּקוּתָא וְקִשּׁוּרָא דִּלְעֵילָּא. וּבְג"כ שֵׁירוּתָא דְּתוּשְׁבַּחְתָּא דְּשִׁירָתָא דָּא אִיהוּ יִשָּׁקֵנִי.

**378.** When the spirit enters the sanctuary of love, the love of the supernal kisses OF ZEIR ANPIN AND MALCHUT OF ATZILUT, is aroused, as it is written: "And Jacob kissed Rachel" (Beresheet 29:11), so that the kisses of the Supernal Love will be done properly. These kisses are the beginning of the arousal of every love, cleaving and bond of above. Therefore, the beginning of the praise of this song is "Let him kiss me."

**379.** מַאן יִשָּׁקֵנִי. הַהוּא דְּסָתִים גּוֹ סְתִימוּ עִלָּאָה. וְאִי תֵּימָא, סְתִימָא דְּכָל סְתִימִין בֵּיה תַּלְיָין נְשִׁיקִין וְנָשִׁיק לְתַתָּא. ת"ח, סְתִימָא דְּכָל סְתִימִין, לֵית מַאן דְּיָדַע לֵיה, וְאִיהוּ גַּלֵּי מִנֵּיה נְהִירוּ חַד דָּקִיק סָתִים, דְּלָא אִתְגְּלֵי בַּר בְּחַד שְׁבִיל דָּקִיק דְּאִתְפָּשַׁט מִגַּוֵּויה, וְאִיהוּ נְהִירוּ דְּנָהִיר לְכֹלָּא. וְדָא אִתְּעָרוּ דְּכָל רָזִין עִלָּאִין. וְאִיהוּ סָתִים. לִזְמְנִין סָתִים, לִזְמְנִין אִתְגַּלְיָא. וְאַף עַל גַּב דְּלָא אִתְגַּלְיָא כְּלָל. וְאִתְּעָרוּ דְּסָלִיקוּ דִּנְשִׁיקִין בֵּיה תַּלְיָין. וּמִגּוֹ דְּאִיהוּ סָתִים, שֵׁירוּתָא דְּתוּשְׁבַּחְתָּא בְּאֹרַח סָתִים אִיהוּ.

**379.** HE QUESTIONS: To whom was it said "Let him kiss me"? HE ANSWERS: It is that which is concealed in a most high concealment, WHICH IS SUPERNAL ABA AND IMA THAT ARE BOTH CALLED 'ABA'. If you ask: Yet the most concealed of all, WHICH IS ARICH ANPIN SUPERNAL, whence are all the kisses, does He kiss downwards TOWARDS MALCHUT? Come and see the most concealed of all, WHICH IS ARICH ANPIN. There is no one who knows it, and it revealed of itself one delicate and concealed light, WHICH IS ABA, that was not revealed except for one delicate path that spread from it TO ILLUMINATE IMA. This is the light that illuminates everything. It is the stimulator of all the supernal secrets and is concealed. Sometimes it is concealed and sometimes revealed, even though it is not revealed at all, and the awakening of the rising of kisses depends on it. It is concealed; THEREFORE, the praise starts in a concealed way THAT HE SAYS, "LET HIM KISS ME WITH THE KISSES OF HIS MOUTH," WHICH IS IN THE THIRD PERSON.

380. וְאִי בֵּיהּ תַּלְיָין מַה בָּעֵי יַעֲקֹב הָכָא, דְּהָא בֵּיהּ תַּלְיָין נְשִׁיקִין. אֶלָּא וַדַּאי הָכִי הוּא. יִשָּׁקֵנִי, הַהוּא דְּסָתִים לְעֵילָּא. וּבַמָּה. בְּהַהוּא רְתִיכָא עִלָּאָה, דְּכָל גַּוְונִין תַּלְיָין וּמִתְחַבְּרָן בֵּיהּ. וְהַאי אִיהוּ יַעֲקֹב. כְּמָה דְּאָמְרֵינָן, דְּבֵיקוּתָא לְאִתְדַּבְּקָא בְּמַלְכָּא בִּבְרָא דִּילֵיהּ הוּא. וְע"ד כְּתִיב מִנְּשִׁיקוֹת פִּיהוּ.

**380.** HE QUESTIONS: The KISSES are dependent upon ABA, IF SO what is Jacob doing here, WHO IS ZEIR ANPIN, if the kisses are dependent upon ABA, AND WHY DOES IT SAY "AND JACOB KISSES RACHEL"? HE ANSWERS: But certainly it is so, THAT JACOB IS THE ONE WHO KISSES, because "Let him kiss me" ALLUDES TO that which is concealed above, WHICH IS ABA. But in what way? Through that supernal Chariot from which all the colors originate and to which they are all attached. This is Jacob, MEANING ZEIR ANPIN, WHICH IS THE CENTRAL COLUMN THAT THE COLORS OF RIGHT AND LIGHT ARE COMBINED IN HIM, AND HIS CHESED, GVURAH AND TIFERET ARE A SUPERNAL CHARIOT. As we have said, this will be done with the cleaving with which the King, WHO IS ABA, cleaves to his son, THAT IS ZEIR ANPIN. HE IS CALLED 'HIS SON', IN ACCORDANCE WITH THE SECRET OF THE PASSAGE: "WHAT IS HIS NAME, AND WHAT IS HIS SON'S NAME, IF YOU CAN TELL" (MISHLEI 30:4). THUS THE ONE WHO KISSES IS JACOB BUT HE DRAWS THEM FROM ABA, TO

WHOM HE IS ATTACHED. Therefore, it is written: "From the kisses of his mouth" (Shir Hashirim 1:2), WHICH IS IN THE THIRD CONCEALED PERSON, BECAUSE IT ALLUDES TO ABA WHO IS CONCEALED.

381. כִּי טוֹבִים דּוֹדֶיךָ, אַהֲדָר לְגַבֵּי שִׁמְשָׁא, דְּאַנְהִיר לָהּ לְסִיהֲרָא, מִגּוֹ נְהִירוּ דְּאִינוּן בּוּצִינִין עִלָּאִין, וְאִיהוּ נָטִיל נְהוֹרָא דְּכֻלְּהוּ, וְאַנְהִיר לְסִיהֲרָא. וְאִינוּן בּוּצִינִין דְּמִזְדַּוְּוגִין בֵּיהּ, מֵאָן אֲתָר נַהֲרִין. הָדָר וְאָמַר מִיַּיִן, מֵהַהוּא יַיִן דְּמִנְטְרָא, מֵהַהוּא יַיִן דְּאִיהוּ חֶדְוָה דְּכָל חֶדְוָון. וּמַאן אִיהוּ הַהוּא יַיִן, דְּיָהִיב חַיִּין וְחֶדְוָה לְכֹלָּא. דָּא אֱלֹהִים חַיִּים, יַיִן, דְּיָהִיב חַיִּין וְחֶדְוָה לְכֹלָּא.

**381.** "For your loves are better than wine" (Ibid.). THE PASSAGE returns to the sun ZEIR ANPIN HIMSELF, AND THEREFORE SPEAKS IN SECOND PERSON, WHICH IS REVEALED, for it illuminates the moon, WHICH IS MALCHUT, from the light of the upper luminaries. It takes the light from all of them and illuminates upon the moon. These lights that are attached in it, from which place do they illuminate? THE PASSAGE repeats and says, "Than (also: 'from') wine", MEANING from that preserved wine, from that wine which is the delight of all the delights. What is that wine that gives life and delight to everyone? This is living Elohim, WHICH IS BINAH, which is the wine that gives life and happiness to all, AND IT IS THE ILLUMINATION OF CHOCHMAH THAT IS DRAWN FROM THE LEFT COLUMN OF BINAH THAT IS COMBINED WITH THE RIGHT.

382. תּוּ מִיַּיִן, מֵהַהוּא שְׁמָא דְּאִקְרֵי יְדֹוָ"ד, דָּא אִיהוּ יַיִן דְּחֶדְוָה דִּרְחִימוּ דְּרַחֲמֵי, וּמִן דָּא, כֻּלְּהוּ נְהִירִין וְחַדָּאן. אָתוּ חַבְרַיָּיא וְנָשִׁיקוּ לֵיהּ בְּרֵישֵׁיהּ.

**382.** Another EXPLANATION of "from wine": It is from that name that is called Yud Hei Vav Hei, MEANING Yud Hei Vav Hei FULLY SPELT WITH YUDS, WHICH NUMERICALLY EQUALS 72, WHICH IS THE SECRET OF SEVENTY JUDGES OF THE SANHEDRIN AND TWO WITNESSES, SEVENTY BEING THE NUMERICAL VALUE OF YAYIN (ENG. 'WINE'). For this is the wine of joy, love, and Mercy, from which all illuminate and rejoice. The friends came and kissed RABBI YOSI on his head.

383. בָּכָה רַבִּי שִׁמְעוֹן, וְאָמַר, יָדַעְנָא וַדַּאי דְּרוּחָא קַדִּישָׁא עִלָּאָה קָא מְכַשְׁכְּשָׁא בְּכוּ, זַכָּאָה דָּרָא דָּא, דְּהָא לָא יְהֵא כְּדָרָא דָּא, עַד זִמְנָא דְּיֵיתֵי מַלְכָּא מְשִׁיחָא. דְּהָא אוֹרַיְיתָא אִתְהַדְרַת לְעַתִּיקוּתָהָא. זַכָּאִין אִינוּן צַדִּיקַיָּא בְּעָלְמָא דֵּין וּבְעָלְמָא דְּאָתֵי.

383. Rabbi Shimon wept and said: I know for sure that the Holy Spirit pulsates and throbs in you. Blessed is this generation, for there will not be another generation like it until the time when King Messiah comes, when the Torah returns to its original glory. Blessed are the righteous in this world and in the World to Come.

## 34. "And this is the offering"

### A Synopsis
Rabbi Elazar tells us that the passage, "And this is the offering, which you shall take of them," is difficult to understand both in the literal meaning and the hidden one. And indeed the explanatory text seems to confuse it further. First, correspondences are drawn between angels, Michael, Gabriel, Uriel and Raphael (Boel when he is in the Seat of Judgment), protecting angels, Attending Serafim, and the gold, silver, brass, blue, purple, scarlet and all of the other offerings. Each of these also has aspects of the Sfirot. We read of "oil of the light" and "oil for the light," which are the luminaries of the upper world, which is male and dominates by day, and the lower world which is female and dominates by night. We read of the seven types of gold, and of silver and brass, and again of the other offerings in the context of the Sfirot. And we learn that it is gold which predominates.

### The Relevance of this Passage
These verses delve deeply into the mysteries of the Torah, for the literal text is devoid of practical meaning and filled with contradiction. Accordingly, we acquire the consciousness and powers of observation to penetrate beyond the surface level of our existence. On a cosmic scale, all is now revealed: the hidden meaning of life, the cause behind the effect, the seed that precedes the tree, the beauty beneath the surface, and the secrets of the Torah. No longer can life seem as senseless and contradictory as the illusory stories of the Torah.

384. וְזֹאת הַתְּרוּמָה אֲשֶׁר תִּקְחוּ מֵאִתָּם. רַבִּי אֶלְעָזָר אָמַר, הַאי קְרָא אוּקְמוּהָ, וְרָזִין דִּילֵיהּ הָא אִתְּמַר. אֲבָל רָזָא דִּקְרָא הָכִי אוֹלִיפְנָא, וְקַשְׁיָין קְרָאֵי, דְּאִי אִינּוּן בְּרָזָא דִּלְתַתָּא קַשְׁיָין אֲהַדְדֵי. וְאִי בְּרָזָא דִּלְעֵילָּא לָא אִינּוּן בְּנְהִירוּ. דַּבֵּר אֶל בְּנֵי יִשְׂרָאֵל וְיִקְחוּ לִי תְּרוּמָה שַׁפִּיר. תִּקְחוּ אֶת תְּרוּמָתִי קַשְׁיָא. וְזֹאת הַתְּרוּמָה אֲשֶׁר תִּקְחוּ מֵאִתָּם קַשְׁיָא וַדַּאי כֹּלָּא, עֵילָּא וְתַתָּא כַּחֲדָא.

384. "And this is the offering, which you shall take of them" (Shemot 25:3). Rabbi Elazar said: We have established this passage and we have already learned its secrets, THAT OFFERING IS THE SECRET OF MALCHUT, AS MENTIONED. But the secret OF: "AND THIS IS THE OFFERING" I have learned this way and the passages are difficult. If they are interpreted

according to the secret of below, MEANING ACCORDING TO THE LITERAL MEANING, they are conflicting, but if according to the secret of above, THAT OFFERING MEANS THE SHECHINAH, they are not clear. BECAUSE IT IS WRITTEN, "Speak to the children of Yisrael that they bring Me an offering" (Shemot 25:2) and this is understood, FOR THE PURPOSE IS THAT IT IS NOT BY THEM, BUT THEY HAVE TO BRING IT. AFTERWARDS IT IS SAID, "OF EVERY MAN WHOSE HEART PROMPTS HIM TO GIVE you shall take My offering" is difficult, FOR HERE IT SEEMS THAT THE OFFERING IS ALREADY IN THEIR POSSESSION AND OTHERS HAVE TO TAKE IT FROM THE CHILDREN OF YISRAEL. AND SO ALSO THE PASSAGE: "And this is the offering which you shall take of them" is difficult, FOR IT ALSO MEANS THAT THE OFFERING IS ALREADY IN THEIR POSSESSION. Everything is DIFFICULT for certain, both above and below, NAMELY, BOTH ACCORDING TO THE LITERAL MEANING AND THE HIDDEN. EVEN ACCORDING TO THE LITERAL MEANING IT IS DIFFICULT, FOR FIRST IT SAYS THAT THE CHILDREN OF YISRAEL SHOULD BRING, AND AFTERWARDS IT SAYS THAT YOU SHALL TAKE OF THEM.

385. אֶלָּא הָכִי אִיהוּ, וְיִקְחוּ לִי תְּרוּמָה. מַאן. בְּנֵי יִשְׂרָאֵל. מֵאֵת כָּל אִישׁ: אִלֵּין מַלְאָכִין עִלָּאִין לְעֵילָא, בְּגִין דְּעָלַיְיהוּ אִיהִי תְּרוּמָה, אֲרָמוּתָא דְּאִינּוּן אָרִימוּ לָהּ תָּדִיר לְגַבֵּי מַלְכָּא עִלָּאָה דְּהָא אִינּוּן סַלְקִין לָהּ תָּדִיר, לְגַבֵּי מַלְכָּא עִלָּאָה. וְכַד יִשְׂרָאֵל זַכָּאִין, אִינּוּן נַטְלִין לָהּ מִנַּיְיהוּ, וְנַחְתִּין לָהּ לְתַתָּא, הַהַ״ד, מֵאֵת כָּל אִישׁ אֲשֶׁר יִדְּבֶנּוּ לִבּוֹ. וּמַאן אִינּוּן. אִינּוּן אַרְבַּע דְּאָרִימוּ לָהּ לְעֵילָא. דְּהַהוּא לֵב אִתְרְעֵי בְּהוּ. וְהַהִיא תְּרוּמָה. אִיהִי זַקְפָּא עָלַיְיהוּ.

385. HE ANSWERS: This is the explanation of, "That they bring Me an offering." Who? The children of Yisrael. "Of every man": These are the supernal angels above, for MALCHUT is an offering (Heb. trumah) to them, MEANING A RAISING (HEB. HARAMAH), for they are constantly raising it before the supernal King, ZEIR ANPIN. They raise it to be united with the supernal King, WHICH IS THE SECRET OF THE FOUR LIVING CREATURES THAT CARRY THE THRONE, WHICH IS THE SECRET OF THE FOUR ANGELS, MICHAEL, GABRIEL, URIEL AND RAPHAEL. When Yisrael are righteous, they take THE SHECHINAH from above THE ANGELS, and bring Her down. This is the meaning of: "Of every man whose heart prompts him

to give." Who are they? They are these four, NAMELY MICHAEL, GABRIEL, URIEL, AND RAPHAEL, who raised Her above. "WHOSE HEART PROMPTS HIM TO GIVE" MEANS that that heart, WHICH IS MALCHUT, favors them and that offering, WHICH IS THE SHECHINAH, is carried by them.

386. וְאע"ג דְּאִיהִי קַיָּימָא עָלַיְיהוּ, וּמַנְחָא עַל גַּבַּיְיהוּ. תִּקְחוּ: תִּסְבּוּן לָהּ מִנַּיְיהוּ לְנַחְתָּהָא לְתַתָּא. וּבַמָה. בְּזִמְנָא דָא, בְּאִינּוּן עוֹבָדִין דְּכַשְׁרָאן, בִּצְלוֹתִין וּבְבָעוּתִין, לְמֶעְבַּד פְּקוּדֵי אוֹרַיְיתָא. בְּהַהוּא זִמְנָא, בְּאִינּוּן גַּוְונִין דְּאִתְחַזְיָין לְתַתָּא כְּגַוְונָא דִלְעֵילָּא, בְּאִינּוּן פּוּלְחָנִין אַחֲרָנִין. וְאִינּוּן גַּוְונִין אַמְשִׁכָאן לְתַתָּא הַהוּא אֲרֹמוּתָא, וְנַצְחָן גַּוְונִין דִּלְתַתָּא, לְאִינּוּן גַּוְונִין דִּלְעֵילָּא, וּמַשְׁכִין לוֹן גַּוְונִין אִלֵּין, לְגַוְונִין עִלָּאִין, וְעָיְילִין אִלֵּין בְּאִלֵּין, וְאִתְעָבִידוּ אִלֵּין גּוּפָא לְאִלֵּין, וְעַל דָּא תִּקְחוּ מֵאִתָּם כְּתִיב.

386. Even though THE SHECHINAH stands over them and dwells upon them, ON THE ANGELS, "you shall take" Her from them to lower Her down. And how? In this time, WE LOWER HER with good deeds, with prayers and beseeching, and by fulfilling the commandments of the Torah. At that time, WHEN THE TABERNACLE WAS BEING BUILT, it was through the colors, GOLD, SILVER...that appear below similar to above, MEANING LIKE THE SUPERNAL SFIROT, and other services. These colors draw below that offering, WHICH IS THE SHECHINAH, and the colors of below triumph over the colors of above, WHICH ARE THE SFIROT. The colors OF BELOW drew the colors OF ABOVE and they entered, these into those, and those OF BELOW became the body for those OF ABOVE. Referring to this, it is written: "You shall take of them."

387. זָהָב דְּאִתְכְּלִיל בְּגַבְרִיאֵל, זָהָב לְעֵילָּא, גַּבְרִי"אֵל נָטִיל לֵיהּ לְתַתָּא. וְשִׁבְעָה זִינֵי זָהָב אִתְפָּרְשָׁאן לְתַתָּא מִן דָּא. וְכֶסֶף לְעֵילָּא, וְאִתְכְּלִיל בְּמִיכָאֵל לְתַתָּא, וְשַׁרְיָא דָּא עַל דָּא. וּנְחֹשֶׁת לְעֵילָּא, וְנָפְקָא מִן זָהָב, בְּגִין דְּזָהָב וְאֶשָּׁא בְּרָזָא חֲדָא קַיְימִין וְאַזְלִין, אֶשָּׁא אַפִּיק נְחֹשֶׁת. וּמֵחֵילָא וְתֻקְפָּא דָּא, אִתְבַּדְרָן נְחָשִׁים שְׂרָפִים דְּנָפְקֵי מֵאֶשָּׁא. וע"ד, נְחֹשֶׁת אִיהוּ סוּמָקָא כְּאֶשָּׁא וְאִתְכְּלִיל בְּאוּרִי"אֵל וְאִתְעֲבִיד דָּא

גּוּפָא לְגַבֵּי דָא.

**387.** Gold that is comprised in Gabriel is gold above, MEANING THE SFIRAH GVURAH, and Gabriel takes it below. This gold is divided below into seven types of gold, WHICH ARE GREENISH GOLD, THE GOLD OF OPHIR, SHEBA GOLD, PRECIOUS GOLD, PURE GOLD, BERYL GOLD. Silver is above, MEANING THE SFIRAH OF CHESED, and is comprised in Michael below and they dwell upon each other. Brass is above, NAMELY THE SFIRAH TIFERET, and it emerges from gold, FOR TIFERET EMERGES FROM GVURAH. Gold and fire pertains to the same mystery, AS BOTH ARE GVURAH, and the fire produced brass, and because of this power and strength, fiery serpents were spread that emerged from fire. Therefore, brass is red like fire, is comprised in Uriel and becomes a body for him.

**388.** וּתְכֵלֶת שַׁרְיָא בְּדָא וּבְדָא, בַּנְּחֹשֶׁת וּבַזָּהָב, וּבְגִין דְּאִתְתַּקַּף בִּתְרֵין סִטְרִין. תְּכֵלֶת אִיהוּ תַּקִּיפָא, וְלֵית מַאן דְּשַׁלְטָא עֲלֵיהּ לְחַיִין, דְּאִיהוּ כָּרְסְיָיא דְּדִינָא לְשַׁרְיָא בֵּיהּ דִּינָא תַּקִּיפָא, וְדָא אִיהוּ בּ״וֹ אֵ״ל, ב״וֹ אֵ״ל: דִּכְתִיב, וְאֵל זוֹעֵם בְּכָל יוֹם. וְכַד אִתְהַדְרָן בְּנֵי נָשָׁא בִּתְיוּבְתָּא שְׁלֵימָתָא, אִתְהַדָּר שְׁמֵיהּ רְפָא״ל, דְּהָא אַסְוָותָא אִזְדַּמָּן לְהוּ מֵהַהוּא דִּינָא קַשְׁיָא.

**388.** Blue dwells in both brass and gold, WHICH INCLUDES THE JUDGMENTS IN TIFERET WHICH IS BRASS AND IN GVURAH WHICH IS GOLD. It prevails on two sides; THEREFORE, blue is severe IN JUDGMENTS, and none can rule to transform it into life. IF HE SEES THE COLOR BLUE IN HIS DREAM, it is the seat of Judgment where severe Judgment dwells. It is THE ANGEL Boel, as it is written: "And an El who has indignation every day" (Tehilim 7:12). When people repent in complete repentance, his name returns to Raphael, because remedy is prepared for them from that severe Judgment.

**389.** וְאַרְגָּמָן: דָּא זָהָב וָכֶסֶף, דְּאִתְהַדְרָן לְאִכְלָלָא כַּחֲדָא, מִיכָאֵל וְגַבְרִיאֵל אִתְכְּלִילוּ דָּא עִם דָּא, מִשְׁלָבָאן דָּא בְּדָא. וְעַל דָּא כְּתִיב, עוֹשֶׂה שָׁלוֹם בִּמְרוֹמָיו. וּבְגִין דְּאִינוּן מִשְׁלָבָאן דָּא בְּדָא, אִתְעֲבִידוּ גּוּפָא חַד.

**389.** Purple is gold and silver, WHICH ARE GVURAH AND CHESED, that returned to be combined together, WHICH ARE Michael and Gabriel that are combined and fitted together. It is written: "He makes peace in His high places" (Iyov 25:2). Because they are fitted together, they become one body, WHICH IS PURPLE. AND IT CORRESPONDS TO THE SFIRAH NETZACH, BECAUSE IN NETZACH, GVURAH AND CHESED RULE TOGETHER.

390. וְתוֹלַעַת שָׁנִי לְעֵילָא, וְאִתְכְּלִיל בְּאוּרִיאֵ״ל כְּמִלְקַדְמִין, לְמֶהֱוֵי אֲחִידוּ, גּוֹ תְּכֵלֶת, וּבְגוֹ אַרְגָּמָן. וְשֵׁשׁ אִיהוּ לְעֵילָא, וְאִתְכְּלִיל כְּמִלְקַדְמִין בְּרָזָא דִרְפָאֵל, לְאִתְאַחֲדָא בַּכֶּסֶף וּבַזָּהָב.

**390.** Scarlet is above IN THE SFIRAH HOD and comprised BELOW in Uriel, as we said earlier, THAT THE ONE BECOMES A BODY FOR THE OTHER so as to be attached to blue and purple, WHICH ARE MALCHUT AND NETZACH. Linen is above IN THE SFIRAH OF YESOD and is comprised, AS WE SAID, in the secret of Raphael. AND THE ONE BECOMES A BODY FOR THE OTHER, so as to be attached to silver and gold, WHICH ARE CHESED AND GVURAH.

391. עַד הָכָא, רָזָא דְז׳ עַמוּדִין לְעֵילָא, גּוֹ ז׳ עַמוּדִים דִּלְתַתָּא. קְלִיפָה גּוֹ קְלִיפָה, לִנְטוּרָא. וְעִזִּים: הָא אוּקִימְנָא דְּהָא אִלֵּין ז׳, מוֹחָא לְמוֹחָא, וְדָא אִיהוּ קְלִיפָה לְמוֹחָא.

**391.** Until here is the secret of the seven pillars of above, WHICH ARE CHESED, GVURAH, TIFERET, NETZACH, HOD AND YESOD, AS MENTIONED EARLIER, within seven pillars of below, WHICH ARE GOLD AND SILVER AND BRASS, ETC. shell within shell, MEANING THAT THEY ARE COVERED BY EACH OTHER AND THOSE OF BELOW BECOME A COVERING OVER THESE OF ABOVE as a protection. We have established that these seven PILLARS are inner side of the inner, MEANING THAT THEY ARE ALL INTERNAL, and goats' hair is a cover to the inner, MEANING THAT IT IS EXTERNAL.

392. וְעוֹרוֹת אֵלִים מְאָדָּמִים, אִלֵּין אִינּוּן מָארֵי תְּרִיסִין, עַיְינִין מְלַהֲטִין בְּטִיסִין דְּנוּרָא, כד״א, וְעֵינָיו כְּלַפִּידֵי אֵשׁ. וְאִקְרוּן רְקִיעִין לְבַר בְּגוֹ

קְלִיפָה. וְעוֹרוֹת תְּחָשִׁים, אִלֵּין אִינּוּן לְגוֹ בְּסִטְרָא קַדִּישָׁא, וְאִתְאַחֲדָן בִּקְדוּשָׁה, וְלָא אִתְאַחֲדָן. כְּמָה דְּאֲמְרָן.

**392.** "And rams' skins dyed red" (Shemot 25:5): These are the protecting angels, WHO PROTECT AGAINST THE OTHER SIDE and have eyes that blaze flames of fire, as it is written: "And his eyes like torches of fire" (Daniel 10:6). They are called 'firmaments' and are outside, within the covering (Heb. *Klipah*). "And badgers' skins" (Shemot 25:5): These are inside in the holy side and they are joined in Holiness, yet are not attached as we said.

**393.** וַעֲצֵי שִׁטִּים, הָא אוֹקִימְנָא דְּאִינּוּן שְׂרָפִים עוֹמְדִים, כד"א שְׂרָפִים עוֹמְדִים מִמַּעַל לוֹ. מַאי מִמַּעַל לוֹ. מִמַּעַל לְהַהִיא קְלִיפָה. וְאִי תֵּימָא, הַאי קְרָא בְּקוּדְשָׁא בְּרִיךְ הוּא אִתְּמַר, וְהָא אִתְּמַר וָאֶרְאֶה אֶת יְיָ', אֶת דַּיְיקָא, כְּגַוְונָא דָּא דִּכְתִיב בְּהַאי קְרָא, דִּכְתִיב, וְשׁוּלָיו מְלֵאִים אֶת הַהֵיכָל, אֶת דַּיְיקָא לְאַסְגָאָה הַהִיא קְלִיפָה. כֵּיוָן דְּאָמַר רָזָא דְּהַהִיא קְלִיפָה, כְּתִיב שְׂרָפִים עוֹמְדִים מִמַּעַל לוֹ, מִמַּעַל לְהַהִיא קְלִיפָה.

**393.** "And acacia wood" (Ibid.): We have established that they are attending Serafim, as it is written: "Serafim stood above him" (Yeshayah 6:2), FOR THEY ARE IN THE WORLD BRIYAH. HE QUESTIONS: What is the meaning of: "above him"? HE ANSWERS: It is above that covering, MEANING THAT NO KLIPAH DOMINATES THEM BY BEING ABOVE THEM, AND THE JUDGMENTS DO NOT BLEMISH ABOVE THE PLACE OF THEIR EXISTENCE, SO THEY ARE IN THE SECRET OF ACACIA WOOD. If you ask whether this passage refers to the Holy One, blessed be He, and THAT "ABOVE HIM" MEANS ABOVE THE HOLY ONE, BLESSED BE HE, IT IS NOT SO. For we have learned: "I saw Hashem" (Ibid. 1). The particle '*Et* (Eng. 'the')' is exact, WHICH MEANS THAT HE SAW MALCHUT THAT IS CALLED 'ET'. Similar to this, it is written in this passage: "And His train filled the temple" (Ibid.). 'Et (the)' is exact, in that it came to include that Klipah, MEANING THAT HIS TRAIN FILLS AND ANNULS THAT KLIPAH THAT CORRESPONDS TO MALCHUT THAT IS CALLED 'ET'. Since it said AND MENTIONED the secret of that Klipah, it wrote: "Serafim stood above him" MEANING above that Klipah.

**394.** שֶׁמֶן לַמָּאוֹר, דָּא מְשַׁח רְבוּת עִלָּאָה, דְּאַתְיָא מִלְעֵילָא. תְּרֵין שֶׁמֶן

אִינּוּן. וְאִינּוּן תְּרֵי, חַד לְעֵילָּא, דְּאִקְרֵי שֶׁמֶן הַמָּאוֹר. וְחַד לְתַתָּא דְּאִקְרֵי שֶׁמֶן לַמָּאוֹר. שֶׁמֶן הַמָּאוֹר אִיהוּ עִלָּאָה, דְּקַיְּימָא בְּוַדַּאי, וְלָא פָּסִיק לְעָלְמִין, וְתָדִיר מַלְיָא רְבוּת קַדְשָׁא, וְכָל בִּרְכָּאן, וְכָל נְהוֹרִין, וְכָל בּוּצִינִין, כֹּלָּא אִתְבָּרְכָאן וְאִתְנַהֲרָן מִתַּמָּן. שֶׁמֶן לַמָּאוֹר, לְזִמְנִין אִתְמַלְיָא וּלְזִמְנִין לָא.

**394.** "Oil for the light" (Shemot 25:6): This is the oil of supernal greatness that comes from above, FROM ABA AND IMA. There are two kinds of oil and they are two LEVELS. One is above, IN ABA AND IMA, and is called 'Oil of the light' and one below is called 'oil for the light'. Oil of the light is supernal, THAT THE OIL is assuredly always in it and never stops. It is always full with holy oil, and all the blessings and all the lights and all the candles are all blessed and illuminate from there. "Oil for the light" IS MALCHUT that is sometimes full and sometimes not.

**395.** תּוּ, הָא תָּנֵינָן, כְּתִיב וַיַּעַשׂ אֱלֹהִים אֶת שְׁנֵי הַמְּאֹרֹת הַגְּדוֹלִים וְגוֹ', וְאַף עַל גַּב דְּהָא אוּקְמוּהָ חַבְרַיָּיא, וְהָכִי אִיהוּ. אֲבָל שְׁנֵי הַמְּאֹרֹת הַגְּדוֹלִים אִלֵּין: שֶׁמֶן הַמָּאוֹר, וְשֶׁמֶן לַמָּאוֹר. עָלְמָא עִלָּאָה, וְעָלְמָא תַּתָּאָה. חַד דְּכַר, וְחַד נוּקְבָא. וְכָל זִמְנָא דִּדְכוּרָא וְנוּקְבָא אַתְיָין כַּחֲדָא, תַּרְוַויְיהוּ קַרְיָין בְּלִישָׁנָא דִּדְכוּרָא. וּבְגִין דְּעָלְמָא עִלָּאָה אִקְרֵי גָּדוֹל, בְּגִינֵיה עָלְמָא תַּתָּאָה דְּאִתְחַבָּר בַּהֲדֵיה בִּכְלָלָא, אִקְרֵי גָּדוֹל.

**395.** Also, IT CAN BE EXPLAINED, for we have learned that it is written: "And Elohim made the two great luminaries…" (Beresheet 1:16), even though the friends have established it and it is so. Yet these two great luminaries are the oil of the light and oil for the light, which are the Upper World, ZEIR ANPIN, and the Lower World, MALCHUT, for the one is male and the other female. Every time male and female come together, they are referred to in the masculine form. The Upper World is called 'great' and, because of it, the attached Lower World is included in it and is also called 'great'. THEREFORE, IT IS WRITTEN: "THE TWO GREAT LUMINARIES."

**396.** כֵּיוָן דְּאִתְפְּרַשׁ דָּא מִן דָּא, אִדְכְּרוּ בִּפְרָט, כָּל חַד וְחַד כַּדְקָא חֲזֵי לֵיה. דָּא אִקְרֵי גָּדוֹל, וְדָא אִקְרֵי קָטָן. וּבְג"כ אָמְרוּ קַדְמָאֵי, דְּלִיהֱוֵי בַּר

נָשׁ זַנְבָּא לְאַרְיָוָתָא, וְלָא רֵישָׁא לְשׁוֹעֲלַיָּא. דְּכַד אִיהוּ קַיְימָא גּוֹ אַרְיָוָתָא, אִקְרֵי כֹּלָּא בִּכְלָלָא דְּאַרְיָוָתָא. זַנְבָּא דְּאַרְיָא אַרְיָא אִיהוּ, בְּלָא פֵּרוּדָא. וְאִי בְּגוֹ שׁוֹעֲלִים, אֲפִילוּ אִיהוּ רֵישָׁא. רֵישָׁא דְּשׁוֹעֲל שׁוֹעֲל אִיהוּ, בְּלָא פֵּרוּדָא, וְשׁוֹעֲל אִקְרֵי.

**396.** When they are separated from each other, each one individually is referred to in a proper way for it; this one is called 'great' and this one is called 'small'. The early sages said that a person should rather be a tail to lions than a head to foxes, because when MALCHUT stood among the lions, WHICH ARE THE SFIROT OF ATZILUT, She is named entirely as the lions, as the tail of a lion is yet a lion inseparably. If MALCHUT is among the foxes, WHICH ARE THE SFIROT OF BRIYAH, MEANING AFTER SHE WAS LESSENED AND DESCENDED TO BRIYAH, even though She is the head OF THE FOX, the head of the fox is yet a fox inseparably and is called 'a fox', BECAUSE SHE BECOMES CROWN OF BRIYAH.

397. וְרָזָא דָּא הַאי קְרָא, דְּהָא בְּקַדְמֵיתָא כַּד יַתְבִין כַּחֲדָא, שְׁנֵי הַמְּאוֹרוֹת הַגְּדוֹלִים אִתְקְרוּן, אע"ג דְּדָא זַנְבָּא לְגַבֵּי דְּעֵלָּאָה. כֵּיוָן דְּדָא אִתְפְּרַשׁ מֵעֵלָּאָה, כִּבְיָכוֹל לְמֶהֱוֵי רֵישָׁא לְשׁוֹעֲלִים, כְּדֵין אִקְרֵי קָטָן. וְעַל רָזָא דָּא שֶׁמֶן הַמָּאוֹר, דְּלָא פָּסִיק לְעָלְמִין, וְקַיְימָא בִּסְלִיקוּ עִלָּאָה לְמִשְׁלַט בִּימָמָא. שֶׁמֶן לַמָּאוֹר פָּסִיק, וְאִקְרֵי קָטָן, וְשָׁלְטָא בְּלֵילְיָא.

**397.** This is the secret OF: 'OIL OF THE LIGHT,' because WHEN ZEIR ANPIN AND MALCHUT SAT TOGETHER at first, they were called 'the two great luminaries', even though MALCHUT was the tail to the above, ZEIR ANPIN. When MALCHUT separated from the above, to be the head to the foxes so to speak, she is called 'small'. According to this secret, the oil of the light never stops and abides in the Upper level to dominate by day, WHICH IS ZEIR ANPIN. "Oil for the light": HIS LIGHT is interrupted and is called 'small', and dominates at night, MEANING MALCHUT.

398. וְחָמֵשׁ בּוּסְמִין אִינּוּן לְגוֹ שֶׁמֶן וּקְטֹרֶת, וְאע"ג דְּאִיהִי חַד אִינּוּן תְּרֵין וְכֹלָּא חַד. אַבְנֵי שֹׁהַם וְגוֹ'. כָּל הָנֵי תְּלֵיסַר אִינּוּן וְאִינּוּן תִּקּוּנָא דְּמַשְׁכְּנָא.

**398.** IT IS WRITTEN: "SPICES FOR THE ANOINTING OIL, AND FOR THE SWEET INCENSE" (SHEMOT 25:6), MEANING five KINDS OF spices are put into the oil and FIVE INTO the incense, even though it is one. THAT IS, IT SEEMS FROM THE PASSAGE THAT THERE IS ONE KIND OF SPICE FOR THE ANOINTING OIL AND FOR THE SWEET INCENSE, YET STILL IN ALL they are two DISTINCTIVE KINDS OF SPICES, FIVE KINDS FOR THE OIL, WHICH ARE THE BEST SPICES: PURE MYRRH, SWEET CINNAMON, SWEET CALAMUS, AND CASSIA. THE FIVE KINDS FOR INCENSE ARE STORAX, ONYCHA, GALBANUM, SWEET SPICES, AND PURE FRANKINCENSE, AND THE SWEET SPICES COMPRISE THEM ALL BUT ARE NOT COUNTED. And it is all one, FOR THEY UNITE AND BECOME ONE. "Onyx stones..." (Shemot 25:7): they are altogether thirteen, MEANING TWELVE STONES TO BE SET AND THE ONYX STONES EQUAL THIRTEEN. They are the adornments of the tabernacle, WHICH IS MALCHUT, THAT BECOME ADORNED IN THE SECRET OF THIRTEEN, WHICH RECEIVES FROM THE TWELVE ACRONYMS OF YUD HEI VAV HEI OF ZEIR ANPIN WITH THE INCLUSION.

399. וְאָהֲדַרְנָא לְמִלֵּי קַדְמָאֵי, זָהָב הָא אִתְּמַר דְּשִׁבְעָה זִינֵי זָהָב אִינּוּן. וְאִי תֵּימָא דְּזָהָב אִיהוּ דִּינָא, וְכֶסֶף אִיהוּ רַחֲמֵי, וְאִסְתַּלָּק זָהָב לְעֵילָא מִנֵּיהּ. לָאו הָכִי, דְּוַדַּאי זָהָב סָלִיק יַתִּיר אִיהוּ עַל כֹּלָּא, אֲבָל זָהָב בְּאֹרַח סְתָם אִיהוּ, וְדָא זָהָב עִלָּאָה, דְּאִיהוּ שְׁבִיעָאָה מִכָּל אִינּוּן זִינֵי זָהָב, וְדָא אִיהוּ זָהָב דְּנָהִיר וְנָצִיץ לְעַיְינִין, וְדָא אִיהוּ דְּכַד נָפִיק לְעָלְמָא, מַאן דְּאִדְבַּק לֵיהּ, טָמִיר לֵיהּ בְּגַוֵּיהּ, וּמִתַּמָּן נַפְקֵי וְאִתְמַשְּׁכָן כָּל זִינֵי זָהָב.

**399.** Let us return to the original subject. We have learned that there are seven kinds of gold. And if you ask: Gold is Judgment, MEANING GVURAH, and silver is Mercy, WHICH IS CHESED, yet gold has risen above it, MEANING THAT THE JUDGMENT HAS BEEN SWEETENED SO MUCH THAT GVURAH IS MORE VALUABLE THAN CHESED. It is not so and assuredly gold is more important than all of them. Yet gold is mentioned in the ordinary meaning, AND NOT THAT IT HAS RISEN MORE THAN CHESED THOUGH SWEETENING. That is supernal Gold, MEANING BINAH BECAUSE OF THE GVURAH THAT IS IN IT, which is the seventh of all kinds of gold. This is the gold that lights and glistens before the eyes. THE SIX LOWER KINDS OF SILVER ARE IN ZEIR ANPIN AND, BECAUSE OF THIS, when it

emerges to the world, one who acquires it hides it by him. From that, all types of gold emerge and are drawn.

400. אֵימָתַי אִקְרֵי זָהָב, מַאן דְּאִקְרֵי זָהָב. כַּד אִיהוּ בִּנְהִירוּ, וְאִסְתַּלָּק בִּיקָר דְּחִילוּ, וְאִיהוּ בְּחֶדְוָה עִלָּאָה, לְמֶחְדֵּי לְתַתָּאֵי. וְכַד אִיהוּ בְּדִינָא, כַּד אִשְׁתַּנֵי מֵהַהוּא גָּוֶון, לְגָוֶון תִּכְלָא אוּכָם וְסוּמָק, כְּדֵין אִיהוּ בְּדִינָא תַּקִּיפָא. אֲבָל זָהָב, בְּחֶדְוָה אִיהוּ, וּבִסְלִיקוּ דִּדְחִילוּ דְּחֶדְוָה קַיְּימָא, וּבְאִתְעֲרוּתָא דְּחֶדְוָה.

400. When is something that is called 'gold' so called? It is when it is lit by the shining light and rises in glory of fear, WHICH ARE THE JUDGMENTS OF THE LEFT COLUMN THAT WERE SWEETENED AND BECAME THE CAUSES OF THE DRAWING OF CHOCHMAH AND THE FEAR WAS TURNED TO BE REST AND GLORY. It abides in supernal joy, to make the lower ones rejoice WITH ITS LIGHT. When it is in Judgment, MEANING UNDER THE DOMINATION OF THE LEFT ONLY, MEANING when it is changed from the color GOLD to the color blue or black or red, then it is under severe Judgment. But gold is in joy and is found when the fear ascends to joy, AS MENTIONED ABOVE, and with the arousing of joy.

401. וְכֶסֶף לְתַתָּא, רָזָא דִּרוֹעָא יְמִינָא, דְּהָא רֵישָׁא עִלָּאָה זָהָב אִיהוּ, דִּכְתִיב אַנְתְּ הוּא רֵישָׁא דְּדַהֲבָא. חֲדוֹהִי וּדְרָעוֹהִי דִּי כְסַף לְתַתָּא. וְכַד אִשְׁתְּלִים כֶּסֶף, כְּדֵין אִתְכְּלִיל בְּזָהָב, וְרָזָא דָּא תַּפּוּחֵי זָהָב בְּמַשְׂכִּיּוֹת כָּסֶף. אִשְׁתְּכַח דְּכֶסֶף אִתְהַדַּר לְזָהָב, וּכְדֵין אִשְׁתְּלִים אַתְרֵיהּ. וְעַ״ד ז׳ זִינֵי זָהָב אִינוּן.

401. Silver is lower THAN GOLD, FOR IT IS the secret of the right arm OF ZEIR ANPIN, THAT IS CHESED, because the supernal Head is of gold, THAT IS BINAH AS MENTIONED, as it is written: "You are this head of gold" (Daniel 2:38) and "its breast and its arms of silver" (Ibid. 32). When the silver is complete, it is included in the gold. This is the secret of: "Apples of gold in ornaments of silver" (Mishlei 25:11). So we find that when the silver reverts to gold, MEANING THAT THE SILVER ORNAMENTS BECOME GOLD, its place is perfected. Therefore, SINCE THE GOLD IS BINAH, there are

seven types of gold, BECAUSE BINAH COMPRISES THE LOWER SEVEN
SFIROT.

402. וּנְחֹשֶׁת נָפְקָא מִזָּהָב, וְאִשְׁתְּנֵי לְגַרְעוֹנָא, דְּרוֹעָא שְׂמָאלָא. וּתְכֵלֶת
יַרְכָא שְׂמָאלָא. וְתוֹלַעַת שָׁנִי, יַרְכָא יְמִינָא, וְאִתְכְּלִיל בִּשְׂמָאלָא. וְשֵׁשׁ,
דָּא נָהָר דְּנָגִיד וְנָפִיק, דְּאִיהוּ נָטִיל כָּל שִׁית סִטְרִין. כְּגַוְונָא דָּא לְתַתָּא,
וְהָא אוּקְמוּהָ וְאִתְּמַר.

**402.** Brass comes from gold and changes TO BECOME inferior to it, because
it is the left arm, NAMELY GVURAH, and blue is the left thigh, NAMELY
HOD. Scarlet is the right thigh, NAMELY NETZACH, and is combined in the
left. And linen is the river that is drawn and flows, WHICH IS YESOD AND IS
CALLED 'LINEN (HEB. SHESH)', because it takes AND COMBINES IN ITSELF
all the six (Heb. shishah) extremities. It is similar below, IN MALCHUT,
AND ALSO ALLUDES TO HER SFIROT. We have already established it and
learned it. AND THIS IS DIFFERENT FROM WHAT WAS EXPLAINED ABOVE.

403. הָא הָכָא שֶׁבַע דְּיוֹבֵל, וְאִינּוּן ז' דִּשְׁמִיטָה. וְאע״ג דְּאִינּוּן שִׁית,
אִינּוּן תְּלֵיסַר, בִּשְׁבִיעָאָה, דְּאִיהוּ רֵישָׁא עֲלַיְיהוּ, הָא תְּלֵיסַר. רֵישָׁא
דְּקַיְימָא עַל כָּל גּוּפָא לְתַתָּא, רֵישָׁא דְּקַיְימָא עַל כָּל שַׁיְיפֵי גּוּפָא, אִיהוּ
זָהָב. מַה בֵּין הַאי לְהַאי. זָהָב עִלָּאָה, אִיהוּ בְּרָזָא סְתִימָא, וּשְׁמָא
דִּילֵיהּ אִיהוּ זָהָב סָגוּר. סָגוּר וְסָתוּם מִכֹּלָּא, וְע״כ אִקְרֵי סָגוּר, דְּאִיהוּ
סָגוּר מֵעֵינָא דְּלָא שַׁלְטָא בֵּיהּ. זָהָב תַּתָּאָה אִיהוּ בְּאִתְגַּלְיָא יַתִּיר.
וּשְׁמָא דִּילֵיהּ אִקְרֵי זָהָב יְרַקְרָק וְכוּ'.

**403.** There are here seven of Jubilee, WHICH IS BINAH THAT INCLUDES
THE SIX SIDES OF ZEIR ANPIN, WHICH ARE GOLD, SILVER, BRASS,
BLUE, PURPLE, AND SCARLET. These are the seven of Sabbatical year,
WHICH IS MALCHUT THAT ALSO INCLUDES THESE SEVEN KINDS THAT
CORRESPOND TO BINAH AND THE SIX SIDES, CHESED, GVURAH,
TIFERET, NETZACH, HOD AND YESOD, AS MENTIONED. Even though
they are six, EXCEPT FOR BINAH, they are thirteen with the seventh, WHICH
IS BINAH, NAMELY CHESED, GVURAH, TIFERET, NETZACH, HOD AND
YESOD OF ZEIR ANPIN AND CHESED, GVURAH, TIFERET, NETZACH,

HOD AND YESOD OF MALCHUT WHICH ARE TWELVE, AND BINAH HERSELF, which is the head over them, equals thirteen. The head that is placed on the whole body below, IN MALCHUT, and the head that stands over all the limbs of the body OF ZEIR ANPIN, is of gold. What is the difference BETWEEN THE HEAD THAT IS ON ZEIR ANPIN AND THE HEAD OF MALCHUT? IT IS because the supernal Gold THAT IS ON ZEIR ANPIN is in a concealed secret, and its name is pure (lit. 'closed') gold, BECAUSE IT IS closed and concealed from everything. Therefore, it is called 'closed', for it is closed to the eye, that cannot take hold of it. BUT the lower gold THAT IS IN MALCHUT is more revealed and is named greenish gold. THE END OF THIS PARAGRAPH IS MISSING AND IS FOUND IN THE NEW ZOHAR.

## 35. Moses, Aaron and Samuel

### A Synopsis

Moses, Aaron and Samuel, we learn here, were three faithful prophets who served in priesthood. Zacharia and Jeremiah were also priests and prophets but did not merit the high supernal level of Aaron. We are reminded that Moses was able to call and God would answer him immediately. Samuel was similarly blessed, and, being very young, also merited the level of youth.

### The Relevance of this Passage

We read here of the faithful prophets of a long ago time, and in doing so, we receive the gift of prophecy. Prophecy, viewed through the lens of Kabbalah, is understood as the ability to perceive the future consequences of our present deeds. Thus, as we reflect upon the names of the prophets, our spiritual awareness and foresight are magnified so that we have vision to always see the end in the beginning; this leads to courage to offer compassion to our friends and foes, and wisdom to refrain from intolerance.

In turn, we are granted a prophetic vision of our immediate future: It is blessed with global peace and tranquillity through a miraculously merciful redemption that exemplifies and honors the sanctity of the Zohar. And though many parallel universes exist, some with pain, others with compassion, it is this universe of peaceful redemption that now becomes our reality.

404. לְשַׁעֲתָא הֲוָה, דִּכְתִּיב וְרוּחַ אֱלֹהִים לָבְשָׁה אֶת זְכַרְיָה. וְא״ת, הָא יִרְמְיָהוּ, דִּכְתִּיב בֵּיה, בְּטֶרֶם אֶצָּרְךָ בַּבֶּטֶן יְדַעְתִּיךָ. וְהָא אַחֲרָנִין. אֶלָּא כֻּלְהוּ לָא זָכוּ לִנְבוּאָה וְלִכְהוּנָה עִלָּאָה כְּאַהֲרֹן, דְּהָא אַהֲרֹן זָכָה בִּנְבוּאָה עִלָּאָה, עַל כָּל שְׁאַר כַּהֲנֵי. זָכָה בִּכְהוּנָה עַל כֻּלְהוּ.

**404.** HERE, THE BEGINNING OF THE ESSAY IS MISSING AND IT IS IN THE NEW ZOHAR, END OF TRUMAH PG. 43, WHERE IT IS SAID THAT AARON MERITED PRIESTHOOD AND PROPHECY AS NO OTHER PRIEST MERITED. AND HE ASKS: YET ZECHARIAH WAS A PRIEST AND A PROPHET, AS IT SAYS CONCERNING HIM, "SHALL PRIEST AND PROPHET BE SLAIN IN THE SANCTUARY OF ADONAI" (EICHAH 2:20)? HIS ANSWER IS WRITTEN HERE: It was for that time AND NOT FOR ALL GENERATIONS, as written, "And the spirit of Elohim came upon Zechariah...WHY DO YOU TRANSGRESS THE COMMANDMENT OF HASHEM?" (II Divrei Hayamim

24:20), MEANING ONLY TEMPORARILY. If you ask: What about Jeremiah, of whom it is written: "Before I formed you in the belly I knew you" (Yirmeyah 1:5)? SO WE SEE THAT HE WAS A PRIEST AND PROPHET, and so there are others, AND NOT ONLY AARON. HE ANSWERS: But they all did not merit prophecy and priesthood like Aaron, because Aaron merited supernal prophecy above all the other priests and he merited supernal priesthood above them all, BEING A HIGH PRIEST.

405. מֹשֶׁה זָכָה בִּנְבוּאָה, וְשִׁמֵּשׁ בִּכְהוּנָה עִלָּאָה. שְׁמוּאֵל זָכָה בְּתַרְוַויְיהוּ. מַה מֹשֶׁה הֲוָה קָרֵי, וְקוּדְשָׁא בְּרִיךְ הוּא אָתִיב לֵיהּ מִיָּד. אוּף שְׁמוּאֵל כְּתִיב בֵּיהּ, הֲלֹא קְצִיר חִטִּים הַיּוֹם אֶקְרָא אֶל יְיָ' וְיִתֵּן קוֹלוֹת וְגוֹ'. אֲבָל לָא סָלִיק לְדַרְגָּא עִלָּאָה כְּמֹשֶׁה. מַה אַהֲרֹן הֲוָה מְשַׁמֵּשׁ בִּכְהוּנָה גַּבֵּי קוּדְשָׁא בְּרִיךְ הוּא, אוּף שְׁמוּאֵל הֲוָה מְשַׁמֵּשׁ קַמֵּי קוּדְשָׁא בְּרִיךְ הוּא, אֲבָל לָא סָלִיק בְּשִׁמּוּשָׁא עִלָּאָה כְּאַהֲרֹן.

405. Moses merited prophecy and served in supernal priesthood, NAMELY, DURING THE SEVEN DAYS OF CONSECRATION AND SO ALSO Samuel merited them both, AS IT IS SAID ABOUT HIM: "AND SAMUEL TOOK A SUCKING LAMB, AND OFFERED IT FOR A BURNT OFFERING" (I SHMUEL 7:9). Just as Moses would call and the Holy One, blessed be He, would answer him immediately, it is also written of Samuel: "Is it not wheat harvest today? I will call to Hashem, that He shall send thunder and rain" (I Shmuel 12:17), yet he did not rise to such a high level as Moses. As Aaron served before the Holy One, blessed be He, Samuel also served before the Holy One, blessed be He, but did not ascend to highest service, TO BE A HIGH PRIEST, like Aaron.

406. וּמִלָּה הָכִי הוּא. תְּלָתָא אִינּוּן דַּהֲווֹ נְבִיאֵי מְהֵימְנֵי, וְשִׁמְּשׁוּ בִּכְהוּנָה. חַד מֹשֶׁה, וְחַד אַהֲרֹן, וְחַד שְׁמוּאֵל. וְאִי תֵּימָא שְׁמוּאֵל לָא מָשִׁיךְ בִּכְהוּנָה, אֶלָּא אַחֲרָא הֲוָה דְּשִׁמֵּשׁ בִּכְהוּנָה, וּמַנּוּ יִרְמְיָהוּ. לָאו הָכִי, דְּהָא כְּתִיב, מִן הַכֹּהֲנִים אֲשֶׁר בַּעֲנָתוֹת. מִן הַכֹּהֲנִים הֲוָה, אֲבָל לָא שִׁמֵּשׁ. וּשְׁמוּאֵל בְּיוֹמֵי דְּעֵלִי שִׁמֵּשׁ. וּמֹשֶׁה זִמְנָא חֲדָא, כָּל אִינּוּן ז' יְמֵי מִלּוּאִים.

**406.** The theory is this: There were three who were faithful prophets and served in priesthood: Moses is one, Aaron is one, and Samuel is one. If you say that Samuel did not continue in priesthood but there was another who served in priesthood, who is Jeremiah, WHO WAS A PRIEST, it is not so, for it is written: "Of the priests who were in Anatot" (Yirmeyah 1:1). He was of the priests but he did not serve IN THE PRIESTHOOD. But Samuel served in the days of Eli, AS IT IS WRITTEN: "AND THE CHILD SAMUEL MINISTERED TO HASHEM BEFORE ELI" (I SHMUEL 3:1) and Moses SERVED one time, namely all the seven days of consecration.

407. שְׁמוּאֵל זָכָה לְנַעַר, דִּכְתִּיב וְהַנַּעַר נָעַר. וּשְׁמוּאֵל מְשָׁרֵת. וּבְגִין דְּקַיְימָא בְּהַאי דַּרְגָּא, וַדַּאי אִיהוּ כְּמֹשֶׁה וְאַהֲרֹן. מַאן דְּנָטִיל לְהַאי נַעַר, וְזָכֵי בֵּיהּ, זָכֵי בְּאִינּוּן דַּרְגִּין עִלָּאִין, דְּקַיְימָן בְּהוּ מֹשֶׁה וְאַהֲרֹן.

**407.** Samuel merited the LEVEL OF youth, WHICH IS THE SECRET OF THE MOCHIN OF THE SMALL FACE OF THE CHERUBS, as it is written: "And the child was young" (I Shmuel 1:24). "And Samuel served…BEING A CHILD GIRDED…" (I Shmuel 2:18). Since he stood in this level, certainly he was like Moses and Aaron, for one who took the level of youth and merited it, merits the highest levels that Moses and Aaron merited.

## 36. "Gold, and silver, and brass"

### A Synopsis

The serpent is spoken of in this passage as both the instigator of evil and also the judgment of evil. Like good, evil is thus also its own reward. The brass from which Moses fashioned the serpent is indicative of a mixed nature, since it is not pure as are silver and gold. The word 'serpent' is from the same root as the word brass, and it explains why Moses made the serpent of brass when commanded by God only to make a fiery serpent. We are told that the cherubs are made of gold, and the tabernacle of gold and silver and bronze. All these symbolic metals have their meanings in the left and right and central columns. The serpent is always ready to do evil, Adam sinned and was driven from the Garden of Eden because of its influence.

### The Relevance of this Passage

As brass is a mixture of metals, not as pure as are gold and silver, man is a mixture of good and evil. The spiritual force emitted here generates thrust, unalterably tilting the scales of human nature toward the side of good, subjugating our evil tendencies and unleashing the power of our soul. The serpent (The Satan) is both a global phenomenon and a distinct part of our being. They are connected. Hence, as we lay waste to the influence of our inner Evil Inclination, we annihilate the universal serpent concurrently, thereby abolishing darkness from the world.

408. כְּרוּבִים אִינּוּן זָהָב, כְּמָה דְּאוּקְמוּהָ, בְּגִין דְּנַפְקֵי מִסִּטְרָא דְּזָהָב, וְלָא אִתְעֲרַב בְּהוּ כֶּסֶף, וְלָא גָּוֶון אַחֲרָא, וְדָא אִיהוּ גָּוֶון זָהָב יְרַקְרַק. בְּמַשְׁכָּן מִתְעָרְבִין גַּוְונִין, זָהָב וְכֶסֶף לְמֵיהַךְ כַּחֲדָא, לְמֶהֱוֵי רָזָא דִּלְעֵילָּא בְּחַד. תּוּ נְחֹשֶׁת לְמֶהֱוֵי בַּהֲדַיְיהוּ, וּלְמֵיזַל בֵּינַיְיהוּ כָּל סִטְרִין, לְאִשְׁתַּכְחָא שְׁלִימוּ בְּכֹלָּא כַּחֲדָא, דִּכְתִיב זָהָב וְכֶסֶף וּנְחֹשֶׁת.

408. The Cherubs were of gold, as we have established, because they are from the side of gold, WHICH IS THE SECRET OF FEAR THAT CHANGED INTO GLORY. Neither silver nor any other color is mixed in with them. This is greenish gold, NAMELY THE GOLD THAT IS AT THE HEAD OF MALCHUT THAT IS CALLED THUS. In the tabernacle, the colors gold and silver are mixed in order to go together, FOR SILVER AND GOLD ARE THEN RIGHT AND LEFT COMBINED WITH EACH OTHER, so that the supernal secret shall be in one. Also MIXED with them is brass, WHICH IS TIFERET, to be with

them and to go with them to all the sides, NAMELY ALL THREE COLUMNS, RIGHT, LEFT, CENTRAL, so that there will be perfection in all of them as one, as it is written: "Gold, and silver, and brass" (Shemot 25:3).

409. ד"א זָהָב וָכֶסֶף. זָהָב דְּאִתְהַדָּר לְכֶסֶף, וְכֶסֶף לְזָהָב, וְכֹלָּא אִתְכְּלִיל כַּחֲדָא, וּבְדוּכְתָּא חֲדָא. בִּתְלַת גַּוְונִין אִתְהַדָּר, כַּד אִצְטְרִיךְ לְחֶדְוָותָא וְלָא דִינָא, זָהָב. כַּד אִצְטְרִיךְ לְרַחֲמֵי, כֶּסֶף. כַּד אִצְטְרִיךְ תְּקִיפָא דְדִינָא, נְחֹשֶׁת.

409. Another explanation for "Gold, and silver" is that gold reverts to silver and silver reverts to gold, FOR THE RIGHT COLUMN WHICH IS SILVER IS COMBINED IN THE LEFT COLUMN WHICH IS GOLD AND SIMILARLY GOLD WITH SILVER. It is all combined together and in one place. They have returned into three colors. When joy is needed and not Judgment, it is gold, LEFT COLUMN. When Mercy is needed, MEANING CHESED, it is silver, RIGHT SIDE. And when the severity of Judgment is needed, IN ORDER TO SUBDUE THE LEFT SO THAT IT SHOULD UNITE WITH THE RIGHT, IT IS brass, WHICH IS THE SECRET OF TIFERET, THE CENTRAL COLUMN.

410. וְעַ"ד אִסְתָּכַּל מֹשֶׁה, בְּעוֹבָדָא דִּנְחַשׁ הַנָּחֹשֶׁת, דִּכְתִיב וַיַּעַשׂ מֹשֶׁה נְחַשׁ נְחֹשֶׁת, וַהֲוָה יָדַע אֲתַר דְּהִתּוּכָא דְּזָהָב בְּהַהוּא נְחֹשֶׁת, בְּגִין דִּנְחָשׁ כְּלִישָׁנָא דִילֵיהּ הוּא, וְאַתְרֵיהּ הֲוָה יָדַע. דְּהָא קוּדְשָׁא בְּרִיךְ הוּא לָא אָמַר לֵיהּ אֶלָּא עֲשֵׂה לְךָ שָׂרָף, וְאִיהוּ אָתָא וְעָבַד נְחַשׁ נְחֹשֶׁת, דִּכְתִיב וַיַּעַשׂ מֹשֶׁה נְחַשׁ נְחֹשֶׁת. מַאי טַעֲמָא.

410. This is how Moses viewed the work of the brass serpent, for it is written: "And Moses made a serpent of brass" (Bemidbar 21:9). He knew the place of the melting of the gold, MEANING THE SUBJUGATION OF THE LEFT SIDE TO THE RIGHT THROUGH THE JUDGMENTS OF that brass, WHICH IS THE CENTRAL COLUMN, because the serpent (Heb. *nachash*) is derived from brass (Heb. *nechoshet*). He knew its place, because the Holy One, blessed be He, just told him to make a fiery serpent, yet he made a brass serpent, as is written: "And Moses made a serpent of brass." What is the reason?

411. אֶלָּא אֲתַר הֲוָה יָדַע, וְעִקָּרָא דְּמִלְתָּא הֲוָה, דְּהָא בְּקַדְמֵיתָא כְּתִיב,

וַיְשַׁלַּח יְיָ' בָּעָם אֶת הַנְּחָשִׁים הַשְּׂרָפִים, וּכְתִיב נָחָשׁ שָׂרָף. עִקְרָא דִּלְהוֹן
נָחָשׁ אִיהוּ. וּבְגִין דְּמֹשֶׁה הֲוָה יָדַע עִקְרָא וְשָׁרְשָׁא וִיסוֹדָא מֵהַהוּא אֲתָר,
עָבַד נָחָשׁ וְאִסְתְּמִיךְ עָלֵיהּ. מ"ט. בְּגִין דְּיִשְׂרָאֵל חָטָאוּ בְּלִישְׁנְהוֹן,
דִּכְתִיב וַיְדַבֵּר הָעָם בֵּאלֹהִים וּבְמֹשֶׁה, וְעַ"ד וַיְשַׁלַּח יְיָ' בָּעָם אֶת
הַנְּחָשִׁים הַשְּׂרָפִים.

**411.** HE ANSWERS: Hashem knew that was the essence of the matter, because it was first written, "And Hashem sent venomous serpents (lit. 'fiery serpents and snakes') among the people" (Ibid. 6), and: "Venomous serpents (Heb. *'nachash* and *saraf'*)" (Devarim 8:15), because their origin was the PRIMORDIAL serpent. Since Moses knew the essence and root and foundation of that place, he made a serpent and laid his hands upon it. What is the reason? Because Yisrael sinned with their tongue, JUST LIKE THE SERPENT, as it is written: "And the people spoke against Elohim, and against Moses" (Bemidbar 21:5). Therefore, "Hashem sent venomous serpents among the people."

412. וּמֹשֶׁה לָא אָזַל אֶלָּא בָּתַר עִקְרָא, וַעֲבַד נָחָשׁ נְחֹשֶׁת, בְּהַהוּא
גַּוְונָא דְּאִצְטְרִיךְ לֵיהּ, דְּהָא אַתְרֵיהּ נְחֹשֶׁת אִיהוּ. וְקוּדְשָׁא בְּרִיךְ הוּא
לָא א"ל מִמַּה יִּתְעֲבִיד, וּמֹשֶׁה אִסְתָּכַּל וַעֲבַד לֵיהּ מִנְחֹשֶׁת, כְּמַה
דְּאִצְטְרִיךְ לְאַתְרֵיהּ. מְנָלָן. דִּכְתִיב וַיַּעַשׂ מֹשֶׁה נְחַשׁ נְחֹשֶׁת וַיְשִׂימֵהוּ עַל
הַנֵּס. מַאי עַל הַנֵּס. עַל הַהוּא רְשִׁימוּ דְּאִיהוּ לְעֵילָּא.

**412.** Moses only followed the source, WHICH IS THE SERPENT, and made a brass serpent in the manner needed, because its place was brass. The Holy One, blessed be He, did not tell him what form to make it, and Moses made it from brass as was necessary for its place. How do we know that? For it is written: "And Moses made a serpent of brass, and put it upon a pole" (Ibid. 9). What is "upon a pole"? MEANING on that mark that is above, WHICH IS THE SECRET OF THE JUDGMENTS OF THE CENTRAL COLUMN WHERE THEIR PLACE IS.

413. וְהָא תְּנֵינָן, בְּכָל אֲתָר הַאי נָחָשׁ אַזְלָא בָּתַר רָזָא דְּאֵשֶׁת חַיִל,
וּבְעָיָא אֵשֶׁת זְנוּנִים לְאִתְתַּקְנָא גַּרְמָהּ כְּגַוְונָא דִּילָהּ, וְלָא יָכִילַת. אֵשֶׁת

חֵיל, הַהוּא רְשִׁימוּ וְאָת דִּילָהּ, אִיהוּ אָת ה', וְהָכִי אִתְחֲזֵי לָהּ. אֶשֶׁת
זְנוּנִים הַהוּא רְשִׁימָא וְאָת דִּילָהּ אִיהוּ כְּהַהוּא גַּוְונָא דְּאִצְטְרִיךְ, וְלָא
אִתְתָּקַן לְמֶהֱוֵי הָכִי, וְאָת דִּילָהּ ק', אָת דִּילָהּ אִתַּתְקְנָא בְּתִקּוּנָא דְּאָת
ה', כְּגַוְונָא דְּקוֹפָא אֵצֶל בְּנֵי נָשָׁא, דְּאַזְלָא בָּתַר בְּנֵי נָשָׁא, וְלָא אִתְתָּקַן
לְמֶעְבַּד הָכִי. כְּגַוְונָא דָּא עֲבַד מֹשֶׁה הַהוּא נָחָשׁ, עַל הַהוּא רְשִׁימוּ
דְּאִתְחֲזֵי לֵיהּ, וְתָדִיר אִתְתָּקַן לְאַבְאָשָׁא, וְעֲלֵיהּ חָב אָדָם, וְאִתְתָּרַךְ
מִגִּנְתָּא דְּעֵדֶן, דַּהֲוָה אֲתַר דִּיוֹרֵיהּ כְּגַוְונָא דְּדִיוּרָא דִּלְעֵילָא.

**413.** We have learned that this serpent always imitates the woman of valor, WHICH IS MALCHUT. The woman of harlotry, THE KLIPAH, wants to adorn herself similarly TO THE WOMEN OF VALOR, but cannot. The mark and letter of the woman of valor is the letter *Hei*, and so it befits her. The mark and letter of the woman of harlotry has to be similar, MEANING *HEI*, but she is not able to. Her letter is *Kof*, because her letter was prepared in the same manner as the letter *Hei*, just like a monkey (Heb. *kof*) by humans, for he follows humans TO IMITATE THEM but cannot do so. In the same way, Moses made that serpent on the mark that befits it. It is always ready to do evil. Adam sinned because of it and was driven from the Garden of Eden, where his dwelling place resembled the dwelling place above.

## 37. "Let there be light"

### A Synopsis

Rabbi Yosi explains here that the Light spoken of is concealed and illuminates only the righteous; it has no purpose in the world. Rabbi Yehuda says that the world is sustained by that Light which is concealed yet sown like a seed. A thread of this Light emerges wherever people are studying Torah. "Yet The Creator will command His steadfast love in the daytime, and in the night His song shall be with me." When Moses erected the tabernacle, a thread of this Light emerged to form a cloud over the Tent of Meeting, and it is what renews the Creation daily, even now. Rabbi Yosi then comments on, "So he set it before them, and they ate, and left some of it over, according to the word of The Creator," which, we learn, means that whoever hears these teachings always finds new meaning and inspiration in them.

### The Relevance of this Passage

The primordial Light spoken of in the phrase, "Let there be light," illuminates us, bringing spiritual renewal and transformation to the world. For the first time in human history, myriad threads of Light are drawn and woven into a blanket that envelopes, warms, and unites all mankind, as our eyes embrace these ancient texts that shine with such splendid spiritual power.

414. כְּתִיב וַיֹּאמֶר אֱלֹהִים יְהִי אוֹר וַיְהִי אוֹר. אָמַר רַבִּי יוֹסִי, הַהוּא אוֹר אִתְגְּנִיז וְאִיהוּ אִזְדָּמַן לְגַבֵּי צַדִּיקַיָּא לְעָלְמָא דְּאָתֵי. כְּמָה דְּאוּקְמוּהָ, דִּכְתִּיב אוֹר זָרוּעַ לַצַּדִּיק. לַצַּדִּיק וַדַּאי סְתָם. וְהַהוּא אוֹר לָא שִׁמֵּשׁ בְּעָלְמָא, בַּר יוֹמָא קַדְמָאָה. וּלְבָתַר אִתְגְּנִיז, וְלָא שִׁמֵּשׁ יַתִּיר.

414. It is written, "And Elohim said, 'Let there be light': and there was light" (Beresheet 1:3). Rabbi Yosi said: This light was concealed and it is designated for the righteous in the World to Come. We have established this according to the words: "Light is sown for the righteous" (Tehilim 97:11). "For the righteous" certainly with no attributes, FOR IT ILLUMINATES TO THE RIGHTEOUS ABOVE AND TO THE RIGHTEOUS BELOW. That light did not serve a purpose in the world except for the first day, and afterwards was concealed and served no more.

415. רַבִּי יְהוּדָה אוֹמֵר, אִלְמָלֵי אִתְגְּנִיז מִכֹּל וָכֹל, לָא קָאִים עָלְמָא

אֲפִילוּ רִגְעָא חֲדָא, אֶלָּא אִתְגְּנִיז וְאִזְדְּרַע כְּהַאי זַרְעָא דְּעָבִיד תּוֹלְדִין
וְזַרְעִין וְאֵיבִין, וּמִנֵּיה אִתְקַיַּים עָלְמָא. וְלֵית לָךְ יוֹמָא, דְּלָא נָפִיק מִנֵּיה
בְּעָלְמָא, וּמְקַיַּים כֹּלָּא דְּבֵיה זָן קוּדְשָׁא בְּרִיךְ הוּא עָלְמָא. וּבְכָל אֲתָר
דְּלָעָאן בְּאוֹרַיְיתָא בְּלֵילְיָא, חַד חוּטָא נָפִיק מֵהַהוּא אוֹר גָּנִיז,
וְאִתְמְשִׁיךְ עַל אִינוּן דְּלָעָאן בָּה, הֲדָא הוּא דִכְתִיב, יוֹמָם יְצַוֶּה יְיָ' חַסְדּוֹ
וּבַלַּיְלָה שִׁירֹה עִמִּי. וְהָא אוֹקִימְנָא.

**415.** Rabbi Yehuda said: Had it been concealed completely, the world could not exist even one moment, but rather it was concealed and sown like this seed THAT IS SOWN and it produced offspring and plants and fruit. The world is sustained from it. There is not even one day, from which nothing comes into the world to maintain everything, because the Holy One, blessed be He, sustains the world with it. A thread of that concealed light emerges wherever that people are occupied with Torah during the night, and it is drawn upon those that are occupied WITH TORAH. This is what is meant by: "Yet Hashem will command His steadfast love in the daytime, and in the night His song shall be with me" (Tehilim 42:9), as we have already established.

**416.** יוֹמָא דְּאִתְקַם מַשְׁכְּנָא לְתַתָּא, מַה כְּתִיב וְלֹא יָכוֹל מֹשֶׁה לָבֹא אֶל
אֹהֶל מוֹעֵד כִּי שָׁכַן עָלָיו הֶעָנָן. מַאי הֶעָנָן. חַד חוּטָא הֲוָה מֵהַהוּא
סִטְרָא דְּאוֹר קַדְמָאָה, דְּנָפַק בְּחֶדְוָה דְּכֹלָּא, עָאלַת לְמַשְׁכְּנָא דִּלְתַתָּא.
וּמֵהַהוּא יוֹמָא. לָא אִתְגְּלֵי, אֲבָל שִׁמּוּשָׁא קָא מְשַׁמֵּשׁ בְּעָלְמָא, וְאִיהוּ
מְחַדֵּשׁ בְּכָל יוֹמָא עוֹבָדָא דִּבְרֵאשִׁית.

**416.** On the day the tabernacle was erected below, it is written: "And Moses was not able to enter into the Tent of Meeting, because the cloud rested on it" (Shemot 40:35). What is "the cloud"? HE ANSWERS: A thread emerged from the side of the primordial light with great joy and entered the tabernacle below, and from that day onward it did not appear again, but it does a service in the world, in renewing daily the work of creation.

**417.** רַבִּי יוֹסִי הֲוָה לָעֵי בְּאוֹרַיְיתָא, וַהֲווֹ עִמֵּיה רַבִּי יִצְחָק וְר' חִזְקִיָּה.
אָמַר ר' יִצְחָק, הָא חֲמֵינָן דְּעוֹבָדָא דְּמַשְׁכְּנָא, כְּגַוְונָא דְּעוֹבָדָא דִּשָׁמַיִם

וָאָרֶץ, וְהָא אִתְּעָרוּ חַבְרַיָּיא בְּרָזִין דִּלְהוֹן זְעֵירוּ, דְּלָא יָכִיל בַּר נָשׁ לְמֵיכַל בְּפוּמֵיהּ, וּלְמֵישַׁט יְדֵיהּ לְגוֹ פוּמֵיהּ וּלְמִבְלַע.

**417.** Rabbi Yosi was occupied with Torah, and Rabbi Yitzchak and Rabbi Chizkiyah were with him. Rabbi Yitzchak said: Behold we see that the work of the tabernacle is similar to the work of the creation of heaven and earth. The friends have already commented about their secrets such a tiny bit that a man cannot eat with his mouth and stretch his hand to his mouth and swallow, MEANING THEY HAVE REVEALED SUCH A SMALL AMOUNT THAT IT IS IMPOSSIBLE TO TASTE IT AND BE SATISFIED WITH IT.

**418.** א״ר יוֹסֵי, מִלִּין אִלֵּין נַסַּלֵּק לוֹן לְגַבֵּי בּוּצִינָא קַדִּישָׁא, דְּאִיהוּ מְתַקֵּן תַּבְשִׁילִין מְתִיקִין, כְּמָה דְּאַתְקִין לוֹן עַתִּיקָא קַדִּישָׁא, סְתִימָא דְּכָל סְתִימִין, וְאִיהוּ אַתְקִין תַּבְשִׁילִין, דְּלֵית בְּהוּ אֲתָר, לְמֵיתֵי אַחֲרָא, לְמִשְׁדֵּי בְּהוּ מִלְחָא. וְתוּ, דְּיָכִיל בַּר נָשׁ לְמֵיכַל וּלְמִשְׁתֵּי וּלְאַשְׁלָמָא כְּרֵסוֹי מִכָּל עֲדוּנִין דְּעָלְמָא וּלְאִשְׁתַּאֲרָא, וּבֵיהּ יִתְקַיַּים, וַיִּתֵּן לִפְנֵיהֶם וַיֹּאכְלוּ וַיּוֹתִירוּ כִּדְבַר יְיָ'.

**418.** Rabbi Yosi said: Let us raise up these issues before the holy luminary that prepares sweet dishes, just like the most concealed Atika Kadisha does. He prepares such dishes that there is no room for another to come and add salt to them. One can eat and drink and fill his stomach with all the delicacies in the world and still leave over, MEANING THAT WHEN HE HEARS THEM HE UNDERSTANDS THEM CLEARLY ENOUGH, YET STILL IN ALL HE WILL LEAVE OVER SOME AND WILL NOT DRAW EVERYTHING THAT THEY CONTAIN. WHENEVER HE REVIEWS THEM, HE FINDS NEW IDEAS OF WHICH HE WAS NOT PREVIOUSLY AWARE. Here is fulfilled: "So he set it before them, and they ate, and left some of it over, according to the word of Hashem" (II Melachim 4:44).

## 38. "And Hashem gave Solomon wisdom"

### A Synopsis

Rabbi Yosi opens the discussion by saying, "And The Creator gave Solomon Wisdom, as He promised him. And there was peace between Chiram and Solomon; and they two made a league together." King Solomon saw that even though his generation was highly spiritualized, it was still not time to reveal to them all the wisdom of the Torah. Yet in the time of Rabbi Shimon, we learn, such concealed things were allowed to be revealed. Rabbi Yosi then worries about how future generations of the world will fare after Rabbi Shimon departs, when wise sages are few and far between, and when even Wisdom itself is forgotten.

### The Relevance of this Passage

The wisdom of Solomon is no longer found in the world's rulers and politicians, who make only war, not peace. By reading this passage, however, we summon forth Solomon's great wisdom and the piety and righteousness of Rabbi Shimon and his entire generation. This spiritual happening reveals to us the secret wisdom of the Torah now instead of later. This great Light removes conflict and hatred from the hearts of powerful men. It stirs truth and compassion in the souls of leaders, warming them to the true spiritual wisdom. And the sphere of influence of the righteous and the wisdom of Solomon extend to the four corners of the globe.

419. פָּתַח וְאָמַר, וַיְיָ', נָתַן חָכְמָה לִשְׁלֹמֹה כַּאֲשֶׁר דִּבֶּר לוֹ וַיְהִי שָׁלוֹם בֵּין חִירָם וּבֵין שְׁלֹמֹה וַיִּכְרְתוּ בְרִית שְׁנֵיהֶם. הַאי קְרָא הָא אִתְּמַר בְּכַמָּה דּוּכְתֵּי. אֲבָל וַיְיָ', אִסְתַּכְּמוּתָא דִּלְעֵילָא וְתַתָּא כַּחֲדָא. וַיְיָ' אִיהוּ וּבֵי דִּינֵיה. נָתַן חָכְמָה, נָתַן: כְּמַאן דְּיָהִיב נְבִזְבְּזָא וּמַתְּנָה לִרְחִימֵיה. כַּאֲשֶׁר דִּבֶּר לוֹ, שְׁלִימוּ דְּחָכְמְתָא, בְּעוּתְרָא, וּבִשְׁלָם, וּבְשֻׁלְטָנוּ, הה"ד כַּאֲשֶׁר דִּבֶּר לוֹ.

419. He opened the discussion saying: "And Hashem gave Solomon wisdom, as He promised him. And there was peace between Chiram and Solomon; and they two made a league together" (I Melachim 5:26). We have learned this passage in many places, but "And Hashem" POINTS OUT the approval of above, ZEIR ANPIN, and below, MALCHUT, as one because "And Hashem" INDICATES Him, ZEIR ANPIN, and His court, MALCHUT. "Gave Solomon wisdom," like one who gives a present and gift to his

friend. "As he promised Him": This is the perfection of wisdom in riches and peace and domination, as it is written, "as He promised him."

420. וַיְהִי שָׁלוֹם בֵּין חִירָם וּבֵין שְׁלֹמֹה, מ"ט. בְּגִין דַּהֲווֹ יַדְעֵי דָּא לְדָא, סְתִימוּ דְּמִלִּין דַּהֲווֹ אַמְרֵי, וּבְנֵי נָשָׁא אַחֲרָנִין לָא הֲווֹ יַדְעֵי לְאִסְתַּכְּלָא וּלְמִנְדַּע בְּהוּ כְּלַל, וּבְגִינַיְיהוּ, אִתְהַדָּר חִירָם לְאוֹדָאָה לִשְׁלֹמֹה בְּכָל מִלּוֹי.

420. "And there was peace between Chiram and Solomon." What is the reason? They understood each other in the vague words they spoke, but other people did not know how to observe them or understand anything. For their sake, Chiram again conceded AND AGREED with Solomon in all his words.

421. שְׁלֹמֹה מַלְכָּא, אִסְתָּכַּל וַהֲוָה חָמֵי, דְּהָא אֲפִילּוּ בְּהַהוּא דָּרָא, דַּהֲוָה שָׁלִים מִכָּל דָּרִין אַחֲרָנִין, לָא הֲוָה רְעוּתָא דְּמַלְכָּא עִלָּאָה, דְּיִתְגְּלֵי חָכְמָה כ"כ עַל יְדֵיהּ, דְּאִתְגְּלֵי אוֹרַיְיתָא דַּהֲוָה סְתִימָא בְּקַדְמֵיתָא, וּפָתַח לָהּ פִּתְחִין. וְאַף עַל גַּב דְּפָתַח, סְתִימִין אִינּוּן, בַּר לְאִינּוּן חַכִּימִין דְּזָכוּ, וּמִתְגַּמְגְּמֵי בְּהוּ, וְלָא יַדְעֵי לְמִפְתַּח בְּהוּ פּוּמָא. וְדָרָא דָּא דְּרַבִּי שִׁמְעוֹן שַׁרְיָא בְּגַוֵּיהּ, רְעוּתָא דְּקוּדְשָׁא בְּרִיךְ הוּא בְּגִינֵיהּ דְּרַבִּי שִׁמְעוֹן, דְּיִתְגַּלְיָין מִלִּין סְתִימִין עַל יְדוֹי.

421. King Solomon looked and saw that even though that generation was more perfect than all the other generations, it was not the desire of the supernal King that so much wisdom should be revealed through it, and that the Torah that was concealed before it would be revealed. AND HE CAME and opened doors. Even though he opened, they are clogged except for those sages who had merit. They stammer in them and cannot speak about them. But it is the desire of the Holy One, blessed be He, that for the sake of Rabbi Shimon, through the generation in which he lives, concealed things should be revealed.

422. אֲבָל תַּוְוהָנָא עַל חַכִּימֵי דָּרָא, הֵיךְ שַׁבְקִין אֲפִילּוּ רִגְעָא חֲדָא, לְמֵיקָם קַמֵּי דְּר"ש לְמִלְעֵי בְּאוֹרַיְיתָא, בְּעוֹד דְּרַבִּי שִׁמְעוֹן קָאִים בְּעָלְמָא, אֲבָל בְּדָרָא דָּא לָא יִתְנְשֵׁי חָכְמְתָא מֵעָלְמָא, וַוי לְדָרָא כַּד

יִסְתַּלַּק אִיהוּ, וְחַכִּימִין יִתְמַעֲטוּן, וְחָכְמְתָא יִתְנְשֵׁי מֵעָלְמָא.

**422.** But I wonder about the sages of the generation. How can they even for one moment forsake standing before Rabbi Shimon and studying Torah, as long as Rabbi Shimon is in this world? In this generation, wisdom will not be forgotten from the world. Woe to the generation when he departs and sages will become fewer and wisdom will be forgotten from the world.

## 39. Blue

### A Synopsis

Rabbi Yitzchak here relates how he once saw Rabbi Shimon speaking about the Torah, when a pillar of cloud, and a light within the pillar, appeared from the sky. This same thing, of course, had once been written about Moses. Rabbi Yitzchak goes on to speak of the second day of Creation, whose aspect is blue. On that same day, we learn, Gehenom was created, emerging from the center of the fire, and with it the emergence of black and filth, mire and dirt.

### The Relevance of this Passage

When blue is an aspect of Creation, it is time for judgment. Drawing upon the merit of Moses and the immeasurable Light of Rabbi Shimon, we annul harsh adjudications and decrees that have been set forth against mankind. We shift the entire world to a destiny of redemption that personifies mercy and miracles, for this is the wish, hope, and prayer of Moses and Rabbi Shimon. And that is the great power of the Zohar.

423. אָמַר ר' יִצְחָק, וַדַּאי הָכִי אִיהוּ, דְּהָא יוֹמָא חַד הֲוֵינָא אָזִיל עִמֵּיהּ בְּאָרְחָא, וּפָתַח פּוּמֵיהּ בְּאוֹרַיְיתָא, וַחֲמֵינָא עַמּוּדָא דַּעֲנָנָא נָעִיץ מֵעֵילָּא לְתַתָּא, וְחַד זִיהֲרָא זָהִיר גּוֹ עַמּוּדָא. דְּחִילְנָא דְּחִילוּ סַגִּי אֲמֵינָא זַכָּאָה אִיהוּ בַּר נָשׁ, דְּהָכִי אִזְדָּמַן לֵיהּ בְּהַאי עָלְמָא.

423. Rabbi Yitzchak said: Indeed it is so, because one day I was going with him on the road, and he opened his mouth with Torah. I saw a pillar of cloud standing from above down, and there was a light shining in the pillar. I became very frightened, and I said, Blessed is the man, that this is prepared for him in this world.

424. מַה כְּתִיב בֵּיהּ בְּמֹשֶׁה, וְרָאָה כָּל הָעָם אֶת עַמּוּד הֶעָנָן עוֹמֵד פֶּתַח הָאֹהֶל וְקָם כָּל הָעָם וְהִשְׁתַּחֲווּ אִישׁ פֶּתַח אָהֳלוֹ. יֵאוֹת הוּא לְמֹשֶׁה, דְּאִיהוּ נְבִיאָה מְהֵימָנָא עִלָּאָה עַל כָּל נְבִיאֵי עָלְמָא, וְדָרָא הַהוּא דְּקַבִּילוּ אוֹרַיְיתָא עַל טוּרָא דְּסִינַי, וְחָמוּ כַּמָּה נִסִּין וְכַמָּה גְּבוּרָאן בְּמִצְרַיִם וְעַל יַמָּא. אֲבָל הָכָא בְּדָרָא דָּא, זְכוּתָא עִלָּאָה דְּרַבִּי שִׁמְעוֹן קָא עָבִיד, לְאִתְחֲזָאָה נִסִּין עַל יְדוֹי.

**424.** It is written about Moses: "And all the people saw the pillar of cloud stand at the door of the Tent, and all the people rose and worshipped, every man in his tent door" (Shemot 33:10). It was appropriate for Moses, who was the faithful prophet above all the prophets of the world. That generation that received the Torah on Mount Sinai saw many miracles and many mighty acts in Egypt and by the sea; THEREFORE, IT IS JUSTIFIED THAT THEY SEE THE PILLAR OF CLOUD. Here in this generation, the great merit of Rabbi Shimon accomplished this, that miracles should be seen through him.

425. וּתְכֵלֶת, אָמַר רַבִּי יִצְחָק, תְּכֵלֶת מֵהַהוּא נוּנָא דְּיַמָּא דְּגִינוֹסַר, דְּאִיהוּ בְּעַדְבֵיה דִּזְבוּלוּן. וְאִצְטְרִיךְ גַּוְונָא דָּא לְעוֹבָדָא דְּמַשְׁכְּנָא לְאִתְחֲזָאָה הַאי גָּוֶון.

**425.** "And blue" (Shemot 25:3): Rabbi Yitzchak said: Blue is from that fish that is in the Sea Genosar, WHICH IS THE SEA OF GALILEE, which is in the portion of Zvulon. This color is needed for the work of the tabernacle to show this color, AS IT IS WRITTEN BEFORE US.

426. פָּתַח וְאָמַר, וַיֹּאמֶר אֱלֹהִים יְהִי רָקִיעַ בְּתוֹךְ הַמַּיִם וִיהִי מַבְדִּיל בֵּין מַיִם לָמָיִם. הַאי רָקִיעַ אִתְבְּרֵי בַּשֵּׁנִי, דְּעוֹבָדָא דָּא מִסִּטְרָא דִּשְׂמָאלָא אִיהוּ. וּבְיוֹמָא תִּנְיָינָא דְּאִיהוּ סְטַר שְׂמָאלָא, אִתְבְּרֵי בֵּיה גֵּיהִנָּם, דְּאִיהוּ נָפִיק מִגּוֹ הַתּוֹכָא דְּנוּרָא דִּשְׂמָאלָא, וּבְיַמָּא אִצְטְבַע בָּה גָּוֶון תְּכֵלָא, דְּאִיהוּ כּוּרְסַיָּיא דְּדִינָא.

**426.** He opened the discussion saying: "And Elohim said, 'Let there be a firmament in the midst of the waters, and let it divide water from water'" (Beresheet 1:6). This firmament was created on the second day, WHICH IS THE LEFT COLUMN, because the work of firmament is from the left side. On the second day, WHICH IS THE LEFT SIDE, Gehenom was created, which emerges from the center of the fire of the left. With it, the sea was colored with the blue color, which is the throne of Judgment, MEANING MALCHUT WHEN IN THE ASPECT OF JUDGMENT.

427. וְנָטִיל הַאי יוֹמָא מַיִם דַּהֲווֹ מִסְּטְרָא דִּימִינָא, וְאִינוּן מַיִם דַּהֲווֹ

מִסְטְרָא דִּימִינָא, לָא אִתְגַּלּוּ אֶלָּא בְּיוֹם שֵׁנִי. בְּיוֹמָא דִּילֵיהּ, לָא אִתְגְּלֵי
מַיִם, אֶלָּא אִתְחַלָּף, בְּגִין דְּאִתְכְּלִיל דָּא בְּדָא, וְאִתְבַּסַּם דָּא בְּדָא. אוֹר
דְּיוֹמָא קַדְמָאָה, נְהִירוּ קַדְמָאָה מִכָּל שִׁיתָא נְהוֹרִין אִיהוּ. וְהַאי אוֹר
בְּסִטְרָא דְּאֶשָּׁא הֲוָה, דִּכְתִיב וְהָיָה אוֹר יִשְׂרָאֵל לְאֵשׁ. וְהַהוּא אוֹר
דְּיִשְׂרָאֵל מִסְטְרָא דִּימִינָא הֲוָה, אִתְכְּלִיל בְּאֶשָּׁא.

**427.** This day, WHICH IS LEFT, took water which is of the right side, BECAUSE WATER IS CHASSADIM. These waters of the right were not revealed until the second day, WHICH IS LEFT. On this day OF THE RIGHT, WHICH IS THE FIRST DAY, the water was not revealed, but rather it changed, FOR THE LIGHT OF THE SIDE OF FIRE THAT PERTAINS TO THE LEFT WAS REVEALED IN IT, AS EXPLAINED BEFORE US. THAT IS because they were combined together and became perfumed the one by the other. AND HE EXPLAINS: The light of the first day was the first light of all the six lights OF THE SIX DAYS OF CREATION. This light was on the side of fire, as it is written: "And the light of Yisrael shall be for a fire" (Yeshayah 10:17). That light ESSENTIALLY is right, and is combined with fire, WHICH IS LEFT.

**428.** וְיוֹמָא קַדְמָאָה מֵאִינּוּן שִׁיתָא יוֹמִין, מַיִם אִיהוּ, וְלָא שִׁמּוּשׁ עוֹבְדָא
דְּמַיִם, אֶלָּא עוֹבְדָא דְּאוֹר, דְּאִיהוּ מִסְטְרָא דְּאֶשָּׁא, דְּאִיהוּ יוֹם שֵׁנִי.
לְאַחֲזָאָה דְּקוּדְשָׁא בְּרִיךְ הוּא לָא בָּרָא עָלְמָא, אֶלָּא עַל שָׁלוֹם, וּבְאֹרַח
שָׁלוֹם הֲוָה כֹּלָּא. יוֹמָא קַדְמָאָה כָּל מַה דַּעֲבַד, מִסְטְרָא דְּחַבְרֵיהּ עָבֵד.
יוֹמָא תִּנְיָינָא בְּסִטְרָא דְּיוֹמָא קַדְמָאָה עֲבַד הַהוּא אוּמָנָא, וְשִׁמֵּשׁ בָּהּ,
דְּכָל חַד חַד שִׁמֵּשׁ בְּעוֹבְדָא דְּחַבְרֵיהּ, לְאַחֲזָאָה, דְּהָא אִתְכְּלִילוּ דָּא בְּדָא.
יוֹמָא תְּלִיתָאָה, הֲוָה בְּסִטְרָא דְּתַרְוַויְיהוּ, וּבֵיהּ הֲוָה אַרְגְּמָן, וְעַל דָּא
כְּתִיב, כִּי טוֹב כִּי טוֹב תְּרֵי זִמְנֵי בְּיוֹמָא תְּלִיתָאָה.

**428.** The first day of these six days is water, WHICH IS CHASSADIM, yet it was not the action of water that was made use of but that of light, which is from the side of fire, which is the second day. That was to show that the Holy One, blessed be He, created the world only upon peace, MEANING BY THE COMBINATION OF THE RIGHT COLUMN AND THE LEFT COLUMN WITH EACH OTHER THROUGH THE THIRD COLUMN THAT MAKES PEACE BETWEEN THEM. Everything was by way of peace. AND THEREFORE,

everything that the first day did was done from the side of his neighbor, THE SECOND DAY. The second day, that craftsman, worked on the side of the first day, because each one performed the actions of its neighbor to show that they were combined together. The third day, WHICH IS THE CENTRAL COLUMN, was from the side of both of them, FOR IT COMBINES TWO COLUMNS, and it was purple, WHOSE COLOR IS A MIXTURE OF WHITE AND RED, WHICH ARE RIGHT AND LEFT. Therefore, it is written twice: "...that it was good" (Beresheet 1:4) on the third day, FOR IT CORRESPONDS TO THE TWO COLUMNS THAT ARE COMBINED IN IT.

429. תְּכֵלֶת, דָּא יוֹמָא תִּנְיָינָא, אִצְטְבַע בְּב׳ גְּווֹנִין סוֹמָק וְאוּכָם. וּתְכֵלֶת, סוֹמָק אִיהוּ דִּילֵיהּ, מִיּוֹמָא תִּנְיָינָא מַמָּשׁ, כְּעֵין גָּווֶן אֶשָּׁא, וְדָא אִיהוּ אֱלֹהִים, וְיָרִית גָּווֶן דְּדַהֲבָא, דְּכֹלָּא גַּוְונָא חֲדָא. תְּכֶלְתָּא נָפִיק מִגּוֹ הַהוּא גָּווֶן סוֹמָק, וְכַד נָחִית לְתַתָּא, אִתְרְחַק גָּווֶן סוֹמָק, וְעָאל גּוֹ הַהוּא אֲתָר דְּאִיהוּ יַמָּא, וְאִצְטְבַע גָּווֶן תְּכֵלָא. הַהוּא סוֹמָקָא עָיֵיל גּוֹ יַמָּא, וְאִתְחַלָּשׁ גָּווֶן דִּילֵיהּ, וְאִתְהַדָּר תְּכֵלָא, וְדָא אִיהוּ אֱלֹהִים, אֲבָל לָאו אִיהוּ תַּקִּיפָא כְּקַדְמָאָה.

429. Blue, WHICH IS MALCHUT FROM THE SIDE OF JUDGMENT, is THE ASPECT OF the second day and it is colored with two colors, red and black. Blue took its red from the very second day, FOR RED IS like the color of fire. This is Elohim, THAT IS THE SECRET OF BINAH AND IS THE SECRET OF GVURAH OF ZEIR ANPIN. Then the color gold inherits, for it is all one color, BECAUSE THE COLOR GOLD IS SIMILAR TO FIRE, ONLY THAT FIRE IS IN SMALLNESS AND GOLD IS IN GREATNESS. Blue emerges from the color red and when it goes down, the color red becomes distant and enters that place which is a sea, MEANING MALCHUT, where it is dyed with the color blue, MEANING THAT IT MIXES WITH THE COLOR BLACK AND BECOMES BLUE. That red enters the sea and the color becomes diluted and returns to the color blue. This is Elohim, WHICH IS MALCHUT, but ITS JUDGMENT is not strong like at first, REFERRING TO THE NAME ELOHIM WHICH IS IN THE LEFT OF ZEIR ANPIN.

430. אוּכָם, גָּווֶן דָּא נָפִיק מֵהַהוּתְכָא דְּסוּמָקָא, כַּד אִתְהַדָּךְ וְאִתְחַלָּשׁ לְתַתָּא בְּהַתּוּכָא דְּזוּהֲמָא, וְנָחִית לְתַתָּא, וְנָפִיק מֵהַהוּא זוּהֲמָא גָּווֶן

סוּמָק, מְזוּהֲמָא תַּקִּיפָא, וּמִגּוֹ זוּהֲמָא תַּקִּיפָא, אִתְהַדָּר לְאוּכָם. וְכֹלָּא מֵהַהוּא סוּמָקָא קַדְמָאָה אִתְהֲדָר. וְכָל דָּא אִתְבְּרֵי בַּשֵּׁנִי, וְהַאי אִקְרֵי אֱלֹהִים אֲחֵרִים.

**430.** The color black emerges from the meltdown of red when it melts and become weakened below in the melting of the filth, NAMELY THE FILTH OF THE SERPENT and goes down. First, there emerges from that filth the color red from strong filth. Because of the hard filth, it again turns into the color black. So we find that it is all drawn from the original red THAT IS IN THE LEFT COLUMN, BECAUSE IT WAS SMITTEN. All this was created in the second day, and this filth is called 'other Elohim'.

**431.** הַאי אוּכָם אִיהוּ חָשׁוּךְ יַתִּיר, דְּלָא אִתְחֲזֵי גָּוֶון דִּילֵיהּ מִגּוֹ חָשׁוּכָא. בּוּצִינָא קַדִּישָׁא הָכִי אָמַר, דְּהַאי גָּוֶון אוּכָם חָשׁוּךְ, בְּאָן אֲתָר אִצְטְבַע. אֶלָּא כַּד הַהוּא סוּמָקָא אִתְהֲדָר בְּגוֹ תִכְלָא, וְאִתְעָרְבוּ גַּוְונִין, אִתְהֲדָר הַתּוּכָא דְּזוּהֲמָא לְגוֹ תְּהוֹמֵי, וְאִתְעֲבֵיד מִתַּמָּן רֶפֶשׁ וָטִיט. כד"א וַיִּגְרְשׁוּ מֵימָיו רֶפֶשׁ וָטִיט. וּמִגּוֹ הַהוּא טִינָא דִּתְהוֹמֵי, נָפַק הַהוּא חָשׁוּךְ דְּאִיהוּ אוּכָם, וְלָא אוּכָם אֶלָּא חָשׁוּךְ יַתִּיר, הה"ד וְחֹשֶׁךְ עַל פְּנֵי תְהוֹם. אֲמַאי אִקְרֵי חֹשֶׁךְ, בְּגִין דִּגְוֶון דִּילֵיהּ חָשׁוּךְ, וְאַחְשִׁיךְ אַנְפֵּי בִּרְיָין. וְדָא אִיהוּ סוּמָק וְאוּכָם, וּבְגִין דָּא לָא כְּתִיב בַּשֵּׁנִי כִּי טוֹב.

**431.** This black is so dark that its color is not observed from within the darkness. The holy luminary, WHO IS RABBI SHIMON, said so. This color black and this darkness, where was it colored? HE SAID: When this red was melted in the blue and the colors RED AND BLUE mixed, the essence of the filth melted into the abysses. Mire and dirt were formed there, as it is written: "And whose waters cast up mire and dirt" (Yeshayah 57:20). This darkness which is black emerged from this dirt of the abysses, which is not really so black as much as it is very dark. This is what is meant by: "And darkness was on the face of the deep" (Beresheet 1:2). Why is it called 'darkness'? Because its color is darkness and it darkened the faces of the creatures, WHICH IS THE SECRET OF THE FILTH OF THE SERPENT THAT CAUSED DEATH TO CREATURES. This is THE BLUE, WHICH IS red and black. Therefore, it is not written in the second day: "that it was good."

## 40. "And, behold, it was very good"

### A Synopsis

Rabbi Yitzchak here explains why the Angel of Death is very good: because fear of the angel and the mystery of death causes people to repent. Then, he tells us, Rabbi Shimon taught him that the Angel of Death is more important than the Angel of Life. The Elohim, we learn, created Adam, who afterwards sinned and was banished from the Garden of Eden. "And The Creator, Elohim, planted a Garden eastward in Eden'" similar to the supernal Garden of Eden above. There follows a glorious description of the Garden of Eden, which is the abode of the holy spirits, both those who have already come to this world and those that have not yet come to this world. All these spirits, we are told, are clothed in garments and have bodies and faces similar to the ones we have in this world. When the time comes to leave this world the Angel of Death strips the spirit of these garments so that he can return to the Garden of Eden and rejoin his other body. There, he can rejoice and observe the secrets he was unable to see when he was in this body. The wicked of the world who do not repent, however, are not given this other body, but are judged in Gehenom of the Earth – hell. A few who contemplated repentance in their hearts but died before they could repent rise from that fire. We learn finally there is no good intention that is lost before God, but that those who did not think of repentance descend into Sheol, never to reappear.

### The Relevance of this Passage

Fear of death is a potent thing that affects people deeply. The Angel of Death is portrayed in black with a sickle, and the sight of this dark entity can cause an awakening of our desire to correct our sins and pursue the path of spirituality. Here we achieve repentance through the purifying forces that light up this passage. This act of repentance is shared with all mankind, ending the reign of the Angel of Death and ensuring a sweet and merciful Final Redemption in our lifetime.

432. וְאִי תֵּימָא, וְהָא כְּתִיב וְהִנֵּה טוֹב מְאֹד דָּא מַלְאָךְ הַמָּוֶת, וְהָכָא אֲמַרְתְ דְּלָא אִתְּמַר בְּגִינֵיהּ כִּי טוֹב. אֶלָּא רָזָא דְּרָזִין הָכָא, דְּהָא וַדַּאי מַלְאַךְ הַמָּוֶת אִיהוּ טוֹב מְאֹד. מ"ט. בְּגִין דְּהָא כָּל בְּנֵי עָלְמָא יַדְעֵי דִּימוּתוּן וְיִתְהַדְּרוּן לְעַפְרָא, וְסַגִּיאִין אִינּוּן דִּמְהַדְּרֵי בְּתִיוּבְתָּא לְמָארֵיהוֹן, בְּגִין דְּחִילוּ דָּא, וְדַחֲלֵי לְמֶחֱטֵי קַמֵּיהּ. סַגִּיאִין דַּחֲלֵי מִן מַלְכָּא, מִגּוֹ דְּתַלְיָא רְצוּעָה לְקַמַיְיהוּ. כַּמָה טָבָא הַהִיא רְצוּעָה לְגַבֵּי

בְּ" נ, דְּעַבְדַּת לוֹן טָבִין וְקָשִׁיטִין, וּמְתַקְּנִין בְּאָרְחַיְיהוּ כַּדְקָא יֵאוֹת. וְעַ"ד וְהִנֵּה טוֹב מְאֹד. מְאֹד וַדַּאי.

**432.** And if you ask: Yet it is written, "And, behold, it was very good" (Beresheet 1:31), which is the Angel of Death, and here you say that it was not written because of him "that it was good" (Ibid. 4). HE ANSWERS: The secret of secrets is here. Certainly, the Angel of Death is very good. What is the reason? It is because all the people of the world know that they will die and return to dust. Therefore, there are many who repent to their Master because of this fear, and fear to sin before Him. Many are those who fear the King because the whips are hanging before them. How good is the whip for people, for it makes them good and true and improve their ways properly. Therefore, "And, behold, it was very good," very good indeed.

433. רָזָא דְּרָזִין, דְּאוֹלִיפְנָא מִגּוֹ בּוּצִינָא קַדִּישָׁא וְהִנֵּה טוֹב, דָּא מַלְאָךְ חַיִּים. מְאֹד, דָּא מַלְאָךְ הַמָּוֶת, דְּאִיהוּ יַתִּיר. אֲמַאי מַלְאָךְ הַמָּוֶת אִיהוּ טוֹב מְאֹד. אֶלָּא כַּד בָּרָא קוּדְשָׁא בְּרִיךְ הוּא עָלְמָא, כֹּלָּא הֲוָה מִתְתַּקָּן עַל לָא יֵיתֵי אָדָם, דְּאִיהוּ מַלְכָּא דְּהַאי עָלְמָא. כֵּיוָן דְּאִתְבְּרֵי אָדָם, עֲבַד לֵיהּ מִתְתַּקָּן בְּאֹרַח קְשׁוֹט, הֲה"ד אֲשֶׁר עָשָׂה הָאֱלֹהִים אֶת הָאָדָם יָשָׁר וְהֵמָּה בִקְשׁוּ חִשְּׁבֹנוֹת רַבִּים, עֲבַד לֵיהּ יָשָׁר, וּלְבָתַר סָרַח, וְאִתְטְרִיד מִגִּנְתָּא דְּעֵדֶן.

**433.** The secret of secrets that I learned from the holy luminary: "And, behold, it was good" is the Angel of Life and "very" is the Angel of Death, who is more IMPORTANT. Why is the Angel of Death "very good"? HE ANSWERS: When the Holy One, blessed be He, created the world, everything was prepared before Adam was created, who was the king of this world. After Adam was created, he prepared it according to the true way, as it is written: "That the Elohim has made man upright; but they have sought out many inventions" (Kohelet 7:29). He made him upright, and afterwards he sinned and was banished from the Garden of Eden.

434. גַּן עֵדֶן אִיהוּ בְּאַרְעָא, נָטִיעַ בְּאִינוּן נְטִיעָן דְּנָטַע לֵיהּ קוּדְשָׁא בְּרִיךְ הוּא, כד"א וַיִּטַּע יְיָ' אֱלֹהִים גַּן בְּעֵדֶן מִקֶּדֶם, אִיהוּ נָטַע לֵיהּ

בְּשְׁמָא שְׁלִים, כְּגַוְונָא עִלָּאָה לְעֵילָא. וְכָל דְּיוּקְנִין עִלָּאִין כֻּלְּהוּ, מְרֻקְמָן
וּמִתְצַיְירִין בְּהַאי גַּן עֵדֶן דִּלְתַתָּא, וְתַמָּן אִינּוּן כְּרוּבִים. לָאו אִינּוּן
גְּלִיפִין בְּגִלִיפוֹי דִּבְנֵי נָשָׁא מִדַּהֲבָא אוֹ מִמִּלָּה אַחֲרָא, אֶלָּא כֻּלְּהוּ
נְהוֹרִין דִּלְעֵילָּא, גְּלִיפִין וּמִתְצַיְירִין בְּצִיּוּרָא מְרֻקְמָא, עוֹבָדֵי יְדֵי אוּמָּנָא
דִּשְׁמָא שְׁלִים דְּקוּדְשָׁא בְּרִיךְ הוּא, וְכֻלְּהוּ מְחַקְּקָן תַּמָּן. וְכָל דְּיוּקְנִין
וְצִיּוּרִין דְּהַאי עָלְמָא, כֻּלְּהוּ מִתְצַיְירָן תַּמָּן, וּגְלִיפָן וּמִתְחַקְּקָן תַּמָּן,
כֻּלְּהוּ כְּגַוְונָא דְּהַאי עָלְמָא.

**434.** The Garden of Eden is planted on earth with those plants that the Holy One, blessed be He, planted, as it is written: "And Hashem Elohim planted a garden eastward in Eden" (Beresheet 2:8). He planted it using the complete name, THAT IS, YUD HEI VAV HEI ELOHIM similar to the supernal Garden OF EDEN above. All the supernal images are embroidered and formed in the Lower GARDEN of Eden, where the Cherubs are. They are not engraved with a human engraving of gold or other matter, but rather are all lights of above, engraved and formed in an embroidered image, the artwork of the Complete Name of the Holy One, blessed be He. They are all engraved there, and all the forms and images of this world, MEANING THE SPIRITS OF PEOPLE, are formed and carved and engraved there, all of them similar to THE WAY THEY WERE in this world.

435. וְאֲתָר דָּא אִיהוּ מָדוֹרָא לְרוּחִין קַדִּישִׁין, בֵּין אִינּוּן דְּאָתוּ לְהַאי
עָלְמָא, בֵּין אִינּוּן דְּלָא אָתוּ לְהַאי עָלְמָא, וְאִינּוּן דִּזְמִינִין לְמֵיתֵי לְהַאי
עָלְמָא. כֻּלְּהוּ רוּחִין מִתְלַבְּשָׁן בִּלְבוּשִׁין וְגוּפִין וּפַרְצוּפִין כְּגַוְונָא דְּהַאי
עָלְמָא, וּמִסְתַּכְּלָן תַּמָּן בְּזִיו יְקָרָא דְּמָארֵיהוֹן, עַד דְּאַתְיָין לְהַאי עָלְמָא.

**435.** This place is the abode of the holy spirits, both those who have already come to this world and those that have not yet come to this world, as well as those who are going to come to this world. They are all spirits that are clothed in garments and bodies and faces similar to this world, and they behold there the splendid glory of their Master until they come to this world.

436. בְּשַׁעֲתָא דְּנַפְקֵי מִתַּמָּן, לְמֵיתֵי לְהַאי עָלְמָא, מִתְפַּשְּׁטִין אִינּוּן
רוּחִין, מֵהַהוּא גּוּפָא וּלְבוּשָׁא דְּתַמָּן, וּמִתְלַבְּשִׁין בְּגוּפָא וּבִלְבוּשָׁא

דְּהַאי עָלְמָא, וְעַבְדִין דִּיּוּרֵיהוֹן בְּהַאי עָלְמָא, בִּלְבוּשָׁא וְגוּפָא דָּא, דְּאִיהוּ מִטִּפָּה סְרוּחָה.

**436.** At the time that they go out from there to come to this world, the spirits separate from that body and the garment of the Garden of Eden, and attire themselves in a body and garment of this world. They make their dwelling place in this world, in this garment and body which is from a putrid drop.

**437.** וְכַד מָטֵי זִמְנֵיהּ לְמֵיהַךְ וּלְנָפְקָא מֵהַאי עָלְמָא, לָא נָפִיק עַד דְּהַאי מַלְאַךְ הַמָּוֶת אַפְשִׁיט לֵיהּ לְבוּשָׁא דְּגוּפָא דָא. כֵּיוָן דְּאִתְפָּשַׁט הַאי גּוּפָא מֵהַהוּא רוּחָא, ע״י דְּהַהוּא מַלְאַךְ הַמָּוֶת, אַזְלָא וּמִתְלַבְּשָׁא בְּהַהוּא גּוּפָא אַחֲרָא דִּבְגִנְתָּא דְּעֵדֶן, דְּאִתְפָּשִׁיט כַּד אָתֵי לְהַאי עָלְמָא. וְלֵית חֵדוּ לְרוּחָא, בַּר בְּהַהוּא גּוּפָא דְּתַמָּן, וְחַדֵּי עַל דְּאִתְפָּשַׁט מֵהַאי גּוּפָא דְּהַאי עָלְמָא, וְאִתְלָבַּשׁ בִּלְבוּשָׁא אַחֲרָא שָׁלִים, כְּגַוְונָא דְּהַאי עָלְמָא, וּבֵיהּ יָתִיב וְאָזִיל וְאִסְתַּכַּל לְמִנְדַּע בְּרָזִין עִלָּאִין, מַה דְּלָא יָכִיל לְמִנְדַּע וּלְאִסְתַּכְּלָא בְּהַאי עָלְמָא בְּגוּפָא דָא.

**437.** When the time comes to go and leave this world, it does not go out until the Angel of Death strips the spirit of this garment. When the body has been stripped from the spirit by the Angel of Death, the spirit goes and becomes attired with the other body that is in the Garden of Eden, which was removed from it when it came into this world. The spirit has no joy except in that body that is there. It rejoices that it was stripped from the body of this world and was clothed in a different garment, which is complete FROM THE GARDEN OF EDEN, WHICH IS SIMILAR to this world. It sits in it and observes in order to know the supernal secrets that IT WAS not able to know and view WHEN IT WAS in this world in this body.

**438.** וְכַד אִתְלַבְּשַׁת נִשְׁמָתָא בְּהַהוּא לְבוּשָׁא דְּהַהוּא עָלְמָא, כַּמָּה עֲדוּנִין, כַּמָּה כִּסּוּפִין דִּילָהּ תַּמָּן. מַה גָּרִים לְגוּפָא דָא, לְאִתְלַבְּשָׁא בֵּיהּ רוּחָא. הֲוֵי אֵימָא הַהוּא דְּאַפְשִׁיט לֵיהּ לְבוּשִׁין אִלֵּין. וְקוּדְשָׁא בְּרִיךְ הוּא עָבִיד טִיבוּ עִם בִּרְיָין, דְּלָא אַפְשִׁיט לֵיהּ לְבַר נָשׁ לְבוּשִׁין אִלֵּין, עַד דְּאַתְקִין לֵיהּ לְבוּשִׁין אַחֲרָנִין יַקִּירִין וְטָבִין מֵאִלֵּין.

**438.** When the soul becomes attired with the garment of that world, IT HAS there many delights and delicacies. Who caused the spirit to be attired with this body THAT IS IN THE GARDEN OF EDEN? Some say it is the one who removed from it the garments of this world, FOR HE IS THE ANGEL OF DEATH. SO WE SEE THAT THE ANGEL OF DEATH IS VERY GOOD. The Holy One, blessed be He, does kindness by the creatures, for He does not remove from the person THE CLOTHES OF THIS WORLD before He prepares for him other garments more precious and better than these IN THE GARDEN OF EDEN.

439. בַּר לְאִינּוּן חַיָּיבֵי עָלְמָא, דְּלָא אַהְדְרוּ בִּתְיוּבְתָּא שְׁלֵימָתָא לְמָארֵיהוֹן, דְּעַרְטִילָאִין אָתוּ לְהַאי עָלְמָא, וְעַרְטִילָאִין יְתוּבוּן תַּמָּן. וְנִשְׁמָתָא אַזְלָא בְּכִסּוּפָא לְגַבֵּי אַחֲרָנִין, דְּלֵית לָהּ לְבוּשִׁין כְּלָל, וְאִתְדָנַת בְּהַהוּא גֵּיהִנָּם דִּבְאַרְעָא, מִגּוֹ הַהוּא אֶשָּׁא דִּלְעֵילָא. וְאִית מִנְהוֹן דִּמְצַפְצְפֵי וְסַלְקֵי, וְאִלֵּין אִינּוּן חַיָּיבֵי עָלְמָא, דְּחַשְׁבֵי בְּלִבַּיְיהוּ תְּשׁוּבָה, וּמִיתוּ, וְלָא יָכִילוּ לְמֶעְבַּד לָהּ. אִלֵּין אִתְדָנוּ תַּמָּן בְּגֵיהִנָּם, וּלְבָתַר מְצַפְצְפֵי וְסַלְקִין.

**439.** Except for those wicked of the world who do not repent with complete repentance to their Master, for naked did they come into this world and naked do they return there. The soul goes in embarrassment of the other SOULS, because it has no clothes at all and it is punished in the terrestrial Gehenom with the fire from above. There are some among them who break through IN GEHENOM AND IMMEDIATELY rise. These are the wicked of the world who contemplated repentance in their hearts, but died before they could repent. These are judged there in Gehenom, and will afterwards break through and rise.

440. חָמֵי כַּמָּה רַחֲמָנוּתָא דְּקוּדְשָׁא בְּרִיךְ הוּא עִם בִּרְיוֹהִי, דַּאֲפִילוּ דְּאִיהוּ חַיָּיבָא יַתִּיר, וְהִרְהֵר תְּשׁוּבָה, וְלָא יָכִיל לְמֶעְבַּד תְּשׁוּבָה, וּמִית, הַאי בְּוַדַּאי, מְקַבֵּל עוֹנְשָׁא, עַד דְּאָזִיל בְּלָא תְּשׁוּבָה. לְבָתַר הַהוּא רְעוּתָא דְּשַׁוֵּי לְמֶעְבַּד תְּשׁוּבָה, לָא אַעְדִּיאַת מִקַּמֵּי מַלְכָּא עִלָּאָה, וְקוּדְשָׁא בְּרִיךְ הוּא אַתְקִין לְהַהוּא חַיָּיבָא דּוּכְתָּא, בִּמְדוֹרָא דִּשְׁאוֹל, וְתַמָּן מְצַפְצְפָא תְּשׁוּבָה. דְּהָא הַהוּא רְעוּתָא נָחִית מִקַּמֵּי קוּדְשָׁא בְּרִיךְ

הוּא, וְתָבַר כָּל גְּזִיזִין דְּתַרְעֵי מָדוֹרֵי גֵּיהִנָּם, וּמָטֵי לְהַהוּא אֲתָר דְּהַהוּא
חַיָּיבָא תַּמָּן, וּבָטַשׁ בֵּיהּ, וְאִתְּעַר לֵיהּ הַהוּא רְעוּתָא כְּמִלְקַדְמִין. וּכְדֵין
מִצְטַצְפָא הַהִיא נִשְׁמְתָא, לְסַלְּקָא מִגּוֹ מָדוֹרָא דִשְׁאוֹל.

**440.** See how great is the mercy of the Holy One, blessed be He, with His creations, for even if one is exceedingly wicked and has contemplated repentance, but died before he could repent, he certainly receives punishment for leaving the world without repentance. But afterwards that desire that he placed in his heart to repent is not absent before the supernal King and the Holy One, blessed be He, prepares a place for that wicked one in the den of the Sheol, from which he breaks through in repentance, because that desire descends before the Holy One, blessed be He, and breaks all the powers of the guards of the gates of the chambers of Gehenom, and reaches that place where the wicked man is. It strikes him, and awakens in him that desire TO REPENT, as he had beforehand, DURING HIS LIFE; then that soul presses to ascend from the chamber of Gehenom.

**441.** וְלֵית רְעוּתָא טָבָא דְּיִתְאָבִיד מִקַּמֵּי מַלְכָּא קַדִּישָׁא. וּבְגִין כָּךְ,
זַכָּאָה אִיהוּ מַאן דִּמְהַרְהֵר הִרְהוּרִין טָבִין לְגַבֵּי מָארֵיהּ, דְּאַף עַל גַּב
דְּלָא יָכִיל לְמֶעְבַּד לוֹן, קוּדְשָׁא בְּרִיךְ הוּא סָלִיק לֵיהּ רְעוּתֵיהּ כְּאִילוּ
עָבִיד. דָּא לְטָב. אֲבָל רְעוּתֵיהּ לְבִישׁ, לָא. בַּר הִרְהוּרָא דכו״ם, וְהָא
אוּקְמוּהָ חַבְרַיָּיא.

**441.** There is no good intention that is lost before the Holy King. Therefore, blessed is he who thinks good thoughts to His Master. Even though he cannot do them, the Holy One, blessed be He, considers his desire as though he actually performed it. This is for good, but the desire for evil, THE HOLY ONE, BLESSED BE HE, DOES NOT CONSIDER AS ACTUALLY DONE, except for thoughts of idol worshipping. And the friends have already established this.

**442.** אִינּוּן דְּלָא הִרְהֲרוּ תְּשׁוּבָה, נַחְתֵּי לִשְׁאוֹל, וְלָא סַלְּקֵי מִתַּמָּן לְדָרֵי
דָרִין. עֲלַיְיהוּ כְּתִיב, כָּלָה עָנָן וַיֵּלַךְ כֵּן יוֹרֵד שְׁאוֹל לֹא יַעֲלֶה. עַל
קַדְמָאֵי כְּתִיב יְיָ׳ מֵמִית וּמְחַיֶּה מוֹרִיד שְׁאוֹל וַיָּעַל.

**442.** Those that did not think of repentance descend into the Sheol and do not ascend from there for generations and generations. About them, it is written: "As the cloud is consumed and vanishes away; so he who goes down to Sheol shall come up no more" (Iyov 7:9). About the former, it is written: "Hashem kills and gives life, He brings down to Sheol and brings up" (I Shmuel 2:6).

## 41. Punishment in Gehenom

### A Synopsis

Rabbi Yehuda begins this discussion by saying that the fire of Gehenom was extinguished until the Evil Inclination appeared, that it burns only with the strength of the heat of the Evil Inclination of the wicked. The text then lists the seven types of wicked people, each of whom has a chamber in Gehenom. An angel rules over that place under the guidance of Dumah, and thousands of angels with him judge the wicked. On the Shabbat, those who observed Shabbat have rest from their punishments, but those who did not observe it continue to burn. Rabbi Yehuda next tells us that the body in the grave is judged until it is decomposed – and this is true for the righteous as well as well as the wicked. Only a very few people are worthy to raise their souls immediately, and these few may therefore be buried in a coffin. He adds that Moses, Aaron and Miriam did not die by the hand of the Destroying Angel, but rather by the hand of God. Those who die in the Holy Land do not die by the hand of the destroyer, but by the hand of the Angel of Mercy. Those who die outside of the Holy Land, we are told, are called 'carcasses', because the Other Side dwells upon them. The rabbi finally explains the four pairs of tenants in Chevron who are not dead, but just sleeping, and are thus hidden in the entrance to the Garden of Eden.

### The Relevance of this Passage

The fires of Hell, we are told, burn only with the strength of the heat of the Evil Inclination of the wicked. The wicked are thus complicit in their own punishment, creating, by their very sins, the fires in which they are burned. Our meditation cools down the hellish fires. And when we pour just a little love into this mixture, the Light of the Zohar extinguishes these fires eternally. The Evil Inclination that dwells in our hearts burns away, meriting us the complete assistance of the Angel of Mercy as we ascend from this world into the next. We ignite a global spiritual transformation, and both Angels, Death and Mercy, are now relieved of their obligations, for bliss becomes our new reality.

443. אָמַר רַבִּי יְהוּדָה, דִּינָא דְּעוֹנְשֵׁי דְּגֵיהִנָּם, הָא אוֹלִיפְנָא, דְּאִיהוּ לְמֵידָן תַּמָּן לְחַיָּיבַיָּא, עַל מָה אִתְדָּנוּ בְּנוּרָא דְּגֵיהִנָּם. אֶלָּא גֵּיהִנָּם אִיהוּ נוּר דָּלִיק יְמָמֵי וְלֵילֵי, כְּגַוְונָא דְּחַיָּיבַיָּא מִתְחַמְּמָן בְּנוּרָא דְּיֵצֶר הָרָע, לְמֶעְבַּר עַל פִּתְגָּמֵי אוֹרַיְיתָא. בְּכָל חֲמוּמָא וַחֲמוּמָא דְּאִינוּן מִתְחַמְּמָן בְּיֵצֶר הָרָע, הָכִי אִתּוֹקַד נוּר דְּגֵיהִנָּם.

**443.** Rabbi Yehuda said: We have learned that the purpose of the punishments of Gehenom is to judge the wicked there. HE QUESTIONS: Why are they sentenced to the punishment of Gehenom? HE ANSWERS: Gehenom is fire that burns days and nights, just like the wicked who warm themselves with the fire of the Evil Inclination to transgress the words of Torah. For every warmth that they warm themselves with the Evil Inclination, so does the fire of Gehenom burn in them.

**444.** זִמְנָא חֲדָא לָא אִשְׁתְּכַח יֵצֶר הָרָע בְּעָלְמָא, דְּאָעִילוּ לֵיהּ גּוֹ גּוּשְׁפַּנְקָא דְּפַרְזְלָא, בְּנוּקְבָּא דִּתְהוֹמָא רַבָּא. וְכָל הַהוּא זִמְנָא, כָּבָה נוּרָא דְּגֵיהִנָּם, וְלָא אִתּוֹקַד כְּלָל. אַהֲדָר יצה"ר לְאַתְרֵיהּ, שָׁארוּ חַיָּיבֵי עָלְמָא לְאִתְחַמְּמָא בֵּיהּ, שָׁארֵי נוּרָא דְּגֵיהִנָּם לְאִתּוֹקְדָא, דְּהָא גֵּיהִנָּם לָא אִתּוֹקַד אֶלָּא בְּחֲמִימוּ דְּתוּקְפָּא דְּיֵצַה"ר דְּחַיָּיבַיָּא. וּבְהַהוּא חֲמִימוּ, נוּרָא דְּגֵיהִנָּם אִתּוֹקַד יְמָמֵי וְלֵילֵי, וְלָא שָׁכִיךְ.

**444.** At one time the Evil Inclination was not present in the world, because they put it into a ring of iron in the hole of the great deep. All that time, the fire of Gehenom was extinguished and did not burn at all. When the Evil Inclination returned to its place and the wicked of the world started to warm up by it, the fire of Gehenom also started to burn. The Gehenom burns only with the strength of the heat of the Evil Inclination of the wicked and, with that heat, the fire of Gehenom burns days and nights and is not quiet.

**445.** שִׁבְעָה פִּתְחִין אִינּוּן לַגֵּיהִנָּם, וְשִׁבְעָה מְדוֹרִין אִינּוּן תַּמָּן. שִׁבְעָה זִינֵי חַיָּיבִין אִינּוּן: רַע. בְּלִיַּעַל. חוֹטֵא. רָשָׁע. מַשְׁחִית. לֵץ. יָהִיר. וְכֻלְּהוּ לְקָבְלַיְיהוּ אִית מְדוֹרִין לַגֵּיהִנָּם, כָּל חַד וְחַד כַּדְקָא חֲזֵי לֵיהּ. וּכְפוּם הַהוּא דַּרְגָּא דְּחָטָא בֵּיהּ הַהוּא חַיָּיבָא, הָכִי יַהֲבִין לֵיהּ מְדוֹרָא בְּגֵיהִנָּם.

**445.** There are seven entrances into Gehenom and there are seven chambers there. There are seven types of wicked people: evil, scoundrel, sinner, wicked, destroyer, buffoon, and arrogant. They all have corresponding chambers in Gehenom, each one as proper for him. They give him a chamber in Gehenom according to the level at which the wicked one sinned.

**446.** וּבְכָל מְדוֹרָא וּמְדוֹרָא, אִית מַלְאָךְ מְמָנָא עַל הַהוּא אֲתָר, תְּחוֹת

יְדָא דְדוּמָה. וְכַמָה אֶלֶף וְרִבּוֹא עִמֵיהּ, דְּדַיְינִין לוֹן לְחַיָּיבַיָא, כָּל חַד
וְחַד כְּמָה דְּאִתְחֲזֵי לֵיהּ בְּהַהוּא מָדוֹרָא דְּאִיהוּ תַּמָן.

**446.** There is an angel appointed over that place under Dumah in every
single chamber. Many thousands and tens of thousands OF ANGELS with
him punish the wicked, each one according to what is proper for him in that
chamber where he is.

**447.** אֶשָׁא דְּגֵיהִנָם לְתַתָּא, מָטֵי מִגּוֹ אֶשָׁא דְּגֵיהִנָם דִּלְעֵילָא, וּמָטֵי
לְהַאי גֵּיהִנָם דִּלְתַתָּא, וְאִתּוֹקַד, בְּהַהוּא אִתְעֲרוּ דְּחֲמִימוּ דְּחַיָּיבַיָא, דְּקָא
מְחַמְמֵי גַּרְמַיְיהוּ גּוֹ יֵצֶר הָרָע, וְכָל אִינוּן מָדוֹרִין דְּלִיקִין תַּמָן.

**447.** The fire of lower Gehenom comes from the fire of upper Gehenom,
NAMELY FROM *NAHAR DINUR* (ENG. 'RIVER OF FIRE'), and comes to the
lower Gehenom to burn with the heat produced by the wicked who warm
themselves with the Evil Inclination. And all these chambers are burning
there.

**448.** אֲתָר אִית בְּגֵיהִנָם, וְדַרְגִּין תַּמָן דְּאִקְרוּן צוֹאָה רוֹתַחַת, וְתַמָן
אִיהוּ זוּהֲמָא דְּנִשְׁמָתִין, אִינוּן דְּמִתְלַכְלְכָן מִכָּל זוּהֲמָא דְּהַאי עָלְמָא.
וּמִתְלַבְּנָן וְסַלְקִין, וְאִשְׁתְּאָרַת הַהוּא זוּהֲמָא תַּמָן, וְאִינוּן דַּרְגִּין בִּישִׁין
דְּאִתְקְרוּן צוֹאָה רוֹתַחַת, אִתְמָנָן עַל הַהוּא זוּהֲמָא. וְנוּרָא דְּגֵיהִנָם
שַׁלְטָא, בְּהַהוּא זוּהֲמָא דְּאִשְׁתְּאָרַת.

**448.** There is a place in Gehenom in which the levels are called 'boiling
excrement'. There is the filth of those souls that have become soiled by all
the filth of this world, and they become cleansed and rise and the filth
remains there. These bad levels that are called 'boiling excrement' are
appointed over that filth, and the fire of Gehenom dominates over the
remaining filth.

**449.** וְאִית חַיָּיבִין, אִינוּן דְּמִתְלַכְלְכָן בְּחוֹבַיְיהוּ תָּדִיר, וְלָא אִתְלַבְּנָן
מִנַּיְיהוּ, וּמִיתוּ בְּלָא תְּשׁוּבָה, וְחָטוּ וְהֶחֱטִיאוּ אַחֲרָנִין, וַהֲווֹ קְשֵׁי קְדָל
תָּדִיר, וְלָא אִתְבָּרוּ קַמֵּי מָארֵיהוֹן בְּהַאי עָלְמָא. אִלֵּין אִתְדָּנוּ תַּמָן

בְּהַהוּא זוּהֲמָא, וּבְהַהִיא צוֹאָה רוֹתַחַת, דְּלָא נָפְקִין מִתַּמָּן לְעָלְמִין. אִינּוּן דִּמְחַבְּלִין אָרְחַיְיהוּ עַל אַרְעָא, וְלָא חַשְׁשׁוּ לִיקָרָא דְּמָארֵיהוֹן בְּהַאי עָלְמָא, כָּל אִינּוּן אִתְדָּנוּ תַּמָּן לְדָרֵי דָרִין, וְלָא נָפְקֵי מִתַּמָּן.

**449.** There are wicked ones who soil themselves by their sins constantly and are not cleansed of them, who died without repenting and sinned and caused others to sin, were always stiff-necked, and were not broken before their Master in this world. They are judged there with that filth and with that boiling excrement and they remain there forever. All these who destroyed their way on earth and do not care about the honor of the Master in this world are judged there for generations and generations and do not leave from there.

**450.** בְּשַׁבָּתֵי וּבְיַרְחֵי וּבִזְמַנֵּי וּבְחַגֵּי, בְּהַהוּא אֲתָר נוּרָא אַשְׁתְּכַךְ, וְלָא אִתְדָּנוּ, אֲבָל לָא נָפְקֵי מִתַּמָּן, כִּשְׁאָר חַיָּיבִין דְּאִית לְהוּ נַיְיחָא. כָּל אִינּוּן דִּמְחַלְּלֵי שַׁבָּתוֹת וּזְמַנֵּי, וְלָא חַיְישֵׁי לִיקָרָא דְּמָארֵיהוֹן כְּלַל, בְּגִין לְמֶטָר לוֹן, אֶלָּא מְחַלְּלֵי בְּפַרְהֶסְיָא, כְּמָה דְּאִינּוּן לָא נַטְרֵי שַׁבָּתֵי וּזְמַנֵּי בְּהַאי עָלְמָא, הָכִי נָמֵי לָא נַטְרִין לֵיה בְּהַהוּא עָלְמָא, וְלֵית לוֹן נַיְיחָא.

**450.** On Shabbat, the first day of the month, festivals and holy days, the fire in that place abates and they are not punished. But they do not go out from there like the other wicked ones who have rest. All those who desecrate Shabbat and Festivals and do not care about the honor of their Master at all, to observe them, but rather desecrate them publicly, OPENLY, just as they do not keep Shabbat and Festivals in this world, so they are not kept in that world and have no rest.

**451.** אָמַר ר' יוֹסִי, לָא תֵּימָא הָכִי, אֶלָּא נַטְרֵי שַׁבָּתֵי וּזְמַנֵּי תַּמָּן בְּגֵיהִנָּם בְּעַל כָּרְחַיְיהוּ. אָמַר רִבִּי יְהוּדָה, אִלֵּין אִינּוּן עכו"ם, דְּלָא אִתְפְּקָדוּ, דְּלָא נַטְרֵי שַׁבָּת בְּהַאי עָלְמָא, נַטְרֵי לֵיה תַּמָּן בַּעַל כָּרְחַיְיהוּ.

**451.** Rabbi Yosi said: Do not speak so. They do observe Shabbat and Festivals there in Gehenom by force, AGAINST THEIR WILL. Rabbi Yehuda said: That refers to idol worshippers, who were not commanded and do not

-273-

observe Shabbat in this world, but do observe it there by force. BUT
WICKED ONES WHO DESECRATE SHABBAT DO NOT HAVE REST THERE.

452. בְּכָל מַעֲלֵי שַׁבְּתָא כַּד יוֹמָא אִתְקַדַּשׁ, כָּרוֹזִין אָזְלִין בְּכָל אִינוּן
מָדוֹרִין דְּגֵיהִנָּם: סְלִיקוּ דִּינָא דְּחַיָּיבַיָּא, דְּהָא מַלְכָּא קַדִּישָׁא אַתְיָא,
וְיוֹמָא אִתְקַדַּשׁ, וְאִיהוּ אַגִּין עַל כֹּלָּא. וּמִיַּד דִּינִין אִסְתַּלָקוּ, וְחַיָּיבַיָּא
אִית לוֹן נַיְיחָא. אֲבָל נוּרָא דְּגֵיהִנָּם לָא אִשְׁתְּכַּךְ, מֵעֲלַיְיהוּ דְּלָא נַטְרֵי
שַׁבָּת לְעָלְמִין. וְכָל חַיָּיבֵי גֵּיהִנָּם שָׁאֲלֵי עֲלַיְיהוּ, מַאי שְׁנָא אִלֵּין דְּלֵית
לוֹן נַיְיחָא, מִכָּל חַיָּיבִין דְּהָכָא. אִינוּן מָארֵיהוֹן דְּדִינָא תַּיְיבִין לוֹן,
אִלֵּין אִינוּן חַיָּיבִין דְּכָפְרוּ בֵּיהּ בְּקוּדְשָׁא בְּרִיךְ הוּא, וְעָבְרוּ עַל אוֹרַיְיתָא
כֹּלָּא, בְּגִין דְּלָא נַטְרוּ שַׁבָּת תַּמָּן, בְּגִין כַּךְ לֵית לְהוֹ נַיְיחִין לְעָלְמִין.

452. At every commencement of Shabbat when the day is sanctified,
announcements are made in all these chambers of Gehenom: Remove the
punishments of the wicked, because the Holy King has come and the day is
sanctified and He protects everyone. Immediately, the punishments depart
and the wicked have rest, but the fire of Gehenom does not depart from
those who never keep the Shabbat. All the wicked ones in Gehenom ask
about them: Why are these different from all the wicked ones that are here,
for they have no rest? The administrators of Judgment answer: They are the
wicked ones who denied the Holy One, blessed be He, and they transgressed
the whole Torah, because they did not observe the Shabbat IN THIS WORLD.
AND ONE WHO DOES NOT OBSERVE THE SHABBAT IS AS THOUGH HE
TRANSGRESSES OVER THE WHOLE TORAH; therefore, they never have rest.

453. וְאִינוּן חַיָּיבִין כֻּלְּהוֹן, נָפְקִין מִדּוּכְתַּיְיהוּ, וְאִתְיְהִיב לוֹן רְשׁוּ
לְמֵיהַךְ לְמֶחֱמֵי בְּהוּ. וּמַלְאַךְ חַד דִּי שְׁמֵיהּ סַנְטְרִי״אֵל, אָזִיל וְאַפִּיק
לְהַהוּא גּוּפָא דִּלְהוֹן, וְעָיֵיל לֵיהּ לַגֵּיהִנָּם, לְעֵינֵיהוֹן דְּחַיָּיבַיָּא, וְחָמָאן לֵיהּ
דְּסַלְקָא תוֹלָעִין, וְנִשְׁמָתָא לֵית לָה נַיְיחָא בְּנוּרָא דְּגֵיהִנָּם.

453. These wicked ones all go out of their place, and they are given
permission to go and see them. One angel, whose name is Santriel, goes and
brings out their body, and carries it to Gehenom before the eyes of the
wicked ones. They see that it is all wormy and that THEIR soul has no rest in
the fire of Gehenom.

454. וְכָל אִינּוּן חַיָּיבַיָּא דְּתַמָּן, סַחֲרִין לְהַהוּא גּוּפָא, וּמַכְרִיזֵי עֲלֵיהּ, דָּא אִיהוּ פְּלַנְיָא חַיָּיבָא, דְּלָא חָיִישׁ לִיקָרָא דְּמָארֵיהּ, כָּפַר בֵּיהּ בְּקוּדְשָׁא בְּרִיךְ הוּא, וְכָפַר בְּכָל אוֹרַיְיתָא כֻּלָּא, וַוי לֵיהּ טָב דְּלָא יִתְבְּרֵי, וְלָא יֵיתֵי לְדִינָא דָּא, וּלְכִסּוּפָא דָּא, הֲדָא הוּא דִכְתִיב, וְיָצְאוּ וְרָאוּ בְּפִגְרֵי הָאֲנָשִׁים הַפֹּשְׁעִים בִּי כִּי תוֹלַעְתָּם לֹא תָמוּת וְאִשָּׁם לֹא תִכְבֶּה וְהָיוּ דֵרָאוֹן לְכָל בָּשָׂר. כִּי תוֹלַעְתָּם לֹא תָמוּת, מִן גּוּפָא. וְאִשָּׁם לֹא תִכְבֶּה, מִן נִשְׁמָתָא. וְהָיוּ דֵרָאוֹן לְכָל בָּשָׂר, וְהָיוּ דִי רָאוֹן, עַד דְּכָל חַיָּיבִין דְּגֵיהִנָּם דְּתַמָּן, יֵימְרוּן, דַּי רְאִיָה דָּא.

**454.** All these wicked ones who are there surround that body and proclaim about it: This is a certain sinner who did not care about the honor of his Master. He denied the Holy One, blessed be He, and denied the whole Torah. Woe is unto him, better had he not been created. Then, he would not come to this punishment and this shame. This is what is written: "And they shall go forth, and look upon the carcasses of the men that have rebelled against Me, for their worm shall not die, neither shall their fire be quenched; and they shall be an abhorrence to all flesh" (Yeshayah 66:24), for "their worm shall not die," MEANING from the body and "neither shall their fire be quenched," MEANING of the soul. "And they shall be an abhorrence (Heb. *deraon*)", meaning they shall be *Dai Raon*, WHICH MEANS that all the wicked ones in Gehenom who are there will say, Enough of this sight (Heb. *day reiyah*), BECAUSE THEY WILL NOT BE ABLE TO BEAR IT.

455. ר' יוֹסֵי אָמַר, וַדַּאי הָכִי הוּא, בְּגִין דְּשַׁבָּת אִיהוּ לָקֳבֵל אוֹרַיְיתָא כֻּלָּא, וְאוֹרַיְיתָא אִיהִי אֵשׁ, בְּגִין דְּעָבְרוּ עַל אֵשׁ דְּאוֹרַיְיתָא, הָא אֵשׁ דְּגֵיהִנָּם דָּלִיק, דְּלָא שָׁכִיךְ מֵעֲלַיְיהוּ לְעָלְמִין.

**455.** Rabbi Yosi said: Certainly it is so, for Shabbat is equal to the whole Torah and the Torah is fire. They transgressed the fire of Torah, so the fire of Gehenom burns them and never abates from them.

456. אָמַר רַבִּי יְהוּדָה, לְבָתַר כַּד נָפִיק שַׁבַּתָּא, אָתֵי הַהוּא מַלְאָךְ, וּמְהַדַּר הַהוּא גּוּפָא לְקִבְרֵיהּ, וְאִתְדָּנוּ תַּרְוַוייהוּ, דָּא לְסִטְרֵיהּ וְדָא

לְסִטְרֵיהּ. וְכָל דָּא, בְּעוֹד דְּגוּפָא קַיְימָא עַל בּוּרְיֵיהּ, דְּהָא כֵּיוָן דְּגוּפָא
אִתְאֲכָל, לֵית לֵיהּ לְגוּפָא כָּל אִלֵּין דִּינִין, וְקוּדְשָׁא בְּרִיךְ הוּא לֹא יָעִיר
כָּל חֲמָתוֹ כְּתִיב בֵּיהּ.

**456.** Rabbi Yehuda said: When the Shabbat departs, that angel, SANTRIEL, comes and returns that body to its grave and they are both punished, this one in his aspect and that one in its aspect. This occurs as long as the body is intact, because once the body is rotten, these punishments no longer apply to it. And of the Holy One, blessed be He, it is written: "Not stirring up all His wrath" (Tehilim 78:38).

457. כָּל חַיָּיבִין דְּעָלְמָא, בְּעוֹד דְּגוּפָא שְׁלִים בְּכָל שַׁיְיפוֹי גּוֹ קִבְרָא,
אִתְדָּנוּ גוּפָא וְרוּחָא, כָּל חַד דִּינָא כַּדְקָא חֲזֵי לֵיהּ. כֵּיוָן דְּגוּפָא אִתְעֲכַּל,
דִּינָא דְּרוּחָא אִשְׁתְּכַח. מַאן דְּאִצְטְרִיךְ לְנָפְקָא, נָפִיק. וּמַאן דְּאִצְטְרִיךְ
לְמֶהֱוֵי עֲלַיְיהוּ נַיְיחָא, אִית לוֹן נַיְיחָא. וּמַאן דְּאִצְטְרִיךְ לְמֶהֱוֵי קַטְמָא
וְעַפְרָא תְּחוֹת רַגְלֵי דְּצַדִּיקַיָּיא. כָּל חַד וְחַד, כַּדְקָא חֲזֵי לֵיהּ, אִתְעֲבֵיד
לֵיהּ.

**457.** For all the wicked of the world, as long as the body is whole with all of its limbs in the grave, the body and spirit are each punished with the punishment that is proper for it. When the body is decomposed, the Judgment of the spirit is ended and whoever has to leave GEHENOM leaves. Whoever needs rest, has rest, and whoever has to be fire and dust under the feet of the righteous, BECOMES SO. Each and every one receives his due proper for him, AFTER HE IS RELEASED FROM HIS PUNISHMENT IN GEHENOM.

458. וְעַל דָּא, כַּמָּה טָב לוֹן, בֵּין לְצַדִּיקֵי, בֵּין לְחַיָּיבֵי, לְמֶהֱוֵי גוּפָא
דִּלְהוֹן דָּבִיק בְּאַרְעָא, וּלְאִתְעֲבָלָא גּוֹ עַפְרָא לִזְמַן קָרִיב, וְלָא לְמֶהֱוֵי
בְּקִיּוּמָא כָּל הַהוּא זִמְנָא סַגִּי, בְּגִין לְאַתְדָּנָא גוּפָא וְנַפְשָׁא וְרוּחָא תָּדִיר.
דְּהָא לֵית לָךְ כָּל צַדִּיק וְצַדִּיק בְּעָלְמָא, דְּלֵית לֵיהּ דִּינָא דְּקִבְרָא. בְּגִין
דְּהַהוּא מַלְאָךְ דִּמְמָנָא עַל קִבְרֵי, קָאִים עַל גּוּפָא, וְדָן לֵיהּ בְּכָל יוֹמָא
וְיוֹמָא. אִם לַצַּדִּיקִים כָּךְ, לַחַיָּיבִים עאכ"ו.

**458.** Therefore, how good it is for both the righteous and wicked that their bodies should cling to earth in order for it to decompose in the dust in a short time, so as not to remain intact a long time, that the body, Nefesh and Ruach may not be punished continuously FOR A LONG TIME. There is no righteous person in the world who does not undergo the punishment of the grave, BECAUSE that angel who is appointed over the graves stands over the body and punishes it every single day. If the righteous have it so, then it is most certainly so for the wicked.

459. וּבְזִמְנָא דְגוּפָא אִתְעַכַּל וְאִתְבְּלֵי בְּעַפְרָא, הָא דִינָא אִשְׁתְּכַךְ מִכֹּלָּא, בַּר מֵאִינוּן חֲסִידֵי קַיָּימִין דְּעָלְמָא, דְּאִינוּן אִתְחֲזוּן לְסַלְּקָא נִשְׁמָתְהוֹן לְהַהוּא אֲתָר עִלָּאָה דְּאִתְחֲזֵי לוֹן, וּזְעִירִין אִינוּן בְּעָלְמָא.

**459.** When the body is consumed and decomposes in the dust, the Judgment abates from them all, MEANING FROM BOTH RUACH AND NEFESH, except for those pious pillars of the world WHO DO NOT HAVE THE PUNISHMENT OF THE GRAVE. THEY MAY BE BURIED IN A COFFIN, for they are worthy to raise their souls IMMEDIATELY to the highest place that is proper for them, but they are very few in the world.

460. כָּל אִינוּן מֵתִין דְּעָלְמָא, כֻּלְּהוּ מֵתִין ע"י דְּמַלְאָכָא מְחַבְּלָא, בַּר אִינוּן דְּמֵתִין בְּאַרְעָא קַדִּישָׁא, לָא מֵתִין עַל יְדוֹי, אֶלָּא ע"י דְּמַלְאָכָא דְרַחֲמֵי דְּשַׁלִּיט בְּאַרְעָא.

**460.** All the deceased in the world die by the hand of the Destroying Angel, except for those who die in the Holy Land. They do not die by his hand, but rather by the hand of the Angel of Mercy who dominates the land.

461. אָמַר רַבִּי יִצְחָק, אִי הָכִי, מַאי שְׁבָחָא אִיהוּ לְמֹשֶׁה וּלְאַהֲרֹן וּמִרְיָם, דִּכְתִיב בְּהוּ ע"פ יְיָ', דְּאִלֵּין לָא מִיתוּ ע"י דְּהַהוּא מַלְאָךְ מְחַבְּלָא, וְאַתְּ אָמְרַתְּ, דְּכוּלֵּי עָלְמָא אִינוּן דְּמִיתוּ בְּאַרְעָא דְיִשְׂרָאֵל, לָא מֵתִין עַל יְדוֹי דְּדָא.

**461.** Rabbi Yitzchak said: If so, why is it praiseworthy in Moses, Aaron, and Miriam, that is written by them THAT THEY DIED, "By the command

-277-

(lit. 'mouth') of Hashem" (Bemidbar 33:38; Devarim 34:5). THIS TEACHES that these do not die by the hand of this Angel Destroyer, yet you say that all those who die in the Land of Yisrael do not die by the hand of this one?

462. אָמַר לֵיהּ, הָכִי הוּא וַדַּאי, וּשְׁבָחָא דְּמֹשֶׁה אַהֲרֹן וּמִרְיָם, הֲוָה יַתִּיר מִכָּל בְּנֵי עָלְמָא, דְּאִינּוּן מִיתוּ לְבַר מֵאַרְעָא קַדִּישָׁא, דְּמֹשֶׁה אַהֲרֹן וּמִרְיָם לְבַר מֵאַרְעָא קַדִּישָׁא מִיתוּ, וְכֻלְּהוּ מִיתוּ ע"י דְּהַהוּא מְחַבְּלָא, בַּר אִינּוּן מֹשֶׁה וְאַהֲרֹן וּמִרְיָם, דְּלָא מִיתוּ אֶלָּא ע"י דְּקוּדְשָׁא בְּרִיךְ הוּא. אֲבָל אִינּוּן דְּמֵתִין בְּאַרְעָא קַדִּישָׁא, לָא מֵתִין ע"י דְּהַהוּא מְחַבְּלָא, דְּהָא אַרְעָא קַדִּישָׁא לָא קַיְּימָא בִּרְשׁוּ אַחֲרָא, אֶלָּא בִּרְשׁוּ דְּקוּדְשָׁא בְּרִיךְ הוּא בִּלְחוֹדוֹי.

462. He said to him: Certainly it is so, that the praise of Moses, Aaron, and Miriam was greater than all the people of the world. For they all died outside of the Holy Land and they all died by the hand of that destroyer, except for Moses, Aaron, and Miriam, who died by the hand of the Holy One, blessed be He. Those who die in the Holy Land do not die by the hand of that destroyer, because the Holy Land is not in the domain of any other, but rather in the domain of the Holy One, blessed be He, Himself.

463 וְע"ד כְּתִיב, יִחְיוּ מֵתֶיךָ נְבֵלָתִי יְקוּמוּן הָקִיצוּ וְרַנְּנוּ שׁוֹכְנֵי עָפָר וְגוֹ'. יִחְיוּ מֵתֶיךָ, אִלֵּין דְּמֵתִין בְּאַרְעָא קַדִּישָׁא, דְּאִינּוּן מֵתִין דִּילֵיהּ, וְלָא מֵאַחֲרָא, דְּלָא שַׁלְטָא תַּמָּן סִטְרָא אַחֲרָא כְּלַל, וְע"ד כְּתִיב מֵתֶיךָ. נְבֵלָתִי יְקוּמוּן, אִינּוּן דְּמִיתוּ בְּאַרְעָא נוּכְרָאָה אַחֲרָא, ע"י דְּהַהוּא מְחַבְּלָא.

463. Therefore, it is written: "The dead men of Your people shall live, my dead body shall arise. Awake and sing, you that dwell in dust..." (Yeshayah 26:19). "The dead men of Your people shall live" are those who die in the Holy Land who are His dead, OF THE HOLY ONE, BLESSED BE HE, and do not die by another, for the Other Side does not dominate there at all. Therefore, it is written: "The dead men of Your people," WHICH MEANS OF THE HOLY ONE, BLESSED BE HE. "My dead body (Heb. *nevelah*) shall arise" is those who died in another foreign land, by the hand of that destroyer.

464. וְעַ"ד אִקְרוּן נְבֵלָה, מַה נְבֵלָה מְטַמְּאָה בְּמַשָּׁא, אוּף אִינּוּן דְּמֵתִין לְבַר מֵאַרְעָא קַדִּישָׁא, מְטַמְּאִין בְּמַשָּׁא. וְעַ"ד אִינּוּן נְבֵלָה. כָּל שְׁחִיטָה דְּאִיפְּסִיל, אִקְרֵי נְבֵילָה, בְּגִין שְׁחִיטָה הָא אִיהִי מִסִּטְרָא אַחֲרָא, וּמִיַּד דְּאִיפְּסִיל שַׁרְיָא עָלָה סִטְרָא אַחֲרָא. וּבְגִין דְּאִיהִי דִּילֵיהּ, וְשַׁרְיָא עָלָהּ אִקְרֵי נְבֵלָה. וְרָזָא דָּא נָבָל הוּא, וְנָבָל שְׁמוֹ וּנְבָלָה עִמּוֹ.

464. Therefore, they are called 'a carcass (Heb. *nevelah*)', FOR IT IS SAID ABOUT THEM "MY DEAD BODY SHALL ARISE." As a carcass brings impurity upon its carriers, these that die outside of the Holy Land also bring impurity upon their carriers; therefore, they are carcasses. Any animal improperly slaughtered is called 'a carcass', because this slaughtering is from the Other Side, since immediately upon disqualification the Other Side dwells upon it, and because it is his own, it is called 'a carcass'. This is what is written: "Naval is his name, and folly (Heb. *nevalah*) is with him" (I Shmuel 25:25), MEANING THAT A CORPSE IS WITH HIM AND MEANING THAT THE OTHER SIDE DWELLS UPON HIM.

465. וְעַ"ד בְּכָל אֲתָר דְּאִיהוּ שַׁרְיָא, אִקְרֵי נְבֵלָה. מְנוּוָל דָּא לָא שַׁרְיָא, אֶלָּא בְּאֲתָר פְּסִילוּ, וְעַ"ד שְׁחִיטָה דְּאַפְסִיל, הָא דִּילֵיהּ הוּא, וְאִקְרֵי עַל שְׁמֵיהּ. וּבְגִין כַּךְ, מֵתִין דְּאִינּוּן לְבַר מֵאַרְעָא קַדִּישָׁא, תְּחוֹת רְשׁוּ אַחֲרָא, וְשַׁרְיָא עָלַיְיהוּ סִטְרָא אַחֲרָא, אִקְרוּן נְבֵלָה.

465. Therefore, wherever THE OTHER SIDE dwells, that place is called '*nevelah*', because this *Menuval* (Eng. 'despicable') dwells only upon a flawed place. Therefore, a slaughtering that has been disqualified is his and is named after him. Therefore, the dead who are outside of the Holy Land under a different domination and upon whom the Other Side dwells are called '*nevelah*'.

466. הָקִיצוּ וְרַנְּנוּ שׁוֹכְנֵי עָפָר, שׁוֹכְנֵי, דַּיְירִין דְּמִיכִין, וְלָא מֵתִין. וּמַאן אִינּוּן. דְּמִיכִין דְּחֶבְרוֹן, דְּאִינּוּן לָא מֵתִין, אֶלָּא דְּמִיכִין. וְעַ"ד כְּתִיב בְּהוּ גּוִיעָה, כְּמַאן דְּגָוַוע, וְאִית בֵּיהּ קִיּוּמָא לְאִנְעֲרָא. אוּף הָכִי אִינּוּן ד' זוּגֵי דְּחֶבְרוֹן, דְּמִיכִין אִינּוּן וְלָא מֵתִין, וְכֻלְּהוּ קַיְימוּ בְּקִיּוּמַיְיהוּ בְּאִינּוּן

גּוּפִין דִּלְהוֹן, וְיַדְעֵי סִתְרִין גְּנִיזִין, יַתִּיר מִשְׁאַר בְּנֵי נָשָׁא. גְּנִיזִין הֲווֹ
תַּמָּן גּוֹ פִּתְחָא דְּג״ע אִינּוּן גּוּפִין דִּלְהוֹן, וְאִלֵּין אִינּוּן שׁוֹכְנֵי עָפָר. וְע״ד
כָּל אִינּוּן דְּנַפְקוּ נִשְׁמָתַיְיהוּ בְּאַרְעָא קַדִּישָׁא, לָא נָפִיק עַל יְדֵי דְּהַהוּא
מְחַבְּלָא, וְלָא שַׁלְטָא תַּמָּן, אֶלָּא עַל יְדֵי דְּמַלְאָכָא דְּרַחֲמֵי, דְּאַרְעָא
קַדִּישָׁא קַיְימָא בְּעַדְבֵיה.

466. "Awake and sing, you that dwell in dust." "You that dwell" MEANS tenants that are sleeping, but not dead, and who are they? They are those who are sleeping in Hebron who are not dead, but just sleeping. Therefore, they are described by 'expiration', like one who expired but has the strength to awaken. Here also, the four pairs of Hebron are asleep and are not dead, and they all are preserved in their bodies and know hidden concealments more than other people. Their bodies are hidden in the entrance to the Garden of Eden, BECAUSE THE ENTRANCE TO THE GARDEN OF EDEN IS IN THE CAVE OF MACHPELAH. These are those "that dwell in dust." Hence, those whose souls departed in the Holy Land do not depart by the hand of that destroyer, for he does not dominate there, but rather by the hand of an angel of Mercy, as the Holy Land is located in His portion.

## 42. There is a place in civilization where people do not die

### A Synopsis

The rabbis here wonder why the destroying angel has no dominion over people while they are in the Temple. They ask Rabbi Shimon, who explains that God created the entire world with the secret of the letters and the engravings of the Holy Name. The letter Tet remained suspended over the place where the Temple would later be. God first threw a stone engraved with its secret of 72 letters into the water; the stone and the water sank under the altar and remained there, maintaining the world. Inside the Temple, we learn, all the letters dwell, and therefore the temple is equal to the whole world. It exists to atone for sins. The destroying angel was never given permission to enter there because he flees from the letter Tet, which supplies the first three Sfirot to the world. Wherever the letter Tet is, we learn, the letter Kof cannot settle, nor can the Other Side dominate. But when a person goes outside the temple, however, the Other Side has permission to dominate him. In Gehenom, we're told finally, the letter Kof dominates.

### The Relevance of this Passage

Only dimly do we perceive the power of letters and words, so how can we imagine that the destroying angel could be kept from his task by the presence of a single letter? Yet in English, it is only a single letter that separates us from God, that keeps us trapped in ourselves: the letter 'I'.

A lone letter can be likened to a single microscopic atom that is capable of releasing unimaginable forces of energy. Here we receive the Light of the letter *Tet* ט, and the power of the Temple bringing us complete protection from pain, refuge from the Angel of Death, and liberation from the bondage of the Other Side. Our darkest, most unwanted traits flee us by virtue of this single letter and the death of death unfolds before our very eyes.

467. אֲתָר אִית בְּיִשׁוּבָא, דְּלָא שַׁלְטָא בֵּיהּ הַהוּא מְחַבְּלָא, וְלָא אִתְיְיהִיב לֵיהּ רְשׁוּ לְאַעֲלָא תַּמָּן, וְכָל אִינוּן דְּדַיְירֵי תַּמָּן, לָא מֵתִין, עַד דְּנַפְקִין לְבַר מִקַּרְתָּא. וְלֵית לָךְ בַּר נָשׁ מִכָּל דְּדַיְירִין תַּמָּן, דְּלָא מֵתִין, וְכֻלְּהוּ מֵתִין כִּשְׁאַר בְּנֵי נָשָׁא, אֲבָל לָאו בְּמָתָא. מ"ט. בְּגִין דְּלָא יַכְלִין לְמֵיתַב תָּדִיר בְּמָתָא, אֶלָּא אִלֵּין נָפְקִין, וְאִלֵּין עָאלִין, וְע"ד כֻּלְּהוּ מֵתִין.

467. There is a place in civilization where that destroyer has no dominion and is not permitted to enter, and those who live there do not die until they

-281-

go out of the city. There is not one there who does not die. They all die like other people, but not in the city. What is the reason? They cannot remain constantly in the city, but they rather go in and out, and therefore they all die.

468. מ״ט לָא שַׁלְטָא תַּמָּן הַהוּא מַלְאָךְ מְחַבְּלָא. אִי תֵּימָא דְּלָא קַיְימָא בִּרְשׁוּתֵיה, הָא אַרְעָא קַדִּישָׁא דְּלָא קַיְימָא בִּרְשׁוּ אָחֳרָא, וּמֵתִין, בְּהַהוּא אָתָר אֲמַאי לָא מֵתִין. אִי תֵּימָא בְּגִין קְדוּשָׁא, לֵית אָתָר בִּקְדוּשָׁה בְּכָל יִשׁוּבָא כְּגַוְונָא דְּאֶרֶץ יִשְׂרָאֵל. וְאִי תֵּימָא, בְּגִין הַהוּא גַּבְרָא דְּבָנֵי לָה. כַּמָה בְּנֵי נָשָׁא הֲווֹ דִּזְכוּתֵיהוֹן יַתִּיר מִדִּילֵיה. אָמַר רַבִּי יִצְחָק, אֲנָא לָא שְׁמַעֲנָא וְלָא אֵימָא.

**468.** What is the reason that the destroying angel does not dominate there? If you say that this is not in his domain, behold the Holy Land that is not located under another domain but people still die. So what is the reason people do not die in this place? And if you say, because of the holiness OF THE PLACE, you do not have a place in the entire civilization that is holy like the Land of Yisrael, and if you say it is because of the merit of the man who built the city, there were many people who merited more than him. Rabbi Yitzchak said: I did not hear anything and I cannot comment.

469. אָתוּ שָׁאִילוּ לֵיהּ לְר״ש, אָמַר לוֹן, וַדַּאי הַהוּא אֲתָר לָא שַׁלְטָא עֲלֵיה מַלְאָךְ הַמָּוֶת, וְקוּדְשָׁא בְּרִיךְ הוּא לָא בָּעֵי דִּבְהַהוּא אֲתָר יְמוּת בַּר נָשׁ לְעָלְמִין, וְאִי תֵּימָא, דְּקֳדָם לָכֵן בְּהַהוּא דּוּכְתָּא, עַד לָא אִתְבְּנֵי, מִיתוּ בֵּיה בְּנֵי נָשָׁא, לָאו הָכִי. אֶלָּא מִיּוֹמָא דְּאִתְבְּרֵי עָלְמָא, אִתְתַּקַּן הַהוּא אֲתָר, לְקִיּוּמָא, וְרָזָא דְּרָזִין הָכָא, לְאִינוּן דְּמִסְתַּכְּלֵי בְּרָזָא דְּחָכְמְתָא.

**469.** They came and asked Rabbi Shimon. He said to them: Certainly the Angel of Death has no dominion over that place, and the Holy One, blessed be He, does not want any person to ever die there. If you say people did die in that place originally before it was built, it is not so. From the day that man was created, that place was established for existence, and the secret of secrets is here for those who view the secret of Wisdom.

470. כַּד בָּרָא קוּדְשָׁא בְּרִיךְ הוּא עָלְמָא, בָּרָא לֵיה בְּרָזָא דְּאַתְוָון,

וְאִתְגַּלְגְּלוּ אַתְוָון, וּבָרָא עָלְמָא, בְּגִלּוּפֵי דִּשְׁמָא קַדִּישָׁא. אִתְגַּלְגְּלוּ
אַתְוָון, וְאַסְחֲרוּ עָלְמָא בְּגִלּוּפֵי וְכַד אִתְגְּלֵי וְאִתְפְּשַׁט עָלְמָא וְאִתְבְּרֵי,
וַהֲווֹ אַתְוָון סַחֲרָן לְמִבְרֵי, אָמַר קוּדְשָׁא בְּרִיךְ הוּא דְּיִסְתַּיֵּים בְּיו״ד,
אִשְׁתְּאָרַת אָת ט׳ בְּהַהוּא דּוּכְתָּא, תַּלְיָא בַּאֲוֵירָא, טֵי״ת, אִיהוּ אָת,
דְּנְהִירוּ חַיִּין, בְּגִין כָּךְ, מַאן דְּחָמֵי טֵי״ת בְּחֶלְמֵיהּ, סִימָנָא טָבָא הוּא
לֵיהּ, וְחַיִּין אִתְתַּקְנוּ לֵיהּ. וְעַל דָּא בְּגִין דַּהֲוָה ט׳ תַּלְיָא עַל גַּבֵּי הַהוּא
אֲתָר, לָא שַׁלְטָא בֵּיהּ מוֹתָא.

**470.** When the Holy One, blessed be He, created the world, He created it with the secret of the letters. The letters rolled and He created the world with the engravings of the Holy Name, and the letters rolled and surrounded the world with engravings. When the world became manifest, expanded and was created, and the letters were circling to create, the Holy One, blessed be He, said that the world should be concluded with *Yud*. The letter *Tet* remained in that place suspended in the air. *Tet* is the letter that illuminates with life; therefore, it is a good sign for one who sees the letter *Tet* in his dream, as life is prepared for him. Therefore, since *Tet* is suspended over that place, death has no dominion there.

471. כַּד בָּעָא קוּדְשָׁא בְּרִיךְ הוּא לְקַיְּימָא עָלְמָא, זָרִיק חַד צְרוֹרָא גּוֹ
מַיָּא, גָּלִיף בְּרָזָא דְּע״ב אַתְוָון, וּמִתַּמָּן שָׁארֵי לְמֵיהַךְ הַהוּא צְרוֹרָא,
וְלָא אַשְׁכַּח אֲתָר לְאִתְקַיְּימָא בֵּיהּ, בַּר אַרְעָא קַדִּישָׁא, וּמַיָּא הֲווֹ אַזְלִין
אֲבַתְרֵיהּ, עַד דְּמָטָא הַהוּא צְרוֹרָא תְּחוֹת הַמִּזְבֵּחַ, וְתַמָּן אִשְׁתְּקַע,
וְאִתְקַיָּים כָּל עָלְמָא.

**471.** When the Holy One, blessed be He, WHO IS THE CENTRAL COLUMN, wanted to maintain the world, MEANING TO DRAW THE FIRST THREE SFIROT INTO THE WORLD THAT ARE CALLED 'EXISTENCE', He threw a stone into the water. HE ENGRAVED by the secret of 72 letters and from there, FROM BINAH this stone started to go, BUT could not find a place to exist except in the Land of Yisrael. Water, WHICH IS THE SECRET OF THE SIX EXTREMITIES OF BINAH, was following THE STONE until that stone reached under the altar. There it sank, and the whole world was maintained from this.

‫472. וְאִי תֵּימָא, אִי הָכִי דִּבְהַהוּא אֲתָר שַׁרְיָין חַיִּים, אֲמַאי לָא אִתְבְּנֵי‬
‫תַּמָּן בֵּי מַקְדְּשָׁא, לְמֵיהַב חַיִּין לְיַתְבָהָא. אֶלָּא הָכָא בְּהַאי אֲתָר‬
‫אִתְקַיַּים בְּגִין אָת חַד דְּשַׁרְיָא עָלֵיהּ. בְּבֵי מַקְדְּשָׁא כָּל אַתְוָון כֻּלְּהוּ‬
‫שַׁרְיָאן בֵּיהּ, וּבְהוּ אִתְבְּרֵי אִיהוּ בִּלְחוֹדוֹי, כְּגַוְונָא דְּכָל עָלְמָא.‬

**472.** If it is so that life dwells in that place, why wasn't the Temple built there to give life to the people who live there? HE ANSWERS: Here in this place, it exists because of one letter that dwells upon it, WHICH IS THE *TET* but in the Temple, all the letters dwell, and THE TEMPLE was created through them alone, equal to the whole world. JUST AS THE WHOLE WORLD WAS CREATED WITH ALL THE LETTERS, WITH EVERY LETTER HAVING A PARTICULAR PLACE, SO WAS THE TEMPLE INDIVIDUALLY CREATED WITH ALL THE LETTERS BY ITSELF.

‫473. וְתוּ, דְּאַרְעָא קַדִּישָׁא יָהִיב חַיִּין וְכַפָּרָה לְיַתְבָהָא בְּהַהוּא עָלְמָא,‬
‫וַאֲתָר דָּא לָאו הָכִי, יָהִיב חַיִּין לְהַהוּא אֲתָר בְּהַאי עָלְמָא, וְלָא בְּעָלְמָא‬
‫דְּאָתֵי. וּבֵי מַקְדְּשָׁא בְּהִפּוּכָא מִתַּמָּן, בְּגִין דְּאִית חוּלָקָא לְיִשְׂרָאֵל‬
‫בְּהַהוּא עָלְמָא, וְלָא בְּעָלְמָא דָּא. וְעַל דָּא קַיְּימָא בֵּי מַקְדְּשָׁא לְכַפָּרָא‬
‫חוֹבִין, וּלְמִזְכֵּי לוֹן לְיִשְׂרָאֵל לְעָלְמָא דְּאָתֵי.‬

**473.** Also, the Holy Land gives life and atonement to its inhabitants in that world, but that place is not so, for it gives life to that place only in this world and not in the World to Come. The Temple is the opposite of that place, because Yisrael have a portion in that world but not in this world. Therefore, the Temple exists to atone for sins and to merit Yisrael for the World to Come.

‫474. ת״ח, טֵי״ת נְהִירוּ דְּחַיִּין בְּכָל אֲתָר, וְעַל דָּא פָּתַח בָּהּ קְרָא כִּי‬
‫טוֹב. דִּכְתִיב וַיַּרְא אֱלֹהִים אֶת הָאוֹר כִּי טוֹב. מֵהַאי אָת, עָרִיק מַלְאָכָא‬
‫מְחַבְּלָא. לָא תֵּימָא עָרִיק, אֶלָּא דְּלָא אִתְיְיהִיב לֵיהּ רְשׁוּ לְאַעֲלָא תַּמָּן.‬

**474.** Come and see: The letter *Tet* is universally the shine of life, FOR IT IS YESOD OF BINAH. Therefore, the passage opens: "That it was good (Heb. *tov*, with *Tet*)", as it is written: "And Elohim saw the light, that it was good"

(Beresheet 1:4). The Destroying Angel flees from this letter AND THE ZOHAR REPEATS AND SAYS, Do not say that he flees, but rather he was not given permission to enter there.

475. אָת דָּא מְשַׁנְיָא מֵאָת ק', ק' לָא מִתְיַישְׁבָא כְּלָל בְּדוּכְתָּא בְּעָלְמָא, וְסִימָנָךְ אִישׁ לָשׁוֹן בַּל יִכּוֹן בָּאָרֶץ אָת טֵי"ת אִתְיַישְׁבָא בְּכָל דּוּכְתָּא, וְאִתְתַּקְנַת לְאִתְיַישְׁבָא כַּדְקָא יֵאוֹת, וּבְג"כ בְּכָל דּוּכְתָּא דְּאָת ט' תַּמָּן, לֵית יְשׁוּבָא לְאָת ק' תַּמָּן לְאִתְיַישְׁבָא בֵּיהּ. וְעַל דָּא אֲתָר דָּא לָא שַׁלְטָא בֵּיהּ כְּלָל סְטְרָא אַחֲרָא, וְיָהִיב חַיִּים דְּהַאי עָלְמָא לְיַתְבֵי תְּחוֹתֵיהּ דְּאָת דָּא, וְלָא יִפּוּק לְבַר, וְכַד נָפִיק לְבַר, אִית רְשׁוּ לִסְטְרָא אַחֲרָא לְשַׁלְטָאה בֵּיהּ. כְּמָה דְּאָת דָּא שַׁלְטָא בְּאֲתָר דָּא, הָכִי נָמֵי שַׁלְטָא אָת אַחֲרָא בְּאֲתָר דְּגֵיהִנָּם, וּמַאן אִיהִי, אָת ק'.

475. This letter is different from the letter *Kof*. The letter *Kof* does not settle at all in any place in the world. You may derive it from: "Let not a slanderous man be established in the earth" (Tehilim 140:12). The letter *Tet* can settle everywhere and is able to settle properly. Wherever the letter *Tet* is, there is no place for the letter *Kof* to settle there. Therefore the Other Side does not dominate at all in this place, FOR HE IS THE ANGEL OF DEATH, and the *Tet* gives life of this world to those who dwell under this letter and do not go outside. Once he goes outside, the Other Side has permission to have power over him, and as this letter dominates in this place TO GIVE LIFE THERE, so does a different letter dominate in the place of Gehenom. Which one is it? It is the letter *Kof*.

## 43. Betzalel knew the permutation of letters

### A Synopsis

In the book of Rabbi Hamnuna Saba (the elder), we learn here, it speaks of the two letters Chet **ח** and Tet **ט**, which are in the word for 'sin'. These letters are withheld from the tribes of Yisrael, so that they should not be marked with sin. In the tabernacle all the letters of the alphabet are engraved, as is the secret of the Holy Name, Yud Hei Vav Hei **י.ה.ו.ה.** (The Tetragrammaton). Betzalel, who knew the Wisdom of joining the letters with which heaven and earth were created, was chosen above by God, and was also chosen below. His name, we are told, means "In the shadow of El." We next read of the meaning of "The son of Uri," and of "the son of Chur," which has two explanations. Finally, we are told that Betzalel was appointed over the tribe of Judah.

### The Relevance of this Passage

The wisdom distilled here concerning the mystical letters *Chet* and *Tet* absolves us of our sins, from the time of Adam to the present moment, while finally doing away with our tendencies to err and commit transgressions. The four-letter Tetragrammaton **י.ה.ו.ה.**, we are told, embodies all the secrets of Creation, the world above and the world below. Thus, the Light that permeates all reality now rejuvenates our soul and uplifts all existence. Our consciousness is liberated from the rational-based, self-centeredness of Satan – the Evil Inclination – by means of the Light of Binah (the son of Chur).

476. וּבְסִפְרָא דְּרַב הַמְנוּנָא סָבָא, הָכָא אִינּוּן תְּרֵין אַתְוָון: ח׳, ט׳. וְעַל דָּא לָא הֲווֹ כְּתִיבִין גּוֹ אַבְנֵי בּוּרְלָא, אַבְנִין דְּאַשְׁלְמוּתָא, וּשְׁבָטִין דְּיִשְׂרָאֵל, תְּרֵין אַתְוָון אִלֵּין אִתְמְנָעוּ מִנַּיְיהוּ, בְּגִין דְּלָא יְהֵא רָשִׁים בְּגַוַּויְיהוּ חֵ״ט.

476. In the book of Rav Hamnuna Saba (the elder), IT IS WRITTEN THAT THE WORD: 'CHET (ENG. 'SIN')' contains the two letters *Chet* and *Tet*. Therefore, they were not written in the Onyx Stones and in the stones to be set, because the tribes of Yisrael had these two letters withheld from them, so that there should not be marked in them *Chet Tet*, MEANING SIN.

477. בְּאֲתָר דְּבֵי מַקְדְּשָׁא תַּלְיָין כָּל אַתְוָון דְּאַלְפָּא בֵּיתָא, בְּרָזִין גְּלִיפָן

דְּשָׁמְהָן קַדִּישִׁין, קְשִׁירִין, מְרֻקְמָן עֲלֵיהּ, וְכָל עָלְמָא דִּלְעֵילָא וְתַתָּא, כֹּלָּא בְּרָזָא דְּאַתְוָון מִתְחַקְּקָן וּגְלִיפָא, וְרָזִין דִּשְׁמָא קַדִּישָׁא עִלָּאָה, עֲלַיְיהוּ אִתְגְּלִיף.

**477.** All the letters of the alphabet are suspended in the site of the Temple in engraved secrets of the Holy Names, bound and embroidered on it. And the entire world of above and below is bordered and engraved in the secret of the letters, and the secret of the supernal Holy Name, NAMELY, YUD HEI VAV HEI is engraved on them.

**478.** בְּמַשְׁכְּנָא אִתְגְּלִיפוּ וְאִתְצָיָירוּ אַתְוָון כַּדְקָא חֲזֵי. דְּהָא בְּצַלְאֵל הֲוָה יָדַע חָכְמְתָא, לְצָרְפָא אַתְוָון דְּאִתְבְּרִיאוּ בְּהוּ שְׁמַיָּא וְאַרְעָא. וְעַל חָכְמְתָא דִּילֵיהּ, אִתְבְּנֵי מַשְׁכְּנָא עַל יְדֵיהּ, וְאִתְבְּרִיר מִכָּל עַמָּא דְּיִשְׂרָאֵל.

**478.** In the tabernacle, the letters were engraved and formed properly, because Betzalel knew the Wisdom of permutating the letters with which the heaven and earth were created. Because of his Wisdom, the tabernacle was build by him and he was chosen from among all the people of Yisrael.

**479.** וּכְמָה דְּאִיהוּ אִתְבְּרִיר לְעֵילָא, הָכִי בָּעָא קוּדְשָׁא בְּרִיךְ הוּא דְּיִתְבְּרִיר לְתַתָּא. לְעֵילָא כְּתִיב, רְאֵה קָרָאתִי בְשֵׁם בְּצַלְאֵל. לְתַתָּא רְאוּ קָרָא יְיָ' בְּשֵׁם בְּצַלְאֵל. וּשְׁמֵיהּ בְּרָזָא עִלָּאָה אִקְרֵי הָכִי בְּצַלְאֵל: בְּצֵל אֵל. וּמַאן אִיהוּ. דָּא צַדִּיק. דְּאִיהוּ יָתִיב בְּצֵל אֵל, הַהוּא דְּאִקְרֵי אֵל עֶלְיוֹן. וְאִיהוּ יָתִיב כְּגַוְונָא דְּהַהוּא אֵל. הַהוּא אֵל נָטִיל שִׁית סְטָרִין, הַהוּא צַדִּיק נָטִיל לוֹן. אוּף הָכִי, הַהוּא אֵל אַנְהִיר לְעֵילָא, הַאי צַדִּיק אַנְהִיר לְתַתָּא. הַהוּא אֵל, כְּלָלָא דְּכֻלְּהוּ שִׁית סְטָרִין. הַהוּא צַדִּיק, כְּלָלָא דְּכֻלְּהוּ שִׁית סְטָרִין.

**479.** He was chosen above and so did the Holy One, blessed be He, want him to be chosen below, as it is written THAT THE HOLY ONE, BLESSED BE HE, SAID TO MOSES, "See I have called by name Betzalel" (Shemot

31:2). MOSES SAID TO YISRAEL, "See, Hashem has called by name Betzalel" (Shemot 35:30). His name is in a supernal secret called 'Betzalel', WHICH MEANS Betzel (Eng. 'in the shadow') of El. Who is he? He is Righteous, MEANING YESOD, who sits in that shadow of El that is called 'supernal El', MEANING TIFERET. He, BETZALEL, is placed like that El, WHO IS TIFERET, as that El takes six extremities, BECAUSE TIFERET TAKES SIX EXTREMITIES, CHESED, GVURAH, TIFERET NETZACH, HOD AND YESOD, and the Righteous, WHO IS YESOD, takes them. So that El illuminates above and this Righteous One illuminates below, TO MALCHUT. That El, WHO IS TIFERET, combines six ends, while that Righteous one is the combination of all six ends.

480. בֶּן אוּרִי: בֶּן אוֹר קַדְמָאָה, דְּבָרָא קוּדְשָׁא בְּרִיךְ הוּא בְּעוֹבָדָא דִּבְרֵאשִׁית. בֶּן חוּר: בֶּן חֵירוּ דְּכֹלָּא. ד"א, בֶּן חוּר: בֶּן חִוָּור מִכָּל גַּוְונִין. וְדָא אִתְמְנֵי לְמַטֵּה יְהוּדָה, כֹּלָּא כַּדְקָא יֵאוֹת.

**480.** "The son of Uri" (Ibid.) MEANS the son of the primordial light (Heb. *or*) that the Holy One, blessed be He, created during the work of Creation. "The son of Chur" (Ibid.) MEANS the son of the freedom (Heb. *cherut*) in everything, NAMELY THE LIGHT OF BINAH, WHICH IS THE SECRET OF FREEDOM. Another explanation: "The son of Chur" means the son who is white (Heb. *chiver*) MEANING white of all the colors, MEANING THAT THE LIGHT OF CHASSADIM, WHICH IS WHITE, IS IN ASCENDANCY IN HIM. And he, BETZALEL, WHO IS YESOD, was appointed over the tribe of Judah, THAT IS THE SECRET OF MALCHUT. Everything is as it should be, BECAUSE YESOD HAS TO BE JOINED WITH MALCHUT.

## 44. Blue, part two

### A Synopsis

All the colors are good if they are seen in a dream, except blue, because it is a throne for executing Judgment of the soul. When the person sees this blue, we learn, he becomes afraid and remembers all the commandments of his Master, and guards himself from sins for fear of the serpent. Therefore, there is blue in the tabernacle. Rabbi Isaac next asks about mercy, and Rabbi Shimon answers that the colors are improved when the cherubs turn their faces toward each other. At that time, even green turns to gold. When the colors are changed, Malchut changes from Judgment to Mercy and from Mercy to Justice, all according to the changing of the colors.

### The Relevance of this Passage

The colors of Creation burst forth. And as they transmute into various shades, tones, and hues, so too does judgment transform into countless acts of the sweetest mercy towards all mankind. We acquire a deep-seated love for our neighbor as all of Malchut is corrected and transformed.

481. כָּל גַּוְונִין טָבִין לְחֶלְמָא, בַּר תִּכְלָא, כְּמָה דְאִתְּמַר. בְּגִין דְּאִיהוּ כֻּרְסְיָיא, לְמֵידָן דִּינִין דְּנִשְׁמָתִין. וְהָא הַאי דַּרְגָּא חִוָּורָא אִיהוּ. אֶלָּא בְּשַׁעֲתָא דְּקַיְּימָא בְּדִינֵי דְּנַפְשָׁאן, כְּדֵין אִיהוּ גָּוֶון תִּכְלָא. וְהָא אוּקִימְנָא.

481. All the colors are good IF THEY ARE SEEN in a dream except blue, because it is a throne, MEANING MALCHUT, for executing Judgment of the souls. HE QUESTIONS: But this level, WHICH IS MALCHUT, is white, AS YOU SAY that it receives FROM YESOD THAT IS CALLED 'THE SON OF CHUR', WHICH MEANS WHITE, MEANING CHESED. HE ANSWERS: At the time that it stands to judge souls, BECAUSE OF THE SINS OF THE LOWER BEINGS, it has the color blue, as we have already established.

482. בְּשַׁעֲתָא דְּחָמֵי בַּר נָשׁ לְהַאי גָּוֶון, אִדְכַּר בַּר נָשׁ לְמֶעְבַּד פִּקּוּדִין דְּמָארֵיהּ. כְּגַוְונָא דִּנְחַשׁ הַנְּחֹשֶׁת, בְּשַׁעֲתָא דַּהֲווֹ חֲמָאן לֵיהּ, הֲווֹ דַּחֲלֵי מִקַּמֵּי דְּקוּדְשָׁא בְּרִיךְ הוּא, וּמְנַטְרָן גַּרְמַיְיהוּ מִכָּל חוֹבִין, וּבְשַׁעֲתָא דְּהַהוּא דְּחִילוּ דְּקוּדְשָׁא בְּרִיךְ הוּא סַלְקָא עֲלַיְיהוּ, מִיַּד אִתְּסְיָין. מַאן

גְּרִים לוֹן לְדַחֲלָא מִקַּמֵּי קוּדְשָׁא בְּרִיךְ הוּא, הַהוּא נָחָשׁ, הַהִיא רְצוּעָה דְּמִסְתַּכְּלָן בָּהּ. אוּף הָכִי תְּכֵלֶת וּרְאִיתֶם אוֹתוֹ וּזְכַרְתֶּם אֶת כָּל מִצְוֹת יְיָ'. מֵהַהוּא דְּחִילוּ דִּילֵיהּ, וְעַל דָּא תְּכֵלֶת בְּמַשְׁכְּנָא.

**482.** When the person sees this color, MEANING BLUE, he is reminded to do all the commandments of his Master as by the brass serpent. For at the moment they saw it, they feared the Holy One, blessed be He, and guarded themselves against all sins. When this fear came over them, they were immediately cured. What caused them to fear the Holy One, blessed be He? It was that serpent, that whip that they saw. Here also, about blue is written: "That you may look upon it, and remember all the commandments of Hashem" (Bemidbar 15:39), which means from the fear of Him. Therefore, there was blue in the tabernacle.

483. אָמַר רַבִּי יִצְחָק, הַאי דְּאָמַר מַר תְּכֵלֶת כֻּרְסְיָיא דְּדִינָא אִיהִי, וְכַד אִיהִי קַיְימָא בְּגַוְונָא דָּא, כְּדֵין אִיהִי כֻּרְסְיָיא לְמֵידָן דִּינֵי נַפְשָׁאן. אֵימָתַי אִיהִי בְּרַחֲמֵי. אָמַר לֵיהּ, בְּשַׁעֲתָא דִּכְרוּבִים מְהַדְּרָן אַנְפַּיְיהוּ דָּא עִם דָּא, וּמִסְתַּכְּלָן אַנְפִּין בְּאַנְפִּין. כֵּיוָן דְּאִינוּן כְּרוּבִים מִסְתַּכְּלָן אַנְפִּין בְּאַנְפִּין כְּדֵין כָּל גַּוְונִין מִתְתַּקְּנָן, וְאִתְהַפָּךְ גַּוֶון תְּכֵלָא לְגַוֶון אַחֲרָא. מִתְהַפָּךְ גַּוֶון יָרוֹק, לְגַוֶון זָהָב.

**483.** Rabbi Yitzchak said: This remark of my master that blue is the Throne of Judgment, and when MALCHUT has this color, it is then a throne to judge on it capital law, ACCORDING TO THIS, when is MALCHUT in Mercy? He said to him: When the Cherubs, WHICH ARE THE SECRET OF MALE AND FEMALE, turn their faces to each other and look face to face, all the colors are improved and the color blue turns into another color. The color green also turns into the color gold.

484. וְעַל דָּא, בְּהִפּוּכָא דְּגַוְונִין, אִתְהַפָּךְ מִדִּינָא לְרַחֲמֵי, וְכֵן מֵרַחֲמֵי לְדִינָא, וְכֹלָּא בְּהִפּוּכָא דְּגַוְונִין. כְּמָה דִּמְסַדְּרִין יִשְׂרָאֵל תִּקּוּנַיְיהוּ לְגַבֵּי קוּדְשָׁא בְּרִיךְ הוּא, הָכִי קַיְימָא כֹּלָּא, וְהָכִי אִתְסַדָּר. וְעַל דָּא כְּתִיב יִשְׂרָאֵל אֲשֶׁר בְּךָ אֶתְפָּאָר, בְּאִינוּן גַּוְונִין דִּכְלִילָן דָּא בְּדָא, שַׁפִּירוּ דְּכֻלְּהוּ.

**484.** When the colors are changed, MALCHUT then changes from Judgment to Mercy and from Mercy to Judgment, all according to the changing of the colors. As the children of Yisrael arrange themselves before the Holy One, blessed be He, so is everything arranged, and so is it set ABOVE. Therefore, it is written: "Yisrael, in whom I will be glorified" (Yeshayah 49:3), for in these colors included one within the other IS the beauty of everything.

## 45. "You shall make a table"

### A Synopsis

Rabbi Yitzchak begins here by explaining that as long as the children of Yisrael were in the Holy Land, they derived their sustenance from a high place, and all the leftovers were sufficient to nourish the rest of the world. But when they were sent into exile, they themselves received only the remnants. Leftovers are given only to dogs and servants, which is exactly what the children of Yisrael have become like in their exile. Next, Rabbi Chiya, Rabbi Shimon, Rabbi Ya'akov (son of Idi) and Rabbi Yesa Junior are traveling, and while they travel they wonder about the meaning of, "But show loyal love to the sons of Barzillay the Giladite, and let them be of those that eat at your table." Rabbi Yesa Junior, the youngest of them, explains the meaning of, "Who gives bread to all flesh: for His steadfast love endures forever." He draws parallels between the brain, the heart and the liver, and Binah, Zeir Anpin and Malchut, and he goes on to speak of how nourishment is sent back and forth between them. Then he mentions the sources of the body as the three worlds Binah, Yetzirah and Asiyah. He explains that, "For he did eat continually at the table of the king" means that all his sustenance and food came from there. Finally, Rabbi Yesa blesses their small meal as they sit down to eat.

### The Relevance of this Passage

As we read this passage, we must ask ourselves: "At whose table are we sitting, and from whom are we deriving our spiritual sustenance?" If it is not from God, then it will never nourish our souls as they need and deserve. If our meals are not blessed with His presence, they are only fit for dogs. Yet if they do derive from God, we shall find ourselves ever-growing in the wisdom that can only come from the Creator. Awareness of this truth emerges in our consciousness. In turn, sustenance, livelihood, and spiritual nourishment flow to us in great abundance, bringing blessings to all mankind.

485. וְעָשִׂיתָ שֻׁלְחָן עֲצֵי שִׁטִּים וְגוֹ'. רַבִּי יִצְחָק פָּתַח, וְאָכַלְתָּ וְשָׂבְעָתָּ וּבֵרַכְתָּ אֶת יְיָ' אֱלֹהֶיךָ וְגוֹ', כַּמָּה זַכָּאִין אִינּוּן יִשְׂרָאֵל, דְּקוּדְשָׁא בְּרִיךְ הוּא אִתְרָעֵי בְּהוּ, וְקָרִיב לוֹן לְגַבֵּיהּ מִכָּל עַמִּין, וּבְגִינֵיהוֹן דְּיִשְׂרָאֵל, יָהִיב מְזוֹנָא וְשָׂבְעָא, לְכָל עָלְמָא, וְאִלְמָלֵא יִשְׂרָאֵל לָא יָהִיב קוּדְשָׁא בְּרִיךְ הוּא מְזוֹנָא לְעָלְמָא, וְהַשְׁתָּא דְּיִשְׂרָאֵל אִינּוּן בְּגָלוּתָא, עאכ"ו דְּנַטְלֵי מְזוֹנָא עַל חַד תְּרֵין.

**485.** "You shall make a table of acacia wood…" (Shemot 25:23). Rabbi Yitzchak opened the discussion saying: "When you have eaten and are replete, then you shall bless Hashem your Elohim…" (Devarim 8:10). How fortunate are Yisrael that the Holy One, blessed be He, favors them and brings them close to Him from among all the nations. Because of them, He gives His sustenance and satisfies the whole world. If it were not for Yisrael, the Holy One, blessed be He, would not give sustenance to the world. Now that they are in exile, surely the whole world receives SUSTENANCE doubly, IN ORDER THAT THE REMAINS SHOULD SUFFICE FOR YISRAEL.

486. בְּזִמְנָא דַּהֲווֹ יִשְׂרָאֵל בְּאַרְעָא קַדִּישָׁא, הֲוָה נָחִית לוֹן מְזוֹנָא מֵאֲתָר עִלָּאָה, וְאִינּוּן יָהֲבֵי חוֹלָק תַּמְצִית לְעַמִּין עוֹבְדֵי כּוֹכָבִים, וְעַמִּין כֻּלְּהוּ לָא אִתְזָנוּ אֶלָּא מִתַּמְצִית וְהַשְׁתָּא דְּיִשְׂרָאֵל אִינּוּן בְּגָלוּתָא, אִתְהַפַּךְ בְּגַוְונָא אַחֲרָא.

**486.** As long as Yisrael were in the Holy Land, sustenance would descend to them from a high place, and they would give a portion of the remnants to the idol worshipping peoples. All the nations were sustained only from the remnants. But now that they are in exile, the situation has changed into a different manner. THE SUSTENANCE REACHES THE NATIONS OF THE WORLD, AND THEY RECEIVE THE REMNANTS FROM THEM.

487. מָתַל לְמַלְכָּא, דְּאַתְקִין סְעוּדָתָא לִבְנֵי בֵּיתֵיהּ, כָּל זִמְנָא דְּאִינּוּן עַבְדֵי רְעוּתֵיהּ, אַכְלֵי סְעוּדָתָא עִם מַלְכָּא, וְיָהֲבֵי לְכַלְבֵּי חוּלָק גַּרְמִין לְמִגְרַר. בְּשַׁעֲתָא דִּבְנֵי בֵּיתֵיהּ לָא עַבְדֵי רְעוּתָא דְּמַלְכָּא, מַלְכָּא יָהִיב כָּל סְעוּדָתָא לְכַלְבֵּי, וְסָלִיק לוֹן גַּרְמֵי.

**487.** For example, a king prepares a meal for his household. As long as they do his bidding, they eat together with the king, and they give the dogs a portion of bones to chew. But when the household does not do the bidding of the king, he gives the entire meal to the dogs, and he gives the bones to them.

488. כְּגַוְונָא דָּא, כָּל זִמְנָא דְּיִשְׂרָאֵל עַבְדֵי רְעוּתָא דְּמָארֵיהוֹן, הָא עַל פָּתוֹרָא דְּמַלְכָּא אִינּוּן אַכְלֵי, וְכָל סְעוּדָתָא אִתַּתְקַן לְהוֹן. וְאִינּוּן,

מֵהַהוּא חֶדְוָה דִּלְהוֹן, יָהֲבֵי גַּרְמֵי דְּאִיהוּ תַּמְצִית לְעוֹבְדֵי כּוֹכָבִים. וְכָל זִמְנָא דְּיִשְׂרָאֵל לָא עַבְדֵי רְעוּתָא דְּמָארֵיהוֹן, אַזְלֵי בְּגָלוּתָא, וְהָא סְעוּדָתָא לְכַלְבֵּי, וְאִסְתַּלַּק לוֹן תַּמְצִית כָּכָה יֵאכְלוּ בְּנֵי יִשְׂרָאֵל אֶת לַחְמָם טָמֵא בַּגּוֹיִם, דְּהָא תַּמְצִית דְּגִעוּלֵיהוֹן אַכְלֵי. וַוי לִבְרָא דְּמַלְכָּא, דְּיָתִיב וּמְצַפֶּה לְפָתוֹרָא דְּעַבְדָּא, מַה דְּאִשְׁתְּאַר מִגּוֹ פָּתוֹרָא אִיהוּ אָכִיל.

**488.** Similarly, as long as the children of Yisrael do the bidding of their Master, they eat at the table of the King and the entire meal is prepared for them. Because of their joy, they give the bones, which are the remains, to the idol worshippers. As long as the children of Yisrael are not doing the bidding of their Master, they go into exile and the meal is given to the dogs, while they are given the remains, AS IT IS WRITTEN: "Thus shall the children of Yisrael eat their bread, unclean, among the nations" (Yechezkel 4:13). They eat the remnants of their abhorrence, MEANING OF THEIR REPUGNANT FOOD. Woe is to the king's son who sits and waits at the table of the servant, and eats what is left of his table.

489. דָּוִד מַלְכָּא אָמַר, תַּעֲרֹךְ לְפָנַי שֻׁלְחָן נֶגֶד צוֹרְרָי דִּשַּׁנְתָּ בַשֶּׁמֶן רֹאשִׁי כּוֹסִי רְוָיָה. תַּעֲרֹךְ לְפָנַי שֻׁלְחָן, דָּא סְעוּדָתָא דְּמַלְכָּא. נֶגֶד צוֹרְרָי, אִינוּן כַּלְבֵּי דְּיַתְבֵי קַמֵּי פָּתוֹרָא, מְצַפָּאן לְחוּלָק גַּרְמִין, וְאִיהוּ יָתִיב עִם מַלְכָּא בְּעֲנוּגָא דִּסְעוּדָתָא בְּפָתוֹרָא.

**489.** King David said, "You prepare a table for me in the presence of my enemies: You anoint my head with oil; my cup runs over" (Tehilim 23:5). "You prepare a table for me," namely the King's meal, "in the presence of my enemies." They are the dogs that sit under the table and wait for the portion of bones, while he sits with the King at His table with the delight of the meal.

490. דִּשַּׁנְתָּ בַשֶּׁמֶן רֹאשִׁי, דָּא רֵישָׁא דִּסְעוּדָתָא, דְּכָל מִשְׁחָא, וְשַׁמְנוּנָא, וְתִקּוּן סְעוּדָתָא, אִתְיְיהִיב בְּקַדְמֵיתָא לִרְחִימָא דְּמַלְכָּא. מַה דְּאִשְׁתְּאַר, לְבָתַר אִתְיְיהִיב לְכַלְבֵּי, וּלְאִינוּן פַּלְחֵי פָּתוֹרָא. כּוֹסִי רְוָיָה,

מַלְיָא כַּסָּא קַמֵּי רְחִימָא דְּמַלְכָּא תָּדִיר, דְּלָא יִצְטְרִיךְ לְמִשְׁאַל. וְעַל רָזָא דָּא, הֲווֹ יִשְׂרָאֵל תָּדִיר, עִם שְׁאַר עַמִּין.

**490.** "You anoint my head with oil": This is the beginning (head) of the meal, for all the oil and fats and the prepared items of the meal are given at the beginning to the friend of the king. Whatever is left over is given afterwards to the dogs and those who serve at the table. "My cup runs over" means that the cup in front of the king's friend is always full and he does not have to request. Upon this secret, the children of Yisrael were consistently IN RELATION with the other nations.

**491.** רַבִּי חִיָּיא הֲוָה אָזִיל לְגַבֵּי דְּרַבִּי שִׁמְעוֹן לִטְבֶרְיָה, וַהֲווֹ עִמֵּיהּ רַבִּי יַעֲקֹב בַּר אִידִי, וְרַבִּי יֵיסָא זְעֵירָא, עַד דַּהֲווֹ אַזְלֵי, אָמַר רַבִּי יֵיסָא לְרַבִּי חִיָּיא, תֵּימָה מָה דִּכְתִּיב, וְלִבְנֵי בַרְזִלַּי הַגִּלְעָדִי תַּעֲשֶׂה חֶסֶד וְהָיוּ בְאוֹכְלֵי שֻׁלְחָנֶךָ וְגוֹ'. אִי הָכִי כָּל טִיבוּ וּקְשׁוֹט, לְמֵיכַל עַל פָּתוֹרֵיהּ וְלָא יַתִּיר, מִדְּקָאָמַר הָכָא וְהָיוּ בְאוֹכְלֵי שֻׁלְחָנֶךָ. וְתוּ, לָאו יְקָרָא דְּמַלְכָּא אִיהוּ, לְמֵיכַל בַּר נָשׁ אָחֳרָא עַל פָּתוֹרֵיהּ דְּמַלְכָּא, וְלָא אִצְטְרִיךְ דָּא, אֶלָּא מַלְכָּא בִּלְחוֹדוֹי, וְכֻלְּהוּ רַבְרְבָנוֹהִי סַחֲרָנֵיהּ, לְתַתָּא מִנֵּיהּ.

**491.** Rabbi Chiya went to Rabbi Shimon in Tiberias with Rabbi Ya'akov bar Idi, and Rabbi Yesa Junior. While they were still traveling, Rabbi Yesa said to Rabbi Chiya: I wonder about the words "But show loyal love to the sons of Barzillay the Giladite, and let them be of those that eat at your table…" (I Melachim 2:7). According to this, all the kindness and truthfulness means to eat at his table and no more, in accordance with the words, "and let them be of those that eat at your table." Also, it is not the honor of the king that someone else eats by his table. It should not be so, rather the king should eat alone and around him all his ministers that are lower than he.

**492.** אָמַר רַבִּי חִיָּיא לָא שְׁמַעְנָא בְּהַאי מִידִי, וְלָא אֵימָא. אֲמַר לְרַבִּי יַעֲקֹב בַּר אִידִי, וְאַתְּ שְׁמַעְתָּ בְּהַאי מִידִי. אֲמַר לֵיהּ, אַתּוּן דְּיָנְקִין בְּכָל יוֹמָא מִדִּבְשָׁא דְּמִשְׁחָא עִלָּאָה, לָא שְׁמַעְתּוּן, כָּל שֶׁכֵּן אֲנָא. אָמַר לֵיהּ לְרַבִּי יֵיסָא, וְאַתְּ שְׁמַעְתָּ מִידִי בְּהַאי. אֲמַר לֵיהּ אע"ג דַּאֲנָא רַבְיָא וּמִיּוֹמִין זְעֵירִין אֲתֵינָא לְגַבַּיְיכוּ, וְלָא זָכֵינָא מִקַּדְמַת דְּנָא, אֲנָא שְׁמַעְנָא.

**492.** Rabbi Chiya said: I have heard nothing about this matter and I make no comment. He said to Rabbi Ya'akov bar Idi, Did you hear anything about this matter? He said to him: You who nurture daily from the honey of the supernal oil, MEANING RABBI SHIMON, if you did not hear, of course I did not. He said to Rabbi Yesa: Did you hear anything about this matter? He said to him: Even though I am a youth, and it has only been a few days since I came to you and before that I had no merit, NONETHELESS I did hear.

493. פָּתַח וְאָמַר נוֹתֵן לֶחֶם לְכָל בָּשָׂר כִּי לְעוֹלָם חַסְדּוֹ. מַאי קָא חָמָא דָוִד דְּסִיּוּם הַלֵּלָא רַבָּא, סִיֵּים הָכִי בְּהַאי קְרָא. אֶלָּא תְּלַת שַׁלִּיטִין אִינּוּן לְעֵילָּא, דְּקוּדְשָׁא בְּרִיךְ הוּא אִשְׁתְּמוֹדְעָא בְּהוּ, וְאִינּוּן רָזָא יַקִּירָא דִּילֵיהּ, וְאִלֵּין אִינּוּן: מוֹחָא, וְלִבָּא, וְכַבְדָּא. וְאִינּוּן בְּהִפּוּכָא דְּהַאי עָלְמָא. לְעֵילָּא, מוֹחָא נָטִיל בְּרֵישָׁא, וּבָתַר יָהִיב לְלִבָּא, וְלִבָּא נָטִיל וְיָהִיב לְכַבְדָּא, וּלְבָתַר כַּבְדָּא יָהִיב חוּלָק לְכָל אִינּוּן מְקוֹרִין דִּלְתַתָּא, כָּל חַד וְחַד כַּדְקָא חֲזִי לֵיהּ. לְתַתָּא, כַּבְדָּא נָטִיל בְּרֵישָׁא, וּלְבָתַר אִיהוּ מְקָרֵב כֹּלָּא לְלִבָּא, וְנָטִיל לִבָּא שְׁפִירוּ דְּמֵיכְלָא. כֵּיוָן דְּנָטִיל, וְאִתְתְּקַף מֵהַהוּא תֵּקְפָּא וּרְעוּ דְּקָא נָטִיל, יָהִיב וְאִתְעַר לְגַבֵּי מוֹחָא. וּלְבָתַר אַהְדָּר כַּבְדָּא, וּפָלִיג מְזוֹנָא לְכָל מְקוֹרִין דְּגוּפָא.

**493.** He opened the discussion saying, "Who gives bread to all flesh: for His steadfast love endures forever" (Tehilim 136:25). HE QUESTIONS: What did David have in mind, that he concluded the great praise with this passage? HE ANSWERS: There are three rulers above through whom the Holy One, blessed be He, is known, and they are the mystery of His glory. They are the brain, the heart, and the liver, MEANING BINAH, ZEIR ANPIN, AND MALCHUT. They are opposite of this world, MEANING FROM THE ASPECT OF THE AWAKENING FROM BELOW THAT ASCENDS FROM THIS WORLD, AS DURING A FAST DAY OR THE LIKE, AS IT IS WRITTEN BEFORE US. Above, the brain receives first and afterwards gives to the heart. Then the heart takes and gives to the liver, and afterwards, the liver gives a portion to all the sources that are below, each one as is proper. Below, THROUGH THE AWAKENING FROM BELOW, the liver, WHICH IS MALCHUT, is first to awaken and later brings it near to the heart, BEING ZEIR ANPIN. The heart takes the best of the food and, after it has received and has become strengthened from the power and desire that it received, it

gives and brings awakening to the brain, WHICH IS BINAH. AND THEN THE SUPPLY IS PROJECTED FROM BINAH TO ZEIR ANPIN, AND FROM ZEIR ANPIN TO MALCHUT, WHICH IS THE LIVER. Afterwards, the liver again distributes sustenance to all the sources of the body, WHICH ARE THE THREE WORLDS BRIYAH, YETZIRAH, AND ASIYAH.

494. בְּיוֹמָא דְּתַעֲנִיתָא, בַּר נָשׁ מְקָרֵב מֵיכְלָא וּמִשְׁתַּיָּא לְגַבֵּי כַּבְדָּא עִלָּאָה, וּמַאי אִיהוּ מְקָרֵב. חֶלְבֵּיהּ וְדָמֵיהּ וּרְעוּתֵיהּ. הַהוּא כַּבְדָּא נָטִיל כֹּלָּא בִּרְעוּתָא. כֵּיוָן דְּכֹלָּא אִיהוּ לְגַבֵּיהּ, נָטִיל וּמְקָרֵב כֹּלָּא לְקֵמֵי לִבָּא, דְּאִיהוּ רַב וְשַׁלִּיט עָלֵיהּ. כֵּיוָן דְּלִבָּא נָטִיל וְאִתְתַּקַּף בִּרְעֲוָא, מְקָרֵב כֹּלָּא לְגַבֵּי מוֹחָא, דְּאִיהוּ שַׁלִּיטָא עִלָּאָה עַל כָּל גּוּפָא, לְבָתַר אַהֲדָר כַּבְדָּא וּמְפַלֵּג חוּלָקִין לְכָל אִינּוּן מְקוֹרִין וְשַׁיְיפִין דִּלְתַתָּא.

**494.** HE EXPLAINS HIS WORDS: On a fast day, man offers food and drink to the supernal liver, WHICH IS MALCHUT, and what does he offer? HE OFFERS his fat and blood and desires. That liver takes it all willingly. Once everything is already by it, it takes and offers it all to the heart, MEANING ZEIR ANPIN, who is superior and dominates it. After the heart has taken and becomes strengthened in will, it offers it all to the brain, WHICH IS BINAH, who is the highest ruler over the whole body THAT IS ZEIR ANPIN. THE SUPPLY RETURNS FROM BINAH TO ZEIR ANPIN AND FROM ZEIR ANPIN TO MALCHUT, WHICH IS LIVER, and afterwards the liver again divides portions to all the sources and limbs below IN BRIYAH, YETZIRAH, AND ASIYAH.

495. בְּזִמְנָא אָחֳרָא, כַּד כֹּלָּא מוֹחָא נָטִיל בְּקַדְמֵיתָא, וּלְבָתַר יָהִיב לְלִבָּא, וְלִבָּא יָהִיב לְכַבְדָּא, וְכַבְדָּא יָהִיב לְכֻלְּהוּ מְקוֹרִין וְשַׁיְיפִין דִּלְתַתָּא, וּלְבָתַר כַּד בָּעֵי לְפַלְגָּא מְזוֹנָא לְהַאי עָלְמָא, בְּרֵישָׁא יָהִיב לְלִבָּא, דְּאִיהוּ מַלְכָּא דִּי בְּאַרְעָא. וּפָתוֹרָא דְּמַלְכָּא, אִתְּעַר בְּקַדְמֵיתָא מִכָּל שְׁאַר בְּנֵי עָלְמָא. זַכָּאָה אִיהוּ, מַאן דְּהֲוֵי בְּחוּשְׁבְּנָא דְּפָתוֹרָא דְּמַלְכָּא, דְּהָא אִשְׁתְּמוֹדְעָא לְאוֹטָבָא לֵיהּ בְּהַהוּא טִיבוּ דִּלְעֵילָּא.

**495.** At a different time, MEANING WHEN THE SUPPLY IS BEING PROVIDED FROM THE SIDE OF AWAKENING FROM ABOVE, the brain first receives all supply, WHICH IS BINAH, from that which is higher than it, WHICH IS

CHOCHMAH. Afterwards, it gives to the heart, WHICH IS ZEIR ANPIN, and the heart gives to the liver, WHICH IS MALCHUT. And the liver gives to all the sources and limbs below, IN BRIYAH, YETZIRAH AND ASIYAH. Afterwards, when it wishes to distribute sustenance to this world, it gives first, MEANING THE CHOICEST AND BEST OF THE SUPPLY, to the heart, who is the king of the earth, NAMELY THE KING OF YISRAEL, and the king's table is stimulated to receive first the other people of the world. Blessed is he who is counted among those of the king's table, for he is recognized ABOVE to do him good with that goodness of above THAT THE KING RECEIVES.

496. וְדָא אִיהוּ טִיבוּ וּקְשׁוֹט, דַּעֲבַד דָּוִד לִבְנֵי בַרְזִילַי, דִּכְתִיב וְהָיוּ בְּאוֹכְלֵי שֻׁלְחָנֶךָ. וְאִי תֵּימָא דְּבְשֻׁלְחָנָא דְמַלְכָּא, אָכִיל בַּר נָשׁ אָחֳרָא בַּר מִנֵּיהּ. לָא. אֶלָּא מַלְכָּא אָכִיל בְּרֵישָׁא, וּבָתַר כָּל עַמָּא. וְאִינּוּן דְּאַכְלֵי עִם מַלְכָּא, בְּשַׁעֲתָא דְּאִיהוּ אָכִיל אִינּוּן דְּחָבִיבִין עֲלֵיהּ מִכֹּלְהוּ, וְאִינּוּן אִתְמְנוּן מִשֻּׁלְחָנָא דְמַלְכָּא.

496. This is kindness and truth that David did for the sons of Barzillay, as it is written: "And let them be of those that eat at your table." If you say at the king's table, another person eats besides him, it is not so. The king eats first, and afterwards all the people. And those who eat with the king during the time that he eats are the ones who are loved by him exceedingly. They are the ones who were appointed TO BE of the king's table.

497. וְאִי תֵּימָא, הָא כְּתִיב, עַל שֻׁלְחַן הַמֶּלֶךְ תָּמִיד הוּא אוֹכֵל. בְּגִין דְּכָל מְזוֹנָא דִּילֵיהּ, לָא עָבֵיד חוּשְׁבְּנָא אָחֳרָא, אֶלָּא עַל שֻׁלְחַן הַמֶּלֶךְ, דְּמִתַּמָּן הֲוָה אָתֵי מְזוֹנָא וּמֵיכְלָא דִּילֵיהּ. וְדָא אִיהוּ עַל שֻׁלְחַן הַמֶּלֶךְ תָּמִיד הוּא אוֹכֵל. אָתָא רַבִּי חִיָּיא, וּנְשָׁקֵיהּ עַל רֵישֵׁיהּ, אָמַר לֵיהּ רַבְיָא אַנְתְּ, וְחָכְמְתָא עִלָּאָה שַׁרְיָא בְּלִבָּךְ. אַדְּהָכִי, חָמוּ לֵיהּ לְרַבִּי חִזְקִיָּה דַּהֲוָה אָתֵי. אֲמַר לֵיהּ רַבִּי חִיָּיא, וַדַּאי בְּחַבְרוּתָא דָּא, קוּדְשָׁא בְּרִיךְ הוּא יִתְחַבַּר עֲלָנָא, דְּהָא מִלִּין חַדְתִּין דְּאוֹרַיְיתָא יִתְחַדְּתוּן הָכָא.

497. If you ask, Is it not written: "For he did eat continually at the table of the king" (II Shmuel 9:13)? SO IT SEEMS THAT HE ATE AT THE TABLE

ACTUALLY? HE ANSWERS: It is because all his food WAS INCLUDED AMONG THOSE WHO ATE AT THE KING'S TABLE, and he made no other reckoning but at the king's table, for his sustenance and food came from there. This is the meaning of: "For he did eat continually at the king's table." Rabbi Chiya came and kissed him on his head, and said to him: You are a youth, but supernal Wisdom dwells in you. In the meantime, they saw that Rabbi Hezekiah had come. Rabbi Chiya said to him: Certainly in this group will the Holy One, blessed be He, join with us, because new words in Torah will be promulgated here.

498. יָתְבוּ לְמֵיכַל. אָמְרוּ, כָּל חַד וְחַד לֵימָא מִלֵּי דְאוֹרַיְיתָא בְּהַאי סְעוּדָתָא, אָמַר רִבִּי יֵיסָא, סְעוּדַת עֲרַאי אִיהִי, וְעַכ״ד סְעוּדָה אִקְרֵי. וְלָא עוֹד, אֶלָּא דְּהַאי אִקְרֵי סְעוּדָתָא דְקוּדְשָׁא בְּרִיךְ הוּא אִתְהֲנֵי מִינָהּ. וְעַל דָּא כְּתִיב, זֶה הַשֻּׁלְחָן אֲשֶׁר לִפְנֵי יְיָ׳, דְּהָא מִלִּין דְּאוֹרַיְיתָא יְסַחֲרוּן לְהַאי אֲתָר.

498. They sat down to eat and said, let each of us say a word of Torah during this meal. Rabbi Yesa said: This is a small meal, but still in all it is called 'a meal'. Even more, this is called 'a meal' from which the Holy One, blessed be He, derives pleasure, as it is written: "This is the table that is before Hashem" (Yechezkel 41:22), because words of Torah surround this place.

## 46. "When you have eaten and are replete, then you shall bless"

### A Synopsis

Rabbi Chiya speaks here about, "And satisfies the desire of every living thing," indicating that the person who has eaten must bless God in order to give joy above. Rabbi Chizkiyah says that even one who is drunk may say the Blessing After a Meal, because the blessing is tied to satisfaction on this level, but a person who is drunk must not pray, because prayer rises higher, to that place where there is neither eating or drinking.

### The Relevance of this Passage

There is a link between our daily bread and our spiritual lives, which on this earthly level, feed each other constantly and interactively. The blessing of a meal awakens divine sparks of Light within the food so that we may nourish both our bodies and our souls. Otherwise, all we receive from the meals we eat is the one percent physical matter of the food. We miss out on the remaining 99 percent – the eternal spiritual nourishment. This passage extracts all the sparks of Light from all the foods eaten by man throughout time. Further, we are uplifted to the highest levels of the spiritual atmosphere, where the Light is so all-embracing that there is no need of food or drink.

499. פָּתַח רַבִּי חִיָּיא וְאָמַר, וְאָכַלְתָּ וְשָׂבָעְתָּ וּבֵרַכְתָּ אֶת יְיָ' אֱלֹהֶיךָ וְגוֹ'. וְכִי עַד לָא אָכִיל בַּר נָשׁ לְשָׂבְעָא, וְיִתְמְלֵי כְּרֵיסֵיהּ, לָא יְבָרֵךְ לֵיהּ לְקוּדְשָׁא בְּרִיךְ הוּא, בְּמַאי נוֹקִים וְאָכַלְתָּ וְשָׂבָעְתָּ, וּבָתַר וּבֵרַכְתָּ. אֶלָּא אֲפִילוּ לָא יֵיכוּל בַּר נָשׁ אֶלָּא כְּזַיִת, וּרְעוּתֵיהּ אִיהוּ עֲלֵיהּ, וְיִשַׁוֵּי לֵיהּ לְהַהוּא מֵיכְלָא עִקָּרָא דְּמֵיכְלֵיהּ, שָׂבְעָא אִקְרֵי. דִּכְתִיב פּוֹתֵחַ אֶת יָדֶךָ וּמַשְׂבִּיעַ לְכָל חַי רָצוֹן. לְכָל חַי אֲכִילָה לָא כְּתִיב, אֶלָּא רָצוֹן. הַהוּא רְעוּתָא דְּשַׁוֵּי עַל הַהוּא מֵיכְלָא, שָׂבְעָא אִקְרֵי, וַאֲפִילוּ דְּלֵית קַמֵּיהּ דְּבַר נָשׁ אֶלָּא הַהוּא זְעֵיר בִּכְזַיִת, וְלָא יַתִּיר הָא רְעוּתָא דְּשָׂבְעָא שַׁוֵּי עֲלֵיהּ. וּבְגִין כַּךְ, וּמַשְׂבִּיעַ לְכָל חַי רָצוֹן, רָצוֹן כְּתִיב, וְלָא אֲכִילָה. וְעַל דָּא וּבֵרַכְתָּ וַדַּאי, וְאִתְחַיָּיב בַּר נָשׁ לְבָרְכָא לֵיהּ לְקוּדְשָׁא בְּרִיךְ הוּא, בְּגִין לְמֵיהַב חֶדְוָה לְעֵילָּא.

499. Rabbi Chiya opened the discussion saying: "When you have eaten and are replete, then you shall bless Hashem your Elohim…" (Devarim 8:10).

-300-

HE QUESTIONS: Before a person eats to satisfaction and fills his stomach, should he not bless the Holy One, blessed be He? How are we to explain the passage: "When you have eaten and are replete" and afterwards, "then you shall bless"? HE ANSWERS: Even if a person eats as much as an olive but desires it, and he considers that eating to be his main food, then this is considered being sated, as it is written, "You open Your hand, and satisfies the desire of every living thing" (Tehilim 145:16). It is not written: 'The food of every living thing,' but rather "The desire of every living thing" TO TEACH that the desire he has for that food is called 'satisfaction'. Even if there is only a small thing in front of the person like an olive and no more, the desire for satiety has been put on it. It is therefore WRITTEN: "And satisfies the desire of every living thing." "Desire" is written and not 'food'. "Then you shall bless" certainly, for the person is obligated to bless the Holy One, blessed be He, in order to give joy above.

500. פָּתַח רַבִּי חִזְקִיָּה, בְּהַאי קְרָא אֲבַתְרֵיהּ וְאָמַר, וְאָכַלְתָּ וְשָׂבָעְתָּ. מֵהָכָא, דְּשִׁכּוֹר שָׁרֵי לֵיהּ לְבָרְכָא בִּרְכָתָא דִּמְזוֹנָא, מַה דְּלֵית הָכִי בִּצְלוֹתָא. דִּצְלוֹתָא לָאו הָכִי, דְּהָא צְלוֹתָא מְעַלְּיָא בְּלָא אֲכִילָה אִיהִי, מַאי טַעֲמָא, בְּגִין דִּצְלוֹתָא סַלְקָא לְעֵילָּא לְעֵילָּא, אֲתַר דְּלֵית בֵּיהּ לָא אֲכִילָה וְלָא שְׁתִיָּה. וְעַל דָּא תָּנֵינָן, עָלְמָא דְּאָתֵי לֵית בֵּיהּ אֲכִילָה וּשְׁתִיָּה וְכוּ'. אֲבָל שְׁאַר דַּרְגִּין דִּלְתַתָּא אִית.

500. After him, Rabbi Chizkiyah opened the discussion with the passage: "When you have eaten and are replete." From here, IT IS UNDERSTOOD that one who is drunk may say the Blessing After a Meal, which is not so pertaining to prayer, for prayer is not so. AND ONE WHO IS DRUNK IS PROHIBITED TO PRAY, because prayer is good without eating. What is the reason? It is because the prayer rises higher, higher to the place where there is neither eating nor drinking, MEANING TO BINAH. Pertaining to this, we learned that there is no eating or drinking in the World to Come, but there is EATING AND DRINKING in the other levels below.

501. בְּבִרְכַּת מְזוֹנָא, אִשְׁתְּכַח גַּוְונָא אַחֲרָא וּמְעַלְּיָא, הַהוּא בִּרְכָתָא דְּאִשְׁתְּכַח בְּשַׂבְעָא. בְּגִין דְּבִרְכַּת מְזוֹנָא, אִיהִי בַּאֲתַר דְּאִית בֵּיהּ אֲכִילָה וּשְׁתִיָּה, וּמִנֵּיהּ נָפַק מְזוֹנָא וְשַׂבְעָא לְתַתָּא, וְעַל דָּא אִצְטְרִיךְ

לְאַחֲזָאָה קָמֵיהּ שָׂבְעָא וְחֶדְוָוה. בַּאֲתַר דִּצְלוֹתָא, לָאו הָכִי, דְּהָא סַלְּקָא
יַתִּיר לְעֵילָא לְעֵילָא וְעַל דָּא, שִׁכּוֹר לָא יְצַלֵי צְלוֹתָא.

**501.** In the blessing after the meal, another method applies; NAMELY, the blessing is tied to satisfaction, since the blessing after food abides where there is food and drink, NAMELY MALCHUT, so it is necessary to show before Him satisfaction and joy. BUT where prayer goes, it is not so, as it ascends higher and higher TO BINAH, where there is no food or drink. So, a drunk man must not pray.

**502.** בְּבִרְכַּת מְזוֹנָא, שִׁכּוֹר שָׁרֵי לֵיהּ לְבָרְכָא בִּרְכַּת מְזוֹנָא. מַשְׁמַע
מֵהַאי קְרָא, דִּכְתִּיב וְאָכַלְתָּ וְשָׂבָעְתָּ וּבֵרַכְתָּ. וְאָכַלְתָּ: זוֹ אֲכִילָה.
וְשָׂבָעְתָּ: זוֹ שְׁתִיָּה דְּהָא שָׂבְעָא, בְּחַמְרָא אִיהִי רְוֵי. חַמְרָא שָׂבְעָא וַדַּאי,
וְדָא אִיהוּ שִׁכּוֹר. דִּכְתִּיב וּבֵרַכְתָּ אֶת דַּיְיקָא, דְּמַשְׁמַע דְּבִרְכַּת מְזוֹנָא
אִצְטְרִיךְ חֶדְוָוה וְשָׂבְעָא. עַל הָאָרֶץ הַטּוֹבָה. מַאי טוֹבָה. שָׂבְעָא. כד"א,
וַנִּשְׂבַּע לֶחֶם וַנִּהְיֶה טוֹבִים בְּגִין כָּךְ אִצְטְרִיךְ חֶדְוָוה וְשָׂבְעָא.

**502.** By the Blessing After a Meal, a drunk person may recite the Blessing After a Meal, as is understood from this passage: "When you have eaten and are replete, then you shall bless." "When you have eaten" refers to eating, "and are replete" refers to drinking, as satiety is with wine, because WITH WINE he becomes sated. In wine, there is certainly satiety and this refers to the drunk, as it is written: "Then you shall bless HASHEM YOUR ELOHIM." Et (the) is precise, FOR IT ALLUDES TO MALCHUT THAT IS CALLED 'ET (THE)', THAT CONTAINS BOTH EATING AND DRINKING. From this, we understand that the Blessing After a Meal requires joy and satisfaction, BECAUSE IT IS WRITTEN: "For the good land" (Devarim 8:10). What is the meaning of 'good'? Satisfaction, as it is written: "For then we had plenty of bread, and were well off" (Yirmeyah 44:17), so it requires joy and satisfaction.

## 47. "You shall make a table," part two

### A Synopsis

Rabbi Yesa begins this discussion by explaining that the table of acacia wood spoken of in scripture stands inside the Tabernacle and should never be left empty of food, even for a moment. This is because blessing and food come out to all the other tables of the world, which are therefore blessed because of it. The table that is set above, we are told, always has the words of Torah spoken over it, and a table that is not blessed by the words of Torah is unclean. Rabbi Yesa next tells us that a happy person is one who has two things on his table: the words of Torah, and a portion of food for the poor. The person can be called 'happy' because he gains great merit from these things. Rabbi Jacob then speaks about Saul, who was chosen for kingship but not for prophecy, since the two gifts are never given together, except in the case of Moses, who alone merited both titles. Samuel, we are told, seemed to merit both titles, too, however, yet he was only a prophet and judge, and this was why the children of Yisrael requested a king. Since kingship settles only upon arousal of the Holy Spirit, we learn, Saul had no prophecy when he ascended to kingship. He had only the awakening of the spirit of understanding with which to execute a true Judgment. As long as he was among the prophets, the prophecy dwelled upon him, but not afterward. Rabbi Jacob next speaks about the table being more important than the bread on it, comparing the table, as the root from which bread can also be said to emerge, to the world, which gives forth plants and fruit and food. He explains why the table is placed on the left, or north, side. The text then speaks of the cleanliness of the body and the intestines, of the need to give the dirty finger bowl water to the Other Side. We learn that the secret of the shew-bread is the twelve faces that are in Zeir Anpin. It is Malchut that draws out food and sustenance from those internal faces.

Rabbi Elazar next tells how God created every person in the similitude of supernal glory. The glory of below was constructed above only by the righteous actions of the people of this world, we learn. The rabbi speaks of the 32 paths of Chochmah and Glory, the three levels of spirit, and the three worlds. The supernal glory, we are told, has within it Briyah, Yetzirah, Asiyah, and so does Man here below. "Let your garments be always white, and let your head lack no oil," means that oil of anointing will never be withheld from Man, for his actions are constantly being whitened. Finally, we hear that a person merits delight in the supernal Eden by giving delight to the souls of the poor through the food upon his table.

### The Relevance of this Passage

Supernal blessings fall upon the tables of all mankind as our eyes fall upon this rich passage. Our thought to share the blessings from this Book of Splendor with the impoverished, at last, removes poverty from the landscape of human civilization while it warms the hearts of the destitute. The Light of prophecy and kingship illumines our souls, elevating our consciousness so that we foresee the future consequences of all our present actions. We receive wisdom to judge others with compassion, with decency, with the sweetest mercy. We acquire courage to judge ourselves with truthfulness and stringency. Finally, sustenance and livelihood come to our world through the words of wisdom that adorn this passage. Poverty is vanquished from our midst and all the world experiences the delights of the supernal Eden.

503. פָּתַח רַבִּי יֵיסָא וְאָמַר וְעָשִׂיתָ שֻׁלְחָן עֲצֵי שִׁטִּים וְגוֹ', שֻׁלְחָן דָּא אִיהוּ קַיְימָא לְגוֹ בְּמַשְׁכְּנָא, וּבִרְכָתָא דִּלְעֵילָּא שַׁרְיָא עֲלֵיהּ, וּמִנֵּיהּ נָפִיק מְזוֹנָא לְכָל עָלְמָא. וְשֻׁלְחָן דָּא לָא אִצְטְרִיךְ לְמֶהֱוֵי בְּרֵיקַנְיָא, אֲפִילוּ רִגְעָא חֲדָא, אֶלָּא לְמֶהֱוֵי עֲלֵיהּ מְזוֹנָא, דְּהָא בִּרְכָתָא לָא אִשְׁתְּכַח עַל אֲתָר רֵיקַנְיָא. וּבְגִין כַּךְ אִצְטְרִיךְ לְמֶהֱוֵי עֲלֵיהּ נַהֲמָא תָּדִיר, דְּלֶהֱוֵי תָּדִיר בִּרְכָתָא עִלָּאָה מִשְׁתַּכְּחָא בֵּיהּ, וּמִגּוֹ הַהוּא שֻׁלְחָן, נַפְקֵי בִּרְכָּאן וּמְזוֹנֵי לְכָל שְׁאַר פָּתוֹרֵי דְּעָלְמָא, דְּאִתְבָּרְכָאן בְּגִינֵיהּ.

503. Rabbi Yesa opened the discussion saying: "You shall make a table of acacia wood…" (Shemot 25:23): This table stands inside the Tabernacle and a supernal blessing dwells upon it. From it emerges food for the whole word, and this table should not be empty even for one moment. There should be food on it, because the blessing is not present in an empty place. Therefore, bread must constantly be on it, in order that the supernal blessing shall always be present in it. And from that table, blessing and food come out to all the other tables of the world, that are blessed due to it.

504. שֻׁלְחָן דְּכָל בַּר נָשׁ אִצְטְרִיךְ לְמֶהֱוֵי הָכִי קַמֵּיהּ, בְּשַׁעֲתָא דְּקָא מְבָרֵךְ לֵיהּ לְקוּדְשָׁא בְּרִיךְ הוּא, בְּגִין דְּתִשְׁרֵי עֲלֵיהּ בִּרְכָתָא מִלְּעֵילָּא, וְלָא יִתְחֲזֵי בְּרֵיקַנְיָא, דְּהָא בִּרְכָּאן דִּלְעֵילָּא לָא שַׁרְיָין בְּאֲתָר רֵיקַנְיָא, דִּכְתִּיב הַגִּידִי לִי מַה יֶּשׁ לָכִי בַּבָּיִת, וְהָא אוּקְמוּהָ חַבְרַיָּיא.

504. The table of every person has to be so before him at the time that he

blesses the Holy One, blessed be He, in order that the blessing from above should dwell upon it and should not appear empty. For the blessings from above do not dwell in an empty place, as it is written: "Tell me, what have you in the house" (II Melachim 4:2), which the friends have already established.

505. שֻׁלְחָן דְּלָא אִתְּמַר עָלֵיהּ מִלֵּי דְּאוֹרַיְיתָא, עָלֵיהּ כְּתִיב, כִּי כָּל שֻׁלְחָנוֹת מָלְאוּ קִיא צוֹאָה בְּלִי מָקוֹם. וְאָסוּר לְבָרְכָא עַל הַהוּא שֻׁלְחָן. מ"ט. בְּגִין דְּאִית שֻׁלְחָן, וְאִית שֻׁלְחָן. שֻׁלְחָן אִיהוּ דְּקָא מְסַדְּרָא קַמֵּיהּ דְּקוּדְשָׁא בְּרִיךְ הוּא לְעֵילָא, וְאִיהוּ קַיְּימָא תָּדִיר לְסַדְּרָא בֵּיהּ פִּתְגָּמֵי אוֹרַיְיתָא, וּלְאַכְלְלָא בֵּיהּ אַתְוָון דְּמִלֵּי דְּאוֹרַיְיתָא, וְאִיהוּ לָקִיט לוֹן לְגַבֵּיהּ, וְכָלִיל כֹּלְּהוּ בְּגַוֵּיהּ, וּבְהוּ אַשְׁתְּלִים, וְחַדֵּי, וְאִית לֵיהּ חֶדְוָה. וְעַל שֻׁלְחָן דָּא כְּתִיב, זֶה הַשֻּׁלְחָן אֲשֶׁר לִפְנֵי יְיָ', לִפְנֵי יְיָ', וְלָא מִלִּפְנֵי יְיָ'.

505. Of a table upon which words of Torah were not spoken, and it is written: "For all tables are full of vomit and filth, so that there is no place clean" (Yeshayah 28:8). It is forbidden to bless over such a table. What is the reason? Because there is a table and there is a table. THERE IS A table that is set above, WHICH IS MALCHUT, before the Holy One, blessed be He, and it is always ready so that words of Torah may be spoken on it, and it should include letters of the words of Torah. It gathers them unto the Holy One, blessed be He, above, who includes all of them in Himself and becomes perfected through them, and He is happy and has joy. About this table, it is written: "This is the table that is before Hashem" (Yechezkel 41:22), WHICH IS MALCHUT and not 'from before Hashem,' WHICH IS FROM ABOVE ZEIR ANPIN, WHICH IS BINAH.

506 שֻׁלְחָן אָחֳרָא אִית, דְּלָא אִית בֵּיהּ חוּלְקָא דְּאוֹרַיְיתָא, וְלֵית לֵיהּ חוּלְקָא בִּקְדוּשָׁה דְּאוֹרַיְיתָא, וְהַהוּא שֻׁלְחָן אִקְרֵי קִיא צוֹאָה, וְדָא אִיהוּ בְּלִי מָקוֹם, דְּלֵית לֵיהּ חוּלְקָא בְּסִטְרָא דִּקְדוּשָׁה כְּלוּם. בְּגִין כָּךְ, שֻׁלְחָן דְּלָא אִתְּמַר עָלֵיהּ מִלֵּי דְּאוֹרַיְיתָא, אִיהוּ שֻׁלְחָן דְּקִיא צוֹאָה. אִיהוּ שֻׁלְחָן דְּטַעֲוָא אָחֳרָא. לֵית בְּהַהוּא שֻׁלְחָן חוּלְקָא בְּרָזָא דֶּאֱלָהָא עִלָּאָה.

506. There is another table that has no part in Torah and has no part in the

holiness of Torah, NAMELY MALCHUT OF KLIPOT, and that table is called 'vomit and filth'. "There is no place," since it has no part in the side of holiness at all. Therefore, a table upon which no words of Torah were said, is a table of vomit and filth, and this is a table of another deity. This table has no part in the secret of Supernal El.

507. שֻׁלְחָן דְּמִלֵי אוֹרַיְיתָא אִתְּמָרוּ עָלֵיהּ, קוּדְשָׁא בְּרִיךְ הוּא נָטִיל הַהוּא שֻׁלְחָן, וְשַׁוֵּי לֵיהּ לְחוּלְקֵיהּ. וְלָא עוֹד, אֶלָּא סוּרְיָ"א רַב מְמָנָא, נָטִיל כָּל אִינּוּן מִלִּין, וְשַׁוֵּי דִּיּוּקְנָא דְּהַהוּא שֻׁלְחָן קַמֵּי קוּדְשָׁא בְּרִיךְ הוּא. וְכָל אִינּוּן מִלִּין דְּאוֹרַיְיתָא דְּאִתְּמָרוּ עָלֵיהּ, סַלְּקִין עַל הַהוּא פָּתוֹרָא, וְאִתְעַטָּר קַמֵּי מַלְכָּא קַדִּישָׁא. מַשְׁמַע דִּכְתִיב זֶה הַשֻּׁלְחָן אֲשֶׁר לִפְנֵי יְיָ' דְּאִתְעַטָּר קַמֵּי קוּדְשָׁא בְּרִיךְ הוּא. שֻׁלְחָן דְּבַר נָשׁ, קַיְּימָא לְדַכְּאָה לֵיהּ לְבַר נָשׁ, מִכָּל חוֹבוֹי.

507. The Holy One, blessed be He, takes a table upon which were said words of Torah, and places it in His portion. Surya, the appointed prince, takes all these words and places the image of that table before the Holy One, blessed be He. All the words of Torah that were said on it come over that table, and it is adorned before the Holy King. This is understood from what is written: "This is the table that is before Hashem," meaning that it is adorned before the Holy One, blessed be He. The table of a person exists to purify the person from all his sins.

508. זַכָּאָה אִיהוּ, מַאן דְּאִלֵּין תְּרֵין קַיְימִין עַל פָּתוֹרֵיהּ. מִלֵּי דְּאוֹרַיְיתָא. וְחוּלְקָא לְמִסְכְּנִין, מֵהַהוּא שֻׁלְחָן. כַּד סַלְּקִין הַהוּא פָּתוֹרָא מִקַּמֵּיהּ דְּבַר נָשׁ, תְּרֵין מַלְאָכִין קַדִּישִׁין אִזְדַּמְנָן תַּמָּן, חַד מִימִינָא, וְחַד מִשְּׂמָאלָא. חַד אָמַר דָּא אִיהוּ שֻׁלְחָן דְּמַלְכָּא קַדִּישָׁא, דִּפְלַנְיָא קָא מְסַדֵּר קָמֵיהּ, מְסַדֵּר יְהֵא תָּדִיר פָּתוֹרָא דָּא, בְּבִרְכָּאן עִלָּאִין, וּמִשְׁחָא וּרְבוּ עִלָּאָה, קוּדְשָׁא בְּרִיךְ הוּא יִשְׁרֵי עֲלוֹי. וְחַד אָמַר, דָּא אִיהוּ שֻׁלְחָן דְּמַלְכָּא קַדִּישָׁא, דִּפְלַנְיָא קָא מְסַדֵּר קָמֵיהּ, דָּא פָּתוֹרָא דִּי עִלָּאֵי וְתַתָּאֵי יְבָרְכוּן לֵיהּ, מְסַדֵּר יְהֵא הַאי פָּתוֹרָא קַמֵּי עַתִּיק יוֹמִין, בְּהַאי עָלְמָא, וּבְעָלְמָא דְּאָתֵי.

**508.** Happy is he who has these two things present on his table: 1) words of Torah and 2) a portion for the poor from that table. When they elevate that table before the person, two holy angels are waiting there, one on the right and one on the left. One says: This is the table of the Holy King that so-and-so arranged before Him, and it shall be set with supernal blessings and supernal oil and supernal greatness, which the Holy One, blessed be He, causes to dwell upon it. And the other ANGEL says: This is the table of the Holy King that so-and-so set before Him, which is a table that those of above and those of below bless. This table shall be set before Atik Yomin in this world and in the World to Come.

509. ר' אַבָּא, כַּד הֲוָה סַלְקִין פָּתוֹרָא מִקַּמֵּיה, הֲוָה חָפֵי לֵיהּ, וַהֲוָה אָמַר סְלִיקוּ הַאי פָּתוֹרָא בִּצְנִיעוּ, דְּלָא יְהֵא בְּכִסּוּפָא קַמֵּי שְׁלוּחֵי מַלְכָּא. שֻׁלְחָן דְּבַר נָשׁ זָכֵי לֵיהּ לְעָלְמָא דְּאָתֵי, וְזָכֵי לֵיהּ לִמְזוֹנָא דְּהַאי עָלְמָא, וְזָכֵי לֵיהּ לְאִשְׁתְּמוֹדְעָא לְטָב קַמֵּי עַתִּיק יוֹמִין, וְזָכֵי לֵיהּ לְאִתּוֹסְפָא חֵילָא וְרִבּוּ בַּאֲתָר דְּאִצְטְרִיךְ. זַכָּאָה אִיהוּ חוּלָקֵיהּ דְּהַהוּא בַּר נָשׁ, בְּהַאי עָלְמָא וּבְעָלְמָא דְּאָתֵי.

**509.** Rabbi Aba said: They would remove the table from before him and cover it, and would say, Remove it modestly so it should not be embarrassed before the messengers of the King. The table of a person gives him merit in the World to Come and attains him food in this world. It merits him to be known for good before Atik Yomin and merits him to add strength and greatness where necessary. Happy is the portion of that man in this world and in the World to Come.

510. רַבִּי יַעֲקֹב אָמַר, כְּתִיב וַיְהִי כָּל יוֹדְעוֹ מֵאִתְּמוֹל שִׁלְשֹׁם וְגוֹ', הֲגַם שָׁאוּל בַּנְּבִיאִים. וְכִי שָׁאוּל בְּחִיר יְיָ' מִקַּדְמַת דְּנָא הֲוָה, דִּכְתִיב, הַרְּאִיתֶם אֲשֶׁר בָּחַר בּוֹ יְיָ', אֲשֶׁר בּוֹחֵר בּוֹ לָא כְּתִיב, אֶלָּא אֲשֶׁר בָּחַר בּוֹ מִקַּדְמַת דְּנָא. וּבְשַׁעֲתָא דְּאָתָא וְעָאל בֵּין נְבִיאֵי וְאִתְנַבֵּי בֵּינַיְיהוּ, אֲמַאי תַּוְוהוּ.

**510.** Rabbi Ya'akov said: It is written, "And it came to pass, when all that knew him before time...Is Saul also one of the prophets" (I Shmuel 10:11). HE QUESTIONS: Saul was chosen by Hashem before this, for it is written,

"Do you see him whom Hashem has chosen?" (Ibid. 24). It is not written: 'chooses', but rather "has chosen," MEANING before now. When he came and entered among the prophets and prophesied among them, why were they surprised?

511. אֶלָּא, כַּד קוּדְשָׁא בְּרִיךְ הוּא אִתְרְעֵי בֵּיה, לָא אִתְרְעֵי בֵּיה אֶלָּא לְמַלְכוּ, אֲבָל לִנְבוּאָה לא. דְּהָא תְּרֵין אִלֵּין, לָא אִתְמְסָרוּ כַּחֲדָא בְּבַר נָשׁ בְּעָלְמָא, בַּר מֹשֶׁה מְהֵימָנָא עִלָּאָה, דְּזָכָה לִנְבוּאָה וּמַלְכוּ כַּחֲדָא, וְלָא אִתְיְהִיב לְבַר נָשׁ אָחֳרָא תַּרְוַויְיהוּ כַּחֲדָא.

511. HE ANSWERS: When the Holy One, blessed be He, selected him, it was only for kingship and not for prophecy, for these two together were never given to one person in the world, except for Moses, the supernal faithful, who merited prophecy and kingship together. They were not given to any other person, both together.

512. וְאִי תֵּימָא, הָא שְׁמוּאֵל דְּזָכָה לְתַרְוַויְיהוּ, לִנְבוּאָה וּמַלְכוּ. לָאו הָכִי. לִנְבוּאָה זָכָה, דִּכְתִּיב וַיֵּדַע כָּל יִשְׂרָאֵל מִדָּן וְעַד בְּאֵר שָׁבַע כִּי נֶאֱמָן שְׁמוּאֵל לְנָבִיא. לְנָבִיא וְלָא לְמֶלֶךְ, דְּאִי מֶלֶךְ הֲוָה, לָא שָׁאֲלוּ יִשְׂרָאֵל מֶלֶךְ. אֲבָל אִיהוּ לָא הֲוָה אֶלָּא נְבִיאָה מְהֵימָנָא, וַהֲוָה דָּאִין דִּינְהוֹן דְּיִשְׂרָאֵל, דִּכְתִּיב וְשָׁפַט אֶת יִשְׂרָאֵל. וְע"ד כַּד הֲוָה שָׁאוּל בִּנְבוּאָה, תַּוְוהוּ עֲלֵיה.

512. And if you ask: There was Samuel, who merited both prophecy and kingship. It is not so. Samuel merited prophecy, as it is written: "And all Yisrael from Dan to Be'er Sheva knew that Samuel was accredited as a prophet" (I Shmuel 3:20), as a prophet but not as a king. He was a prophet and judge, for had he been a king, Yisrael would not have requested a king. He was only a faithful prophet, and he judged the sentence of Yisrael, as it is written: "He judged Yisrael" (I Shmuel 7:17). Therefore, when Saul was in prophecy, they were surprised about him.

513. וְאִי תֵּימָא, אֲמַאי שָׁרָא עֲלֵיה נְבוּאָה, הוֹאִיל וְזָכָה לְמַלְכוּ. אֶלָּא תַּרְוַויְיהוּ לָא זָכָה בְּהוּ כַּחֲדָא. וּבְגִין דְּמַלְכוּ אִתְיְשַׁב עַל אִתְעֲרוּתָא

דְּרוּחַ קַדְשָׁא, הֲוָה בְּאִתְעָרוּ דִּנְבוּאָה קֹדֶם לָכֵן. אֲבָל כַּד סָלִיק לְמַלְכוּ,
לָא הֲוָה בֵּיהּ נְבוּאָה, אֶלָּא אִתְּעָרוּ דְּרוּחַ סׇכְלְתָנוּ, לְמֶֽעְדָּן קְשׁוֹט, אִתְּעַר
עֲלֵיהּ, דְּהָכִי אִתְחֲזֵי לְמַלְכָּא. וּבְעוֹד דַּהֲוָה גּוֹ אִינּוּן נְבִיאֵי, שָׁרָא עֲלֵיהּ
נְבוּאָה, לְבָתַר דְּאִתְפְּרַשׁ מִנַּיְיהוּ, לָא הֲוָה בֵּיהּ נְבוּאָה.

**513.** If you ask: Why did Saul merit prophecy since he already merited kingship? HE ANSWERS: He did not merit them both together, because the kingship settles ONLY upon the awakening of the Holy Spirit, BUT NOT PROPHECY; THEREFORE, he had the waakening of prophecy beforehand. When he ascended to kingship, he had no prophecy, just an awakening of the spirit of understanding with which to execute a true judgment was upon him, for this is fitting for a king. As long as he was among the prophets, the prophecy dwelt upon him, but after he left them, he had no prophecy.

**514.** וַאֲנָא, מַאן יָהִיב לִי אִתְעָרוּתָא דְּרוּחַ קַדְשָׁא, לְמֶהֱוֵי בְּגוֹ נְבִיאֵי
מְהֵימְנֵי, תַּלְמִידֵי דְּרַבִּי שִׁמְעוֹן בֶּן יוֹחַאי, דְּעֶלָּאִין וְתַתָּאִין זָעִין מִנֵּיהּ,
כ״שׁ אֲנָא, לְמֶהֱוֵי בֵּינַיְיכוּ.

**514.** And I, SAID RABBI YA'AKOV BAR IDI, who has awakened in me the Holy Spirit, to be among faithful prophets, the disciples of Rabbi Shimon, that the higher and lower beings tremble before him, and all the more so I MERITED to be among you.

**515.** פָּתַח וְאָמַר, וְעָשִׂיתָ שֻׁלְחָן וְגוֹ׳. שֻׁלְחָן דָּא אִיהוּ לְתַתָּא, לְשַׁוָּאָה
עֲלֵיהּ לֶחֶם דְּאַפְּיָא מַאן עָדִיף דָּא מִן דָּא, לֶחֶם אוֹ שֻׁלְחָן. אִי תֵּימָא
דְּכֹלָּא אִיהוּ חַד. הָא שֻׁלְחָן מִתְסַדְּרָא לְגַבֵּי הַהוּא לֶחֶם. וְתוּ, שֻׁלְחָן
לְתַתָּא וְלֶחֶם עֲלֵיהּ. לָאו הָכִי, אֶלָּא שֻׁלְחָן אִיהוּ עִקָּרָא, בְּסִדּוּרָא
דִּילֵיהּ, לְקַבְּלָא בִּרְכָּאן דִּלְעֵילָּא וּמְזוֹנָא לְעָלְמָא. וּמֵרָזָא דְּהַאי שֻׁלְחָן,
נָפִיק מְזוֹנָא לְעָלְמָא כְּמָה דְּאִתְיְהִיב בֵּיהּ מִלְּעֵילָּא.

**515.** He opened the discussion saying: "You shall make a table..." This table is below to place upon it the baked bread. HE QUESTIONS: What is more important, the bread or the table? If you say that they are equal, IT IS

NOT SO, for the table is set for the bread, and also the table is below and the bread is on it. HE ANSWERS: It is not so, for the table is essentials, set to receive blessings from above and food for the world. From the secret of this table, WHICH IS THE SECRET OF MALCHUT, food emerges to the world as it is given from above.

516. וְהַהוּא לֶחֶם, אִיהוּ אִיבָּא דְּקָא נָפִיק מֵהַאי שֻׁלְחָן לְאַחֲזָאָה דְּהָא מִשֻּׁלְחָן דָּא, נַפְקֵי פֵּרִין וְאָבִין וּמְזוֹנָא לְעָלְמָא. אִי לָא אִשְׁתְּכַח כֶּרֶם, עֲנָבִין אִיבָּא דְּאִינּוּן דְּנַפְקֵי מִנֵּיהּ, לָא יְהוֹן מִשְׁתַּכְּחִין. אִי אִילָנָא לָא יְהֵא, אִיבָּא לָא יִשְׁתְּכַּח בְּעָלְמָא, בְּגִין כַּךְ, שֻׁלְחָן אִיהוּ עִקָּרָא, מְזוֹנָא דְּנָפִיק מִנֵּיהּ, אִיהוּ הַהוּא לֶחֶם הַפָּנִים.

516. Bread is the fruit and food that emerges from this table, to show that fruits, plants, and food for the world all emerge from this table. If the world had no vineyards, there would be no grapes, for these are the fruits that grow from it. If there were no trees, the world would have no fruits. Therefore, the table is the root and the food that emerges from it is the shewbread.

517. וְכַהֲנֵי הֲווֹ לַקְטֵי אִיבָּא דְּשֻׁלְחָן מֵע"ש לע"ש, לְאַחֲזָאָה דְּהָא מְזוֹנָא עִלָּאָה נָפִיק מִגּוֹ הַהוּא דְּשֻׁלְחָן. בְּגִין הַהוּא לֶחֶם דַּהֲווֹ לַקְטֵי כַּהֲנֵי, אִתְבְּרְכָא כָּל מְזוֹנָא וּמְזוֹנָא דְּאַכְלֵי וְשָׁתָאן, דְּלָא לְקַטְרְגָּא בְּהוּ יֵצֶר הָרָע, דְּהָא יֵצֶר הָרָע לָא אִשְׁתְּכַח, אֶלָּא מִגּוֹ מֵיכְלָא וּמִשְׁתְּיָא. הה"ד, פֶּן אֶשְׂבַּע וְכִחַשְׁתִּי וְגוֹ', דְּמִגּוֹ מֵיכְלָא וּמִשְׁתְּיָא יֵצֶר הָרָע מִתְרַבֵּי בִּמְעוֹי דְּבַר נָשׁ.

517. The priests would gather the fruits of the table every Shabbat Eve to show that the supernal food comes from that table. And because of that bread that the priests would gather, all the food that they ate and drank was blessed, so that the Evil Inclination could not accuse them, because the Evil Inclination is present only in the midst of eating and drinking. This is what is meant by: "Lest I become sated, and deny You..." (Mishlei 30:9), for the Evil Inclination of a person grows in one's intestines due to eating and drinking.

518. לֶחֶם דָּא, מְזוֹנָא דְּקָא נָפִיק מִגּוֹ שֻׁלְחָן, מְבָרֵךְ מְזוֹנָא דְּכַהֲנֵי, דְּלָא יִשְׁתְּכַּח בְּהוּ מְקַטְרְגָא לְקַטְרְגָא לוֹן, לְמִפְלַח בְּלִבָּא שְׁלִים לְקוּדְשָׁא בְּרִיךְ הוּא. וְדָא אִצְטְרִיךְ לְכַהֲנֵי יַתִּיר מִכָּל עָלְמָא. וּבְגִין כַּךְ, שֻׁלְחָן אִיהוּ עִקָּרָא, וְאֵיבָא וּמְזוֹנָא דְּקָא נָפִיק מִנֵּיה, אִיהוּ הַהוּא לֶחֶם.

**518.** This bread, which is the food that emerges from the table, blesses the food of the priests, so that there will be no accuser to accuse them and that they would serve the Holy One, blessed be He, with a whole heart. This is more necessary for the priests than for the rest of the world. Therefore, the table is the root, WHICH IS THE SECRET OF MALCHUT, and the fruit and food that come from it is that bread, NAMELY THE SHEWBREAD.

519. שֻׁלְחָן דָּא, אִצְטְרִיךְ סִדּוּרָא דִּילֵיהּ לְאִתְתַּקְּנָא, בְּסִטְרָא דְּצָפוֹן, דִּכְתִיב וְהַשֻּׁלְחָן תִּתֵּן עַל צֶלַע צָפוֹן. מ"ט. בְּגִין דְּמִתַּמָּן שֵׁירוּתָא דְּחֶדְוָה. שְׂמָאלָא נָטִיל מִימִינָא תָּדִיר בְּקַדְמֵיתָא, וּלְבָתַר אִיהוּ אִתְּעַר לְגַבֵּי נוּקְבָא, וּבָתַר קָרִיבַת לֵיהּ יְמִינָא לְגַבֵּיהּ, וְאִתְדַּבְּקַת בֵּיהּ.

**519.** The setting of this table has to be prepared on the north side, WHICH IS THE SECRET OF LEFT, as it is written: "And you shall put the table on the north side" (Shemot 26:35). What is the reason? It is because there is the source of joy. The left always receives from the right first and then it is aroused and supplies the Nukva, WHICH IS THE SECRET OF THE TABLE. Afterwards the right draws near her, THE NUKVA, AND CLINGS TO HER.

520. מַיִם אִינּוּן מִימִינָא, וְאִיהוּ חֶדְוָה, מִיַּד יָהִיב לִשְׂמָאלָא, וְאִתְדַּבְּקוּ בֵּיהּ אִינּוּן מַיִם, וְחַדְאָן לֵיהּ. וּבָתַר אִתְכְּלִיל אִיהוּ לִימִינָא, וְאִתְּעַר לְנוּקְבָא בְּהַהוּא חֶדְוָה. וְסִימָנָךְ, מַאן דְּנָטִיל מַיָּא בִּידֵיהּ יְמִינָא בְּמָאנָא, קַדְמָאָה לְאַרְקָא מַיָּא בִּשְׂמָאלָא אִיהוּ, וְלָא מִשְּׂמָאלָא לִימִינָא, דְּהָא מַיָּא מִימִינָא נָטִיל לוֹן שְׂמָאלָא.

**520.** AND THE ZOHAR BRINGS PROOF AND SAYS: Water is from the right, MEANING CHASSADIM, and it is joy. Immediately, THE RIGHT gives THE WATER to the left and the water cleaves unto it and causes it joy, MEANING

THAT THE CHOCHMAH WHICH IS IN THE LEFT BECOMES ATTIRED IN
CHASSADIM OF THE RIGHT. After it is included in the right, it arouses the
Nukva with that joy, MEANING THAT IT SUPPLIES HER CHOCHMAH THAT
IS COMBINED WITH CHASSADIM. You can derive it from THE WASHING OF
HANDS, FOR one who takes water in a vessel TAKES with the right hand
AND THEN TRANSFERS IT TO THE LEFT HAND, and the first to pour the
water is the left, ONTO THE RIGHT HAND. It is not THAT THE WATER
COMES FROM the left onto the right, because the left received the water
from the right hand.

**521.** וּבג״כ מַיָּא לָא אִשְׁתְּכָחוּ, אֶלָּא מִסִּטְרָא דִשְׂמָאלָא. כֵּיוָן דְּנָטִילוּ
מַיָּא לְגַבֵּיהּ, הָא אִתְּעֲרוּ לְגַבֵּי נוּקְבָא בְּאִינּוּן מַיִם. וְע״ד גְּבוּרוֹת גְּשָׁמִים
תְּנֵינָן. וּבְגִין כָּךְ וְהַשֻּׁלְחָן תִּתֵּן עַל צֶלַע צָפוֹן, דְּמֵהַהוּא סְטָר אִיבִּין
אִשְׁתְּכָחוּ בֵּיהּ יַתִּיר, מִסִּטְרָא אַחֲרָא. בְּאִתְּעֲרוּ דְּחֶדְוָה דִּילֵיהּ
בְּקַדְמֵיתָא, כד״א שְׂמאלוֹ תַּחַת לְרֹאשִׁי לְבָתַר וִימִינוֹ תְּחַבְּקֵנִי.

**521.** Therefore, there is water, WHICH IS CHASSADIM, only on the left side,
IN ORDER TO BE COMBINED AND PERFECTED IN CHOCHMAH OF THE
LEFT. Once water is taken to the left, it becomes aroused AND SUPPLIES to
the Nukva. Therefore, we have learned of the powers of the rains, FOR
EVEN THOUGH THE WATER IS CHASSADIM FROM THE RIGHT, IT COMES
ONLY FROM THE LEFT WHICH IS GVURAH. Therefore, "And you shall put
the table on the north side," because fruits are more abundant from that side,
WHICH IS THE RIGHT, than from the other side, THE RIGHT through its
becoming aroused first with its joy OF THE LEFT, as it is written: "His left
hand is under my head" and afterwards, "His right hand embraces me" (Shir
Hashirim 2:6).

**522.** שֻׁלְחָן דְּבַר נָשׁ אִצְטְרִיךְ לְאִשְׁתְּכָחָא בִּנְקִיּוּתָא דְּגוּפָא, דְּלָא
יִתְקְרַב לְמֵיכַל מְזוֹנָא דִּילֵיהּ, אֶלָּא בִּנְקִיּוּתָא דְּגַרְמֵיהּ. וְע״ד אִצְטְרִיךְ
בַּר נָשׁ, לְפַנָּאָה גַּרְמֵיהּ בְּקַדְמֵיתָא, עַד לָא יֵיכוּל מְזוֹנָא דְּשֻׁלְחָנָא
דַּכְיָא, דְּהַהוּא מְזוֹנָא דְּאַתְקִין לֵיהּ, בֵּיהּ אִתְרְעֵי קוּדְשָׁא בְּרִיךְ הוּא,
בְּגִין דְּלָא יִתְקְרַב עַל הַהוּא שֻׁלְחָן קִיא צוֹאָה, דְּאִיהוּ מֵרָזָא דְּסט״א
וְסט״א לָא יְקַבֵּל מֵהַהוּא מְזוֹנָא דְּשֻׁלְחָן דָּא כְּלוּם.

**522.** The table of a person must be clean, for the body should approach to eat its food only with self-cleanliness. A person has to evacuate first, before he eats the food of the pure table, because the Holy One, blessed be He, wants the food that he prepares for Him, in order that he should not approach the table of vomit and filth, which is from the secret of the Other Side, so that the Other Side will not receive anything from the food of this table.

523. לְבָתַר דְּאָכִיל ב"נ, וְאִתְעַנַּג, אִצְטְרִיךְ לְמֵיהַב חוּלָקָא דְּתַמְצִית לְהַהוּא סִטְרָא. וּמַאן אִיהוּ. מַיִם אַחֲרוֹנִים. הַהוּא זוּהֲמָא דִּידָין, דְּאִצְטְרִיךְ לְמֵיהַב לְהַהוּא סִטְרָא, חוּלָקָא דְּאִצְטְרִיךְ לֵיהּ. וְע"ד וַדַּאי אִינּוּן חוֹבָה, חוֹבָה אִינּוּן, וּבַאֲתָר דְּחוֹבָה שַׁרְיָין. וְאִיהוּ חִיּוּבָא עַל בַּר נָשׁ, לְמֵיהַב לֵיהּ חוּלָקָא דָּא. וְע"ד לָא אִצְטְרִיךְ לְבָרְכָא כְּלַל, דְּהָא בְּרָכָה לָאו אִיהוּ בְּהַהוּא סִטְרָא.

**523.** After the person has eaten and received pleasure, he must give the part of the remnants to that side, TO THE KLIPOT. What is it? It is the 'fingerbowl water' that dirt of the hands that he must give to that side, for it is the portion that it needs. It is certainly an obligation, because it is obligatory and they dwell in a place of obligation, NAMELY THE KLIPOT, for it is obligatory upon every person to give it this portion. Therefore, it is not necessary to make a blessing at all OVER THE 'FINGERBOWL WATER', because there is no blessing on that side.

524. וּבְגִין כַּךְ אִצְטְרִיךְ בַּר נָשׁ, דְּלָא יָהִיב מְזוֹנָא דְּע"ג פָּתוֹרֵיהּ, לְהַהוּא קִיא צוֹאָה, וְכ"ש בְּמֵעוֹי, וְכ"ש דְּאִיהוּ טַב לְבַר נָשׁ וּבְרִיאוּ וְתִקּוּנָא דְּגוּפֵיהּ. וְעַל דָּא, שֻׁלְחָן אִיהוּ לְמֵיכַל בֵּיהּ בְּדַכְיוּ, כְּמָה דְּאִתְּמַר.

**524.** Therefore, a person must BE VERY CAREFUL not to give the food that is on his table to that filthy vomit, and all the more so his intestines SHOULD BE CLEAN. Of course, that is good for the health and well-being of his body. Therefore, the table should be eaten upon in purity, as we have learned.

525. שֻׁלְחָן דָּא דְּקַיְּימָא בְּבֵי מַקְדְּשָׁא, בְּגִין לְאִשְׁתַּכְּחָא בֵּיהּ מְזוֹנָא,

וּלְאַפָּקָא מִנֵּיהּ מְזוֹנָא, וַע״ד אֲפִילּוּ רִגְעָא חֲדָא, לָא אִצְטְרִיךְ לְקַיְּימָא בְּרֵיקַנְיָא. שֻׁלְחָן אָחֳרָא, אִיהוּ שֻׁלְחָן דְּרֵיקַנְיָא, וְלָא אִצְטְרִיךְ לְמֵיהַב לֵיהּ דּוּכְתָּא בַּאֲתָר קַדִּישָׁא. וְעַל דָּא, שֻׁלְחָן דְּמַקְדְּשָׁא, אֲפִילּוּ רִגְעָא חֲדָא לָא יָתִיב בְּלָא מְזוֹנָא. וְיִצְטְרַךְ דְּלָא יִשְׁתְּכַּח אֲתָר גְּרִיעַ, דְּהָא בִּרְכָתָא דִלְעֵילָּא לָא מִשְׁתַּכְּחָא בַּאֲתָר גְּרִיעַ, דָּא שֻׁלְחָן דְּקַמֵּיהּ דְּקוּדְשָׁא בְּרִיךְ הוּא. שֻׁלְחָן דְּבַר נָשׁ דְּקָא מְבָרֵךְ עֲלֵיהּ לְקוּדְשָׁא בְּרִיךְ הוּא, אוּף הָכִי לָא אִצְטְרִיךְ לְמֶהֱוֵי בְּרֵיקַנְיָא, דְּהָא לֵית בִּרְכָתָא בַּאֲתָר רֵיקַנְיָא.

**525.** This table stands in the Temple, so that there would be food on it and to take out food from it, and it should not be empty even for one moment. The other table, OF THE OTHER SIDE, is the table of emptiness, and it should not be given a place in a holy site. Therefore, the table of the Temple should not remain without food for even one moment and there must not be a defective place, because the blessing from above is not present in a place that is defective AND LACKING. This is the table that is before the Holy One, blessed be He. And the table that the person blesses before the Holy One, blessed be He, must also not be empty, because there is no blessing in an empty place.

**526.** נַהֲמֵי דְּעַל גַּבֵּי שֻׁלְחָן דְּקוּדְשָׁא בְּרִיךְ הוּא, אִינּוּן תְּרֵיסַר. וְהָא אוּקִימְנָא רָזָא דִּנְהָמֵי, דְּאִינּוּן רָזָא דְּפָנִים. וְעַל דָּא אִקְרֵי לֶחֶם הַפָּנִים, דְּהָא מְזוֹנָא וְסִפּוּקָא דְּעָלְמָא, מֵאִינּוּן פָּנִים עִלָּאִין קָאַתְיָיא. וּבְגִין כַּךְ, לֶחֶם דָּא, אִיהוּ פְּנִימָאָה דְּכֹלָּא, אִיהוּ בְּרָזָא עִלָּאָה, כִּדְקָא יֵאוֹת.

**526.** There are twelve loaves of bread that is on the table of the Holy One, blessed be He, WHICH IS MALCHUT. We have established the secret of the bread, which is the secret of the face, MEANING THE TWELVE FACES THAT ARE IN ZEIR ANPIN, WHICH ARE CHESED AND GVURAH, TIFERET AND MALCHUT, WHICH ARE THE FOUR FACES OF THE LIVING CREATURES, THE FACE OF THE LION, FACE OF THE OX, THE FACE OF THE EAGLE, THE FACE OF MAN. EACH ONE OF THEM IS COMBINED OF THREE FACES, NAMELY LION, OX, AND EAGLE, AND THEY ARE TWELVE FACES. Therefore, they are called 'the Shew (lit. 'face') Bread', because the food

and sustenance of the world, WHICH IS MALCHUT, comes from these supernal faces OF ZEIR ANPIN. Therefore, this bread is the inner part of everything, WHICH IS THE FOOD OF MALCHUT, AND IT is in the supernal secret OF ZEIR ANPIN, as is proper.

527. לֶחֶם הַפָּנִים, מֵיכְלָא דְּאִינוּן פָּנִים, מְזוֹנָא וְסִפּוּקָא דְּנָפִיק לְעָלְמָא, מִנַּיְיהוּ אָתֵי, וְשַׁרְיָא עַל הַהוּא פָּתוֹרָא, וּבְגִין דִּשְׁלְחָן דָּא, מְקַבְּלָא מְזוֹנָא וְסִפּוּקָא מֵאִינוּן פָּנִים דִּלְעֵילָא, וְאִיהִי אַפִּיקַת מְזוֹנִין וְסִפּוּקִין מֵאִינוּן פָּנִים פְּנִימָאִין, וּמְזוֹנָא דְּאַפִּיקַת, אִיהוּ הַהוּא לֶחֶם, כִּדְקָאמְרָן, חוֹם הֲוָה מִתְקְרֵב, וְחוֹם הֲוָה מִתְעֲדֵי מִתַּמָּן, וְהָא אוּקְמוּהָ, דִּכְתִיב, בְּיוֹם הִלָּקְחוֹ וּבְגִין שְׁלְחָן דָּא אִית לְבַר נָשׁ לְנַטְרָא רָזִין דִּשְׁלְחָן דִּילֵיהּ בְּכָל אִינוּן גַּוְונִין כִּדְקָאמְרָן.

527. The Shew (lit. 'face') Bread THAT WAS IN THE TEMPLE is the food of these faces THAT ARE IN MALCHUT, MEANING THAT IT IS DRAWN FROM THE FOOD THAT SHE RECEIVES FROM THE TWELVE FACES OF ZEIR ANPIN, AS MENTIONED ABOVE. The food and sustenance that emerge to the world, come from them and dwell on that table THAT IS IN THE TEMPLE. This table, WHICH IS MALCHUT, receives food and sustenance from these supernal faces, THE TWELVE FACES OF ZEIR ANPIN, and it is MALCHUT that draws out food and sustenance from these internal faces OF ZEIR ANPIN. The food that She draws out is that bread that was mentioned, THAT WAS IN THE TEMPLE; THEREFORE, THAT BREAD IS CALLED 'SHEW (FACE) BREAD'. Hot BREAD was placed upon the table, and it was removed from there warm. We have already established this in relation to the verse: "On the day when it was taken away" (I Shmuel 21:7). Because of this table, a person should keep the secrets of his table in all the manners that we have said.

528. רַבִּי אֶלְעָזָר פָּתַח וְאָמַר, בְּכָל עֵת יִהְיוּ בְגָדֶיךָ לְבָנִים וְשֶׁמֶן עַל רֹאשְׁךָ אַל יֶחְסָר. הַאי קְרָא אוּקְמוּהָ וְאִתְּמַר, אֲבָל ת״ח, קוּדְשָׁא בְּרִיךְ הוּא בָּרָא לֵיהּ לְבַר נָשׁ בְּרָזָא דְּחָכְמְתָא, וְעָבֵד לֵיהּ בְּאוּמְנוּתָא סַגִּי, וְנָפַח בְּאַפּוֹי נִשְׁמָתָא דְּחַיֵּי, לְמִנְדַּע וּלְאִסְתַּכְּלָא בְּרָזִין דְּחָכְמְתָא, לְמִנְדַּע בִּיקָרָא דְּמָארֵיהּ, כד״א, כֹּל הַנִּקְרָא בִשְׁמִי וְלִכְבוֹדִי בְּרָאתִיו

יְצַרְתִּיו אַף עֲשִׂיתִיו. וְלִכְבוֹדִי בְּרָאתִיו דַּיְיקָא, וְרָזָא דָּא וְלִכְבוֹדִי
בְּרָאתִיו אוֹלִיפְנָא, דְּהָא כָּבוֹד דִּלְתַתָּא רָזָא דְּכוּרְסְיָיא קַדִּישָׁא לָא
אִתְתָּקַן לְעֵילָא, אֶלָּא מִגּוֹ תִּקּוּנָא דִּבְנֵי עָלְמָא.

**528.** Rabbi Elazer opened the discussion saying: "Let your garments be always white; and let your head lack no oil" (Kohelet 9:8). This passage has been established and we have learned it. The Holy One, blessed be He, created man with the secret of Wisdom and made him with great craftsmanship. He breathed into him the soul of life, so he would know and behold the mysteries of Wisdom and know the glory of his Master, as it is written: "Every one that is called by My Name, for I have created him for My glory; I have formed him; yea, I have made him" (Yeshayah 43:7). "For I have created him for My glory" is precise, and I have learned this secret of: "For I have created him for My glory". The glory of below, which is the secret of the Holy Throne, NAMELY MALCHUT, was constructed above only by the workings of the people of THIS world.

**529.** כַּד אִינּוּן בְּנֵי נָשָׁא, זַכָּאִין וַחֲסִידִין, וְיַדְעֵי לְתַקָּנָא תִּקּוּנֵי, הה"ד
וְלִכְבוֹדִי בְּרָאתִיו. בְּגִין דְּהַאי כְבוֹדִי, לְתַקָּנָא לֵיהּ בְּעַמּוּדִין תַּקִּיפִין,
וּלְקַשְׁטָא לֵיהּ בְּתִקּוּנָא וְקִשׁוּטָא דִּלְתַתָּא, בְּגִין דְּהַאי כְבוֹדִי יִסְתָּלַק,
בִּזְכוּ דְּצַדִּיקַיָּיא דִּי בְּאַרְעָא.

**529.** When people are righteous and pious and know how to make corrections FOR THE SAKE OF THE GLORY, WHICH IS MALCHUT, AS MENTIONED ABOVE, it is written: "For I have created him for My glory," MEANING for the sake of this glory of mine, so that they should establish it with strong pillars, WHICH ARE CHESED, GVURAH AND TIFERET, and adorn it with ornaments and adornment from below. MEANING THAT THEY WILL RAISE MAYIN NUKVIN (FEMALE WATERS) FROM BELOW IN ORDER TO DRAW MOCHIN INTO HER THAT ARE CALLED 'ADORNMENTS', in order that this glory of mine should be raised through the merit of the righteous that are on earth.

**530.** בְּגִין כַּךְ בְּרָאתִיו. כְּגַוְונָא דִּכְבוֹד עִלָּאָה, דְּתִקּוּנִין אִלֵּין בֵּיהּ.
בְּרִיאָה לְסִטַר שְׂמָאלָא. וְעַל דָּא, הוֹאִיל וְאָדָם אִיהוּ בְּאַרְעָא, וְאִית לֵיהּ

לְתַקְּנָא הַהוּא כְּבוֹדִי עֲבָדִית בֵּיהּ תִּקּוּנִין דִּכְבוֹד עִלָּאָה, דְּאִית בֵּיהּ אוּף
הָכִי בְּרִיאָה, וְעַל דָּא בְּרָאתִיו.

530. Therefore, "I have created him" similar to supernal glory, WHICH IS
BINAH THAT BECAME CHOCHMAH AGAIN, FOR THIS CHOCHMAH IS
CALLED '32 PATHS OF CHOCHMAH AND GLORY' (HEB. *KAVOD*),
NUMERICALLY IN 32. These adornments are in him, FOR HE HAS Briyah
(Eng. 'creation') on the left side, MEANING THE LEFT COLUMN OF BINAH,
FROM WHICH IS DRAWN CHOCHMAH. Since man is on the earth and he has
to amend My glory, THAT IS MALCHUT, I made in him the vessels for the
supernal glory, WHICH IS BINAH, for there is IN MAN creation too.
Therefore, "I have created him" AND IT IS THE ASPECT NESHAMAH.

531. בְּהַהוּא כָּבוֹד עִלָּאָה, אִית בֵּיהּ יְצִירָה, וְע"ד יְצַרְתִּיו, תִּקּוּנָא דָּא
יָהֲבִית בֵּיהּ בְּאָדָם, לְמֶהֱוֵי אִיהוּ בְּאַרְעָא, כְּגַוְונָא דְּהַהוּא כָּבוֹד עִלָּאָה.
בְּהַהוּא כָּבוֹד עִלָּאָה, אִית בֵּיהּ עֲשִׂיָּיה, וְעַל דָּא אוּף הָכִי בְּבַר נָשׁ,
כְּתִיב עֲשִׂיתִיו, לְמֶהֱוֵי אִיהוּ כְּגַוְונָא דְּהַהוּא כָּבוֹד עִלָּאָה, דִּמְתַקֵּן וּבָרִיךְ
לִכְבוֹד תַּתָּאָה.

531. That supernal glory, WHICH IS BINAH, contains Yetzirah (Eng.
'formation'), WHICH IS THE LIGHT OF CHASSADIM, AND THE ASPECT OF
RUACH THAT IS DRAWN FROM THE RIGHT COLUMN OF BINAH.
Therefore, "I have formed him," and I have placed this aspect in man, so
that he should be on earth in the likeness of the supernal glory, WHICH IS
BINAH. That supernal glory has Asiyah in it, WHICH IS MALCHUT AND THE
ASPECT OF NEFESH. It is also written of man: "I have made him," so that
he should be in the likeness of that supernal glory that perfects and blesses
the lower glory, WHICH IS MALCHUT.

532. מְנָלָן, דְּהַהוּא כָּבוֹד עִלָּאָה אִית בֵּיהּ תְּלַת אִלֵּין, דִּכְתִיב בֵּיהּ,
יוֹצֵר אוֹר וּבוֹרֵא חֹשֶׁךְ עוֹשֶׂה שָׁלוֹם. יוֹצֵר אוֹר, הָא יְצִירָה. וּבוֹרֵא חֹשֶׁךְ,
הָא בְּרִיאָה. עוֹשֶׂה שָׁלוֹם הָא עֲשִׂיָּה. וְדָא אִיהוּ כָּבוֹד עִלָּאָה, דְּקָא
מְתַקֵּן וּבָרִיךְ וְסָפִיק בְּכָל צָרְכָיו לִכְבוֹד תַּתָּאָה.

**532.** How do we know that within the supernal glory, WHICH IS BINAH, there are these three, BRIYAH, YETZIRAH AND ASIYAH? It is written, "I form the light, and create darkness, I make peace" (Yeshayah 45:7). "I form the light" refers to Yetzirah and "creates darkness" refers to Briyah. SINCE IT IS THE LEFT SIDE OF BINAH, AS MENTIONED, IT CONTAINS DARKNESS BEFORE IT JOINS THE RIGHT COLUMN. "I make peace" refers to Asiyah, and this is the supernal glory, that prepares and blesses and supplies all the needs of the lower glory, WHICH IS MALCHUT.

533. כְּגַוְונָא דָא, בָּרָא אָדָם בְּאַרְעָא, דְּאִיהוּ כְּגַוְונָא דְּהַהוּא כָּבוֹד עִלָּאָה, לְתַקְּנָא לְהַאי כָּבוֹד, וּלְאִתְכַּלְלָא מִכָּל סִטְרִין. כָּבוֹד עִלָּאָה אִית בֵּיהּ תְּלַת אִלֵּין, אָדָם לְתַתָּא אִית בֵּיהּ תְּלַת אִלֵּין. וּלְאִתְכַּלְלָא הַהוּא כָּבוֹד תַּתָּאָה, מֵעֵילָּא וּמִתַּתָּא, לְמֶהֱוֵי שְׁלִים בְּכָל סִטְרִין. זַכָּאָה אִיהוּ בַּר נָשׁ, דְּזָכֵי בְּעוֹבָדוֹי לְמֶהֱוֵי כְּגַוְונָא דָא.

**533.** Similarly, He created Man upon earth, who is similar to that supernal glory, so that he should arrange this glory, WHICH IS MALCHUT, so it would be combined from all sides. The supernal glory has in it these three, BRIYAH, YETZIRAH AND ASIYAH, and Man below has in him these three, BRIYAH, YETZIRAH AND ASIYAH. In this way, this glory, MALCHUT, will be comprised of above and below, MEANING FROM BINAH AND FROM MAN, to be perfect on all sides. Happy is the person that merits through his actions to be like this.

534. וְעַל דָּא כְּתִיב, בְּכָל עֵת יִהְיוּ בְגָדֶיךָ לְבָנִים וְשֶׁמֶן עַל רֹאשְׁךָ אַל יֶחְסָר. מַה לִכְבוֹד עִלָּאָה, הַהוּא מִשְׁחָא רְבוּת קַדְשָׁא לָא אִתְמְנַע מִנֵּיהּ, מֵרָזָא דְּעָלְמָא דְּאָתֵי. אוּף הָכִי לְבַר נָשׁ, דְּעוֹבָדוֹי מִתְלַבְּנָן תָּדִיר, הַהוּא מְשַׁךְ רְבוּת קַדְשָׁא, לָא יִתְמְנַע מִנֵּיהּ תָּדִיר.

**534.** In reference to this, it is written: "Let your garments be always white; and let your head lack no oil" (Kohelet 9:8). Just as the supernal glory is not withheld from the holy oil of anointing, WHICH IS THE SECRET OF THE FLOW FROM ABA THAT IS DESTINED FOR THE WORLD TO COME, WHICH IS BINAH, so is man, whose actions are constantly being whitened. That oil of anointing will never be withheld from him, WHICH IS THE FLOW FROM ABA.

535. בְּמַאי זָכֵי בַּר נָשׁ, לְאִתְעַדְּנָא בְּהַהוּא עִדּוּנָא עִלָּאָה. בְּשֻׁלְחָן
דִּילֵיהּ. כְּמָה דְּאִיהוּ מְעַדֵּן עַל פָּתוֹרֵיהּ נַפְשָׁאן דְּמִסְכְּנֵי, דִּכְתִיב וְנֶפֶשׁ
נַעֲנָה תַּשְׂבִּיעַ, מַה כְּתִיב בַּתְרֵיהּ, אָז תִּתְעַנַּג עַל יְיָ' וְגוֹ', דְּאוֹף הָכִי
קוּדְשָׁא בְּרִיךְ הוּא רָוֵי לֵיהּ, בְּכָל אִינּוּן עִדּוּנִין דְּמִשְׁח רְבוּת קוּדְשָׁא
עִלָּאָה, דְּנָגִיד וְאִתְמְשַׁךְ תָּדִיר לְהַהוּא כָּבוֹד עִלָּאָה, כְּתִיב וְנֶפֶשׁ נַעֲנָה
תַּשְׂבִּיעַ, מַה כְּתִיב בַּתְרֵיהּ, אָז תִּתְעַנַּג עַל יְיָ'.

535. How does a person merit to delight in that supernal delight in Eden, WHICH IS THE BOUNTY OF ABA, upon his table? This is just as he gives delight upon his table to the souls of the poor, as it is written: "And satisfy the afflicted soul" (Yeshayah 58:10). Afterwards, it is written: "Then shall you delight yourself in Hashem" (Ibid. 14), for the Holy One, blessed be He, satiates him with all these delights of the supernal holy anointing oil that flows and is drawn constantly to that supernal glory, as it is written, "And satisfy the afflicted soul," which is followed by, "Then shall you delight yourself in Hashem."

## 48. "It is a time to act for Hashem"

### A Synopsis
Rabbi Yosi and Rabbi Chiya are traveling here on the road when Rabbi Chiya states, "It is a time to act for The Creator. They have made void Your Torah," means that as long as people are occupied with Torah then all is well in heaven and earth. If they neglect the Torah, however, His strength wanes, and all the righteous must work even harder to do good in order to re-empower God, along with His camps and legions. At this moment, a mule-driver joins the discussion, surprising the rabbis with his insight. He speaks of "a time to love, and a time to hate," and says that when the children of Yisrael are not occupied with Torah that time itself is imperfect, incomplete and void of Light. Then, "it is a time to act for The Creator." Rabbi Yosi and Rabbi Chiya then get off their own mules and walk with the mule-driver.

### The Relevance of this Passage
The purpose here is to empower the righteous in their study of Torah, which exponentially multiplies the volume of Light in the world. Our efforts prevent the righteous from further suffering on our behalf as the infinite Light of the Zohar overwhelms the darkness and purifies mankind with untold leniency and loving kindness. Such is the loftiness of the soul of Rabbi Shimon. Moreover, we abolish the hatred (along with its roots) that festers in a man's heart.

536. ר׳ יוֹסִי וְר׳ חִיָּיא הֲוָה אַזְלֵי בְּאוֹרְחָא, וַהֲוָה חַד טַיָּיעָא טָעִין אֲבַתְרַיְיהוּ, א״ר יוֹסִי לְר׳ חִיָּיא, אִית לָן לְאִתְעַסְּקָא וּלְאִשְׁתַּדְּלָא בְּמִלֵּי דְאוֹרַיְיתָא, דְּהָא קוּדְשָׁא בְּרִיךְ הוּא אָזִיל לְקַמָּן, וְעַל דָּא עִידָן הוּא, לְמֶעְבַּד לֵיהּ תִּקּוּנָא בַּהֲדָן בְּהַאי אָרְחָא.

536. Rabbi Yosi and Rabbi Chiya were traveling on the road and a donkey-driver was driving his donkeys behind them. Rabbi Yosi said to Rabbi Chiya: We should be occupied and endeavoring with words of Torah, because the Holy One, blessed be He, is going before us. Therefore, it is time to adorn Him, so that he WILL be with us on this road.

537. פָּתַח רַבִּי חִיָּיא וְאָמַר עֵת לַעֲשׂוֹת לַיְיָ׳ הֵפֵרוּ תוֹרָתֶךְ, הַאי קְרָא אִתְּמַר, וְאוּקְמוּהָ חַבְרַיָּיא. אֲבָל עֵת לַעֲשׂוֹת לַיְיָ׳, בְּכָל זִמְנָא דְּאוֹרַיְיתָא

מִתְקַיְּימָא בְּעָלְמָא, וּבְנֵי נָשָׁא מִשְׁתַּדְּלָן בָּהּ, כְּבְיָכוֹל, קוּדְשָׁא בְּרִיךְ הוּא
חַדֵּי בְּעוֹבָדֵי יְדוֹי, וְחַדֵּי בְּעָלְמִין כֻּלְּהוּ, וּשְׁמַיָּא וְאַרְעָא קַיְּימֵי
בְּקִיּוּמַיְּיהוּ. וְלָא עוֹד, אֶלָּא קוּדְשָׁא בְּרִיךְ הוּא כָּנִישׁ כָּל פָּמַלְיָא דִּילֵיהּ,
וְאָמַר לוֹן, חָמוּ עַמָּא קַדִּישָׁא דְּאִית לִי בְּאַרְעָא, דְּאוֹרַיְיתִי מִתְעַטְּרָא
בְּגִינֵיהוֹן. חָמוּ עוֹבָדֵי יְדַי, דְּאַתּוּן אֲמַרְתּוּן מָה אֱנוֹשׁ כִּי תִזְכְּרֶנּוּ. וְאִינּוּן
כַּד חֲמָאן חֶדְוָה דְּמָארֵיהוֹן בְּעַמֵּיהּ, מִיָּד פַּתְחֵי וְאָמְרֵי, וּמִי כְעַמְּךָ
כְּיִשְׂרָאֵל גּוֹי אֶחָד בָּאָרֶץ.

**537.** Rabbi Chiya opened the discussion saying: "It is a time to act for Hashem. They have made void Your Torah" (Tehilim 119:126). The friends have established this verse. "It is a time to act for Hashem" means that, as long as the Torah is existent in the world and people are occupied with it, the Holy One, blessed be He, so to speak rejoices with the works of His hands and rejoices with all the worlds. And heaven and earth remain intact. Moreover, the Holy One, blessed be He, gathers His entire court and says to them, 'See the holy nation that I have on earth, that the Torah is crowned for due to them. See the works of My hands, that you said about them: "What is man, that You are mindful of him"' (Tehilim 8:5). When they see their Master's joy with His people, they immediately say, "And what one nation in the earth is like Your people, like Yisrael?" (II Shmuel 7:23).

**538.** וּבְשַׁעֲתָא דְּיִשְׂרָאֵל מִתְבַּטְּלֵי מֵאוֹרַיְיתָא, כְּבְיָכוֹ״ל, תָּשַׁשׁ חֵילֵיהּ,
דִּכְתִיב צוּר יְלָדְךָ תֶּשִׁי. וּכְדֵין כְּתִיב, וְכָל צְבָא הַשָּׁמַיִם עוֹמְדִים עָלָיו
וְעַל דָּא עֵת לַעֲשׂוֹת לַיְיָ׳, אִינּוּן צַדִּיקַיָּיא דְּאִשְׁתָּאֲרָן, אִית לוֹן לְחַגְרָא
חַרְצִין, וּלְמֶעְבַּד עוֹבָדִין דְּכַשְׁרָאן, בְּגִין דְּקוּדְשָׁא בְּרִיךְ הוּא יִתְתְּקַף
בְּהוּ, בְּצַדִּיקַיָּיא, וּמַשְׁרְיָין וְאוֹכְלְסִין דִּילֵיהּ. מ״ט. בְּגִין דְּהֵפֵרוּ תּוֹרָתֶךָ,
וְלָא מִשְׁתַּדְּלֵי בָּהּ בְּנֵי עָלְמָא, כִּדְקָא יָאוֹת.

**538.** When the children of Yisrael are neglectful of the Torah, His strength wanes so to speak, as it is written: "Of the Rock that begot you, you are unmindful" (Devarim 32:18). Then it is written: "And all host of heaven standing" AS HE SAID TO THEM, "WHO WILL ENTICE ACHAV..." (II Divrei Hayamim 18:18-19). Therefore, "it is a time to act for Hashem," for these righteous who have remained should gird their loins and do good works, so

that the Holy One, blessed be He, should be strengthened through them, by the righteous as well as His camps and legions. What is the reason? "They have made void Your Torah," and people in world are not properly occupied with it.

539. הַהוּא טַיָּיעָא דַּהֲוָה טָעִין אֲבַתְרַיְיהוּ, אָמַר לוֹן בְּמָטוּ מִנַּיְיכוּ, שְׁאֶלְתָּא חֲדָא בָּעֵינָא לְמִנְדַּע. אָמַר רַבִּי יוֹסִי, וַדַּאי אָרְחָא מִתְתַּקְּנָא קַמָּן, שָׁאִיל שְׁאֶלְתָּךְ. אָמַר, הַאי קְרָא, אִי כְּתִיב יֵשׁ לַעֲשׂוֹת, אוֹ נַעֲשֶׂה, הֲוָה אֲמֵינָא הָכִי. מַאי עֵת. וְתוּ, לַעֲשׂוֹת לַיְיָ', לִפְנֵי יְיָ' אִצְטְרִיךְ, מַאי לַעֲשׂוֹת לַיְיָ'. אָמַר רַבִּי יוֹסִי, בְּכַמָּה גַּוְונִין אָרְחָא מִתְתַּקְּנָא קַמָּן. חַד, דַּהֲוֵינָן תְּרֵין, וְהַשְׁתָּא הָא אֲנַן תְּלָתָא, וּשְׁכִינְתָּא אִתְכְּלִילַת בַּהֲדָן. וְחַד דַּחֲשִׁיבְנָא דְּלָא הֲוֵית אֶלָּא כְּאִילָנָא יַבֵּשְׁתָּא, וְאַנְתְּ רַעֲנָנָא כְּזֵיתָא. וְחַד, דְּיָאוֹת שָׁאֶלְתָּ, וְהוֹאִיל וְשָׁרִית מִלָּה, אֵימָא.

539. The donkey-driver who was driving the donkeys behind them said: I beg of you, I wish to know the answer to one question. Rabbi Yosi said: Surely the way is yet to be traveled before us; ask your question. He said: If this verse were written: 'We should act' or 'Let us act,' then I would recite it likewise; but what is the meaning of: "It is a time" and "to act for Hashem?" It should read: 'Before Hashem'. Rabbi Yosi said: The way is prepared for us in many manners. Once we were two and now we are three, for the Shechinah is included with us. Another is that I thought that you were simply like a dried-out tree, but you are really fresh like an olive tree. Another is that you asked well. Since you started the matter, speak up.

540. פָּתַח וְאָמַר עֵת לַעֲשׂוֹת לַיְיָ' הֵפֵרוּ תּוֹרָתֶךָ. עֵת לַעֲשׂוֹת לַיְיָ', אִית עֵת. וְאִית עֵת. עֵת לֶאֱהֹב וְעֵת לִשְׂנֹא. עֵת אִיהוּ לְעֵילָא, דְּהַהוּא עֵת, רָזָא דִּמְהֵימְנוּתָא אִיהוּ. וְדָא אִקְרֵי עֵת רָצוֹן, וְהַאי אִיהוּ דְּאִתְחַיָּיב בַּר נָשׁ לְמִרְחַם לַיְיָ' תָּדִיר, כד״א וְאָהַבְתָּ אֵת יְיָ' אֱלֹהֶיךָ, וְע״ד, עֵת לֶאֱהֹב, דָּא אִיהוּ עֵת דְּאִתְחַיָּיב בַּר נָשׁ לֶאֱהֹב.

540. He opened the discussion saying: "It is a time to act for Hashem. They have made void your Torah." "A time to act for Hashem" MEANS that there is a time and there is a time: "A time to love, and a time to hate" (Kohelet

3:8). 'Time' refers to above, for time is the secret of Faith; NAMELY, MALCHUT THAT IS CALLED 'TIME'. It is called 'a time of goodwill', which means that a person is obliged to love Hashem always, as it is written: "And you shall love Hashem your Elohim" (Devarim 6:5). And therefore, "a time to love" is the time that the person is obliged to love.

541. וְאִית עֵת אָחֳרָא, דְּאִיהוּ רָזָא דֶּאֱלֹהִים אֲחֵרִים, וְאִתְחַיָּיב בַּר נָשׁ לְמִשְׂנָא לֵיהּ, וְלָא יִתְמְשַׁךְ לְבֵיהּ אֲבַתְרֵיהּ, וְע״ד עֵת לִשְׂנֹא, וּבְגִין כָּךְ כְּתִיב דַּבֵּר אֶל אַהֲרֹן אָחִיךָ וְאַל יָבֹא בְכָל עֵת אֶל הַקֹּדֶשׁ.

541. There is another time, which is the secret of other Elohim when the person is obliged to hate, and his heart should not be drawn after it. Therefore, there is "a time to hate" as it is written: "Speak to Aaron your brother, that he come not at all times (lit. 'time') into the Holy Place" (Vayikra 16:2).

542. בְּזִמְנָא דְּיִשְׂרָאֵל מִשְׁתַּדְּלֵי בְּאוֹרַיְיתָא, וּפְקוּדֵי אוֹרַיְיתָא, הַהוּא עֵת רָזָא דִּמְהֵימְנוּתָא קַדִּישָׁא, מִתַּתְקְנָא בְּתִקּוּנָהָא, וּמִתְקַשְּׁטָא בִּשְׁלֵימוּתָא, כְּדְקָא יֵאוֹת. וּבְזִמְנָא דְּיִשְׂרָאֵל מִתְבַּטְּלֵי מֵאוֹרַיְיתָא, כִּבְיָכוֹל הַהוּא עֵת, לָאו אִיהוּ בְּתִקּוּנָהָא, וְלָא אִשְׁתְּכַחַת בִּשְׁלִימוּ, וְלָא בִּנְהוֹרָא וּכְדֵין עֵת לַעֲשׂוֹת לַיְיָ׳.

542. When the children of Yisrael are occupied with Torah and with the commandments of the Torah, that time, which is the secret of the holy Faith, NAMELY MALCHUT, is well established and is adorned to perfection as proper. But during the time the children of Yisrael are not occupied with Torah, so to speak, that time is not in its perfection, and is not complete and without light. Then "it is a time to act for Hashem."

543. מַאי לַעֲשׂוֹת. כד״א אֲשֶׁר בָּרָא אֱלֹהִים לַעֲשׂוֹת. מַאי לַעֲשׂוֹת. דְּאִשְׁתָּאֲרוּ גּוּפֵי דְּשֵׁידֵי, דְּאִתְקַדַּשׁ יוֹמָא, וְלָא אִתְעֲבִידוּ, וְאִשְׁתָּאֲרוּ לַעֲשׂוֹת, רוּחִין בְּלָא גּוּפֵי. אוּף הָכָא עֵת לַעֲשׂוֹת, אִשְׁתְּאַר בְּלָא תִּקּוּנָא, וּבְלָא שְׁלִימוּ. מ״ט. מִשּׁוּם דְּהֵפֵרוּ תוֹרָתֶךָ, בְּגִין דְּאִתְבַּטָּלוּ יִשְׂרָאֵל לְתַתָּא מִפִּתְגָּמֵי אוֹרַיְיתָא. בְּגִין דְּהַהוּא עֵת, הָכִי קַיְימָא, אוֹ סַלְקָא, אוֹ

נַחְתָּא, בְּגִינֵיהוֹן דְּיִשְׂרָאֵל.

**543.** HE QUESTIONS: What is the meaning of "to act" IN "A TIME TO ACT FOR HASHEM"? HE ANSWERS: It is written, "Which Elohim created and performed (lit. 'to act')" (Beresheet 2:3). What is there to act? It means that there remained the bodies of the demons that were not made, because the day had become sanctified and they remained yet to be done, for they were spirits without bodies. Here also, "a time to act": The time remained without perfection and without completion, for what reason? Because "they have made void Your Torah" and the children of Yisrael below neglected the words of Torah. That time is either elevated or it is lowered because of the children of Yisrael. IF THEY ARE OCCUPIED WITH TORAH IT IS ELEVATED, BUT IF THEY ARE IDLED FROM TORAH IT DESCENDS.

**544.** אָתוּ ר׳ יוֹסִי וְרַבִּי חִיָּיא וּנְשָׁקוּהוּ בְּרֵישֵׁיה. אָמַר ר׳ יוֹסִי, וַדַּאי לֵית אַנְתְּ כְּדַאי, לְטַיְיעָא אֲבַתְרָן. זַכָּאָה אָרְחָא דָא, דְּזָכֵינָן לְמִשְׁמַע דָא, זַכָּאָה דָרָא דְּרַבִּי שִׁמְעוֹן שָׁארֵי בְּגַוֵּיה, דַּאֲפִילוּ בֵּינֵי טוּרַיָּא, חָכְמְתָא אִשְׁתְּכַחַת תַּמָּן. נָחֲתוּ רַבִּי יוֹסִי וְרַבִּי חִיָּיא, וְאָזְלוּ תְּלָתְהוֹן בְּאָרְחָא.

**544.** Rabbi Yosi and Rabbi Chiya came and kissed him on his head. Rabbi Yosi said: Certainly, it is not according to your honor to lead donkeys behind us. Blessed is this way, where we merited to hear this. Blessed is the generation in which Rabbi Shimon lives, for even among the mountains there is Wisdom. Rabbi Yosi and Rabbi Chiya alighted from their donkeys and the three walked on their way.

## 49. A time of goodwill

### A Synopsis

The mule-driver continues from the previous section, speaking about, "But as for me, let my prayer be to You, The Creator, in an acceptable time (a time of goodwill): Elohim, in the greatness of Your steadfast love hear me, in the truth of Your salvation." He comments that a favorable time is when the congregation is praying. "But as for me," refers to King David. He then explains that a prayer of Redemption in a time of goodwill brings together time and favor. This prayer is said during the Minchah of Shabbat, we learn, because at that time all anger is removed and Judgment is aroused only in order to be sweetened with Chesed and Mercy, and there is joy in everything. The mule-driver next says that Moses died during the time of the Shabbat Minchah; therefore at this time the gates of the Holy Study Hall are locked and everyone has to justify himself before God. Moses, the Faithful Shepherd, Joseph the Righteous and King David all died at this same time, so there are three justification prayers. When Moses died, the light of the sun darkened and the Written Torah was barred. When Joseph died, all the springs dried up and all the tribes went into exile. When King David died, the moon herself gathered in her light, which was gathered up by the Oral Torah. Then, we are told, the lights of Torah were concealed and there was much confusion and many arguments among the scholars, thus, the rabbis decreed severe fasts and locked the gates of the Torah.

### The Relevance of this Passage

By invoking the three qualities of Moses, Joseph, and David, Faithfulness, Righteousness, and Kingship, we magnify these sublime qualities within our fellow man and ourselves. Judgments are repealed as we repent and meditate upon this mystical text. The iniquities of man and the sins of our own past are accounted for and compassionately corrected by the unfathomable greatness of Moses, Joseph, and David, and through the forbearance they engender.

545. פָּתַח הַהוּא טַיָּיעָא וְאָמַר וַאֲנִי תְפִלָּתִי לְךָ יְיָ' עֵת רָצוֹן אֱלֹהִים בְּרָב חַסְדֶּךָ עֲנֵנִי בֶּאֱמֶת יִשְׁעֶךָ, תָּנֵינָן, אֵימָתַי אִקְרֵי עֵת רָצוֹן. בְּשַׁעְתָּא דְּצִבּוּר קָא מְצַלָּאן. שַׁפִּיר אִיהוּ, וְהָכִי אִיהוּ וַדַּאי. דְּהָא כְּדֵין, צִבּוּרָא מְסַדְּרֵי וּמַתְקְנֵי תִּקּוּנָא דְּהַאי עֵת, וּכְדֵין אִיהוּ עֵת רָצוֹן, וְאִצְטְרִיךְ לְמִשְׁאַל שְׁאֶלְתָּא, דִּכְתִיב אֱלֹהִים בְּרָב חַסְדֶּךָ עֲנֵנִי בֶּאֱמֶת יִשְׁעֶךָ דְּהָא כְּדֵין אִצְטְרִיךְ לְמִשְׁאַל שְׁאֶלְתָּא.

-325-

**545.** That donkey-driver opened the discussion saying: "But as for me, let my prayer be to You, Hashem, in an acceptable time (a time of goodwill): Elohim, in the greatness of Your steadfast love hear me, in the truth of Your salvation" (Tehilim 69:14). We have learned that a favorable time is when the congregation is praying, then it is appropriate. It is certainly so, for the congregation sets out and prepares the establishing of that time. Then it is a favorable time when it is proper to make requests, as it is written: "Elohim, in the greatness of Your steadfast love hear me, in the truth of Your salvation." For then it is the time to make requests.

546. וַאֲנִי תְפִלָּתִי לְךָ יְיָ׳, הָא הָכָא רָזָא דִיחוּדָא. וַאֲנִי: דָא דָוִד מַלְכָּא, אֲתָר דְּאִקְרֵי גְּאוּלָה. תְּפִלָּתִי: דָא תְּפִלָּה. וְהָכָא אִיהוּ סְמִיכָא לִגְאוּלָה, דְּאִיהוּ חַד. כַּד אִיהוּ סָמֵךְ גְּאוּלָה לִתְפִלָּה, כְּדֵין אִיהוּ עֵת רָצוֹן. עֵת רָצוֹן: אוּף הָכִי, כְּלָלָא אִיהוּ כַּחֲדָא, עֵת חַד, רָצוֹן חַד, אִתְכְּלִילוּ דָא בְּדָא, וַהֲווֹ חַד. וְדָוִד מַלְכָּא בָּעָא לְיַחֲדָא בְּהַאי קְרָא, יְחוּדָא חֲדָא.

**546.** "But as for me, let my prayer be to You, Hashem." Here is the secret of the unison: "But as for me" refers to King David, NAMELY MALCHUT THAT IS CALLED 'I'. It is the place that is called 'Redemption', WHICH IS MALCHUT WHEN JOINED WITH YESOD, "my prayer" refers to prayer, NAMELY PLAIN MALCHUT. Here THAT HE SAYS "ME...MY PRAYER," the Amidah prayer is adjacent to redemption for they are one, FOR THEY ARE BOTH THE ASPECT OF MALCHUT. When one brings together redemption to the Amidah prayer, then it is a time of goodwill. A time of goodwill is also one inclusion together. Time is one, NAMELY MALCHUT, and favor is one, FOR IT IS THE SECRET OF THE FAVOR THAT BECOMES REVEALED FROM KETER, and they are combined together to become one. King David wanted to form one unity through this verse, AS WE HAVE SAID.

547. וְאִי תֵּימָא, אֲמַאי אִתְמְנֵי הַאי קְרָא, בִּצְלוֹתָא דְּמִנְחָה דְּשַׁבָּת. יָאוֹת אִיהוּ לְמֶהֱוֵי בְּשַׁבָּת בְּהַהוּא צְלוֹתָא דְּמִנְחָה, וְלָא בִּצְלוֹתָא דְּחוֹל, דְּוַדַּאי לָאו צְלוֹתָא דְּמִנְחָה דְּשַׁבָּת כְּחוֹל. בְּגִין דְּהָא בְּחוֹל בְּשַׁעֲתָא דְּמִנְחָה, תַּלְיָא דִּינָא בְּעָלְמָא, וְלָאו אִיהוּ עֵת רָצוֹן. אֲבָל בְּשַׁבָּת, דְּכָל רוּגְזָא אִתְעֲדֵי, וְכֹלָּא אִתְכְּלִיל כַּחֲדָא, וְאַע״ג דְּדִינָא אִתְּעַר, אִתְבַּסְּמוּתָא אִיהוּ, וְעַ״ד אִצְטְרִיךְ קְרָא דִיחוּדָא, לְיַחֲדָא כָּל דַּרְגִּין, דְּכַד

הֲוֵי יְחוּדָא, דִּינָא אִתְחַבָּר וְאִתְכְּלִיל בְּרַחֲמֵי, וְאִתְבַּסַם כֹּלָא, וּכְדֵין עֵת רָצוֹן כְּתִיב. עֵת רָצוֹן, כָּלִיל כֹּלָא כַּחֲדָא. וְדִינָא אִתְבְּסַם בְּהַהוּא זִמְנָא, וַהֲוֵי חֶדְוָה בְּכֹלָא.

**547.** If you ask: Why was this verse selected TO BE SAID during the Minchah of Shabbat? HE ANSWERS: It is proper for it to be in the Minchah service of Shabbat and not in the weekday service, for it is certain that Minchah service of Shabbat is unlike the weekday prayer because Judgment is suspended over the world during the weekday at the time of Minchah, and it is not a time of goodwill. However, during Shabbat, when all anger is removed and everything is combined together, FOR THE JUDGMENT AND CHESED ARE ONE, Judgment is aroused, but it is in order to be sweetened, MEANING ONLY IN ORDER TO REVEAL THE SWEETNESS THAT IT CONTAINS. Therefore, a verse of unity is needed to unite all the grades, for when there is unity, Judgment joins and combines with Mercy and everything is sweetened, as it is written: "A time of goodwill." "A time of goodwill" shows that everything, JUDGMENT AND CHESED, is combined together, that Judgment is sweetened at that time, and there is joy in everything.

**548.** מֹשֶׁה אִסְתַּלָּק מֵעָלְמָא, בְּהַהוּא שַׁעֲתָא דִּצְלוֹתָא דְּמִנְחָה דְּשַׁבָּת, בְּשַׁעֲתָא דְּעֵת רָצוֹן אִשְׁתְּכַח. וּבְהַהִיא שַׁעֲתָא רַעֲוָא הֲוָה לְעֵילָא, וְצַעֲרָא לְתַתָּא, וְעַ"ד נִנְעֲלוּ תַּרְעִין בְּשַׁבָּת, מִשַּׁעֲתָא דְּמִנְחָה וּלְעֵילָא. מַאן תַּרְעִין נִנְעֲלוּ. תַּרְעִין דְּבֵי מִדְרָשָׁא, בְּגִין לְאַדְכְּרָא לְמֹשֶׁה רַעְיָא מְהֵימָנָא, דְּאוֹרַיְיתָא אִתְבַּטְלָא בְּגִינֵיהּ.

**548.** Moses departed from the world, at the time of the Shabbat Minchah, at the time when there was "a time of goodwill." At that moment favor was above and pain was below, BECAUSE OF THE DEATH OF MOSES. Therefore, during Shabbat the gates are locked from the time of Minchah and further. Which gates are locked? The gates of the Holy Study Hall, in order to memorialize Moses, the Faithful Shepherd, for the Torah was voided because of him, BECAUSE HE DIED.

**549.** בְּהַהוּא זִמְנָא, בֵּי מִדְרָשָׁא דְּמֹשֶׁה אִתְבְּטִיל, כָּל שְׁכֵן אַחֲרָנִין.

מַאן חָמֵי תַּרְעִין דְּבֵי מִדְרָשָׁא דְּמֹשֶׁה דְּנִנְעֲלוּ, דְּלָא נִנְעֲלוּ אַחֲרָנִין כֻּלְּהוּ. אוֹרַיְיתָא דְּמֹשֶׁה עֲצִיבָא עָלֵיהּ בְּהַהוּא זִמְנָא, מַאן לָא עָצִיב. בְּגִ״כ כָּל תַּרְעֵי דְּבֵי מִדְרָשֵׁי נִנְעֲלוּ, וְאִצְטְרִיכוּ כֹּלָּא לְצַדְּקָא לֵיהּ לְקוּדְשָׁא בְּ״ה בְּאֹרַח שְׁבָחָא, וְהַיְינוּ צִדְקָתְךָ כְּהַרְרֵי אֵל.

**549.** At the time THAT HE DIED, the Study Hall of Moses and THE STUDY HALLS of others became nullified. Whoever saw the doors of Moses's Study Hall were locked, while all the others be not locked? If Moses's Torah mourned for him at that time, who did not mourn? Therefore, all the gates of the Study Hall are locked, and everyone has to justify the Holy One, blessed be He, by way of praise, THAT WE RECITE THEN: "Your righteousness is like the great mountains" (Tehilim 36:7).

**550.** תְּלָתָא אִינּוּן דְּאִסְתָּלָקוּ מֵעָלְמָא בְּהַאי זִמְנָא, וְכֻלְּהוּ כְּלִילָן בְּמֹשֶׁה. חַד, מֹשֶׁה נְבִיאָה מְהֵימָנָא עִלָּאָה. וְחַד, יוֹסֵף צַדִּיקָא. וְחַד, דָּוִד מַלְכָּא. בְּגִינֵי כַּךְ, תְּלַת צִדּוּקֵי דִּינֵי הָכָא, חַד אִיהוּ דְּיוֹסֵף זַכָּאָה, קָדִים לְכָל הָנֵי, וְדָא אִיהוּ צִדְקָתְךָ כְּהַרְרֵי אֵל מִשְׁפָּטֶיךָ תְּהוֹם רַבָּה וְגו׳, דָּא יוֹסֵף, דְּאִיהוּ בִּלְחוֹדוֹי כְּהַרְרֵי אֵל, כְּכֻלְּהוּ טוּרִין עִלָּאִין. וְחַד מֹשֶׁה נְבִיאָה מְהֵימָנָא, וְדָא אִיהוּ דִּכְתִּיב, וְצִדְקָתְךָ אֱלֹהִים עַד מָרוֹם אֲשֶׁר עָשִׂיתָ גְדוֹלוֹת, בְּגִין דְּאִיהוּ נָטִיל לְכָל סִטְרִין, יְמִינָא וּשְׂמָאלָא. וְחַד אִיהוּ דָּוִד מַלְכָּא, וְדָא אִיהוּ דִּכְתִּיב, צִדְקָתְךָ צֶדֶק לְעוֹלָם וְתוֹרָתְךָ אֱמֶת, לְעוֹלָם: דָּא דָּוִד מַלְכָּא.

**550.** There were three who departed from the world at that time, and they are all included in Moses. They are Moses, the Faithful Shepherd, Joseph the Righteous, and King David. Therefore, there are here three justification prayers. One is for Joseph the Righteous, who preceded all these, and this is: "Your righteousness is like the great mountains; Your Judgments are a great deep…" This refers to Joseph the Righteous, for he alone is like the great mountains, like all the supernal Mountains, WHICH ARE CHESED, GVURAH, TIFERET, NETZACH AND HOD OF ZEIR ANPIN, FOR JOSEPH, WHO IS YESOD, IS COMBINED OF THEM ALL. Another is Moses, the Faithful Prophet, and this is what is written: "Your righteousness also, Elohim, reaches the high heavens, who have done great things" (Tehilim

71:19) because he IS ZEIR ANPIN, WHICH IS THE CENTRAL COLUMN THAT takes all the sides, THE RIGHT SIDE AND THE LEFT SIDE, AND MEDIATES BETWEEN THEM. The other is King David, as it is written: "Your righteousness is an everlasting righteousness, and Your Torah is Truth" (Tehilim 119:142). "Everlasting (lit. 'for the world')" refers to King David, WHO IS THE SECRET OF MALCHUT THAT IS CALLED 'WORLD'.

551. כְּדֵין אִתְכְּנִישׁ כֹּלָּא בְּהַאי זִמְנָא, תּוֹרָה שֶׁבִּכְתָב, וְתוֹרָה שבע״פ. וע״ד בְּהַאי זִמְנָא נִנְעָלוּ תַּרְעֵי דְּאוֹרַיְיתָא, וְנִנְעָלוּ תַּרְעֵי דְּכָל עָלְמָא, בְּהַאי זִמְנָא. בְּשַׁעֲתָא דְּמִית יוֹסֵף צַדִּיקָא, יָבְשׁוּ מְקוֹרִין וּמַבּוּעִין, וְכֻלְּהוּ שִׁבְטִין נַפְלוּ בְּגָלוּתָא, פָּתְחוּ עִלָּאֵי וְאָמְרוּ, צִדְקָתָךְ כְּהַרְרֵי אֵל מִשְׁפָּטֶיךָ תְּהוֹם רַבָּה וְגוֹ'. בְּשַׁעֲתָא דְּמִית מֹשֶׁה, אִתְחֲשָׁךְ שִׁמְשָׁא בְּטִיהֲרָא, וְאִנְעָלַת תּוֹרָה שֶׁבִּכְתָב, נְהוֹרָא דְּאַסְפַּקְלַרְיָאה דְּנַהֲרָא. בְּשַׁעֲתָא דְּמִית דָּוִד מַלְכָּא, כְּנִישַׁת סִיהֲרָא נְהוֹרָהָא וְאוֹרַיְיתָא דִּבְעַל פֶּה כְּנִישַׁת נְהוֹרָהָא.

551. When everything was gathered at that time, the Written Torah, WHICH IS MOSES, and the Oral Torah, THAT IS DAVID, the gates of Torah were locked and all the gates of the world were locked at that time. At the moment that Joseph the Righteous died, the sources and springs dried up, and all the tribes fell into exile. Those above opened with the words: "Your righteousness is like the great mountains, Your Judgments are a great deep." At that moment that Moses died, the light of the sun darkened at midday and the Written Torah was barred, which is the light of the shining mirror, WHICH IS ZEIR ANPIN. At the moment that King David died, the moon, WHICH IS MALCHUT, gathered in its light and the Oral Torah gathered in its light.

552. וּמֵהַהוּא זִמְנָא אִתְגְּנִיזוּ נְהוֹרִין דְּאוֹרַיְיתָא, וְאַסְגִּיאוּ מַחֲלוֹקֶת עַל מִשְׁנָה, וְחַכִּימַיָּא בְּמַחֲלוֹקֶת, וְכֻלְּהוּ תַּקִּיפֵי לִבָּא בְּעִרְבּוּבְיָא. וְעַל דָּא, חֶדְוָה דְּאוֹרַיְיתָא לָאו אִיהוּ בְּהַהוּא זִמְנָא, בְּכָל דָּרִין דְּעָלְמָא. וּמָה אִנּוּן חוּמְרֵי דְּתַעֲנִיּוֹת דְּגָזְרוּ רַבָּנָן, כַּד מִית פְּלוֹנִי, גָּזְרוּ תַּעֲנִית. כַּד הֲוָה כַּךְ, גָּזְרוּ כַּךְ. וְכַד הֲוָה כְּנִישׁוּ יַתִּיר דְּחֶדְוָה דְּתוֹרָה דִּבְכְתָב וְתוֹרָה דִּבְעַל פֶּה, בְּהַהוּא זִמְנָא, עאכ״ו דְּאִצְטְרִיךְ לְמִנְעַל תַּרְעֵי דְּאוֹרַיְיתָא

בְּהַהוּא זִמְנָא. וּבג"כ אַמְרֵינָן הָנֵי צְדוּקֵי דִּינָא, כְּמָה דְּאִתְּמַר. חֲדוּ רַבִּי יוֹסִי וְרַבִּי חִיָּיא, וּנְשָׁקוּהוּ בְּרֵישֵׁיה כְּמִלְּקַדְמִין, אָמְרוּ זַכָּאָה חוּלְקָנָא בְּהַאי אָרְחָא.

**552.** Since that time the lights of Torah were concealed, and arguments multiplied in the Mishnah. The scholars argued and all those of stout heart were confused; therefore, there was no joy of the Torah at that time throughout the generations of the world. This is the cause of the severe fasts that the Rabbis decreed. When a certain person died they decreed a fast, when something happened they decreed so. When the joy of the Written Torah and the Oral Torah was most gathered up at that time, it is so much more necessary to lock the gates of the Torah. Therefore, we say the Justifications of the Judgments, as we have mentioned. Rabbi Yosi and Rabbi Chiya rejoiced and kissed him on his head as before. They said: Happy is our portion on this way.

## 50. "Wisdom strengthens the wise"

### A Synopsis

The mule-driver of previous sections here says that, "Wisdom strengthens the wise more than ten rulers who are in the city," refers to Moses. When Moses ascended Mount Sinai to receive the Torah, the firmaments and the supernal camps of the angels rose against him because he was going to lower the Torah to the earth and take their goodness and joy from them. But Moses strengthened himself. The Torah shields those who study it with the courage and strength derived from "ten rulers", which are the Ten Commandments. The ten rules are, we learn, the ten kinds of wisdom found in the Torah, which is the secret of the ten Sfirot in ten engraved Names. In one Name of 22 engraved letters, we are told, the secrets of the world to come are combined and cannot be understood, yet, nonetheless, the Holy One bequeathed to the righteous a longing for that time.

### The Relevance of this Passage

A deep longing for eternal world peace stirs within our hearts, and the effect is a miraculous positive change in human civilization. We are strengthened with goodness and compassion, for these are the traits of the Torah and the power of the Zohar. We secure a swift and sweet redemption of man, bringing the world to come into the here and now.

553. תּוּ פָּתַח וְאָמַר. הַחָכְמָה תָּעוֹז לֶחָכָם מֵעֲשָׂרָה שַׁלִּיטִים אֲשֶׁר הָיוּ בָּעִיר. הַחָכְמָה תָּעוֹז לֶחָכָם, דָּא מֹשֶׁה, כַּד סָלִיק לְטוּרָא דְסִינַי לְקַבְּלָא אוֹרַיְיתָא, אִזְדַּעֲזָעוּ כָּל אִינּוּן רְקִיעִין, וְכָל אִינּוּן מַשְׁרְיָין עִלָּאִין, וְאָמְרוּ קָמֵיהּ, מָארֵיהּ דְּעָלְמָא, וּמַה כָּל טוּבָא, וְכָל חֶדְוָה דִּילָן, לָאו אִיהוּ אֶלָּא בְּאוֹרַיְיתָא, וְאַתְּ בָּעֵי לְנַחְתָּא לָהּ בְּאַרְעָא. אִתְכְּנִישׁוּ עַל מֹשֶׁה לְאוֹקְדֵיהּ בְּנוּרָא, אִתְתַּקַּף מֹשֶׁה וְכוּ', כְּמָה דְּאוּקְמוּהָ חַבְרַיָּיא, דְּקוּדְשָׁא בְּרִיךְ הוּא אָמַר לֵיהּ לְמֹשֶׁה וְכוּלֵי.

553. Again he opened the discussion saying: "Wisdom strengthens the wise more than ten rulers who are in the city" (Kohelet 7:19). "Wisdom strengthens the wise" refers to Moses. When he ascended Mount Sinai to receive the Torah, all the firmaments and all the supernal camps OF ANGELS trembled. They said before Him, Master of the world, behold all our goodness and joy is only in the Torah, and you want to lower it to earth. They gathered against Moses to burn him with fire. Moses strengthened

himself, as the friends have established that the Holy One, blessed be He, said to Moses, etc.

554. אֲבָל הַחָכְמָה תָּעוֹז לְחָכָם, כָּל מָאן דְּאִתְעַסָּק בְּאוֹרַיְיתָא, וְאִשְׁתַּדַּל בָּה לִשְׁמָהּ, אִתְתַּקַּף בָּה בְּאוֹרַיְיתָא, בְּשַׁעְתָּא דְּאִצְטְרִיךְ לְמֶהֱוֵי לֵיהּ תֶּקְפָּא וְחֵילָא, לְאַגָּנָא עָלֵיהּ בְּשַׁעְתָּא דְּאִצְטְרִיךְ. וְהַהוּא תֶּקְפָּא וְחֵילָא מֵאָן אֲתָר אִתְתַּקַּף. הֲדָר וְאָמַר, מֵעֲשָׂרָה שַׁלִּיטִים. אִינּוּן עֶשֶׂר אֲמִירָן דִּכְתִּיבִין בָּה בְּאוֹרַיְיתָא, דְּאִינּוּן שַׁלִּיטִין עִלָּאִין, דְּב"נ אִתְתַּקַּף בְּהוֹ בְּהַאי עָלְמָא, וּבְעָלְמָא דְּאָתֵי כָּל רָזִין דְּעָלְמָא, וְכָל פִּקּוּדִין, וְכָל חָכְמְתָא דְּעֵילָא וְתַתָּא, בְּהוֹ תַּלְיָא, וּבְהוֹ אִתְכְּלִיל כֹּלָּא, וְכֹלָּא אִיהוּ בְּאוֹרַיְיתָא. זַכָּאָה חוּלָקֵיהּ מָאן דְּאִשְׁתַּדַּל בְּאוֹרַיְיתָא, לְמֶהֱוֵי מִתְתַּקַּף בְּתֶקְפָּא לְעָלְמָא דְּאָתֵי.

554. "Wisdom strengthens the wise" means that everyone who is occupied with Torah and endeavors in it for its own sake, receives strength from the Torah that protects him, when he needs courage and strength. From which place does he receive that courage and strength to strengthen himself? THE VERSE repeats, saying, from "ten rulers," those are the Ten Commandments that are written in the Torah which are supernal Rules that the person strengthen himself with them in this world and in the World to Come. All the secrets of the world and all the commandments and all the Wisdom of above and below depend upon them and everything is included in them and everything is in the Torah. Happy is the portion of he who is occupied with Torah, so as to become strengthened with courage in the World to Come.

555. עֲשָׂרָה שַׁלִּיטִין, עֶשֶׂר זִינֵי חָכְמְתָא אִינּוּן בָּה בְּאוֹרַיְיתָא, בְּעֶשֶׂר שְׁמָהָן גְּלִיפָן, וְאִתְכְּלִילוּ בִּשְׁמָא חַד, דְּעֶשְׂרִין וְתְרֵין אַתְוָון גְּלִיפִין, רָזִין דְּעָלְמָא דְּאָתֵי, בְּאִינּוּן זִיהֲרִין, דְּלָא שַׁלְטָא עֵינָא לְמֶחֱמֵי, וַאֲפִילוּ בְּסָכְלְתָנוּ לְמִנְדַּע, וּלְאִסְתַּכְּלָא בְּהַהוּא עִדּוּנָא, וְכִסּוּפָא, דְּקוּדְשָׁא ב"ה אַחְסִין לוֹן לְצַדִּיקַיָּיא לְעָלְמָא דְּאָתֵי. כד"א לֹא רָאֲתָה אֱלֹהִים זוּלָתְךָ יַעֲשֶׂה לִמְחַכֵּה לוֹ.

555. The ten rules are the ten kinds of Wisdom that are in the Torah, WHICH

IS THE SECRET OF THE TEN SFIROT, in ten engraved names; NAMELY, THE TEN NAMES THAT ALLUDE TO THE TEN SFIROT OF EHEYEH. In one Name of 22 engraved letters, THE NAME *ALEPH-NUN-KOF-TAV-FINAL MEM* OF THE BLESSING OF THE PRIESTS, the secrets of the World to Come are combined, in these lights that the eye cannot see, NOR even with understanding know and behold that delight, or the longing that the Holy One, blessed be He, bequeathed to the righteous for the World to Come, as it is written: "Neither has the eye seen, that an Elohim beside You, should do such a thing for him that waits for him" (Yeshayah 64:3).

## 51. The food of the souls

### A Synopsis

The mule-driver from previous sections says that the merit gained from a person's table in this world enables him to eat on another table of delight in the world to come. There is a table there because food and pleasure are eaten by the souls in that world just as the ministering angels eat. The supernal angels eat manna, the food that comes from the dew of the world above, a food from the light of the Holy Anointing Oil itself. The souls of the righteous are nourished from thence in the Garden of Eden, and there also they become clothed. During Shabbat and Festivals, the souls take off their garments and ascend to see the glory of their Master. He next explains the meaning of: "And it shall come to pass, that every new moon, and every Shabbat, shall all flesh come to bow down to the ground before Me', says The Creator."

The rabbis ask the mule-driver his name, which is Chanan. Finally, they all stop at the next village, which is also named Chanan, and they sit down at table blessed with the words of Torah.

### The Relevance of this Passage

The spiritual foundation upon which we build our life determines our place of standing in the world to come. A life devoted to the procurement of spiritual assets, as opposed to the material kind, reaps untold pleasures in the world to come.

This simple truth holds true in this world as well. Indulging our avaricious impulses, while neglecting the needs of our soul, spawns a future of difficulty, a tomorrow built of despair, a destiny born of darkness. The building blocks of spirituality are erected here, ingrained into our being, so that we eat *foods* of indescribable delights in the Garden of Eden.

556. פָּתוֹרָא דְּבַר נָשׁ, מְזַכֵּי לֵיהּ לְמֵיכַל עַל פָּתוֹרָא אָחֳרָא, בְּעֶדוּנָא דְּהַהוּא עָלְמָא, כד"א כִּי עַל שֻׁלְחָן הַמֶּלֶךְ תָּמִיד הוּא אוֹכֵל. וְדָוִד מַלְכָּא הֲוָה אָמַר, תַּעֲרֹךְ לְפָנַי שֻׁלְחָן נֶגֶד צוֹרְרָי, וְדָא אִיהוּ אִתְּסַדְּרוּתָא דְּפָתוֹרָא בְּהַהוּא עָלְמָא, דְּהָא כְּדֵין אִיהוּ עִדוּנָא וְכִסּוּפָא, דְּנִשְׁמָתָא אִתְהֲנֵי בְּהוּ, בְּעָלְמָא דְּאָתֵי.

556. The table of a person merits him to eat on another table in the delight of that world, THE WORLD TO COME, as it is written: "For he did eat

continually at the table of the king" (II Shmuel 9:13). King David used to say, "You prepare a table before me in the presence of my enemies" (Tehilim 23:5), and this is the preparation of the table in that world, for then there is delight and desire with which the soul has pleasure in the World to Come.

557. וְכִי פָּתוֹרָא אִית לוֹן לְנִשְׁמָתִין בְּהַהוּא עָלְמָא. אִין. דְּהָא מְזוֹנָא וְסִפּוּקָא דְּעֵדוּנָא אַכְלֵי בְּהַהוּא עָלְמָא, כְּגַוְוֹנָא דְּמַלְאֲכֵי עִלָּאֵי אַכְלֵי. וְכִי מַלְאֲכֵי עִלָּאֵי אַכְלֵי. אִין. כְּגַוְוֹנָא דִּלְהוֹן אָכְלוּ יִשְׂרָאֵל בְּמַדְבְּרָא. וְהַהוּא מְזוֹנָא, רָזָא אִיהוּ לְטַלָּא, דְּנָגִיד וְאִתְמְשַׁךְ מֵעֵילָא, מֵרָזָא דְּעָלְמָא דְּאָתֵי, וְאִיהוּ מְזוֹנָא דִּנְהִירוּ מְשַׁח רְבוּת קַדְשָׁא, וְנִשְׁמָתְהוֹן דְּצַדִּיקַיָּא אִתְּזָנוּ מִתַּמָּן בְּגִנְתָּא דְּעֵדֶן, וְאִתְהֲנוּן תַּמָּן. דְּהָא תַּמָּן נִשְׁמָתְהוֹן דְּצַדִּיקַיָּא, מִתְלַבְּשָׁן בְּגִנְתָּא דְּעֵדֶן דִּלְתַתָּא, כְּגַוְוֹנָא דְּהַאי עָלְמָא.

557. HE QUESTIONS: Is there a table for the souls in that world? HE ANSWERS: Yes, because food and the supply of pleasure are eaten by the souls in that world just as the ministering angels eat. HE QUESTIONS: Do the supernal angels eat? HE ANSWERS: Yes, and similar to that eating did the children of Yisrael eat in the desert, NAMELY THE MANNA. That food is the secret of the dew that flows and is drawn from above from the secret of the World to Come, WHICH IS BINAH. It is a food from the light of the Holy Anointing Oil. The souls of the righteous are nourished from there in the Garden of Eden and they gain pleasure there, because the souls of the righteous are clothed there in the Lower Garden of Eden just as they WERE CLOTHED in this world.

558. וּבְשַׁבָּתֵי וּבִזְמַנֵּי, מִתְפַּשְּׁטָאן, וְסַלְקִין לְמֶחֱמֵי בִּיקָרָא דְּמָארֵיהוֹן, וּלְאִתְעַדְּנָא בְּעֵדוּנָא עִלָּאָה כַּדְקָא יֵאוֹת, דִּכְתִיב וְהָיָה מִדֵּי חֹדֶשׁ בְּחָדְשׁוֹ וּמִדֵּי שַׁבָּת בְּשַׁבַּתּוֹ יָבֹא כָל בָּשָׂר לְהִשְׁתַּחֲוֹת לְפָנַי אָמַר יְיָ'. וְכִי כָּל בָּשָׂר יֵיתֵי, לָאו הָכִי הֲוָה לֵיהּ לְמִכְתַּב, אֶלָּא כָּל רוּחַ אוֹ כָּל נִשְׁמָה, מַהוּ כָּל בָּשָׂר. אֶלָּא קוּדְשָׁא בְּרִיךְ הוּא עֲבַד לֵיהּ לְב"נ בְּהַאי עָלְמָא, כְּגַוְוֹנָא דִּיקָרָא דִּכְבוֹד עִלָּאָה לְעֵילָא. הַהוּא כְּבוֹד עִלָּאָה, אִיהוּ

רוּחַ לְרוּחַ, וְנִשְׁמְתָא לַנְּשָׁמָה, עַד דְּמָטֵי לְחַד אֲתָר לְתַתָּא דְּאִקְרֵי גּוּף, וּבְהַאי עָיֵיל חַד רוּחַ דִּמְקוֹרָא דְּחַיִּים, דְּאִקְרֵי כֹּל, בְּדָא אִיהוּ כָּל טוּבָא, וְכָל מְזוֹנָא, וְכָל סִפּוּקָא, דְּהַהוּא גּוּף. וְרָזָא דָּא, וְיִתְרוֹן אֶרֶץ בַּכֹּל הִיא הַאי כָּל אִיהוּ רוּחַ לְהַהוּא גּוּף.

**558.** During Shabbat and Festivals, THE SOULS take off THEIR GARMENTS and ascend to see the glory of their Master and to delight with the supernal Delight properly, as it is written: "'And it shall come to pass, that every new moon, and every Shabbat, shall all flesh come to bow down to the ground before Me,' says Hashem" (Yeshayah 66:23). HE QUESTIONS: Will all flesh come? It must not be so, instead it should have been written: 'Every spirit or every soul.' What is the meaning of "all flesh?" HE ANSWERS: The Holy One, blessed be He, has made for Man in this world the likeness of the honor of the supernal glory above, WHICH IS THE SECRET OF WISDOM OF THE 32 PATHS, AS MENTIONED ABOVE. That supernal glory is a spirit to spirit, AS IT ILLUMINATES UPON ZEIR ANPIN WHICH IS CALLED 'SPIRIT', and a soul to soul, AS IT ILLUMINATES TO BINAH THAT IS CALLED 'SOUL', until it reaches a place below that is called 'body', NAMELY MALCHUT. It inserts in it one spirit of the source of life that is called 'all', WHICH IS YESOD. This is the secret of: "Moreover, land has an advantage for everyone (lit. 'all')." (Kohelet 5:8). 'All' is a spirit for that body.

**559.** כְּגַוְונָא דָּא בַּר נָשׁ בְּהַאי עָלְמָא, אִיהוּ גּוּף, וְרוּחַ דְּשַׁלְטָא בֵּיהּ, כְּגַוְונָא דְּהַהוּא רוּחַ עִלָּאָה, דְּאִקְרֵי כֹּל, דְּשַׁלְטָא עַל גּוּפָא לְעֵילָּא, וְדָא הוּא דְּאִקְרֵי כָּל בָּשָׂר, וְעַ״ד כְּתִיב, יָבֹא כָל בָּשָׂר לְהִשְׁתַּחֲוֹות לְפָנַי אָמַר יְיָ'. עַל הַהוּא עִדּוּנָא כְּתִיב, עַיִן לֹא רָאָתָה אֱלֹהִים זוּלָתְךָ יַעֲשֶׂה לִמְחַכֵּה לוֹ.

**559.** Similarly, man in this world is a body and the spirit that rules over him resembles that Supernal Spirit called 'all' that rules over the body above, WHICH IS MALCHUT. This spirit, THAT IS IN THE BODY OF MAN, is called 'all flesh' as it is written: "'Shall all flesh come to bow down to the ground before Me,' says Hashem" (Kohelet 5:8). In reference to this delight, it is written: "Neither has the eye seen, that an Elohim beside You, should do such a thing for him that waits for him" (Yeshayah 64:3).

560. חֲדוּ חַבְרַיָּיא בְּאָרְחָא. כַּד מָטוּ לְגוֹ טוּרָא חַד אָמַר ר' חִיָּיא לְהַהוּא טַיָּיעָא, מָה שְׁמֶךָ. אָמַר לֵיהּ חָנָן. א״ל קוּדְשָׁא בְּרִיךְ הוּא יְחֻנֶּנְךָ, וְיִשְׁמַע לְקוֹלֶךָ בְּשַׁעֲתָא דְּתִצְטְרִיךְ לֵיהּ. אָמַר רַבִּי יוֹסִי, וַדַּאי הָא נָטֵי שִׁמְשָׁא, וְהָכִי בָּתַר טוּרָא דָּא, אִית כְּפַר חַד עַל שְׁמָךְ, דְּאִקְרֵי כְּפַר חָנָן, נָבִית תַּמָּן בְּגִין יְקָרָא דִּשְׁמֶךָ. כַּד מָטוּ לְהָתָם, עָאלוּ לְבֵית אוּשְׁפִּיזַיְיהוּ, וְסִדְּרוּ קַמַיְיהוּ פָּתוֹרָא, בְּכַמָּה זִינִין לְמֵיכַל. אָמַר ר' חִיָּיא, וַדַּאי פָּתוֹרָא דָּא, כְּגַוְונָא דְּעָלְמָא דְּאָתֵי, וְאִית לָן לְסַלְּקָא הַאי פָּתוֹרָא, וּלְאַעֲטְרָא לֵיהּ בְּמִלִּין דְּאוֹרַיְיתָא.

560. The friends rejoiced on the way. When they reached a certain mountain, Rabbi Chiya said to this donkey-driver: What is your name? He said to him: "Chanan." He said to him: May the Holy One, blessed be He, be gracious unto you (Heb. *yechonencha*) and hear your voice when you need Him. Rabbi Yosi said: For certain the sun is setting and past this mountain there is a village named after you, for it is called 'Village of Chanan'. Let us lodge there in honor of your name. When they arrived there, they came to their lodging and prepared before them the table with many kinds of food. Rabbi Chiya said: This table is in the likeness of the World to Come, and it is incumbent upon us to elevate this table and adorn it with words of Torah.

## 52. The center of the World

### A Synopsis

Here, Rabbi Yosi discusses: "When you have eaten and are replete, then you shall bless The Creator your Elohim for the good land which He has given you." He says the Holy Land is the center of the world, and in the center of that is Jerusalem, and in the center of that is the Holy of Holies. Everywhere on earth is nourished from this one place. In the wilderness where the Other Side dominates, we learn, the children of Yisrael wandered for forty years. If they had been righteous during that time they would have removed the Other Side from the world, but instead they strengthened it. Moses died on Mount Avarim and was buried by the Shechinah. We are next told that Moses dominated the mountain, and that he showed those who die in the wilderness will rise at the resurrection of the dead. Rabbi Yosi then tells us that God sent a goat to a mountain called Azazel, which is the stronghold of the Other Side. Finally, we learn that if one who delights at his table worries about the holiness of the Holy Land and the sanctuary of the King that has been destroyed, he will be remembered by God as though he re-built the ruins of the Temple.

### The Relevance of this Passage

A reading of this passage enjoins our souls to the Holy of Holies, the wellspring and fountainhead of all spiritual nourishment. This sacred connection is critical if our prayers are to be answered, if our lives are to be renewed with passion, peace, prosperity, and blessedness.

The Temple is a refuge from death itself, such is the resplendence of this Light. Thus, a heartfelt visual embrace of this text rebuilds the spiritual Temple, as if by our own hands. The long hidden Light begins to shine and death dies. Evil is laid to waste and goodness fills the land. The dead are readied for Resurrection in a process that will embody sweet mercy and disburden.

561. פָּתַח ר' יוֹסִי וְאָמַר, וְאָכַלְתָּ וְשָׂבָעְתָּ וּבֵרַכְתָּ אֶת יְיָ' אֱלֹהֶיךָ עַל הָאָרֶץ הַטּוֹבָה אֲשֶׁר נָתַן לָךְ. אִי בְּאַרְעָא דְיִשְׂרָאֵל מִבָּרְכֵינָן, לְבַר מֵאַרְעָא מְנָלָן. דְּהָא בְּגַוְוּנָא דָּא לָא אִצְטְרִיךְ. אֶלָּא, קוּדְשָׁא בְּרִיךְ הוּא כַּד בָּרָא עָלְמָא, פָּלִיג אַרְעָא, יִשׁוּבָא אִיהוּ לִסְטַר חַד, וְחָרְבָּא אִיהוּ לִסְטַר אָחֳרָא. פָּלִיג יִשׁוּבָא, וְאַסְחַר עָלְמָא סַחֲרָנֵיהּ דִּנְקוּדָה חֲדָא. וּמָאן אִיהוּ, דָּא אַרְעָא קַדִּישָׁא, אַרְעָא קַדִּישָׁא אֶמְצָעִיתָא דְּעָלְמָא. וּבְאֶמְצָעִיתָא דְאַרְעָא קַדִּישָׁא, אִיהוּ יְרוּשְׁלֵם. אֶמְצָעִיתָא דִירוּשְׁלֵם

אִיהוּ בֵּית קֹדֶשׁ הַקֳּדָשִׁים, וְכָל טִיבוּ וְכָל מְזוֹנָא דְּכָל יְשׁוּבָא, תַּמָּן נָחִית מִלְעֵילָא. וְלֵית לָךְ אֲתָר בְּכָל יְשׁוּבָא דְּלָא אִתְּזַן מִתַּמָּן.

**561.** Rabbi Yosi opened the discussion with the verse: "When you have eaten and are replete, then you shall bless Hashem your Elohim for the good land which He has given you" (Devarim 8:10). HE QUESTIONS: If we bless in the land of Yisrael, how do we know THAT WE HAVE TO BLESS outside of the Land of Yisrael? FOR IT SEEMS that in this circumstance, OUTSIDE OF THE LAND OF YISRAEL, it is not necessary to bless. HE ANSWERS: When the Holy One, blessed be He, created the world, He divided the earth. The PLACE OF habitation was on one side and THE PLACE of desolation was on the other side. And He divided the inhabited PLACE, and circled the world around one point. What is it? It is the Holy Land, because the Holy Land is the center of the world and in the center of the Holy Land is Jerusalem, and the center of Jerusalem is the Holy of Holies. Every goodness and all the food of the entire habitation descend there from above and there is not one place inhabited that is not nourished from there.

**562.** פָּלִיג חַרְבָּא. וְלָא אִשְׁתְּכַח חַרְבָּא תַּקִּיפָא בְּכָל עָלְמָא, בַּר הַהוּא מִדְבָּר, דְּתַבְרוּ חֵילֵיהּ וְתָקְפֵּיהּ יִשְׂרָאֵל אַרְבְּעִים שָׁנָה, כְּמָה דְּאַתְּ אָמֵר הַמּוֹלִיכָךְ בַּמִּדְבָּר הַגָּדוֹל וְהַנּוֹרָא. בְּהַהוּא מַדְבְּרָא, שַׁלְטָא סִטְרָא אָחֳרָא, וּבְעַל כָּרְחֵיהּ אַזְלוּ יִשְׂרָאֵל עֲלֵיהּ, וְתָבְרוּ חֵילֵיהּ, אַרְבְּעִין שְׁנִין. וְאִי יִשְׂרָאֵל יִשְׁתַּכְּחוּ זַכָּאִין בְּאִינּוּן אַרְבְּעִין שְׁנִין, הֲוָה מִתְעַבְּרָא הַהוּא סִטְרָא אָחֳרָא מֵעָלְמָא, וּמִדְּקָא אַרְגִּיזוּ לֵיהּ לְקוּדְשָׁא בְּרִיךְ הוּא כָּל אִינּוּן זִמְנִין, אִתְתְּקַף הַהוּא סִטְרָא אָחֳרָא, וְנַפְלוּ כֻּלְּהוּ תַּמָּן תְּחוֹת רְשׁוּתֵיהּ.

**562.** He divided the desolate place, and there was no greater desolation in the entire world as in that wilderness, that the children of Yisrael broke its strength and power for forty years, as it is written: "…who led you through that great and terrible wilderness" (Ibid. 15). The Other Side dominates in that wilderness and, against its will, the children of Yisrael walked on it and smashed its strength forty years. Had they been righteous during the forty years, they would have removed the Other Side from the world, but because they angered the Holy One, blessed be He, so many times, the Other Side grow strong. They all fell under its power there.

563. וְאִי תֵּימָא, וְהָא מֹשֶׁה דְּסָלִיק עַל כָּל בְּנֵי עָלְמָא, הֵיךְ מִית תַּמָּן. לָאו הָכִי, דְּהָא מֹשֶׁה מְהֵימָנָא לָא הֲוָה בִּרְשׁוּתֵיה, אֶלָּא בְּהַר הָעֲבָרִים. מַאי הָעֲבָרִים. פְּלוּגְתָּא. דְּאִתְפְּלְגוּ עָלֵיהּ שַׁלִּיטִין עִלָּאִין דִּלְעֵילָּא, וְלָא אִתְמְסַר בִּידָא דִּמְמָנָא וְשַׁלִּיטָא אָחֳרָא, וְאִשְׁתְּאַר הָכִי, עַד דְּאָתָא מֹשֶׁה עַבְדָּא מְהֵימָנָא, וְשַׁלִּיט עָלֵיהּ, וְאִתְקְבַר תַּמָּן, וְלָא אִתְעֲסָק בֵּיהּ בְּקָבוּרְתֵּיהּ, בַּר קוּדְשָׁא בְּרִיךְ הוּא בִּלְחוֹדוֹי, דִּכְתִּיב וַיִּקְבֹּר אוֹתוֹ בַגָּי.

563. If you ask: Behold Moses, who was elevated over all the people of the world, how did he die there? HE ANSWERS: It was not so, for Moses was not under the jurisdiction OF THE OTHER SIDE, but rather on the Mount Avarim. What means Avarim? Quarrels, FROM THE EXPRESSION WRATH (HEB. *EVRA*) AND FURY. The supernal rulers of above quarreled over it, FOR THEY WANTED TO DOMINATE THE MOUNTAIN, but it was handed not to any other ruler and it remained so until Moses, the Faithful Servant, came and dominated it. Moses was buried there, and no one took part in his burial except the Holy One, blessed be He, alone, as it is written: "And he buried him in the valley" (Devarim 34:6).

564. וַיִּקְבֹּר אֹתוֹ, מַאן. הַהוּא דִּכְתִּיב בֵּיהּ בְּאֹרַח סָתִים, וְאֶל מֹשֶׁה אָמַר, וְלָא כְּתִיב מַאן אִיהוּ. וַיִּקְרָא אֶל מֹשֶׁה, וְלָא כְּתִיב מַאן אִיהוּ. אוּף הָכָא וַיִּקְבּוֹר אֹתוֹ, וְלָא כְּתִיב מַאן אִיהוּ, אֶלָּא וַדַּאי הַאי אֲתָר יְדִיעָא אִיהוּ לְגַבֵּי חַבְרַיָּיא. וְעַל דָּא, בְּהַהוּא טוּרָא לָא שַׁלִּיט עָלֵיהּ, בַּר מֹשֶׁה בִּלְחוֹדוֹי, וְאִיהוּ אִתְקְבַר תַּמָּן. וּבְגִין לְמִנְדַע לְכָל דָּרִין אַחֳרָנִין דְּעָלְמָא, דְּאִינּוּן מֵתֵי מִדְבָּר יְקוּמוּן, הַהוּא רַעֲיָא דִּלְהוֹן אַשְׁרֵי לֵיהּ בְּגַוַּויְיהוּ, לְמֶחֱוֵי כֻּלְּהוּ בְּאִתְעָרוּתָא דְּקִיּוּמָא לְעָלְמָא דְּאָתֵי.

564. "And he buried him…" HE QUESTIONS: Who is the one WHO BURIED HIM? HE ANSWERS: The one of whom it is written in a non-descriptive way, "And he said to Moses" (Shemot 24:1) and similarly, "And…called to Moses" (Vayikra 1:1). It did not write who he is. "And he buried him": It is not written who he is. But certainly this place is known to the friends, THAT IT IS THE SHECHINAH CALLED 'PLACE', FOR IT IS THE SHECHINAH WHEREVER IT IS SAID JUST 'HE'. Therefore, no one dominated in this mountain except Moses himself, and he was buried there. He did it so that

all the generations of the world would know that those who died in the wilderness will rise AT THE RESURRECTION OF THE DEAD. The Holy One, blessed be He, caused their shepherd to dwell among them, so that they all will be present in the rising to existence of the World to Come.

565. וְאִי תֵּימָא, אִי הָכִי דְּהַהוּא מַדְבְּרָא אִיהוּ תֻּקְפָּא דְּסִטְרָא אָחֳרָא, הֵיךְ פָּקִיד קוּדְשָׁא בְּרִיךְ הוּא, עַל הַהוּא שָׂעִיר, לְשַׁדְּרָא לֵיהּ לְטוּרָא אָחֳרָא, דְּאִקְרֵי עֲזָאזֵל, הֲוָה לוֹן לְשַׁדְּרָא לֵיהּ לְהַהוּא טוּרָא דְּאַזְלֵי יִשְׂרָאֵל בְּמַדְבְּרָא בֵּיהּ. אֶלָּא, כֵּיוָן דְּהָא אָזְלוּ בֵּיהּ יִשְׂרָאֵל אַרְבְּעִין שְׁנִין, הָא אִתְּבַּר תֻּקְפֵּיהּ. וְתֻקְפֵּיהּ אִתְתַּקַּף בַּאֲתָר דְּלָא עָבַר בֵּיהּ גְּבַר תַּמָּן לְעָלְמִין, וּבְהַהוּא טוּרָא, הָא הֲוָה דִּיּוּרֵיהוֹן דְּיִשְׂרָאֵל תַּמָּן אַרְבְּעִין שְׁנִין.

565. If you ask: If that wilderness is the strength of the Other Side, how could the Holy One, blessed be He, command that this goat shall be sent to a different mountain that is called 'Azazel'? They should have sent it to that mountain that Yisrael went over in the wilderness, for there is the place of the strength of the Other Side. HE ANSWERS: Since the children of Yisrael had already gone there forty years, its power was broken. And its power grew strong in a place where nobody ever passed before. Yet that mountain THAT IS IN THE WILDERNESS THAT YISRAEL WALKED IN was the dwelling place of Yisrael for forty years.

566. אֲבָל בְּהַאי שָׂעִיר, הַהוּא אֲתָר אִיהוּ טִנָּרָא תַּקִּיפָא עִלָּאָה, וּתְחוֹת עֻמְקָא דְּהַהוּא טִנָּרָא, דְּבַר נָשׁ לָא יָכִיל לְמֵיעַל תַּמָּן, אִיהוּ שַׁלִּיט יַתִּיר לְמֵיכַל טַרְפֵּיהּ, בְּגִין דְּיִתְעֲבַר מֵעֲלַיְיהוּ דְּיִשְׂרָאֵל, וְלָא יִשְׁתְּכַח בְּהוּ מְקַטְרְגָא עֲלַיְיהוּ בְּיִשׁוּבָא.

566. But that place, WHERE THEY SEND that goat, is a supernal strong rock, and under the depths of that rock, where no man can enter, THE OTHER SIDE dominates exceedingly to eat its prey. Then it will be removed from Yisrael and there will be accuser against them will in the inhabited region.

567. שׁוּלְטָנוּתֵיהּ דְּרָזָא דִּמְהֵימְנוּתָא, גּוֹ אֶמְצָעִיתָא דִּנְקוּדָה דְּכָל

אַרְעָא קַדִּישָׁא, בְּבֵי קֹדֶשׁ הַקֳּדָשִׁים. וְאע״ג דְּהַשְׁתָּא לָאו אִיהוּ בְּקִיּוּמָא, בְּזַכוּתֵיהּ כָּל עָלְמָא אִתְּזַן, וּמְזוֹנָא וְסִפּוּקָא מִתַּמָּן נָפְקָא לְכֹלָּא, בְּכָל אֲתָר סִטְרָא דְּיִשּׁוּבָא. וּבְגִין כַּךְ, אע״ג דְּיִשְׂרָאֵל הַשְׁתָּא לְבַר מֵאַרְעָא קַדִּישָׁא, עִם כָּל דָּא מֵחֵילָא וְזָכוּתָא דְּאַרְעָא, אִשְׁתְּכַח מְזוֹנָא וְסִפּוּקָא לְכָל עָלְמָא. וע״ד כְּתִיב וּבֵרַכְתָּ אֶת יְיָ׳ אֱלֹהֶיךָ עַל הָאָרֶץ הַטּוֹבָה אֲשֶׁר נָתַן לָךְ. עַל הָאָרֶץ הַטּוֹבָה וַדַּאי, דְּהָא בְּגִינָהּ מְזוֹנָא וְסִפּוּקָא אִשְׁתְּכַח בְּעָלְמָא.

**567.** The dominion of the secret of Faith is found in the central point of the whole Holy Land, in the Holy of Holies, and even though it does not exist today, NONETHELESS, in its merit the whole world is fed. Food and sustenance emit from there to all, in every inhabited place. Therefore, even though Yisrael are outside the Holy Land, because of the strength and merit of the Land there is food and sustenance in the world. Therefore, it is written: "And you shall bless Hashem your Elohim for the good land that He has given you," "the good land" certainly, for there is found food and sustenance in the world because of it.

**568.** מַאן דְּאִתְעַדָּן עַל פָּתוֹרֵיהּ וּמִתְעַנַּג בְּאִינּוּן מֵיכְלִין, אִית לֵיהּ לְאַדְכְּרָא וּלְדַאֲגָא עַל קְדוּשָׁה דְּאַרְעָא קַדִּישָׁא, וְעַל הֵיכָלָא דְּמַלְכָּא דְּקָא אִתְחֲרִיב. וּבְגִין הַהוּא עֲצִיבוּ דְּאִיהוּ קָא מִתְעַצַּב עַל פָּתוֹרֵיהּ, בְּהַהוּא חֶדְוָה וּמִשְׁתְּיָא דְּתַמָּן, קוּדְשָׁא בְּרִיךְ הוּא חָשִׁיב עָלֵיהּ כְּאִלּוּ בָּנָה בֵּיתֵיהּ, וּבָנָה כָּל אִינּוּן חַרְבֵּי דְּבֵי מַקְדְּשָׁא, זַכָּאָה חוּלָקֵיהּ.

**568.** One who delights at his table and has pleasure in foods should remember and care for the holiness of the Holy Land, and the sanctuary of the King that has been destroyed. Because he was sad about his table there, in the midst of joy and feasting, the Holy One, blessed be He, considers for him as though he built His house, and built all these ruins of the Temple. Happy is his portion.

## 53. A Cup of Blessing

### A Synopsis

Here, Rabbi Yosi says that the Cup of Blessing becomes blessed from Chesed, Gvurah and Tiferet of Zeir Anpin that are the three patriarchs; therefore a cup is necessary only when there are three men together. The Cup of Blessing, which, we learn, is Malchut, is perfected by the ten Sfirot. It should be looked at because: "The eyes of The Creator your Elohim are always upon it." It is the secret of Faith, and must always be guarded because it is for the Cup's sake that the table is blessed during the prayer after meals. Rabbi Yosi says again that the table must never be empty because the blessing does not exist on an empty table. Just so, wisdom is given to the wise.

### The Relevance of this Passage

As our eyes drink the Light of these verses, our souls partake of the Cup of Blessing. We receive sustenance so that we may tithe, spiritual nourishment so that we may persevere the spiritual path, and appreciation of God's endless goodness so that we may protect and forever keep all that is sacred and precious in our lives. By the virtue of the Patriarchs our tables are kept full so that we may now take possession of all these blessings.

569. כּוֹס שֶׁל בְּרָכָה, לָא הֲוֵי אֶלָּא בִּתְלָתָא. בְּגִין דְּהָא מֵרָזָא דִּתְלַת אֲבָהָן קָא מִתְבָּרְכָא, וְע"ד לָא אִצְטְרִיךְ כּוֹס אֶלָּא בִּתְלָתָא. כּוֹס שֶׁל בְּרָכָה אִצְטְרִיךְ לְמֵיהַב לֵיהּ בִּימִינָא וּבִשְׂמָאלָא, וּלְקַבְּלָא לֵיהּ בֵּין תַּרְוַויְיהוּ, בְּגִין דְּאִתְיְהִיב בֵּין יְמִינָא וּשְׂמָאלָא. וּלְבָתַר יִשְׁתְּבִיק לֵיהּ בִּימִינָא, דְּהָא מִתַּמָּן אִתְבָּרְכָא.

569. The Cup of Blessing is used only when there are three WHO ATE TOGETHER. It is blessed from the secret of the three Patriarchs, FOR MALCHUT, WHICH IS THE SECRET OF THE CUP OF BLESSING, IS BLESSED FROM CHESED, GVURAH AND TIFERET OF ZEIR ANPIN THAT ARE CALLED 'PATRIARCHS'. Therefore, a cup is necessary only when there are three men. One should give the Cup of Blessing with the right and left HANDS, and receive it in both, because MALCHUT is given between the right and left OF ZEIR ANPIN. Afterwards one should leave it only in his right hand, because from there it is blessed, MEANING FROM THE LIGHT OF THE CHASSADIM THAT ARE IN THE RIGHT OF ZEIR ANPIN.

570. עֲשָׂרָה דְבָרִים נֶאֶמְרוּ בְּכוֹס שֶׁל בְּרָכָה, וְכֻלְהוּ הֲווֹ כַּדְקָא יָאוֹת, בְּגִין דְּתִקּוּנֵי דְכוֹס שֶׁל בְּרָכָה עֲשָׂרָה אִינּוּן, וְהָא אוּקְמוּהָ חַבְרַיָּא. כּוֹס שֶׁל בְּרָכָה אִצְטְרִיךְ לְאַשְׁגָּחָא בֵּיהּ בְּעֵינָא, בְּגִין דִּכְתִיב עֵינֵי יְיָ׳ אֱלֹהֶיךָ בָּהּ, וְלָא אִצְטְרִיךְ לְאִתְנָשֵׁי מֵעֵינָא, אֶלָּא לְאַשְׁגָּחָא בֵּיהּ.

**570.** Ten things were said about the Cup of Blessing and they are all proper, because the Cup of Blessing, WHICH IS MALCHUT, is perfected by ten, NAMELY THE TEN SFIROT, as the friends have established. It is necessary to look at the Cup of Blessing with the eyes, because it is written: "The eyes of Hashem your Elohim are always upon it" (Devarim 11:12) ON THE LAND WHICH IS MALCHUT, THAT IS CALLED 'CUP OF BLESSING'. It should not be removed from the eye, but should rather be looked at.

571. כּוֹס שֶׁל בְּרָכָה, אִתְבְּרַךְ בְּהַהוּא בִּרְכָתָא, דְּקָא מְבָרֵךְ בַּר נָשׁ עֲלֵיהּ לְקוּדְשָׁא בְּרִיךְ הוּא, בְּגִין דְּאִיהוּ רָזָא דִמְהֵימְנוּתָא, וְאִצְטְרִיךְ לְנַטְרָא לֵיהּ בִּנְטִירוּ עִלָּאָה, כְּמַאן דְּאִיהוּ חֲשִׁיבוּתָא דְמַלְכָּא, דְּהָא בְּגִינֵיהּ, אִתְבְּרַךְ פָּתוֹרֵיהּ, בְּשַׁעֲתָא דְבִרְכָתָא דִמְזוֹנָא, דְּהַהוּא בַּר נָשׁ מְבָרֵךְ.

**571.** The Cup of Blessing is blessed with the blessing that the person makes over it to the Holy One, blessed be He, because it is the secret of Faith, NAMELY MALCHUT. It must be guarded with the highest guard, as it is the importance of the King, and it is for its sake that the table is blessed during the blessing after the meal that one blesses.

572. פָּתוֹרֵיהּ אִצְטְרִיךְ דְּלָא יְהֵא בְּרֵיקַנְיָא, דְּהָא לֵית בִּרְכָתָא מִשְׁתַּכְּחָא עַל פָּתוֹרָא רֵיקַנְיָא, כְּמָה דְאוּקְמוּהָ, דִּכְתִיב, הַגִּידִי לִי מַה יֶּשׁ לָכְי בַבָּיִת וְגוֹ'. וְעַ"ד פָּתוֹרָא לָא אִצְטְרִיךְ לְאִתְחֲזָאָה בְּרֵיקַנְיָא, דְּהָא בִּרְכָאן עִלָּאִין לָא שַׁרְיָין, אֶלָּא בַּאֲתַר שָׁלִים. וְרָזָא דָא וּבְלֵב כָּל חֲכַם לֵב נָתַתִּי חָכְמָה, וּכְתִיב יָהֵב חָכְמְתָא לְחַכִּימִין. וְעַל רָזָא דְנָא שֻׁלְחָן דְּלֶחֶם הַפָּנִים, דִּכְתִיב וְנָתַתָּ עַל הַשֻּׁלְחָן לֶחֶם פָּנִים לְפָנַי תָּמִיד.

**572.** The table OF A PERSON must never be empty, because the blessing is not present on an empty table, as we have established: "Tell me, what have

you in the house" (II Melachim 4:2). Therefore, the table should not appear empty, because the supernal blessings dwell only in a whole place. This is the secret of: "And in the hearts of all that are wise hearted I have put wisdom" (Shemot 31:6), MEANING AFTER HE HAS BEEN PERFECTED WITH WISDOM, HE IS GIVEN WISDOM. "He gives Wisdom to the wise" (Daniel 2:21). Upon this secret is based the table of the shewbread, THAT IT IS NEVER EMPTY, as it is written: "And you shall set upon the table shewbread before Me always" (Shemot 25:30).

## 54. A candlestick, shekels, the month

### A Synopsis

One cannot summarize the dozens of pieces of information given in this section with regard to the menorah, about the meaning of the letters and musical tones. The arms and branches of the candlestick are compared to the Sfirot and to the relationship of Zeir Anpin and Malchut. Malchut, we are told, serves Zeir Anpin in order to reveal all the aspects of Zeir Anpin that are called Sfirah. Rabbi Shimon says to the Faithful Shepherd (Moses) that Malchut is like a sacrifice of higher and lesser value, depending on whether one is wealthy, average, or poor. If one is very wealthy, all good that is done is to one's merit in the world to come. If one is of average wealth, one is serving two worlds, and thus merits half a shekel in the world to come. If one is poor, the sacrifice is of lower value. Yet, we find, God descends to dwell with he who makes himself a contrite and humble spirit for the Shechinah's sake. From the day a person inherits his soul, which comprises the Holy One and His Shechinah, he is called 'a son'. The soul has five names: Neshamah, Ruach, Nefesh, Chayah and Yechidah. Rabbi Shimon next says that, "and you shall love The Creator ' with all your might" means 'with all your money'. He then praises the Faithful Shepherd, and requests that he arise once more and complete the commandments of His master.

### The Relevance of this Passage

This passage again reveals the many layers of meaning that are symbolized by sacred objects in Scripture, and it helps us to more fully comprehend the depth and richness of the Torah. The menorah can be said to have meaning at the physical level, the verbal level, the alphabetical and numerical and geometrical levels, the cosmological level, and the spiritual level. All of these meanings become operational through the simple act of lighting the menorah, although their inner workings remain unobservable to the naked eye. Endowed with this awareness, this section fires up the Light that was revealed when the menorah was lit in the ancient Tabernacle, and it shines upon us with great intensity. All of our spiritual actions will now achieve their maximum effect in the upper world, because we realize that a vast spiritual machinery is set into motion by a simple physical action, such as lighting a menorah or reading a passage of the Holy Zohar. This consciousness is, ultimately, our key.

רעיא מהימנא

573. תַּנָּאִין וְאָמוֹרָאִין אִתְכְּנָשׁוּ כֻּלְּכוּ, דְּהָא קָא מָטוּ שַׁעֲתָא, לְתַקְּנָא

בֵּיה מָאנֵי מַלְכָּא, לְאַנְהָרָא לְאִתְתַּקְּנָא קַמֵיה, דְּאִינוּן: מַשְׁכְּנָא, מְנַרְתָּא, פָּתוֹרָא, מַדְבְּחָא, כִּיּוֹר, וְכַנּוֹ, אָרוֹן, וְכַפֹּרֶת, וּכְרוּבִים, וְכֹלָּא בְּשֶׁקֶל. וּבְגִין דָּא מָנֵי לְיִשְׂרָאֵל, זֶה יִתְּנוּ.

### Ra'aya Meheimna (the Faithful Shepherd)

**573.** All gather, Tanaim and Amoraim, because the time has come to perfect the vessels of the King, and to illuminate so that they should be perfected before Him, for they are the Tabernacle, the candlestick, table, basin, and its stand, ark, cover, and the Cherubs. It is all PERFECTED with a shekel, AS SHALL BE WRITTEN BEFORE US. Therefore, He commanded Yisrael: "This they shall give" (Shemot 30:13).

**574.** קָם תָּנָא חֲדָא וְאָמַר, רַעְיָא מְהֵימָנָא וַדַּאי הָכִי הוּא, וְלָךְ מָנֵי לְמֶעְבַּד כֻּלְּהוּ, הֲדָא הוּא דִכְתִיב, וְעָשִׂיתָ מְנוֹרָה. וְעָשִׂיתָ שֻׁלְחָן. וְהָכִי בְּכֹלָּא, וּרְאֵה וְעָשֵׂה, וּמִכֹּלָּא לָא אִתְקָשֵׁי לָךְ לְמֶעְבַּד, אֶלָּא תְּלַת מִלִּין דִּרְשִׁימִין בְּאַתְוָון דִּשְׁמֶךְ, מְ"נוֹרָה, שְׁ"קָלִים, הַ"חֹדֶשׁ. אֲמַאי אִתְקָשֵׁי לָךְ.

**574.** One Tana arose and said: Faithful Shepherd, certainly it is so. You were commanded to make everything, as it is written: "And you shall make a candlestick" (Shemot 25:31), "You shall make a table" (Ibid. 23) and so in everything, you should observe and make. Of all of them, you had difficulty in making only three things that are marked in the letters of your Name, which are the candlestick (**M**enorah), **Sh**ekels and this (**Hei**) month. Why did you find it difficult?

**575.** א"ל, סָבָא סָבָא, אַתּוּן מְפִיקִין קוּשְׁיָא דָא דְּאִתְקָשֵׁי לִי, מִן מְקֹשָׁה תֵּיעָשֶׂה הַמְּנוֹרָה. וַדַּאי מָאנָא דְּקוּדְשָׁא בְּרִיךְ הוּא, אִיהִי שְׁכִינְתָּא, דְּאִיהִי מָאנָא לְשַׁמְּשָׁא לְבַעְלָהּ, אִיהִי מְנַרְתָּא דִּילֵיהּ, דְּאִתְּמַר בֵּיה, שֶׁבַע בַּיּוֹם הִלַּלְתִּיךָ, דְּאִינוּן: הַגְּדוּלָה, וְהַגְּבוּרָה, וְהַתִּפְאֶרֶת, וְהַנֵּצַח, וְהַהוֹד, יְסוֹד, וּמַלְכוּת. שֶׁבַע כְּלִילָא.

**575.** He said to him: Old man, you learn this difficulty that I had from the

verse: "Of beaten work (or derived from: difficult) shall the candlestick be made" (Ibid.), BECAUSE "SHALL THE CANDLESTICK BE MADE" PURPORTS THAT IT SHOULD BE MADE BY ITSELF, THAT MOSES WAS NOT ABLE TO MAKE IT. Certainly, the vessel of the Holy One, blessed be He, is the Shechinah, which is a vessel to serve her husband, ZEIR ANPIN. She is his candlestick, as it is written: "Seven times a day I praise You" (Tehilim 119:164). They are "the greatness, and the power (Heb. *Gvurah*), and the glory (Heb. *Tiferet*), and the victory (Heb. *Netzach*), and the majesty (Heb. *Hod*)" (I Divrei Hayamim 29:11), Yesod and Malchut, which comprises seven.

576. מִשְּׁבַע דַּרְגִּין אִלֵּין, שְׁלֹשֶׁת קְנֵי מְנוֹרָה מִצִּדָּהּ הָאֶחָד, גּוּפָא וּתְרֵין דְּרוֹעֵי דְמַלְכָּא. אִיהוּ נֵר מִצְוָה, לְאַנְהָרָא בְּהוֹן. וּשְׁלֹשָׁה קְנֵי מְנוֹרָה מִצִּדָּהּ הַשֵּׁנִי, אִינּוּן תְּרֵין שׁוֹקִין, וּבְרִית. וְאִיהוּ נֵר מַעֲרָבִית, לְאַנְהָרָא בְּהוֹן. מְנַרְתָּא דְּמַלְכָּא אִתְקְרִיאַת, וְאִיהִי נֵר לְאַנְהָרָא בֵּיהּ נֵר מִצְוָה, דְּאִתְּמַר בֵּיהּ מִצְוַת יְיָ' בָּרָה מְאִירַת עֵינָיִם.

576. From these seven grades IS THE CANDLESTICK COMPOSED. "Three branches of the candlestick out of one side" (Shemot 25:32) ARE the body, NAMELY TIFERET, and the two arms of the King, WHICH ARE CHESED AND GVURAH. She is MALCHUT. SHE IS the candle for a precept with which to illuminate upon them, BEING THEIR FOURTH. "And three branches of the candlestick out of the second side" are two thighs, WHICH ARE NETZACH AND HOD, the covenant, WHICH IS YESOD, and She, MALCHUT, is the western candle to illuminate them. The king's candlestick is called 'MALCHUT', being a candle that lights the candle with which one fulfills a precept, BEING A FOURTH TO THE ABOVE MENTIONED CHESED, GVURAH AND TIFERET, WHENCE SHE RECEIVES CHOCHMAH, as written: "The commandment of Hashem is pure, enlightening the eyes" (Tehilim 19:9).

577. וּמַאן רֵישָׁא דִּמְנַרְתָּא, בִּינָה ה' עִלָּאָה, דְּאִית לָהּ תְּלַת קָנִין, בְּדִיּוּקְנָא דָּא ה', תְּלַת וָוֵי"ן, דְּאִינּוּן תְּלַת אֲבָהָן. ה' תִּנְיָינָא, ג' קָנִים תִּנְיָינִין בְּדִיּוּקְנָא דָּא ה', דְּאִינּוּן נֶצַח הוֹד יְסוֹד. ו' מְנַרְתָּא דְּאֶמְצָעִיתָא בֵּין יָ"ה. עַל שְׁמֵיהּ אִתְקְרֵי בִּינָה. אִיהוּ כָּלִיל ו' קָנִין לְתַתָּא, בְּחוּשְׁבָּן ו', בּוֹ' קָנִין דִּילֵיהּ.

**577.** What is the head (or top) of the candlestick? It is Binah, the supernal *Hei*, NAMELY THE FIRST THREE SFIROT OF BINAH, THE SUPERNAL ABA AND IMA, who has IN HER SEVEN LOWER SFIROT, WHICH ARE YISRAEL–SABA AND TEVUNAH, three branches in this shape of *Hei*, which is composed of three *Vav*'s that are the three Patriarchs, CHESED, GVURAH AND TIFERET. The second *Hei* HAS a second set of three branches in the shape of *Hei*, which are Netzach, Hod, and Yesod. *Vav* is the center of the candlestick, NAMELY ZEIR ANPIN, which is the son of *Yud* and *Hei*, BECAUSE ZEIR ANPIN IS THE CENTRAL COLUMN THAT MEDIATES BETWEEN THE TWO COLUMNS OF BINAH. Binah is so called after him, BECAUSE BINAH IS MADE UP OF THE LETTERS *BEN* (ENG. 'THE SON OF') *YUD-HEI*. ZEIR ANPIN includes six branches below, IN HIS PLACE, which amounts to *Vav* (= 6) in his six branches.

578. י' אֵשֶׁת חַיִל עֲטֶרֶת בַּעְלָה, תָּגָא דְסֵפֶר תּוֹרָה, כְּצוּרַת ז' מִסִּטְרָא דְעָלְמָא דְּאָתֵי, לָאו אִיהִי מָאנָא לְגַבֵּיהּ, וְלָאו מְשַׁמְּשָׁא לְגַבֵּיהּ, אֶלָּא עֲטָרָה עַל רֵישֵׁיהּ. אֲבָל בְּעָלְמָא דֵין, אִיהִי כְּגַוְונָא דָא, הוּהִ"י אִיהוּ מָאנָא תְּחוֹתֵיהּ, שַׁמּוּשָׁא דִּילֵיהּ, בְּכָל סְפִירָה דִּילֵיהּ, בְּכָל אֵבֶר דִּילֵיהּ, בְּכָל מִדָה דִּילֵיהּ.

**578.** *Yud* is "A virtuous woman is a crown to her husband" (Mishlei 12:4), the crown of the Torah scroll, WHICH IS ZEIR ANPIN, in the shape of a *Zayin*, WHICH IS A *YUD* ON TOP OF A *VAV*, NAMELY A CROWN OVER *VAV*, WHICH IS ZEIR ANPIN, from the aspect of the World to Come, WHICH IS BINAH; MALCHUT is not a vessel to it, and now serves him only as a crown on his head. In this world, BEING MALCHUT FROM HER OWN ASPECT, She is like this *Hei-Vav-Hei-Yud*, WHICH PERMUTATION SHOWS that She is a vessel under him AND serves him in every Sfirah of his, in his every limb, and in his every attribute. MEANING THAT MALCHUT SERVES ZEIR ANPIN IN ORDER TO REVEAL ALL THE ASPECTS OF ZEIR ANPIN THAT ARE CALLED SFIRAH, LIMB AND ATTRIBUTE.

579. וּבְגִין דָּא, י' דָא, לְזִמְנִין אִיהִי תְּחוֹתוֹהִי, לְזִמְנִין עַל רֵישֵׁיהּ, לְזִמְנִין בְּאֶמְצָעִיתָא. עַל רֵישֵׁיהּ יְהוָֹ"ה אֶבֶן מָאֲסוּ הַבּוֹנִים הָיְתָה לְרֹאשׁ פִּנָּה. וְדָא לְהַעֲלוֹת נֵר תָּמִיד, דְּאִיהוּ י' עַל הוָֹ"ה מִסִּטְרָא דִמְנַרְתָּא. בְּאֶמְצָעִיתָא, מַחֲצִית הַשָּׁקֶל, הֲהָ"ד, זֶה יִתְּנוּ, כְּגַוְונָא דָא

הוי״ה. בְּסוֹפָא, בְּמַשְׁכְּנָא, כְּגַוְונָא דָּא הוה״י, חָמֵשׁ אַמּוֹת אֹרֶךְ, מִסְּטְרָא דְּה׳ עִלָּאָה, וְה׳ אַמּוֹת רֹחַב, מִסְּטְרָא דְּה׳ תַּתָּאָה. וְאַמָּה: ו׳. וַחֲצִי הָאַמָּה: י׳. וְכֹלָּא אִתְרְמִיז בְּאָת ו׳.

**579.** Therefore this *Yud*, WHICH IS MALCHUT, is sometimes under ZEIR ANPIN and sometimes on top and sometimes in the center. HE EXPLAINS: On top IS THE SECRET OF THE *YUD* of Yud Hei Vav Hei, IN THE SECRET OF THE VERSE, "The stone which the builders rejected has become the head stone of the corner" (Tehilim 118:22). This is "to cause the lamps to burn continually" (Vayikra 24:2), which is *Yud* on *Hei-Vav-Hei* from the side of the candlestick. In the center OF ZEIR ANPIN, it is half a shekel, MEANING THAT SHE IS AS LARGE AS HIM AND THEY ARE BOTH TWO HALVES OF THE BODY. FOR ZEIR ANPIN IS THE ASPECT OF THE RIGHT HALF OF BINAH AND MALCHUT IS THE ASPECT OF THE LEFT PART OF BINAH. Then it is CALLED 'HALF A SHEKEL', as it is written: "This they shall give...HALF A SHEKEL AFTER THE SHEKEL OF THE SANCTUARY" (Shemot 30:13), thus *Hei-Vav-Yud-Hei*. In the end OF ZEIR ANPIN, in the tabernacle, she *Hei-Vav-Hei-Yud*. AND THIS IS THE SECRET OF "five cubits long" (Shemot 27:1) from the first *Hei*, and "five cubits broad" from the lower *Hei*. 'Cubit' is the secret of *Vav*, WHICH IS ZEIR ANPIN, and half of cubit is *Yud*, WHICH IS MALCHUT THAT STANDS AT THE END. Everything is alluded to in the letter *Vav*, WHICH IS ZEIR ANPIN, OR HIS CROWN, OR IN HIS CENTER OR AT HIS END.

**580.** וְדָא אִיהוּ רָזָא, אֲנִי רִאשׁוֹן וַאֲנִי אַחֲרוֹן וּמִבַּלְעָדַי אֵין אֱלֹהִים דְּאִתְרְמִיז בְּהַאי שְׁמָא, יוֹ״ד הֵ״י וָי״ו הֵ״י וְכָל שֵׁם דְּשַׁלִּיט ה׳ עַל י׳ נוּקְבָא אִיהוּ, מִסְּטְרָא דִּשְׂמָאלָא. וְאע״ג דְּמִסְּטְרָא דְּאָת י׳ אִיהִי בְּרֵישָׁא, בָּתַר דְּבִתְרֵין הֵהִי״ן אִיהִי בְּסוֹפָא, כְּגַוְונָא דָּא הֵ״י הֵ״י, אִתְּדָן לְרוֹב, וְנוּקְבָא אִיהִי. אֶלָּא י׳ עַל ה׳ תָּגָא, תְּחוֹת ה׳, שִׁמּוּשׁ. כ״ש תְּחוֹת ו׳.

**580.** This is the secret of: "I am the first, and I am the last; and beside Me there is no Elohim" (Yeshayah 44:6), "I AM THE FIRST" IS THE SECRET OF MALCHUT WHEN IT IS A CROWN ON THE HEAD OF ZEIR ANPIN, WHILE "AND I AM THE LAST" IS WHEN SHE IS A POINT AT THE END OF ZEIR ANPIN. "AND BESIDE ME THERE IS NO ELOHIM" IS WHEN SHE IS IN THE CENTER OF ZEIR ANPIN, MEANING FOURTH TO THE PATRIARCHS AFTER

CHESED, GVURAH AND TIFERET. She is alluded to in this Name, *Yud-Vav -Dalet, Hei-Yud, Vav-Yud-Vav, Hei-Yud,* WHERE *YUD* IS AT THE BEGINNING AND *YUD* IN THE CENTER OF THE *VAV* – AND *YUD* AT THE END OF THE *HEI* – every Name in which *Hei* dominates *Yud* is a female from the left. And even though *Yud* at the beginning of the Name IS MALE, STILL-IN-ALL, SINCE after the two *Hei*'s of the Name, it is at the end, such as *Hei-Yud,* *Hei-Yud,* it is judged according to the majority, as a female. The *Yud* that is upon *Hei* is a crown, under *Hei* a vessel, and all the more so under *Vav.*

581. וּבְגִין דְּלָא עֲבִידְנָא קָצוּץ וּפֵרוּד בְּיִחוּדָא דִּלְעֵילָא, דְּכֹלָּא יְחוּדָא חַד, נִתְקַשֶּׁה לִי לְמֶעְבַּד. וְקוּדְשָׁא בְּרִיךְ הוּא דְּיָדַע כָּל מַחֲשַׁבְתִּין, אָמַר, בָּתַר דְּדָא לְטוֹב אִתְכַּוָּון, דְּלָא לְמֶעְבַּד קָצוּץ וּפֵרוּד, תֵּ"יעָשֶׂה הַמְּנ"וֹרָה, תֵּיעָשֶׂה מֵעַצְמָהּ כְּגַוְונָא דִשְׁכִינְתָּא, תֵּיעָשֶׂה מֵעַצְמוֹ דְּקוּדְשָׁא בְּרִיךְ הוּא, בְּלָא פֵּרוּדָא. שְׁאָר מָאנִין דִּבְהוֹן אִיהִי שְׁכִינְתָּא שִׁמּוּשׁ, וַיַּעַשׂ בְּצַלְאֵל.

581. I do not make any division or separation in the Supernal Unity, THAT IS IN BINAH, and it is all one unison. THEREFORE, it was difficult for me to produce THE THREE THINGS, THE CANDLESTICK, THE SHEKELS, AND THE NEW MOON, WHICH ARE THE SECRET OF MALCHUT. FOR IN THE CANDLESTICK, THERE IS THE ASPECT OF THE CROWN OF ZEIR ANPIN AND IN THE SHEKELS AND NEW MOON IT IS CONSIDERED TO BE IN HIS CENTER. The Holy One, blessed be He, who knows all thoughts, said, 'His intention was good not to make division and separation.' THEREFORE, let the candlestick be made by itself, just like the Shechinah is made from the self of the Holy One, blessed be He, without division. Of the other vessels of the Tabernacle, by which the Shechinah is at the service, NAMELY AT THE END OF ZEIR ANPIN, IT IS SAID: "And Betzalel made" (Shemot 37:1). AND IT WAS NOT NECESSARY THAT IT BE MADE BY ITSELF.

582. וּבְכָל אֲתָר דִּשְׁכִינְתָּא תַּתָּאָה אִיהִי עֲטָרָא דְּעַמּוּדָא דְּאֶמְצָעִיתָא, כַּד נְטִילַת מִן בִּינָה, דְּאִיהוּ עָלְמָא דְּאָתֵי, וַדַּאי לֵית יְדִיעָה לְבּ"ן. בְּקוּדְשָׁא בְּרִיךְ הוּא, וְלָא בְּכָל מִדּוֹת דִּילֵיהּ, עַד דְּיֵעוּל בְּהַאי תַּרְעָא, דְּאִתְּמַר עָלָהּ זֶה הַשַּׁעַר לַיְיָ', בְּאוֹת ל'.

582. Wherever the lower Shechinah is a crown in the central pillar, WHICH

IS ZEIR ANPIN, THAT IS when she is taken from Binah, which is the World to Come, it is certain THAT THEN man has no knowledge of the Holy One, blessed be He, and all his attributes. BINAH HAS THEN BEEN REDUCED TO THE SIX ENDS until he enters that gate, about which is said: "This is the gate of Hashem" (Tehilim 118:20) MEANING through the letter *Lamed*, WHICH ALLUDES TO A TOWER THAT FLIES IN THE AIR.

583. אִיהִי כְּלִילָא מִכָּל סְפִירָה, וּמִכָּל אַתְוָון דִּשְׁמָהָן, מְפוֹרָשִׁים וְנִסְתָּרִים. אִיהִי נְקוּדָה בְּכָל אָת וְאָת, שִׁמּוּשָׁא תְּחוֹת בַּעְלָהּ. וְאִיהִי עֲטָרָה עַל רֵישֵׁיהּ, מִסִּטְרָא דִּילָהּ דְּטַעֲמֵי. כְּגוֹן סְגוֹל נְקוּדָה תְּחוֹת יַרְכֵי מַלְכָּא, וְהָאָרֶץ הֲדוֹם רַגְלָי. וְאִיהִי בְּאֶמְצָעִיתָא, עִמֵּיהּ, מַחֲצִית הַשֶּׁקֶל, בְּשׁוּרֵק. וְאִיהִי עֲטָרָה עַל רֵישֵׁיהּ, מִסִּטְרָא דִּסְגוֹלְתָּא.

583. FROM THE ASPECT OF HER BEING IN THE CENTER OF ZEIR ANPIN, she is combined from all the Sfirot and all the letters of the expressed and hidden Names, FOR SHE RECEIVES FROM THEM ALL AND THEY ARE INCLUDED IN HER. AND FROM THE ASPECT OF WHICH SHE IS AT THE END OF ZEIR ANPIN, she is a dot under every single letter, because she serves under her husband, ZEIR ANPIN, FOR FROM THERE IS SHE BUILT-UP TO UNITE WITH ZEIR ANPIN. AND FROM THE ASPECT OF her being a crown on the head OF ZEIR ANPIN, she is from the side of the musical tones THAT ARE MARKED ABOVE THE LETTERS. HE EXPLAINS: She is a dot like the dot of Segol that is below the knees of the King, MEANING BELOW NETZACH HOD AND YESOD OF ZEIR ANPIN THAT ARE CALLED 'KNEES', as it is written, "and the earth is My footstool" (Yeshayah 66:1), MEANING MALCHUT THAT IS CALLED 'EARTH'. She is in the center WITH ZEIR ANPIN, for then she is called 'half-a-shekel', HALF A BODY AS EXPLAINED EARLIER, and this is in the point of the Shuruk, which is in the center of the *Vav*. She is a crown on his head from the side OF THE MUSICAL NOTE THAT IS CALLED 'segulta', WHICH IS ABOVE THE LETTERS.

584. זַרְקָא מַקַּף שׁוֹפָר, הוֹלֵךְ סְגוֹלְתָּא, בְּהַהוּא זִמְנָא אִיהִי כֶּתֶר עַל רֵישָׁא דְּמַלְכָּא, כֶּתֶר יִתְּנוּ לְךָ יְיָ' אֱלֹהֵינוּ. אִיהִי יְדִיעַת הַהוּא דְּאִתְּמַר בֵּיהּ, בַּמּוּפְלָא מִמְּךָ אַל תִּדְרוֹשׁ וּבַמְכֻסֶּה מִמְּךָ אַל תַּחְקוֹר. דְּבָהּ אִשְׁתְּמוֹדַע, דְּאִיהוּ רִאשׁוֹן לְעֵילָא בְּתָגָא, דְּהַיְינוּ סְגוֹלְתָּא וְאִיהוּ

אַחֲרוֹן, בִּסְגוֹל. וּמִבַּלְעָדָיו אֵין אֱלֹהִים, בְּשׁוּרֵק. וְכֹלָּא בָּהּ אִשְׁתְּמוֹדַע.

**584.** Zarka, Makaf, Shofar, Holech, Segulta: When we cast and bring close MALCHUT TO BINAH THAT IS CALLED 'SHOFAR', SHE TURNS INTO THE SEGULTA OF THE MUSICAL TONES. Then she is a crown on the head of the King, ZEIR ANPIN, AS MENTIONED ABOVE, FOR THIS IS THE MEANING OF: 'A crown is given to you, Hashem our Elohim'. She is known then by what is said of her, 'Search not into that which is concealed from you, and inquire not into that which is hidden from you.' We know that it is 'first' above in Keter, which is Segulta, WHICH IS ABOVE THE LETTERS. It is the 'last' in the Segol, WHICH IS BELOW THE LETTERS, 'and beside him there is no Elohim' in the Shuruk, WHICH IS IN THE CENTER OF THE LETTERS, FOR THEN SHE ILLUMINATES WITH THE SHINE OF CHOCHMAH. Everything is known through her.

**585.** מַאן דְּאִתְדַּבַּק בָּהּ לְתַתָּא, אִיהִי מְסַלְּקָא לֵיהּ לְעֵילָּא. וּמַאן דְּבָעֵי לְאִסְתַּלְּקָא עֲלָהּ לְאַדְבְּקָא לְעֵילָּא מִינָהּ, אִיהִי מַשְׁפִּילַתוּ לְתַתָּא מִינָהּ, וְלֵית לֵיהּ חוּלָקָא בָּהּ. וּבְגִין דְּיַעֲקֹב אִשְׁתְּמוֹדַע בָּהּ, אוֹלִיף לָהּ לִבְנוֹי, וּמָנֵי דְּלָא יְבַקְּשׁוּן לְסַלְּקָא לְדַרְגָּא לְעֵילָּא מִינָהּ, דְּאִיהִי כֹּלָּא, עֵילָּא וְתַתָּא וְאֶמְצָעִיתָא. הֲה"ד, וְזֹאת אֲשֶׁר דִּבֶּר לָהֶם אֲבִיהֶם.

**585.** Whoever cleaves UNTO MALCHUT from below THE LETTERS, she raises him above, FOR SHE IS BUILT FROM THERE TO UNITE FACE-TO-FACE WITH ZEIR ANPIN. Yet she lowers below her he who desires to ascend above her to understand her from above THE LETTERS, and he has no part in her, BECAUSE WHEN SHE IS ABOVE IN SUPERNAL ABA AND IMA, SHE CANNOT BE UNDERSTOOD. Because Jacob received knowledge through her, MEANING FROM THE ASPECT OF BELOW THE LETTERS, he taught her to his children, and commanded them not to ascend to a level that is above her. She is everything, FOR SHE IS COMBINED OF THEM ALL, from above and from below and in the middle. It is written: "And this is that which their father spoke to them" (Beresheet 44:28), NAMELY MALCHUT THAT IS CALLED 'THIS'. FOR HE TOLD TO THEM NOT TO RISE ABOVE HER.

**586.** נָבִיא דַּהֲוָה אִשְׁתְּמוֹדַע בָּהּ, צָוַוח וְאָמַר לְמָארֵי תּוֹרָה חֲכָמִים

בְּאוֹרַיְיתָא, וַעֲתִירִין בָּהּ, וּשְׂמֵחִים בְּחֶלְקָם. צָוַוח לְגַבַּיְיהוּ וְאָמַר, כֹּה
אָמַר יְיָ' אַל יִתְהַלֵּל וְגוֹ', כִּי אִם בְּזֹאת יִתְהַלֵּל הַמִּתְהַלֵּל הַשְׂכֵּל וְיָדוֹעַ
אוֹתִי. דָּוִד דַּהֲוָה יָדַע בָּהּ אָמַר, אִם תַּחֲנֶה עָלַי מַחֲנֶה וְגוֹ', בְּזֹאת אֲנִי
בוֹטֵחַ. וְיִרְמְיָה חָזָא גָּלוּתָא אָרִיךְ, וְסָמָאֵל וְנָחָשׁ וְכָל מְמָנָן דְּשַׁבְעִין
אוּמִין בְּרִבּוֹ רִבְּוָון, דְּנַחְתֵּי עַל יִשְׂרָאֵל, וְחָזָא הַאי קְרָא דְּאָמַר קוּדְשָׁא
בְּרִיךְ הוּא, וְאַף גַּם זֹאת בִּהְיוֹתָם בְּאֶרֶץ אוֹיְבֵיהֶם וְגוֹ', אָמַר נָבִיא זֹאת
אָשִׁיב אֶל לִבִּי עַל כֵּן אוֹחִיל. וַאֲשֶׁר לֹא שָׁת לִבּוֹ גַּם לָזֹאת, עָלֵיהּ
אִתְּמַר וּכְסִיל לָא יָבִין אֶת זֹאת. וְזֹאת לִיהוּדָה וַיֹּאמַר שְׁמַע יְיָ' קוֹל
יְהוּדָה, בְּגִין דְּנָטִיר מַאי דְּמָנֵי לֵיהּ אֲבוֹי זָכָה לְמַלְכוּ. וְדָוִד בְּגִינָהּ
אִסְתַּלָּק לְמַלְכוּ, דְּטָרַח כָּל יוֹמוֹי עָלָהּ.

**586.** The prophet who recognized her cried and said to the Torah scholars and the Sages of the Torah: Those who are wealthy with it, MEANING that they are happy with their portion, FOR ONE WHO IS HAPPY WITH HIS PORTION IS WEALTHY. He cried toward them and said, "Thus says Hashem, 'Let not the wise man glory…but let him that glories glory in this, that he understands and knows Me'" (Yirmeyah 9:22-23), MEANING MALCHUT THAT IS CALLED 'THIS' AND NOT ABOVE HER. David, who knew her, said "Though a host should camp against me…even then I will be confident (lit. 'in this')" (Tehilim 27:3). Jeremiah saw the length of the exile, as well as Samael and the Serpent and all the princes of the seventy nations that were swooping down upon Yisrael by tens of thousands, and he saw the verse that the Holy One, blessed be He, said, "And yet for all that (lit. 'this'), when they are in the land of their enemies…" (Vayikra 26:44). The prophet said, "This I recall to my mind, therefore I have hope" (Eichah 3:21), FOR MALCHUT THAT IS CALLED 'THIS' IS WITH THEM IN EXILE; THEREFORE, HE AWAITS SALVATION. Of him who "neither did he set his heart even to this" (Shemot :23), it is written: "Nor does a fool understand this" (Tehilim 92:7) and also, "And this is the blessing of Judah. And he said, 'Hear Hashem, the voice of Judah'" (Devarim 33:7). Judah observed what his father commanded him, AS MENTIONED EARLIER; THEREFORE, he merited kingship. David rose because of it to kingship, for he endeavored all his days to PERFECT it.

**587.** אָמַר בּוּצִינָא קַדִּישָׁא, עָלָהּ אִתְּמַר, וְזֹאת הַתּוֹרָה אֲשֶׁר שָׂם מֹשֶׁה

וְגוֹ'. בָּהּ אַזְהַרְתְּ לְיִשְׂרָאֵל, בְּשַׁעְתָּא מִיתָתָךְ. בָּהּ בְּרֶכֶת לְיִשְׂרָאֵל, בְּכָל שֵׁבֶט וְשֵׁבֶט. הַהַ"ד וְזֹאת הַבְּרָכָה אֲשֶׁר בֵּרַךְ מֹשֶׁה וְגוֹ', וּבְגִין דָּא אוֹקְמוּהָ חַבְרַיָּיא מָארֵי מַתְנִיתִין, דִּכְתִיב, זֹאת הַתּוֹרָה אָדָם כִּי יָמוּת בָּאֹהֶל, וְאָמְרוּ עָלָהּ מַאי כִּי יָמוּת בָּאֹהֶל, אֶלָּא אֵין הַתּוֹרָה מִתְקַיֶּימֶת, אֶלָּא בְּמִי שֶׁמֵּמִית עַצְמוֹ עָלֶיהָ, וְלֵית מִיתָה אֶלָּא עוֹנִי, דְּעָנִי חָשׁוּב כְּמֵת.

587. Said the holy luminary, RABBI SHIMON, TO THE FAITHFUL SHEPHERD: It is said, "And this is the Torah which Moses set..." (Devarim 4:44). You admonished Yisrael with it at the time of your death and you did bless every single tribe of Yisrael with it, as it is written: "And this is the blessing which Moses...blessed" (Devarim 33:1). Therefore, the scholars, the masters of the Mishnah, explained it in relation to the verse: "This is the Torah, when a man dies in a tent" (Bemidbar 19:14). Pertaining to this, they said: What is the meaning of "dies in a tent?" The Torah is maintained only in one who kills himself for its sake. Death means poverty, for a poor man is considered as dead.

588. דְּאִיהוּ קָרְבָּן עוֹלֶה וְיוֹרֵד. מִסִּטְרָא דְּעָשִׁיר עוֹלֶה וַדַּאי, דְּאִסְתַּלָּק עָלֵיהּ. דְּכָל עֲתִירִין, כָּל טִיבוּ דְּעָבְדִין, כֻּלְּהוֹן לְזַכָּאָה לְהוֹן לְעָלְמָא דְּאָתֵי, וְתַמָּן אִיהִי תָּגָא עַל רֵישַׁיְיהוּ. בֵּינוֹנִי, דְּפָלַח לְמִזְכֵּי בִּתְרֵין עָלְמִין, אִיהוּ מַחֲצִית הַשֶּׁקֶל עִמֵּיהּ בְּעָלְמָא דְּאָתֵי, כְּגוֹן מַצָּה דְּאִתְפְּלִיג, חֶצְיָהּ תַּחַת הַמַּפָּה לַאֲפִיקוֹמָן בָּתַר סְעוּדָה. וְחֶצְיָהּ לְמִצְוָה קֹדֶם סְעוּדָה. וּמִסִּטְרָא דָּא נֶאֱמַר בְּאֶסְתֵּר, מַה שְּׁאֵלָתֵךְ וְיִנָּתֵן לָךְ וּמַה בַּקָּשָׁתֵךְ עַד חֲצִי הַמַּלְכוּת וְתֵעָשׂ.

588. MALCHUT is like a sacrifice of higher and lesser value. From the side of the wealthy one, it is certainly of higher value for it goes high above him, because all the good that the wealthy people do is all to their merit in the World to Come. There it is a crown on their heads, AND THIS IS FROM THE ASPECT OF IT BEING A CROWN OVER ZEIR ANPIN. The average man, who serves in order to merit two worlds, MEANING ALSO THIS WORLD, it is with him half a shekel in the World to Come, like Matzah that is broken in two, half under the napkin for Afikomen and half TO EAT to fulfill a commandment before the meal. From this side, it is said: "What is your

petition? And it shall be granted you: and what is your request? Even to half the kingdom it shall be performed" (Ester 5:6), AND THIS FROM THE ASPECT THAT SHE IS IN THE MIDDLE OF ZEIR ANPIN.

589. אֲבָל מַאן דְּאִיהוּ עָנִי, דְּמֵמִית גַּרְמֵיהּ בְּגִינָהּ, כְּגַוְונָא דִּילָךְ רַעְיָא מְהֵימְנָא, אִיהוּ קָרְבָּן יוֹרֵד תְּחוֹתָךְ, וַאֲמַאי. בְּגִין דְּמַאן דְּאַשְׁפִּיל גַּרְמֵיהּ בְּגִין שְׁכִינְתֵּיהּ, דְּקוּדְשָׁא בְּרִיךְ הוּא אִיהוּ נָחִית עֲלֵיהּ, וְהַאי הוּא דְּאָמַר דָּוִד, כִּי רָם יְיָ' וְשָׁפָל יִרְאֶה. וְהַנָּבִיא אָמַר, כִּי כֹה אָמַר רָם וְנִשָּׂא שׁוֹכֵן עַד וְקָדוֹשׁ שְׁמוֹ וְגוֹ' וְאֶת דַּכָּא וּשְׁפַל רוּחַ. דְּאַף עַל גַּב דַּאֲנָא מָרוֹם וְקָדוֹשׁ אֶשְׁכּוֹן, בְּגִין הַהוּא דְּאִתְעֲבֵיד דַּכָּא וּשְׁפַל רוּחַ בְּגִין שְׁכִינְתִּי, לְסַלְקָא לָהּ מִשִּׁפְלוּת דִּילָהּ עֲטָרָא לְרֵישֵׁיהּ, אֲנָא נָחִית לְדַיְירָא עִמֵּיהּ. וּבָתַר דְּבַעְלָהּ דִּשְׁכִינְתָּא נָחִית עַל בַּר נָשׁ, אִיהִי נְחִיתַת מֵעַל רֵישֵׁיהּ, וְיַהֲבַת אַתְרָא דְּרֵישָׁא לְבַעְלָהּ, וּנְחִיתַת לְרַגְלוֹי דְּמַלְכָּא. וְרָזָא דְּמִלָּה, הַשָּׁמַיִם כִּסְאִי וְהָאָרֶץ הֲדוֹם רַגְלָי.

589. But for one who is a poor, who endangers his life for its (her) sake, as is your quality, Faithful Shepherd, she, MALCHUT, is a sacrifice of lower value (lit. 'descending') under you, FOR SHE BECOMES A POINT UNDER YESOD OF ZEIR ANPIN, WHICH IS THE ASPECT OF FAITHFUL SHEPHERD. Why is it so? Because one who humbles himself for the sake of the Shechinah, the Holy One, blessed be He, descends to him. This is what David meant by: "Though Hashem be high, yet He takes note of the lowly" (Tehilim 138:6), and the prophet said, "For thus says the high and lofty one, that inhabits eternity, whose Name is holy...yet with him also that is of a contrite and humble spirit" (Yeshayah 57:15). Even though 'I dwell on high and in a holy place,' yet due to him who makes himself a contrite and humble spirit for the Shechinah's sake, in order to elevate Her from Her humbleness AND TO MAKE HER a crown for his head, I descend to dwell with him. After the husband of the Shechinah, WHICH IS ZEIR ANPIN, descends upon the man, She lowers Herself from his head, allows the space of the head to her husband, ZEIR ANPIN, and descends to the legs of the King, NAMELY UNDER HIS NETZACH, HOD AND YESOD THAT ARE CALLED 'LEGS'. The secret of the matter is: "The heaven is My throne, and the earth is my footstool" (Yeshayah 66:1); NAMELY, MALCHUT THAT IS CALLED 'EARTH'.

590. דְּמִיּוֹמָא דְּיָרִית בַּר נָשׁ נִשְׁמָתָא, כְּלִילָא מְקוּדְשָׁא בְּרִיךְ הוּא וּשְׁכִינְתֵּיה, מֵהַהִיא שַׁעֲתָא אִתְקְרֵי בֵּן. אָמַר חַד תָּנָא, וְכִי מֵהַהוּא יוֹמָא דְּיָרִית בַּר נָשׁ נִשְׁמָתָא, כְּלִילָא מְקוּדְשָׁא בְּרִיךְ הוּא וּשְׁכִינְתֵּיה, יִתְקְרֵי בְּרֵיהּ מנ״ל. מֵהַאי קְרָא דְּאָמַר דָּוִד בְּסֵפֶר תְּהִלִּים, אֲסַפְּרָה אֶל חֹק יְיָ׳ אָמַר אֵלַי בְּנִי אַתָּה אֲנִי הַיּוֹם יְלִדְתִּיךָ.

590. From the day that the person inherits the soul, which comprises the Holy One, blessed be He, and His Shechinah, he is called 'a son'. One Tana said: Is it so that from the day that the person inherits a soul that comprises of the Holy One, blessed be He, and His Shechinah, he is called 'a son'? From where do we know this? It is from this verse that David said in the book of Tehilim, "I will tell of the decree: Hashem has said to me, 'You are My son; this day have I begotten you'" (Tehilim 2:7), FOR THIS OCCURS BY EVERY PERSON AT THE MOMENT THAT HE ATTAINS THE SOUL.

591. א״ל בּוּצִינָא קַדִּישָׁא, רַעְיָא מְהֵימְנָא, מַאי הַיּוֹם יְלִדְתִּיךָ. אֶלָּא בְּגִינָךְ אָמַר דָּוִד בְּרוּחַ קֻדְשָׁא, אֲנִי הַיּוֹם יְלִדְתִּיךָ. הֵן עוֹד הַיּוֹם גָּדוֹל, בְּהַהוּא דְּאִתְּמַר בֵּיהּ, וְלָא קָם נָבִיא עוֹד בְּיִשְׂרָאֵל כְּמֹשֶׁה. אַנְתְּ קַיֶּימֶת בִּשְׁכִינְתָּא וְאָהַבְתָּ אֵת יְיָ׳ אֱלֹהֶיךָ בְּכָל לְבָבְךָ, דְּהַיְינוּ גּוּפָא. וּבְכָל נַפְשְׁךָ, דְּהַיְינוּ נִשְׁמָתָא. דַּחֲמֵשׁ שְׁמָהָן אִית לָהּ: נִשְׁמָה. רוּחַ. נֶפֶשׁ. חַיָּה. יְחִידָה. וּבְכָל מְאֹדֶךָ, בְּכָל מָמוֹנָא דִּילָךְ. קוּדְשָׁא בְּרִיךְ הוּא וּשְׁכִינְתֵּיה לָא יָזוּז מִינָךְ בְּכָל אִלֵּין.

591. The holy luminary, RABBI SHIMON said to him: Faithful Shepherd, what is the meaning of "this day have I begotten you"? IT WOULD HAVE SUFFICED TO SAY "YOU ARE MY SON" TO CONVEY THAT I HAVE BEGOTTEN YOU. But because of you did David say with the Holy Spirit "this day have I begotten you." FOR "I" REFERS TO THE SHECHINAH AND "THIS DAY" REFERS TO THE FAITHFUL SHEPHERD WHICH IS TIFERET, AS IT IS WRITTEN: "It is yet high day" (Beresheet 29:7), for him, of whom it is said, "And there arose not a prophet in Yisrael like Moses" (Devarim 34:10). THEREFORE, HE IS CALLED 'HIGH DAY'. You lived in the Shechinah, "and you shall love Hashem your Elohim with all your heart" (Devarim 6:5), namely the body "and with all your soul (Heb. *Nefesh*)"

namely the soul. For it has five names, Neshamah, Ruach, Nefesh, Chayah, Yechidah. "And with all your might", namely with all your money. The Holy One, blessed be He, and His Shechinah do not budge from you in all of these things.

592. אַנְתְּ חַשַׁבְתְּ, דַּאֲפִילוּ הֲווֹ כָּל עָלְמִין תְּחוֹת רְשׁוּתָךְ, הֲוֵית יָהִיב לְאַקָמָא לִשְׁכִינְתָּא בְּקוּדְשָׁא בְּרִיךְ הוּא, וּלְאַמְלָכָא לֵיהּ בִּשְׁכִינְתֵּיהּ עַל כָּל מְמָנָן דְּאוּמִין דְּעָלְמָא, וּלְבָתַר לְסַלְקָא לֵיהּ וּשְׁכִינְתֵּיהּ. בְּדִיוּקְנָא דִּילָךְ כְּלִילָא מִכָּל מִדּוֹת טָבִין, בְּכָל עָלְמִין, וּבְמַשְׁרְיָין עִלָּאִין וְתַתָּאִין, וְעַל כָּל יִשְׂרָאֵל.

**592.** You thought that even if all the worlds would be under your jurisdiction, you would give them in order to raise the Shechinah to the Holy One, blessed be He, to crown Him with His Shechinah over all the Princes of the nations of the world, and afterwards to elevate Him and His Shechinah. Your form is comprised of all good traits, throughout the worlds and the companies of the supernal angels, and the lower beings, and all Yisrael.

593. מַחֲשָׁבָה טוֹבָה הַקוּדְשָׁא בְּרִיךְ הוּא מְצָרְפָהּ לְמַעֲשֶׂה. בָּתַר דְּאַנְתְּ בְּרֵיהּ, עַל כָּל דְּחָשַׁבְתְּ לְמָרָךְ, יְקַיֵּים עַל יָדָךְ, וְלָא תָזוּז מִנֵּיהּ לְעָלְמִין, אֶלָּא תְּהֵא בְּדִיוּקְנֵיהּ בְּכֹלָּא. וְאַנְתְּ בְּגָלוּתָא גָּנִיז מִבְּנֵי נָשָׁא. וְאַנְתְּ מֵעָלְמָא דָא, שְׁלִיחָא דְּקוּדְשָׁא בְּרִיךְ הוּא לְמֵימַר מִלִּין אִלֵּין קָדָמָךְ, וַאֲנָא מְצֻוֶּוה מִנֵּיהּ, דְּלָא לְמֵזַז מִינָךְ בְּכָל עֵת וְשַׁעֲתָא דְּאַנְתְּ בָּעֵי. אֲנָא וְכָל תַּנָּאִין וְאָמוֹרָאִין דִּמְתִיבְתָּאן. קוּם אַשְׁלִים פִּקּוּדִין דְּמָרָךְ.

**593.** The Holy One, blessed be He, attaches a good thought to action. Since you are His son, everything that you thought of for the sake of your Master, He fulfills through you. You will not stir from Him forever, but will remain in His image in everything. You are concealed from humans during the time of exile. But I, from this world, am a messenger from the Holy One, blessed be He, to say these words before you, and I am commanded by Him not to stir from you at anytime that you desire. I and all the Tanaim and Amorain of our Yeshivah REQUEST OF YOU to arise and complete the commandments of your Master.

## 55. "And they shall make an ark"

### A Synopsis

Here, Rabbi Shimon speaks about the Torah and the ark. The supernal ark is the Shechinah, and the Holy One and His Shechinah are a unity. The rabbi maintains that the Torah is more beloved than anything; then he shows that the Ark and the ink with which the Torah is written are both made from wood, commenting that the world to come is the 'inside,' and the letters of Torah, though black on the outside, are white on the inside, as are the Torah scholars and holy sages.

### The Relevance of this Passage

The Ark and the Torah are the two most sacred artifacts and symbols in Scripture; yet they remain the least understood. The ancient Kabbalists, however, revealed the inner significance of these two divine instruments. When Moses received the Tablets on Mount Sinai, the energy and spiritual Light that was revealed during the event literally vanquished all forms of darkness throughout the world. Death, chaos, pain, and suffering were extinguished, overwhelmed by the luminous radiance.

The term "Tablets" is a code describing a unique instrument that was fashioned to generate divine energy in our physical world. In the language of the 21st Century, one might envision the Tablets as a spiritual "nuclear power plant."

Just as a city is equipped with transformer substations that bring electrical energy from the local power station to our homes, the term *Ten Commandments* really signifies ten transformers that channel spiritual energy into our physical world. Both electrical and spiritual energy operate under similar principles. Both require physical tools to manifest and express their power in the material realm.

Moses had attained the highest level of consciousness. This truth is the deeper significance behind the concept of Moses "climbing to the top of the mountain." By virtue of his lofty level, Moses was able to control the raw forces of energy in the spiritual domain. He left the 600,000 Israelites at the foot of the mountain so that he could activate the tablets, thus bringing a final end to death and chaos.

During Moses' absence, two wicked and powerful alchemists infiltrated this gathering of 600,000 strong, and convinced the Israelites that Moses was dead, presumably from an overdose of "spiritual radiation." These hateful souls knew their days were over if the Israelites and the world remained connected to the energy flowing from this mountain. It would mean the end of evil and the dawn of immortality.

Consequently, they devised a cunning plan. They enlisted the help of a rabble-rousing faction that had split from the Israelites. The two alchemists and the rebel group were known as the "Mixed Multitude."

The Mixed Multitude convinced other Israelites to help them manufacture another instrument capable of generating a large supply of spiritual current. Activating this second source of spiritual power was the key to their insidious strategy.

Gold, being the finest conductor of electrical current, was also recognized as a powerful conductor of spiritual current. Thus, they built an apparatus constructed of gold, known by the code term "Golden Calf." Powering up the Golden Calf unleashed an additional surge of energy into the cosmos that literally blew out the circuits of the Tablets. The Light suddenly went out. Death was reborn, and evil returned to our midst. The Tablets, however, still retained an afterglow. Moses put the glowing Tablets into the Ark, along with the scroll of the Torah. Though not operating at peak capacity, this divine apparatus could help mankind replenish the Light that previously showered Sinai and the world.

All the Torahs and arks that now dwell in the synagogues of the world are wired and connected to the original Ark. Each week, when the ark in a synagogue is opened and the Torah is read, a portion of the Light that once illuminated Sinai is restored into the world. Unfortunately, the majority of Torahs in the world today are invalid. But thankfully, by the grace of God, when we read the verses that expound upon these mysteries, the Light of Sinai is replenished by connecting us to the supernal ark.

Moreover, whereas a synagogue is under the constraint of time and space, the supernal ark and the Zohar operate in a timeless realm, above physical laws. Thus, all the Light destined to be revealed now bathes the world with a complete luminous radiance that extinguishes death and decay in a merciful manner. The immortality that was lost on Sinai is hereby regained and the mixed-multitude is forever banished, blotted out by this ultimate illumination of Light.

594. פָּתַח וְאָמַר, וְעָשׂוּ אֲרוֹן עֲצֵי שִׁטִּים. ס"ת, עַמּוּדָא דְּאֶמְצָעִיתָא. אֲרוֹן דִּילֵיהּ, שְׁכִינְתָּא. מִבַּיִת וּמִחוּץ תְּצַפֶּנּוּ, לְקוּדְשָׁא בְּרִיךְ הוּא בִּשְׁכִינְתֵּיהּ, מִלְּבַר וּמִלְּגוֹ וְכֹלָּא חַד. מַה דְּלָאו הָכִי בְּאָרוֹן דְּהַאי עָלְמָא, דְּאוֹרַיְיתָא מִלְּגוֹ מִין אֶחָד, וְאָרוֹן מִין אַחֲרָא. דָּא בִּכְתִיבַת דְּיוֹ, וְדָא עֵץ מְצוּפֶּה זָהָב. דְּוַדַּאי אוֹרַיְיתָא חֲבִיבָא מִכֹּלָּא, הַהֲ"ד, לָא יַעַרְכֶנָּה זָהָב וּזְכוּכִית.

**594.** He opened the discussion with the verse: "And they shall make an ark of Acacia wood" (Shemot 25:10). The Book of Torah is the Central Pillar, NAMELY ZEIR ANPIN. Its ark is the Shechinah and "inside and outside shall he overlay it" (Ibid. 11); namely the Holy One, blessed be He, with His Shechinah THAT COVERS HIM from "outside and inside." THE HOLY ONE, BLESSED BE HE, AND HIS SHECHINAH are all one. This is not so with the ark in this world, for the Torah which is inside is one kind and the ark is another kind. The one is written with ink and the other is wood overlaid with gold. Certainly the Torah is more beloved than everything, as it is written: "Gold and glass cannot equal it" (Iyov 28:17).

עד כאן רעיא מהימנא

595. וּמִסִּטְרָא אַחֲרָא אֲפִילּוּ בְּהַאי עָלְמָא, אַחֲזֵי דְּכֹלָּא חַד, דְּיוֹ וְעֵץ, דִּדְיוֹ מִתַּפּוּחִים, דְּאִתְעֲבִידוּ בְּעֵץ אִינּוּן, וְעוֹד, דְּיוֹ אוּכָם מִלְּבַר, וְחִוָּור מִלְּגוֹ. הָכִי אִינּוּן מָארֵי תּוֹרָה וְחַכָּמִים, אוּכָמִים בְּהַאי עָלְמָא דְּאִיהוּ לְבַר, שַׁפִּירִין בְּהַהוּא עָלְמָא דְּאָתֵי, דְּאִיהוּ מִלְּגוֹ. וּבְגִין דָּא, דְּיוֹ, לִישָׁנָא דַּיּוֹ לְעֶבֶד לִהְיוֹת כְּרַבּוֹ. דְּיוֹ: יוֹ"ד יָדוֹ, חָכְמָה וּתְבוּנָה וָדַעַת דְּכָתַב בַּר נָשׁ בְּיָדוֹ בִּדְיוֹ.

**595.** From a different view even, THE TORAH AND THE ARK THAT ARE in this world show that it is all one, ink and wood, LIKE THE HOLY ONE, BLESSED BE HE, AND HIS SHECHINAH, because ink is made of apples, which are of wood, NAMELY OF GALLNUTS. SO WE FIND THAT A TORAH SCROLL THAT IS WRITTEN WITH INK IS ONE KIND WITH THE ARK THAT IS MADE OF WOOD, FOR THIS IS THE SECRET OF THE HOLY ONE, BLESSED BE HE, AND HIS SHECHINAH. Moreover, ink, NAMELY THE LETTERS, is black on the outside and white on the inside, as are the Torah scholars and sages black in this world, which is outside. They are beautiful in the World to Come, which is in the inside. Therefore, ink (Heb. *dyo*) is the same expression as 'Dayo (Eng. 'sufficient') for a servant to be like his master.' Dyo CONTAINS THE LETTERS IN *YUD* OR THE LETTERS OF 'yado' (Eng. 'his hand') THAT ALLUDE TO Chochmah, Binah and Da'at, WHICH IS THE SECRET OF *YUD*, for a man writes with his hand.

**End of Ra'aya Meheimna (the Faithful Shepherd)**

## 56. "And look that you make them after their pattern"

### A Synopsis
Here, Rabbi Yosi says that the title verse is referring to the tabernacle. God gave Moses detailed instructions for constructing the tabernacle, and also gave him a vision of how the tabernacle of Metatron would look in the future. The tabernacle above did not come into existence until the tabernacle below was complete. Rabbi Yosi then tells us that there are two tabernacles and two priests: of the latter, one is the primordial Light (Chesed of Zeir Anpin) and the other is Michael the High Priest.

### The Relevance of this Passage
Our physical world is an exact reflection of the upper world, thus the well-known Kabbalistic phrase, "As Above, so Below." The forces of the upper world influence and animate all events in this physical world, except for the actions of man. Our deeds in the lower world cause a stirring in the upper world. Thus, by reading this section, we reconnect ourselves to the tabernacle below and the supernal tabernacle above, forever ensuring our ties to the Light of the Creator. We make contact with the angel Matatron, Michael, and the Sfirah of Binah and Chesed, which bring an abundance of Mercy and inner guidance into our lives.

596. פָּתַח רַבִּי יוֹסֵי וְאָמַר, בְּאִינּוּן רָזִין עִלָּאִין דְּמַשְׁכְּנָא כְּתִיב, וּרְאֵה וַעֲשֵׂה בְּתַבְנִיתָם וְגוֹ', וּכְתִיב וַהֲקֵמֹתָ אֶת הַמִּשְׁכָּן כְּמִשְׁפָּטוֹ וְגוֹ', אוֹלִיפְנָא דְּאָמַר לֵיהּ קוּדְשָׁא בְּרִיךְ הוּא לְמֹשֶׁה, כָּל תִּקּוּנִין, וְכָל דְּיוּקְנִין דְּמַשְׁכְּנָא, כָּל חַד וְחַד כַּדְקָא חֲזֵי לֵיהּ, דְּחָמָא לֵיהּ לִמְטַטְרוֹ"ן, דְּקָא מְשַׁמֵּשׁ לְכַהֲנָא רַבָּא לְגוֹ. וְאִי תֵּימָא, וְהָא לָא אִתְּקַם מַשְׁכְּנָא לְעֵילָּא, עַד יוֹמָא דְּאִתְּקַם מַשְׁכְּנָא לְתַתָּא, וְלָא שִׁמֵּשׁ הַהוּא נַעַר דִּלְעֵילָּא, עַד יוֹמָא דְּשִׁמְּשׁוּ לְתַתָּא, בְּהַאי מַשְׁכְּנָא אַחֲרָא.

596. Rabbi Yosi opened the discussion saying: Of these mysteries of the Tabernacle, it is written, "And look that you make them after their pattern…" (Shemot 25:40) and it is written: "And you shall rear up the Tabernacle according to its fashion…" (Shemot 26:30). We have learned that the Holy One, blessed be He, spoke to Moses of all the forms and all the constructions of the Tabernacle, each one as it should be, and showed him THE ANGEL, Metatron, who serves the High Priest inside. If you ask: But the Tabernacle above was not erected until the day that the Tabernacle

was erected below, and that youth, METATRON, did not serve above until
the day that they served below in the other Tabernacle?

597. אֶלָּא וַדַּאי הָכִי הוּא, דְּהָא מַשְׁכְּנָא לָא אִתְּקַם לְעֵילָא, עַד
דְּאִתְּקַם מַשְׁכְּנָא לְתַתָּא, אֲבָל חָמָא מֹשֶׁה חֵיזוּ דְּכָל מַשְׁכְּנָא, וְלָא הֲוָה
מִתְסַדֵּר בְּקִיּוּמֵיהּ, עַד דְּאִתְּקַם מַשְׁכְּנָא לְתַתָּא, וְחָמָא לֵיהּ לִמְטַטְרוֹ"ן
מְשַׁמֵּשׁ לְבָתַר, לָאו דַּהֲוָה אִיהוּ מְשַׁמֵּשׁ, אֶלָּא דַּהֲוָה מְשַׁמֵּשׁ לְבָתַר,
וְלָאו בְּהַהוּא זִמְנָא. אָמַר לֵיהּ קוּדְשָׁא בְּרִיךְ הוּא לְמֹשֶׁה, חָמֵי מַשְׁכְּנָא,
וְחָמֵי נַעַר, כֹּלָּא מִתְעַכֵּב עַד דְּיִתְּקַם הָכָא לְתַתָּא.

**597.** HE ANSWERS: Certainly it is so that the Tabernacle was not erected
above until it was erected below. Moses saw above the appearance of the
whole Tabernacle, but it was not arranged completely until the Tabernacle
was erected below, and he saw Metatron, who he served afterwards. AND
HE DID NOT SEE HIM actually serving but rather as he would be serving
later on, but not at that time. The Holy One, blessed be He, said to Moses,
'See the Tabernacle and see the youth, METATRON, but it will all be
delayed until the Tabernacle will be erected below.'

598. וְאִי תֵּימָא, אִי הָכִי, מְטַטְרוֹן אִיהוּ דְּקָא מְשַׁמֵּשׁ. אֶלָּא וַדַּאי
מַשְׁכְּנָא דִּילֵיהּ אִיהוּ, וּמִיכָאֵל כַּהֲנָא רַבָּא, אִיהוּ דְּקָא מְשַׁמֵּשׁ גּוֹ הַהוּא
מַשְׁכְּנָא דִּמְטַטְרוֹן. כְּגַוְונָא דִּמְשַׁמֵּשׁ כַּהֲנָא רַבָּא עִלָּאָה לְעֵילָא, גּוֹ
מַשְׁכְּנָא אַחֲרָא סְתִימָא דְּלָא אִתְגַּלְיָיא, בְּרָזָא דְּעָלְמָא דְּאָתֵי. תְּרֵין
מַשְׁכְּנִין אִינּוּן. חַד אִיהוּ סְתִימָא עִלָּאָה. וְחַד הַאי מַשְׁכְּנָא דִּמְטַטְרוֹן.
תְּרֵי כַּהֲנֵי אִינּוּן, חַד אוֹר קַדְמָאָה. וְחַד מִיכָאֵל כַּהֲנָא רַבָּא לְתַתָּא.

**598.** If you ask: Metatron serves in the Tabernacle above AND NOT
MICHAEL? HE ANSWERS: The tabernacle is of Metatron and Michael the
High Priest is the one who serves in the Tabernacle of Metatron, as the High
Priest serves above in another Tabernacle that is concealed and not revealed,
which is the secret of the World to Come, WHICH IS BINAH. There are two
tabernacles. One is concealed, BINAH, and one is the Tabernacle of
Metatron. There are two priests, MEANING THE ATTRIBUTES OF CHESED
THAT IS CALLED 'PRIEST'. One is the primordial light, NAMELY CHESED
OF ZEIR ANPIN, and one is Michael, the High Priest below

## 57. Three Names included as one

### A Synopsis

Rabbi Shimon here discloses some concealed secrets of the supernal tabernacle, Binah, which is built on twelve pearls or supernal limbs. He speaks then of the three names which are combined together and which interpenetrate each other from the Right, Left and Central Columns of Zeir Anpin. The Right Column, Chesed, holds the Alef and Lamed of El. The Left Column, Gvurah, takes those letters and adds Hei-Yud-Mem to form Elohim. Mercy is included with them. The Central Column of Zeir Anpin takes all these and adds Nun-Vav to form Eloheinu, 'Our Elohim'. We can see that the Right Column is included in the Left; but the Left Column is also included in the Right by virtue of the fact that they take letters from the World to Come (Binah) to form Mem-Yud-Mem, Mayim, or 'water'. Rabbi Shimon also explains here how letters are formed and congealed and cocooned.

### The Relevance of this Passage

The mention of "Twelve Pearls" indicates the root of the twelve constellations. Thus, we receive power to ascend above the plane of the planets and their respective astrological influences. At this moment we alter our destiny for the better, guaranteeing a redemption that is free of negative influences, judgments, and any form of pain.

When the Zohar discourses on the Three Columns, we are strengthened in our souls so that our behavioral actions embody balance. We receive mercy (Right Column), and it forever tempers and sweetens our acts of judgment towards others. We arouse judgment (Left Column), and it balances excessive mercy, so that we offer tough love in the appropriate measure and time. We receive emotional strength to always resist our selfish desires (Central Column), so that we enjoin our soul to the Supernal Realm, the source of all sustenance and blessing. Finally, the powers of Creation, embodied by the Hebrew letters, bring complete order, balance, and rejuvenation to all existence.

599. מִכָּאן רָזִין סְתִימִין דְּבֵי מַשְׁכְּנָא, מִפּוּמָא דְבוּצִינָא. מַשְׁכְּנָא עִלָּאָה, אִתְבְּנֵי עַל תְּרֵיסַר מַרְגְּלִיטִין, שַׁיְיפִין עִלָּאִין, יְמִינָא וּשְׂמָאלָא, שְׂמָאלָא וִימִינָא.

599. From here, concealed secrets of the Tabernacle are disclosed by the mouth of the Luminary, WHO IS RABBI SHIMON. The supernal Tabernacle,

WHICH IS BINAH, is built on twelve pearls, supernal limbs, WHICH ARE THREE COLUMNS AND MALCHUT THAT RECEIVES THEM. EACH ONE OF THESE FOUR IS COMBINED OF THREE COLUMNS, TOTALING TWELVE, and are comprised, the right within the left and the left within the right.

600. תְּלַת שְׁמָהָן אִינוּן כְּלִילָן כַּחֲדָא, וְדָא עָיֵיל בְּדָא, וְדָא עָיֵיל בְּדָא. א״ל, קַדְמָאָה וְאִתְסְדַר בִּימִינָא. א, אִיהוּ קַדְמָאָה דְּאִיהִי יְמִינָא, וְאַגְלִים וְאִתְצָיָיר בְּרָזָא דִּימִינָא, וְכַד עָיֵיל וְקָא מְשַׁמֵּשׁ לְגוֹ אִתְאֲחָד בַּהֲדֵיהּ ל, וְאִקְרֵי בְּרָזָא דִּילֵיהּ א״ל, דְּהָא ל׳ מֵרָזָא דִּלְעֵילָא גוֹ קֹדֶשׁ הַקֳּדָשִׁים נָפַק.

600. There are three Names that are combined together. THEY ARE EL, ELOHIM, AND ELOHEINU (ENG. 'OUR ELOHIM'), AS SHALL BE EXPLAINED, and each penetrates the other. El is the first Name, as is set on the right OF ZEIR ANPIN, WHICH IS THE SECRET OF CHESED. THE SYSTEM IS AS FOLLOWS: *Aleph*, which is first, is to the right, NAMELY CHESED. It was turned into a shapeless lump, then was sculpted in the secret of the right. SMALLNESS IS CONSIDERED AS IF IT WERE AN UNFINISHED FORM, FOR IT IS A FORMLESS LUMP NOT YET COMPLETED, WHILE GREATNESS IS CONSIDERED SHAPED. When it entered and served internally, NAMELY IN BINAH THAT IS CALLED 'SUPERNAL TABERNACLE', the *Lamed* joined it. In its secret, it is called 'El (*Aleph-Lamed*)', because the *Lamed* emerged from the secret of above inside the Holy of Holies, WHICH IS BINAH, BECAUSE THE *LAMED* ALLUDES TO THE SECRET OF TOWER THAT FLIES IN THE AIR, NAMELY BINAH.

601. לָאו דְּתַמָּן אַגְלִים, אֶלָּא וַדַּאי כַּד נָפַק אַגְלִים, כִּשְׁאַר אַתְוָון, דְּכַד נָפְקוּ מֵרָזָא דְּעָלְמָא דְּאָתֵי, אַגְלִימוּ וְאִתְצָיָירוּ. אוּף הָכִי הַאי ל׳, אע״ג דְּאִיהוּ רָזָא דִּלְעֵילָא, לָא אַגְלִים, עַד דְּנָפַק לְבַר, וּכְדֵין א״ל. וְדָא רָזָא דִּימִינָא.

601. The *Lamed* became cocooned there IN BINAH, and it is certain that when it emerged from there, it became cocooned like the other letters, that became cocooned and shapen after emerging from the secret of the World to Come, WHICH IS BINAH. BECAUSE BEFORE THE LETTERS ENTER THE

CENTRAL COLUMN, THEY ARE MOIST AND AFTER THEY EMERGE FROM THERE TO THE SECRET OF THE FIRMAMENT – WHICH IS THE CENTRAL COLUMN, THEY CONGEAL AND BECOME COCOONED. That *Lamed* also, even though it is a supernal secret, ALLUDING TO BINAH, THE SECRET OF THE TOWER THAT FLIES IN THE AIR, it did not become cocooned until it emerged outside. Then it is the Name El, which is to the right OF ZEIR ANPIN.

602. שְׂמָאלָא כָּלִיל בְּגַוֵּיה לִימִינָא, וְנָטִיל הַאי שְׁמָא לְגַבֵּיה, וְאִתְכְּלִיל בַּהֲדֵיה, וְכַד אִתְכְּלִיל בַּהֲדֵיה אִקְרֵי אִיהוּ אֱלֹהִים. וְאִי תֵּימָא, הָא אַקְדִּים שְׂמָאלָא בְּרָזָא דְּעָלְמָא דְּאָתֵי.

**602.** The left includes within it the right, and takes this Name, EL (*ALEPH-LAMED*), to itself and combines with it. When it is included with it, it is called 'Elohim' (*Aleph-Lamed-Hei-Yud-final Mem*). HE QUESTIONS: And if you say: Behold the left came first in the secret of the World to Come?

603. וַדַּאי הָכִי הוּא. אֶלָּא, כַּד נָפְקוּ דַּרְגִּין, בְּרָזָא דְּאַתְוָון מִגּוֹ עָלְמָא דְּאָתֵי, בָּעָא שְׁמָא דָּא לְאִתְחֲזָאָה וּלְאִתְבְּנֵי, לְאַחֲזָאָה עַל הַהוּא אֲתָר דְּנָפְקֵי מִתַּמָּן, וְאִתְבְּנֵי שְׁמָא דָּא, כְּגַוְונָא דָּא. אֱ"ל בְּקַדְמֵיתָא בְּסִטְרָא דִּימִינָא, אִתְכְּלִיל גּוֹ שְׂמָאלָא, וְנָטִיל לֵיה שְׂמָאלָא, וְאִקְרֵי אֱלֹהִים, וְדָא אִיהוּ רָזָא דִּימִינָא, בִּשְׁמָא דֶּאֱלֹהִים, וְעַל רָזָא דָּא, בְּכָל אֲתָר דְּאִיהוּ דִּינָא, תַּמָּן אִיהוּ רַחֲמֵי, דְּהָא כָּלִיל אִיהוּ דִּינָא, וְהָא אִתְבְּנֵי וְאִתְחֲזֵי.

**603.** HE ANSWERS: Certainly it is so, but when the grades emerge in the secret of letters from the World to Come, WHICH IS BINAH, the name ELOHIM has to be revealed and erected, and point at that place from where they emerged, MEANING AT THE ORDER OF THEIR EMERGING IN BINAH. THEREFORE, this name was erected in this way: First *Aleph* and *Lamed* on the right side became included LATER within the left and the left took it, AND BECAME JOINED WITH ITS LETTERS, *HEI, YUD, MEM,* and is called 'Elohim'. AS THEY EMERGED IN BINAH SO DID THEY EMERGE IN ZEIR ANPIN. This is the secret of the right, WHICH IS EL THAT IS PRESENT in the Name Elohim. According to that secret IS FOUND that there is Mercy

wherever there is Judgment, BECAUSE JUDGMENT, WHICH IS LEFT, includes it, and is erected and visible in it.

604. הַהוּא דְּנָפַק מִתַּמָּן, אֶמְצָעִיתָא, נָטִיל לְתַרְוַוייְהוּ, וְאִשְׁתָּלִים, וְאִקְרֵי אֱלֹהֵינוּ. הָא הָכָא שְׁלִימוּ דְּאִתְחֲזֵי מֵרָזָא דְּעָלְמָא עִלָּאָה, וְכֹלָּא אִתְכְּלִיל דָּא בְּדָא. כֵּיוָן דְּהַאי אֶמְצָעִיתָא אִשְׁתָּלִים, שָׁרָא עֲלֵיהּ שְׁמָא קַדִּישָׁא, מַפְתְּחָא דְּכֹלָּא, דְּאִקְרֵי יְהוֹ״ה, וּכְדֵין נָטִיל לְכָל סִטְרִין, עֵילָּא וְתַתָּא, יְמִינָא וּשְׂמָאלָא, וּלְכָל סִטְרִין אַחֲרָנִין. וְעַל דָּא, כַּד אִשְׁתָּלִים מֵרָזָא דִּתְרֵין סִטְרִין מִימִינָא וּשְׂמָאלָא, אִקְרֵי אֱלֹהֵינוּ, הָא הָכָא יְמִינָא וּשְׂמָאלָא וְאֶמְצָעִיתָא בִּכְלָלָא דִּשְׁמָא דָּא. וְדָא אִתְחֲזֵי וְאִתְבְּנֵי. רָזָא דְּאַתְוָון נָפְקוּ מִתַּמָּן, כְּגַוְונָא דָּא אִתְבְּנֵי וְאִתְחֲזֵי, כָּל חַד וְחַד.

**604.** The one that emerged from there, FROM BINAH, IN THE SENSE OF THE CENTRAL COLUMN OF ZEIR ANPIN, receives them both, NAMELY THE NAME EL AND THE NAME ELOHIM, and is completed to be called 'Eloheinu' (Eng. 'Our Elohim'). Here is the completeness that appears from the secret of the Supernal World, WHICH IS BINAH. It is all combined one with the other, BECAUSE THERE ARE HERE IN THE NAME ELOHEINU SIX LETTERS: *ALEPH-LAMED* ON THE RIGHT – *HEI-YUD* ON THE LEFT AND *NUN-VAV* IN THE CENTER AND THEY ARE COMBINED TOGETHER. Since this Central COLUMN is completed, the Holy Name dwells upon it, which is the key to everything that is called Yud Hei Vav Hei, Then THE CENTRAL COLUMN takes all the sides, the upper and lower, WHICH ARE NETZACH HOD, right and left, WHICH ARE CHESED AND GVURAH, and all the other directions, WHICH ARE EAST AND WEST. Therefore, when it is completed with the secret of the two sides, NAMELY WITH THE TWO COLUMNS, from right and left, it is called 'Eloheinu', for there is right, left and center in this name, AS MENTIONED. It is visible and erected as is the secret of letters that emerge from there erected and visible, each and every one, AS WILL BE EXPLAINED.

605. הָא אִתְכְּלִיל יְמִינָא בִּשְׂמָאלָא, וְנָטִיל שְׂמָאלָא שְׁמָא דִּימִינָא, יְמִינָא אָן כָּלִיל בְּגַוֵּיהּ שְׂמָאלָא, לְמֶהֱוֵי נָטִיל יְמִינָא רָזָא דִּשְׂמָאלָא. אֶלָּא, כַּד אִתְכְּלִיל יְמִינָא בִּשְׂמָאלָא, וְנָטִיל שְׂמָאלָא שְׁמָא רָזָא

דִּימִינָא, שְׁמָא אֵ"ל. יְמִינָא כָּלִיל בְּגַוֵּיהּ שְׂמָאלָא, וְאִיהוּ הִי"ם.

**605.** HE ASKS: The right is indeed included in the left, for the left receives the name of the right, WHICH IS EL, BUT where is the left included in the right, so that right should receive the meaning of the left? HE ANSWERS: The right is included in the left and the left received the Name of the meaning of the right, WHICH IS the name El. The right also included in itself the left, which is *Hei-Yud- final Mem*.

606. אֲמַאי הָכִי. אֶלָּא בְּשַׁעֲתָא דְּאִתְבְּנֵי הַהוּא אֲתָר דְּנַפְקוּ מִתַּמָּן, נָטִיל לִשְׂמָאלָא תְּרֵין אַתְוָון, יְמִינָא נָטִיל חַד, מֵרָזָא דְּעָלְמָא דְּאָתֵי. שְׂמָאלָא תְּרֵין, וְאִיהוּ הִי"ם. כְּדֵין יְמִינָא כָּלִיל בְּגַוֵּיהּ לִשְׂמָאלָא, וְנָטִיל לְאָת בַּתְרָאָה ם, וְנָטִיל י' דַּהֲוָה בִּשְׂמָאלָא, ם אִיהוּ בִּשְׁלִימוּ מֵ"ם, וְאִתְבְּנֵי הָכִי מַיִם, בְּהַהוּא י' דְּנָטִיל יַתִּיר. כְּדֵין יְמִינָא כָּלִיל לֵיהּ לִשְׂמָאלָא בְּגַוֵּיהּ.

**606.** HE QUESTIONS: Why is it so? HOW COULD THE RIGHT BE INCLUDED IN THE LEFT? HE ANSWERS: When that place whence they emerged was erected, NAMELY IN THE THREE COLUMNS OF BINAH, the left received two letters, OUT OF THE LETTERS *HEI-YUD-FINAL MEM* WHICH ARE IN THE LEFT COLUMN OF BINAH, and the right took one letter OF THE LETTERS *HEI-YUD-FINAL MEM* that are in the World to Come, WHICH IS BINAH. The left took two, which are *HEI-YUD* of *Hei-Yud-final Mem*. Then the right included the left in itself and took the last letter OF *HEI-YUD-FINAL MEM* – WHICH IS *Mem*. It also took the *Yud*, which was to the left; the *Mem* it received is fully spelled *Mem-Mem*. Together with the *Yud* it received, the word Mayim (Eng. 'water', *Mem-Yud-final Mem*) was constructed. Then does the right include the left within it.

## 58. The letters

### A Synopsis

Here, Rabbi Shimon speaks at length, telling how all the letters formed, rolled, combined, conceived new letters and thus participated in the creation of everything: fire, water, air, all the Sfirot, the light, the goatskin covering on the tabernacle, the perfection of the tabernacle, sound, the Garden, and the waters. He tells how all the seven names coming from the name of Mem-Bet in 42 letters are the secret of: "In the beginning Elohim created the heaven and the earth. And the earth was without form and void'" We also learn the meanings of: "And darkness was on the face of the deep," "Let there be light, and there was light," "the laver and its pedestal," "Let there be a firmament in the midst of the waters," "The voice of The Creator is upon the waters, the El of Glory'," "Let the earth bring forth grass," and "Let the waters under the heaven be gathered together to one place."

### The Relevance of this Passage

The Hebrew letters are the instruments of Creation. They are genetic strands of cosmic DNA. The letters transcend religion, race, geography, and the very concept of language. They are instruments of power.

This truth is found within the Hebrew word for "letter," which means "pulse" or "vibration," indicating a flow of energy. By virtue of their shapes, sounds, and sequences, Hebrew letters radiate a wide range of forces. Their influence is universal, their scope, sweeping. Their power is shared with all mankind, though this penetrating truth has been concealed for millennia. Their sacred energy removes rash and intolerant emotions, fear, and anxiety from our beings. Their spiritual influence cleanses destructive impulses from our natures. The Light they emit purifies our hearts.

All these spiritual benefits, and more, are now bequeathed to us in this majestic passage discoursing on the Creation of the spiritual and physical cosmos.

607. לְבָתַר אִתְבָּנוּן אַתְוָון, א' דַּהֲוָה בְּקַדְמֵיתָא בְּסִטְרָא דִימִינָא, אוֹלִיד וְאַפִּיק אָת ש', כָּלִיל בִּתְלַת סִטְרִין, וְאִשְׁתַּתַּף בְּאָת א', וְאִתְעֲבֵיד אֵשׁ. תּוּ אַעֲדוּ אַתְוָון אִלֵּין, גּוֹ בְּטִישׁוּ דִתְרֵין סִטְרִין אִלֵּין, וְאִתְקְרִיבוּ כַּחֲדָא בְּמַחְלוֹקֶת, וּמִגּוֹ מַחֲלוֹקֶת דָּא דְּמַיִם בְּאֵשׁ, וְאֵשׁ בְּמַיִם, אוֹלִידוּ אַתְוָון וְאַפִּיקוּ אָת ר' וְאָת ו' וְאָת ח' וְאִתְעֲבֵידוּ רוּחַ,

וְעָאל בֵּין תְּרֵין סִטְרִין, וּכְדֵין אִתְיַישָׁבוּ אַתְוָון קַדְמָאֵי בְּדוּכְתַּיְיהוּ, כָּל חַד וְחַד בִּשְׁלִימוּ.

**607.** Afterwards, the letters are erected in such a way that the *Aleph* that was originally on the right side, begot and brought forth IN THE LEFT the letter *Shin*, WHICH IS COMBINED OF THE THREE SIDES – RIGHT LEFT AND CENTER. THEREFORE, IT CONTAINS THREE *VAV*'S and it jpined with the letter *Aleph*, and THE COMBINATION Esh (Eng. 'fire') was made ON THE LEFT. Some more letters were conceived by the blows of the two sides, RIGHT AND LEFT, and they approached each other in controversy, FOR THE RIGHT IS MADE OF WATER AND THE LEFT OF FIRE. From this controversy of fire with water and water with fire, they bore letters and they brought forth the letter *Resh* and the letter *Vav* and the letter *Chet* to become Ruach (Eng. 'air'). THE RUACH entered between the two sides, WHICH ARE WATER AND FIRE, AND MEDIATED AND COMBINED THE ONE WITH THE OTHER, and then the original letters settled in their places, each one in perfection.

**608.** תּוּ אַתְוָון אַעֲדוּ, וְאִתְגַּלְגְּלוּ כַּחֲדָא, א' אַפִּיק מ', דְּאִיהוּ מִסִּטְרָא דִּילֵיהּ בִּימִינָא, דְּהָא בִּימִינָא אִתְיַישָׁב. מ' אַפִּיק שׁ' בְּגִין דְּהָא מ' כְּלִילָא אִיהִי, בְּקַדְמֵיתָא הֲוַת מִשְּׂמָאלָא, וְאִתְכְּלִיל לְבָתַר בִּימִינָא וְאִשְׁתְּלִים בִּתְרֵין סִטְרִין, כֵּיוָן דְּאִשְׁתְּלִים, אַעֲדוּ וְאוֹלִידוּ כַּחֲדָא, וְאִתְכְּלָלוּ בִּתְרֵין סִטְרִין.

**608.** More letters were conceived and they rolled together. The *Aleph* brought forth *Mem* that is from the right side, because it settled in the right, AND NOW THE *ALEPH* BROUGHT IT OUT TO THE ASPECT OF THE LEFT SIDE – the *Mem* brought forth the *Shin* TO THE ASPECT OF THE CENTRAL COLUMN, because the *Mem* was originally included in the left, BECAUSE IT WAS A CLOSED FINAL *MEM* IN THE NAME ELOHIM ON THE LEFT. Afterwards, it became combined in the right, FOR THE *ALEPH* TOOK IT AND MADE IT INTO AN OPEN *MEM* SO WE FIND THAT it is completed on two sides, ON THE RIGHT AND ON THE LEFT – and once it was completed, BOTH THE SIDES IN IT CONCEIVED and bore together THE LETTER *SHIN* that is combined of the two sides. IT IS THE SECRET OF THE CENTRAL COLUMN THAT COMBINES WITHIN ITSELF RIGHT AND LEFT – FOR THE THREE BRANCHES OF THE *SHIN* ALLUDE TO THEM.

609. אִתְתְּקְפוּ אַתְוָון אמ״ש תְּלַת אִלֵּין, וְאַעֲדוּ וְאוֹלִידוּ תְּלַת אַחֲרָנִין, גּוֹ גִּלְגּוּלָא. מ׳ אִתְתְּקַן וְאַעֲדֵי וְאוֹלִיד ר׳. א׳ אַעֲדֵי וְאוֹלִיד ו׳. ש׳ אַעֲדֵי וְאוֹלִיד ח׳, וְאִשְׁתַּכְלַל כֹּלָא.

**609.** Those three letters, *Aleph*, *Mem*, *Shin*, grew stronger, conceived and begot three others while revolving. The *Mem* was constructed and conceived and bore *Resh*. The *Aleph* conceived and bore *Vav*. The *Shin* conceived and bore the letter *Chet*, and then they were accomplished together.

610. תּוּ אַעֲדוּ אַתְוָון אִלֵּין רָזָא אמ״ש, וְאִתְגַּלְגְּלוּ כְּמִלְּקַדְמִין, א׳ אַעֲדֵי וְאוֹלִיד וְאַפִּיק אֶת ב׳ בְּסִטְרָא דְּמַעֲרָב, כְּדֵין אִתְיַישָּׁב אִיהוּ בְּסִטְר דָּרוֹם. מ׳ אַעֲדֵי וְאוֹלִיד וְאַפִּיק אֶת ד׳ בְּסִטְרָא דְּצָפוֹן, כְּדֵין אִסְתַּלָּק אִיהוּ בֵּין צָפוֹן וְדָרוֹם, וְתַלְיָא בַּאֲוִירָא. ש׳ אַעֲדֵי וְאוֹלִיד וְאַפִּיק אֶת ג׳, וְאִתְיַישָּׁב בְּסִטְרָא דְּמִזְרָח, וְאִיהוּ אִסְתַּלָּק בֵּין מַעֲרָב וּמִזְרָח, וְתַלְיָא בַּאֲוִירָא. אִשְׁתְּכָחוּ תְּרֵין אַתְוָון מ״ש, תַּלְיָין בַּאֲוִירָא.

**610.** The letters of the secret of *Aleph-Mem-Shin* again conceived and revolved as before. The *Aleph* conceived and bore the letter *Bet* on the West side, WHICH IS MALCHUT. Then THE *ALEPH* settled on the South side, WHICH IS CHESED. The *Mem* conceived and bore the letter *Dalet* on the North side, WHICH IS GVURAH, and THE *MEM* ascended between North and South, where it is suspended in the air. The *Shin* conceived and bore the letter *Gimel* and settled in the East side, WHICH IS TIFERET, and THE *SHIN* ascended between West and East and is suspended in the air. So we find the two letters *Mem* and *Shin* are suspended in the air.

611. א׳ דְּאִשְׁתְּאַר, אִסְתַּלָּק בְּדוּכְתֵּיה, וְסָלִיק לְעֵילָא, וְאִתְעַטָּר בֵּיה י״ה. בְּאִלֵּין אִתְתְּקַף, וְאַעֲדֵי וְאוֹלִיד ה״ו, וְקָאֵים בְּדוּכְתֵּיה, כְּדֵין אִתְעַטָּר, וְאַנְהִיר, וּפָשִׁיט נְהִירוּ, וְאוֹלִיד נְהִירוּ, וְאַפִּיק אֶת ט׳, בַּטִּישׁוּ דְּקָא בָּטַשׁ וְנָהִיר רָזָא דְּעָלְמָא עִלָּאָה, בִּנְהִירוּ.

**611.** The *Aleph* that remained IN THE VESSEL OF CHESED OF THE BODY

was elevated in its place and ascended above TO THE PLACE OF CHOCHMAH, BINAH, DA'AT, WHICH IS THE SECRET OF *YUD-HEI* OF THE NAME YUD HEI VAV HEI. It was crowned there with *Yud-Hei*. In these, *YUD-HEI,* THE *ALEPH* grew stronger to conceive and bore *Hei-Vav,* AND THE NAME YUD HEI VAV HEI WAS COMPLETED, and remained in its place, IN CHESED OF THE BODY. AND THE NAME YUD HEI VAV HEI ILLUMINATED WITHIN THE BODY; *YUD-HEI-VAV* IN CHESED, GVURAH AND TIFERET OF THE BODY AND THE LAST *HEI* IN MALCHUT. Then THE *ALEPH* was crowned and illuminated and expanded in its light and bore light and brought forth the letter *Tet,* which is the striking with which the mystery of the Supernal World, WHICH IS BINAH, struck and illuminated in the light OF CHESED, GVURAH AND TIFERET.

612. כְּדֵין אִסְתַּלָק א', וְנָטִיל מִגּוֹ אֲוִירָא מ"ש, וְאִתְחַבְּרוּ בַּהֲדֵיהּ, וַהֲווֹ אמ"ש כְּמִלְקַדְמִין, וְאִתְיַישַׁב א' בְּסִטְרָא דְּדָרוֹם, ש' בְּסִטְרָא דְּמִזְרָח, מ' בְּסִטְרָא דְּצָפוֹן. סַלְקָא ג' דַּהֲוָה בְּסִטְרָא דְּמִזְרָח, וְאַעֲדֵי וְאוֹלִיד צ"ת. אָתָא ב' דַּהֲוָה בְּסְטַר מַעֲרָב, וְסָלִיק וְאִתְחַבַּר בֵּין צ"ת. סְלִיקוּ א' ו', דָּא מִסְטַר דָּרוֹם וְדָא מִסְטַר מִזְרָח, וְאִתְחַבְּרוּ תַּרְוַויְיהוּ בַּהֲדֵי ב' בֵּין צ"ת, וְאַנְהִיר שְׁמָא צְבָאוֹת.

**612.** Then the *Aleph* was elevated and took to it *Mem* and *Shin* that were in the air. They joined it and became THE COMBINATION OF *Aleph-Mem-Shin* as before. The *Aleph* settled in the South side, WHICH IS CHESED, the *Shin* in the East side, WHICH IS TIFERET and the *Mem* in the North side, WHICH IS GVURAH. The *Gimel* that was in the East side ascended and conceived and bore *Tzadi-Tav.* And the *Bet,* which was in the West side, WHICH IS MALCHUT, came and ascended and joined between *Tzadi* and *Tav. Aleph* and *Vav* ascended, the one from the South and the other from the East, NAMELY *ALEPH* FROM THE SOUTH AND *VAV* FROM THE EAST, and were both joined with the *Bet* between the letters *Tzadi* and *Tav.* THEY JOINED and the Name Tzva'ot illuminated (*Tzadi-Bet-Aleph-Vav-Tav*).

613. כַּד אִתְנְהִיר שְׁמָא דָּא גּוֹ מַשְׁכְּנָא, אַעֲדוּ אַתְוָון וְאוֹלִידוּ ז' ב' נ'. סְלִיקוּ אמ"ש כְּמִלְקַדְמִין, וְאַעֲדוּ וְאוֹלִידוּ ס' ע' פ'.

**613.** When this name, TZVA'OT, illuminated in the Tabernacle, WHICH IS

MALCHUT, the letters conceived and bore *Zayin-Bet-Nun*. The letters *Aleph-Mem-Shin* ascended as before, MEANING THAT THEY ILLUMINATED IN CHESED, GVURAH AND TIFERET as MENTIONED ABOVE. They conceived and bore *Samech-Ayin-Pe*, WHICH ARE THE SFIROT TIFERET, NETZACH AND HOD.

614. אִשְׁתְּאַר ק' יְחִידָאי, וְסַלְקָא וְנַחְתָּא, קַיְּימָא גּוֹ נוּקְבָּא דִּתְהוֹמָא רַבָּא, חָמָא לֵהּ קוּדְשָׁא בְּרִיךְ הוּא, דְּקָא מִתְעַרְבְּבָא, בְּלָא גּוּפָא וְלָא צִיּוּרָא, וְלָא עָיֵיל לְמַשְׁכְּנָא. עָבֵד לֵהּ חוֹפָּאָה לְמַשְׁכְּנָא. וּמַאי נִיהוּ. יְרִיעוֹת עִזִּים לְאֹהֶל עַל הַמִּשְׁכָּן, כד"א, וְעָשִׂיתָ יְרִיעֹת עִזִּים לְאֹהֶל עַל הַמִּשְׁכָּן, לְאֹהֶל וְלָא אֹהֶל. קוּ"ף וְלָא אָדָם.

614. The Kof remained alone, but went up and down and then stood in the hole of the great abyss. The Holy One, blessed be He, saw that it was confused and without a body or form, and that it did not enter the Tabernacle WHICH IS MALCHUT. So He made it into a cover on the Tabernacle. What is it? It is the curtain of goats' hair to be a covering over the Tabernacle, as it is written: "And you shall make curtains of goats' hair to be a covering (lit. 'tent') upon the tabernacle" (Shemot 26:7). IT IS WRITTEN a tent yet it is not a tent, BUT A COVER FOR THE TENT, for it is a monkey (Heb. *Kof*) and not a human.

615. תּוּ אִתְגַּלְגְּלוּ אַתְוָון כְּמִלְּקַדְמִין, גּוֹ עוֹבָדָא דְּמַשְׁכְּנָא, אמ"ש, ש' אִתְגַּלְגְּלָא וְאִתְיָישְׁבָא בְּסִטַר מִזְרָח, וְאִשְׁתְּאַר ג' תַּלְיָיא בַּאֲוִירָא. מ' אִתְגַּלְגְּלָא וְאִתְיָישְׁבָא בְּסִטַר צָפוֹן, וְנָפַק ד' וְאִתְחַבַּר גּוֹ שׁ' בְּהַהוּא סִטְרָא. א' אִתְגַּלְגַּל וְאִתְיָישֵׁב וְסָלִיק לְגַבֵּי י', וְסַלְקָא וְאִתְתַּקְפָא בַּהֲדֵיהּ, וְנָטִיל לֵיהּ, וְאִתְחַבַּר גּוֹ בְּחִבּוּרָא חֲדָא שַׁדָּ"י. כַּד שְׁמָא דָּא אִתְתַּקַּן גּוֹ מַשְׁכְּנָא, כְּדֵין קִיּוּמָא וְקַיְּימָא אִיהוּ מִגּוֹ מַשְׁכְּנָא דִּלְתַתָּא.

615. Again the letters *ALEPH-MEM-SHIN* rolled into the building of the Tabernacle as before, the *Shin* on the East side, and the *Gimel*, THAT WAS IN THE EAST, remained suspended in the air. FOR FROM IT EMERGED THE NAME TZVA'OT and the *Mem* rolled and settled in the North side, BECAUSE IN ORDER TO ILLUMINATE IN NETZACH, HOD AND YESOD, THE LETTERS

ALEPH-MEM-SHIN HAVE TO BE CLOTHED IN CHESED, GVURAH AND
TIFERET. The *Dalet* emerged, WHICH WAS IN THE NORTH, and joined the
*Shin* on that side AND THE COMBINATION *SHIN-DALET* (ENG. 'DEMON')
WAS FORMED. The *Aleph* rolled and settled ON THE SOUTH SIDE, and
ascended to THE HEAD OF the *Yud* THAT IS THERE. It ascended and became
strengthened with it and took it, AND JOINED IT WITH *SHIN-DALET*, the
Name Shadai (*Shin-Dalet-Yud*) was unified into one, WHICH ILLUMINATES
IN THE SFIRAH YESOD. When this Name was established in the
Tabernacle, WHICH IS MALCHUT, it (she) can exist and is situated within
the lower Tabernacle, MEANING THAT ITS EXISTENCE DEPENDS UPON THE
ERECTION OF THE LOWER TABERNACLE.

616. תּוּ אַתְוָון אִתְגַּלְגְּלוּ כְּמִלְּקַדְמִין, לְאִתְיַישְּׁבָא מַשְׁכְּנָא, סְלִיקוּ
אַתְוָון, א' בְּרֵישָׁא, ת' לְבָתַר, א"ת. ב' בְּרֵישָׁא, ש' לְבָתַר, אִתְחַלְּפוּ
אַתְוָון, אב"ג ית"ץ, אִתְגַּלְגְּלוּ בְּגִלּוּפֵי קַדְשָׁא א' ק'. א' אַפִּיק ק'.
לְנַטְרָא מַשְׁכְּנָא. ק', אַפִּיק ר'. ר' אַפִּיק ע' קר"ע.

616. Again the letters ALEPH-MEM-SHIN rolled as before, in order to settle
in the Tabernacle, and the letters ascended, first the *Aleph* and then the *Tav*,
AND THE COMBINATION OF *Aleph-Tav* WAS FORMED; first the *Bet* and then
the *Shin* AND THE COMBINATION OF *BET-SHIN* WAS FORMED. The
COMBINATIONS OF the letters exchanged BY MEANS OF THE ATBASH
CIPHER, AND THEN EMERGED *Aleph-Bet-Gimel-Yud-Tav-Tzadi*. They
turned through the holy engravings, *Aleph* to *Kof*, THE *ALEPH* OF THE
ATBASH CIPHER brought forth *Kof* to guard the Tabernacle, AS MENTIONED
ABOVE. The *Kof* brought forth the *Resh*, the *Resh* brought it forth *Ayin* AND
THESE BECAME THE COMBINATION OF *Kof-Resh-Ayin*.

617. רָזָא דָא, וְאֶת עוֹרוֹת גְּדָיֵי הָעִזִּים הִלְבִּישָׁה עַל יָדָיו וְעַל חֶלְקַת
צַוָּארָיו. כְּגַוְונָא דָא, וְעָשִׂיתָ יְרִיעַת עִזִּים לְאֹהֶל עַל הַמִּשְׁכָּן. דְּהָא
חוּלְקָא דָא, אִצְטְרִיךְ לְאַחֲזָאָה לְבַר, לְנַטְרָא הַהִיא דִּלְגָאו, וְעַל רָזָא דָא
אַלְבִּישַׁת לֵיהּ לְיַעֲקֹב לְבַר. שט"ן קר"ע, אַתְוָון אִינּוּן רְשִׁימָן לְבַר, בְּגִין
נְטוּרָא דְמַשְׁכְּנָא, דְּאִיהוּ רָזָא דִּבְרִית קַדִּישָׁא, וְאִתְפָּרְעָא עָרְלָה לְבָתַר
בְּחוּפָּאָה דָא.

**617.** This secret OF THE NAME *KOF-RESH-AYIN*, IS THE SECRET OF THE VERSE: "And she put the skins of the kids of the goat upon his hands, and upon the smooth of his neck" (Beresheet 27:16) and similarly, "And you shall make curtains of goats' hair to be a covering upon the tabernacle." FOR THE NAME *KOF-RESH-AYIN*, WHOSE SOURCE IS *KOF*, CONTAINS THE HARSH (HEB. *AZIM*) AND SEVERE JUDGMENTS THAT ARE CALLED 'GOATS (HEB. *IZIM*)'. THEREFORE, this part must be visible on the outside to guard what is inside, SO THAT THE EXTERNAL FORCES DO NOT GAIN NOURISHMENT FROM IT, AS HAS BEEN EXPLAINED EARLIER. The letters OF THE NAME *Sin-Tet-Nun – Kof-Resh-Ayin*, WHICH IS THE SECOND NAME OF THE NAME OF *MEM-BET* (42) AFTER *ALEPH-BET-GIMEL YUD-TAV- TZADI* MENTIONED EARLIER, are marked outside THE TABERNACLE in order to guard the Tabernacle, which is the secret of the holy covenant, the foreskin was uncovered through this cover.

618. תּוּ אִתְגַּלְגְּלוּ אַתְוָון, וְאַפִּיק א״ת ב״ש, שְׁקוּצִי״ת בְּרֵאשִׁית בָּרָא אֱלֹהִים אֵת הַשָּׁמַיִם וְאֵת הָאָרֶץ וְהָאָרֶץ הָיְתָה תֹהוּ וְגוֹ'. בְּגִלְגּוּלָא דָא וְהָאָרֶץ הָיְתָה תֹהוּ וָבֹהוּ בְּאַתְוָון קר״ע שט״ן. וְחֹשֶׁךְ עַל פְּנֵי תְהוֹם ג' אַפִּיק ר', ד' ק' עַד הָכָא אַתְוָון, אִתְגַּלְגְּלוּ, וּבְטִישׁוּ דָּא בְּדָא לְתִקּוּנָא גּוֹ מַשְׁכְּנָא.

**618.** Again the letters rolled and brought forth THE COMBINATIONS OF the Atbash cipher UP TO *Shin-Kof-Vav Tzadi-Yud-Tav*. THE MEANING IS THAT THE ATBASH CIPHER BROUGHT FORTH ALL THE SEVEN NAMES COMING FROM THE NAME OF *MEM-BET* (42 LETTERS) OF 'ANA B'KOACH,' UNTIL *SHIN-KOF-VAV TZADI-YUD-TAV*. THESE ARE '*ALEPH-BET-GIMEL YUD-TAV-TZADI*,' '*KOF-RESH-AYIN SIN-TET-NUN*,' '*NUN-GIMEL-DALET YUD-CAF-SHIN*,' '*BET-TET-RESH TZADI-TAV-GIMEL*,' '*CHET-KOF-BET TET-NUN-AYIN*,' '*YUD-GIMEL-LAMED PE-ZAYIN-KOF*,' '*SHIN-KOF-VAV TZADI-YUD-TAV*.' THEY ARE THE SECRET OF THE 42 LETTERS OF: "In the beginning Elohim created the heaven and the earth. And the earth was without form and void (Heb. *bohu*)..." (Beresheet 1:1) UNTIL THE *BET* OF BOHU. FOR THESE 42 LETTERS ARE THE SECRET OF THE NAME OF *MEM-BET* (42). In this cycle OF THE LETTERS, it is the secret of "And the earth was without form and void" because of the letters *Kof-Resh-Ayin Sin-Tet-Nun*, MEANING BY THE STRENGTH OF THE SEVERE JUDGMENTS THAT IT CONTAINS. THERE BECOMES: "And darkness was on the face of the

deep" (Ibid. 2) The *Gimel* brought forth *Resh* and the *Dalet-Kof* AND THESE BECAME THE COMBINATIONS *GIMEL=RESH DALET=KOF* – until here, AFTER THERE EMERGED THE FOUR COMBINATIONS OF *ALEPH =TAV BET=SHIN GIMEL=RESH DALET=KOF*, the letters rolled and struck one another to be established in the Tabernacle. THE REASON IS THAT THE PERMUTATION OF THE ATBASH CIPHER, CONTAINS ELEVEN COMBINATIONS: *ALEPH=TAV*; *BET=SHIN*; *GIMEL=RESH*; *DALET=KOF*; *HEI=TZADI*; *VAV=PE*; *ZAYIN=AYIN*; *CHET=SAMECH*; *TET=NUN*; *YUD= MEM* AND *CAF=LAMED* – WHICH ARE DIVIDED INTO THREE COLUMNS, RIGHT, LEFT AND CENTRAL. THE FIRST FOUR, *ALEPH=TAV BET=SHIN GIMEL=RESH* AND *DALET=KOF* ARE THE RIGHT COLUMN. THEREFORE, THEY ARE CONSIDERED AS ESTABLISHING THE TABERNACLE.

619. אִינּוּן אֲמַ"שׁ אַפִּיקוּ תּוֹלְדִין, ה' צ' ו' פ' אַתְוָון דְּתַלְיָין גּוֹ אֲוִירָא, וּבְטִישׁוּ בְּאִינּוּן אַחֲרָנִין וְאַפִּיקוּ צִיּוּרָא דְּמַשְׁכְּנָא ז' ע'. עַד הָכָא קַיְּימָא וְחֹשֶׁךְ עַל פְּנֵי תְהוֹם כֻּלְּהוּ בְּסִטְרוֹי ח' אָתָא ס' וְאִתְחַבָּר בַּהֲדֵיהּ, כְּדֵין יְהִי אוֹר וַיְהִי אוֹר.

**619.** These THREE LETTERS, *Aleph-Mem-Shin*, brought forth offspring *Hei-Tzadi-Vav-Pe*, FOR IN THE CONTINUATION OF THE ATBASH CIPHER, these are the letters that are suspended in the air. They struck others and brought forth the form of the Tabernacle *Zayin-Ayin*, WHICH IS THE SEVENTH COMBINATION OF THE ATBASH CIPHER. Until here, IT IS RELATED TO THE SECRET OF THE VERSE: "And darkness upon the face of the deep." All of them, NAMELY ALL THE THREE PREVIOUSLY MENTIONED COMBINATIONS, *HEI=TZADI VAV=PE* AND *ZAYIN=AYIN* are at its side, MEANING THE SIDE OF DARKNESS – IT IS BY REASON THAT THESE THREE COMBINATIONS ARE IN THE LEFT COLUMN OF THE ATBASH CIPHER, AND BEFORE THE LEFT JOINS WITH THE RIGHT, IT IS WHOLLY DARK. The *Samech* came and joined with the letter *Chet*, AND THE COMBINATION *CHET-SAMECH* WAS FORMED – WHICH IS AT THE FIRST OF THE FOUR COMBINATIONS OF THE CENTRAL COLUMN, WHICH ARE *CHET= SAMECH TET=NUN YUD=MEM* AND *CAF=LAMED* – then it is said, "'Let there be light', and there was light" (Beresheet 1:3), BECAUSE THE LIGHT COMES FROM THE CENTRAL COLUMN AFTER IT MEDIATES AND JOINS TOGETHER THE TWO COLUMNS, RIGHT AND LEFT.

620. אִתְגַּלְגְּלוּ אַתְוָון כְּמִלְּקַדְמִין, אב״ג ית״ץ, אַעְדּוּ וְאוֹלִידוּ וְאַפִּיקוּ צִיּוּרָא גּוֹ רָזִין דְּמַשְׁכְּנָא, בִּכְלָלָא חֲדָא בְּרָזָא א׳ ל׳ ב׳ ם׳, דְּהָא אָת א׳ אַעְדֵּי, וְאוֹלִיד בְּרָזָא דְּחֵילָא וְתוּקְפָּא, אָת ל׳. אִתְגַּבַּר בְּתוּקְפֵּיהּ, וְאִסְתַּלָּק בִּיקָרֵיהּ, וְאוֹלִיד אָת ב׳, כְּדֵין אַעְדִּיאוּ וְאוֹלִידוּ אַתְוָון אִתְחַבְּרוּ אַחֲרָנִין אִלֵּין מ׳ אִתְחַבַּר בְּגִלּוּפֵיהּ בְּאָת ב׳, כְּדֵין נַפְקֵי בְּחִבּוּרָא עַד ט״ר י״ש כ״ת לְמֶהֱוֵי אַתְוָון סַלְקִין בְּאַתְרַיְיהוּ, גּוֹ צֵרוּפָא דְּרָזָא דְּמַשְׁכְּנָא. אֶת הַכִּיּוֹר וְאֶת כַּנּוֹ.

**620.** The letters *Aleph-Bet-Gimel-Yud-Tav-Tzadi* rolled as before, and conceived and bore and brought forth one form of the secrets of the Tabernacle in one inclusion in the secret of THE PERMUTATED Albam CIPHER. The *Aleph* conceived and bore the letter *Lamed* by means of strength and might AND THE COMBINATION *ALEPH=LAMED* WAS FORMED. THE *ALEPH* strengthened in its might and ascended in its glory and bore the letter *Bet*. Then they conceived and bore the letters, and these other LETTERS joined, the *Mem* joined through its engraving with the letter *Bet*, AND THE COMBINATION *BET=MEM* WAS FORMED. So they emerged in pairs up to the combinations Tet=Resh, *Yud=Shin*, *Caf=Tav*, so that the letters should rise to their places in the combination of the secret of the Tabernacle. THIS IS THE SECRET OF: "The laver and its pedestal" (Shemot 38:16), FOR THE LAVER IS NETZACH AND ITS PEDESTAL IS HOD.

621. יְהִי רָקִיעַ בְּתוֹךְ הַמָּיִם, דְּהָא מַיִין סְלִיקוּ וְנַחְתּוּ בְּרָזָא דְּאַתְוָון א״ל. א׳ אַפִּיק ו׳. ו׳ אַפִּיק ק׳. אָת ל׳ סָלִיק אִתְגְּלִיפוּ אַתְוָון בְּגִלּוּפַיְיהוּ, בְּחִבּוּרָא חֲדָא, קוֹל יְיָ׳ עַל הַמַּיִם א״ל וְכוּ׳, אִלֵּין אַתְוָון א״ל, דְּהָא אִלֵּין אַעְדּוּ וְאוֹלִידוּ וְאַפִּיקוּ אַתְוָון, גּוֹ צִיּוּרִין דְּמַשְׁכְּנָא.

**621.** "Let there be a firmament in the midst of the waters" (Beresheet 1:6). The waters were ascending BY THE SUPERNAL WATERS and descending BY THE LOWER WATERS in the secret of the letters *Aleph-Lamed*. The *Aleph* OF EL brought forth a *Vav* and the *Vav* brought forth *Kof* and the letter *Lamed* OF EL ascended TO THEM. The letters were engaged in the engraving in one joint, VOICE (HEB. *KOL*, *KOF-VAV-LAMED*). THEREFORE, THE UPPER WATERS WERE DIVIDED FROM THE LOWER WATERS THROUGH THE

LETTERS *KOF-VAV-LAMED*. THIS IS WHAT IS WRITTEN: "The voice of Hashem is upon the waters, The El OF GLORY..." (Tehilim 29:3). These letters, *Aleph-Lamed*, THAT ARE IN THE VERSE "THE EL OF GLORY" conceived and bore and were engraved in the imprint by means of the letters, so as to produce the drawings of the Tabernacle.

622. אמ"ש אַעָדוּ וְאוֹלִידוּ וְאִתְגְּלִיפוּ בְּגִלוּפֵי רָזִין דְּאַתְוָון, לְאַפָּקָא צִיּוּרִין דְּמַשְׁכְּנָא, א' אַפִּיק ג', ש' אַפִּיק ן', לְחַבְּרָא גּוֹ אָת ג' בְּרָזָא גַּן. תַּדְשֵׁא הָאָרֶץ דֶּשֶׁא עֵשֶׂב וְגוֹ'. אִתְגַּלְגְּלוּ אַתְוָון כְּמִלְּקַדְּמִין אמ"ש, בְּרָזָא ב"ם בְּאִלֵּין כְּנִישׁוּ מַיָּא לַאֲתָר חַד, דִּכְתִיב יִקָּווּ הַמַּיִם מִתַּחַת הַשָּׁמַיִם אֶל מָקוֹם אֶחָד.

**622.** THE THREE LETTERS, *Aleph-Mem-Shin*, conceived and bore and became engraved in the imprint of the letters, so as to produce the drawings of the Tabernacle WHICH IS MALCHUT. The *Aleph* brought forth *Gimel*. The *Shin* brought forth *final Nun* and joined it with *Gimel*, in the secret of Gan (garden, *Gimel- final Nun*), WHICH IS THE THIRD PAIR OF THE Albam cipher IN THE SECRET OF THE VERSE: "Let the earth bring forth grass" (Beresheet 1:11). The letters *Aleph-Mem-Shin* rolled again by means of *Bet=Mem* OF THE ALBAM CIPHER, in these waters that gathered into one place, as it is written: "Let the waters under the heaven be gathered together to one place" (Ibid. 9).

## 59. Sh'ma Yisrael

### A Synopsis

Here, Rabbi Chiya and Rabbi Yosi are again traveling on the road. Rabbi Yosi opens a discussion with the words of the reading of Sh'ma: "Hear O Yisrael, The Creator our Elohim, The Creator is One," and, "Hear O Yisrael; this day you are become the people," and, "Hear O Yisrael, you are to pass over the Jordan this day." He then asks why the word "Hear" is used so many times, and says the union of Shem (name) with Ayin (seventy) is necessary. He next speaks of the seventy Names in the secret of the supernal chariot, the 72 Names of the three verses, the seventy members of the Sanhedrin plus the two witnesses. Sh'ma Yisrael, we learn, alludes to Malchut (that is called Shem) when he unites with Zeir Anpin (which is called Yisrael). Next, Rabbi Yosi tells us that "this day you are become a people" means that you broke your heart in order to serve God. The "Hear O Yisrael" of the unison is, we learn, the secret of above and below, the secret of people accepting upon themselves the yoke of the heavenly kingdom, Malchut. At this moment of acceptance the Shechinah comes and rests on the person's head and bears him witness before God. Because the person recites and unites the Name of the Holy One, the Shechinah blesses him with seven blessings, and calls to him, "You are my servant, Yisrael, in whom I will be glorified."

### The Relevance of this Passage

Two great sages traveling upon a road indicates the journey of their souls through celestial corridors in the upper world, where they behold secrets of the universe. One secret collected on this excursion concerns the sh'ma, which essentially enjoins our world (and our souls) to the upper world. The purpose of this revelation is to unify the two worlds, and this effect is achieved now.

The sh'ma emits a Light of healing, a divine radiance that nourishes 248 parts of our spiritual and physical bodies. Thus, in the act of meditatively perusing this passage, we receive Light that heals all our physical ailments and the spiritual nutrients that forever strengthen our soul. The sages speak of the 72 Names of God so that we may draw upon their miraculous power to achieve our personal transformations. This miraculous change touches all mankind to facilitate the unification of the lower world with the upper. The Shechinah is spoken of so that we

| | | | | | | | |
|---|---|---|---|---|---|---|---|
| והו | ילי | סיט | עלם | מהש | ללה | אכא | כהת |
| הזי | אלד | לאו | ההע | יזל | מבה | הרי | הקם |
| לאו | כלי | לוו | פהל | נלך | ייי | מלה | חהו |
| נתה | האא | ירת | שאה | ריי | אום | לכב | ושר |
| יוו | להו | כוק | מנד | אני | חעם | רהע | ייי |
| ההה | מיכ | וול | ילה | סאל | ערי | עשל | מיה |
| וול | דני | החש | עמם | ננא | נית | מבה | פוי |
| מום | היי | יבמ | ראה | חבו | איע | מנק | דמב |

may permanently fortify our immune system and forever shield this world from the dark forces of the night.

623. רַבִּי חִיָּיא וְרַבִּי יוֹסֵי הֲווֹ אַזְלֵי בְּאָרְחָא, עַד דַּהֲווֹ אַזְלֵי א״ר יוֹסֵי, נִפְתַּח בְּעִידוֹנִין, וְנֵימָא מִלֵּי דְּאוֹרַיְיתָא. פָּתַח ר' יוֹסֵי בְּמִלֵּי דִּקְרִיאַת שְׁמַע וְאָמַר, כְּתִיב שְׁמַע יִשְׂרָאֵל יְיָ' אֱלֹהֵינוּ יְיָ' יְיָ' אֶחָד. וּכְתִיב שְׁמַע יִשְׂרָאֵל הַיּוֹם הַזֶּה נִהְיֵיתָ לְעָם. וּכְתִיב שְׁמַע יִשְׂרָאֵל אַתָּה עוֹבֵר הַיּוֹם אֶת הַיַּרְדֵּן. כָּל הָנֵי שְׁמַע שְׁמַע דְּקָאָמַר מֹשֶׁה אֲמַאי. דְּהָא שְׁמַע יִשְׂרָאֵל דְּיִחוּדָא יָאוֹת. הָנֵי אַחֲרָנִין אֲמַאי.

**623.** Rabbi Chiya and Rabbi Yosi were traveling on the road. While they were still traveling, Rabbi Yosi said: Let us start with delicacies and let us say words of Torah. Rabbi Yosi opened the discussion with the words of the reading of Sh'ma and said: It is written, "Hear O Yisrael, Hashem our Elohim, Hashem is One" (Devarim 6:4), "hearken, O Yisrael; this day you are become the people" (Devarim 27:9), and "Hear O Yisrael, you are to pass over the Jordan this day" (Devarim 9:1). What is the need for all these 'Hear's' that Moses said. "Hear O Yisrael, Hashem our Elohim, Hashem is One" is meant for unison and is good, but why the other ones?

624. אֶלָּא כֻּלְּהוּ לְדַרְשָׁא קָאָתוּ, שְׁמַע יִשְׂרָאֵל דְּיִחוּדָא וַדַּאי הַאי לְדַרְשָׁא קָא אָתְיָא, וְהָכָא רָמִיז וְאִתְחֲזֵי יִחוּדָא דְּחָכְמְתָא עִלָּאָה. שְׁמַע, ע' מֵאַתְוָון רַבְרְבָן אִיהִי, אֲמַאי. אֶלָּא רֶמֶז קָא רָמִיז בִּכְלָלָא חֲדָא, לְאַכְלְלָא עֵילָא וְתַתָּא כַּחֲדָא בְּיִחוּדָא חֲדָא, שְׁמַע: שֵׁם ע'. הָכָא אִתְכְּלִיל הַאי שֵׁם בְּאִינּוּן ע' שְׁמָהָן עִלָּאִין, לְאַכְלְלָא לוֹן, דְּהָא שֵׁם אִתְבָּרְכָא מִנַּיְיהוּ, וְאִתְכְּלִיל בְּהוּ. וְאִצְטְרִיךְ לְאַכְלְלָא לוֹן כַּחֲדָא בְּיִחוּדָא חַד, וּלְשַׁוָּאָה רְעוּתֵיהּ בְּהוּ.

**624.** HE ANSWERS: They all should be interpreted. The "Hear (Heb. *Sh'ma*) O Yisrael" of the unison should certainly be interpreted, for here it alludes to and reflects the unison of the Supernal Chochmah. In Sh'ma (*Shin-Mem-Ayin*), the *Ayin* is of the large letters, for it refers to an inclusion that includes what is above and below in one unity. Because Sh'ma IS COMPOSED OF THE LETTERS OF shem (Eng. 'Name') and *Ayin*. For here

this name, WHICH IS MALCHUT THAT IS CALLED 'NAME', is comprised in the seventy (=Ayin) supernal Names OF ZEIR ANPIN, in order to combine them. For the name, WHICH IS MALCHUT, is blessed by them and is become a part of them. They have to be combined as one, MEANING IN ONE WORD SH'MA, in one unity, and one has to pay attention in them.

625. דְּהָא וַדַּאי ע' שְׁמָהָן אִינּוּן בְּרָזָא דִּרְתִּיכָא עִלָּאָה, וּמֵהַאי רְתִיכָא עִלָּאָה, אִתְבָּרְכָא הַאי שֵׁם, וְאִתְכְּלִיל בְּגַוַוייהוּ, וּלְבָתַר יִשְׂרָאֵל בִּכְלָל. אֲבָל הָא תָּנֵינָן, דָּא יִשְׂרָאֵל סָבָא, לְמֶהֱוֵי יִשְׂרָאֵל בִּכְלָלָא חֲדָא, הַהוּא אֲתָר דְּבֵקוּתָא דְּכֹלָּא. וְעַל דָּא שְׁמַע יִשְׂרָאֵל, הַשְׁתָּא אִתְדָּבְּקַת אִתְּתָא בְּבַעְלָהּ, וַהֲוֵי כֹּלָּא בִּכְלָלָא חֲדָא, וְדָא שְׁמַע יִשְׂרָאֵל דְּיִחוּדָא. לְבָתַר קָא מְיַחֵד תְּלַת סִטְרִין, יְיָ' אֱלֹהֵינוּ יְיָ' אֶחָד, לְמֶהֱוֵי כֹּלָּא חַד.

**625.** Certainly the seventy Names are in the secret of the supernal Chariot, WHICH ARE CHESED, GVURAH AND TIFERET OF ZEIR ANPIN OF THE CHEST AND ABOVE, WHICH ARE A VEHICLE FOR BINAH, NAMELY 72 NAMES OF THE THREE VERSES: "AND...REMOVED...AND IT CAME...AND ...STRETCHED OUT" (SHEMOT 14:19-21). THIS IS THE SECRET OF SEVENTY (THE HEBREW LETTER AYIN) MEMBERS OF THE SANHEDRIN PLUS THE TWO WITNESSES. And this Name is blessed by that supernal Chariot, WHICH IS MALCHUT, and becomes a part of them. Afterwards, AFTER THE WORD SH'MA, the word Yisrael without attributes is recited, NAMELY ZEIR ANPIN. Yet we have learned it is Yisrael Saba, MEANING that Yisrael, WHICH IS ZEIR ANPIN, should be in one unity with that place to which everyone is attached. ZEIR ANPIN, WHICH IS CALLED 'YISRAEL' IN GENERAL, SHOULD BE ATTACHED WITH YISRAEL SABA, MEANING THAT HE ASCENDS AND BECOMES A GARMENT TO IT. Hence "Sh'ma Yisrael," WHICH ALLUDES that now the wife cleaves with her husband; NAMELY, MALCHUT THAT IS CALLED 'SHEM' WITH ZEIR ANPIN THAT IS CALLED 'YISRAEL'. Everything is in one inclusion, and this is THE MEANING OF "Sh'ma Yisrael" of the unison. Afterwards, the three sides unite, which are: "Hashem our Elohim, Hashem is One", WHICH ARE ABA AND IMA AND ZEIR ANPIN, so that all becomes one.

626. שְׁמַע יִשְׂרָאֵל דְּכֻלְּהוּ שְׁאַר, לָאו אִינּוּן כְּהַאי גַּוְונָא, אֲבָל כֻּלְּהוּ אַחֲרָנִין לִדְרָשָׁא קָאֲתוּ, וְכֻלְּהוּ בְּאֲתָר אַחֲרָא אִתְדָּבְּקוּ, שְׁמַע יִשְׂרָאֵל

אַתָּה עֹבֵר הַיּוֹם. שְׁמַע יִשְׂרָאֵל הַיּוֹם הַזֶּה נִהְיֵיתָ לְעָם. וְכֻלְּהוּ בְּדַרְגָּא תַּתָּאָה אִתְדְּבָקוּ.

**626.** "Hear O Yisrael" in all the other PLACES are not in this manner, but they all are to be interpreted and they are all attached in a different place. "Hear O Yisrael, you are to pass over the Jordan this day" (Devarim 9:1); "and hearken, O Yisrael; this day you are become the people" (Devarim 27:9) They are all attached in the lower level, WHICH IS MALCHUT THAT IS CALLED 'HEARING'.

**627.** שְׁמַע יִשְׂרָאֵל הַיּוֹם הַזֶּה נִהְיֵיתָ לְעָם, שְׁמַע יִשְׂרָאֵל יָאוֹת. הַיּוֹם הַזֶּה נִהְיֵיתָ לְעָם מַהוּ. הָיִיתָ מִבְּעֵי לֵיהּ, מַאי נִהְיֵיתָ. אֶלָּא בְּכָל אֲתָר עָם, כַּד אִתְבָּרוּ לִבַּיְיהוּ לְפֻלְחָנָא, כד"א נִהְיֵיתִי וְנֶחֱלֵיתִי. וְדָא הוּא דִּכְתִיב, שִׁמְעוּנִי אַחַי וְעַמִּי. אִי אַחַי, לָמָּה עַמִּי, וְאִי עַמִּי, לָמָּה אַחַי. אֶלָּא אָמַר דָּוִד, אִי בִּרְעוּתָא אַתּוּן אַחַי, וְאִי לָאו אַתּוּן עַמִּי, לְתַבְרָא לִבַּיְיכוּ לְפוּלְחָנִי. כָּךְ הַיּוֹם הַזֶּה נִהְיֵיתָ לְעָם, תָּבַרְתְּ לִבָּךְ לְפֻלְחָנָא דְּקוּדְשָׁא בְּרִיךְ הוּא.

**627.** "Hearken, O Yisrael; this day you are become the people," HE QUESTIONS: "Hearken, O Yisrael" is well and good, but "this day have you are become the people," what is ITS MEANING? It should have said, 'You were,' so what is the meaning of "are become"? HE ANSWERS: Every place that 'people' is mentioned, it alludes to the fact that these hearts were broken to the service OF THE HOLY ONE, BLESSED BE HE. THEREFORE, IT IS SAID, "YOU ARE BECOME (HEB. *NIHYETAH*)," as it is written: "I fainted (Heb. *nihyeti*) and was sick" (Daniel 8:27). This is the meaning of: "Hear me, My brethren, and My people" (I Divrei Hayamim 28:2). HE QUESTIONS: If it is "My brethren," why did it say "My people"? And if "My people," then why "My brethren"? HE ANSWERS: But David said, 'If you will do it willingely, you are My brethren,' but if not, then you are 'My people,' that must break your hearts in My service.' Thus, "this day have you become a people" (Devarim 27:9), MEANING that you broke your heart so as to serve the Holy One, blessed be He.

**628.** שְׁמַע יִשְׂרָאֵל אַתָּה עֹבֵר הַיּוֹם אֶת הַיַּרְדֵּן, כֹּלָּא בְּדַרְגָּא תַּתָּאָה,

אִיהוּ, וְשָׁמַע יִשְׂרָאֵל דְּיִחוּדָא הוּא דַּרְגָּא עִלָּאָה. מַה בֵּין הַאי לְהַאי. אֶלָּא הַהוּא שָׁמַע יִשְׂרָאֵל דְּיִחוּדָא, לָא הֲוֵי בְּכֻלְּהוּ כְּהַאי גַּוְונָא, דְּהָא אִיהוּ הֲוֵי רָזָא דְּעֵילָּא וְתַתָּא. וְאִיהוּ רָזָא לְקַבְּלָא עֲלַיְיהוּ עוֹל מַלְכוּת שָׁמַיִם, בְּכָל סִטְרָא, בְּגִין דְּיִצְטְרִיךְ לֵיהּ לְבַר נָשׁ, לְמֶהֱוֵי זַמִּין בְּהַהִיא שַׁעֲתָא, לְיַחֲדָא שְׁמָא דְּקוּדְשָׁא בְּרִיךְ הוּא, וּלְקַבְּלָא עֲלֵיהּ עוֹל מַלְכוּת שָׁמַיִם.

**628.** "Hear O Yisrael, you are to pass over the Jordan this day." It is all in the lower level, WHICH IS MALCHUT. And "Hear O Yisrael" of the unison is the upper level, WHICH IS ZEIR ANPIN THAT IS INCLUDED IN YISRAEL SABA, AS MENTIONED ABOVE. What is the difference between them? In "Hear O Yisrael" of the unison , not all of them have it in this manner, because it is the secret of above, OF YISRAEL–SABA AND TEVUNAH, and of below, ZEIR ANPIN AND MALCHUT. It is the secret of accepting upon themselves the yoke of the Heavenly Kingdom in anything. The person has to be ready at that time to declare the unity of the Name of the Holy One, blessed be He, ZEIR ANPIN, and to accept upon himself the yoke of the Heavenly Kingdom, WHICH IS MALCHUT.

629. וּבְשַׁעֲתָא דְּאָתֵי בַּר נָשׁ לְקַבְּלָא עֲלֵיהּ עוֹל מַלְכוּת שָׁמַיִם, כְּדֵין שְׁכִינְתָּא אַתְיָא וְשַׁרְיָא עַל רֵישֵׁיהּ, וְקַאִים עֲלֵיהּ כְּסָהִיד, לְסָהֲדָא סַהֲדוּתָא קָמֵי מַלְכָּא קַדִּישָׁא, דְּהַאי אִיהוּ דְּקָא מְיַחֵד שְׁמֵיהּ תְּרֵי זִמְנֵי בְּיוֹמָא, וּשְׁמֵיהּ אִתְיַחֵד עֵילָּא וְתַתָּא כַּדְקָא יֵאוֹת. וְעַל דָּא ע' מִשְׁמַע יִשְׂרָאֵל מֵאַתְוָון רַבְרְבָן, וְד' נָמֵי מֵאַתְוָון רַבְרְבָן, לְמֶהֱוֵי עַד קָמֵי מַלְכָּא קַדִּישָׁא. וְהָא אוּקְמוּהָ, יְדוֹ"ד אֱלֹהֵינוּ יְדוֹ"ד, וְדָא הוּא רָזָא דְּיִחוּדָא בִּתְלַת סִטְרִין, כְּמָה דְּאוּקְמֵיהּ בּוּצִינָא קַדִּישָׁא, וְאִתְּעַר בֵּיהּ בְּכַמָּה דּוּכְתֵּי, וְלֵית לָן רְשׁוּ לְאִתְּעָרָא בֵּיהּ יַתִּיר.

**629.** At the moment that the person comes to accept upon himself the yoke of the Heavenly Kingdom, then the Shechinah comes and rests on his head and stands over him as a witness. She bears witness before the Holy King that this one unites His name twice daily and His name is united above and below properly. Therefore, the *Ayin* of 'Sh'ma Yisrael' is of the large letters and the *Dalet* OF ECHAD (ENG. 'ONE'), is also of the large letters, WHICH

ARE THE LETTERS *AYIN-DALET* (ED, ENG 'WITNESS'), MEANING to be a witness before the Holy King. We have already established that "Hashem our Elohim, Hashem" is the secret of the unison on three sides, NAMELY, ABA, IMA, AND ZEIR ANPIN, and this is the secret of the unity in three sides, as the holy luminary has established and has asserted it in many places. We have no permission to assert it any more.

630. וְדַאי הַאי בַּר נָשׁ, דְּקָא מְיַחֵד שְׁמָא דְּקוּדְשָׁא בְּרִיךְ הוּא עֵילָא וְתַתָּא כַּדְקָא יֵאוֹת, שְׁכִינְתָּא אַתְיָא וְשַׁרְיָא עַל רֵישֵׁיה, וּמְבָרֵךְ לֵיהּ בְּשֶׁבַע בִּרְכָּאן, וְקָרֵי עָלֵיה, וַיֹּאמֶר לִי עַבְדִּי אַתָּה יִשְׂרָאֵל אֲשֶׁר בְּךָ אֶתְפָּאָר.

630. The Shechinah comes and rests upon the head of that person who unites the Name of the Holy One, blessed be He, above and below properly, and blesses him with seven blessings, CORRESPONDING TO THE SEVEN SFIROT. She calls to him, "And said to me, 'You are my servant, Yisrael, in whom I will be glorified'" (Yeshayah 49:3).

## 60. "To you it was shown, that you might know"

### A Synopsis

Rabbi Chiya opens this discussion with: "To you it was shown, that you might know that The Creator He is the Elohim'." He says the children of Yisrael lost all knowledge of their faith when they were in Egypt, until Moses taught them about the supernal Elohim in the world. Then they saw many miracles, were given the Torah, and learned the ways of God. The entire secret of the faith is, we are told, suspended upon this verse: "Know therefore this day, and consider it in your heart, that The Creator He is Elohim in heaven above, and upon the earth beneath, there is no other." The secret of secrets is that Zeir Anpin, which is Yud Hei Vav Hei, and Elohim, which is Malchut, are One.

### The Relevance of this Passage

Just as a stone is made of the same material as the mountain from which it is hewn, the soul of man is a spark of the divine Light. Therein lies the secret of the profound oneness that underlies this physical reality. The essence of The Creator, and our souls, is an unending desire to impart goodness, joy, and delight.

Thus, when we resist our wanton, self-seeking desires and use them in the service of others (sharing), we attain oneness with The Creator. The stone merges with the mountain. The faith to live by this truth awakens in our hearts. The strength to conquer our avaricious tendencies is born within us. Trust, conviction, and knowledge of The Creator are emblazoned in our minds. Our ultimate transformation and the final evolutionary stage of humanity are achieved. Mankind now embodies a *Desire to Receive for the Sake of Sharing,* and oneness is achieved between the Light and the Vessel.

631. רַבִּי חִיָּיא פָּתַח אֲבַתְרֵיהּ וְאָמַר, אַתָּה הָרְאֵתָ לָדַעַת כִּי יְיָ' הוּא הָאֱלֹהִים וְגוֹ', הַאי קְרָא אִית לְאִסְתַּכְּלָא בֵּיהּ, אַתָּה הָרְאֵתָ, מַאי הָרְאֵתָ. אֶלָּא כַּד נָפְקוּ יִשְׂרָאֵל מִמִּצְרַיִם, לָא הֲווֹ יַדְעֵי בְּרָזָא דִמְהֵימְנוּתָא דְּקוּדְשָׁא בְּרִיךְ הוּא כְּלוּם, בְּגִין דְּכֻלְּהוּ הֲווֹ פָּלְחֵי פּוּלְחָנָא נוּכְרָאָה בְּגָלוּתָא, וְאַנְשׁוּ כָּל עִקָּרָא דִמְהֵימְנוּתָא דַּהֲוָה בְּהוּ בְּקַדְמֵיתָא, דִּירִיתוּ כָּל אִינּוּן תְּרֵיסַר שִׁבְטִין מֵאֲבוּהוֹן יַעֲקֹב.

631. Rabbi Chiya opened the discussion after him saying: "To you it was shown, that you might know that Hashem He is the Elohim…" (Devarim

4:35). This verse should be viewed closely. What is the meaning of: "To you it was shown?" HE ANSWERS: When the children of Yisrael went forth from Egypt, they knew nothing through the secret of the Faith in the Holy One, blessed be He, because they all worshipped idols in exile. They forgot all the roots of the Faith that they had originally that the twelve tribes inherited from their father Jacob.

632. וְכַד אָתָא מֹשֶׁה, אוֹלִיף לוֹן דְּאִית אֱלוֹהַּ עִלָּאָה בְּעָלְמָא, כְּמָה דְּאוּקְמוּהָ. לְבָתַר חָמוּ כָּל אִינּוּן נִסִּין וּגְבוּרָן דְּעַל יַמָּא, וְכָל נִסִּין וּגְבוּרָן דְּעָבֵד לְהוּ בְּמִצְרַיִם. לְבָתַר חָמוּ כַּמָּה גְבוּרָן, בְּמָנָא וּבְמַיָּא וְאִתְיְהִיבַת לוֹן אוֹרַיְיתָא, וְאוֹלִיפוּ אָרְחֵי דְּקוּדְשָׁא בְּרִיךְ הוּא, עַד דְּמָטֵי לְעִדָּנָא דָּא.

632. When Moses came, he taught them that there was a supernal Elohim in the world, as we have established. Afterwards, they saw all the miracles and mighty deeds by the sea, and all the miracles and mighty deeds that He performed for them in Egypt. Then they saw many mighty deeds with the manna and with the water, the Torah was given to them, and they learned the ways of the Holy One, blessed be He, until they came to that time.

633. אָמַר לוֹן מֹשֶׁה, עַד הַשְׁתָּא אִצְטְרִיכְנָא לְמֵילַף לְכוּ, כְּמָה דְּיַלְפִין לְרַבְיָא. וְדָא הוּא אַתָּה הָרְאֵתָ לָדַעַת, וְאוֹלִיפַת עַד הָכָא, לָדַעַת לְמִנְדַּע וּלְאַסְתַּכְּלָא וּלְמֵיעַל בְּרָזָא דִּמְהֵימְנוּתָא. וּמַאי אִיהִי. כִּי יְיָ' הוּא הָאֱלֹהִים.

633. Moses said to them: Until now, I had to teach you as one teaches a child. This is the meaning of: "To you it was shown, that you might know," for I taught you until now the knowledge to know, behold and enter the secret of Faith, which is that Hashem He is the Elohim'.

634. אִי תֵּימָא מִלָּה זְעֵירָא הִיא לְמִנְדַּע, הָא כְּתִיב וְיָדַעְתָּ הַיּוֹם וַהֲשֵׁבֹתָ אֶל לְבָבֶךָ כִּי יְיָ' הוּא הָאֱלֹהִים בַּשָּׁמַיִם מִמַּעַל וְעַל הָאָרֶץ מִתַּחַת אֵין עוֹד. הָכָא תַּלְיָא כָּל רָזָא דִּמְהֵימְנוּתָא, לְמִנְדַּע מִגּוֹ דָּא, רָזָא דְּכָל רָזִין, לְמִנְדַּע סְתִימוּ דְּכָל סְתִימִין, יְהֹוָ"ה אֱלֹהִים שֵׁם מָלֵא, וְכֹלָּא חַד. אַתָּה הָרְאֵתָ לָדַעַת, הָכָא רָזָא דְּרָזִין לְאִינּוּן יַדְעֵי מִדִּין.

-386-

**634.** If you wonder whether it is a small matter to know this, behold it is written: "Know therefore this day, and consider it in your heart, that Hashem He is the Elohim in heaven above, and upon the earth beneath, there is no other" (Ibid. 39). The entire secret of the Faith, deriving the secret of all secrets from this and knowing the most concealed of all, is stems from THIS VERSE. Yud Hei Vav Hei Elohim is a full name, FOR YUD HEI VAV HEI IS ZEIR ANPIN AND ELOHIM IS MALCHUT, and it indicates that it is all one. "To you it was shown, that you might know…THAT HASHEM HE IS THE ELOHIM…": Here is the secret of secrets to those who know the law; NAMELY, THE SECRET THAT ZEIR ANPIN, WHICH IS YUD HEI VAV HEI, AND ELOHIM, WHICH IS MALCHUT, ARE ONE.

## 61. "Then I was by Him, as a nursling"

### A Synopsis

Rabbi Chiya speaks here about the relationship between a king and a craftsman who together make a palace. He says the Torah is the craftsman whom the Holy One used to create the world. Before the world was created, the Torah preceded it by two thousand years. The Holy One looked into the Torah, saw what was to be created, and created it. He created man to be occupied with Torah, for which the world exists. Now, everyone who looks into the Torah and is occupied with it causes the world to remain in existence. Like Adam, we are told, all people before they come to this world stand before God in the same form and existence as they are in the world. At the moment a soul is about to descend to this world, God calls the appointed angel who has authority over the soul, and asks the angel to bring her into His presence. Then the soul comes clothed in the form of this world, and the Holy King makes her swear that she will be occupied with Torah when she descends to this world. It is better for one not to be born, we are told, than to come to this world and not try to know God.

### The Relevance of this Passage

Here we learn that the Torah predated the world and was indeed the pattern for all Creation. Traditionally, the Torah is viewed as a religious canon in which the fundamental laws of moral and physical conduct are inscribed. Scholars view the Torah as a document of recorded history, or a collection of stories that expound upon God's relationship with man.

Kabbalistically, these descriptions miss the mark. The author of the Zohar, the eminent Kabbalist Rabbi Shimon bar Yochai, ridicules those who see only stories and tales in this sacred instrument. The scroll is not an attempt to define the proper morals by which a man should live. Humanity will never seek out positive change, nor will a man persevere on the spiritual path when the vague concepts of morality and ethics are the primary motivation and reward. Lacking the Kabbalistic knowledge concerning the Torah, the scroll becomes a fruitless symbol of tradition, instead of an awesome instrument of power.

What is the power of the Torah when viewed through the lens of Kabbalah? It is the personal and universal power to change; to transform; to elevate; to grow; to become God(like). Toward that end, the scroll emits spiritual influences that envelope us with: healing, so that we share it with others; prosperity, so that we may tithe and give to the poor; assistance in the removal of envy, so that we may love others unconditionally; the ability to attract one's soul-mate, so that

we may complete our souls; and the courage to conquer our deepest fears, so that we may climb the highest mountains.

This most potent passage evokes this ancient memory, recalling our promise to God to delve, heart and soul, into the Torah's mysteries. And at this moment, here and now, we are honoring our commitment, igniting the full power of the Torah, and completing the purpose of Creation.

635. זַכָּאִין אִינוּן כָּל אִינוּן דְּמִשְׁתַּדְּלֵי בְּאוֹרַיְיתָא. וּבְגִין דְּכַד בְּרָא קוּדְשָׁא בְּרִיךְ הוּא עָלְמָא, אִסְתְּכַּל בָּהּ בְּאוֹרַיְיתָא, וּבְרָא עָלְמָא, וּבְאוֹרַיְיתָא אִתְבְּרֵי עָלְמָא, כְּמָה דְּאוּקְמוּהָ, דִּכְתִּיב וָאֶהְיֶה אֶצְלוֹ אָמוֹן, אַל תִּקְרֵי אָמוֹן אֶלָּא אוּמָן.

**635.** Happy are all those who are occupied with Torah, for when the Holy One, blessed be He, created the world, He looked into the Torah and thus created the world. He did create the world with Torah and with Torah was the world created, as we have established. It is written: "then I was by Him, as a nursling (Heb. *amon*)" (Mishlei 8:30). Do not pronounce it 'amon' but rather 'umon (Eng. 'a craftsman')' FOR TORAH IS THE CRAFTMANSHIP OF THE WORLD.

636. וְכִי אוֹרַיְיתָא אוּמָנָא הֲוָה. אִין. לְמַלְכָּא דְּבָעֵי לְמֶעְבַּד פַּלְטְרִין, אִי לָא שַׁוֵּי לְגַבֵּיהּ אוּמָנָא, לָא יָכִיל לְמֶעְבַּד פְּלַטְרִין. כֵּיוָן דִּפְלַטְרִין וְאִתְעֲבֵידוּ, לָא סָלִיק שְׁמָא, אֶלָּא דְּמַלְכָּא. אִלֵּין פְּלַטְרִין דְּעָבֵד מַלְכָּא, מַלְכָּא שַׁוֵּי בְּאִינוּן פְּלַטְרִין מַחֲשָׁבָה.

**636.** HE QUESTIONS: Is the Torah a craftsman? HE ANSWERS: Yes, SIMILAR to a king who wishes to build a palace. If he does not take a craftsman, he cannot make the palace. Once the palace is built, it is not known AFTER THE NAME OF THE CRAFTSMAN, but rather by the name of the king. For people say these are the palaces that the king made, BY REASON that the king gave the idea for all these palaces.

637. כָּךְ קוּדְשָׁא בְּרִיךְ הוּא, בָּעֵי לְמִבְרֵי עָלְמָא, אִסְתְּכַּל בְּאוּמָנָא, וְאע״ג דְּאוּמָנָא עֲבַד פְּלַטְרִין, לָא סָלִיק שְׁמָא אֶלָּא דְּמַלְכָּא, אִלֵּין

פְּלַטְרִין דַּעֲבַד מַלְכָּא, וַדַּאי מַלְכָּא בָּנָה פְּלַטְרִין. אוֹרַיְיתָא צֹוַוחַת
וְאָהְיֶה אֶצְלוֹ אָמוֹן, בִּי בָּרָא קוּדְשָׁא בְּרִיךְ הוּא עָלְמָא, דְּעַד אִתְבְּרֵי
עָלְמָא, אַקְדִּימַת אוֹרַיְיתָא תְּרֵין אַלְפֵי שְׁנִין לְעָלְמָא, וְכַד בָּעָא קוּדְשָׁא
בְּרִיךְ הוּא לְמִבְרֵי עָלְמָא, הֲוָה מִסְתַּכַּל בָּה בְּאוֹרַיְיתָא, בְּכָל מִלָּה
וּמִלָּה, וְעָבֵד לְקֳבְלָהּ אוּמָנוּתָא דְּעָלְמָא. בְּגִין דְּכָל מִלִּין וְעוֹבָדִין דְּכָל
עָלְמִין, בְּאוֹרַיְיתָא אִינּוּן. וְע"ד קוּדְשָׁא בְּרִיךְ הוּא הֲוָה מִסְתַּכַּל בָּה,
וּבָרָא עָלְמָא.

**637.** So the Holy One, blessed be He, wanted to create the world. He looked to the craftsman, WHICH IS THE TORAH and, although the craftsman made the palace, it is credited to the name of the king, for people say these are the palaces that the king made. Certainly, the king built the palace. The Torah cries, 'Then I was by Him, as a craftsman,' for the Holy One, blessed be He, created the world with me. Before the world was created, the Torah preceded the world by two thousand years. When the Holy One, blessed be He, wanted to create the world, He looked into every single word in the Torah, and created the craft in the world correspondingly, because all the things and words of the worlds are in the Torah. Therefore, the Holy One, blessed be He, looked into it and so created the world.

**638.** לָאו דְּאוֹרַיְיתָא בָּרָא עָלְמָא, אֶלָּא קוּדְשָׁא בְּרִיךְ הוּא,
בְּאִסְתַּכְּלוּתָא דְּאוֹרַיְיתָא בָּרָא עָלְמָא. אִשְׁתְּכַח דְּקוּדְשָׁא בְּרִיךְ הוּא
אִיהוּ אוּמָנָא, וְאוֹרַיְיתָא לְקֳבְלֵיהּ וּלְגַבֵּיהּ אוּמָנָא, שֶׁנֶּאֱמַר וָאֶהְיֶה אֶצְלוֹ
אָמוֹן, וָאֶהְיֶה אָמוֹן לָא כְּתִיב, אֶלָּא אֶצְלוֹ, הוֹאִיל וְקוּדְשָׁא בְּרִיךְ הוּא
אִסְתַּכַּל בָּה, אֶצְלוֹ הֲוָה אוּמָנָא.

**638.** Not that the Torah created the world, but rather the Holy One, blessed be He, by His looking into the Torah, created the world. So we find that the Holy One, blessed be He, is the craftsman and the Torah in relation to Him and by Him is a craft, as it is written: "Then I was by Him, as a nursling (Heb. *amon*)." It does not say 'I was as amon,' but "I was by Him as amon." The Holy One, blessed be He, looked into it, so it was by Him a craft.

**639.** וְאִי תֵּימָא מַאן יָכִיל לְמֶהֱוֵי אוּמָנָא לְגַבֵּיהּ. אֶלָּא אִסְתַּכְּלוּתָא

-390-

דְּקוּדְשָׁא בְּרִיךְ הוּא בְּגַוְונָא דָא, בְּאוֹרַיְיתָא, כְּתִיב בָּה, בְּרֵאשִׁית בָּרָא אֱלֹהִים אֶת הַשָּׁמַיִם וְאֵת הָאָרֶץ, אִסְתָּכַּל בְּהַאי מִלָּה, וּבְרָא אֶת הַשָּׁמַיִם. בְּאוֹרַיְיתָא כְּתִיב בָּה, וַיֹּאמֶר אֱלֹהִים יְהִי אוֹר, אִסְתָּכַּל בְּהַאי מִלָּה, וּבְרָא אֶת הָאוֹר. וְכֵן בְּכָל מִלָּה וּמִלָּה דִּכְתִּיב בָּה בְּאוֹרַיְיתָא, אִסְתָּכַּל קוּדְשָׁא בְּרִיךְ הוּא, וְעָבֵד הַהִיא מִלָּה, וְעַ"ד כְּתִיב וָאֶהְיֶה אֶצְלוֹ אָמוֹן. כְּגַוְונָא דָא כָּל עָלְמָא אִתְבְּרֵי.

**639.** And if you ask: Who can be a craftsman next to the Holy One, blessed be He? The looking of the Holy One, blessed be He, was in this manner. It is written in the Torah: "In the beginning Elohim created the heaven and the earth" (Beresheet 1:1). He looked at this and created the heaven. In the Torah, it is written: "And Elohim said, 'Let there be light'" (Ibid. 3). He looked at this word and created the light, and so with every single word that is written in the Torah, the Holy One, blessed be He, looked and created that thing. Therefore it is written: "Then I was by Him as a craftsman." The whole world was created in the same way.

**640.** כֵּיוָן דְּאִתְבְּרֵי עָלְמָא, כָּל מִלָּה וּמִלָּה לָא הֲוָה מִתְקַיֵּים, עַד דְּסָלִיק בִּרְעוּתָא לְמִבְרֵי אָדָם, דִּיהֱוֵי מִשְׁתַּדַּל בְּאוֹרַיְיתָא, וּבְגִינָהּ אִתְקַיֵּים עָלְמָא. הַשְׁתָּא כָּל מַאן דְּאִסְתָּכַּל בָּהּ בְּאוֹרַיְיתָא, וְאִשְׁתַּדַּל בָּהּ, כִּבְיָכוֹל, הוּא מְקַיֵּים כָּל עָלְמָא. קוּדְשָׁא בְּרִיךְ הוּא אִסְתָּכַּל בְּאוֹרַיְיתָא, וּבְרָא עָלְמָא. בַּר נָשׁ מִסְתַּכַּל בָּהּ בְּאוֹרַיְיתָא וּמְקַיֵּים עָלְמָא. אִשְׁתְּכַח דְּעוֹבָדָא וְקִיּוּמָא דְּכָל עָלְמָא, אוֹרַיְיתָא אִיהִי. בְּגִין כַּךְ זַכָּאָה אִיהוּ בַּר נָשׁ דְּאִשְׁתַּדַּל בְּאוֹרַיְיתָא, דְּהָא אִיהוּ מְקַיֵּים עָלְמָא.

**640.** Once the world was created, nothing persevered until it arose in His desire to create man, to be occupied with Torah, for which the world exists. Now, everyone who looks into the Torah and is occupied with it causes the world to remain in existence. The Holy One, blessed be He, looked into the Torah and created the world. Man looks into the Torah and causes it to exist, so we see that the existence and the sustenance of the entire world is the Torah. Therefore, Happy is the man who is occupied in Torah, for he keeps the world in existence.

641. בְּשַׁעֲתָא דְסָלִיק בִּרְעוּתָא דְקוּדְשָׁא בְּרִיךְ הוּא לְמִבְרֵי אָדָם, קָאִים קַמֵּיה בְּדִיוּקְנֵיה וְקִיוּמֵיה, כְּמָה דְאִיהוּ בְּהַאי עָלְמָא. וַאֲפִילוּ כָּל אִינוּן בְּנֵי עָלְמָא, עַד לָא יֵיתוּן בְּהַאי עָלְמָא, כֻּלְהוּ קַיְימִין בְּקִיוּמַיְיהוּ וּבְתִקוּנַיְיהוּ כְּגַוְונָא דְקַיְימִין בְּהַאי עָלְמָא, בְּחַד אוֹצַר דְתַמָּן כָּל נִשְׁמָתִין דְעָלְמָא מִתְלַבְּשָׁן בְּדִיוּקְנַיְיהוּ.

**641.** At the time that the desire arose in the Holy One, blessed be He, to create Adam, he stood before Him in his form and existence as he is in the world. All the people of the world, before they come to this world, stand in their complete existence, as they are present in this world in one treasury, where all the souls of the world are clothed in their form.

642. וּבְשַׁעֲתָא דִזְמִינִין לְנַחְתָּא בְּהַאי עָלְמָא, קָרֵי קוּדְשָׁא בְּרִיךְ הוּא לְחַד מְמָנָא, דִי מְנֵי קוּדְשָׁא בְּרִיךְ הוּא בִּרְשׁוּתֵיה כָּל נִשְׁמָתִין דִזְמִינִין לְנַחְתָּא לְהַאי עָלְמָא, וְאָמַר לֵיה, זִיל אַיְיתֵי לִי רוּחַ פְּלוֹנִי. בְּהַהִיא שַׁעֲתָא אַתְיָא הַהוּא נִשְׁמָתָא, מִתְלַבְּשָׁא בְּדִיוּקְנָא דְהַאי עָלְמָא, וְהַהוּא מְמָנָא אַחְזֵי לָה קַמֵּי מַלְכָּא קַדִישָׁא.

**642.** At the moment that they are about to descend to this world, the Holy One, blessed be He, calls one appointed angel in whose authority the Holy One, blessed be He, places all the souls that are to descend to this world. And He says to him: Bring me the spirit of so-and-so. At that moment, the soul comes clothed in the form of this world, and that appointed angel presents it before the Holy King.

643. קוּדְשָׁא בְּרִיךְ הוּא אָמַר לָה, וְאוֹמֵי לָה, דְכַד תֵּיחוֹת לְהַאי עָלְמָא, דְתִשְׁתַּדַל בְּאוֹרַיְיתָא, לְמִנְדַע לֵיה, וּלְמִנְדַע בְּרָזָא דִמְהֵימְנוּתָא. דְכָל מַאן דְהַוֵי בְּהַאי עָלְמָא, וְלָא אִשְׁתַּדַל לְמִנְדַע לֵיה, טַב לֵיה דְלָא יִתְבְּרֵי. בְּג"כ אִתְחֲזֵי קַמֵּי מַלְכָּא קַדִישָׁא, לְמִנְדַע בְּהַאי עָלְמָא, וּלְאִשְׁתַּדְלָא בֵּיה בְּקוּדְשָׁא בְּרִיךְ הוּא, בְּרָזָא דִמְהֵימְנוּתָא.

**643.** The Holy One, blessed be He, says to it and makes it swear that it should be occupied with Torah when it descends to this world, to know it

and to know the secret of the Faith. For everyone who was in this world, and did not try to know Him, it is better created. Therefore, it appears before the King THROUGH THAT APPOINTED ANGEL AS MENTIONED BEFORE, so as to know HIM in this world and to endeavor in the Holy One, blessed be He, in the secret of the Faith.

## 62. "To you it was shown, that you might know," part two

### A Synopsis

Rabbi Chiya says here that the secret of the Torah is to know and to behold this world in the secret of Faith. He then reminds us that the general principle of the whole secret of Faith is "That you might know that The Creator He is the Elohim." This is of course the knowledge of above and below, Malchut below being both the Faith and the name Elohim. He speaks of the Written Torah, which is Yud Hei Vav Hei or Zeir Anpin, and of the Oral Torah, which is Malchut and the name Elohim. It is all one. The Written Torah is general and the Oral Torah is specific because Malchut is one specific Sfirah of the ten Sfirot of Zeir Anpin. Rabbi Chiya then says there are two precepts of the Torah: one, Yud Hei Vav Hei, is 'remember', and the other, Elohim, is 'keep'. The secret of 'remember' has 248 positive precepts, we learn, and the secret of 'keep' has 365 negative precepts. And it is all one.

### The Relevance of this Passage

Here we receive faith for those times when we are drowning in doubt. We tie our souls to the upper world through the power of the Tetragrammaton, Yud Hei Vav Hei ‫י.ה.ו.ה.‬, and Divinity flows into our lives. The truth of the Creator is invoked in the hearts of all mankind so that we are all deeply committed to walk the spiritual path of Torah, illuminated by Kabbalah.

644. הה"ד אַתָּה הָרְאֵתָ לָדַעַת, אִתְחֲזִיאַת עַל יְדָא דְּהַהוּא מְמָנָא, קָמֵי קוּדְשָׁא בְּרִיךְ הוּא. לָדַעַת לְמִנְדַע וּלְאִסְתַּכְּלָא בְּהַאי עָלְמָא, בְּרָזָא דִּמְהֵימְנוּתָא, בְּרָזָא דְּאוֹרַיְיתָא. וְכָל מַאן דַּהֲוָה בְּהַאי עָלְמָא, וְלָא אִשְׁתָּדַל בְּאוֹרַיְיתָא לְמִנְדַע לֵיהּ, טַב לֵיהּ דְּלָא אִתְבְּרֵי, דְּהָא בְּגִין דָּא אַיְיתֵי לֵיהּ קוּדְשָׁא בְּרִיךְ הוּא לְבַר נָשׁ בְּהַאי עָלְמָא.

644. "To you it was shown, that you might know" by that appointed angel that is before the Holy One, blessed be He, "That you might know": To know and to behold this world by means of the Faith, by means of the Torah. Everyone who was in this world that did not occupy himself with Torah, to know it, it would be better for him not to have been created, since the Holy One, blessed be He, brought man into this world for that reason.

645. לָדַעַת כִּי יְיָ' הוּא הָאֱלֹהִים. דָּא אִיהוּ כְּלָלָא דְּכָל רָזָא
דִּמְהֵימְנוּתָא, דְּכָל אוֹרַיְיתָא, כְּלָלָא דְּעֵילָא וְתַתָּא, וְרָזָא דָּא אִיהוּ
כְּלָלָא דְּכָל רָזָא דִּמְהֵימְנוּתָא, וְהָכִי הוּא וַדַּאי. כְּלָלָא דְּכָל אוֹרַיְיתָא,
דָּא אִיהוּ רָזָא דְּתוֹרָה שֶׁבִּכְתָב, וְדָא אִיהוּ רָזָא דְּתוֹרָה שֶׁבְּעַל פֶּה, וְכֹלָּא
חַד, כְּלָלָא דְּרָזָא דִּמְהֵימְנוּתָא, בְּגִין דְּאִיהוּ שֵׁם מָלֵא, דְּאִיהוּ רָזָא
דִּמְהֵימְנוּתָא, וּמַאן אִיהוּ. ה' אֶחָד וּשְׁמוֹ אֶחָד, יְיָ' אֶחָד שְׁמַע יִשְׂרָאֵל
יְיָ' אֱלֹהֵינוּ יְיָ' אֶחָד. דָּא אִיהוּ יִחוּדָא חַד. וּשְׁמוֹ אֶחָד, בשכמל"ו, הָא
יִחוּדָא אַחֲרָא לְמֶהֱוֵי שְׁמֵיהּ חַד. וְרָזָא דָּא יְיָ' הוּא הָאֱלֹהִים, דָּא כְּתִיב,
כַּד אִינּוּן בְּיִחוּדָא חֲדָא.

645. 'That you might know that Hashem He is the Elohim': This is the
general principle of the whole secret of the Faith of the entire Torah, the
comprising of that which is above and below. This secret is the principle
comprehending the whole secret of the Faith, WHICH IS MALCHUT, so it is
certainly THAT THE NAME ELOHIM IS MALCHUT. The inclusion of the
entire Torah is the secret of the Written Torah, NAMELY THE NAME YUD
HEI VAV HEI, WHICH IS ZEIR ANPIN THAT IS CALLED 'THE WRITTEN
TORAH'. This is the secret of the Oral Torah, WHICH IS MALCHUT, WHICH
IS THE NAME ELOHIM. It is all one, and this is the totality of the secret of
the Faith, because "HASHEM HE IS THE ELOHIM" is the complete Name,
which is the secret of the Faith THAT IS CALLED 'NAME'. FOR IN THIS
UNION IT IS FULL AND WHOLE. What is it? He is "Hashem shall be One,
and His Name One" (Zecharyah 14:9). "Hashem shall be one" is the secret
of "Hear O Yisrael, Hashem our Elohim, Hashem is One." This is one
unison. "And His Name One" IS THE SECRET OF: 'Blessed is the Name of
the glory of His kingdom forever and ever.' For this is another unison, so
that His Name should be one, WHICH IS MALCHUT. This is the secret of:
"Hashem He is the Elohim" (I Melachim 18:39), which is written when they
are in one unity.

646. וְאִי תֵּימָא, אִי הָכִי, כְּגַוְונָא דִּכְתִיב יְיָ' אֶחָד וּשְׁמוֹ אֶחָד, לָאו
אִיהוּ יְיָ' הוּא הָאֱלֹהִים, דְּאִי כְּתִיב יְיָ' אֶחָד וּשְׁמוֹ הוּא אֶחָד, הֲוָה
אֲמֵינָא הָכִי. אֲבָל לָא כְּתִיב, אֶלָּא יְיָ' אֶחָד, וּשְׁמוֹ אֶחָד, וְאִצְטְרִיךְ
לְמֵימַר כְּגַוְונָא דָּא יְיָ' הוּא, הָאֱלֹהִים הוּא, וְאִתְחֲזֵי יְיָ' אֶחָד וּשְׁמוֹ אֶחָד.

**646.** And if you say THAT IF "HASHEM HE IS THE ELOHIM" is similar to WHAT IS WRITTEN: "Hashem shall be One, and His Name One," yet it is not SIMILAR TO THE VERSE, "Hashem He is the Elohim." For it were written: 'Hashem shall be One, and His Name is One,' I would agree, but it is written, "Hashem shall be One, and His Name One." It should have been said HERE: 'Hashem He is, the Elohim He is,' then it would have looked like, "Hashem shall be one, and His name One."

647. אֶלָּא כֹּלָּא חַד, דְּכַד מִתְיַיחֲדָן תְּרֵין שְׁמָהָן אִלֵּין, דָּא בְּיִחוּדָא חַד, וְדָא בְּיִחוּדָא חַד, כְּדֵין תְּרֵין שְׁמָהָן אִלֵּין אִתְעֲבִידוּ חַד, וְאִתְכְּלִילוּ דָּא בְּדָא, וַהֲוֵי כֹּלָּא שְׁמָא שְׁלִים, בְּיִחוּדָא חֲדָא, וּבְכֵן יְיָ' הוּא הָאֱלֹהִים, דְּהָא כְּדֵין אִתְכְּלִיל כֹּלָּא דָּא בְּדָא, לְמֶהֱוֵי חַד. וְעַד דְּאִתְיַחֲדוּ כָּל חַד, דָּא בִּלְחוֹדוֹי, וְדָא בִּלְחוֹדוֹי, לָא אִתְכְּלִילוּ דָּא בְּדָא, לְמֶהֱוֵי כֹּלָּא חַד.

**647.** HE ANSWERS: It is all one, because when these two names are unified, the one in one unison and the other in another unison, AS IT IS WRITTEN, "HASHEM IS ONE AND HIS NAME ONE," both the names become one and are combined one within the other. It all becomes a complete name in one unison. Thus, "Hashem He is the Elohim," because everything is combined with each other to become one. As long as they are not all joined, and are each one by itself, they are not included one with the other, so that they would all become one.

648. כְּלָלָא דְּכָל אוֹרַיְיתָא הָכִי אִיהוּ וַדַּאי, דְּהָא אוֹרַיְיתָא אִיהִי תּוֹרָה שֶׁבִּכְתָב, וְאִיהוּ תּוֹרָה שֶׁבְּעַל פֶּה. תּוֹרָה שֶׁבִּכְתָב, דָּא אִיהוּ דִּכְתִיב יְיָ'. תּוֹרָה דבע"פ, דָּא הוּא דִּכְתִיב הָאֱלֹהִים. וּבְגִין דְּאוֹרַיְיתָא אִיהוּ רָזָא דִּשְׁמָא קַדִּישָׁא, אִקְרֵי הָכִי תּוֹרָה שֶׁבִּכְתָב וְתוֹרָה דבע"פ, דָּא כְּלָל, וְדָא פְּרָט. כְּלָל אִצְטְרִיךְ לִפְרָט, וּפְרָט אִצְטְרִיךְ לִכְלָל, וְאִתְיַיחֲדוּ דָּא בְּדָא, לְמֶהֱוֵי כֹּלָּא חַד.

**648.** THE ZOHAR EXPLAINS ITS PREVIOUS WORDS, WHICH SAY THAT "HASHEM HE IS THE ELOHIM" COMPRISES the generality of the entire Torah. For assuredly the Torah is the Written Torah and the Oral Torah; the Written Torah as it is written: "Hashem", WHICH IS ZEIR ANPIN THAT IS

CALLED 'THE WRITTEN TORAH', and the Oral Torah as it is written, "The Elohim," NAMELY MALCHUT THAT IS CALLED 'ORAL TORAH' AND CALLED 'ELOHIM'. Because the Torah is the secret of the Holy Name, "HASHEM HE IS THE ELOHIM," it is called 'the Written Torah' and 'Oral Torah'. The one, WRITTEN TORAH, is general, and the other ORAL TORAH, is specific, BECAUSE ZEIR ANPIN IS GENERAL AND MALCHUT IS SPECIFIC, BECAUSE MALCHUT IS ONE SPECIFIC Sfirah OF THE TEN Sfirot OF ZEIR ANPIN. The general rule needs the specific, and the specific needs the general, and they join one with the other to be all one.

649. וְעַל דָּא, כְּלָלָא דְּאוֹרַיְיתָא אִיהוּ כְּלָלָא דְּעֵילָא וְתַתָּא, בְּגִין דִּשְׁמָא דָא לְעֵילָא, וּשְׁמָא דָא לְתַתָּא, דָּא רָזָא דְּעָלְמָא עִלָּאָה, וְדָא רָזָא דְּעָלְמָא תַּתָּאָה, וְעַל דָּא כְּתִיב, אַתָּה הָרְאֵתָ לָדַעַת כִּי יְיָ' הוּא הָאֱלֹהִים. דָּא אִיהוּ כְּלָלָא דְּכֹלָא, וְדָא אִצְטְרִיךְ בַּר נָשׁ לְמִנְדַּע בְּהַאי עָלְמָא.

649. Therefore, the general rule of the Torah is that of above ZEIR ANPIN, and below, MALCHUT, because this Name YUD HEI VAV HEI is above IN ZEIR ANPIN and the other name ELOHIM is below IN MALCHUT. The one is the secret of the upper world and the other is the secret of the lower world. Therefore, it is written: "To you it was shown, that you might know that Hashem He is the Elohim" This comprehends everything and this is what man must know in this world.

650. וְאִי תֵּימָא, פִּקוּדֵי אוֹרַיְיתָא אָן אִינּוּן הָכָא בִּכְלָלָא דָּא. אֶלָּא דָּא אִיהוּ זָכוֹר, וְדָא אִיהוּ שָׁמוֹר, וְכָל פִּקוּדֵי אוֹרַיְיתָא בְּהָנֵי כְּלִילָן, בְּרָזָא דְּזָכוֹר וּבְרָזָא דְּשָׁמוֹר, וְכֹלָא אִיהוּ חַד.

650. If you ask: Where are the precepts of the Torah in this generality OF "HASHEM HE IS THE ELOHIM?" HE ANSWERS: The one, YUD HEI VAV HEI, is 'remember' and the other, ELOHIM, is 'keep', and all the precepts of the Torah are included in these, in the secret of 'remember' THAT INCLUDES 248 POSITIVE PRECEPTS, and in the secret 'keep' THAT INCLUDES 365 NEGATIVE PRECEPTS, THAT TOGETHER ARE 613 PRECEPTS OF THE TORAH. And it is all one.

## 63. Tefilin

### A Synopsis

Rabbi Yosi here explains that the Evening Service is obligatory because Zeir Anpin (day) and Malchut (night) must be joined in unison. He says that "And you shall love" is right, and "And it shall come to pass, if you hearken" is left; this is more specific than the general unity or joining of left and right in Sh'ma Yisrael. This unity, we are told, is similar to the head Tfilin and the hand Tefilin. The head Tefilin with its four paragraphs is congruent with the three names, "The Creator our Elohim, The Creator" in the Sh'ma Yisrael. Rabbi Yosi then tells us that the left and right columns of the paragraphs, and of the three names, both join with Da'at in the Central Column as the union of Chochmah and Binah. The hand Tefilin is the unity of the head Tfilin with Malchut, and the secret of this unity, we learn, is 'Blessed'. All blessings flow from the upper point, Chochmah, which is male, to the World to Come, Binah, which is female. Binah is therefore called 'Baruch', and also 'a blessing'. Rabbi Shimon comments that the unity of Zeir Anpin (the head Tefilin) and Malchut (the hand Tefilin) is set in order by way of Chochmah, Binah, the right of Da'at and the left of Da'at.

### The Relevance of this Passage

Tefilin is an antenna. In it, we see the power of joining left and right and above and below. As a battery requires both a positive and negative pole to produce power, Tefilin generates metaphysical power by incorporating the positive (right) and negative (left) spiritual poles permeating the planet and the heavens. This joining is also germane to the connection of the evening service. Our reading stirs the forces generated through the laying of Tefilin and the performance of the evening service.

Our Evil Inclination and the dark forces that dominate the night are crushed, so great is the Light channeled by the Zohar. Chochmah unites with Binah, the upper world enjoins our world, our bodies are tuned to our souls, and all that exists shines with resplendent Light.

651. פָּתַח רַבִּי יוֹסֵי וְאָמַר, הָא דִּתְנֵינָן דִּצְלוֹתָא דְּעַרְבִית חוֹבָה אִיהִי וַדַּאי, בְּגִין דִּקְרִיאַת שְׁמַע דְּעַרְבִית חוֹבָה, וְקוּדְשָׁא בְּרִיךְ הוּא אִתְיַחַד בְּלֵילְיָא, כְּמָה דְּאִתְיַחַד בִּימָמָא, וּמִדַּת לֵילְיָא אִתְכְּלִיל בִּימָמָא, וּמִדַּת יְמָמָא אִתְכְּלִיל בְּלֵילְיָא, וְאִתְעֲבֵיד יִחוּדָא חֲדָא. וּמַאן דְּאָמַר רְשׁוּת, בְּגִין אֵמוּרִין וּפְדָרִין דְּמִתְאַכְּלֵי בְּלֵילְיָא וְהָא אוּקִימְנָא.

-398-

**651.** Rabbi Yosi opened the discussion saying: We have learned that the Evening Service is obligatory. It is certainly an obligation, because the Evening reading of Sh'ma is obligatory, for the Holy One, blessed be He, unites WITH MALCHUT during the night just as He unites during the day. The aspect of night, WHICH IS MALCHUT, is included in the day, WHICH IS ZEIR ANPIN, and the aspect of day is included in the night. And one unison is formed. If one says THAT THE EVENING SERVICE is voluntary, it is because IT CORRESPONDS to the portions of the sacrifices and the fat that are consumed on the altar during the night, FOR THERE IS NO OBLIGATION THAT THEY SHOULD BE BURNT DURING THE NIGHT, as we have already established.

652. כְּתִיב וְאָהַבְתָּ אֵת יְיָ׳ אֱלֹהֶיךָ בְּכָל לְבָבְךָ וּבְכָל נַפְשְׁךָ וְגוֹ׳, הַאי קְרָא אוּקִימְנָא לֵיהּ, וְאוּקְמוּהָ חַבְרַיָּיא. אֲבָל אִית לְשָׁאֲלָא, אִי בְּהַאי יִחוּדָא דִּשְׁמַע יִשְׂרָאֵל, אִתְכְּלִיל כֹּלָּא, יְמִינָא וּשְׂמָאלָא, אַמַּאי לְבָתַר וְאָהַבְתָּ וְהָיָה אִם שָׁמֹעַ, דְּהָא בְּיִחוּדָא אִתְכְּלִילוּ. אֲבָל הָתָם בִּכְלָל, וְהָכָא בִּפְרָט, וְהָכִי אִצְטְרִיךְ.

**652.** It is written: "And you shall love Hashem your Elohim with all your heart, and with all your soul, and with all your might" (Devarim 6:5). We already established this verse and the friends have established it, but it could be asked: In this unison of 'Sh'ma Yisrael', everything is included, right and left, BECAUSE YUD HEI VAV HEI IS RIGHT AND OUR ELOHIM IS LEFT. Why IS IT NECESSARY TO SAY afterwards "And you shall love," WHICH IS RIGHT, and "And it shall come to pass, if you hearken" (Devarim 11:13), WHICH IS LEFT. They were already included in the unity OF 'SH'MA YISRAEL'. HE ANSWERS: They are ALLUDED TO in general there IN 'SH'MA YISRAEL', but here IN, "AND YOU SHALL LOVE" AND "AND IT SHALL COME TO PASS, IF YOU HEARKEN," they are specified. This is the way it should be.

653. וּבְרָזָא דְּיִחוּדָא דָּא אִתְעָרְנָא בֵּיהּ, יִחוּדָא דָּא אִיהוּ כְּגַוְונָא דִּתְפִלִּין דְּרֵישָׁא, וּתְפִלִּין דִּדְרוֹעָא. בִּתְפִלִּין דְּרֵישָׁא ד׳ פָּרְשִׁיָּין, וְהָא אִתְּמַר, וְהָכָא תְּלַת שְׁמָהָן אִינּוּן. הָתָם בִּתְפִילִּין דְּרֵישָׁא, ד׳ פָּרְשִׁיָּין, כָּל חַד וְחַד בִּלְחוֹדוֹי, וְהָכָא תְּלַת שְׁמָהָן, מַה בֵּין הַאי לְהַאי.

**653.** In the secret of this unison, we have observed that this unity is similar to the head Tefilin and the hand Tefilin. In the head Tefilin, there are four paragraphs, as we have learned, and here in SH'MA YISRAEL, there are three names, HASHEM, OUR ELOHIM, HASHEM. In the head Tefilin, there are four paragraphs, each one by itself, and here are three names. What is the difference between them?

654. אֶלָּא אִינּוּן ד' פַּרְשִׁיָּין, הָא אִתְּעֲרוּ בְּהוּ, חַד, נְקוּדָה קַדְמָאָה עִלָּאָה. וְחַד, רָזָא דְּעָלְמָא דְּאָתֵי. וְחַד, יְמִינָא. וְחַד, שְׂמָאלָא. אִלֵּין רָזָא דִּתְפִלִּין דְּרֵישָׁא. וְהָכָא, בְּרָזָא דִּיְחוּדָא דָּא, תְּלַת שְׁמָהָן, וְאִינּוּן כְּגַוְונָא דְּאִינּוּן ד' פַּרְשִׁיוֹת. יְיָ' קַדְמָאָה, דָּא נְקוּדָה עִלָּאָה, רֵאשִׁיתָא דְּכֹלָּא. אֱלֹהֵינוּ רָזָא דְּעָלְמָא דְּאָתֵי. יְיָ' בַּתְרָאָה, כְּלָלָא דִּימִינָא וּשְׂמָאלָא כַּחֲדָא, בִּכְלָלָא חֲדָא, וְאֵלֵּין אִינּוּן תְּפִלִּין דְּרֵישָׁא, וְדָא אִיהוּ יְחוּדָא קַדְמָאָה.

**654.** HE ANSWERS: They have observed about these four paragraphs that the one PARAGRAPH, "SANCTIFY" (SHEMOT 13:2), is the first upper point, NAMELY CHOCHMAH AND THE RIGHT COLUMN. Another PARAGRAPH "AND IT SHALL BE WHEN HASHEM SHALL BRING YOU" (IBID. 11), is the secret of the World to Come, WHICH IS BINAH AND THE LEFT COLUMN. One PARAGRAPH "AND IT SHALL COME TO PASS, IF YOU HEARKEN," is the secret of the right OF THE MOCHIN OF DA'AT and the final PARAGRAPH, "AND IT SHALL BE IF YOU HEARKEN," is the secret of the left OF THE MOCHIN OF DA'AT. BECAUSE DA'AT, WHICH IS THE CENTRAL COLUMN, COMBINES CHOCHMAH AND BINAH, WHICH ARE RIGHT AND LEFT. This is the secret of the head Tefilin and here in the secret of the unity OF 'SH'MA YISRAEL' are three names, which are like the four paragraphs. The first Yud Hei Vav Hei is the upper point, which is the beginning of everything, WHICH IS CHOCHMAH AND THE RIGHT COLUMN. Our Elohim is the secret of the World to Come, NAMELY BINAH AND THE LEFT COLUMN, the last Yud Hei Vav Hei is the combination of right and left together in one combination, NAMELY DA'AT, WHICH IS THE CENTRAL COLUMN, THAT COMBINES RIGHT AND LEFT. This is ALSO the unity of the head Tefilin. SO WE SEE THAT THEY ARE BOTH EQUAL. This is the first unity, NAMELY 'SH'MA YISRAEL...', WHICH IS THE UPPER UNITY THAT PRECEDES THE LOWER UNITY, WHICH IS: "BLESSED IS THE NAME OF THE GLORY OF HIS KINGDOM..."

655. תְּפִלִּין דִּדְרוֹעָא, כְּלָלָא דְּכָל הָנֵי כַּחֲדָא, וְדָא אִיהוּ רָזָא בשכמל"ו. הָכָא כְּלָלָא דְּאִינּוּן תְּפִלִּין דְּרֵישָׁא, דְּאִתְכְּלִילוּ גּוֹ תְּפִלִּין דִּדְרוֹעָא.

655. The hand Tefilin is the combination of all these four PARAGRAPHS together, FOR THEY ARE NOT PLACED IN FOUR INDIVIDUAL COMPARTMENTS LIKE IN THE HEAD TEFILIN, BUT RATHER ARE ALL IN ONE COMPARTMENT. This is the secret OF THE UNITY of: 'Blessed is the Name of the glory of His kingdom forever and ever,' WHICH IS THE LOWER UNITY OF MALCHUT. Here, IN THE LOWER UNITY, is the inclusion of the head Tefilin, WHICH IS CHOCHMAH, BINAH AND DA'AT OF ZEIR ANPIN, which are included in the hand Tefilin, WHICH IS MALCHUT.

656. וְרָזָא דָּא, בָּרוּךְ: דָּא רָזָא דִּנְקוּדָה עִלָּאָה, דְּאִיהוּ בָּרוּךְ, דְּכָל בִּרְכָאן נַבְעִין מִתַּמָּן. וְאִי תֵּימָא עָלְמָא דְּאָתֵי אִקְרֵי בָּרוּךְ. לָאו הָכִי, דְּהָא נְקוּדָה עִלָּאָה אִיהוּ דְּכַר, עָלְמָא דְּאָתֵי נוּקְבָא. אִיהוּ בָּרוּךְ וְאִיהִי בִּרְכָה. בָּרוּךְ דְּכַר. בִּרְכָה נוּקְבָּא. וְעַל דָּא בָּרוּךְ אִיהוּ נְקוּדָה עִלָּאָה, שֵׁם: דָּא עָלְמָא דְּאָתֵי, דְּאִיהוּ שֵׁם גָּדוֹל, כד"א וּמַה תַּעֲשֵׂה לְשִׁמְךָ הַגָּדוֹל. כְּבוֹד: דָּא כָּבוֹד עִלָּאָה, דְּאִיהוּ יְמִינָא וּשְׂמָאלָא.

656. The secret of this UNITY is 'Blessed'. This is the secret of the upper point, which is blessed, for all the blessings flow from there, WHICH IS CHOCHMAH. If you ask if the World to Come, WHICH IS BINAH, is called 'Blessed'. It is not so, because the upper point is male, and the World to Come is female; THEREFORE, it is called 'Blessed' and she is called 'a blessing'. Therefore, 'blessed' is the upper point, CHOCHMAH, 'Name' is the World to Come, WHICH IS BINAH, which is a Great Name, as it is written: "And what will You do for Your Great Name" (Yehoshua 7:9). Glory refers to upper Glory, WHICH IS ZEIR ANPIN, that combines right and left.

657. וְכֻלְּהוּ כְּלִילָן בְּהַאי תְּפִלָּה שֶׁל יַד, דְּאִיהוּ מַלְכוּתוֹ, וְנָטִיל כֹּלָּא בְּגַוֵּיהּ, וּבְהַאי מַלְכוּתוֹ אִתְכְּלִילָן בֵּיהּ עָלְמִין כֻּלְּהוּ, לְמֵיזַן לוֹן, וּלְסַפְּקָא לוֹן, בְּכָל מַה דְּאִצְטְרִיכוּ וְעַל דָּא לְעוֹלָם וָעֶד.

**657.** All of them, CHOCHMAH, BINAH, AND ZEIR ANPIN, are combined in the hand Tfilah, which is His kingdom that takes everything into it. All the worlds are combined in His kingdom to nourish them, and to sustain them with all their needs. Hence "forever (Lit. 'for the world') and ever" WHICH SHOWS IT SUSTAINS ALL THE WORLDS.

658. וְדָא אִיהוּ יִחוּדָא דִּתְפִלִין דְּרֵישָׁא, וּתְפִלִין דִּדְרוֹעָא, וּכְגַוְונָא דְּרָזָא דְּיִחוּדָא דִּתְפִלִין, הָכִי אִיהוּ יִחוּדָא דְּכֹלָּא, וְדָא אִיהוּ בְּרִירָא דְּמִלָּה. וְהָא סָדַרְנָא יִחוּדָא דָּא קָמֵי בּוֹצִינָא קַדִּישָׁא, וְאָמַר לִי, דְּהָא בַּד' גַּוְונִין אִתְסְדַּר יִחוּדָא, וְדָא בְּרִירָא מִכֵּלְּהוּ, וְהָכִי אִיהוּ וַדַּאי, וְכֵלְּהוּ רָזָא דִּמְהֵימְנוּתָא, אֲבָל סְדוּרָא דִּתְפִלִין, דָּא אִיהוּ יִחוּדָא עִלָּאָה, כְּדְקָא יָאוּת.

**658.** This is the unity of the head Tefilin, WHICH IS ZEIR ANPIN, and of the hand Tefilin, WHICH IS MALCHUT. As it is the secret of the unison of the Tefilin, so is it the unison of everything. This is the clarification of the matter, and I have arranged this unity before the holy luminary, RABBI SHIMON, who said to me that in four manners is the unity set in order, WHICH ARE CHOCHMAH, BINAH, THE RIGHT OF DA'AT, AND THE LEFT OF DA'AT. This order is clearer than all of them. It is certainly so, and they are all the secret of the Faith, WHICH IS MALCHUT THAT RECEIVES THEM, but the order OF THE UNITY of the Tefilin is the upper unity, OF ZEIR ANPIN, as appropriate.

## 64. "And you shall love Hashem your Elohim"

### A Synopsis
Rabbi Yosi says here that the Right, Chesed, arouses love for the Holy One; the Holy One moves His right hand toward he who loves Him, and receives him with love. Rabbi Yosi goes on to explain that "If He sets His heart upon man, if He gather to Himself his spirit and soul" shows that everything in the world depends only upon desire. Love for the Holy One becomes aroused in three ways, we learn: "with all your heart, and with all your soul, and with all your might." Rabbi Yosi next lists the thirteen precepts that are in the right, explaining that "If you walk in My statutes" the right, or love, shall predominate; if you do not, the left or Judgment shall prevail.

### The Relevance of this Passage
We need only *desire* His Light in order to learn how to love Him and draw beneficence to our souls. Desire is the catalyst the sets the Light into motion, where it naturally flows from above to below. These ancient verses evoke our love and a deep-seated desire for Light, causing Him to radiate throughout the terrestrial realm with awe-inspiring luminance. The *Desire to Receive this Light for the Sake of Sharing with Others* ignites within our hearts and souls. The effect of this is nothing short of miraculous.

659. וּמְגּוֹ דְּאִתְכְּלִילוּ יְמִינָא וּשְׂמָאלָא בְּרָזָא דִשְׁמָא קַדִּישָׁא בְּאֹרַח כְּלָל, אִצְטְרִיךְ לְבָתַר לְאַפָּקָא לוֹן בְּאֹרַח פְּרָט, אֲבָל לָאו בְּאֹרַח יְחוּדָא, דְּהָא יְחוּדָא בַּקְרָא קַדְמָאָה אִיהוּ, לְמֶהֱוֵי יְדֹו"ד אֶחָד בִּתְפִלִּין דְּרֵישָׁא, וּשְׁמוֹ אֶחָד בִּתְפִלִּין דִּדְרוֹעָא, וַהֲוֵי כֹּלָּא חַד. כֵּיוָן דְּיִחוּדָא דָּא אִתְסָדַּר כֹּלָּא בִּכְלָלָא מֵרֵישָׁא דִּנְקוּדָה עִלָּאָה, אִצְטְרִיךְ לְבָתַר לְאַתְעָרָא מֵרֵישָׁא דִּנְהוֹרָא קַדְמָאָה, דְּאִיהוּ רֵישָׁא דְּכֹלָּא.

659. Since the right and the left were combined by means of the Holy Name in a general way, NAMELY IN 'SH'MA YISRAEL' AND 'BLESSED IS THE NAME...', it is necessary afterwards to bring them out in a specified way, MEANING IN: "AND YOU SHALL LOVE" AND IN, "AND IT SHALL COME TO PASS, IF YOU HEARKEN," but not by the way of unification, because unity appears in the first verse, IN 'SH'MA YISRAEL' so that Hashem should be one in the head Tefilin, and His name one in the hand Tefilin, and will all be one. Since this unity was arranged altogether in general, from the top of the

supernal point, WHICH IS CHOCHMAH, it is necessary afterwards to arouse the first light from the top, WHICH IS CHESED OF ZEIR ANPIN, for it is the first of everything, OF THE SFIROT OF ZEIR ANPIN.

660. וְאָהַבְתָּ דָּא רֵאשִׁיתָא דִּימִינָא, לְמִרְחַם לֵיהּ לְקוּדְשָׁא בְּרִיךְ הוּא בִּרְחִימוּ דְּאִתְדַּבְּקוּתָא דִּילֵיהּ, וּמַאן אִיהוּ, דְּאִיהוּ אִתְּעַר רְחִימוּ. מַאן דְּרָחִים לֵיהּ לְקוּדְשָׁא בְּרִיךְ הוּא, אִיהוּ אִתְּעַר יְמִינָא דִּילֵיהּ לְגַבֵּיהּ. וּמְקַבֵּל לֵיהּ בִּרְחִימוּ. כָּל מִלִּין דְּעָלְמָא לָא תַּלְיָין אֶלָּא בִּרְעוּתָא, רוּחַ אַמְשִׁיךְ רוּחַ וְאַיְיתֵי רוּחַ וְסִימָנָךְ דָּא אִם יָשִׂים אֵלָיו לִבּוֹ רוּחוֹ וְנִשְׁמָתוֹ אֵלָיו יֶאֱסֹף.

660. The paragraph: "And you shall love" is the starting point of the right, NAMELY THE SFIRAH OF CHESED, to love the Holy One, blessed be He, with a devotional love. Who is it THAT AROUSES THE LOVE? It is the right, WHICH IS CHESED, which arouses love. THE HOLY ONE, BLESSED BE HE, arouses His right hand toward he who loves the Holy One, blessed be He, and receives him with love. All the things in the world depend only upon desire, spirit shows spirit and brings spirit, and you may derive this from: "If He sets His heart upon man, if He gather to Himself his spirit and soul" (Iyov 34:14).

661. כַּד אִתְּעַר בַּר נָשׁ רְחִימוּ לְגַבֵּי קוּדְשָׁא בְּרִיךְ הוּא, אִתְּעֲרוּתָא דִּימִינָא לָא אִתְּעַר, אֶלָּא בִּתְלַת גַּווֹנִין, כד"א, בְּכָל לְבָבְךָ. וּבְכָל נַפְשְׁךָ. וּבְכָל מְאֹדֶךָ. הָא תְּלַת גַּווֹנִין הָכָא. דְּלָא תֵּימָא אוֹ הַאי אוֹ הַאי, דְּהָא לָא כְּתִיב אוֹ בְּכָל לְבָבְךָ, אוֹ בְּכָל נַפְשְׁךָ, אוֹ בְּכָל מְאֹדֶךָ. אֶלָּא כֻּלְּהוּ אִצְטְרִיךְ, לִבָּא וְנַפְשָׁא וּמָמוֹנָא. וּכְדֵין קוּדְשָׁא בְּרִיךְ הוּא אִתְּעַר יְמִינֵיהּ לְגַבֵּיהּ, וּפָשִׁיט לֵיהּ לְקַבְּלֵיהּ, וּמְקַבְּלָא לֵיהּ.

661. When the person arouses love toward the Holy One, blessed be He, the awakening of the right, WHICH IS LOVE, is aroused only in three manners, as it is written: "with all your heart, and with all your soul, and with all your might" (Devarim 6:5), so we have three manners. You should not say either this or that, for it is not written: 'Either with all your heart, or with all your soul, or with all your might.' Rather, heart, soul and money are all

necessary. Then the Holy One, blessed be He, arouses toward him His right hand, extends it to him and receives him.

662. וְעַל דָּא כְּתִיב, נְאֻם יְיָ' לַאדֹנִי שֵׁב לִימִינִי. וְרָזָא דְּהַאי קְרָא, הָא אִתְעַרְנָא בֵּיהּ, דְּדָוִד מַלְכָּא עַל דַּרְגָּא דִּילֵיהּ קָאָמַר, כַּד אִתְקְשַׁר בִּימִינָא. תְּלֵיסַר פְּקוּדִין הָכָא בִּימִינָא, וְאָהַבְתָּ אֵת יְיָ' אֱלֹהֶיךָ, הָא חֲדָא. בְּכָל לְבָבְךָ, תְּרֵין. וּבְכָל נַפְשְׁךָ, ג'. וּבְכָל מְאֹדֶךָ, אַרְבַּע. וְשִׁנַּנְתָּם לְבָנֶיךָ, חֲמִשָּׁא. וְדִבַּרְתָּ בָּם, הָא שִׁיתָא. בְּשִׁבְתְּךָ בְּבֵיתֶךָ, הָא שִׁבְעָה. וּבְלֶכְתְּךָ בַדֶּרֶךְ, תְּמַנְיָא. וּבְשָׁכְבְּךָ, הָא תִּשְׁעָה. וּבְקוּמֶךָ, הָא עֲשָׂרָה. וּקְשַׁרְתָּם לְאוֹת עַל יָדֶךָ, הָא חַד סַר. וְהָיוּ לְטֹטָפֹת בֵּין עֵינֶיךָ, הָא תְּרֵיסַר. וּכְתַבְתָּם עַל מְזוּזֹת בֵּיתֶךָ וּבִשְׁעָרֶיךָ, הָא תְּלֵיסַר.

**662.** Of this it is written: "Hashem says to my master, 'Sit you at My right hand'" (Tehilim 110:1). We have remarked about the secret of this verse that King David said it in reference to his level, WHICH IS MALCHUT, when she is tied to the right. There are thirteen precepts here in the right. "And you shall love Hashem your Elohim" is one, "with all your heart" two, "and with all your soul," three. "With all your might" is four, "and you shall teach them diligently to your children" (Devarim 6:7) is five, "and you shall talk of them" (Ibid.) is six. "When you sit in your house" (Ibid.) is seven. "And when you walk by the way" (Ibid.) is eight. "And when you lie down" (Ibid.) is nine. "And when you rise up" (Ibid.) is ten. "And you shall bind them as a sign upon your arm" (Ibid. 8) is eleven. "And they shall be as frontlets between your eyes" (Ibid.) is twelve. "And you shall write them on the doorposts of your house, and on your gates" (Ibid. 9) is thirteen.

663. תְּלֵיסַר פְּקוּדִין אִלֵּין, תַּלְיָין בִּימִינָא, וּשְׂמָאלָא אִתְכְּלִיל בִּימִינָא, וְהָכִי אִצְטְרִיךְ, וּבְכָל זִמְנָא דִּשְׂמָאלָא אִתְעַר, יְמִינָא שָׁארֵי בֵּיהּ בְּרֵישָׁא. וּבְגִין דָּא, אִם יִזְכּוּן, שְׂמָאלָא אִתְכְּלִיל בִּימִינָא. וְאִי לָאו, יְמִינָא אִתְכְּלִיל בִּשְׂמָאלָא, וְשַׁלְטָא שְׂמָאלָא. וְסִימָנָא דָּא, אִם בְּרֵישָׁא, כְּגוֹן אִם בְּחֻקּוֹתַי תֵּלֵכוּ. וּבְכָל אֲתָר, שְׂמָאלָא אִתְעַר בִּרְחִימוּ בְּרָזָא דִּימִינָא, וּלְבָתַר אִתְתַּקַּף דִּינֵיהּ, כְּמָה דְּאִצְטְרִיךְ. וְכַךְ אִצְטְרִיךְ בְּכָל אֲתָר, וְהָא אִתְעָרוּ חַבְרַיָּיא, בְּהָנֵי מִלִּין. אָתָא רִבִּי חִיָּיא וּנְשָׁקֵיהּ.

**663.** These thirteen precepts are come from the right, and the left is included in the right, which is as it should be. Whenever the left is aroused, the right starts with it first. Therefore if they have merit, then the left combines with the right. If not, then the right is combined with the left and the left dominates. The reason for this is from the verse: "If you walk in My statutes" (Vayikra 26:3). The left is always aroused with love by the secret of the right and afterwards, its Judgment becomes overpowering, as should be always. The friends have already explained these words. Rabbi Chiya came and kissed him.

## 65. "Moreover you shall make the tabernacle with ten curtains"

### A Synopsis

Rabbi Yosi opens this discussion by saying the ten curtains are the ten Sfirot. He goes on to show the unity of the tabernacle even though it has ten limbs, then the unity of a person even though he has many external and internal limbs, and lastly the unity of the Torah even though it has many precepts. The precepts of the Torah, we learn, are one in the secret of Adam, which is male and female, Zeir Anpin and Nukva. Someone who diminishes even one precept in the Torah diminishes the image of the Faith, Malchut. In closing, Rabbi Yosi says that the children of Yisrael are likewise one in that they are one nation.

### The Relevance of this Passage

Scientists have for a long time been studying subatomic particles, observing by way of instruments their births and movements and deaths, the seemingly random nature of their appearance and disappearance, and the mysterious linking of pairs of charged particles. A reading of this section awakens our awareness of unity in diversity, an inner understanding of the mystery of the Many-in-One, the union of the parts, and the order that underlies chaos. The Light generated here induces this awareness in the collective consciousness of all mankind, banishing the barriers that cause disunity and create chaos. Everyday, everywhere, people the world over feel a new-sprung sense of compassion, love, and unconditional unity with their neighbor, unprecedented in human history.

664. פָּתַח וְאָמַר וְאֶת הַמִּשְׁכָּן תַּעֲשֶׂה עֶשֶׂר יְרִיעוֹת וְגוֹ׳, הָא הָכָא רָזָא דְּיִחוּדָא, דְּהָא תִּקּוּנָא דְּמַשְׁכְּנָא מִכַּמָּה דַּרְגִּין אִיהוּ, דִּכְתִּיב בֵּיהּ וְהָיָה הַמִּשְׁכָּן אֶחָד. לְאִתְחֲזָאָה דְּכָל שַׁיְיפִין דְּגוּפָא, כֻּלְּהוּ רָזָא דְּגוּפָא חַד.

**664.** He opened the discussion saying: "Moreover you shall make the tabernacle with ten curtains…" (Shemot 26:1). Here is the mystery of unison, BECAUSE THE TEN CURTAINS CORRESPOND TO THE TEN SFIROT. The perfection of the Tabernacle is made of numerous grades, as it is written: "That the Tabernacle shall be one" (Ibid. 6), in order to show that all the limbs of the body of the Tabernacle are the secret of one body.

665. בְּבַר נָשׁ אִית בֵּיהּ כַּמָּה שַׁיְיפִין עִלָּאִין וְתַתָּאִין, אִלֵּין פְּנִימָאִין

לְגוֹ, וְאִלֵּין בְּאִתְגַּלְיָא לְבַר, וְכֻלְּהוּ אִקְרוּן גּוּפָא חֲדָא, וְאִקְרֵי בַּר נָשׁ
חַד, בְּחִבּוּרָא חֲדָא. אוּף הָכִי מַשְׁכְּנָא, כֻּלְּהוּ שַׁיְיפִין כְּגַוְונָא דִלְעֵילָא,
וְכַד אִתְחַבָּרוּ כֹּלָּא כַּחֲדָא, כְּדֵין כְּתִיב וְהָיָה הַמִּשְׁכָּן אֶחָד.

665. SIMILAR in a person that has many limbs, some superior and some lower ones, some are internal and others are visible externally, but they are all called 'one body'. And he is considered 'one person with one connection'. So it is with the tabernacle that all the limbs are similar to the above, and when they are all connected as one, it is written: "that the Tabernacle shall be one."

666. פִּקּוּדֵי אוֹרַיְיתָא, כֹּלָּא שַׁיְיפִין וְאֵבָרִין, בְּרָזָא דִלְעֵילָא. וְכַד
מִתְחַבְּרִין כֻּלְּהוּ כְּחַד, כְּדֵין כֻּלְּהוּ סַלְּקָן לְרָזָא חַד. רָזָא דְמַשְׁכְּנָא,
דְּאִיהוּ אֵבָרִין וְשַׁיְיפִין, כֻּלְּהוּ סַלְּקִין לְרָזָא דְּאָדָם, כְּגַוְונָא דְּפִקּוּדֵי
אוֹרַיְיתָא, דְּהָא פִּקּוּדֵי אוֹרַיְיתָא, כֻּלְּהוּ בְּרָזָא דְּאָדָם, דְּכַר וְנוּקְבָּא, דְּכַד
מִתְחַבְּרָן כַּחֲדָא, אִינּוּן חַד, רָזָא דְּאָדָם. מַאן דְּגָרַע אֲפִילוּ פִּקּוּדָא חֲדָא
דְּאוֹרַיְיתָא, כְּאִלּוּ גָּרַע דִּיּוּקְנָא דִמְהֵימְנוּתָא, דְּהָא כֻּלְּהוּ שַׁיְיפִין וְאֵבָרִין
בְּדִיּוּקְנָא דְּאָדָם, וּבְגִין כָּךְ כֹּלָּא סַלְקָא בְּרָזָא דְּיִחוּדָא.

666. The precepts of the Torah are all parts and limbs by a supernal secret, and when they all connect and become one, they all amount to be one place. The secret of the Tabernacle is that it is limbs and organs that all amount to the secret of man, like the precepts of the Torah because the precepts of the Torah are all in the secret of man, WHICH MEANS male and female, WHICH ARE ZEIR ANPIN AND NUKVA. When they join together, they are one in the secret of man, WHO IS THE SECRET OF YUD HEI VAV HEI SPELLED FULLY WITH *ALEPH*'S, WHICH IS THE NUMERICAL VALUE OF 'ADAM'. Someone who diminishes even one precept in the Torah, it is as though he has diminished the image of the Faith, WHICH IS MALCHUT, for all the limbs are together in the secret of man. Therefore, everything amounts to the secret of unity.

667. וְעַל דָּא, יִשְׂרָאֵל אִינּוּן גּוֹי אֶחָד, דִּכְתִיב וְאַתֵּן צֹאנִי צֹאן מַרְעִיתִי
אָדָם אַתֶּם. וּכְתִיב מִי כְעַמְּךָ כְּיִשְׂרָאֵל וְגוֹ'.

**667.** Therefore, the children of Yisrael are all one nation, for it is written about them: "But you My flock, the flock of My pasture, are men (lit. 'man')" (Yechezkel 34:31) and "And what one nation in the earth is like Your people" (II Shmuel 7:23).

## 66. "With all your heart, and with all your soul, and with all your might"

### A Synopsis

Rabbi Yitzchak here asks why "and with all your soul" is necessary when the scripture already says: "with all your heart," since love is aroused only from the heart. He then says that "with all your heart" means both the good heart and the evil heart, or evil inclination. Next, he asks why the word "all" is in "with all your soul." Rabbi Elazar answers that the soul includes Nefesh, Ruach and Neshamah, adding that "all your might" means all your belongings. Love for God means to give Him all of this, and to love Him in everything. He then says that it is even possible for a person to love God with the evil inclination, for when this is subdued to Him, and the person breaks the evil inclination, he is showing love for God. He next tells of the enticer, who is doing the will of the Holy One by tempting people from the true path and thus enabling them to show righteousness. The enticer deserves praise, we learn, for he does the Holy One's command, and enables the righteous to inherit their supernal treasures in the world to come. Just as the side of life becomes strengthened when people do good, the other side, the evil inclination, becomes strengthened when the evil ones listen to him and he dominates them. Man, we are told finally, constantly becomes stronger with God: "Happy is the man whose strength is in You; in whose heart are Your highways."

### The Relevance of this Passage

The ultimate act of deception by the enticer – the negative angel, the Satan – is to convince a man that he (the Satan) does not really exist. Consequently, we believe that our self-indulgent desires, our covetous aspirations, and our egocentric wants originate from within our being. This is a mistake. He has convinced us that our enemy is some other person or some external problem instead of our own untamed, uncertain nature. All the while, he hides in the shadows of our minds, lurking in the dark recesses of our beings, so that we might never know he exists.

In truth, these selfish desires and negative, uncertain thoughts are implanted within us by the angel Satan. Yet, the Zohar reveals a deeply profound reason for his existence: so that a man, through his own effort, can triumph over him, rejecting the momentary, illusionary pleasure that the Satan provides, for the authentic, eternal Light of the

Creator. In this way a man becomes the cause and creator of his own Light. He expresses the Godly nature that dwells within his soul.

This portion of text accomplishes many things. We grasp the role of evil in the world, perhaps the most perplexing and disturbing of all theological questions. We unlock our ability to recognize our Evil Inclination as a separate and distinct entity, unattached to our true soul consciousness.

We kindle Light and it extinguishes darkness, exterminating the very roots of evil. And, by virtue of the above, we become the cause and creators of our own Light; thus, we fulfill our purpose in this world.

668. רַבִּי יִצְחָק הֲוָה שְׁכִיחַ קַמֵּיה דְּרַבִּי אֶלְעָזָר, אָמַר לֵיה, וַדַּאי רְחִימוּ דְּקוּדְשָׁא בְּרִיךְ הוּא דְּבַר נָשׁ רָחִים לֵיה, לָא אִתְּעַר אֶלָּא מִלִּבָּא, בְּגִין דְּלִבָּא אִיהוּ אִתְעֲרוּתָא לְאִתְעֲרָא לְגַבֵּיה רְחִימוּ, אִי הָכִי, אֲמַאי כְּתִיב בְּכָל לְבָבְךָ, וּלְבָתַר וּבְכָל נַפְשְׁךָ. דְּמַשְׁמַע דִּתְרֵין גְּוְונִין אִינּוּן חַד לִבָּא, וְחַד נַפְשָׁא, אִי לִבָּא הוּא עִקָּרָא, מַאי בָּעֵי נַפְשָׁא. אָמַר לֵיה, וַדַּאי לִבָּא וְנַפְשָׁא תְּרֵין אִינּוּן, וְאִתְאַחֲדָן לְחַד. דְּהָא לִבָּא וְנַפְשָׁא וּמָמוֹנָא, כֻּלְּהוּ אִתְאַחֲדָן דָּא בְּדָא, וְלִבָּא אִיהוּ עִקָּרָא וִיסוֹדָא דְּכֹלָּא.

668. Rabbi Yitzchak was present before Rabbi Elazar and said to him: Certainly, the love of the Holy One, blessed be He, that a person feels for Him is aroused only from the heart, for the heart is a place of awakening to arouse toward Him love. HE QUESTIONS: If so, why is it written: "With all your heart" and afterwards "and with all your soul," so it seems that there are two manners IN LOVE, one in the heart and one in the soul? If the heart is the essence, why is the soul necessary? He said to him: The heart and the soul are two and they join into one, for heart and soul and money all unite together, but the heart is the essence and foundation of everything.

669. וְהָא דְּאִתְּמַר בְּכָל לְבָבְךָ, בִּתְרֵין לְבֵין אִיהוּ, דְּאִינְהוּ תְּרֵין יְצָרִין, חַד יְצָרָא טָבָא, וְחַד יְצָרָא בִּישָׁא, וּתְרֵין אִלֵּין כָּל חַד וְחַד לֵב אִקְרֵי בַּל, דָּא אִקְרֵי לֵב טוֹב, וְדָא אִקְרֵי לֵב רָע. וּבְגִין כַּךְ אִיהוּ לְבָבְךָ, דְּאִינּוּן תְּרֵין, יֵצֶר הַטּוֹב וְיֵצֶר הָרָע.

669. We have learned that "with all your heart" MEANS with two hearts,

which are two inclinations, the Good Inclination and the Evil Inclination. Of these two, which are each called 'the heart', one is called 'good heart' and one is called 'evil heart'. Therefore, IT SAYS, "your heart" WITH TWO *BET*'S AND IT DOESN'T SAY 'YOUR HEART' WITH ONE *BET*, which SHOWS two, the Good Inclination and the Evil Inclination.

**670.** וּבְכָל נַפְשְׁךָ, וּבְנַפְשְׁךָ מִבָּעֵי לֵיהּ, מַאי וּבְכָל נַפְשְׁךָ, הַאי בְּכָל אֲמַאי. אֶלָּא לְאַכְלָלָא נפ״ש ורו״ח ונשמ״ה, דָּא אִיהוּ וּבְכָל נַפְשְׁךָ, בְּכָל מַה דְּאָחִיד הַאי נֶפֶשׁ. וּבְכָל מְאֹדֶךָ, אוּף הָכִי כַּמָּה זִינִין אִינוּן דְּמָמוֹנָא, כֻּלְּהוּ מְשַׁנְיָין אִלֵּין מֵאִלֵּין, וְעַ״ד כְּתִיב בְּכָל. רְחִימוּ דְקוּדְשָׁא בְּרִיךְ הוּא, לְמִמְסַר לֵיהּ כָּל דָּא, לְמִרְחַם לֵיהּ בְּכָל חַד וְחַד.

**670.** HE QUESTIONS: It should have said, 'And with your soul.' Why does it say, "And with all your soul"? Why is 'all' said?" HE ANSWERS: It comes to include Nefesh, Ruach and Neshamah, for this is the meaning of, "And with all your soul" all that pertains to this soul "and with all your might." WHY DOES IT SAY 'ALL'? IT IS because there are many kinds of substance, for they are all different one from another, NAMELY SILVER, PRECIOUS STONES AND SO ON. Therefore, it says, "and with all YOUR MIGHT" MEANING WITH ALL HIS BELONGINGS, because the love for the Holy One, blessed be He, means to give Him all this, and to love Him in everything.

**671.** וְאִי תֵּימָא, בְּיֵצֶר הָרָע הֵיךְ יָכִיל בַּר נָשׁ לְמִרְחַם לֵיהּ, דְּהָא יֵצֶר הָרָע מְקַטְרְגָא אִיהוּ, דְּלָא יִקְרַב בַּר נָשׁ לְפוּלְחָנָא דְקוּדְשָׁא בְּרִיךְ הוּא, וְהֵיךְ יִרְחִים לֵיהּ בֵּיהּ. אֶלָּא, דָּא אִיהוּ פוּלְחָנָא דְקוּדְשָׁא בְּרִיךְ הוּא יַתִּיר, כַּד הַאי יֵצֶר הָרָע אִתְכַּפְיָא לֵיהּ, בְּגִין רְחִימוּ דְּקָא מְרַחַם לֵיהּ לְקוּדְשָׁא בְּרִיךְ הוּא. דְּכַד הַאי יֵצֶר הָרָע אִתְכַּפְיָא, וְתָבַר לֵיהּ הַהוּא בַּר נָשׁ, דָּא אִיהוּ רְחִימוּ דְּקוּדְשָׁא בְּרִיךְ הוּא, בְּגִין דְּיִדִיעַ לְקָרְבָא לְהַהוּא יֵצֶר הָרָע, לְפוּלְחָנָא דְקוּדְשָׁא בְּרִיךְ הוּא.

**671.** If you ask: How is it possible for a person to love THE HOLY ONE, BLESSED BE HE, with the Evil Inclination, for the Evil Inclination persecutes so that the person should not approach the service of the Holy

One, blessed be He? So how is it possible to love HIM with it? HE ANSWERS: This is an even MORE PRECIOUS MANNER of serving Hashem, for when this Evil Inclination is subdued to Him and that person breaks him, this is the love of the Holy One, blessed be He. Because he knows how to bring close the Evil Inclination to the service of the Holy One, blessed be He.

672. הָכָא אִיהוּ רָזָא לְמָארֵי מִדִּין. כָּל מַה דַּעֲבַד קוּדְשָׁא בְּרִיךְ הוּא עֵילָּא וְתַתָּא, כֹּלָּא אִיהוּ בְּגִין לְאַחֲזָאָה יְקָרָא דִּילֵיה, וְכֹלָּא אִיהוּ לְפוּלְחָנֵיה. וְכִי מַאן חָמֵי עַבְדָּא, דְּלֶהֱוֵי מְקַטְרְגָא דְּמָארֵיה, וּבְכָל מַה דִּרְעוּתֵיה דְּמָארֵיה, אִתְעָבֵיד אִיהוּ מְקַטְרְגָא, רְעוּתֵיה דְּקוּדְשָׁא בְּרִיךְ הוּא, דִּיהוֹן בְּנֵי נָשָׁא תָּדִיר בְּפוּלְחָנֵיה, וְיֵהַכוּן בְּאָרַח קְשׁוֹט, בְּגִין לְמִזְכֵּי לוֹן בְּכַמָּה טָבִין, הוֹאִיל וּרְעוּתֵיה דְּקוּדְשָׁא בְּרִיךְ הוּא בְּהַאי, הֵיךְ אַתְיָא עַבְדָּא בִּישָׁא, וְאִשְׁתְּכַח מְקַטְרְגָא מִגּוֹ רְעוּתֵיה דְּמָארֵיה, וְאַסְטֵי לִבְנֵי נָשָׁא לְאָרַח בִּישׁ, וְאַדְחֵי לוֹן מֵאָרַח טָב, וְעָבֵיד לוֹן דְּלָא יַעַבְדוּן רְעוּתָא דְּמָארֵיהוֹן, וְאַסְטֵי לִבְנֵי נָשָׁא לְאָרַח בִּישׁ.

672. Here is the secret of those who know Judgment. For everything that the Holy One, blessed be He, made above and below is all only to show His honor, and everything is for His service. Who saw a servant go against his master?! Whatever is the will of his master, he becomes an inciter NOT TO DO THE WILL OF HIS MASTER. The will of the Holy One, blessed be He, is that people should be constantly in His service, and that they should go in the true path in order to merit much good. Since this is the will of the Holy One, blessed be He, how could an evil servant come and incite against the will of his Master? And he turns people to the evil path and thrusts them from the good path and causes them not to do the will of their Master, and turns people to the evil path?

673. אֶלָּא, וַדַּאי רְעוּתֵיה דְּמָארֵיה עָבֵיד. לְמַלְכָּא דַּהֲוָה לֵיה בַּר יְחִידָאי, וַהֲוָה רָחִים לֵיה יַתִּיר, וּפָקִיד עֲלֵיה בִּרְחִימוּ, דְּלָא יִקְרַב גַּרְמֵיה לְאִתְּתָא בִּישָׁא, בְּגִין דְּכָל מַאן דְּיִקְרַב לְגַבָּהּ, לָאו כְּדַאי אִיהוּ לְאַעֲלָא גּוֹ פַּלְטְרִין דְּמַלְכָּא. אוֹדֵי לֵיה הַהוּא בְּרָא, לְמֶעְבַּד רְעוּתֵיה דַּאֲבוֹי בִּרְחִימוּ.

**673.** HE ANSWERS: Certainly he is doing the will of his master. It is LIKE a king who had an only son, and he loved him exceedingly. And he commanded him with love not to come close to an evil woman, because anyone who approaches her is not worthy to enter the king's palace. That son promised that he would lovingly do the will of his father.

674. בְּבֵיתָא דְמַלְכָּא, לְבַר, הֲוַת חֲדָא זוֹנָה, יָאָה בְּחֵיזוּ, וּשְׁפִירָא בְּרֵיוָא. לְיוֹמִין אָמַר מַלְכָּא, בְּעֵינָא לְמֶחֱמֵי רְעוּתֵיה דִּבְרִי לְגַבָּאי. קָרָא לָה לְהַהִיא זוֹנָה, וְאָמַר לָה זִילִי וּתְפַתִּי לִבְרִי, לְמֶחֱמֵי רְעוּתֵיה דִּבְרִי לְגַבָּאי. הַהִיא זוֹנָה מַאי עַבְדַת, אַזְלַת אֲבַתְרֵיה דִּבְרֵיה דְּמַלְכָּא שָׁרְאַת לְחַבְּקָא לֵיה וּלְנַשְׁקָא לֵיה, וּלְפַתֵּי לֵיה בְּכַמָּה פִתּוּיִין. אִי הַהוּא בְּרָא יָאוֹת, וְאָצִית לְפִקוּדָא דַּאֲבוֹי, גָּעַר בָּה, וְלָא אָצִית לָה, וְדָחֵי לָה מִנֵּיה. כְּדֵין אָבוֹי חַדֵּי בִּבְרֵיה, וְאָעִיל לֵיה לְגוֹ פַּרְגּוֹדָא דְהֵיכָלֵיה, וְיָהִיב לֵיה מַתְּנָן וּנְבִזְבְּזָא וִיקָר סַגִּיא. מַאן גָּרִים כָּל הַאי יְקָר לְהַאי בְּרָא, הֲוֵי אֵימָא הַהִיא זוֹנָה.

**674.** Outside of the king's palace was a harlot who was very beautiful to behold. After a few days, the king said: I want to see the wishes of my son toward me. He called that harlot and told her: Go and entice my son, in order to test the wishes of my son toward me. What did that harlot do? She went after the king's son and started to embrace him and kiss him and entice him with all kinds of enticements. If that son is proper and observes the commands of his father, he scolds her and does not listen to her and thrusts her away from him. Then the father rejoices with his son, brings him into the inner sanctum of his palace, and gives him presents and gifts and great honor. Who caused all this honor for that son? We must say that it was the harlot.

675. וְהַהִיא זוֹנָה אִית לָה שְׁבָחָא בְּהַאי אוֹ לָאו. וַדַּאי שְׁבָחָא אִית לָה מִכָּל סִטְרִין. חַד, דְּעָבְדַת פִּקוּדָא דְמַלְכָּא. וְחַד, דְּגָרְמַת לֵיה לְהַהוּא בְּרָא, לְכָל הַהוּא טִיבוּ, לְכָל הַאי רְחִימוּ דְּמַלְכָּא לְגַבֵּיה. וְעַ״ד כְּתִיב, וְהִנֵּה טוֹב מְאֹד. וְהִנֵּה טוֹב, דָּא מַלְאָךְ חַיִּים. מְאֹד, דָּא מַלְאַךְ הַמָּוֶת, דְּאִיהוּ וַדַּאי טוֹב מְאֹד, לְמַאן דְּאָצִית פִּקוּדִין דְּמָארֵיה. וְתָא חֲזֵי, אִי

לָא יְהֵא הַאי מְקַטְרְגָא, לָא יַרְתוּן צַדִּיקַיָּא הָנֵי גְּנְזַיָּא עִלָּאִין, דִּזְמִינִין לְיַרְתָא לְעָלְמָא דְּאָתֵי.

**675.** HE QUESTIONS: Does that harlot deserve praise for this or not? HE SAYS: Certainly she deserves praise from all aspects, for she did the king's command and she brought that son all the good, all this love of the king toward him. Therefore, it is written: "And, behold, it was very good" (Beresheet 1:31). "And, behold, it was good" refers to the Angel of Life, while 'very' refers to the Angel of Death, THE EVIL INCLINATION, who is certainly very good, for he who fulfills the command of his master. Come and see: if there would not be this enticer, then the righteous would not inherit those supernal treasures that are their share in the World to Come.

**676.** זַכָּאִין אִינּוּן דְּאִעְרָעוּ בְּהַאי מְקַטְרְגָא, וְזַכָּאִין אִינּוּן דְּלָא אִעְרָעוּ בֵּיהּ. זַכָּאִין אִינּוּן דְּאִעְרָעוּ בֵּיהּ, וְאִשְׁתְּזִיבוּ מִנֵּיהּ, דִּבְגִינֵיהּ יַרְתִין כָּל אִינּוּן טָבִין, וְכָל אִינּוּן עִדּוּנִין, וְכָל אִינּוּן כִּסּוּפִין דְּעָלְמָא דְּאָתֵי, דַּעֲלֵיהּ כְּתִיב עַיִן לָא רָאָתָה אֱלֹהִים זוּלָתְךָ.

**676.** Blessed are those who met this enticer and blessed are those who did not meet this enticer. HE EXPLAINS: Blessed are those who met him, NAMELY THOSE that were saved from him, for because of him they inherit all that good and all those delights, and all those pleasures of the World to Come. About them, it is written: "Neither has the eye seen, (that) an Elohim, beside You" (Yeshayah 64:3).

**677.** וְזַכָּאִין אִינּוּן דְּלָא אִעְרָעוּ בֵּיהּ, דִּבְגִינֵיהּ יַרְתִין גֵּיהִנָּם, וְאִטְרָדוּ מֵאֶרֶץ הַחַיִּים, דְּהָא אִינּוּן חַיָּיבַיָּא דְּאִעְרָעוּ בֵּיהּ, הֲווֹ צַיְיתִין לֵיהּ, וְאִתְמַשְׁכוּ אֲבַתְרֵיהּ. וְעַל דָּא אִית לְצַדִּיקַיָּא לְמֶחֱזַק לֵיהּ טָבִין דְּהָא בְּגִינֵיהּ יַרְתִין כָּל אִינּוּן טָבָאן וְעִדּוּנִין וְכִסּוּפִין לְעָלְמָא דְּאָתֵי.

**677.** Blessed are those who did not meet him, MEANING THEY DID NOT STUMBLE BECAUSE OF HIM — for they would have inherited Gehenom and would have been banished from the Land of the Living. For those wicked ones who met him and would have listened to him, all would be drawn after

him. Therefore, the righteous have to recognize his good, for they inherit all the good and delights and pleasures of the World to Come because of him.

678. תּוֹעַלְתָּא דְּהַאי מְקַטְרְגָא. כַּד חַיָּיבַיָּא צַיְיתִין לֵיהּ מַאי אִיהִי. אֶלָּא, אע״ג דְּלֵית לֵיהּ תּוֹעַלְתָּא, פְּקוּדָא דְּמָארֵיהּ אִיהוּ עָבִיד. וְתוּ, דְּהָא אִתְתָּקַף בְּגִין הַאי, הוֹאִיל וְאִיהוּ רָע, אִתְתָּקַף כַּד עָבֵיד בִּישׁ. חַיָּיבָא לָא אִתְתָּקַף עַד דְּקָטִיל בַּר נָשׁ, כֵּיוָן דְּקָטִיל בְּנֵי נָשָׁא, כְּדֵין אִתְתָּקַף וְאִתְגַּבַּר בְּחֵילֵיהּ, וְאִית לֵיהּ נַיְיחָא. כַּךְ הַהוּא מְקַטְרְגָא, דְּאִתְקְרֵי מַלְאַךְ הַמָּוֶת, לָא אִתְגַּבַּר בְּחֵילֵיהּ, עַד דְּאַסְטֵי לִבְנֵי נָשָׁא, וּמְקַטְרֵג לוֹן, וְקָטִיל לוֹן, כְּדֵין אִית לֵיהּ נַיְיחָא, וְאִתְתָּקַף וְאִתְגַּבַּר בְּחֵילֵיהּ.

**678.** HE QUESTIONS: What is the benefit of the enticer when the wicked listen to him? HE ANSWERS: He has no benefit, NEVERTHELESS he does the command of his Master. He becomes stronger because of this, for since he is evil, he gains strength when they do evil. The wicked does not become strengthened until he kills a person, and when he has slain people then he grows strong and mighty with his power, and he has satisfaction. So it is with that enticer, NAMELY THE EVIL INCLINATION who is called the Angel of Death, who does not grow in strength with his power until he instigates people and persecutes them and kills them. Then he has satisfaction and becomes strong and mighty with his power.

679. כְּמָה דְּאִתְתָּקַף סִטְרָא דְּחַיִּים, כַּד בְּנֵי נָשָׁא טָבִין, וְיֶהֱכוּן בְּאֹרַח מֵישָׁר. אוּף הָכִי, הַאי מְקַטְרְגָא אִתְתָּקַף וְאִתְגַּבַּר, כַּד חַיָּיבַיָּא צַיְיתִין לֵיהּ, וְשָׁלִיט עָלַיְיהוּ. רַחֲמָנָא לִישֵׁזְבָן. וְזַכָּאִין אִינּוּן דְּזַכָּאָן לְנַצְחָא לֵיהּ, וּלְאַכְפְּיָא לֵיהּ, לְמִזְכֵּי בְּגִינֵיהּ לְעָלְמָא דְּאָתֵי, וְאִתְתָּקַף בַּר נָשׁ בְּמַלְכָּא קַדִּישָׁא תָּדִיר, ע״ד וַדַּאי אִתְּמַר, אַשְׁרֵי אָדָם עוֹז לוֹ בָךְ מְסִלּוֹת בִּלְבָבָם, זַכָּאִין אִינּוּן בְּהַאי עָלְמָא וּבְעָלְמָא דְּאָתֵי.

**679.** Just as the side of life becomes strengthened when people are good and go in the straight path, this enticer also becomes stronger and mightier when

the evil listen to him and he dominates them. May the Merciful one save us. Blessed are they who merit to be victorious over him and to subdue him, so as to merit through him the World to Come. Man constantly grows stronger with the Holy King, as is certainly said, "Happy is the man whose strength is in You; in whose heart are Your highways" (Tehilim 84:6). Blessed are they in this world and in the World to Come.

## 67. The righteous are the face of the Shechinah

### A Synopsis

When Rabbi Elazar encounters Rabbi Yosi, Rabbi Yehuda and Rabbi Chiya on the road, he tells them he sees the face of the Shechinah. This, we learn, is because when one sees the righteous or pious they represent Her face since She hides within them.

### The Relevance of this Passage

Here we draw the Light of righteousness into our souls so that our faces shine with the radiance of the Shechinah. Further, would any of us, if we met an Angel on the road, recognize the Holy Spirit in him? Would we even register the Angel's presence, as used to ignoring strangers as we are? The Light of this passage ensures that when we gaze into the faces of strangers or friends or family, we recognize the presence of the Shechinah and the spark of Light that lives within all men. Thus, the goal of "Love thy Neighbor" is readily achieved and we complete our purpose in life.

680. רַבִּי יוֹסִי וְרַבִּי יְהוּדָה וְרַבִּי חִיָּיא, הֲווֹ אַזְלֵי בְּאָרְחָא, פָּגַע בְּהוּ ר' אֶלְעָזָר, עַד דְּחָמוּ לֵיהּ, נָחֲתוּ מִן חֲמָרֵי כֻּלְּהוּ. אָמַר רַבִּי אֶלְעָזָר, וַדַּאי אַנְפֵּי שְׁכִינְתָּא חֲמֵינָא, דְּהָא כַּד חָמֵי ב"נ צַדִּיקַיָּא, אוֹ זַכָּאִין דִּי בְּדָרָא, וְאִעֲרַע בְּהוּ, וַדַּאי אִינּוּן אַנְפֵּי שְׁכִינְתָּא. וְאַמַּאי אִקְרוּן אַנְפֵּי שְׁכִינְתָּא. בְּגִין דִּשְׁכִינְתָּא אִסְתַּתְּרַת בְּגַוַוְיְיהוּ, אִיהִי בִּסְתִימוּ, וְאִינּוּן בְּאִתְגַּלְיָא. בְּגִין דִּשְׁכִינְתָּא אִינּוּן דִּקְרִיבִין לָהּ, אִקְרוּן פָּנִים דִּילָהּ. וּמַאן אִינּוּן. אִינּוּן דְּאִיהִי אִתְתַּקְנַת בַּהֲדַיְיהוּ, לְאִתְחֲזָאָה לְגַבֵּי מַלְכָּא עִלָּאָה. וְהוֹאִיל וְאַתּוּן הָכָא, וַדַּאי שְׁכִינְתָּא אִתְתַּקְנַת עֲלַיְיכוּ, וְאַתּוּן פָּנִים דִּילָהּ.

680. Rabbi Yosi, Rabbi Yehuda and Rabbi Chiya were traveling on the road and Rabbi Elazar met them. As soon as they saw him, they all got off their donkeys. Rabbi Elazar said: For certain, I see the face of the Shechinah. When one sees the righteous or the pious of the generation and meets them, certainly they represent the face of Shechinah. Why are they called 'the face of Shechinah'? It is because the Shechinah hides within them. THE SHECHINAH is concealed in them, but they are visible. Therefore, those who are close to Her are called 'Her face'. Who are those THAT ARE CLOSE

TO HER? They are those with whom She prepares to appear before the supernal King, ZEIR ANPIN, MEANING WHO ELEVATE MAYIN NUKVIN (FEMALE WATERS) TO UNITE THE HOLY ONE, BLESSED BE HE, WITH HIS SHECHINAH. Now that you are here, certainly the Shechinah is positioned over you, and you are Her face.

## 68. "Let me go, for the day breaks"

### A Synopsis

Here, Rabbi Elazar tells how Jacob wrestled all night with the Appointed Angel of Esau, Samael – though until dawn he thought he was wrestling with Esau. He struck the Angel, who said "Let me go, for the day breaks," because the Angel and his female, Lilit have dominion only at night. We are then told that when morning arrived Samael and his friends entered the hole of the great Abyss in the North. Another explanation of "Let me go, for the day breaks," is that night stands for the exile of the children of Yisrael, during which the wicked idol-worshipping kingdom dominates them until morning, the Redemption, arrives, and the Holy One illuminates for them. Jacob, we next learn, would not let the Angel go unless He blessed him, which He did. Jacob saw in Esau's face the exact image that he saw in Samael, because, we are told, whatever a person is connected to is reflected in his face. And again Rabbi Elazar tells the three rabbis that because the Shechinah is with them, he sees their faces are like Hers.

### The Relevance of this Passage

Strength to wrestle and conquer our own fears and dark side is bestowed upon us. This radiance shines into our darkest moments so that what we see illuminated before us is always the truth, not just a shadow of the truth. Moreover, this Light relinquishes the hold of the two negative angels, Samael and Lilit, over all mankind, freeing us forever from their deadly grip. Now that we have total control and dominance over the root of evil – through the greatness and spiritual prowess of Jacob – we are free to complete our personal ascension and actuate the Final Redemption in a softhearted and merciful manner.

681. פָּתַח וְאָמַר, קַח נָא אֶת בִּרְכָתִי אֲשֶׁר הֻבָאת לָךְ וְגוֹ', כַּד חָמָא יַעֲקֹב לְסָמָאֵל, מְקַטְרְגָא בְּהַהוּא לֵילְיָא, חָמָא לֵיהּ בְּהַהוּא דְּיוּקְנָא דְּעֵשָׂו, וְלָא אִשְׁתְּמוֹדַע בֵּיהּ עַד דְּסָלִיק צַפְרָא. כֵּיוָן דְּסָלִיק צַפְרָא, וְאַשְׁגַּח בֵּיהּ, חָמָא לֵיהּ בְּאַנְפִּין סְתִימִין וְאִתְגַּלְיָין. אִסְתְּכַּל בְּהַהוּא דְּיוּקְנָא, דַּהֲוָה כְּדִיוּקְנָא דְּעֵשָׂו, מִיַּד אַשְׁגַּח וְיָדַע דַּהֲוָה מִמְּנָא דְּעֵשָׂו. אַתְקִיף בֵּיהּ מַה כְּתִיב, וַיֹּאמֶר שַׁלְּחֵנִי כִּי עָלָה הַשָּׁחַר. וְחַבְרַיָּיא אִתְּעָרוּ, דִּבְגִין דְּמָטָא זִמְנֵיהּ לְזַמְּרָא וּלְשַׁבְּחָא לֵיהּ לְקוּדְשָׁא בְּרִיךְ הוּא, וְעַ"ד כִּי עָלָה הַשָּׁחַר.

**681.** He opened the discussion saying: "Take, I pray you, my blessing that is brought to you…" (Beresheet 33:11). When Jacob saw the accuser, Samael, that night, WHO WRESTLED WITH HIM AT THE PASSAGE OF YABOK, he saw him in the image of Esau but did not recognize him until the dawn rose. As soon as the dawn rose, he saw him with his face both visible and concealed. He viewed his image that was like the image of Esau and immediately realized that he was the minister of Esau, NAMELY SAMAEL. He struck him. It is written: "And he said, 'Let me go, for the day breaks'" (Beresheet 32:27) and the friends retorted that it was because his time had arrived to sing and praise to the Holy One, blessed be He. Therefore, it says, "For the day breaks."

682. וְהָכָא אִית לְאִסְתַּכְּלָא, דְּוַדַּאי שָׁלְטָנוּתָא דִּילֵיהּ לָאו אִיהוּ אֶלָּא בְּלֵילְיָא, גּוֹ חֲשׁוֹכָא, וְרָזָא דָּא מִפַּחַד בַּלֵּילוֹת דָּא פַּחְדָּא דְּגֵיהִנָּם. וּמַה דְּאָמַר בַּלֵּילוֹת. ר"ל אִיהוּ וְנוּקְבֵיהּ. וּבְגִינֵי כַּךְ לָא שַׁלִּיט אֶלָּא בְּלֵילְיָא.

**682.** Here we must look into that, for certainly his dominion is only during the night in the darkness. This is the secret of: "Because of the fear by night (lit. 'nights')" (Shir Hashirim 3:8), which is the fear of Gehenom. And he said, "the nights" IN THE PLURAL, because it refers to SAMAEL and his female, LILIT. Therefore, he has power only during the night.

683. וְדָא דְּאָמַר וַיֹּאמֶר שַׁלְּחֵנִי כִּי עָלָה הַשָּׁחַר. מַאי כִּי עָלָה הַשָּׁחַר. בְּגִין דְּכַד אָתֵי צַפְרָא, וְאִתְעֲבַר שָׁלְטָנוּ דְּחֲשׁוֹכָא דְּלֵילְיָא, כְּדֵין עָאל אִיהוּ וְאָכְלוּסֵיהּ בְּנוּקְבָא דִּתְהוֹמָא רַבָּא, דְּלִסְטַר צָפוֹן, עַד דְּעָאל לֵילְיָא, וְאִשְׁתְּרוּ כַּלְבֵּי, וְשַׁלְטֵי וּמְשַׁטְטֵי בְּלֵילְיָא, עַד דְּאָתֵי צַפְרָא. וְעַל דָּא הֲוָה דָּחִיק לוֹמַר, שַׁלְּחֵנִי כִּי עָלָה הַשָּׁחַר, דְּהָא לָא שַׁלִּיט בִּימָמָא.

**683.** He said: "Let me go, for the day breaks." What is the point of "for the day breaks?" HE ANSWERS: When the morning arrived and the domination of the darkness of the night was removed, he and his friends entered the hole of the great abyss that is in the North until the night arrived. And the dogs were freed, NAMELY THE OTHER SIDE, from their chains and dominate and float about during the night, until the morning arrives. Therefore, SAMAEL

was pressing and saying, "Let me go, for the day breaks," because he does not dominate during the day.

684. כְּגַוְונָא דָּא גָּלוּתָא דְּיִשְׂרָאֵל, דְּאִיהוּ בְּלֵילְיָא, וְאִקְרֵי לַיְלָה. מַלְכָּא עכו"ם חַיָּיבָא שַׁלְטָא עֲלַיְיהוּ דְּיִשְׂרָאֵל, עַד דְּיֵיתֵי צַפְרָא וְיַנְהִיר לוֹן קוּדְשָׁא בְּרִיךְ הוּא, וְיִתְעֲבָר שְׁלְטָנֵיהוֹן, וְעַל דָּא כִּי עָלָה הַשַּׁחַר, דְּחִיק הֲוָה בִּידֵיה, וְתָשַׁשׁ חֵילֵיה, דְּהָא אִתְעֲבָר לֵילְיָא וְעַל דָּא אִתְתְּקַף יַעֲקֹב בֵּיה, וְחָמָא דְּיוּקְנֵיה כְּדִיוּקְנָא דְּעֵשָׂו, אֲבָל לָא בְּאִתְגַּלְיָא כָּל כָּךְ. וּכְדֵין אוֹדֵי לֵיה עַל בִּרְכָּאן.

684. Similar to this is the exile of the children of Yisrael, which is THE ASPECT of night, and is called 'night'. The wicked idol-worshipping kingdom dominates over Yisrael until the morning arrives, WHICH IS THE REDEMPTION. The Holy One, blessed be He, will illuminate for them, and the dominance of the IDOL-WORSHIPPING KINGDOM will be removed. Therefore, he said, "For the dawn breaks" because he was pressured and his strength was weakened, because the night had passed. Therefore, Jacob overpowered him and saw that his image was like the image of Esau, but not so clear. AND SAMAEL HAD TO approve the blessings THAT HIS FATHER GAVE HIM, BECAUSE HE SAID TO HIM, "I WILL NOT LET YOU GO, UNLESS YOU BLESS ME" (BERESHEET 32:27) AND, "AND HE BLESSED HIM THERE" (IBID. 30).

685. מַה כְּתִיב לְבָתַר, כִּי עַל כֵּן רָאִיתִי פָנֶיךָ כִּרְאֹת פְּנֵי אֱלֹהִים וַתִּרְצֵנִי. דְּחָמָא בְּאִינּוּן אַנְפִּין דְּעֵשָׂו כְּדִיוּקְנָא דְּאִתְחֲזֵי לֵיה סָמָא"ל מַמָּשׁ, דְּהָא בְּכָל אֲתָר דְּב"נ אִתְקַשַּׁר, הָכִי אִתְחֲזֵי בְּאַנְפּוֹי. וְאַתּוּן קַדִּישֵׁי עֶלְיוֹנִין שְׁכִינְתָּא בַּהֲדַיְיכוּ, וְאַנְפִּין דִּלְכוֹן כְּאִינּוּן אַנְפִּין דִּילָה, זַכָּאִין אַתּוּן. אֲמַר אִי אָרְחָא חֲדָא הֲוֵינָא אַזְלֵי בַּהֲדַיְיכוּ, הֲוֵינָא יַתְבֵי עִמְּכוֹן, הַשְׁתָּא דְּאַתּוּן לְאָרְחַיְיכוּ, וַאֲנָא לְאָרְחִי, אִתְפְּרַשׁ מִנַּיְיכוּ בְּמִילֵּי דְּאוֹרַיְיתָא.

685. It is written afterwards: "For truly I have seen your face, as though I had seen the face of Elohim, and you were pleased with me" (Beresheet

33:10). He saw in Esau's face the exact image that he saw in Samael, because whoever is connected to, is reflected in his face. The Shechinah is with you, Supernal Holy Ones. Therefore, your faces are like Her face. Blessed are you. He said: If I were going on the same path with you, I would then sit with you, but now that you are going on your way and I on my way, I will separate from you with the words of Torah.

## 69. "Unless Hashem builds the house"

### A Synopsis

Rabbi Elazar opens a discussion of: "A song of ascents for Solomon. Unless The Creator builds the house, they who build it labor in vain; unless The Creator keeps the city, the watchman stays awake in vain." He then comments that King David said this for his son, Solomon, when Nathan the prophet foretold that Solomon would build the Holy Temple. Another explanation of the verse, we learn, is that unless the King, who is Binah, builds the house with the seven pillars of Chesed, Gvurah, Tiferet, Netzach, Hod, Yesod and Malchut of Zeir Anpin, they who build it shall labor in vain. The tabernacle can only be guarded by a youth, who was first Joshua (in the youthful aspect of Metatron), then the child Samuel. God alone guards the Holy Temple, and He guards the righteous as they travel, as is written: "The Creator shall preserve your going out and your coming in."

### The Relevance of this Passage

In effect, Rabbi Elazar's discourse concerns how to draw the Light of the Creator to our own homes. King David, we are told, composed verses that spoke of the necessity of having the Creator's Light imbued at the seed level of the building of the Temple. Otherwise, all the construction and safeguards would be for naught. For us, this means that our own temples, our homes and communities, must be imbued with this Light. Otherwise, there is no chance for protection and blessing, regardless of what we might do on a physical level.

Without our constant awareness of this need for Light, we are left vulnerable to the forces of chaos. Here we travel back to the seed level of our homes, our communities, and the entire world, and we inject them with the awesome Light of The Creator. The radiance banishes all the darkness and forces of chaos that have wreaked havoc upon our lives since the dawn of humanity.

686. פָּתַח וְאָמַר שִׁיר הַמַּעֲלוֹת לִשְׁלֹמֹה אִם יְיָ' לֹא יִבְנֶה בַיִת שָׁוְא עָמְלוּ בוֹנָיו בּוֹ אִם יְיָ' לֹא יִשְׁמָר עִיר שָׁוְא שָׁקַד שׁוֹמֵר. וְכִי שְׁלֹמֹה אָמַר תּוּשַׁבַּחְתָּא דָּא כַּד בָּנָה בֵּי מַקְדְּשָׁא. לָאו הָכִי, דְּהָא דָוִד מַלְכָּא א"ל בְּגִין שְׁלֹמֹה מַלְכָּא בְּרֵיהּ, כַּד אָתָא נָתָן לְגַבֵּיהּ, וְא"ל עַל שְׁלֹמֹה דְּאִיהוּ יִבְנֵי בֵּי מַקְדְּשָׁא. וּלְבָתַר דָּוִד מַלְכָּא אַחֲזֵי לִשְׁלֹמֹה בְּרֵיהּ דִּיוּקְנָא דְּבֵי מַקְדְּשָׁא. כֵּיוָן דְּחָמָא דָוִד דִּיוּקְנָא דְּבֵי מַקְדְּשָׁא, וְכָל תִּקּוּנוֹי, אָמַר שִׁירָתָא עַל שְׁלֹמֹה בְּרֵיהּ, וְאָמַר אִם יְיָ' לֹא יִבְנֶה בַיִת וְגו'.

**686.** He opened the discussion saying: "A song of ascents for Solomon. Unless Hashem builds the house, they who build it labor in vain, unless Hashem keeps the city, the watchman stays awake in vain" (Tehilim 127:1). HE QUESTIONS: Did Solomon then say this praise when he built the Temple? HE ANSWERS: It was not so, but rather King David said it for his son, King Solomon, when Natan the prophet came to him and told him about Solomon that he would build the Temple. Afterwards King David showed his son, Solomon, the form of the Temple. When David saw the form of the Temple and all its trappings, he recited praise for Solomon his son, and said, "Unless Hashem builds the house…"

687. ד"א שִׁיר הַמַּעֲלוֹת לִשְׁלֹמֹה, לְמַלְכָּא דִשְׁלָמָא דִילֵיה. וְהַאי שִׁירָתָא אִיהוּ שִׁירָתָא וְתוּשְׁבַּחְתָּא עַל כָּל שְׁאַר שִׁירָתָא, וְשִׁירָתָא הֲדָא סַלְקָא עַל כֻּלְּהוּ. אִם יְיָ' לֹא יִבְנֶה בַיִת, דְּחָמָא דָוִד מַלְכָּא, כָּל אִינּוּן עַמּוּדִין שִׁבְעָה, דְּהַאי בֵּית קָאֵים עָלַיְיהוּ, דְּאִינּוּן קַיְימֵי שׁוּרִין שׁוּרִין, לְמִבְנֵי הַאי בַּיִת. לְעֵילָא מִכֻּלְּהוּ קַיְימָא מָארֵיהּ דְּבֵיתָא דְּאָזִיל עַל גַּבַּיְיהוּ, וְיָהִיב לוֹן חֵילָא וְתוּקְפָּא, לְכָל חַד וְחַד כַּדְקָא יֵאוֹת.

**687.** Another explanation for: "A song of ascents for Solomon." It MEANS to the King that the peace is His, THAT IS ZEIR ANPIN. This song is a song and praise above all the other songs, and this song rises above all of them. "Unless Hashem builds the house," MEANING King David saw all these seven pillars, WHICH ARE CHESED, GVURAH, TIFERET NETZACH, HOD, YESOD AND MALCHUT OF ZEIR ANPIN, upon which this house, MALCHUT, stands, for they stand row by row in order to build this house. Above them all stands the Master of the house, THAT IS BINAH, who goes over them and gives strength and courage to each and every one accordingly.

688. וְע"ד אָמַר דָּוִד, אִי הַאי מַלְכָּא דִשְׁלָמָא כֹּלָּא דִילֵיה, דְּאִיהוּ מָארֵיהּ דְּבֵיתָא, לָא בָּנֵי לְהַאי בֵּיתָא, שָׁוְא עָמְלוּ בוֹנָיו בּוֹ, אִינּוּן קַיְימִין דְּקַיְימִין לְמִבְנֵי עַל הַאי בֵּיתָא. אִם יְיָ' לֹא יִשְׁמָר עִיר, דָּא מַלְכָּא דִשְׁלָמָא כֹּלָּא דִילֵיה. שָׁוְא שָׁקַד שׁוֹמֵר, דָּא אִיהוּ חַד קַיְימָא דְּעָלְמָא אִתְתָּקַּן עָלֵיה, וּמַנּוּ. צַדִּיק, דְּהָא אִיהוּ נָטִיר לָהּ לְהַאי עִיר.

**688.** In reference to this, David said: Unless the King, that the whole peace is His, WHO IS BINAH, who is the landlord, build the house, "they who build it labor in vain." These are the pillars CHESED, GVURAH, TIFERET NETZACH, HOD, YESOD AND MALCHUT OF ZEIR ANPIN who will build this house. "Unless Hashem keeps the city," that is, the King that the whole peace is His, WHO IS BINAH, "the watchman stays awake in vain," who is a pillar, upon which the world, MALCHUT, is built. What is it? It is the Righteous, NAMELY YESOD OF ZEIR ANPIN, who watches over the city, MALCHUT.

689. מַשְׁכְּנָא דְּעָבֵד מֹשֶׁה, יְהוֹשֻׁעַ הֲוָה קָאֵים תָּדִיר וְנָטִיר לֵיהּ, דְּהָא לֵית נְטִירוּ דִּילֵיהּ בַּר בֵּיהּ דְּאִקְרֵי נַעַר, דִּכְתִיב וּמְשָׁרְתוֹ יְהוֹשֻׁעַ בֶּן נוּן נַעַר לֹא יָמִישׁ מִתּוֹךְ הָאֹהֶל. לְבָתַר הַאי מַשְׁכְּנָא לָא הֲוָה נָטִיר, אֶלָּא בְּגִין נַעַר אַחֲרָא, דִּכְתִיב וְהַנַּעַר שְׁמוּאֵל מְשָׁרֵת, בְּגִין דְּלֵית נְטִירוּ דְּמַשְׁכְּנָא, אֶלָּא בְּנַעַר. וּמַאן אִיהוּ שׁוֹמֵר דָּא. הַהוּא דְּנָטִיר מַשְׁכְּנָא דְּאִקְרֵי הָכִי נַעַר מְטַטְרוֹ"ן.

**689.** Joshua stood constantly and guarded the Tabernacle that Moses made, WHICH IS MALCHUT OF THE ASPECT OF MOCHIN OF THE SIX ENDS. It could be guarded only by him, for he is called 'a youth', WHICH IS THE ASPECT OF METATRON, as it is written: "But his servant Joshua, the son of Nun, a young man, did not depart out of the tent" (Shemot 33:11). Afterwards, this Tabernacle was guarded only by another youth, as it is written: "And the child Samuel ministered" (I Shmuel 3:1), because the Tabernacle can be guarded only by a youth. Who is this guard? He is the one who guards the SUPERNAL Tabernacle, WHICH IS MALCHUT OF THE ASPECT OF MOCHIN OF THE SIX EXTREMITIES, who is called so BY THE NAME 'youth', who is Metatron.

690. אֲבָל אַתּוּן קַדִּישֵׁי עֶלְיוֹנִין, לָאו נְטִירוּ דִּלְכוֹן כִּנְטִירוּ דְּמַשְׁכְּנָא, אֶלָּא נְטִירוּ דִּלְכוֹן כִּנְטִירוּ דְּבֵי מַקְדְּשָׁא, קוּדְשָׁא בְּרִיךְ הוּא בִּלְחוֹדוֹי, דִּכְתִיב אִם יְיָ' לֹא יִשְׁמָר עִיר שָׁוְא שָׁקַד שׁוֹמֵר, דְּהָא בְּכָל זִמְנָא דְּצַדִּיקַיָּא אַזְלֵי בְּאָרְחָא, קוּדְשָׁא בְּרִיךְ הוּא נָטִיר לוֹן תָּדִיר, דִּכְתִיב יְיָ' יִשְׁמָר צֵאתְךָ וּבוֹאֶךָ.

**690.** Guarding you, supernal Holy Ones, is not like the guarding of the Tabernacle, but guarding you is like the keeping of the Temple. The Holy One, blessed be He, alone guards it, as it is written: "Unless Hashem keeps the city, the watchman stays awake in vain." Similarly, all the time that the righteous are going on the road, the Holy One, blessed be He, guards them constantly, as it is written: "Hashem shall preserve your going out and your coming in" (Tehilim 121:8).

691. אַזְלוּ אֲבַתְרֵיהּ, וְאוֹזְפוּהוּ תְּלַת מִלִּין, וְאַהַדְּרוּ לְאָרְחַיְיהוּ קָרוּ עֲלֵיהּ, כִּי מַלְאָכָיו יְצַוֶּה לָךְ לִשְׁמָרְךָ בְּכָל דְּרָכֶיךָ, עַל כַּפַּיִם יִשָּׂאוּנְךָ וְגוֹ'. יִשְׂמַח אָבִיךָ וְאִמֶּךָ וְתָגֵל יוֹלַדְתֶּךָ.

**691.** They went after him and escorted him three miles, and then returned their way. They declared about him: "For He shall give His angels charge over you, to keep you in all your ways. They shall bear you up in their hands…" (Tehilim 91:11). "Let your father and your mother be glad, and let her who bore you rejoice" (Mishlei 23:25).

## 70. "In multitude of people is the glory of the king"

### A Synopsis

Here, Rabbi Yehuda discusses: "In the multitude of people is the glory of the king, but in the lack of people is the downfall of the prince." He says that while other nations have more people than Yisrael, they mix with each other, and therefore because the children of Yisrael do not mix, there is no nation in the world as great and numerous as Yisrael. When people are praying in the synagogue, it is to the king's glory. When they do not come and pray, the supernal appointees and legions are lowered, because the praises are required to be said above and below simultaneously. "The downfall of the prince," then, we learn, refers to these supernal beings. Yet even ten people in the synagogue are sufficient to praise God and to make comrades of the supernal legions.

### The Relevance of this Passage

The greatness and size of Yisrael is a metaphor alluding to the internal Vessel – the magnitude of *desire to receive* – that exists within the souls of the children of Yisrael. Prior to the Creation of the world, a single, unified soul – the Vessel – existed in the Endless World. This one infinite soul was comprised of all the souls of humanity, and its essential nature was desire. The one Vessel shattered into countless pieces of all sizes and spilled into our world. Thus, each broken fragment represents a different measure and intensity of desire. The largest pieces of the shattered Vessel are called *children of Yisrael.* Thus, the Israelites have the capacity to draw the greatest amount of Light into this world by virtue of the intensity of their desire. Thus, they are also accountable for the quantity of darkness that engulfs the world.

"Prayer in the synagogue" is not about worship or offering praise to the Creator. Rather, it denotes the path of spiritual transformation (of which prayer is but a tool to help effect change within a man's nature). Hence, we are being told that the children of Yisrael must embrace spiritual transformation to bring Light to all the nations of the world. Light is created when an Israelite resists his selfish and intense *desire to receive for the self alone* and, instead, *receives for the purpose of sharing with others*.

Prayer is one procedure that helps reveal Light as it diminishes the drive of the ego. Ten men are required in a synagogue during prayer, for they correspond to the Ten Sfirot, which creates circuitry. A reading of this passage awakens our momentous responsibility to bring Light to others. We are inspired to perform acts of caring, and we summon the courage to practice self-denial. Our meditation here is

a great act of sharing; thus it nourishes all the nations of the world with spiritual Light, ending conflict and crumbling the seeds of intolerance.

692. וְאֶת הַמִּשְׁכָּן תַּעֲשֶׂה עֶשֶׂר יְרִיעוֹת וְגוֹ'. רַבִּי יְהוּדָה פָּתַח, בְּרָב עַם הַדְרַת מֶלֶךְ וּבְאֶפֶס לְאֹם מְחִתַּת רָזוֹן. בְּרָב עַם הַדְרַת מֶלֶךְ, אִלֵּין אִינּוּן יִשְׂרָאֵל, דִּכְתִיב בְּהוּ כִּי עַם קָדוֹשׁ אַתָּה לַיְיָ' אֱלֹהֶיךָ. וְאִינּוּן עַמָּא דְּסַלְקִין לְכַמָּה אַלְפִין, וּלְכַמָּה רִבְּוָון, וְכַד אִינּוּן סַגִּיאִין בְּחוּשְׁבָּנֵיהוֹן, יְקָרָא דְּקוּדְשָׁא בְּרִיךְ הוּא אִיהוּ. דְּהָא עִלָּאִין וְתַתָּאִין מְשַׁבְּחָן שְׁמֵיהּ דְּמַלְכָּא עִלָּאָה, וּמְשַׁבְּחָן לֵיהּ בְּגִין עַמָּא קַדִּישָׁא דָּא. הה"ד רַק עַם חָכָם וְנָבוֹן הַגּוֹי הַגָּדוֹל הַזֶּה.

692. "Moreover, you shall make the tabernacle with ten curtains…" (Shemot 26:1). Rabbi Yehuda opened the discussion saying: "In the multitude of people is the glory of the king, but in the lack of people is the downfall of the prince" (Mishlei 14:28). "In the multitude of people is the glory of the king" refers to Yisrael, about whom it is written: "For you are a holy people to Hashem your Elohim" (Devarim 7:6). They are a people that number many thousands and ten thousands, and when their numbers are great, it is the glory of the Holy One, blessed be He, because those above and those below praise the Name of the supernal King because of this holy nation. This is what is meant by: "Surely this great nation is a wise and understanding people" (Devarim 4:6).

693. וְאִי תֵּימָא, הָא כְּתִיב, כִּי אַתֶּם הַמְעַט מִכָּל הָעַמִּים, אֶלָּא, מִכָּל הָעַמִּים וַדַּאי, אֲבָל מֵעַמָּא חַד יַתִּיר סַגִּיאִין אִינּוּן. דְּהָא לֵית עַמָּא בְּכָל עָלְמָא רַב וְסַגִּי כְּיִשְׂרָאֵל. וְאִי תֵּימָא הָא בְּנֵי יִשְׁמָעֵאל, וְהָא בְּנֵי אֱדוֹם, הָא כַּמָּה אִינּוּן. וַדַּאי הָכִי סַגִּיאִין אִינּוּן, אֲבָל כָּל שְׁאַר עַמִּין כֻּלְּהוּ מִתְעָרְבֵי אִלֵּין בְּאִלֵּין, בְּגִין אִית לְעַם דָּא, בְּעָם דָּא, וּלְאִלֵּין בְּנִין בְּעָם אַחֲרָא, וְאִלֵּין בְּאַחֲרָא. ובג"כ לֵית עַמָּא בְּכָל עָלְמָא, רַב סַגִּי כְּיִשְׂרָאֵל, עַמָּא בְּרִירָא וִיחִידָאָה, אִלֵּין בְּאִלֵּין, בְּלָא עִרְבּוּבְיָא אַחֲרָא כְּלַל, דִּכְתִיב כִּי עַם קָדוֹשׁ אַתָּה לַיְיָ' אֱלֹהֶיךָ, וּבְךָ בָּחַר יְיָ', וע"ד בְּרָב עַם הַדְרַת מֶלֶךְ, הַדּוּרָא אִיהוּ דְּמַלְכָּא עִלָּאָה קוּדְשָׁא בְּרִיךְ הוּא.

**693.** If you ask: But it is written, "Because you were more (also: few) in number than all the other peoples" (Devarim 7:7). HE ANSWERS: "Than all the other people": They are certainly the fewest, but of any of these people they are more numerous, for in the whole world there is no nation as great and numerous as Yisrael. If you ask: Behold the Ishmelites and the Edomites, who are numerous. HE ANSWERS: For sure numerous, but all the other nations mix one with the other. This nation has children in this nation and this nation has children in another nation, BUT THE CHILDREN OF YISRAEL DO NOT MIX WITH OTHER NATIONS AND NO NATIONS MIX WITH THEM. Therefore, there is no nation in the world as great and numerous as Yisrael. A select and unique people are they. Among them, there is no intermingle at all, as it is written: "For you are a holy people to Hashem your Elohim, Hashem your Elohim has chosen you…" Hence "in the multitude of people is the glory of the king," namely the glory of the supernal King, the Holy One, blessed be He.

694. תּוּ בְּזִמְנָא דְקוּדְשָׁא בְּרִיךְ הוּא אָתֵי לְבֵי כְּנִישְׁתָּא, וְכָל עַמָּא אַתְיָין כַּחֲדָא, וּמְצַלָּאן, וְאוֹדָן, וּמְשַׁבְּחָן לֵיהּ לְקוּדְשָׁא בְּרִיךְ הוּא, כְּדֵין הַדּוּרָא דְמֶלֶךְ אִיהוּ, דְמֶלֶךְ סְתָם דָּא מַלְכָּא קַדִּישָׁא. דְּאִתְתָּקַן בִּשְׁפִירוּ וּבְתִקּוּנָא לְסַלְּקָא לְעֵילָא.

**694.** WE SHOULD EXPLAIN THIS PASSAGE. When the Holy One, blessed be He, comes to the synagogue and all the people come together and pray and give thanks and praise the Holy One, blessed be He, it is the King's glory. A 'king' without attributes is the Holy King, THAT IS THE HOLY ONE, BLESSED BE HE, that is perfected with beauty and perfection to ascend above, to ABA AND IMA.

695. וּבְאֶפֶס לְאֹם מְחִתַּת רָזוֹן, וְכַד אִיהוּ אַקְדִּים לְבֵי כְּנִישְׁתָּא, וְעַמָּא לָא אַתְיָין לְצַלָּאָה וּלְשַׁבְּחָא לֵיהּ לְקוּדְשָׁא בְּרִיךְ הוּא, כְּדֵין כָּל הַהוּא שֻׁלְטָנוּתָא דִלְעֵילָא, וְכָל אִינּוּן מְמָנָן וּמַשִׁרְיָין עִלָּאִין, כֻּלְהוּ אִתְבָּרוּ מֵהַהוּא עִלּוּיָא דְמִתְתַּקְנֵי בְּתִקּוּנֵי הַהוּא מֶלֶךְ.

**695.** "But in the lack of people is the downfall of the prince." This is when THE HOLY ONE, BLESSED BE HE, comes earlier to the synagogue, but the

people did not come to pray and praise the Holy One, blessed be He. Then all the dominions of above and the supernal appointees and legions are cut from the elevation of preparing the adornments of that King, WHO IS THE HOLY ONE, BLESSED BE HE.

696. מ״ט. בְּגִין דִּבְהַהִיא שַׁעֲתָא, דְּיִשְׂרָאֵל לְתַתָּא קָא מְסַדְּרֵי צְלוֹתְהוֹן וּבְעוּתְהוֹן, וּמְשַׁבְּחָן לְמַלְכָּא עִלָּאָה. כָּל אִינּוּן מַשִׁרְיָין עִלָּאִין, מְסַדְּרִין שְׁבָחִין, וּמִתַּתְקְנָן בְּהַהוּא תִּקּוּנָא קַדִּישָׁא, בְּגִין דְּמַשִׁרְיָין עִלָּאִין כֻּלְּהוּ חַבְרִין אִינּוּן בְּיִשְׂרָאֵל לְתַתָּא, לְשַׁבְּחָא לְקוּדְשָׁא בְּרִיךְ הוּא כַּחֲדָא, לְמֶהֱוֵי סְלוּקָא דְּקוּדְשָׁא בְּרִיךְ הוּא עֵילָּא וְתַתָּא כַּחֲדָא.

696. What is the reason THAT THEY ARE CUT FROM THEIR LOFTY PLACES? Because when Yisrael below arrange their prayers and requests and are supporting the supernal King, all these supernal legions arrange praises and support that Holy Perfection. For all the supernal legions are friends with Yisrael below to praise the Holy One, blessed be He, together, so that the elevating of the Holy One, blessed be He, should be done above and below together.

697. וְכַד אִינּוּן מִזְדַּמְּנָן לְמֶהֱוֵי חַבְרִים בְּהוּ בְּיִשְׂרָאֵל, וְיִשְׂרָאֵל לְתַתָּא לָא אַתְיָין לְסַדְּרָא צְלוֹתְהוֹן וּבְעוּתְהוֹן וּלְשַׁבְּחָא לְמָארֵיהוֹן, כֻּלְּהוּ מַשִׁרְיָין קַדִּישִׁין, שְׁלְטָנוּתָא עִלָּאָה אִתְבָּרוּ מִתִּקּוּנֵיהוֹן, דְּהָא לָא סַלְקִין בִּסְלוּקָא, וְלָא יַכְלִין לְשַׁבְּחָא לְמָארֵיהוֹן כַּדְקָא יֵאוֹת. בְּגִין דְּשִׁבְחֵי דְּקוּדְשָׁא בְּרִיךְ הוּא, אִצְטְרִיךְ לְמֶהֱוֵי כַּחֲדָא עֵילָּא וְתַתָּא, עִלָּאִין וְתַתָּאִין בְּשַׁעֲתָא חֲדָא, וְע״ד מְחִתַּת רָזוֹן וְלָא מְחִתַּת מֶלֶךְ.

697. When THE ANGELS are bidden to be comrades with the people of Yisrael, TO PRAISE THE HOLY ONE, BLESSED BE HE, TOGETHER, and the children of Yisrael below do not come to set their prayers and requests and to praise their Master, then all the holy legions of the supernal dominion are cut from their perfection. They are not elevated and they cannot praise their Master properly, because the praises of the Holy One, blessed be He, have to be recited together above and below by those of above and those of below at the same time. Therefore it says, "The downfall of the prince" and not

'the downfall of the king' BECAUSE THIS PERTAINS ONLY TO THE COMPANIES OF ANGELS AND NOT TO THE KING HIMSELF.

698. וַאֲפִילוּ דְּלָא אַסְגִּיאוּ בְּבֵי כְּנִשְׁתָּא, אֶלָּא עֲשָׂרָה, בְּאִינּוּן עֲשָׂרָה מִזְדַּמְּנָן מַשִׁרְיָין עִלָּאִין, לְמֶהֱוֵי עִמְּהוֹן חַבְרִים. מ"ט בְּגִין דְּכָל תִּקּוּנֵי דְּהַהוּא מֶלֶךְ, אִינּוּן בַּעֲשָׂרָה, וְעַל דָּא דִּי בַּעֲשָׂרָה, אִי לָאו אִינּוּן יַתִּיר.

698. Even if they were not many that came to the synagogue and just ten, the supernal legions would come to be comrades with these ten to praise THE HOLY ONE, BLESSED BE HE. What is the reason? It is because all the perfections of that King are done with ten. Therefore, ten is sufficient if there are no more.

## 71. Wherever letters are added, it causes a lessening

### A Synopsis

Rabbi Yehuda begins here by saying that 'ten' can be written with the *Hei*, which is the Shechinah, or without it: *eser*, *asarah*. She is not included in 'twelve' at all. Twelve, the higher number, *Shtei asar*, is spelled without the *Ayin* of the evil eye, we learn, and when that letter is added the number is reduced by one to eleven, *Ashtei asar*. Wherever letters are added, we are then told, it serves as subtraction. Even adding *Yud* to Amnon's name and referring to him as 'Aminon' decreases his honor.

### The Relevance of this Passage

When the Evil Eye (envious stares and glances of ill-will) is permitted to shed its influence, it literally banishes the Light that is present. It has drastic effects upon people and situations. Evil Eye is banished from the world through the forces summoned here. The desire to cast Evil Eye is also eliminated from our being.

We learn that quite often when a person adds, he actually takes away, as per the well-known adage: *Less is more*. This truth is often seen in religion. A person becomes caught up in the religious aspect of faith, performing more and more rites and rituals in the name of holiness, but he grows to be more intolerant of others. This is the difference between a spiritual path and a religious one. Here we receive the wisdom and consciousness to seek out spiritual righteousness as opposed to self-righteousness born of religiosity. This dangerous holier-than-thou consciousness is purged from human consciousness, engendering tolerance and respect among all of God's children.

699. וְתָ"ח בַּמִּשְׁכָּן מַה כְּתִיב, וְאֶת הַמִּשְׁכָּן תַּעֲשֶׂה עֶשֶׂר יְרִיעוֹת, עֶשֶׂר: בְּגִין דְּתִקּוּנָא דְּמַשְׁכְּנָא, בַּעֲשָׂרָה אִיהוּ, לְמֶהֱוֵי כַּדְקָא יָאוֹת. עֶשֶׂר, מ"ט עֶשֶׂר, וְלָא עֲשָׂרָה. אֶלָּא עֶשֶׂר, בְּכָל אֲתַר אִיהוּ בְּלָא שְׁכִינְתָּא, דְּלָאו אִיהִי בְּחוּשְׁבְּנָא כְּגַוְונָא דָּא עוֹמֵד עַל שְׁנֵי עָשָׂר בָּקָר, שְׁכִינְתָּא לָאו אִיהִי בְּחוּשְׁבְּנָא, דְּהָא אִיהִי קַיְימָא לְעֵילָא, דִּכְתִיב וְהַיָּם עֲלֵיהֶם מִלְמָעְלָה. וּבְאִלֵּין דּוּכְתֵּי דִּרְמִיזֵי לְרָזָא דִּלְעֵילָא דְּחָסֵר מִנְּהוֹן, הָא שְׁכִינְתָּא יַתִּיר עַל הַהוּא חוּשְׁבְּנָא, דְּלָאו אִיהִי בְּחוּשְׁבְּנָא.

699. Come and see what is written of the Tabernacle: "Moreover you shall make the tabernacle with ten curtains" (Shemot 26:1). THE NUMBER ten is

because the perfection of the Tabernacle, WHICH IS MALCHUT, is by ten, AS MENTIONED EARLIER IN THE LAST ESSAY, so that everything will be proper. HE QUESTIONS: HE SAYS TEN (Heb. *eser*, fem.). What is the reason THAT IT SAYS ten (Heb. *eser* fem.) and not ten (Heb. *asarah*, masc.)? HE ANSWERS: For every place THAT IT IS WRITTEN ESER WITHOUT THE *HEI* refers to THE TEN SFIROT without the Shechinah, FOR THE SHECHINAH ENCIRCLES THEM FROM ABOVE because She is not counted WITH THE TEN. Similarly, "it stood upon twelve oxen (Heb. *shnei asar*)" (I Melachim 7:25). SINCE THE WORD TEN IS WRITTEN WITHOUT *HEI*, the Shechinah is not in the number TWELVE, since She stands over them from above as it is written: "And the sea was set above upon them" (Ibid.), MEANING THE SHECHINAH THAT IS CALLED 'SEA'. In those places that allude to what is missing above them, the Shechinah is extranumerary, not included in the count.

700. לְסִטְרָא אַחֲרָא, יָהֲבֵי חוּשְׁבָּנָא יַתִּיר, וְאִיהִי בְּמִנְיָינָא בִּגְרִיעוּ, כְּגוֹן עֶשְׁתֵּי, וְהָא אוּקְמוּהָ. וּבְכָל אֲתָר דְּאַתְוָון אִתּוֹסְפָן, כְּגַוְונָא דָא, אִיהוּ לִגְרִיעוּתָא. כְּגוֹן הַאֲמִינוֹן אָחִיךָ, דְּסַגְיָא אַמְנוֹן. וּבְסִטְרָא דִּקְדוּשָׁא, גָּרַע אָת וְאִיהוּ תּוֹסֶפֶת.

**700.** The Other Side is given an addition to the number, and it decreases in number. For example, Ashtei ASAR (=eleven) is spelled with *Ayin* THAT IS ADDED TO THE NUMBER SHTEI ASAR (=TWELVE), THUS REDUCING THE NUMBER FROM TWELVE TO ELEVEN. THIS IS AN INDICATION OF WHAT IS LACKING FROM ABOVE, FOR THE ADDED *AYIN* IS THE SECRET OF THE EVIL EYE (HEB. *AYIN*), as we have already established. Wherever letters are added in this manner, it serves as subtraction. For example: "Has Aminon your brother" (II Shmuel 13:20). It would have been sufficient TO SAY Amnon AND THE REASON THE *YUD* WAS ADDED IS TO LESSEN HIS HONOR. However, a letter is deducted on the holy side and it is really an addition, MEANING THAT BY DEDUCTING THE *AYIN* FROM ASHTEI ESREH, THE NUMBER ELEVEN BECOMES TWELVE.

## 72. The Seven Firmaments

### A Synopsis

Here, Rabbi Chiya discusses: "Who covers Himself with Light as with a garment, who stretches out the heavens like a curtain," saying that God created the Heavens from fire and water, expanded and spread out like a curtain. The seven firmaments, we are told, correspond to seven Sfirot, and there is one firmament above them, Tevunah, which cannot be viewed but only understood. Above that, there is one which no one can see or know. Then, Rabbi Chiya says, there are ten firmaments, which are the ten curtains of the tabernacle and also ten Sfirot. Next, Rabbi Yosi says there are nine firmaments, and that the Shechinah is the tenth. He adds that Rabbi Shimon revealed the secrets of all the firmaments, seven above and seven below. The seven firmaments contain stars and constellations, which guide the world.

### The Relevance of this Passage

The stars and the heavens rule our cosmos, scattering across our vision like bright diamonds, opening our hearts to the million sparks of love that fly to us from God. However, the seven heavenly bodies that adorn our strip of galaxy also exert negative influences. The lower Seven Sfirot control the planets and stars. Thus, by connecting to them here, we ascend above planetary influence and immediately begin directing our own fate. The destiny of mankind makes a quantum shift, from an apocalyptic finale to a Final Redemption that is founded upon compassion, mercy, and pleasantness. This miraculous turn of events occurs by virtue of the love of Rabbi Shimon, author of this heavenly tome.

701. רַבִּי חִיָּיא פָּתַח וְאָמַר, עוֹטֶה אוֹר כַּשַּׂלְמָה נוֹטֶה שָׁמַיִם כַּיְרִיעָה. הַאי קְרָא אוּקְמוּהָ, דְּכַד בָּרָא קוּדְשָׁא בְּרִיךְ הוּא עָלְמָא, אִתְעַטָּף בְּהַהוּא אוֹר קַדְמָאָה, וּבָרָא בֵּיה שָׁמַיִם.

**701.** Rabbi Chiya opened the discussion saying: "Who covers Himself with light as with a garment, who stretches out the heavens like a curtain" (Tehilim 104:2). This verse has been established. When the Holy One, blessed be He, created the world, He covered Himself with that first light THAT WAS IN THE CREATION, and created with it the heaven.

702. וְת"ח, אוֹר וְחֹשֶׁךְ לָאו כַּחֲדָא הֲוֵי. אוֹר מִסְּטְרָא דִּימִינָא, וְחֹשֶׁךְ

מִסִטְרָא דִּשְׂמָאלָא. מַאי עֲבַד קוּדְשָׁא בְּרִיךְ הוּא, שִׁתֵּף לוֹן כַּחֲדָא, וּבָרָא מִנְּהוֹן שָׁמַיִם. מַאי שָׁמַיִם. אֵשׁ וּמַיִם. שִׁתְּפָן כַּחֲדָא, וְעָבִיד שְׁלָם בֵּינַיְיהוּ.

**702.** Come and see: Light and darkness were not together, because light is from the side of the Right COLUMN and darkness is from the side of the Left COLUMN. What did the Holy One, blessed be He, WHO IS BINAH, do? He joined them together and created the heaven from them, WHICH IS THE SECRET OF ZEIR ANPIN, BECAUSE ZEIR ANPIN IS THE SECRET OF THE CENTRAL COLUMN AND MEDIATES BETWEEN BOTH COLUMNS, RIGHT AND LEFT, WHICH ARE FIRE AND WATER. What are Heavens? (Heb. *shamayim*). IT IS COMPOSED OF *Esh* and *Mayin* (Eng. 'fire and water'), which He joined together, and made peace between them.

703. וְכַד אִתְכְּלִילוּ כַּחֲדָא, וּמָתַח לוֹן, כַּיְרִיעָה מָתַח לוֹן, וְעָבִיד מִנְּהוֹן אָת וי' וְדָא אִקְרֵי יְרִיעָה. דְּהָא אָת דָּא אִתְפָּשִׁיט מִנֵּיהּ נְהִירוּ, וְאִתְעֲבִידוּ יְרִיעוֹת, הה"ד וְאֶת הַמִּשְׁכָּן תַּעֲשֶׂה עֶשֶׂר יְרִיעוֹת.

**703.** When they were combined together, FIRE AND WATER, He expanded them and spread them like a curtain, AS IT IS WRITTEN: "WHO STRETCHES OUT THE HEAVENS LIKE A CURTAIN." And He made of them the letter *Vav* OF THE NAME YUD HEI VAV HEI, NAMELY ZEIR ANPIN. This is called 'a curtain' or 'curtains', because light spread from this letter *Vav* TO MALCHUT, and curtains were made. This is what is meant by: "Moreover you shall make the Tabernacle with ten curtains.

704. וְשֶׁבַע רְקִיעִין אִינּוּן מְתִיחִין, גְּנִיזִין בְּגִנְזוֹי עִלָּאָה, כְּמָה דְּאוּקְמוּהָ. וְחַד רְקִיעָא דְּקַיְּימָא עֲלַיְיהוּ, וְהַהוּא רְקִיעַ לֵית בֵּיהּ גָּוֶון, וְלֵית לֵיהּ אֲתָר בְּאִתְגַּלְיָא וְלָא קַיְּימָא לְאִסְתַּכְּלָא בֵּיהּ, וְהַאי רְקִיעַ אִיהוּ גָּנִיז, וְנָהִיר לְכֻלְּהוּ, וְנָטִיל לוֹן בְּמַטְלָנֵיהוֹן, כָּל חַד וְחַד כַּדְקָא חֲזֵי לֵיהּ. אֶלָּא קַיְּימָא בְּסוּכְלְתָנוּ.

**704.** These seven firmaments expanded and are concealed in the supernal Storehouse, WHICH ARE THE SEVEN SFIROT OF ZEIR ANPIN: CHESED, GVURAH, TIFERET NETZACH, HOD, YESOD AND MALCHUT, FOR

CHOCHMAH IS COVERED AND CONCEALED IN THEM, WITHIN THE LIGHT OF CHASSADIM THAT ILLUMINATES UPON THEM FROM BINAH, as we have established. There is one firmament above them, WHICH IS TEVUNAH, and that firmament has neither color nor a revealed place in it IN THE ILLUMINATION OF CHOCHMAH. Nor can it be viewed. And this firmament is concealed and illuminates all THE SEVEN FIRMAMENTS, causing them to journey, each and every one as is proper for it. IT CANNOT BE VIEWED, it can only be understood.

705. מֵהַאי רָקִיעַ וּלְהָלְאָה, לֵית מַאן דְּיֵדַע וְיִשְׁגַּח, וְאִית לֵיהּ לְבַר נָשׁ לְמִסְתַּם פּוּמֵיהּ, וּדְלָא לְמַלְלָא וּלְאִסְתַּכְּלָא בְּסוּכְלְתָנוּ. מַאן דְּיִסְתַּכַּל אַהֲדָר לַאֲחוֹרָא, דְּלֵית מַאן דְּיָכִיל לְמִנְדַּע.

705. From that firmament and higher, MEANING HIGHER THAN YISRAEL-SABA, AND TEVUNAH, there is no one who can know or observe. A person should close his mouth in order not to talk and observe with understanding. One who will observe will go backwards, because there is none who can understand THERE.

706. עֶשֶׂר יְרִיעוֹת אִינּוּן, דְּאִינּוּן עֲשָׂרָה רְקִיעִין. וּמַאן אִינּוּן יְרִיעוֹת דְּמַשְׁכְּנָא דְּאִינּוּן עֶשֶׂר. וְקַיְימָן לְמִנְדַּע לְחַכִּימֵי לִבָּא. מַאן דְּיִנְדַּע בְּהוּ, אִסְתַּכַּל בְּחָכְמְתָא סַגִּיא, וּבְרָזִין דְּעָלְמָא, וְאִסְתַּכַּל לְעֵילָא בְּהַהוּא אֲתָר, דְּכָל חַד וְחַד אִתְדַּבָּק בֵּיהּ, בַּר תְּרֵין אִינּוּן דְּקַיְימָן בִּימִינָא וּבִשְׂמָאלָא, וְאִינּוּן גְּנִיזִין בַּהֲדֵי שְׁכִינְתָּא.

706. There are ten curtains, which are ten firmaments, and who are they? They are the curtains of the Tabernacle, WHICH IS MALCHUT, which are ten, NAMELY TEN SFIROT. They can be comprehended by the wise-hearted, BECAUSE CHOCHMAH IS REVEALED IN MALCHUT BUT NOT HIGHER THAN HER. One who knows them, observes great Wisdom and the secrets of the world, and looks up into that place to which each and everyone is attached, except for two FIRMAMENTS that stand on the right and left, WHICH ARE HER CHOCHMAH AND BINAH that are hidden with the Shechinah.

707. רַבִּי יוֹסֵי אָמַר תֵּשַׁע רְקִיעִין אִינּוּן, וּשְׁכִינְתָּא אִיהִי עֲשִׂירָאָה. דְּאִי

תֵּימָא בְּגִין דִּכְתִּיב עֶשֶׂר, בַּר מִשְּׁכִינְתָּא אִיהוּ. אִי הָכִי, שְׁכִינְתָּא חַד סְרֵי אִיהִי דְּקַיְּימָא עַל עֶשֶׂר. אֶלָּא וַדַּאי תֵּשַׁע אִינוּן, וְאִינּוּן תֵּשַׁע יוֹמִין שֶׁבֵּין ר"ה לְיוֹם הַכִּפּוּרִים, וְאִיהִי עֲשִׂירָאָה. כְּגַוְונָא דָא, מִשְׁכָּן אִיהוּ עֶשֶׂר יְרִיעוֹת.

**707.** Rabbi Yosi said: There are nine firmaments and the Shechinah is the tenth. If you say that since it is written Eser (Eng. 'ten') WITHOUT *Hei*, they are ten besides the Shechinah. Yet if so, then there are eleven Sfirot in the Shechinah, as She is one SFIRAH and is supernumerary to ten SFIROT. YET IT IS KNOWN THAT THERE ARE TEN SFIROT AND NOT ELEVEN, AS IT IS WRITTEN IN THE SEFER YETZIRAH (ENG. 'THE BOOK OF FORMATION'). But certainly there are nine, which are the nine days between Rosh Hashanah and Yom Kippur, and She is the tenth. Similarly, the Tabernacle is made of ten curtains.

708. אִינּוּן עֶשֶׂר רְקִיעִין רָזָא דְּרָזִין דְּלָא אִתְמְסַר בַּר לְאִינּוּן דְּיַדְעֵי חָכְמְתָא, וְכֹלָּא אִיהוּ בְּרָזִין דְּבוּצִינָא קַדִּישָׁא, דְּאִיהוּ גַּלֵּי רָזָא דְּכָל רְקִיעָא וּרְקִיעָא, וְאִינּוּן שַׁמָּשִׁין דִּמְשַׁמְּשֵׁי בְּכָל חַד וְחַד. שְׁבַע רְקִיעִין אִינּוּן לְעֵילָּא, שְׁבַע רְקִיעִין אִינּוּן לְתַתָּא, כְּגַוְונָא דִלְעֵילָּא. שְׁבַע רְקִיעִין אִינּוּן, דִּבְהוּ כֹּכְבַיָּא וּמַזָּלֵי לְאַנְהָגָא עָלְמָא דָא כְּפוּם אָרְחֵיהּ, כְּמָה דְּאִצְטְרִיךְ לֵיהּ.

**708.** These ten firmaments are the mystery of mysteries that is handed only to those who know Wisdom, and it is all in the secrets of the Holy luminary, RABBI SHIMON, who revealed the secret of every single firmament and those who minister in each and every one. There are seven firmaments above, IN ZEIR ANPIN, and there are seven firmaments below, IN MALCHUT, like above, AND THE SEVENTH FIRMAMENT, WHICH IS CHESED, INCLUDES THE FIRST THREE SFIROT. Therefore, there are ten, AS MENTIONED ABOVE. There are seven firmaments, which contain stars and constellations with which to lead this world according to its way, as is needed.

## 73. "Extol Him who rides upon the clouds"

### A Synopsis

Rabbi Yosi here continues discussing the firmaments. He says "the clouds" means the seventh firmament, that of Chesed, which is called Aravot because it is mixed from fire and water. He "who rides upon the clouds" is the eighth and higher firmament, Binah. Aravot includes within itself all the other six Sfirot, and that is the secret of the Supernal Chariot. Because those who enter the presence of this firmament must enter with only joy, the High Priest must enter the Holy Sanctuary only with joy. Rabbi Yosi next asks what the person in dire straits is to do if he cannot pray with joy, being full of sadness. He answers that those who pray with tears awaken the compassion of God. Then we learn that Binah is called 'Yah', because he is joy and he causes joy and he is the higher firmament. And when this firmament dominates, we are told, it revokes any punishment that had been decreed for a person who is in sadness yet still fasts on the Sabbath. Rabbi Elazar next says he thinks that "Him who rides upon the clouds" refers to Arich Anpin, who is the most hidden and most ancient of all, whose name is 'Yah', and who rides upon Aba and Ima, who are Yud-Hei. Even though Arich Anpin cannot be grasped or understood, Aba and Ima are the first level that emerged from Him. The name of Zeir Anpin, Yud Hei Vav Hei, is not as great because it has more letters, but, nonetheless, it is still the Great Name, which is used for Amen, to draw from Him.

Rabbi Elazar then tells us again how the precepts of the Torah are the limbs of the body, that every one of the limbs is important, and that neglecting even one precept of the Torah makes a blemish. He next discusses the union of the supernal limbs, whose secret is 'remember', and the lower limbs, whose secret is 'keep'. We are reminded that anyone who completes the precepts of the Torah will inherit two worlds, this world and the world to come. Then, Rabbi Chiya and Rabbi Aba rise at midnight to study Torah, and the daughter of the innkeeper stands nearby to light a candle for them and listen to their words.

### The Relevance of this Passage

Depression and gloom cause the Shechinah to depart our presence. Hence, true joy is kindled in our hearts so that the Shechinah envelops us in all her splendor. We are told that genuine tears of sadness (not selfishness) cause our prayers to be answered. In turn, the gates of mercy are opened to us by the lamenting prayers of the righteous who have cried and spilled tears on our behalf throughout history. We are

connected to the highest, most hidden realms of the spiritual atmosphere that shines immeasurable rays of Light into our dimension.

Meditating upon this section while making the conscious effort to share this Light with all mankind brings us blessing, helping our world now to become the world to come.

709. בְּכֻלְּהוּ שְׁבִיעָאָה עָדִיף, בַּר תְּמִינָאָה, דְּקָא מַדְבַּר לְכֻלְּהוּ, וְקַיְּימָא עַל כֻּלְּהוּ. כְּתִיב סֹלּוּ לָרוֹכֵב בָּעֲרָבוֹת, מַאן רוֹכֵב בָּעֲרָבוֹת, וּמַאן אִינוּן עֲרָבוֹת. אֶלָּא, עֲרָבוֹת דָּא רְקִיעָא שְׁבִיעָאָה, אֲמַאי אִתְקְרֵי עֲרָבוֹת. עַל דְּאִיהוּ כָּלִיל מֵאֶשָּׁא וּמַיָּא כַּחֲדָא, וּמִסִּטְרָא דְּדָרוֹם, וּמִסִּטְרָא דְּצָפוֹן, וְאִיהוּ מְעוּרָב מִתְּרֵין סִטְרִין.

709. Among them all, the seventh is the most valuable, WHICH IS CHESED, except for the eighth FIRMAMENT, WHICH IS BINAH, who leads all seven firmaments and stands upon them all. It is written: "Extol Him who rides upon the clouds" (Tehilim 68:5). HE QUESTIONS: Who is the one who rides the clouds and what are the clouds (Heb. *aravot*)? HE ANSWERS: 'Aravot' is the seventh firmament, WHICH IS THE FIRST SFIRAH OF ZEIR ANPIN THAT IS CALLED 'CHESED', AND INCLUDES ALL THE SFIROT OF ZEIR ANPIN THAT ARE BELOW IT. Why is it called 'Aravot'? Because it is mixed (Heb. *me'orav*) of fire and water together, NAMELY from the south, WHICH IS WATER, and from the north, WHICH IS FIRE. It is mixed of the two sides AND THE ONE WHO RIDES ON THE CLOUDS IS THE EIGHTH FIRMAMENT, BINAH.

710. וְאִי תֵּימָא, אִי הָכִי, שְׁתֵּי עֲרָבוֹת דְּקָא מִתְחַבְּרָן בְּלוּלָב, וְתָנֵינָן עֲרָבוֹת, הֲדָא הוּא דִכְתִיב סֹלּוּ לָרוֹכֵב בָּעֲרָבוֹת. אִי הָכִי, מַאן יָהִיב יַרְכִּין בְּגוּפָא, אוֹ גוּפָא בְּיַרְכִּין, דְּהָא דָּא עָבִיד פֵּרִין וְאֵיבִין, וְדָא לָא עָבִיד פֵּרִין וְאֵיבִין.

710. If you ask: If so, what about the two Aravot (Eng. 'willow branches) that are joined with the Lulav (Eng. 'palm leaf'), we have learned that this is what is written, "Extol Him who rides upon the Aravot." AND THEY ARE NETZACH AND HOD THAT ARE CALLED 'THIGHS'. HE QUESTIONS: Who gave thighs, WHICH ARE NETZACH AND HOD, in the body, WHICH IS CHESED, GVURAH AND TIFERET, and who gave a body, WHICH IS

CHESED, GVURAH AND TIFERET, in the thighs THAT ARE NETZACH AND HOD – MEANING, HERE YOU SAY THAT ARAVOT ARE CHESED OF ZEIR ANPIN, WHICH IS CONSIDERED THE BODY OF ZEIR ANPIN AND THERE YOU SAY THAT THEY ARE NETZACH AND HOD, WHICH ARE THE THIGHS THAT ARE OUTSIDE OF ITS BODY. WHO COMPARES THEM, seeing that this one, NAMELY THE BODY, produces fruit and this one, NAMELY NETZACH AND HOD which are thighs, does not produce fruit.

711. אֶלָּא, וַדַּאי כֹּלָּא הוּא רָזָא דַּעֲרָבוֹת דְּבָלוּלָב, אִינוּן עֲרָבוֹת דְּבָלוּלָב, חַד אֵשׁ, וְחַד מַיִם. בְּרָזָא דָא דְּכֻלְּהוּ, וְאִיהוּ שְׁבִיעָאָה אִיהוּ אֵשׁ וּמַיִם כָּלִיל כַּחֲדָא, בְּרָזָא חֲדָא, וּבְגִין דַּעֲרָבוֹת אִיהוּ רָזָא כְּלָלָא דְּכֻלְּהוּ שִׁית אַחֲרָנִין, אִיהוּ רָזָא דִּרְתִיכָא עִלָּאָה, וְקוּדְשָׁא בְּרִיךְ הוּא אִתְרְעֵי בְּהַאי רְקִיעַ, יַתִּיר מִכֻּלְּהוּ רְקִיעִין, וְתִיאוּבְתֵּיהּ תָּדִיר לְאַתְקְנָא לְהַהוּא רְקִיעָא, בִּשְׁפִירוּ עִלָּאָה. וְע״ד, סֹלּוּ לָרֹכֵב בָּעֲרָבוֹת לְהַהוּא דְּרֹכֵב בָּעֲרָבוֹת. וּמַאן אִיהוּ. הַהוּא רָקִיעַ טָמִיר וְגָנִיז, דְּקַיְימָא ע״ג חֵיוָתָא, דְּאִיהוּ רֹכֵב בָּעֲרָבוֹת.

711. HE ANSWERS: But certainly it all resembles the secret of Aravot (willow branches) of the Lulav (palm leaf), for one of these willow branches of the Lulav, WHICH ARE NETZACH AND HOD, is fire, WHICH IS HOD, and the other is water, WHICH IS NETZACH. They all pertain to the same secret, FOR THE ONE IS COMPLETELY WATER AND THE OTHER IS COMPLETELY FIRE AND THEY ARE NOT MIXED ONE WITH THE OTHER, FOR THEY ARE TWO SFIROT EACH WITH INDIVIDUAL DOMINION. It is the seventh FIRMAMENT, WHICH IS CHESED, which combines fire and water together in one secret, FOR IT IS ONE SFIRAH, AND SO WE FIND THAT IT COMBINES WITHIN ITSELF THE TWO ARAVOT OF THE LULAV IN ACTUALITY. Because the firmament Aravot includes within itself all the other six SFIROT, WHICH ARE GVURAH, TIFERET, NETZACH, HOD, YESOD AND MALCHUT, AS THE HIGHEST ONE INCLUDES ALL THOSE THAT ARE LOWER THAN IT, that is the secret of the supernal Chariot. The Holy One, blessed be He, WHO IS BINAH, desires this firmament more than all the firmaments and His desire is always to perfect this firmament with the highest beauty. On this, it is said, "Extol Him who rides upon Aravot," MEANING He who rides on Aravot. Who is he? This firmament that stands over the living creatures, NAMELY BINAH THAT STANDS ABOVE CHESED, GVURAH AND TIFERET

OF ZEIR ANPIN THAT ARE CALLED 'LIVING CREATURES', for it is He who rides on the clouds.

712. וְעִלְזוּ לְפָנָיו. מִלְּפָנָיו לָא כְּתִיב, אֶלָּא לְפָנָיו, דְּהָא לֵית מַאן דְּיִנְדַּע בֵּיהּ כְּלוּם. אֲבָל לְפָנָיו, מַאן דְּעָיֵיל לְקַמֵּיהּ דְּהַאי רְקִיעַ, אִצְטְרִיךְ לְמֵיעַל בְּחֶדְוָה, וְלָא בַּעֲצִיבוּ כְּלַל, בְּגִין דְּהַאי רְקִיעָא גָּרִים, דְּתַמָּן לָא שַׁרְיָא עֲצִיבוּ וְרוּגְזָא כְּלַל, דְּהָא תַּמָּן כֹּלָּא אִיהוּ בְּחֶדְוָה.

**712.** "And rejoice before Him" (Ibid.): It is not written, 'From before Him' but rather "before Him," BECAUSE 'FROM BEFORE HIM' IMPLIES BEFORE BINAH, WHICH IS CHOCHMAH and there is nobody who can know anything in Him. But "before Him," WHICH IS BINAH THAT RIDES UPON THE CLOUDS, one who enters before this firmament must enter with joy and without any sadness at all, because this firmament causes it so that neither sadness nor anger can dwell at all, because everything there is with joy. THEREFORE, IT SAYS, "AND REJOICE BEFORE HIM."

713. וְעַל דָּא, כֹּהֵן גָּדוֹל דְּקַיְּימָא לְקַמֵּיהּ, לָא הֲוָה עָאל לְבֵי קוּדְשָׁא, בַּר בְּחֶדְוָה, וּלְאַחֲזָאָה חֶדְוָה, דְּהָא אַתְרָא גָּרִים. וְעַל דָּא כְּתִיב, עִבְדוּ אֶת יְיָ' בְּשִׂמְחָה בֹּאוּ לְפָנָיו בִּרְנָנָה. דְּהָא אִצְטְרִיךְ דְּלָא לְאַחֲזָאָה בָּהּ עֲצִיבוּ.

**713.** Therefore, the High Priest who stands before Him enters the Holy Sanctuary only in joy and expresses joy, because the place causes it. Of this, it is written: "Serve Hashem with gladness, come before His presence with singing" (Tehilim 100:2), because one should not show sadness in it.

714. וְאִי תֵּימָא, אִי הָכִי, הַאי מַאן דְּאִיהוּ בְּצַעֲרָא וּבְדוֹחֲקָא, דְּלָא יָכִיל לְמֶחֱדֵי לְבֵּיהּ, וּמִגּוֹ דּוֹחֲקֵיהּ אִית לֵיהּ לְמִתְבַּע רַחֲמִין, קַמֵּי מַלְכָּא עִלָּאָה, אִי הָכִי, לָא יְצַלֵּי צְלוֹתָא כְּלַל, וְלָא יֵיעוּל בַּעֲצִיבוּ כְּלַל, דְּהָא לָא יָכִיל לְמֶחֱדֵי לְבֵּיהּ, וּלְאַעֲלָא קַמֵּיהּ בְּחֶדְוָה, מַאי תַּקּוּנָא אִית לֵיהּ לְהַאי בַּר נָשׁ.

**714.** And if you ask: One who is in pain and in dire straits, who cannot feel

joy in his heart, and because of his dire straits he has to ask for Mercy from the supernal King. If so, then he shouldn't pray his prayer at all and should not enter with any sadness at all, because he cannot gladden his heart and enter before Him with joy. What remedy does this person have?

715. אֶלָּא וַדַּאי הָא תָּנֵינָן, כָּל תַּרְעִין נִנְעֲלוּ וְאִסְגִּירוּ, וְתַרְעִין דְּדִמְעִין לָא אִסְגִּירוּ, וְלֵית דִּמְעָה אֶלָּא מִגּוֹ צַעֲרָא וְעֲצִיבוּ. וְכָל אִינּוּן דִּמְמָנָן עַל אִינּוּן תַּרְעִין, כֻּלְּהוּ מִתְבְּרִין גְּזִיזִין וּמַנְעוּלִין, וְעַיְילִין אִינּוּן דִּמְעִין, וְהַהִיא צְלוֹתָא עָאלַת קָמֵי מַלְכָּא קַדִּישָׁא.

**715.** HE ANSWERS: Surely we have learned that all the gates are closed and locked, but the gates of tears are not closed. Tears come only from pain and sadness, and all those who are appointed over the gates break the obstacles on the roads and the locks. They bring in these tears and that prayer enters before the Holy King.

716. כְּדֵין הַהוּא אֲתָר אִית לֵיהּ דּוֹחֲקָא, מֵהַהוּא עֲצִיבוּ וְדוֹחֲקָא דְּהַהוּא בַּר נָשׁ, כד"א בְּכָל צָרָתָם לֹא צָר. תִּיאוּבְתֵּיהּ דְּהַהוּא עָלְמָא עִלָּאָה, לְגַבֵּי הַאי אֲתָר, כִּדְכוּרָא דְּתִיאוּבְתֵּיהּ תָּדִיר לְגַבָּהּ דְּנוּקְבָּא. כַּד מַלְכָּא עָאל לְגַבֵּי מַטְרוֹנִיתָא, אַשְׁכַּח לָהּ בַּעֲצִיבוּ, כְּדֵין כָּל מָה דְּאִיהִי בָּעָאת, בִּידָהָא אִתְמְסָר, וְהַהוּא בַּר נָשׁ, וְהַהִיא צְלוֹתָא, לָא אַהֲדָר בְּרֵיקַנְיָא, וְקוּדְשָׁא בְּרִיךְ הוּא חַיִּיס עָלֵיהּ. זַכָּאָה חוּלָקֵיהּ דְּהַהוּא בַּר נָשׁ, דְּאוֹשִׁיד דִּמְעִין קָמֵי קוּדְשָׁא בְּרִיךְ הוּא, בִּצְלוֹתֵיהּ.

**716.** Then, that place, NAMELY MALCHUT, is distressed by the sadness and distress of that person, as it is written: "In all their affliction He is afflicted" (Yeshayah 63:9), BECAUSE THE PAIN OF THE PERSON TOUCHES THE SHECHINAH. The longing of the Supernal World, WHICH IS ZEIR ANPIN, to this place, WHICH IS MALCHUT, is like a male whose longing is always toward the female. Therefore, when the King, WHO IS ZEIR ANPIN, comes to the Matron, WHO IS MALCHUT, and finds Her sad, he gives over to Her hands whatever She desires. That person or that prayer do not return empty, and the Holy One, blessed be He, has Mercy on him. Blessed is the portion

of that person who pours out tears before the Holy One, blessed be He, in his prayer.

717. כְּגַוְונָא דָא בְּשַׁבָּת, מַאן דְּיָתִיב בְּתַעֲנִיתָא בְּשַׁבָּת, מִגּוֹ צַעֲרֵיהּ אַחְזֵי עֲצִיבָא, וּבְשַׁבָּת שַׁלְטָא הַהוּא רְקִיעָא עִלָּאָה, הַהוּא דְּאִתְחֲזֵי בְּחֶדְוָה, וְאִיהוּ חֶדְוָה וְחַדֵּי לְכֹלָּא. הַהוּא דְּיָתִיב בַּעֲצִיבוּ, בְּגִין דְּאִיהוּ שַׁלְטָא, אַפִּיק לְהַהוּא בַּר נָשׁ מֵהַהוּא עוֹנָשָׁא דְּאִתְגְּזַר עָלֵיהּ, וְהָא אִתְּמַר, סֹלּוּ: הָבוּ יְקַר, וְרוֹמְמוּ לְהַהוּא דְּרוֹכֵב בָּעֲרָבוֹת, דְּאִיהוּ חֶדְוָה וְחַדֵּי כֹּלָּא, רְקִיעָא עַל גַּבֵּי חֵיוָתָא בְּיָ"הּ שְׁמוֹ וַדַּאי, דְּהָא בְּהַהוּא אֲתָר שְׁמָא דָא אִתְכְּלִיל. וְעִלְזוּ לְפָנָיו, בְּגִין דְּלָא אִצְטְרִיךְ לְאַחֲזָאָה קַמֵּיהּ עֲצִיבוּ, כְּמָה דְאִתְּמַר.

717. It is similar on Shabbat. There is one who fasts on Shabbat and expresses sadness because of his pain, yet during Shabbat that supernal Firmament dominates, WHICH IS BINAH, that one that appears with joy, and causes everyone to rejoice. As for that PERSON, who is in sadness, once this FIRMAMENT dominates, it revokes that punishment that was deemed against that person. We have already learned this. AND THIS IS WHAT IS SAID: "Extol…" WHICH MEANS to give honor and exaltation to He who rides on the clouds, for He is joy and causes joy for everyone and He is the firmament which is above the Living Creatures, NAMELY BINAH, AS EXPLAINED EARLIER. "Yah is His Name" (Tehilim 68:5): Certainly, because in this place is this Name included, BECAUSE BINAH IS CALLED 'YAH'. "And rejoice before him," meaning not to expresses sadness before Him, as explained.

718. רַבִּי אֶלְעָזָר אָמַר, הַאי קְרָא, הָכִי אִצְטְרִיךְ לְמֵימַר, סֹלּוּ לָרוֹכֵב עַל עֲרָבוֹת, מַאי בָּעֲרָבוֹת. בְּיָהּ שְׁמוֹ, בֵּיהּ הוּא מִבָּעֵי לֵיהּ, מַאי שְׁמוֹ. אֶלָּא הַאי קְרָא, עַל סְתִימָא דְּכָל סְתִימִין, עַתִּיקָא דְּכָל עַתִּיקִין אִתְּמַר. הַהוּא דְּלָא אִתְגַּלְיָא, וְלָא אִתְיְדַע כְּלָל, דְּאִיהוּ רוֹכֵב בָּעֲרָבוֹת. וְאִי תֵּימָא, דְּאִיהוּ אַתְיָא וְרָכִיב בֵּיהּ, אִי הָכִי, אע"ג דְּסָתִים הוּא בַּאֲתָר דָּא קַיְימָא לְאִתְגַּלְיָא.

**718.** Rabbi Elazar said: This passage should have said, "Extol Him who rides upon the clouds" AND THIS PURPORT WOULD BE BINAH THAT RIDES UPON ZEIR ANPIN. What then is the meaning of "upon the clouds." AND ALSO with "Yah is His Name": It should have said, 'Yah is He', IF IT REFERS TO BINAH. What is the meaning of "His Name"? This verse is said about the most concealed of all and the most ancient of all, NAMELY ARICH ANPIN THAT IS MORE CONCEALED THAN THE CONCEALED SUPERNAL ABA AND IMA AND MORE ANCIENT THAN THEY. He is not revealed and not known at all, BECAUSE ITS CHOCHMAH IS CONCEALED ENTIRELY, AND DOES NOT ILLUMINATE BENEATH IT AT ALL, and rides upon the clouds, WHICH ARE ABA AND IMA, WHO ARE YUD-HEI. And if you ask: Since He comes and rides on *Yud-Hei*, even though He is concealed, can He be revealed in this place?

719. אֶלָּא סוֹלוּ לָרוֹכֵב בָּעֲרָבוֹת, דָּא אִיהוּ עַתִּיקָא דְּכָל עַתִּיקִין, סְתִימָא דְּכָל סְתִימִין, דְּלָא יְדִיעַ. וּבַמֶּה אִיהוּ רוֹכֵב, בַּעֲרָבוֹת, בְּיָ"ה, דְּאִיהוּ רָזָא קַדְמָאָה דְּנָפִיק מִנֵּיה וְדָא אִיהוּ שְׁמֵיה, מֵהַהוּא סְתִימָא, דְּלָא יְדִיעַ, שְׁמָא דִּילֵיה הוּא יָ"ה. לָאו דְּאִיהוּ הוּא, אֶלָּא אִיהוּ הוּא, בְּגִין דְּהַהוּא פְּרוֹכְתָּא דְּאִתְפְּרְסָא וְנָפִיק מִקַּמֵיה. אֲבָל הַאי פְּרוֹכְתָּא אִיהוּ שְׁמוֹ, וְדָא אִיהוּ רְתִיכָא דִּילֵיה, וְלָא אִתְיְדַע כְּלָל.

**719.** HE ANSWERS: But "Extol Him who rides upon the clouds" refers to the most ancient of all, the most concealed of all, which cannot be grasped, AND WILL NOT BE REVEALED. Upon what does He ride? The clouds, *Yud-Hei*, NAMELY ABA AND IMA, which is the secret of the first LEVEL that emerged from Him, BECAUSE ABA AND IMA EMERGED FROM ARICH ANPIN. This is "His Name" of that which is concealed that is not known, BECAUSE His Name is *Yud-Hei*. THEREFORE, THE VERSE SAYS, "YAH IS HIS NAME" and not THAT ABA AND IMA THEMSELVES are HIS NAME. Rather, ABA AND IMA are HIS NAME because of that curtain that separated and emerged before Him. That curtain is His Name, BECAUSE MALCHUT IS CALLED 'NAME' and this is His Chariot, MEANING THROUGH THAT CURTAIN HE IS CLOTHED IN ABA AND IMA, AND THEREFORE is not known at all, BECAUSE IT IS NOT REVEALED BY THEM.

720. וְדָא אִיהוּ שְׁמוֹ הַגָּדוֹל, בְּגִין דְּאִית שְׁמֵיה דְּלָאו אִיהוּ כָּל כָּךְ

גָּדוֹל, בְּהַאי אע״ג דְּאִית בֵּיהּ תּוֹסֶפֶת אַתְוָון. דָּא אִיהוּ שְׁמָא רַבָּא, וְעַל דָּא בְּהַאי שְׁמָא, אֲנָן מַפִּיקִין אָמֵן, דְּאִיהוּ מִנֵּיהּ. בְּהַאי אַזְלָא אָמֵן בְּכָל זִמְנָא, וּבִשְׁמָא אַחֲרָא לָאו הָכִי.

**720.** And this is His "Great Name," NAMELY ABA AND IMA WITH MALCHUT OF ARICH ANPIN THAT ARE ENCLOTHED IN THEM. There is a Name that is not as great as He, NAMELY THE NAME YUD HEI VAV HEI, WHICH IS ZEIR ANPIN, even though He has more letters, BECAUSE ABA AND IMA ARE CALLED ONLY BY THE TWO LETTERS *YUD-HEI* ALONE. STILL IN ALL, it is the Great Name. Therefore, with this Name we utter and say Amen, which is DRAWN from Him. With this NAME, Amen goes on continuously, BECAUSE THE UNION OF ABA AND IMA IS NEVER INTERRUPTED. With the other Name, WHICH IS ZEIR ANPIN THAT IS CALLED YUD HEI VAV HEI, it is not so, BECAUSE THE PAIRING OF THE MALE AND FEMALE IS INTERRUPTED BY THE SIN OF THE LOWER BEINGS.

**721.** אָמֵן יְהֵא שְׁמֵיהּ רַבָּא מְבָרַךְ, דְּכַד הַאי שְׁמָא אִתְתָּקַן, כֹּלָּא אִיהוּ בִּשְׁלִימוּ, וְכָל עָלְמִין חַדָּאן בְּחַדוּ. בְּהַאי שְׁמָא, כְּלִילָן עִלָּאִין וְתַתָּאִין. בְּהַאי שְׁמָא, כְּלִילָן שִׁית מֵאָה וּתְלֵיסַר פְּקוּדֵי אוֹרַיְיתָא, דְּאִינוּן כְּלָלָא דְּכָל רָזִין עִלָּאִין וְתַתָּאִין. כְּלָלָא דְּעָלְמָא דִּדְכוּרָא לְעֵילָא, וּכְלָלָא דְּעָלְמָא דְּנוּקְבָא לְתַתָּא.

**721.** THIS THAT WE SAY: 'Amen, May His Great Name be blessed FOREVER AND FOR ALL ETERNITY'. For when this Name is perfected, everything is complete, and all the worlds rejoice. And in the Name are included the higher and lower beings. In this Name are included the 613 precepts of the Torah, which are the inclusion of all the secrets, the upper and the lower. It is the combination of the Male World above, WHICH IS ZEIR ANPIN, and the Female World below, WHICH IS MALCHUT.

**722.** וְכֻלְּהוּ פְּקוּדִין, כֻּלְּהוּ שַׁיְיפִין וְאֵבָרִין, לְאִתְחֲזָאָה בְּהוּ רָזָא דִּמְהֵימְנוּתָא. מַאן דְּלָא יַשְׁגַּח וְלָא אִסְתְּכַל בְּרָזִין דִּפְקוּדֵי אוֹרַיְיתָא, לָא יָדַע, וְלָא אִסְתְּכַל, הֵיךְ מִתְתַּקְנָן שַׁיְיפִין בְּרָזָא עִלָּאָה. שַׁיְיפִין דְּגוּפָא כֻּלְּהוּ, מִתְתַּקְנָן עַל רָזָא דִּפְקוּדֵי אוֹרַיְיתָא, וְאע״ג דְּאִית שַׁיְיפִין,

דְּאִינוּן רַבְרְבִין וְעִלָּאִין, כֻּלְּהוּ זְעִירִין וְרַבְרְבִין, אִי אִתְנְטִיל חַד מִנַּיְיהוּ, אֲפִילוּ זְעֵירָא דְּבַר נָשׁ, אִקְרֵי מָארֵיהּ דְּמוּמָא, כ״שׁ וְכ״שׁ הַהוּא דְּגָרַע אֲפִילוּ חַד פִּקּוּדָא מֵאִינוּן פִּקּוּדֵי אוֹרַיְיתָא, דְּאָטִיל מוּמָא בְּאֲתָר דְּלָא אִצְטְרִיךְ.

**722.** All the precepts are organs and limbs to express through them the secret of the Faith, WHICH IS THE SECRET OF THE SHECHINAH. One who does not notice and observe the secrets of the precepts of the Torah does not know and CANNOT observe how to perfect the limbs in the supernal secret. The limbs of the body are all established upon the secret of the precepts of the Torah, BECAUSE THE 248 LIMBS CORRESPOND TO THE 248 POSITIVE PRECEPTS AND THE 365 VEINS CORRESPOND TO THE 365 NEGATIVE PRECEPTS. Even though there are certain limbs that are big and vital, AND THERE ARE SOME WHICH ARE SMALL AND INFERIOR, if any of them, either big or small, is removed, even the smallest in the person, he is considered blemished. He who diminishes even one precept of the precepts of the Torah makes a blemish in a place where there should not be any.

723. תָּא חֲזֵי, מַה כְּתִיב, וַיִּקַּח יְיָ׳ אֱלֹהִים אֶת הָאָדָם וַיַּנִּחֵהוּ בְגַן עֵדֶן לְעָבְדָהּ וּלְשָׁמְרָהּ. וְתָנֵינָן, לְעָבְדָהּ וּלְשָׁמְרָה אִלֵּין קָרְבָּנִין, וְכֹלָּא חַד. אֲבָל דָּא רָזָא דְּפִקּוּדֵי אוֹרַיְיתָא, לְעָבְדָהּ: אִלֵּין רמ״ח שַׁיְיפִין עִלָּאִין. וּלְשָׁמְרָה: אִלֵּין תְּלַת מְאָה וְשִׁתִּין וְחָמֵשׁ שַׁיְיפִין תַּתָּאִין. אִלֵּין עִלָּאִין דְּזָכוֹר. וְאִלֵּין תַּתָּאִין דְּשָׁמוֹר, וְכֹלָּא חַד.

**723.** Come and see what is written: "And Hashem Elohim took the man, and put him into the Garden of Eden to till it and to keep it" (Beresheet 2:15). We have learned that "to till it and to keep it" refers to the offerings, and it is all one. But this is the secret of the precepts of the Torah. "To till it": These are the 248 supernal Limbs, "and to keep it" are the 365 lower limbs, NAMELY THE 365 SINEWS. Those higher ones pertain to 'remember,' WHICH IS ZEIR ANPIN, and those lower ones pertain to 'keep,' WHICH IS MALCHUT. And it is all one.

724. זַכָּאָה אִיהוּ מַאן דְּזָכֵי לְאַשְׁלָמָא לוֹן. פִּקּוּדִין דְּאוֹרַיְיתָא, גָּרִים

לְבַר נָשׁ לְאַשְׁלָמָא רוּחֵיהּ וְנִשְׁמָתֵיהּ בְּהַאי עָלְמָא, וּבְעָלְמָא דְּאָתֵי.
אוֹרַיְיתָא מְזַכָּה לְבַר נָשׁ, לְאַחְסָנָא תְּרֵין עָלְמִין, עָלְמָא דָּא וְעָלְמָא
דְּאָתֵי. כָּל מַאן דְּאִשְׁתָּדַּל בְּאוֹרַיְיתָא, אִשְׁתָּדַּל בַּחַיִּים. חַיִּים בְּהַאי
עָלְמָא, וְחַיִּים בְּעָלְמָא דְּאָתֵי. אִשְׁתְּזִיב מִכָּל עוֹנָשִׁין בִּישִׁין, דְּלָא יַכְלִין
לְשַׁלְטָאָה עָלֵיהּ. אִי בְּאִשְׁתַּדְּלוּתָא הָכִי. כ"ש מַאן דְּעָבֵיד עוֹבָדָא.

**724.** Blessed is he who is worthy of completing the precepts of the Torah. He causes man to perfect his spirit and soul in this world and in the World to Come. The Torah merits the person to inherit two worlds, this world and the World to Come. Everyone who endeavors in Torah endeavors in life, life in this world and life in the World to Come and is spared from all the bad punishments, which cannot dominate him. If by endeavoring IN TORAH it is so, so much more so for he who acts AND FULFILLS THE PRECEPTS OF THE TORAH.

## 74. "For the commandment is a candle; and Torah is light"

### A Synopsis

Rabbi Yosi here explains that it is necessary to perform a deed to prepare the candle, and it is necessary to be occupied with Torah to light the candle in order to merit the supernal light from which the candle is lit. He goes on to discuss the reproofs of instruction that the Holy One brings upon a person to purify him of his sins.

Another explanation of the candle is that it is the Oral Torah, which only illuminates through the Written Torah, which is the light. The candle is a commandment or precept that women merit, the candle of Shabbat, but only men can merit through Torah and illuminate the candle. Next, we hear of a father and daughter who are bitterly unhappy because her new husband doesn't even know how to say the prayer after a meal, and does not merit Torah. The young man sits before Rabbi Yosi, who proclaims that either the light of Torah will emerge from him, or else a son will emerge from him. The young man laughs and explains that because he is young and respectful he decided that he should not speak before the older wiser men for two months, but now the time has come. He says that the "the commandments" refers to Malchut, which is a candle waiting to be kindled by Zeir Anpin. He speaks of her two arms and the 248 supernal limbs, which add to 250, or *resh-nun*; 'candle' is *nun-resh*. And Torah is 'Light', because Torah is from the right side, which is the first light that was created. When the left is combined in it, we learn, there is perfection in everything.

### The Relevance of this Passage

Here we are purified and corrected of sin, so that our souls flicker like the flame of a candle. Our 248 limbs are warmed and nurtured by the supernal candlelight that radiates from the Torah. And just as one candle can light millions of others without diminishing its own flame, the spiritual Light we now reveal is shared with all the souls of this planet, flooding the entire globe with the Light of the Creator. As mankind basks in the glow, peace takes hold and tranquillity spreads throughout the land.

725. רַבִּי חִיָּיא וְר' אַבָּא, שָׁרוּ בְּבֵי אוּשְׁפִּיזַיְיהוּ, קָמוּ בְּפַלְגוּת לֵילְיָא, לְאִשְׁתַּדְּלָא בְּאוֹרַיְיתָא. בְּרַתֵּיה דְּאוּשְׁפִּיזָא, קָמַת וְאַנְהֵירַת לוֹן שְׁרַגָּא, וּלְבָתַר קַיְימַת אֲבַתְרַיְיהוּ לְמִשְׁמַע מִלִּין דְּאוֹרַיְיתָא.

**725.** Rabbi Chiya and Rabbi Aba were dwelling in their lodging. They rose at midnight to occupy themselves with Torah. The daughter of the innkeeper arose, lit a candle for them, and stood behind them in order to hear words of Torah.

726. פָּתַח רַבִּי יוֹסִי וְאָמַר, כִּי נֵר מִצְוָה וְתוֹרָה אוֹר וְדֶרֶךְ חַיִּים תּוֹכְחוֹת מוּסָר. כִּי נֵר מִצְוָה, כָּל מַאן דְּאִשְׁתַּדַּל בְּהַאי עָלְמָא, בְּאִינּוּן פְּקוּדִין דְּאוֹרַיְיתָא, אִתְסְדַר קָמֵיהּ בְּכָל פִּקּוּדָא וּפִקּוּדָא חַד שְׁרָגָּא, לְאַנְהָרָא לֵיהּ בְּהַהוּא עָלְמָא. וְתוֹרָה אוֹר, מַאן דְּאִתְעַסָּק בְּאוֹרַיְיתָא, זָכֵי לְהַהוּא נְהוֹרָא עִלָּאָה, דְּאַדְלִיקַת שְׁרָגָּא מִנֵּיהּ, דְּהָא שְׁרָגָּא בְּלָא נְהוֹרָא לָא כְּלוּם. נְהוֹרָא בְּלָא שְׁרָגָּא, אוּף הָכִי לָא יָכִיל לְאַנְהָרָא. אִשְׁתְּכַח דְּכֹלָּא דָּא לְדָא אִצְטְרִיךְ. אִצְטְרִיךְ עוֹבָדָא לְאַתְקְנָא שְׁרָגָּא. וְאִצְטְרִיךְ לְמִלְעֵי בְּאוֹרַיְיתָא, לְאַנְהָרָא שְׁרָגָּא. זַכָּאָה אִיהוּ מַאן דְּאִתְעַסָּק בָּהּ בִּנְהוֹרָא וּבִשְׁרָגָּא.

**726.** Rabbi Yosi opened the discussion saying: "For the commandment is a candle; and Torah is light; and reproofs of instruction are the way of life" (Mishlei 6:23). "For the commandment is a candle" MEANS THAT whoever endeavors in this world in the precepts of the Torah, one candle is prepared to shine for him in that world by every precept. "And Torah is light" MEANS he who is occupied with Torah merits that supernal light from which the candle is lit, because a candle without light is nothing. Light without a candle can also not illuminate, so we find that they both depend upon each other. It is necessary to perform a deed to prepare the candle and it is necessary to be occupied with Torah to light the candle. Blessed is he who is occupied with the light and the candle.

727. וְדֶרֶךְ חַיִּים תּוֹכְחוֹת מוּסָר, אֹרַח חַיִּים לְאַעֲלָא בֵּיהּ לְעָלְמָא דְּאָתֵי, אִינּוּן תּוֹכְחוֹת, דְּמְקַבֵּל בַּר נָשׁ לְאַעֲדָאָה גַּרְמֵיהּ מֵאֹרַח בִּישׁ, וּלְמֵיהַךְ בְּאָרְחָא טָבָא. תּוּ וְדֶרֶךְ חַיִּים, אִינּוּן תּוֹכְחוֹת מוּסָר, דְּאַיְיתֵי קוּדְשָׁא בְּרִיךְ הוּא עָלֵיהּ דְּבַר נָשׁ, לְדַכְּאָה לֵיהּ מֵחוֹבוֹי בְּאִינּוּן תּוֹכְחוֹת. זַכָּאָה אִיהוּ מַאן דְּקַבִּיל לְהוּ בִּרְעוּ דְּלִבָּא.

**727.** "And reproofs of instruction are the way of life", MEANING "the way of

life" with which to enter into the World to Come. These are the reproofs that a person receives in order to remove himself from the path of evil and to go in the path of good. It CAN BE EXPLAINED that "the way of life" is the reproofs of instruction that the Holy One, blessed be He, brings upon the person to purify him of his sins with these reproofs. Blessed is he who accepts them with a willing heart.

728. דָּבָר אַחֵר כִּי נֵר מִצְוָה, דָּא שְׁרָגָּא בּוּצִינָא דְּדָוִד, דְּאִיהוּ נֵר מִצְוָה אוֹרַיְיתָא דִּבְעַל פֶּה, דְּאִצְטְרִיךְ לְאִתְתַּקְּנָא תָּדִיר, וְאִיהִי לָא נַהֲרָא אֶלָּא מִגּוֹ תּוֹרָה שֶׁבִּכְתָב, דְּהָא אוֹרַיְיתָא דִּבְעַל פֶּה לֵית לָהּ נְהִירוּ, אֶלָּא מִגּוֹ תּוֹרָה שֶׁבִּכְתָב, דְּאִיהִי אוֹר לְאַנְהָרָא.

728. Another explanation, "For the commandment is a candle": This is the candle, the luminary of David, which is a candle lit to perform a precept, the Oral Torah, NAMELY MALCHUT, that must be constantly attended to. She does not illuminate except through the Written Torah, WHICH IS ZEIR ANPIN, because the Oral Torah possesses light only through the Written Torah, which is a light for illumination.

729. אַשְׁגַּח אֲבַתְרֵיהּ, וְחָמָא בְּרַתֵּיהּ דְּאוּשְׁפִּיזָא קָיְימָא אֲבַתְרַיְיהוּ, אָמַר כִּי נֵר מִצְוָה, מַאי נֵר. דָּא נֵר דְּאִיהִי מִצְוָה דְּנָשִׁין זַכְיָין בֵּיהּ, וְאִיהִי נֵר דְּשַׁבָּת, דְּאַף עַל גַּב דְּנָשִׁין לָא זַכָּאן בְּאוֹרַיְיתָא, הָא גּוּבְרִין זַכְיָין בְּאוֹרַיְיתָא, וְנַהֲרִין לְהַאי שְׁרָגָּא, דְּנָשִׁין מְתַתְּקְנָן בְּהַאי מִצְוָה. נָשִׁין בְּתִקּוּנָא דְּהַאי נֵר. גּוּבְרִין בְּאוֹרַיְיתָא, לְאַנְהָרָא לְהַאי נֵר, תִּקּוּנָא דְּמִצְוָה דְּנָשִׁין אִתְחַיִּיבוּ בְּהוּ.

729. He looked behind and saw the daughter of the innkeeper standing behind them. He said, "For the commandment is a candle." What is a candle? It is a candle that is a precept that women merit, and it is the candle of Shabbat. Although women do not merit through Torah, but men do, the latter illuminate that candle that women perfect with this precept. Women, through the perfection of this candle, and the men, through Torah, kindle and light this candle, which is the perfection of the precept that women are obligated to do.

730. שָׁמְעַת הַהִיא אִתְּתָא וּבָכָאת, אַדְהָכִי קָם אֲבוּהַ דְּאִתְּתָא, דַּהֲוַת תַּמָּן, וְעָאל בֵּינַיְיהוּ, וְחָמָא בְּרַתֵּיה קַיְּימַת אֲבַתְרַיְיהוּ וּבָכָאת, שָׁאִיל לָהּ אֲבוּהַ. סָחַת לֵיה עוֹבָדָא. שָׁרֵי אֲבוּהַ דְּאִתְּתָא אוּף אִיהוּ וּבָכָה. אָמַר לֵיה רַבִּי יוֹסֵי, דִּילְמָא חֲתָנָךְ בַּעְלָהּ דִּבְרַתִּיךְ, לָא זָכָה בְּאוֹרַיְיתָא. אָמַר לֵיה וַדַּאי הָכִי הוּא, וְעַל דָּא וַדַּאי בָּכֵינָן, אֲנָא וּבְרַתִּי תָּדִיר.

730. That woman heard it and wept. In the meantime, the father of the woman who was there rose and came among them. He saw his daughter standing behind them weeping. Her father asked her, and she told him the story. Then the father of the woman also started to weep. Rabbi Yosi said to him: Perhaps your son-in-law, the husband of your daughter did not merit Torah. He said to him: It is indeed so. And that is why my daughter and I weep constantly.

731. וּבְגִין דַּחֲמֵינָא, לֵיה יוֹמָא חַד, דְּדָלִיג מֵאִגְּרָא דָּא, לְמִשְׁמַע קַדִּישׁ בַּהֲדֵי צִבּוּרָא, סָלִיק בִּרְעוּתָא דִּילִי, לְמֵיהַב לֵיה בְּרַתִּי, וּתֵכֶף דְּנַפְקוּ צִבּוּרָא מִבֵּי כְּנִישְׁתָּא, יְהִיבְנָא לֵיה בְּרַתִּי. דַּאֲמֵינָא בְּדִלּוּגָא דָּא דְּאָתָא לְמִשְׁמַע קַדִּישׁ, גַּבְרָא רַבָּא לֶיהֱוֵי בְּאוֹרַיְיתָא, וְאע״ג דְּאִיהוּ רַבְיָא, וְלָא יְדַעְנָא בֵּיה מִקַּדְמַת דְּנָא. וְהַשְׁתָּא אֲפִילוּ בִּרְכַּת מְזוֹנָא לָא יָדַע, וְלָא יָכִילְנָא בַּהֲדֵיה לְמִלְעֵי בֵּין חַבְרַיָּיא, דְּיוֹלִיף קְרִיאַת שְׁמַע, אוֹ בִּרְכַּת מְזוֹנָא.

731. Because the day I saw him jump from this attic to hear Kaddish with the congregation, I got the desire to give him my daughter in marriage, and immediately after the congregation left the synagogue I gave him my daughter. For I said, by that jump with which he came to hear the Kaddish IT IS KNOWN that he will be a learned man in Torah. Even though he was a youth and I did not know him previously, I GAVE HIM MY DAUGHTER. But now he doesn't even know how TO BLESS the blessing after the meal and I cannot even learn with him among the scholars, so he should learn Sh'ma or the blessing after the meal.

732. אָמַר לֵיה אַעְבַּר לֵיה בְּאָחֳרָא, אוֹ דִּלְמָא בְּרָא יוֹלִיד דְּלֶהֱוֵי גַּבְרָא רַבָּא. אַדְהָכִי קָם אִיהוּ, וְדָלֵג עֲלַיְיהוּ וְיָתִיב לְקַמַּיְיהוּ. אִסְתָּכַּל בֵּיה רַבִּי

יוֹסֵי, אָמַר, וַדַּאי אֲנָא חֲמֵינָא בְּהַאי רַבְיָא, דִּנְהוֹרָא דְּאוֹרַיְיתָא יִפּוּק
לְעָלְמָא מִנֵּיהּ. אוֹ בְּרָא דְּיוֹקִים מִנֵּיהּ. חָיֵיךְ הַהוּא רַבְיָא, וְאָמַר, רַבּוֹתַי
אֵימָא קַמַּיְיכוּ חַד מִלָּה.

**732.** Rabbi Yosi said to him: Exchange him for another, or perhaps he will bear a son who will be great in Torah. In the meantime, THE SON-IN-LAW OF THE INNKEEPER arose and jumped to them. Rabbi Yosi looked at him intently and said: Certainly, I see in this youth that the light of Torah will emerge from him into the world or else a son will emerge from him. That youth laughed and said: My masters, I will speak before you of one subject.

733. פָּתַח וְאָמַר צָעִיר אֲנִי לְיָמִים וְאַתֶּם יְשִׁישִׁים עַל כֵּן זָחַלְתִּי וָאִירָא
מֵחַוּת דֵּעִי אֶתְכֶם. הַאי קְרָא אִתְּעֲרוּ בֵּיהּ עַמּוּדֵי עָלְמָא. אֲבָל אֱלִיהוּא
דִּכְתִּיב בֵּיהּ מִמִּשְׁפַּחַת רָם, אִתְּעֲרוּ, דְּהָא מִזַּרְעָא דְּאַבְרָהָם קָאָתָא.
וְשַׁפִּיר. אֲבָל אֱלִיהוּא כַּהֲנָא הֲוָה, וּמִזַּרְעָא דִּיחֶזְקֵאל נְבִיאָה הֲוָה, כְּתִיב
הָכָא בֶּן בַּרַכְאֵל הַבּוּזִי, וּכְתִיב הָתָם יְחֶזְקֵאל בֶּן בּוּזִי הַכֹּהֵן.

**733.** He opened the discussion saying: "I am young, and you are very old; therefore I was afraid, and dared not declare my opinion to you" (Iyov 32:6). The pillars of the world have remarked upon this verse. About Elihu, it is written: "of the family Ram" (Ibid. 2). It was then remarked that he was said to have come from the seed of Abraham, and it is good. But Elihu was a priest and was from the seed of Ezekiel the prophet, because it is written: "Son of Barachel the Buzite" (Ibid.) and also, "Ezekiel the priest, the son of Buzi" (Yechezkel 1:3).

734. וְאִי תֵּימָא בְּגִין דִּכְתִּיב בּוּזִי, בּוּז מִשְׁפָּחוֹת הֲוָה. לָאו הָכִי, הָדַר
וְאָמַר מִמִּשְׁפַּחַת רָם, עִלָּאָה עַל כֹּלָּא. אֲמַאי אִקְרֵי בּוּזִי. עַל דְּמְבַזֶּה
גַּרְמֵיהּ לְגַבֵּי מַאן דְּגָדוֹל מִנֵּיהּ, וְעַל דָּא סָלִיק בִּשְׁמָא עִלָּאָה, בּוּזִי, דָּא
דְּאִקְרֵי אָדָם שְׁלֵימָא בְּכֹלָּא, מַה דְּלָא אִקְרֵי הָכִי בַּר נָשׁ אַחֲרָא, הֲדָא
הוּא דִכְתִּיב וְאַתָּה בֶּן אָדָם, וְעַל דְּסָלִיק בִּשְׁמָא דָּא, אִקְרֵי רָם, עִלָּאָה
עַל כֹּלָּא.

**734.** If you say: Because it is written Buzi, he was "the contempt (Heb. *buz*)

-453-

of families" (Iyov 31:34), it is not so, because it says afterwards "of the family of Ram," meaning higher (Heb. *ram*) above all. Why is he called 'Buzi'? It is because he shames himself before one who is greater than him. Therefore, he is called by the lofty name of Buzi, with which was named he who was perfect in everything, such as no one was called, MEANING EZEKIEL. It is written: "And you, son of man" (Yechezkel 2:6). Because ELIHU was called by that name, Buzi, he was also called 'Ram', meaning higher above all.

735. וְעַל דָּא אָמַר צָעִיר אֲנִי לְיָמִים. לְיָמִים, מִיָּמִים מִבָּעֵי לֵיהּ, מַאי לְיָמִים. אֶלָּא אָמַר צָעִיר אֲנִי, וְאַזְעִירְנָא גַּרְמֵי לְיָמִים, לְגַבֵּי בַּר נָשׁ דְּאִית לֵיהּ יוֹמִין סַגִּיאִין. מ"ט. בְּגִין דְּאָמַרְתִּי דְּיָמִים יְדַבֵּרוּ. וְעַל דָּא צָעִיר אֲנִי, וְאַזְעִירְנָא גַּרְמֵי לְגַבֵּי יָמִים. וְאַתֶּם יְשִׁישִׁים, חֲמֵינָא לְכוּ יְשִׁישִׁים. עַל כֵּן זָחַלְתִּי וָאִירָא מֵחַוֹּת דֵּעִי אֶתְכֶם. אוּף אֲנָא, אָמַרְתִּי יָמִים יְדַבֵּרוּ וְרֹב שָׁנִים יוֹדִיעוּ חָכְמָה. וַדַּאי. אָכֵן רוּחַ הִיא בֶאֱנוֹשׁ וְנִשְׁמַת שַׁדַּי תְּבִינֵם. וְעַל דָּא בְּגִין דַּאֲנָא רַבְיָא, שַׁוֵּינָא בִּרְעוּתִי דְּלָא לְמַלְּלָא עַד תְּרֵין יַרְחִין, וְעַד יוֹמָא דָא אִשְׁתְּלִימוּ. וְהַשְׁתָּא דְּאַתּוּן הָכָא, אִית לְמִפְתַּח בְּאוֹרַיְיתָא קַמַּיְיכוּ.

735. Therefore, he said, "I am young (lit. 'young in days')." HE QUESTIONS: He says "in days," but should have said 'of days.' What is "in days"? But he said, "I am young," meaning I have made myself small "in days" before one who has many days. What is the reason? Because I said that "days should speak" (Iyov 32:7). Therefore, "I am young" meaning that I belittled myself before "days." "And you are old": I saw that you are old, so "I am afraid, and dared not declare my opinion to you. Also I said, "Days should speak and multitude of years should teach wisdom." Certainly, "But there is a spirit in man: and the breath of Shadai gives them understanding" (Ibid. 8). Therefore, since I am a youth, I decided not to speak for two months, and today they have completed. Now that you are here, it is proper to open with words of Torah before you.

736. פָּתַח וְאָמַר, כִּי נֵר מִצְוָה וְתוֹרָה אוֹר וְדֶרֶךְ חַיִּים תּוֹכְחוֹת מוּסָר. כִּי נֵר מִצְוָה דָּא אִיהִי מִשְׁנָה, כד"א וְהַתּוֹרָה וְהַמִּצְוָה. וְהַתּוֹרָה: זוֹ תּוֹרָה שֶׁבִּכְתָב. וְהַמִּצְוָה: זוֹ מִשְׁנָה. דְּאִיהִי נֵר שְׁרָגָא, דְּקַיְּימָא לְאַדְלְקָא.

**736.** He opened the discussion saying: "For the commandment is a candle; and Torah is light; and the reproofs of instruction are the way of life." "For the commandment is a candle" refers to Mishnah as is said: "And the Torah, and the commandments" (Shemot 24:12). "Torah" is the Written Torah, ZEIR ANPIN, and 'the commandments' refers to Mishnah, NAMELY MALCHUT, which is a candle, MEANING a candle that is waiting to be kindled, BECAUSE MALCHUT HAS NO LIGHT ON HER OWN AND NEEDS ZEIR ANPIN TO KINDLE HER AND ILLUMINATE HER.

737. נֵר אֲמַאי אִקְרֵי נֵר. אֶלָּא כַּד מְקַבְּלָא מֵבֵּין תְּרֵין דְּרוֹעִין, רמ"ח שַׁיְיפִין עִלָּאִין, אִיהוּ פְּתָחַת לְגַבַּיְיהוּ תְּרֵין דְּרוֹעִין דִּילָהּ, כְּדֵין אִתְכְּלִילוּ אִלֵּין תְּרֵין דְּרוֹעִין בְּהוּ, וְאִקְרֵי נֵר. וְתוֹרָה אוֹר, דְּקָא נָהִיר לְהַהוּא נֵר וְאַדְלִיקַת מִנֵּיהּ מִסִּטְרָא דְּאוֹר קַדְמָאָה, דְּאִיהוּ יְמִינָא. דְּהָא אוֹרַיְיתָא מֵהַהוּא סְטְרָא דְּיְמִינָא דְּאוֹר קַדְמָאָה אִתְיְהִיבַת, דִּכְתִיב מִימִינוֹ אֵשׁ דָּת לָמוֹ, מִסְּטְרָא דְּיְמִינָא אִתְיְהִיבַת, וְאע"ג דְּאִתְכְּלִיל בֵּיהּ שְׂמָאלָא, דְּהָא כְּדֵין אִיהוּ שְׁלִימוּ דְּכֹלָּא.

**737.** HE QUESTIONS: MALCHUT IS CALLED 'candle', but why is She called 'candle'? HE ANSWERS: WHEN MALCHUT receives from between the two arms OF ZEIR ANPIN, WHICH IS THE SECRET OF THE TWO COLUMNS RIGHT AND LEFT, the 248 supernal Limbs, WHICH ARE THE CHASSADIM OF THE 248 POSITIVE PRECEPTS, She opens to them Her two arms, WHICH ARE HER TWO COLUMNS, RIGHT AND LEFT. These two arms become combined WITH THE 248 LIMBS AND BECOME THE NUMERICAL VALUE OF 250 (=*RESH-NUN*). THEREFORE, it is called 'a candle (Heb. *ner*, *Nun-Resh*)'. "And Torah is light" BECAUSE THE TORAH illuminates this candle and THE CANDLE is kindled from the side of the First Light, which is right, because Torah is from the right side, WHICH IS the First Light that was given. About this, it is written: "From His right hand went a fiery law for them" (Devarim 33:2). It is given from the right, even though the left is combined with it, because WHEN THE LEFT IS COMBINED IN IT, there is perfection in everything.

## 75. 207 on the right, 103 on the left

### A Synopsis
The young man from the previous section continues by explaining that the first Light is combined with the 207 worlds hidden on the right under Binah. There are also 103 worlds on the left side, adding to 310 worlds that God prepares constantly for the righteous. The Light of the right is Chesed, and it produces offspring for every single day, otherwise the world would not be able to exist. It is written: "For I have said, the world is built by love."

### The Relevance of this Passage
The Sfirah of Chesed correlates to the Right Column attribute of mercy, which tempers and sweetens judgment. If our world were balanced towards the Left (Judgment). it would be immediately destroyed. Thus, out of Love for his Creation, God injected mercy (Chesed) into the cosmos, which gives a man *time* to repent and change his ways before judgments can be executed. In this moment, we rouse the forces of mercy, using it to atone for our sins, complete our spiritual path, and cause unceasing fulfillment to fill all existence.

738. אוֹר דָּא אִתְכְּלִיל בְּמָאתָן וְשִׁבְעָה עָלְמִין, דְּאִינּוּן גְּנִיזִין בְּסִטְרָא דְּהַהוּא אוֹר, וְאִתְפָּשַׁט בְּכֻלְּהוּ. תְּחוֹת כּוּרְסַיָּיא עִלָּאָה טְמִירָא, שַׁרְיָין אִינּוּן עוֹלָמוֹת, מִסִּטְרָא דְּהַהוּא יְמִינָא. תְּלַת מֵאָה וְעֶשֶׂר אִינּוּן, מָאתָן וְשִׁבְעָ, אִינּוּן בְּסִטְרָא דִּימִינָא. מֵאָה וּתְלַת, אִינּוּן בְּסִטְרָא דִּשְׂמָאלָא. וְאִינּוּן תְּלַת מֵאָה וָעֶשֶׂר. וְאִלֵּין אִינּוּן דְּקוּדְשָׁא בְּרִיךְ הוּא מְתַקֵּן תָּדִיר לְצַדִּיקַיָּא, וּמֵאִלֵּין מִתְפַּשְּׁטָן כַּמָּה וְכַמָּה אוֹצְרֵי חֶמְדָּה, וְכֻלְּהוּ גְּנִיזִין לְאִתְעַדְנָא מִנְהוֹן צַדִּיקַיָּא לְעָלְמָא דְּאָתֵי וְעַל אִלֵּין כְּתִיב לְהַנְחִיל אוֹהֲבַי יֵשׁ וְאוֹצְרוֹתֵיהֶם אֲמַלֵּא וְעַל אִלֵּין כְּתִיב עַיִן לֹא רָאָתָה אֱלֹהִים זוּלָתְךָ וְגוֹ'.

738. This light is combined with the 207 worlds, which are hidden under that light, and it spreads in all of them. Below the concealed supernal Throne, WHICH IS BINAH, these 207 worlds dwell at that right side. There are 310, 207 on the right side and 103 from the left side, and together they equal 310. They are the ones that the Holy One, blessed be He, prepares constantly for the righteous, and from these spread many, many treasures of

delight. They are all hidden for the righteous to delight with in the World to Come. Of this, it is written: "That I may cause those who love me to inherit substance (Heb. *yesh*, Yud-Shin); and I will fill their treasures" (Mishlei 8:21). About all these, it is written: "Neither has the eye seen, (that) an Elohim beside You…" (Yeshayah 64:3).

739. י"ש: אִלֵּין, תְּלַת מֵאָה וַעֲשַׂר עוֹלָמוֹת, גְּנִיזִין תְּחוֹת עָלְמָא דְאָתֵי, אִינוּן מָאתָן וְשֶׁבַע דְּאִינוּן מִסִּטְרָא דְּיְמִינָא, אִקְרוּן אוֹר קַדְמָאָה. בְּגִין דַּאֲפִילוּ אוֹר שְׂמָאלָא אִקְרֵי אוֹר. אֲבָל אוֹר קַדְמָאָה אִיהוּ זַמִּין לְמֶעְבַּד תּוֹלְדִין לְעָלְמָא דְאָתֵי. וְאִי תֵּימָא לְעָלְמָא דְאָתֵי וְלָא יַתִּיר. אֶלָּא אֲפִילוּ בְּכָל יוֹמָא וְיוֹמָא דְּאִי לָא הֲוָה הַאי אוֹר, עָלְמָא לָא יָכִיל לְמֵיקָם, דִּכְתִיב אָמַרְתִּי עוֹלָם חֶסֶד יִבָּנֶה.

**739.** *Yud-Shin* (= 310) are the 310 worlds that are concealed under the World to Come, NAMELY UNDER BINAH. These 207 worlds, which are on the right side, are called 'First Light', because even the light of the left is called 'light', IT IS A DIM LIGHT THAT PRODUCES NO OFFSPRING. SINCE THE LIGHT OF THE RIGHT PRECEDES THE LIGHT OF THE LEFT, THE LIGHT OF THE RIGHT, WHICH IS CHESED, PRECEDES THE LIGHT OF THE LEFT CALLED 'THE FIRST LIGHT'. But the First Light will produce offspring in the World to Come. And if you say that this is true only for the World to Come, WHICH IS BINAH, and no more, yet it produces offspring every single day, MEANING EVEN FOR THE LEVELS OF ZEIR ANPIN THAT IS CALLED 'DAY'. For if this light would not be IN ZEIR ANPIN, then the world, WHICH IS MALCHUT, would not be able to exist, as it is written: "For I have said, the world is built by love (Heb. *chesed*)" (Tehilim 89:3), MEANING WITH THE FIRST LIGHT THAT IS CALLED 'CHESED'.

## 76. "Light is sown" constantly

### A Synopsis

The young man from previous sections continues, telling how God, by the hand of his righteous gardener, sowed light in his Garden of Eden (Malchut) in rows and rows. This act produced fruit that constantly nourishes the world. Even during the time of exile, after the river stopped coming into the Garden of Eden and the gardener no longer entered there, still the Light constantly re-sows itself and produces fruits. Similarly, the Torah is sown constantly in the world, producing offspring and fruit, nourishing the world. The young man adds that "reproofs of instruction" signifies God places over a desired way of life one who smites, thus through suffering people are led to the right way. And once again we hear of the secret of 'keep' and 'remember', and how Malchut and Zeir Anpin need each other for perfection.

### The Relevance of this Passage

What wonderful, sparkling images come before us when the sages speak of God's Gardener dropping seeds of Light into long, soft furrows in the ground, and then of the Light sprouting and bringing forth fruit. Each of our souls is a garden where seeds of Light have been planted since the dawn of creation. The Light of this passage tends the garden, nurturing the Light-seeds so that our souls now blossom like a blooming orchard of fruit trees on a sun-drenched summer's day.

740. הַאי אוֹר זָרַע לֵיהּ קוּדְשָׁא בְּרִיךְ הוּא בְּגִנְתָּא דְּעֶדְנוֹי, וְעָבִיד לֵיהּ שׁוּרִין שׁוּרִין, עַל יְדוֹי דְּהַאי צַדִּיק, דְּאִיהוּ גַּנָּנָא דְּגִנְתָּא, וְנָטִיל לְהַאי אוֹר, וְזָרַע לֵיהּ זְרוּעָא דִּקְשׁוֹט. וְעָבִיד לֵיהּ שׁוּרִין בְּגִנְתָּא וְאוֹלִיד וְאַצְמַח וְעָבִיד פֵּרִין, וּמִנַּיְיהוּ אִתְזַן עָלְמָא, הה"ד אוֹר זָרוּעַ לַצַּדִּיק וְגוֹ'.

740. The Holy One, blessed be He, sowed this light in His Garden of Eden, WHICH IS MALCHUT, and formed it in rows, MEANING THAT HE DIVIDED IT ACCORDING TO THE COLUMNS, by the hand of this righteous, who is the gardener of the Garden, who took this light and sowed it a true seed. And He formed it in rows in the Garden of Eden, WHICH IS MALCHUT. It sprouted and produced fruit, and from there is the world nourished. This is what is meant by: "Light is sown for the righteous" (Tehilim 97:11).

741. וּכְתִיב וּכְגַנָּה זֵרוּעֶיהָ תַצְמִיחַ. מַאן זֵרוּעֶיהָ. אִלֵּין זְרוּעֵי דְאוֹר

קַדְמָאָה, דְּאִיהוּ זָרוּעַ תָּדִיר, הַשְׁתָּא אוֹלִיד וְעָבִיד אֵיבִין, וְהַשְׁתָּא זָרוּעַ
אִיהוּ, בְּקַדְמֵיתָא, עַד לָא יֵיכוּל עָלְמָא אִיבָּא דָא, אוֹלִיד זְרוּעָה דָא
וְיָהִיב אִיבָּא וְלָא שָׁכִיךְ. וְעַל דָּא, כָּל עָלְמִין אִתְזָנוּ בְּסִפּוּקָא דְּהַהוּא
גִּנְּתָא, דְּאִקְרֵי צַדִּיק, דְּלָא שָׁכִיךְ וְלָא פָּסִיק לְעָלְמִין.

**741.** It is written: "And as a garden causes the things that are sown in it to spring forth" (Yeshayah 61:11). HE QUESTIONS: What are "the things that are sown in it?" HE ANSWERS: These are the things that were sown by the First Light, which is sown constantly. Now it bears and produces fruits, and now it is again sown as before, before the world eats up this fruit that this plant produces, so we find that it produces fruit incessantly. Therefore, the world is fed by the supply of that Garden, which is called 'Righteous', NAMELY YESOD OF ZEIR ANPIN, that neither rests nor pauses forever.

**742.** בַּר בְּזִמְנָא דְּיִשְׂרָאֵל בְּגָלוּתָא. וְאִי תֵּימָא בְּזִמְנָא דְּגָלוּתָא כְּתִיב,
אָזְלוּ מַיִם מִנִּי יָם וְנָהָר יֶחֱרַב וְיָבֵשׁ, הֵיךְ עָבֵיד תּוֹלְדִין. אֶלָּא כְּתִיב
זָרוּעַ, זָרוּעַ אִיהוּ תָּדִיר, וּמִיּוֹמָא דְּאַפְסִיק הַהוּא נָהָר. בְּגִנְּתָא לָא עָאל
בֵּיהּ הַהוּא גַּנָּנָא. וְהַהוּא אוֹר דְּאִיהוּ זָרוּעַ תָּדִיר, עָבֵיד אֵיבִין וּמִנֵּיהּ
וּמִגַּרְמֵיהּ אִזְדְּרַע כְּקַדְמֵיתָא, וְלָא שָׁכִיךְ תָּדִיר. בְּגִנְּתָא דְּעָבֵיד תּוֹלְדִין,
וּמֵהַהוּא זָרוּעַ נָפִיל בֵּיהּ בְּאַתְרֵיהּ, וּמִגַּרְמֵיהּ עָבֵיד תּוֹלְדִין
כְּדִבְקַדְמֵיתָא. וְאִי תֵּימָא, דְּאִינּוּן תּוֹלְדִין וְאֵיבִין הֲווֹ כְּמָה דַּהֲוָה בְּזִמְנָא
דְּגִנְּתָא תַּמָּן. לָאו הָכִי. אֲבָל לָא אִתְמָנַע זָרוּעַ דָּא לְעָלְמִין.

**742.** Except during the time that the children of Yisrael are in exile. If you ask: During the time of exile, it is said, "The waters fail from the sea" (Iyov 14:11), WHICH IS MALCHUT THAT IS CALLED 'SEA' and the river is parched, and dries up" (Ibid.) WHICH IS YESOD THAT IS CALLED 'A RIVER' THAT EMERGES FROM EDEN. IF SO, how can it produce offspring? HE ANSWERS: But it is written "is sown", WHICH MEANS that constantly it is sown, EVEN DURING THE TIME OF EXILE. From the day that that river stopped coming into the Garden of Eden, WHICH IS YESOD THAT IS CALLED 'GARDENER', that gardener no longer entered there. That light that is constantly being sown produces fruits, because from it and by itself it is sown as before, and it never ceases. THIS IS LIKE a garden that produces

offspring, and from its PREVIOUS planting it falls back to its place, MEANING THAT DURING THE HARVESTING OF THE FIELD, SEEDS FALL TO THE GROUND, and produce offspring by itself, as before. If you remark that the offspring and the fruits are the same as when that gardener was there, it is not so. Yet this sowing is never interrupted.

743. כְּגַוְונָא דָא וְתוֹרָה אוֹר, אוֹרַיְיתָא דְּאִתְיְיהִיבַת מִסְטְרָא דְּהַהוּא אוֹר קַדְמָאָה, הָכִי אִזְדְרַע תָּדִיר בְּעָלְמָא, וְעָבִיד תּוֹלְדִין וְאֵיבִין, וְלָא שָׁכִיךְ לְעָלְמִין, וּמֵהַהוּא אִיבָא דִּילֵיה אִתְזָן עָלְמָא.

743. Similarly, "And Torah is light" (Mishlei 6:23). The Torah was given from the side of that First Light and so is it sown constantly in the world, producing offspring and fruits. It never stops, and from its fruit the world is nourished.

744. וְדֶרֶךְ חַיִּים תּוֹכְחוֹת מוּסָר. תְּרֵין אָרְחִין אִינּוּן, חַד אֹרַח חַיִּים, וְחַד בְּהִפּוּכָא מִנֵּיהּ. סִימָנָא דְּאֹרַח חַיִּים מַאן אִיהוּ. תּוֹכְחוֹת מוּסָר. דְּכַד בָּעָא קוּדְשָׁא בְּרִיךְ הוּא לְנַטְרָא לְהַאי אֹרַח חַיִּים, שַׁוֵּי עָלֵיהּ הַהוּא דְּאַלְקֵי, וְעָבֵיד תּוֹכְחוֹת מוּסָר לִבְנֵי עָלְמָא. וּמַאן אִיהוּ. הַאי דִּכְתִּיב וְאֶת לַהַט הַחֶרֶב הַמִּתְהַפֶּכֶת לִשְׁמֹר אֶת דֶּרֶךְ עֵץ הַחַיִּים וְעַל דָּא, דֶּרֶךְ חַיִּים אִיהוּ תּוֹכְחוֹת מוּסָר. וּמַאן דְּאִית בֵּיהּ תּוֹכָחוֹת, וַדַּאי דְּמִתְעָרֵי לֵיהּ לְמֵהַךְ בְּהַהוּא אֹרַח חַיִּים, דְּשָׁארֵי תַּמָּן תּוֹכְחוֹת מוּסָר.

744. "And reproofs of instruction are the way of life" (Mishlei 6:23). There are two ways, one is the way of life and one is the opposite of it. What is the sign of the way of life? It is "reproofs of instruction," for when the Holy One, blessed be He, wishes to guard the way of life, He places over it one who smites and makes reproofs of instruction for the people of the world. Who is he? He is that of which is written: "And the bright blade of a revolving sword to guard the way to the Tree of Life" (Beresheet 3:24). Therefore, "reproofs of instruction are the way of life," for one who receives reproof, MEANING SUFFERINGS, is surely awakened to walk that way of life, for there dwell reproofs of instruction.

745. הַאי קְרָא לָאו רֵישֵׁיהּ סֵיפֵיהּ וְלָאו סֵיפֵיהּ רֵישֵׁיהּ. אֶלָּא כֹּלָּא רָזָא

דִּמְהֵימְנוּתָא דְּהַאי קְרָא. כִּי נֵר מִצְוָה, דָּא רָזָא דְּשָׁמוֹר. וְתוֹרָה אוֹר,
דָּא רָזָא דְּזָכוֹר, וְדֶרֶךְ חַיִּים תּוֹכְחוֹת מוּסָר, אִלֵּין גְּזִרִין וְעוֹנָשִׁין
דְּאוֹרַיְיתָא, וְכֹלָּא רָזָא דִּמְהֵימְנוּתָא. וְאִצְטְרִיךְ דָּא לְדָא, וּלְמֶהֱוֵי רָזָא
דְּכֹלָּא כַּדְקָא יָאוֹת.

745. The verse, "FOR THE COMMANDMENT IS A CANDLE...": Its beginning is not like its end and its end is not like its beginning, BECAUSE IT STARTS WITH THE LIGHT OF TORAH AND PRECEPTS AND ENDS WITH REPROOFS OF INSTRUCTION. HE ANSWERS: All that is in this verse pertains to the secret of the Faith, WHICH IS THE SECRET OF MALCHUT. "For the commandment is a candle" is the secret of 'keep', WHICH IS MALCHUT, and "Torah is light" is the secret of 'remember', WHICH IS ZEIR ANPIN. "And reproofs of instruction are the way of life": These are the decrees and punishments in the Torah. It is all the secret of the Faith, NAMELY FOR THE PERFECTION OF MALCHUT, and they need each other so that the secret of it all is well established.

## 77. Light, Water, Firmament

### A Synopsis

The young man continues, discussing the Light from the right, namely Chesed, the aspect of Aaron the Priest, and Light from the left, which two were only joined together and perfected when Elohim divided the Light from the darkness. We learn that by the Left Column the evil inclination emerges. Next we read of how the five levels Chesed, Gvurah, Tiferet, Netzach and Hod were in Light, in water and in firmament, each of which was therefore mentioned five times. By these three was the secret of Adam formed and made into engravings, which were Light from the Right Column, water from the Left Column, and the firmament from the Central Column. This is similar to the form of man at birth: he is first seed, which is the Light of all the limbs of the body; the Light spreads and becomes water, after which the form of the body spreads into these waters; as soon as the form and shape of the body is formed and engraved, that expansion consolidates and is called 'firmament'. After it congeals, it is written: "And Elohim called the firmament heaven." Next, we are told, after the body was purified and cleansed, the moisture that was drawn and left over from it comprised the bad and troubled waters from which were formed the male and female of the Other Side. As soon as the inciter emerged, the curse emerged into the world, and the Light of the moon was decreased. The youth then explains the emergence of the first Adam, Zeir Anpin in Atzilut, who was formed without a female; the second Adam, the man of Briyah, was formed and engraved from the seed of the first Adam within the female, Malchut of Atzilut. The 22 letters from Aleph to Zayin emerged from the first Light, and the body of the first Adam was formed and engraved in them. The youth tells of the measure in the firmament and the joining of the letters of the first Light with the waters and the congealing of the two columns. And then, we learn, this first Adam joined with the Nukva to beget a second Adam of Briya.

### The Relevance of this Passage

Because the verses speak of the mighty gestation of Light, water and the firmament, and of the Three Columns, our personal attributes of judgment (Left), compassion (Right), and self-restraint (Central) are strengthened and balanced in the appropriate measure. If we can possibly extend mercy to our most undeserving of enemies, judgment cannot befall us. But how many of us, in truth, have the capability and willpower to offer mercy to our most mean-spirited of foes?

The sacred words adorning this passage awaken such mercy within us. As we now offer forbearance and compassion to others, these qualities

are returned to us in equal measure. Additionally, we attain dominion over our Evil Inclination (Left Column) and connect ourselves to the embryonic state of Creation, when all was pure and free of sin. This cleanses our soul and completes our life's purpose.

746. וְעַל רָזָא דָּא דְּהַאי אוֹר, דְּדָלִיק וְנָהִיר לְהַאי נֵר, כְּתִיב בֵּיה בְּאַהֲרֹן, בְּהַעֲלוֹתְךָ אֶת הַנֵּרוֹת, בְּגִין דְּהוּא אָתֵי מִסְּטְרָא דְּהַאי אוֹר. אוֹר דָּא כְּתִיב בֵּיה, יְהִי אוֹר וַיְהִי אוֹר. כֵּיוָן דְּאָמַר יְהִי אוֹר, אֲמַאי כְּתִיב וַיְהִי אוֹר, דְּהָא בְּוַיְהִי כֵן סַגְיָא. אֶלָּא, יְהִי אוֹר, דָּא אוֹר קַדְמָאָה, דְּאִיהוּ יְמִינָא, וְאִיהוּ לְקֵץ הַיָּמִין. וַיְהִי אוֹר, דְּמִימִינָא נָפְק שְׂמָאלָא, וּמֵרָזָא דִּימִינָא נָפְק שְׂמָאלָא, וְע"ד וַיְהִי אוֹר, דָּא שְׂמָאלָא.

**746.** In relation to the secret of that light that kindles and illuminates this candle, WHICH IS MALCHUT, it is written of Aaron: "When you light the lamps" (Bemidbar 8:2). It comes from the side of that light, about which is written: "'Let there be light', and there was light" (Beresheet 1:3). HE QUESTIONS: Once it is written, "Let there be light," why is it necessary to add, "And there was light?" It would have been sufficient to say, "And it was so." HE ANSWERS: "Let there be light" is the First Light which is right (Heb. *yamin*), NAMELY CHESED THE ASPECT OF AARON THE PRIEST. This is "the end of days (Heb. *yamin*)." "And there was light" is the left that emerges from the right, because the left emerges from the secret of the right. Therefore, "and there was light" refers to the left.

747. מִכָּאן דְּוַיְהִי קַדְמָאָה דְּאוֹרַיְיתָא, בְּסִטְרָא דִּשְׂמָאלָא הֲוָה. וּבְגִין כָּךְ לָאו אִיהוּ סִימָן בְּרָכָה. מ"ט. בְּגִין דְּבֵיה נָפַק הַהוּא חֹשֶׁךְ דְּאַחֲשִׁיךְ אַנְפֵּי עָלְמָא. וְסִימָנָא דָּא כַּד אִתְגְּלֵי רָזָא דְּעֶשָׂו וְעוֹבְדוֹי, בְּהַאי וַיְהִי הֲוָה, דִּכְתִיב וַיְהִי עֵשָׂו אִישׁ יֹדֵעַ צַיִד. אִתְקַיָּים בְּוַיְהִי אִישׁ יֹדֵעַ צַיִד, לְפַתָּאָה בְּנֵי עָלְמָא, דְּלָא יַהֲכוּן בְּאֹרַח מֵישָׁר.

**747.** From here IS UNDERSTOOD that: "And it came to pass (Heb. *vayehi*)" that is mentioned in the Torah is of the left side. Therefore, 'vayehi' is not a sign of blessing. What is the reason? It is because by THE LEFT COLUMN emerges that darkness that darkened the face of the world, WHICH IS THE ANGEL OF DEATH, THE EVIL INCLINATION. This is how we come by it:

when the secret of Esau and his actions were revealed, it was done so by 'vayehi' as it is written, "And (Heb. *vayehi*) Esau was a cunning hunter" (Beresheet 25:27). And by 'vayehi' it was fulfilled "a cunning hunter" who knew how to entice hearts, to seduce people of the world, and not to go in the straight path.

748. וַיַּרְא אֱלֹהִים אֶת הָאוֹר כִּי טוֹב, דָּא אִיהוּ עַמּוּדָא דְּקָאֵים בְּאֶמְצָעִיתָא, וְקָאֵים וְאָחִיד בְּסִטְרָא דָּא, וּבְסִטְרָא דָּא. כַּד הֲוָה שְׁלִימוּ דִּתְלַת סִטְרִין, כְּתִיב בֵּיהּ כִּי טוֹב, מָה דְּלָא הֲוָה בְּהָנֵי אַחֲרָנִין, בְּגִין דְּלָא הֲוָה שְׁלִימוּ עַד אוֹר תְּלִיתָאָה, דְּאַשְׁלִים לְכָל סִטְרִין, וְכֵיוָן דְּאָתָא תְּלִיתָאָה דָּא, כְּדֵין אַפְרִישׁ מַחֲלוֹקֶת דִּימִינָא וּשְׂמָאלָא, דִּכְתִיב וַיַּבְדֵּל אֱלֹהִים בֵּין הָאוֹר וּבֵין הַחֹשֶׁךְ.

**748.** "And Elohim saw the light, that it was good" (Beresheet 1:4). This is the pillar that stands in the center, MEANING THE CENTRAL COLUMN, that stands and is attached to this side and that side, FOR IT MEDIATES AND UNITES RIGHT AND LEFT WITH EACH OTHER. When perfection of these sides was affected, NAMELY THREE COLUMNS, it IS WRITTEN "that it was good." This did not happen with the other TWO COLUMNS, RIGHT AND LEFT, THAT ARE ALLUDED TO IN "LET THERE BE LIGHT" AND "AND THERE WAS LIGHT," AND IT IS NOT SAID BY THEM. "AND IT WAS GOOD" because there was no perfection until the third light OF THE CENTRAL COLUMN that completed all the sides. Once this third came, the division of right and left was enunciated, as it is written: "And Elohim divided the light from the darkness" (Ibid.), FOR THE RIGHT IS THE SECRET OF LIGHT AND THE LEFT IS THE SECRET OF DARKNESS. THE CENTRAL COLUMN MADE PEACE BETWEEN THEM AND THEY WERE INCLUDED, THE ONE WITH THE OTHER, FOR THROUGH THIS THEY WERE BOTH PERFECTED.

749. וְעַל דְּאִינּוּן חָמֵשׁ דַּרְגִּין, דְּאִתְפָּרְשׁוּ וְאִתְמְשָׁכוּ מֵהַאי אוֹר קַדְמָאָה, כְּתִיב אוֹר חָמֵשׁ זִמְנִין, וְכֻלְּהוּ הֲווֹ מִסִּטְרָא דִּימִינָא, וְאִתְכְּלִילוּ בֵּיהּ, וְכַד אִתְכְּלִילוּ בְּסִטַר שְׂמָאלָא, אִתְכְּלִילוּ בְּרָזָא דְּמַיִם, דְּנָטִיל מִימִינָא, וּבְגִין כַּךְ כְּתִיב מַיִם חָמֵשׁ זִמְנִין. וְכַד אִשְׁתְּלִימוּ בְּרָזָא דְּאֶמְצָעִיתָא, כְּתִיב רָקִיעַ חָמֵשׁ זִמְנִין, וְעַ"ד תְּלַת אִינּוּן אוֹר. מַיִם.

רְקִיעַ. לָקֳבֵל תְּלַת דַּרְגִּין אִלֵּין, דְּכֻלְּהוּ חָמֵשׁ דַּרְגִּין אִתְכְּלִילוּ בְּהוּ, וְעַל דָּא בְּכֻלְּהוּ כְּתִיב חָמֵשׁ זִמְנִין, בְּכָל חַד וְחַד.

**749.** Because they were five levels that separated and were drawn from this First Light, THAT ARE CHESED, GVURAH, TIFERET NETZACH AND HOD, 'light' is therefore mentioned IN THE FIRST DAY five times. They were all from the right side, FOR ALL THE FIVE SFIROT, CHESED, GVURAH, TIFERET, NETZACH AND HOD, ARE UNDER THE DOMINATION OF THE RIGHT, WHICH IS CHESED. When they were combined in the left side, they were combined in the secret of waters that flow from the right, BECAUSE THE RIGHT MELTS THE FROZENNESS OF THE LEFT AND TURNS IT INTO FLOWING WATERS. Therefore, water was mentioned BY THE SECOND DAY OF CREATION, WHICH IS LEFT, five times, CORRESPONDING TO CHESED, GVURAH, TIFERET, NETZACH AND HOD OF THE LEFT COLUMN. When RIGHT AND LEFT were perfected in the secret of the Central COLUMN, CALLED 'FIRMAMENT', "firmament" was mentioned five times, CORRESPONDING TO CHESED, GVURAH, TIFERET, NETZACH AND HOD OF THE CENTRAL COLUMN. Therefore, these three, light, water, firmament, correspond to these three levels, RIGHT, LEFT, AND CENTRAL, for in each one of them are comprehended the five levels, CHESED, GVURAH, TIFERET, NETZACH AND HOD. Therefore, they are all mentioned five times each; NAMELY LIGHT, WATER, AND FIRMAMENT.

750. הָכָא רָזָא דְּרָזִין, בְּאִלֵּין תְּלָתָא, אִתְצַיַּיר וְאִתְגְּלִיף בְּגִלּוּפֵי רָזָא דְּיוּקְנָא דְּאָדָם, דְּאִיהוּ אוֹר בְּקַדְמֵיתָא, לְבָתַר מַיִם, לְבָתַר אִתְפָּשַׁט בְּגַוַּוְויְיהוּ רָקִיעַ, דְּאִיהוּ גְּלִיפָא דְּגְלִיפוּ דְּיוּקְנָא דְּאָדָם.

**750.** Here lies the mystery of mysteries: By these three, light, water, firmament , the secret of the form of man was formed and made into engravings, which was light at first FROM THE RIGHT COLUMN, and afterwards water FROM THE LEFT COLUMN. Afterwards, THE CENTRAL COLUMN spread among them, which is the firmament, which is the engraving of the imprint of the form of man.

751. כְּגַוְונָא דְּגְלִיפוּ צִיּוּרָא דְּדִיּוּקְנָא דְּאָדָם בְּתוֹלַדְתֵּיהּ. דְּהָא בְּתוֹלַדְתָּא דְּבַר נָשׁ, בְּקַדְמֵיתָא זֶרַע, דְּאִיהוּ אוֹר, דְּהָא נְהִירוּ דְּכָל

שַׁיְיפֵי גוּפָא, אִיהוּ הַהוּא זֶרַע, וּבְגִין כַּךְ אִיהוּ אוֹר, וְהַהוּא אוֹר אִקְרֵי
זֶרַע, דִּכְתִיב אוֹר זָרוּעַ, הַהוּא זֶרַע מַמָּשׁ. לְבָתַר הַהוּא זֶרַע דְּאִיהוּ אוֹר
אִתְפָּשַׁט וְאִתְעָבֵיד מַיִם, בַּלְחוּתָא דִּילֵיהּ, אַגְלִיף יַתִּיר, וְאִתְפָּשַׁט
פְּשִׁיטוּ גוֹ אִינוּן מַיִם, פְּשִׁיטוּ דְּגוּפָא לְכָל סִטְרִין. כֵּיוָן דְּאִתְצַיָּיר,
וְאִגְלִיף צִיּוּרָא וּדְיוּקְנָא דְּגוּפָא, אַקְרִישׁ הַהוּא פְּשִׁיטוּ, וְאִקְרֵי רְקִיעַ.
וְדָא אִיהוּ רָקִיעַ בְּתוֹךְ הַמַּיִם. וּלְבָתַר דְּאַקְרִישׁ, כְּתִיב וַיִּקְרָא אֱלֹהִים
לָרָקִיעַ שָׁמָיִם. דְּהָא אַקְרִישׁ הַהוּא לְחוּתָא דְּגוּפָא, דַּהֲוָה גוֹ אִינוּן מַיִם.

**751.** AND IT IS SIMILAR to the engraving of the form of man when born. At the birth of a person, he is first seed, which is light, for that seed is the light of all the limbs of the body; therefore, it is light. That light is called 'seed', as written: "Light is sown" (Tehilim 97:11), namely that actual seed. Afterwards, that seed that is called 'light' spreads and becomes water. By the moisture of the water, it becomes further engraved and the form of the body expands into these waters, growing to all sides. As soon as the form and shape of the body is formed and engraved, that expansion consolidates and is called 'firmament'. That is "a firmament in the midst of the waters" (Beresheet 1:6) and, after it congeals, it is written: "And Elohim called the firmament heaven" (Ibid. 8), because the moisture of the body that was in the water has congealed.

752. כֵּיוָן דְּאִבְרִיר גוּפָא, וְאִנָּקֵי בִּנְקִיּוּ, הַהוּא לְחוּתָא דְּאִתְנְגִיד
וְאִשְׁתְּאַר, הֲוָה פְּסוֹלֶת דְּקָא אִתְעֲבַד גּוֹ הַתּוּכָא, וְאִינוּן מַיִם הָרָעִים
עֲכוּרִין, וּמִנַּיְיהוֹן אִתְעָבֵיד פְּסוֹלֶת, מְקַטְרְגָא לְכָל עָלְמָא, דְּכַר וְנוּקְבָּא.
לְבָתַר כַּד נַחֲתוּ אִינוּן מַיִם עֲכוּרִין, וְאִתְהַתְּכוּ לְתַתָּא בְּסִטַר שְׂמָאלָא,
נָפְקוּ לְקַטְרְגָא כָּל עָלְמָא. זַכָּאָה אִיהוּ מַאן דְּאִשְׁתְּזִיב מִנַּיְיהוֹן.

**752.** As soon as the body is purified and has been cleansed, the moisture that was drawn and left over from it is the refuse that is made by melting. This is the bad and troubled waters, from which is formed the refuse that incites the whole world, NAMELY THE OTHER SIDE, AND male and female WERE FORMED. When the troubled waters flow down and melt on the left side, THE MALE AND FEMALE OF THE OTHER SIDE emerge to instigate the whole world. Fortunate is he who is saved from them.

753. כֵּיוָן דְּנָפִיק מְקַטְרְגָא, כְּתִיב יְהִי מְאֹרֹת חָסֵר ו' וְאִתְמַשְׁכָא אִסְכְּרָה בְּרַבְיֵי, וְחָסֵר נְהוֹרָא דְּסִיהֲרָא. לְבָתַר וְהָיוּ לִמְאוֹרֹת, בִּשְׁלִימוּ תַּרְוַוְיְיהוּ כַּחֲדָא. בְּמַאן. בְּהַהוּא רְקִיעַ הַשָּׁמַיִם, דְּהָא כַּד סַלְקָא וְאִתְחַבְּרָא בְּהַהוּא רְקִיעַ הַשָּׁמַיִם, כְּדֵין וְהָיוּ לִמְאוֹרֹת, נְהוֹרִין שְׁלֵימִין תַּרְוַוְיְיהוּ כַּחֲדָא דְּלָא פְּגִימֵי כְּלַל.

753. As soon as the inciter has emerged, it is written: "Let there be lights (Heb. *meorot*)" (Beresheet 1:14) without *Vav*, WHICH IS AN EXPRESSION OF DESTRUCTION AND CURSE (HEB. *ME'EROT*), through which the sickness of croup is drawn to children. The light of the moon was decreased. Afterwards, IT IS WRITTEN: "And let them be for lights (Heb. *me'orot* with *Vav*)" (Ibid. 15), meaning completely both together. How WERE THEY COMPLETED? By the firmament of that heaven, WHICH IS THE CENTRAL COLUMN, WHICH IS TIFERET OF ZEIR ANPIN. When MALCHUT ascended and was attached to the firmament of heaven, then "let them be for lights" for both together were perfect luminaries, entirely unblemished. BECAUSE ZEIR ANPIN, WHICH IS THE SECRET OF THE SUN AND RIGHT COLUMN, AND MALCHUT, WHICH IS THE SECRET OF THE MOON AND THE LEFT COLUMN, COMBINED AND BECAME COMPLETED BY EACH OTHER THROUGH THE CENTRAL COLUMN, WHICH IS TIFERET OF ZEIR ANPIN.

754. שָׁארֵי חַיִּיךְ הַאי רַבְיָא וְחַדֵּי. אָמַר לוֹן הַאי דַּאֲמֵינָא דְּאִתְבְּרִיר הָכָא רָזָא דְּאָדָם, בְּאוֹר דְּאִיהוּ זֶרַע, וּלְבָתַר אִתְעֲבֵיד מַיִם, וּמִגּוֹ אִינּוּן מַיִם, אִתְפָּשַׁט רְקִיעַ, דִּיּוּקְנָא דְּאָדָם כְּמָה דְּאִתְעָרְנָא. תֵּינַח כַּד אִתְעֲבֵיד דָּא לְגוֹ מֵעוֹי דְּאִתְּתָא, דְּהָא לָא אִתְצַיָּיר זַרְעָא, אֶלָּא בְּגוֹ מֵעוֹי דְּנוּקְבָּא, לְאִתְפָּשְׁטָא בָּהּ דִּיּוּקְנָא דְּאָדָם, וְהָכָא אִי אִלֵּין חָמֵשׁ דַּרְגִּין, אִינּוּן דִּיּוּקְנָא דְּאָדָם, בְּאָן אֲתַר אִתְצַיָּיר וְאִתְפָּשַׁט הַאי דִּיּוּקְנָא, בְּגוֹ אִינּוּן מַיִם.

754. That youth started to laugh and rejoiced. He said to them: That which I said is that here was purified the secret of man through the light that is seed. Then it becomes water, and from this water expands the firmament, which is the form of man. As I commented, this is correct when it is done in the belly of a women, because the seed forms only in the belly of a female for the

form of man to grow in her. Here are these five levels, CHESED, GVURAH, TIFERET, NETZACH, HOD AND YESOD OF LIGHT, WATER, AND FIRMAMENT, which are the image of man. According to this, in which place was formed and expanded this form in the water?

755. אִי תֵּימָא גּוֹ נוּקְבָּא הֲוֹו דָּא עָלְמָא דְּאָתֵי, לָאו הָכִי, דְּהָא לָא אִתְצָיַּיר צִיּוּרָא וְדִיוּקְנָא, עַד דְּנַפְקוּ אַתְוָון לְבַר, וּלְבָתַר אִתְגְּלִימוּ. וְתוּ דְּהָא עָלְמָא דְּאָתֵי הֲוָה אוּמָּנָא, דִּכְתִּיב וַיֹּאמֶר אֱלֹהִים יְהִי אוֹר וַיְהִי אוֹר. וַיֹּאמֶר אֱלֹהִים יְהִי רָקִיעַ, הָא אוּמָּנָא הֲוָה.

755. If you say that it was formed in a female, which is the World to Come, NAMELY BINAH, it is not so. Because proper form and image are not formed until they emerged FROM BINAH and afterwards they were formed and consolidated. The World to Come, WHICH IS BINAH, is also the craftsman OF ALL THE CREATION AND IS THE SECRET OF ELOHIM THAT IS MENTIONED THERE, as it is written: "And Elohim said, 'Let there be light,' and there was light" AND ALSO, "And Elohim said, 'Let there be a firmament.'" So BINAH is the craftsman, THE ONE WHO FORMS, THAT MAKES THE SHAPE OF LIGHT, WATER, AND FIRMAMENT, SO HOW CAN YOU SAY THAT THE SHAPE AND FORM ARE MADE IN BINAH?

756. אִי תֵּימָא בְּנוּקְבָּא דִּלְתַתָּא, לָאו הָכִי, דְּהָא עַד לָא הֲוֹת, וְכַד נָפַק הַאי דִּיוּקְנָא דְּאָדָם, נוּקְבֵיה נַפְקַת בַּהֲדֵיה. הָא לָא אִתְצָיַּיר דִּיוּקְנָא דְּאָדָם בָּהּ. אִי הָכִי, בְּאָן אֲתַר אִתְצָיַּיר וְאִתְגְּלִיף הַאי זֶרַע, לְמֶהֱוֵי גְּלִיפוּ דִּיוּקְנָא דְּאָדָם.

756. If you say that THE FIGURE OF MAN WAS FORMED in the lower female, NAMELY MALCHUT, it is not so. MALCHUT was not yet in existence BECAUSE AFTERWARDS, when this figure of man emerged THAT IS IN LIGHT, WATER, FIRMAMENT, WHICH IS ZEIR ANPIN, the woman emerged with him, so the figure of man was not formed in her. If so, in which place was formed and engraved that seed OF LIGHT, WATER, FIRMAMENT, to become an engraving of the shape of man?

757. אֶלָּא דָּא רָזָא עִלָּאָה, אָדָם קַדְמָאָה אִתְצָיַּיר וְאִתְגְּלִיף בְּלָא

נוּקְבָּא. אָדָם תִּנְיָינָא, מֵחֵילָא וְזַרְעָא דְּהַאי, אַגְלִיף וְאִתְצַיַיר גּוֹ נוּקְבָּא.

**757.** HE ANSWERS: This is a supernal secret. The first man, NAMELY ZEIR ANPIN OF ATZILUT, WHICH IS THE SECRET OF LIGHT, WATER, FIRMAMENT, was engraved and formed without a woman. The second man, NAMELY THE MAN OF BRIYAH, from the strength and seed of THE FIRST MAN was engraved and formed within the woman, WHICH IS MALCHUT OF ATZILUT.

**758.** אָדָם קַדְמָאָה, גְּלִיפוּ דְּצִיּוּרָא וּדְיוּקְנָא דְּגוּפָא, לָא הֲוָה בְּנוּקְבָּא, וּבְלָא צִיּוּרָא כְּלָל הֲוָה. וְאִתְצַיַיר וְאִגְלִיף לְתַתָּא מֵעָלְמָא דְּאָתֵי, בְּלָא דְּכוּרָא, וּבְלָא נוּקְבָּא, אִינּוּן אַתְוָון אַגְלִימוּ גּוֹ מְשִׁחָתָא, וְאִתְצַיַיר וְאִגְלִיף בְּהוּ רָזָא דְּאָדָם. וְאַתְוָון בְּאֹרַח מֵישָׁר, בְּסִדּוּרָא דִּלְהוֹן, מֵרָזָא דְּאוֹר קַדְמָאָה, שָׁרִיאוּ לְאִתְגַּלְפָא וּלְאִתְצַיְּירָא, וְאִזְדְּרַע הַאי אוֹר בְּגַוֵּיהּ גּוֹ מְשִׁחָתָא. כַּד מָטָא גּוֹ מְשִׁחָתָא, אִתְהַדָּר מַיָּא, גּוֹ מַיָּא, אִתְפָּשַׁט רָקִיעַ צִיּוּרָא דְּאָדָם, דְּיוּקְנָא כִּדְקָא חֲזִי.

**758.** THE ZOHAR EXPLAINS HIS WORDS. The engraving of the form and shape of the body of the first man, WHO IS ZEIR ANPIN, was not in the woman, and was entirely without form, MEANING THAT HE DID NOT FORM AND CONSOLIDATE WHILE STILL IN BINAH TO A DEGREE THAT HE COULD BE CONSIDERED 'A FORM'. He was formed and engraved below the World to Come, NAMELY BELOW BINAH without Male and without Female. Only these letters, NAMELY THE 22 LETTERS OF ZEIR ANPIN THAT ARE DIVIDED INTO THREE COLUMNS were embodied and consolidated in measure, WHICH IS CALLED 'FIRMAMENT', FOR IT WAS THE CAUSE OF THE CONGEALMENT OF THE LETTERS. The secret of man was formed and engraved in them. And the letters in straightforward order, in the order they emerged from the First Light THAT WAS IN BINAH, WHICH IS THE SECRET OF SEVEN LETTERS FROM *ALEPH* TO *ZAYIN* WHICH IS THE SECRET OF THE RIGHT COLUMN, WERE DRAWN TO THE MEASURE IN THE FIRMAMENT. And they commenced to be engraved and formed. This light was sown IN THE FIRMAMENT, WHICH IS ZEIR ANPIN, in the measure. After THE LIGHT, WHICH IS THE RIGHT COLUMN, reached the measure, THE LEFT COLUMN WAS DRAWN INTO IT. AND THERE THE LIGHT

REVERTED to water in the waters. AFTERWARDS, the firmament expanded, WHICH IS THE ACTUAL CENTRAL COLUMN, BY STRENGTH OF THE TWO COLUMNS THAT ILLUMINATED AND WERE INCLUDED IN IT, properly into the form of man, MEANING THAT IT BECAME EMBODIED AND CONGEALED AS MUCH AS NECESSARY. FOR THE TWO COLUMNS, RIGHT AND LEFT WERE CONSOLIDATED.

759. לְבָתַר דְּאִתְקַשְׁטַת נוּקְבָּא לְגַבֵּיה, וְאִתְהַדְרוּ אַנְפִּין בְּאַנְפִּין, הַאי דִּיּוּקְנָא דְּאָדָם, עָאל בְּתִיאוּבְתָּא לְגַבֵּי נוּקְבָּא, וְתַמָּן אַגְלִיף וְאִתְצָיָיר כְּגַוְונָא דִּילֵיה, וְעָלֵיה כְּתִיב וַיּוֹלֶד בִּדְמוּתוֹ כְּצַלְמוֹ וְגוֹ', הַאי אִתְצַיָיר גּוֹ נוּקְבָּא, מַה דְּלָא הֲוָה הַהוּא קַדְמָאָה, דְּאִתְצַיָיר הַהוּא קַדְמָאָה בְּגַוֵּיה בִּמְדִידוּ גּוֹ מְשִׁחָתָא כְּמָה דְּאִתְּמַר.

759. After the Nukva was adorned, MEANING THAT SHE WAS CONSTRUCTED BY ABA AND IMA, and ZEIR ANPIN AND NUKVA were again face to face, this form of man, WHICH IS ZEIR ANPIN, came with the longing to Nukva. There IN NUKVA became engraved and formed THE SECOND MAN OF BRIYAH according to his form. About him, it is written: "And he begot a son in his own likeness, after his image…" (Beresheet 5:3), BECAUSE THE FIRST MAN BELOW CORRESPONDS TO ZEIR ANPIN AND THE SECOND MAN, NAMELY HIS SON, SETH, CORRESPONDS TO THE SECOND MAN OF ABOVE. This one became formed in a female, NAMELY THE NUKVA OF ZEIR ANPIN, unlike that first one, WHICH IS ZEIR ANPIN, because that first one became formed by himself by the gauge that is in the measure.

## 78. Cain, Abel, Seth, Enosh, Mahalalel

### A Synopsis

The young man tells us of the first generations, of how the letters formed and combined to make Cain and Abel and Seth and Enosh and Mahalalel. And the sin that was in them because of the serpent began to be straightened out in Mahalalel, yet it was not improved until the children of Yisrael stood on Mt. Sinai and received the Torah. Only then were candle and Light repaired together. The world, however, was still in pain and sadness until Noah came. Next, the young man says that he comes from Babylon and is the son of Rabbi Safra. He was banished to their land and was afraid to speak of Torah because everyone there was so knowledgeable in it. Rabbi Yosi wept, and they all rise to kiss the young man's head. The young man also explains that he has not joined yet with his wife, although it would have been lawful, because he did not yet know the prayer after the meal.

### The Relevance of this Passage

The drama of mortal existence began with temptation, disobedience, expulsion, jealousy, and murder, the same ills that still beset us today. Connecting with this passage corrects the sins of the recent and distant past. As the goodness and wisdom of the young husband were hidden, the goodness and wisdom of our souls have been concealed through the ages. These ancient texts awaken the righteousness within us so the Light that shone on Mount Sinai reappears, and the knowledge of the Torah's deep mysteries immediately circulates throughout our world, ushering in the age of the Messiah, immortality and boundless joy.

760. כְּגַוְונָא דָּא לְתַתָּא. לְתַתָּא מַה כְּתִיב, וְהָאָדָם יָדַע אֶת חַוָּה אִשְׁתּוֹ וַתַּהַר וַתֵּלֶד אֶת קַיִן, שָׁרְיאַת קוֹף לְאוֹלְדָּא, בִּמְעָהָא, בְּחֵילָא וְסִיּוּעָא דְּאָדָם לְבָתַר דְּהָא קַבִּילַת זוּהֲמָא מִגּוֹ הַאי קוֹף. וְעַל דָּא לָא כְּתִיב הָכָא וַיּוֹלֶד, אֶלָּא יָדַע וַתַּהַר וַתֵּלֶד, וְנָפַק פְּסוֹלֶת גּוֹ נוּקְבָּא.

760. Pertaining to below, WHAT IS WRITTEN: "And Adam knew Eve, his wife; and she conceived, and bore Cain" (Beresheet 4:1). The *Kof* (of Cain), WHOSE LEG WAS CLOTHED WITH THE KLIPOT IN THE SECRET OF THE PASSAGE: "HER FEET GO DOWN TO DEATH" (MISHLEI 5:5) started to bear IN THE BELLY OF EVE with the strength and support of Adam after it had already received filth from this *Kof*. FIRST, THE SERPENT CAME,

WHICH IS THE SECRET OF *KOF*, UPON EVE AND INSERTED FILTH INTO HER AND THEN ADAM CAME UPON HER. Therefore, it is not written: 'And he begot,' but rather "And ADAM knew...And she conceived, and bore" and the refuse emerged of the female, EVE.

761. וַתּוֹסֶף לָלֶדֶת אֶת אָחִיו אֶת הָבֶל, וּבְהַאי נָמֵי לָא כְּתִיב וַיּוֹלֶד, וְאע״ג דְּמִסְטְרָא דִּדְכוּרָא הֲוָה. אֲבָל מְקַטְרְגָא תָּשַׁש וְתָבַר חֵילֵיה, דְּהָא בְּאָת קוֹף שָׁרִיאוּ אַתְוָון לְאוֹלָדָא.

**761.** "And she again bore his brother Abel" (Beresheet 4:2). It is not written: 'And he begot,' even though he was on the male side, NAMELY THE RIGHT SIDE, AS MENTIONED ABOVE, because the prosecutor weakened and his strength was broken, because from the letter *Kof* OF CAIN, the letters started begeting.

762. כֵּיוָן דְּאִתְבְּרִיר פְּסוֹלֶת, שָׁרִיאוּ אַתְוָון לְאוֹלָדָא מֵרָזָא דְּאָת ש״ת. תִּקּוּנָא דְּכַר וְנוּקְבָא, בְּאִסְתַּכְּמוּתָא כַּחֲדָא. וּכְדֵין כְּתִיב וַיּוֹלֶד בִּדְמוּתוֹ כְּצַלְמוֹ וַיִּקְרָא אֶת שְׁמוֹ שֵׁת, וְלָא כְּתִיב וַתִּקְרָא. וַיִּקְרָא אִיהוּ, וְלָא אִיהִי. אִיהוּ קָרָא שְׁמֵיה שֵׁת, תִּקּוּנָא דְּכַר וְנוּקְבָּא כַּחֲדָא, דַּהֲווֹ בְּאִסְתַּכְּמוּתָא חֲדָא.

**762.** After the refuse IN CAIN was sorted, the letters started to bear from the secret of the letters *Shin-Tav*, WHICH ARE the perfection of Male and Female in mutual agreement. BECAUSE *SHIN* IS THE THREE COLUMNS OF ZEIR ANPIN, THAT IS MALE AND THE *TAV* IS FEMALE, NAMELY MALCHUT, it is written: "And he begot in his likeness, after his image, and called his name Seth (*Shin-Tav*)" (Beresheet 5:3). It is not written that 'she called' AS EARLIER TO SHOW that he called and not she. He called his name Seth and that which is written earlier, "SHE CALLED" IS BECAUSE THE NAME SETH is the perfection of Male and Female mutually, for they were in mutual agreement.

763. תּוּ אִתְגַּלְגְּלוּ אַתְוָון, וְאַהַדְרוּ לְאוֹלָדָא אֶלֶף דְּאָדָם, וְאִינּוּן אַתְוָון בַּאֲתָר דְּאִיהוּ סִיּוּם שְׁמֵיה. וּמַאן אִיהוּ. נ', וּלְבָתַר ו' לָא ה', דְּהָא

אִתְעֲדִיאַת בְּהֶבֶל. בְּגִין כַּךְ נָטִיל אֶת אָחֳרָא אֲבַתְרֵיהּ ו', סַיֵּים
בְּשֵׁירוּתָא דְּשֵׁת ש', וְאִקְרֵי אֱנוֹשׁ.

**763.** The letters rolled some more and again bore *Aleph* of Adam. What are these letters that are where his name ends? *Nun*, THAT IS AFTER *MEM* OF ADAM, and the *Vav*, THAT IS AFTER *DALET* OF ADAM, but not *Hei*, WHICH IS AFTER *DALET*, because this *Hei* conceived with Abel. THUS THE LETTERS *ALEPH-NUN-Vav* emerged, ending with the beginning of the name Seth, WHICH IS *Shin*. And he was called 'Enosh' (*Aleph-Nun-Vav-Shin*).

**764.** אֱנוֹשׁ מַה בֵּין שְׁמָא דָּא לִשְׁמָא דְּאָדָם. אֶלָּא אֱנוֹשׁ לָאו אִיהוּ
בְּתָקְפָּא הֲוָה, תִּקּוּנָא דְּקַדְמָאֵי הֲוָה, מָה אֱנוֹשׁ כִּי תִזְכְּרֶנּוּ. וּכְתִיב מָה
אֱנוֹשׁ כִּי תְגַדְּלֶנּוּ וְגו', וַתִּפְקְדֶנּוּ לִבְקָרִים לִרְגָעִים תִּבְחָנֶנּוּ. וְעַל דָּא
כְּתִיב וַיְיָ' חָפֵץ דַּכְּאוֹ הֶחֱלִי, תְּבִירוּ דְּגוּפָא, וְתָקְפָּא דְּנַפְשָׁא, אוֹרִית שֵׁת
לֶאֱנוֹשׁ יְרוּתָא דַּהֲוָה לֵיהּ לְקַבְּלָא. וְאִיהוּ אוּף הָכִי אוֹרִית לִבְנוֹ.

**764.** HE QUESTIONS: What is the difference between this name and the name Adam? HE ANSWERS: Enosh had not his own strength, but was rather the perfection of the earlier ones, ADAM AND SETH, as it is written: "What is man (Heb. *Enosh*), that You are mindful of him?" (Tehilim 8:5) and: "What is man (Heb. Enosh), that You should magnify him…and that You should remember him every morning, and try him every moment?" (Iyov 7:17-18). About this, it is written: "But it pleased Hashem to crush him by disease" (Yeshayah 53:10), because the breaking of the body and the strength of the soul is what Seth bequeathed to his son Enosh. This was an inheritance that he should have received FOR HIMSELF, but he bequeathed it also to his son, NAMELY MAHALALEL.

**765.** תּוּ אִתְגַּלְגְּלוּ אַתְוָון לְאַתְקְנָא עֲקִימָא, וְאִתְהַדְּרוּ לְאוֹלָדָא. קֵינָן.
הַאי תִּקּוּנָא דְּקֵינָן, וְאִתְתַּקַּן תְּחוֹתֵיהּ, וְאִתְהַדְּרוּ אַתְוָון לְבַסְּמָא עָלְמָא
מֵעֲקִימוּ דַּהֲוָה. מַהֲלַלְאֵל מ' סוֹפָא דְּאַתְוָון דְּאָדָם. ה' וְל' תִּקּוּנָא
דְּאַתְוָון דְּהֶבֶל, וּבְגִין דְּלָא הֲוָה חַיָּיבָא כְּקַיִן, לָא אִתְחַלְּפוּ אַתְוָון
מִשְּׁמֵיהּ בַּר חַד. דְּבַאֲתַר ב' הֲוָה א' לְמֶהֱוֵי תִּקּוּנָא יַתִּיר.

**765.** The letters rolled further in order to straighten out the deviation, THAT BECAME DEVIATED BY THE SIN OF ADAM, AND CAIN, AND ABEL, and they then begot Keinan, because Keinan is the perfection for Cain, FOR KEINAN IS COMPOSED OF THE LETTERS OF CAIN. He was perfected instead of him and the letters reverted to improving the world from the deviation. Mahalalel, THE SON OF KEINAN, the *Mem* OF MAHALALEL is the last of the letters of Adam. *Hei* and *Lamed* are the perfection of the letters of Abel (*Hei-Bet-Lamed*). Since Abel was not a sinner like Cain, the letters of his name were not changed, IN MAHALALEL, except for one LETTER ALONE, for in place of the *Bet* OF ABEL, there was an *Aleph* IN MAHALALEL in order to be perfected even further.

766. עַד הָכָא אִתְבְּסַם עָלְמָא, וְאִתְתְּקַן עֲקִימָא מְשֵׁירוּתָא דֶּאֱנוֹשׁ. בַּר חוֹבָא דְּאָדָם, דְּלָא אִתְבְּסַם, עַד דְּקָיְימוּ יִשְׂרָאֵל בְּטוּרָא דְּסִינַי, אֲבָל תְּקוּנָא דְּעֲקִימוּ דְּקַיִן וְהֶבֶל אִתְתְּקַן וְאִתְבְּסַם אֲבָל עָלְמָא הֲוָה בְּצַעֲרָא וְעִצְבוֹנָא, עַד דְּאָתָא נֹחַ דִּכְתִּיב זֶה יְנַחֲמֵנוּ מִמַּעֲשֵׂנוּ וּמֵעִצְּבוֹן יָדֵינוּ מִן הָאֲדָמָה אֲשֶׁר אֵרְרָהּ יְיָ'. וְחוֹבָא דְּאָדָם לָא אִתְבְּסַם, עַד דְּקָיְימוּ יִשְׂרָאֵל עַל טוּרָא דְּסִינַי, וְקַבִּילוּ אוֹרַיְיתָא, וְכַד יִשְׂרָאֵל קַבִּילוּ אוֹרַיְיתָא, כְּדֵין נֵר וְאוֹר אִתְתַּקַן כַּחֲדָא.

**766.** Until now the world was improved and the deviation that started with Enosh was repaired. Only the sin of Adam that was not improved until the children of Yisrael stood on Mount Sinai, but the deviation on Cain and Abel was repaired and improved. Yet the world was in pain and sadness until Noah came, as it is written: "This one shall comfort us for our work and the toil of our hands, because of the ground which Hashem has cursed" (Beresheet 5:29). The sin of Adam was not improved until the children of Yisrael stood on Mount Sinai and received the Torah and, when they received the Torah, candle and light, WHICH ARE MALCHUT AND ZEIR ANPIN AS MENTIONED EARLIER, were then repaired together.

767. וְהַשְׁתָּא רַבּוֹתַי, אֲנָא מִבָּבֶל, וּבְרָא דְּרַב סַפְרָא אֲנָא, וְלָא זָכֵינָא לְאִשְׁתְּמוֹדְעָא לְאַבָּא, וְאַטְרִידְנָא הָכָא, וְדָחִילְנָא, דְּהָא יַתְבֵי אַרְעָא דָּא, אִינּוּן אַרְיְיוָון בְּאוֹרַיְיתָא, וְשַׁוֵּינָא עֲלַי דְּלָא אֵימָא מִילֵי דְּאוֹרַיְיתָא קָמֵי בַּ"נ, עַד תְּרֵין יַרְחִין, וְיוֹמָא דָּא אִשְׁתְּלִימוּ. זַכָּאָה חוּלְקִי

-474-

דְּאִתְעַרְעָתוּן הָכָא. אָרִים רַבִּי יוֹסִי קָלֵיהּ וּבְכֵי, וְקָמוּ כֻּלְּהוּ וּנְשָׁקוּהוּ בְּרֵישֵׁיהּ. אָמַר רַבִּי יוֹסִי זַכָּאָה חוּלָקָנָא דְּזָכֵינָא בְּהַאי אָרְחָא, לְמִשְׁמַע מִלֵּי דְּעַתִּיק יוֹמִין מִפּוּמָךְ, מַה דְּלָא זָכֵינָן לְמִשְׁמַע עַד הַשְׁתָּא.

767. And now, Sirs, I am from Babylon and I am the son of Rabbi Safra, but I did not merit to know my father, and I have been banished here. I feared because the inhabitants of this land are like lions in Torah, and I took upon myself not to say words of Torah before any man for two months. Today have these two months elapsed. Blessed is my portion that I met you here. Rabbi Yosi raised his voice and wept, and they all rose and kissed him on his head. Rabbi Yosi said: Blessed is my portion that I merited this way to hear the words of Atik Yomin from your mouth, which I did not merit until now.

768. יָתִיבוּ כֻּלְּהוּ, אָמַר לוֹן רַבּוֹתַי, מִדְּחָמֵינָא צַעֲרָא דְּהַאי חָמֵי וּבְרַתֵּיהּ, דְּדַחֲקֵי וּמִצְטַעֲרֵי בְּנַפְשַׁיְיהוּ, דְּלָא יָדַעְנָא בִּרְכַּת מְזוֹנָא. אֲמֵינָא לוֹן, דְּעַד דְּאֶנְדַּע בִּרְכַּת מְזוֹנָא, לָא אִתְחַבַּר בְּאִנְתְּתִי, כְּאָרַח כָּל בְּנֵי עָלְמָא, וְאע״ג דְּיָכִילְנָא לְשַׁמְּשָׁא בָּהּ בְּלָא חוֹבָה, לָא בְּעֵינָא לְמֶעְבַּד עַל דַּעְתַּיְיהוּ, הוֹאִיל וְלָא הֲוֵינָא יָכִיל לְמֵימַר מִדִּי, עַד תְּרֵין יַרְחִין. חֲדוּ רַבִּי יוֹסִי וְרַבִּי חִיָּיא וְחָמוֹי וּבְרַתֵּיהּ, וּבְכוּ מִסַּגְאוּ חֶדְוָה. אָמַר רַבִּי יוֹסִי, בְּמָטוּ מִינָךְ, כֵּיוָן דְּשָׁרִיאַת, אַנְהִיר לָן יְמָמָא, זַכָּאָה חוּלָקָנָא בְּאָרַח דָּא.

768. They all sat down and he said to them: Sirs, when I saw the pain of my father-in-law and his daughter, who were pressed and were pained because I did not know the blessing after the meal, I said to them: Until I know the blessing after the meal I will not join with my wife, as is the way of all the people. Even though I could live with her conjugally without sin, I did not want to deceive them, because I could say nothing for two months. Rabbi Yosi and Rabbi Chiya and his father-in-law and daughter rejoiced, and wept for excessive joy. Rabbi Yosi said: I beg of you, since you started, illuminate for us the day. Blessed is our portion on this way.

# 79. Secrets of the blessing after the meal

## A Synopsis

The youth again opens the discussion and announces that one verse says, "And you shall eat before The Creator your Elohim" and another verse says, "And rejoice before The Creator your Elohim." These verses, we then learn, were fulfilled when the children of Yisrael dwelt in the Holy Land and appeared before God in the Temple. A person must give to the poor, we are told, even as God gives him food, and he should not be a glutton because gluttony is from the Other Side. During the meal, he should be occupied solely with Torah. Next, the young man speaks of the Cup of Blessing: a person should bless with it only with joy, in the presence of three people who have eaten together. We further read that we must aim the desire above, to God, when we say, 'And by whose goodness we live,' because the world is built by that goodness, as it is written: "For I have said, the world is built by Chesed" and is nourished by it.

When we read "Who sustains the entire world with His goodness, with grace, with kindness (Chesed), and with Mercy" and, "Who gives bread to all flesh, for His steadfast love (Chesed) endures forever," it means that He provides food for the righteous and the wicked: this is called the Blessing of the Right, because Gvurah and Judgment are not included in the Blessing after the meal. Therefore, we are told, the left hand should not assist the right to hold the cup. The second blessing is the blessing of the Land. The spread of goodness is thankfulness. The young man then tells us of the right and left of Netzach and Hod, and how Hod is the result of the spread of Love; in this instance both Netzach and Hod come from the right. There is no left in the Blessing after a meal because the Other Side has no part in the food of Yisrael. After the Land of the Living is blessed and receives food, we ask for Mercy for everyone. On Shabbat when there is no Judgment, we say, 'May it please you to strengthen us.' We say who is good and does good, and the one who recites the Blessing after a meal receives the blessings before everyone else, and has a long life. Thus the right performs salvation from the inciter. When the young man finishes speaking, Rabbi Yosi declares a feast and the rabbis gather everyone together for rejoicing, finally calling the young man's wife 'a Bride'.

## The Relevance of this Passage

On one level, "eat before the Creator your Elohim" pertains to the sparks of Light contained in the foods we eat. Blessing our food ensures that we receive both spiritual and physical nourishment, so that even the act of eating becomes a sacred tool for spiritual

transformation. Hence, we are now connected to the Temple and to the Torah, which help us elevate holy sparks in the foods we consume.

We are inspired to give a portion of our sustenance to the needy, and our gluttonous cravings are subjugated. All the blessings and goodness derived from the eating of God's food, especially during the Sabbath, are summoned forth so that we may feast upon the Light, share it with others, and enjoy long, sumptuous sips from the Cup of Blessing.

The cumulative Light aroused from all the blessings and Torah study of the righteous throughout history, during and after their meals, ignites in this spectacular moment of meditation. All judgments are therefore annulled. Mercy envelops mankind. Poverty is at last purged from the landscape of civilization. And the angel Satan is deprived of his meals, starved until he withers away, becoming nothing more than a long forgotten relic of the past.

769. פָּתַח הַהוּא רַבְיָא בְּבִרְכַּת מְזוֹנָא וְאָמַר, כָּתוּב אֶחָד אוֹמֵר וְאָכַלְתָּ לִפְנֵי יְיָ' אֱלֹהֶיךָ, וְכָתוּב אֶחָד אוֹמֵר וְשָׂמַחְתָּ לִפְנֵי יְיָ' אֱלֹהֶיךָ. הָנֵי קְרָאֵי כַּד יִשְׂרָאֵל הֲווֹ שָׁרָאן בְּאַרְעָא קַדִּישָׁא, וְאִתְחֲזוּן קַמֵּי קוּדְשָׁא בְּרִיךְ הוּא בְּבֵי מַקְדְּשָׁא, הֲווֹ מִתְקַיְּימֵי. הַשְׁתָּא הֵיךְ מִתְקַיְּימֵי, מַאן יָכִיל לְמֵיכַל לִפְנֵי יְיָ' וּלְמֶחֱדֵי לִפְנֵי יְיָ'.

**769.** That youth opened the discussion with the blessing after the meal and said: One verse says, "And you shall eat before Hashem your Elohim" (Devarim 4:23) and another verse says, "And rejoice before Hashem your Elohim" (Devarim 27:7). These verses were fulfilled when the children of Yisrael dwelt in the Holy Land and appeared before the Holy One, blessed be He, in the Temple. How are they fulfilled today? Who can eat before Hashem and who can rejoice before Hashem?

770. אֶלָּא וַדַּאי הָכִי הוּא, בְּקַדְמֵיתָא כַּד יָתִיב בַּר נָשׁ עַל פָּתוֹרֵיהּ לְמֵיכַל, מְבָרֵךְ עַל נַהֲמָא הַמּוֹצִיא. מַאי טַעֲמָא הַמּוֹצִיא, וְלָא מוֹצִיא, דְּהָא כְּתִיב בּוֹרֵא הַשָּׁמַיִם, וְלָא כְּתִיב הַבּוֹרֵא. עוֹשֵׂה אֶרֶץ, וְלָא כְּתִיב הָעוֹשֵׂה אֶרֶץ. מַאי טַעֲמָא הָכָא הַמּוֹצִיא.

**770.** HE ANSWERS: Certainly it is so. At the beginning, when a person sits down at his table to eat, he makes the blessing for bread, "Hamotzi." What

is the reason we say, "who brings (Heb. *hamotzi*) forth bread" and not 'he who brings (Heb. *hamotzi*) forth bread,' WITHOUT THE DEFINITE ARTICLE *HEI*? It is written: "He creates (lit. 'creator') the heavens" (Yeshayah 42:5), but not written: 'He who creates (lit. 'the creator').' "He has made (lit. 'maker') the earth" (Yirmeyah 10:12) and is not written 'He who has made (the maker) the earth.' What is the reason that here we say Hamotzi (Lit. 'the bringer')?

771. אֶלָּא כָּל מִלִּין דְּאִינּוּן מֵרָזָא דְּעָלְמָא עִלָּאָה, סְתִירָא אִסְתַּתְּרָא ה' מִתַּמָּן, לְאִתְחֲזָאָה דְּהָא מֵעָלְמָא גְּנִיזָא וּסְתִירָא אִיהוּ. וְכָל מִלִּין דְּאִינּוּן מֵעָלְמָא תַּתָּאָה דְּאִתְגַּלְיָא יַתִּיר, כְּתִיב בֵּה, דִּכְתִיב הַמּוֹצִיא בְּמִסְפָּר צְבָאָם הַקּוֹרֵא לְמֵי הַיָּם, כֻּלְּהוּ מֵרָזָא דְּעָלְמָא תַּתָּאָה אִיהוּ. וְאִי אִכְתִיב בִּשְׁמָא אִיהוּ בֵה', כְּגוֹן הָאֵל הַגָּדוֹל, וְהָכָא דְּאִיהוּ בְּאִתְגַּלְיָא מֵרָזָא דְּעָלְמָא תַּתָּאָה אִיהוּ, כֵּיוָן דִּמְבָרֵךְ בַּר נָשׁ, שְׁכִינְתָּא אַתְיָא קָמֵיה.

771. HE ANSWERS: The *Hei* is hidden from all the things that come from the upper concealed world, WHICH IS BINAH, AS THERE IS NO DEFINITE ARTICLE (*HEI*) THERE. THIS SHOWS THAT IT COMES FROM THE HIDDEN AND CONCEALED WORLD. All the things that are from the lower world, WHICH IS MALCHUT that is more revealed, are written with a *Hei*, as it is written: "That (*Hei*) brings out their host by number" (Yeshayah 40:26). "That (*Hei*) calls for the waters of the sea" (Amos 5:8). They are all from the secret of the Lower World. If a Name is written, it is also with a *Hei*, such as "the great El" for example. And here where He is revealed WITH A *HEI*, IT IS BECAUSE it is from the secret of the lower world, because when a person is blessing, the Shechinah comes before him.

772. וּמַה דְּאָמַר וְאָכַלְתָּ לִפְנֵי יְיָ' אֱלֹהֶיךָ. הָכָא אִתְכְּלִיל לְמַלְּלָא בְּמִלֵּי דְּאוֹרַיְיתָא, דְּהָכִי אִצְטְרִיךְ הוֹאִיל וְקוּדְשָׁא בְּרִיךְ הוּא קָמֵיה, לְקַיְּימָא דִּכְתִיב, זֶה הַשֻּׁלְחָן אֲשֶׁר לִפְנֵי יְיָ'. וּכְתִיב וְאָכַלְתָּ שָׁם לִפְנֵי יְיָ' אֱלֹהֶיךָ.

772. "And you shall eat before Hashem your Elohim" is included here, in speaking words of Torah. So it should be, because the Holy One, blessed be He, is standing before him, as it is written: "This is the table that is before Hashem" (Yechezkel 41:22) and, "And you shall eat there before Hashem your Elohim" (Devarim 14:26).

773. הוֹאִיל וְקָאִים ב״נ קַמֵּי מָארֵיה, אִצְטְרִיךְ נָמֵי לְמֵיחַן לְמִסְכְּנֵי, לְמֵיתַן לוֹן, כְּמָה דְּאִיהוּ יָהִיב לֵיה לְמֵיכַל. כְּמַאן דְּאָכִיל קַמֵּי מַלְכָּא קַדִּישָׁא וְאִצְטְרִיךְ דְּלָא יִשְׁתְּכַח בַּלְעָן עַל פָּתוֹרֵיה, דְּהָא בִּלְעָנוּ מִסְטְרָא אָחֳרָא הֲוֵי, וְרָזָא דָּא הַלְעִיטֵנִי נָא, אֹרַח בִּלְעָנוּ, וְהָכִי אִצְטְרִיךְ לְסִטְרָא אָחֳרָא, וּכְתִיב וּבֶטֶן רְשָׁעִים תֶּחְסָר. וְע״ד וְאָכַלְתָּ לִפְנֵי יְיָ׳ אֱלֹהֶיךָ כְּתִיב, וְלָא לִפְנֵי סִטְרָא אָחֳרָא. וְאִצְטְרִיךְ דְּלָא יִתְעַסַּק בְּמִלִּין בְּטֵלִין, וּבְצָרְכֵי סְעוּדָה וְאִצְטְרִיךְ לְאִתְעַסְּקָא בְּמִלִּין דְּאוֹרַיְיתָא, דְּהָא כַּד מִלִּין דְּאוֹרַיְיתָא אִתְּמָרוּ עַל פָּתוֹרָא, יָהִיב הַהוּא בַּר נָשׁ תֶּקְפָּא לְמָארֵיה.

773. Because the person is standing before his Master, he must also favor the poor, to give them just as THE HOLY ONE, BLESSED BE HE, gives him to eat. HE SHOULD BE like one who is eating before the Holy King, and he should not be a glutton at his table, because gluttony is from the Other Side. This is the secret of: "Give me to swallow, I pray you" (Beresheet 25:30), which is by way of gluttony, which is a requirement of the Other Side, as it is written: "But the belly of the wicked shall feel want" (Mishlei 13:25). Therefore, it is written: "And you shall eat before Hashem your Elohim" and not before the Other Side. One should not be occupied with frivolous things and the preparations for the meal, but should be occupied with words of Torah, for one gives strength to his Master when words of Torah are spoken at the table.

774. וְשָׂמַחְתָּ לִפְנֵי יְיָ׳ אֱלֹהֶיךָ, דָּא אִיהוּ בְּכוֹס שֶׁל בְּרָכָה, כַּד בָּרִיךְ בַּר נָשׁ בְּכוֹס שֶׁל בְּרָכָה, אִצְטְרִיךְ לְמֶחֱדֵי וּלְאַחֲזָאָה חֶדְוָה וְלָא עֲצִיבוּ כְּלַל, כֵּיוָן דְּנָטִיל בַּר נָשׁ כּוֹס שֶׁל בְּרָכָה, קוּדְשָׁא בְּרִיךְ הוּא קָאִים עַל גַּבֵּיה, וְאִיהוּ אִצְטְרִיךְ לְאַעֲטְפָא רֵישֵׁיה בְּחֶדְוָה. וּלְבָרְכָא עַל הַכּוֹס בְּמוֹתַב תְּלָתָא, נְבָרֵךְ שֶׁאָכַלְנוּ מִשֶּׁלּוֹ.

774. "And rejoice before Hashem your Elohim." This refers to the Cup of Blessing. When a person blesses with the Cup of Blessing, he should rejoice and express joy and no sadness at all. As soon as the person has taken the Cup of Blessing, the Holy One, blessed be He, stands over him, and he should cover his head joyfully and bless over the cup in the presence of

three people WHO ATE TOGETHER, 'Let us bless Him, of His bounty we have eaten.'

775. וּבְטוּבוֹ חָיִינוּ, דָּא אִצְטְרִיךְ רְעוּתָא לְעֵילָא לְגַבֵּי עַתִּיקָא דְעַתִּיקִין, וְע״ד אִיהִי בְּאֹרַח סָתִים. וּבְטוּבוֹ, וְלָא מְטוּבוֹ. וּבְטוּבוֹ: דָּא יְמִינָא עִלָּאָה. וּמְטוּבוֹ: דָּא דַרְגָּא אַחֲרָא, דְּאָתֵי מִסִּטְרָא דִּימִינָא, וְאִיהוּ דַּרְגָּא לְתַתָּא מִנֵּיה, בְּגִין דִּבְהַהוּא טוֹב אִתְבְּנֵי עָלְמָא, וּבֵיה אִתְּזַן.

775. 'And by whose goodness we live': Here we must AIM the desire up to the most ancient of all. Therefore, it is in a concealed way, as it says, 'BY WHOSE GOODNESS' AND DOES NOT SAY, 'BY YOUR GOODNESS.' HE SAYS, 'By whose goodness' and not 'goodness,' because 'by whose goodness' is the supernal Right, WHICH IS THE SFIRAH CHESED and 'from whose goodness' is a different level below that comes from the right side. It is a level that is lower than it, NAMELY THE SFIRAH OF YESOD. THEREFORE, he must say, 'By whose goodness,' because the world is built by that goodness, WHICH IS CHESED. AS IT IS WRITTEN: "FOR I HAVE SAID, THE WORLD IS BUILT BY CHESED" (TEHILIM 89:3) and is nourished by it.

776. אֲמַאי אִקְרֵי טוֹב וַאֲמַאי אִקְרֵי חֶסֶד. טוֹב אִיהוּ, כַּד כָּלִיל כֹּלָּא בְּגַוֵּיה, וְלָא אִתְפָּשַׁט לְנַחְתָּא לְתַתָּא. חֶסֶד כַּד נַחְתָּא לְתַתָּא. וְעָבִיד טִיבוּ בְּכָל בִּרְיָין, בְּצַדִּיקֵי וּבְרַשִׁיעֵי וְלָא חָיֵישׁ, וְאע״ג דְּדַרְגָּא חַד הוּא. מְנָלָן דִּכְתִיב אַךְ טוֹב וָחֶסֶד יִרְדְּפוּנִי, אִי טוֹב לָמָה חֶסֶד, וְאִי חֶסֶד לָמָה טוֹב, דְּהָא בְּחַד סַגְיָא אֶלָּא טוֹב כָּלִיל כֹּלָּא בְּגַוֵּיה, וְלָא אִתְפָּשַׁט לְתַתָּא. חֶסֶד נָחִית וְאִתְפָּשַׁט לְתַתָּא, וְזָן כֹּלָּא צַדִּיקֵי וְרַשִׁיעֵי כַּחֲדָא.

776. HE QUESTIONS: Why is it called 'goodness' and why 'Chesed', WHICH ARE TWO NAMES? HE ANSWERS: 'Goodness' is when THE SFIRAH contains everything within itself and THE LIGHT does not spread to descend downward. Chesed is when THE LIGHT descends below and does good for all the creations, the righteous and the wicked without hesitation, BECAUSE IT DOES NOT CONTAIN JUDGMENTS. Even though both of them, GOODNESS AND CHESED, are one level as written: "Surely goodness and

kindness (Heb. *chesed*) shall follow me" (Tehilim 23:6). AND WE CAN ASK, If IT SAYS 'goodness,' WHY DOES IT SAY 'kindness,' and if IT SAYS 'kindness,' why DOES IT SAY 'goodness'? It would be sufficient to say one OF THEM. But, AS MENTIONED ABOVE, 'goodness' means that it retains everything within itself and does not SPREAD down. Chesed descends and spreads down and nourishes everything, the righteous and wicked alike.

777. וְהָכָא כֵּיוָן דְּאָמַר וּבְטוּבוֹ חַיִּינוּ, הָדַר וְאָמַר וְאָמַר אֶת הַזָּן אֶת הָעוֹלָם כֻּלּוֹ בְּטוּבוֹ בְּחֶסֶד, הה"ד נוֹתֵן לֶחֶם לְכָל בָּשָׂר כל"ח. וְע"ד הַזָּן אֶת הַכֹּל, לְצַדִּיקֵי וּלְרַשִׁיעֵי לְכֹלָּא. דָּא אִקְרֵי בִּרְכַּת יָמִין. שְׂמֹאל לָאו אִיהוּ בְּבִרְכַּת מְזוֹנָא. וּבְגִין כָּךְ שְׂמָאלָא לָא תְּסַיֵּיעַ לִימִינָא.

777. Here it says: "And by whose goodness we live," WHICH IS POSSIBLE TO EXPLAIN THAT THE FLOW DOES NOT DESCEND TO THE RIGHTEOUS AND THE WICKED. Therefore, it says again, 'Who sustains the entire world with His goodness, with grace, with kindness (Heb. *chesed*), and with Mercy.' This is the meaning of: "Who gives bread to all flesh, for His steadfast love (Heb. *chesed*) endures forever" (Tehilim 136:25). Therefore, IT SAYS: 'He provides food for all,' namely for the righteous and the wicked, for everyone. This is called 'the Blessing of the Right', WHICH IS CHESED. The Left, WHICH IS GVURAH AND JUDGMENT, is not included in the Blessing after a meal. Therefore, the left HAND should not assist the right HAND TO HOLD THE CUP.

778. דְּכֵיוָן דְּבָרִיךְ בִּרְכַּת זִמּוּן, אִצְטְרִיךְ לְדַבְּקָא אֶרֶץ הַחַיִּים בַּיָּמִין, לְאִתְזָנָא מִתַּמָּן, וּלְפַרְנְסָא וּלְמֵיהַב מְזוֹנָא לְכֹלָּא, וְעַל דָּא תִּנְיָינָא בִּרְכַּת הָאָרֶץ, וְאִצְטְרִיךְ לְאַדְכְּרָא בָּהּ בְּרִית וְתוֹרָה, עַל בְּרִיתָךְ שֶׁחָתַמְתָּ בִּבְשָׂרֵנוּ, וְעַל תּוֹרָתָךְ שֶׁלִּמַּדְתָּנוּ, לְאַחֲזָאָה דְּמֵהַהוּא טוֹב אִתְּזַן בְּרִית וְתוֹרָה, דְּאִיהוּ תִּקּוּנָא דְּהַאי טוֹב.

778. After he is reciting the Blessing after a Meal, we have to attach the Land of the living, WHICH IS MALCHUT, to the right, so it is nourished from there to sustain and give nourishment to all. Therefore, the second BLESSING is the Blessing of the Land. We should to mention in it covenant and Torah, NAMELY 'for Your covenant which You have sealed in our flesh;

for Your Torah which You have taught us' to show that the covenant and the Torah are nourished from this goodness, which is the perfection of this goodness.

779. מִכָּאן אוֹלִיפְנָא, דְּנָשִׁים פְּטוּרוֹת מִבִּרְכַּת מְזוֹנָא לְאַפָּקָא יְדֵי חוֹבָה, דְּהָא לֵית בְּהוּ תּוֹרָה וּבְרִית. וְלַחְתּוֹם עַל הָאָרֶץ וְעַל הַמָּזוֹן, הָא דִּדְבֵקוּתָא כַּחֲדָא בְּחֶסֶד, עַל הָאָרֶץ דָּא אִיהִי אֶרֶץ הַחַיִּים. וְעַל הַמָּזוֹן דָּא אִיהוּ חֶסֶד, הָא כְּלִילוּ דָּא בְּדָא בִּדְבֵיקוּתָא חֲדָא.

**779.** From here, we learn that women are exempt from the Blessing after a meal in order to fulfill their obligation, because there is no Torah and covenant in them. One should conclude: 'For the land and for the sustenance,' as their joining together is with Chesed. 'For the land' refers to the Land of the living, MALCHUT, 'and for the sustenance' refers to Chesed. They are combined together in one union.

780. אִתְפַּשְׁטוּתָא דְּטוֹב אִיהוּ הוֹדָאָה דְּאִקְרֵי חֶסֶ"ד, וְעַ"ד אִיהוּ אוֹמֵר, נוֹדֶה לְךָ, עַל כָּךְ וְעַל כָּךְ נִסִּין וְאָתִין דְּאִתְעָבִידוּ מִסִּטְרָא דְּטוֹב. וְאִי תֵּימָא וְהָא כְּתִיב נְעִימוֹת בִּימִינְךָ, נֵצַח, הָא אִיהוּ מִסִּטְרָא דְּיָמִין. לָאו הָכִי, אֶלָּא כָּל חַד וְחַד אַחְזֵי עַל הַהוּא אֲתָר דְּנָפִיק מִנֵּיהּ.

**780.** The spread of goodness is thankfulness (Heb. *hoda'ah*) that is called 'Chesed', FOR WHEN THE GOODNESS SPREADS DOWN WE THANK HIM FOR THIS. Therefore, it says: We offer thanks to You for this and for these miracles and signs that have been done for us from the side of goodness. If you ask: Yet it is written, "At Your right hand are pleasures for ever more (Heb. *netzach*)" (Tehilim 16:11), we see that NETZACH is on the right AND NOT HOD. HE ANSWERS: Each one points out the place it emerged from, FOR NETZACH (ENG. 'VICTORY') IS THE RESULT OF WARS, AND WARS ARE LEFT, AND HOD IS THE RESULT OF THE EXPANSION OF CHESED, WHICH IS RIGHT.

781. וְאִי תֵּימָא נֵצַח בַּיָּמִין, הָא כְּתִיב נְעִימוֹת, וּכְתִיב וּנְעִים זְמִירוֹת יִשְׂרָאֵל, וְדָא שְׂמָאלָא. וְכָל שְׂמָאלָא אִתְכְּלִיל בְּרָזָא דִּימִינָא. אֲבָל

הוֹדָאָה אוֹדֵי עַל יְמִינָא, לְאַחֲזָאָה דְּהָא מִנֵּיה נָפְקָא, וְדָא פְּשִׁיטוּ דְּטוֹב, דְּאִתְפָּשַׁט בְּאֶרֶץ הַחַיִּים.

**781.** If you say that: Netzach is right, as it is written, 'pleasures', NAMELY "AT YOUR RIGHT HAND ARE PLEASURES FOR EVER MORE" and, "The sweet singer of Yisrael" (II Shmuel 23:1) AND 'SINGER' is left. SO WE SEE THAT NETZACH IS LEFT. HE ANSWERS: All the left is included in the secret of the right, FOR NETZACH IS RIGHT AND PLEASURES WHICH ARE LEFT ARE INCLUDED IN IT. As for thankfulness, one is thankful for THE GOODNESS THAT IS IN the right to show that HOD emerges from there, FOR IT IS THE RESULT OF THE EXPANSION OF GOODNESS FROM THE RIGHT. This is the expansion of the goodness that expanded in the Land of the living, WHICH IS MALCHUT.

782. מ"ט לֵית הָכָא שְׂמָאלָא, בְּגִין דְּלֵית חוּלָקָא לְסִטְרָא אַחֲרָא בִּמְזוֹנָא דְּיִשְׂרָאֵל. וְאִי אִתְּעַר שְׂמָאלָא, סִטְרָא אַחֲרָא יִתְּעַר עִמֵּיה, וְהָא אִיהוּ זַבִּין בְּכֵרוּתֵיה וְחוּלָקֵיה לְיַעֲקֹב אֲבוּנָא. וְהָא אֲנַן יָהִיבְנָא לֵיה חוּלָקֵיה, לְהַהוּא מְקַטְרְגָא בְּזוּהֲמָא דְּמַיִין בַּתְרָאִין, וְאִי לֵית זוּהֲמָא, הָא חוּלָקֵיה דְּהַהוּא מֵיכְלָא, דְּקַרִיבוּ בֵּיה יְדִין.

**782.** What is the reason there is no left here, IN THE BLESSING AFTER A MEAL, BUT THE RIGHT ALONE. It is because the Other Side has no part in the food of Yisrael. If the left would be aroused, then the Other Side would be aroused with it, AS IT IS DRAWN FROM THE LEFT. It has already sold itsbirthright and portion to Jacob the patriarch. Therefore, we give the prosecutor his portion with the filth of the 'last waters.' And if there was no filth ON THE HANDS THAT WERE WASHED, then his portion is in the food that his hand touched, BECAUSE THEY HAVE SOME RESIDUE OF FOOD ON THEM.

783. וְעַל דָּא לֵית לֵיה חוּלָקָא בַּהֲדָן. וְהוֹאִיל וְלֵית לֵיה חוּלָקָא בַּהֲדָן, דְּהָא נָטַל חוּלָקֵיה, לֵית לָן לְאִתְּעֲרָא שְׂמָאלָא כְּלָל. דְּלָא יִתְּעַר מְקַטְרְגָא וְיִטוֹל תְּרֵין חוּלָקִין, חַד לְתַתָּא, וְחַד לְעֵילָא, כִּבְכוֹר. דְּהָא זַבִּין בְּכֵרוּתֵיה לְיַעֲקֹב אֲבוּנָא. חוּלָקֵיה אִיהוּ לְתַתָּא, וְלֵית לֵיה לְעֵילָא

כְּלוּם. יִשְׂרָאֵל נַטְלֵי לְעֵילָא, וְעֵשָׂו נָטִיל לְתַתָּא, וְע"ד לָא יִתְקְרַב שְׂמָאלָא כְּלָל, בְּבִרְכַּת מְזוֹנָא.

**783.** Therefore, it, THE OTHER SIDE, has no part with us, SINCE ITS PART IS IN THE LEFT THAT CONTAINS NO RIGHT. IT HAS NO PART IN THE FOOD, WHICH IS CHESED, AS EXPLAINED IN THE ADJACENT ESSAY. Since it has no part with us, as it has already taken its part IN THE LEFT, we should not arouse the Left at all, in order not to arouse the inciter TO NURTURE FROM HIS FOOD. AND THEN he will receive two portions like a first-born, one below, and one above. His portion is below, and he has nothing above. Yisrael took above and Esau took below. Therefore, the Left should not approach at all in the Blessing after a Meal.

784. כֵּיוָן דְּמִתְבָּרְכָא הַאי אֶרֶץ הַחַיִּים מִסִּטְרָא דִּימִינָא, וּמְקַבֵּל מְזוֹנָא, כְּדֵין בָּעֵינָן רַחֲמִין עַל כֹּלָּא. רַחֵם יְיָ' אֱלֹהֵינוּ עַל יִשְׂרָאֵל עַמָּךְ וְעַל יְרוּשָׁלַיִם עִירָךְ וְגוֹ', דְּהָא מֵהַהוּא מְזוֹנָא וְסִפּוּקָא דְּאֶרֶץ הַחַיִּים, נִזְכֵּי בָּה אֲנָן וּבֵי מַקְדְּשָׁא. דְּיִתְבְּנֵי בֵּי מַקְדְּשָׁא לְתַתָּא בְּאִינּוּן רַחֲמִים.

**784.** After the Land of the living is blessed from the right side and receives food, AS MENTIONED ABOVE, we ask for Mercy for everyone, AND SAY: 'Have Mercy, Hashem our Elohim, upon Yisrael Your people and upon Jerusalem Your city' etc. From that food and sustenance that is in the Land of the living, WHICH IS MALCHUT, shall we ourselves receive from them, NAMELY YISRAEL YOUR PEOPLE, and the Temple will be rebuilt below through His Mercy, NAMELY 'AND UPON JERUSALEM YOUR CITY...'

785. וּבְשַׁבָּת דְּלָא אִשְׁתְּכַח דִּינָא, לְמֶהֱוֵי נֶצַח וְהוֹד כְּלַל חֲסָדִים, אוֹמֵר רְצֵה וְהַחֲלִיצֵנוּ לְמֶהֱוֵי תַּרְוַויְיהוּ, חַסְדֵי דָּוִד הַנֶּאֱמָנִים, וְע"ד אַל תְּהִי צָרָה וְיָגוֹן וְכוּ', דְּהָא רְצֵה וּמוֹדִים, אִינּוּן חָסִיד דָּוִד, וְשִׂים שָׁלוֹם דְּקָאֲמָרָן בִּצְלוֹתָא, בְּבִרְכַּת עוֹשֶׂה שָׁלוֹם בִּמְרוֹמָיו הוּא בְּרַחֲמָיו יַעֲשֶׂה שָׁלוֹם עָלֵינוּ.

**785.** On Shabbat, when there is no Judgment, in order for Netzach and Hod to be included with Chassadim, AS WAS SAID ABOVE THAT NETZACH IS

THE RIGHT INCLUDED IN THE LEFT, AND IS A RESULT OF JUDGMENT, NAMELY WARS. HOD IS A RESULT OF THE EXPANSION OF CHASSADIM DOWN. THUS THEY ARE NOT ACTUALLY CHASSADIM BUT CONTAIN CHASSADIM. BUT ON SHABBAT WHEN THERE IS NO JUDGMENT we say, 'May it please You to strengthen us,' FOR 'PLEASE' IS NETZACH AND 'STRENGTHEN' IS HOD, because they are both NETZACH AND HOD, "The sure loving promises CHASSADIM of David" (Yeshayah 55:3), NAMELY ACTUAL CHASSADIM. Therefore, 'let there be no distress, sadness…' for then 'May it please you (Heb. *retzeh*)' and 'we thankfully acknowledge, (Heb. *mochin*)' NAMELY NETZACH AND HOD, the Chassadim of David, exist WITHOUT ANY MIXTURES OF JUDGMENT AT ALL. 'Bestow peace', that we say in the Amidah Prayer, in the blessing of 'He who makes peace in His heavens, may He make peace for us' IS YESOD THAT PROVIDES THE CHASSADIM OF DAVID MENTIONED EARLIER TO DAVID, WHO IS MALCHUT.

786. הַטּוֹב וְהַמֵּטִיב, דְּכֹלָּא אָתֵי מִסִּטְרָא דִּימִינָא, וְלָא מִסְטַר שְׂמָאלָא כְּלוּם. מַאן דִּמְבָרֵךְ בִּרְכַּת מְזוֹנָא, אִיהוּ נָטִיל בִּרְכָאן בְּקַדְמֵיתָא מִכֵּלְּהוּ, וְאִתְבְּרַךְ בְּכָל בִּרְכַּת מְזוֹנָא, וְעַל דָּא אִית לֵיהּ אַרְכָּא דְחַיִּין. מַאן דְּנָטִיל כּוֹס שֶׁל בְּרָכָה, וְקָא מְבָרֵךְ עָלֵיהּ, כְּתִיב כּוֹס יְשׁוּעוֹת אֶשָּׂא. מַאן יְשׁוּעוֹת דָּא יְמִינָא, דְּאִיהוּ מוֹשִׁיעַ מִכָּל מְקַטְרְגִין דְּעָלְמָא, דִּכְתִיב וַתּוֹשַׁע לוֹ יְמִינוֹ, וּכְתִיב הוֹשִׁיעָה יְמִינְךָ וַעֲנֵנִי.

**786.** AFTERWARDS WE SAY 'who is good and does good', BECAUSE everything comes from the right side and nothing from the left side. The one who recites the Blessing after a Meal receives the blessings before all of them, NAMELY BEFORE THOSE WHO ANSWER AFTER HIM, and is blessed in the Blessing after a Meal. Therefore, he has a long life. It is written about the one who takes the Cup of Blessing and blesses over it: "I will raise the cup of salvations" (Tehilim 116:13). What are the salvations? This refers to the right that saves from all the inciters in the world, as it is written: "His right hand…gained Him the victory" (Tehilim 98:1) and, "Save with Your right hand, and answer me" (Tehilim 60:7).

787. אַדְהָכִי הֲוָה נָהִיר יְמָמָא, קָמוּ כֻּלְּהוּ וּנְשָׁקוּהוּ. א"ר יוֹסֵי, וַדַּאי הִלּוּלָא אִיהוּ יוֹמָא דָא, וְלָא נֵיפוּק מֵהָכָא, עַד דְּיִתְעֲבִיד הִלּוּלָא בְּכָל

אַנְשֵׁי מָתָא, דָּא הוּא הַלּוּלָא דְּקוּדְשָׁא בְּרִיךְ הוּא אִתְרְעֵי בֵּיה. נַטְלוּ לָה
לְאִנְתְּתֵיה, וּבָרִיכוּ לָה בְּכַמָּה בִּרְכָאן, עַבְדוּ דַּאֲבוּהָ יְתַקֵּן בֵּיתָא אָחֳרָא
לְחֶדְוָה, כְּנִישׁוּ כָּל אַנְשֵׁי מָתָא לְהַהִיא חֶדְוָתָא, וְקָרְאוּ לָה כַּלָּה. וְחַדּוּ
עִמְּהוֹן כָּל הַהוּא יוֹמָא, וְאִיהוּ חַדֵי עִמְּהוֹן בְּמִלֵּי דְּאוֹרַיְיתָא.

**787.** In the meantime, the day dawned and they all rose and kissed him. Rabbi Yosi said: Today is certainly a feast day, and we will not leave here until a feast is prepared for all the people of the city. This is a feast that the Holy One, blessed be He, favors. They took his wife, blessed her with numerous blessings and required that her father designate another house for the joyous event. They gathered all the people of the city for that joyous event and called HIS WIFE a bride. They rejoiced with them all that night, and he rejoiced with them with words of Torah.

## 80. The seven blessings of the bride

### A Synopsis

The young husband tells us here of the marriage canopy for the Bride, and the marriage canopy for the Other Bride, the Shechinah. He speaks about the Seven Blessings that elevate the Bride of below and the Bride of Above. Ten kinds of joy are combined: joy, happiness, groom, bride, gladness, jubilation, cheer, love and delight, peace and friendship, so the Bride is the perfection of everything. The rabbis place the youth at their head, and with great happiness they tell Rabbi Shimon everything about him. Rabbi Shimon relates how he blessed the young man's father, Rabbi Safra, that he would have a son who would excel at Torah, but the father died before he could see it.

### The Relevance of this Passage

The union of soul mates, of male and female, of the upper and lower worlds, is the ultimate objective of our existence. Thus, if we are single (a half of one soul), the blessings arising from this text direct us to our true soul mate (the other half of our soul). If we are married, our relationship is divinely enriched, placing our marriage upon a foundation of spirituality. All of this Light, at last, causes the upper and lower worlds to join together in spiritual wedlock, their ultimate and eternal unification bringing joy, happiness, and jubilation to all mankind.

788. פָּתַח אִיהוּ עַל פָּתוֹרָא וְאָמַר, וְעָשִׂיתָ אֶת הַקְּרָשִׁים לַמִּשְׁכָּן עֲצֵי שִׁטִּים עוֹמְדִים. כְּתִיב הָכָא עוֹמְדִים. וּכְתִיב הָתָם שְׂרָפִים עוֹמְדִים. מַה לְהַלָּן שְׂרָפִים, אוּף הָכָא נָמֵי שְׂרָפִים. אִלֵּין קְרָשִׁים קַיְימָן בְּתִקּוּנֵי דְכַלָּה, וְסָחֲרָן סָחֲרָנָא דְחוּפָּה, לְמִשְׁרֵי בְּהַהִיא חוּפָּה רוּחַ עִלָּאָה, כְּגַוְונָא דָא כַּלָּה לְתַתָּא, אִצְטְרִיךְ לְתַקְּנָא חוּפָּה לְחוּפָּאָה בְּתִקּוּנוֹ שַׁפִּירוּ, לִיקָרָא דְכַלָּה אַחֲרָא, דְּאַתְיָא לְמִשְׁרֵי תַּמָּן בְּחֶדְוָה, לְכַלָּה תַּתָּאָה.

788. The YOUTH, MEANING THE HUSBAND, opened the discussion saying: "And you shall make boards for the Tabernacle of acacia wood standing up" (Shemot 26:15). It says here "standing up" and elsewhere "Seraphim stood above" (Yeshayah 6:2). Just as there are Seraphim there, so also THE BOARDS here ARE THE SECRET OF Seraphim. These SERAPHIM THAT ARE CALLED 'boards' stand as implements of the Bride, WHO IS THE

SHECHINAH, around the Chupah (Eng. 'marriage canopy'), WHICH IS THE COVER THAT IS ABOVE THE BOARDS, so that the Supernal Spirit shall dwell upon that canopy, NAMELY ZEIR ANPIN. Ii is the same way with the bride below, as it is necessary to prepare a canopy as a cover in beautiful ornaments in honor of the other Bride, WHICH IS THE SHECHINAH, that comes to dwell there in joy upon the lower bride.

789. וּבְגִין יְקָרָא דְּהַהִיא כַּלָּה עִלָּאָה, אִצְטְרִיךְ לְמֶעְבַּד חוּפָּאָה דִּשְׁפִירוּ, בְּכָל תִּקּוּנֵי דִּשְׁפִירוּ, לְזַמְּנָא לְכַלָּה עִלָּאָה, לְהַהִיא חֶדְוָה. כְּגַוְונָא דָּא בְּכָל גְּזִירוּ דִּבְרִית לְתַתָּא, אִצְטְרִיךְ לְאַתְקָּנָא כָּסָא אַחֲרָא בִּשְׁפִירוּ, לְמָארֵי קִנְאָה דִּבְרִית קַיָּימָא דְּאָתֵי תַּמָּן. אוּף הָכָא בְּכָל חוּפָּה, אִצְטְרִיךְ תִּקּוּנֵי שְׁפִירוּ, לְחוּפָּאָה לְחוּפָּה לִיקָרָא דְּכַלָּה סְתָם.

789. In honor of the supernal Bride, we should to make a beautiful canopy with beautiful decorations to invite the supernal Bride, WHO IS THE SHECHINAH, to this canopy. Just as in every covenant of circumcision below, we should to decorate a beautiful second chair for he who is zealous for the sign of the covenant who comes there, NAMELY ELIYAHU, similarly here, we should to have beautiful decorations to cover the canopy, in honor of a Bride, THAT IS THE SHECHINAH.

790. דְּהָא דָּא, כְּגַוְונָא דְּדָא קַיְימָא. דָּא סַלְקָא בְּשֶׁבַע בִּרְכָּאן, וְדָא סַלְקָא בְּשֶׁבַע בִּרְכָּאן. וְכַד סַלְקָא בְּשֶׁבַע בִּרְכָּאן כְּדֵין אִקְרֵי כַּלָּה. וְעַל דָּא אָסִיר לְשַׁמְּשָׁא בָּהּ עַד דְּאִתְכְּלִילַת בְּאִינּוּן שֶׁבַע בִּרְכָּאן, כְּגַוְונָא עִלָּאָה.

790. This one, THE BRIDE BELOW, is similar to that one, THE BRIDE ABOVE, and the one OF BELOW is elevated with Seven Blessings, while the other OF ABOVE is elevated with Seven Blessings. Therefore, it is prohibited to cohabit with her until she has been included with these Seven Blessings, as is with the one of above.

791. אִינּוּן שֶׁבַע בִּרְכָּאן, יָרְתָּא כַּלָּה, מְרוּחָא עִלָּאָה, אֲתָר דְּכָל בִּרְכָּאן נַגְדִּין מִתַּמָּן. שִׁית בִּרְכָּאן אִינּוּן דְּכַלָּה אִתְבָּרְכָא מִנַּיְיהוּ, וְאַתְּ אֲמַרְתְּ

דְּאִינּוּן שֶׁבַע. אֶלָּא שְׁבִיעָאָה אִיהוּ דְּקָא מְקַיֵּים כֹּלָּא.

**791.** The Bride, WHO IS THE SHECHINAH, inherits these Seven Blessings from the Supernal Spirit, THAT IS ZEIR ANPIN, the place from where all the blessings are drawn. HE QUESTIONS: There are six blessings, NAMELY CHESED, GVURAH, TIFERET, NETZACH, HOD AND YESOD OF ZEIR ANPIN, that the Bride is blessed with, yet you say there are seven. HE ANSWERS: The seventh one establishes them all, FOR THE SEVENTH BLESSING CORRESPONDS TO BINAH.

792. רוּבָּא דְּבִרְכָּאן עַל הַיַּיִן אֲמַאי. אֶלָּא דְּאִיהוּ סִטְרָא דְּחַדֵּי לְכֹלָּא, עַל הַהוּא יַיִן דְּאִתְנְטִיר בָּעֲנָבוֹי תָּדִיר. וּבְגִין כַּךְ בִּרְכָה קַדְמָאָה דְּאִינּוּן שֶׁבַע, אִיהוּ רָזָא יַיִן. עָבִיד פְּרִי בֵּין לְעֵילָא בֵּין לְתַתָּא. גֶּפֶן נָטִיל כֹּלָּא, וְאַפִּיק אִיבָּא לְעָלְמָא, וְאִתְּעָרוּ דְּחֶדְוָה שְׂמָאלָא אִיהוּ, דִּכְתִּיב שְׂמָאלוֹ תַּחַת לְרֹאשִׁי וּלְבָתַר וִימִינוֹ תְּחַבְּקֵנִי. וְהַהוּא אִילָנָא דְּחַיֵּי עָבִיד פֵּירִין וְאֵיבִין בְּאִתְעָרוּתָא דָּא, וְדָא אִיהִי בִּרְכָה קַדְמָאָה דְּכֹלָּא.

**792.** HE QUESTIONS: Why are most blessings recited over wine? HE ANSWERS: WINE is the aspect that causes everyone to rejoice, the wine that is always kept in its grapes. Therefore, the first blessing of those seven BLESSINGS is the secret of wine, NAMELY 'WHO CREATES THE FRUIT OF THE VINE (HEB. *BORE PRI HAGEFEN*),' because wine produces fruits both above IN BINAH and below IN MALCHUT. The vine, WHICH IS MALCHUT, receives everything and brings forth fruits to the world, FOR AFTER RECEIVING THE ASPECT OF WINE, MALCHUT IS NAMED LOWER CHOCHMAH. AND BEFORE SHE RECEIVES CHOCHMAH, SHE IS NOT ABLE TO GIVE BIRTH. The arousing of joy, MEANING THE BEGINNING OF THE UNION OF ZEIR ANPIN AND MALCHUT, is the left, as it is written: "His left hand is under my head" (Shir Hashirim 2:6) and afterwards, "And His right hand embraces me" (Ibid.) That Tree of Life, WHICH IS ZEIR ANPIN, produces fruits and plants with this arousal OF THE LEFT, BECAUSE BEFORE IT RECEIVES CHOCHMAH FROM THE LEFT OF BINAH, IT CANNOT BEGET. Therefore, it is the first blessing of them all.

793. תִּנְיָינָא שֶׁהַכֹּל בָּרָא לִכְבוֹדוֹ, רָזָא דִּבְרִית קַדִּישָׁא, חֶדְוָה דְּחִבּוּרָא,

דְּנָטִיל כָּל בִּרְכָאן מֵרָזָא דִימִינָא, לְמֶעְבַּד אֵיבִין בְּהַהוּא גֶּפֶן, דְּהָא בְּקַדְמֵיתָא הַהוּא פְּרִי נָחִית מִלְעֵילָא, אֹרַח שַׁיְיפִין, וְנָגִיד לִבְרִית קַדִּישָׁא, לְנַגְדָּא לֵיה בְּהַהוּא גֶּפֶן, וְדָא מִסִּטְרָא דִימִינָא, דְּהָא לֵית אִיבָּא מִשְׁתַּכְחָא אֶלָּא בִּימִינָא. שְׂמָאלָא אִתְּעַר וִימִינָא עָבִיד.

**793.** The second blessing is: 'That He has created everything (all) for His honor'. This is the secret of the Holy Covenant, NAMELY YESOD OF ZEIR ANPIN THAT IS CALLED 'ALL'. This is the joy of the union that receives all the blessings from the secret of the right, THAT IS CHESED, to produce fruits by that vine, WHICH IS MALCHUT THAT IS CALLED 'HIS HONOR'. That fruit first descends from above, FROM BINAH, through the limbs, WHICH ARE THE SFIROT OF ZEIR ANPIN, and is drawn to the Holy Covenant, WHICH IS YESOD, to be drawn to that vine, WHICH IS MALCHUT. This is from the right side, WHICH IS CHESED, because fruits are to be found only on the right. The left arouses THE BEARING OF THE FRUITS and the right produces THE FRUITS. FRUITS REFER TO THE SOULS OF THE RIGHTEOUS.

794. לְבָתַר כָּלִיל שְׂמָאלָא בִּימִינָא, וִימִינָא בִּשְׂמָאלָא, לְמֶהֱוֵי רָזָא דְּאָדָם. וּבְגִין כַּךְ תְּלִיתָאָה אִיהוּ יוֹצֵר הָאָדָם. וְעַ״ד יַעֲקֹב, דְּאִיהוּ עַמּוּדָא דְּאֶמְצָעִיתָא, דִּיּוּקְנָא דְּאָדָם הֲוָה.

**794.** Afterwards, the left is included in the right and the right in the left in order to become the secret of man, WHICH IS THE CENTRAL COLUMN, TIFERET. Therefore, the third BLESSING is 'the Creator of Man'. Jacob, who is the Central pillar, was the image of Adam (man), FOR THE IMAGE OF ADAM POINTS TOWARD THE CENTRAL COLUMN, AS RIGHT AND LEFT ARE COMBINED IN HIM.

795. רְבִיעָאָה, אִיהוּ עַמּוּדָא חֲדָא, דְּיַרְכָּא יְמִינָא. חֲמִישָׁאָה, שׁוֹשׁ תָּשִׂישׂ וְתָגֵל עֲקָרָה דְּבֵיתָא, בְּחֶדְוָה בְּקִבּוּץ וּכְנִישׁוּ דִּבְנָהָא, מֵאַרְבַּע סִטְרֵי עָלְמָא, וְדָא רָזָא דְּיַרְכָּא אַחֲרָא, דְּאִתְחַבַּר בְּיַרְכָּא שְׂמָאלָא, לְמֵיזַל וּלְמִיכְנַשׁ לְכָל סִטְרִין, וּכְנִישׁוּ דִּבְנִין, וּרְחִימוּ, לְמֵיעַל לוֹן בֵּין בִּרְכִּין.

**795.** The fourth BLESSING, NAMELY 'WHO CREATED,' is one pillar of the right thigh, NAMELY THE SFIRAH OF NETZACH. The fifth blessing is: 'May the barren one (Heb. *akarah*) rejoice', NAMELY the mistress (Heb. *akarah*) of the house, MALCHUT, and be happy at the ingathering of her children from the four winds of the world. This is the secret of the other thigh, WHICH IS NETZACH, that joined in the left thigh, WHICH IS HOD, to go to all sides, gather the children and bring them between the knees, WHICH ARE NETZACH AND HOD.

796. וּבְאִינּוּן תְּרֵין, דִּנְבִיאִים שַׁרְיָין בְּגַוַּוייהוּ, חֶדְוָה דְּעִקָּרָא דְּבֵיתָא. מ"ט. בְּגִין דְּהָא שְׁתֵּי עֲרָבוֹת, לָא עַבְדִּין אֵיבָּא וּפֵירִין, וּכְנִישׁוּ דִּבְנִין לְגַבַּיְיהוּ, אִינּוּן פֵּירִין וְאֵיבִין דִּלְהוֹן, וְלָא אִתְּעֲרוּ כְּנִישׁוּ דִּבְנָהָא לְגַבָּהָא, בַּר בַּנְבִיאִים.

**796.** And in these two, NETZACH AND HOD between whom the prophets dwell, AND RECEIVE THEIR PROPHECY FROM THEM, abides the joy of the Mistress of the House, WHICH IS MALCHUT. What is the reason? It is because two willow branches (Heb. *aravot*), WHICH ARE NETZACH AND HOD, do not produce verdure and fruits and the ingathering of the children to them is their fruits and verdure, WHICH THEY BRING TO THE MISTRESS OF THE HOUSE THAT IS MALCHUT. The ingathering of the children is aroused only by prophets, WHO ARE NETZACH AND HOD. THEREFORE, THIS BLESSING: 'MAY THE BARREN ONE REJOICE AND BE HAPPY AT THE INGATHERING OF HER CHILDREN', IS IN HOD.

797. שְׁתִיתָאָה שָׂמֵחַ תְּשַׂמַּח רֵעִים הָאֲהוּבִים, אֲתָר דִּרְעוּתָא וְחֶדְוָה וְאַחְוָה אִשְׁתְּכַח, עַמּוּדָא דְּכָל עָלְמָא דְּאִקְרֵי צַדִּיק, וְצַדִּיק וְצֶדֶק רֵעִים וַאֲהוּבִים אִינּוּן, דְּלָא אִתְעֲדוּן דָּא מִן דָּא. עַד הָכָא שִׁית בִּרְכָאן, דְּכַלָּה אִתְבָּרְכַת מִנַּיְיהוּ.

**797.** The sixth blessing is: 'Grant abundant joy to the loving friends'. It is the place where there are favor, joy, and delight, NAMELY the pillar of the entire world that is called 'Righteous', WHICH IS YESOD. And righteous and righteousness, WHICH ARE YESOD AND MALCHUT, are friends and beloved, as they do not turn away one from the other. BECAUSE THIS

BLESSING ALSO INCLUDES MALCHUT, IT SAYS 'LOVING FRIENDS.' Until here are the six blessings by which the bride is blessed.

‎798. שְׁבִיעָאָה אִיהוּ מְקַיֵּים כֹּלָּא, וּמֵהַאי שְׁבִיעָאָה מִתְבָּרְכָאן כֹּלָּא וַדַּאי, כְּלָלָא דְּעֶשֶׂר אֲמִירָן, בְּגִין דְּדָא, כָּלִיל עֵילָּא וְתַתָּא. וְעַ"ד כָּלִיל בְּהַאי, י׳ זִינֵי דְּחֶדְוָה, שָׂשׂוֹן, שִׂמְחָה, חָתָן, וְכַלָּה, גִּילָה, רִיצָה, אַהֲבָה, וְאַחֲוָה, שָׁלוֹם, וְרֵיעוּת, לְמֶהֱוֵי כַּלָּה שְׁלִימוּ דְּכֹלָּא.

**798.** The seventh BLESSING establishes them all, and all are blessed from that seventh one, WHICH IS BINAH, WHICH IS THE SOURCE OF ALL MOCHIN. Certainly it is the combination of the ten sayings, NAMELY THE TEN SFIROT, for it comprehends that which is above and below, NAMELY THE FIRST THREE SFIROT AND SEVEN LOWER ONES WHICH ARE THE TEN SFIROT. Therefore, ten kinds of joy are combined in it: 'joy; happiness; groom; bride; gladness; jubilation; cheer; love and delight; peace and friendship', so that the Bride shall be perfected in everything.

‎799. זַכָּאִין אִינּוּן יִשְׂרָאֵל, דְּאִינּוּן זָכוּ לְתַתָּא, כְּגַוְונָא דִלְעֵילָּא. עָלַיְיהוּ כְּתִיב, וּמִי כְעַמְּךָ כְּיִשְׂרָאֵל גּוֹי אֶחָד בָּאָרֶץ. חֲדוּ כֻּלְּהוּ כָּל הַהוּא יוֹמָא בְּמִלִּין דְּאוֹרַיְיתָא, וְכָל בְּנֵי מָתָא עַבְדוּ לֵיהּ רֵישָׁא עָלַיְיהוּ. לְיוֹמָא אַחֲרָא, קָמוּ רִבִּי יוֹסִי וְרִבִּי חִיָּיא וּבָרְכוּ לוֹן, וְאָזְלוּ לְאָרְחַיְיהוּ.

**799.** Blessed are the children of Yisrael, for they merit below as above. About them, it is written: "And what one nation in the earth is like your people, like Yisrael" (II Shmuel 7:23). They all rejoiced that entire day with words of Torah, and all the inhabitants of that city placed him, THE YOUTH, as their head. On the next day, Rabbi Yosi and Rabbi Chiya arose and blessed them and went on their way.

‎800. כַּד מָטוּ לְגַבֵּיהּ דְּר"ש, זָקַף עֵינוֹי וְחָמָא לוֹן. אָמַר לוֹן מִסְתַּכֵּל הֲוֵינָא בְּכוּ יוֹמָא דָא, וַחֲמֵינָא לְכוּ תְּרֵין יוֹמִין וְחַד לֵילְיָא, דַּהֲוֵיתוּן לְגַבֵּי מַשְׁכְּנָא דְּהַהוּא נַעַר מְטַטְרוֹן, וְהַהוּא נַעַר הֲוָה אוֹלִיף לְכוּ רָזִין עִלָּאִין בְּחֶדְוָה דְּאוֹרַיְיתָא, זַכָּאָה חוּלָקֵכוֹן בָּנַי.

**800.** When they arrived before Rabbi Shimon, he raised his eyes and saw them. He said to them: I viewed you today and I saw that you were two days and one night in the Tabernacle of the youth Metatron, and that youth taught you supernal secrets with the joy of Torah. Blessed is your portion, my sons.

801. סְדָרוּ מִלִּין כֻּלְּהוּ קַמֵּיה, וְסָחוּ לֵיה עוֹבָדָא, אָמַר לוֹן זַכָּאִין אַתּוּן, וְזַכָּאָה חוּלָקִי, דְּהָא אַדְכַּרְנָא יוֹמָא חַד דַּהֲוָה אָזִיל עִמִּי בְּאָרְחָא רַב סָפְרָא אֲבוֹי, וּבָרִיכִית לֵיה כַּד אִתְפְּרַשׁ מִנִּי, דְּיֶהֱא לֵיה בַּר אַרְיָא בְּאוֹרַיְיתָא, וְלָא בָּרִיכִית לֵיה דְּאִיהוּ יִזְכֵּי בֵּיה. זַכָּאָה חוּלָקֵכוֹן בָּנַי, עֲלַיְיכוּ כְּתִיב וְכָל בָּנַיִךְ לִמּוּדֵי יְיָ׳.

**801.** They related before him all the words and told him the whole story. He said to them: Blessed are you and blessed is my portion, for I remember that one day his father, Rabbi Safra, was traveling with me on the road. When he separated from me, I blessed him that he should have a son who will be a lion in Torah, but I did not bless him so that he should merit to see him thus. THEREFORE, HE DIED AND DID NOT KNOW HIM. Blessed is your portion, my sons. About you, it is written: "And all your children shall be taught of Hashem" (Yeshayah 54:13).

## 81. "And all your children shall be taught of Hashem"

### A Synopsis

Rabbi Shimon explains here that when children are studying Torah, the Shechinah gives them strength and courage, and the Holy One assists them: this is the meaning of, "And all your children shall be taught of The Creator." But another meaning emerges as Rabbi Shimon and Rabbi Chiya encounter a child who answers them with a prophecy. The child says that prophecy stems from the aspects of Netzach and Hod, but only for the children of Yisrael, not for other people.

### The Relevance of this Passage

The Light of the Shechinah shining here imbues the children of our world with courage and strength and a love of spirituality. And because all of us are children of our parents and children of the Light, we, too, are strengthened so that we have the boldness to reject the temptations of material existence and the wisdom to walk in the way of the Creator. The innocence of childhood blossoms in our souls. And the prophecy associated with children that causes gems of wisdom to come out from the mouths of babes, emerges in our consciousness.

802. ד"א וְכָל בָּנַיִךְ לִמּוּדֵי יְיָ'. וְכִי כָּל בְּנִין דְּאִינּוּן דְּיִשְׂרָאֵל, כֻּלְּהוּ אוֹלִיף לוֹן קוּדְשָׁא בְּרִיךְ הוּא אוֹרַיְיתָא. אִין. דְּהָא בְּשַׁעֲתָא דְּאִינּוּן יְנוֹקֵי לָעָאן בְּאוֹרַיְיתָא, שְׁכִינְתָּא אַתְיָא וְיָהִיב לוֹן חֵילָא וְתִקְפָּא לְמִלְעֵי בְּאוֹרַיְיתָא, דְּאִלְמָלֵא סִיּוּעָא דְּקוּדְשָׁא בְּרִיךְ הוּא, לָא יַכְלִין אִינּוּן יְנוֹקֵי לְמִסְבַּל.

802. Another explanation of: "And all your children shall be taught of Hashem" (Yeshayah 54:13). FOR IT CAN BE ASKED: Are all the children of Yisrael taught Torah by the Holy One, blessed be He? HE SAYS: Yes, because when these children are studying Torah, the Shechinah comes and gives them strength and courage to study Torah. If not for the assistance of the Holy One, blessed be He, the children could not tolerate it.

803. רַבִּי שִׁמְעוֹן הֲוָה שְׁכִיחַ יוֹמָא חַד גַּבֵּי פִּתְחָא דְּלוֹד, וְרַבִּי חִיָּיא בַּהֲדֵיהּ, פָּגַע בֵּיהּ חַד יְנוּקָא, אָמַר רַבִּי שִׁמְעוֹן וַדַּאי דְּקוּדְשָׁא בְּרִיךְ הוּא

אִתְּעַר בְּעָלְמָא הַשְׁתָּא לְיוֹמִין זְעִירִין, גִּלְגּוּלָא רַבָּא לְמַלְכֵי אַרְעָא אִלֵּין בְּאִלֵּין. וַדַּאי בְּעוֹד דְּאִינּוּן מְקַטְרְגִין אִלֵּין עַל אִלֵּין, יִשְׂרָאֵל יְהוֹן גּוֹ רְוָוחָא.

**803.** Rabbi Shimon was at the gate of Lod one day, with Rabbi Chiya. A child came to him. Rabbi Shimon said: Surely the Holy One, blessed be He, will arouse in the world in a few days a great revolution, MEANING GREAT WARS, among the kings of the world, one with another. It is definite that while they are oppressing each other, the children of Yisrael will be peaceful.

**804.** אָמַר הַהוּא יַנּוּקָא, וְהָא בְּיוֹמָא דָא שַׁאֲרֵי אִתְּעָרוּתָא דָא, דְּהָא בְּהַאי יוֹמָא דָמִין סַגִּיאִין אוּשְׁדִין בְּעָלְמָא. א״ל רַבִּי חִיָּיא, מְנָא לֵיהּ לְהַאי יַנּוּקָא. אָמַר רַבִּי שִׁמְעוֹן, לְזִמְנִין נְבוּאָה נָפִיל בְּפוּם יַנּוּקָן, וּמִתְנַבְּאֵי יַתִּיר מֵחַד נְבִיאָה.

**804.** That boy said: Behold, this awakening has started today, for much blood has been spilled today in the world. Rabbi Chiya said to him: How does this boy know this? Rabbi Shimon said: Sometimes prophecy comes by the mouths of children, and they prophesy more then a prophet.

**805.** אָמַר הַהוּא יַנּוּקָא, וְכִי תַּוְוהָא אִיהוּ בְּיַנּוּקֵי לְמֶהֱוֵי לוֹן נְבוּאָה, וְהָא קְרָא שְׁלִים אִיהוּ. מְנָלָן. דִּכְתִיב וְכָל בָּנַיִךְ לִמּוּדֵי יְיָ'. אִינּוּן וַדַּאי לִמּוּדֵי יְיָ', וּנְבוּאָה מִנְּהוֹן נָפְקָא, מַה דְּלֵית הָכִי לְכָל עָלְמָא, אֶלָּא לְיִשְׂרָאֵל בִּלְחוֹדוֹי, דִּכְתִיב בְּהוּ וְכָל בָּנַיִךְ לִמּוּדֵי יְיָ', וּבְגִינֵי כַּךְ מִנְּהוֹן נָפְקָא נְבוּאָה. אָתָא רַבִּי שִׁמְעוֹן וּנְשָׁקֵיהּ אָמַר מְיוּמָאי לָא שְׁמַעֲנָא דָא, בַּר הַשְׁתָּא.

**805.** The boy said: Is it any wonder that children prophecy? There is a whole verse to support this. How do we know this? From the verse: "And all your children shall be taught of Hashem." Assuredly, they are "taught of Hashem," MEANING IN THE ASPECTS OF NETZACH AND HOD KNOWN AS "TAUGHT OF HASHEM," as prophecy stems from there. This is not so with

the whole world but for the children of Yisrael alone, as it is written: "And all your children shall be taught of Hashem." Therefore, prophecy comes from them. Rabbi Shimon came and kissed him. He said: I have never heard this except just now.

## 82. "And you shall make boards"

### A Synopsis
Rabbi Shimon here says that the boards in "And you shall make boards for the Tabernacle of acacia wood standing up" are like the Seraphim standing each with their six wings. All the hosts of heaven stand, and all the supernal angels are occasionally called 'Seraphim'.

### The Relevance of this Passage
The tabernacle was the Vessel necessary for the Light to express itself on this planet. Here Rabbi Shimon reveals supernal secrets behind the construction of the tabernacle. His purpose in doing so is to construct a personal tabernacle, an internal vessel, for the reader through his holy words so that God's Light can rest upon us. Moreover, this action connects our planet to the original Tabernacle, allowing God's Light to inhabit the entire world, causing the demise of death, suffering, pain, and torment. Expect nothing less when such a magnificent instrument is wielded in the hands of so noble a sage.

806. דָּא פְּקוּדָא דְּקוּדְשָׁא בְּרִיךְ הוּא לְמֹשֶׁה: וְעָשִׂיתָ אֶת הַקְּרָשִׁים לַמִּשְׁכָּן עֲצֵי שִׁטִּים עוֹמְדִים. וּכְתִיב שְׂרָפִים עוֹמְדִים מִמַּעַל לוֹ שֵׁשׁ כְּנָפַיִם וְגוֹ', עוֹבָדָא דְּמַשְׁכְּנָא בְּאִינּוּן קְרָשִׁים, כְּגַוְונָא דְּאִינּוּן שְׂרָפִים, אִלֵּין עוֹמְדִים, וְאִלֵּין עוֹמְדִים.

806. This was the commandment of the Holy One, blessed be He, to Moses: "And you shall make boards for the Tabernacle of acacia wood standing up" (Shemot 26:15). It is written: "Seraphim stood above Him, each one had six wings..." (Yeshayah 6:2). For the construction of the Tabernacle with these boards resembled these Seraphim. The ones were standing and the others were standing.

807. וְאִי תֵּימָא, וְהָא כָּל חַיָּילֵי שְׁמַיָּא אִינּוּן עוֹמְדִים כֻּלְּהוּ, כד"א וְנָתַתִּי לְךָ מַהְלְכִים בֵּין הָעוֹמְדִים הָאֵלֶּה, וּכְתִיב וְכָל צְבָא הַשָּׁמַיִם עוֹמְדִים עָלָיו וְגוֹ', דְּהָא כֻּלְּהוּ מַשִׁרְיָין עִלָּאִין לֵית לְהוּ קְפִיצִין, וְכֻלְּהוּ קַיְימֵי בְּקִימָה. אֶלָּא וַדַּאי כֻּלְּהוּ קַיְימִין, וּלְזִמְנִין אִלֵּין אִקְרוּן שְׂרָפִים, וּלְזִמְנִין סַלְּקִין בִּשְׁמָא אַחֲרָא, אֲבָל אִלֵּין כֻּלְּהוּ בְּחַד שְׁמָא קַיְימֵי.

**807.** If you say that all the hosts of heaven stand, as it is written: "Then I will give you access among these who stand by" (Zecharyah 3:7) and "all the host of heaven standing by Him..." (I Melachim 22:19). Do all the supernal camps have no joints, NAMELY KNEES TO KNEEL AND SIT, so they all stand? HE ANSWERS: Surely they all stand. They are sometimes called 'Seraphim' and sometimes with a different name, but these IN THE VERSE "SERAPHIM STOOD ABOVE HIM" always bear the same name, SERAPHIM. AND THE COMPARISON OF THE BOARDS OF THE TABERNACLE TO SERAPHIM IS TRUE WITH ALL THE SUPERNAL ANGELS, BECAUSE THEY ARE ALL REFERRED TO AS SERAPHIM OCCASIONALLY BUT THEY ARE NOT EXACTLY LIKE THE SERAPHIM IN THE VERSE: "SERAPHIM STOOD ABOVE HIM..."

## 83. "Hashem is my shepherd; I shall not want"

### A Synopsis

Here, Rabbi Shimon tells us that the Shechinah came and dwelled on David and inspired him to recite this praise to God and to request sustenance from Him. When God brings food to the world, the Shechinah takes from it first, so it is for her sake that food descends to all the worlds. "The Creator is my shepherd," we learn, also means that He sustains a person with everything he needs.

### The Relevance of this Passage

The Light of sustenance and abundance shines upon us through the merit of King David. We learn from David that one should meditate upon this passage with great desire, requesting The Creator to fill all of our needs, for if one does not ask, one cannot receive. Thus, ask for everything good, the totality of Light, the Final Redemption, the annulment of judgments, and infinite loving kindness, through it all.

808. וְהַאי קְרָא אוּקְמוּהָ, כְּתִיב מִזְמוֹר לְדָוִד יְיָ׳ רֹעִי לָא אֶחְסָר. הָא אִתְּמַר, מַה בֵּין מִזְמוֹר לְדָוִד, וּבֵין לְדָוִד מִזְמוֹר. וְהָכָא, שְׁכִינְתָּא קַדְמָא וְאַתְיָא, וְשָׁרָאת עֲלֵיה בְּקַדְמֵיתָא. יְיָ׳ רֹעִי, וְכִי אֲמַאי שְׁכִינְתָּא קַדְמָא הָכָא, וְהָא דָוִד אִצְטְרִיךְ לְאַקְדְּמָא אִיהוּ בְּקַדְמֵיתָא, הוֹאִיל וּבָעֵי מְזוֹנֵיה מֵעִם קוּדְשָׁא בְּרִיךְ הוּא.

808. This verse has been established, for it is written: "A Psalm of David, Hashem is my shepherd; I shall not want" (Tehilim 23:1), for we have learned the difference between "A Psalm of David" and "To David a psalm." "A PSALM OF DAVID" SHOWS THAT THE SHECHINAH DWELT UPON HIM AND THEN HE SANG, AND "TO DAVID A PSALM" SHOWS THAT FIRST HE SANG, THEN THE SHECHINAH DWELT UPON HIM. Here by "Hashem is my shepherd," the Shechinah preceded and came and dwelt upon him first, FOR IT IS WRITTEN: "A PSALM OF DAVID." HE QUESTIONS: Why did the Shechinah precede here, BY "HASHEM IS MY SHEPHERD?" David should have preceded, since he asked for his sustenance from the Holy One, blessed be He.

809. אֶלָּא, וַדַּאי שְׁכִינְתָּא קַדְמָא וְאַתְיָא, וְשָׁרָאת עֲלֵיה, וְאִתְּעֲרַת לֵיה לְשַׁבְּחָא לְמַלְכָּא שְׁבָחָא דָא, וּלְמִבְעֵי מְזוֹנֵי מִקְּמֵי מַלְכָּא, דְּהָא הָכִי

אִצְטְרִיךְ עַל מִלָּה דִּמְזוֹנָא דְּבָעֵיָא אִיהִי וּרְעוּתָא דִּילָהּ, דְּכָל בְּנֵי עָלְמָא יִבְעוּן מְזוֹנֵי. בְּגִין דְּכַד קוּדְשָׁא בְּרִיךְ הוּא בָּעֵי לְנַחְתָּא מְזוֹנֵי לְעָלְמָא, אִיהִי נַטְלָא בְּקַדְמֵיתָא, וְעָלָהּ נַחְתֵּי מְזוֹנֵי לְעָלְמִין כֻּלְּהוּ. וּבְגִינֵי כָּךְ אִיהִי אַקְדִּימַת לְמִלָּה דָּא דִּמְזוֹנֵי, וְשַׁרְאַת עָלֵיהּ דְּדָוִד.

**809.** HE ANSWERS: Surely the Shechinah preceded and came and dwelt upon him, and aroused him to recite this praise to the King and request sustenance of the King. This is the way it should be concerning food, FOR THE SHECHINAH desires it and Her wish is that all the inhabitants of the world should pray for food, because when the Holy One, blessed be He, desires to bring down food to the world, THE SHECHINAH takes first. For Her sake, food descends to all the worlds, BECAUSE IT IS IMPOSSIBLE THAT THOSE BELOW SHOULD RECEIVE ANYTHING UNLESS THOSE ABOVE RECEIVE FIRST, AS MENTIONED ABOVE. Therefore, THE SHECHINAH preceded in this matter of food and dwelt upon David.

810. יְיָ' רֹעִי, יְיָ' רַעְיָא דִּילִי, כְּהַאי רַעְיָא דְּמַדְבַּר עָאנָא דִּילֵיהּ בַּאֲתַר דְּדִשְׁאִין וַעֲשָׂבִין, דְּלָא מְחַסַּר בֵּיהּ כָּל מִדְעַם. אוּף הָכִי קוּדְשָׁא בְּרִיךְ הוּא, הוּא אִיהוּ, רַעְיָא דִּילִי, לְמֵיזָן לִי בְּכָל מָה דַּאֲנָא אִצְטְרִיךְ. ד"א יְיָ' רֹעִי, תַּנְיָנָן, דְּקַשְׁיִין מְזוֹנוֹתָיו דְּב"נ קַמֵּי קוּדְשָׁא בְּרִיךְ הוּא, כִּקְרִיעַת יַם סוּף. הָכָא תְּרֵין גַּוְונִין אִינּוּן, וְתַרְוַויְיהוּ בְּאֹרַח קְשׁוֹט.

**810.** "Hashem is my shepherd" just like the shepherd who leads his sheep to the place that has herbage and grasses, where nothing is lacking. The Holy One, blessed be He, is also my Shepherd to sustain one with everything I need. Another explanation FOR "Hashem is my shepherd": We have learned that man's sustenance is as difficult to obtain as the splitting of the Red Sea. These here are two manners, TWO EXPLANATIONS, and they are both true.

## 84. Man's sustenance is difficult to obtain as the splitting of the Red Sea

### A Synopsis

Rabbi Shimon explains here that even though it is difficult for God to see the wicked and the sinners, still He feeds and sustains everyone according to the supernal Chesed that is drawn and flows over all the inhabitants of the world. With it He feeds and sustains all the righteous, and the pious, and the wicked, and all the people of the world, and all the beasts and animals of the field, and the birds of the heavens – from the horns of the buffalo to the eggs of lice. So why, we are asked, was this as difficult for God as the splitting of the Red Sea, which should have been easy for Him? Rabbi Shimon explains that when the children of Yisrael called for God to part the sea, the minister of Egypt spoke and reminded Him of the sins committed by them, and that He should judge them accordingly and let them drown. Yet, we are told, God split the sea for them because of the righteousness of Abraham, who rose up early in the morning to fulfill His commandments.

### The Relevance of this Passage

Here we learn again that God shines His Light on the just and the unjust, that the rains fall on the righteous and the wicked, that sustenance is given to everyone. In this way, each of us is enabled to play out destiny, to exercise free will, to move toward or away from God in the space He has made for us. And, we learn, He will always show mercy, even when we have sinned.

On a deeper level, Kabbalah informs us that Moses and the children of Israel split the Red Sea by virtue of their own transformations of character. As the Red Sea stood before them, and the Egyptian army raced towards them from behind, doubt and uncertainty gripped the Israelites. Nevertheless, using the power of the 72 Names of God to transcend their own fears and uncertainties, the Israelites walked into the sea until the waters filled their nostrils. This immense display of trust was a miracle of human nature. In turn, their behavioral actions ignited a miracle of Mother Nature, the seas parted as the waters rose to the heavens.

Though we all sin, we utilize this passage and the righteousness of Abraham to accomplish our own miracles of nature – to forever change our ways and correct all the sins of our past. This miraculous occurrence causes miracles of nature. And there is no greater miracle than the world's liberation from the clutches of the angel Satan (metaphorically represented as Yisrael fleeing the Egyptians through the parted Red Sea).

## 84. Man's sustenance is difficult to obtain
## as the splitting of the Red Sea

Granted, this is a feat as difficult as parting an ocean, but the strength, power, and Light of Abraham are here, with the *72 Names*, to support us, so it is a *fait accompli* the moment our eyes and hearts embrace these ancient verses.

‏811. חַד בְּגִין דְּקוּדְשָׁא בְּרִיךְ הוּא כָּל עוֹבָדוֹי בְּדִינָא וּקְשׁוֹט, וְעַל דִּינָא וּקְשׁוֹט אִתְקַיַּים עַל עָלְמָא. וּבְכָל יוֹמָא וְיוֹמָא וּבְכָל זִמְנָא וְזִמְנָא, דָּן כָּל עָלְמָא בְּדִינָא לְצַדִּיקֵי וּלְרַשִׁיעֵי וּלְכָל בְּנֵי עָלְמָא, כד"א כִּי צַדִּיק יְיָ' צְדָקוֹת אָהֵב. וְכַד אִיהוּ דָּן בְּנֵי נָשָׁא, וְחָמֵי בְּנֵי נָשָׁא כַּמָּה חַיָּיבִין, וְכַמָּה חַטָּאִין קַמֵּיהּ, כְּדֵין קָשֶׁה בְּעֵינוֹי לְמֵיהַב לוֹן מְזוֹנָא בְּכָל זִמְנָא, בְּגִין דְּאִית לֵיהּ לְמֵיזָן חַיָּיבַיָּא, וּלְאִינּוּן דְּחַטָּאן.

**811.** One EXPLANATION is that all the actions of the Holy One, blessed be He, are according to Justice and Truth, and the entire world is supported on Justice and Truth. Every day and all the time, He judges the righteous, the wicked and all the inhabitants of the world with Justice, as it is written: "For Hashem is righteous, He loves righteousness" (Tehilim 11:7). When He judges the people and sees how many are wicked and how many are sinners before Him, it is difficult for Him to give them food constantly, because He has to feed the wicked and those that sin.

‏812 וְאִיהוּ עָבֵיד עִמְּהוֹן לְגוֹ מְשׁוּרַת הַדִּין, וְזָן וּמְפַרְנֵס לוֹן כְּפוּם חֶסֶד עִלָּאָה, דְּאִתְמְשַׁךְ וְאִתְנְגִיד עַל כָּל בְּנֵי עָלְמָא, וּבֵהּ אִיהוּ זָן וּמְפַרְנֵס לְכֹלָּא, לְצַדִּיקֵי וּלְחֲסִידֵי וּלְרַשִׁיעֵי, וּלְכָל אִינּוּן בְּנֵי עָלְמָא, וּלְכָל חֵיוָן וּבְעִירֵי חַקְלָא, וְעוֹפֵי שְׁמַיָּא, מִקַּרְנֵי רְאֵמִים עַד בֵּיצֵי כַלְמֵי, וְלָא אִשְׁתְּאַר בְּעָלְמָא, דְּאִיהוּ לָא זָן וּמְפַרְנֵס לְכֹלָּא, אַף עַל גַּב דְּקָשֶׁה קַמֵּיהּ, לְפוּם עוֹבָדִין דִּבְנֵי עָלְמָא, כִּקְרִיעַת יַם סוּף.

**812.** Yet He deals with them mercifully, and feeds and sustains them according to the supernal Chesed that is drawn and flows over all the inhabitants of the world. With it, He feeds and sustains all the righteous and pious and the wicked and all the people of the world and all the beasts and animals of the field and the birds of the heavens, from the horns of the buffalo to the eggs of lice. There is nothing left in the world that is not fed,

but He sustains everything, even though it is difficult for Him due to the actions of the people of the world, as is the splitting of the Red Sea.

813. וְכִי קְרִיעַת יַם סוּף קָשֶׁה קַמֵּיה, וְהָכְתִיב גּוֹעֵר בַּיָּם וַיַּבְּשֵׁהוּ, הַקּוֹרֵא לְמֵי הַיָּם וַיִּשְׁפְּכֵם עַל פְּנֵי הָאָרֶץ, וְהָא כֵּיוָן דְּסָלִיק רְעוּתָא קַמֵּיה, כֹּלָּא קַמֵּיה כְּאַיִן הוּא חָשִׁיב, וְאַתְּ אַמְרַתְּ דִּקְרִיעַת יַם סוּף קָשֶׁה קַמֵּיה.

813. HE QUESTIONS: Was the splitting of the Red Sea difficult for Him? Is it not written: "He rebukes the sea and makes it dry" (Nachum 1:4)? "He calls for the waters of the sea, and pours them out upon the face of the earth" (Amos 5:8) and, as soon as the desire arises before Him, everything is as nothing before Him, and you say that splitting the Red Sea is difficult to perform before Him?

814. אֶלָּא בְּזִמְנָא דְּיִשְׂרָאֵל אַעְבָּרוּ לְגַבֵּי יַמָּא, וּבָעָא קוּדְשָׁא בְּרִיךְ הוּא לְמִקְרַע לוֹן יַמָּא דְּסוּף, אָתָא רַהַב הַהוּא מְמָנָא דְּעַל מִצְרַיִם, וּבָעָא דִּינָא מִקַּמֵּי קוּדְשָׁא בְּרִיךְ הוּא. אָמַר קַמֵּיה, מָארֵיה דְּעָלְמָא, אֲמַאי אַתְּ בָּעֵי לְמֶעְבַּד דִּינָא עַל מִצְרַיִם, וּלְמִקְרַע יַמָּא לְיִשְׂרָאֵל, הָא כֻּלְּהוּ חַיָּיבִין קַמָּךְ, וְכָל אָרְחָךְ בְּדִינָא וּקְשׁוֹט. אִלֵּין פַּלְחֵי כּו"ם וְאִלֵּין פַּלְחֵי כּו"ם. אִלֵּין בְּגִלּוּי עֲרָיוֹת, וְאִלֵּין בְּגִלּוּי עֲרָיוֹת. אִלֵּין אוֹשְׁדֵי דָמִין, וְאִלֵּין אוֹשְׁדֵי דָמִין.

814. HE ANSWERS: When the children of Yisrael approached the sea and the Holy One, blessed be He, wanted to split the Red Sea for them, Rahav, the minister of Egypt, came and requested Justice from the Holy One, blessed be He. Rahav said before Him, Master of the Universe: Why do You want to punish Egypt and split the sea for Yisrael? Are they not all wicked before You? Your ways are with Justice and Truth, but these worship idols and these worship idols, and these sin with incest and these sin with incest. These spill blood and these spill blood.

815. בְּהַהִיא שַׁעְתָּא הֲוָה קָשֶׁה קַמֵּיה, לְמֶעְבַּר עַל אֹרַח דִּינָא. וְהָא יִשְׂרָאֵל הֲווֹ נַטְלֵי עַל יַמָּא, דִּכְתִּיב וַיֹּאמֶר יְיָ' אֶל מֹשֶׁה מַה תִּצְעַק אֵלַי

## 84. Man's sustenance is difficult to obtain
## as the splitting of the Red Sea

דַּבֵּר אֶל בְּנֵי יִשְׂרָאֵל וְיִסָּעוּ, וַהֲוָה קָשֶׁה קַמֵּיה לְמֶעֱבַּר עַל דִּינָא,
וּלְמִקְרַע לוֹן יַמָּא דְסוּף, וְאִלְמָלֵא דְּאַשְׁגַּח קוּדְשָׁא בְּרִיךְ הוּא בִּזְכוּת
אַבְרָהָם, דְּאַקְדִּים בְּצַפְרָא לְמֶעֱבַּד פִּקּוּדָא דְּמָארֵיה, וּרְעוּתָא דִילֵיה,
כִּדְכְתִיב וַיַּשְׁכֵּם אַבְרָהָם בַּבֹּקֶר, כֻּלְּהוּ אִתְאֲבִידוּ בְּיַמָּא, בְּגִין דִּבְכָל
הַהוּא לֵילְיָא, בְּדִינָא הֲוָה קוּדְשָׁא בְּרִיךְ הוּא עֲלַיְיהוּ דְיִשְׂרָאֵל.

**815.** At that moment, it was difficult for Him to disregard Justice. Here the children of Yisrael were driving toward the sea, as it is written: "And Hashem said to Moses, 'Why do you cry to me? speak to the children of Yisrael, that they go forward'" (Shemot 14:15). But it was difficult for Him disregard Judgment and split the Red Sea for them. Had not the Holy One, blessed be He, looked to the Merit of Abraham, who preceded in the early morning to fulfill the commandment of his Master and His desire, as it is written: "And Abraham rose up early in the morning" (Beresheet 22:3), they would all have been lost in the sea, because the Holy One, blessed be He, was judging Yisrael all that night.

816. דְּתָנֵינָן, מַאי דִכְתִיב וְלֹא קָרַב זֶה אֶל זֶה כָּל הַלָּיְלָה. מְלַמֵּד דְּאָתוּ
מַלְאֲכֵי עִלָּאֵי לְשַׁבְּחָא בְּהַהוּא לֵילְיָא קַמֵּי קוּדְשָׁא בְּרִיךְ הוּא, אָמַר לוֹן,
וְכִי עוֹבְדֵי יְדַי טַבְעִין בְּיַמָּא, וְאַתּוּן מְשַׁבְּחָן קַמָּאי, מִיַּד וְלֹא קָרַב זֶה
אֶל זֶה כָּל הַלָּיְלָה. מַה כְּתִיב, וַיְהִי בְּאַשְׁמֹרֶת הַבֹּקֶר, אַשְׁגַּח קוּדְשָׁא
בְּרִיךְ הוּא בִּזְכוּתָא דְּאַבְרָהָם, דְּאַקְדִּים בְּצַפְרָא לְמֶעֱבַּד רְעוּתֵיה
דְּמָארֵיה, כִּדְכְתִיב וַיַּשְׁכֵּם אַבְרָהָם בַּבֹּקֶר. כְּדֵין אַהֲדַר יַמָּא, וְעָרְקוּ מַיִין
קַמַּיְיהוּ דְיִשְׂרָאֵל.

**816.** We have learned that it is written: "...so that one came not near the other all the night" (Shemot 14:20), which teaches that the Archangels came to praise before the Holy One, blessed be He, that night. He said to them: 'The works of my hands are drowning in the sea and you sing praises before Me?' Immediately, "one came not near the other all the night" BECAUSE "ONE TO ANOTHER" IS SAID ABOUT THE ANGELS WHO PRAISE THE HOLY ONE, BLESSED BE HE, AS IT IS WRITTEN: "AND ONE CRIED TO ANOTHER, AND SAID, 'HOLY...'" It is written: "And it was come to pass,

that in the morning watch" (Shemot 14:24), the Holy One, blessed be He, observed the merit of Abraham, who rose up early in the morning to do the will of his Master, as it written, "And Abraham rose up early in the morning." Then the sea turned back and the water fled from before the children of Yisrael.

817. דִּכְתִּיב וַיָּשָׁב הַיָּם לִפְנוֹת בֹּקֶר לְאֵיתָנוֹ, וְתָנֵינָן, לְאֵיתָנוֹ: לִתְנָאוֹ. לְהַהוּא תְּנַאי דְּהִתְנָה עִמֵּיהּ קוּדְשָׁא בְּרִיךְ הוּא, כַּד בָּרָא עָלְמָא, לְאֵיתָנוֹ, כְּתִיב הָכָא לְאֵיתָנוֹ, וּכְתִיב הָתָם מַשְׂכִּיל לְאֵיתָן הָאֶזְרָחִי, וְעַל דָּא לִפְנוֹת בֹּקֶר, בְּהַהוּא זִמְנָא דְּאַקְדִּים אַבְרָהָם לְמֶעְבַּד רְעוּתָא דְּמָארֵיהּ, כְּדֵין אִתְקְרַע יַמָּא, וְע"ד קָשֶׁה הֲוָה קַמֵּיהּ קְרִיעַת יַם סוּף.

817. It is also written: "And the sea returned to its strength (Heb. *leeitano*) when the morning appeared" (Ibid. 27). We learned that "leeitano" MEANS *litnao* (Eng. 'to its conditioning'), to that condition that the Holy One, blessed be He, made with it when He created the world. FOR HE HAD MADE A CONDITION THAT IT SHOULD SPLIT FOR YISRAEL, BECAUSE *EITANO* (ENG. 'ITS STRENGTH') IS SPELLED WITH THE SAME LETTERS AS *TNAI* (ENG. 'CONDITION'). BUT WE SHOULD ADD that it is written here: 'leeitano', while there it is written: "Maskil of Eitan the Ezrachite" (Tehilim 89:1), WHO IS ABRAHAM. HERE ALSO *EITANO* ALLUDES TO ABRAHAM. THEREFORE, THE TORAH SAYS: "when the morning appeared." At that same time, Abraham got up early in the morning to do the will of his Master, then the sea was split. Therefore, the splitting of the sea was difficult for Him.

## 85. Match-making is difficult before the Holy One, blessed be He, like splitting the Red Sea

### A Synopsis

When the Red Sea parted, we learn, some people were saved and some were killed. Someone dies and there is weeping, yet his wife is given to another and there is singing. And sometimes a wicked person gets a good woman. Rabbi Shimon says here that there are concealed secrets in all this, yet, nonetheless, it is all according to the law. He then tells us that 'before the Holy One' refers to Malchut; these things are difficult for Her because they are not under Her authority; she receives everything from the Holy One. Rabbi Shimon next questions the meaning of, "And that soul will be cut off from before Me," and decides that it means that the soul will be cut off from all the delights of the world to come, which is Binah. Then we read of Jonah: "And Yonah rose to flee to Tarshish from before The Creator," and, "for the men knew that he had fled from before The Creator." How is it possible to flee from God? Rabbi Shimon explains that this means Jonah was afraid to be in the Holy Land so that the spirit of prophecy should not come upon him. He then speaks of the role of the Shechinah, who dwells in the Holy Land, and who rested on King David before he said, "Yud Hei Vav Hei is my shepherd; I shall not want." When the Shechinah receives food above for all the worlds, all the angels delight and awaken and raise their wings to cover their faces when She comes to deliver their food to them, so that they do not gaze upon Her. There are three companies of worshipping angels, we are told, who fit into each other like the tendons in the standing boards of acacia in the tabernacle.

Rabbi Shimon next discusses, "For the merchandise of it is better than the merchandise of silver, and its gain than fine gold," and, "He makes me to lie down in green pastures; He leads me beside the still waters." "He restores my soul," we learn, means the soul of David, which is Malchut, who wishes to amend his level properly. The righteous will rest in the world to come with these "still waters" that are drawn and emerge from Eden.

### The Relevance of this Passage

Here we see that there is an underlying and hidden, yet lawful, reason for life and death, good and evil, grieving and rejoicing. We are told that these things are not hard for the Holy One but they are hard for Malchut, and from this we see that it is only because our understanding is so much lower than God's that we have difficulty accepting the seeming inequities of the world. This difficulty is

ultimately caused by the existence of time. Kabbalah defines time as the distance between cause and effect.

It is the separation between action and reaction; the measurement between conduct and recompense; the space between deed and dividend; and the chasm between crime and consequence. Because of time's existence, we believe mistakenly that goodness goes unrewarded, that evil goes unpunished, and that life lacks true justice. The world appears chaotic and random; when in reality, there is an exquisite and elegant order, the law of cause and effect, beneath the turmoil. Through David, we correct the sins of our past, rectifying and restoring all Malchut. All the waters of earth become still and the green pastures upon our earth welcome us as the Light of the Shechinah reaches her maximum intensity.

818. כְּגַוְונָא דָא, קָשִׁין זִווּגִין קָמֵי קוּדְשָׁא בְּרִיךְ הוּא כִּקְרִיעַת יַם סוּף, מַה קְרִיעַת יַם סוּף קָטִיל לְאַלֵּין בְּהַאי סִטְרָא, וּמְקַיֵּים לְאַלֵּין בְּהַאי סִטְרָא, אוּף הָכָא בְּזִווּגִין, כְּתִיב מוֹצִיא אֲסִירִים בַּכּוֹשָׁרוֹת, וְתָנֵינָן בְּכִי וְשִׁירוֹת, מַיְית הַאי, וְיָהִיב אִתְּתֵיה לְהַאי וּלְזִמְנִין לַחַיָּיבָא, מִזְדַּמְּנָא לֵיה אִתְּתָא מְעַלְיָא. אֲבָל רָזִין סְתִימִין אִינּוּן בְּכֹלָּא וְכֹלָּא הוּא בְּדִינָא, וּמַה דְּאִתְעֲרוּ חַבְרַיָּיא בְּהָא, וַדַּאי הָכִי הוּא.

**818.** Similarly, match-making is difficult before the Holy One, blessed be He, like the splitting of the Red Sea; just as by the splitting of the Red Sea, these are killed on the one hand while others are kept alive on the other hand. By match-making, it is also written: "He brings out the prisoners into prosperity (Heb. *bakosharot*)" (Tehilim 68:7). We have learned that IT IS SPELLED WITH THE LETTERS of weeping and singing (Heb. *bechi veshirot*), because this one dies AND THERE IS WEEPING, and He gives his wife to another AND THERE IS SINGING. Sometimes a wicked person gets a good woman; THEREFORE, MATING IS DIFFICULT BEFORE HIM LIKE THE SPLITTING OF THE RED SEA. There are concealed secrets in it all, and it is all according to the law. And what the friends have remarked ABOUT THIS, TO EXPLAIN WHY ONE IS THRUST ASIDE BEFORE ANOTHER, certainly it is so.

819. וּמַה דְּאִתְעֲרוּ לְפְנֵי, וְלֹא מִלְּפָנֵי לְפְנֵי הַהוּא דְּקָאִים לְפָנֵי קָמֵיה דְּקוּדְשָׁא בְּרִיךְ הוּא, וְשִׁמֵּשׁ קַמֵּיה, וְעַ"ד לָא אָמְרוּ דְּקַשִׁין זִווּגִין לְקוּדְשָׁא בְּרִיךְ הוּא. וְכֵן קָשִׁין מְזוֹנוֹתָיו שֶׁל אָדָם לְקוּדְשָׁא בְּרִיךְ הוּא,

## 85. Match-making is difficult before the Holy One, blessed be He, like splitting the Red Sea

אֶלָּא לִפְנֵי וּלְהַאי קַשְׁיָין כָּל הָנֵי, דְּהָא לָאו בִּרְשׁוּתֵיהּ קַיְימֵי, אע״ג דְּאִיהוּ עָבֵיד, בִּרְשׁוּתָא אַחֲרָא עָבֵיד.

**819.** And the remark that we were taught about 'before', MEANING THAT 'MATCH-MAKING IS DIFFICULT BEFORE THE HOLY ONE, BLESSED BE HE,' instead of 'from before the Holy One, blessed be He,' it is because 'before' refers to that which stands before the Holy One, blessed be He, and serves before Him, NAMELY MALCHUT THAT RECEIVES FROM THE HOLY ONE, BLESSED BE HE. Therefore, it was not said that match-making is difficult for the Holy One, blessed be He, and similarly, IT WAS NOT SAID that man's food is difficult to obtain for the Holy One, blessed be He. Rather it is before the Holy One, blessed be He, WHICH IS MALCHUT, because all these things are difficult FOR MALCHUT, for they are not under Her authority even though She does accomplish it but this is under another's authority. BECAUSE SHE RECEIVES EVERYTHING FROM THE HOLY ONE, BLESSED BE HE, IT IS APPROPRIATE TO SAY THAT THESE THINGS ARE DIFFICULT FOR HER.

820. כְּתִיב וְנִכְרְתָה הַנֶּפֶשׁ הַהִיא מִלְּפָנָי. מַאי מִלְּפָנָי. אֶלָּא דָּא עָלְמָא דְּאָתֵי, הַהוּא דְּכָל חַיִּין קַיְימִין תַּמָּן. דָּבָר אַחֵר, דָּא צִנּוֹרָא עִלָּאָה, נָהָר דְּלָא פַּסְקִין מֵימוֹי לְעָלְמִין. וְכֹלָּא חַד, וְדָא אִיהוּ דְּנָטִיל כָּל עֶדוּנִין דְּעָלְמָא דְּאָתֵי. וּמֵאִינּוּן עֶדוּנִין עִלָּאִין תִּשְׁתְּצֵי, מֵאֲתָר דְּהַהוּא נֹעַם יְיָ׳ תַּמָּן, וְדָא אִיהוּ מִלְּפָנָי.

**820.** It is written: "And that soul will be cut off from before Me" (Vayikra 22:3). HE QUESTIONS: What is the meaning of "from before Me"? HE ANSWERS: It refers to the World to Come, MEANING BINAH, where all life forms are present. Another explanation: This is the supernal Channel, the river whose waters will never be interrupted, WHICH IS YESOD OF ZEIR ANPIN. It is all one, because this YESOD OF ZEIR ANPIN receives all the delights of the World to Come, WHICH IS BINAH. AND THE VERSE: "AND THAT SOUL WILL BE CUT OFF FROM BEFORE ME" MEANS THAT THE SOUL will be cut off from all these supernal delights that are in the place where the pleasantness of Hashem is, NAMELY BINAH. That is THE MEANING OF "from before Me," BEFORE THE HOLY ONE, BLESSED BE HE, FOR THE

HOLY ONE, BLESSED BE HE, RECEIVES FROM HER, BINAH, THAT PROVIDES TO ZEIR ANPIN THAT IS CALLED 'THE HOLY ONE, BLESSED BE HE'.

821. וְאִי תֵּימָא, אִי הָכִי, הָא כְּתִיב, וַיָּקָם יוֹנָה לִבְרוֹחַ תַּרְשִׁישָׁה מִלִּפְנֵי יְיָ' כִּי יָדְעוּ הָאֲנָשִׁים כִּי מִלִּפְנֵי יְיָ' הוּא בּוֹרֵחַ, וְתָנֵינָן מ"ט אֲזַל יוֹנָה וּבָרַח, וְכִי מַאן יֵיכוּל לְמִבְרַח מִקַּמֵּי קוּדְשָׁא בְּרִיךְ הוּא, אֶלָּא הֲוָה אָזִיל וּבָרַח לְנַפְקָא מֵאַרְעָא קַדִּישָׁא, דְּהָא שְׁכִינְתָּא לָא שַׁרְיָא לְבַר מֵאַרְעָא דְּיִשְׂרָאֵל, וּבְגִין דְּלָא תִּשְׁרֵי עֲלוֹי שְׁכִינְתָּא, הֲוָה בָּרַח בְּאַרְעָא קַדִּישָׁא, דְּהָא שְׁכִינְתָּא אִיהִי שַׁרְיָא תַּמָּן, כְּמָה דְאַתְּ אָמַר אֶשְׁתְּךָ כְּגֶפֶן פּוֹרִיָּה בְּיַרְכְּתֵי בֵיתֶךָ. גֶּפֶן פּוֹרִיָּה דָּא שְׁכִינְתָּא, מַה שְׁכִינְתָּא הֲוָה סְתִימָא לְגוֹ בְּבֵית קוה"ק, אוּף הָכִי אִתְּתָא צְנִיעָא, לָא נָפְקָא מִתַּרְעָא דְּבֵיתָהּ לְבַר. וּבְגִינֵי כַּךְ הֲוָה בָּרַח יוֹנָה לְבַר מֵאַרְעָא קַדִּישָׁא, וְהָא הָכָא כְּתִיב מִלִּפְנֵי, וְלָא כְּתִיב לִפְנֵי.

**821.** If you ask: If so, it is written, "And Jonah rose to flee to Tarshish from before Hashem" (Yonah 1:3) and "for the men knew that he had fled from before Hashem" (Ibid. 10). We have learned what is the reason Jonah fled. Is it then possible to flee from the Holy One, blessed be He? But he fled in order to go out of the Holy Land, since the Shechinah does not dwell outside the Land of Yisrael, and in order that the Shechinah should not dwell upon him, he fled from the Holy Land. The Shechinah dwells there, as it is written: "Your wife shall be like a fruitful vine in the recesses of your house" (Tehilim 128:3). "A fruitful vine" is the Shechinah. Just as the Shechinah is concealed inside, in the Holy of Holies, similarly, a modest woman does not go out from the entrance of her house outside. THEREFORE, THE TORAH COMPARES THE WOMAN TO THE SHECHINAH, and Jonah fled outside of the Holy Land. HE QUESTIONS: Here it is "from before" and it does not say 'before', AND STILL IN ALL, IT MEANS THE SHECHINAH AND NOT BINAH?

822. אֶלָּא וַדַּאי הָכִי הוּא, מִלִּפְנֵי, דְּהָא רוּחַ נְבוּאָה לָא אַתְיָא מִגּוֹ שְׁכִינְתָּא, אֶלָּא מִלִּפְנֵי. אִינּוּן תְּרֵין דַּרְגִּין דִּנְבִיאִים, דְּקָא שַׁרְיָין עַל שְׁכִינְתָּא, וּמֵהַהוּא אֲתָר דָּחִיל לְמֶהֱוֵי תַּמָּן בְּאַרְעָא קַדִּישָׁא, וְע"ד

## 85. Match-making is difficult before the Holy One, blessed be He, like splitting the Red Sea

מִלְּפָנַי. כִּי מִלְּפְנֵי יְיָ' הוּא בּוֹרֵחַ, וְלָא לִפְנֵי יְיָ', דְּהָא הֲוָה יָדַע דִּנְבוּאָה לָא הֲוָה אָתֵי אֶלָּא מִלְּפָנַי.

**822.** HE ANSWERS: It is certainly so, "from before" MEANING BEFORE THE SHECHINAH, because the spirit of prophecy does not come from the Shechinah but rather "from before" MEANING BEFORE THE SHECHINAH, which are the two levels of prophets, WHICH ARE NETZACH AND HOD, that dwell upon the Shechinah. From that place, NETZACH AND HOD, he was afraid to be in the Holy Land so that the prophecy should not dwell upon him. Therefore, it says, "from before Me" because "he fled from before Hashem" and not 'before Hashem,' WHICH WOULD MEAN THE SHECHINAH. Because he knew that prophecy comes only from "from before Me," WHICH IS NETZACH AND HOD.

823. וּבְגִינֵי כַּךְ קָשִׁין זִוּוּגִין, קַשִּׁין מְזוֹנוֹתָיו שֶׁל אָדָם לִפְנֵי הַקּוּדְשָׁא בְּרִיךְ הוּא, וְעַ"ד דָּוִד מַלְכָּא תָּלֵי מְזוֹנוֹתָיו לְעֵילָּא, בְּגִין דִּלְעֵילָּא לָא פָּסִיק לְעָלְמִין. אֲבָל הָכָא פָּסִיק, דְּהָא לָא תַּלְיָן בֵּיהּ מְזוֹנוֹת. לְעֵילָּא אִינּוּן. וְעַ"ד כְּתִיב, יְיָ' רֹעִי לָא אֶחְסָר, לָא יִפְסְקוּן מְזוֹנוֹת מִנִּי לְעָלְמִין, בְּגִין דְּהַהוּא נָהָר דְּנָגִיד וְנָפִיק מֵעֵדֶן לָא פָּסִיק לְעָלְמִין, וּבְגִ"ד קַדְמָא שְׁכִינְתָּא עַל דָּא.

**823.** Because of this, matings and food of people are difficult before the Holy One, blessed be He, WHICH IS THE SHECHINAH, AS MENTIONED. Therefore, King David aspired for his food higher THAN THE SHECHINAH, FOR HE SAID "HASHEM IS MY SHEPHERD...", WHICH IS ZEIR ANPIN. Above, the flow is never interrupted, but it can be interrupted here BY THE SHECHINAH, because the food is not dependent upon Her but higher IN ZEIR ANPIN. Therefore, it is written: "Hashem is my shepherd; I shall not want," WHICH MEANS THAT food will never be interrupted from me, because that river which is drawn and emerges from Eden, WHICH IS ZEIR ANPIN THAT RECEIVES FROM ABA AND IMA, never has its flow interrupted. Therefore, the Shechinah preceded AND RESTED ON HIM, AND AFTERWARDS HE SAID PRAISE.

824. ת"ח, בְּשַׁעֲתָא דְּהַאי אֲתָר מְקַבְּלָא מְזוֹנָא מִלְעֵילָּא, כֻּלְּהוּ

דְּמִקַדְּשֵׁי לְמָארֵיהוֹן, כֻּלְּהוּ מִתְעַדְּנִין, וּמִתְעָרִין, וְסַלְּקִין גַּדְפִּין, כַּד אַתְיָא שְׁכִינְתָּא בְּהַהוּא מְזוֹנָא, בְּגִין דְּלָא יִסְתַּכְּלוּן בָּהּ.

**824.** Come and see: When that place, THE SHECHINAH, receives food above, FROM ZEIR ANPIN, FOR THE WORLDS, all THE ANGELS who sanctify their Master delight and awaken and raise their wings TO COVER THEIR FACE when the Shechinah comes with their food TO THEM, in order that they should not gaze upon THE SHECHINAH.

825. וְאִינּוּן תְּלַת מַשִׁרְיָין בְּסַלִּיקוּ חַד, קָרָאן וְאַמְרֵי קָדוֹשׁ. קָרָאן אִלֵּין לְמַשִׁרְיָיתָא תִּנְיָינָא, וְסַלְּקִין גַּדְפִּין אִלֵּין קַדְמָאֵי, וְאִלֵּין תִּנְיָינֵי, וְאַמְרִין אִלֵּין תִּנְיָינֵי קָדוֹשׁ. קָרָאן אִלֵּין לְמַשִׁרְיָיתָא תְּלִיתָאָה, וְסַלְּקִין גַּדְפִּין תְּלַת מַשִׁרְיָין כַּחֲדָא, וְכֻלְּהוּ אַמְרֵי קָדוֹשׁ יְיָ' צְבָאוֹת מְלֹא כָל הָאָרֶץ כְּבוֹדוֹ. וְעַ"ד כֻּלְּהוּ מְשֻׁלָּבָן דָּא בְּדָא, אִלֵּין עָאלִין לְגוֹ אִלֵּין, וְאִלֵּין עָאלִין לְגוֹ אִלֵּין, מְשֻׁלָּבָן דָּא בְּדָא, כְּמָה דְּאַתְּ אָמַר מְשֻׁלָּבוֹת אִשָּׁה אֶל אֲחוֹתָהּ כֵּן תַּעֲשֶׂה לְכָל קַרְשֵׁי הַמִּשְׁכָּן.

**825.** There are three companies OF ANGELS on one level, who call and say: 'Holy'. These call to the second company and the first and the second ones raise their wings, and the second ones say: 'Holy'. Then these call to the third company and all three companies in unison raise their wings and all say: 'Holy is Hashem Tzva'ot, the whole earth is full of His glory'. Therefore, ALL THREE COMPANIES are fitted one into the other, interpenetrating each other, as we say BY THE BOARDS: "Connected one with the other, thus shall you make the boards for the tabernacle" (Shemot 26:17).

826. קְרָשִׁים קַיְימֵי תָּדִיר בְּקִיּוּמַיְיהוּ, וְלָא מִתְכַּפְפֵי, כְּגַוְונָא דְּאִינּוּן עוֹמְדִים, דְּלָא מִתְכַּפְפֵי דְּלֵית לוֹן קְפִיצֵי, וְקַיְימֵי תָּדִיר בְּלָא יְשִׁיבָה, וְעַ"ד כְּתִיב בַּקְּרָשִׁים עוֹמְדִים.

**826.** The boards always stand erect and do not bend, like these who stand, MEANING THE SERAPHIM, who do not bend, because they have no knees to kneel. They stand constantly without sitting, so it is written of the boards: "standing up."

## 85. Match-making is difficult before the Holy One, blessed be He, like splitting the Red Sea

827. מָה כְּתִיב, שְׁתֵּי יָדוֹת לַקֶּרֶשׁ הָאֶחָד, אוּף הָכִי, בִּתְרֵי גְּוָונֵי אִינּוּן כְּלִילָן כָּל חַד וְחַד מִנַּיְיהוּ, הַהוּא דִּילֵיהּ וּדְחַבְרֵיהּ, וְחַבְרֵיהּ אוּף הָכִי בֵּיהּ, וְעַל דָּא דָּא מְשַׁלְּבָן דָּא עִם דָּא.

**827.** It is written: "Two tenons shall there be in one board" (Ibid.). Here also, JUST AS BY THE SERAPHIM, each including two aspects, WHICH ARE THE TWO TENONS, each one has its own aspect and that of its neighbor, and the same with its neighbor. Therefore, they are fitted one with the other.

828. כְּגַוְונָא דָּא כְּתִיב בְּאוֹרַיְיתָא, כִּי טוֹב סַחְרָהּ מִסְּחַר כֶּסֶף וּמֵחָרוּץ תְּבוּאָתָהּ, דָּא אוֹלִיף לְדָא, וְדָא אוֹלִיף לְדָא, אִתְעֲבִידוּ מְשַׁלְּבָן דָּא עִם דָּא. דָּא נָטִיל דִּילֵיהּ וּדְחַבְרֵיהּ, וְדָא נָטִיל דִּילֵיהּ וּדְחַבְרֵיהּ, וּמְשַׁלְּבָן דָּא בְּדָא.

**828.** It is similarly written in the Torah: "For the merchandise of it is better than the merchandise of silver, and its gain than fine gold" (Mishlei 3:14). The one teaches the other and the other teaches the former, so they become fitted one to the other. The one takes his own portion and that of his neighbor, and the other takes his own portion and the portion of his neighbor, MEANING HIS REWARD AND THE REWARD OF HIS FRIEND WITH WHOM HE IS STUDYING, and they are fitted together. THEREFORE: "FOR THE MERCHANDISE OF IT IS BETTER THAN THE MERCHANDISE OF SILVER," BECAUSE THERE ONE TAKES THE MERCHANDISE AND THE OTHER TAKES THE VALUE OF THE SILVER, BUT HERE EACH ONE IS INTERCONNECTED WITH HIS FRIEND. FOR EACH ONE HAS THE MERCHANDISE AND ALSO THE VALUE HE RECEIVES FROM HIS FRIEND WITH WHOM HIS IS STUDYING.

829. כְּתִיב בִּנְאוֹת דֶּשֶׁא יַרְבִּיצֵנִי עַל מֵי מְנוּחוֹת יְנַהֲלֵנִי. נְאוֹת דֶּשֶׁא, אִלֵּין אִינּוּן מְקוֹרִין עִלָּאִין, דְּכָל מְזוֹנָא וְסִפּוּקָא אַתְיָא מִנַּיְיהוּ. נְאוֹת אִלֵּין אִקְרוּן נְאוֹת יַעֲקֹב. נְאוֹת דֶּשֶׁא, בְּגִין דְּאִית נְאוֹת לְבַר דְּאִקְרוּן נְאוֹת מִדְבָּר, וְעַ"ד בִּנְאוֹת דֶּשֶׁא. וְאִי תֵּימָא הָא כְּתִיב תַּדְשֵׁא הָאָרֶץ דֶּשֶׁא, דְּהָא אִיהוּ לְתַתָּא. אֶלָּא דֶּשֶׁא מֵאִינּוּן נְאוֹת אַתְיָא דְּאִתְיְילִיד

וְאַצְמַח מִנַּיְיהוּ, וְעַ״ד בִּנְאוֹת דֶּשֶׁא יַרְבִּיצֵנִי.

**829.** It is written: "He makes me to lie down in green pastures; He leads me beside the still waters" (Tehilim 23:2). 'Green pastures' refers to the supernal sources, WHICH ARE THE SFIROT OF ZEIR ANPIN, from which all food and sustenance come. THEY ARE CALLED 'pastures (Heb. *neot*)', BECAUSE THESE SFIROT OF ZEIR ANPIN are called "the habitations (Heb. *neot*) of Jacob" (Eichah 2:2). AND THEY ARE CALLED 'green pastures', because there are external pastures that are called "the pastures of the wilderness" (Yoel 2:22). Therefore, HE CALLS THESE OF HOLINESS BY THE NAME: 'green (Heb. *deshe*) pastures'. Yet you may argue it is written, "Let the earth bring forth grass (Heb. *deshe*)" (Beresheet 1:11). So we see that 'DESHE' is below, IN THE EARTH THAT IS MALCHUT? HE ANSWERS: But "deshe" comes for these pastures, where it is born and grows, AND THEY COME TO MALCHUT. Therefore, IT SAYS, "He makes me to lie down in green pastures."

830. עַל מֵי מְנוּחוֹת יְנַהֲלֵנִי, אִלֵּין מַיִין דְּנַיְיחָא, דְּקָא נַגְדִּין מֵהַהוּא אֲתַר דְּנָגִיד וְנָפִיק מֵעֵדֶן, וְאִינּוּן מַיִין אִקְרוּן מֵי מְנוּחוֹת. נַפְשִׁי יְשׁוֹבֵב דָּא הוּא נֶפֶשׁ דָּוִד, וְלָא בָּעָא דָּוִד לְאַתְקָנָא אֶלָּא לְהַהוּא דַּרְגָּא דִּילֵיהּ כַּדְקָא יָאוֹת. בְּאִלֵּין מֵי מְנוּחוֹת, זְמִינִין צַדִּיקַיָּא לְנַיְיחָא לְעָלְמָא דְּאָתֵי, דִּכְתִיב וְנָחֲךָ יְיָ׳ תָּמִיד וְגוֹ׳.

**830.** "He leads me beside the still waters." These are the waters of stillness that are drawn from that place that is drawn and emerges from Eden, WHICH IS BINAH, and these waters are called 'still waters'. "He restores my soul" (Tehilim 23:3): This is the soul of David, WHICH IS MALCHUT, and the only reason that David wants this is to amend his level properly. With these "still waters" will the righteous rest in the World to Come, as it is written: "And Hashem lead you continually…" (Yeshayah 58:11).

## 86. The stars

### A Synopsis
It would not be wise to make a synopsis of this long and exquisite passage. Each reader must read the entire section for himself, in order to delight in the beauty of its imagery and to gain some understanding of its profound teaching.

### The Relevance of this Passage
Here we are treated to an entirely new vision of the role of the stars, in everything from the growth of plants to the governance of all human activity. When we read this section with its unforgettable imagery we are filled with a sense of mystery, and also with a lust for knowledge that burns as brightly as the stars. Though a bounty of celestial wisdom is distilled here, foremost to the reader is the knowledge that man, alone, can steer the stars and direct his destiny. Distant stars of war and stern judgments are subdued by our efforts here. Stars used by the wicked to propagate evil are snuffed out and rendered powerless. Stars of mercy sparkle, stars of joy flash, and stars of peace gleam to ignite our personal redemptions and the immediate arrival of Heaven on earth.

831. וְעָשִׂיתָ קַרְסֵי נְחֹשֶׁת חֲמִשִּׁים וְגוֹ'. רַבִּי אֶלְעָזָר וְרַבִּי אַבָּא הֲווֹ יַתְבֵי לֵילְיָא חַד. כַּד רָמַשׁ לֵילְיָא, עָאלוּ גּוֹ גִּנָּא דְעַל יַמָּא דִּטְבֶרְיָא. אַדְהָכִי, חָמוּ תְּרֵין כֹּכְבַיָּא דְנַטְלֵי, דָּא מֵהָכָא, וְדָא מֵהָכָא, וְאַעֲרָעוּ דָּא בְּדָא וְאִטְמָרוּ.

831. "And you shall make fifty clasps of brass…" (Shemot 26:11). Rabbi Elazar and Rabbi Aba were sitting one night. When it became dark, they entered a garden that was by the Sea of Tiberias. In the meantime, they saw two stars that were moving, one from one side and the other from the other side. Then they met and disappeared.

832. אָמַר רַבִּי אַבָּא, כַּמָּה רַבְרְבָן עוֹבָדֵי דְקוּדְשָׁא בְּרִיךְ הוּא, בִּשְׁמַיָּא מִלְעֵילָא, וּבְאַרְעָא מִלְרַע. מַאן יָכִיל לְמִנְדַּע בְּאִלֵּין תְּרֵין כֹּכְבַיָּא, דְּנַפְקוּ חַד מֵהָכָא, וְחַד מֵהָכָא וְאַעֲרָעוּ דָּא בְּדָא, וְאִטְמָרוּ. א״ל רַבִּי אֶלְעָזָר וְכִי לָא חֲמֵינָא לוֹן, הָא אַשְׁגַּחְנָא בְּהוּ, וְאַשְׁגַּחְנָא בְּכַמָּה עוֹבָדִין אַחֲרָנִין דְּקוּדְשָׁא בְּרִיךְ הוּא עָבֵיד תָּדִיר.

**832.** Rabbi Aba said: How great are the works of the Holy One, blessed be He, in the heavens above and on the earth below. Who can understand these two stars that came out each from a different side, met and then disappeared. Rabbi Elazar said to him: Have we not seen them? For we observed them and we have observed other actions that the Holy One, blessed be He, does constantly.

833. פָּתַח וְאָמַר גָּדוֹל אֲדוֹנֵינוּ וְרַב כֹּחַ וְגוֹ' גָּדוֹל וְרַב וְעִלָּאָה אִיהוּ קוּדְשָׁא בְּרִיךְ הוּא. וְכִי לָא יָדַעְנָא דְקוּדְשָׁא בְּרִיךְ הוּא גָּדוֹל אִיהוּ וְרַב כֹּחַ, מַאי שְׁבָחָא דְּדָוִד הָכָא.

**833.** He opened the discussion with the verse: "Great is our Master, and of great power" (Tehilim 147:5). HE QUESTIONS: The passage tells that the Holy One, blessed be He, is great, mighty and supernal. Don't I know that the Holy One, blessed be He, is great and mighty? What is the reason for David's praise here?

834. אֶלָּא בְּכָל אֲתָר אִיהוּ אָמַר גָּדוֹל יְיָ', וְהָכָא אָמַר גָּדוֹל אֲדוֹנֵינוּ. מ"ט. אֶלָּא הָתָם דְּאִיהוּ אָמַר גָּדוֹל יְיָ' וּמְהֻלָּל מְאֹד. בְּדַרְגָּא עִלָּאָה קָאָמַר. וְהָכָא דִּכְתִיב גָּדוֹל אֲדוֹנֵינוּ בְּדַרְגָּא תַּתָּאָה קָאָמַר, דְּאִיהוּ אֲדוֹן כָּל הָאָרֶץ. מָה כְּתִיב לְעֵילָא מֵהַאי קְרָא, מוֹנֶה מִסְפָּר לַכּוֹכָבִים לְכֻלָּם שֵׁמוֹת יִקְרָא. אִי כָּל בְּנֵי עָלְמָא מִיּוֹמָא דְאִתְבְּרֵי אָדָם, יִתְכַּנְּשׁוּן לְמִמְנֵי כֹּכְבַיָּא, לָא יַכְלִין, כד"א וּסְפוֹר הַכּוֹכָבִים אִם תּוּכַל לִסְפּוֹר אוֹתָם. וְקוּדְשָׁא בְּרִיךְ הוּא מַה כְּתִיב בֵּיהּ, מוֹנֶה מִסְפָּר לַכּוֹכָבִים לְכֻלָּם שֵׁמוֹת יִקְרָא. מ"ט. בְּגִין דִּכְתִיב גָּדוֹל אֲדוֹנֵינוּ וְרַב כֹּחַ וְגוֹ'. כְּמָה דְלֵית מִסְפָּר לְכֹכְבֵי שְׁמַיָּא, בַּר מִנֵּיהּ. אוּף הָכִי אִיהוּ כְּתִיב בֵּיהּ, וְלִתְבוּנָתוֹ אֵין מִסְפָּר.

**834.** HE ANSWERS: He always says "great is Hashem," but here he says "great is our Master." What is the reason? When he says, "Great is Hashem, and greatly to be praised" (Tehilim 145:3), he is speaking of the higher level, ZEIR ANPIN, but where it is written: "Great is our Master," he is talking about the lower level, WHICH IS MALCHUT, the Master of the whole world. What is written before this verse? "He counts the number of the

stars; He calls them all by their names" (Tehilim 147:4). If all the people from the time that Adam was created would gather to count the stars, they would not be able to do it, as it says, "And count the stars, if you be able to number them" (Beresheet 15:5). What is written about the Holy One, blessed be He? "He counts the number of the stars; He calls them all by their names" What is the reason? It is written: "Great is our Master, and of great power." Just as there are none who can count the stars except the Holy One, blessed be He, so is it written pertaining to Him: "His understanding is infinite" (Tehilim 147:5).

835. תָּא חֲזֵי, כְּתִיב הַמּוֹצִיא בְמִסְפָּר צְבָאָם וְגוֹ׳, כֻּלְּהוּ חַיָּילִין וּמַשְׁרְיָין וְכֹכְבַיָּא, קוּדְשָׁא בְּרִיךְ הוּא אַפִּיק לוֹן בִּשְׁמָא, כָּל חַד וְחַד, וְלָא גָּרַע אֲפִילוּ חַד. בְּכָל כֹּכְבַיָּא וּמַזָּלֵי דִרְקִיעִין כֻּלְּהוּ, אִתְמְנוּן נְגִידִין וּפְקִידִין לְשַׁמָּשָׁא עָלְמָא, כָּל חַד וְחַד כַּדְקָא חֲזֵי לֵיהּ. וְלֵית לָךְ עִשְׂבָּא זְעֵירָא בְּכָל עָלְמָא, דְּלָא שַׁלְטָא עֲלֵיהּ כֹּכְבָּא וּמַזָּלָא בִּרְקִיעָא, וְעַל הַהוּא כֹּכְבָּא מְמָנָא חַד, דְּקָא מְשַׁמֵּשׁ קַמֵּיהּ דְּקוּדְשָׁא בְּרִיךְ הוּא, כָּל חַד וְחַד כַּדְקָא חֲזֵי לֵיהּ.

835. Come and see: It is written, "That brings out their host by number" (Yeshayah 40:26), MEANING that the Holy One, blessed be He, brought forth all the hosts and companies and stars, each one by name and none was missing. Throughout the stars and constellations of all the firmaments, leaders, and supervisors were appointed to minister the world, each one as is worthy for him. There is not even one small blade of grass in the world that does not have a star and constellation in the firmament that rules over it, and over each and every star is an appointee that serves before the Holy One, blessed be He, as is proper for Him.

836. כָּל כֹּכְבַיָּא דְּבִרְקִיעִין כֻּלְּהוּ מְשַׁמְּשֵׁי עַל הַאי עָלְמָא, וְכֻלְּהוּ פְּקִידָן לְשַׁמָּשָׁא כָּל מִלָּה וּמִלָּה לְאִינוּן דִּבְהַאי עָלְמָא, וְלָא צַמְחִין וְלָא מִגַּדְּלִין עֲשָׂבִין וְאִלָנִין וּדְשָׁאִין, וְעִשְׂבֵּי בָרָא, בַּר בְּחֵיזוּ דְּכֹכְבַיָּא דְּקָא קַיְימֵי עָלַיְיהוּ, וְאִתְחֲזוּן עָלַיְיהוּ אַנְפִּין, בְּאַנְפִּין כָּל חַד וְחַד כְּמָה דְּאִתְחֲזֵי לֵיהּ.

836. All the stars in the firmament are in charge over this world, and they

are all appointed to attend to every single thing for those that are in this world. No grass, trees or vegetables grow without the supervision of the stars that stand over them and appear to them face-to-face, each one as is proper for it.

837. רוֹב מַשִׁרְיָין דְּכֹכְבַיָּא וּמַזָּלֵי, כֻּלְּהוּ נָפְקִין בְּרֵאשִׁיתָא דְּלֵילְיָא, עַד תְּלַת שַׁעֲתֵי חָסֵר רְבִיעָא. מִתַּמָּן וּלְהָלְאָה לָא נָפְקִין בַּר זְעִירִין. וְאִינוּן כֹּכְבַיָּא כֻּלְּהוּ לָא מְשַׁמְּשֵׁי לְבַטָּלָה, וְלָא אִתְחֲזוּן לְבַטָּלָה. וְאִית כֹּכְבַיָּא דְּקָא מְשַׁמְּשֵׁי כָּל לֵילְיָא, בְּגִין לְאַצְמָחָא וּלְגַדְּלָא כָּל אִינוּן מִלִּין דְּאִתְפְּקָדוּ עֲלַיְיהוּ. וְאִית כֹּכְבַיָּא דְּקָא מְשַׁמְּשֵׁי עַד פַּלְגוּת לֵילְיָא, וְצָמְחִין וּמְגַדְּלִין מֵרֵאשִׁיתָא דְּלֵילְיָא, עַד הַהִיא שַׁעֲתָא, כָּל אִינוּן מִלִּין דְּאִתְפְּקָדוּ עֲלַיְיהוּ, וְאִית כֹּכְבַיָּא דְּקָא מְשַׁמְּשֵׁי זְעֵיר מְלֵילְיָא, דְּכֵיוָן דְּאִתְחֲזֵי בַּהֲדֵי הַהוּא עִשְׂבָּא, אוֹ הַהוּא דְּשָׁאָה, מִיָּד אַשְׁלִים שִׁמּוּשֵׁיהּ, וְלָא אִצְטְרִיךְ יַתִּיר בְּהַהוּא לֵילְיָא. וְהָא אִינוּן לָא קַיְימִין לְבַטָּלָה, כֵּיוָן דְּאַשְׁלִימוּ שִׁמּוּשַׁיְיהוּ, לָא אִתְחֲזוּן יַתִּיר בְּהַאי עָלְמָא, וְעָיְילִין לְאַתְרַיְיהוּ.

837. Most of the companies of stars and constellations come out at the beginning of the night, until three hours minus a quarter. From there onwards only small stars come out. And all these stars do not work for no reason and do not appear in vain. There are some stars that serve the entire night, in order to cause all those things that are under their responsibility to sprout and grow. There are certain stars that serve until midnight, and they cause to sprout and grow from the beginning of the night until that time all those things that were assigned to them. There are also stars that serve a short period of the night, for their service is completed after they have appeared to that grass or plant. They do not have to serve further that night, for they do not stand idly. As soon as they conclude their service, they are no longer seen in the world but enter their place.

838. בְּסִפְרָא דְּחָכְמְתָא עִלָּאָה דִּבְנֵי קֶדֶם, אַמְרֵי עַל כָּל אִינוּן כֹּכְבַיָּא דְּשַׁרְבִיטָא, דְּקָא מְשַׁדְּרֵי שַׁרְבִיטָא בִּרְקִיעָא, אַמְרֵי דַּעֲשָׂבִין אִינוּן בְּאַרְעָא, מֵאִינוּן דְּאַקְרוּן סַמֵּי דְּחַיֵּי, וְאַבְנִין יַקִּירָן אִית בְּאַרְעָא, וְזָהָב שָׁחוּט דְּמִגַּדְּלָא גּוֹ טוּרֵי רָמָאי, בִּזְעֵיר מַיִּין דְּחַפְיָא עֲלֵיהּ, וְלָא חַפְיָא

אֶלָּא דְּנָגִיד עָלֵיהּ, וְשָׁלְטָאן עַל כָּל אִלֵּין כֹּכְבַיָּא דְּשַׁרְבִיטָא, וּמִגַּדְלֵי אִלֵּין בְּגִינַיְיהוּ.

**838.** In the Book of Supernal Wisdom of the people of the East, they talk about the comets that have a scepter behind them in the sky, MEANING THAT A LONG TAIL OF LIGHT IS ATTACHED AND EMANATES FROM THOSE STARS. They say that there are grasses on the earth of those that are called 'the spice of life', and there are precious stones in the earth and hammered gold that is formed in the high mountains with a bit of water, that covers it yet does not cover it. But it is drawn over it. The comets rule over them, and they grow through them.

839. וְכָל תִּקּוּנָא וּגְדוּלָא דִּלְהוֹן, לָאו אִיהוּ אֶלָּא בְּחֵיזוּ וְנֹגְהָא דְּהַהוּא שַׁרְבִיטָא, דְּקָא מְשַׁדַּר הַהוּא כֹּכְבָא, גּוֹ רְקִיעָא, וּכְדֵין אִתְתַּקָּנָן וּמִתְגַּדְּלָן כָּל אִינּוּן מִלִּין.

**839.** All their development and growth is only through the shine of that tail that the star extends into the firmament, and then all these things are perfected.

840. מַרְעִין אִית בִּבְנֵי נָשָׁא, כְּגוֹן יְרוֹקִין וְקַסְטִירִין. דְּאַסְוָותָא דִּלְהוֹן לָא תָּלֵי, אֶלָּא בְּחַד מַרְאֶה דְּפַרְזְלָא קָלִיל נָצִיץ לְעַיְינִין, וְאִית לֵיהּ לְמָארֵיהּ דְּמָרַע לְאִסְתַּכְּלָא בֵּיהּ. וְלָא אִתְּסֵי בְּהַאי עַד דְּאַעֲבַר הַהוּא מַרְאֶה לִסְטְרָא דָּא וּלְסִטְרָא דָּא, כְּגַוְונָא דְּשַׁרְבִיטָא, דְּיוֹשִׁיט נְצִיצוּ דִּבְרַק לְאַנְפּוֹי, וּבְהַהוּא אוֹשִׁיטוּ דְּבַרְק דְּקָא נָצִיץ לְעַיְינִין, אָתֵי לֵיהּ אַסְוָותָא. אוֹף הָכִי, כָּל אִינּוּן דְּשַׁלְטֵי עֲלַיְיהוּ אִינּוּן כֹּכְבַיָּא, לֵית לוֹן תִּקּוּנָא וּגְדוּלָא בַּמֶּה דְּאִתְחֲזֵי, בַּר הַהוּא פְּשִׁיטוּ דְּשַׁרְבִיטָא, וּבְהַאי מִתַּתְקְנֵי, בְּחֵיזוּ, בִּגְווֹן, בְּחֵילָא, כְּמָה דְּאִתְחֲזֵי.

**840.** There are illnesses among people, namely jaundice and infection, WHICH ARE TYPES OF SICKNESSES, AND THEY SEEM TO BE SICKNESS OF THE GALL IN WHICH THEIR FACES BECOME GREENISH. Their only remedy is the mirror of glittering metal that sparkles in the eyes, NAMELY A MIRROR THAT IS MADE OF POLISHED METAL, and the ill person has to stare at it.

The ill person is not cured until the mirror is moved from one side to the other, AND THE MIRROR has to reflect a spark of flash similar to a comet onto his face. When that flash sparks in the eyes, the remedy is effected. In this case also, all those ruled by the stars develop and grow only due to the expansion of the comet, and they develop this in appearance, color and strength, as it should be.

841. וְשַׁפִּיר אִיהוּ, דְּהָא כְּגַוְונָא דָא, רָמִיז בְּסִפְרָא דִּשְׁלֹמֹה מַלְכָּא, בְּחָכְמְתָא דְּאַבְנִין יְקִירִין, דְּאִי חָסֵר מִנְּהוֹן נְגְהָא דִּנְצִיצוּ וּלְהִיטוּ דְּכֹכְבַיָּא יְדִיעָן, לָא מִגַּדְלִין, וְלָא מִתַקְּנֵי לוֹן לְעָלְמִין, וְכֹלָּא אַתְקִין קוּדְשָׁא בְּרִיךְ הוּא לְתִקּוּנָא דְּעָלְמָא, כד״א לְהָאִיר עַל הָאָרֶץ, בְּכָל מַה דְּאִצְטְרִיךְ בְּהַאי עָלְמָא לְתַקְּנָא לֵיהּ.

841. It is good, because the like of it is alluded to in the book of King Solomon. HE SAYS: In the science of precious stones, if there would have been lacking the shine of the sparkle and flaming of certain stars, they would never grow or develop. The Holy One, blessed be He, prepared all this in the development of the world, as written: "To give light upon the earth" (Beresheet. 1:15), MEANING THEY SHINE ON AND PERFECT anything in the world that needs perfecting.

842. כְּתִיב וְעָשִׂיתָ קַרְסֵי נְחֹשֶׁת חֲמִשִּׁים, וּכְתִיב וְעָשִׂיתָ חֲמִשִּׁים קַרְסֵי זָהָב, וּתְנֵינָן, מַאן דְּלָא חָמָא אִינּוּן קְרָסִים בְּמַשְׁכְּנָא, לָא חָמָא נְהִירוּ דְּכֹכְבַיָּא בִּרְקִיעָא, בְּגִין דִּבְהַהוּא חֵיזוּ, וּבְהַהוּא גַוְונָא, דָּמְיָין לְכָל מַאן דְּאִסְתְּכַּל בְּהוּ.

842. It is written: "And you shall make fifty clasps of brass" and "you shall make fifty golden clasps" (Shemot 26:6). We have learned that one who has never seen the clasps in the Tabernacle has never seen the light of the stars in the sky, because THE CLASPS OF THE TABERNACLE were similar in appearance and manner OF THE STARS to all who viewed them.

843. כֹּכְבַיָּא אִית בִּרְקִיעָא, דְּאִלֵּין נַפְקֵי מֵהַהוּא רְקִיעָא, דְּכָל כֹּכְבַיָּא אֲדוּקִין תַּמָּן. בְּהַהוּא רְקִיעָא אִית מְאָה חַלּוֹנֵי מַשְׁקוֹפִין, מִנְּהוֹן לִסְטַר מִזְרָח, וּמִנְּהוֹן לִסְטַר דָּרוֹם. וּבְכָל חַלּוֹנָא וְחַלּוֹנָא כֹּכְבָא חַד.

**843.** There are stars in the sky that emerge from that firmament wherein all the stars are kept, WHICH IS THE SECOND FIRMAMENT WHEREIN THE SUN, MOON, STARS AND CONSTELLATIONS ARE SET, AND THIS FIRMAMENT IS THE THIRD FIRMAMENT THAT EMERGES FROM IT. In that firmament, there are one hundred framed windows, some on the East and some on the South, and in every window there is one star.

844. וְכַד שִׁמְשָׁא אָזִיל בְּאִינּוּן חַלּוֹנִין וּמַשְׁקוֹפִין דִּי בִּרְקִיעָא נָצִיץ בְּנִצִיצוּ, וְאִלֵּין כֹּכְבַיָּא נַפְקֵי לְאִתְנַצְצָא מֵהַהוּא נְצִיצוּ דְּשִׁמְשָׁא וְאִצְטָבְעוּ, מִנְהוֹן סוּמָקִין כְּגַוְּונָא דִּנְחֹשֶׁת, וּמִנְהוֹן יְרוֹקִין כְּגַוְּונָא דְּזָהָב, וְעַל דָּא, אִלֵּין סוּמָקִין, וְאִלֵּין יְרוֹקִין. חַמְשִׁים אִינּוּן בְּאִינּוּן חַמְשִׁים חַלּוֹנִין, וַחֲמִשִּׁים אִינּוּן בְּאִינּוּן חַלּוֹנִין אַחֲרָנִין. דְּלִסְטַר מִזְרָח אִינּוּן יְרוֹקִין, דְּלִסְטַר דָּרוֹם אִינּוּן סוּמָקִין, בְּהוּ אִתְאֲחַד סִיּוּמָא דְּמַשְׁכְּנָא.

**844.** When the sun travels through these windows and frames in the firmament and sparkles, those stars emerge to sparkle from the sun's sparkle, and become colored, some red like bronze and some yellow like gold. Therefore, some are red and some are yellow. There are fifty STARS in these fifty windows, and fifty in the other fifty windows. On the East side, they are yellow and on the South side they are red. With them were joined the ending of the Tabernacle.

845. בְּכָל אִינּוּן כֹּכְבַיָּא דְּנַפְקֵי מֵהַהוּא רְקִיע, מִתְעָרְבֵי אִינּוּן כֹּכְבַיָּא בְּלֵילְיָא, וְנַצְצֵי וּמְלַהֲטֵי וְשַׁלְטֵי בְּהַאי עָלְמָא. מִנְהוֹן עַל נְחֹשֶׁת, מִנְהוֹן עַל זָהָב יְרַקְרַק, וְאִתְתַּקָּנָן וּמִגַּדְלָן עַל חֵילָא דִּלְהוֹן.

**845.** The night stars are intermingled in all these stars that emerge from that firmament, and they sparkle and flame and rule this world. Some DOMINATE over bronze, some over yellow-gold, which develop and grow with their strength.

846. אִלֵּין כֹּכְבַיָּא שַׁלְטֵי בְּכָ"ה וּפַלְגָּא נְקוּדִין דְּלֵילְיָא, דְּאִינּוּן רִגְעֵי שַׁעֲתָא, וְאִינּוּן דִּמְגַּדְלֵי נְחֹשֶׁת דְּאִינּוּן סוּמָקֵי וְלַהֲטֵי וְנַצְצֵי. וְכַד אוֹשִׁיטוּ תְּלָת זִמְנִין נְצִיצוּ לְסִטְרָא דְּמִזְרָח, אוֹ חֲמֵשׁ, אוֹ שְׁבַע, מַלְכֵי

עַמִּין יֵיתוּן עַל הַהוּא סִטְרָא, וְכָל עֲתְרָא וְדַהֲבָא יִסְתַּלָּק מֵהַהוּא סִטְרָא. וְאִי נְצִיצוּ חַד, תְּרֵין, אַרְבַּע, שִׁית, דָּא בָּתַר דָּא, אֵימָתָא וּפַחֲדָא יִפּוֹל, וְיִשְׁרֵי עַל הַהוּא סִטְרָא. בָּטִישׁ נְצִיצוּ וְשָׁכִיךְ, בָּטִישׁ נְצִיצוּ וְשָׁכִיךְ, יִתְעֲרוּ קְרָבֵי, וְלָא יִתְעַבִידוּ, דְּהָא בְּהַהוּא זִמְנָא, אִתְעֲרוּתָא הוּא לְעֵילָא קַמֵּי קוּדְשָׁא בְּרִיךְ הוּא, בְּאִינוּן מְמָנָן דְּעָלְמָא דְּשַׁלְטִין עַל שְׁאַר עַמִּין, וְכֵן כְּגַוְוּנָא דָּא בְּסִטְרָא אַחֲרָא.

**846.** These stars rule over twenty five and a half points of the night, which are the minutes of the hour. Some produce bronze and some are red, and they flash and glitter. When they emit sparks three times toward the East, or five TIMES or seven, the kings of the nations come against that side and all riches and gold move out of that side. If that sparkle is once, twice, four or six times, one after the other, fear and terror then fall and dwell upon that side. If the sparkle throbs and then is quiet, wars are threatened but are not effected, because there is then an arousing among the Patrons of the world that dominate over the other nations before the Holy One, blessed be He. It is the same on the other side, WEST.

847. פָּתַח וְאָמַר, לֶהֱוֵא שְׁמֵיהּ דִּי אֱלָהָא מְבָרַךְ מִן עָלְמָא וְעַד עָלְמָא דִּי חָכְמְתָא וּגְבוּרְתָא דִּילֵיהּ הִיא. וְהוּא מְהַשְׁנֵא עִדָּנַיָּא וְזִמְנַיָּא. וְכֹלָא אִיהוּ בִּרְשׁוּתֵיהּ, וְאַפִּיק לְעַמֵּיהּ קַדִּישָׁא, מֵחֵילָא וּרְשׁוּתָא דְּכֹכָבַיָּא וּמַזָּלֵי, בְּגִין דְּאִינוּן טַעֲוָון אַחֲרָן וְלָא בְּאִלֵּין חוּלָקָא דְּיַעֲקֹב, כִּי אִם בְּיוֹצֵר הַכֹּל הוּא.

**847.** He opened the discussion with the verse: "Blessed be the Name of Elohim forever and ever, for wisdom and might are His, and He changes the times and the seasons" (Daniel 2:20-21). Everything is in His jurisdiction, and He removed His holy people from the control of the stars and constellations, because they are other Elohim. The portion of Jacob is not with them but rather "the former of all things" (Yirmeyah 10:16) IS HIS PORTION.

848. רָקִיעַ אִית לְעֵילָא, עַל כָּל אִלֵּין רְקִיעִין, וְאִיהוּ טָמִיר וְגָנִיז, וְחוֹתָמָא דְּגוּשְׁפַּנְקָא דְּמַשְׁכְּנָא שַׁלְטָא עַל הַאי רָקִיעַ, וְהַאי רָקִיעַ אִקְרֵי

אִדְרָא דְמַשְׁכְּנָא, וּבְהַאי רָקִיעַ כָּל אִינּוּן חַלּוֹנִין, מִסִּטְרָא דָא, וּמִסִּטְרָא דָא, וְאָחִיד כָּל אִינּוּן סְדוּרִין דְמַשְׁכְּנָא. שִׁית חַלּוֹנִין אִינּוּן רַבְרְבִין עַל כֻּלְּהוּ, וְחַד סָתִים לְשַׁלְטָא עֲלַיְיהוּ.

**848.** There is a firmament above all these firmaments, NAMELY THE FIRMAMENT OF BINAH, WHICH IS HIGHER THAN THE SEVEN FIRMAMENTS, WHICH ARE CHESED, GVURAH, TIFERET, NETZACH, HOD, YESOD AND MALCHUT, ABOUT WHOM IS SAID, "OUT OF WHOSE WOMB CAME THE ICE" (IYOV 38:29). It is concealed and hidden and is sealed with the ring of the Tabernacle, NAMELY THE SUPERNAL TABERNACLE WHICH IS BINAH, AND THE SEAL OF THE RING IS THE SECRET OF MALCHUT OF THE ATTRIBUTE OF JUDGMENT THAT IS CONCEALED IN THIS FIRMAMENT, WHICH CAUSES IT TO BE HIDDEN AND CONCEALED AND UNKNOWN. This firmament is known as Idra DeMishkena, NAMELY THE CHAMBER OF THE SUPERNAL TABERNACLE, and in this firmament are all these HUNDRED windows, MENTIONED EARLIER, of this side and of that side. FROM THEM ARE THEY DRAWN TO THE THIRD FIRMAMENT OF BELOW, and it is attached to all parts of the LOWER Tabernacle, WHICH IS MALCHUT. There are six windows greater than all of them, WHICH ARE CHESED, GVURAH, TIFERET NETZACH, HOD AND YESOD, and one closed, WHICH CORRESPONDS TO THE SEAL OF THE RING THAT WAS MENTIONED, WHICH IS MALCHUT OF THE LOCK, which dominates them, CONCEALS AND COVERS THEM FROM THE CONCEIVING OF THOSE BELOW.

849. חַלּוֹנָא חַד, אִקְרֵי חַלּוֹן זָהֲרָא, וּבֵיהּ נָפְקָא כֹּכְבָא חֲדָא, דְּאִקְרֵי לְחַכִּימֵי י"ד, וְדָא אִיהוּ הַתּוּכָא דְּקָא מְהַתֵּךְ לְתַתָּא בְּשָׁלְטָנוּתָא דִּיהוּדָה. לָאו דְּאִית לֵיהּ חוּלָקָא בֵּיהּ, דְּהָא לֵית לַשְׁבָטִין דְּיִשְׂרָאֵל חוּלָקָא וְאַחֲסָנָא בְּהוּ, אֶלָּא שִׁבְטָא דִּיהוּדָה שַׁלְטָא עַל הַאי, וְלָאו אִיהוּ עֲלֵיהּ.

**849.** One window, OF THE SEVEN LARGE WINDOWS, is called 'the Light Window', WHICH CORRESPONDS TO CHESED. Through it emerges a star called by the sages Yad (Eng. 'Hand'), which is the POWER OF melting that melts downward, IN ORDER TO REMOVE THE JUDGMENTS THAT ARE IN IT

under the dominion of Judah. Not that Judah has a part in it, since the tribes have no part or possession in THE STARS to worship them, but rather the tribe Judah rules over these JUDGMENTS and not they over him.

850. וְכַד אַסְטוּ בְּנֵי יְהוּדָה אָרְחַיְיהוּ מִבָּתַר קוּדְשָׁא בְּרִיךְ הוּא, אָזְלוּ לְמִנְדַע בָּתַר חֲלוֹנָא דָא, וְהַאי כֹּכָבָא. וְאָמְרוּ דְּהַאי יְדָא דְּקָא מְנַצַּח לִשְׁאַר עַמִּין, דִּכְתִּיב בֵּיהּ יָדְךָ בְּעֹרֶף אוֹיְבֶיךָ, וְאָזְלוּ אֲבַתְרֵיהּ וְעַבְדוּ לֵיהּ שִׁמּוּשָׁא וּפֻלְחָנָא, וְעַל דָּא כְּתִיב, וַיַּעַשׂ יְהוּדָה הָרַע בְּעֵינֵי יְיָ'.

850. When the children of Judah turned away from the Holy One, blessed be He, and followed after this window and the star for understanding, they said that the Yad (Eng. 'hand') triumphs over the other nations, as it is written: "Your hand shall be on the neck of your enemies" (Beresheet 49:8). They followed it and served it, and about this is written: "And Judah did evil in the sight of Hashem" (I Melachim 14:22).

851. הַאי כֹּכָבָא כַּד נָפִיק פָּשִׁיט חַד יָד בַּחֲמֵשׁ אֶצְבְּעָן, נָהִיר וְנָצִיץ בְּהַהוּא חַלּוֹן. מָאֲרֵיהוֹן דְּקוּסְמִין וְחֲרָשִׁין, דַּחֲלֵי מֵהַאי אֲתָר, בְּגִין דִּבְשַׁעֲתָא דְּהַאי שַׁלְטָא, כֻּלְּהוּ קָסְמִין וְחֲרָשִׁין מִתְבַּלְבְּלֵי, וְלָא אַצְלַח בִּידַיְיהוּ.

851. When this star emerges, it stretches out one hand, WHICH IS THE SECRET OF CHESED THAT IS CALLED 'RIGHT HAND', with five fingers, WHICH ARE CHESED, GVURAH, TIFERET, NETZACH AND HOD THAT ARE IN IT, and illuminates and sparkles in that window. Then the sorcerers and magicians fear that place, because all the sorcerers and magicians are confused and their magic does not thrive during the time that it dominates.

852. וְאִי תֵּימָא, הוֹאִיל וְאִיהוּ הַאי רָקִיעַ טְמִירָא, הֵיךְ יַדְעֵי לֵיהּ. אֶלָּא סִימָנָא אִית לוֹן לְבַר, וְיַדְעֵי דְּהָא שַׁלְטָא כֹּכָבָא דָא, וְדַחֲלֵי תָּדִיר מִנֵּיהּ, וְלָא אַצְלַח בִּידֵיהוֹן, אִינּוּן קָסְמִין וְחֲרָשִׁין. וְעַל דָּא אִית זִמְנִין דְּאַצְלְחוּ בֵּיהּ בְּנֵי נָשָׁא, וְאִית זִמְנִין דְּלָא אַצְלָחוּ בֵּיהּ. וּבְגִין דָּא אִינּוּן מָאֲרֵי קוּסְמִין וְחֲרָשִׁין מִתְמַעֲטֵי מֵעָלְמָא, בְּגִין דְּלָא יַדְעִין עִקָּרָא, כַּד חֲמָאן

-523-

דְּלָא אַצְלַח בִּידַיְיהוּ. וְעַל דָּא אִינוּן קַדְמָאֵי הֲוֹו יַדְעֵי, וּמִסְתַּכְּלָן לְבַר בְּהַהוּא סִימָנָא, דְּקָא יַדְעֵי.

**852.** If you ask: Since this firmament is concealed, AS MENTIONED THAT IT IS IN BINAH, how do THE SORCERERS know about it, TO BECOME CONFUSED BY IT? HE ANSWERS: They have a sign in the outer part OF THE HOLINESS from which they know that star is ruling. They constantly fear it, and their sorcery and magic do not succeed in it. There are times when people are successful in it and there are times when people are not successful. Therefore, the sorcerers and magicians are becoming less numerous in the world because they do not know the source when they see that the magic is not successful by them. Therefore, the ancient MAGICIANS knew THE SOURCE, for they would gaze at that sign THAT WAS ON THE EXTERIOR OF THE HOLINESS of which they knew.

853. חַלּוֹנָא תִּנְיָינָא, אִקְרֵי חַלּוֹן טוּפְרָא, בְּגִין דְּאִיהוּ כְּגַוְונָא דְּטוּפְרָא, וּבֵיהּ נָפְקָא כֹּכָבָא חַד, דְּאִקְרֵי לְחַכִּימִין צִפְעוֹן, דְּהָא דָּא שַׁלְטָא בְּשׁוּלְטָנָא תַּקִּיף בְּדִינָא בְּרֵישָׁא וְזַנְבָא, אִית לֵיהּ כְּצִפְעוֹן כְּמִין לְקַטְלָא.

**853.** The second window, WHICH IS GVURAH, is called 'the Window of Nail (Heb. *tziporen*)' because it is similar to the Nail, NAMELY THE LEFT COLUMN THAT IS CALLED 'TZIPOREN'. Through it emerges a star that is called by the scholars 'Tziph'on (Eng. 'viper')', because it dominates with harsh Judgment and with its head and tail, like a viper that lies in wait to kill.

854. מֵהַהוּא חַלּוֹן, נַפְקֵי שִׁית מֵאָה אֶלֶף רִבּוֹא רוּחִין, דְּשַׁלְטִין עַל אִינוּן טוּפְרִין דִּבְנֵי נָשָׁא, כַּד אִזְדַרְקָן בְּאִתְגַּלְיָא. בְּהַאי עַבְדֵי חֲרָשִׁין וְקָסְמִין, כָּל אִינוּן דְּיַדְעֵי לוֹן. בְּהַהִיא שַׁעֲתָא דְּהַאי כֹּכָבָא שַׁלְטָא, כָּל אִינוּן דְּזַרְקֵי טוּפְרֵי, אוֹ עַבְדֵי חֲרָשִׁין בְּהוֹן, גָּרִים מוֹתָא לְכָל עָלְמָא, וְסָלִיק חֲרָשִׁין בִּידַיְיהוּ דְּאִינוּן דְּעַבְדֵי לוֹן.

**854.** From that window emerge TO BELOW six billion spirits that rule over the nails of people when they are thrown away openly. All those who know how to perform sorcery and magic with them at the time that this star dominates. All those who throw away their nails or perform magic with

them bring death to the whole world. And the magic that they perform is successful in it.

855. חַלּוֹנָא תְּלִיתָאָה, אִקְרֵי חַלּוֹן חוֹשְׁנָא, וּבֵיהּ נָפְקָא כֹּכָבָא חֲדָא, וְאִקְרֵי נֹגַ"הּ דְּבוֹסִי"נָא, הַאי אִיהוּ נְצִיצוּ דְּנָצִיץ, וְקַיְּימָא עַל כָּל רוּחָא, וְנַיְיחָא וְשֵׁיזָבוּתָא וְטִיבוּתָא בֵּיהּ. לֵית בֵּיהּ קַטְרוּגָא כְּלַל, כַּד אִיהוּ שַׁלְטָא, כָּל נַיְיחָא, וְכָל נְהִירוּ שַׁלְטָא בְּעָלְמָא, שַׁלְוָה שָׂבְעָא וְכֹלָּא שַׁלִּיט בְּעָלְמָא.

**855.** The third window, WHICH IS TIFERET, is called 'the Window of the Breastplate', BECAUSE TIFERET IS CALLED 'BREASTPLATE'. Through it emerges a star called 'the Nig'ha DeBusina', THE SHINE OF THE LAMP. This is a sparkle that sparkles despite all winds, and peace and deliverance are in it, SINCE IT IS THE CENTRAL COLUMN THAT UNITES RIGHT AND LEFT TOGETHER AND THEREBY REMOVES ALL THE JUDGMENTS THAT ARE IN THEM. It bears no accusation at all. When it dominates, all peace and all light rule the world, and tranquillity and satisfaction and all GOOD rule the world.

856. חַלּוֹנָא רְבִיעָאָה, אִיהוּ חַלּוֹן דְּאִקְרֵי גְּבִיעַ, וּבֵיהּ נָפְקָא כֹּכָבָא חַד, דְּאִקְרֵי לְחַכִּימִין אֶשְׁכּוֹל הַכֹּפֶר, בְּגִין דְּהָכִי נָפִיק כְּאֶשְׁכּוֹל, נָצִיץ נְצִיצִין כַּעֲנָבִין בְּכוֹפְרָא, בְּהַאי אִתְּעָרוּ דְּרַחֲמֵי אִתְּעַר בְּעָלְמָא, מַרְחִיק וּמַקְרִיב, תּוֹלְדִין סַגִּיאִין אַסְגִּיאוּ בְּעָלְמָא. בְּנֵי עָלְמָא לָא קַפְדֵי כַּד אִצְטְרִיכוּ דָּא לְדָא, שְׁלָמָא וְחֶדְוָה אִתְּעַר בְּעָלְמָא.

**856.** The fourth window, WHICH IS YESOD, is called 'the Window of the Goblet', BECAUSE IT RECEIVES AND PROVIDES WINE, WHICH IS THE SECRET OF THE ILLUMINATION OF THE LEFT THAT IS SWEETENED BY THE RIGHT TO MALCHUT. Through it emerges a star that is called 'the cluster of the henna' by the sages, because it emerges AND ILLUMINATES like a cluster and sparkles like grapes IN A CLUSTER of the henna. Through it is aroused Mercy in the world. It keeps THE JUDGMENTS at a distance and brings close MERCT. Many children are born into the world, and people are not particular when they need one another. Peace and joy are aroused in the world.

857. חַלּוֹנָא חֲמִישָׁאָה, אִיהוּ חַלּוֹן דְּאִקְרֵי בְּאֵר, עַל דִּי כֹּכְבָא דְּנָפִיק בֵּיהּ, עָאל וְנָפִיק שָׁאִיב כַּדְלֵי, לָא שָׁכִיךְ לְעָלְמִין. בְּהַאי חַכִּימֵי לִבָּא לָא יַכְלִין לְמֵיקָם בְּאֹרַח קְשׁוֹט, בְּגִין דְּלָא קָאֵים בְּקִיּוּמָא, וְלָא שָׁכִיךְ לְעָלְמִין. וְעַ"ד אִתְדַּחֲקָן גַּרְמַיְיהוּ, לְעַיְּינָא בְּהַאי אֲתָר, וּלְמֵידַן דִּינָא.

**857.** The fifth window, WHICH IS NETZACH, is a window called 'a Well', because of the star that emerges from it. It enters and emerges and draws sustenance like a pail FROM A WELL, and never ceases. The wise-hearted could never trully understand this star, because it is never stationary and is never quiet. Therefore, THE WISE-HEARTED had difficulty studying this place and making conclusions.

858. חַלּוֹנָא שְׁתִיתָאָה, אִיהוּ חַלּוֹן דְּאִקְרֵי נֹגָהָא, וְנָפְקָא בֵּיהּ כֹּכְבָא חַד, דְּאִקְרִין גִּזְרוֹן, בְּגִין דְּכַד הַאי שַׁלְטָא, עָלְמָא קָאֵים בְּדִינָא, וְכַמָּה גְּזֵרִין, וּבְכַמָּה עוֹנָשִׁין, וּבְכָל יוֹמָא וְיוֹמָא מִתְחַדְּשָׁן גְּזֵרִין עַל עָלְמָא, וְעַד לָא יְסַיְּימוּן אִלֵּין, הָא אַחֲרָנִין מִתְחַדְּשִׁין, וְהַאי לָא שַׁלְטָא כ"כ בְּעָלְמָא.

**858.** The sixth window IS HOD. This is a window that is called 'Nog'ha' (brightness) and a star emerges from it called 'Gizron' (Eng. 'decree'). When it rules, the world is under Judgment, under many decrees and many punishments. Every single day, there are new decrees against the world and new ones are formed before these Judgments are completely executed. This star does not rule much in the world.

859. אֲבָל סָמוּךְ לְיוֹמֵי מְשִׁיחָא, יְשְׁלוֹט הַאי חַלּוֹנָא, בְּהַאי כֹּכְבָא, עַל עָלְמָא. וְעַ"ד יִשְׁלְטוּן חַיָּין בִּישִׁין עַל עָלְמָא, וְיִתְחַדְּתוּן זִינִין בִּישִׁין, דָּא בָּתַר דָּא, וְיִשְׂרָאֵל יְהוֹן בְּעָקוּ. וְכַד יִתְדַּחֲקוּן גּוֹ חֲשׁוֹכָא דְּגָלוּתָא, כְּדֵין יַנְהֵר לוֹן קוּדְשָׁא בְּרִיךְ הוּא נְהִירוּ דִּימָמָא, וִיקַבְּלוּן מַלְכוּתָא קַדִּישֵׁי עֶלְיוֹנִין, וְיִתְבַּטֵּל מַלְכוּתָא מִידָא דְּעַמְמִין עוֹבְדֵי כּוֹכָבִים, וְיִשְׁלְטוּן עֲלַיְיהוּ יִשְׂרָאֵל, וְיִתְקַיֵּים וְהָיָה אוֹר הַלְּבָנָה וְגוֹ'.

**859.** Close to the days of Messiah, the window with this star shall rule the

world. Therefore, wild animals will rule the world and new evil species will be formed one after the other, and the children of Yisrael will be in distress. When they will be pressed in the darkness of exile, the Holy One, blessed be He, will light up for them the light of day, WHICH IS REDEMPTION, and the supernal Holy Ones will accept the kingdom. Rulership will be annulled from the idol-worshipping nations and Yisrael will rule over them. Then will be fulfilled: "Moreover the light of the moon shall be as the light of the sun…" (Yeshayah 30:26).

860. וּכְדֵין חַלוֹנָא שְׁבִיעָאָה יִתְפְּתַח בְּכָל עָלְמָא, וְכֹכְבָא דִּילֵיהּ אִיהוּ כֹּכְבָא דְּיַעֲקֹב, וְהַאי אִיהוּ דְּקָאָמַר בִּלְעָם, דָּרַךְ כֹּכָב מִיַּעֲקֹב, וְכֹכְבָא דָּא יְהֵא נָהִיר אַרְבְּעִין יוֹמִין. וְכַד יִתְגְּלֵי מַלְכָּא מְשִׁיחָא, וְיִתְכַּנְּשׁוּן לְגַבֵּי מַלְכָּא מְשִׁיחָא כָּל עַמִּין דְּעָלְמָא, כְּדֵין יִתְקַיֵּים קְרָא דִּכְתִּיב, שֹׁרֶשׁ יִשַׁי אֲשֶׁר עֹמֵד לְנֵס עַמִּים אֵלָיו גּוֹיִם יִדְרֹשׁוּ וְהָיְתָה מְנוּחָתוֹ כָּבוֹד.

860. Then the seventh window will be opened to the whole world, and its star is the star of Jacob. This is what Bila'am said, "There shall come a star out of Jacob" (Bemidbar 24:17), and this star will illuminate for forty days. When King Messiah will be revealed and all the nations of the world will gather before him, this passage will be fulfilled: "That the root of Yishai, that stands for a banner of the peoples, to it shall the nations seek, and his resting place shall be glorious" (Yeshayah 11:10).

## 87. The three watches of the night

### A Synopsis

Rabbi Shimon opens this discussion with the verse: "But none says, 'Where is Eloha my maker (lit. 'makers'), who gives songs in the night.'" By 'makers', we learn, the Scripture means that Eloha includes both Zeir Anpin and His court, Malchut. Malchut is constantly praising all night in order to receive His joyous supernal Light. All the stars are thankful and praise God during the entire time that they are visible in the sky, because the supernal angels who are appointed over the stars are all thankful and praise in watches during the three parts of the night. We next learn that in order to unite with their Master, the angels must push the Other Side outside, and they do this by bringing sleep to the inhabitants of the world, which attracts the Other Side downward. Evil spirits float around until midnight, we are told. Rabbi Shimon then tells of the angels that stand outside, spoken of in "Who makes the winds (spirits) His messengers," and the angels who are fire that stand inside, spoken of in "the flames of fire His ministers." The supernal angels praise God only after they have pushed the impurity outside. The master over all the companies of angels is the candle of David, who is Malchut. Next, Rabbi Shimon offers an alternative explanation for the opening verse, where the secret is that the spirit of man is composed of male and female, as in "And Elohim said, 'Let us make man in our image, after our likeness.'" Following this, Rabbi Elazar and Rabbi Aba arise at midnight to study Torah. At midnight the Holy One is aroused through love for the Congregation of Yisrael, and He sees the good deeds they performed that day, inhaling their sweet savor. Then the light illuminates, the trees in the Garden of Eden sing praises, and the righteous experience there the delights of the World to Come.

### The Relevance of this Passage

The Light of the Creator travels though numerous dimensions before manifesting in our physical realm. A vast "communication" network runs throughout these dimensions, transporting this Light. This network incorporates what we commonly refer to as angels. Angels are the interface through which a man interacts with the awesome Light of the Creator. However, our senses of perception are, by design, restricted and limited. Much remains hidden from the thoughts of men and women.

Consequently, the force called "angel" remains unobservable to the naked eye and illogical to the rational mind. Like the unseen wind, however, its influence is very real. Positive actions of sharing, tolerance, and compassion ignite positive angels in our lives. Behavior

that embodies selfishness, intolerance, hatred, and self-indulgence rouses negative forces of darkness.

David, we are told, ruled over all the angels. Thus, here we are given the power to govern all the angels, to have them do our bidding, so that we attract the Light of The Creator into our lives. We animate positive angels and bring forth countless blessings. We expel all negative angels and dissolve all blockages. The Light that illuminates after midnight, when two saintly sages engage in Torah study, shines here, endowing us with the power to triumph over the Other Side, especially during the evening hours when the influence of the dark force reaches its maximum power. This is the final end of darkness and all Creation rejoices in turn!

861. פָּתַח ר״ש וְאָמַר, וְלֹא אָמַר אַיֵּה אֱלוֹהַּ עֹשָׂי נֹתֵן זְמִרוֹת בַּלָּיְלָה. הַאי קְרָא אוּקְמוּהָ וְאִתְּמַר, אֲבָל עֹשָׂי, עוֹשֵׂי מִבָּעֵי לֵיהּ, מַאן עֹשָׂי. אֶלָּא שְׁמָא דֶּאֱלוֹהַּ שְׁמָא כָּלִיל אִיהוּ דְּאִתְחֲזֵי הוּא וּבֵי דִינֵיהּ. דָּא שְׁמָא שְׁלִים אִיהוּ, דְּכָלִיל דְּכַר וְנוּקְבָּא: א״ל ו״ה וּבְגִינֵי כַּךְ עֹשָׂי.

861. Rabbi Shimon opened the discussion with the verse: "But none says, 'Where is Eloha my maker (lit. 'makers'), who gives songs in the night'" (Iyov 35:10). This passage has been established and we have studied it. The Scripture says "my makers" IN THE PLURAL instead of 'my maker' IN THE SINGULAR. Who are "my makers," IN PLURAL? HE ANSWERS: The name Eloha is an inclusive name that denotes Him, WHO IS ZEIR ANPIN, and His court, WHICH IS MALCHUT. This is a complete name that includes male and female, WHICH CONTAINS THE LETTERS *El-Vav-Hei*. THEREFORE IT IS WRITTEN: "my makers" IN PLURAL, BECAUSE IT INCLUDES BOTH LEVELS.

862. נֹתֵן זְמִרוֹת בַּלָּיְלָה, בְּגִין דְּדָא אִיהוּ דְּקָא מְשַׁבַּחַת תָּדִיר לְגַבֵּי מַלְכָּא דִּשְׁלָמָא דִּילֵיהּ, כְּגַוְונָא דְּבוּצִינָא דְּלָא שָׁכִיךְ תָּדִיר, בְּגִין לְקַבְּלָא נְהוֹרָא חֶדְוָה עִלָּאָה, מִסְּגִיאוּת חֶדְוָה דִּילֵיהּ. וְעַ״ד נֹתֵן זְמִרוֹת בַּלָּיְלָה.

862. "Who gives songs in the night": WHY IN THE NIGHT? IT IS because MALCHUT THAT IS CALLED 'NIGHT', constantly praises the King that the Peace is His, WHO IS ZEIR ANPIN, like a candle that is never placid, BUT ALWAYS WAVERS HERE AND THERE. SIMILARLY, MALCHUT IS

CONSTANTLY PRAISING IN ORDER TO RECEIVE THE SUPERNAL JOYOUS LIGHT OF ZEIR ANPIN, BECAUSE OF THIS GREAT JOY THAT IS AROUSED BY THE RECITED PRAISES. Therefore it says, "who gives songs in the night."

863. כָּל אִינּוּן כֹּכְבַיָּא דְּקָא מְנַהֲרָן בִּרְקִיעָא, כֻּלְּהוּ אוֹדָאן וּמְשַׁבְּחָן לְקוּדְשָׁא בְּרִיךְ הוּא, בְּכָל הַהוּא זִמְנָא דְּאִתְחֲזוּן בִּרְקִיעָא, בְּגִין דְּמַלְאֲכֵי עִלָּאֵי, כֻּלְּהוּ אוֹדָאן וּמְשַׁבְּחָן אַשְׁמוּרוֹת, בִּתְלַת פַּלְגֵי דַּהֲוֵי לֵילְיָא.

**863.** All these stars that illuminate in the firmament are thankful and praise the Holy One, blessed be He, during the entire time that they are visible in the sky, because the supernal angels, WHO ARE APPOINTED OVER THE STARS, are all thankful and praise in watches during the three parts into which the night is divided.

864. בְּלֵילְיָא אִתְפַּלְּגָן כַּמָּה סִטְרִין. בְּרֵאשִׁיתָא דְּלֵילְיָא, כַּד רָמַשׁ לֵילְיָא וְאִתְחֲשַׁךְ, כָּל אִינּוּן רוּחִין בִּישִׁין וְזִינִין בִּישִׁין, כֻּלְּהוּ מִתְבַּדְּרָן וּמְשַׁטְטֵי בְּכָל עָלְמָא. וְאִתְפָּרְשַׁת סִטְרָא אַחֲרָא, וְתָבְעֵי אָרְחֵי דְּבֵי מַלְכָּא, מִכָּל אִינּוּן סִטְרִין קַדִּישִׁין.

**864.** During the night, various sides are divided. At the beginning of the night, when the night sets in and it becomes dark, all these evil spirits and evil species scatter and float throughout the whole world, and the Other Side separates and demands the ways of the King from all these holy sides.

865. כֵּיוָן דְּהַהוּא סִטְרָא אַחֲרָא אִתְּעַר, כָּל בְּנֵי עָלְמָא טַעֲמֵי טַעֲמָא דְּמוֹתָא, חַד מִשִּׁתִּין בְּמוֹתָא, וְשַׁלְטָא עֲלַיְיהוּ. כְּדֵין כֵּיוָן דִּמְסָאֲבוּ אִתְפָּרְשָׁא מִלְּעֵילָּא, וְשַׁלְטָא וְנַחְתָּא לְתַתָּא, כְּדֵין אִתְפָּרְשָׁן תְּלַת מַשִׁרְיָין לְשַׁבְּחָא לֵיהּ לְקוּדְשָׁא בְּרִיךְ הוּא, בִּתְלַת סִטְרִין דְּלֵילְיָא, כְּמָה דְּאִתְּעָרוּ בְּהַאי חַבְרַיָּא.

**865.** As soon as the Other Side is aroused, all the inhabitants of the world taste death, MEANING THAT SLEEP FALLS UPON THEM, which is one-sixtieth

of death, AND THE OTHER SIDE dominates them. Since the impurity is separated from above and descended to dominate below, three companies of angels separate to praise the Holy One, blessed be He, in the three parts of the night, as the friends have remarked.

866. בְּעוֹד דְּאִינּוּן מְשַׁבְּחִין לְקוּדְשָׁא בְּרִיךְ הוּא, סְטְרָא אַחֲרָא אַזְלָא וּמְשַׁטְּטָא לְתַתָּא, בְּכָל סְטְרֵי עָלְמָא, וְעַד דְּסִטְרָא אַחֲרָא לָא אִתְעֲבַּר מִתַּמָּן, לָא יַכְלִין אִינּוּן לְאִתְיַיחֲדָא בְּמָארֵיהוֹן.

866. While they are still praising the Holy One, blessed be He, the Other Side goes and flies below to all directions of the world. As long as the Other Side is not removed from there, the angels cannot be united with their Master.

867. רָזָא לְחַכִּימִין, מַלְאֲכֵי עֶלְיוֹנִין, וְיִשְׂרָאֵל לְתַתָּא, כֻּלְּהוּ דְּחָקֵי בְּהַהוּא סְטְרָא אַחֲרָא. מַלְאָכִין עִלָּאִין כַּד בָּעָאן לְאִתְיַיחֲדָא בְּמָארֵיהוֹן, לָא יַכְלִין עַד דְּדַחְיָין לָהּ לְבַר. מַה עַבְדִין, נַחְתִּין שִׁיתִּין רִבּוֹא דְּמַלְאֲכֵי קַדִּישֵׁי, וַאֲפִילּוּ שֵׁינָתָא עַל כָּל בְּנֵי עָלְמָא, כֵּיוָן דְּאִיהִי נַחְתָּא, דְּקָא דַּחְיָין לָהּ לְבַר, וְיָהֲבֵי לָהּ כָּל עָלְמָא דָּא בְּהַהִיא שֵׁינָתָא, כְּדֵין אִיהִי שַׁלְטָא עֲלַיְיהוּ, וּמְקַבְּלִין מִסְאֲבוּ מִינָהּ. בַּר בְּאַרְעָא דְּיִשְׂרָאֵל בִּלְחוֹדָהָא, דְּלָא שַׁלְטָא תַּמָּן. כֵּיוָן דְּאִיהִי אִתְפָּרְשָׁא מִנַּיְיהוּ, עָאלִין לְקַמֵּי מָארֵיהוֹן, וּמְשַׁבְּחָן וְאוֹדָאן קַמֵּיהּ.

867. This is a secret for the sages. The angels above and the children of Yisrael below all reject that Other Side. When the supernal angels wish to unite with their Master, they cannot do it until they push THE OTHER SIDE outside. What do they do? About six hundred thousand holy angels descend and throw down sleep upon all the inhabitants of the world. Once THE OTHER SIDE has descended, because they pushed it out and give it this world entirely in that sleep, then THE OTHER SIDE rules over them, PEOPLE, and they become impure by it, except in the Land of Yisrael alone, for THE OTHER SIDE does not rule there. As soon as THE OTHER SIDE separates from them, the angels come before their Master, and praise and give thanks before Him.

868. כְּגַוְונָא דָא יִשְׂרָאֵל לְתַתָּא, לָא יַכְלִין לְאִתְיַיחֲדָא בְּמָארֵיהוֹן, עַד דְּדַחְיָין לְהַהוּא סִטְרָא אַחֲרָא מִנַּיְיהוּ, וְיָהֲבֵי לָהּ חוּלָקָא בְּמָה דְּאִתְעַסְקַת, וּלְבָתַר, אִינּוּן מִתְקָרְבֵי לְגַבֵּי מָארֵיהוֹן, וְלָא אִשְׁתְּכַח מְקַטְרְגָא עֵילָא וְתַתָּא.

868. Similarly, Yisrael below cannot become united with their Master until they push away the Other Side from them, and give it a portion to keep it occupied, WHICH IS THE SECRET OF THE SCAPE GOAT. Afterwards, they approach their Master, and there is no accuser is present above or below.

869. וְאִי תֵּימָא תִּינַח לְתַתָּא, אֲבָל לְעֵילָא מַאי קַטְרוּגָא תַּמָּן. אֶלָּא לְעֵילָא, בְּגִין דְּאִיהוּ רוּחַ מְסָאֲבָא, וְאִינּוּן רוּחִין קַדִּישִׁין, עַד דִּמְשַׁדְּרֵי רוּחָא מְסָאֲבָא מִבֵּינַיְיהוּ, לָא יַכְלִין לְקָרְבָא לְגַבֵּי מָארֵיהוֹן, דְּהָא קוּדְשָׁא גּוֹ מְסָאֲבָא, לָא מִתְעָרַב לְעָלְמִין. וְכֵן כְּגַוְונָא דָא, יִשְׂרָאֵל לְתַתָּא, לָא מִתְעָרְבִין בְּאוּמִין עכו"ם דְּעָלְמָא. וּתְרֵין סִטְרִין, עֶלָּאִין וְתַתָּאִין, כַּד בַּעְיָין לְקָרְבָא לְגַבֵּי מַלְכָּא קַדִּישָׁא, דַּחְיָין לָהּ לְבַר.

869. If you ask: This is all applicable below, WITH HUMANS, but above WITH ANGELS, what kind of accusation is possible there, BECAUSE OF WHICH THEY ARE OBLIGED TO PUSH THE OTHER SIDE DOWNWARDS, AS MENTIONED? HE ANSWERS: Above, it is because THE OTHER SIDE is an impure spirit and they, THE ANGELS, are Holy Spirits. THEREFORE, until they send away the Other Side from among them, they cannot approach their Master, because holiness and impurity can never mix. Similarly, the children of Yisrael below do not mix with the nations of the world who worship idols. When both sides, those above, THE ANGELS, and those below, YISRAEL, desire to approach the King, they push THE OTHER SIDE out.

870. וְעַל דָּא, כַּד עָיֵיל לֵילְיָא, וּמַלְאָכִין קַדִּישִׁין עֶלָּאִין, כַּד מִסְתַּדְּרָן שׁוּרִין לְקָרְבָא לְגַבֵּי מָארֵיהוֹן, דַּחְיָין לֵיהּ לְהַהוּא סִטְרָא לְבַר בְּקַדְמֵיתָא, וּלְבָתַר עָאלִין בְּקוּדְשָׁא.

870. Therefore, when night arrives and the holy supernal angels arrange

themselves in lines to approach their Master, they first push the Other Side out, and afterwards come into the sanctuary.

871. לְמַלְכָּא, דַּהֲווֹ לֵיהּ אַבְנִין יַקִּירִין בְּחַד תֵּיבוּתָא, מִתְגַּלְפָא בְּקוּסְטְרוֹי. וְהַהוּא מַלְכָּא הֲוָה חַכִּים. בְּגִין דְּלָא יִתְקְרַב כָּל מַאן דְּבָעֵי, לְגַבֵּי הַהוּא תֵּיבוּתָא דְּאַבְנִין יַקִּירָן וּמַרְגְּלָן דְּתַמָּן, נָטַל בְּחָכְמָתֵיהּ, חַד חִוְיָא תַּקִּיפָא, וְכָרִיךְ לֵיהּ סָחֲרָנֵיהּ דְּהַהוּא תֵּיבוּתָא, כָּל מַאן דְּבָעֵי לְאוֹשָׁטָא יְדֵיהּ לְגַבֵּי תֵּיבוּתָא, הָא חִוְיָא דָּלִיג עָלֵיהּ, וְקָטִיל לֵיהּ.

871. THIS IS SIMILAR to a king who had precious stones in a locked chest in his fortress. That king was wise and in his great wisdom, he took a strong snake and wrapped it around that chest in order that not everyone who so wished could approach that chest with precious gems and pearls. If anyone would try to put his hand to that box, the snake would pounce upon him and kill him.

872. חַד רְחִימָא הֲוָה לְמַלְכָּא, אָמַר לֵיהּ מַלְכָּא, כָּל זִמְנָא דְּאַתְּ בָּעֵי לְאֵעֲלָא וּלְאִשְׁתַּמְּשָׁא בְּתֵיבוּתָא, תַּעֲבִיד כַּךְ וְכַךְ לְגַבֵּי הַהוּא חִוְיָא, וְתִפְתַּח תֵּיבוּתָא, וּתְשַׁמֵּשׁ בִּגְנִיזִין דִּילִי. כַּךְ קוּדְשָׁא בְּרִיךְ הוּא, כָּרִיךְ חִוְיָא סָחֲרָנֵיהּ דְּקֻדְשָׁא, אָתָאן מַלְאָכִין עִלָּאִין לְאֵעֲלָא גּוֹ קֻדְשָׁא, הָא חִוְיָא תַּמָּן, וְדַחֲלֵי לְאִסְתַּאֲבָא בֵּיהּ.

872. The king had a close friend and the king said to him: Whenever you want to enter and make use of that chest, you may do such and such to the snake. Then you can open the chest and help yourself to my treasure. The Holy One, blessed be He, does also wrap a snake around the sanctuary, NAMELY THE OTHER SIDE THAT APPROACHES ANGELS, WHEN THE ILLUMINATION OF THE LEFT DOMINATES DURING THE BEGINNING OF NIGHT. When the supernal angels come to enter the sanctuary, the snake is there and they fear becoming impure through it. THEREFORE, THEY CAUSE SLEEP TO FALL UPON PEOPLE, FOR THEN THE OTHER SIDE GOES BELOW AND SEPARATES FROM THEM, AND THE ANGELS CAN ENTER THE SANCTUARY AND RECITE POETRY, AS MENTIONED.

873. ת"ח, כְּתִיב עוֹשֶׂה מַלְאָכָיו רוּחוֹת מְשָׁרְתָיו אֵשׁ לוֹהֵט, עוֹשֶׂה

מַלְאָכָיו רוּחוֹת, אִלֵּין מַלְאָכִין דְּקַיְימִין לְבַר. מְשָׁרְתָיו אֵשׁ לֹהֵט, אִלֵּין מַלְאָכִין דְּקַיְימִין לְגוֹ, אִיהוּ רוּחָא מְסָאֲבוּ, וְאִינּוּן רוּחַ. רוּחַ בְּרוּחַ לָא עָיֵיל דָּא בְּדָא. רוּחַ מְסָאֲבוּ בְּרוּחַ קַדְּשָׁא לָא אִתְעָרְבֵי דָּא בְּדָא. וּבְג"כ אִינּוּן דְּאִקְרוּן רוּחַ, לָא יַכְלִין לְאַעֲלָא לְגוֹ, בְּגִין הַהוּא רוּחָא מְסָאֲבוּ. אִינּוּן דִּלְגוֹ, אִינּוּן אֵשׁ, וְהַהוּא אֵשׁ דָּחֵי לְהַהוּא מְסָאֲבוּ דְּלָא עָיֵיל לְגוֹ. וּבְג"כ כֹּלָּא דַּחְיָין לֵיהּ לְבַר לְמְסָאֲבוּ, דְּלָא יִתְעָרַב בַּהֲדַיְיהוּ. וְעַל דָּא, מַלְאֲכֵי עִלָּאֵי קָא מְשַׁבְּחָן לֵיהּ לְקוּדְשָׁא בְּרִיךְ הוּא, בָּתַר דְּדַחְיָין לֵיהּ לְמְסָאֲבוּ לְבַר.

**873.** Come and see: It is written, "Who makes the winds (or: spirits) His messengers, the flames of fire His ministers" (Tehilim 104:4). "Who makes the spirits His messengers": These are the angels that stand outside, while "the flames of fire His ministers" are the angels that stand inside. SO WE REALIZE THAT THE OTHER SIDE is the impure spirit, AND THESE ANGELS WHO SAY PRAISE DURING THE NIGHT ARE THE EXTERNAL ANGELS. And they are a spirit, and one spirit does not enter another. The impure spirit and the Holy Spirit do not mix together. Therefore, those that are called 'spirit', WHICH ARE THE EXTERNAL ANGELS, cannot enter inside because of that impure spirit. SO THEY PUSH IT DOWN AS MENTIONED. The angels that are inside, who are fire, that fire pushes away that impure spirit, so it does not enter inside. They all push the impure spirit outside so it does not mix with them. Therefore, the supernal angels praise the Holy One, blessed be He, only after they have pushed impurity out.

874. תְּלַת אַשְׁמוּרוֹת אִינּוּן בְּלֵילְיָא, לָקֳבְלֵיהוֹן תְּלַת מַשִׁרְיָין, דְּקָא מִתְפַּלְּגֵי לְשַׁבְּחָא לְקוּדְשָׁא בְּרִיךְ הוּא, כְּמָה דְּאִתְּמַר. וְע"ד הַאי רְבּוֹן דְּכֻלְּהוּ, אִיהוּ נֵר דְּדָוִד דְּלָא שָׁכִיךְ לְעָלְמִין, אֶלָּא תָּדִיר אוֹדֵי וּמְשַׁבַּח לֵיהּ לְמַלְכָּא עִלָּאָה, וְע"ד נוֹתֵן זְמִירוֹת בַּלָּיְלָה.

**874.** There are three watches during the night, corresponding to three companies OF ANGELS who divide to praise the Holy One, blessed be He, as we have learned. Therefore, the master over them all is the candle of David, NAMELY MALCHUT, that is never quiet, but is rather constantly thanking and praising the supernal King, ZEIR ANPIN. Therefore, IT IS WRITTEN: "Who gives songs in the night."

875. ד"א, וְלָא אָמַר אַיֵּה אֱלוֹהַּ עוֹשָׂי, כְּמָה דְּאִתְּמַר, בְּגִין דְּהָא מְעֵילָא וּמִתַּתָּא אִתְכְּלִיל בַּר נָשׁ, וְאִתְעָבֵיד, כְּמָה דְּאִיהוּ גוּפָא מִתְּרֵין סִטְרִין, מִגּוֹ דְּכַר וְנוּקְבָּא, אוּף הָכִי רוּחָא. רוּחַ אִיהוּ כָּלִיל, מִגּוֹ דְּכַר וְנוּקְבָּא. וְעַל רָזָא דְּנָא אִתְתָּקַן בַּר נָשׁ בְּגְלִיפוֹי, בְּגוּפָא וְרוּחָא. וּבְגִין דְּאִיהוּ כָּלִיל בְּרָזָא דָא, וּבְעוֹבָדָא דָא, כְּמָה דְּאִתְּמַר, ע"ד כְּתִיב, וַיֹּאמֶר אֱלֹהִים נַעֲשֶׂה אָדָם בְּצַלְמֵנוּ כִּדְמוּתֵנוּ וְהָא אִתְּמַר.

**875.** Another explanation OF THE VERSE: "But none says, 'Where is Eloha my maker ('makers'), who gives songs in the night'" IS WRITTEN AS 'MAKERS' IN PLURAL. It is as we have learned that since man is made and comprised of above and below, just like the body comes out from male and female, so it is with the spirit. The spirit of man is composed of male and female, NAMELY OF ZEIR ANPIN AND MALCHUT. By these means is man perfected in his engravings of body and spirit. Since he pertains to this secret and this action, OF MALE AND FEMALE, as we have learned, it is written: "And Elohim said, 'Let us make man in our image, after our likeness'" (Beresheet 1:26), WHICH IS IN THE PLURAL AND REFERS TO ZEIR ANPIN AND MALCHUT. And we have already learned this. THEREFORE IT ALSO SAYS, "WHERE IS ELOHA MY MAKERS" IN THE PLURAL, NAMELY BOTH ASPECTS OF ZEIR ANPIN AND MALCHUT THAT EFFECTED MAN.

876. בְּלֵילְיָא הָא אֲמַרְתְּ, דְּהָא בְּרֵאשִׁיתָא דְּלֵילְיָא, כָּל אִינּוּן זִינִין וְרוּחִין בִּישִׁין מִתְעָרֵי בְּעָלְמָא, הֵיךְ אִיהוּ יָכִיל לְמֶהֱוֵי, דְּאִי הָכִי, הָא תָּנֵינָן, דְּמִסְּטְרָא דְּצָפוֹן נַפְקֵי כָּל הָנֵי זִינִין בִּישִׁין, וְאִתְּמַר דְּכַד אִתְּעַר רוּחַ צָפוֹן בְּפַלְגוּת לֵילְיָא, דְּהָא כְּדֵין כָּל אִינּוּן רוּחִין בִּישִׁין, וְסִטְרִין בִּישִׁין, אִתְכַּנָּשׁוּ מֵעָלְמָא, וְעָאלִין גּוֹ נוּקְבָּא דִּתְהוֹמָא רַבָּא, אִי הָכִי הָא בְּסִטְרָא דְּדָרוֹם דְּאִיהוּ יְמִינָא, אֲמַאי מְשַׁטְּטֵי אִינּוּן זִינִין בִּישִׁין בְּרֵישׁ לֵילְיָא, דְּקָא שַׁלְטָא רוּחַ דָּרוֹם.

**876.** During the night, you say that in the beginning of the night all these types of evil spirits are aroused in the world. How can this be, for we have learned that all these evil types emerge from the North, WHICH IS LEFT, and

we have learned that when the North Wind is aroused at midnight, all these evil spirits and evil aspects gather together from the whole world and enter through the hole of the Great Abyss. If so then in the South Side, which is the Right, WHICH IS CHESED, why do these evil types rove around in the beginning of the night when the South Wind dominates? IT SHOULD BE THE OPPOSITE THAT DURING THE BEGINNING OF THE NIGHT WHEN THE SOUTH WIND DOMINATES, THE OTHER SIDE SHOULD BE REMOVED FROM THE WORLD AND AT MIDNIGHT WHEN THE NORTH WIND DOMINATES, THEY SHOULD AGAIN DOMINATE IN THE WORLD?

877. אֶלָּא וַדַּאי, אִלְמָלֵא הַהוּא סִטְרָא דְּדָרוֹם, דְּקָא מְעַכֵּב וְדָחְיָיא לְהַהוּא סִטְרָא בִּישָׁא, הֲוָה מְטַשְׁטֵשׁ כּוּלֵי עָלְמָא, וְלָא יָכִיל עָלְמָא לְמִסְבַּל. אֲבָל כַּד אִתְּעַר הַהוּא סִטְרָא אַחֲרָא, לָא אִתְּעַר אֶלָּא בְּסִטַר רוּחַ מַעֲרָב, דְּקָא שַׁלְטָא בְּרֵישׁ לֵילְיָא, וְעָלְמָא אִיהוּ כֹּלָא כָּנִישׁ. וְעַ״ד קוּדְשָׁא בְּרִיךְ הוּא אַקְדִּים הוּא אַסְוָותָא לְעָלְמָא, בְּגַוְונָא דָא כְּמָה דְּאִתְּמַר. זַכָּאִין אִינּוּן יִשְׂרָאֵל בְּהַאי עָלְמָא וּבְעָלְמָא דְּאָתֵי דְּקוּדְשָׁא בְּרִיךְ הוּא אִתְרְעֵי בְּהוּ מִכָּל שְׁאַר עַמִּין דְּעָלְמָא.

877. HE ANSWERS: But surely, were it not for the South Side that detains and pushes away the Other Side, THEN THE OTHER SIDE would trouble the whole world, and the world could not tolerate it. When the Other Side is aroused TO DOMINATE THE WORLD, it is aroused only from the West Side, WHICH IS MALCHUT, that dominates during the beginning of the night and gathers the whole world. Therefore, the Holy One, blessed be He, precedes with a remedy for the world BY THE SLEEP, as we have learned. Blessed are the children of Yisrael in this world and in the World to Come, that the Holy One, blessed be He, has chosen them of all the other nations of the world.

878. עָאלוּ לְבֵיתָא רַבִּי אֶלְעָזָר וְרַבִּי אַבָּא. כַּד אִתְפְּלַג לֵילְיָא, קָמוּ לְמִלְעֵי בְּאוֹרַיְיתָא. אָמַר רַבִּי אַבָּא, הַשְׁתָּא וַדַּאי אִיהוּ עִידָן רְעוּתָא לְקוּדְשָׁא בְּרִיךְ הוּא, וְהָא זִמְנִין סַגִּיאִין אִתְּעָרְנָא הַאי, דְּקוּדְשָׁא בְּרִיךְ הוּא בְּשַׁעֲתָא דְּאִתְפְּלַג לֵילְיָא, עָאל גּוֹ אִינּוּן צַדִּיקַיָּיא בְּגִנְתָא דְּעֵדֶן, וְאִשְׁתַּעֲשַׁע בְּהוּ. זַכָּאָה אִיהוּ מַאן דְּאִשְׁתַּדַּל בְּאוֹרַיְיתָא, בְּהַהִיא זִמְנָא.

**878.** Rabbi Elazar and Rabbi Aba entered the house. At midnight, they rose to study Torah. Rabbi Aba said: It is certainly a favorable time for the Holy One, blessed be He. Many times, we have remarked about this, that at midnight, the Holy One, blessed be He, enters the Garden of Eden with the righteous and delights Himself with them. Blessed is he who studies Torah at that time.

879. אָמַר רַבִּי אֶלְעָזָר, הָא דְּאִשְׁתַּעֲשַׁע קוּדְשָׁא בְּרִיךְ הוּא גּוֹ צַדִּיקַיָּא בְּגִנְתָּא דְּעֵדֶן, הֵיךְ אִשְׁתַּעֲשַׁע. אֶלָּא בְּהַהוּא זִמְנָא דְּאִתְפְּלַג לֵילְיָא, קוּדְשָׁא בְּרִיךְ הוּא אִתְּעַר בִּרְחִימוּ דִּשְׂמָאלָא, לְגַבֵּי כְּנֶסֶת יִשְׂרָאֵל, דְּהָא לֵית רְחִימוּ אֶלָּא מִסִּטְרָא דִּשְׂמָאלָא. וּכְנֶסֶת יִשְׂרָאֵל לֵית לָהּ דּוֹרוֹנָא לְמִקְרַב לְגַבֵּי מַלְכָּא, אוֹ חֲשִׁיבוּ מֵעַלְיָא, אֶלָּא בְּאִינּוּן רוּחִין דְּצַדִּיקַיָּא, דְּקוּדְשָׁא בְּרִיךְ הוּא חָמֵי לוֹן מִתְעַטְּרָן, בְּכַמָּה עוֹבָדִין טָבִין, וּבְכַמָּה זַכְיָין דְּעַבְדוּ בְּהַהוּא יוֹמָא, וְקוּדְשָׁא בְּרִיךְ הוּא נִיחָא לֵיהּ מִכָּל קָרְבָּנִין וְעִלָוָון, דְּקוּדְשָׁא בְּרִיךְ הוּא אָרַח בְּהוּ רֵיחַ נִיחֹחַ, דְּקָא עַבְדֵי יִשְׂרָאֵל.

**879.** Rabbi Elazar said: When the Holy One, blessed be He, delights Himself with the righteous, how does He delight Himself? HE ANSWERS: At midnight, the Holy One, blessed be He, is aroused through the love of the Left for the Congregation of Yisrael, WHICH IS MALCHUT. Love is only in the Left, MEANING THAT CHOCHMAH OF THE LEFT IS CLOTHED WITH THE CHASSADIM OF THE CENTRAL COLUMN, AND THEN CHOCHMAH IS COMPLETED. The Congregation of Yisrael has no present to offer the King or a beautiful and distinguished thing, except for these spirits of the righteous, for the Holy One, blessed be He, sees them adorned with many good deeds and many merits that they performed that day. They are accepted more favorably than all the offerings and burnt sacrifices, for the Holy One, blessed be He, smells in them the sweet savor that the children of Yisrael produce.

880. כְּדֵין נְהִירִין אִתְנְהִיר, וְכֹל אִילָנִין דְּגִנְתָּא דְּעֵדֶן אָמְרוּ שִׁירָתָא, וְצַדִּיקַיָּא מִתְעַטְּרָן תַּמָּן בְּאִינּוּן עִדּוּנִין דְּעָלְמָא דְּאָתֵי. כַּד אִתְּעַר בַּר נָשׁ בְּהַהִיא שַׁעֲתָא לְמִלְעֵי בְּאוֹרַיְיתָא, נָטִיל חוּלָקֵיהּ עִמְּהוֹן דְּצַדִּיקַיָּא דִּי בְּגוֹ גִּנְתָּא, חַד שְׁמָא גְּלִיפָא דִּתְלָתִין וּתְרֵין אַתְוָון, אִתְעַטַּר בְּהוּ תַּמָּן,

וְאִיהוּ גּוֹ רָזִין דְּצַדִּיקַיָּא.

**880.** Then the light lights up, FOR THE LIGHT OF CHOCHMAH IS LIT UP AFTER BEING CLOTHED IN CHASSADIM OF THE CENTRAL COLUMN. All the trees in the Garden of Eden sing songs of praise and the righteous become adorned there with the delights of the World to Come, WHICH ARE THE ILLUMINATION OF CHOCHMAH THAT IS CALLED 'EDEN'. When a person wakes FROM HIS SLEEP at that time to study Torah, He takes his portion with the righteous in the Garden of Eden. One Name which is engraved with 32 letters, WHICH IS THE SECRET OF THE 32 PATHS OF CHOCHMAH, adorns the righteous there, and this pertains to the secret of the righteous.

## 88. "I will praise Hashem with my whole heart"

### A Synopsis
Here, Rabbi Elazar shows how Yah (Yud-Hei) is included with Halelu (praise) in Haleluyah. He then speaks of the secret of the alphabet shown by King David in his praises, namely the supernal letters, and the letters of Malchut, and the secret of 32 paths of Chochmah. Praising God with one's whole heart, we are told, means with both the Good and the Evil Inclinations. We should give thanks to God for good and for evil, and, furthermore, say this thanks before everyone.

### The Relevance of this Passage
Here, Zohar is taking us deeper into a teaching that has been slowly but steadily intensifying throughout 'Trumah' – the nature of evil. When we are told that we should give thanks for evil, we probably feel a shock wave of protest run through us. Are we not here to defeat and overcome evil? How can we give thanks for such blackness? In each act of victory over evil, man achieves a state of divinity. He unleashes the Godly spark of Light flickering in his soul. This truth can be seen in our physical world. Muscle tissue requires resistance and strain in order to grow stronger. A lit candle requires darkness to give it value and worth. Likewise, the soul of man requires burden and lightlessness in order to realize its full splendor.

When evil has run its course, and man has fully triumphed over the darkness, the soul will be strengthened to its maximum potential. We will have evolved to the highest level – the state of God. This has been the journey of over 5761 years, thus far. Two paths to this ultimate divine place have always existed, the path of torment and the softhearted path of spirituality. Both paths strengthen the soul and achieve the same outcome. But the path of torment is known all too well, while the path of spirituality remains the least traveled, until now. By utilizing the awesome spiritual influence of the Zohar, we *now* choose the path of Light. We fully correct our souls and complete the spiritual evolution of all mankind in a compassionate way, so there is no further need of darkness and challenge

881. פָּתַח רַבִּי אֶלְעָזָר וְאָמַר, הַלְלוּיָה אוֹדֶה יְיָ' בְּכָל לֵבָב וְגוֹ', הַלְלוּיָה, הָא אִתְּמַר וְאִתְּעָרוּ בֵּיהּ חַבְרַיָּיא, וְהָכִי אִיהוּ, דְּדָא אִיהוּ שְׁבָחָא דְּקָא סַלְּקָא עַל כָּל אִינּוּן שִׁירִין וְתוּשְׁבְּחָן דְּאָמַר דָּוִד, בְּעֶשֶׂר זִינֵי תוּשְׁבְּחָן דְּאִיהוּ אָמַר, בְּגִין דְּאִיהוּ כָּלִיל שְׁמָא וְשֻׁבְחָא בְּחַד, וְאִיהוּ כְּלָלָא דִשְׁמָא קַדִישָׁא עִלָּאָה.

**881.** Rabbi Elazar opened the discussion saying: "Haleluyah. I will praise Hashem with my whole heart" (Tehilim 111:1). "Haleluyah (lit. 'praise Yah')": We have learned this and the friends remarked about it. So it is, for this is a praise that transcends all the songs and praises that David said, among the ten various praises he said, Because it includes the Name YAH (*YUD-HEI*), and the praise 'HALLELU' (LIT. 'PRAISE') together. This is the entirety of the Holy Supernal Name YUD HEI VAV HEI, BECAUSE THE NAME *YUD-HEI* IS THE WHOLE OF THE NAME YUD HEI VAV HEI.

882. אוֹדֶה יְיָ׳ בְּכָל לֵבָב, בְּכָל אֲתָר דְּאָמַר דָּוִד מַלְכָּא, רָזָא דְּאַלְפָּא בֵּיתָא, אִיהוּ רָזָא דְּאַתְוָון גְּלִיפָן, דְּנָפְקִין בְּגִלּוּפֵי דִתְלָתִין וּתְרֵין שְׁבִילִין. וְאִית אַתְוָון עִלָּאִין, מֵרָזָא דְּעָלְמָא עִלָּאָה. וְאִית אַתְוָון אָחֳרָנִין, דְּאִינּוּן אַתְוָון זְעִירִין. וְהָכָא אִיהוּ רָזָא דְּאַלְפָּא בֵּיתָא, דְּעָלְמָא תַּתָּאָה.

**882.** "I will praise Hashem with my whole heart." Wherever King David mentioned the secret of the alphabet, MEANING WHEN HE ARRANGED THE BEGINNING OF THE SENTENCES IN THE ORDER OF THE *ALEPHBET*, it is the secret of the engraved letters that emanate in the engravings of the 32 paths, NAMELY THE 32 PATHS OF CHOCHMAH. There are supernal letters from the secret of the Supernal World, WHICH IS BINAH, and there are other letters which are small letters, WHICH ARE FROM MALCHUT. Here is the secret of the alphabet of the lower world, WHICH IS MALCHUT.

883. אוֹדֶה יְיָ׳ בְּכָל לֵבָב: בְּיִצְרָא טָבָא וּבְיִצְרָא בִּישָׁא דְּאִיהוּ שָׁרֵי בְּגַוֵּיה. דְּהָא עַל כֹּלָּא אִית לְאוֹדָאָה לֵיהּ לְקוּדְשָׁא בְּרִיךְ הוּא, בְּיִצְרָא טָבָא וּבְיִצְרָא בִּישָׁא. דְּהָא מִסִּטְרָא דְּיִצְרָא טָבָא אָתֵי טוֹב לְבַר נָשׁ, וְאִית לְבָרְכָא לֵיהּ לְקוּדְשָׁא בְּרִיךְ הוּא הַטּוֹב וְהַמֵּטִיב. וּבְסִטְרָא דְּיִצְרָא בִּישָׁא, אָתֵי קַטְרוּגָּא לְבַר נָשׁ, וְאִית לְאוֹדָאָה לְקוּדְשָׁא בְּרִיךְ הוּא, בְּכָל מַה דְּאָתֵי עַל בַּר נָשׁ, מִסִּטְרָא דָּא וּמִסִּטְרָא דָּא.

**883.** "I will praise Hashem with my whole heart," meaning with the Good Inclination and Evil Inclination that dwell in him. We must thank the Holy One, blessed be He, for everything, both with the Good Inclination and the Evil Inclination. Good comes for the person from the side of the Good

Inclination, and it behooves us to bless the Holy One, blessed be He, with the blessing of 'who is good and does good'. From the side of evil come accusations against the person, and it behooves one to thank the Holy One, blessed be He, for everything that may come unto a person from either side.

884. בְּסוֹד יְשָׁרִים וְעֵדָה, בְּסוֹד יְשָׁרִים: בְּאִינּוּן דְּרָזָא דְּקוּדְשָׁא בְּרִיךְ הוּא אִינּוּן יַדְעֵי. דְּהָא כָּל רָזִין דְּקוּדְשָׁא בְּרִיךְ הוּא אִינּוּן יַדְעֵי, וְאִינּוּן רָזָא דִּילֵיהּ, וְעַל דָּא בְּסוֹד יְשָׁרִים. וְעֵדָה: אַלֵּין אִינּוּן יִשְׂרָאֵל, כַּד מִתְכַּנְּשֵׁי בַּעֲשָׂרָה, לְאוֹדָאָה לֵיהּ לְקוּדְשָׁא בְּרִיךְ הוּא, וּבג"כ, אִית לְאוֹדָאָה לֵיהּ לְקוּדְשָׁא בְּרִיךְ הוּא, עַל טָב וְעַל בִּישׁ, וּלְפַרְסְמָא קַמֵּי כֹּלָּא. דְּאִי תֵּימָא הָא אִיהוּ יָדַע, אֲמַאי אִצְטְרִיךְ לְפַרְסְמָא. אֶלָּא בְּדָא, אִתְיָיקַר קוּדְשָׁא בְּרִיךְ הוּא בְּעָלְמָא לְפַרְסְמָא נִסָּא. וְעַל דָּא קוּדְשָׁא בְּרִיךְ הוּא כְּתִיב בֵּיהּ, וְהִתְגַּדִּלְתִּי וְהִתְקַדִּשְׁתִּי וְגוֹ'.

**884.** "In the assembly of the upright, and in the congregation" (Ibid.): "In the assembly (lit. 'secret') of the upright" refers to those who know the secret of the Holy One, blessed be He, as they know all the secrets of the Holy One, blessed be He, as they are His secret IN GENERAL. Referring to this, HE SAYS: "in the secret of the upright." "The congregation" is the children of Yisrael when they gather in a group of ten to thank the Holy One, blessed be He. Therefore, we should give thanks to the Holy One, blessed be He, for good and for evil and publicize it before everyone. If you ask: THE HOLY ONE, BLESSED BE HE, knows, so why is it necessary to publicize? The Holy One, blessed be He, is glorified in the world by this PUBLICIZING. THEREFORE, WE SHOULD publicize the miracle and THEREFORE, it is written of the Holy One, blessed be He: "Thus will I magnify Myself and sanctify Myself..." (Yechezkel 38:23).

## 89. "Let every soul praise Yah"

### A Synopsis

Here, Rabbi Yehuda says that all souls come from the holy body, Malchut, and dwell within in humans. He speaks again of the fountains of Wisdom that emerge into 32 paths, and of the Holy Spirit, in which all the spirits are included.

Rabbi Yitzchak then tells us how profoundly moved Rabbi Shimon had been when speaking of this, and how he had told of the treasures of the supernal King, the key which is Yesod, the supernal Engravings, and the treasury of the Images (Malchut). Moses died and approached the Fiftieth Gate, we learn, without revealing these secrets to Yisrael.

### The Relevance of this Passage

This passage speaks of the paradise that is obtained by the souls of the wise after death. The joy, so fierce that it causes Rabbi Shimon to weep, is the joy of returning to paradise. It is the moment when the burden of physical existence drops forever from one's soul, when the anguish and woe is cleared from one's sobbing heart, and when everything is made eternally young and joyful again. The notion of "death" has spiritual connotations, relevant to the here and now. In the moment we choose to ascend to a higher spiritual level, our old self dies. Thus, the world to come, paradise, along with its abundant joyful treasures, pertains to the next level of spirituality which, potentially, lies in the very next moment, should we choose it. In this passage we choose it. Death itself dies and paradise appears before our eyes. The burden of physical existence is forever lifted.

885. רַבִּי יְהוּדָה פָּתַח וְאָמַר, כֹּל הַנְּשָׁמָה תְּהַלֵּל יָהּ. תָּנָא, כָּל נִשְׁמָתִין אָתוּ מֵהַאי גּוּפָא קַדִּישָׁא, וְאִתְעָרוּ בִּבְנֵי נָשָׁא. וּמֵאָן אֲתָר. מֵהַהוּא אֲתָר דְּאִקְרֵי יָד. מֵאָן אֲתָר דָּא אָמַר רַבִּי יְהוּדָה דִּכְתִיב מָה רַבּוּ מַעֲשֶׂיךָ יְיָ' כֻּלָּם בְּחָכְמָה עָשִׂיתָ. תָּנָא, מֵהַאי חָכְמְתָא דְּמַבּוּעוֹי נָפְקִין לִתְלָתִין וּתְרֵין שְׁבִילִין, אִשְׁתְּכָלַל כֹּלָּא, וְכָל מָה דְּאִית לְעֵילָא וְתַתָּא, וְהוּא אִתְקְרֵי רוּחָא קַדִּישָׁא, דְּכָל רוּחִין אִשְׁתְּכָלָלוּ בֵּיהּ.

885. Rabbi Yehuda opened the discussion with the verse: "Let every soul praise Yah" (Tehilim 150:6). We have learned that all souls come from this holy body, NAMELY MALCHUT, WHICH IS A BODY TO ZEIR ANPIN, and dwell within humans. HE QUESTIONS: From which place is it, MEANING

FROM WHICH ASPECT? HE ANSWERS: It is from the place that is called 'hand', NAMELY MALCHUT. HE QUESTIONS: What is the aspect of this place? Rabbi Yehuda said: It is written, "Hashem, how manifold are Your works. In Wisdom have You made them all" (Tehilim 104:24) and we have learned of that Chochmah (Wisdom), that Her fountains flow into 32 paths. Everything is included, everything that is above and below, WHICH IS MALCHUT, WHICH IN HER ALONE IS CHOCHMAH revealed, AND NOT IN ANY OTHER LEVEL. It is called 'the Holy Spirit' in which all spirits are included.

886. אָמַר רַבִּי יִצְחָק, בְּיוֹמָא דַּהֲוָה רַבִּי שִׁמְעוֹן פָּרִישׁ מִלָּה דָּא, עֵינוֹי נַבְעִין מַיָּא, וַהֲוָה אָמַר, כָּל גִּנְזַיָּיא דְּמַלְכָּא עִלָּאָה, אִתְמְסָרָן בְּחַד מַפְתְּחָא, וְאִתְגַּלְיָיא בְּקַזְפִיטָן דְּקוּרְדִּיטֵי גְּלִיפִין עִלָּאִין.

886. Rabbi Yitzchak said: During the day that Rabbi Shimon was explaining this subject, his eyes were gushing tears. He said: All the treasures of the supernal King are given over with one key, WHICH IS YESOD. The supernal Engravings, WHICH ARE THE SUPERNAL CONCEALED THINGS THAT ARE REVEALED THROUGH YESOD IN MALCHUT WHEREIN IS THE PLACE OF REVELATION, are revealed by the keeper of the treasury of the Images, THAT IS YESOD, THE HUSBAND OF MALCHUT THAT IS CALLED 'THE TREASURY OF THE IMAGES'.

887. אֶלָּא הָכִי תָּאנָא, מַאן יָכִיל לְאִשְׁתְּמוֹדְעָא וּלְאִתְכַּלְלָא מַה דִּגְנִיז בְּדָא מַבּוּעָא. דְּהָא מֹשֶׁה לָא גַּלֵּי דָּא בְּיוֹמוֹי, כַּד הֲוָה גַּלֵּי רָזָא עֲמִיקְתָּא לְיִשְׂרָאֵל, וְאַף עַל גַּב דְּכֹלָּא הֲוָה מִתְגַּלְיָיא עַל יְדוֹי. אֶלָּא בְּהַהִיא שַׁעֲתָא דְּבָעֵא קוּדְשָׁא בְּרִיךְ הוּא לְסַלְקָא לֵיה לִמְתִיבְתָּא קַדִּישָׁא עִלָּאָה, וּלְטַמְרָא לֵיה מִבְּנֵי נָשָׁא, דִּכְתִיב בֶּן מֵאָה וְעֶשְׂרִים שָׁנָה אָנֹכִי הַיּוֹם. הַיּוֹם מַמָּשׁ, דְּהַהוּא יוֹמָא אִשְׁתְּלִימוּ יוֹמוֹי, לְאִתְקָרְבָא לַאֲתַר דָּא, דִּכְתִיב הֵן קָרְבוּ יָמֶיךָ קָרְבוּ מַמָּשׁ.

887. We have learned, who can comprehend and grasp what is concealed in this fountain, WHICH IS YESOD, for Moses did not reveal in his lifetime, while he revealed deep secrets to Yisrael, NAMELY THE FIFTIETH GATE, even though everything was revealed through him. When the Holy One,

blessed be He, wanted to elevate him to the supernal Holy Yeshivah and conceal him from people, as it is written: "I am 120 years old this day" (Devarim 31:2). It is on the very day OF HIS DEMISE, because on that day (the count of) his days was completed, to approach this place, THE FIFTIETH GATE, as it is written: "Behold, your days approach" (Ibid. 14). They actually approached, IN THAT THEY APPROACHED THE FIFTIETH GATE.

## 90. Moses did not die

### A Synopsis

Rabbi Shimon says here that from our point of view death is called 'death', but from the view of those above, life is increased to one who dies. So Moses did not die, and neither did Jacob, because he had a complete Faith. When Jacob was renamed 'Israel', we learn, it meant the perfection of everything, which is the lack of death.

### The Relevance of this Passage

Death dies. All is perfected and made eternal through Jacob and Moses. Mercy and loving kindness envelop the entire metamorphose. End of story.

888. דְּתַנְיָא אָמַר רַבִּי שִׁמְעוֹן, מֹשֶׁה לָא מִית. וְאִי תֵּימָא הָא כְּתִיב וַיָּמָת שָׁם מֹשֶׁה. כַּךְ בְּכָל אֲתָר לְצַדִּיקַיָּא קָרֵי בְּהוּ מִיתָה. מַאי מִיתָה. מִסִּטְרָא דִּילָן אִקְרֵי הָכִי. דְּתַנְיָא אָמַר רַבִּי שִׁמְעוֹן, וְכֵן תָּנָא, דְּמַאן דְּאִיהוּ בִּשְׁלִימוּתָא דִּמְהֵימְנוּתָא קַדִּישָׁא תַּלְיָיא בֵּיה, לָא תַּלְיָיא בֵּיה מִיתָה וְלָא מִית. כְּמָה דַּהֲוָה בְּיַעֲקֹב דִּמְהֵימְנוּתָא שְׁלֵימָתָא הֲוָה בֵּיה.

**888.** We have learned that Rabbi Shimon said: Moses did not die. If you ask, yet it is written: "And Moses died there" (Devarim 34:5). And so every place where death is mentioned by the righteous, what is death? From our view, it is called so, BUT FROM THE VIEW OF THOSE ABOVE, TO THE CONTRARY, HIS LIFE INCREASED. For we have learned that Rabbi Shimon said: He taught that the Holy Faith is suspended from one who is perfect. Death is not attached to him and he doesn't die, as it was with Jacob, who had a complete Faith. THEREFORE, JACOB THE PATRIARCH DID NOT DIE.

889. דְּאָמַר ר' שִׁמְעוֹן, לֹא יִקָּרֵא שִׁמְךָ עוֹד יַעֲקֹב כִּי אִם יִשְׂרָאֵל יִהְיֶה שְׁמֶךָ, וַיִּקְרָא אֶת שְׁמוֹ יִשְׂרָאֵל. מַאי יִשְׂרָאֵל. שְׁלֵימוּתָא דְכֹלָּא. דִּכְתִיב וְאַתָּה אַל תִּירָא עַבְדִּי יַעֲקֹב וְאַל תֵּחַת יִשְׂרָאֵל כִּי הִנְנִי מוֹשִׁיעֲךָ מֵרָחוֹק וְאֶת זַרְעֲךָ מֵאֶרֶץ שִׁבְיָם וְגוֹ'.

**889.** For Rabbi Shimon said: "Your name shall not be called any more Jacob, but Yisrael shall be your name, and he called his name Yisrael" (Beresheet 35:10). What means Yisrael? The perfection of everything,

WHICH IS THE LACK OF DEATH. It is written: "Therefore fear you not, My servant Jacob, says Hashem; neither be dismayed, Yisrael: for, lo, I will save you from afar, and your seed from the land of their captivity..." (Yirmeyah 30:10).

890. א״ר יְהוּדָה מֵהָכָא, כִּי אִתְּךָ אָנִי, דַּיְיקָא, זַכָּאָה חוּלְקֵיהּ, דְּמָארֵיהּ אָמַר לֵיהּ כֵּן. כִּי אִתִּי אַתָּה לָא כְּתִיב, אֶלָּא כִּי אִתְּךָ אָנִי, דְּמָארֵיהּ אָתֵי לְאִתְחַבְּרָא דִּיוּרֵיהּ עֲמֵיהּ.

**890.** Rabbi Yehuda said: From the following IS DERIVED THAT JACOB DID NOT DIE, as it is written, "For I am with you" (Ibid. 11). "I" is exact, FOR IT POINTS OUT TO MALCHUT THAT IS CALLED 'I.' Blessed is the portion of him, whose Master speaks thus to him. It is not written, 'For you are with me', FOR THEN IT WOULD IMPLY THAT HE WAS ATTACHED TO THE HOLY ONE, BLESSED BE HE, ABOVE BUT NOT WHEN HE WAS IN HIS PLACE BELOW. Rather "for I am with you," WHICH POINTS OUT that his Master came to join and dwell with him.

891. אר״ש שַׁפִּיר קָאֲמַר ר' אַבָּא דְּאֲמַר וְשָׁב יַעֲקֹב וְשָׁקַט וְשַׁאֲנַן וְאֵין מַחֲרִיד. וְשָׁב יַעֲקֹב: לְאִתְקְרֵי בִּשְׁמָא אַחֲרָא, דִּכְתִּיב לֹא יִקָּרֵא שִׁמְךָ עוֹד יַעֲקֹב כִּי אִם יִשְׂרָאֵל.

**891.** Rabbi Shimon said: Rabbi Aba has spoken well ABOUT THE VERSE, "And Jacob shall return, and shall be quiet and at ease, and none shall make him afraid" (Ibid. 10). "And Jacob shall return" MEANS he shall return to being called by a different name, as it is written: "Your name shall not be called any more Jacob, but Yisrael."

892. ד״א וְשָׁב יַעֲקֹב, לְאֲתָר דְּאִתְנְסִיב מִתַּמָּן. וְשָׁקַט, בְּעוֹלָם הַזֶּה. וְשַׁאֲנַן, בְּעוֹלָם הַבָּא. וְאֵין מַחֲרִיד מִמַּלְאַךְ הַמָּוֶת. דְּמַשְׁמַע דְּכֹלָּא הֲוָה בֵּיהּ. ר' יִצְחָק אָמַר, חַבְרַיָּיא הָא אוּקְמוּהָ, דִּכְתִּיב וְאֶת זַרְעֲךָ מֵאֶרֶץ שִׁבְיָם, מַה זַרְעוֹ בַּחַיִּים, אַף הוּא בַּחַיִּים.

**892.** Another explanation for: "And Jacob shall return" MEANING "AND

JACOB SHALL RETURN" to the place from where he was taken "and shall be quiet" NAMELY in this world. "And at ease," NAMELY in the World to Come. "And none shall make him afraid," NAMELY of the Angel of Death. The implication is that he had everything in him, FOR JACOB DID NOT DIE. Rabbi Yitzchak said: The friends have established it, as it is written, "And your seed from the land of their captivity" (Ibid. 10). Just as his seed is alive, so is he alive. HENCE, JACOB DID NOT DIE.

## 91. Circumcision, redemption of the firstborn son and marriage

### A Synopsis

Rabbi Yehuda tells us here that bad things will come to the people in the world who do not take advantage of the Torah that their Master left for them. He then says there are three things that a person is obligated to do for his son: circumcision, redemption, and to marry him to a woman. This is because God did these things for Yisrael. Also, we are told, He carried them like the eagle who carries its children on its wings.

### The Relevance of this Passage

Our meditation purifies our children and redeems all the world's children who grace us with their innocence. By this action, we are carried upward on our own strong wings, and the men and women, sons and daughters of this world, find their soul mates and unite in completion. And then our entire world unites with our Creator in a Final Redemption that exemplifies the loving kindness of this holy book.

893. וְהַבְּרִיחַ הַתִּיכוֹן בְּתוֹךְ הַקְּרָשִׁים מַבְרִיחַ מִן הַקָּצֶה אֶל הַקָּצֶה. רַבִּי יְהוּדָה פָּתַח אַשְׁרֶיךָ אֶרֶץ שֶׁמַּלְכֵּךְ בֶּן חוֹרִים וְשָׂרַיִךְ בָּעֵת יֹאכֵלוּ. וּכְתִיב, אִי לָךְ אֶרֶץ שֶׁמַּלְכֵּךְ נָעַר וְשָׂרַיִךְ בַּבֹּקֶר יֹאכֵלוּ. וַוי לְעָלְמָא דְּלָא מַשְׁגְּחָן בְּפוּלְחָנָא דְּמָארֵיהוֹן, דְּהָא מָארֵיהוֹן אַשְׁגַּח בְּגִינֵיהוֹן לְאוֹטָבָא לְהוּ, דְּאָנַח קַמַּיְיהוּ פִּתְגָּמֵי אוֹרַיְיתָא, וְלָא מַשְׁגְּחָן.

893. "And the middle bar in the midst of the boards shall reach from end to end" (Shemot 26:28). Rabbi Yehuda opened the discussion saying: "Happy are you, O land, when your king is a free man, and your princes eat in due season" (Kohelet 10:17) and, "Woe to you, O land, when your king is a child, and your princes dine in the morning" (Ibid. 16). Woe is to the people in the world that do not care the service of their Master, because their Master endeavors to do good for them, for He has left words of Torah before them but they do pay attention to them.

894. דְּתָנֵינָן, תְּלַת מִלִּין בָּעֵי בַּר נָשׁ לְמֶעְבַּד לִבְרֵיהּ, מִילָה, וּפִדְיוֹן, וּלְנַסְבָּא לֵיהּ אִנְתּוּ. וְכֹלָּא עָבֵיד קוּדְשָׁא בְּרִיךְ הוּא לְיִשְׂרָאֵל. מִילָה: דִּכְתִיב וְשׁוּב מוֹל אֶת בְּנֵי יִשְׂרָאֵל שֵׁנִית. וּכְתִיב וּבֶן שְׁמֹנַת יָמִים יִמּוֹל

לָכֶם כָּל זָכָר. פִּדְיוֹן. דִּכְתִיב וַיִּפְדְּךָ מִבֵּית עֲבָדִים מִיַּד פַּרְעֹה מֶלֶךְ מִצְרָיִם. לְנַסְבָא לֵיהּ אַנְתּוּ: דִּכְתִיב זָכָר וּנְקֵבָה בָּרָא אוֹתָם, וּכְתִיב וַיְבָרֶךְ אוֹתָם אֱלֹהִים וַיֹּאמֶר לָהֶם אֱלֹהִים פְּרוּ וּרְבוּ. תּוּ, אַטִּיל לְהוּ כְּהַאי נִשְׁרָא, דְּאַטִּיל לִבְנוֹי עַל גַּדְפּוֹי, דִּכְתִיב וָאֶשָּׂא אֶתְכֶם עַל כַּנְפֵי נְשָׁרִים.

**894.** We have learned that there are three things that a person is obligated to do for his son: circumcision; redemption; marry him to a woman. The Holy One, blessed be He, did all this with Yisrael. Circumcision, as it is written: "And circumcise again the children of Yisrael a second time" (Yehoshua 5:2) and, "And he that is eight days old shall be circumcised among you, every male" (Beresheet 17:12). Redemption, as it is written: "And redeemed you out of the house of bondmen, from the land of Pharaoh, King of Egypt" (Devarim 7:8). To marry him to a woman, as it is written: "Male and female He created them" (Beresheet 1:27) and, "And Elohim blessed them, and Elohim said to them, be fruitful and multiply" (Ibid. 28). Also, He carried them like an eagle who carries its young on its wings, as it is written: "And how I bore you on eagles' wings" (Shemot 19:4).

## 92. Until Jacob people died without sickness

### A Synopsis

Rabbi Yosi tells us that Rabbi Huna went up to the Holy Land and found the rabbis discussing this passage: "And I will punish Bel in Babylon, and I will take out of his mouth that he has swallowed up; and the nations shall not flow together any more to him." Rabbi Huna tries to make himself heard, but no one will listen until Rabbi Yudai asks him to speak. Rabbi Huna then explains that Jacob asked God if a person could be sick for a few days before death so he could put his affairs in order and repent of his sins. Thus, God granted this wish to Jacob, and he was the first person to fall sick before dying.

### The Relevance of this Passage

Here, the reader proactively repents of his wrongdoings and brings order to his affairs without having to go through pain and illness just to comprehend the importance of penitence. Moreover, just as Jacob had the power to bring sickness to this world so that a man could avoid suffering in the World to Come, we now draw upon Jacob's righteousness and awesome power to achieve the reverse effect, the end of sickness, the cessation of suffering, the demise death. The gateway to the World to Come is now open'

895. אָמַר רַבִּי יוֹסִי, כֹּלָּא הוּא יֵאוֹת, אֲבָל אוֹרַיְיתָא דְּאַהֲדָר קַמַּיְיהוּ דְּיִשְׂרָאֵל, וְאוֹלִיף לוֹן, יַתִּיר מִכֹּלָּא. תָּא חֲזֵי, לֵית שְׁבָחָא דְּבַר נָשׁ בְּהַאי עָלְמָא וּבְעָלְמָא דְּאָתֵי, כְּשִׁבְחָא דְּאוֹרַיְיתָא דִּכְתִּיב בָּהּ בִּי מְלָכִים יִמְלֹכוּ.

895. Rabbi Yosi said: It is all nice, but the Torah that was given before the children of Yisrael and taught to them is more IMPORTANT than everything. Come and see: There is no praise for a person in this world and in the World to Come like the praise of Torah, as it is written of it: "By me kings reign" (Mishlei 8:15).

896. דְּהָא תָּנֵינָן כַּד סָלִיק רַב הוּנָא לְהָתָם, אַשְׁכַּח רַבָּנָן דַּהֲווֹ עַסְקֵי בְּהַאי קְרָא, דִּכְתִּיב, וּפָקַדְתִּי עַל בֵּל בְּבָבֶל וְהוֹצֵאתִי אֶת בִּלְעוֹ מִפִּיו וְלֹא יִנְהֲרוּ אֵלָיו עוֹד גּוֹיִם. וְרַב הוּנָא לָא הֲווֹ מַשְׁגִּיחִין בֵּיהּ, דְּהָא לָא אִשְׁתְּמוֹדְעָן לֵיהּ בְּקַדְמֵיתָא, בְּגִין דַּהֲוָה זְעֵיר. עָאל לְבֵי מִדְרָשָׁא,

וְאַשְׁכַּח רַבָּנָן דַּהֲווֹ אַמְרֵי, הַאי קְרָא אִית לְאִסְתַּכְּלָא בֵּיהּ, אִי טַעֲוָתֵיהּ
וְדַחַלְתֵּיהּ דִּנְבוּכַדְנֶצַּר הֲוָה שְׁמֵיהּ בֵּל, הָא כְּתִיב בֵּיהּ, וְעַד אַחֲרִין עַל
קֳדָמַי דָּנִיֵּאל דִּי שְׁמֵהּ בֵּלְטְשַׁאצַּר כְּשֵׁם אֱלָהִי. וְעוֹד, מַאי וְהוֹצֵאתִי אֶת
בִּלְעוֹ מִפִּיו.

**896.** We have learned that when Rav Huna went up TO THE HOLY LAND, he found the Rabbis occupied with this passage that says: "And I will punish Bel in Babylon, and I will take out of his mouth which he has swallowed up; and the nations shall not flow together any more to him" (Yirmeyah 51:44). Rav Huna STOOD BUT they didn't notice him, because they did not recognize him at first and because he was small. He came to the study hall and he heard the sages saying that this verse THAT WAS JUST MENTIONED must be examined to see whether the name of the idol and object of fear of Nebuchadnezzar was Bel. AND THEREFORE HE SAID: "AND I WILL PUNISH BEL," yet it is written, "But at last Daniel came in before me, whose name is Beltshatzar, according to the name of my Elohim" (Daniel 4:5). SO WE SEE THAT HIS IDOL'S NAME WAS BELTSHATZAR. Also, what does this mean: "And I will take out of his mouth which he has swallowed up"?

**897.** קָם רַב הוּנָא בֵּינֵי קַיְימֵי דְּעַמּוּדֵי, וְאָמַר אִילּוּ הֲוֵינָא בְּאַתְרַי,
דָּרִישְׁנָא לֵיהּ לְהַאי פְּסוּקָא. לָא אַשְׁגָחוּ בֵּיהּ. קָם תִּנְיָינוּת, וְאָמַר מִלָּה
דָּא. אָתָא רַבִּי יוֹדָאי בַּר רַב, וְאוֹתְבֵיהּ קַמֵּיהּ. אָמַר לֵיהּ, אֵימָא בְּרִי
אֵימָא, דְּמִלֵּי אוֹרַיְיתָא כְּתִיב בְּהוּ, בְּרֹאשׁ הוֹמִיּוֹת תִּקְרָא וְגוֹ'.

**897.** Rav Huna stood up between the foundation of the pillars and said: If I were in my own place, I would explain this verse. They paid him no attention. He stood up and repeated it a second time. Rabbi Yudai, the son of Rav, came over and sat him down in front of him. He said to him: Speak my son, speak, because concerning the words of Torah is written, "She cries in the chief place of concourse…" (Mishlei 1:21).

**898.** פָּתַח וְאָמַר, הָכִי תָּנֵינָן, בְּיוֹמֵי קַדְמָאֵי עַד לָא אָתָא יַעֲקֹב, הֲוָה
בַּר נָשׁ שָׁלוּ בְּבֵיתֵיהּ, מָטָא זִמְנֵיהּ, מִית בְּלָא מַרְעִין, כֵּיוָן דְּאָתָא יַעֲקֹב,

בָּעָא קָמֵיהּ דְּקוּדְשָׁא בְּרִיךְ הוּא, אָמַר לֵיהּ, מָרֵי דְּעָלְמָא, אִי נִיחָא
קָמָךְ, דְּלִנְפּוֹל בַּר נָשׁ בְּבֵי מַרְעֵיהּ, תְּרֵין אוֹ תְּלַת יוֹמִין, וּלְבָתַר יִתְכְּנַשׁ
לְעַמֵּיהּ, וְיַפְקֵד לְבֵיתֵיהּ, וְיֵתוּב מֵחוֹבוֹי. אָמַר לֵיהּ שַׁפִּיר. אַתְּ הוּא
סִימָנָא בְּעָלְמָא. ת״ח, מָה כְּתִיב בֵּיהּ וַיְהִי אַחֲרֵי הַדְּבָרִים הָאֵלֶּה וַיֹּאמֶר
לְיוֹסֵף הִנֵּה אָבִיךָ חוֹלֶה. חֹלֶה כְּתִיב מַה דְּלָא הֲוָה לְבַר נָשׁ מִן קַדְמַת
דְּנָא.

**898.** He opened the discussion saying: We have learned that in the early days, before Jacob came, a person was peacefully in his home, WITHOUT ANY SICKNESS – when his time came TO DIE, he died without any sickness. When Jacob came, he asked of the Holy One, blessed be He: Master of the Universe, if it is favorable before You, let a person fall into illness for two or three days. Then he should be gathered unto his people, SO THAT HE WOULD BE ABLE to arrange for his family and repent his sins. THE HOLY ONE, BLESSED BE HE, told him, 'Fine, you will be an example for the world,' MEANING THAT IT WILL START WITH YOU. Come and see what is written concerning him: "And it came to pass after these things, that one told Joseph, Behold your father is sick (Heb. *choleh*)" (Beresheet 48:1). The word choleh is spelled WITHOUT A *VAV* – WHICH SHOWS THAT IT WAS NEW, and that no person had this before.

## 93. Up until Hezekiah, there was no sick person, who was cured

### A Synopsis

We learn here that, after Jacob died, everyone who became ill also died, until Hezekiah. When he became ill he prayed to God, saying that if people were healed from illness, they would thank God and return to their lives with repentance. God took his point, and granted his request, beginning with Hezekiah. At this time also the sun turned back ten degrees, we learn, and time turned back five full hours, so the Elohim of Hezekiah performed two miracles on one day. God swore to Hezekiah that three kings would descend from him, we are then told. The first of these kings was Nebuchadnezzar, who made an idol and caused everyone to worship it. From the temple he took a vessel that was engraved with the letters of the Holy Name and placed it in the mouth of the idol, which then spoke great things. Daniel came and commanded the idol, saying, 'I am the messenger of the supernal Master. I decree upon you to leave here.' Then the vessel came out of the idol's mouth and the idol fell to the ground and broke. Rabbi Huna then concludes by saying that all this is the meaning of: "And I will take out of his mouth that he has swallowed up; and the nations shall not flow together any more to him."

### The Relevance of this Passage

The Light of healing shines brightly here, brighter still, when we fill our hearts with contriteness and make a conscious effort to share this radiance with others in need of healing. Doing so achieves eternal well-being for the body and soul of man.

899. בָּתַר דְּשָׁכִיב, לָא הֲוָה בַּר נָשׁ דַּהֲוָה לֵיהּ מַרְעִין, דְּלָא מִית. עַד דְּאָתָא חִזְקִיָּה, מָה כְּתִיב בֵּיהּ, בַּיָּמִים הָהֵם חָלָה חִזְקִיָּהוּ לָמוּת וְגוֹ'. תָּא חֲזֵי, מָה כְּתִיב וַיַּסֵּב חִזְקִיָּהוּ פָּנָיו אֶל הַקִּיר וַיִּתְפַּלֵּל אֶל יְיָ', אָמַר לֵיהּ, אִי נִיחָא קָמָךְ דְּיִתְּסוּן בְּנֵי נָשָׁא מִבֵּי מַרְעֵיהוֹן, וְיוֹדוּן שְׁמָךְ, וְיִשְׁתְּמוֹדְעוּן, וִיתוּבוּן לְבָתַר בִּתְיוּבְתָּא שְׁלֵימָתָא, וְיִשְׁתַּכְּחוּן בְּנֵי עָלְמָא זַכָּאִין קֳדָמָךְ. אָמַר לֵיהּ קוּדְשָׁא בְּרִיךְ הוּא, יָאוֹת הוּא אַתְּ תְּהֵא סִימָנָא בְּעָלְמָא, וְכָךְ הוּא, מַאי דְּלָא הֲוָה מִקַּדְמַת דְּנָא. הֲדָא הוּא דִכְתִּיב, מִכְתָּב לְחִזְקִיָּהוּ מֶלֶךְ יְהוּדָה בַּחֲלוֹתוֹ וַיְחִי מֵחָלְיוֹ. וְתָאנָא, הַהוּא יוֹמָא אִתְחֲזַר שִׁמְשָׁא עֶשֶׂר דַּרְגִּין.

899. After he died, there was no person IN THE WORLD who became ill and

did not die from that illness until Hezekiah came. What is written about him? "In those days Hezekiah fell mortally sick…" (Yeshayah 38:1). Come and see what is written: "Then Hezekiah turned his face toward the wall, and prayed to Hashem" (Ibid. 2). He said TO THE HOLY ONE, BLESSED BE HE: Does it please You that people should be healed from their illness, and they should thank Your Name and recognize, and return later on in complete repentance. The inhabitants of the world will be meritorious in Your eyes. The Holy One, blessed be He, said to him, 'It pleases Me, and you will be a sign to the world,' THAT IT WILL START WITH YOU. So it was, what never was before. This is what is meant by: "The writing of Hezekiah King of Judah when he had been sick, and was recovered of his sickness" (Ibid. 9). We learned that the sun turned BACKWARD ten degrees.

900. וְתָאנָא, מְרוֹדָךְ בַּלְאֲדָן הֲוָה אָכִיל כָּל יוֹמָא בַּד' שַׁעֲתֵי, וְנָאִים עַד תֵּשַׁע שַׁעֲתֵי, וְהַהוּא יוֹמָא נָאִים עַד ט' שַׁעֲתֵי, כַּד אִתְּעַר חָמָא שִׁמְשָׁא דְּקָאֵים בַּד' שַׁעֲתֵי, אָמַר מַאי הַאי, בְּקָטוֹלָא דְּקוּנְטִירָא קוֹנְטְרוֹי אַנְקְטַרְתּוּן. אָמְרוּ לֵיהּ לָמָּה. אָמַר, דְּנָאִימְנָא יוֹמָא חַד, וּתְלָתוּת יוֹמָא. א"ל, לָאו הָכִי, אֶלָּא אֱלָהָא דְּחִזְקִיָה עֲבַד יוֹמָא דֵּין תְּרֵין נִיסִין. אָסֵי לְחִזְקִיָה מִבֵּי מַרְעֵיהּ, וְאַחְזַר שִׁמְשָׁא לְעִדָנָא דָּא. אָמַר וְכִי אִית בְּעָלְמָא אֱלָהָא רַבָּא בַּר מֵאֱלָהִי. אָמְרוּ, אֱלָהָא דְּחִזְקִיָהוּ.

**900.** We also learned that Merodach Baladan used to always eat daily at the fourth hour OF THE DAY, and also that he slept until the ninth hour OF THE DAY. That day TOO, he slept until the ninth hour. When he awoke, he saw that the sun stood at the fourth hour OF THE DAY. He said: What is this. Is this a plot to starve me with hunger? They said to him: Why? He said: For I have slept one and a third days, BECAUSE HE THOUGHT THAT THIS WAS THE FOURTH HOUR OF THE NEXT DAY AND THAT HE HAD SLEPT ONE FULL DAY FROM FOUR HOURS AND A THIRD OF THE SECOND DAY, BECAUSE IT WAS ALREADY AT THE FOURTH HOUR OF THE SECOND DAY. They said to him that it was not so, but that the Elohim of Hezekiah performed two miracles on that day. One is that He cured Hezekiah of his illness and the second is that He returned the sun to this hour. He said: Is there a great Elohim in this world except for my Elohim? And they said: The Elohim of Hezekiah.

901. קָם וְכָתַב כְּתָבוֹי, שְׁלָם לְחִזְקִיָהוּ מַלְכָּא דִּיהוּדָה וּשְׁלָם לֶאֱלָהֵיהּ

וּשְׁלָם לִירוּשְׁלֵם קַרְתָּא קַדִּישָׁא. לְבָתַר אַמְלִיךְ וְקָם מִכֻּּרְסָיֵהּ, וּפָסַע
תְּלַת פְּסִיעָן, וְכָתַב אַחֲרָנִין, שְׁלָם לֶאֱלָהָא רַבָּא דְּבִירוּשְׁלֵם וּשְׁלָם
לְחִזְקִיָּהוּ מַלְכָּא דִּיהוּדָה וּשְׁלָם לִירוּשְׁלֵם קַרְתָּא קַדִּישָׁא. א"ל קוּדְשָׁא
בְּרִיךְ הוּא, אַנְתְּ פָּסַעְתְּ בְּגִין יְקָרִי תְּלַת פְּסִיעָן, חַיֶּיךְ מִינָךְ יִפְּקוּן תְּלַת
מַלְכִין שַׁלִּיטִין, קַסְטִירִין רוֹפִינִין דְּשַׁלִּיטִין בְּכָל עָלְמָא, וְקַדְמָאָה
מִנַּיְיהוּ נְבוּכַדְנֶצַּר הֲוָה.

**901.** He arose and wrote his letter: 'Peace to Hezekiah, the King of Judah, and peace to his Elohim and peace to Jerusalem, the Holy City. 'Afterwards, he changed his mind, arose from his throne, took three steps and wrote another letter: 'Peace to the Great Elohim in Jerusalem and peace to Hezekiah, the King of Judah, and peace to Jerusalem, the Holy City. 'The Holy One, blessed be He, said to him, 'You took three steps in My honor. I swear that three kings will descend from you, rulers and princes who will rule over the whole world.' And the first of them was Nebuchadnezzar.

902. ת"ח, מַאי א"ל דָּנִיֵּאל, אַנְתְּ הוּא רֵאשָׁה דִּי דַהֲבָא. וּבַתְרָךְ תְּקוּם
מַלְכוּ אָחֳרִי אֲרַע מִינָךְ וּמַלְכוּ תְּלִיתָאָה אָחֳרִי וְגוֹ'. מַה כְּתִיב נְבוּכַדְנֶצַּר
מַלְכָּא עֲבַד צְלֵם דִּי דְהַב רוּמֵיהּ אַמִּין שִׁתִּין פְּתָיֵהּ אַמִּין שִׁית. אָמַר
נְבוּכַדְנֶצַּר צַלְמָא דַּחֲמֵינָא, הֲוָה רֵישָׁא דִּי דַהֲבָא, מְעוֹי דִכְסֶף, אֲנָא
אַעֲבִיד כֹּלָּא דְּדַהֲבָא, דִּלְהֱוֵי קַזְפִירָא דְדַהֲבָא בְּרֵישָׁא.

**902.** Come and see what Daniel said to Nebuchadnezzar: "You are this head of gold. And after you shall arise another kingdom inferior to you, and another third kingdom of brass..." (Daniel 2:38-39). What is written? "Nebuchadnezzar the king made an image of gold, whose height was sixty cubits: and the breadth of which was six cubits" (Daniel 3:1). Nebuchadnezzar said, 'The idol that I saw IN THE DREAM had a head of gold and his innards were silver. I shall make it entirely of gold and there shall be a golden crown on its head.'

903. וְתָאנָא, הַהוּא יוֹמָא כָּנַשׁ כָּל אוּמַיָּא וְעַמְמַיָּא וְלִישָׁנַיָּיא לְמִפְלַח
לְהַהוּא צַלְמָא, וְנָטַל מָאנָא מִמָּאנֵי מַקְדְּשָׁא, דַּהֲוָה גָּלִיף בֵּיהּ שְׁמָא

קַדִּישָׁא, וְעָיֵיל לֵיהּ בְּפוּמֵיהּ דְּהַהוּא צַלְמָא וּבְהַהִיא שַׁעֲתָא, הֲוָה מְמַלֵּל
רַבְרְבָן, עַד דְּאָתָא דָּנִיֵּאל, וְקָרִיב גַּבֵּי דְּהַהוּא צַלְמָא, וְאָמַר אֲנָא
שְׁלִיחָא דְּמָארֵא עִלָּאָה, גּוֹזְרַנִי עָלָךְ לְמֶפַּק מֵהָכָא. אַדְכַּר שְׁמָא
קַדִּישָׁא, וְנָפַק הַהוּא מָאנָא, וְנָפַל צַלְמָא וְאִתְּבַּר. הַיְינוּ דִּכְתִּיב
וְהוֹצֵאתִי אֶת בִּלְעוֹ מִפִּיו וְלֹא יִנְהֲרוּ אֵלָיו עוֹד גּוֹיִם. קָם ר׳ יְהוּדָה
וּנְשָׁקֵיהּ עַל רֵישֵׁיהּ, אָמַר אִי לָא דְּקָרִיבְנָא בְּקוּטְפַיְיא הָכָא, לָא
אִשְׁתְּמוֹדַעְנָא בָּךְ. וַהֲווֹ דַּחֲלִין קַמֵּיהּ מֵהַהוּא יוֹמָא.

**903.** We learned that he gathered all the nations and peoples and tongues on that day to worship that idol. And he took a vessel of the vessels of the Temple upon which was engraved the Holy Name, and placed it in the mouth of that idol. At that moment, the idol spoke great things until Daniel came and approached that idol, saying, 'I am the messenger of the supernal Master. I decree upon you to leave here.' When he mentioned the Holy Name, that vessel came out of the idol's mouth, and the idol fell and broke. This is the meaning of that which is written: "And I will take out of his mouth which he has swallowed up; and the nations shall not flow together any more to him" (Yirmeyah 51:44). Rabbi Yehuda got up and kissed RAV HUNA on his head. He said: If I had not brought you close to the friends here, we would not recognize you. From that day onwards, they were in awe of him.

## 94. "Happy are you, O land, when your king is a free man"

### A Synopsis

Rabbi Yosi says here that this verse refers to Moses when he freed the children of Yisrael from slavery in Egypt. By 'land' he means the earth, Malchut, which is sutained from the heavens, Zeir Anpin. Rabbi Yosi then discusses the destruction of the Holy Temple and the Holy Land, and explains that when God wants to judge the world He first has a trial above, and then the verdict is established below. Rabbi Shimon next says that "And the middle bar in the midst of the boards shall reach from end to end" refers to Jacob, who united Malchut and Zeir Anpin through Rachel and Leah. "And Jacob was a plain man", we learn, means he was whole, and completes supernal Chesed and supernal Gvurah in Binah, and the two Columns in Zeir Anpin. Chochmah, we are told, includes everything. The patriarchs, Abraham and Isaac, include everything, too, and Jacob combines both of them.

### The Relevance of this Passage

Our Evil Inclination, the ego, has been the foundation of turmoil, pain, and all unhappiness. The Other Side tells us that we are self-governing, free, and independent, but in truth, we have been enslaved to its will and command. We are under the delusion that we act freely. In reality, we have been held captive by its desires. We are imprisoned by our reactive whims and self-absorbed desires. We are enslaved to our careers, jobs, and shallow relationships. We are incarcerated by our need for other people's acceptance. The ego is a ball and chain that has anchored us to this physical dimension, its material trappings and its inevitable turmoil.

For this reason, fulfillment has always been a rare commodity. Our moments of happiness and true freedom are fleeting. This segment of Zohar unlocks the chains of the Other Side, offering us the greatest freedom a man can attain, freedom from the self. The Zohar's spiritual influences impress us with wisdom to finally recognize life's true and lasting pleasures, closeness with the Creator, marriage, children, friendship, and the strength to forever resist trading them away for transient pleasures born of self-indulgence. This wisdom, and the ultimate freedom it now provides, flows to us from Abraham, Isaac, Jacob, and Moses.

904. תָּאנָא אַשְׁרֶיךָ אֶרֶץ שֶׁמַּלְכֵּךְ בֶּן חוֹרִים וְשָׂרַיִךְ בָּעֵת יֹאכֵלוּ. ר' יוֹסִי אוֹקִים לְהַאי קְרָא, בְּמֹשֶׁה, בְּשַׁעֲתָא דְּאַפִּיק לְהוּ לְיִשְׂרָאֵל מִמִּצְרַיִם, וַעֲבַד לוֹן בְּנֵי חוֹרִין. וְשָׂרַיִךְ בָּעֵת יֹאכֵלוּ, דִּכְתִיב וַאֲכַלְתֶּם אוֹתוֹ בְּחִפָּזוֹן

פֶּסַח הוּא לַיְיָ'.

**904.** We have studied: "Happy are you, O land, when your king is a free man, and your princes eat in due season" (Kohelet 10:17). Rabbi Yosi established this verse to refer to Moses at the time that he took the children of Yisrael out of Egypt and made them free people. "And your princes eat in due season" as it is written: "And you shall eat it in haste; it is Hashem's Pesach" (Shemot 12:11).

**905.** אָמַר ר' שִׁמְעוֹן בַּר יוֹחָאי, וְכִי לָא אֲמֵינָא דְּמִלוֹי דִּשְׁלֹמֹה מַלְכָּא, דְּכֻלְּהוּ בְּגוֹ, לְגוֹ הֵיכְלָא קַדִּישָׁא הֲווֹ. וְהַאי דְּאַמְרִיתוּ כֹּלָּא שַׁפִּיר הֲוָה, וְלִדְרָשָׁא הוּא דְאָתָא, אֲבָל הַאי קְרָא, לְעֵילָא בְּהֵיכְלָא קַדִּישָׁא הוּא.

**905.** Rabbi Shimon bar Yochai said, Did I not say that the words of King Solomon are all inside the sanctuary of the King? What you said is all well, and it required for an argument to be based upon it, but this verse is above in the Supernal Sanctuary, WHICH IS MALCHUT.

**906.** תָּאנָא, אַשְׁרֵיךְ אֶרֶץ שֶׁמַּלְכֵּךְ בֶּן חוֹרִים. מַאי אֶרֶץ. אֶרֶץ סְתָם. דְּתַנְיָא, מ"ד הִשְׁלִיךְ מִשָּׁמַיִם אֶרֶץ תִּפְאֶרֶת יִשְׂרָאֵל. אֶלָּא הַאי אֶרֶץ, הִיא רָזָא, בְּגוֹ כִּתְרֵי מַלְכָּא קַדִּישָׁא, דִּכְתִיב בֵּיהּ בְּיוֹם עֲשׂוֹת יְיָ' אֱלֹהִים אֶרֶץ וְשָׁמָיִם. וְהַאי אֶרֶץ, וְכָל מַה דְּיָנִיק וְאִתְּזָן, מֵהַהוּא אֲתָר דְּאִקְרֵי שָׁמַיִם הוּא, וְלָא אִתְּזָנַת אַרְעָא דָא, אֶלָּא מִשְּׁלִימוּתָא קַדִּישָׁא, דְּאִקְרֵי שָׁמָיִם.

**906.** We have studied: "Happy are you, O land, when your king is a free man." What land is this? It means just land, NAMELY MALCHUT, for we have learned that it is written: "He has cast down from heaven to earth (or: land) the beauty of Yisrael" (Eichah 2:1). Behold, this land is a secret among the crowns of the Holy King, NAMELY THE SFIROT, of which is written: "In the day that Hashem Elohim made the earth and the heavens" (Beresheet 2:4). FOR ELOHIM IS BINAH, HEAVEN IS ZEIR ANPIN AND EARTH IS MALCHUT. On this earth. All that is nourished is from that place called 'heavens', because this earth is sustained only from the holy perfection called 'heavens'.

907. וּבְשַׁעֲתָא דְּבָעָא קוּדְשָׁא בְּרִיךְ הוּא לְאַחֲרָבָא בֵּיתֵיה דִּלְתַתָּא, וְאַרְעָא קַדִּישָׁא דִּלְתַתָּא, אַעֲבָר לְהַאי אַרְעָא קַדִּישָׁא דִּלְעֵילָּא בְּקַדְמֵיתָא, וְנָחִית לֵיה מֵהַהוּא דַּרְגָּא דַּהֲוָה יַנְקָא מִשָּׁמַיִם קַדִּישָׁא, וּלְבָתַר חָרִיב לְהַאי דִּלְתַתָּא, הֲדָ"א הִשְׁלִיךְ מִשָּׁמַיִם אֶרֶץ בְּקַדְמֵיתָא, וּלְבָתַר וְלֹא זָכַר הֲדֹם רַגְלָיו. דְּתַנְיָא. כַּךְ אָרְחוֹי דְּקוּדְשָׁא בְּרִיךְ הוּא, כַּד בָּעֵי לְמֵידַן עָלְמָא, בְּקַדְמֵיתָא עָבֵיד דִּינָא לְעֵילָּא, וּלְבָתַר אִתְקַיַּים לְתַתָּא, דִּכְתִיב יִפְקוֹד יְיָ' עַל צְבָא הַמָּרוֹם בַּמָּרוֹם בְּקַדְמֵיתָא, וּלְבָתַר וְעַל מַלְכֵי הָאֲדָמָה עַל הָאֲדָמָה.

**907.** When the Holy One, blessed be He, wanted to destroy His house below, NAMELY THE TEMPLE, and the terrestrial Holy Land, He first removed the celestial Holy Land, WHICH IS MALCHUT, lowered it from that level from which it was nourishing, which is the Holy Heavens, NAMELY ZEIR ANPIN, and destroyed the terrestrial one. This is what is meant by: "He cast down from heavens (to) earth" (Eichah 2:1) first, and afterwards: "And remembered not His footstool" (Ibid.), WHICH IS THE TERRESTRIAL TEMPLE AND THE HOLY LAND CALLED 'HIS FOOTSTOOL'. We have learned that these are the ways of the Holy One, blessed be He. When He wants to judge the world, first He has a trial above and then verdict is carried below, as it is written: "Hashem shall punish the host of the high ones on high" and afterwards: "The kings of the earth upon the earth" (Yeshayah 24:21).

908. א"ר שִׁמְעוֹן, אַשְׁרֵיךְ אֶרֶץ שֶׁמַּלְכֵּךְ בֶּן חוֹרִין, דְּזָן לָךְ בִּסְגִיאוּת כֹּלָּא, בְּלָא דְּחִילוּ דְּאַחֲרָא, וּמֵהַהוּא מַלְכָּא עִלָּאָה אִתְּזַן כֹּלָּא. וְשָׂרַיִךְ בָּעֵת יֹאכֵלוּ, כְּד"א כָּעֵת יֵאָמֵר לְיַעֲקֹב וּלְיִשְׂרָאֵל מַה פָּעַל אֵל, אִי לָךְ אֶרֶץ שֶׁמַּלְכֵּךְ נָעַר כְּד"א וְנָתַתִּי נְעָרִים שָׂרֵיהֶם. דְּוַוי לְאַרְעָא כַּד יַנְקָא מִשְּׂמָאלָא. וְשָׂרַיִךְ בַּבֹּקֶר יֹאכֵלוּ, בְּהַהוּא קַדְרוּתָא, וְעַד לָא נָהִיר, וְלָא שַׁלְטָא מַה דְּשַׁלְטָא.

**908.** Rabbi Shimon said: "Happy are you, O land, when your king is a free man" REFERS TO ZEIR ANPIN, who sustains you with abundance without

fear of another. From that supernal King all are sustained. "And your princes eat in due season" is as written: "In due time Jacob and Yisrael are told what El has performed" (Bemidbar 23:23), FOR THEY ARE THE PRINCES. "Woe to you, O land, when your king is a child" (Kohelet 10:16) is as written: "And I will give children to be their princes" (Yeshayah 3:4). Woe is unto the land if it nourishes from the left, WHICH IS CALLED 'CHILD'. "And your princes dine in the morning" (Ibid.), that is, in that darkness OF THE LEFT as long as that which should rule does not illuminate or rule, NAMELY THE CENTRAL COLUMN THAT UNITES RIGHT AND LEFT.

909. תָּנָא אָמַר רַבִּי שִׁמְעוֹן, וְהַבְּרִיחַ הַתִּיכוֹן בְּתוֹךְ הַקְּרָשִׁים מַבְרִיחַ מִן הַקָּצֶה אֶל הַקָּצֶה, דָּא הוּא יַעֲקֹב קַדִּישָׁא שְׁלֵימָא, כְּמָה דְּאוּקִימְנָא, דִּכְתִיב וְיַעֲקֹב אִישׁ תָּם יוֹשֵׁב אֹהָלִים. יוֹשֵׁב אֹהֶל לָא כְּתִיב, אֶלָּא יוֹשֵׁב אוֹהָלִים, תְּרֵי, דְּאָחִיד לְהַאי וְאָחִיד לְהַאי. אַף הָכָא כְּתִיב, וְהַבְּרִיחַ הַתִּיכוֹן בְּתוֹךְ הַקְּרָשִׁים, מַבְרִיחַ מִן הַקָּצֶה אֶל הַקָּצֶה, דְּאָחִיד לְהַאי וְאָחִיד לְהַאי.

909. We have learned that Rabbi Shimon said: "And the middle bar in the midst of the boards shall reach from end to end" (Shemot 26:28). This refers to holy and perfect Jacob, as we have established. It is written: "And Jacob was a plain man, dwelling in tents" (Beresheet 25:27). It is not written 'tent,' but rather "tents," WHICH MEANS two, for he is attached to this one and that one, NAMELY IN MALCHUT THAT IS ABOVE THE CHEST OF ZEIR ANPIN THAT IS CALLED 'LEAH' AND IN MALCHUT BELOW THE CHEST OF ZEIR ANPIN CALLED 'RACHEL'. It is also written here: "And the middle bar in the midst of the boards shall reach from end to end," so that it is attached here and held there, TO LEAH AND RACHEL, MEANING THROUGHOUT THE STATURE OF ZEIR ANPIN FROM END TO END.

910. דְּתָנֵינָן, מַאי אִישׁ תָּם. כְּתַרְגּוּמוֹ, שְׁלִים. שְׁלִים מִכֹּלָּא, שְׁלִים לִתְרֵין סִטְרִין, לְעַתִּיקָא קַדִּישָׁא, וְלִזְעֵיר אַפִּין. שְׁלִים לְחֶסֶד עִלָּאָה וְלִגְבוּרָה עִלָּאָה, וְאַשְׁלִים לְהַאי וּלְהַאי.

910. What is meant by 'a plain man?' It is translated into Aramaic as 'whole', for he is whole in everything and completes both aspects, Atika

Kadisha and Zeir Anpin. HE IS THE CENTRAL COLUMN WHO MEDIATES AND COMPLETES BOTH COLUMNS, RIGHT AND LEFT, THAT ARE IN BINAH THAT IS SOMETIMES CALLED 'ATIKA KADISHA', AND THE TWO COLUMNS IN ZEIR ANPIN. This is because he completes Supernal Chesed and Supernal Gvurah, NAMELY THE TWO COLUMNS, RIGHT AND LEFT, THAT ARE IN BINAH, and he completes the one and the other, BINAH AND ZEIR ANPIN.

911. א"ר שִׁמְעוֹן, חֲמֵינָא דְּהָא חָכְמָתָא כְּלַל כֹּלָּא. וְחֶסֶד עִלָּאָה נָפְקָא מֵחָכְמָה. גְּבוּרָה, דְּהוּא דִּינָא תַּקִיפָא, נָפְקָא מִבִּינָה. יַעֲקֹב אַשְׁלִים לִתְרֵין סְטְרִין וַאֲבָהָן כְּלַל כֹּלָּא, וְיַעֲקֹב כְּלַל כֹּלָּא אֲבָהָתָא.

911. Rabbi Shimon said: I see that Chochmah includes everything and Supernal Chesed, THAT IS IN ZEIR ANPIN WHICH IS THE RIGHT COLUMN, emerges from Chochmah. Gvurah, which is strong Judgment, emerges from Binah. Jacob completes both sides, FOR HE MEDIATES BETWEEN CHESED AND GVURAH AND UNITES AND COMPLETES THEM. The Patriarchs, ABRAHAM AND ISAAC, NAMELY, CHESED AND GVURAH OF ZEIR ANPIN, include everything, and Jacob is the combination of the Patriarchs, BECAUSE HE COMBINES BOTH OF THEM.

## 95. Chochmah united with its paths

### A Synopsis

Rabbi Shimon speaks about the mechanism of the delivery of wisdom to the world, and of the delivery of the wise back to paradise. He tells of fifty gates, 32 paths, the secret of the 22 and the power of 72 and the way in which these things are accomplished. The Sfirah of Binah is expounded upon. He reminds us of the joining of everything through Jacob, and of the fertilization of one of God's qualities with another, for "In Wisdom have you made them all."

### The Relevance of this Passage

Even in the most complex and unfathomable sections of Trumah, like this one, a meaning can be discerned, though it would take years of study to understand the symbolism and the numerology intellectually and grasp all of its spiritual benefits. Nevertheless, certain ideas clearly stand out: 22 corresponds to the 22 primordial forces of Creation, which express themselves through the very pages of this book, namely the 22 Letters of the Hebrew alphabet. Thus, here we are touching the pure, primeval Light of Creation and it purifies our hearts and souls. 72 denotes the 72 Names of God, telling us that we are now receiving the power to perform feats of wonder concerning the ultimate transformation of human nature. The word "Binah" is itself a portal, a priceless passkey to the supernal fountainhead where we now dip ourselves into the pure, pristine wellspring of Light, and reemerge, cleansed in body and soul.

And the great name of Jacob, who is the Central Column force incarnate, ignites our own Central Column, the divine gift of free will, the autonomous choice a man has to reject the base drives born of ego. Our ego is herewith overthrown by the will of our soul. And the Satan is crushed by the cosmic Central Column power of Jacob.

912. תָּאנָא בָּטַשׁ חָכְמָה בִּשְׁבִילוֹי, וְכָנִיף בְּרוּחָא לְמַיָּא, וְאִתְכְּנִפוּ מַיָּא לְאֲתָר חַד, וְאִתְפְּתָחוּ חַמְשִׁין תַּרְעִין דְּבִינָה. מֵאִלֵּין שְׁבִילִין, נָפְקֵי עֲשָׂרָה כִּתְרִין, בְּקַרְנִיטֵי זְהִירִין, וְאִשְׁתָּאֲרוּ עֶשְׂרִין וּתְרֵין שְׁבִילִין. בָּטַשׁ הַהוּא רוּחָא בְּאִינּוּן שְׁבִילִין, וְאִתְפְּתָחוּ חַמְשִׁין תַּרְעִין דְּבִינָה, וְאִתְגְּלִיפוּ עֶשְׂרִין וּתְרֵין, בְּחַמְשִׁין תַּרְעִין דְּיוּבְלָא, וְאִתְעַטָּרוּ בְּשַׁבְעִין וּתְרֵין אַתְוָון דִּשְׁמָא קַדִּישָׁא. אִלֵּין אִתְפְּתָחוּ לִסְטְרוֹי.

912. We have studied that Chochmah united with its paths and gathered

with its wind, MEANING ITS SEVEN LOWER SFIROT, WHICH ARE CALLED
'WIND', the waters, and the waters gathered into one place. The fifty gates of
Binah opened. From these 32 paths, ten crowns emerged, WHICH ARE THE
TEN SFIROT OF THE FIRST THREE SFIROT OF CHOCHMAH, with glorious
crowns and there remain 22 paths, WHICH IS THE SECRET OF THE SEVEN
LOWER SFIROT OF CHOCHMAH, BEING THE SECRET OF 22 LETTERS.
THEREFORE, WHEN that wind beat upon the paths IN ORDER TO GATHER
THE WATERS TO ONE PLACE, AS MENTIONED, the fifty Gates of Binah
opened, WHICH IS THE SECRET OF THE FIRST THREE SFIROT OF BINAH.
And 22 opened, WHICH ARE THE LOWER SEVEN SFIROT in the fifty Gates
of Jubilee, MEANING IN THESE FIFTY GATES OF BINAH. THESE 22 OF
BINAH ARE crowned with the *Ayin-Bet* (72) letters of the Holy Name, THAT
ILLUMINATE WITH THE ILLUMINATION OF CHOCHMAH, and opened to its
aspect. BUT UPON THE FIFTY GATES OF BINAH, WHICH ARE THE FIRST
THREE SFIROT OF BINAH, THE NAME *MEM-BET* (42) ILLUMINATES, AS
MENTIONED NEARBY.

913. וְאִתְעַטָּרוּ עֶשְׂרִין וּתְרֵין כִּתְרִין דְּרַחֲמֵי, דִּכְלִילָן בְּעַתִּיק יוֹמִין,
דְּנָהִיר לוֹן כָּל חַד בְּסִטְרוֹי. אִתְעַטָּרוּ חַמְשִׁין גְּלִיפִין, בְּמ״ב אַתְוָון
קַדִּישִׁין דִּשְׁמָא קַדִּישָׁא, דִּבְהוֹן אִתְבְּרֵי שְׁמַיָּא וְאַרְעָא. וְאִתְגְּלִיפוּ
בְּגְלוּפֵיהוֹן, תְּמַנְיָא תַּרְעִין, דְּאִינּוּן תְּמַנְיָא אַתְוָון דְּרַחֲמֵי, דִּכְתִיב יְיָ׳ יְיָ׳
אֵל רַחוּם וְחַנּוּן, דְּנָפְקָא מֵעַתִּיקָא קַדִּישָׁא, לִזְעֵירָא, וּמִתְחַבְּרָן בְּאִלֵּין
כִּתְרִין קַדִּישִׁין, חָכְמָה וּבִינָה עִלָּאִין דְּסַלְקִין. נָפְקָא חֶסֶד עִלָּאָה מֵהַאי
סִטְרָא, וְדִינָא דִּגְבוּרָה מֵהַאי סִטְרָא, אָתָא זְכוּתָא דְּיַעֲקֹב, וְאַשְׁלִים
אַתְרְוַויְיהוּ וְאָחִיד לוֹן. דְּהָא הוּא שְׁלֵימוּתָא עִלָּאָה.

913. The 22 crowns of Mercy were adorned, WHICH ARE THE SEVEN
LOWER SFIROT that are included in Atik Yomin, who illuminates upon
them each one in his aspect. THEY ILLUMINATE IN COVERED CHASSADIM.
FROM THEM are adorned fifty engravings, WHICH ARE THE FIFTY GATES
OF BINAH, with the 42 holy letters of the Holy Name, with which heaven
and earth were created. They were engraved into eight gates, which are the
eight letters of Mercy, as it is written: "Hashem, Hashem, El, Merciful and
Gracious..." (Shemot 34:6). THESE ARE THE EIGHT NAMES that emerge
from Atika Kadisha, that emerge into ZEIR ANPIN. The Supernal Chochmah
and Binah join these holy crowns and ascend, MEANING THAT THEY

ILLUMINATE FROM BELOW UPWARDS. And Supernal Chesed emerges from this side, MEANING FROM CHOCHMAH. The Judgment of Gvurah emerges from this side, FROM BINAH, and the merit of Jacob, WHICH IS THE SECRET OF THE CENTRAL COLUMN, TIFERET, comes and unites them ONE WITH THE OTHER, for this is the supernal perfection.

914. תָּאנָא א״ר שִׁמְעוֹן, בג״כ יִשְׂרָאֵל אִתְקְרֵי. דְּתָאנָא יַעֲקֹב תַּתָּאָה. יִשְׂרָאֵל עִלָּאָה. יַעֲקֹב לָאו שְׁלֵימוּתָא יִשְׂרָאֵל שְׁלֵימוּתָא דְּכֹלָּא. וְכֵן תָּאנָא, נְאֻם דָּוִד בֶּן יִשַׁי, דָּוִד לָאו שְׁלֵימוּתָא, דְּהָא בַּתְרָאָה הוּא. יִשַׁי יְסוֹד עִלָּאָה הוּא, וּשְׁלֵימוּתָא. וְהַיְינוּ דְּתָנֵינָן, לָא גָּלוּ יִשְׂרָאֵל מֵאַרְצָם עַד שֶׁכָּפְרוּ בְּקוּדְשָׁא בְּרִיךְ הוּא, וּבְמַלְכוּתָא דְּבֵית דָּוִד, דִּכְתִיב, אֵין לָנוּ חֵלֶק בְּדָוִד וְלֹא נַחֲלָה בְּבֶן יִשַׁי אִישׁ לְאֹהָלָיו יִשְׂרָאֵל. מַאי אִישׁ לְאֹהָלָיו. אֲתַר דְּעכו״ם שַׁרְיָא בְּגַוַּוייהוּ, הַיְינוּ לֵאלֹהָיו.

**914.** We have learned that Rabbi Shimon said: This is the reason that he is called 'Yisrael'. We have learned that Jacob is below, MEANING THE ASPECT OF FROM THE CHEST DOWN OF ZEIR ANPIN. Yisrael is above, MEANING FROM THE CCHEST UP OF ZEIR ANPIN. Jacob is not perfection, but Yisrael is complete perfection, and we have learned: "The saying of David the son of Yishai" (II Shmuel 23:1). David is not perfection because he is last, FOR HE IS THE LAST SFIRAH, MALCHUT, WHOSE PERFECTION LIES ONLY IN YESOD. Yishai is Yesod, which is highest, is perfect. This is what we learned, that the children of Yisrael were not exiled from their land until they denied the Holy One, blessed be He, and the Kingdom of David, WHICH ARE YESOD AND MALCHUT, as it is written: "We have no part in David" (II Shmuel 20:1), WHICH IS MALCHUT, "Neither have we inheritance in the son of Yishai," WHICH IS YESOD, "every man to his tents, O Yisrael" (Ibid.). What is the meaning of "each man to his tents (Heb. *ohalav*)", meaning to his deity (Heb. *Elohav*), which is the place where idol worshipping dwells among them.

915. אָמַר ר׳ יְהוּדָה, כַּד שַׁרְיָא חָכְמְתָא לְגַלְפָּא גְּלִיפָא בְּכֻלְּהוּ כִּתְרִין, מֵאָן כִּתְרָא שָׁאֲרֵי מֵהַהוּא דְּאִתְקְרֵי בִּינָה. בְּבִינָה אִתְכְּלִיל כֹּלָּא. וּבג״כ אִתְפַּתָּחוּ בָּהּ חַמְשִׁין תַּרְעִין, וְאִשְׁתְּכַח דְּכֹלָּא בְּחָכְמָה אִתְגְּלִפוּ, הה״ד כֻּלָּם בְּחָכְמָה עָשִׂיתָ.

**915.** Rabbi Yehuda said: When Chochmah started to engrave on in all the crowns, NAMELY THE SFIROT, from which crown did it start? HE ANSWERS: From THAT CROWN that is called 'Binah', as everything is included in Binah BECAUSE THE REVELATION OF CHOCHMAH STARTED IN IT. Therefore, fifty gates were opened in it, so it appears that everything was engraved with Chochmah. This is what is ment by: "In wisdom have you made them all" (Tehilim 104:24).

## 96. "Who has measured the waters in the hollow of his hand"

### A Synopsis

Rabbi Elazar says here that water is Chesed. Rabbi Shimon then replies that water is Binah, but that they are the same thing. He next explains the meanings in "and meted out heaven with the span," "and comprehended the dust of the earth as a measure," "and weighed the mountains in scales," and "and the hills in a balance." Rabbi Elazar then summarizes by saying that it is implied that Jacob, who is Tiferet, emerges from harsh Judgment because Isaac had harsh Judgment in his portion. Rabbi Shimon extends this argument by adding that Isaac (Gvurah) emerged from Chesed, therefore in all the levels Judgment emerges from Mercy and Mercy from Judgment: it is recognized that it is all one and that they all come from one. Rabbi Elazar, we find, thinks that it appears there is no perfection unless one is attached to the other, so that the Central Column, Mercy, unites Chesed and Judgment. He next says we have learned that it is not considered such a great distance between Chesed and Judgment, except from our viewpoint. Rabbi Yehuda then concludes by saying that all the candles illuminate from one, from Ein Sof (Infinity); all the candles are one, and we must not distinguish between them, for one who separates them is in turn separated from eternal life himself.

### The Relevance of this Passage

In this section, we read that God's judgment is achieved through understanding, measurement, and weighing and balancing, with the exercise of loving kindness and mercy. Spiritually, we are being taught that Light is an endless, infinite Force whose sole essence is goodness. This Light never stands in judgment of us. Nor does this boundless Force execute punishment. Good fortune and reward, judgment and punishment, are the result of the manner in which we knowingly or unknowingly interact with the Light that permeates all existence.

As a model, the force of electricity can bring great light and benefit to a city, comfort and security to a community. Or it can bring destruction if our fingers carelessly touch raw current. In the case of the latter, it is meaningless to say electricity punished us. The Zohar is providing us with the schematic of the cosmos, the blueprint of the soul.

It is our behavior, the blend and balance of judgment and mercy, that we extend to others that determines how much judgment and mercy the cosmos reflects back to us. Thus, we learn that a man offers compassion because he will one day need it. And a man bestows mercy for the times when he seeks it. Jacob, as the Central Column

force, embodies the wisdom of balance, the perfection of sharing and receiving, judgment and mercy. Jacob creates a circuit of Light through the union of opposite forces, much like the filament in a bulb that unites, through resistance, the positive and negative poles to produce ordinary light. The wisdom and will to embody such balanced behavior is bequeathed to us through Jacob. The entire world is herewith measured, balanced, unified, and illuminated by the supernal candle, the Creator of the cosmos. And because mercy now grows in our heart, this is all achieved with boundless benevolence.

916. תָּאנָא, כְּתִיב מִי מָדַד בְּשָׁעֲלוֹ מַיִם וְגוֹ'. בְּשָׁעֲלוֹ מַיִם. מַאן מַיִם. דָּא הוּא בִּינָה. ר' אֶלְעָזָר מַתְנֵי הָכִי, דָּא חֶסֶד. א"ל ר"ש, כֹּלָּא בְּחַד מַתְקְלָא סַלְקָא. וְשָׁמַיִם בַּזֶּרֶת תִּכֵּן, מַאן שָׁמַיִם. תִּפְאֶרֶת. דִּכְתִּיב תִּפְאֶרֶת יִשְׂרָאֵל. וְכָל בַּשָּׁלִישׁ עֲפַר הָאָרֶץ. דָּא הוּא גְּבוּרָה. וְשָׁקַל בַּפֶּלֶס הָרִים, אִלֵּין אִינּוּן שְׁאַר כִּתְרִין, דְּאִקְרוּן טוּרֵי אֲפַרְסְמוֹנָא דַּכְיָא. וּגְבָעוֹת בְּמֹאזְנָיִם, אִלֵּין שְׁאַר רְתִיכִין תַּתָּאִין מִנַּיְיהוּ.

**916.** We have learned that it is written: "Who has measured the waters in the hollow of his hand" (Yeshayah 40:12). What is water? Binah. Rabbi Elazar taught it this way: that this is Chesed. Rabbi Shimon said to him: They are all the same, FOR CHESED IS DRAWN FROM BINAH, "and meted out heaven with the span" (Ibid.). What is "heaven"? It is Tiferet, as it is written: "The beauty (Heb. *Tiferet*) of Yisrael" (Eichah 2:1). THEREFORE, THE WORD 'METED' IS USED, THE IMPLICATION BEING THAT IT IS ARRANGED FOR SPLENDOR AND BEAUTY. "And comprehended the dust of the earth in a measure" (Yeshayah 40:12) is Gvurah, MEANING THE LEFT COLUMN, FOR BEFORE IT IS INCLUDED IN THE RIGHT, IT DOES NOT ILLUMINATE AND IS LIKE THE DUST OF THE EARTH. "And weighed the mountains in scales" (Ibid.): These are the other crowns, MEANING SFIROT, that are called 'mountains of pure balsam', WHICH ARE NETZACH, HOD AND YESOD. "And the hills in a balance?" (Ibid.): These are the rest of the Chariots below them, NAMELY THOSE IN MALCHUT AND BRIYAH, YETZIRAH AND ASIYAH.

917. תָּא חֲזִי, בְּשָׁעֲלוֹ, מַאי שָׁעֲלוֹ. דָּא רוּחַ חָכְמְתָא דְּהָכִי תָּנֵינָן, שַׁעֲלָא דְּקִיטְרֵי בְּקִיזְפָא שְׁקִיעָן.

**917.** Come and see: It is written, "in the hollow of his hand." What is "the hollow of his hand"? HE ANSWERS: This is the spirit of Chochmah, for we have learned a knotted path is overcome by a palanquin.

‎918. וְשָׁמַיִם בַּזֶרֶת תִּכֵּן, מַאן זֶרֶת. אִלֵּין אִינּוּן חַמְשִׁין תַּרְעִין דְּאִתְפַּתְחוּ וְאִתְפַּזָרוּ לְכָל סִטְרִין, כד"א וְזֵרִיתִי פֶרֶשׁ עַל פְּנֵיכֶם וְגוֹ'. וְכָל בַּשָּׁלִישׁ, מַאן שָׁלִישׁ. רַחֲמֵי. שְׁלֵימוּתָא דְּכֹלָּא. וְשָׁקַל בַּפֶּלֶס, מַאי פֶּלֶס, אָמַר ר' שִׁמְעוֹן, דִּכְתִיב מֹאזְנֵי צֶדֶק. אַבְנֵי צֶדֶק. תּוּ אָמַר רַבִּי שִׁמְעוֹן, הָנֵי מִילֵי בְּשִׁיעוּרָא דְּיוֹצֵר כֹּלָּא אוּקִימְנָא.

**918.** "And meted out heaven with the span": What is a span? HE ANSWERS: These are the fifty gates OF BINAH that were opened and scattered to all directions, BECAUSE THE WORD 'SPAN (HEB. ZERET)' MEANS SCATTERING, as is said, "And spread (Heb. zreti) dung upon your faces" (Malachi 2:3). "And comprehended in a measure (Heb. shalish)" (Yeshayah 40:12): What is shalish? NAMELY Mercy, WHICH IS THE CENTRAL COLUMN, TIFERET, THAT INCLUDES WITHIN ITSELF THREE (HEB. SHLOSHAH) COLUMNS, which is the completion of everything. "And weighed the mountains in scales": What means scales? Rabbi Shimon said: As it is written, "Just balances, just weights" (Vayikra 19:36), WHICH ARE NETZACH AND HOD. Rabbi Shimon also said: I have established these subjects in the lecture about 'who forms everything'.

‎919. אָמַר רַבִּי אֶלְעָזָר, ש"מ, דְּיַעֲקֹב מִגּוֹ דִּינָא קַשְׁיָא נָפִיק, דְּהָא יִצְחָק דִּינָא קַשְׁיָא, אָחִיד לְחוּלָקֵיה. אָמַר לֵיה ר' שִׁמְעוֹן, וְדָא הוּא בִּלְחוֹדוֹי, וְהָא יִצְחָק מִגּוֹ חֶסֶד נָפַק, וְהָכִי כֻּלְּהוּ, דִּינָא מִגּוֹ רַחֲמֵי נָפְקָא, וְרַחֲמֵי מִדִּינָא. אַבְרָהָם יָרִית אַחֲסָנָא דְּחֶסֶד, נָפַק יִצְחָק בְּדִינָא מִגּוֹ חֶסֶד. יַעֲקֹב נָפַק בְּרַחֲמֵי, מִגּוֹ דִּינָא קַשְׁיָא, וְכָךְ הוּא לְעֵילָא, דָּא מִן דָּא, וְיָנְקָא דָּא מִן דָּא, עַד דְּאִשְׁתְּמוֹדַע כֹּלָּא דְּהוּא חַד, וּמֵחַד תַּלְיָין כֻּלְּהוּ, וְכֹלָּא אִשְׁתְּכַח חַד. בְּרִיךְ שְׁמֵיה לְעָלַם וּלְעָלְמֵי עָלְמִין.

**919.** Rabbi Elazar said: Here it is implied that Jacob, WHO IS TIFERET, emerges from harsh Judgment, FROM GVURAH, WHICH IS HIS OPPOSITE, because Isaac, WHO IS GVURAH, had harsh Judgment in his portion. Rabbi

Shimon said to him: Is that all? Indeed Isaac, WHO IS GVURAH, emerged from Chesed, and so in all THE LEVELS, Judgment emerges from Mercy and Mercy from Judgment. Abraham inherited an inheritance of Chesed, and Isaac emerged with Judgment from Chesed. Jacob emerged with Mercy from harsh Judgment, WHO IS ISAAC, and so it is above IN THE LEVELS OF ATZILUT. One EMERGES from another and one nourishes from the other, NAMELY GVURAH FROM CHESED AND CHESED FROM GVURAH, until it is recognized that it is all one and they are all come from one and they are all really one. Blessed be His Name forever and ever.

920. אָמַר רַבִּי אֶלְעָזָר, אִשְׁתְּמוֹדַע, דְּלֵית שְׁלֵימוּתָא אֶלָּא כַּד אָחִיד דָּא מִן דָּא, וְדָא אָחִיד בְּתַרְוַויְיהוּ, לְשַׁכְלָלָא כֹּלָּא, כְּגוֹן יַעֲקֹב, וְהַיְינוּ דִּכְתִּיב מַבְרִיחַ מִן הַקָּצֶה אֶל הַקָּצֶה.

920. Rabbi Elazar said: It appears that there is no perfection unless one is attached to the other, CHESED TO JUDGMENT AND JUDGMENT TO CHESED and THE CENTRAL COLUMN WHICH IS MERCY, is attached to both of them, FOR IT UNITES THE TWO COLUMNS, CHESED AND JUDGMENT, to fasten them all. This is like Jacob, WHO IS THE CENTRAL COLUMN, as written: "Shall reach from end to end" (Shemot 26:28). THAT IS THE MIDDLE BAR, WHICH IS THE SECRET OF THE CENTRAL COLUMN THAT REACHES FROM THE END OF CHESED TO THE END OF HARSH JUDGMENT, EVEN THOUGH THEY ARE OPPOSITES FROM ONE ANOTHER. STILL IT REACHES THEM AND UNITES THEM THE ONE WITH THE OTHER.

921. תָּאנָא, כּוֹלֵי הַאי לָא אִתְקְרֵי אֶלָּא מִסִּטְרָא דִּילָן, וּמִסִּטְרָא דִּילָן אִשְׁתְּמוֹדַע כֹּלָּא. דְּהָא בְּהַאי לְעֵילָא כֹּלָּא בְּחַד מַתְקְלָא סַלְקָא. לָא שָׁנֵי, וְלָא יִשְׁתַּנֵּי, כְּמָה דִּכְתִּיב אֲנִי יְיָ' לָא שָׁנִיתִי. אָמַר רַבִּי יְהוּדָה, כֻּלְּהוֹן בּוּצִינִין נְהִירִין מֵחַד, וּמֵחַד תַּלְיָין, וּבוּצִינִין אִינְהוּ חַד כֹּלָּא. דְּהָא לָא בָּעוּ לְאִתְפָּרְשָׁא, וּמַאן דְּפָרִישׁ לוֹן, כְּאִלּוּ אִתְפְּרַשׁ מִן חַיֵּי עָלְמָא.

921. We have learned that it is not considered such A GREAT DISTANCE BETWEEN CHESED and JUDGMENT, except from our viewpoint and everything shows from our side, AS WE SAID ABOVE. Because everything

above rises in one manner, it neither changes nor will it change, as it is written: "For I am Hashem, I do not change" (Malachi 3:6). Rabbi Yehuda said: All the candles illuminate from one, FROM THE BLESSED ENDLESS LIGHT, and they depend upon one. All the candles are one, and one must not distinguish BETWEEN THEM, for one who separates between them is separated from eternal life.

## 97. "And He rode upon a Cherub, and did fly"

### A Synopsis

Rabbi Yitzchak speaks here of two Cherubs called 'youths': Metatron and Sandalphon, and how God settles upon them. Rabbi Yosi then tells us that if the two Cherubs turn their faces away from each other, there is no peace in the world. This, we learn, is because there is then no pairing above, and Rabbi Yitzchak points out that a similar idea is conveyed in "the nakedness of your father, or the nakedness of your mother, shall you not uncover." He says that in the old days people cared about Torah, but now only a few are left who do, and these few holy ones are those with whom God Himself prays.

### The Relevance of this Passage

The verses, "Two Cherubs who turn their faces away from each other" and "The nakedness of your mother or the nakedness of your father" pertain to the disjoining of the Right and Left Columns. This separation creates a dangerous imbalance that inevitably prevents peace in our lives. The root of evil is the Left Column – the *Desire to Receive for the Self Alone*. Left unchecked, its appetite is unappeasable. Like a black hole in deep space, it consumes everything in its vicinity, leaving blackness in its wake. If the Right Column Force of sharing is left unchecked, it will give ceaselessly. However, lacking any aspect of the Left (Desire to Receive), it will never be replenished. Eventually its resources are depleted, and it ends up empty, feeling a tremendous lack.

The Central Column unites these two opposite forces by *resisting* the *Desire to Receive* and transforming it into the *Desire to Receive for the Sake of Sharing.* Jacob and the righteous souls, past and present, who love Torah now activate the complete consciousness of Central Column (the will to resist our selfish drives and instead think about the next person), which brings the full compliment of Light and genuine peace to the world.

922. אָמַר ר' יִצְחָק, כְּתִיב וְנָתַתִּי נְעָרִים שָׂרֵיהֶם וְתַעֲלוּלִים יִמְשְׁלוּ בָם, הַיְינוּ דִּכְתִיב וְעָשִׂיתָ שְׁנַיִם כְּרוּבִים זָהָב. כְּתִיב יוֹשֵׁב הַכְּרוּבִים, וּכְתִיב וַיִּרְכַּב עַל כְּרוּב וַיָּעֹף. יוֹשֵׁב הַכְּרוּבִים, כַּד שַׁרְיָא לְאִתְיַישְּׁבָא בִּשְׁלֵימוּתָא, כְּתִיב יוֹשֵׁב הַכְּרוּבִים. וְכַד לָא שַׁרְיָא, וְלָא אִתְיַישְּׁבָא מַלְכָּא בְּכֻרְסְיָא, כְּתִיב וַיִּרְכַּב עַל כְּרוּב חַד, דְּלָא אִתְיַישְּׁבָא מַלְכָּא בְּכֻרְסְיֵיה. יוֹשֵׁב הַכְּרוּבִים תְּרֵי.

**922.** Rabbi Yitzchak said: It is written, "And I will make youngsters their princes, and babes shall rule over them" (Yeshayah 3:4). This is in accordance with the verse: "And you shall make two Cherubs of gold" (Shemot 25:18) THAT ARE METATRON AND SANDALPHON, WHO ARE CALLED 'YOUTHS'. It is written: "who sits upon the Cherubs" (I Shmuel 4:4) and also, "And He rode upon a Cherub, and did fly" (II Shmuel 22:11), MEANING ONLY ON ONE CHERUB? HE ANSWERS: When THE HOLY ONE, BLESSED BE HE, wishes to settle upon them entirely, it is written: "Who sits upon the Cherubs," THAT HE SETTLES ON THEM BOTH TOGETHER. But when the King does not dwell and is not seated on the throne, MEANING WHEN THERE IS NO UNION ABOVE BETWEEN MALE AND FEMALE, it is written: "And He rode upon a Cherub." This is because the King, WHO IS ZEIR ANPIN, is not seated on His throne, THAT IS MALCHUT. BUT "Who sits on the Cherubs" would imply two.

923. אָמַר רַבִּי יוֹסֵי, וַוי לְעָלְמָא, כַּד חַד כְּרוּב אַהְדַּר אַנְפֵּיה מֵחַבְרֵיה, דְּהָא כְּתִיב וּפְנֵיהֶם אִישׁ אֶל אָחִיו, כַּד הֲוָה שְׁלָמָא בְּעָלְמָא. אָמַר רַבִּי יִצְחָק, הָא תָּנֵינָן עֶרְוַת אָבִיךָ וְעֶרְוַת אִמְּךָ לֹא תְגַלֵּה, וַוי לְמַאן דִּגְלֵי עֶרְיָיתְהוֹן. כְּגַוְונָא דָּא כְּתִיב בְּיַעֲקֹב, מַבְרִיחַ מִן הַקָּצֶה אֶל הַקָּצֶה. זַכָּאָה חוּלָקֵהוֹן דְּיִשְׂרָאֵל, דְּקוּדְשָׁא בְּרִיךְ הוּא מִשְׁתְּבַּח בְּתִשְׁבְּחָתַיְיהוּ כְּגַוְונָא דִלְעֵילָא, דִּכְתִיב יִשְׂרָאֵל אֲשֶׁר בְּךָ אֶתְפָּאָר.

**923.** Rabbi Yosi said: Woe is to the world when one cherub turns his face away from his neighbor, FOR THIS SHOWS THAT THERE IS NO UNION ABOVE OF RIGHT AND LEFT. It is written: "And their faces shall look one to another" (Shemot 25:20) at the time that there is peace in the world. IT IS IMPLIED THAT IF THEY DO NOT FACE EACH OTHER, THERE IS NO PEACE IN THE WORLD. Rabbi Yitzchak said: We have learned that "the nakedness of your father, or the nakedness of your mother, shall you not uncover" (Vayikra 18:7), MEANING THAT ONE SHOULD NOT SIN BY SEPARATING THE UNION OF MALE AND FEMALE WHO ARE YOUR FATHER AND MOTHER. Woe is to he who uncovers their nakedness, MEANING IF HE BLEMISHES THEM. THEREFORE, IT IS NOT NECESSARY TO DERIVE THIS FROM: "AND THEIR FACES ONE TO ANOTHER." Similar to this, it is written by Jacob: 'Shall reach from end to end,' MEANING THAT HE UNITES RIGHT AND LEFT TOGETHER. Blessed is the portion of Yisrael that the Holy One, blessed be He, praises Himself with their praise as above, IN TIFERET, as it

is written: "Yisrael in whom I will be glorified" (Yeshayah 49:3).

924. תָּאנָא אָמַר רַבִּי יִצְחָק, בְּיוֹמֵי קַדְמָאֵי, הֲוָה בַּר נָשׁ אָמַר לְחַבְרֵיהּ, אֵימָא לִי מִלָּה חֲדָא דְאוֹרַיְיתָא, וְטוֹל מָנֶה כְּסַף. הַשְׁתָּא אָמַר בַּר נָשׁ לְחַבְרֵיהּ, טוֹל מָנֶה כְּסַף וְאִשְׁתְּדַּל בְּאוֹרַיְיתָא, וְלֵית מַאן דְּיִשְׁגַּח, וְלֵית מַאן דְּיַרְכִּין אוּדְנֵיהּ, בַּר אִינּוּן זְעִירִין קַדִּישֵׁי עֶלְיוֹנִין, דְּקוּדְשָׁא בְּרִיךְ הוּא מִשְׁתְּבַּח בְּהוּ, דִּכְתִּיב וְעַמֵּךְ כֻּלָּם צַדִּיקִים לְעוֹלָם יִרְשׁוּ אָרֶץ נֵצֶר מַטָּעַי מַעֲשֵׂה יָדַי לְהִתְפָּאֵר.

**924.** We have learned that Rabbi Yitzchak said: In the early days, a person would say to his neighbor, 'Tell me a word of Torah, and receive a coin of silver.' Now a person says to his neighbor, 'Receive a coin of silver and study Torah.' No one cares and no one pays attention, except for these few holy ones with whom the Holy One, blessed be He, praises Himself, as it is written: "Your people also shall be all righteous, they shall inherit the land forever; they shall be the branch of My planting, the work of My hands, that I may be glorified" (Yeshayah 60:21).

## 98. "The hooks of the pillars"

### A Synopsis

Rabbi Yitzchak speaks here about the forms of the supernal pillars, Netzach and Hod, and the hooks from which are suspended the pillars below. The two pillars are united and watered, we are told, by the spinal column, Tiferet, that stands over them. Lastly, we learn that the hooks (*vavim*) are six within six, so that there are *vav's* above in Chesed, Gvurah and Tiferet and *vav's* below in Netzach, Hod and Yesod.

### The Relevance of this Passage

Essentially, this passage speaks of how Light flows. Tiferet is the upper Central Column, and Yesod is the lower Central Column residing between Netzach and Hod. This is the critical channel that needs to be opened for us to receive the Light. The Zohar now opens up Netzach and Hod, through the unifying power of Yesod, so that an abundance of Light floods our world, opening up the hearts of man to the true Creator.

925. וָוֵי הָעַמּוּדִים וַחֲשֻׁקֵיהֶם כָּסֶף. רִבִּי יִצְחָק אָמַר, וָוֵי הָעַמּוּדִים, הָא אֲמֵינָא כָּל אִינּוּן דְּמִתְאַחֲדָן מִקִּטְרֵי קַיְימִין עִלָּאִין, אִקְרוּן וָוֵי הָעַמּוּדִים. וְכָל אִינּוּן דִּלְתַתָּא, תַּלְיָין מֵאִינּוּן וָוִים. מַאי וָוִים. שַׁתָּא בְּגוֹ שַׁתָּא, וּמִתְאַחֲדָן וּמִתְשַׁקְיָין מֵחוּטָא דְּשִׁדְרָה, דְּקָאִים עֲלַיְיהוּ. וּבְסִפְרָא דִּצְנִיעוּתָא תָּאנָא, וָוִים לְעֵילָּא, וָוִים לְתַתָּא, וְכֻלְּהוּ בְּמַתְקְלָא חַד סַלְּקִין.

925. "The hooks of the pillars and their joints shall be of silver" (Shemot 27:10). Rabbi Yitzchak said: "The hooks of the pillars": I say all these that are joined with the forms of the supernal pillars, WHICH ARE NETZACH AND HOD, are called 'the hooks of the pillars'. All those of below are suspended from these hooks. What are hooks (Heb. *vavim*)? They are six within six, BECAUSE VAVIM (VAV'S) ARE TWO TIMES SIX (= *VAV*), FOR THE SIX EXTREMITIES ARE COMBINED OF EACH OTHER AND EACH ONE HAS SIX. THEREFORE, NETZACH IS SIX AND HOD IS SIX. They are united and watered by the spinal column, WHICH IS TIFERET that stands over them, FOR TIFERET STANDS OVER NETZACH AND HOD. In Safra De'tzniuta (Eng. 'the hidden book'), we learned that there are *Vav's* above, IN

CHESED, GVURAH AND TIFERET, and *Vav*'s below, IN NETZACH, HOD AND YESOD. They all are interpreted in the same way, MEANING THAT THERE IS NO DISPUTE HERE.

# Safra Det'zniuta

# Names of the articles

## 1. First Chapter

### A Synopsis

Rabbi Shimon says that the Concealed Book consists of five chapters, contained in a great chamber, that fill the entire earth. However, only one who has entered wisdom and come out from it in peace can see the entire wisdom in that book. He tells a parable to illustrate his point about one who grasps the generality of wisdom but does not know the delights and delicacies that derive from that generality. The Concealed Book weighs on scales, the great scales at the head of Atik that balance all things. We learn of the death of the ancient kings and the earth having been made void at that time, and of the 6,000 years that the world exists. Though the ancient world was destroyed in twelve hours the thirteenth will be established with mercy and be renewed as before. During the seventh millennium, "Hashem alone shall be exalted on that day." Rabbi Shimon compares the first vision of Ezekiel to the first verses of Beresheet that tell the story of creation. The essence of all the Sfirot in this context are brought into the discussion. The Concealed Book tells of the creation of things in a way that is hidden to the common man; warning is given against anyone who would try to tell of it without understanding. But the righteous is the foundation of the world, and there is wisdom in righteousness which is vital to the structure of the world.

1. מַאן צְנִיעוּתָא דְסִפְרָא. אָמַר רְבִּי שִׁמְעוֹן, חֲמִשָּׁה פְּרָקִין אִינוּן דִּכְלִילָן בְּהֵיכָל רַב, וּמַלְיָין כָּל אַרְעָא. אָמַר ר' יְהוּדָה, אִי כְּלִילָן הָנֵי, מִכָּלְהוּ עֲדִיפֵי. אָמַר ר' שִׁמְעוֹן, הָכִי הוּא, לְמַאן דְּעָאל וְנָפַק, וּלְמָאן דְּלָא עָאל וְנָפַק לָאו הָכִי.

**1.** HE ASKS: What is the Concealed Book? Rabbi Shimon said: There are five chapters, contained in a great chamber, which fill the entire earth. Rabbi Yehuda said: If these include THE ENTIRE WISDOM, THEN they are the best AND THERE IS NO NEED TO STUDY FURTHER. Rabbi Shimon said: This is true for one who has entered WISDOM and came out FROM IT IN PEACE. HE CAN SEE HERE THE INCORPORATION OF THE ENTIRE WISDOM, but it is not so for one who did not enter WISDOM and emerge FROM IT IN PEACE.

2. מַתְלָא, לְבַר נָשׁ דַּהֲוָה הַיּוּרֵיהּ בֵּינֵי טוּרִין, וְלָא יָדַע בְּדִיּוּרֵי מָתָא.

זָרַע חִטִין. וְאָכִיל חִטֵי בְּגוּפַיְיהוּ. יוֹמָא חַד עָאל לְמָתָא, אַקְרִיבוּ לֵיהּ
נַהֲמָא טָבָא. אָמַר הַהוּא בַּר נָשׁ, דְּנָא לָמָה. אָמְרוּ נַהֲמָא הוּא לְמֵיכַל.
אָכַל וְטָעַם לְחָדָּא לְחִכֵּיהּ. אָמַר וּמִמָּה אִתְעָבֵיד דָּא. אָמְרוּ מֵחִטִּין.
לְבָתַר אַקְרִיבוּ לֵיהּ גְּרִיצִין דְּלִישִׁין בְּמִשְׁחָא. טָעַם מִנַּיְיהוּ, אָמַר וְאִלֵּין
מִמָּה אִתְעָבִידוּ. אָמְרוּ מֵחִטִּין. לְבָתַר אַקְרִיבוּ לֵיהּ טְרִיקֵי מַלְכִין,
דְּלִישִׁין בְּדוּבְשָׁא וּמִשְׁחָא. אָמַר וְאִלֵּין מִמָּה אִתְעָבִידוּ. אָמְרוּ מֵחִטִּין.
אָמַר וַדַּאי אֲנָא מָארֵי דְּכָל אִלֵּין, דַּאֲנָא אָכִיל עִקְּרָא דְּכָל אִלֵּין דְּאִיהוּ
חִטָּה. בְּגִין הַהוּא דַּעְתָּא מֵעִדוּנֵי עָלְמָא לָא יָדַע וְאִתְאֲבִידוּ מִנֵּיהּ. כָּךְ,
מַאן דְּנָקִיט כְּלָלָא, וְלָא יָדַע בְּכֻלְּהוּ עִדוּנִין דִּמְהַנְיָין, דְּנָפְקִין מֵהַהוּא
כְּלָלָא.

**2.** This is likened to a man who lived in the mountains and was not acquainted with the city inhabitants. He sowed wheat, and then he ate the wheat just as it was. One day, he came to the city, where he was served with good bread. That person said, 'What is this?' They answered him, 'This is bread to be eaten.' He ate and it was delicious to his palate. He said, 'What is this made from?' They said, 'It is made from wheat. Afterwards, they served him cookies mixed with oil. He tasted them. He asked, 'And what are these made from?' They answered, 'From wheat.' Afterwards, they offered him food fit for kings kneaded with oil and honey. He said, 'What are these made from?' They told him, 'From wheat'. He said, 'I certainly have all these, because I eat the essence of all these, which is wheat.' Because of this opinion, he did not learn how to make all these delicacies and he did not know of the delights of the world – thus, they were lost to him. It is also so with one who grasps the generality of wisdom, but does not know the delights and delicacies that derive from that generality.

**3.** תָּאנָא. סִפְרָא דִּצְנִיעוּתָא, סִפְרָא, דְּשָׁקִיל בְּמַתְקְלָא. דְּעַד דְּלָא הֲוָה
מַתְקְלָא, לָא הֲווֹ מַשְׁגִּיחִין אַפִּין בְּאַפִּין, וּמַלְכִין קַדְמָאִין מִיתוּ,
וְזִיּוּנֵיהוֹן לָא אִשְׁתַּכְּחוּ, וְאַרְעָא אִתְבַּטְּלַת.

**3.** We have learned that the Concealed Book is a book that weighs on scales, THAT IS, THE BOOK THAT SPEAKS OF THE WEIGHT OF THE LIGHTS ON SCALES IS CALLED 'THE CONCEALED BOOK', BECAUSE THE WISDOM IN

THE SCALES ILLUMINATES FROM BELOW UPWARDS WHICH IS THE WAY OF CONCEALMENT. THIS IS THE SECRET OF, "BUT WITH THE LOWLY (ALSO: 'CONCEALED') IS WISDOM" (MISHLEI 11:2). Before there was a balance, THE RIGHT AND THE LEFT – WHICH IS THE SECRET OF MALE AND FEMALE – did not look AT EACH OTHER face to face. The ancient kings died and had no weapon, and the earth – WHICH IS THE SECRET OF MALCHUT – was made void.

4. עַד דְּרֵישָׁא דְּכְסוּפָא דְּכָל כְּסוּפִין, לְבוּשֵׁי דִּיקָר אַתְקִין, וְאַחֲסִין.

4. Until the head, the most delectable of all delectations – WHICH IS THE HEAD OF THE NUKVA OF ATIK, CALLED 'THE UNKNOWN HEAD' – prepared precious garments and bequeathed THEM TO ALL.

5. הַאי מַתְקְלָא תָּלֵי בַּאֲתָר דְּלָא הֲוָה, אִתְקָלוּ בֵּיה אִינּוּן דְּלָא אִשְׁתַּכְּחוּ. מַתְקְלָא קָאֵים בְּגוּפֵיה. לָא אִתְאֲחַד, וְלָא אִתְחֲזֵי. בֵּיה סְלִיקוּ, וּבֵיה סָלְקִין דְּלָא הֲווֹ, וַהֲווֹ, וְיְהֶוְיָין.

5. These scales are hung in a place where they were not before, MEANING AT THE HEAD OF ATIK. In them were weighed those who had no WEAPONS – NAMELY, THE KINGS. BUT THE ESSENCE OF the scales lies in the body, MEANING THE CENTRAL COLUMN THAT IS TIFERET, WHERE JUDGMENT LIES. THIS JUDGMENT does not unite and is not visible IN THE SCALES. IN THESE SCALES, THE LIGHTS OF THE LEFT ascend FROM BELOW UPWARD, and in them rise those that were not, those that were, and those that will be.

6. סִתְרָא גּוֹ סִתְרָא, אִתְתְּקַן וְאִזְדְּמַן, בְּחַד גּוּלְגַּלְתָּא, מַלְיָיא טַלָּא דִּבְדוֹלְחָא. קְרוּמָא דְּאַוִּירָא אִזְדְּכַּךְ וְסָתִים, אִינּוּן עָמָר נְקִי תַּלְיָין בְּשִׁקּוּלָא. רְעוּתָא דְּרַעֲוִין אִתְגַּלְיָיא בִּצְלוֹתָא דְּתַתָּאֵי. אַשְׁגָּחָא פְּקִיחָא דְּלָא נָאֵים, וְנָטִיר תְּדִירָא. אַשְׁגָּחוּתָא דְתַתָּא בְּאַשְׁגָּחוּתָא דִּנְהִירוּ דְּעֵילָּאָה. תְּרֵין נוּקְבִין דְּפַרְדַּשְׁקָא, דְּאִתְעַר רוּחָא לְכֹלָא.

6. Concealment was installed within concealment and settled in a skull, NAMELY, KETER OF ARICH ANPIN, full of crystal dew, WHICH IS CONCEALED CHOCHMAH OF ARICH ANPIN. The membrane of air THAT IS

BETWEEN THE SKULL AND CONCEALED CHOCHMAH was purified and hidden. The HAIRS OF THE HEAD OF ARICH ANPIN THAT ARE CALLED 'pure wool' are on the scale. The Will of All Wills is revealed ON THE FOREHEAD OF ARICH ANPIN through the prayers of the lower beings. Supervision from the open EYE that never sleeps and guards constantly IS INSTALLED IN THE EYES OF ARICH ANPIN, and the supervision OF THE LOWER DEPENDS on this supernal supervision OF ARICH ANPIN. The royal viceroy has two nostrils – WHICH IS THE SECRET OF THE NOSE that revives the spirit OF LIFE in everything.

7. בְּרֵאשִׁית בָּרָא אֱלֹהִים אֵת הַשָּׁמַיִם וְאֵת הָאָרֶץ, שִׁיתָא בְּרֵאשִׁית עֲלַיְיהוּ, כּוּלְהוּ לְתַתָּא, וְתַלְיָין מִשִּׁבְעָה דְּגוּלְגַּלְתָּא עַד יְקִירוּ דִּיקִירוּתָא, וְהָאָרֶץ תִּנְיָינָא לָאו בְּחוּשְׁבָּן וְהָא אִתְּמַר. וּמֵהַהִיא דְּאִתְלַטְיָיא נָפְקָא, דִּכְתִיב מִן הָאֲדָמָה אֲשֶׁר אֵרְרָהּ יְיָ'. הָיְתָה תֹהוּ וָבֹהוּ וְחֹשֶׁךְ עַל פְּנֵי תְהוֹם וְרוּחַ אֱלֹהִים מְרַחֶפֶת עַל פְּנֵי הַמָּיִם. תְּלֵיסַר, תַּלְיָין בִּתְלֵיסָר יְקִירוּ דְּיַקִירוּתָא.

7. "In the beginning Elohim created the heaven and the earth" (Beresheet 1:1). These are six WORDS, CORRESPONDING TO CHESED, GVURAH, TIFERET, NETZACH, HOD AND YESOD, and "In the beginning," WHICH IS BINAH, is above them. All of them are below, IN BINAH AND IN ZEIR ANPIN, and are suspended AND COME DOWN from the seven features of the Skull. THEY SPREAD to the most precious, THE THIRTEEN FEATURES OF THE BEARD OF ARICH ANPIN, FROM WHICH IS INFERRED THE SECOND VERSE, NAMELY, "WAS WITHOUT FORM AND VOID..." (IBID. 2), WHICH CONTAINS THIRTEEN WORDS AS SHALL BE EXPLAINED. The second OCCURRENCE OF "the earth" – THE WORD "EARTH" WITH WHICH THE SECOND VERSE STARTS – is not counted AMONG THESE THIRTEEN WORDS, as we learned, because it emerged from the earth that was damaged ON ACCOUNT OF THE SIN OF THE TREE OF KNOWLEDGE OF GOOD AND EVIL, FOR MALCHUT OF THE ATTRIBUTE OF HARSH JUDGMENT WAS MIXED IN IT, as it is written, "because of the ground which Hashem has cursed" (Beresheet 5:29). THEREFORE, IT IS NOT COUNTED WITH THE THIRTEEN AND THEY START WITH THE WORD "WAS" – "was without form and void, and darkness was on the face of the deep, and a wind from Elohim moved over the surface of the waters..." WHICH ARE THIRTEEN WORDS.

AND THESE thirteen words are derived from the thirteen features of the most precious, WHICH IS THE BEARD OF ARICH ANPIN, WHICH ARE EXPLAINED LATER.

8. שִׁיתָא אַלְפֵי שְׁנִין, תַּלְיָין בְּשִׁיתָא קַדְמָאֵי, שְׁבִיעָאָה עָלַיְיהוּ, דְּאִתְתָּקַף בִּלְחוֹדוֹי. וְאִתְחָרִיב כֹּלָּא בִּתְרֵיסַר שַׁעֲתֵּי, דִּכְתִיב הָיְתָה תֹהוּ וָבֹהוּ וְגוֹ'. תְּלֵיסַר יְקִים לוֹן בְּרַחֲמֵי, וּמִתְחַדְּשָׁן בְּקַדְמֵיתָא, וְקָמוּ כָּל אִינּוּן שִׁיתָא. בְּגִין דִּכְתִיב בָּרָא, וּלְבָתַר כְּתִיב הָיְתָה, דְּהָא הֲוַת וַדַּאי, וּלְבַסּוֹף תֹהוּ וָבֹהוּ וְחֹשֶׁךְ, וְנִשְׂגַּב יְיָ' לְבַדּוֹ בַּיּוֹם הַהוּא.

8. The 6,000 years THAT THE WORLD EXISTS derive AND EXPAND from the first six WORDS, WHICH ARE: "CREATED... ELOHIM...THE...HEAVEN ...AND...EARTH." The seventh, WHICH IS BINAH, is above them and alone is strengthened, NAMELY THE WORD, "IN THE BEGINNING" THAT PRECEDED THEM. Everything was destroyed in twelve hours, as written, "was without form and void..." The thirteenth will be established BY THOSE TWELVE HOURS with mercy, and they are renewed as before. These six will arise AGAIN, because it is written, "created" and afterwards, it is written, "was," WHICH IMPLIES THAT NOW IT IS NOT ANYMORE. This is because it certainly was DURING THE 6,000 YEARS and in the end, DURING THE SEVENTH MILLENNIUM, it is "without form and void, and darkness..." BECAUSE IT WAS DESTROYED. THIS IS THE MEANING OF, "And Hashem alone shall be exalted on that day" (Yeshayah 2:11), NAMELY DURING THE SEVENTH MILLENNIUM.

9. גְּלוּפֵי דְּגְלִיפִין כְּחֵיזוּ דְּחִוְיָא אָרִיךְ, וּמִתְפַּשֵּׁט לְכָאן וּלְכָאן, זַנְבָא בְּרֵישָׁא. רֵישָׁא אָחִיד אַכַּתְפִין, אַעֲבַּר וְזָעִים, נָטַר וְגָנִיז. חַד לְאֶלֶף יוֹמִין זְעִירִין אִתְגַּלְיָיא, קוּלְטְרָא בִּקְטְרוֹי, סַנְפִּירָא בְּעַדְבוֹי, אִתְחַבַּר רֵישֵׁיהּ בְּמַיִּין דְּיַמָּא רַבָּא, דִּכְתִיב שִׁבַּרְתָּ רָאשֵׁי תַנִּינִים עַל הַמָּיִם. תְּרֵין הֲווֹ, חַד אִתְחֲזֵרֵי, תַּנִּינָם כְּתִיב חָסֵר. רָאשֵׁי, כד"א וּדְמוּת עַל רָאשֵׁי הַחַיָּה רָקִיעַ.

9. The imprints of the engravings look like a long snake, which extends this way and that, so the tail is at the head and the head joins the shoulders. It

passes and it is wrathful, it guards and conceals. Once in a thousand small days is providence revealed through its doings. The fin UPON WHICH THE WORLD IS SITUATED IS in its lot. Its head is broken in the waters of the Great Sea, as is written: "You did break the heads of the sea serpents (Heb. *taninim*) in the waters" (Tehilim 74:13). There were two but one returned, for '*Taninim*' is spelled without Yud, WHICH IS THE MARK OF PLURAL. EVEN THOUGH IT IS SPELLED "HEADS", IT IS SINGULAR, as is written, "And over the heads (Heb. *rashei*) of the living creature was the likeness of a firmament" (Yechezkel 1:22). IT SAYS '*RASHEI*' WITH A YUD EVEN THOUGH IT WAS THE HEAD OF A SINGLE CREATURE. HERE ALSO ABOUT THE SEA SERPENT, EVEN THOUGH IT SAYS HEADS IT REALLY MEANS THE HEAD OF ONE SERPENT.

10. וַיֹּאמֶר אֱלֹהִים יְהִי אוֹר וַיְהִי אוֹר, הַיְינוּ דִכְתִיב כִּי הוּא אָמַר וַיֶּהִי, הוּא בִּלְחוֹדוֹי. לְבָתַר אִתְחַזְרוּ חַד יהו"י יה"ו וי' בַּתְרָאָה שְׁכִינְתָּא לְתַתָּא. כְּמָה דְה' שְׁכִינְתָּא אִשְׁתְּכַח וּבְחַד מַתְקָלָא אִתְקָלוּ.

10. "And Elohim said, Let there be (Heb. *yehi*) light; and there was (Heb. *vayehi*) light" (Beresheet 1:3). This is similar to, "For He spoke, and it was (Heb. *vayehi*)" (Tehilim 33:9). THE WORD "AND IT WAS" IS COUPLED BY SAYING TO SHOW THAT "*VAYEHI*" is by itself AND THE WORD "*YEHI* (LIT. 'LIGHT')" IS BY ITSELF, BECAUSE *YEHI* IS ABA AND RIGHT COLUMN, AND *VAYEHI* IS IMA AND LEFT COLUMN. Later RIGHT AND LEFT became one again THROUGH THE CENTRAL COLUMN, WHICH IS THE SECRET OF ZEIR ANPIN THAT RECONCILED THEM. *YEHI* (YUD-HEI-YUD) AND *VAYEHI* (VAV-YUD-HEI-YUD) UNITED AND FROM THEM WAS MADE THE PERMUTATION Yud Hei Vav Yud, BECAUSE IDENTICAL LETTERS ARE NOT COUNTED TWICE. Yud Hei Vav ARE THE SECRET OF ABA AND IMA AND ZEIR ANPIN THAT RECONCILES AND UNITES THEM. The last Yud OF YUD HEI VAV YUD is the lower Shechinah like Hei IS the Shechinah and they are weighed in the same scales.

11. וְהַחַיּוֹת רָצוֹא וָשׁוֹב, דִּכְתִיב וַיַּרְא אֱלֹהִים אֶת הָאוֹר כִּי טוֹב. אָמְרוּ צַדִּיק כִּי טוֹב. הַאי, בְּמַתְקְלֵיהּ סַלְקָא. קַדְמָאָה בִּלְחוֹדוֹי. וְכֹלָּא לְחַד אִתְחֲזָרֵי. אֲחַתָא וּמוֹדַעְתָּא כְּלִילָן דָּא בְּדָא בְּיו"ד ה"א, כִּתְרֵין רְחִימִין דְּמִתְחַבְּקָן.

**11.** "And the living creatures ran and returned" (Yechezkel 1:14), resembles, "And Elohim saw the light, that it was good" (Beresheet 1:4). THIS IS THE MEANING OF, "Say of the righteous, that it shall be well (or: 'good') with him" (Yeshayah 3:10). This verse, "AND ELOHIM SAW THE LIGHT THAT IT WAS GOOD" goes up on the scales. But in the first verse, "LET THERE BE LIGHT; AND THERE WAS LIGHT," THE RIGHT AND LEFT were separate, but now they all became one again AFTERWARDS THROUGH THE CENTRAL COLUMN. The sister, WHICH IS CHOCHMAH, and kinswoman, WHICH IS THE SECRET OF BINAH, THAT ARE ALLUDED TO IN, "LET THERE BE LIGHT; AND THERE WAS LIGHT," AS MENTIONED ABOVE, have been included through it, each with the other in the secret of Yud Hei, WHICH IS CHOCHMAH AND BINAH. They are beloved and embracing crowns. THE REASON THAT CHOCHMAH AND BINAH ARE CALLED 'SISTER AND KINSWOMAN' IS IN ACCORDANCE WITH THE VERSE, "SAY TO WISDOM, YOU ARE MY SISTER, AND CALL UNDERSTANDING YOUR KINSWOMAN" (MISHLEI 7:4).

12. שִׁיתָא נָפְקִין מֵעַנְפָּא דְּשַׁרְשָׁא דְּגוּפָא, לִישָׁן מְמַלֵּל רַבְרְבָן. לִישָׁן דָּא, סָתִים בֵּין יוּ״ד וְהֵ״א, דִּכְתִיב זֶה יֹאמַר לַה' אָנִי וְזֶה יִקְרָא בְּשֵׁם יַעֲקֹב וְזֶה יִכְתּוֹב יָדוֹ לַיְיָ' וּבְשֵׁם יִשְׂרָאֵל יְכַנֶּה יְכַנֶּה מַמָּשׁ. זֶה יֹאמַר לַה' אָנִי: אֲחָתָא. וְכֹלָּא אִתְּמַר בֵּיה״ו. כֹּלָּא כְּלִילָן בְּלִישָׁן סָתִים לְאִימָא. דְּהָא אִתְפַּתְּחַת לֵיהּ דְּנָפִיק מִינָהּ. אַבָּא יָתִיב בְּרֵישָׁא, אִימָא בְּאֶמְצָעִיתָא וּמִתְכַּסְיָיא מִכָּאן וּמִכָּאן וַוי לְמַאן דְּגַלֵּי עֲרָיָיתְהוֹן.

**12.** Six SFIROT – CHESED, GVURAH, TIFERET, NETZACH, HOD AND YESOD – come out from the branch of the root of the body, which is a tongue that speaks great things. This tongue is concealed between Yud Vav Dalet and Hei Aleph, WHICH ARE CHOCHMAH AND BINAH, AS WRITTEN, "One shall say, I am Hashem's; and another shall call himself by the name of Jacob; and another shall subscribe with his hand to Hashem, and surname himself by the name of Yisrael" (Yeshayah 44:5), actually surname himself. "One shall say, I am Hashem's" – this is the sister, NAMELY CHOCHMAH, WHICH IS FORBIDDEN (FOR INTERCOURSE) LIKE A SISTER, BECAUSE IT IS INCOMPREHENSIBLE. "AND ANOTHER SHALL CALL HIMSELF BY THE NAME OF JACOB" – THIS IS THE KINSWOMAN, WHICH IS BINAH, WHEREIN THE ILLUMINATION OF CHOCHMAH BEGINS. THEREFORE, IT SAYS "BY THE NAME OF JACOB," BECAUSE NAME DENOTES

COMPREHENSION, "AND ANOTHER SHALL SUBSCRIBE WITH HIS HAND TO HASHEM" IS DA'AT. "AND SURNAME HIMSELF BY THE NAME OF YISRAEL" IS THE SPREADING OF DA'AT TO ZEIR ANPIN, AND THEN ZEIR ANPIN IS CALLED 'YISRAEL', MEANING ACTUALLY SURNAME AS MENTIONED. It is all expressed in Yud Hei Vav, NAMELY IN CHOCHMAH, BINAH AND DA'AT. All THOSE THREE – CHOCHMAH, BINAH AND DA'AT – are included in the secret tongue in Ima, FOR DA'AT THAT MEDIATES BETWEEN THE TWO COLUMNS, CHOCHMAH AND BINAH THAT ARE IN IMA, INCLUDES WITHIN ITSELF CHOCHMAH, BINAH AND DA'AT, because she was opened by it and it emerges from her. Aba sits at the head, Ima in the center, and is covered from this way and that way. Woe to the one who uncovers their nakedness.

וַיֹּאמֶר אֱלֹהִים יְהִי מְאֹרֹת בִּרְקִיעַ הַשָּׁמַיִם, שַׁלִּיט דְּכַר בְּנוּקְבָּא. 13. דִּכְתִּיב וְצַדִּיק יְסוֹד עוֹלָם, נָהִיר יוֹ"ד בִּתְרֵין, וְנָהִיר וּמְעַבֵּר לְנוּקְבָּא. אִתְיְיחַד יוֹ"ד בִּלְחוֹדוֹי, סָלִיק בְּדַרְגּוֹי לְעֵילָּא לְעֵילָּא. אִתְחַשְּׁכָא נוּקְבָא, וְאִתְנְהִירַת אִימָא וּמִתְפַּתְּחָא בְּתַרְעוֹי. אָתָא מַפְתְּחָא דְּכָלִיל בְּשִׁית, וּמְכַסְיָא פִתְחָהָא, וְאָחִיד לְתַתָּא לְהַאי וּלְהַאי, וַוי לְמַאן דְּגַלֵּי פִּתְחָהָא.

13. "And Elohim said, Let there be luminaries in the firmament of heaven" (Beresheet 1:14). THIS INDICATES THAT the Male, WHICH IS ZEIR ANPIN, shall rule over the Female, WHICH IS MALCHUT. THEREFORE, THE MALE IS CALLED 'THE GREAT LUMINARY' AND THE FEMALE, 'THE SMALL LUMINARY', as is written, "And the righteous is an everlasting foundation (or: 'the foundation of the world')" (Mishlei 10:25). THE RIGHTEOUS, WHO IS YESOD (LIT. 'FOUNDATION') OF ZEIR ANPIN, IS YESOD OF MALCHUT THAT IS CALLED 'WORLD'. IT IS IMPLIED THAT THE WORLD WOULD NOT EXIST WERE IT NOT FOR THE RIGHTEOUS, AND THEREFORE HE RULES OVER IT. AND HE EXPLAINS WHY IT IS SO, SAYING, Yud, WHICH IS CHOCHMAH AND SUPERNAL ABA AND IMA, illuminated both HEIS, and illuminated and impregnated THE FIRST HEI WITH the Female. Then Yud unified within itself, SEPARATING FROM THE HEI, ascended in its levels high up and the Nukva became dark. Ima shone and opened her gates. Then came the Key that included six SFIROT, WHICH IS ZEIR ANPIN, that covered the entrance OF IMA and joined below with the one and the other, MEANING WITH BOTH THE NUKVA AND WITH IMA. Woe to him who exposes the entrance.

## 2. Second Chapter

### A Synopsis

Here the Beard of Faith is explained. This beard is not mentioned in the Torah, being too precious to be spoken of there; all thirteen of its characteristics are outlined here. There are thirteen springs, nine of which flow down to water the body, Zeir Anpin – the other four are guarded and do not flow down. In the month of Tishrei, these thirteen features are in the upper world, Binah, and the thirteen gates of Mercy open there. The movement of the letters Yud Hei Vav Hei are described as they pertain above in the head of Arich Anpin and below in Zeir Anpin. This is followed by the seven features of the Skull of Zeir Anpin, that was formed from the air (the light of Chassadim from Aba) and a spark (the light of Gvurot from Ima). These features are the dew of two colors, three spaces of engraved letters, the hairs over the ears, a non-luminous forehead, eyes of three colors, the nose with three flames, and the ears curved level to hear good and evil. We hear an explanation of the difference between "I" and "He" as written in verses like, "I am Hashem, that (lit. 'He') is My name"; "He" is used for one who is hidden and not present, who is not visible to the eye, who has no name. This section closes with the statement that Yisrael Saba and Tevunah, which are Binah, are called 'Mother'.

‫14. פִּרְקָא תִּנְיָינָא. דִּיקְנָא מְהֵימְנוּתָא. דִּיקְנָא לָא אִדְכַּר בְּגִין דְּהִיא יַקִּירוּתָא דְּכֹלָּא מֵאַדְנִין נָפְקַת, בְּסַחֲרָנָהָא דְּבֹסִיטָא, סָלִיק וְנָחִית חוּטָא חִוָּורָא. בִּתְלֵיסַר מִתְפְּרַשׁ.‬

**14.** Second Chapter. In it is explained the Beard of Faith. The beard is not mentioned IN THE TORAH, PROPHETS OR THE WRITINGS, FOR IT IS WRITTEN, "THE EYES OF HASHEM," "THE EARS OF HASHEM," AND ALSO "HIS CHEEKS ARE LIKE A BED OF SPICES" (SHIR HASHIRIM 5:13), BUT THERE IS NO MENTION OF THE BEARD, because it is most precious and it comes out from the ears WHERE THE BEARD STARTS. It encircles the shape of the face, as a white strand going up and down around the face, MEANING THAT THE BEARD IN GENERAL LOOKS LIKE A WHITE STRAND WITH WHITE HAIRS AROUND THE FACE. SOME OF THEM GO UP, SHINING FROM BELOW UPWARDS, WHILE SOME GO DOWN, SHINING FROM ABOVE DOWNWARDS. It is explained in thirteen CHARACTERISTICS.

15. בְּיְקִירָא דְּבִיְקִירוּתָא הַהִיא, כְּתִיב לֹא עָבַר בָּהּ אִישׁ וְלֹא יָשַׁב אָדָם שָׁם. אָדָם לְבַר הוּא. אָדָם לָא כָּלִיל הָכָא. כְּ"שׁ אִישׁ. בִּתְלֵיסַר נְבִיעִין מַבּוּעִין מִתְפָּרְשָׁן, אַרְבַּע בִּלְחוֹדוֹי אִסְתָּמַרוּ. תִּשְׁעָה אַשְׁקְיּוּן לְגוּפָא.

**15.** Concerning that most precious, NAMELY THE BEARD, it is written, "Through a land that no man (Heb. *ish*) passed through, and where no man (Heb. *adam*) dwelt" (Yirmeyah 2:6). ZEIR ANPIN IS CALLED 'ADAM' AND YESOD OF ZEIR ANPIN IS CALLED 'ISH'. Adam is outside ARICH ANPIN, FOR ZEIR ANPIN THAT IS CALLED 'ADAM' WRAPS ARICH ANPIN ON THE OUTSIDE FROM THE NAVEL DOWN, and all the more so *ish*, WHICH IS YESOD OF ZEIR ANPIN THAT IS EVEN OUTSIDE ZEIR ANPIN. NETZACH, HOD AND YESOD ARE OUTSIDE THE TORSO AND, ALL THE MORE SO, OUTSIDE OF ARICH ANPIN; THEREFORE, THEY HAVE NO SHARE IN THIS BEARD OF ARICH ANPIN. THE BEARD is explained by thirteen springs and only four OF THE FEATURES are guarded, SO AS NOT TO FLOW DOWN TO ZEIR ANPIN. Nine OF THE FEATURES water the body, WHICH IS ZEIR ANPIN.

16. מִקַּמֵּי פִּתְחָא דְּאָדְנִין, שָׁארֵי יָקִירוּ לְאִתַתָּקֵן, נָחִית בִּשְׁפִּירוּ בְּרֵישָׁא דְּשִׂפְוָון. מֵהַאי רֵישָׁא לְהַאי רֵישָׁא קָאִים. אָרְחָא דְּנָפִיק תְּחוֹת תְּרֵין נוּקְבִין דְּפַרְדַשְׁקָא, לְאַעְבְּרָא חוֹבָה, דִּכְתִיב וְתִפְאַרְתּוֹ עֲבוֹר עַל פָּשַׁע. תְּחוֹת שִׂפְוָון אֲסַחַר שַׂעֲרָא לְרֵישָׁא אַחֲרָא. אָרְחָא אַחֲרָא נָפִיק תְּחוֹתוֹי. חָפֵי תַּקְרוּבְתָּא דְּבוּסְמָא, לְרֵישָׁא דִּלְעֵילָא. תְּרֵין תַּפּוּחִין אִתְחֲזָן לְאַנְהָרָא בּוּצִינִין. מַזָּלָא דְּכֹלָּא, תַּלְיָיא עַד לִבָּא, בֵּיהּ תַּלְיָין עִלָּאִין וְתַתָּאִין.

**16.** THE FIRST FEATURE IS THAT the precious, WHICH IS THE BEARD, starts to form in front of the opening of the ears, MEANING OPPOSITE THE OPENINGS OF THE EARS, and descends beautifully DOWNWARDS TO THE BEGINNING OF THE LIPS. 2) THERE ARE HAIRS at the top of the lips, from the top OF THE RIGHT LIP to the top OF THE LEFT LIP. 3) There is a path CLEAR OF HAIR that emerges below the two nostrils to remove sins, as it is written, "And it is His glory (Heb. *tiferet*) to pass over transgressions" (Mishlei 19:11). 4) THE HAIRS below the lips again become another top. 5) Another path, FREE OF HAIR, emerges under it, MEANING IN THE MIDDLE

OF THE HAIRS AT THE LOWER LIP. 6) An offering of spices, MEANING HAIRS, covers THE FACE FROM BELOW to the top OF THE UPPER LIP. 7) Two apples, MEANING THE CHEEKS THAT ARE FREE OF HAIR, are visible to light the candles. 8) From the overall Mazal, MEANING THE HAIRS THAT SPREAD AND hang as far as the heart, extend the upper and lower beings, MEANING THE UPPER EXPANSE OF THE BEARD THAT IS CALLED 'SUPERNAL MAZAL'.

17. אִינּוּן דְּתַלְיָין לָא נָפְקִין דָּא מִן דָּא. חַפְיָין זְעִירִין עַל גְּרוֹנָא דִּיקִירוּ. רַבְרְבִין, מִתְשַׁעֲרִין בְּשִׁיעוּרָא שְׁלִים. שִׂפְוָון אִתְפְּנוּן מִכָּל סִטְרִין, זַכָּאָה לְמַאן דְּנָשִׁיק מֵאִינּוּן נְשִׁיקִין. בְּהַהִיא מַזָּלָא דְּכֹלָּא נַגְדִין תְּלֵיסַר מְשִׁיחִין דַּאֲפַרְסְמוֹנָא דַּכְיָא. כֹּלָּא בְּהַאי מַזָּלָא שְׁכִיחַ, וְסָתִים.

17. THE NINTH FEATURE IS THAT the SHORT HAIRS that hang BETWEEN THE HAIRS OF THE UPPER EXPANSE OF THE BEARD do not stick out one from the other, FOR THEY ARE ALL THE SAME SIZE. THE TENTH CHAREACTERISTIC IS the short HAIRS that cover the neck CLOSE TO the precious BEARD. THE ELEVENTH FEATURE IS long HAIRS that are in full length THAT HANG OVER THE NECK. THE TWELFTH FEATURE IS the lips, free of hair from all sides. Blessed is he who kisses with these kisses. THE THIRTEENTH FEATURE IS THAT in the overall Mazal flow thirteen RIVERS of fine balsam tree oil. Everything is in this Mazal, which is concealed, NAMELY THE LOWER EXPANSE OF THE BEARD THAT IS CALLED 'THE LOWER MAZAL'.

18. בְּזִמְנָא דְּמָטָא תִּשְׁרֵי, יַרְחָא שְׁבִיעָאָה, מִשְׁתַּכְחֵי אִלֵּין תְּלֵיסַר בְּעָלְמָא עִלָּאָה וּמִתְפַּתְּחֵי תְּלֵיסַר תַּרְעֵי דְּרַחֲמֵי, בְּהַהוּא זִמְנָא דִּרְשׁוּ יְיָ בְּהִמָּצְאוֹ כְּתִיב.

18. When Tishrei arrives, which is the seventh month, these thirteen FEATURES are in the upper world, WHICH IS BINAH, and the thirteen Gates of Mercy open there. Concerning that time, IT IS WRITTEN, "Seek Hashem while He may be found" (Yeshayah 55:6).

19. וַיֹּאמֶר אֱלֹהִים תַּדְשֵׁא הָאָרֶץ דֶּשֶׁא עֵשֶׂב מַזְרִיעַ זֶרַע עֵץ פְּרִי וְגוֹ',

הַיְינוּ דִכְתִיב וְעִנִּיתֶם אֶת נַפְשׁוֹתֵיכֶם בְּתִשְׁעָה לַחֹדֶשׁ בָּעֶרֶב. אֲדֹנָי יְדֹו״ד אַתָּה הַחִלּוֹתָ לְהַרְאוֹת אֶת עַבְדְּךָ אֶת גָּדְלֶךָ. יהו״ה שְׁלִים בְּסִטְרוֹי. וְהָכָא בִּרְחִישׁוּתָא דָּא דְאַרְעָא, לָא שְׁלִים.

**19.** "And Elohim said, Let the earth bring forth grass, herb yielding seed, and fruit tree yielding fruit after its kind..." (Beresheet 1:11). This is the meaning of, "You shall afflict your souls" (Vayikra 16:31) in the ninth of the month at evening. It is also written, "Adonai Hashem, You have begun to show Your servant Your greatness" (Devarim 3:24). HERE THE NAME Yud Hei Vav Hei is whole on all sides, MEANING THAT IT ILLUMINATES ON THE RIGHT SIDE AND THE LEFT SIDE TOGETHER. THEREFORE, IT IS WRITTEN, ADONAI YUD HEI VAV HEI AND 'YOUR GREATNESS'. But here, with the awakening of the earth, it is incomplete, FOR ONLY THE LEFT SIDE ILLUMINATES WITHOUT THE RIGHT SIDE.

**20.** יה״י לָא כְּתִיב, קָרֵינָן יו״ד עִלָּאָה יו״ד תַּתָּאָה, וַיִּיצֶר י׳ עִלָּאָה י׳ תַּתָּאָה, יְהִי י׳ עִלָּאָה, י׳ תַּתָּאָה. ה׳ בְּגַוְויְיהוּ. כְּלָלָא דִשְׁלִימוּ. שְׁלִים, וְלָא לְכָל סְטָר. אִתְעֲקַר מֵהַאי אֲתָר שְׁמָא דָא, וְאִשְׁתִּיל בְּאַחֲרָא, כְּתִיב וַיִּטַּע יְיָ׳ אֱלֹהִים.

**20.** It is not written HERE 'let there be (Heb. *yehi*) GRASS AND HERB', WHERE we read an upper Yud and a lower Yud, IN ACCORDANCE WITH THE SECRET OF "*Vayyitzer* (lit. 'And He formed')" (Beresheet 2:19) SPELLED WITH TWO YUDS, the upper Yud BEING UPPER CHOCHMAH and the lower Yud BEING LOWER CHOCHMAH, NAMELY THE NUKVA. THIS IS THE SECRET OF THE TWO YUDS AT THE BEGINNING AND THE END OF THE PERMUTATION YUD ALEPH HEI DALET VAV NUN HEI YUD. *Yehi* CONTAINS upper Yud and lower Yud with Hei between them, FOR HEI IS THE SECRET OF BINAH, FROM WHICH THE LOWER YUD RECEIVES CHOCHMAH. And that is overall perfection, FOR THEN IT RECEIVES CHOCHMAH, WHICH IS perfect, though not from every side BUT ONLY FROM THE LEFT. THEREFORE, this name is uprooted – NAMELY THE NUKVA WHICH IS CALLED 'NAME' – and is planted in a different place as it is written: "And Hashem Elohim planted a garden in Eden..." (Ibid. 8).

**21.** ה׳ בֵּין יו״ד לְיו״ד דְּיְה״י, נָשְׁבָא דְּפַרְדַּשְׁקָא דְעַתִּיקָא, לִזְעֵירָא

דְּאַנְפִּין בְּלָא רוּחָא לָא אִתְקַיְּים. בְּהֵ"א, אִשְׁתַּכְלַל הֵ"א עִלָּאָה הֵ"א
תַּתָּאָה, דִּכְתִיב אֲהָה אֲדֹנָי אֱלֹהִים.

**21.** ANOTHER EXPLANATION: The Hei WRITTEN between the two Yuds of 'Yehi', ALLUDES TO the blowing OF THE SPIRIT (OR: 'WIND') OF CHOCHMAH from the nose of Arich Anpin to Zeir Anpin. Without the spirit OF CHOCHMAH it cannot exist. By the Hei THAT ALLUDES TO THE NOSE OF ARICH ANPIN, the upper Hei OF THE NAME YUD HEI VAV HEI and the lower Hei OF THE NAME YUD HEI VAV HEI were perfected, MEANING THAT THE UPPER HEI, WHICH IS BINAH, RECEIVES CHOCHMAH IN ITS LEFT COLUMN FROM THE NOSE OF ARICH ANPIN AND TRANSFERS TO THE LOWER HEI, WHICH IS THE NUKVA. THEN THE TWO HEI'S ARE TOGETHER, as is written, "Ah (spelled Aleph Hei Hei) Adonai Elohim" (Yirmeyah 1:6). THIS INDICATES THAT WHENEVER THE TWO HEI'S ARE TOGETHER, WHEN THE LOWER HEI RECEIVES CHOCHMAH FROM THE LEFT COLUMN OF THE UPPER HEI, IT IS SAID, ALEPH HEI HEI, WHICH ALLUDES TO A TIME OF TROUBLE. THE NUKVA IS THEN IN TROUBLE, FOR SHE IS DESOLATE AND SERE, AS MENTIONED.

**22.** בְּקִיטְפוֹי דְּקַטְפִין, בְּרוּחָא דְּמַתְקְלִין, יה"ו. י' עִלָּאָה דְּאִתְעַטָּר בְּקִטְרָא דְּעַתִּיקָא, הוּא קְרוּמָא עִלָּאָה דְּאִזְדַכַּךְ וְסָתִים. הֵ"א עִלָּאָה, דְּאִתְעַטָּר בְּרוּחָא דְּנוּקְבִין דְּפַרְדַשְׁקָא, דְּנָפִיק לְאַחֲיָיא. ו' עִלָּאָה, בּוֹצִינָא דְּקַרְדִּינוּתָא דְּאִתְעַטָּר בְּסִטְרוֹי, מִתְפַּשְּׁטָן אַתְוָון לְבָתַר, וְאִתְכְּלִילוּ בִּזְעֵירָא דְּאַפִּין. כְּמָה דְּשַׁרְיָא בְּגוּלְגַלְתָּא, אִשְׁתַּכְּחוּ מִתְפַּשְּׁטָן בְּכָל גּוּפָא, לְשַׁכְלָלָא כֹּלָּא. בַּעֲמַר נְקָא. כַּד תָּלֵי תַּלְיָין אִלֵּין אַתְוָון. כַּד אִתְגַּלֵּי לִזְעֵירָא מִתְיַישְּׁבָן בֵּיהּ אִלֵּין אַתְוָון, וְאִתְקְרֵי בְּהוֹן.

**22.** In the cluster of clusters, in the spirit of the scales, WHICH IS ZEIR ANPIN, IN WHOM LIES THE SCALE AS MENTIONED, AND WHO IS CALLED 'A CLUSTER', AS IS WRITTEN, "MY BELOVED IS TO ME AS A CLUSTER OF HENNA" (SHIR HASHIRIM 1:14) THERE IS Yud-Hei-Vav. HE EXPLAINS: The upper Yud, WHICH IS ABA AND IMA, CALLED 'ABA', is adorned with the bond of Atik, which is a lofty membrane that is purified and hidden. The upper Hei was adorned with the spirit of the two openings of the royal viceroy that emerged to revive, MEANING TO BESTOW CHOCHMAH THAT IS

CALLED 'LIFE'. The upper Vav IS THE CENTRAL COLUMN, AND DA'AT, WHEREIN LIES the hard spark that is crowned on its sides. The letters YUD-HEI-VAV expand afterwards and become part of Zeir Anpin IN ACCORDANCE WITH THE SECRET OF 'THREE EMERGE FROM ONE, ONE EXISTS IN THREE'. Just as YUD-HEI-VAV dwell in the Skull OF ARICH ANPIN, they also spread throughout the body OF ARICH ANPIN, NAMELY ITS SEVEN LOWER SFIROT, CHESED, GVURAH, TIFERET, NETZACH, HOD, YESOD AND MALCHUT, to complete everything. When these letters YUD-HEI-VAV are suspended, THAT IS, CONCEALED, THEY ARE in pure wool. When they appear to Zeir Anpin, the letters YUD-HEI-VAV rest on Him, and He is named after them.

23. יוֹ״ד דְּעַתִּיקָא סָתִים בְּעִטְרוֹי, בְּגִין שְׂמָאלָא אִשְׁתְּכַח ה״ה אִתְפְּתַח בְּאַחֲרָא וְאִינְקִיב בִּתְרֵין נוּקְבִין, וְאִשְׁתְּכַח בְּתִקּוּנִין. וָ״ו אִתְפְּתַח בְּאַחֲרָא, דִּכְתִיב הוֹלֵךְ לְדוֹדִי לְמֵישָׁרִים. בְּבוּצִינָא דְּקַרְדִּינוּתָא לְמִכְסְיָא פִּתְחָא.

23. The Yud OF YUD HEI VAV HEI in Atik is concealed with its crowns, because the Left is present, WHICH CAN BE RESOLVED ONLY BY THE SCALE. The Hei is opened by another Hei, NAMELY THE HEI OF ZEIR ANPIN, WHEREIN IS THE PLACE OF REVELATION. THEREFORE, HEI, WHEN FULLY SPELLED, IS SPELLED WITH ANOTHER HEI, NAMELY HEI-HEI. IT IS composed of two females, BECAUSE THE LAST HEI, WHICH IS MALCHUT, IS included IN IT and acquired its features. Vav is opened by another Vav that is in Zeir Anpin, as written, "goes to my beloved directly" (Shir Hashirim 7:11), AS THE SUPERNAL FEATURES GO TO MY BELOVED, THAT IS ZEIR ANPIN. FOR IN HIM IS the hard spark to cover the entrance of Ima. THEREFORE, VAV FULLY SPELLED IS SPELLED WITH ANOTHER VAV, NAMELY VAV-VAV.

24. ו׳ לְעֵילָא ו׳ לְתַתָּא, ה׳ לְעֵילָא ה׳ לְתַתָּא. י׳ לְעֵילָא וּבָהּ לָא אִשְׁתָּתַּף אַחֲרָא, וְלָא סָלִיק בַּהֲדָהּ, בַּר רְמִיזָא דְּרָמִיז כַּד אִתְגַּלְיָין תְּרֵין וּמִתְחַבְּרָן בְּחַד דַּרְגָּא, חַד רִגְשָׁא בְּגִין לְאִתְפָּרְשָׁא, ו״ד כְּלִילָן בְּיוֹ״ד וָוִי כַּד אִסְתַּלָּק הַאי, וְאִתְגַּלְיָין.

24. THUS THERE IS Vav above IN THE HEAD AND THERE IS Vav below IN ZEIR ANPIN. THERE IS Hei above IN THE HEAD AND THERE IS Hei below IN ZEIR ANPIN; THIS IS WHY THEY ARE DOUBLED IN FULL SPELLING, AS MENTIONED, BECAUSE ABOVE THEY ARE CONCEALED AND BELOW THEY ARE REVEALED. Yud is above, but no other YUD partakes in it – AS IN THE CASE OF HEI AND VAV – or comes out WITH IT WHEN PRONOUNCED, except by allusion, BECAUSE VAV-DALET IN THE FULL SPELLING OF YUD HAVE THE SAME NUMERICAL VALUE AS YUD (= 10). THIS IS AN ALLUSION THAT IT INCLUDES A SECOND, LOWER YUD, meaning that two were revealed IN YUD – SUPERNAL ABA AND IMA, who join in one level, trembling together in order to separate FROM THE LEFT. AND THIS IS Vav Dalet that are included in Yud Vav Dalet, YUD BEING SUPERNAL ABA AND VAV DALET SUPERNAL IMA. Woe when ABA, YUD, departs, AND VAV DALET are revealed.

25. אִינּוּן בּוּסְמִין דְּטִיפְסָא שְׁרִיקִין, דְּעַבְרֵי לָא מִתְעַכְּבָא בְּדוּכְתָּא, וְהַחַיּוֹת רָצוֹא וָשׁוֹב. בְּרַח לְךָ אֶל מְקוֹמֶךָ. אִם תַּגְבִּיהַ כַּנֶּשֶׁר וְאִם בֵּין כּוֹכָבִים שִׂים קִנֶּךָ מִשָּׁם אוֹרִידְךָ.

25. These spices – MEANING THE ILLUMINATIONS OF CHOCHMAH CALLED 'SPICES' AND 'SCENT' – of the red engravings, WHICH ARE ALL THE ASPECTS OF THE LEFT COLUMN, WHICH ARE RED, that pass through TO ILLUMINATE, do not mingle at the place, BUT RATHER RETURN IMMEDIATELY TO THEIR PLACE, AS WRITTEN, "And the living creatures ran and returned" (Yechezkel 1:14), AS THEY IMMEDIATELY RETURN TO THEIR PLACE. LIKEWISE, "Flee to your place" (Bemidbar 24:11), means that he hastens to return to his place. This is the secret of the verse, "Though you do soar aloft like the eagle, and though you do set your nest among the stars" (Ovadyah 1:4), "from there I will bring you down" (Ibid.).

26. וַתּוֹצֵא הָאָרֶץ דֶּשֶׁא. אֵימָתַי. כַּד שְׁמָא אִתְנְטַע. וּכְדֵין אֲוִירָא נָפִיק, וְנִצוֹצָא אִזְדְּמָן. חַד גּוּלְגַּלְתָּא אִתְפָּשַׁט בְּסִטְרוֹי, טַלָּא מָלֵי עָלַהּ, דִּתְרֵי גְּווֹנֵי.

26. "And the earth brought forth grass" (Beresheet 1:12). When DID THIS OCCUR? IT WAS when the name, WHICH IS THE NUKVA, was planted. AND

SO FROM ABA AND IMA, emerged air, WHICH IS THE LIGHT OF CHASSADIM FROM ABA, and a spark, WHICH IS THE LIGHT OF GVUROT FROM IMA. WHEN THE AIR AND THE SPARK JOINED TOGETHER, a Skull extended from them, WHICH IS KETER OF ZEIR ANPIN at its sides. Dew filled over it, THE SKULL, of two colors, NAMELY WHITE AND RED IN THE SECRET OF, "FOR YOUR DEW IS THE DEW OF LIGHT" (YESHAYAH 26:19), WHICH ARE THE LIGHTS OF CHESED AND GVURAH. AND THIS IS THE FIRST OF THE SEVEN FEATURES OF THE SKULL OF ZEIR ANPIN.

27. תְּלַת חַלָלִין דְּאַתְוָון רְשִׁימִין, אִתְגַּלְיָין בֵּיהּ. אוּכְמִין כְּעוֹרְבָא תַּלְיָין עַל נוּקְבִין עֲמִיקִין, דְּלָא יָכִיל לְמִשְׁמַע יְמִינָא וּשְׂמָאלָא. הָכָא חַד אָרְחָא לְעֵילָא דַּקִיק.

27. SECOND FEATURE: Three spaces of engraved letters, NAMELY YUD-HEI-VAV, appear in it. THIRD FEATURE: HAIRS, black as a raven, hang over the deep openings OF THE EARS, and one cannot hear from the right or the left, BECAUSE THE HAIRS, WHICH ARE JUDGMENTS, BLOCK THEM. Here, IN RELATION TO THE HAIRS ON THE SKULL OF ZEIR ANPIN, THERE IS ABOVE one thin path, NAMELY THE PATH AT THE CENTER OF THE HEAD THAT DIVIDES THE HAIRS INTO RIGHT AND LEFT.

28. מִצְחָא דְּלָא נָהִיר, קְטָטוּתָא דְּעָלְמָא. בַּר כַּד רַעֲוָא אַשְׁגַּח בֵּיהּ. עַיְינִין דִּתְלַת גְּוָונֵי, לְמִרְתַּת קַמַּיְיהוּ אִתְסְחָן בְּחֶלְבָּא דְּנָהִיר. כְּתִיב עֵינֶיךָ תִּרְאֶינָה יְרוּשָׁלַיִם נָוֶה שַׁאֲנָן, וּכְתִיב צֶדֶק יָלִין בָּהּ. נָוֶה שַׁאֲנָן, עַתִּיקָא דְּסָתִים, עֵינֶךָ כְּתִיב.

28. THE FOURTH FEATURE IS a non-luminous forehead, FROM WHICH ARE DRAWN JUDGMENT AND strife to the world except AT TIMES OF GREATNESS, when the will OF THE FOREHEAD OF ARICH ANPIN supervises THE FOREHEAD OF ZEIR ANPIN. THE FIFTH FEATURE IS eyes of three colors – WHICH ARE BLACK, RED AND GREEN – which are to be feared, BECAUSE ALL THESE COLORS ALLUDE TO JUDGMENTS, FOR RED IS LEFT AND GREEN IS THE CENTRAL COLUMN AND BLACK IS MALCHUT. DURING GREATNESS, they wash in luminous milk, WHICH IS THE SECRET OF CHESED THAT FLOWS from Atika, as is written, "Your eyes shall see Jerusalem a quiet habitation" (Yeshayah 33:20), MEANING FREE OF

JUDGMENT. It is also written, "Righteousness lodged in it" (Yeshayah 1:21), SO THERE IS IN IT JUDGMENT THAT IS CALLED 'RIGHTEOUSNESS'. HE ANSWERS: IT SAYS "quiet habitation," WHEN THE EYE OF the hidden Atik SHINES IN ACCORDANCE WITH THE MEANING OF "WASHED IN MILK" (SHIR HASHIRIM 5:12), because it is spelled *Eynecha* (lit. 'your eyes') WITHOUT YUD, THE MARK OF PLURAL. IN ATIKA, THERE IS NO LEFT AND BOTH EYES ARE CONSIDERED AS THE RIGHT EYE.

29. חוֹטָמָא פַּרְצוּפָא דִזְעֵירָא, לְאִשְׁתְּמוֹדְעָא. תְּלַת שַׁלְהוֹבִין מִתּוֹקְדִין בְּנוּקְבוֹי. דַּרְגָּא עֲקִימָא, לְמִשְׁמַע טָב וּבִישׁ.

**29.** THE SIXTH FEATURE IS the nose of the face that is short for identification, BECAUSE THE FACE IS RECOGNIZED BY THE NOSE, AS OUR SAGES HAVE SAID, 'WITNESS CAN TESTIFY ONLY WHEN THERE IS A FACE TOGETHER WITH A NOSE'. Three flames burn in its nostrils, WHICH ARE THE THREE ASPECTS OF JUDGMENT – JUDGMENT DRAWN FROM BINAH, FROM MALCHUT AND FROM THE LEFT COLUMN. THE SEVENTH FEATURE IS curved level to hear good and evil, MEANING THE EARS DURING GREATNESS, AFTER THE HAIR THAT BLOCKED THEM IS REMOVED, AS MENTIONED. FOR THEN THEY ARE OPENED TO HEAR GOOD AND EVIL TO DO GOOD FOR THE GOOD PEOPLE AND TO PUNISH THE EVIL, AND TO RECEIVE THE PRAYERS OF THE LOWER BEINGS.

30. כְּתִיב אֲנִי יְיָ' הוּא שְׁמִי. וּכְתִיב אֲנִי אָמִית וַאֲחַיֶּה. וּכְתִיב וַאֲנִי אֶשָּׂא וַאֲנִי אֶסְבּוֹל. הוּא עָשָׂנוּ וְלוֹ אֲנַחְנוּ. וְהוּא בְּאֶחָד וּמִי יְשִׁיבֶנּוּ. הוּא אִקְרֵי מַאן דְּסָתִים וְלָא שְׁכִיחַ, הוּא מַאן דְּלָא אִזְדַּמָּן לְעֵינָא. הוּא מַאן דְּלָא אִקְרֵי בִּשְׁמָא.

**30.** It is written, "I am Hashem, that (lit. 'He') is My name" (Yeshayah 42:8), SPOKEN IN THE FIRST PERSON "I," AND THE THIRD PERSON, "HE," IN ONE CLAUSE. IT SHOULD HAVE SAID, 'I AM, HASHEM IS MY NAME.' YET IT SAYS, "I" AND "HE," ARE TWO NAMES, as written, "I kill and I make alive" (Devarim 32:39), and it is also written, "And I will bear; and I will carry" (Yeshayah 46:4). SO WE SEE THAT "I" IS A NAME, MEANING THE NAME OF MALCHUT, AND "HE" IS ALSO A NAME. It is written, "He has made us and we are His" (Tehilim 100:3), AND "But He is

unchangeable, and who can turn Him" (Iyov 23:13). SO WE SEE THAT HE IS ALSO CALLED BY THE NAME "HE," BECAUSE "He" is used for one who is hidden and not present. "He" is used for one who is not visible to the eye, MEANING THAT HE IS NOT READY TO RECEIVE CHOCHMAH THAT IS CALLED 'EYE'. He is used for one who has no name, NAMELY BINAH, WHICH IS YISRAEL SABA AND TEVUNAH.

31. הוּא, ה' כָּלִיל ו'. ו' כָּלִיל א'. וְלָא כָּלִיל ה'. אָלֶף אָזִיל לִי', י' אָזִיל לִי', דְּסָתִים מִכָּל סְתִימִין, דְּלָא מִתְחַבְּרָן בֵּיהּ ו"ד. וַוי כַּד לָא נָהִיר י' בו"ד.

**31.** HE EXPLAINS THE IMPLICATIONS OF THE THREE LETTERS HEI VAV ALEPH (HE), ACCORDING TO WHAT HE SAID ABOVE THAT CONCEALED CHOCHMAH, ABA AND IMA AND YISRAEL-SABA AND TEVUNAH ARE EACH CALLED "He." HE SAYS, Hei OF *HU* (LIT. 'HE'-HEI VAV ALEPH) includes Vav, Vav includes Aleph OF *HU*, but does not include Hei OF *HU*. Aleph goes towards Yud, Yud goes towards the most concealed Yud, to which the Vav Dalet OF YUD FULLY SPELLED are not attached. Woe is when the Yud does not illuminate on Vav Dalet.

32. כַּד אִסְתַּלָּק י' מִן ו"ד בְּחוֹבֵי עָלְמָא, עֶרְיָיתָא דְּכֹלָּא אִשְׁתְּכַח, ע"ד כְּתִיב עֶרְוַת אָבִיךָ לֹא תְגַלֵּה. וְכַד אִסְתָּלִיק יו"ד מִן הֵ"א, ע"ד כְּתִיב וְעֶרְוַת אִמְּךָ לֹא תְגַלֵּה אִמְּךָ הִיא לֹא תְגַלֵּה עֶרְוָתָהּ. אִמְּךָ הִיא וַדַּאי, כִּי אִם לַבִּינָה תִקְרָא וְגוֹ'.

**32.** When Yud departed from Vav Dalet because of the sins of the world, the nakedness of them all was revealed. And about this is written, "The nakedness of your father... shall you not uncover" (Vayikra 18:7); it is written, "or the nakedness of your mother shall you not uncover, SUPERNAL ABA AND IMA, YUD, THAT ARE BOTH CONSIDERED 'ABA'. She is your mother, you shall not uncover her nakedness" (Ibid.), BECAUSE YISRAEL -SABA AND TEVUNAH ARE BOTH CALLED BY THE NAME 'IMA'. She is surely your mother as is written, "if (Heb. *im*) you cry after wisdom (Binah)" (Mishlei 2:3), FOR YISRAEL-SABA AND TEVUNAH, WHICH ARE BINAH, ARE CALLED 'MOTHER' (HEB. *EM*).

## 3. Third Chapter

### A Synopsis

We hear that the Beard was concealed in the scriptures because everything that is hidden and not revealed is lofty and precious. Here the nine features of the Beard are listed, together with the nine clauses beginning in Tehilim 118:5 with "Out of my distress I called on Yah"; it is also stated that these nine features are in the secret of the verse, "And the earth brought forth grass, herb yielding seed after its kind, and tree yielding fruit, whose seed was in itself, after its kind." There are thirteen features of the Beard in the supernal one, Arich Anpin; the lower, Zeir Anpin, appears in nine features of the Beard. The addition of thirteen plus nine yields 22, which is the 22 letters that were engraved through them. Now the discussion turns to various interpretations of the verse, "And Elohim said, Let the waters swarm abundantly with moving creatures that have life." As one explanation is the movement of the lips during prayer, we are told that the prayer in which a person requests something of God is arranged in nine ways. It is said that great attention is necessary in all these nine manners of prayer. God will honor anyone who meditates properly on them, giving him everything he needs in this world and in the World to Come.

We are told that "And Elohim said, Let Us make man" referred not only to man on earth but also supernal man, both male and female; when the one is completed, the other is completed.

33. פִּרְקָא תְּלִיתָאָה תִּשְׁעָה תִּקּוּנִין יַקִּירִין אִתְמְסָרוּ לְדִיקְנָא כָּל מָה דְּאִתְטְמַר וְלָא אִתְגַּלְיָיא עִלָּאָה וְיַקִּירָא אִשְׁתְּכַח. וְהָא גְּנִזֵיהּ קְרָא.

**33.** Third Chapter. Nine precious features were granted to the beard. Everything that is hidden and not revealed is lofty and precious. THE BEARD was concealed in the Scriptures, FOR THERE IS NO MENTION OF THE BEARD SUCH AS, "THE EYES OF HASHEM," "THE EARS OF HASHEM" AND "HIS CHEEKS ARE LIKE A BED OF SPICES" (SHIR HASHIRIM 5:13). BUT THERE IS NO MENTION OF THE BEARD, AND THAT IS BECAUSE IT IS LOFTY AND PRECIOUS.

34. תִּיקוּנָא קַדְמָאָה דְּדִיקְנָא, נִימִין עַל נִימִין מִקַּמֵּי פִּתְחָא דְּאָדְנִין עַד רֵישָׁא דְּפוּמָא. מֵרֵישָׁא הַאי, עַד רֵישָׁא אַחֲרָא אִשְׁתְּכַח. מִתְּחוֹת תְּרֵין

נוּקְבִּין אָרְחָא מַלְיָיא דְּלָא אִתְחֲזְיָיא. עַלְעִין אִתְחַפְיָין מֵהַאי גִּיסָא
וּמֵהַאי גִּיסָא. בְּהוּ אִתְחַזְיָין תַּפּוּחִין סוּמָקִין כְּוַורְדָּא. בְּחַד חוּטָא תַּלְיָין
אוּכְמִין תַּקִּיפִין עַד חַדּוֹי. שִׂפְוָון סוּמָקִין כְּוַורְדָּא אִתְפְּנוּן.

**34.** The first feature of the beard: Hairs upon hairs EMERGE from before the opening of the ears to the top of the mouth, MEANING THE UPPER LIP. THE SECOND FEATURE: It is from this top OF THE LIP to the other top OF THE LIP. THE THIRD FEATURE: THERE IS a path below the two nostrils OF THE NOSE so full OF HAIR that it is invisible. THE FOURTH FEATURE: The cheeks are covered WITH HAIR on one side and the other side. THE FIFTH FEATURE: In them TWO apples OF THE FACE are seen, red as a rose. THE SIXTH FEATURE: on one thread hangs coarse black HAIR down to the chest. THE SEVENTH FEATURE: The lips are free OF HAIR and are as red as a rose.

35. זְעִירִין נַחְתִּין בְּגְרוֹנָא, וּמְחַפְּיָין קְדָלָא. רַבְרְבִין וּזְעִירִין כְּגִידִין
נַחְתִּין בְּשִׁקּוּלָא. בְּאֵלֵין אִשְׁתְּכַח גִּיבָּר וְתַקִּיף מַאן דְּאִשְׁתְּכַח.

**35.** THE EIGHTH FEATURE: Short HAIRS travel down the neck and cover the nape. THE NINTH FEATURE: HAIRS both long and short, HARD as sinews descend equally, MEANING THAT THEY EQUALLY MINGLE WITH EACH OTHER. One who has these nine features is mighty and strong, NAMELY ZEIR ANPIN.

36. כְּתִיב מִן הַמֵּצַר קָרָאתִי יָהּ. תִּשְׁעָה אָמַר דָּוִד עַד כָּל גּוֹיִם סְבָבוּנִי,
לְאַסְחֲרָא וּלְאַגָּנָא עֲלוֹי. וַתּוֹצֵא הָאָרֶץ דֶּשֶׁא עֵשֶׂב מַזְרִיעַ זֶרַע לְמִינֵהוּ
וְעֵץ עוֹשֶׂה פְּרִי אֲשֶׁר זַרְעוֹ בוֹ לְמִינֵהוּ. תִּשְׁעָה אִלֵּין אִתְעֲקָרוּ מִשְּׁמַיָא
שְׁלִים, וְאַשְׁתִּילוּ לְבָתַר בִּשְׁמָא שְׁלִים, דִּכְתִיב וַיִּטַּע יְיָ' אֱלֹהִים. תִּקּוּנִין
דְּדִיקְנָא בִּתְלֵיסַר אִשְׁתְּכָּחָן אִיהִי, דְּהִיא עִלָּאָה. תַּתָּאָה, בְּתִשְׁעָה
אִתְחֲזוּן. כ"ב אַתְוָון אִתְגְּלִיפוּ בְּגִינֵיהוֹן.

**36.** It is written, "Out of my distress I called on Yah" (Tehilim 118:5). David recited nine clauses until "all nations compassed me about" (Ibid. 10), in order to surround HIMSELF WITH THEM and protect himself. THEY CORRESPOND TO THE NINE FEATURES OF THE BEARD OF ZEIR ANPIN.

1. "OUT OF MY DISTRESS I CALLED ON YAH." 2. "YAH ANSWERED ME WITH LIBERATION." 3. "HASHEM IS ON MY SIDE, I WILL NOT FEAR." 4. "HASHEM TAKES MY PART WITH THOSE WHO HELP ME." 5. "IT IS BETTER TO TAKE REFUGE IN HASHEM." 6. A SECOND "IT IS BETTER TO TAKE REFUGE IN HASHEM." TOGETHER WITH THE THREE TIMES 'MAN' IS MENTIONED, WHICH ALLUDE TO THREE FEATURES, THEY ARE NINE, AND THESE NINE FEATURES ARE IN THE SECRET OF THE VERSE, "And the earth, brought forth grass, herb yielding seed after its kind, and tree, yielding fruit, whose seed was in itself, after its kind" (Beresheet 1:12). These nine FEATURES OF THE BEARD were uprooted from a whole name, NAMELY FROM THE THIRTEEN FEATURES OF THE BEARD OF ARICH ANPIN, AND CAME TO ZEIR ANPIN. Afterwards, they were AGAIN planted in a complete name, as is said, "And Hashem Elohim planted", WHICH IS THE FULL NAME OF ATIK AND ZEIR ANPIN. There are thirteen features of the Beard in the supernal one, NAMELY ARICH ANPIN. The lower, WHICH IS ZEIR ANPIN, appears in nine features OF THE BEARD, AND THIRTEEN PLUS NINE EQUALS 22. These are the 22 letters that were engraved through them.

37. עַל הַאי, חֶלְמָא דְּאָחִיד דִּיקְנָא דְּב"ן עִלָּאָה בִּידֵיהּ, שְׁלִים בְּמָארֵיהּ. שַׂנְאִין תְּחוֹתוֹי יִכְנְעוּן. כ"ש דִּיקְנָא עִלָּאָה דְּנָהִירָא בְּתַתָּאָה, דְּעִלָּאָה רַב חֶסֶד אִקְרֵיהּ, בִּזְעֵירָא חֶסֶ"ד סְתָם, כַּד אִצְטְרִיךְ נְהִירוּ אַנְהַר וְאִקְרֵי רַב חֶסֶד.

37. Therefore, IF ONE SEES IN a dream that he was holding in his hand the beard of an important man, then he is at peace with his Master and his enemies shall be subdued under him. The upper Beard, OF ARICH ANPIN, that illuminates to the lower BEARD OF ZEIR ANPIN is more so, because the upper Beard is called 'abundant in Chesed', while in Zeir Anpin it is CALLED plain 'Chesed'. When he needs light, the upper Beard then illuminates and HE TOO is called abundant in Chesed.

38. וַיֹּאמֶר אֱלֹהִים יִשְׁרְצוּ הַמַּיִם שֶׁרֶץ נֶפֶשׁ חַיָּה, כְּלוֹמַר, חַ"י יָ"ה אִתְפַּשַּׁט נְהִירוּ דְּדָא בְּדָא, כֹּלָּא אִתְרַחֲשׁוּן בְּזִמְנָא חֲדָא, מַיִם טָבָאן מַיִם בִּישָׁן. בְּגִין דְּאָמַר יִשְׁרְצוּ, אִתְכְּלָלוּ דָּא בְּדָא. חַיָּה עִלָּאָה, חַיָּה תַּתָּאָה. חַיָּה טָבָא. חַיָּה בִּישָׁא.

**38.** "And Elohim said, Let the waters swarm abundantly with moving creatures that have life (Heb. *nefesh chayah*)" (Beresheet 1:20), meaning Chai (lit. 'living') Yud Hei, BECAUSE CHAYAH INCLUDES THE LETTERS OF CHAI AND YUD HEI. CHAI IS YESOD OF ZEIR ANPIN, YUD HEI ARE ABA AND IMA, AND "LET THE WATERS SWARM" MEANS THAT the light of one should spread into the other, MEANING THAT THE LIGHT OF YUD HEI WILL SPREAD INTO CHAI, YESOD OF ZEIR ANPIN. THUS LIVING NEFESH WILL EMERGE, WHICH ARE THE NUKVA AND ALSO THE NEFESH OF ADAM. Everything swarmed at the same time, both good waters OF HOLINESS and evil waters OF THE OTHER SIDE. Once He said, "Let the waters swarm", they were intermingled and a supernal living creature (Heb. *chayah*), NAMELY THE NUKVA, a lower living creature, NAMELY THE NEFESH OF ADAM, a good living creature, WHICH IS THE NUKVA, and an evil living creature, WHICH IS LILIT, came out. FOR "LIVING CREATURE THAT MOVES" (IBID. 21) IS LILIT, AS MENTIONED ABOVE.

39. ד״א יִשְׁרְצוּ הַמַּיִם, תַּרְגּוּם יְרַחֲשׁוּן. כְּלוֹמַר, כַּד מְרַחֲשִׁין בְּשִׂפְוָותֵיהּ פִּתְגָּמֵי צְלוֹתָא, בְּזַכּוּתָא, וּבְנִקְיוּת דַּעְתָּא, וּבְמַיָּא הֲוָה רָחִישׁ נַפְשָׁא חַיָּתָא. וְכַד בָּעֵי בַּר נָשׁ לְסַדְּרָא צְלוֹתֵיהּ לְמָארֵיהּ, וְשִׂפְוָותֵיהּ מְרַחֲשָׁן בְּהַאי גַּוְונָא מִתַּתָּא לְעֵילָּא, לְסַלְּקָא יְקָרָא דְמָארֵיהּ, לְאַתָר דְּשַׁקְיוּ דַּעֲמִיקוּ דְבֵירָא, נָגִיד וְנָפִיק. לְבָתַר יַנְגִיד לְאַמְשָׁכָא מִלְּעֵילָּא לְתַתָּא, מֵהַהוּא שַׁקְיָא דְּנַחְלָא, לְכָל דַּרְגָּא וְדַרְגָּא, עַד דַּרְגָּא בַּתְרָאָה לְאַמְשָׁכָא נְדָבָה לְכֹלָּא מֵעֵילָּא לְתַתָּא. לְבָתַר בָּעֵי לְקַשְּׁרָא קִשְׁרָא בְּכֹלָּא, קִשְׁרָא דְכַוָּונָה דִמְהֵימָנוּתָא וְיַעְבְּדוּן כָּל מִשְׁאֲלוֹהִי, בֵּין שְׁאֶלְתָּא דְצִבּוּרָא, בֵּין שְׁאֶלְתָּא דִיְחִידָא.

**39.** According to another explanation, "Let the waters swarm," is translated into Aramaic as 'move', meaning that his lips move with words of prayer purely and with a clear mind. The living Nefesh moves in CLEANSING AND PURIFYING waters, for when a person wishes to set out his prayer to his Master, his lips move thus: from below upwards, in order to elevate the glory of his Master to the place of the water source of the deep well, WHICH IS BINAH. Later, it will flow and draw from above downwards, from that water source of the river, WHICH IS BINAH, to each and every grade down to the last grade, WHICH IS MALCHUT, so that it may draw willingly for

everyone from above downwards. Afterwards, He has to connect everything, NAMELY TO UNITE ALL THE GRADES IN BLESSED ENDLESS LIGHT, in a connection of devotion of Faith; and so all his requests, individual and communal, will be fulfilled.

40. וּשְׁאֶלְתָּא דְּאִית לְבַר נָשׁ לְשַׁאֲלָא מִמָּארֵיהּ, הֵן מְסוּדְּרוֹת בַּט' גְּווֹנֵי, אִית בְּאַלְפָא בֵּיתָא, וְאִית בְּאַדְכַּר מְכִילוֹהִי דְּקוּדְשָׁא בְּרִיךְ הוּא, רַחוּם וְחַנּוּן וְגוֹ'. אִית בִּשְׁמָהָן יַקִּירָן דְּקוּדְשָׁא בְּרִיךְ הוּא, כְּגוֹן אֶהְיֶה יָהּ יְהוּ אֵל אֱלֹהִים יְיָ' צְבָאוֹת שַׁדַּי אֲדֹנָי. אִית בְּע"ס, כְּגוֹן: מ' י' ה' נ' ת' ג' ח' ב' ח' כ'. אִית בְּאַדְכַּר צַדִּיקַיָּא, כְּגוֹן הָאָבוֹת וְהַנְּבִיאִים וְהַמְּלָכִים. אִית בְּשִׁירֵי וּבְתוּשְׁבְּחָתֵּי, דְּאִית בְּהוֹן קַבָּלָה אֲמִתִּית. וְעֵילָּא מִנְּהוֹן מַאן דְּיָדַע לְתַקֵּן תִּקּוּנִין לְמָארֵיהּ, כַּדְקָא יֵאוֹת. וְאִית בִּידִיעָה סַלְּקָא מִתַּתָּא לְעֵילָּא, וְאִית מַאן דְּיָדַע לְהַמְשִׁיךְ שִׁפְעָא מֵעֵילָא לְתַתָּא.

40. The prayer in which a person asks of his Master is arranged in nine ways: 1) THE PRAYER is ARRANGED ACCORDING to the alphabet. 2) It is ARRANGED by mentioning the attributes of the Holy One, blessed be He: Merciful, Kind, etc. 3) It is ARRANGED by the precious names of the Holy One, blessed be He, namely, Eheyeh, Yah, Yud Hei Vav, El, Elohim, Yud Hei Vav Hei, Tzva'ot, Shadai, Adonai. 4) It is ARRANGED according to the ten Sfirot, which are Malchut, Yesod, Hod, Netzach, Tiferet, Gvurah, Chesed, Binah, Chochmah, Keter. 5) There is mentioning of the righteous, namely the patriarchs, the prophets and the kings. 6) It includes hymns and praises that have true acceptance. 7) And above all that, one who knows how to prepare corrections for his Master properly. 8) There is knowledge of how to raise from below upwards. 9) And there is one who knows how to draw plenty from above downwards.

41. וּבְכָל ט' גְּווֹנֵי אִלֵּין, צְרִיכָא כַּוָּנָה כַּוָּנָה גְּדוֹלָה, וְאִי לָא עֲלֵיהּ קְרָא דִּכְתִיב וּבוֹזֵי יֵקָלּוּ. וּבְכַוָּנַת אָמֵן, דְּהוּא כָּלִיל תְּרֵין שְׁמָהָן יְהֹו"ה אֲדֹנָ"י. וְהָאֶחָד גָּנִיז טוּבֵיהּ וּבִרְכוֹהִי, בְּאוֹצָר הַנִּקְרָא הֵיכָל, וְהוּא רָמוּז בְּפָסוּק וְה' בְּהֵיכַל קָדְשׁוֹ הַס מִפָּנָיו וּלְדָא רָמְזוּ רַז"ל, כָּל טוּב הָאָדָם בְּבֵיתוֹ, שֶׁנֶּאֱמַר בְּכָל בֵּיתִי נֶאֱמָן הוּא, וּמִתַּרְגְּמִינָן בְּכָל דְּעַמֵּי.

**41.** In all these nine manners OF PRAYER, great attention is necessary. If not, it is said about him, "and they that despise Me shall be lightly esteemed" (I Shmuel 2:30). And on meditating on answering Amen, ONE HAS TO DIRECT HIS THOUGHT that he is combining the two names Yud Hei Vav Hei Adonai, WHOSE NUMERICAL VALUE IS 91 AS IS THAT OF AMEN. And one NAME, WHICH IS YUD HEI VAV HEI, ZEIR ANPIN, hides its goodness and blessings in the treasury called 'sanctuary', WHICH IS ADONAI, MALCHUT. This is alluded to in the passage, "But Hashem is in His Temple; let all the earth keep silence before Him" (Chavakuk 2:20). To this the sages alluded, 'All the goodness of man lies in his house', BECAUSE THE NUMERICAL VALUE OF MAN (HEB. *ADAM*) IS 45, THAT OF THE NAME OF YUD HEI VAV HEI, FULLY SPELLED WITH ALEPH, AND ALL HIS GOODNESS IN HIS HOUSE, WHICH IS ADONAI, MALCHUT, as is said, "In all My house he is trusted" (Bemidbar 12:7), which is translated into Aramaic as, "in all My people," MEANING MALCHUT.

42. וְאִי מְכַוֵּון בְּכָל חַד וְחַד מט׳ גְּווֵנֵי כַּדְקָא יֵאוֹת, דָּא הוּא בַּר נָשׁ דְּאוֹקִיר לִשְׁמָא דְּמָארֵיהּ לִשְׁמָא קַדִּישָׁא, וְעַל דָּא כְּתִיב כִּי מְכַבְּדַי אֲכַבֵּד וּבוֹזַי יֵקַלּוּ, אֲכַבֵּד בְּעָלְמָא דֵּין, לְקַיֵּים וּלְמֶעְבַּד כָּל צָרְכוֹי. וְיֶחֱזוּן כָּל עַמְמֵי אַרְעָא, אֲרֵי שְׁמָא דְּה׳ אִתְקְרֵי עָלֵיהּ, וְיִדְחֲלוּן מִנֵּיהּ. וּבְעָלְמָא דְּאָתֵי, יִזְכֵּי לְמֵיקַם בִּמְחִיצַת חֲסִידִים, אַף עַל פִּי דְּלָא קָרֵי כָּל צוֹרְכֵיהּ, כֵּיוָן דְּזָכָה לְאַשְׁגָּחָא יְדִיעַת מָארֵיהּ, וְאִיכְוַון בֵּיהּ כַּדְקָא יֵאוֹת.

**42.** If one meditates on each of the nine manners OF PRAYER, such is a person who honors the name of his Master, His Holy Name. Of this, it is written, "for them that honor Me will I honor, and they that despise Me shall be lightly esteemed." I shall honor him in this world to fulfill and maintain all his needs. All the nations of the world will see that he is named after Yud Hei Vav Hei, and they will fear him. In the World to Come, he shall stand in the proximity of the pious, MEANING IN THE SECTION OF THE PIOUS, even if he did not study the Torah as much as necessary, since he merited to behold the knowledge of his Master and had the proper intention.

43. מַאי וּבוֹזַי יֵקַלּוּ. דָּא הוּא מַאן דְּלָא יָדַע לְאַחֲדָא שְׁמָא קַדִּישָׁא, וּלְקַשְׁרָא קִשְׁרָא דִּמְהֵימְנוּתָא, וּלְאַמְשָׁכָא לְאֲתַר דְּאִצְטְרִיךְ, וּלְאוֹקִיר שְׁמָא דְּמָארֵיהּ טָב לֵיהּ דְּלָא אִתְבְּרֵי. וכ״ש מַאן דְּלָא אִתְכַּוֵּון בְּאָמֵן.

וְעַל דָּא, כָּל מַאן דְּמַרְחִישׁ בְּשִׂפְוָותֵיה בִּנְקִיוּתָא דְּלִבָּא, בְּמַיָּא דִּמְנַקֵי,
מַאי כְּתִיב בַּהֲדֵיה, וַיֹּאמֶר אֱלֹהִים נַעֲשֶׂה אָדָם, כְּלוֹמַר, בִּשְׁבִיל אָדָם
דְּיָדַע לְאַחֲדָא צֶלֶם וּדְמוּת כַּדְקָא יֵאוֹת, וְיִרְדּוּ בִדְגַת הַיָּם.

(עד כאן ד"א)

43. What is the meaning of, "and they that despise Me shall be lightly
esteemed"? This refers to one who does not know how to unify the Holy
Name or tie the bond of Faith, and cause a flowing to the place that needs it
and to honor his Master's name. It were better had he not been created,
especially one who does not have proper meditation on Amen. For it is
written of everyone who moves his lips with a clean heart and with
cleansing waters, "And Elohim said, Let us make man" (Beresheet 1:26).
This relates to a person who knows how to properly unite image and
likeness, WHICH ARE ZEIR ANPIN THAT IS CALLED 'IMAGE' AND THE
NUKVA THAT IS CALLED 'LIKENESS'. "and let them have dominion over the
fish of the sea."

**(End of the other explanation from verse 39)**

44. וַיֹּאמֶר אֱלֹהִים נַעֲשֶׂה אָדָם. הָאָדָם לָא כְּתִיב, אֶלָּא אָדָם סְתָם,
לְאַפָּקָא אָדָם דִּלְעֵילָא. דְּאִתְעֲבִיד בִּשְׁמָא שְׁלִים. כַּד אִשְׁתְּלִים דָּא,
אִשְׁתְּלִים דָּא. אִשְׁתְּלִים דְּכַר וְנוּקְבָּא לְאַשְׁלְמָא כֹּלָּא. יְדֹוָ"ד סְטְרָא
דִּדְכַר. אֱלֹהִים סְטְרָא דְּנוּקְבָּא. אִתְפָּשַׁט דְּכוּרָא, וְאִתְתְּקַן בְּתִקּוּנוֹי
כְּאָמָא, בְּפוּמֵיה דְּאָמָה. מַלְכִין דְּאִתְבְּטָלוּ, הָכָא אִתְקַיָּימוּ.

44. "And Elohim said, Let us make man." It is not written, 'The man',
WHICH WOULD HAVE IMPLIED ONLY THE FIRST MAN, but man in general,
MEANING in order to bring forth AND PERFECT ALSO supernal man, THAT
IS, MALE AND FEMALE THAT ARE CALLED 'MAN' that is made now with a
whole name, YUD HEI VAV HEI ELOHIM. For when the one is completed,
then the other is completed, MEANING THAT WHEN THE LOWER MAN IS
COMPLETED THE UPPER MAN IS COMPLETED. He is perfected with male
and female, so as to complete everything. Yud Hei Vav Hei is CALLED 'the
aspect of male', WHICH IS ZEIR ANPIN, Elohim is CALLED 'the female

aspect', WHICH IS MALCHUT, IN SUCH A WAY THAT YUD HEI VAV HEI ELOHIM IS A FULL NAME. The male, ZEIR ANPIN, expands and is built with his implements like Ima at the mouth of the penis, MEANING WITH THE CORONA OF YESOD. The SEVEN kings that were gone exist here, THROUGH YESOD OF ZEIR ANPIN, WHICH IS THE CENTRAL COLUMN.

45. דִּינִין דִּדְכוּרָא תַּקִּיפִין בְּרֵישָׁא, בְּסוֹפָא נַיְיחִין. דְּנוּקְבָּא בְּאִיפְּכָא. וְי״ה קוּנְטִירִין דְּקִיטוּרָא בְּעִטְפוֹי שְׁקִיעִין. י׳ זְעֵירָא בְּגַוָּוהָא אִשְׁתְּכַח.

**45.** THE MALE IS THE SECRET OF THE RIGHT COLUMN, WHICH IS MAINLY OF CHASSADIM. THEREFORE, Judgments of the male are strong at the beginning, and are benign at the end. It is the opposite by the female, SINCE SHE IS OF THE LEFT COLUMN IN THE ASPECT OF CHOCHMAH WITHOUT CHASSADIM, WHICH IS DARKNESS THAT DOESN'T ILLUMINATE, and fifteen hard judgments of smoke are submerged in her lap. There is a small Yud in her, WHICH IS THE SECRET OF LOWER CHOCHMAH THAT IS CALLED 'YUD', WHICH, BEING MALCHUT, IS SMALL.

46. אִי אִתְבְּסָמוּ דִּינִין, בָּעָא עַתִּיקָא. אָתָא חִוְיָא עַל נוּקְבָּא, וְקִינָא דְּזוּהֲמָא אִתְתָּקַן בְּגַוָּוה, לְמֶעְבַּד מָדוֹרָא בִּישָׁא. דִּכְתִיב וַתַּהַר וַתֵּלֶד אֶת קַיִן. קִינָא דְּמָדוֹרָא דְּרוּחִין בִּישִׁין וְעָלְעוּלִין וְקַטְפוּרִין.

**46.** Atika wanted to see if the Judgments OF THE NUKVA were mollified, ADAM AND HIS WIFE JOINED TOGETHER. The serpent came upon Eve WITH THE TEMPTATION OF THE TREE OF KNOWLEDGE OF GOOD AND EVIL. A nest of filth was formed in her, IN THE FEMALE, and became the dwelling place of evil, for it is written, "And she conceived, and bore Cain" (Beresheet 4:1), WHICH MEANS a nest (Heb. *ken*) and dwelling place of storms, demons and evil spirits.

47. אַתְקִין בֵּיה בְּהַאי אָדָם, כְּתָרִים, בִּכְלָל וּפְרָט, אִתְכְּלָלוּ בִּפְרָט וּכְלָל, שׁוֹקִין וּדְרוֹעִין, יְמִינָא וּשְׂמָאלָא.

**47.** He prepared crowns in this man, in general and in particular. They were included in the particular and in the general, NAMELY the legs and arms, which are right and left, MEANING GENERAL AND PARTICULAR IN THE ARMS, AND PARTICULAR AND GENERAL IN THE LEGS.

48. דָּא אִתְפְּלַג בְּסִטְרוֹי אִתְתַּקַן דְּכַר וְנוּקְבָּא יה״ו. י׳ דְּכַר. ה׳ נוּקְבָּא.
ו׳ כְּתִיב זָכָר וּנְקֵבָה בְּרָאָם וַיְבָרֶךְ אוֹתָם וַיִּקְרָא שְׁמָם אָדָם. דְּיוּקְנָא
וּפַרְצוּפָא דְּאָדָם יָתִיב עַל כָּרְסְיָא, וּכְתִיב וְעַל דְּמוּת הַכִּסֵּא דְּמוּת
כְּמַרְאֵה אָדָם עָלָיו מִלְמָעְלָה.

48. When THE CENTRAL COLUMN divides to its sides, NAMELY TO THE RIGHT SIDE AND TO THE LEFT SIDE, male and female are formed by THE SECRET OF Yud Hei Vav, for Yud, WHICH IS THE RIGHT SIDE, is male and Hei, WHICH IS THE LEFT SIDE, is female. OF Vav it is written, "male and female He created them. And Elohim blessed them" (Beresheet 1:27-28). And he called their name 'Adam', so that the image and face of Adam sits on the throne THAT IS THE NUKVA, as is written, "And upon the likeness of the throne was the likeness as the appearance of a man above upon it" (Yechezkel 1:26). THUS VAV INCLUDES MALE AND FEMALE TOGETHER, IN ACCORDANCE WITH THE SECRET OF MAN SITTING UPON THE THRONE.

## 4. Fourth Chapter

### A Synopsis

This chapter tells us that Atika is hidden but Zeir Anpin, who is partially hidden, is revealed in Malchut. He cannot be comprehended in His own place, but He can be comprehended in a different place. When lower man descended in the image and likeness, there were two spirits in him from his two sides, because man combines right and left: the holy Neshamah and the living Nefesh. When he sinned the left expanded from above downwards. The theme of 'two' is carried throughout the rest of this chapter, in connection with the Holy Names, the climbing scales that go up and down, Male and Female, the two equal crowns of Dalet and Vav, two men to spy secretly, two women, two who were embracing above. All these allusions to two result again in the statement that it is necessary to unite the right and the left and the central columns together, for the healing of Hashem is drawn by this unity.

49. פִּרְקָא רְבִיעָאָה. עַתִּיקָא, טָמִיר וְסָתִים. זְעֵירָא דְּאַנְפִּין, אִתְגַּלְיָיא וְלָא אִתְגַּלְיָיא. דְּאִתְגַּלְיָיא, בְּאַתְוָון כְּתִיב. דְּאִתְכַּסְיָיא, סָתִים בְּאַתְוָון, דְּלָא מִתְיַישְׁבָן בְּאַתְרוֹי, בְּגִין דְּאִיהוּ לָא אִתְיְישָׁבוּ בֵּיה עִלָּאִין וְתַתָּאִין.

49. Fourth Chapter. Atika, WHICH IS KETER, is covered and hidden. Zeir Anpin is revealed yet not revealed, MEANING THAT THE REVELATION STARTS IN HIM AND THAT REVELATION IS IN MALCHUT. The revealed, WHICH IS ZEIR ANPIN, is spelled with letters, MEANING THAT IT IS EXPRESSED IN THE LETTERS OF THE NAME THAT IS CALLED 'YUD HEI VAV HEI', WHICH MEANS, 'WAS, IS AND WILL BE, FOR EVERYTHING IS REVEALED IN HIM. That which is covered, THAT IS, ATIKA, is concealed of letters, FOR IT IS CALLED 'EHEYEH' (LIT. 'I SHALL BE'), IN THE FUTURE TENSE, WHICH MEANS THAT He cannot be comprehended in His place BUT IN A DIFFERENT PLACE. Because He is, the upper and lower beings cannot comprehend Him, FOR EVEN THE UPPER BEINGS DO NOT GRASP HIM.

50. וַיֹּאמֶר אֱלֹהִים תּוֹצֵא הָאָרֶץ נֶפֶשׁ חַיָּה לְמִינָהּ בְּהֵמָה וָרֶמֶשׂ וְגוֹ', הַיְינוּ דִּכְתִיב אָדָם וּבְהֵמָה תּוֹשִׁיעַ יְיָ'. חַד בִּכְלָלָא דְּאַחֲרָא מִשְׁתַּכְּחָא. בְּהֵמָה בִּכְלָלָא דְּאָדָם. אָדָם כִּי יַקְרִיב מִכֶּם קָרְבָּן לַיְיָ' מִן הַבְּהֵמָה, מִשּׁוּם דְּאִתְכְּלָל בִּכְלָלָא דְּאָדָם

**50.** "And Elohim said, Let the earth bring forth living creatures after their kind, cattle and creeping things..." (Beresheet 1:24). This is the meaning of, "Hashem, You preserve man and beast" (Tehilim 36:7). One is contained in the other, namely the living creatures is included in man, as is written, "If any man of you bring an offering to Hashem, of the cattle..." (Vayikra 1:2). IT IS USEFUL FOR HIM, because the living creatures is included in the secret of man.

**51.** כַּד נָחַת אָדָם דִּלְתַתָּא בְּדִיּוּקְנָא עִלָּאָה, אִשְׁתְּכָחוּ תְּרֵין רוּחִין מִתְּרֵין סִטְרִין, דִּימִינָא וּשְׂמָאלָא כָּלִיל אָדָם. דִּימִינָא, נִשְׁמָתָא קַדִּישָׁא. דִּשְׂמָאלָא נֶפֶשׁ חַיָּה. חָב אָדָם אִתְפָּשַׁט שְׂמָאלָא, וְאִתְפָּשַׁטוּ אִינּוּן בְּלָא גּוּפָא.

**51.** When the lower man descended in the upper form NAMELY IN IMAGE AND LIKENESS, there were two spirits in him from HIS two sides, because man combines right and left. The right is of the holy Neshamah and the left is of the living Nefesh. When he sinned, then the left expanded from above downwards, WHICH IS THE SIN OF THE TREE OF KNOWLEDGE OF GOOD AND EVIL THAT DREW THE ILLUMINATION OF THE LEFT, WHICH IS CHOCHMAH, FROM ABOVE DOWNWARDS. Then those who have no body expanded.

**52.** כַּד מִתְדַּבְּקִין דָּא בְּדָא, אִתְיַילְדָן כְּהַאי חַיָּה דְּאוֹלִידַת סַגִּיאִין בְּקִטְרָא חֲדָא. כ״ב אַתְוָון סְתִימִין, כ״ב אַתְוָון אִתְגַּלְיָין, י׳ סָתִים, י׳ גַּלְיָיא. סָתִים וְגַלְיָיא, בְּמַתְקְלָא דְּטַפְסִין, אִתְקָלוּ.

**52.** HERE HE CONCLUDES EXPLAINING THE ABOVE-MENTIONED ARTICLE THAT SAYS THAT ZEIR ANPIN IS REVEALED YET IS NOT REVEALED. HE EXPLAINS: When THE RIGHT AND LEFT OF BINAH joined together, 22 concealed letters were born, like when an animal bears many at one time. THEY ARE THE ENTIRETY OF THE LIGHTS OF ZEIR ANPIN, THE SECRET OF THE RIGHT, and 22 revealed letters, WHICH ARE THE GENERALITY OF THE LETTERS OF THE NUKVA OF ZEIR ANPIN. THEY ARE THE SECRET OF THE TWO YUDS AT THE BEGINNING AND END OF 'YUD ALEPH HEI DALET VAV NUN HEI YUD,' WHICH IS THE PERMUTATION OF YUD HEI VAV HEI ADONAI, WHICH ARE MALE AND FEMALE. Yud AT THE BEGINNING, THE

YUD OF YUD HEI VAV HEI, WHICH IS ZEIR ANPIN, is concealed, AS THE
ILLUMINATION OF CHOCHMAH IS NOT REVEALED IN IT. BUT Yud AT THE
END, WHICH IS OF ADONAI, is revealed, AS THE ILLUMINATION OF
CHOCHMAH IS REVEALED IN IT. The concealed and revealed, RIGHT AND
LEFT, ARE WEIGHED in the climbing scales, MEANING THAT THE PANS OF
THE SCALES CLIMB UP AND DOWN. THIS IS THE SECRET OF THE
CENTRAL COLUMN THAT BALANCES BOTH LIGHTS, RIGHT AND LEFT, SO
THAT THEY WOULD HAVE THE SAME WEIGHT AND UNITE WITH EACH
OTHER.

53. י' נָפְקִין מִנֵּיהּ דְּכַר וְנוּקְבָּא ו"ד, בְּהַאי אֲתַר, ו' דְּכַר, ד' נוּקְבָּא.
בְּגִין דָּא, ד"ו תְּרֵין. ד"ו דְּכַר וְנוּקְבָּא. ד"ו תְּרֵין קַפְלִין. י' בִּלְחוֹדוֹי
דְּכַר. ה' נוּקְבָּא. ה' ד' הֲוַת בְּקַדְמֵיתָא, וּמִדְּאִתְעַבְּרַת בּוֹ' בְּגַוָּהּ, אַפִּיקַת
ו', אִתְחֲזֵי יו"ד בְּחֵיזְוֵיהּ כְּלָלָא דיה"ו. מִדְּאַפִּיקַת יו"ד דְּהוּא דְּכַר
וְנוּקְבָּא, אִתְיַישְׁבַת לְבָתַר, וּמְכַסְיָיא לְאִמָּא.

53. Male and female emerge from Yud, WHICH ARE Vav and Dalet OF THE
FULLY SPELLED YUD. In this place Vav is male and Dalet is female,
INSTEAD OF VAV HEI AS IN OTHER PLACES. Hence *Du* (Dalet Vav)
MEANS IN HEBREW two, BECAUSE Dalet Vav are male and female. Dalet
and Vav are two EQUAL crowns. Yud in itself is male. Hei is female. Hei
was Dalet originally, MEANING THE DALET OF THE FULLY SPELLED YUD,
AS EXPLAINED. When it conceived Vav within it, IT BECAME HEI,
MEANING VAV WITHIN DALET. AFTERWARDS, it brought forth AND BORE
the Vav, WHICH IS THE SECRET OF YUD HEI VAV OF THE NAME. And the
Yud appears in its form, which is the entirety of Yud Hei Vav. BEFORE,
THE YUD WAS COMPOUNDED OF VAV DALET AND AFTERWARDS, THE
DALET CONCEIVED WITH THE VAV AND BECAME HEI AND AFTERWARDS
BORE THE VAV. After Yud, which is of male and female, produced HEI
VAV, WHICH ARE IMA AND ZEIR ANPIN, VAV was afterwards settled, THAT
IS, RECEIVED MOCHIN, and covered Ima, WHICH IS HEI.

54. וַיִּרְאוּ בְּנֵי הָאֱלֹהִים אֶת בְּנוֹת הָאָדָם, הַיְינוּ דִכְתִיב שְׁנַיִם אֲנָשִׁים
מְרַגְּלִים חֶרֶשׁ לֵאמֹר, מַאי בְּנוֹת הָאָדָם. דִּכְתִּיב אָז תָּבֹאנָה שְׁתַּיִם
נָשִׁים זוֹנוֹת אֶל הַמֶּלֶךְ. בְּגִינֵיהוֹן כְּתִיב, כִּי רָאוּ כִּי חָכְמַת אֱלֹהִים
בְּקִרְבּוֹ וְגוֹ'. אָז תָּבֹאנָה וְלָא בְּקַדְמֵיתָא. בְּקִיסְטְרָא דְּקִיטוּרֵי דְּפִיגָּאן,

תְּרֵין מִתְחַבְּקָן הֲווֹ לְעֵילָא, לְתַתָּא נַחְתוּ יַרְתוּ עַפְרָא, אִבְּדוּ חוּלָקָא
טָבָא דַּהֲוָה בְּהוּ. עָטְרָא דְּחֶמְלָא, וְאִתְעַטָּר בְּקוּסְטָא דְּעִנְבָא.

**54.** "And the sons of Elohim saw the daughters of men" (Beresheet 6:2). This resembles the verse, "Two men to spy secretly, saying" (Yehoshua 2:1). What is the meaning of "the daughters of men"? It is written, "Then came two women, that were harlots, to the king" (I Melachim 3:16), because of them, it is written, "for they saw that the wisdom of Elohim was in him..." (Ibid. 28). "Then came", but not before. When the image of the unripe fig dominated, MEANING THE EATING OF UNRIPE FRUIT, two were embracing above. When they descended, they inherited dust. They lost the good portion that they possessed from the crown of Mercy, and became crowned with the aspect of grapes.

55. וַיֹּאמֶר יְיָ' אֶל מֹשֶׁה מַה תִּצְעַק אֵלָי. אֵלַי דַּיְיקָא. דַּבֵּר אֶל בְּנֵי
יִשְׂרָאֵל וְיִסָּעוּ. וְיִסָּעוּ דַּיְיקָא.

**55.** "And Hashem said to Moses, Why do you cry to Me?" (Shemot 14:15). "To Me" is precise. "Speak to the children of Yisrael, that they go forward" (Ibid.); "that they go forward" is precise.

56. בְּמַזָּלָא הֲוָה תַּלְיָ, דְּבָעָא לְאוֹקִיר דּוּקְנֵיהּ. וְהַיָּשָׁר בְּעֵינָיו תַּעֲשֶׂה
וְהַאֲזַנְתָּ לְמִצְוֹתָיו וְשָׁמַרְתָּ כָּל חֻקָּיו עַד כָּאן. כִּי אֲנִי יְיָ' רֹפְאֶיךָ, לְהַאי
דַּוְקָא.

**56.** It depended upon Mazal, for he wanted to glorify the Beard. FOR THEN THE ILLUMINATION OF CHOCHMAH WAS DRAWN FROM THE SUPERNAL MAZAL, WHICH IS THE SECRET OF THE EIGHTH OF THE THIRTEEN FEATURES OF THE BEARD THAT IS CALLED 'MAZAL'. THIS IS THE MEANING OF, "And will do that which is right in His sight" (Shemot 15:26). THIS IS THE LEFT COLUMN, IN WHICH CHOCHMAH IS DRAWN THAT IS CALLED 'HIS SIGHT'. "And will give ear to His commandments" (Ibid.), MEANS THE RIGHT COLUMN INTO WHICH CHASSADIM ARE DRAWN FROM BINAH CALLED 'EARS'. THEREFORE, IT SAYS, "GIVE EAR". "And keep all His statutes" (Ibid.) REFERS TO THE CENTRAL COLUMN, WHICH KEEPS

THE STATUTES, SO THE RIGHT IS DRAWN FROM ABOVE DOWNWARDS AND THE LEFT ONLY FROM BELOW UPWARDS. Up to here, MEANING IT IS NECESSARY UP TO HERE TO DRAW AND UNITE THE THREE COLUMNS TOGETHER, "for I am Hashem that heals you," FOR MY HEALING IS DRAWN BY THIS UNITY, precisely OF THE THREE COLUMNS.

## 5. Fifth Chapter

### A Synopsis

Rabbi Shimon begins by explaining the seven levels, that culminate in the souls of Adam and Eve outside of Atzilut. Zeir Anpin concealed His face from them because of their sin of the Tree of Knowledge of Good and Evil. After this we read about the verses in Beresheet that tell of the creation of the heavens and the earth, the firmament and the waters. The part played by various letters and the significant numerology are explored as well. Rabbi Shimon turns to the question of the Nefilim, speaking about those who fell from the grades of Atzilut. When Solomon came he corrected those who were not holy with his wisdom. The text now reviews the main points spoken of in all the five chapters, the characteristics of the beard and skull of Arich Anpin in particular, with emphasis on the numbers thirteen, nine and seven. We read that Malchut shelters under the shade of Yesod of Zeir Anpin, that rules over the Tree of Knowledge of Good and Evil. He who does good walks among the seven pillars (the lower seven Sfirot) and merits the four living creatures – Lion, Ox, Eagle and Man. Rabbi Shimon speaks about the Angel Metatron who was Enoch, and then about the courts of law – four above and four below. He tells us that there are different kinds of judgment, some more harsh and some less harsh. The last section here speaks about "And it came to pass when men began to multiply on the face of the earth"; we learn that "men" alludes to supernal man, namely Moses. Various references are made to "horn," one that is used for anointing and one, the horn of Jubilee, the first Hei of Yud Hei Vav Hei, that blows the breath of life into everything.

When the first Hei appears to the lower Hei, namely Binah to Malchut, then the name is considered full, Adonai Elohim. And when it becomes perfect, in the future to come, then "Hashem alone shall be exalted on that day."

57. פִּרְקָא חֲמִישָׁאָה הוֹי גּוֹי חוֹטֵא עַם כֶּבֶד עָוֹן זֶרַע מְרֵעִים בָּנִים וְגוֹ'. שִׁבְעָה דַּרְגִּין יוֹד ה' ו' ה' ה' י' אַפִּיק ו' ד' ה' הוי, ה' אַפִּיק ו' ו' אַפִּיק ה' ו"ד לְבַר אַסְתִּיר אָדָם דְּכַר וְנוּקְבָּא דְּאִינוּן ד"ו דִּכְתִיב בָּנִים מַשְׁחִיתִים.

57. Fifth Chapter. It is written, "Oh (Heb. *Hoy* - Hei Vav Yud) sinful nation, a people laden with iniquity, a seed of evildoers, children that deal

corruptly..." (Yeshayah 1:4). THERE ARE seven levels, ONE COMING OUT OF THE OTHER, Yud Vav Dalet, Hei, Vav, Hei Hei. HE EXPLAINS: Yud brought forth Vav Dalet OF THE FULLY SPELLED YUD, AND THE DALET CONCEIVED VAV AND BECAME Hei, FOR THEN YUD BECOMES Hei Vav Yud. THESE ARE THE FOUR LEVELS, YUD, VAV, DALET, HEI. AND AFTERWARDS Hei bore the Vav, WHICH IS THE FIFTH LEVEL, and the Vav, WHICH IS ZEIR ANPIN, brought forth Hei FROM INSIDE ATZILUT WHICH IS THE NUKVA AND THE SIXTH LEVEL, AND BROUGHT FORTH Dalet Vav, THE SOULS OF ADAM AND EVE outside OF ATZILUT, AS THEY ARE THE SEVENTH LEVEL. It hid male and female of Adam being Dalet Vav OUTSIDE ATZILUT, MEANING THAT HE CONCEALED HIS FACE FROM THEM, as is written ABOUT THEM, "children that deal corruptly," BECAUSE THEY SINNED BY THE TREE OF KNOWLEDGE OF GOOD AND EVIL.

**58.** בְּרֵאשִׁית בָּרָא. בְּרֵאשִׁית מַאֲמָר. בָּרָא חֲצִי מַאֲמָר. אָב וּבֵן. סָתִים וְגַלְיָא. עֵדֶן עִלָּאָה דְּסָתִים וְגָנִיז. עֵדֶן תַּתָּאָה, נָפִיק לְמַטְלָנוֹי וְאִתְגַּלְיָא יְהֹוָה. יָהּ. אֱלֹהִים. אֶת. אֲדֹנָי אֶהְיֶה. יְמִינָא וּשְׂמָאלָא כַּחֲדָא אִשְׁתַּתְּפוּ, הַשָּׁמַיִם. וְאֵת, דִּכְתִיב וְהַתִּפְאֶרֶת וְהַנֵּצַח אִינוּן כַּחֲדָא אִשְׁתַּתְּפוּ. הָאָרֶץ, דִּכְתִיב מָה אַדִּיר שִׁמְךָ בְּכָל הָאָרֶץ. מְלֹא כָל הָאָרֶץ כְּבוֹדוֹ.

**58.** "In the beginning created": "*Beresheet*" (lit. 'In the beginning') is a saying, THAT IS, A COMPLETE LEVEL. "*Bara*" (lit. 'created') is half a saying, MEANING HALF A LEVEL. THEY ARE Father and Son, concealed and revealed, the upper Eden that is concealed and hidden and the lower Eden that emerges to its journeys IN THREE PLACES. Then are revealed Yud Hei Vav Hei, Yah, MEANING A SAYING AND HALF A SAYING ARE REVEALED THROUGH THE JOURNEY. "Elohim the (Heb. *Et*)" THAT FOLLOW "IN THE BEGINNING CREATED", MEAN Adonai Eheyeh, BECAUSE '*ET*' IS THE SECRET OF MALCHUT THAT IS CALLED 'ADONAI', AND 'ELOHIM' THE SECRET OF BINAH, Right and Left joined together. THIS IS THE SECRET OF "the heavens," WHICH IS TIFERET THAT INCLUDES CHESED AND GVURAH, WHICH ARE RIGHT AND LEFT "and the (Heb. *ve'et*)" IS NETZACH, HOD, AND YESOD, as written, "And the glory (Tiferet) and the victory (Netzach), ETC." (I Divrei Hayamim 29:11) that joined together. FOR "HEAVENS" IS TIFERET AND "AND THE" IS NETZACH AND HOD. "FOR ALL THAT IS IN HEAVEN AND ON EARTH" (IBID.) IS YESOD. "The earth" IS THE LAST MALCHUT, as written, "how majestic is Your name in

all the earth" (Tehilim 8:2). "The whole earth is full of His glory" (Yeshayah 6:3), WHERE EARTH MEANS MALCHUT.

59. יְהִי רָקִיעַ בְּתוֹךְ הַמַּיִם לְהַבְדִּיל בֵּין הַקֹּדֶשׁ וּבֵין קֹדֶשׁ הַקֳּדָשִׁים, עַתִּיקָא לִזְעֵירָא, אִתְפְּרַשׁ, וְאִתְדְּבַק. לָא אִתְפְּרַשׁ מַמָּשׁ פּוּמָא מְמַלֵּל רַבְרְבָן.

59. "Let there be a firmament in the water" (Beresheet 1:6) to divide between the Holy, WHICH IS ZEIR ANPIN, and the Holy of Holies, WHICH ARE ARICH ANPIN AND ABA AND IMA. THE FIRMAMENT DIVIDES between Atik, WHICH IS ARICH ANPIN, and Zeir Anpin. It is divided FROM ARICH ANPIN VIA THE FIRMAMENT yet clings AS IT IS NOT ACTUALLY DIVIDED by the mouth that speaks great things.

60. אַנְתִּיק וְאִתְעַטָּר בְּכִתְרִין זְעִירִין, בַּחֲמִשָּׁה זִינִין מַיִם, וּכְתִיב וְנָתַן עָלָיו מַיִם חַיִּים. הוּא אֱלֹהִים חַיִּים וּמֶלֶךְ עוֹלָם. אִתְהַלֵּךְ לִפְנֵי יְיָ' בְּאַרְצוֹת הַחַיִּים. וְהָיְתָה נֶפֶשׁ אֲדֹנִי צְרוּרָה וְגוֹ'. וְעֵץ הַחַיִּים בְּתוֹךְ הַגָּן. י"ה, יו"ד ה"א, אֶהְיֶה בֵּין מַיִם לָמָיִם. מַיִם שְׁלֵימִין, וּמַיִם דְּלָא שְׁלֵימִין. רַחֲמִין שְׁלֵימִין, רַחֲמִין דְּלָא שְׁלֵימִין.

60. ZEIR ANPIN is severed to be crowned with small crowns in five kinds of LIVING water, MEANING IN THE SFIROT – CHESED, GVURAH, TIFERET, NETZACH, HOD OF IMA, WHICH IS THE SECRET OF FIVE HUNDRED YEARS THAT ARE CALLED 'LIVING WATERS OR LIFE', as it is written, "And running (or: 'living') water shall be put thereto" (Bemidbar 19:17), WHICH IS CHESED. "He is the living Elohim, and an everlasting King" (Yirmeyah 10:10), IS GVURAH. "I shall walk before Hashem in the lands of the living" (Tehilim 116:9), IS NETZACH. "Yet the soul of my Master shall be bound in the bond of life with Hashem your Elohim" (I Shmuel 25:29), IS HOD. "And the Tree of Life also in the midst of the Garden" (Beresheet 2:9), IS TIFERET. Yud Hei IS CHOCHMAH AND BINAH, Yud Vav Dalet, Hei Aleph IS CHOCHMAH BINAH OF ZEIR ANPIN HIMSELF, WHICH IS THE SECRET OF YUD HEI VAV HEI FULLY SPELLED WITH ALEPH'S. Eheyeh IS THE SECRET OF KETER. THEY ARE THE DIVISION between waters and waters, for the UPPER waters ABOVE THE FIRMAMENT, WHICH ARE YUD HEI,

Yud Vav Dalet, Hei Aleph, and Eheyeh are whole, while the lower beings below the firmament are waters that are not whole. Above the firmament, there is complete mercy and below the firmament, there is incomplete mercy.

61. וַיֹּאמֶר יְיָ׳ לֹא יָדוֹן רוּחִי בָאָדָם לְעוֹלָם בְּשַׁגַּם הוּא בָשָׂר. וַיֹּאמֶר יְיָ׳, כַּד אִתְיַישְׁבָא בִּזְעֵירָא. מִכָּאן דָבָר בְּשֵׁם אָמְרוּ. דְעַתִּיקָא סָתִים קָאֲמַר לֹא יָדוֹן רוּחִי בָאָדָם דִלְעֵילָא, מִשׁוּם דִבְהַהוּא רוּחָא דְאִתְנְשָׁבָא מִתְּרֵין נוּקְבִין דְפַרְדַשְׁקָא, מָשִׁיךְ לְתַתָּאֵי.

61. "And Hashem said, My spirit shall not abide in man for ever for that he also is flesh" (Beresheet 6:3). "And Hashem said," meaning when He settled and became clothed with Zeir Anpin. From here we derive that 'one quotes one', because concealed Atik that is Arich Anpin, said, "My spirit shall not abide" in supernal man, Zeir Anpin. For with that spirit (also: 'wind') that blows from the two nostrils of the nose of Arich Anpin, it draws life to those below, which is the secret of the light of Chochmah that is called 'life.'

62. וּבְג״כ כְּתִיב וְהָיוּ יָמָיו מֵאָה וְעֶשְׂרִים שָׁנָה. יו״ד שְׁלִים וְלָא שְׁלִים. י׳ בִּלְחוֹדוֹי מֵאָה. תְּרֵין אַתְוָון תְּרֵין זִמְנִין, מֵאָה וְעֶשְׂרִים שָׁנָה. י׳ בִּלְחוֹדוֹי כַּד אִתְגַּלְיָא בִּזְעֵירָא, אִתְמְשַׁךְ בְּעֶשֶׂר אַלְפִין שְׁנִין. מִכָּאן כְּתִיב, וַתָּשֶׁת עָלַי כַּפֶּכָה.

62. Therefore it is written, "and His days shall be a hundred and twenty years" (Ibid.), because Yud Vav Dalet is the secret of Chochmah and life. It is whole yet not whole. Yud in itself is one hundred, meaning ten Sfirot, each including ten, amounting to one hundred. The two letters Vav Dalet that are not whole are twice ten. Together they amount to a hundred and twenty years. Yud in itself, when it is revealed in Zeir Anpin, spreads to ten thousand years, because each of the Sfirot of Chochmah expands to a thousand. Now it is written, "You laid Your hand upon me" (Tehilim 139:5), meaning that his height was diminished to one hundred cubits. He received the light of life from the Yud, which is whole and not whole,

BECAUSE THE VAV DALET, WHICH ARE NOT WHOLE, ARE CONNECTED WITH THE YUD, AS MENTIONED.

63. הַנְּפִילִים הָיוּ בָאָרֶץ, הַיְינוּ דִּכְתִּיב וּמִשָּׁם יִפָּרֵד וְהָיָה לְאַרְבָּעָה רָאשִׁים. מֵאֲתָר דְּאִתְפְּרַשׁ גִּנְתָא, אִקְרֵי הַנְּפִילִים, דִּכְתִּיב וּמִשָּׁם יִפָּרֵד. הָיוּ בָאָרֶץ בַּיָּמִים הָהֵם, וְלָא לְבָתַר זִמְנָא. עַד דְּאָתָא יְהוֹשֻׁעַ, וּבְנֵי הָאֱלֹהִים אִסְטַמָרוּ.

63. "There were *Nefilim* (lit. 'fallen ones') in the earth in those days" (Beresheet 6:4). This is as is written, "And from thence it was parted, and branched into four streams" (Beresheet 2:10), for ever since the place where the Garden parted, WHICH IS MALCHUT OF ATZILUT, it is called 'fallen,' MEANING THROUGHOUT THE THREE WORLDS OF BRIYAH, YETZIRAH AND ASIYAH. FOR ALL THOSE THAT FELL THERE FROM THE GRADES OF ATZILUT ARE CALLED 'FALLEN', as is written, "And from thence it was parted." "There were...in the earth in those days," but not afterwards until Joshua came and the children of Elohim were hidden, NAMELY THE TWO SECRET SPIES, ABOUT WHIOM IT IS WRITTEN, "AND HID THEM" (YEHOSHUA 2:4).

64. עַד דְּאָתָא שְׁלֹמֹה וּבְנוֹת הָאָדָם אִתְכְּלָלָא, הה"ד, וְתַעֲנוּגוֹת. תַּעֲנֻגֹת קָאֵרֵי בְּנֵי הָאָדָם דְּאִתְרְמִיוּ מֵהַאי רוּחִין אַחֲרָנִין, דְּלָא אִתְכְּלָלוּ בְּחָכְמָה עִלָּאָה. דִּכְתִּיב וַיְיָ' נָתַן חָכְמָה לִשְׁלֹמֹה. וּכְתִיב וַיֶּחְכַּם מִכָּל הָאָדָם. מִשּׁוּם דְּהָנֵי לָא אִתְכְּלָלוּ בְּאָדָם.

64. Until Solomon came and the daughters of men were incorporated IN HOLINESS, as is written, "and the delights of the sons of men" (Kohelet 2:8). The word "delights" has a feminine suffix INSTEAD OF A MASCULINE ONE, BECAUSE IT REFERS TO THE DAUGHTERS OF MAN MENTIONED EARLIER, "TWO WOMEN THAT WERE HARLOTS." "Sons of men," FROM THE WORDS "THE DELIGHTS OF THE SONS OF MEN", REFER TO THE SONS OF MEN that were cast from other spirits IN ATZILUT, and were not included in supernal Chochmah. It is written, "And Hashem gave Solomon wisdom" (I Melachim 5:26) and, "For he was wiser than all men" (Ibid. 11). It is because HE CORRECTED ALL THESE MEN, who were not included in man OF HOLINESS.

65. וַיְיָ' נָתַן חָכְמָה, ה' עֵלָאָה. וַיֶּחְכַּם, דְּמִינָהּ אִתְחַכַּם לְתַתָּא. הֵמָה הַגִּבּוֹרִים אֲשֶׁר מֵעוֹלָם, עוֹלָם דִּלְעֵילָא. אַנְשֵׁי הַשֵּׁם, דְּאִתְנְהֲגָן בִּשְׁמָא. מַאי שְׁמָא. שְׁמָא קַדִּישָׁא, דְּאִתְנְהַגָן בֵּיהּ דְּלָא קַדִּישִׁין לְתַתָּא, וְלָא אִתְנְהֲגָן אֶלָּא בִּשְׁמָא. אַנְשֵׁי הַשֵּׁם סְתָם, וְלָא אַנְשֵׁי הֲוָיָ"ה. לָאו מִסְתִּים סְתִימָא, אֶלָּא גְרִיעוּתָא, וְלָא גְרִיעוּתָא אַנְשֵׁי הַשֵּׁם סְתָם, מִכְּלָלָא דְּאָדָם נָפְקוּ, כְּתִיב אָדָם בִּיקָר בַּל יָלִין, אָדָם בִּיקָר, בִּיקָרוּ דְּמַלְכָּא, בַּל יָלִין, בְּלָא רוּחָא.

65. "And Hashem gave Solomon wisdom," MEANING THAT HE GAVE HIM the upper Hei, WHICH IS BINAH. "For he was wiser," because from it, FROM BINAH, he became wise below. "the same were mighty men of old (or: 'from the world')" (Beresheet 6:4), meaning from the upper world, THE WORLD OF ATZILUT FROM WHICH THEY FELL AS MENTIONED, "men of renown (lit. 'name')" (Ibid.) who made use of the name. What is the name? It is the Holy Name, MEANING MALCHUT THAT IS CALLED 'NAME', and they used it, those unholy beings, MEANING THAT THE NEFILIM USED IT TO DRAW CHOCHMAH FROM ABOVE DOWNWARDS, WHICH IS NOT HOLY FOR IT IS FORBIDDEN TO DO SO. They utilized only the name, WHICH IS MALCHUT. IT IS SAID "men of name", in general, instead of 'men of Yud Hei Vav Hei', WHICH IS ZEIR ANPIN. It is not because the verse is ambiguous, MEANING THAT THE VERSE DOES NOT MENTION ANY PARTICULAR NAME, but it is rather diminishing yet not diminishing. IT IS DIMINISHING BECAUSE IT IS LESS THAN THE NAME YUD HEI VAV HEI, BUT IT IS ALSO NOT A LESSENING BECAUSE IT IS MALCHUT THAT IS CALLED 'NAME', AND IT COULD NOT BE WRITTEN IN ANY OTHER WAY. "Men of renown" is general; they are no longer part of humanity, as it is written, "Nevertheless man abides not in honor" (Tehilim 49:13). "Honor" REFERS TO the glory of the King, WHICH IS MALCHUT THAT IS CALLED 'NAME' AND IS THE GLORY OF ZEIR ANPIN. SINCE MAN MAKES USE OF THE NAME, WHICH IS MALCHUT, he "abides not," MEANS WHEN HE WAS without spirit.

66. תְּלֵיסַר מַלְכֵי קְרָבָא, בְּשִׁבְעָה. שִׁבְעָה. מַלְכִין בְּאַרְעָא, אִתְחֲזִיאוּ נָצְחֵי קְרָבָא. תִּשְׁעָה דְּסַלְּקִין בְּדַרְגִּין, דְּרַהֲטִין בִּרְעוּתְהוֹן, וְלֵית דִּימְחֵי בִּידֵיהוֹן. חֲמִשָּׁה מַלְכִין קַיְימִין בְּבֶהִילוּ, לְקַמֵּי אַרְבַּע לָא יַכְלִין לְמֵיקַם.

**66.** HE NOW REVIEWS MOST OF THE MAIN POINTS THAT HE SPOKE OF IN ALL THE FIVE CHAPTERS WITH A FEW ADDITIONS VERY BRIEFLY. HE SAYS, Thirteen warring kings, NAMELY THE THIRTEEN FEATURES OF THE BEARD OF ARICH ANPIN in seven, MEANING THAT THE THIRTEEN RECEIVE FROM THE SEVEN FEATURES OF THE SKULL OF ARICH ANPIN. Seven kings, NAMELY THE SEVEN FEATURES OF THE SKULL OF ZEIR ANPIN, WHEN THEIR LIGHT SPREADS in the earth, WHICH IS MALCHUT, appear to be victorious in war. Nine ascend the grades and run as they wish, NAMELY NINE FEATURES OF THE BEARD OF ZEIR ANPIN THAT ASCEND AND RUN THROUGHOUT THE GRADES. There is no one to detain them. Five kings stand in confusion and cannot stand before four.

67. אַרְבַּע מַלְכִין נָפְקִין לְקַדְמוּת אַרְבַּע, בְּהוֹן תַּלְיָין כַּעֲנָבִין בְּאִתְכְּלָא צְרִירָן בְּהוֹ שִׁבְעָה רְהִיטִין. סָהֲדִין סָהֲדוּתָא וְלָא קַיְימִין בְּדוּכְתַּיְיהוּ. אִילָנָא דְמִבְסָם יָתִיב בְּגוֹ. בַּעֲנָפוֹי אֲחִידָן וּמְקַנְּנָן צִפֳּרִין. תְּחוֹתוֹי תַּטְלֵל חֵיוָתָא דְשַׁלִּיטָא בְּהַהוּא אִילָנָא בִּתְרֵי כְּבִישִׁין, לְמֵהַךְ בְּשִׁבְעָה סַמְכִין סָחֲרָנֵיהּ, בְּאַרְבַּע חֵיוָון, מִתְגַּלְגְּלִין בְּאַרְבַּע סִטְרִין.

**67.** HE SAYS, Four kings come out AND ARE BORN towards the four KINGS, they cling to them like grapes to a bunch. Seven runners are incorporated in them, WHICH ARE CHESED, GVURAH, TIFERET, NETZACH, HOD, YESOD AND MALCHUT WITHIN THE WHOLE MALCHUT. WHEN CHOCHMAH IS REVEALED IN IT, THEY RUN AND HASTEN IN THE SECRET OF, "AND THE LIVING CREATURES RAN AND RETURNED" (YECHEZKEL 1:14). They give testimony when they are not in their places, BECAUSE WHEN THEY REVEAL THE ILLUMINATION OF CHOCHMAH THAT IS CALLED 'TESTIMONY', THEY ARE FORCED TO DESCEND FROM THEIR PLACE. The aromatic tree, WHICH IS YESOD OF ZEIR ANPIN, PROVIDES CHASSADIM TO MALCHUT AND CHOCHMAH BECOMES SCENTED WITH CHASSADIM. It is settled among THE SEVEN SFIROT OF MALCHUT. Among its branches THAT SPREAD FROM IT, birds take hold and nest. Under YESOD OF ZEIR ANPIN, the living creature, WHICH IS MALCHUT, shelters in its shade. It rules over that tree that has two ways, THE TREE OF KNOWLEDGE OF GOOD AND EVIL. IF ONE GAINS MERIT IT IS GOOD AND IF ONE DOES NOT, IT IS EVIL. AND IF HE MERITS, GOOD DOMINATES. THEN HE walks among the seven pillars – WHICH ARE CHESED, GVURAH, TIFERET, NETZACH, HOD, YESOD AND MALCHUT OF THE NUKVA, WHICH IS THE SECRET OF

THE ILLUMINATION OF CHASSADIM that surround THE TREE OF KNOWLEDGE OF GOOD AND EVIL AND RULE OVER IT. HE MERITS the four living creatures: Lion, Ox, Eagle, Man, WHICH ARE NETZACH, HOD, YESOD AND MALCHUT, WHICH IS THE SECRET OF THE LOWER CHARIOT, that revolve in the four directions.

68. חִוְיָא דְּרָהִיט בש״ע דְּלוּגִין, דָּלִיג עַל טוּרִין, מְקַפֵּץ עַל גִּבְעָתָא, דִּכְתִיב מְדַלֵּג עַל הֶהָרִים מְקַפֵּץ עַל הַגְּבָעוֹת. זְנָבֵיה בְּפוּמֵיה, בְּשִׁנּוּי, נָקִיב בִּתְרֵין גִּיסִין. כַּד נָטִיל גִּיסְטְרָא אִתְעֲבֵיד לִתְלַת רוּחִין.

**68.** The snake that runs with 370 leaps, "Leaping on the mountains, skipping on the hills" (Shir Hashirim 2:8), his tail in his mouth, between his teeth, pierced in two sides. While moving, he ceases and his body is divided into three aspects.

69. כְּתִיב וַיִּתְהַלֵּךְ חֲנוֹךְ אֶת הָאֱלֹהִים. וּכְתִיב חֲנוֹךְ לַנַּעַר עַל פִּי דַרְכּוֹ. לַנַּעַר הַיָּדוּעַ. אֶת הָאֱלֹהִים, וְלָא אֶת יְיָ'. וְאֵינֶנּוּ, בְּשֵׁם זֶה, כִּי לָקַח אוֹתוֹ אֱלֹהִים לְהִקָּרֵא בִּשְׁמוֹ.

**69.** It is written, "And Enoch walked with the Elohim" (Beresheet 5:24) and also, "Train (Heb. *chanoch*) up a child in the way he should go" (Mishlei 22:6), MEANING that certain child THAT IS THE ANGEL METATRON. THIS IS THE MEANING OF THE VERSE. ENOCH BECAME A CHILD, METATRON; "with the Elohim", REFERS TO MALCHUT and not with Yud Hei Vav Hei WHICH IS ZEIR ANPIN, BECAUSE HE BECAME A SERVANT OF MALCHUT. "And he was not" (Beresheet 5:24) MEANS THAT he was not under the name Enoch, "for the Elohim took him" to be called in His name, FOR HE BECAME AN ANGEL OF ELOHIM.

70. תְּלַת בָּתֵּי דִינִין, אַרְבַּע אִינּוּן. אַרְבַּע בָּתֵּי דִינִין דִּלְעֵילָא. אַרְבַּע לְתַתָּא. דִּכְתִיב לֹא תַעֲשׂוּ עָוֶל בַּמִּשְׁפָּט בַּמִּדָּה בַּמִּשְׁקָל וּבַמְּשׂוּרָה. דִּינָא קַשְׁיָא. דִּינָא דְּלָא קַשְׁיָא, דִּינָא בְּשִׁקּוּלָא, דִּינָא דְּלָא בְּשִׁקּוּלָא. דִּינָא רַפְיָא. דַּאֲפִילוּ לָא הַאי וְלָא הַאי.

**70.** The three courts of law are four. There are four courts of law above and four courts of law below, as it is written, "You shall not do unrighteousness in judgment, in length, in weight, or in measure" (Vayikra 19:35). FOR JUDGMENT IS THE RIGHT COLUMN, LENGTH IS THE LEFT COLUMN, WEIGHT IS THE CENTRAL COLUMN AND MEASURE IS MALCHUT. AND HE EXPLAINS THAT THERE IS harsh judgment, judgment that is not harsh, there is the judgment of weight, a judgment that is not in EQUAL weight. There is light judgment that has neither HARSH JUDGMENT nor JUDGMENT THAT IS NOT HARSH.

‎71. וַיְהִי כִּי הֵחֵל הָאָדָם לָרֹב עַל פְּנֵי הָאֲדָמָה. הֵחֵל הָאָדָם לָרֹב. הַיְינוּ דִכְתִּיב בְּשַׁגַּם וְגוֹ', הָאָדָם דִּלְעֵילָּא. וּכְתִיב עַל פְּנֵי הָאֲדָמָה. וּמֹשֶׁה לָא יָדַע כִּי קָרַן עוֹר פָּנָיו, הַיְינוּ דִכְתִּיב כָּתְנוֹת עוֹר.

**71.** "And it came to pass when men began to multiply on the face of the earth" (Beresheet 6:1): "Men began to multiply," as is written, "for that he also (Heb. *beshagam*) is flesh" (Ibid. 3). BESHAGAM IS COMPOSED OF THE SAME LETTERS AS MOSES. BOTH HAVE SHIN AND MEM, AND BET AND GIMEL OF THE FORMER EQUAL HEI OF THE LATTER (IN NUMERICAL VALUE). THEREFORE, THE VERSE SAYS "MEN," WHICH ALLUDES TO supernal man, NAMELY MOSES WHO IS A CHARIOT TO ZEIR ANPIN, and it is written "on the face of the earth" EVEN THOUGH THE LEVEL OF MOSES WAS ABOVE IN ZEIR ANPIN THAT IS CALLED 'HEAVEN'. THIS IS THE MEANING OF THE VERSE, "Moses knew not that the skin of his face shone" (Shemot 34:29). This is the meaning of, "coats of skin" (Beresheet 3:21), WHICH MEANS COATS FROM MALCHUT.

‎72. קֶרֶן, דִּכְתִּיב וַיִּקַּח שְׁמוּאֵל אֶת קֶרֶן הַשֶּׁמֶן. לֵית מְשִׁיחָא אֶלָּא בְּקֶרֶן, וּבִשְׁמְךָ תָּרוּם קַרְנֵנוּ. שָׁם אַצְמִיחַ קֶרֶן לְדָוִד. הַיְינוּ עֲשִׁירָאָה דְּמַלְכָּא. וְאַתְיָא מִן יוֹבְלָא דְּהִיא אִימָא, דִּכְתִּיב וְהָיָה בִמְשׁוֹךְ בְּקֶרֶן הַיּוֹבֵל. קֶרֶן בְּיוֹבְלָא אִתְעַטָּר עֲשִׁירָאָה בְּאִימָא. קֶרֶן, דְּנָטִיל קֶרֶן וְרֵוַח לְאַתְבָא רוּחֵיהּ לֵיהּ.

**72.** AND THE VERSE, "THE SKIN OF HIS FACE shone (Heb. *karan*)": "KARAN" RESEMBLES the words, "And Samuel took the horn (Heb. *keren*)

of oil" (I Shmuel 16:13). Kings are anointed only with a horn, as it is written, "And in your favor our horn shall be exalted" (Tehilim 89:18), and also, "There will I make the horn of David to shoot up" (Tehilim 132:17). This refers to the tenth of the king, WHICH IS MALCHUT, THE TENTH SFIRAH OF ZEIR ANPIN. It comes from Jubilee, which is Ima, as is written, "And it shall come to pass, that when they make a long blast with the ram's horn (*Keren* of the Jubilee)" (Yehoshua 6:5). The *Keren*, WHICH IS MALCHUT, is crowned with *Jubilee*, NAMELY the tenth is crowned with Ima, WHICH IS BINAH THAT CLOTHES IT, SO IT BECOMES LIKE BINAH. AND IT IS CALLED '*Keren*', SINCE MALCHUT takes *Keren* FROM BINAH, JUBILEE, and the spirit IN IT, so that the spirit OF BINAH should return to it, NAMELY ITS MOCHIN.

73. וְהַאי קֶרֶן דְּיוֹבְלָא הוּא. וְיוֹבֵל ה'. וה' נְשִׁיבָא דְּרוּחָא לְכֹלָּא. וְכֹלָּא תַּיְיבִין לְאַתְרַיְיהוּ, דִּכְתִּיב אֲהָהּ יְיָ' אֱלֹהִים, כַּד אִתְחֲזֵי ה' לה' יְיָ' אֱלֹהִים אִתְקְרֵי שֵׁם מָלֵא וּכְתִיב וְנִשְׂגַּב יְיָ' לְבַדּוֹ בַּיּוֹם הַהוּא. ע"כ סָתִים וְאִתְעַטַּר צְנִיעוּתָא דְּמַלְכָּא, דְּהַיְינוּ סִפְרָא דִּצְנִיעוּתָא. זַכָּאָה מַאן דְּעָאל וְנָפַק וְיָדַע שְׁבִילוֹי וְאָרְחוֹי.

73. This horn is of Jubilee, and Jubilee IS IMA, NAMELY the FIRST Hei OF YUD HEI VAV HEI, and THIS Hei blows the breath of life into everything. They all return to their places, NAMELY AS IS WRITTEN, "IT SHALL BE A JUBILEE FOR YOU, YOU SHALL RETURN EVERY MAN TO HIS POSSESSION" (VAYIKRA 25:10). It is written, "*Ah* (spelled Aleph Hei Hei) Adonai Elohim" (Yirmeyah 1:6), MEANING ELOHIM IS SPELLED AS YUD HEI VAV HEI WITH THE VOWELING OF ELOHIM, WHICH IS BINAH, AND ADONAI IS MALCHUT. When the FIRST Hei appears to the LOWER Hei, NAMELY BINAH TO MALCHUT, WHEN THEY BOTH ARE CLOTHED WITH EACH OTHER, the name is considered full, Adonai Elohim. AND WHEN THIS ATTIREMENT WILL BE PERMANENT, NAMELY IN THE FUTURE TO COME, THEN it is written, "And Hashem alone shall be exalted on that day" (Yeshayah 2:17). Until here the concealment of the King has been hidden and crowned, namely the Concealed Book. Blessed is he who enters WISDOM and comes out, and knows its paths and ways.

(סליק פרשת תרומה)

**End of Trumah**

# NOTES

# NOTES

# NOTES

# NOTES

# NOTES

# NOTES

# NOTES

# NOTES

# NOTES

# NOTES

# NOTES

# NOTES

# NOTES

# NOTES

# NOTES

# NOTES